FREQUENTLY USED SYMBOLS AND ABBREVIATIONS (CONTINUED)

Symbol	Definition
k_r	Cost of Retained Earnings
k_s	Required Return on Common Stock
m	Number of times per year interest is compounded
M	Bond's Par Value
M/B	Market/Book Ratio
MACRS	Modified Accelerated Cost Recovery System
MNC	Multinational Company
MRP	Materials Requirement Planning
n	• Number of Outcomes Considered
	• Number of Periods—Typically, Years
	• Years to Maturity
N	Number of Days Payment Can Be Delayed by Giving up the Cash Discount
N_d	Net Proceeds from the Sale of Debt (Bond)
N_n	Net Proceeds from the Sale of New Common Stock
N_p	Net Proceeds from the Sale of the Preferred Stock
NCAI	Net Current Asset Investment
NFAI	Net Fixed Asset Investment
NOPAT	Net operating profits after taxes
NPV	Net Present Value
O	Order Cost Per Order
OC	Operating Cycle
OCF	Operating Cash Flow
P	Price (value) of asset
P_0	Value of Common Stock
$PBDT_t$	Profits Before Depreciation and Taxes in year t
PD	Preferred Stock Dividend
P/E	Price/Earnings Ratio
PMT	Amount of Payment
Pr	Probability
PV	Present Value
PVA_n	Present Value of an n-Year Annuity
$PVIF_{i,n}$	Present Value Interest Factor for a Single Amount Discounted at i Percent for n Periods
$PVIFA_{i,n}$	Present Value Interest Factor for an Annuity When Interest is Discounted Annually at i Percent for n Periods
Q	• Order Quantity in Units
	• Sales Quantity in Units
R_F	Risk-Free Rate of Interest
RADR	Risk-Adjusted Discount Rate
ROA	Return on Total Assets
ROE	Return on Common Equity
S	Usage in Units per Period
SML	Security Market Line
t	Time
T	Firm's Marginal Tax Rate
V	Value of an Asset or Firm
V_C	Value of Entire Company
V_D	Value of All Debt
V_P	Value of Preferred Stock
V_S	Value of Common Stock
VC	Variable Operating Cost per Unit
w_j	• Proportion of the Portfolio's Total Dollar Value Represented by Asset j
	• Proportion of a Specific Source of Financing j in the Firm's Capital Structure
WACC	Weighted Average Cost of Capital
WMCC	Weighted Marginal Cost of Captial
YTM	Yield to Maturity
ZBA	Zero Balance Account
σ	Standard Deviation
Σ	Summation Sign

TABLE A-4 Present Value Interest Factors for a One-Dollar Annuity Discounted at i Percent for n Periods: $PVIFA_{i,n} = \sum_{t=1}^{n} \frac{1}{(1+i)^t}$

Period	1%	2%	3%	4%	5%	6%	7%	8%	9%	10%	11%	12%	13%	14%	15%	16%	17%	18%	19%	20%	25%	30%	35%
1	.990	.980	.971	.962	.952	.943	.935	.926	.917	.909	.901	.893	.885	.877	.870	.862	.855	.847	.840	.833	.800	.769	.741
2	1.970	1.942	1.913	1.886	1.859	1.833	1.808	1.783	1.759	1.736	1.713	1.690	1.668	1.647	1.626	1.605	1.585	1.566	1.547	1.528	1.440	1.361	1.289
3	2.941	2.884	2.829	2.775	2.723	2.673	2.624	2.577	2.531	2.487	2.444	2.402	2.361	2.322	2.283	2.246	2.210	2.174	2.140	2.106	1.952	1.816	1.696
4	3.902	3.808	3.717	3.630	3.546	3.465	3.387	3.312	3.240	3.170	3.102	3.037	2.974	2.914	2.855	2.798	2.743	2.690	2.639	2.589	2.362	2.166	1.997
5	4.853	4.713	4.580	4.452	4.329	4.212	4.100	3.993	3.890	3.791	3.696	3.605	3.517	3.433	3.352	3.274	3.199	3.127	3.058	2.991	2.689	2.436	2.220
6	5.795	5.601	5.417	5.242	5.076	4.917	4.767	4.623	4.486	4.355	4.231	4.111	3.998	3.889	3.784	3.685	3.589	3.498	3.410	3.326	2.951	2.643	2.385
7	6.728	6.472	6.230	6.002	5.786	5.582	5.389	5.206	5.033	4.868	4.712	4.564	4.423	4.288	4.160	4.039	3.922	3.812	3.706	3.605	3.161	2.802	2.508
8	7.652	7.326	7.020	6.733	6.463	6.210	5.971	5.747	5.535	5.335	5.146	4.968	4.799	4.639	4.487	4.344	4.207	4.078	3.954	3.837	3.329	2.925	2.598
9	8.566	8.162	7.786	7.435	7.108	6.802	6.515	6.247	5.995	5.759	5.537	5.328	5.132	4.946	4.772	4.607	4.451	4.303	4.163	4.031	3.463	3.019	2.665
10	9.471	8.983	8.530	8.111	7.722	7.360	7.024	6.710	6.418	6.145	5.889	5.650	5.426	5.216	5.019	4.833	4.659	4.494	4.339	4.192	3.570	3.092	2.715
11	10.368	9.787	9.253	8.760	8.306	7.887	7.499	7.139	6.805	6.495	6.207	5.938	5.687	5.453	5.234	5.029	4.836	4.656	4.486	4.327	3.656	3.147	2.752
12	11.255	10.575	9.954	9.385	8.863	8.384	7.943	7.536	7.161	6.814	6.492	6.194	5.918	5.660	5.421	5.197	4.988	4.793	4.611	4.439	3.725	3.190	2.779
13	12.134	11.348	10.635	9.986	9.394	8.853	8.358	7.904	7.487	7.103	6.750	6.424	6.122	5.842	5.583	5.342	5.118	4.910	4.715	4.533	3.780	3.223	2.799
14	13.004	12.106	11.296	10.563	9.899	9.295	8.745	8.244	7.786	7.367	6.982	6.628	6.302	6.002	5.724	5.468	5.229	5.008	4.802	4.611	3.824	3.249	2.814
15	13.865	12.849	11.938	11.118	10.380	9.712	9.108	8.560	8.061	7.606	7.191	6.811	6.462	6.142	5.847	5.575	5.324	5.092	4.876	4.675	3.859	3.268	2.825
16	14.718	13.578	12.561	11.652	10.838	10.106	9.447	8.851	8.313	7.824	7.379	6.974	6.604	6.265	5.954	5.668	5.405	5.162	4.938	4.730	3.887	3.283	2.834
17	15.562	14.292	13.166	12.166	11.274	10.477	9.763	9.122	8.544	8.022	7.549	7.120	6.729	6.373	6.047	5.749	5.475	5.222	4.990	4.775	3.910	3.295	2.840
18	16.398	14.992	13.754	12.659	11.690	10.828	10.059	9.372	8.756	8.201	7.702	7.250	6.840	6.467	6.128	5.818	5.534	5.273	5.033	4.812	3.928	3.304	2.844
19	17.226	15.679	14.324	13.134	12.085	11.158	10.336	9.604	8.950	8.365	7.839	7.366	6.938	6.550	6.198	5.877	5.584	5.316	5.070	4.843	3.942	3.311	2.848
20	18.046	16.352	14.878	13.590	12.462	11.470	10.594	9.818	9.129	8.514	7.963	7.469	7.025	6.623	6.259	5.929	5.628	5.353	5.101	4.870	3.954	3.316	2.850
21	18.857	17.011	15.415	14.029	12.821	11.764	10.836	10.017	9.292	8.649	8.075	7.562	7.102	6.687	6.312	5.973	5.665	5.384	5.127	4.891	3.963	3.320	2.852
22	19.661	17.658	15.937	14.451	13.163	12.042	11.061	10.201	9.442	8.772	8.176	7.645	7.170	6.743	6.359	6.011	5.696	5.410	5.149	4.909	3.970	3.323	2.853
23	20.456	18.292	16.444	14.857	13.489	12.303	11.272	10.371	9.580	8.883	8.266	7.718	7.230	6.792	6.399	6.044	5.723	5.432	5.167	4.925	3.976	3.325	2.854
24	21.244	18.914	16.936	15.247	13.799	12.550	11.469	10.529	9.707	8.985	8.348	7.784	7.283	6.835	6.434	6.073	5.746	5.451	5.182	4.937	3.981	3.327	2.855
25	22.023	19.524	17.413	15.622	14.094	12.783	11.654	10.675	9.823	9.077	8.422	7.843	7.330	6.873	6.464	6.097	5.766	5.467	5.195	4.948	3.985	3.329	2.856
30	25.808	22.396	19.601	17.292	15.373	13.765	12.409	11.258	10.274	9.427	8.694	8.055	7.496	7.003	6.566	6.177	5.829	5.517	5.235	4.979	3.995	3.332	2.857
35	29.409	24.999	21.487	18.665	16.374	14.498	12.948	11.655	10.567	9.644	8.855	8.176	7.586	7.070	6.617	6.215	5.858	5.539	5.251	4.992	3.998	3.333	2.857
40	32.835	27.356	23.115	19.793	17.159	15.046	13.332	11.925	10.757	9.779	8.951	8.244	7.634	7.105	6.642	6.233	5.871	5.548	5.258	4.997	3.999	3.333	2.857
45	36.095	29.490	24.519	20.720	17.774	15.456	13.606	12.108	10.881	9.863	9.008	8.283	7.661	7.123	6.654	6.242	5.877	5.552	5.261	4.999	4.000	3.333	2.857
50	39.196	31.424	25.730	21.482	18.256	15.762	13.801	12.233	10.962	9.915	9.042	8.304	7.675	7.133	6.661	6.246	5.880	5.554	5.262	4.999	4.000	3.333	2.857

Using the Calculator to Compute the Present Value of an Annuity

Before you begin, make sure to clear the memory, ensure that you are in the *end mode* and that your calculator is set for *one payment per year*, and set the number of decimal places that you want (usually two for dollar-related accuracy).

SAMPLE PROBLEM You want to know what the present value will be of an annuity of $700 received at the end of each year for 5 years, given a discount rate of 8%.

Hewlett-Packard HP 12C,
17 BII, and 19 BII[a]

Input	Function
700	PMT
5	N
8	I%YR
	PV

Solution[b]
(2794.90)

Texas Instruments,
BA-35, BAII,
and BAII Plus[c]

Input	Function
700	PMT
5	N
8	%i
	CPT
	FV

Solution[d]
(2794.90)

[a]For the 12C, you would use the `n` key instead of the `N` key and use the `i` key instead of the `I%YR` key.

[b]The minus sign that precedes the solution should be ignored.

[c]For the Texas Instruments BAII, you would use the `2nd` key instead of the `CPT` key; for the Texas Instruments BAII Plus, you would use the `I/Y` key instead of the `%i` key.

[d]If a minus sign precedes the solution, it should be ignored.

© 2006 Pearson Education, Inc. All rights reserved.

TABLE A-2 Present Value Interest Factors for One Dollar Discounted at i Percent for n Periods: $PVIF_{i,n} = \dfrac{1}{(1+i)^n}$

Period	1%	2%	3%	4%	5%	6%	7%	8%	9%	10%	11%	12%	13%	14%	15%	16%	17%	18%	19%	20%	25%	30%	35%
1	.990	.980	.971	.962	.952	.943	.935	.926	.917	.909	.901	.893	.885	.877	.870	.862	.855	.847	.840	.833	.800	.769	.741
2	.980	.961	.943	.925	.907	.890	.873	.857	.842	.826	.812	.797	.783	.769	.756	.743	.731	.718	.706	.694	.640	.592	.549
3	.971	.942	.915	.889	.864	.840	.816	.794	.772	.751	.731	.712	.693	.675	.658	.641	.624	.609	.593	.579	.512	.455	.406
4	.961	.924	.888	.855	.823	.792	.763	.735	.708	.683	.659	.636	.613	.592	.572	.552	.534	.516	.499	.482	.410	.350	.301
5	.951	.906	.863	.822	.784	.747	.713	.681	.650	.621	.593	.567	.543	.519	.497	.476	.456	.437	.419	.402	.328	.269	.223
6	.942	.888	.837	.790	.746	.705	.666	.630	.596	.564	.535	.507	.480	.456	.432	.410	.390	.370	.352	.335	.262	.207	.165
7	.933	.871	.813	.760	.711	.665	.623	.583	.547	.513	.482	.452	.425	.400	.376	.354	.333	.314	.296	.279	.210	.159	.122
8	.923	.853	.789	.731	.677	.627	.582	.540	.502	.467	.434	.404	.376	.351	.327	.305	.285	.266	.249	.233	.168	.123	.091
9	.914	.837	.766	.703	.645	.592	.544	.500	.460	.424	.391	.361	.333	.308	.284	.263	.243	.225	.209	.194	.134	.094	.067
10	.905	.820	.744	.676	.614	.558	.508	.463	.422	.386	.352	.322	.295	.270	.247	.227	.208	.191	.176	.162	.107	.073	.050
11	.896	.804	.722	.650	.585	.527	.475	.429	.388	.350	.317	.287	.261	.237	.215	.195	.178	.162	.148	.135	.086	.056	.037
12	.887	.789	.701	.625	.557	.497	.444	.397	.356	.319	.286	.257	.231	.208	.187	.168	.152	.137	.124	.112	.069	.043	.027
13	.879	.773	.681	.601	.530	.469	.415	.368	.326	.290	.258	.229	.204	.182	.163	.145	.130	.116	.104	.093	.055	.033	.020
14	.870	.758	.661	.577	.505	.442	.388	.340	.299	.263	.232	.205	.181	.160	.141	.125	.111	.099	.088	.078	.044	.025	.015
15	.861	.743	.642	.555	.481	.417	.362	.315	.275	.239	.209	.183	.160	.140	.123	.108	.095	.084	.074	.065	.035	.020	.011
16	.853	.728	.623	.534	.458	.394	.339	.292	.252	.218	.188	.163	.141	.123	.107	.093	.081	.071	.062	.054	.028	.015	.008
17	.844	.714	.605	.513	.436	.371	.317	.270	.231	.198	.170	.146	.125	.108	.093	.080	.069	.060	.052	.045	.023	.012	.006
18	.836	.700	.587	.494	.416	.350	.296	.250	.212	.180	.153	.130	.111	.095	.081	.069	.059	.051	.044	.038	.018	.009	.005
19	.828	.686	.570	.475	.396	.331	.277	.232	.194	.164	.138	.116	.098	.083	.070	.060	.051	.043	.037	.031	.014	.007	.003
20	.820	.673	.554	.456	.377	.312	.258	.215	.178	.149	.124	.104	.087	.073	.061	.051	.043	.037	.031	.026	.012	.005	.002
21	.811	.660	.538	.439	.359	.294	.242	.199	.164	.135	.112	.093	.077	.064	.053	.044	.037	.031	.026	.022	.009	.004	.002
22	.803	.647	.522	.422	.342	.278	.226	.184	.150	.123	.101	.083	.068	.056	.046	.038	.032	.026	.022	.018	.007	.003	.001
23	.795	.634	.507	.406	.326	.262	.211	.170	.138	.112	.091	.074	.060	.049	.040	.033	.027	.022	.018	.015	.006	.002	.001
24	.788	.622	.492	.390	.310	.247	.197	.158	.126	.102	.082	.066	.053	.043	.035	.028	.023	.019	.015	.013	.005	.002	.001
25	.780	.610	.478	.375	.295	.233	.184	.146	.116	.092	.074	.059	.047	.038	.030	.024	.020	.016	.013	.010	.004	.001	.001
30	.742	.552	.412	.308	.231	.174	.131	.099	.075	.057	.044	.033	.026	.020	.015	.012	.009	.007	.005	.004	.001	*	*
35	.706	.500	.355	.253	.181	.130	.094	.068	.049	.036	.026	.019	.014	.010	.008	.006	.004	.003	.002	.002	*	*	*
40	.672	.453	.307	.208	.142	.097	.067	.046	.032	.022	.015	.011	.008	.005	.004	.003	.002	.001	.001	.001	*	*	*
45	.639	.410	.264	.171	.111	.073	.048	.031	.021	.014	.009	.006	.004	.003	.002	.001	.001	.001	*	*	*	*	*
50	.608	.372	.228	.141	.087	.054	.034	.021	.013	.009	.005	.003	.002	.001	.001	.001	*	*	*	*	*	*	*

Using the Calculator to Compute the Present Value of a Single Amount

Before you begin, make sure to clear the memory, ensure that you are in the *end mode* and that your calculator is set for *one payment per year*, and set the number of decimal places that you want (usually two for dollar-related accuracy).

SAMPLE PROBLEM You want to know the present value of $1,700 to be received at the end of 8 years, assuming an 8% discount rate.

Hewlett-Packard HP 12C, 17 BII, and 19 BII[a]

Solution[b]
918.46

Texas Instruments, BA-35, BAII, and BAII Plus[c]

Solution[d]
918.46

[a] For the 12C, you would use the `n` key instead of the `N` key and use the `i` key instead of the `I%YR` key.
[b] The minus sign that precedes the solution should be ignored.
[c] For the Texas Instruments BAII, you would use the `1/Y` key instead of the `2nd` key instead of the `N` key; for the Texas Instruments BAII Plus, you would use the `%i` key.
[d] If a minus sign precedes the solution, it should be ignored.

© 2006 Pearson Education, Inc. All rights reserved.

TABLE A-1 Future Value Interest Factors for One Dollar Compounded at *i* Percent for *n* Periods: $FVIF_{i,n} = (1 + i)^n$

Period	1%	2%	3%	4%	5%	6%	7%	8%	9%	10%	11%	12%	13%	14%	15%	16%	20%	25%	30%	35%
1	1.010	1.020	1.030	1.040	1.050	1.060	1.070	1.080	1.090	1.100	1.110	1.120	1.130	1.140	1.150	1.160	1.200	1.250	1.300	1.350
2	1.020	1.040	1.061	1.082	1.102	1.124	1.145	1.166	1.188	1.210	1.232	1.254	1.277	1.300	1.322	1.346	1.440	1.562	1.690	1.822
3	1.030	1.061	1.093	1.125	1.158	1.191	1.225	1.260	1.295	1.331	1.368	1.405	1.443	1.482	1.521	1.561	1.728	1.953	2.197	2.460
4	1.041	1.082	1.126	1.170	1.216	1.262	1.311	1.360	1.412	1.464	1.518	1.574	1.630	1.689	1.749	1.811	2.074	2.441	2.856	3.321
5	1.051	1.104	1.159	1.217	1.276	1.338	1.403	1.469	1.539	1.611	1.685	1.762	1.842	1.925	2.011	2.100	2.488	3.052	3.713	4.484
6	1.062	1.126	1.194	1.265	1.340	1.419	1.501	1.587	1.677	1.772	1.870	1.974	2.082	2.195	2.313	2.436	2.986	3.815	4.827	6.053
7	1.072	1.149	1.230	1.316	1.407	1.504	1.606	1.714	1.828	1.949	2.076	2.211	2.353	2.502	2.660	2.826	3.583	4.768	6.275	8.172
8	1.083	1.172	1.267	1.369	1.477	1.594	1.718	1.851	1.993	2.144	2.305	2.476	2.658	2.853	3.059	3.278	4.300	5.960	8.157	11.032
9	1.094	1.195	1.305	1.423	1.551	1.689	1.838	1.999	2.172	2.358	2.558	2.773	3.004	3.252	3.518	3.803	5.160	7.451	10.604	14.894
10	1.105	1.219	1.344	1.480	1.629	1.791	1.967	2.159	2.367	2.594	2.839	3.106	3.395	3.707	4.046	4.411	6.192	9.313	13.786	20.106
11	1.116	1.243	1.384	1.539	1.710	1.898	2.105	2.332	2.580	2.853	3.152	3.479	3.836	4.226	4.652	5.117	7.430	11.642	17.921	27.144
12	1.127	1.268	1.426	1.601	1.796	2.012	2.252	2.518	2.813	3.138	3.498	3.896	4.334	4.818	5.350	5.936	8.916	14.552	23.298	36.644
13	1.138	1.294	1.469	1.665	1.886	2.133	2.410	2.720	3.066	3.452	3.883	4.363	4.898	5.492	6.153	6.886	10.699	18.190	30.287	49.469
14	1.149	1.319	1.513	1.732	1.980	2.261	2.579	2.937	3.342	3.797	4.310	4.887	5.535	6.261	7.076	7.987	12.839	22.737	39.373	66.784
15	1.161	1.346	1.558	1.801	2.079	2.397	2.759	3.172	3.642	4.177	4.785	5.474	6.254	7.138	8.137	9.265	15.407	28.422	51.185	90.158
16	1.173	1.373	1.605	1.873	2.183	2.540	2.952	3.426	3.970	4.595	5.311	6.130	7.067	8.137	9.358	10.748	18.488	35.527	66.541	121.713
17	1.184	1.400	1.653	1.948	2.292	2.693	3.159	3.700	4.328	5.054	5.895	6.866	7.986	9.276	10.761	12.468	22.186	44.409	86.503	164.312
18	1.196	1.428	1.702	2.026	2.407	2.854	3.380	3.996	4.717	5.560	6.543	7.690	9.024	10.575	12.375	14.462	26.623	55.511	112.454	221.822
19	1.208	1.457	1.753	2.107	2.527	3.026	3.616	4.316	5.142	6.116	7.263	8.613	10.197	12.055	14.232	16.776	31.948	69.389	146.190	299.459
20	1.220	1.486	1.806	2.191	2.653	3.207	3.870	4.661	5.604	6.727	8.062	9.646	11.523	13.743	16.366	19.461	38.337	86.736	190.047	404.270
21	1.232	1.516	1.860	2.279	2.786	3.399	4.140	5.034	6.109	7.400	8.949	10.804	13.021	15.667	18.821	22.574	46.005	108.420	247.061	545.764
22	1.245	1.546	1.916	2.370	2.925	3.603	4.430	5.436	6.658	8.140	9.933	12.100	14.713	17.861	21.644	26.186	55.205	135.525	321.178	736.781
23	1.257	1.577	1.974	2.465	3.071	3.820	4.740	5.871	7.258	8.954	11.026	13.552	16.626	20.361	24.891	30.376	66.247	169.407	417.531	994.653
24	1.270	1.608	2.033	2.563	3.225	4.049	5.072	6.341	7.911	9.850	12.239	15.178	18.788	23.212	28.625	35.236	79.496	211.758	542.791	1342.781
25	1.282	1.641	2.094	2.666	3.386	4.292	5.427	6.848	8.623	10.834	13.585	17.000	21.230	26.461	32.918	40.874	95.395	264.698	705.627	1812.754
30	1.348	1.811	2.427	3.243	4.322	5.743	7.612	10.062	13.267	17.449	22.892	29.960	39.115	50.949	66.210	85.849	237.373	807.793	2619.936	8128.426
35	1.417	2.000	2.814	3.946	5.516	7.686	10.676	14.785	20.413	28.102	38.574	52.799	72.066	98.097	133.172	180.311	590.657	2465.189	9727.598	36448.051
45	1.565	2.438	3.781	5.841	8.985	13.764	21.002	31.920	48.325	72.888	109.527	163.985	244.629	363.662	538.752	795.429	3657.176	22958.844	134102.187	*
50	1.645	2.691	4.384	7.106	11.467	18.419	29.456	46.900	74.354	117.386	184.559	288.996	450.711	700.197	1083.619	1670.669	9100.191	70064.812	497910.125	*

Using the Calculator to Compute the Future Value of a Single Amount

Before you begin, be certain to clear the memory, ensure that you are in the *end mode* and that your calculator is set for *one payment per year*, and set the number of decimal places that you want (usually two for dollar-related accuracy).

SAMPLE PROBLEM You place $800 in a savings account at 6% compounded annually. What is your account balance at the end of 5 years?

Hewlett-Packard HP 12C,
17 BII, and 19 BII[a]

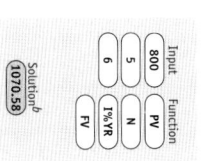

Texas Instruments,
BA-35, BAII
and BAII Plus[c]

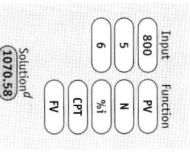

[a] For the 12C, you would use the [n] key instead of the [N] key and use the [i] key instead of the [I%YR] key.
[b] The minus sign that precedes the output should be ignored.
[c] For the Texas Instruments BAII, you would use the [I/Y] key instead of the [%i] key for the Texas Instruments BAII Plus, you would use the [I/Y] key instead of the [%i] key.
[d] If a minus sign precedes the solution, it should be ignored.

© 2006 Pearson Education, Inc. All rights reserved.

TABLE A-3 Future Value Interest Factors for a One-Dollar Ordinary Annuity Compounded at i Percent for n Periods: $FVIFA_{i,n} = \sum_{t=1}^{n}(1+i)^{t-1}$

Period	1%	2%	3%	4%	5%	6%	7%	8%	9%	10%	11%	12%	13%	14%	15%	16%	20%	25%	30%	35%
1	1.000	1.000	1.000	1.000	1.000	1.000	1.000	1.000	1.000	1.000	1.000	1.000	1.000	1.000	1.000	1.000	1.000	1.000	1.000	1.000
2	2.010	2.020	2.030	2.040	2.050	2.060	2.070	2.080	2.090	2.100	2.110	2.120	2.130	2.140	2.150	2.160	2.200	2.250	2.300	2.350
3	3.030	3.060	3.091	3.122	3.152	3.184	3.215	3.246	3.278	3.310	3.342	3.374	3.407	3.440	3.472	3.506	3.640	3.813	3.990	4.172
4	4.060	4.122	4.184	4.246	4.310	4.375	4.440	4.506	4.573	4.641	4.710	4.779	4.850	4.921	4.993	5.066	5.368	5.766	6.187	6.633
5	5.101	5.204	5.309	5.416	5.526	5.637	5.751	5.867	5.985	6.105	6.228	6.353	6.480	6.610	6.742	6.877	7.442	8.207	9.043	9.954
6	6.152	6.308	6.468	6.633	6.802	6.975	7.153	7.336	7.523	7.716	7.913	8.115	8.323	8.535	8.754	8.977	9.930	11.259	12.756	14.438
7	7.214	7.434	7.662	7.898	8.142	8.394	8.654	8.923	9.200	9.487	9.783	10.089	10.405	10.730	11.067	11.414	12.916	15.073	17.583	20.492
8	8.286	8.583	8.892	9.214	9.549	9.897	10.260	10.637	11.028	11.436	11.859	12.300	12.757	13.233	13.727	14.240	16.499	19.842	23.858	28.664
9	9.368	9.755	10.159	10.583	11.027	11.491	11.978	12.488	13.021	13.579	14.164	14.776	15.416	16.085	16.786	17.518	20.799	25.802	32.015	39.696
10	10.462	10.950	11.464	12.006	12.578	13.181	13.816	14.487	15.193	15.937	16.722	17.549	18.420	19.337	20.304	21.321	25.959	33.253	42.619	54.590
11	11.567	12.169	12.808	13.486	14.207	14.972	15.784	16.645	17.560	18.531	19.561	20.655	21.814	23.044	24.349	25.733	32.150	42.566	56.405	74.696
12	12.682	13.412	14.192	15.026	15.917	16.870	17.888	18.977	20.141	21.384	22.713	24.133	25.650	27.271	29.001	30.850	39.580	54.208	74.326	101.840
13	13.809	14.680	15.618	16.627	17.713	18.882	20.141	21.495	22.953	24.523	26.211	28.029	29.984	32.088	34.352	36.786	48.496	68.760	97.624	138.484
14	14.947	15.974	17.086	18.292	19.598	21.015	22.550	24.215	26.019	27.975	30.095	32.392	34.882	37.581	40.504	43.672	59.196	86.949	127.912	187.953
15	16.097	17.293	18.599	20.023	21.578	23.276	25.129	27.152	29.361	31.772	34.405	37.280	40.417	43.842	47.580	51.659	72.035	109.687	167.285	254.737
16	17.258	18.639	20.157	21.824	23.657	25.672	27.888	30.324	33.003	35.949	39.190	42.753	46.671	50.980	55.717	60.925	87.442	139.109	218.470	344.895
17	18.430	20.012	21.761	23.697	25.840	28.213	30.840	33.750	36.973	40.544	44.500	48.883	53.738	59.117	65.075	71.673	105.930	173.636	285.011	466.608
18	19.614	21.412	23.414	25.645	28.132	30.905	33.999	37.450	41.301	45.599	50.396	55.749	61.724	68.393	75.836	84.140	128.116	218.045	371.514	630.920
19	20.811	22.840	25.117	27.671	30.539	33.760	37.379	41.446	46.018	51.158	56.939	63.439	70.748	78.968	88.211	98.603	154.739	273.556	483.968	852.741
20	22.019	24.297	26.870	29.778	33.066	36.785	40.995	45.762	51.159	57.274	64.202	72.052	80.946	91.024	102.443	115.379	186.687	342.945	630.157	1152.200
21	23.239	25.783	28.676	31.969	35.719	39.992	44.865	50.422	56.764	64.002	72.264	81.698	92.468	104.767	118.809	134.840	225.024	429.681	820.204	1556.470
22	24.471	27.299	30.536	34.248	38.505	43.392	49.005	55.456	62.872	71.402	81.213	92.502	105.489	120.434	137.630	157.414	271.028	538.101	1067.265	2102.234
23	25.716	28.845	32.452	36.618	41.430	46.995	53.435	60.893	69.531	79.542	91.147	104.602	120.203	138.295	159.274	183.600	326.234	673.626	1388.443	2839.014
24	26.973	30.421	34.426	39.082	44.501	50.815	58.176	66.764	76.789	88.496	102.173	118.154	136.829	158.656	184.166	213.976	392.480	843.032	1805.975	3833.667
25	28.243	32.030	36.459	41.645	47.726	54.864	63.248	73.105	84.699	98.346	114.412	133.333	155.616	181.867	212.790	249.212	471.976	1054.791	2348.765	5176.445
30	34.784	40.567	47.575	56.084	66.438	79.057	94.459	113.282	136.305	164.491	199.018	241.330	293.192	356.778	434.738	530.306	1181.865	3227.172	8729.805	23221.258
35	41.659	49.994	60.461	73.651	90.318	111.432	138.234	172.314	215.705	271.018	341.583	431.658	546.663	693.552	881.152	1120.699	2948.294	9856.746	32422.090	104134.500
40	48.885	60.401	75.400	95.024	120.797	154.758	199.630	259.052	337.872	442.580	581.812	767.080	1013.667	1341.979	1779.048	2360.724	7343.715	30088.621	120389.375	*
45	56.479	71.891	92.718	121.027	159.695	212.737	285.741	386.497	525.840	718.881	986.613	1358.208	1874.086	2590.464	3585.031	4965.191	18280.914	91831.312	447005.062	*
50	64.461	84.577	112.794	152.664	209.341	290.325	406.516	573.756	815.051	1163.865	1668.723	2399.975	3459.344	4994.301	7217.488	10435.449	4596.094	*	*	*

Using the Calculator to Compute the Future Value of an Ordinary Annuity

Before you begin, be certain to clear the memory, ensure that you are in the *end mode* and that your calculator is set for *one payment per year*, and set the number of decimal places that you want (usually two for dollar-related accuracy).

SAMPLE PROBLEM You want to know what the future value will be at the end of 5 years if you place five end-of-year deposits of $1,000 in an account paying 7% annually. What is your account balance at the end of 5 years?

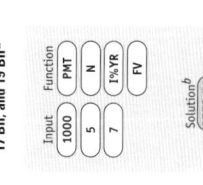

Hewlett-Packard HP 12C, 17 BII, and 19 BII[a]

Input: 1000, 5, 7
Function: PMT, N, I%YR, FV
Solution[b]: 5750.74

Texas Instruments, BA-35, BAII, and BAII Plus[c]

Input: 1000, 5, 7
Function: PMT, N, %i, CPT, FV
Solution[d]: 5750.74

[a]For the 12C, you would use the [n] key instead of the [N] key and use the [i] key instead of the [I%YR] key.
[b]The minus sign that precedes the solution should be ignored.
[c]For the Texas Instruments BAII, you would use the [2nd] key instead of the [CPT] key; for the Texas Instruments BAII Plus, you would use the [I/Y] key instead of the [%i] key.
[d]If a minus sign precedes the solution, it should be ignored.

© 2006 Pearson Education, Inc. All rights reserved.

Principles of Managerial Finance

Brief

The Addison-Wesley Series in Finance

Copeland/Weston
*Financial Theory
and Corporate Policy*

Dufey/Giddy
Cases in International Finance

Eakins
*Finance: Investments,
Institutions, and Management*

Eiteman/Stonehill/Moffett
Multinational Business Finance

Gitman
Principles of Managerial Finance

Gitman
*Principles of Managerial Finance
—Brief Edition*

Gitman/Joehnk
Fundamentals of Investing

Gitman/Madura
Introduction to Finance

Hughes/MacDonald
International Banking: Text and Cases

Madura
Personal Finance

Marthinsen
*Risk Takers: Uses and Abuses
of Financial Derivatives*

McDonald
Derivatives Markets

Megginson
Corporate Finance Theory

Melvin
International Money and Finance

Mishkin/Eakins
Financial Markets and Institutions

Moffett
Cases in International Finance

Moffett/Stonehill/Eiteman
Fundamentals of Multinational Finance

Rejda
*Principles of Risk Management
and Insurance*

Solnik/McLeavey
International Investments

Principles of Managerial Finance

Brief Fourth Edition

Lawrence J. GITMAN

San Diego State University

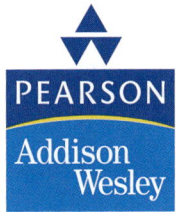

Boston San Francisco New York
London Toronto Sydney Tokyo Singapore Madrid
Mexico City Munich Paris Cape Town Hong Kong Montreal

Editor-in-Chief: Denise Clinton
Senior Acquisitions Editor: Donna Battista
Senior Project Manager: Mary Clare McEwing
Development Editor: Ann Torbert
Managing Editor: Jim Rigney
Senior Production Supervisor: Nancy Fenton
Executive Marketing Manager: Stephen Frail
Media Producer: Bethany Tidd
Supplements Editor: Kirsten Dickerson
Digital Assets Manager: Jason Miranda
Permissions Editor: Dana Weightman
Project Coordination, Text Design, Art Studio,
    and Electronic Page Makeup: Thompson Steele, Inc.
Design Manager: Regina Hagen Kolenda
Cover Designer: Regina Hagen Kolenda
Cover Photographs: Masterfile
Senior Manufacturing Buyer: Hugh Crawford

For permission to use copyrighted material, grateful acknowledgment is made to the copyright holders on p. CR-1, which is hereby made part of this copyright page.

Library of Congress Cataloging-in-Publication Data

Gitman, Lawrence J.
    Principles of managerial finance : brief / Lawrence J. Gitman.—4th ed.
        p. cm.
    Includes bibliographical references and index.
    ISBN 0-321-26760-5 (brief 4th ed. : alk. paper)
    1. Corporations—Finance. 2. Business enterprises—Finance.   I. Title.
HG4011.G52 2005
658.15—dc22

2004060133

© 2006 by Lawrence J. Gitman

All rights reserved. No part of this publication may be reproduced, stored in a retrieval system, or transmitted, in any form or by any means, electronic, mechanical, photocopying, recording, or otherwise, without the prior written permission of the publisher.

For information on obtaining permission for the use of material from this work, please submit a written request to Pearson Education, Inc., Rights and Contracts Department, 75 Arlington Street, Suite 300, Boston, MA 02116 or fax your request to (617) 848-7047. Printed in the United States.

ISBN 0-321-26760-5

2 3 4 5 6 7 8 9 10—QWT—09 08 07 06 05

Dedicated to the memory of my mother, Dr. Edith Gitman, who instilled in me the importance of education and hard work

Gitman's Proven Teaching/Learning System

Users of *Principles of Managerial Finance, Brief* have praised the effectiveness of the book's teaching/learning system, which has been hailed as one of its hallmarks. The system, driven by a set of carefully developed learning goals, has been retained and polished in the Fourth Edition. Key elements of the teaching/learning system are illustrated and described in the "walkthrough" of features on the pages that follow. Both students and instructors are encouraged at the start of the semester to acquaint themselves with the many useful learning features the book offers.

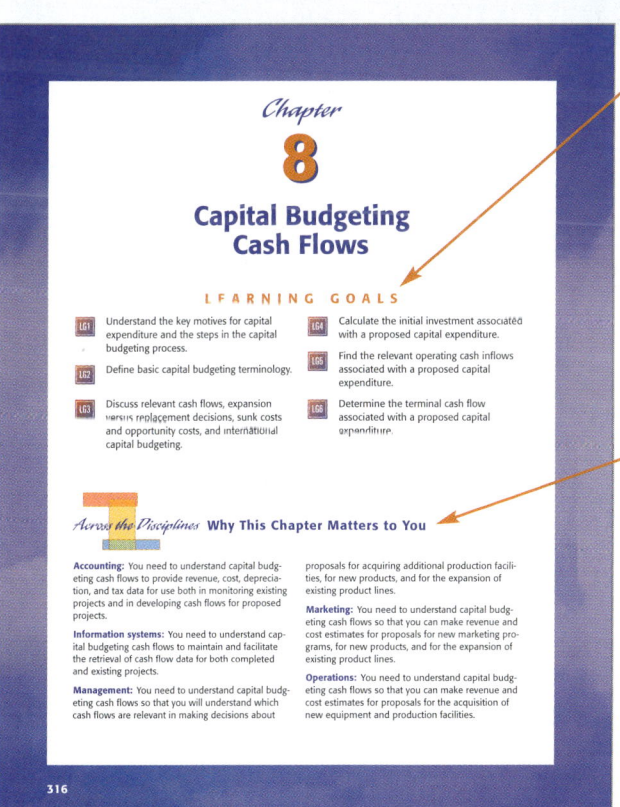

Six **Learning Goals** at the start of the chapter anchor the most important concepts and techniques to be learned in the chapter. The learning goal icons reappear next to related text sections and again in the chapter-end summary, end-of-chapter homework materials, and supplements such as the Study Guide, Test Bank, and FinanceWorks.

Every chapter opens with a feature that discusses the intersection of the finance topics covered in the chapter with the concerns of other major business disciplines. **Across the Disciplines** shows students majoring in accounting, information systems, management, marketing, and operations why the chapter matters to them, and it encourages them to appreciate the numerous cross-disciplinary interactions that routinely occur in business.

Learning goal icons appear next to first-level text headings. The learning goal icon ties chapter content to learning goals.

 The Capital Budgeting Decision Process

Long-term investments represent sizable outlays of funds that commit a firm to some course of action. Consequently, the firm needs procedures to analyze and properly select its long-term investments. It must be able to measure cash flows and apply appropriate decision techniques. As time passes, fixed assets may become obsolete or may require an overhaul; at these points, too, financial deci-

Examples are an important component of the book's learning system. Clearly set off from the text, they provide an immediate and concrete demonstration of how to apply financial concepts, tools, and techniques.

Examples in certain chapters, most notably in Chapter 4, demonstrate the time value of money techniques. These examples show the use of time lines, factor tables, financial calculators, and spreadsheets.

Spreadsheet solutions accompany most calculator solutions and show the inputs, solutions, and cell formulas of the spreadsheets. In this edition, spreadsheet solutions have been added in Chapters 6 and 10.

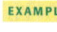

EXAMPLE

As noted, Pam Valenti wishes to find the present value of $1,700 to be received 8 years from now, assuming an 8% opportunity cost.

Table Use The present value interest factor for 8% and 8 years, $PVIF_{8\%,8\,yrs}$, found in Table A–2, is 0.540. Using Equation 4.12, $1,700 \times 0.540 = \$918$. The present value of the $1,700 Pam expects to receive in 8 years is $918.

Calculator Use Using the calculator's financial functions and the inputs shown at the left, you should find the present value to be $918.46. The value obtained with the calculator is more accurate than the values found using the equation or the table, although for the purposes of this text, these differences are insignificant.

Spreadsheet Use The present value of the single future amount also can be calculated as shown on the following Excel spreadsheet.

	A	B
1	PRESENT VALUE OF A SINGLE AMOUNT	
2	Future value	$1,700
3	Interest rate, pct per year compounded annually	8%
4	Number of years	8
5	Present value	$918.46

Entry in Cell B5 is =–PV(B3,B4,0,B2). The minus sign appears before PV to change the present value to a positive amount.

Key equations are printed in blue throughout the text to help readers identify the most important mathematical relationships. The variables used in these equations are for convenience printed on the front endpapers of the book.

factor for an initial principal of $1 compounded at i percent for n periods is referred to as $FVIF_{i,n}$.

$$\text{Future value interest factor} = FVIF_{i,n} = (1+i)^n \quad (4.5)$$

By finding the intersection of the annual interest rate, i, and the appropriate periods, n, you will find the future value interest factor that is relevant to a particular problem.[2] Using $FVIF_{i,n}$ as the appropriate factor, we can rewrite the general equation for future value (Equation 4.4) as follows:

$$FV_n = PV \times (FVIF_{i,n}) \quad (4.6)$$

This expression indicates that to find the future value at the end of period n of an initial deposit, we have merely to multiply the initial deposit, PV, by the appropriate future value interest factor.[3]

For help in study and review, **key terms** and their definitions appear in the margin when they are first introduced. These terms are also boldfaced in the index and appear in the Glossary.

discounting cash flows
The process of finding present values; the inverse of compounding interest.

The Concept of Present Value

The process of finding present values is often referred to as **discounting cash flows**. It is concerned with answering the following question: If I can earn i percent on my money, what is the most I would be willing to pay now for an opportunity to receive FV_n dollars n periods from today?

This process is actually the inverse of compounding interest. Instead of finding the future value of present dollars invested at a given rate, discounting determines the present value of a future amount, assuming an opportunity to earn a certain return on the money. This annual rate of return is variously referred to as the *discount rate, required return, cost of capital,* and *opportunity cost*. These terms will be used interchangeably in this text.

Marginal hints add useful ideas, comments, and pieces of information to enrich the text discussion and help student learning.

Hint Anyone familiar with an electronic spreadsheet, such as Excel, realizes that most of the time-value-of-money calculations can be performed expeditiously by using the special functions contained in the spreadsheet.

Electronic Spreadsheets

Like financial calculators, electronic spreadsheets have built-in routines that simplify time value calculations. We provide in the text a number of spreadsheet solutions that identify the cell entries for calculating time values. The value for each variable is entered in a cell in the spreadsheet, and the calculation is programmed using an equation that links the individual cells. If values of the variables are changed, the solution automatically changes as a result of the equation linking the cells. In the spreadsheet solutions in this book, the equation that determines the calculation is shown at the bottom of the spreadsheet.

Review Questions, which appear at the end of each major section of the chapter, challenge you to stop and test your understanding of key concepts, tools, techniques, and practices before you move on to the next section.

In Practice boxes offer insight into important topics in finance, through the experiences of real companies, both large and small. There are two categories of boxes.

Focus on Ethics boxes in nine chapters help you appreciate important ethical issues in finance.

Focus on Practice boxes take a corporate focus that relates a business event to a specific financial concept or technique.

Both types of boxes will provide you with a solid grounding in the practice of finance in the real world.

The Summary begins with **Focus on Value**, which explains how the chapter's content relates to the firm's goal of maximizing owner wealth. This feature helps reinforce understanding of the link between the financial manager's actions and share value.

The **Review of Learning Goals** restates each learning goal and summarizes the key material that was presented to support mastery of that goal.

> **REVIEW OF LEARNING GOALS**
>
> Key formulas and decision criteria for this chapter are summarized in Table 9.10 (see page 382).
>
> **LG1** Calculate, interpret, and evaluate the payback period. The payback period is the amount of time required for the firm to recover its initial investment, as calculated from cash inflows. Shorter payback periods are preferred. The payback period is relatively easy to calculate, has simple intuitive appeal, considers cash flows, and measures risk exposure. Its weaknesses include lack of linkage to the wealth maximization goal, failure to consider time value explicitly, and the fact that it ignores cash flows that occur after the payback period.
>
> NPV and IRR yield the same accept–reject decisions, but often provide conflicting rankings.
>
> **LG3** Use net present value profiles to compare the NPV and IRR techniques in light of conflicting rankings. A net present value profile graphs projects' NPVs for various discount rates. NPV profiles are useful for comparing projects, especially when NPV and IRR rankings conflict. On a purely theoretical basis, NPV is preferred over IRR because NPV assumes the more conservative reinvestment rate and does not exhibit the mathematical problem of multiple IRRs that often occurs when IRRs are calculated for nonconventional cash flows. In prac-

Self-Test Problems, keyed to the learning goals, give you an opportunity to strengthen your understanding of topics by doing a sample problem. Solutions are provided in Appendix B at the back of the book.

> **SELF-TEST PROBLEMS** (SOLUTIONS IN APPENDIX B)
>
> **LG2 LG5** ST4–1 **Future values for various compounding frequencies** Delia Martin has $10,000 that she can deposit in any of three savings accounts for a 3-year period. Bank A compounds interest on an annual basis, bank B compounds interest twice each year, and bank C compounds interest each quarter. All three banks have a stated annual interest rate of 4%.
> a. What amount would Ms. Martin have at the end of the third year, leaving all interest paid on deposit, in each bank?
> b. What *effective annual rate* (*EAR*) would she earn in each of the banks?
> c. On the basis of your findings in parts **a** and **b**, which bank should Ms. Martin deal with? Why?
> d. If a fourth bank (bank D), also with a 4% stated interest rate, compounds interest continuously, how much would Ms. Martin have at the end of the third year? Does this alternative change your recommendation in part c? Explain why or why not.

New! **Warm-Up Exercises** follow the Self-Test Problems. These short, numerical exercises, also keyed to the learning goals, give you practice in applying tools and techniques presented in the chapter.

> **WARM-UP EXERCISES**
>
> **LG2** E4–1 Assume a firm makes a $2,500 deposit into its money market account. If this account is currently paying 0.7%, (yes, that's right, less than 1%!), what will the account balance be after 1 year?
>
> **LG2 LG5** E4–2 If Bob and Judy combine their savings of $1,260 and $975, respectively, and deposit this amount into an account that pays 2% annual interest, compounded monthly, what will the account balance be after 4 years?
>
> **LG3** E4–3 Gabrielle just won $2.5 million in the state lottery. She is given the option of receiving a total of $1.3 million now or she can elect to be paid $100,000 at the end of each of the next 25 years. If Gabrielle can earn 5% annually on her investments, from a strict economic point of view which option should she take?

A comprehensive set of **Problems**, keyed to the learning goals, contains more than one problem for each concept, tool, or technique. A short descriptor at the beginning of the problem identifies the concept or technique. Difficulty identifiers appear in the margin next to each problem. Problems labeled as "Integrative" tie together related topics. Guideline answers to selected end-of-chapter problems appear in Appendix C.

> **PROBLEMS**
>
> **LG1** P4–1 **Using a time line** The financial manager at Starbuck Industries is considering
> BASIC an investment that requires an initial outlay of $25,000 and is expected to result in cash inflows of $3,000 at the end of year 1, $6,000 at the end of years 2 and 3, $10,000 at the end of year 4, $8,000 at the end of year 5, and $7,000 at the end of year 6.
> a. Draw and label a time line depicting the cash flows associated with Starbuck Industries' proposed investment.
> b. Use arrows to demonstrate, on the time line in part **a**, how compounding to find future value can be used to measure all cash flows at the end of year 6.
> c. Use arrows to demonstrate, on the time line in part **b**, how discounting to find present value can be used to measure all cash flows at time zero.
> d. Which of the approaches—future value or present value—do financial managers rely on most often for decision making? Why?
>
> P4–2 **Future value calculation** *Without referring to tables or to the preprogrammed function on your financial calculator*, use the basic formula for future value along with the given interest rate, *i*, and the number of periods, *n*, to calculate

New! The last item in the chapter problems is an **Ethics Problem**. The ethics problem gives you another opportunity to think about and apply ethics principles to financial situations.

> **LG6** P4–57 **ETHICS PROBLEM** A manager at a "check into cash" business (see *In*
> INTERMEDIATE *Practice* box on page 165) defends his business practice as simply "charging what the market will bear." "After all," says the manager, "we don't force people to come in the door." How would you respond to this ethical defense of the payday-advance business?

x

CHAPTER 4 CASE

Funding Jill Moran's Retirement Annuity

Sunrise Industries wishes to accumulate funds to provide a retirement annuity for its vice president of research, Jill Moran. Ms. Moran, by contract, will retire at the end of exactly 12 years. Upon retirement, she is entitled to receive an annual end-of-year payment of $42,000 for exactly 20 years. If she dies prior to the end of the 20-year period, the annual payments will pass to her heirs. During the 12-year "accumulation period" Sunrise wishes to fund the annuity by making equal, annual, end-of-year deposits into an account earning 9% interest. Once the 20-year "distribution period" begins, Sunrise plans to move the accumulated monies into an account earning a guaranteed 12% per year. At the end of the distribution period, the account balance will equal zero. Note that the first deposit will be made at the end of year 1 and that the first distribution payment will be received at the end of year 13.

Chapter Cases call for application of concepts and techniques to a more complex realistic situation than in the regular problems. These cases help strengthen practical application of financial tools and techniques.

SPREADSHEET EXERCISE

At the end of 2005, Uma Corporation was considering undertaking a major long-term project in an effort to remain competitive in its industry. The production and sales departments determined the potential annual cash flow savings that could accrue to the firm if it acts soon. Specifically, they estimate that a mixed stream of future cash flow savings will occur at the end of the years 2006 through 2011. The years 2012 through 2016 will see consecutive and equal cash flow savings at the end of each year. The firm estimates that its discount rate over the first 6 years will be 7%. The expected discount rate over the years 2012 through 2016 will be 11%.

The project managers will find the project acceptable if it results in present cash flow savings of at least $860,000. The following cash flow savings data are supplied to the finance department for analysis:

New! Every chapter includes a **Spreadsheet Exercise**. This exercise gives you an opportunity to use Excel® software to create one or more spreadsheets with which to analyze a financial problem. The spreadsheet to be created often is modeled on a table in the chapter or a spreadsheet template that can be viewed at the book's Web site.

WEB EXERCISE

Mortgage interest rates vary daily. Over a period of time, mortgage interest rates have followed definite trends based on federal interest rate policies and economic conditions. Historical interest rate information is available on the Web.

TO DO

a. For this Web exercise, direct your Internet browser to www.mbaa.org/, the home page of the Mortgage Bankers Association. View the current mortgage interest rates listed on the right side of the screen. Now direct your browser to the Mortgage and Market Data link at the top of the page, highlighting Interest rates. This page contains data for mortgage rates over the past decades. Study and comment on the levels of interest rates over the recent past. The Freddie Mac Average Rate for 30-Year Fixed Rate Mortgages, 1971—present (Monthly) link is a good place to start. How do interest rates recently—in the past year, for example—compare with those that prevailed during the 1970s, 1980s, and 1990s? Do you see any trends in the level of interest rates?

A **Web Exercise** at the end of the chapter links the chapter topic to a related site on the Internet and asks you to use information there to answer questions. These exercises capture your interest while teaching about finance-related sites.

Brief Contents

Detailed Contents — xv
Preface — xxvii
To the Student — xxxviii

Part 1 Introduction to Managerial Finance — 1

1. The Role and Environment of Managerial Finance — 2
2. Financial Statements and Analysis — 39
3. Cash Flow and Financial Planning — 91

Part 2 Important Financial Concepts — 135

4. Time Value of Money — 136
5. Risk and Return — 195
6. Interest Rates and Bond Valuation — 235
7. Stock Valuation — 274

Part 3 Long-Term Investment Decisions — 315

8. Capital Budgeting Cash Flows — 316
9. Capital Budgeting Techniques: Certainty and Risk — 352

Part 4 Long-Term Financial Decisions — 401

10. The Cost of Capital — 402
11. Leverage and Capital Structure — 437
12. Dividend Policy — 479

Part 5 Short-Term Financial Decisions — 509

13. Working Capital and Current Assets Management — 510
14. Current Liabilities Management — 549

Appendixes

A. Financial Tables — A-1
B. Solutions to Self-Test Problems — B-1
C. Answers to Selected End-of-Chapter Problems — C-1

Web Chapter: Financial Markets and Institutions
on the book's Web site www.aw-bc.com/gitman
Web Chapter: International Managerial Finance
on the book's Web site www.aw-bc.com/gitman

Glossary — G-1
Credits — CR-1
Index — I-1

Contents

Preface   xxvii
To the Student   xxxviii

Part 1

Introduction to Managerial Finance   1

Chapter 1
The Role and Environment of Managerial Finance   2

Finance and Business   3
What Is Finance?   3
Major Areas and Opportunities in Finance   3
Legal Forms of Business Organization   4
Why Study Managerial Finance?   7
Review Questions   8

The Managerial Finance Function   8
Organization of the Finance Function   8
Relationship to Economics   9
Relationship to Accounting   10
Primary Activities of the Financial Manager   11
Review Questions   11

Goal of the Firm   12
Maximize Profit?   12
Maximize Shareholder Wealth   13
Corporate Governance   14
The Role of Ethics   15
The Agency Issue   17
Review Questions   18

Financial Institutions and Markets   19
Financial Institutions   19
Financial Markets   20
The Relationship Between Institutions and Markets   20
The Money Market   20
The Capital Market   22
In Practice Focus on Practice: Warren Buffett—The Oracle of Omaha   25
Review Questions   25

Business Taxes   26
Ordinary Income   26
Capital Gains   29
Review Questions   30

Using This Text — 30
- Summary — 30
- Self-Test Problem — 32
- Warm-Up Exercises — 32
- Problems — 33

Chapter 2
Financial Statements and Analysis — 39

The Stockholders' Report — 40
- The Letter to Stockholders — 40
- The Four Key Financial Statements — 41
- Notes to the Financial Statements — 45
- Consolidating International Financial Statements — 46
- *In Practice* Focus on Ethics: Investors and Sox Declare War on Accounting Misdeeds — 47
- Review Questions — 47

Using Financial Ratios — 48
- Interested Parties — 48
- Types of Ratio Comparisons — 48
- Cautions About Using Ratio Analysis — 50
- Categories of Financial Ratios — 51
- Review Questions — 52

Liquidity Ratios — 52
- Current Ratio — 52
- Quick (Acid-Test) Ratio — 52
- Review Question — 53

Activity Ratios — 53
- Inventory Turnover — 54
- Average Collection Period — 54
- Average Payment Period — 55
- Total Asset Turnover — 55
- Review Question — 56

Debt Ratios — 56
- Debt Ratio — 57
- Times Interest Earned Ratio — 58

Chapter 1 Case: Assessing the Goal of Sports Products, Inc. — 36
Spreadsheet Exercise — 37
Web Exercise — 38

- Fixed-Payment Coverage Ratio — 58
- Review Questions — 59

Profitability Ratios — 59
- Common-Size Income Statements — 59
- Gross Profit Margin — 60
- Operating Profit Margin — 61
- Net Profit Margin — 61
- Earnings per Share (EPS) — 61
- Return on Total Assets (ROA) — 62
- Return on Common Equity (ROE) — 62
- Review Questions — 63

Market Ratios — 63
- Price/Earnings (P/E) Ratio — 63
- Market/Book (M/B) Ratio — 63
- Review Question — 64

A Complete Ratio Analysis — 64
- Summarizing All Ratios — 64
- DuPont System of Analysis — 68
- Review Questions — 71
- Summary — 71
- Self-Test Problems — 73
- Warm-Up Exercises — 74
- Problems — 75
- Chapter 2 Case: Assessing Martin Manufacturing's Current Financial Position — 86
- Spreadsheet Exercise — 88
- Web Exercise — 90

Chapter 3
Cash Flow and Financial Planning 91

Analyzing the Firm's Cash Flow 92
Depreciation 92
Developing the Statement of Cash Flows 95
Operating Cash Flow 98
Free Cash Flow 101
Review Questions 102

The Financial Planning Process 102
Long-Term (Strategic) Financial Plans 103
Short-Term (Operating) Financial Plans 103
Review Questions 104

Cash Planning: Cash Budgets 104
The Sales Forecast 104
Preparing the Cash Budget 105
In Practice Focus on Practice: Cash Forecasts: Easier Said Than Done 106
Evaluating the Cash Budget 110
Coping with Uncertainty in the Cash Budget 111
Review Questions 112

Profit Planning: Pro Forma Statements 112
Preceding Year's Financial Statements 113
Sales Forecast 113
Review Question 114

Preparing the Pro Forma Income Statement 114
Considering Types of Costs and Expenses 115
Review Questions 116

Preparing the Pro Forma Balance Sheet 117
Review Questions 119

Evaluation of Pro Forma Statements 119
Review Questions 119
Summary 120
Self-Test Problems 121
Warm-Up Exercises 123
Problems 124
Chapter 3 Case: Preparing Martin Manufacturing's 2007 Pro Forma Financial Statements 131
Spreadsheet Exercise 132
Web Exercise 133

Part 2

Important Financial Concepts 135

Chapter 4
Time Value of Money 136

The Role of Time Value in Finance 137
Future Value Versus Present Value 137
Computational Tools 138
Basic Patterns of Cash Flow 140
Review Questions 141

Single Amounts 141
Future Value of a Single Amount 141
Present Value of a Single Amount 145
Comparing Present Value and Future Value 147
Review Questions 148

Annuities 148
Types of Annuities 149
Finding the Future Value of an Ordinary Annuity 150
Finding the Present Value of an Ordinary Annuity 151
Finding the Present Value of a Perpetuity 153
Review Questions 154

Mixed Streams 154
Future Value of a Mixed Stream 154
Present Value of a Mixed Stream 156
Review Question 158

Compounding Interest More Frequently Than Annually 158
Semiannual Compounding 158
Quarterly Compounding 159
A General Equation for Compounding More Frequently Than Annually 160
Using Computational Tools for Compounding More Frequently Than Annually 161
Continuous Compounding 162
Nominal and Effective Annual Rates of Interest 163
Review Questions 164
In Practice Focus on Ethics: How Fair Is "Check into Cash"? 165

Special Applications of Time Value 165
Determining Deposits Needed to Accumulate a Future Sum 166
Loan Amortization 167
Finding Interest or Growth Rates 168
Finding an Unknown Number of Periods 171
Review Questions 172

Summary 173
Self-Test Problems 175
Warm-Up Exercises 176
Problems 177
Chapter 4 Case: Funding Jill Moran's Retirement Annuity 192
Spreadsheet Exercise 192
Web Exercise 193

Chapter 5
Risk and Return — 195

Risk and Return Fundamentals — 196
Risk Defined — 196
Return Defined — 196
Risk Aversion — 198
Review Questions — 199

Risk of a Single Asset — 199
Risk Assessment — 199
Risk Measurement — 201
Review Questions — 205

Risk of a Portfolio — 205
Correlation — 205
Diversification — 206
Correlation, Diversification, Risk, and Return — 208
International Diversification — 209
In Practice Global Focus: An International Flavor to Risk Reduction — 210
Review Questions — 211

Risk and Return: The Capital Asset Pricing Model (CAPM) — 211
Types of Risk — 211
The Model: CAPM — 212
Review Questions — 218
Summary — 219
Self-Test Problems — 221
Warm-Up Exercises — 222
Problems — 223
Chapter 5 Case: Analyzing Risk and Return on Chargers Products' Investments — 232
Spreadsheet Exercise — 233
Web Exercise — 234

Chapter 6
Interest Rates and Bond Valuation — 235

Interest Rates and Required Returns — 236
Interest Rate Fundamentals — 236
Term Structure of Interest Rates — 238
Risk Premiums: Issuer and Issue Characteristics — 240
Review Questions — 241

Corporate Bonds — 242
Legal Aspects of Corporate Bonds — 242
Cost of Bonds to the Issuer — 243
General Features of a Bond Issue — 244
Interpreting Bond Quotations — 245
Bond Ratings — 246
In Practice Focus on Ethics: Can We Trust the Bond Raters? — 247
Popular Types of Bonds — 247
International Bond Issues — 248
Review Questions — 250

Valuation Fundamentals — 250
Key Inputs — 250
The Basic Valuation Model — 251
Review Questions — 253

Bond Valuation — 253
Bond Fundamentals — 253
Basic Bond Valuation — 253
Bond Value Behavior — 255

Yield to Maturity (YTM)	258	Problems	265
Semiannual Interest and Bond Values	260	Chapter 6 Case: Evaluating Annie Hegg's Proposed Investment in Atilier Industries Bonds	271
Review Questions	261		
Summary	262		
Self-Test Problems	264	Spreadsheet Exercise	272
Warm-Up Exercises	264	Web Exercise	273

Chapter 7
Stock Valuation 274

Differences Between Debt and Equity Capital 275
Voice in Management 275
Claims on Income and Assets 275
Maturity 276
Tax Treatment 276
Review Question 276

Common and Preferred Stock 276
Common Stock 277
Preferred Stock 280
Issuing Common Stock 282
Interpreting Stock Quotations 286
Review Questions 288

Common Stock Valuation 288
In Practice Focus on Ethics: Do Investors Now Require a "Credibility Premium"? 289
Market Efficiency 289
The Basic Stock Valuation Equation 291
Free Cash Flow Valuation Model 294

Other Approaches to Common Stock Valuation 296
Review Questions 298

Decision Making and Common Stock Value 298
Changes in Expected Return 298
Changes in Risk 299
Combined Effect 300
Review Questions 300
Summary 300
Self-Test Problems 303
Warm-Up Exercises 303
Problems 304
Chapter 7 Case: Assessing the Impact of Suarez Manufacturing's Proposed Risky Investment on Its Stock Value 311
Spreadsheet Exercise 312
Web Exercise 313

Part 3

Long-Term Investment Decisions 315

Chapter 8
Capital Budgeting Cash Flows 316

The Capital Budgeting Decision Process 317
Motives for Capital Expenditure 317
Steps in the Process 317
Basic Terminology 318
Review Questions 320

The Relevant Cash Flows 321
In Practice Focus on Ethics: How Accurate Are Cash Flows? 321
Major Cash Flow Components 322
Expansion Versus Replacement Decisions 322
Sunk Costs and Opportunity Costs 323
International Capital Budgeting and Long-Term Investments 324
Review Questions 324

Finding the Initial Investment 325
Installed Cost of a New Asset 325
After-Tax Proceeds from Sale of Old Asset 326
Change in Net Working Capital 328
Calculating the Initial Investment 329
Review Questions 330

Finding the Operating Cash Inflows 330
Interpreting the Term *After-Tax* 330
Interpreting the Term *Cash Inflows* 331
Interpreting the Term *Incremental* 332
Review Questions 334

Finding the Terminal Cash Flow 334
Proceeds from Sale of Assets 335
Taxes on Sale of Assets 335
Change in Net Working Capital 335
Review Question 336

Summarizing the Relevant Cash Flows 337
Review Question 337
Summary 337
Self-Test Problems 339
Warm-Up Exercises 340
Problems 340
Chapter 8 Case: Developing Relevant Cash Flows for Clark Upholstery Company's Machine Renewal or Replacement Decision 349
Spreadsheet Exercise 350
Web Exercise 351

Chapter 9
Capital Budgeting Techniques: Certainty and Risk 352

Capital Budgeting Techniques 353
Bennet Company's Relevant Cash Flows 353
Payback Period 354
Net Present Value (NPV) 357
Internal Rate of Return (IRR) 359
Review Questions 362

Comparing NPV and IRR Techniques 362
Net Present Value Profiles 362
Conflicting Rankings 363
Which Approach Is Better? 364
Review Questions 365

Additional Considerations: Real Options and Capital Rationing 366
Recognizing Real Options 366
Choosing Projects Under Capital Rationing 368
Review Questions 370

Behavioral Approaches for Dealing with Risk 370
Sensitivity and Scenario Analysis 371
Decision Trees 372
Simulation 372
International Risk Considerations 373
Review Questions 375

Risk-Adjusted Discount Rates 375
Determining Risk-Adjusted Discount Rates (RADRs) 376
In Practice Focus on Ethics: Warren Buffett Versus California Earthquake Authority 377
RADRs in Practice 379
Review Questions 380
Summary 381
Self-Test Problems 383
Warm-Up Exercises 384
Problems 386
Chapter 9 Case: Making Norwich Tool's Lathe Investment Decision 397
Spreadsheet Exercise 398
Web Exercise 399

Long-Term Financial Decisions 401

Chapter 10
The Cost of Capital 402

An Overview of the Cost of Capital 403
Some Key Assumptions 403
In Practice Focus on Ethics: Creative Accounting and Cost of Capital at WorldCom 404
The Basic Concept 404
Specific Sources of Capital 405
Review Questions 406

The Cost of Long-Term Debt 407
Net Proceeds 407
Before-Tax Cost of Debt 407
After-Tax Cost of Debt 410
Review Questions 410

The Cost of Preferred Stock — 410
Preferred Stock Dividends — 410
Calculating the Cost of Preferred Stock — 411
Review Question — 411

The Cost of Common Stock — 411
Finding the Cost of Common Stock Equity — 411
The Cost of Retained Earnings — 413
The Cost of New Issues of Common Stock — 414
Review Questions — 415

The Weighted Average Cost of Capital — 415
Calculating the Weighted Average Cost of Capital (WACC) — 415
Weighting Schemes — 416
Economic Value Added (EVA®) — 417
Review Questions — 418

The Marginal Cost and Investment Decisions — 418
The Weighted Marginal Cost of Capital (WMCC) — 418
The Investment Opportunities Schedule (IOS) — 421
Using the WMCC and IOS to Make Financing/Investment Decisions — 421
Review Questions — 423
Summary — 423
Self-Test Problem — 425
Warm-Up Exercises — 426
Problems — 427
Chapter 10 Case: Making Star Products' Financing/Investment Decision — 433
Spreadsheet Exercise — 435
Web Exercise — 436

Chapter 11
Leverage and Capital Structure — 437

Leverage — 438
Breakeven Analysis — 439
Operating Leverage — 442
In Practice Focus on Practice: Adobe's Operating Leverage — 445
Financial Leverage — 446
Total Leverage — 448
Review Questions — 451

The Firm's Capital Structure — 451
Types of Capital — 451
External Assessment of Capital Structure — 452
Capital Structure of Non-U.S. Firms — 452
Capital Structure Theory — 454
The Optimal Capital Structure — 457
Review Questions — 459

The EBIT–EPS Approach to Capital Structure — 459
Presenting a Financing Plan Graphically — 459
Comparing Alternative Capital Structures — 461
Considering Risk in EBIT–EPS Analysis — 462
The Basic Shortcoming of EBIT–EPS Analysis — 463
Review Question — 464

Choosing the Optimal Capital Structure — 464
Linkage — 464
Estimating Value — 465
Maximizing Value Versus Maximizing EPS — 465
Some Other Important Considerations — 466
Review Questions — 466

Summary	467	Chapter 11 Case: Evaluating McGraw Industries' Capital Structure	476
Self-Test Problems	469	Spreadsheet Exercise	477
Warm-Up Exercises	470	Web Exercise	478
Problems	471		

Chapter 12
Dividend Policy — 479

Dividend Fundamentals — 480
Cash Dividend Payment Procedures — 480
Tax Treatment of Dividends — 482
Dividend Reinvestment Plans — 482
Review Questions — 482

The Relevance of Dividend Policy — 483
The Residual Theory of Dividends — 483
Arguments for Dividend Irrelevance — 485
Arguments for Dividend Relevance — 486
Review Questions — 486

Factors Affecting Dividend Policy — 486
Legal Constraints — 487
Contractual Constraints — 488
Internal Constraints — 488
Growth Prospects — 488
Owner Considerations — 488
In Practice Focus on Ethics: Were Ford Managers Hoarding Cash? — 489
Market Considerations — 490
Review Question — 490

Types of Dividend Policies — 490
Constant-Payout-Ratio Dividend Policy — 491
Regular Dividend Policy — 491
Low-Regular-and-Extra Dividend Policy — 492
Review Question — 493

Other Forms of Dividends — 493
Stock Dividends — 493
Stock Splits — 495
Stock Repurchases — 496
Review Questions — 497
Summary — 498
Self-Test Problem — 499
Warm-Up Exercises — 500
Problems — 501
Chapter 12 Case: Establishing General Access Company's Dividend Policy and Initial Dividend — 506
Spreadsheet Exercise — 507
Web Exercise — 508

Part 5

Short-Term Financial Decisions 509

Chapter 13
Working Capital and Current Assets Management 510

Net Working Capital Fundamentals 511
Net Working Capital 511
The Tradeoff Between Profitability and Risk 512
Review Questions 513

The Cash Conversion Cycle 514
Calculating the Cash Conversion Cycle 514
Funding Requirements of the Cash Conversion Cycle 515
Strategies for Managing the Cash Conversion Cycle 518
Review Questions 518

Inventory Management 518
Differing Viewpoints About Inventory Level 519
Common Techniques for Managing Inventory 519
In Practice Focus on Practice: RFID: The Wave of the Future 523
International Inventory Management 523
Review Questions 524

Accounts Receivable Management 524
Credit Selection and Standards 524
Credit Terms 529
Credit Monitoring 531
Review Questions 533

Management of Receipts and Disbursements 534
Float 534
Speeding Up Collections 534
Slowing Down Payments 535
Cash Concentration 535
Zero-Balance Accounts 536
Investing in Marketable Securities 537
Review Questions 537

Summary 539

Self-Test Problems 540

Warm-Up Exercises 541

Problems 542

Chapter 13 Case: Assessing Roche Publishing Company's Cash Management Efficiency 546

Spreadsheet Exercise 547

Web Exercise 548

Chapter 14
Current Liabilities Management 549

Spontaneous Liabilities 550
Accounts Payable Management 550
In Practice Focus on Ethics: Amazon Stays Ethical to Avoid Biting the Hands that Feed It 554
Accruals 554
Review Questions 555

Unsecured Sources of Short-Term Loans 555
Bank Loans 555
Commercial Paper 560
International Loans 561
Review Questions 562

Secured Sources of Short-Term Loans 562
Characteristics of Secured Short-Term Loans 563
The Use of Accounts Receivable as Collateral 564
The Use of Inventory as Collateral 566
Review Questions 567
Summary 568
Self-Test Problem 571
Warm-Up Exercises 572
Problems 572
Chapter 14 Case: Selecting Kanton Company's Financing Strategy and Unsecured Short-Term Borrowing Arrangement 578
Spreadsheet Exercise 579
Web Exercise 580

Appendixes
A Financial Tables A-1
B Solutions to Self-Test Problems B-1
C Answers to Selected End-of-Chapter Problems C-1

Web Chapter: Financial Markets and Institutions on the book's Web site
www.aw-bc.com/gitman
Web Chapter: International Managerial Finance on the book's Web site
www.aw-bc.com/gitman

Glossary G-1
Credits CR-1
Index I-1

Preface

The desire to write *Principles of Managerial Finance* came out of my experience teaching the introductory managerial finance course early in my academic career. When I began teaching full time, I was not very far removed from my own undergraduate studies and therefore could appreciate the difficulties some of my students were having with the textbook we used. They wanted a book that spoke to them in plain English. They wanted a book that tied concepts to reality. And they wanted not just description, but demonstration of concepts, tools, and techniques. Recognizing that, I decided that I would write an introductory finance text that would effectively resolve these concerns.

Three years later, in 1976, the first edition of *Principles* was published. Its initial market success was driven by its conversational tone, wide use of examples set off in the text, and coverage of short-term finance. Building on these strengths, over several editions, numerous translations, and more than half a million U.S. users, I've continued to listen carefully to feedback from both professors and students, from adopters, nonadopters, and practitioners. My thanks to all of those people, without whose input I could not have as effectively refined and improved the text over the years.

As before, my goal in the fourth Brief Edition of *Principles* is to satisfy the needs of professors and students. Like the first edition, the fourth still uses plain English, ties concepts to reality, and demonstrates concepts, tools, and techniques. It incorporates a proven learning system, which integrates pedagogy with concepts and practical applications. It concentrates on the concepts, techniques, and practices that are needed to make keen financial decisions in an increasingly competitive business environment. The strong pedagogy and generous use of examples make the text an easily accessible resource for long-distance learning and self-study programs.

The fourth Brief Edition has been specifically designed to fit the one-term financial management course. It is intended for those professors who want to provide students with a thorough introduction to corporate finance that focuses on the fundamental concepts, tools, techniques, and practices of financial management. I've "right-sized" the book for the one-term course by eliminating from my longer *Principles* book topics that will be covered in subsequent courses. Specifically, I've eliminated the chapter on corporate mergers and the separate chapter on international managerial finance, although discussions and examples of international finance appear in appropriate chapter discussions throughout. In addition, the chapter from the longer book that contains discussion of hybrid and derivative securities is not included in this Brief Edition. Also, coverage of capital budgeting in the Brief Edition is presented in two chapters, compared to three chapters in the longer book. Finally, presentation of many topics has been streamlined throughout. The resulting presentation thoroughly covers all basic topics, yet is four chapters and about 250 pages shorter than *Principles of Managerial Finance*, Eleventh Edition, upon which it is based.

The text's organization, described in detail in the following pages, conceptually links the firm's actions and its value as determined in the securities market. Each major decision area is presented in terms of both risk and return factors and their potential impact on the owners' wealth. A "Focus on Value" element at the end of each chapter helps reinforce the student's understanding of the link between the financial manager's actions and share value.

Although the text is sequential, instructors can assign almost any chapter as a self-contained unit. This flexibility enables instructors to customize the text to various teaching strategies and course lengths.

We live in a world in which both international and ethical considerations cannot be divorced from the study of business in general and finance in particular. As in prior editions, discussions of international dimensions of chapter topics are integrated throughout the book. A marginal icon of a globe highlights such discussions. In each chapter in which international coverage is included, the international material is integrated into learning goals and end-of-chapter materials. In addition, for those who want to spend more time addressing the topic, a separate chapter on international finance is available at the book's Web site, www.aw-bc.com/gitman.

The business failures and scandals of recent years, and attempts to forestall or fix such problems by means of the Sarbanes-Oxley Act of 2002, have renewed the need for the study and application of ethics in business. Therefore, in the fourth Brief Edition, we have included in nine chapters an *In Practice* box that focuses on ethical issues. These boxes address some of the most significant ethical issues that financial managers face as they attempt to sail the sometimes-rough waters of the business world.

In organizing each chapter, I have adhered to a managerial decision-making perspective, relating decisions to the firm's overall goal of wealth maximization. Once a particular concept has been developed, its application is illustrated by an example. These examples demonstrate, and solidify in the student's thought, financial decision-making considerations and their consequences.

In response to suggestions of the book's users and reviewers, I have added to the already rich homework assignments two new types of assignment materials: short, numerical Warm-Up Exercises, and a Spreadsheet Exercise. In addition, a Group Exercise for each chapter is available at the book's Web site, www.aw-bc.com/gitman. These new materials expand and enrich the opportunities for instructors and students in today's classroom environment.

From classroom to boardroom, the fourth Brief Edition of *Principles of Managerial Finance* can help users get to where they want to be. I hope that your review of this new edition confirms my belief that it is better than ever—more relevant, more accurate, and more effective than its prior edition. I hope you agree that *Principles of Managerial Finance, Brief,* Fourth Edition, meets your needs for the one-term managerial finance course.

Revised Content

As we made plans to publish the fourth Brief Edition, we carefully assessed market feedback about content changes that would better meet the needs of professors teaching the course. As a result, the chapter sequence remains the same as in the previous edition. A number of new topics have been added at appropriate places, and existing discussions have been updated and/or smoothed. We now use a 365-day year for calculations throughout the text.

For those instructors who expressed a desire to assign an entire chapter on financial institutions and markets as a foundational structure in the managerial finance course, we have made available online at the book's Web site, www.aw-bc.com/gitman, a complete chapter on institutions and markets. A chapter on international managerial finance is also available at the Web site.

The following list details the chapter-by-chapter content changes in the new edition.

Chapter 1   The Role and Environment of Managerial Finance
- Expanded discussion of the role of the corporate board of directors.
- New section on corporate governance, including the influence of individual and institutional investors and discussion of the *Sarbanes-Oxley Act of 2002*.
- Revision of business taxation discussion to reflect the *Jobs and Growth Tax Relief Reconciliation Act of 2003*.
- New *In Practice* box on Warren Buffett, the "Oracle of Omaha."
- Discussion of EVA® moved out of Chapter 1 (and in to Chapter 10).

Chapter 2   Financial Statements and Analysis
- New text discussion on the Public Company Accounting Oversight Board (PCAOB).
- New *In Practice* ethics box on how investors and the Sarbanes-Oxley Act have declared war on accounting misdeeds.

Chapter 3   Cash Flow and Financial Planning
- New text explanation of the classification of decreases and increases in cash balances.
- New discussion and example of net operating profits after taxes (NOPAT) and its role in calculating operating cash flow (OCF) and free cash flow (FCF).
- Revised *In Practice* box on some real-world aspects of cash forecasting.

Chapter 4   Time Value of Money
- New *In Practice* ethics box about interest rates involved in the "payday loan" business.

Chapter 5   Risk and Return
- New *In Practice* box about reducing risk through international diversification.

Chapter 6 Interest Rates and Bond Valuation
- New *In Practice* ethics box about the trustworthiness of bond ratings agencies.
- Spreadsheet examples added for calculations of basic bond valuation, bond values at differing required returns, yield to maturity, and bond value with semiannual interest.

Chapter 7 Stock Valuation
- New *In Practice* ethics box about whether investors require a "credibility premium."
- New text section on behavioral finance.

Chapter 8 Capital Budgeting Cash Flows
- New *In Practice* ethics box about the accuracy of cash flow estimates in practice.
- Streamlined discussion of the tax calculation necessary to find initial investment and terminal value.
- Revision of the calculation of operating cash inflows for consistency with net operating profits after taxes (NOPAT) and operating cash flow (OCF) discussions introduced in Chapter 3.

Chapter 9 Capital Budgeting Techniques: Certainty and Risk
- New text section on multiple IRRs.
- New *In Practice* ethics box about incorrect risk evaluation by the California Earthquake Authority.

Chapter 10 The Cost of Capital
- New *In Practice* ethics box about "creative accounting" and the cost of capital at WorldCom.
- Spreadsheet example added for calculation of the before-tax cost of debt of a corporate bond.
- New discussion of economic value added (EVA®).

Chapter 11 Leverage and Capital Structure
- Revised *In Practice* box about operating leverage at Adobe Systems.
- Linkage of net operating profits after taxes (NOPAT), introduced in Chapter 3, with finding optimal capital structure.

Chapter 12 Dividend Policy
- New figure to illustrate the dividend-payment time line.
- New text discussion of the tax treatment of dividends, based on the *Jobs and Growth Tax Relief Reconciliation Act of 2003*.
- Revised *In Practice* ethics box about how much cash managers should retain for growth prospects.

Chapter 13 Working Capital and Current Assets Management

- New *In Practice* box on the use of radio frequency indentification (RFID) technology to monitor inventory and supply chain operations.
- Revised and expanded section on MRP systems to include MRPII and ERP systems.
- Revised section on aging of accounts receivable, including a new example of an aging schedule.

Chapter 14 Current Liabilities Management

- Revised *In Practice* ethics box on the ethical issues of stretching accounts payable.

Supplements to the Fourth Edition

The *PMF* Teaching/Learning System includes a variety of useful supplements for teachers and for students.

Teaching Tools for Instructors

The key teaching tools available to instructors are the *Instructor's Manual*, testing materials, and *PowerPoint Lecture Presentations*.

Instructor's Manual Compiled by Frederick P. Schadler, East Carolina University. This comprehensive resource pulls together the teaching tools so that instructors can use the textbook easily and effectively in the classroom. Each chapter provides an overview of key topics and detailed answers and solutions to all review questions, Warm-Up Exercises, end-of-chapter problems, and chapter cases, plus suggested answers to all critical thinking questions in boxes, Ethics Problems, Group Exercises on the Web, and Web Exercises. At the end of the manual are practice quizzes and solutions. The complete Instructor's Manual, including Spreadsheet Exercises, is available online from the catalogue for this textbook (found at www.aw-bc.com) and on the Instructor's Resource CD-ROM.

Testing Material Created by Daniel J. Borgia, Florida Gulf Coast University. Thoroughly revised to accommodate changes in the text, the Test Bank consists of a mix of true/false, multiple-choice, and essay questions. Each test question includes identifiers for type of question, skill tested by learning goal, level of difficulty, and—new to this edition—key topic tested plus, where appropriate, the formula(s) or equation(s) used in deriving the answer. The Test Bank is available in both printed and electronic formats, including Windows or Macintosh *TestGen* files and Microsoft Word files. The Test Bank and TestGen are available online at www.aw-bc.com and on the Instructor's Resource CD-ROM.

Instructors can download the *TestGen* version of the Test Bank into *QuizMaster,* an online testing program for Windows and Macintosh that enables users to conduct timed or untimed exams at computer workstations. After completing tests, students can see their scores and view or print a diagnostic report of those topics or objectives requiring more attention. When installed on a local area network, *QuizMaster* allows instructors to save the scores on disk, print study diagnoses, and monitor progress of students individually or by class section and by all sections of the course.

PowerPoint Lecture Presentation Created by Daniel J. Borgia, Florida Gulf Coast University. Available for Windows or Macintosh on the Instructor's

Resource CD-ROM, this presentation combines lecture notes with art from the textbook. The PowerPoint Lecture Presentation is available online at www.aw-bc.com and on the Instructor's Resource CD-ROM.

Instructor's Resource CD-ROM Electronic files of the *Instructor's Manual, Test Bank*, and *PowerPoint Lecture Presentation* are available on one convenient CD-ROM, compatible with both Windows and Macintosh computers. The electronic versions allow instructors to customize the support materials to their individual classroom needs. All the resources on the Instructor's Resource CD-ROM are also available online at www.aw-bc.com.

Learning Tools for Students

Beyond the book itself, students have access to several resources for success in this course: FinanceWorks, *Study Guide*, and the *Principles of Managerial Finance, Brief,* Fourth Edition Web site.

FinanceWorks Packaged with new copies of this text at no additional cost, the Student Access Kit for FinanceWorks opens the door to a powerful Web-based diagnostic testing and tutorial system designed specifically for the Gitman, *Principles of Managerial Finance* textbooks. With FinanceWorks, instructors can create, edit, and assign online homework, and test and track all student work in the online gradebook. FinanceWorks allows students to take practice tests correlated to the textbook and receive a customized study plan based on the test results. The problems in FinanceWorks are based on the even-numbered end-of-chapter problems. However, because the FinanceWorks problems have algorithmically generated values, no student will have the same homework as another, and there is an unlimited opportunity for practice and testing. Students get the help they need, when they need it, from the robust tutorial options, including "View an Example" and "Help Me Solve This," which breaks the problem into its steps and links to the relevant textbook page.

Students can use FinanceWorks with no instructor intervention. However, to take advantage of the full capabilities of FinanceWorks, including assigning homework and tracking student progress in the automated gradebook, instructors will want to set up their class. Please contact your local sales representative to request an Instructor Quick Start Guide for FinanceWorks. You can find your representative using the rep locator at www.aw-bc.com/replocator.

Study Guide Prepared by Stanley G. Eakins, East Carolina University. The *Study Guide* is an integral component of the *PMF* Learning System. It offers many tools for studying finance. Each chapter contains the following features: chapter summary enumerated by learning goals; topical chapter outline, also broken down by learning goals for quick review; sample problem solutions; study tips; a full sample exam with the answers at the end of the chapter; and a financial dictionary of key terms.

Principles of Managerial Finance, Brief, Fourth Edition Web Site The Web site to accompany this textbook, located at www.aw-bc.com/gitman, contains many additional resources. For each chapter on the Web site you will find

- eThemes of the Times: a collection of *New York Times* articles keyed to the chapter, along with review questions
- Web Cases, which ask students to use the Web to find information and solve finance problems
- Web Exercises from the textbook
- Spreadsheet templates
- Group Exercises
- Self-Assessment Quizzes
- Case Studies in Finance, updated by Michael Seiler of Hawaii Pacific University

In addition to the chapter resources, you will find

- Two new Web chapters: (1) "Financial Markets and Institutions," from the text *Introduction to Finance* by Lawrence J. Gitman and Jeff Madura, and (2) "International Managerial Finance," from *Principles of Managerial Finance*, Eleventh Edition, by Lawrence J. Gitman
- An online glossary, both as review flashcards and as a quick-reference document
- A Financial Calculator Guide
- Our Online Career Center

In addition to the Web site, the course content is available in CourseCompass™, Blackboard, and WebCT. The CourseCompass™ course also contains an electronic version of the text, including live Web Exercises and links to additional online resources. CourseCompass™ is a nationally hosted, dynamic, interactive online course management system powered by Blackboard, leaders in the development of Internet-based learning tools. This easy-to-use and customizable program enables professors to tailor content and functionality to meet individual course needs. To see a demo, visit www.coursecompass.com. Please contact your local sales representative for more information on obtaining course content in these various formats.

Acknowledgments

To My Colleagues, Friends, and Family

No textbook can consistently meet market needs without continual feedback from colleagues, students, practitioners, and members of the publishing team. Once again, I invite colleagues to relate their classroom experiences using this book and its package to me in care of the Acquisitions Editor in Finance, Addison-Wesley Publishing Company, 75 Arlington Street, Suite 300, Boston, Massachusetts 02116. Your constructive criticism will help me to continue to improve the textbook and its Teaching/Learning System still further.

Addison-Wesley and former publisher HarperCollins sought the advice of a great many excellent reviewers, all of whom strongly influenced various aspects of this book. The following individuals provided extremely thoughtful and useful comments for the preparation of the fourth edition:

Ronnie J. Clayton, *Jacksonville State University*
Mario A. Dipp, *San Diego State University, Imperial Valley Campus*
Linda U. Hadley, *Columbus State University*
Richard Harvey, *Fairmont State College*
Zahid Iqbal, *Texas Southern University*
Jim Keys, *Florida International University*
Balasundram Maniam, *Sam Houston State University*
Stanley Martin, *University of Colorado, Boulder*
Kiseok Nam, *University of Texas-Pan American*
Susanne Polley, *State University of New York, Cortland*
Joseph V. Stanford, *Bridgewater State College*
Alan Wong, *Indiana University Southeast*

My special thanks go to the following individuals who analyzed the manuscript in previous editions:

Saul W. Adelman
M. Fall Ainina
Gary A. Anderson
Ronald F. Anderson
James M. Andre
Gene L. Andrusco
Antonio Apap
David A. Arbeit
Allen Arkins
Saul H. Auslander
Peter W. Bacon
Richard E. Ball
Thomas Bankston
Alexander Barges
Charles Barngrover
Michael Becker
Scott Besley
Douglas S. Bible
Charles W. Blackwell
Russell L. Block
Calvin M. Boardman
Paul Bolster
Robert J. Bondi
Jeffrey A. Born
Jerry D. Boswell
Denis O. Boudreaux
Kenneth J. Boudreaux
Wayne Boyet
Ron Braswell
Christopher Brown
William Brunsen
Samuel B. Bulmash
Francis E. Canda
Omer Carey
Patrick A. Casabona
Robert Chatfield
K. C. Chen
Roger G. Clarke
Terrence M. Clauretie
Mark Cockalingam
Thomas Cook
Maurice P. Corrigan
Mike Cudd
Donnie L. Daniel
Prabir Datta
Joel J. Dauten
Lee E. Davis
Richard F. DeMong

Peter A. DeVito
James P. D'Mello
R. Gordon Dippel
Carleton Donchess
Thomas W. Donohue
Shannon Donovan
Vincent R. Driscoll
Betty A. Driver
Lorna Dotts
David R. Durst
Dwayne O. Eberhardt
Ronald L. Ehresman
Ted Ellis
F. Barney English
Greg Filbeck
Ross A. Flaherty
Rich Fortin
Timothy J. Gallagher
George W. Gallinger
Gerald D. Gay
R. H. Gilmer
Anthony J. Giovino
Philip W. Glasgo
Jeffrey W. Glazer
Joel Gold
Ron B. Goldfarb
Dennis W. Goodwin
David A. Gordon
J. Charles Granicz
C. Ramon Griffin
Reynolds Griffith
Lewell F. Gunter
Melvin W. Harju
Phil Harrington
George F. Harris
George T. Harris
John D. Harris
R. Stevenson Hawkey
Roger G. Hehman
Harvey Heinowitz
Glenn Henderson
Russell H. Hereth
Kathleen T. Hevert
J. Lawrence Hexter
Douglas A. Hibbert
Roger P. Hill
Linda C. Hittle
James Hoban
Hugh A. Hobson
Keith Howe
Kenneth M. Huggins
Jerry G. Hunt
Mahmood Islam
James F. Jackson
Stanley Jacobs
Dale W. Janowsky
Jeannette R. Jesinger
Nalina Jeypalan
Timothy E. Johnson
Roger Juchau
Ashok K. Kapoor
Daniel J. Kaufman, Jr.
Joseph K. Kiely
Terrance E. Kingston
Thomas M. Krueger
Lawrence Kryzanowski
Harry R. Kuniansky
Richard E. La Near
William R. Lane
James Larsen
Rick LeCompte
B. E. Lee
Scott Lee
Michael A. Lenarcic
A. Joseph Lerro
Thomas J. Liesz
Alan Lines
Christopher K. Ma
James C. Ma
Dilip B. Madan
Judy Maese
James Mallet
Timothy A. Manuel
Brian Maris
Daniel S. Marrone
William H. Marsh
John F. Marshall
Linda J. Martin
Stanley A. Martin
Charles E. Maxwell
Timothy Hoyt
McCaughey
Jay Meiselman
Vincent A. Mercurio
Joseph Messina
John B. Mitchell
Daniel F. Mohan
Charles Mohundro
Gene P. Morris
Edward A. Moses
Tarun K. Mukherjee
William T. Murphy
Randy Myers
Lance Nail
Donald A. Nast
G. Newbould
Charles Ngassam
Gary Noreiko
Dennis T. Officer
Kathleen J. Oldfather
Kathleen F. Oppenheimer
Richard M. Osborne
Jerome S. Osteryoung
Prasad Padmanabahn
Roger R. Palmer
Don B. Panton
John Park
Ronda S. Paul
Bruce C. Payne
Gerald W. Perritt
Gladys E. Perry
Stanley Piascik
Gregory Pierce
Mary L. Piotrowski
D. Anthony Plath
Jerry B. Poe
Gerald A. Pogue
Ronald S. Pretekin
Fran Quinn
Rich Ravichandran
David Rayone
Walter J. Reinhart
Jack H. Reubens
Benedicte Reyes
William B. Riley, Jr.
Ron Rizzuto
Gayle A. Russell
Patricia A. Ryan
Murray Sabrin
Kanwal S. Sachedeva
R. Daniel Sadlier
Hadi Salavitabar
Gary Sanger
William L. Sartoris
Carl J. Schwendiman
Carl Schweser
Jim Scott
John W. Settle
Richard A. Shick
A. M. Sibley
Surendra S. Singhvi
Stacy Sirmans
Barry D. Smith

Gerald Smolen
Ira Smolowitz
Jean Snavely
Joseph V. Stanford
John A. Stocker
Lester B. Strickler
Elizabeth Strock
Sankar Sundarrajan
Philip R. Swensen
S. Tabriztchi
John C. Talbott
Gary Tallman
Harry Tamule
Richard W. Taylor
Rolf K. Tedefalk
Richard Teweles
Kenneth J. Thygerson
Robert D. Tollen
Emery A. Trahan
Pieter A. Vandenberg
Nikhil P. Varaiya
Oscar Varela
Kenneth J. Venuto
James A. Verbrugge
Ronald P. Volpe
John M. Wachowicz, Jr.
William H. Weber III
Herbert Weinraub
Jonathan B. Welch
Grant J. Wells
Larry R. White
Peter Wichert
C. Don Wiggins
Howard A. Williams
Richard E. Williams
Glenn A. Wilt, Jr.
Bernard J. Winger
Tony R. Wingler
I. R. Woods
John C. Woods
Robert J. Wright
Richard H. Yanow
Seung J. Yoon
Charles W. Young
Philip J. Young
Joe W. Zeman
J. Kenton Zumwalt
John T. Zeitlow
Tom Zwirlein

My special thanks go to all members of the book team whose vision, creativity, and ongoing support helped me to engineer the elements of the Teaching/Learning System: to Michael J. Woodworth of Purdue University for the *In Practice: Focus on Practice* boxes; to John Zietlow of Lee University and Edward Zajicek of Winston-Salem State University for the *In Practice: Focus on Ethics* boxes; to William Mosher of Clark University for the Warm-Up Exercises, Web Exercises, and online Group Exercises; to Steven Lifland of High Point University for the new in-chapter spreadsheet examples and the end-of-chapter Spreadsheet Exercises; to Bernard W. Weinrich of St. Louis Community College, Forest Park Campus, for preparing the marginal annotations; to Daniel J. Borgia of Florida Gulf Coast University for revising the *Test Banks* and the *PowerPoint Lecture Presentation*; to Fred Schadler of East Carolina University for updating the *Instructor's Manual;* to Stan Eakins of East Carolina University for revising the *Study Guide;* and to Michael Seiler of Hawaii Pacific University for updating the Case Studies in Finance on the book's Web site. I'm pleased by and proud of all their efforts.

A hearty round of applause also goes to the publishing team assembled by Addison-Wesley—including Donna Battista, Mary Clare McEwing, Gina Kolenda, Nancy Fenton, Bethany Tidd, Dana Weightman, Jason Miranda, Kirsten Dickerson, Stephen Frail, and others who worked on the book—for the inspiration and the perspiration that define teamwork. A standing ovation is due Ann Torbert, whose development expertise contributed to the book's standard of excellence. An equally resounding ovation is due Nancy Freihofer and all the people at Thompson Steele, Inc., whose dedication, care, and hard work nutured this book into existence. Also, special thanks to the formidable Addison-Wesley sales force in finance, whose ongoing efforts keep the business fun!

Finally, and most important, many thanks to my wife, Robin, and to our children, Zachary and Jessica, for patiently providing support, understanding, and good humor throughout the revision process. To them, I will be forever grateful.

Lawrence J. Gitman
La Jolla, California

To the Student

Because you have a good many options for getting your assigned reading materials, I appreciate your choosing this textbook as the best means for learning. You should not be disappointed. When I wrote the first edition of this book, I was not far removed from my undergraduate studies and therefore set out to write a book that would meet the needs of students. Through its various editions over the years, I have been careful to maintain that student focus.

In the textbook I have put together an effective learning system. It integrates a variety of learning tools with the concepts, tools, techniques, and practical applications you'll need to learn about managerial finance. We have carefully listened to the compliments and complaints of students and of professors who have used earlier editions of this textbook in their coursework, and we have worked hard to present the most important concepts and practices of managerial finance in a clear and interesting way.

This book is loaded with features designed to motivate your study of finance and to help you learn the course material. For an overview and explanation of those features, go to pages vii–xi ("Gitman's Proven Teaching/Learning System"). The page views and descriptions there will walk you through the features included in the book.

Some words of advice about a few specific features: First, pay attention to the learning goals, which will help you focus attention on what material you need to learn, where you can find it in the chapter, and whether you've mastered it by the end of the chapter.

Second, at the end of each major text section are Review Questions. You may be tempted to rush past those questions, but try to resist doing so. Pausing briefly to test your understanding of the key concepts, tools, techniques, and practices in the section you've just read will help you cement your understanding of that material. Give yourself an honest assessment of whether you've understood what you've read. If you haven't, go back (even briefly) and review anything that seemed unclear.

Third, look for (or make) opportunities to talk with classmates or friends about what you're reading and learning in the course. Being able to talk about the concepts and techniques of finance demonstrates how much you've learned, uncovers things you haven't yet understood fully, and gives you valuable practice for class and (eventually) the business world. While you're talking, don't neglect to discuss the issues raised in the *Focus on Ethics* boxes in the book, which look at some of the types of opportunities to do right (or not) that people in business sometimes face.

Packaged with new copies of the text at no additional cost, the Student Access Kit for FinanceWorks opens the door to a powerful Web-based diagnostic testing and tutorial system designed specifically for this text. FinanceWorks allows you to take practice tests correlated to the textbook and receive a customized study plan based on your results. The problems in FinanceWorks are based on the even-numbered end-of-chapter problems. However, because the FinanceWorks problems have algorithmically generated values, no student will have the same homework as another. Thus there is an unlimited opportunity for practice and testing. You will get the help you need, when you need it, from the robust tutorial options, including "View an Example" and "Help Me Solve This," which breaks the problem into steps and links to the relevant textbook page.

Given today's rapidly changing technology, who knows what might be available next? We are striving to keep pace with your needs and interests, and want to hear your ideas for improving the teaching and learning of finance. Please feel free to share your ideas with us by e-mailing finance@aw-bc.com.

I wish you all the best in this course, and in your academic and professional careers.

Lawrence J. Gitman
San Diego State University

Part 1

Introduction to Managerial Finance

Chapter 1
The Role and Environment of Managerial Finance

Chapter 2
Financial Statements and Analysis

Chapter 3
Cash Flow and Financial Planning

Chapter 1

The Role and Environment of Managerial Finance

LEARNING GOALS

LG1 Define *finance*, its major areas and opportunities, and the legal forms of business organization.

LG2 Describe the managerial finance function and its relationship to economics and accounting.

LG3 Identify the primary activities of the financial manager.

LG4 Explain the goal of the firm, corporate governance, the role of ethics, and the agency issue.

LG5 Understand financial institutions and markets, and the role they play in managerial finance.

LG6 Discuss business taxes and their importance in financial decisions.

Across the Disciplines Why This Chapter Matters to You

Accounting: You need to understand the relationships between the firm's accounting and finance functions; how the financial statements you prepare will be used for making investment and financing decisions; ethical behavior by those responsible for a firm's funds; what agency costs are and why the firm must bear them; and how to calculate the tax effects of proposed transactions.

Information systems: You need to understand the organization of the firm; why finance personnel require both historical and projected data to support investment and financing decisions; and what data are necessary for determining the firm's tax liability.

Management: You need to understand the legal forms of business organization; the tasks that will be performed by finance personnel; the goal of the firm; the issue of management compensation; the role of ethics in the firm; the agency problem; and the firm's relationship to various financial institutions and markets.

Marketing: You need to understand how the activities you pursue will be affected by the finance function, such as the firm's cash and credit management policies; the role of ethics in promoting a sound corporate image; and the role the financial markets play in the firm's ability to raise capital for new projects.

Operations: You need to understand the organization of the firm and of the finance function in particular; why maximizing profit is not the main goal of the firm; the role of financial institutions and markets in financing the firm's production capacity; and the role of ethics and the agency problem.

CHAPTER 1   The Role and Environment of Managerial Finance

The field of finance directly affects the lives of every person and every organization. Many areas for study and a large number of career opportunities are available in finance. The purpose of this chapter is to acquaint you with the study of finance, the managerial finance function, and the goal of the firm, including corporate governance issues. The chapter also describes financial institutions and markets, and business taxation. Finance will affect your working life in whatever area of study you choose to concentrate.

Finance and Business

The field of finance is broad and dynamic. It directly affects the life of every person and of every organization. There are many areas and career opportunities in the field of finance. Basic principles of finance, such as those you will learn in this textbook, can be universally applied in business organizations of different types.

What Is Finance?

finance
The art and science of managing money.

Finance can be defined as the art and science of managing money. Virtually all individuals and organizations earn or raise money and spend or invest money. Finance is concerned with the process, institutions, markets, and instruments involved in the transfer of money among individuals, businesses, and governments.

Major Areas and Opportunities in Finance

The major areas of finance can be summarized by reviewing the career opportunities in finance. These opportunities can, for convenience, be divided into two broad areas: financial services and managerial finance.

Financial Services

financial services
The area of finance concerned with the design and delivery of advice and financial products to individuals, business, and government.

Financial services is the area of finance concerned with the design and delivery of advice and financial products to individuals, business, and government. It involves a variety of interesting career opportunities within the areas of banking and related institutions, personal financial planning, investments, real estate, and insurance. Career opportunities available in each of these areas are described at this textbook's Web site www.aw-bc.com/gitman.

Managerial Finance

managerial finance
Concerns the duties of the *financial manager* in the business firm.

financial manager
Actively manages the financial affairs of any type of business, whether financial or nonfinancial, private or public, large or small, profit-seeking or not-for-profit.

Managerial finance is concerned with the duties of the financial manager in the business firm. **Financial managers** actively manage the financial affairs of any type of businesses—financial and nonfinancial, private and public, large and small, profit-seeking and not-for-profit. They perform such varied financial tasks as planning, extending credit to customers, evaluating proposed large expenditures, and raising money to fund the firm's operations. In recent years, changing economic, competitive, and regulatory environments have increased the importance and complexity of the financial manager's duties. Today's financial manager is more actively involved in developing and implementing corporate strategies aimed at "growing the firm" and improving its competitive position. As a result, many top executives have come from the finance area.

 Another ongoing trend has been the globalization of business activity. U.S. corporations have dramatically increased their sales, purchases, investments, and fund raising in other countries, and foreign corporations have likewise increased their corresponding activities in the United States. These changes have increased the need for financial managers who can manage cash flows in different currencies and protect against the risks that naturally arise from international transactions. Although these changes make the managerial finance function more complex, they can lead to a more rewarding and fulfilling career.

Legal Forms of Business Organization

The three most common legal forms of business organization are the *sole proprietorship*, the *partnership*, and the *corporation*. Other specialized forms of business organization also exist. Sole proprietorships are the most numerous. However, corporations are overwhelmingly dominant with respect to business receipts and net profits. Corporations are given primary emphasis in this textbook.

Sole Proprietorships

sole proprietorship
A business owned by one person and operated for his or her own profit.

unlimited liability
The condition of a sole proprietorship (or general partnership) allowing the owner's total wealth to be taken to satisfy creditors.

A **sole proprietorship** is a business owned by one person who operates it for his or her own profit. About 75 percent of all business firms are sole proprietorships. The typical sole proprietorship is a small business, such as a bike shop, personal trainer, or plumber. The majority of sole proprietorships are found in the wholesale, retail, service, and construction industries.

Typically, the proprietor, along with a few employees, operates the proprietorship. He or she normally raises capital from personal resources or by borrowing and is responsible for all business decisions. The sole proprietor has **unlimited liability**; his or her total wealth—not merely the amount originally invested—can be taken to satisfy creditors. The key strengths and weaknesses of sole proprietorships are summarized in Table 1.1 (see page 5).

Partnerships

partnership
A business owned by two or more people and operated for profit.

articles of partnership
The written contract used to formally establish a business partnership.

A **partnership** consists of two or more owners doing business together for profit. Partnerships account for about 10 percent of all businesses, and they are typically larger than sole proprietorships. Finance, insurance, and real estate firms are the most common types of partnership. Public accounting and stock brokerage partnerships often have large numbers of partners.

Most partnerships are established by a written contract known as **articles of partnership**. In a *general* (or *regular*) *partnership*, all partners have unlimited liability, and each partner is legally liable for *all* of the debts of the partnership. Strengths and weaknesses of partnerships are summarized in Table 1.1.

Corporations

corporation
An artificial being created by law (often called a "legal entity").

Hint Many small corporations, as well as small proprietorships and partnerships, have no access to financial markets. In addition, whenever the owners take out a loan, they usually must personally cosign the loan.

A **corporation** is an artificial being created by law. Often called a "legal entity," a corporation has the powers of an individual in that it can sue and be sued, make and be party to contracts, and acquire property in its own name. Although only

TABLE 1.1 Strengths and Weaknesses of the Common Legal Forms of Business Organization

	Sole proprietorship	Partnership	Corporation
Strengths	• Owner receives all profits (and sustains all losses) • Low organizational costs • Income included and taxed on proprietor's personal tax return • Independence • Secrecy • Ease of dissolution	• Can raise more funds than sole proprietorships • Borrowing power enhanced by more owners • More available brain power and managerial skill • Income included and taxed on partner's personal tax return	• Owners have *limited liability*, which guarantees that they cannot lose more than they invested • Can achieve large size via sale of ownership (stock) • Ownership (stock) is readily transferable • Long life of firm • Can hire professional managers • Has better access to financing • Can offer attractive retirement plans
Weaknesses	• Owner has *unlimited liability*—total wealth can be taken to satisfy debts • Limited fund-raising power tends to inhibit growth • Proprietor must be jack-of-all-trades • Difficult to give employees long-run career opportunities • Lacks continuity when proprietor dies	• Owners have *unlimited liability* and may have to cover debts of other partners • Partnership is dissolved when a partner dies • Difficult to liquidate or transfer partnership	• Taxes generally higher, because corporate income is taxed, and dividends paid to owners are also taxed at a maximum 15% rate • More expensive to organize than other business forms • Subject to greater government regulation • Lacks secrecy, because stockholders must receive financial reports

stockholders
The owners of a corporation, whose ownership, or *equity*, is evidenced by either common stock or preferred stock.

common stock
The purest and most basic form of corporate ownership.

dividends
Periodic distributions of earnings to the stockholders of a firm.

board of directors
Group elected by the firm's stockholders and typically responsible for developing strategic goals and plans, setting general policy, guiding corporate affairs, approving major expenditures, and hiring/firing, compensating, and monitoring key officers and executives.

about 15 percent of all businesses are incorporated, the corporation is the dominant form of business organization in terms of receipts and profits. It accounts for nearly 90 percent of business receipts and 80 percent of net profits. Although corporations are involved in all types of businesses, manufacturing corporations account for the largest portion of corporate business receipts and net profits. The key strengths and weaknesses of large corporations are summarized in Table 1.1.

The owners of a corporation are its **stockholders**, whose ownership, or *equity*, is evidenced by either common stock or preferred stock.[1] These forms of ownership are defined and discussed in Chapter 7; at this point it is enough to say that **common stock** is the purest and most basic form of corporate ownership. Stockholders expect to earn a return by receiving **dividends**—periodic distributions of earnings—or by realizing gains through increases in share price.

As noted in the upper portion of Figure 1.1 (see page 6), control of the corporation is structured as a democracy. The stockholders (owners) vote periodically to elect members of the board of directors and to decide other issues such as amending the corporate charter. The **board of directors** is typically responsible for developing strategic goals and plans, setting general policy, guiding corporate affairs, approving major expenditures, and hiring/firing, compensating, and monitoring key officers and executives. The directors typically include both "inside

---
1. Some corporations do not have stockholders but rather have "members" who often have rights similar to those of stockholders—that is, they are entitled to vote and receive dividends. Examples include mutual savings banks, credit unions, mutual insurance companies, and a whole host of charitable organizations.

FIGURE 1.1

Corporate Organization
The general organization of a corporation and the finance function (which is shown in yellow)

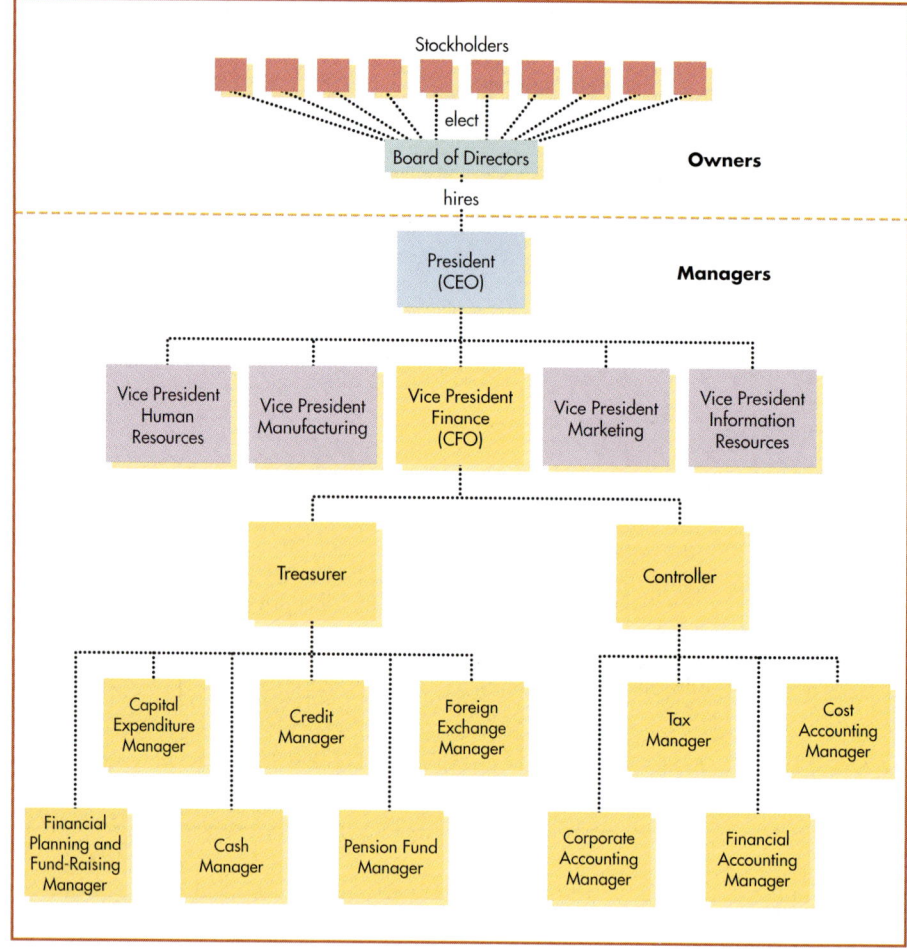

directors," such as key corporate executives, and "outside directors," such as executives from other companies, major shareholders, and national or community leaders. Outside directors for major corporations are generally paid an annual fee of $15,000 to $25,000 or more. Also, they are frequently granted options to buy a specified number of shares of the firm's stock at a stated—and often attractive—price.

The **president or chief executive officer (CEO)** is responsible for managing day-to-day operations and carrying out the policies established by the board of directors. The CEO is required to report periodically to the firm's directors.

It is important to note the division between owners and managers in a large corporation, as shown by the dashed horizontal line in Figure 1.1. This separation and some of the issues surrounding it will be addressed in the discussion of *the agency issue* later in this chapter.

president or chief executive officer (CEO)
Corporate official responsible for managing the firm's day-to-day operations and carrying out the policies established by the *board of directors*.

Other Limited Liability Organizations

A number of other organizational forms provide owners with limited liability. The most popular are **limited partnerships (LPs), S corporations (S corps), limited liability corporations (LLCs)**, and **limited liability partnerships (LLPs)**. Each represents a specialized form or blending of the characteristics of the organizational forms described previously. What they have in common is that their owners enjoy limited liability, and they typically have fewer than 100 owners. Each of these limited liability organizations is described at the book's Web site (www.aw-bc.com/gitman).

Why Study Managerial Finance?

An understanding of the concepts, techniques, and practices presented throughout this text will fully acquaint you with the financial manager's activities and decisions. Because most business decisions are measured in financial terms, the financial manager plays a key role in the operation of the firm. People in all areas of responsibility—accounting, information systems, management, marketing, operations, and so forth—need a basic understanding of the managerial finance function.

Okay, so you're not planning to major in finance! You still will need to understand the activities of the financial manager to improve your chance of success in your chosen business career. All managers in the firm, regardless of their job descriptions, work with financial personnel to justify labor requirements, negotiate operating budgets, deal with financial performance appraisals, and sell proposals at least partly on the basis of their financial merits. Clearly, those managers who understand the financial decision-making process will be better able to address financial concerns and will therefore more often get the resources they need to attain their own goals. The "Across the Disciplines" element that appears on each chapter-opening page should help you understand some of the many interactions between managerial finance and other business careers. These features should help you understand the importance of finance to all business careers.

As you study this text, you will learn about the career opportunities in managerial finance, which are briefly described in Table 1.2. Although this text focuses

TABLE 1.2 **Career Opportunities in Managerial Finance**

Position	Description
Financial analyst	Primarily prepares the firm's financial plans and budgets. Other duties include financial forecasting, performing financial comparisons, and working closely with accounting.
Capital expenditures manager	Evaluates and recommends proposed asset investments. May be involved in the financial aspects of implementing approved investments.
Project finance manager	In large firms, arranges financing for approved asset investments. Coordinates consultants, investment bankers, and legal counsel.
Cash manager	Maintains and controls the firm's daily cash balances. Frequently manages the firm's cash collection and disbursement activities and short-term investments; coordinates short-term borrowing and banking relationships.
Credit analyst/manager	Administers the firm's credit policy by evaluating credit applications, extending credit, and monitoring and collecting accounts receivable.
Pension fund manager	In large companies, oversees or manages the assets and liabilities of the employees' pension fund.
Foreign exchange manager	Manages specific foreign operations and the firm's exposure to fluctuations in exchange rates.

Review Questions

1–1 What is *finance*? Explain how this field affects the life of everyone and of every organization.

1–2 What is the *financial services* area of finance? Describe the field of *managerial finance*.

1–3 Which legal form of business organization is most common? Which form is dominant in terms of business receipts and net profits?

1–4 Describe the roles and the basic relationship among the major parties in a corporation—stockholders, board of directors, and president. How are corporate owners compensated?

1–5 Briefly name and describe some organizational forms other than corporations that provide owners with limited liability.

1–6 Why is the study of managerial finance important regardless of the specific area of responsibility one has within the business firm?

The Managerial Finance Function

People in all areas of responsibility within the firm must interact with finance personnel and procedures to get their jobs done. For financial personnel to make useful forecasts and decisions, they must be willing and able to talk to individuals in other areas of the firm. For example, when considering a new product, the financial manager needs to obtain sales forecasts, pricing guidelines, and advertising and promotion budget estimates from marketing personnel. The managerial finance function can be broadly described by considering its role within the organization, its relationship to economics and accounting, and the primary activities of the financial manager.

Organization of the Finance Function

The size and importance of the managerial finance function depend on the size of the firm. In small firms, the finance function is generally performed by the accounting department. As a firm grows, the finance function typically evolves into a separate department linked directly to the company president or CEO through the chief financial officer (CFO). The lower portion of the organizational chart in Figure 1.1 (on page 6) shows the structure of the finance function in a typical medium-to-large-size firm.

Reporting to the CFO are the treasurer and the controller. The **treasurer** (the chief financial manager) is commonly responsible for handling financial activities, such as financial planning and fund raising, making capital expenditure decisions, managing cash, managing credit activities, managing the pension fund, and

treasurer
The firm's chief financial manager, who is responsible for the firm's financial activities, such as financial planning and fund raising, making capital expenditure decisions, and managing cash, credit, the pension fund, and foreign exchange.

CHAPTER 1 The Role and Environment of Managerial Finance

controller
The firm's chief accountant, who is responsible for the firm's accounting activities, such as corporate accounting, tax management, financial accounting, and cost accounting.

Hint A *controller* is sometimes referred to as a *comptroller*. Not-for-profit and governmental organizations frequently use the title of comptroller.

foreign exchange manager
The manager responsible for monitoring and managing the firm's exposure to loss from currency fluctuations.

marginal cost–benefit analysis
Economic principle that states that financial decisions should be made and actions taken only when the added benefits exceed the added costs.

managing foreign exchange. The **controller** (the chief accountant) typically handles the accounting activities, such as corporate accounting, tax management, financial accounting, and cost accounting. The treasurer's focus tends to be more external, the controller's focus more internal. *The activities of the treasurer, or financial manager, are the primary concern of this text.*

If international sales or purchases are important to a firm, it may well employ one or more finance professionals whose job is to monitor and manage the firm's exposure to loss from currency fluctuations. A trained financial manager can "hedge," or protect against such a loss, at reasonable cost by using a variety of financial instruments. These **foreign exchange managers** typically report to the firm's treasurer.

Relationship to Economics

The field of finance is closely related to economics. Financial managers must understand the economic framework and be alert to the consequences of varying levels of economic activity and changes in economic policy. They must also be able to use economic theories as guidelines for efficient business operation. Examples include supply-and-demand analysis, profit-maximizing strategies, and price theory. The primary economic principle used in managerial finance is **marginal cost–benefit analysis,** the principle that financial decisions should be made and actions taken only when the added benefits exceed the added costs. Nearly all financial decisions ultimately come down to an assessment of their marginal benefits and marginal costs.

EXAMPLE

Amy Chen is a financial manager for Nord Department Stores, a large chain of upscale department stores operating primarily in the western United States. She is currently trying to decide whether to replace one of the firm's online computers with a new, more sophisticated one that would both speed processing and handle a larger volume of transactions. The new computer would require a cash outlay of $80,000, and the old computer could be sold to net $28,000. The total benefits from the new computer (measured in today's dollars) would be $100,000. The benefits over a similar time period from the old computer (measured in today's dollars) would be $35,000. Applying marginal cost–benefit analysis, Amy organizes the data as follows:

Benefits with new computer	$100,000	
Less: Benefits with old computer	35,000	
(1) Marginal (added) benefits		$65,000
Cost of new computer	$ 80,000	
Less: Proceeds from sale of old computer	28,000	
(2) Marginal (added) costs		52,000
Net benefit [(1) − (2)]		$13,000

Because the marginal (added) benefits of $65,000 exceed the marginal (added) costs of $52,000, Amy recommends that the firm purchase the new computer to replace the old one. The firm will experience a net benefit of $13,000 as a result of this action.

Relationship to Accounting

The firm's finance (treasurer) and accounting (controller) activities are closely related and generally overlap. Indeed, managerial finance and accounting are often not easily distinguishable. In small firms the controller often carries out the finance function, and in large firms many accountants are closely involved in various finance activities. However, there are two basic differences between finance and accounting; one is related to the emphasis on cash flows and the other to decision making.

Emphasis on Cash Flows

The accountant's primary function is to develop and report data for measuring the performance of the firm, assess its financial position, comply with and file reports required by securities regulators, and file and pay taxes. Using certain standardized and generally accepted principles, the accountant prepares financial statements that recognize revenue at the time of sale (whether payment has been received or not) and recognize expenses when they are incurred. This approach is referred to as the **accrual basis.**

The financial manager, on the other hand, places primary emphasis on *cash flows,* the intake and outgo of cash. He or she maintains the firm's solvency by planning the cash flows necessary to satisfy its obligations and to acquire assets needed to achieve the firm's goals. The financial manager uses this **cash basis** to recognize the revenues and expenses only with respect to actual inflows and outflows of cash. Regardless of its profit or loss, *a firm must have a sufficient flow of cash to meet its obligations as they come due.*

accrual basis
In preparation of financial statements, recognizes revenue at the time of sale and recognizes expenses when they are incurred.

cash basis
Recognizes revenues and expenses only with respect to actual inflows and outflows of cash.

EXAMPLE

Thomas Yachts, a small yacht dealer, sold one yacht for $100,000 in the calendar year just ended. The yacht was purchased during the year at a total cost of $80,000. Although the firm paid in full for the yacht during the year, at year-end it has yet to collect the $100,000 from the customer. The accounting view and the financial view of the firm's performance during the year are given by the following income and cash flow statements, respectively.

Accounting View (accrual basis)		Financial View (cash basis)	
Thomas Yachts Income Statement for the Year Ended 12/31		Thomas Yachts Cash Flow Statement for the Year Ended 12/31	
Sales revenue	$100,000	Cash inflow	$ 0
Less: Costs	80,000	Less: Cash outflow	80,000
Net profit	$ 20,000	Net cash flow	($80,000)

In an accounting sense Thomas Yachts is profitable, but in terms of actual cash flow it is a financial failure. Its lack of cash flow resulted from the uncollected account receivable of $100,000. Without adequate cash inflows to meet its obligations, the firm will not survive, regardless of its level of profits. ■

As the example shows, accrual accounting data do not fully describe the circumstances of a firm. Thus the financial manager must look beyond financial

> **Hint** The primary emphasis of accounting is on accrual methods; the primary emphasis of financial management is on cash flow methods.

statements to obtain insight into existing or developing problems. Of course, accountants are well aware of the importance of cash flows, and financial managers use and understand accrual-based financial statements. Nevertheless, the financial manager, by concentrating on cash flows, should be able to avoid insolvency and achieve the firm's financial goals.

Decision Making

The second major difference between finance and accounting has to do with decision making. Accountants devote most of their attention to the *collection and presentation of financial data*. Financial managers evaluate the accounting statements, develop additional data, and *make decisions* on the basis of their assessment of the associated returns and risks. Of course, this does not mean that accountants never make decisions or that financial managers never gather data. Rather, the primary focuses of accounting and finance are distinctly different.

Primary Activities of the Financial Manager

> **Hint** Technically, financial managers make recommendations with regard to decisions that are ultimately made by the CEO and/or corporate board of directors.

In addition to ongoing involvement in financial analysis and planning, the financial manager's primary activities are making investment decisions and making financing decisions. Investment decisions determine both the mix and the type of assets held by the firm. Financing decisions determine both the mix and the type of financing used by the firm. These sorts of decisions can be conveniently viewed in terms of the firm's balance sheet, as shown in Figure 1.2. However, the decisions are actually made on the basis of their cash flow effects on the overall value of the firm.

FIGURE 1.2

Financial Activities
Primary activities of the financial manager

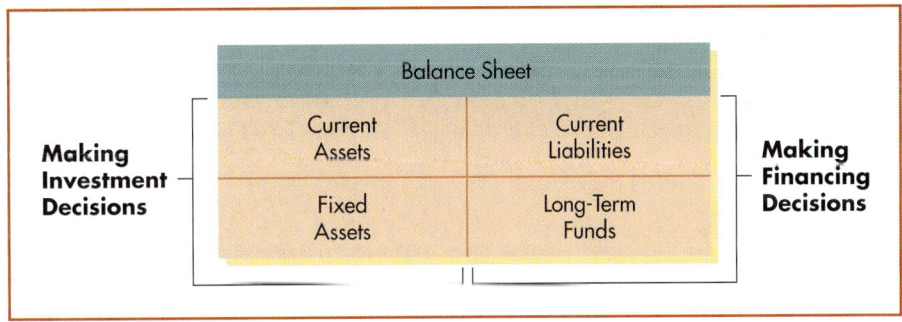

Review Questions

1–7 What financial activities is the treasurer, or financial manager, responsible for handling in the mature firm?

1–8 What is the primary economic principle used in managerial finance?

1–9 What are the major differences between accounting and finance with respect to emphasis on cash flows and decision making?

1–10 What are the two primary activities of the financial manager that are related to the firm's balance sheet?

Goal of the Firm

As noted earlier, the owners of a corporation are normally distinct from its managers. Actions of the financial manager should be taken to achieve the objectives of the firm's owners, its stockholders. In most cases, if financial managers are successful in this endeavor, they will also achieve their own financial and professional objectives. Thus financial managers need to know what the objectives of the firm's owners are.

Maximize Profit?

Some people believe that the firm's objective is always to maximize profit. To achieve this goal, the financial manager would take only those actions that were expected to make a major contribution to the firm's overall profits. For each alternative being considered, the financial manager would select the one that is expected to result in the highest monetary return.

Corporations commonly measure profits in terms of **earnings per share (EPS)**, which represent the amount earned during the period on behalf of each outstanding share of common stock. EPS are calculated by dividing the period's total earnings available for the firm's common stockholders by the number of shares of common stock outstanding.

> **earnings per share (EPS)**
> The amount earned during the period on behalf of each outstanding share of common stock, calculated by dividing the period's total earnings available for the firm's common stockholders by the number of shares of common stock outstanding.

EXAMPLE

Nick Bono, the financial manager of Harpers, Inc., a producer of marine engine components, is choosing between two investments, Rotor and Valve. The following table shows the EPS that each investment is expected to have over its 3-year life.

	Earnings per share (EPS)			
Investment	Year 1	Year 2	Year 3	Total for years 1, 2, and 3
Rotor	$1.40	$1.00	$0.40	$2.80
Valve	0.60	1.00	1.40	3.00

In terms of the profit maximization goal, Valve would be preferred over Rotor, because it results in higher total earnings per share over the 3-year period ($3.00 EPS compared with $2.80 EPS).

But is profit maximization a reasonable goal? No. It fails for a number of reasons: It ignores (1) the timing of returns, (2) cash flows available to stockholders, and (3) risk.

Timing

Because the firm can earn a return on funds it receives, *the receipt of funds sooner rather than later is preferred*. In our example, in spite of the fact that the total earnings from Rotor are smaller than those from Valve, Rotor provides much greater earnings per share in the first year. The larger returns in year 1 could be reinvested to provide greater future earnings.

Cash Flows

Profits do *not* necessarily result in cash flows available to the stockholders. Owners receive cash flow in the form of either cash dividends paid them or the proceeds from selling their shares for a higher price than initially paid. Greater EPS do not necessarily mean that a firm's board of directors will vote to increase dividend payments.

Furthermore, higher EPS do not necessarily translate into a higher stock price. Firms sometimes experience earnings increases without any correspondingly favorable change in stock price. Only when earnings increases are accompanied by increased future cash flows would a higher stock price be expected.

Risk

Profit maximization also disregards **risk**—the chance that actual outcomes may differ from those expected. A basic premise in managerial finance is that a tradeoff exists between return (cash flow) and risk. *Return and risk are, in fact, the key determinants of share price, which represents the wealth of the owners in the firm.*

Cash flow and risk affect share price differently: Higher cash flow is generally associated with a higher share price. Higher risk tends to result in a lower share price because the stockholder must be compensated for the greater risk. In general, stockholders are **risk-averse**—that is, they want to avoid risk. When risk is involved, stockholders expect to earn higher rates of return on investments of higher risk and lower rates on lower-risk investments. The key point, which will be fully developed in Chapter 5, is that differences in risk can significantly affect the value of an investment.

Because profit maximization does not achieve the objectives of the firm's owners, it should *not* be the primary goal of the financial manager.

Maximize Shareholder Wealth

The goal of the firm, and therefore of all managers and employees, is *to maximize the wealth of the owners for whom it is being operated*. The wealth of corporate owners is measured by the share price of the stock, which in turn is based on the timing of returns (cash flows), their magnitude, and their risk.

When considering each financial decision alternative or possible action in terms of its effect on the share price of the firm's stock, *financial managers should accept only those actions that are expected to increase share price*. Figure 1.3 (see page 14) depicts this process. Because share price represents the owners' wealth in the firm, maximizing share price will maximize owner wealth. Note that *return (cash flows) and risk are the key decision variables in maximizing owner wealth*. It is important to recognize that earnings per share, because they are viewed as an indicator of the firm's future returns (cash flows), often appear to affect share price.

What About Stakeholders?

Although maximization of shareholder wealth is the primary goal, many firms broaden their focus to include the interests of *stakeholders* as well as shareholders. **Stakeholders** are groups such as employees, customers, suppliers, creditors,

---

risk
The chance that actual outcomes may differ from those expected.

Hint The relationship between risk and return is one of the most important concepts in the book. Investors who seek to avoid risk will *always* require a bigger return for taking bigger risks.

risk-averse
Seeking to avoid risk.

stakeholders
Groups such as employees, customers, suppliers, creditors, owners, and others who have a direct economic link to the firm.

FIGURE 1.3

Share Price Maximization
Financial decisions and share price

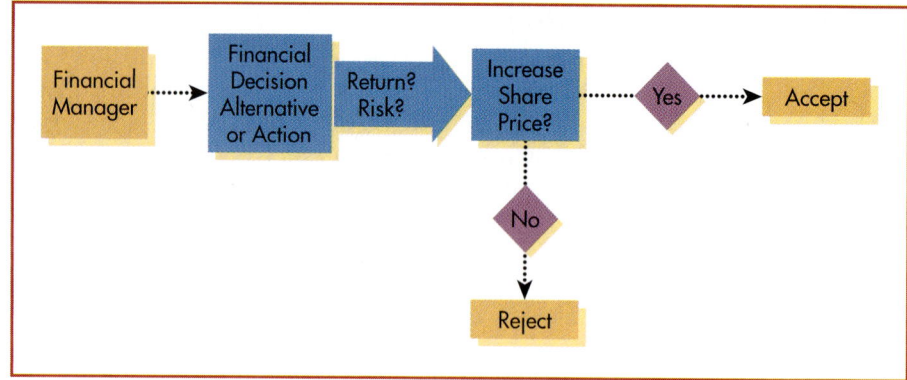

owners, and others who have a direct economic link to the firm. A firm with a *stakeholder focus* consciously avoids actions that would prove detrimental to stakeholders. The goal is not to maximize stakeholder well-being but to preserve it.

The stakeholder view does not alter the goal of maximizing shareholder wealth. Such a view is often considered part of the firm's "social responsibility." It is expected to provide long-run benefit to shareholders by maintaining positive stakeholder relationships. Such relationships should minimize stakeholder turnover, conflicts, and litigation. Clearly, the firm can better achieve its goal of shareholder wealth maximization by fostering cooperation with its other stakeholders, rather than conflict with them.

Corporate Governance

corporate governance
The system used to direct and control a corporation. Defines the rights and responsibilities of key corporate participants, decision-making procedures, and the way in which the firm will set, achieve, and monitor its objectives.

The system used to direct and control a corporation is referred to as **corporate governance.** It defines the rights and responsibilities of the key corporate participants such as the shareholders, board of directors, officers and managers, and other stakeholders, and the rules and procedures for making corporate decisions. It also typically specifies the structure through which the company sets objectives, develops plans for achieving them, and establishes procedures for monitoring performance.

Figure 1.1 on page 6 depicts the typical corporate governance structure, in which the stockholders (owners) elect a board of directors (their representatives), who in turn hire officers and managers (professional managers) to operate the firm in a manner consistent with the goals, plans, and policies established and monitored by the board on behalf of the shareholders. Typically, the board's policies specify ethical practices and provide for the protection of stakeholder interests.

Individual Versus Institutional Investors

individual investors
Investors who buy relatively small quantities of shares so as to meet personal investment goals.

institutional investors
Investment professionals, such as insurance companies, mutual funds, and pension funds, that are paid to manage other people's money and that trade large quantities of securities.

Clearly, the corporate board's first responsibility is to the shareholders. To better understand this responsibility it is helpful to differentiate between the two broad classes of owners—individuals and institutions. **Individual investors** are investors who buy relatively small quantities of shares so as to earn a return on idle funds, build a source of retirement income, or provide financial security. **Institutional investors** are investment professionals that are paid to manage other people's money. They hold and trade large quantities of securities for individuals, businesses, and governments. Institutional investors include banks, insurance companies, mutual funds, and pension funds, which invest large sums of money to earn competitive returns for their clients/plan participants.

Institutional investors tend to have a much greater influence on corporate governance than do individual investors. Simply stated, because they own large amounts of common stock and have the resources to buy and sell large blocks of shares, institutional investors are able to maintain management's attention. If a large institutional investor sells or buys a sizable block of shares, the share price will likely be driven down or up, respectively. Clearly, these large investors speak in a much louder voice than does the individual investor.

The Sarbanes-Oxley Act of 2002

Beginning in 2000, numerous corporate misdeeds were uncovered and disclosed by various regulatory bodies. The misdeeds derived from two main types of issues: (1) false disclosures in financial reporting and other information releases, and (2) undisclosed conflicts of interest between corporations and their analysts, auditors, and attorneys and between corporate directors, officers, and shareholders. In response to these fraudulent disclosures and conflicts of interest, in July 2002 Congress passed the **Sarbanes-Oxley Act of 2002** (commonly called **SOX**).

Sarbanes-Oxley focused on eliminating the many disclosure and conflict of interest problems that had surfaced. It did the following: established an oversight board to monitor the accounting industry; tightened audit regulations and controls; toughened penalties against executives who commit corporate fraud; strengthened accounting disclosure requirements and ethical guidelines for corporate officers; established corporate board structure and membership guidelines; established guidelines with regard to analyst conflicts of interest; mandated instant disclosure of stock sales by corporate executives; and increased securities regulation authority and budgets for auditors and investigators. Although it is too soon to know the full effect of SOX, most commentators believe it will be effective in eliminating fraudulent disclosures and conflicts of interest by corporations.

Sarbanes-Oxley Act of 2002 (SOX)
An act aimed at eliminating corporate disclosure and conflict of interest problems. Contains provisions about corporate financial disclosures and the relationships among corporations, analysts, auditors, attorneys, directors, officers, and shareholders.

The Role of Ethics

In recent years, the ethics of actions taken by certain businesses have received major media attention. Examples include aircraft manufacturer Boeing Co.'s receiving billions of dollars of contracts with the Pentagon as a result of its questionable dealings with an Air Force acquisitions official, who later became a Boeing vice president and in 2004 was sentenced to nine months in prison for her actions; auditing firm KPMG's 2004 agreement to pay $115 million, one of the largest settlements ever paid by an auditing firm, to settle a shareholder lawsuit claiming they had failed in their audit work for Lernout & Hauspie Speech Products NV, a now-defunct Belgian maker of speech-recognition software; the late 2002 agreement by ten of Wall Street's largest firms to pay $1.4 billion to settle allegations by state and federal regulators that they provided misleading stock advice to investors for the benefit of their coprorate invesment banking clients; an agreement by financial services company American Express Co. in early 2002 to pay $31 million to settle a sex- and age-discrimination lawsuit filed on behalf of more than 4,000 women who said they were denied equal pay and promotions; and energy company Enron Corp.'s key executives indicating to employee-shareholders in mid-2001 that the firm's then-depressed stock price would soon recover while, at the same time, selling their own shares and, not long after, taking the firm into bankruptcy.

Clearly, these and similar actions have raised the question of **ethics**—standards of conduct or moral judgment. Today, the business community in general and the financial community in particular are developing and enforcing ethical standards. The goal of these ethical standards is to motivate business and market participants to adhere to both the letter and the spirit of laws and regulations concerned with business and professional practice. Most business leaders believe businesses actually strengthen their competitive positions by maintaining high ethical standards.

ethics
Standards of conduct or moral judgment.

Considering Ethics

Robert A. Cooke, a noted ethicist, suggests that the following questions be used to assess the ethical viability of a proposed action.[2]

1. Is the action arbitrary or capricious? Does it unfairly single out an individual or group?
2. Does the action violate the moral or legal rights of any individual or group?
3. Does the action conform to accepted moral standards?
4. Are there alternative courses of action that are less likely to cause actual or potential harm?

Clearly, considering such questions before taking an action can help to ensure its ethical viability.

Today, an increasing number of firms are directly addressing the issue of ethics by establishing corporate ethics policies and requiring employee compliance with them. A major impetus toward the development of corporate ethics policies has been the *Sarbanes-Oxley Act of 2002* described earlier. Frequently, employees are required to sign a formal pledge to uphold the firm's ethics policies. Such policies typically apply to employee actions in dealing with all corporate stakeholders, including the public. Many companies also require employees to participate in ethics seminars and training programs. To provide further insight into the ethical dilemmas and issues sometimes facing the financial manager, there are *In Practice* boxes that focus on ethics in many of the chapters throughout this book.

Ethics and Share Price

An effective ethics program is believed to enhance corporate value. An ethics program can produce a number of positive benefits. It can reduce potential litigation and judgment costs; maintain a positive corporate image; build shareholder confidence; and gain the loyalty, commitment, and respect of the firm's stakeholders. Such actions, by maintaining and enhancing cash flow and reducing perceived risk, can positively affect the firm's share price. *Ethical behavior is therefore viewed as necessary for achieving the firm's goal of owner wealth maximization.*[3]

---

2. Robert A. Cooke, "Business Ethics: A Perspective," in *Arthur Andersen Cases on Business Ethics* (Chicago: Arthur Andersen, September 1991), pp. 2 and 5.

3. For an excellent discussion of this and related issues by a number of finance academics and practitioners who have given a lot of thought to financial ethics, see James S. Ang, "On Financial Ethics," *Financial Management* (Autumn 1993), pp. 32–59.

The Agency Issue

We have seen that the goal of the financial manager should be to maximize the wealth of the firm's owners. Thus managers can be viewed as *agents* of the owners who have hired them and given them decision-making authority to manage the firm. Technically, any manager who owns less than 100 percent of the firm is to some degree an agent of the other owners. This separation of owners and managers is shown by the dashed horizontal line in Figure 1.1 on page 6.

In theory, most financial managers would agree with the goal of owner wealth maximization. In practice, however, managers are also concerned with their personal wealth, job security, and fringe benefits. Such concerns may make managers reluctant or unwilling to take more than moderate risk if they perceive that taking too much risk might jeopardize their jobs or reduce their personal wealth. The result is a less-than-maximum return and a potential loss of wealth for the owners.

Hint A stockbroker confronts the same issue. If she gets you to buy and sell more stock, it's good for *her*, but it may *not* be good for you.

The Agency Problem

From this conflict of owner and personal goals arises what has been called the **agency problem**, the likelihood that managers may place personal goals ahead of corporate goals. Two factors—market forces and *agency costs*—serve to prevent or minimize agency problems.

agency problem
The likelihood that managers may place personal goals ahead of corporate goals.

Market Forces One market force is major shareholders, particularly large *institutional investors* such as life insurance companies, mutual funds, and pension funds. These holders of large blocks of a firm's stock exert pressure on management to perform, by communicating their concerns to the firm's board. They often threaten to exercise their voting rights or liquidate their holdings if the board does not respond positively to their concerns.

Another market force is the *threat of takeover* by another firm that believes it can enhance the target firm's value by restructuring its management, operations, and financing. The constant threat of a takeover tends to motivate management to act in the best interests of the firm's owners.

agency costs
The costs borne by stockholders to maintain a *governance structure* that minimizes agency problems and contributes to the maximization of owner wealth.

Agency Costs To minimize agency problems and contribute to the maximization of owners' wealth, stockholders incur **agency costs**. These are the costs of maintaining a *corporate governance* structure that monitors management behavior, ensures against dishonest acts of management, and gives managers the financial incentive to maximize share price.

incentive plans
Management compensation plans that tend to tie management compensation to share price; the most popular incentive plan involves the grant of *stock options*.

The most popular, powerful, and expensive approach is to *structure management compensation* to correspond with share price maximization. The objective is to give managers incentives to act in the best interests of the owners. In addition, the resulting compensation packages allow firms to compete for and hire the best managers available. The two key types of compensation plans are incentive plans and performance plans.

stock options
An incentive allowing managers to purchase stock at the market price set at the time of the grant.

Incentive plans tend to tie management compensation to share price. The most popular incentive plan is the granting of **stock options** to management. These options allow managers to purchase stock at the market price set at the time of the grant. If the market price rises, managers will be rewarded by being able to resell the shares at the higher market price.

performance plans
Plans that tie management compensation to measures such as EPS, growth in EPS, and other measures of return. *Performance shares* and/or *cash bonuses* are used as compensation under these plans.

Many firms also offer **performance plans,** which tie management compensation to measures such as earnings per share (EPS), growth in EPS, and other

performance shares
Shares of stock given to management for meeting stated performance goals.

cash bonuses
Cash paid to management for achieving certain performance goals.

measures of return. **Performance shares,** shares of stock given to management as a result of meeting the stated performance goals, are often used in these plans. Another form of performance-based compensation is **cash bonuses,** cash payments tied to the achievement of certain performance goals.

The Current View of Management Compensation

The execution of many compensation plans has been closely scrutinized in recent years. Both individuals and institutional stockholders, as well as the Securities and Exchange Commission (SEC), continue to publicly question the appropriateness of the multimillion-dollar compensation packages that many corporate executives receive. For example, the three highest-paid CEOs in 2003 were (1) Reuben Mark of Colgate-Palmolive, who earned $141.1 million; (2) Steven P. Jobs of Apple Computer, who earned $74.8 million; and (3) George David of United Technologies, who earned $70.5 million. Tenth on the same list was Richard M. Kovacevich of Wells Fargo, who earned $35.9 million. During 2003, the compensation of the average CEO of a major U.S. corporation increased by about 9 percent from 2002. CEOs of 365 of the largest U.S. companies surveyed by *Business Week*, using data from Standard & Poor's EXECUCOMP, earned an average of $8.1 million in total compensation; the average for the 20 highest paid CEOs was $46.5 million.

Recent studies have failed to find a strong relationship between CEO compensation and share price. During the past few years, publicity surrounding these large compensation packages (without corresponding share price performance) has driven down executive compensation. Contributing to this publicity is the SEC requirement that publicly traded companies disclose to shareholders and others both the amount of compensation to their highest-paid executives and the method used to determine it. At the same time, new compensation plans that better link managers' performance with regard to shareholder wealth to their compensation are being developed and implemented.

Unconstrained, managers may have other goals in addition to share price maximization, but much of the evidence suggests that share price maximization—the focus of this book—is the primary goal of most firms.

Review Questions

1–11 For what three basic reasons is profit maximization inconsistent with wealth maximization?

1–12 What is *risk?* Why must risk as well as return be considered by the financial manager who is evaluating a decision alternative or action?

1–13 What is the goal of the firm and, therefore, of all managers and employees? Discuss how one measures achievement of this goal.

1–14 What is *corporate governance?* How has the *Sarbanes-Oxley Act of 2002* affected it? Explain.

1–15 Describe the role of corporate ethics policies and guidelines, and discuss the relationship that is believed to exist between ethics and share price.

1–16 How do market forces—both shareholder activism and the threat of takeover—act to prevent or minimize the *agency problem?* What role do *institutional investors* play in shareholder activism?

1–17 Define *agency costs*, and explain their relationship to a firm's *corporate governance* structure. How can the firm *structure management compensation* to minimize agency problems? What is the current view with regard to the execution of many compensation plans?

Financial Institutions and Markets

Most successful firms have ongoing needs for funds. They can obtain funds from external sources in three ways. The first source is through a *financial institution* that accepts savings and transfers them to those that need funds. A second source is through *financial markets,* organized forums in which the suppliers and demanders of various types of funds can make transactions. A third source is through *private placement.* Because of the unstructured nature of private placements, here we focus primarily on the role of financial institutions and financial markets in facilitating business financing.

Financial Institutions

financial institution
An intermediary that channels the savings of individuals, businesses, and governments into loans or investments.

Hint Think about how inefficient it would be if each individual saver had to negotiate with each potential user of savings. Institutions make the process very efficient by becoming intermediaries between savers and users.

Financial institutions serve as intermediaries by channeling the savings of individuals, businesses, and governments into loans or investments. Many financial institutions directly or indirectly pay savers interest on deposited funds; others provide services for a fee (for example, checking accounts for which customers pay service charges). Some financial institutions accept customers' savings deposits and lend this money to other customers or to firms; others invest customers' savings in earning assets such as real estate or stocks and bonds; and some do both. Financial institutions are required by the government to operate within established regulatory guidelines.

Key Customers of Financial Institutions

The key suppliers of funds to financial institutions and the key demanders of funds from financial institutions are individuals, businesses, and governments. The savings that individual consumers place in financial institutions provide these institutions with a large portion of their funds. Individuals not only supply funds to financial institutions but also demand funds from them in the form of loans. However, individuals as a group are the *net suppliers* for financial institutions: They save more money than they borrow.

Business firms also deposit some of their funds in financial institutions, primarily in checking accounts with various commercial banks. Like individuals, firms borrow funds from these institutions, but firms are *net demanders* of funds: They borrow more money than they save.

Governments maintain deposits of temporarily idle funds, certain tax payments, and Social Security payments in commercial banks. They do not borrow funds *directly* from financial institutions, although by selling their debt securities to various institutions, governments indirectly borrow from them. The government, like business firms, is typically a *net demander* of funds: It typically borrows more than it saves. We've all heard about the federal budget deficit.

Major Financial Institutions

The major financial institutions in the U.S. economy are commercial banks, savings and loans, credit unions, savings banks, insurance companies, mutual funds, and pension funds. These institutions attract funds from individuals, businesses, and governments, combine them, and make loans available to individuals and businesses. Descriptions of the major financial institutions are found at the textbook's Web site at www.aw-bc.com/gitman.

Financial Markets

financial markets
Forums in which suppliers of funds and demanders of funds can transact business directly.

private placement
The sale of a new security issue, typically bonds or preferred stock, directly to an investor or group of investors.

public offering
The nonexclusive sale of either bonds or stocks to the general public.

primary market
Financial market in which securities are initially issued; the only market in which the issuer is directly involved in the transaction.

secondary market
Financial market in which preowned securities (those that are not new issues) are traded.

Financial markets are forums in which suppliers of funds and demanders of funds can transact business directly. Whereas the loans and investments of institutions are made without the direct knowledge of the suppliers of funds (savers), suppliers in the financial markets know where their funds are being lent or invested. The two key financial markets are the money market and the capital market. Transactions in short-term debt instruments, or marketable securities, take place in the *money market*. Long-term securities—bonds and stocks—are traded in the *capital market*.

To raise money, firms can use either private placements or public offerings. **Private placement** involves the sale of a new security issue, typically bonds or preferred stock, directly to an investor or group of investors, such as an insurance company or pension fund. Most firms, however, raise money through a **public offering** of securities, which is the nonexclusive sale of either bonds or stocks to the general public.

All securities are initially issued in the **primary market.** This is the only market in which the corporate or government issuer is directly involved in the transaction and receives direct benefit from the issue. That is, the company actually receives the proceeds from the sale of securities. Once the securities begin to trade between savers and investors, they become part of the **secondary market.** The primary market is the one in which "new" securities are sold. The secondary market can be viewed as a "preowned" securities market.

The Relationship Between Institutions and Markets

Financial institutions actively participate in the financial markets as both suppliers and demanders of funds. Figure 1.4 depicts the general flow of funds through and between financial institutions and financial markets; private placement transactions are also shown. The individuals, businesses, and governments that supply and demand funds may be domestic or foreign. We next briefly discuss the money market, including its international equivalent—the *Eurocurrency market*. We then end this section with a discussion of the capital market, which is of key importance to the firm.

The Money Market

money market
A financial relationship created between suppliers and demanders of *short-term funds*.

The **money market** is created by a financial relationship between suppliers and demanders of *short-term funds* (funds with maturities of one year or less). The money market exists because some individuals, businesses, governments, and

FIGURE 1.4

Flow of Funds
Flow of funds for financial institutions and markets

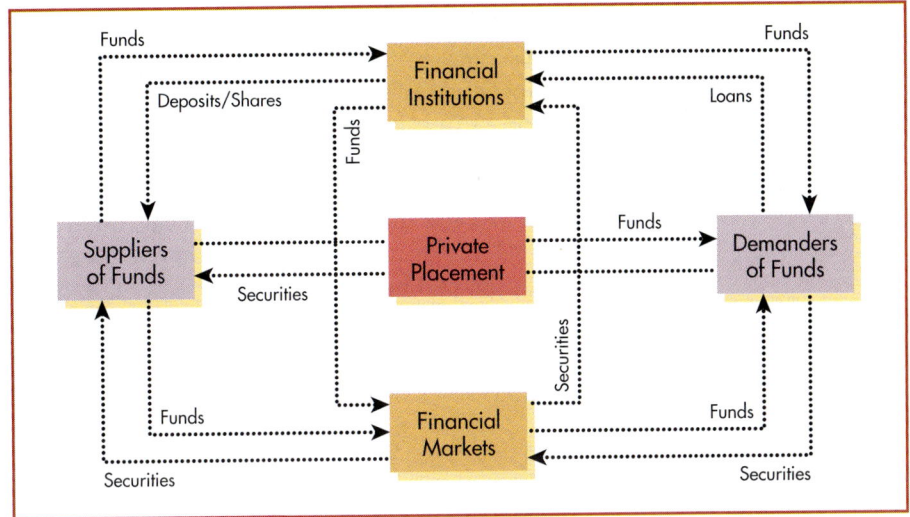

marketable securities
Short-term debt instruments, such as U.S. Treasury bills, commercial paper, and negotiable certificates of deposit issued by government, business, and financial institutions, respectively.

financial institutions have temporarily idle funds that they wish to put to some interest-earning use. At the same time, other individuals, businesses, governments, and financial institutions find themselves in need of seasonal or temporary financing. The money market brings together these suppliers and demanders of short-term funds.

Most money market transactions are made in **marketable securities**—short-term debt instruments, such as U.S. Treasury bills, commercial paper, and negotiable certificates of deposit issued by government, business, and financial institutions, respectively. (Marketable securities are described in Chapter 13.)

The Operation of the Money Market

The money market is not an actual organization housed in some central location. How, then, are suppliers and demanders of short-term funds brought together? Typically, they are matched through the facilities of large New York banks and through government securities dealers. A number of stock brokerage firms purchase money market instruments for resale to customers. Also, financial institutions purchase money market instruments for their portfolios so as to provide attractive returns on their customers' deposits and share purchases. Additionally, the Federal Reserve banks become involved in loans from one commercial bank to another; these loans are referred to as transactions in **federal funds.**

federal funds
Loan transactions between commercial banks in which the Federal Reserve banks become involved.

In the money market, businesses and governments demand short-term funds (borrow) by *issuing* a money market instrument. Parties that supply short-term funds (invest) *purchase* the money market instruments. To issue or purchase a money market instrument, one party must go directly to another party or use an intermediary, such as a bank or brokerage firm, to make the transaction. The secondary (resale) market for marketable securities is no different from the primary (initial issue) market with respect to the basic transactions that are made. Individuals also participate in the money market as purchasers and sellers of money market instruments. Although individuals do not issue marketable securities, they may sell them in the money market to liquidate them prior to maturity.

Hint Remember that the *money market* is for short-term fund raising and is represented by current liabilities on the balance sheet. The *capital market* is for long-term fund raising and is reflected by long-term debt and equity on the balance sheet.

The Eurocurrency Market

Eurocurrency market
International equivalent of the domestic money market.

The international equivalent of the domestic money market is called the **Eurocurrency market.** This is a market for short-term bank deposits denominated in U.S. dollars or other easily convertible currencies. Historically, the Eurocurrency market has been centered in London, but it has evolved into a truly global market.

Eurocurrency deposits arise when a corporation or individual makes a bank deposit in a currency other than the local currency of the country where the bank is located. If, for example, a multinational corporation were to deposit U.S. dollars in a London bank, this would create a Eurodollar deposit (a dollar deposit at a bank in Europe). Nearly all Eurodollar deposits are *time deposits*. This means that the bank would promise to repay the deposit, with interest, at a fixed date in the future—say, in 6 months. During the interim, the bank is free to lend this dollar deposit to creditworthy corporate or government borrowers. If the bank cannot find a borrower on its own, it may lend the deposit to another international bank. The rate charged on these "interbank loans" is called the **London Interbank Offered Rate (LIBOR),** and it is the base rate that is used to price all Eurocurrency loans.

London Interbank Offered Rate (LIBOR)
The base rate that is used to price all Eurocurrency loans.

The Eurocurrency market has grown rapidly, primarily because it is an unregulated, wholesale, and global market that fills the needs of both borrowers and lenders. Investors with excess cash to lend are able to make large, short-term, and safe deposits at attractive interest rates. Likewise, borrowers are able to arrange large loans, quickly and confidentially, also at attractive interest rates.

The Capital Market

capital market
A market that enables suppliers and demanders of *long-term funds* to make transactions.

The **capital market** is a market that enables suppliers and demanders of *long-term funds* to make transactions. Included are securities issues of business and government. The backbone of the capital market is formed by the various *securities exchanges* that provide a forum for bond and stock transactions.

Key Securities Traded: Bonds and Stocks

The key capital market securities are *bonds* (long-term debt) and both *common stock* and *preferred stock* (equity, or ownership).

bond
Long-term debt instrument used by business and government to raise large sums of money, generally from a diverse group of lenders.

Bonds are long-term debt instruments used by business and government to raise large sums of money, generally from a diverse group of lenders. *Corporate bonds* typically pay interest *semiannually* (every 6 months) at a stated *coupon interest rate.* They have an initial *maturity* of from 10 to 30 years, and a *par,* or *face, value* of $1,000 that must be repaid at maturity. Bonds are described in detail in Chapter 6.

EXAMPLE

Lakeview Industries, a major microprocessor manufacturer, has issued a 9 percent coupon interest rate, 20-year bond with a $1,000 par value that pays interest semiannually. Investors who buy this bond receive the contractual right to $90 annual interest (9% coupon interest rate × $1,000 par value) distributed as $45 at the end of each 6 months (1/2 × $90) for 20 years, plus the $1,000 par value at the end of year 20.

As noted earlier, shares of *common stock* are units of ownership, or equity, in a corporation. Common stockholders earn a return by receiving dividends—peri-

preferred stock
A special form of ownership having a fixed periodic dividend that must be paid prior to payment of any dividends to common stockholders.

odic distributions of earnings—or by realizing increases in share price. **Preferred stock** is a special form of ownership that has features of both a bond and common stock. Preferred stockholders are promised a fixed periodic dividend that must be paid prior to payment of any dividends to common stockholders. In other words, preferred stock has "preference" over common stock. Preferred and common stock are described in detail in Chapter 7.

Major Securities Exchanges

securities exchanges
Organizations that provide the marketplace in which firms can raise funds through the sale of new securities and purchasers can resell securities.

Securities exchanges provide the marketplace in which firms can raise funds through the sale of new securities and purchasers of securities can easily resell them when necessary. Many people call securities exchanges "stock markets," but this label is misleading because bonds, common stock, preferred stock, and a variety of other investment vehicles are all traded on these exchanges. The two key types of securities exchanges are the organized exchange and the over-the-counter exchange. In addition, important markets exist outside the United States.

organized securities exchanges
Tangible organizations that act as *secondary markets* where outstanding securities are resold.

Organized Securities Exchanges **Organized securities exchanges** are tangible organizations that act as *secondary markets* where outstanding securities are resold. Organized exchanges account for about 62 percent of the *total dollar volume* (about 46 percent of the *total share volume*) of domestic shares traded. The best-known organized exchanges are the New York Stock Exchange (NYSE) and the American Stock Exchange (AMEX), both headquartered in New York City. There are also regional exchanges, such as the Chicago Stock Exchange and the Pacific Exchange.

Most exchanges are modeled after the New York Stock Exchange, which is the dominant *organized* U.S. exchange. For a firm's securities to be listed for trading on an organized exchange, a firm must file an application for listing and meet a number of requirements. For example, to be eligible for listing on the NYSE, a firm must have at least 2,200 stockholders owning 100 or more shares; a minimum of 1.1 million shares of publicly held stock outstanding; pretax earnings of at least $6.5 million over the previous 3 years, with no loss in the previous 2 years; and a minimum market value of public shares of $100 million. Clearly, only large, widely held firms are candidates for NYSE listing.

To make transactions on the "floor" of the New York Stock Exchange, an individual or firm must own a "seat" on the exchange. There are a total of 1,366 seats on the NYSE, most of which are owned by brokerage firms. Trading is carried out on the floor of the exchange through an *auction process*. The goal of trading is to fill *buy orders* at the lowest price and to fill *sell orders* at the highest price, thereby giving both purchasers and sellers the best possible deal.

Once placed, an order to buy or sell can be executed in minutes, thanks to sophisticated telecommunication devices. New Internet-based brokerage systems enable investors to place their buy and sell orders electronically. Information on publicly traded securities is reported in various media, both print, such as the *Wall Street Journal,* and electronic, such as MSN Money (www.moneycentral.msn.com).

over-the-counter (OTC) exchange
An intangible market for the purchase and sale of securities not listed by the organized exchanges.

The Over-the-Counter Exchange The **over-the-counter (OTC) exchange** is an intangible market for the purchase and sale of securities not listed by the organized exchanges. OTC traders, known as *dealers,* are linked with the purchasers and sellers of securities through the *National Association of Securities Dealers Automated Quotation (Nasdaq) system.*

This sophisticated telecommunications network provides current bid and ask prices on thousands of actively traded OTC securities. The *bid price* is the highest price offered by a dealer to purchase a given security, and the *ask price* is the lowest price at which the dealer is willing to sell the security. The dealer in effect adds securities to his or her inventory by purchasing them at the bid price and sells securities from the inventory at the ask price. The dealer expects to profit from the *spread* between the bid and ask prices. Unlike the auction process on the organized securities exchanges, the prices at which securities are traded in the OTC market result from both competitive bids and negotiation.

Unlike the organized exchanges, the OTC handles *both* outstanding securities and new public issues, making it both a *secondary* and a *primary market*. The OTC accounts for about 38 percent of the *total dollar volume* (about 54 percent of the *total share volume*) of domestic shares traded.

International Capital Markets Although U.S. capital markets are by far the world's largest, there are important debt and equity markets outside the United States. In the **Eurobond market,** corporations and governments typically issue bonds denominated in dollars and sell them to investors located outside the United States. A U.S. corporation might, for example, issue dollar-denominated bonds that would be purchased by investors in Belgium, Germany, or Switzerland. Through the Eurobond market, issuing firms and governments can tap a much larger pool of investors than would be generally available in the local market.

The foreign bond market is another international market for long-term debt securities. A **foreign bond** is a bond issued by a foreign corporation or government that is denominated in the investor's home currency and sold in the investor's home market. A bond issued by a U.S. company that is denominated in Swiss francs and sold in Switzerland is an example of a foreign bond. Although the foreign bond market is much smaller than the Eurobond market, many issuers have found it to be an attractive way of tapping debt markets in Germany, Japan, Switzerland, and the United States.

Finally, the **international equity market** allows corporations to sell blocks of shares to investors in a number of different countries simultaneously. This market enables corporations to raise far larger amounts of capital than they could raise in any single national market. International equity sales have also proven to be indispensable to governments that have sold state-owned companies to private investors during recent years.

The Role of Securities Exchanges

Securities exchanges create continuous liquid markets in which firms can obtain needed financing. They also create **efficient markets** that allocate funds to their most productive uses. This is especially true for securities that are actively traded on major exchanges, where the competition among wealth-maximizing investors determines and publicizes prices that are believed to be close to their true value. See the *In Practice* box on the facing page for the story of one legendary stock price, and the equally legendary man who brought it about.

The price of an individual security is determined by the demand for and supply of the security. The competitive market created by the major securities

Eurobond market
The market in which corporations and governments typically issue bonds denominated in dollars and sell them to investors located outside the United States.

foreign bond
Bond that is issued by a foreign corporation or government and is denominated in the investor's home currency and sold in the investor's home market.

international equity market
A market that allows corporations to sell blocks of shares to investors in a number of different countries simultaneously.

efficient market
A market that allocates funds to their most productive uses as a result of competition among wealth-maximizing investors that determines and publicizes prices that are believed to be close to their true value.

In Practice FOCUS ON PRACTICE

WARREN BUFFETT: THE ORACLE OF OMAHA

In early 1980, investors could buy one share of Berkshire Hathaway Class A (BRKA) common stock for $285. That may have seemed expensive at the time, but by mid-2004 the price of just one share had climbed to more than $86,500. The wizard behind this phenomenal growth in shareholder value is the Chairman of **Berkshire Hathaway,** Warren Buffett, nicknamed the "Oracle of Omaha."

Born in 1930, Buffett practiced his entrepreneurial skills as a teenager by delivering newspapers in Omaha, Nebraska, and he made his first stock purchase at the age of 11. Buffett studied economics at Columbia University, under two professors, Benjamin Graham and David Dodd, who were proponents of value investing. Graham was particularly noted for advocating the principle of intrinsic business value, the measure of a company's true worth independent of the stock price.

After finishing his formal education, Buffett began his investment career in earnest. While running several investment partnerships, he purchased a struggling New Bedford, Massachusetts, textile mill called Berkshire Hathaway. By deploying the company's capital in other ventures, Berkshire Hathaway soon became an investment vehicle rather than a textile mill. Indeed, the original textile mill assets were disposed of in 1985.

In the years since then, Buffett has pursued a strategy of buying up entire companies or taking a large stock position if he feels a company's stock is underpriced relative to the true value of its assets. For example, consider some of Berkshire Hathaway's holdings in mid-2004: 8.2 percent of **Coca-Cola** (since 1994), 11.8 percent of **American Express Company** (1998), 9.5 percent of **Gillette** (1989), and 18.1 percent of **The Washington Post** (1973). Ignoring hot investment trends, Buffett looks for undervalued companies with low overhead, high growth potential, strong market share, and a low ratio of the stock price to the company's earnings (called the *P/E ratio;* see Chapter 2).

Berkshire Hathaway's annual report is a "must-read" for many investors, due to the popularity of Buffet's annual letter to shareholders with his homespun take on such topics as investing, corporate governance, and corporate leadership. Berkshire Hathaway's annual shareholder meetings in Omaha have turned into a cult-like gathering each year, with thousands traveling to listen to Buffett answer questions from shareholders. One question that has been firmly answered is the question of Buffett's ability to create shareholder value.

■ *The share price of BRKA has never been split to make the shares more affordable to average investors. Why might the company refuse to split its shares?*

exchanges provides a forum in which share prices are continuously adjusted to changing demand and supply.

For an in-depth, chapter-length discussion of financial institutions and financial markets, see the online chapter at the book's Web site (www.aw-bc.com/gitman).

Review Questions

1–18 Who are the key participants in the transactions of financial institutions? Who are *net suppliers* and who are *net demanders?*

1–19 What role do *financial markets* play in our economy? What are *primary* and *secondary* markets? What relationship exists between financial institutions and financial markets?

1–20 What is the *money market*? How does it work?
1–21 What is the *Eurocurrency market*? What is the *London Interbank Offered Rate (LIBOR)* and how is it used in this market?
1–22 What is the *capital market*? What are the primary securities traded in it?
1–23 What role do securities exchanges play in the capital market? How does the *over-the-counter exchange* operate? How does it differ from the *organized securities exchanges*?
1–24 Briefly describe the international capital markets, particularly the *Eurobond market* and the *international equity market*.
1–25 What are *efficient markets*? What determines the price of an individual security in such a market?

Business Taxes

Taxes are a fact of life, and businesses, like individuals, must pay taxes on income. The income of sole proprietorships and partnerships is taxed as the income of the individual owners; corporate income is subject to corporate taxes. Regardless of their legal form, all businesses can earn two types of income: ordinary and capital gains. Under current law, these two types of income are treated differently in the taxation of individuals; they are not treated differently for entities subject to corporate taxes. Frequent amendments are made to the tax code. As this book goes to press (Dec. 2004), a bill, which is likely to pass, is before Congress that proposes cuts to the top corporate tax rate from the current 35% to 34% in 2005 and 2006 and a further reduction to 32% starting in 2007.

Ordinary Income

ordinary income
Income earned through the sale of a firm's goods or services.

The **ordinary income** of a corporation is income earned through the sale of goods or services. Ordinary income is currently taxed subject to the rates depicted in the corporate tax rate schedule in Table 1.3.

TABLE 1.3 Corporate Tax Rate Schedule

Range of taxable income	Tax calculation: Base tax + (Marginal rate × amount over base bracket)
$ 0 to $ 50,000	$ 0 + (15% × amount over $ 0)
50,000 to 75,000	7,500 + (25 × amount over 50,000)
75,000 to 100,000	13,750 + (34 × amount over 75,000)
100,000 to 335,000	22,250 + (39 × amount over 100,000)
335,000 to 10,000,000	113,900 + (34 × amount over 335,000)
10,000,000 to 15,000,000	3,400,000 + (35 × amount over 10,000,000)
15,000,000 to 18,333,333	5,150,000 + (38 × amount over 15,000,000)
Over 18,333,333	6,416,667 + (35 × amount over 18,333,333)

EXAMPLE

Webster Manufacturing, Inc., a small manufacturer of kitchen knives, has before-tax earnings of $250,000. The tax on these earnings can be found by using the tax rate schedule in Table 1.3:

$$\begin{aligned} \text{Total taxes due} &= \$22{,}250 + [0.39 \times (\$250{,}000 - \$100{,}000)] \\ &= \$22{,}250 + (0.39 \times \$150{,}000) \\ &= \$22{,}250 + \$58{,}500 = \underline{\$80{,}750} \end{aligned}$$

From a financial point of view, it is important to understand the difference between average and marginal tax rates, the treatment of interest and dividend income, and the effects of tax deductibility.

Average Versus Marginal Tax Rates

average tax rate
A firm's taxes divided by its taxable income.

The **average tax rate** paid on the firm's ordinary income can be calculated by dividing its taxes by its taxable income. For firms with taxable income of $10,000,000 or less, the average tax rate ranges from 15 to 34 percent, reaching 34 percent when taxable income equals or exceeds $335,000. For firms with taxable income in excess of $10,000,000, the average tax rate ranges between 34 and 35 percent. The average tax rate paid by Webster Manufacturing, Inc., in the preceding example was 32.3 percent ($80,750 ÷ $250,000). As a corporation's taxable income increases, its average tax rate approaches and finally reaches 34 percent. It remains at that level up to $10,000,000 of taxable income, beyond which it rises toward and reaches 35 percent at $18,333,333.

marginal tax rate
The rate at which *additional income* is taxed.

The **marginal tax rate** represents the rate at which *additional income* is taxed. In the current corporate tax structure, the marginal tax rate on income up to $50,000 is 15 percent; from $50,000 to $75,000 it is 25 percent; and so on, as shown in Table 1.3. Webster Manufacturing's marginal tax rate is currently 39 percent because its next dollar of taxable income (bringing its before-tax earnings to $250,001) would be taxed at that rate. To simplify calculations in the text, *a fixed 40 percent tax rate is assumed to be applicable to ordinary corporate income.*

EXAMPLE

If Western Manufacturing's earnings go up to $300,000, the marginal tax rate on the additional $50,000 of income will be 39 percent. The company will therefore have to pay additional taxes of $19,500 (0.39 × $50,000). Total taxes on the $300,000, then, will be $100,250 ($80,750 + $19,500). To check this figure using the tax rate schedule in Table 1.3, we would get a total tax liability of $22,500 + [0.39 × ($300,000 − $100,000)] = $22,250 + $78,000 = $100,250— the same value obtained by applying the marginal tax rate to the added income and adjusting the known tax liability.

The *average tax rate* tends to be most useful in evaluating taxes historically, and the *marginal tax rate* is more frequently used in financial decision making. Given our focus on financial decision making, *the tax rates used throughout this text are assumed to represent marginal tax rates.*

Interest and Dividend Income

In the process of determining taxable income, any *interest received* by the corporation is included as ordinary income. Dividends, on the other hand, are treated

double taxation
Occurs when the already once-taxed earnings of a corporation are distributed as cash dividends to stockholders, who must pay taxes of up to a maximum rate of 15 percent on them.

intercorporate dividends
Dividends received by one corporation on common and preferred stock held in other corporations.

differently. This different treatment moderates the effect of **double taxation**, which occurs when the already once-taxed earnings of a corporation are distributed as cash dividends to stockholders, who must pay taxes of up to a maximum rate of 15 percent on them. Therefore, dividends that the firm receives on common and preferred stock held in other corporations, and representing less than 20 percent ownership in them, are subject to a 70 percent exclusion for tax purposes.[4]

Because of the dividend exclusion, only 30 percent of these **intercorporate dividends** are included as ordinary income. The tax law provides this exclusion to avoid *triple taxation*. Triple taxation would occur if the first and second corporations were taxed on income before the second corporation paid dividends to its shareholders, who must then pay taxes up to a maximum rate of 15 percent on them. The dividend exclusion in effect eliminates most of the potential tax liability from the dividends received by the second and any subsequent corporations.

EXAMPLE

Checker Industries, a major manufacturer of molds for the plastics industry, during the year just ended received $100,000 in interest on bonds it held and $100,000 in dividends on common stock it owned in other corporations. The firm is subject to a 40% marginal tax rate and is eligible for a 70% exclusion on its intercorporate dividend receipts. The after-tax income realized by Checker from each of these sources of investment income is found as follows:

	Interest income	Dividend income
(1) Before-tax amount	$100,000	$100,000
Less: Applicable exclusion	0	(0.70 × $100,000) = 70,000
Taxable amount	$100,000	$ 30,000
(2) Tax (40%)	40,000	12,000
After-tax amount [(1) − (2)]	$ 60,000	$ 88,000

As a result of the 70% dividend exclusion, the after-tax amount is greater for the dividend income than for the interest income. Clearly, the dividend exclusion enhances the attractiveness of stock investments relative to bond investments made by one corporation in another.

Tax-Deductible Expenses

In calculating their taxes, corporations are allowed to deduct operating expenses, as well as interest expense. The tax deductibility of these expenses reduces their after-tax cost. The following example illustrates the benefit of tax deductibility.

EXAMPLE

Two companies, Debt Co. and No Debt Co., both expect in the coming year to have earnings before interest and taxes of $200,000. Debt Co. during the year will have to pay $30,000 in interest. No Debt Co. has no debt and therefore will

---

4. The exclusion is 80% if the corporation owns between 20% and 80% of the stock in the corporation paying it dividends; 100% of the dividends received are excluded if it owns more than 80% of the corporation paying it dividends. For convenience, we are assuming here that the ownership interest in the dividend-paying corporation is less than 20%.

have no interest expense. Calculation of the earnings after taxes for these two firms is as follows:

	Debt Co.	No Debt Co.
Earnings before interest and taxes	$200,000	$200,000
Less: Interest expense	30,000	0
Earnings before taxes	$170,000	$200,000
Less: Taxes (40%)	68,000	80,000
Earnings after taxes	$102,000	$120,000
Difference in earnings after taxes		$18,000

Whereas Debt Co. had $30,000 more interest expense than No Debt Co., Debt Co.'s earnings after taxes are only $18,000 less than those of No Debt Co. ($102,000 for Debt Co. versus $120,000 for No Debt Co.). This difference is attributable to the fact that Debt Co.'s $30,000 interest expense deduction provided a tax savings of $12,000 ($68,000 for Debt Co. versus $80,000 for No Debt Co.).

This amount can be calculated directly by multiplying the tax rate by the amount of interest expense (0.40 × $30,000 = $12,000). Similarly, the $18,000 *after-tax cost* of the interest expense can be calculated directly by multiplying one minus the tax rate by the amount of interest expense [(1 − 0.40) × $30,000 = $18,000]. ∎

The tax deductibility of certain expenses reduces their actual (after-tax) cost to the profitable firm. Note that both for accounting and tax purposes *interest is a tax-deductible expense, whereas dividends are not*. Because dividends are not tax deductible, their after-tax cost is equal to the amount of the dividend. Thus a $30,000 cash dividend has an after-tax cost of $30,000.

Capital Gains

capital gain
The amount by which the sale price of an asset exceeds the asset's initial purchase price.

If a firm sells a capital asset (such as stock held as an investment) for more than its initial purchase price, the difference between the sale price and the purchase price is called a **capital gain**. For corporations, capital gains are added to ordinary corporate income and taxed at the regular corporate rates, with a maximum marginal tax rate of 39 percent. To simplify the computations presented in the text, as for ordinary income, *a fixed 40 percent tax rate is assumed to be applicable to corporate capital gains*.

EXAMPLE

Loos Company, a manufacturer of pharmaceuticals, has pretax operating earnings of $500,000 and has just sold for $150,000 an asset that was purchased 2 years ago for $125,000. Because the asset was sold for more than its initial purchase price, there is a capital gain of $25,000 ($150,000 sale price − $125,000 initial purchase price). The corporation's taxable income will total $525,000 ($500,000 ordinary income plus $25,000 capital gain). Because this total exceeds $335,000, the capital gain will be taxed at the 34% rate (see Table 1.3), resulting in a tax of $8,500 (0.34 × $25,000). ∎

Review Questions

1–26 Describe the tax treatment of *ordinary income* and that of *capital gains*. What is the difference between the *average tax rate* and the *marginal tax rate*?

1–27 Why might the *intercorporate dividend* exclusion make corporate stock investments by one corporation in another more attractive than bond investments?

1–28 What benefit results from the tax deductibility of certain corporate expenses?

Using This Text

The organization of this textbook links the firm's activities to its value, as determined in the securities markets. The activities of the financial manager are described in the five parts of the book. Each major decision area is presented in terms of both return and risk factors and their potential effects on owners' wealth. Coverage of international events and topics is integrated into the chapter discussions.

The text has been developed around a group of learning goals—six per chapter. Mastery of these goals results in a broad understanding of managerial finance. These goals have been carefully integrated into a learning system. Each chapter begins with a numbered list of learning goals. Next to each major text heading is a "toolbox," which notes by number the specific learning goal(s) addressed in that section. At the end of each section of the chapter (positioned before the next major heading) are review questions that test your understanding of the material in that section. At the end of each chapter, the chapter summaries, self-test problems, warm-up exercises, and problems are also keyed by number to each chapter's learning goals. By linking all elements to the learning goals, the integrated learning system facilitates your mastery of the goals.

Each chapter ends with a case that integrates the chapter materials, and can be used to synthesize and apply related concepts and techniques. Following the chapter case, you will find a spreadsheet exercise and a Web exercise. These exercises will help you apply the chapter material and polish needed business skills by using Excel Software and mining the Web for financial information.

SUMMARY

FOCUS ON VALUE

Chapter 1 established the primary goal of the firm—**to maximize the wealth of the owners for whom the firm is being operated.** For public companies, which are the focus of this text, value at any time is reflected in the stock price. Therefore, management should act only on those alternatives or opportunities that are expected to create value for owners by increasing the stock price. Doing this requires management to consider the returns (magnitude and timing of cash flows) and the risk of each proposed action and their combined effect on value.

REVIEW OF LEARNING GOALS

LG1 **Define *finance*, its major areas and opportunities, and the legal forms of business organization.** Finance is the art and science of managing money. It affects the life of every person and of every organization. Major opportunities in financial services exist within banking and related institutions, personal financial planning, investments, real estate, and insurance. Managerial finance is concerned with the duties of the financial manager in the business firm. It offers numerous career opportunities. The recent trend toward globalization of business activity has created new demands and opportunities in managerial finance.

The legal forms of business organization are the sole proprietorship, the partnership, and the corporation. The corporation is dominant in terms of business receipts and profits, and its owners are its common and preferred stockholders. Stockholders expect to earn a return by receiving dividends or by realizing gains through increases in share price.

LG2 **Describe the managerial finance function and its relationship to economics and accounting.** All areas of responsibility within a firm interact with finance personnel and procedures. The financial manager must understand the economic environment and relies heavily on the economic principle of marginal cost–benefit analysis to make financial decisions. Financial managers use accounting but concentrate on cash flows and decision making.

LG3 **Identify the primary activities of the financial manager.** The primary activities of the financial manager, in addition to ongoing involvement in financial analysis and planning, are making investment decisions and making financing decisions.

LG4 **Explain the goal of the firm, corporate governance, the role of ethics, and the agency issue.** The goal of the financial manager is to maximize the owners' wealth, as evidenced by stock price.

Profit maximization ignores the timing of returns, does not directly consider cash flows, and ignores risk, so it is an inappropriate goal. Both return and risk must be assessed by the financial manager who is evaluating decision alternatives. The wealth-maximizing actions of financial managers should also reflect the interests of stakeholders, groups who have a direct economic link to the firm.

The corporate governance structure is used to direct and control the corporation by defining the rights and responsibilities of the key corporate participants. Both individual and institutional investors hold the stock of most companies, but the institutional investors tend to have much greater influence on corporate governance. The Sarbanes-Oxley Act of 2002 (SOX) was passed to eliminate fraudulent financial disclosure and conflict of interest problems. Positive ethical practices help a firm and its managers to achieve the firm's goal of owner wealth maximization. SOX has provided impetus toward such practices.

An agency problem results when managers, as agents for owners, place personal goals ahead of corporate goals. Market forces, in the form of shareholder activism and the threat of takeover, tend to prevent or minimize agency problems. Institutional investors often exert pressure on management to perform. Firms incur agency costs to maintain a corporate governance structure that monitors managers' actions and provides incentives for them to act in the best interests of owners. Stock options and performance plans are examples of such agency costs.

LG5 **Understand financial institutions and markets, and the role they play in managerial finance.** Financial institutions serve as intermediaries by channeling into loans or investments the savings of individuals, businesses, and governments. The financial markets are forums in which suppliers and demanders of funds can transact business directly. Financial institutions actively participate in the financial markets as both suppliers and demanders of funds.

In the money market, marketable securities (short-term debt instruments) are traded, typically through large New York banks and government securities dealers. The Eurocurrency market is the international equivalent of the domestic money market.

In the capital market, transactions in long-term debt (bonds) and equity (common and preferred stock) are made. The organized securities exchanges provide secondary markets for securities. The over-the-counter (OTC) exchange offers a secondary market for securities and is a primary market in which new public issues are sold. Important international debt and equity markets are the Eurobond market and the international equity market. The securities exchanges create continuous liquid markets for needed financing and allocate funds to their most productive uses.

Discuss business taxes and their importance in financial decisions. Corporate income is subject to corporate taxes. Corporate tax rates are applicable to both ordinary income (after deduction of allowable expenses) and capital gains. The average tax rate paid by a corporation ranges from 15 to 35 percent. Corporate taxpayers can reduce their taxes through certain provisions in the tax code: intercorporate dividend exclusions and tax-deductible expenses. A capital gain occurs when an asset is sold for more than its initial purchase price; it is added to ordinary corporate income and taxed at regular corporate tax rates. (For convenience, we assume a 40 percent marginal tax rate in this book.)

Self-Test Problem (Solution in Appendix B)

ST1–1 **Corporate taxes** Montgomery Enterprises, Inc., had operating earnings of $280,000 for the year just ended. During the year the firm sold stock that it held in another company for $180,000, which was $30,000 above its original purchase price of $150,000, paid 1 year earlier.
  a. What is the amount, if any, of capital gains realized during the year?
  b. How much total taxable income did the firm earn during the year?
  c. Use the corporate tax rate schedule given in Table 1.3 to calculate the firm's total taxes due.
  d. Calculate both the *average tax rate* and the *marginal tax rate* on the basis of your findings.

Warm-Up Exercises

E1–1 Ann and Jack have been partners for several years. Their firm, A & J Tax Preparation, has been very successful, as the pair agree on most business-related questions. One disagreement, however, concerns the legal form of their business. Ann has tried for the past 2 years to get Jack to agree to incorporate. She believes that there is no downside to incorporating and sees only benefits. Jack strongly disagrees; he thinks that the business should remain a partnership forever.
First, take Ann's side and explain the positive side to incorporating the business. Next, take Jack's side and state the advantages to remaining a partnership. Lastly, what information would you want if you were asked to make the decision for Ann and Jack?

E1–2 You have been made treasurer for a day at AIMCO, Inc. AIMCO develops technology for video conferencing. A manager of the satellite division has asked you to authorize a capital expenditure in the amount of $10,000. The manager states that this expenditure is necessary to continue a long-running project designed to use satellites to allow video conferencing anywhere on the planet. The manager admits that the satellite concept has been surpassed by recent technological advances in telephony, but he feels that AIMCO should continue the project. His reasoning is based on the fact that $2.5 million has already been spent over the past 15 years on this project. Although the project has little chance to be viable, the manager believes it would be a shame to waste the money and time already spent.

Use marginal cost–benefit analysis to make your decision regarding whether you should authorize the $10,000 expenditure to continue the project.

E1–3 The end-of-the-year parties at Yearling, Inc., are known for their extravagance. Management provides the best food and entertainment to thank the employees for their hard work. During the planning for this year's bash, a disagreement broke out between the treasurer's staff and the controller's staff. The treasurer's staff contended that the firm was running low on cash and might have trouble paying its bills over the coming months; they requested that cuts be made to the budget for the party. The controller's staff felt that any cuts were unwarranted as the firm continued to be very profitable.

Can both sides be right? Explain your answer.

E1–4 Recently, some branches of Donut Shop, Inc., have dropped the practice of allowing employees to accept tips. Customers who once said, "Keep the change," now have to get used to waiting for their nickels. Management even instituted a policy of requiring that the change be thrown out if a customer drives off without it. As a frequent customer who gets coffee and doughnuts for the office, you notice that the lines are longer and that more mistakes are being made in your order. Explain why tips could be viewed as similar to stock options and why the delays and incorrect orders could represent a case of agency cost. If tips are gone forever, how could Donut Shop reduce these agency costs?

E1–5 Reston, Inc., has asked your corporation, Pruro, Inc., for financial assistance. As a long-time customer of Reston, your firm has decided to give that assistance. The question you are debating is whether Pruro should take Reston stock with a 5% dividend yield or a promissory note paying 5%.

Assuming payment is guaranteed and the dollar amounts for annual interest and dividend income are identical, which option will result in greater after-tax income for the first year?

Problems

BASIC

P1–1 Liability comparisons Merideth Harper has invested $25,000 in Southwest Development Company. The firm has recently declared bankruptcy and has $60,000 in unpaid debts. Explain the nature of payments, if any, by Ms. Harper in each of the following situations.

a. Southwest Development Company is a sole proprietorship owned by Ms. Harper.
b. Southwest Development Company is a 50–50 partnership of Ms. Harper and Christopher Black.
c. Southwest Development Company is a corporation.

P1–2 **Marginal cost–benefit analysis and the goal of the firm** Ken Allen, capital budgeting analyst for Bally Gears, Inc., has been asked to evaluate a proposal. The manager of the automotive division believes that replacing the robotics used on the heavy truck gear line will produce total benefits of $560,000 (in today's dollars) over the next 5 years. The existing robotics would produce benefits of $400,000 (also in today's dollars) over that same time period. An initial cash investment of $220,000 would be required to install the new equipment. The manager estimates that the existing robotics can be sold for $70,000. Show how Ken will apply marginal cost–benefit analysis techniques to determine the following:
a. The marginal (added) benefits of the proposed new robotics.
b. The marginal (added) cost of the proposed new robotics.
c. The net benefit of the proposed new robotics.
d. What should Ken Allen recommend that the company do? Why?
e. What factors besides the costs and benefits should be considered before the final decision is made?

P1–3 **Accrual income versus cash flow for a period** Thomas Book Sales, Inc., supplies textbooks to college and university bookstores. The books are shipped with a proviso that they must be paid for within 30 days but can be returned for a full refund credit within 90 days. In 2006, Thomas shipped and billed book titles totaling $760,000. Collections, net of return credits, during the year totaled $690,000. The company spent $300,000 acquiring the books that it shipped.
a. Using accrual accounting and the preceding values, show the firm's net profit for the past year.
b. Using cash accounting and the preceding values, show the firm's net cash flow for the past year.
c. Which of these statements is more useful to the financial manager? Why?

P1–4 **Identifying agency problems, costs, and resolutions** Explain why each of the following situations is an agency problem and what costs to the firm might result from it. Suggest how the problem might be dealt with short of firing the individual(s) involved.
a. The front desk receptionist routinely takes an extra 20 minutes of lunch to run personal errands.
b. Division managers are padding cost estimates so as to show short-term efficiency gains when the costs come in lower than the estimates.
c. The firm's chief executive officer has secret talks with a competitor about the possibility of a merger in which (s)he would become the CEO of the combined firms.
d. A branch manager lays off experienced full-time employees and staffs customer service positions with part-time or temporary workers to lower employment costs and raise this year's branch profit. The manager's bonus is based on profitability.

CHAPTER 1   The Role and Environment of Managerial Finance   35

BASIC

P1–5 **Corporate taxes** Tantor Supply, Inc., is a small corporation acting as the exclusive distributor of a major line of sporting goods. During 2006 the firm earned $92,500 before taxes.
   a. Calculate the firm's tax liability using the corporate tax rate schedule given in Table 1.3.
   b. How much are Tantor Supply's 2006 after-tax earnings?
   c. What was the firm's *average tax rate*, based on your findings in part **a**?
   d. What is the firm's *marginal tax rate*, based on your findings in part **a**?

BASIC

P1–6 **Average corporate tax rates** Using the corporate tax rate schedule given in Table 1.3, perform the following:
   a. Calculate the tax liability, after-tax earnings, and average tax rates for the following levels of corporate earnings before taxes: $10,000; $80,000; $300,000; $500,000; $1.5 million; $10 million; and $20 million.
   b. Plot the average tax rates (measured on the *y* axis) against the pretax income levels (measured on the *x* axis). What generalization can be made concerning the relationship between these variables?

BASIC

P1–7 **Marginal corporate tax rates** Using the corporate tax rate schedule given in Table 1.3, perform the following:
   a. Find the marginal tax rate for the following levels of corporate earnings before taxes: $15,000; $60,000; $90,000; $200,000; $400,000; $1 million; and $20 million.
   b. Plot the marginal tax rates (measured on the *y* axis) against the pretax income levels (measured on the *x* axis). Explain the relationship between these variables.

INTERMEDIATE

P1–8 **Interest versus dividend income** During the year just ended, Shering Distributors, Inc., had pretax earnings from operations of $490,000. In addition, during the year it received $20,000 in income from interest on bonds it held in Zig Manufacturing and received $20,000 in income from dividends on its 5% common stock holding in Tank Industries, Inc. Shering is in the 40% tax bracket and is eligible for a 70% dividend exclusion on its Tank Industries stock.
   a. Calculate the firm's tax on its operating earnings only.
   b. Find the tax and the after-tax amount attributable to the interest income from Zig Manufacturing bonds.
   c. Find the tax and the after-tax amount attributable to the dividend income from the Tank Industries, Inc., common stock.
   d. Compare, contrast, and discuss the after-tax amounts resulting from the interest income and dividend income calculated in parts **b** and **c**.
   e. What is the firm's total tax liability for the year?

INTERMEDIATE

P1–9 **Interest versus dividend expense** Michaels Corporation expects earnings before interest and taxes to be $40,000 for this period. Assuming an ordinary tax rate of 40%, compute the firm's earnings after taxes and earnings available for common stockholders (earnings after taxes and preferred stock dividends, if any) under the following conditions:
   a. The firm pays $10,000 in interest.
   b. The firm pays $10,000 in preferred stock dividends.

P1-10 **Capital gains taxes** Perkins Manufacturing is considering the sale of two non-depreciable assets, X and Y. Asset X was purchased for $2,000 and will be sold today for $2,250. Asset Y was purchased for $30,000 and will be sold today for $35,000. The firm is subject to a 40% tax rate on capital gains.
a. Calculate the amount of capital gain, if any, realized on each of the assets.
b. Calculate the tax on the sale of each asset.

P1-11 **Capital gains taxes** The following table contains purchase and sale prices for the nondepreciable capital assets of a major corporation. The firm paid taxes of 40% on capital gains.

Asset	Purchase price	Sale price
A	$ 3,000	$ 3,400
B	12,000	12,000
C	62,000	80,000
D	41,000	45,000
E	16,500	18,000

a. Determine the amount of capital gain realized on each of the five assets.
b. Calculate the amount of tax paid on each of the assets.

P1-12 **ETHICS PROBLEM** What does it mean to say that managers should maximize shareholder wealth "subject to ethical constraints"? What ethical considerations might enter into decisions that result in cash flow and stock price effects that are less than they might otherwise have been?

CHAPTER 1 CASE

Assessing the Goal of Sports Products, Inc.

Loren Seguara and Dale Johnson both work for Sports Products, Inc., a major producer of boating equipment and accessories. Loren works as a clerical assistant in the Accounting Department, and Dale works as a packager in the Shipping Department. During their lunch break one day, they began talking about the company. Dale complained that he had always worked hard trying not to waste packing materials and efficiently and cost-effectively performing his job. In spite of his efforts and those of his co-workers in the department, the firm's stock price had declined nearly $2 per share over the past 9 months. Loren indicated that she shared Dale's frustration, particularly because the firm's profits had been rising. Neither could understand why the firm's stock price was falling as profits rose.

Loren indicated that she had seen documents describing the firm's profit-sharing plan under which all managers were partially compensated on the basis of the firm's profits. She suggested that maybe it was profit that was important to management, because it directly affected their pay. Dale said, "That doesn't make sense, because the stockholders own the firm. Shouldn't management do what's best for stockholders? Something's wrong!" Loren responded, "Well, maybe that explains why the company hasn't concerned itself with the stock price. Look, the only profits that stockholders receive are in the form of cash dividends, and this firm has never paid dividends during its 20-year history. We as stockholders therefore don't directly benefit from profits. The only way we benefit is for the stock price to rise." Dale chimed in, "That probably explains why the firm is being sued by state and federal environmental officials for dumping pollutants in the adjacent stream. Why spend money for pollution control? It increases costs, lowers profits, and therefore lowers management's earnings!"

Loren and Dale realized that the lunch break had ended and they must quickly return to work. Before leaving, they decided to meet the next day to continue their discussion.

TO DO

a. What should the management of Sports Products, Inc., pursue as its overriding goal? Why?
b. Does the firm appear to have an *agency problem*? Explain.
c. Evaluate the firm's approach to pollution control. Does it seem to be *ethical*? Why might incurring the expense to control pollution be in the best interests of the firm's owners despite its negative effect on profits?
d. Does the firm appear to have an effective *corporate governance* structure? Explain any shortcomings.
e. On the basis of the information provided, what specific recommendations would you offer the firm?

SPREADSHEET EXERCISE

Assume that Monsanto Corporation is considering the renovation and/or replacement of some of its older and outdated carpet-manufacturing equipment. Its objective is to improve the efficiency of operations in terms of both speed and reduction in the number of defects. The company's finance department has compiled pertinent data that will allow it to conduct a marginal cost–benefit analysis for the proposed equipment replacement.

The cash outlay for new equipment would be approximately $600,000. The net book value of the old equipment and its potential net selling price is $250,000. The total benefits from the new equipment (measured in today's dollars) would be $900,000. The benefits of the old equipment over a similar period of time (measured in today's dollars) would be $300,000.

TO DO

Create a spreadsheet to conduct a marginal cost–benefit analysis for Monsanto Corporation and determine the following:

a. The marginal (added) benefits of the proposed new equipment.
b. The marginal (added) cost of the proposed new equipment.
c. The net benefit of the proposed new equipment.
d. What would you recommend that the firm do? Why?

WEB EXERCISE

The World Wide Web (a part of the larger Internet) has become such a powerful force in every aspect of our society that to ignore its potential would lessen your learning experience. As a source of timely information, the Web is unrivaled. Anyone in the world now has the ability to do in-depth research into almost any topic with just a few mouse clicks. The Web exercise in each chapter of this book will continue the work done within the chapter, applying real-world and real-time data to the subjects taught therein. A relatively brief "deliverable" is attached with the assigned searches. These documents are meant to serve as verification of your time spent online. The chapter, its examples and problems, and Web exercises should all be seen as tools through which overlap reinforces the key elements of the material.

TO DO

Go to the SEC's Web site at www.sec.gov/. There, click on the link under Filings and Forms for Descriptions of SEC Forms (commonly called "Edgar"). Scroll down to Table 3 Securities and Exchange Act. Summarize several of the more pertinent reports listed in this table. More importantly, after returning to the SEC's home page, locate examples of these forms as filed by a corporation of your choosing. Catalogue what you notice regarding these filings.

> **Remember to check the book's Web site at**
> **www.aw-bc.com/gitman**
> **for additional resources, including additional Web exercises.**

Chapter 2

Financial Statements and Analysis

LEARNING GOALS

LG1 Review the contents of the stockholders' report and the procedures for consolidating international financial statements.

LG2 Understand who uses financial ratios, and how.

LG3 Use ratios to analyze a firm's liquidity and activity.

LG4 Discuss the relationship between debt and financial leverage and the ratios used to analyze a firm's debt.

LG5 Use ratios to analyze a firm's profitability and its market value.

LG6 Use a summary of financial ratios and the DuPont system of analysis to perform a complete ratio analysis.

Across the Disciplines   Why This Chapter Matters to You

Accounting: You need to understand the stockholders' report and preparation of the four key financial statements; how firms consolidate international financial statements; and how to calculate and interpret financial ratios for decision making.

Information systems: You need to understand what data are included in the firm's financial statements to design systems that will supply such data to those who prepare the statements and to those in the firm who use the data for ratio calculations.

Management: You need to understand what parties are interested in the stockholders' report and why; how the financial statements will be analyzed by those both inside and outside the firm to assess various aspects of performance; the caution that should be exercised in using financial ratio analysis; and how the financial statements affect the value of the firm.

Marketing: You need to understand the effects your decisions will have on the financial statements, particularly the income statement and the statement of cash flows, and how analysis of ratios, especially those involving sales figures, will affect the firm's decisions about levels of inventory, credit policies, and pricing decisions.

Operations: You need to understand how the costs of operations are reflected in the firm's financial statements and how analysis of ratios, particularly those involving assets, cost of goods sold, or inventory, may affect requests for new equipment or facilities.

generally accepted accounting principles (GAAP)
The practice and procedure guidelines used to prepare and maintain financial records and reports; authorized by the *Financial Accounting Standards Board (FASB).*

All companies gather financial data about their operations and report this information in financial statements for interested parties. These statements are widely standardized, and so we can use the data in them to make comparisons between firms and over time. Analysis of certain items of financial data can identify areas where the firm excels and, also, areas of opportunity for improvement. This chapter reviews the content of financial statements and explains categories of financial ratios and their use.

The Stockholders' Report

Financial Accounting Standards Board (FASB)
The accounting profession's rule-setting body, which authorizes *generally accepted accounting principles (GAAP).*

Public Company Accounting Oversight Board (PCAOB)
A not-for-profit corporation established by the *Sarbanes-Oxley Act of 2002* to protect the interests of investors and further the public interest in the preparation of informative, fair, and independent audit reports.

Securities and Exchange Commission (SEC)
The federal regulatory body that governs the sale and listing of securities.

stockholders' report
Annual report that publicly owned corporations must provide to stockholders; it summarizes and documents the firm's financial activities during the past year.

letter to stockholders
Typically, the first element of the annual stockholders' report and the primary communication from management.

Every corporation has many and varied uses for the standardized records and reports of its financial activities. Periodically, reports must be prepared for regulators, creditors (lenders), owners, and management. The guidelines used to prepare and maintain financial records and reports are known as **generally accepted accounting principles (GAAP)**. These accounting practices and procedures are authorized by the accounting profession's rule-setting body, the **Financial Accounting Standards Board (FASB)**. The *Sarbanes-Oxley Act of 2002*, enacted in an effort to eliminate the many disclosure and conflict of interest problems of corporations, established the **Public Company Accounting Oversight Board (PCAOB)**, which is a not-for-profit corporation that oversees auditors of public corporations. The PCAOB is charged with protecting the interests of investors and furthering the public interest in the preparation of informative, fair, and independent audit reports. The expectation is that it will instill confidence in investors with regard to the accuracy of the audited financial statements of public companies.

Publicly owned corporations with more than $5 million in assets and 500 or more stockholders[1] are required by the **Securities and Exchange Commission (SEC)**—the federal regulatory body that governs the sale and listing of securities—to provide their stockholders with an annual **stockholders' report**. The stockholders' report summarizes and documents the firm's financial activities during the past year. It begins with a letter to the stockholders from the firm's president and/or chairman of the board.

The Letter to Stockholders

The **letter to stockholders** is the primary communication from management. It describes the events that are considered to have had the greatest effect on the firm during the year. It also generally discusses management philosophy, strategies, and actions, as well as plans for the coming year. Links at this book's Web site (www.aw-bc.com/gitman) will take you to some representative letters to stockholders.

---

1. Although the Securities and Exchange Commission (SEC) does not have an official definition of *publicly owned*, these financial measures mark the cutoff point it uses to require informational reporting, regardless of whether the firm publicly sells its securities. Firms that do not meet these requirements are commonly called "closely owned" firms.

The Four Key Financial Statements

The four key financial statements required by the SEC for reporting to shareholders are (1) the income statement, (2) the balance sheet, (3) the statement of stockholders' equity, and (4) the statement of cash flows.[2] The financial statements from the 2006 stockholders' report of Bartlett Company, a manufacturer of metal fasteners, are presented and briefly discussed. Note that an abbreviated form of the statement of stockholders' equity—the statement of retained earnings—is described in the following discussions.

Income Statement

income statement
Provides a financial summary of the firm's operating results during a specified period.

The **income statement** provides a financial summary of the firm's operating results during a specified period. Most common are income statements covering a 1-year period ending at a specified date, ordinarily December 31 of the calendar year. Many large firms, however, operate on a 12-month financial cycle, or *fiscal year*, that ends at a time other than December 31. In addition, monthly income statements are typically prepared for use by management, and quarterly statements must be made available to the stockholders of publicly owned corporations.

Hint Some firms, such as retailers and agricultural firms, end their fiscal year at the end of their operating cycle rather than at the end of the calendar year—for example, retailers at the end of January and agricultural firms at the end of September.

Table 2.1 (see page 42) presents Bartlett Company's income statements for the years ended December 31, 2006 and 2005. The 2006 statement begins with *sales revenue*—the total dollar amount of sales during the period—from which the *cost of goods sold* is deducted. The resulting *gross profits* of $986,000 represent the amount remaining to satisfy operating, financial, and tax costs. Next, *operating expenses*, which include selling expense, general and administrative expense, lease expense, and depreciation expense, are deducted from gross profits.[3] The resulting *operating profits* of $418,000 represent the profits earned from producing and selling products; this amount does not consider financial and tax costs. (Operating profit is often called *earnings before interest and taxes*, or *EBIT*.) Next, the financial cost—*interest expense*—is subtracted from operating profits to find *net profits* (or *earnings*) *before taxes*. After subtracting $93,000 in 2006 interest, Bartlett Company had $325,000 of net profits before taxes.

Next, taxes are calculated at the appropriate tax rates and deducted to determine *net profits* (or *earnings*) *after taxes*. Bartlett Company's net profits after taxes for 2006 were $231,000. Any preferred stock dividends must be subtracted from net profits after taxes to arrive at *earnings available for common stockholders*. This is the amount earned by the firm on behalf of the common stockholders during the period.

Dividing earnings available for common stockholders by the number of shares of common stock outstanding results in *earnings per share (EPS)*. EPS represent the number of dollars earned during the period on behalf of each outstanding share of common stock. In 2006, Bartlett Company earned $221,000

---

2. Whereas these statement titles are consistently used throughout this text, it is important to recognize that in practice, companies frequently use different titles. For example, General Electric uses "Statement of Earnings" rather than "Income Statement" and "Statement of Financial Position" rather than "Balance Sheet." Both Nextel and Qualcomm use "Statement of Operations" rather than "Income Statement."

3. Depreciation expense can be, and frequently is, included in manufacturing costs—cost of goods sold—to calculate gross profits. Depreciation is shown as an expense in this text to isolate its effect on cash flows.

TABLE 2.1 Bartlett Company Income Statements ($000)

	For the years ended December 31	
	2006	2005
Sales revenue	$3,074	$2,567
Less: Cost of goods sold	2,088	1,711
Gross profits	$ 986	$ 856
Less: Operating expenses		
Selling expense	$ 100	$ 108
General and administrative expenses	194	187
Lease expense[a]	35	35
Depreciation expense	239	223
Total operating expense	$ 568	$ 553
Operating profits	$ 418	$ 303
Less: Interest expense	93	91
Net profits before taxes	$ 325	$ 212
Less: Taxes (rate = 29%)[b]	94	64
Net profits after taxes	$ 231	$ 148
Less: Preferred stock dividends	10	10
Earnings available for common stockholders	$ 221	$ 138
Earnings per share (EPS)[c]	$ 2.90	$ 1.81
Dividend per share (DPS)[d]	$ 1.29	$ 0.75

[a] Lease expense is shown here as a separate item rather than being included as part of interest expense, as specified by the FASB for financial reporting purposes. The approach used here is consistent with tax reporting rather than financial reporting procedures.

[b] The 29% tax rate for 2006 results because the firm has certain special tax write-offs that do not show up directly on its income statement.

[c] Calculated by dividing the earnings available for common stockholders by the number of shares of common stock outstanding—76,262 in 2006 and 76,244 in 2005. Earnings per share in 2006: $221,000 ÷ 76,262 = $2.90; in 2005: $138,000 ÷ 76,244 = $1.81.

[d] Calculated by dividing the dollar amount of dividends paid to common stockholders by the number of shares of common stock outstanding. Dividends per share in 2006: $98,000 ÷ 76,262 = $1.29; in 2005: $57,183 ÷ 76,244 = $0.75.

dividend per share (DPS)
The dollar amount of cash distributed during the period on behalf of each outstanding share of common stock.

for its common stockholders, which represents $2.90 for each outstanding share. The actual cash **dividend per share (DPS)**, which is the dollar amount of cash distributed during the period on behalf of each outstanding share of common stock, paid in 2006 was $1.29.

Balance Sheet

balance sheet
Summary statement of the firm's financial position at a given point in time.

The **balance sheet** presents a summary statement of the firm's financial position at a given point in time. The statement balances the firm's *assets* (what it owns) against its financing, which can be either *debt* (what it owes) or *equity* (what was provided by owners). Bartlett Company's balance sheets as of December 31 of 2006 and 2005 are presented in Table 2.2. They show a variety of asset, liability (debt), and equity accounts.

TABLE 2.2 Bartlett Company Balance Sheets ($000)

	December 31 2006	December 31 2005
Assets		
Current assets		
Cash	$ 363	$ 288
Marketable securities	68	51
Accounts receivable	503	365
Inventories	289	300
Total current assets	$1,223	$1,004
Gross fixed assets (at cost)[a]		
Land and buildings	$2,072	$1,903
Machinery and equipment	1,866	1,693
Furniture and fixtures	358	316
Vehicles	275	314
Other (includes financial leases)	98	96
Total gross fixed assets (at cost)	$4,669	$4,322
Less: Accumulated depreciation	2,295	2,056
Net fixed assets	$2,374	$2,266
Total assets	$3,597	$3,270
Liabilities and Stockholders' Equity		
Current liabilities		
Accounts payable	$ 382	$ 270
Notes payable	79	99
Accruals	159	114
Total current liabilities	$ 620	$ 483
Long-term debt (includes financial leases)[b]	$1,023	$ 967
Total liabilities	$1,643	$1,450
Stockholders' equity		
Preferred stock—cumulative 5%, $100 par, 2,000 shares authorized and issued[c]	$ 200	$ 200
Common stock—$2.50 par, 100,000 shares authorized, shares issued and outstanding in 2006: 76,262; in 2005: 76,244	191	190
Paid-in capital in excess of par on common stock	428	418
Retained earnings	1,135	1,012
Total stockholders' equity	$1,954	$1,820
Total liabilities and stockholders' equity	$3,597	$3,270

[a]In 2006, the firm has a 6-year financial lease requiring annual beginning-of-year payments of $35,000. Four years of the lease have yet to run.
[b]Annual principal repayments on a portion of the firm's total outstanding debt amount to $71,000.
[c]The annual preferred stock dividend would be $5 per share (5% × $100 par), or a total of $10,000 annually ($5 per share × 2,000 shares).

An important distinction is made between short-term and long-term assets and liabilities. The **current assets** and **current liabilities** are *short-term* assets and liabilities. This means that they are expected to be converted into cash (current assets) or paid (current liabilities) within 1 year or less. All other assets and liabilities, along with stockholders' equity, which is assumed to have an infinite life, are considered *long-term*, or *fixed*, because they are expected to remain on the firm's books for more than 1 year.

As is customary, the assets are listed from the most liquid—*cash*—down to the least liquid. *Marketable securities* are very liquid short-term investments, such as U.S. Treasury bills or certificates of deposit, held by the firm. Because they are highly liquid, marketable securities are viewed as a form of cash ("near cash"). *Accounts receivable* represent the total monies owed the firm by its customers on credit sales made to them. *Inventories* include raw materials, work in process (partially finished goods), and finished goods held by the firm. The entry for *gross fixed assets* is the original cost of all fixed (long-term) assets owned by the firm.[4] *Net fixed assets* represent the difference between gross fixed assets and *accumulated depreciation*—the total expense recorded for the depreciation of fixed assets. (The net value of fixed assets is called their *book value*.)

Like assets, the liabilities and equity accounts are listed from short-term to long-term. Current liabilities include *accounts payable,* amounts owed for credit purchases by the firm; *notes payable,* outstanding short-term loans, typically from commercial banks; and *accruals,* amounts owed for services for which a bill may not or will not be received. (Examples of accruals include taxes due the government and wages due employees.) **Long-term debt** represents debt for which payment is not due in the current year. *Stockholders' equity* represents the owners' claims on the firm. The *preferred stock* entry shows the historical proceeds from the sale of preferred stock ($200,000 for Bartlett Company).

Next, the amount paid by the original purchasers of common stock is shown by two entries: common stock and paid-in capital in excess of par on common stock. The *common stock* entry is the *par value* of common stock. **Paid-in capital in excess of par** represents the amount of proceeds in excess of the par value received from the original sale of common stock. The sum of the common stock and paid-in capital accounts divided by the number of shares outstanding represents the original price per share received by the firm on a single issue of common stock. Bartlett Company therefore received about $8.12 per share [($191,000 par + $428,000 paid-in capital in excess of par) ÷ 76,262 shares] from the sale of its common stock.

Finally, **retained earnings** represent the cumulative total of all earnings, net of dividends, that have been retained and reinvested in the firm since its inception. It is important to recognize that retained earnings *are not cash* but rather have been utilized to finance the firm's assets.

Bartlett Company's balance sheets in Table 2.2 show that the firm's total assets increased from $3,270,000 in 2005 to $3,597,000 in 2006. The $327,000 increase was due primarily to the $219,000 increase in current assets. The asset increase, in turn, appears to have been financed primarily by an increase of

---

[4]. For convenience the term *fixed assets* is used throughout this text to refer to what, in a strict accounting sense, is captioned "property, plant, and equipment." This simplification of terminology permits certain financial concepts to be more easily developed.

CHAPTER 2   Financial Statements and Analysis   45

TABLE 2.3	Bartlett Company Statement of Retained Earnings ($000) for the Year Ended December 31, 2006	
Retained earnings balance (January 1, 2006)		$1,012
Plus: Net profits after taxes (for 2006)		231
Less: Cash dividends (paid during 2006)		
Preferred stock	$10	
Common stock	98	
Total dividends paid		108
Retained earnings balance (December 31, 2006)		$1,135

$193,000 in total liabilities. Better insight into these changes can be derived from the statement of cash flows, which we will discuss shortly.

Statement of Retained Earnings

The *statement of retained earnings* is an abbreviated form of the statement of stockholders' equity. Unlike the **statement of stockholders' equity,** which shows all equity account transactions that occurred during a given year, the **statement of retained earnings** reconciles the net income earned during a given year, and any cash dividends paid, with the change in retained earnings between the start and the end of that year. Table 2.3 presents this statement for Bartlett Company for the year ended December 31, 2006. The statement shows that the company began the year with $1,012,000 in retained earnings and had net profits after taxes of $231,000, from which it paid a total of $108,000 in dividends, resulting in year-end retained earnings of $1,135,000. Thus the net increase for Bartlett Company was $123,000 ($231,000 net profits after taxes minus $108,000 in dividends) during 2006.

Statement of Cash Flows

The **statement of cash flows** is a summary of the cash flows over the period of concern. The statement provides insight into the firm's operating, investment, and financing cash flows and reconciles them with changes in its cash and marketable securities during the period. Bartlett Company's statement of cash flows for the year ended December 31, 2006, is presented in Table 2.4 (see page 46). Further insight into this statement is included in the discussion of cash flow in Chapter 3.

Notes to the Financial Statements

Included with published financial statements are explanatory notes keyed to the relevant accounts in the statements. These **notes to the financial statements** provide detailed information on the accounting policies, procedures, calculations, and transactions underlying entries in the financial statements. Common issues addressed by these notes include revenue recognition, income taxes, breakdowns of fixed asset accounts, debt and lease terms, and contingencies. Professional securities analysts use the data in the statements and notes to develop estimates of the value of securities that the firm issues, and these estimates influence the

---

statement of stockholders' equity
Shows all equity account transactions that occurred during a given year.

statement of retained earnings
Reconciles the net income earned during a given year, and any cash dividends paid, with the change in retained earnings between the start and the end of that year. An abbreviated form of the *statement of stockholders' equity.*

statement of cash flows
Provides a summary of the firm's operating, investment, and financing cash flows and reconciles them with changes in its cash and marketable securities during the period.

notes to the financial statements
Footnotes detailing information on the accounting policies, procedures, calculations, and transactions underlying entries in the financial statements.

TABLE 2.4   Bartlett Company Statement of Cash Flows ($000) for the Year Ended December 31, 2006

Cash Flow from Operating Activities		
Net profits after taxes	$231	
Depreciation	239	
Increase in accounts receivable	(138)[a]	
Decrease in inventories	11	
Increase in accounts payable	112	
Increase in accruals	45	
Cash provided by operating activities		$500
Cash Flow from Investment Activities		
Increase in gross fixed assets	($347)	
Change in business interests	0	
Cash provided by investment activities		(347)
Cash Flow from Financing Activities		
Decrease in notes payable	($20)	
Increase in long-term debts	56	
Changes in stockholders' equity[b]	11	
Dividends paid	(108)	
Cash provided by financing activities		(61)
Net increase in cash and marketable securities		$92

[a]As is customary, parentheses are used to denote a negative number, which in this case is a cash outflow.

[b]Retained earnings are excluded here, because their change is actually reflected in the combination of the "net profits after taxes" and "dividends paid" entries.

actions of investors and therefore the firm's share value. The *In Practice* box on the facing page discusses some common corporate accounting misdeeds, their potential impact on investors, and how SOX has helped to eliminate them.

Consolidating International Financial Statements

So far, we've discussed financial statements involving only one currency, the U.S. dollar. The issue of how to consolidate a company's foreign and domestic financial statements has bedeviled the accounting profession for many years. The current policy is described in **Financial Accounting Standards Board (FASB) Standard No. 52**, which mandates that U.S.-based companies translate their foreign-currency-denominated assets and liabilities into dollars, for consolidation with the parent company's financial statements. This is done by converting all of a U.S. parent company's foreign-currency-denominated assets and liabilities into dollar values using the exchange rate prevailing at the fiscal year ending date (the current rate). Income statement items are treated similarly. Equity accounts, on the other hand, are translated into dollars by using the exchange rate that prevailed when the parent's equity investment was made (the historical rate). Retained earnings are adjusted to reflect each year's operating profits or losses.

Financial Accounting Standards Board (FASB) Standard No. 52
Mandates that U.S.-based companies translate their foreign-currency-denominated assets and liabilities into dollars, for consolidation with the parent company's financial statements. This is done by using the *current rate (translation) method.*

In Practice **FOCUS ON ETHICS**

INVESTORS AND SOX DECLARE WAR ON ACCOUNTING MISDEEDS

If you are a student at Rutgers University, you may have taken the new course "Cooking the Books," which is entirely focused on financial fraud. If you study business at Seton Hall University (ex-Tyco CFO Dennis Kozlowski's alma mater), you may enroll in a class showing how accounting numbers can be altered by manipulation. New courses such as these may help deter future accounting fiascos: According to Professors Richard McKenzie (University of California at Irvine) and Tibor Machan (Chapman University), knowing which accounting and finance practices are proper is key to keeping companies honest, as is the personal integrity of accountants and financial managers.

Financial statements are often misstated—and not just by the Tycos, Enrons, and WorldComs of the business world. The SEC has implemented a special effort to prevent fraudulent earnings-management practices. Marianne Jennings, an expert in this area, asserts that common techniques used by corporate accountants to increase or reduce a year's revenues or expenses include the following: writing down inventory, writing up inventory valuation to meet profit target, recording supplies or expenses early, delaying invoices, selling excess assets, and deferring expenditures. Arthur Levitt, chairman of the SEC, also sees evidence of "cookie jar reserves"—a practice in which unrealistic assumptions are used to overstate or understate expenses for the period, so as to reduce earnings in some years and to increase earnings in "down years." The result is a more stable yearly pattern of earnings.

What about the auditors of the financial statements in these cases, you ask? One study of 33 companies that experienced accounting problems indicated that 31 of those companies were handed a clean bill of health by their auditors. When an independent research firm called RateFinancials studied the annual stockholders' reports and other financial documents of 120 major companies, it estimated that as many as one-third do not accurately depict their true financial condition in one or more of their financial reports.

Is shareholder wealth being maximized by these practices? Jennings cites evidence that when earnings manipulation is discovered, the companies' stock prices drop by 9 percent, on average. For the 33 companies cited previously, shareholder wealth dropped from $1.8 trillion to $527 billion following the revelation of the accounting misdeeds.

Investors were cheered by the passage in 2002 of the Sarbanes-Oxley Act (SOX), whose subtitle is "The Public Company Accounting Reform and Investor Protection Act" (discussed in Chapter 1). Included in SOX are provisions for criminal penalties for altering documents, requirement for a code of ethics for the senior financial officers, requirement for the CEO and CFO to sign off on annual reports, new requirements for auditor independence, and certification of a company's internal controls. More accurate and truthful information will reduce the uncertainty of the information flow that investors appraise in valuing stock.

Sources: Marianne M. Jennings, "Earning Management: The Ethical Issues Remain," *Corporate Finance Review* 3(5), pp. 39–41 (March/April 1999); Jennifer Oladip, "Business Ethics 101," *The Columbus Dispatch*, July 28, 2002, pp. F1–F2; Bruce Meyerson, "Efforts at Transparency Too Obscure for Words," *Seattle Times*, June 23, 2004. Accessed online at: www.seattletimes.nwsource.com.

■ *Of the provisions listed for SOX, which one do you think will have the greatest effect on the accuracy and trustworthiness of financial statements? Defend your answer.*

Review Questions

2–1 What roles do GAAP, the FASB, and the PCAOB play in the financial reporting activities of public companies?

2–2 Describe the purpose of each of the four major financial statements.

2–3 Why are the notes to the financial statements important to professional securities analysts?

Using Financial Ratios

The information contained in the four basic financial statements is of major significance to a variety of interested parties who regularly need to have relative measures of the company's operating efficiency. *Relative* is the key word here, because the analysis of financial statements is based on the use of *ratios* or *relative values*. **Ratio analysis** involves methods of calculating and interpreting financial ratios to analyze and monitor the firm's performance. The basic inputs to ratio analysis are the firm's income statement and balance sheet.

ratio analysis
Involves methods of calculating and interpreting financial ratios to analyze and monitor the firm's performance.

Interested Parties

Hint Management should be the most interested party of this group. Managers not only have to worry about the financial situation of the firm, but they are also critically interested in what the other parties think about the firm.

Ratio analysis of a firm's financial statements is of interest to shareholders, creditors, and the firm's own management. Both current and prospective shareholders are interested in the firm's current and future levels of risk and return, which directly affect share price. The firm's creditors are interested primarily in the short-term liquidity of the company and its ability to make interest and principal payments. A secondary concern of creditors is the firm's profitability; they want assurance that the business is healthy. Management, like stockholders, is concerned with all aspects of the firm's financial situation, and it attempts to produce financial ratios that will be considered favorable by both owners and creditors. In addition, management uses ratios to monitor the firm's performance from period to period.

Types of Ratio Comparisons

Ratio analysis is not merely the calculation of a given ratio. More important is the *interpretation* of the ratio value. A meaningful basis for comparison is needed to answer such questions as "Is it too high or too low?" and "Is it good or bad?" Two types of ratio comparisons can be made: cross-sectional and time-series.

Cross-Sectional Analysis

cross-sectional analysis
Comparison of different firms' financial ratios at the same point in time; involves comparing the firm's ratios to those of other firms in its industry or to industry averages.

benchmarking
A type of *cross-sectional analysis* in which the firm's ratio values are compared to those of a key competitor or group of competitors that it wishes to emulate.

Cross-sectional analysis involves the comparison of different firms' financial ratios at the same point in time. Analysts are often interested in how well a firm has performed in relation to other firms in its industry. Frequently, a firm will compare its ratio values to those of a key competitor or group of competitors that it wishes to emulate. This type of cross-sectional analysis, called **benchmarking**, has become very popular.

Comparison to industry averages is also popular. These figures can be found in the *Almanac of Business and Industrial Financial Ratios*, *Dun & Bradstreet's Industry Norms and Key Business Ratios*, *Business Month*, *FTC Quarterly Reports*, *RMA Annual Statement Studies*, *Value Line*, and industry sources.[5] A sample from one available source of industry averages is given in Table 2.5.

---

5. Cross-sectional comparisons of firms operating in several lines of business are difficult to perform. Weighted-average industry average ratios based on the firm's product-line mix can be used or, if data are available, analysis of the firm on a product-line basis can be performed to evaluate a multiproduct firm.

TABLE 2.5 Industry Average Ratios (2003) for Selected Lines of Business[a]

Line of business (number of concerns reporting)[b]	Current ratio (X)	Quick ratio (X)	Sales to inventory (X)	Collection period (days)	Total assets to sales (%)	Total liabilities to net worth (%)	Return on sales (%)	Return on total assets (%)	Return on net worth (%)
Department stores (143)	4.9 2.6 1.6	1.4 0.6 0.2	6.6 4.6 3.5	1.8 6.1 21.2	32.0 43.8 64.9	25.1 76.6 176.9	2.8 1.0 0.1	6.8 2.3 0.1	16.2 4.5 0.2
Electronic computers (76)	2.3 1.6 1.2	1.5 0.9 0.7	31.6 11.3 6.8	27.4 40.9 68.5	24.6 58.9 104.1	54.3 114.3 238.3	3.4 0.5 (9.7)	7.3 1.3 (10.4)	20.6 4.6 (20.6)
Grocery stores (455)	2.6 1.6 1.1	1.0 0.5 0.2	29.6 19.6 13.9	1.1 2.9 6.9	15.3 21.3 31.2	48.5 105.2 277.3	2.2 1.0 0.3	9.4 4.4 1.4	24.8 10.0 3.5
Motor vehicles (42)	2.9 1.7 1.2	1.1 0.7 0.5	11.4 8.3 5.5	16.1 24.1 40.5	27.8 37.4 47.3	56.4 150.8 357.2	4.2 1.5 0.2	10.3 4.1 0.8	26.9 9.6 1.2

[a]These values are given for each ratio for each line of business. The center value is the median, and the values immediately above and below it are the upper and lower quartiles, respectively.
[b]Standard Industrial Classification (SIC) codes for the lines of business shown are, respectively: SIC #5311, SIC #3571, SIC #5411, SIC #3711.
Source: "Industry Norms and Key Business Ratios," Copyright © 2003 Dun & Bradstreet, Inc. Reprinted with permission.

Hint Industry averages are not particularly useful for analyzing firms with multiproduct lines. In the case of multiproduct firms, it is difficult to select the appropriate benchmark industry.

Many people mistakenly believe that as long as the firm being analyzed has a value "better than" the industry average, it can be viewed favorably. However, this "better than average" viewpoint can be misleading. Quite often a ratio value that is far better than the norm can indicate problems that, on more careful analysis, may be more severe than had the ratio been worse than the industry average. It is therefore important to investigate significant deviations *to either side* of the industry standard.

EXAMPLE In early 2007, Mary Boyle, the chief financial analyst at Caldwell Manufacturing, a producer of heat exchangers, gathered data on the firm's financial performance during 2006, the year just ended. She calculated a variety of ratios and obtained industry averages. She was especially interested in inventory turnover, which reflects the speed with which the firm moves its inventory from raw materials through production into finished goods and to the customer as a completed sale. Generally, higher values of this ratio are preferred, because they indicate a quicker turnover of inventory. Caldwell Manufacturing's calculated inventory turnover for 2006 and the industry average inventory turnover were as follows:

	Inventory turnover, 2006
Caldwell Manufacturing	14.8
Industry average	9.7

Mary's initial reaction to these data was that the firm had managed its inventory significantly *better than* the average firm in the industry. The turnover was nearly 53% faster than the industry average. Upon reflection, however, she realized that a very high inventory turnover could also mean very low levels of inventory. The consequence of low inventory could be excessive stockouts (insufficient inventory). Discussions with people in the manufacturing and marketing departments did, in fact, uncover such a problem: Inventories during the year were extremely low, the result of numerous production delays that hindered the firm's ability to meet demand and resulted in lost sales. A ratio that initially appeared to reflect extremely efficient inventory management was actually the symptom of a major problem.

Time-Series Analysis

time-series analysis
Evaluation of the firm's financial performance over time using financial ratio analysis.

Time-series analysis evaluates performance over time. Comparison of current to past performance, using ratios, enables analysts to assess the firm's progress. Developing trends can be seen by using multiyear comparisons. Any significant year-to-year changes may be symptomatic of a major problem.

Combined Analysis

The most informative approach to ratio analysis combines cross-sectional and time-series analyses. A combined view makes it possible to assess the trend in the behavior of the ratio in relation to the trend for the industry. Figure 2.1 depicts this type of approach using the average collection period ratio of Bartlett Company, over the years 2003–2006. This ratio reflects the average amount of time (in days) it takes the firm to collect bills, and lower values of this ratio generally are preferred. The figure quickly discloses that (1) Bartlett's effectiveness in collecting its receivables is poor in comparison to the industry, and (2) Bartlett's trend is toward longer collection periods. Clearly, Bartlett needs to shorten its collection period.

Cautions About Using Ratio Analysis

Before discussing specific ratios, we should consider the following cautions about their use:

1. Ratios that reveal large deviations from the norm merely indicate *symptoms* of a problem. Additional analysis is typically needed to isolate the *causes* of the problem. The fundamental point is this: Ratio analysis directs attention to potential areas of concern; it does not provide conclusive evidence as to the existence of a problem.
2. A single ratio does not generally provide sufficient information from which to judge the *overall* performance of the firm. Only when a group of ratios is used can reasonable judgments be made. However, if an analysis is concerned only with certain *specific* aspects of a firm's financial position, one or two ratios may suffice.
3. The ratios being compared should be calculated using financial statements dated at the same point in time during the year. If they are not, the effects of *seasonality* may produce erroneous conclusions and decisions. For example, comparison of the inventory turnover of a toy manufacturer at the end of

FIGURE 2.1

Combined Analysis
Combined cross-sectional and time-series view of Bartlett Company's average collection period, 2003–2006

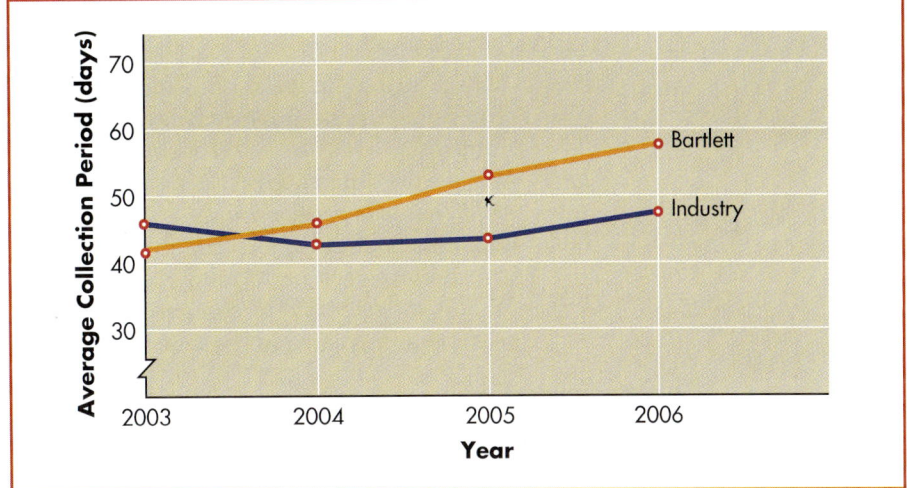

June with its end-of-December value can be misleading. Clearly, the seasonal impact of the December holiday selling season would skew any comparison of the firm's inventory management.

4. It is preferable to use *audited financial statements* for ratio analysis. If the statements have not been audited, the data contained in them may not reflect the firm's true financial condition.
5. The financial data being compared should have been developed in the same way. The use of differing accounting treatments—especially relative to inventory and depreciation—can distort the results of ratio comparisons, regardless of whether cross-sectional or time-series analysis is used.
6. Results can be distorted by *inflation,* which can cause the book values of inventory and depreciable assets to differ greatly from their true (replacement) values. Additionally, inventory costs and depreciation write-offs can differ from their true values, thereby distorting profits. Without adjustment, inflation tends to cause older firms (older assets) to appear more efficient and profitable than newer firms (newer assets). Clearly, in using ratios, care must be taken when comparing older to newer firms or a firm to itself over a long period of time.

Categories of Financial Ratios

Financial ratios can be divided for convenience into five basic categories: liquidity, activity, debt, profitability, and market ratios. Liquidity, activity, and debt ratios primarily measure risk. Profitability ratios measure return. Market ratios capture both risk and return.

As a rule, the inputs necessary for an effective financial analysis include, at a minimum, the income statement and the balance sheet. We will use the 2006 and 2005 income statements and balance sheets for Bartlett Company, presented earlier in Tables 2.1 and 2.2, to demonstrate ratio calculations. Note, however, that the ratios presented in the remainder of this chapter can be applied to almost any company. Of course, many companies in different industries use ratios that focus on aspects peculiar to their industry.

Review Questions

2–4 With regard to financial ratio analysis, how do the viewpoints held by the firm's present and prospective shareholders, creditors, and management differ?

2–5 What is the difference between *cross-sectional* and *time-series* ratio analysis? What is *benchmarking*?

2–6 What types of deviations from the norm should the analyst pay primary attention to when performing cross-sectional ratio analysis? Why?

2–7 Why is it preferable to compare ratios calculated using financial statements that are dated at the same point in time during the year?

Liquidity Ratios

liquidity
A firm's ability to satisfy its short-term obligations *as they come due.*

The **liquidity** of a firm is measured by its ability to satisfy its short-term obligations *as they come due.* Liquidity refers to the solvency of the firm's *overall* financial position—the ease with which it can pay its bills. Because a common precursor to financial distress and bankruptcy is low or declining liquidity, these ratios can provide early signs of cash flow problems and impending business failure. The two basic measures of liquidity are the current ratio and the quick (acid-test) ratio.

Current Ratio

current ratio
A measure of liquidity calculated by dividing the firm's current assets by its current liabilities.

The **current ratio**, one of the most commonly cited financial ratios, measures the firm's ability to meet its short-term obligations. It is expressed as follows:

$$\text{Current ratio} = \frac{\text{Current assets}}{\text{Current liabilities}}$$

The current ratio for Bartlett Company in 2006 is

$$\frac{\$1,223,000}{\$620,000} = 1.97$$

Generally, the higher the current ratio, the more liquid the firm is considered to be. A current ratio of 2.0 is occasionally cited as acceptable, but a value's acceptability depends on the industry in which the firm operates. For example, a current ratio of 1.0 would be considered acceptable for a public utility but might be unacceptable for a manufacturing firm. The more predictable a firm's cash flows, the lower the acceptable current ratio. Because Bartlett Company is in a business with a relatively predictable annual cash flow, its current ratio of 1.97 should be quite acceptable.

Quick (Acid-Test) Ratio

quick (acid-test) ratio
A measure of liquidity calculated by dividing the firm's current assets minus inventory by its current liabilities.

The **quick (acid-test) ratio** is similar to the current ratio except that it excludes inventory, which is generally the least liquid current asset. The generally low liquidity of inventory results from two primary factors: (1) many types of inventory cannot be easily sold because they are partially completed items, special-purpose items, and the like; and (2) inventory is typically sold on credit, which means that it becomes an account receivable before being converted into cash. The quick ratio is calculated as follows:[6]

$$\text{Quick ratio} = \frac{\text{Current assets} - \text{Inventory}}{\text{Current liabilities}}$$

The quick ratio for Bartlett Company in 2006 is

$$\frac{\$1,223,000 - \$289,000}{\$620,000} = \frac{\$934,000}{\$620,000} = 1.51$$

A quick ratio of 1.0 or greater is occasionally recommended, but as with the current ratio, what value is acceptable depends largely on the industry. The quick ratio provides a better measure of overall liquidity only when a firm's inventory cannot be easily converted into cash. If inventory is liquid, the current ratio is a preferred measure of overall liquidity.

Review Question

2–8 Under what circumstances would the current ratio be the preferred measure of overall firm liquidity? Under what circumstances would the quick ratio be preferred?

Activity Ratios

activity ratios
Measure the speed with which various accounts are converted into sales or cash—inflows or outflows.

Activity ratios measure the speed with which various accounts are converted into sales or cash—inflows or outflows. With regard to current accounts, measures of liquidity are generally inadequate because differences in the *composition* of a firm's current assets and current liabilities can significantly affect its "true" liquidity. It is therefore important to look beyond measures of overall liquidity and to assess the activity (liquidity) of specific current accounts. A number of ratios are available for measuring the activity of the most important current accounts, which include inventory, accounts receivable, and accounts payable.[7] The efficiency with which total assets are used can also be assessed.

---

6. Sometimes the quick ratio is defined as (cash + marketable securities + accounts receivable) ÷ current liabilities. If a firm were to show as current assets items other than cash, marketable securities, accounts receivable, and inventories, its quick ratio might vary, depending on the method of calculation.

7. For convenience, the activity ratios involving these current accounts assume that their end-of-period values are good approximations of the average account balance during the period—typically 1 year. Technically, when the month-end balances of inventory, accounts receivable, or accounts payable vary during the year, the average balance, calculated by summing the 12 month-end account balances and dividing the total by 12, should be used instead of the year-end value. If month-end balances are unavailable, the average can be approximated by dividing the sum of the beginning-of-year and end-of-year balances by 2. These approaches ensure a ratio that on the average better reflects the firm's circumstances. Because the data needed to find averages are generally unavailable to the external analyst, year-end values are frequently used to calculate activity ratios for current accounts.

Inventory Turnover

inventory turnover
Measures the activity, or liquidity, of a firm's inventory.

Inventory turnover commonly measures the activity, or liquidity, of a firm's inventory. It is calculated as follows:

$$\text{Inventory turnover} = \frac{\text{Cost of goods sold}}{\text{Inventory}}$$

Applying this relationship to Bartlett Company in 2006 yields

$$\text{Inventory turnover} = \frac{\$2,088,000}{\$289,000} = 7.2$$

The resulting turnover is meaningful only when it is compared with that of other firms in the same industry or to the firm's past inventory turnover. An inventory turnover of 20.0 would not be unusual for a grocery store, whereas a common inventory turnover for an aircraft manufacturer is 4.0.

average age of inventory
Average number of days' sales in inventory.

Inventory turnover can be easily converted into an **average age of inventory** by dividing it into 365—the assumed number of days in a year.[8] For Bartlett Company, the average age of inventory in 2006 is 50.7 days (365 ÷ 7.2). This value can also be viewed as the average number of days' sales in inventory.

Average Collection Period

average collection period
The average amount of time needed to collect accounts receivable.

The **average collection period**, or average age of accounts receivable, is useful in evaluating credit and collection policies.[9] It is arrived at by dividing the average daily sales[10] into the accounts receivable balance:

$$\text{Average collection period} = \frac{\text{Accounts receivable}}{\text{Average sales per day}}$$

$$= \frac{\text{Accounts receivable}}{\frac{\text{Annual sales}}{365}}$$

The average collection period for Bartlett Company in 2006 is

$$\frac{\$503,000}{\frac{\$3,074,000}{365}} = \frac{\$503,000}{\$8,422} = 59.7 \text{ days}$$

On the average, it takes the firm 59.7 days to collect an account receivable.

The average collection period is meaningful only in relation to the firm's credit terms. If Bartlett Company extends 30-day credit terms to customers, an average collection period of 59.7 days may indicate a poorly managed credit or collection department, or both. It is also possible that the lengthened collection

---

8. Unless otherwise specified, a 365-day year is used throughout this textbook. This assumption makes the calculations more realistic than would use of a 360-day year consisting of twelve 30-day months.

9. The average collection period is sometimes called the *days' sales outstanding (DSO)*. A discussion of the evaluation and establishment of credit and collection policies is presented in Chapter 13.

10. The formula as presented assumes, for simplicity, that all sales are made on a credit basis. If this is not the case, *average credit sales per day* should be substituted for average sales per day.

period resulted from an intentional relaxation of credit-term enforcement in response to competitive pressures. If the firm had extended 60-day credit terms, the 59.7-day average collection period would be quite acceptable. Clearly, additional information is needed to evaluate the effectiveness of the firm's credit and collection policies.

Average Payment Period

average payment period
The average amount of time needed to pay accounts payable.

The **average payment period**, or average age of accounts payable, is calculated in the same manner as the average collection period:

$$\text{Average payment period} = \frac{\text{Accounts payable}}{\text{Average purchases per day}}$$

$$= \frac{\text{Accounts payable}}{\frac{\text{Annual purchases}}{365}}$$

The difficulty in calculating this ratio stems from the need to find annual purchases,[11] a value not available in published financial statements. Ordinarily, purchases are estimated as a given percentage of cost of goods sold. If we assume that Bartlett Company's purchases equaled 70 percent of its cost of goods sold in 2006, its average payment period is

$$\frac{\$382,000}{\frac{0.70 \times \$2,088,000}{365}} = \frac{\$382,000}{\$4,004} = 95.4 \text{ days}$$

This figure is meaningful only in relation to the average credit terms extended to the firm. If Bartlett Company's suppliers have extended, on average, 30-day credit terms, an analyst would give Bartlett a low credit rating. Prospective lenders and suppliers of trade credit are most interested in the average payment period because it provides insight into the firm's bill-paying patterns.

Total Asset Turnover

total asset turnover
Indicates the efficiency with which the firm uses its assets to generate sales.

Hint The higher the cost of the new assets, the larger the denominator and thus the smaller the ratio. Therefore, because of inflation and the use of historical costs, firms with newer assets will tend to have lower turnovers than those with older assets.

The **total asset turnover** indicates the efficiency with which the firm uses its assets to generate sales. Total asset turnover is calculated as follows:

$$\text{Total asset turnover} = \frac{\text{Sales}}{\text{Total assets}}$$

The value of Bartlett Company's total asset turnover in 2006 is

$$\frac{\$3,074,000}{\$3,597,000} = 0.85$$

This means the company turns over its assets 0.85 times per year.

---

11. Technically, annual *credit* purchases—rather than annual purchases—should be used in calculating this ratio. For simplicity, this refinement is ignored here.

Review Question

2–9 To assess the firm's average collection period and average payment period ratios, what additional information is needed, and why?

Debt Ratios

The *debt position* of a firm indicates the amount of other people's money being used to generate profits. In general, the financial analyst is most concerned with long-term debts, because these commit the firm to a stream of contractual payments over the long run. The more debt a firm has, the greater its risk of being unable to meet its contractual debt payments and becoming bankrupt. Because creditors' claims must be satisfied before the earnings can be distributed to shareholders, current and prospective shareholders pay close attention to the firm's ability to repay debts. Lenders are also concerned about the firm's indebtedness. Management obviously must be concerned with indebtedness.

In general, the more debt a firm uses in relation to its total assets, the greater its *financial leverage*. **Financial leverage** is the magnification of risk and return introduced through the use of fixed-cost financing, such as debt and preferred stock. The more fixed-cost debt a firm uses, the greater will be its expected risk and return.

financial leverage
The magnification of risk and return introduced through the use of fixed-cost financing, such as debt and preferred stock.

EXAMPLE

Patty Akers is in the process of incorporating her new business. After much analysis she determined that an initial investment of $50,000—$20,000 in current assets and $30,000 in fixed assets—is necessary. These funds can be obtained in either of two ways. The first is the *no-debt plan*, under which she would invest the full $50,000 without borrowing. The other alternative, the *debt plan*, involves investing $25,000 and borrowing the balance of $25,000 at 12% annual interest. Regardless of which alternative she chooses, Patty expects sales to average $30,000, costs and operating expenses to average $18,000, and earnings to be taxed at a 40% rate. Projected balance sheets and income statements associated with the two plans are summarized in Table 2.6. The no-debt plan results in after-tax profits of $7,200, which represent a 14.4% rate of return on Patty's $50,000 investment. The debt plan results in $5,400 of after-tax profits, which represent a 21.6% rate of return on Patty's investment of $25,000. The debt plan provides Patty with a higher rate of return, but the risk of this plan is also greater, because the annual $3,000 of interest must be paid before receipt of earnings.

The example demonstrates that *with increased debt comes greater risk as well as higher potential return*. Therefore, the greater the financial leverage, the greater the potential risk and return. A detailed discussion of the impact of debt on the firm's risk, return, and value is included in Chapter 11. Here, we emphasize the use of financial debt ratios to assess externally a firm's debt position.

TABLE 2.6 Financial Statements Associated with Patty's Alternatives

	No-debt plan	Debt plan
Balance Sheets		
Current assets	$20,000	$20,000
Fixed assets	30,000	30,000
Total assets	$50,000	$50,000
Debt (12% interest)	$ 0	$25,000
(1) Equity	50,000	25,000
Total liabilities and equity	$50,000	$50,000
Income Statements		
Sales	$30,000	$30,000
Less: Costs and operating expenses	18,000	18,000
Operating profits	$12,000	$12,000
Less: Interest expense	0	$0.12 \times \$25,000 = $ 3,000
Net profits before taxes	$12,000	$ 9,000
Less: Taxes (rate = 40%)	4,800	3,600
(2) Net profits after taxes	$ 7,200	$ 5,400
Return on equity [(2) ÷ (1)]	$\frac{\$7,200}{\$50,000} = 14.4\%$	$\frac{\$5,400}{\$25,000} = 21.6\%$

There are two general types of debt measures: measures of the degree of indebtedness and measures of the ability to service debts. The **degree of indebtedness** measures the amount of debt relative to other significant balance sheet amounts. A popular measure of the degree of indebtedness is the debt ratio.

The second type of debt measure, the **ability to service debts,** reflects a firm's ability to make the payments required on a scheduled basis over the life of a debt.[12] The firm's ability to pay certain fixed charges is measured using **coverage ratios.** Typically, higher coverage ratios are preferred, but too high a ratio (above industry norms) may result in unnecessarily low risk and return. In general, the lower the firm's coverage ratios, the less certain it is to be able to pay fixed obligations. If a firm is unable to pay these obligations, its creditors may seek immediate repayment, which in most instances would force a firm into bankruptcy. Two popular coverage ratios are the times interest earned ratio and the fixed-payment coverage ratio.

degree of indebtedness
Measures the amount of debt relative to other significant balance sheet amounts.

ability to service debts
The ability of a firm to make the payments required on a scheduled basis over the life of a debt.

coverage ratios
Ratios that measure the firm's ability to pay certain fixed charges.

Debt Ratio

debt ratio
Measures the proportion of total assets financed by the firm's creditors.

The **debt ratio** measures the proportion of total assets financed by the firm's creditors. The higher this ratio, the greater the amount of other people's money being used to generate profits. The ratio is calculated as follows:

$$\text{Debt ratio} = \frac{\text{Total liabilities}}{\text{Total assets}}$$

---

12. The term *service* refers to the payment of interest and repayment of principal associated with a firm's debt obligations. When a firm services its debts, it pays—or fulfills—these obligations.

The debt ratio for Bartlett Company in 2006 is

$$\frac{\$1,643,000}{\$3,597,000} = 0.457 = 45.7\%$$

This value indicates that the company has financed close to half of its assets with debt. The higher this ratio, the greater the firm's degree of indebtedness and the more financial leverage it has.

Times Interest Earned Ratio

times interest earned ratio
Measures the firm's ability to make contractual interest payments; sometimes called the *interest coverage ratio*.

The **times interest earned ratio**, sometimes called the *interest coverage ratio*, measures the firm's ability to make contractual interest payments. The higher its value, the better able the firm is to fulfill its interest obligations. The times interest earned ratio is calculated as follows:

$$\text{Times interest earned ratio} = \frac{\text{Earnings before interest and taxes}}{\text{Interest}}$$

The figure for *earnings before interest and taxes* is the same as that for *operating profits* shown in the income statement. Applying this ratio to Bartlett Company yields the following 2006 value:

$$\text{Times interest earned ratio} = \frac{\$418,000}{\$93,000} = 4.5$$

The times interest earned ratio for Bartlett Company seems acceptable. A value of at least 3.0—and preferably closer to 5.0—is often suggested. The firm's earnings before interest and taxes could shrink by as much as 78 percent [(4.5 − 1.0) ÷ 4.5], and the firm would still be able to pay the $93,000 in interest it owes. Thus it has a good margin of safety.

Fixed-Payment Coverage Ratio

fixed-payment coverage ratio
Measures the firm's ability to meet all fixed-payment obligations.

The **fixed-payment coverage ratio** measures the firm's ability to meet all fixed-payment obligations, such as loan interest and principal, lease payments, and preferred stock dividends.[13] As is true of the times interest earned ratio, the higher this value, the better. The formula for the fixed-payment coverage ratio is

$$\text{Fixed-payment coverage ratio} = \frac{\text{Earnings before interest and taxes} + \text{Lease payments}}{\text{Interest} + \text{Lease payments} + \{(\text{Principal payments} + \text{Preferred stock dividends}) \times [1/(1 - T)]\}}$$

where T is the corporate tax rate applicable to the firm's income. The term $1/(1 - T)$ is included to adjust the after-tax principal and preferred stock dividend pay-

---

13. Although preferred stock dividends, which are stated at the time of issue, can be "passed" (not paid) at the option of the firm's directors, it is generally believed that the payment of such dividends is necessary. *This text therefore treats the preferred stock dividend as a contractual obligation, to be paid as a fixed amount, as scheduled.*

ments back to a before-tax equivalent that is consistent with the before-tax values of all other terms. Applying the formula to Bartlett Company's 2006 data yields

$$\frac{\text{Fixed-payment}}{\text{coverage ratio}} = \frac{\$418{,}000 + \$35{,}000}{\$93{,}000 + \$35{,}000 + \{(\$71{,}000 + \$10{,}000) \times [1/(1 - 0.29)]\}}$$

$$= \frac{\$453{,}000}{\$242{,}000} = 1.9$$

Because the earnings available are nearly twice as large as its fixed-payment obligations, the firm appears safely able to meet the latter.

Like the times interest earned ratio, the fixed-payment coverage ratio measures risk. The lower the ratio, the greater the risk to both lenders and owners; the greater the ratio, the lower the risk. This ratio allows interested parties to assess the firm's ability to meet additional fixed-payment obligations without being driven into bankruptcy.

Review Questions

2–10 What is *financial leverage*?

2–11 What ratio measures the firm's *degree of indebtedness*? What ratios assess the firm's *ability to service debts*?

Profitability Ratios

There are many measures of profitability. As a group, these measures enable the analyst to evaluate the firm's profits with respect to a given level of sales, a certain level of assets, or the owners' investment. Without profits, a firm could not attract outside capital. Owners, creditors, and management pay close attention to boosting profits because of the great importance placed on earnings in the marketplace.

Common-Size Income Statements

common-size income statement
An income statement in which each item is expressed as a percentage of sales.

A popular tool for evaluating profitability in relation to sales is the **common-size income statement**. Each item on this statement is expressed as a percentage of sales. Common-size income statements are especially useful in comparing performance across years. Three frequently cited ratios of profitability that can be read directly from the common-size income statement are (1) the gross profit margin, (2) the operating profit margin, and (3) the net profit margin.

Common-size income statements for 2006 and 2005 for Bartlett Company are presented and evaluated in Table 2.7 (see page 60). These statements reveal that the firm's cost of goods sold increased from 66.7 percent of sales in 2005 to 67.9 percent in 2006, resulting in a worsening gross profit margin. However, thanks to a decrease in total operating expenses, the firm's net profit margin rose from 5.4 percent of sales in 2005 to 7.2 percent in 2006. The decrease in expenses

TABLE 2.7 Bartlett Company Common-Size Income Statements

	For the years ended December 31 2006	For the years ended December 31 2005	Evaluation[a] 2005–2006
Sales revenue	100.0%	100.0%	same
Less: Cost of goods sold	67.9	66.7	worse
(1) Gross profit margin	32.1%	33.3%	worse
Less: Operating expenses			
Selling expense	3.3%	4.2%	better
General and administrative expenses	6.8	6.7	better
Lease expense	1.1	1.3	better
Depreciation expense	7.3	9.3	better
Total operating expense	18.5%	21.5%	better
(2) Operating profit margin	13.6%	11.8%	better
Less: Interest expense	3.0	3.5	better
Net profits before taxes	10.6%	8.3%	better
Less: Taxes	3.1	2.5	worse[b]
Net profits after taxes	7.5%	5.8%	better
Less: Preferred stock dividends	0.3	0.4	better
(3) Net profit margin	7.2%	5.4%	better

[a]Subjective assessments based on data provided.

[b]Taxes as a percentage of sales increased noticeably between 2005 and 2006 because of differing costs and expenses, whereas the average tax rates (taxes ÷ net profits before taxes) for 2005 and 2006 remained about the same—30% and 29%, respectively.

more than compensated for the increase in the cost of goods sold. A decrease in the firm's 2006 interest expense (3.0 percent of sales versus 3.5 percent in 2005) added to the increase in 2006 profits.

Gross Profit Margin

gross profit margin
Measures the percentage of each sales dollar remaining after the firm has paid for its goods.

The **gross profit margin** measures the percentage of each sales dollar remaining after the firm has paid for its goods. The higher the gross profit margin, the better (that is, the lower the relative cost of merchandise sold). The gross profit margin is calculated as follows:

$$\text{Gross profit margin} = \frac{\text{Sales} - \text{Cost of goods sold}}{\text{Sales}} = \frac{\text{Gross profits}}{\text{Sales}}$$

Bartlett Company's gross profit margin for 2006 is

$$\frac{\$3,074,000 - \$2,088,000}{\$3,074,000} = \frac{\$986,000}{\$3,074,000} = 32.1\%$$

Hint This is a very significant ratio for small retailers, especially during times of inflationary prices. If the owner of the firm does not raise prices when the cost of sales is rising, the gross profit margin will erode.

This value is labeled (1) on the common-size income statement in Table 2.7.

Operating Profit Margin

operating profit margin
Measures the percentage of each sales dollar remaining after all costs and expenses *other than* interest, taxes, and preferred stock dividends are deducted; the "pure profits" earned on each sales dollar.

The **operating profit margin** measures the percentage of each sales dollar remaining after all costs and expenses *other than* interest, taxes, and preferred stock dividends are deducted. It represents the "pure profits" earned on each sales dollar. Operating profits are "pure" because they measure only the profits earned on operations and ignore interest, taxes, and preferred stock dividends. A high operating profit margin is preferred. The operating profit margin is calculated as follows:

$$\text{Operating profit margin} = \frac{\text{Operating profits}}{\text{Sales}}$$

Bartlett Company's operating profit margin for 2006 is

$$\frac{\$418,000}{\$3,074,000} = 13.6\%$$

This value is labeled (2) on the common-size income statement in Table 2.7.

Net Profit Margin

net profit margin
Measures the percentage of each sales dollar remaining after all costs and expenses, *including* interest, taxes, and preferred stock dividends, have been deducted.

The **net profit margin** measures the percentage of each sales dollar remaining after all costs and expenses, *including* interest, taxes, and preferred stock dividends, have been deducted. The higher the firm's net profit margin, the better. The net profit margin is calculated as follows:

$$\text{Net profit margin} = \frac{\text{Earnings available for common stockholders}}{\text{Sales}}$$

Bartlett Company's net profit margin for 2006 is

$$\frac{\$221,000}{\$3,074,000} = 7.2\%$$

Hint The net profit margin is sometimes defined as net profits after taxes divided by sales. The formula used here places greater emphasis on the common stockholders.

This value is labeled (3) on the common-size income statement in Table 2.7.

The net profit margin is a commonly cited measure of the firm's success with respect to earnings on sales. "Good" net profit margins differ considerably across industries. A net profit margin of 1 percent or less would not be unusual for a grocery store, whereas a net profit margin of 10 percent would be low for a retail jewelry store.

Earnings per Share (EPS)

Hint EPS represents the dollar amount earned *on behalf of* each outstanding share of common stock—not the amount of earnings *actually distributed* to shareholders.

The firm's *earnings per share (EPS)* is generally of interest to present or prospective stockholders and management. As we noted earlier, EPS represents the number of dollars earned during the period on behalf of each outstanding share of common stock. Earnings per share is calculated as follows:

$$\text{Earnings per share} = \frac{\text{Earnings available for common stockholders}}{\text{Number of shares of common stock outstanding}}$$

Bartlett Company's earnings per share in 2006 is

$$\frac{\$221,000}{76,262} = \$2.90$$

This figure represents the dollar amount earned *on behalf of* each outstanding share of common stock. The dollar amount of cash *actually distributed* to each shareholder is the *dividend per share (DPS)*, which, as noted in Bartlett Company's income statement (Table 2.1), rose to $1.29 in 2006 from $0.75 in 2005. EPS is closely watched by the investing public and is considered an important indicator of corporate success.

Return on Total Assets (ROA)

return on total assets (ROA)
Measures the overall effectiveness of management in generating profits with its available assets; also called the *return on investment (ROI)*.

The **return on total assets (ROA)**, often called the *return on investment (ROI)*, measures the overall effectiveness of management in generating profits with its available assets. The higher the firm's return on total assets, the better. The return on total assets is calculated as follows:

$$\text{Return on total assets} = \frac{\text{Earnings available for common stockholders}}{\text{Total assets}}$$

Hint Some firms use this measure as a simple decision technique for evaluating proposed fixed-asset investments.

Bartlett Company's return on total assets in 2006 is

$$\frac{\$221,000}{\$3,597,000} = 6.1\%$$

This value indicates that the company earned 6.1 cents on each dollar of asset investment.

Return on Common Equity (ROE)

return on common equity (ROE)
Measures the return earned on the common stockholders' investment in the firm.

The **return on common equity (ROE)** measures the return earned on the common stockholders' investment in the firm. Generally, the higher this return, the better off are the owners. Return on common equity is calculated as follows:

$$\text{Return on common equity} = \frac{\text{Earnings available for common stockholders}}{\text{Common stock equity}}$$

This ratio for Bartlett Company in 2006 is

$$\frac{\$221,000}{\$1,754,000} = 12.6\%$$

Note that the value for common stock equity ($1,754,000) was found by subtracting the $200,000 of preferred stock equity from the total stockholders' equity of $1,954,000 (see Bartlett Company's 2006 balance sheet in Table 2.2). The calculated ROE of 12.6 percent indicates that during 2006 Bartlett earned 12.6 cents on each dollar of common stock equity.

Review Questions

2–12 What three ratios of profitability are found on a *common-size income statement*?

2–13 What would explain a firm's having a high gross profit margin and a low net profit margin?

2–14 Which measure of profitability is probably of greatest interest to the investing public? Why?

Market Ratios

market ratios
Relate a firm's market value, as measured by its current share price, to certain accounting values.

Market ratios relate the firm's market value, as measured by its current share price, to certain accounting values. These ratios give insight into how well investors in the marketplace feel the firm is doing in terms of risk and return. They tend to reflect, on a relative basis, the common stockholders' assessment of all aspects of the firm's past and expected future performance. Here we consider two popular market ratios, one that focuses on earnings and another that considers book value.

Price/Earnings (P/E) Ratio

price/earnings (P/E) ratio
Measures the amount that investors are willing to pay for each dollar of a firm's earnings; the higher the P/E ratio, the greater the investor confidence.

The **price/earnings (P/E) ratio** is commonly used to assess the owners' appraisal of share value. The P/E ratio measures the amount that investors are willing to pay for each dollar of a firm's earnings. The level of this ratio indicates the degree of confidence that investors have in the firm's future performance. The higher the P/E ratio, the greater the investor confidence. The P/E ratio is calculated as follows:

$$\text{Price/earnings (P/E) ratio} = \frac{\text{Market price per share of common stock}}{\text{Earnings per share}}$$

If Bartlett Company's common stock at the end of 2006 was selling at $32.25, using the EPS of $2.90, the P/E ratio at year-end 2006 is

$$\frac{\$32.25}{\$2.90} = 11.1$$

This figure indicates that investors were paying $11.10 for each $1.00 of earnings. The P/E ratio is most informative when applied in cross-sectional analysis using an industry average P/E ratio or the P/E ratio of a benchmark firm.

Market/Book (M/B) Ratio

market/book (M/B) ratio
Provides an assessment of how investors view the firm's performance. Firms expected to earn high returns relative to their risk typically sell at higher M/B multiples.

The **market/book (M/B) ratio** provides an assessment of how investors view the firm's performance. It relates the market value of the firm's shares to their book—strict accounting—value. To calculate the firm's M/B ratio, we first need to find the *book value per share of common stock*:

$$\frac{\text{Book value per share}}{\text{of common stock}} = \frac{\text{Common stock equity}}{\text{Number of shares of common stock outstanding}}$$

Substituting the appropriate values for Bartlett Company from its 2006 balance sheet, we get

$$\text{Book value per share of common stock} = \frac{\$1,754,000}{76,262} = \$23.00$$

The formula for the market/book ratio is

$$\text{Market/book (M/B) ratio} = \frac{\text{Market price per share of common stock}}{\text{Book value per share of common stock}}$$

Substituting Bartlett Company's end of 2006 common stock price of $32.25 and its $23.00 book value per share of common stock (calculated above) into the M/B ratio formula, we get

$$\text{Market/book (M/B) ratio} = \frac{\$32.25}{\$23.00} = 1.40$$

This M/B ratio means that investors are currently paying $1.40 for each $1.00 of book value of Bartlett Company's stock.

The stocks of firms that are expected to perform well—improve profits, increase their market share, or launch successful products—typically sell at higher M/B ratios than the stocks of firms with less attractive outlooks. Simply stated, firms expected to earn high returns relative to their risk typically sell at higher M/B multiples. Clearly, Bartlett's future prospects are being viewed favorably by investors, who are willing to pay more than its book value for the firm's shares. Like P/E ratios, M/B ratios are typically assessed cross-sectionally, to get a feel for the firm's risk and return compared to peer firms.

Review Question

2–15 How do the *price/earnings (P/E) ratio* and the *market/book (M/B) ratio* provide a feel for the firm's risk and return?

A Complete Ratio Analysis

Analysts frequently wish to take an overall look at the firm's financial performance and status. Here we consider two popular approaches to a complete ratio analysis: (1) summarizing all ratios and (2) the DuPont system of analysis. The summary analysis approach tends to view *all aspects* of the firm's financial activities to isolate key areas of responsibility. The DuPont system acts as a search technique aimed at finding the *key areas* responsible for the firm's financial condition.

Summarizing All Ratios

We can use Bartlett Company's ratios to perform a complete ratio analysis using both cross-sectional and time-series analysis approaches. The 2006 ratio values calculated earlier and the ratio values calculated for 2004 and 2005 for Bartlett

Company, along with the industry average ratios for 2006, are summarized in Table 2.8 (see pages 66 and 67), which also shows the formula used to calculate each ratio. Using these data, we can discuss the five key aspects of Bartlett's performance—liquidity, activity, debt, profitability, and market.

Liquidity

The overall liquidity of the firm seems to exhibit a reasonably stable trend, having been maintained at a level that is relatively consistent with the industry average in 2006. The firm's liquidity seems to be good.

Activity

Bartlett Company's inventory appears to be in good shape. Its inventory management seems to have improved, and in 2006 it performed at a level above that of the industry. The firm may be experiencing some problems with accounts receivable. The average collection period seems to have crept up above that of the industry. Bartlett also appears to be slow in paying its bills; it pays nearly 30 days slower than the industry average. This could adversely affect the firm's credit standing. Although overall liquidity appears to be good, the management of receivables and payables should be examined. Bartlett's total asset turnover reflects a decline in the efficiency of total asset utilization between 2004 and 2005. Although in 2006 it rose to a level considerably above the industry average, it appears that the pre-2005 level of efficiency has not yet been achieved.

Debt

Bartlett Company's indebtedness increased over the 2004–2006 period and is currently above the industry average. Although this increase in the debt ratio could be cause for alarm, the firm's ability to meet interest and fixed-payment obligations improved, from 2005 to 2006, to a level that outperforms the industry. The firm's increased indebtedness in 2005 apparently caused a deterioration in its ability to pay debt adequately. However, Bartlett has evidently improved its income in 2006 so that it is able to meet its interest and fixed-payment obligations at a level consistent with the average in the industry. In summary, it appears that although 2005 was an off year, the company's improved ability to pay debts in 2006 compensates for its increased degree of indebtedness.

Profitability

Bartlett's profitability relative to sales in 2006 was better than the average company in the industry, although it did not match the firm's 2004 performance. Although the *gross* profit margin was better in 2005 and 2006 than in 2004, higher levels of operating and interest expenses in 2005 and 2006 appear to have caused the 2006 *net* profit margin to fall below that of 2004. However, Bartlett Company's 2006 net profit margin is quite favorable when compared to the industry average.

The firm's earnings per share, return on total assets, and return on common equity behaved much as its net profit margin did over the 2004–2006 period. Bartlett appears to have experienced either a sizable drop in sales between 2004 and 2005 or a rapid expansion in assets during that period. The exceptionally

TABLE 2.8 Summary of Bartlett Company Ratios (2004–2006, Including 2006 Industry Averages)

Ratio	Formula	Year 2004[a]	Year 2005[b]	Year 2006[b]	Industry average 2006[c]	Evaluation[d] Cross-sectional 2006	Evaluation[d] Time-series 2004–2006	Evaluation[d] Overall
Liquidity								
Current ratio	$\dfrac{\text{Current assets}}{\text{Current liabilities}}$	2.04	2.08	1.97	2.05	OK	OK	OK
Quick (acid-test) ratio	$\dfrac{\text{Current assets} - \text{Inventory}}{\text{Current liabilities}}$	1.32	1.46	1.51	1.43	OK	good	good
Activity								
Inventory turnover	$\dfrac{\text{Cost of goods sold}}{\text{Inventory}}$	5.1	5.7	7.2	6.6	good	good	good
Average collection period	$\dfrac{\text{Accounts receivable}}{\text{Average sales per day}}$	43.9 days	51.2 days	59.7 days	44.3 days	poor	poor	poor
Average payment period	$\dfrac{\text{Accounts payable}}{\text{Average purchases per day}}$	75.8 days	81.2 days	95.4 days	66.5 days	poor	poor	poor
Total asset turnover	$\dfrac{\text{Sales}}{\text{Total assets}}$	0.94	0.79	0.85	0.75	OK	OK	OK
Debt								
Debt ratio	$\dfrac{\text{Total liabilities}}{\text{Total assets}}$	36.8%	44.3%	45.7%	40.0%	OK	OK	OK
Times interest earned ratio	$\dfrac{\text{Earnings before interest and taxes}}{\text{Interest}}$	5.6	3.3	4.5	4.3	good	OK	OK
Fixed-payment coverage ratio	$\dfrac{\text{Earnings before interest and taxes} + \text{Lease payments}}{\text{Int.} + \text{Lease pay.} + \{(\text{Prin.} + \text{Pref. div.}) \times [1/(1-T)]\}}$	2.4	1.4	1.9	1.5	good	OK	good

CHAPTER 2   Financial Statements and Analysis   67

		Year			Industry average 2006[c]	Evaluation[d]		
Ratio	Formula	2004[a]	2005[b]	2006[b]		Cross-sectional 2006	Time-series 2004–2006	Overall
Profitability								
Gross profit margin	$\dfrac{\text{Gross profits}}{\text{Sales}}$	31.4%	33.3%	32.1%	30.0%	OK	OK	OK
Operating profit margin	$\dfrac{\text{Operating profits}}{\text{Sales}}$	14.6%	11.8%	13.6%	11.0%	good	OK	good
Net profit margin	$\dfrac{\text{Earnings available for common stockholders}}{\text{Sales}}$	8.2%	5.4%	7.2%	6.2%	good	OK	good
Earnings per share (EPS)	$\dfrac{\text{Earnings available for common stockholders}}{\text{Number of shares of common stock outstanding}}$	$3.26	$1.81	$2.90	$2.26	good	OK	good
Return on total assets (ROA)	$\dfrac{\text{Earnings available for common stockholders}}{\text{Total assets}}$	7.8%	4.2%	6.1%	4.6%	good	OK	good
Return on common equity (ROE)	$\dfrac{\text{Earnings available for common stockholders}}{\text{Common stock equity}}$	13.7%	8.5%	12.6%	8.5%	good	OK	good
Market								
Price/earnings (P/E) ratio	$\dfrac{\text{Market price per share of common stock}}{\text{Earnings per share}}$	10.5	10.0[e]	11.1	12.5	OK	OK	OK
Market/book (M/B) ratio	$\dfrac{\text{Market price per share of common stock}}{\text{Book value per share of common stock}}$	1.25	0.85[e]	1.40	1.30	OK	OK	OK

[a] Calculated from data not included in the chapter.
[b] Calculated by using the financial statements presented in Tables 2.1 and 2.2.
[c] Obtained from sources not included in this chapter.
[d] Subjective assessments based on data provided.
[e] The market price per share at the end of 2005 was $18.36.

high 2006 level of return on common equity suggests that the firm is performing quite well. The firm's above-average returns—net profit margin, EPS, ROA, and ROE—may be attributable to the fact that it is more risky than average. A look at market ratios is helpful in assessing risk.

Market

Investors have greater confidence in the firm in 2006 than in the prior two years, as reflected in the price/earnings (P/E) ratio of 11.1. However, this ratio is below the industry average. The P/E ratio suggests that the firm's risk has declined but remains above that of the average firm in its industry. The firm's market/book (M/B) ratio has increased over the 2004–2006 period, and in 2006 it exceeds the industry average. This implies that investors are optimistic about the firm's future performance. The P/E and M/B ratios reflect the firm's increased profitability over the 2004–2006 period: Investors expect to earn high future returns as compensation for the firm's above-average risk.

In summary, the firm appears to be growing and has recently undergone an expansion in assets, financed primarily through the use of debt. The 2005–2006 period seems to reflect a phase of adjustment and recovery from the rapid growth in assets. Bartlett's sales, profits, and other performance factors seem to be growing with the increase in the size of the operation. In addition, the market response to these accomplishments appears to have been positive. In short, the firm seems to have done well in 2006.

DuPont System of Analysis

DuPont system of analysis
System used to dissect the firm's financial statements and to assess its financial condition.

The **DuPont system of analysis** is used to dissect the firm's financial statements and to assess its financial condition. It merges the income statement and balance sheet into two summary measures of profitability: return on total assets (ROA) and return on common equity (ROE). Figure 2.2 depicts the basic DuPont system with Bartlett Company's 2006 monetary and ratio values. The upper portion of the chart summarizes the income statement activities; the lower portion summarizes the balance sheet activities.

Dupont Formula

DuPont formula
Multiplies the firm's *net profit margin* by its *total asset turnover* to calculate the firm's *return on total assets (ROA)*.

The DuPont system first brings together the *net profit margin*, which measures the firm's profitability on sales, with its *total asset turnover*, which indicates how efficiently the firm has used its assets to generate sales. In the **DuPont formula**, the product of these two ratios results in the *return on total assets (ROA)*:

$$ROA = \text{Net profit margin} \times \text{Total asset turnover}$$

Substituting the appropriate formulas into the equation and simplifying results in the formula given earlier,

$$ROA = \frac{\text{Earnings available for common stockholders}}{\text{Sales}} \times \frac{\text{Sales}}{\text{Total assets}} = \frac{\text{Earnings available for common stockholders}}{\text{Total assets}}$$

CHAPTER 2   Financial Statements and Analysis   69

FIGURE 2.2   **Dupont System of Analysis**
The DuPont system of analysis with application to Bartlett Company (2006)

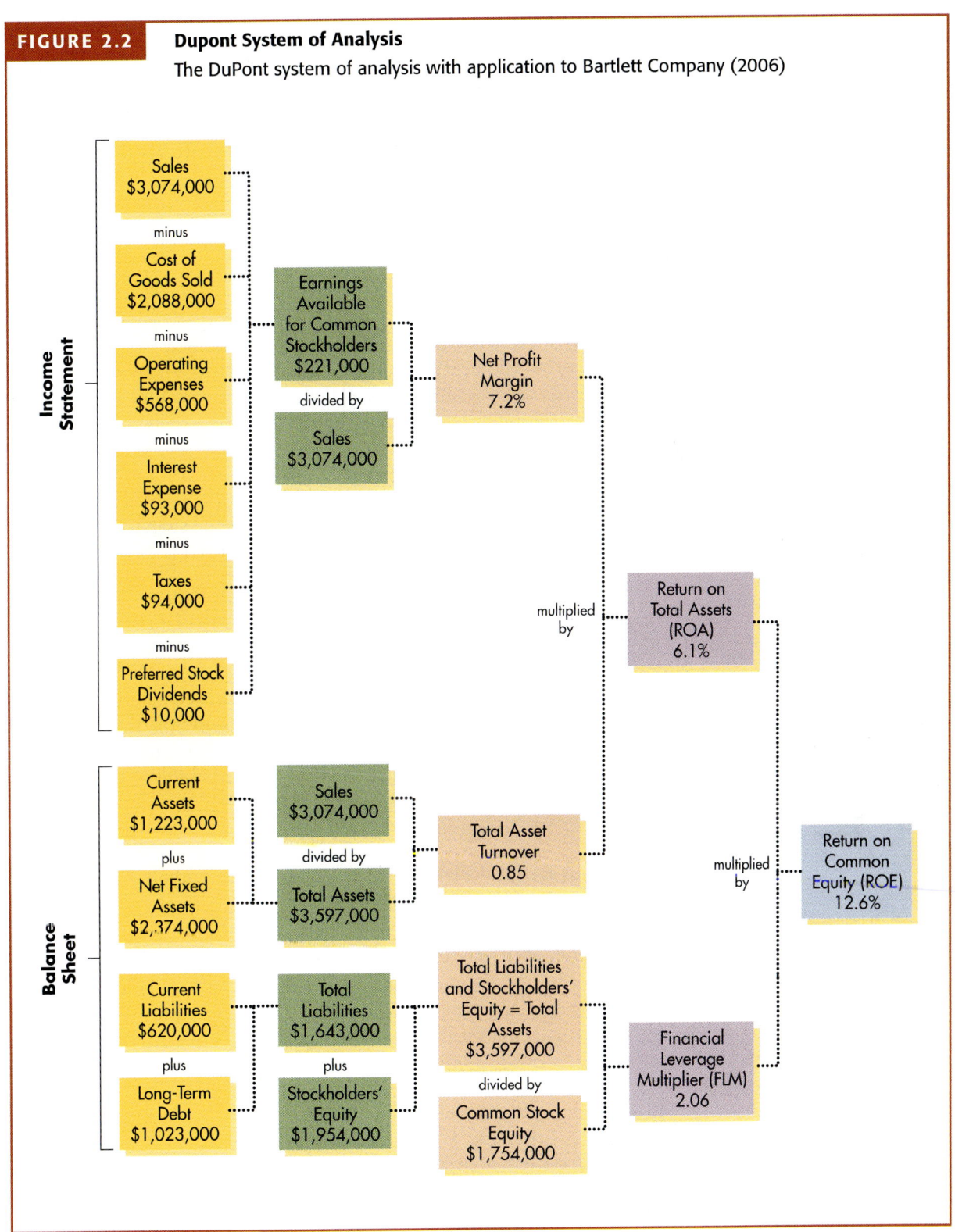

When the 2006 values of the net profit margin and total asset turnover for Bartlett Company, calculated earlier, are substituted into the DuPont formula, the result is

$$ROA = 7.2\% \times 0.85 = 6.1\%$$

This value is the same as that calculated directly in an earlier section (page 62). The DuPont formula enables the firm to break down its return into profit-on-sales and efficiency-of-asset-use components. Typically, a firm with a low net profit margin has a high total asset turnover, which results in a reasonably good return on total assets. Often, the opposite situation exists.

Modified Dupont Formula

modified DuPont formula
Relates the firm's *return on total assets (ROA)* to its *return on common equity (ROE)* using the *financial leverage multiplier (FLM)*.

The second step in the DuPont system employs the **modified DuPont formula**. This formula relates the firm's *return on total assets (ROA)* to its *return on common equity (ROE)*. The latter is calculated by multiplying the return on total assets (ROA) by the **financial leverage multiplier (FLM)**, which is the ratio of total assets to common stock equity:

financial leverage multiplier (FLM)
The ratio of the firm's total assets to its common stock equity.

$$ROE = ROA \times FLM$$

Substituting the appropriate formulas into the equation and simplifying results in the formula given earlier,

$$ROE = \frac{\text{Earnings available for common stockholders}}{\text{Total assets}} \times \frac{\text{Total assets}}{\text{Common stock equity}} = \frac{\text{Earnings available for common stockholders}}{\text{Common stock equity}}$$

Use of the financial leverage multiplier (FLM) to convert the ROA into the ROE reflects the impact of financial leverage on owners' return. Substituting the values for Bartlett Company's ROA of 6.1 percent, calculated earlier, and Bartlett's FLM of 2.06 ($3,597,000 total assets ÷ $1,754,000 common stock equity) into the modified DuPont formula yields

$$ROE = 6.1\% \times 2.06 = 12.6\%$$

The 12.6 percent ROE calculated by using the modified DuPont formula is the same as that calculated directly (page 62).

Applying the Dupont System

The advantage of the DuPont system is that it allows the firm to break its return on equity into a profit-on-sales component (net profit margin), an efficiency-of-asset-use component (total asset turnover), and a use-of-financial-leverage component (financial leverage multiplier). The total return to owners therefore can be analyzed in these important dimensions.

The use of the DuPont system of analysis as a diagnostic tool is best explained using Figure 2.2. Beginning with the rightmost value—the ROE—the financial analyst moves to the left, dissecting and analyzing the inputs to the formula to isolate the probable cause of the resulting above-average (or below-average) value.

EXAMPLE

For the sake of demonstration, let's ignore all industry average data in Table 2.8 and assume that Bartlett's ROE of 12.6 % is actually below the industry average. Moving to the left in Figure 2.2, we would examine the inputs to the ROE—the ROA and the FLM—relative to the industry averages. Let's assume that the FLM is in line with the industry average, but the ROA is below the industry average. Moving farther to the left, we examine the two inputs to the ROA—the net profit margin and total asset turnover. Assume that the net profit margin is in line with the industry average, but the total asset turnover is below the industry average. Moving still farther to the left, we find that whereas the firm's sales are consistent with the industry value, Bartlett's total assets have grown significantly during the past year. Looking farther to the left, we would review the firm's activity ratios for current assets. Let's say that whereas the firm's inventory turnover is in line with the industry average, its average collection period is well above the industry average.

We can readily trace the possible problem back to its cause: Bartlett's low ROE is primarily the consequence of slow collections of accounts receivable, which resulted in high levels of receivables and therefore high levels of total assets. The high total assets slowed Bartlett's total asset turnover, driving down its ROA, which then drove down its ROE. By using the DuPont system of analysis to dissect Bartlett's overall returns as measured by its ROE, we found that slow collections of receivables caused the below-industry-average ROE. Clearly, the firm needs to better manage its credit operations.

Review Questions

2–16 Financial ratio analysis is often divided into five areas: *liquidity, activity, debt, profitability,* and *market* ratios. Differentiate each of these areas of analysis from the others. Which is of the greatest concern to creditors?

2–17 Describe how you would use a large number of ratios to perform a complete ratio analysis of the firm.

2–18 What three areas of analysis are combined in the *modified DuPont formula*? Explain how the *DuPont system of analysis* is used to dissect the firm's results and isolate their causes.

SUMMARY

FOCUS ON VALUE

Financial managers review and analyze the firm's financial statements periodically, both to uncover developing problems and to assess the firm's progress toward achieving its goals. These actions are aimed at **preserving and creating value for the firm's owners.** Financial ratios enable financial managers to monitor the pulse of the firm and its progress toward

REVIEW OF LEARNING GOALS

LG1 **Review the contents of the stockholders' report and the procedures for consolidating international financial statements.** The annual stockholders' report, which publicly owned corporations must provide to stockholders, documents the firm's financial activities of the past year. It includes the letter to stockholders and various subjective and factual information, as well as four key financial statements: the income statement, the balance sheet, the statement of stockholders' equity (or its abbreviated form, the statement of retained earnings), and the statement of cash flows. Notes describing the technical aspects of the financial statements follow. Financial statements of companies that have operations whose cash flows are denominated in one or more foreign currencies must be translated into dollars in accordance with *FASB Standard No. 52*.

LG2 **Understand who uses financial ratios, and how.** Ratio analysis enables stockholders and lenders and the firm's managers to evaluate the firm's financial performance. It can be performed on a cross-sectional or a time-series basis. Benchmarking is a popular type of cross-sectional analysis. Key cautions for applying financial ratios are as follow: (1) Ratios with large deviations from the norm merely indicate symptoms of a problem. (2) A single ratio does not generally provide sufficient information. (3) The ratios being compared should be calculated using financial statements dated at the same point in time during the year. (4) Audited financial statements should be used. (5) Data should be checked for consistency of accounting treatment. (6) Inflation and different asset ages can distort ratio comparisons.

LG3 **Use ratios to analyze a firm's liquidity and activity.** Liquidity, or the ability of the firm to pay its bills as they come due, can be measured by the current ratio and the quick (acid-test) ratio. Activity ratios measure the speed with which accounts are converted into sales or cash—inflows or outflows. The activity of inventory can be measured by its turnover; that of accounts receivable by the average collection period; and that of accounts payable by the average payment period. Total asset turnover measures the efficiency with which the firm uses its assets to generate sales.

LG4 **Discuss the relationship between debt and financial leverage and the ratios used to analyze a firm's debt.** The more debt a firm uses, the greater its financial leverage, which magnifies both risk and return. Financial debt ratios measure both the degree of indebtedness and the ability to service debts. A common measure of indebtedness is the debt ratio. The ability to pay fixed charges can be measured by times interest earned and fixed-payment coverage ratios.

LG5 **Use ratios to analyze a firm's profitability and its market value.** The common-size income statement, which shows all items as a percentage of sales, can be used to determine gross profit margin, operating profit margin, and net profit margin. Other measures of profitability include earnings per share, return on total assets, and return on common equity. Market ratios include the price/earnings ratio and the market/book ratio.

LG6 **Use a summary of financial ratios and the DuPont system of analysis to perform a complete ratio analysis.** A summary of all ratios—liquidity, activity, debt, profitability, and market—can be used to perform a complete ratio analysis using cross-sectional and time-series analysis. The DuPont system of analysis is a diagnostic tool used to find the key areas responsible for the firm's financial performance. It enables the firm to break the return on common equity into three components: profit on sales, efficiency of asset use, and use of financial leverage.

Self-Test Problems (Solutions in Appendix B)

   ST2–1 Ratio formulas and interpretations Without referring to the text, indicate for each of the following ratios the formula for calculating it and the kinds of problems, if any, the firm is likely to have if that ratio is too high relative to the industry average. What if the ratio is too low relative to the industry average? Create a table similar to the one that follows and fill in the empty blocks.

Ratio	Too high	Too low
Current ratio =		
Inventory turnover =		
Times interest earned =		
Gross profit margin =		
Return on total assets =		
Price/earnings (P/E) ratio =		

   ST2–2 Balance sheet completion using ratios Complete the 2006 balance sheet for O'Keefe Industries using the information that follows it.

O'Keefe Industries
Balance Sheet
December 31, 2006

Assets		Liabilities and Stockholders' Equity	
Cash	$32,720	Accounts payable	$120,000
Marketable securities	25,000	Notes payable	_____
Accounts receivable	_____	Accruals	20,000
Inventories	_____	Total current liabilities	_____
Total current assets	_____	Long-term debt	_____
Net fixed assets	_____	Stockholders' equity	$600,000
Total assets	$_____	Total liabilities and stockholders' equity	$_____

The following financial data for 2006 are also available:
(1) Sales totaled $1,800,000.
(2) The gross profit margin was 25%.
(3) Inventory turnover was 6.0.
(4) There are 365 days in the year.
(5) The average collection period was 40 days.
(6) The current ratio was 1.60.
(7) The total asset turnover ratio was 1.20.
(8) The debt ratio was 60%.

WARM-UP EXERCISES

E2–1 You are a summer intern at the office of a local tax-preparer. To test your basic knowledge of financial statements, your manager, who graduated from your alma mater 2 years ago, gives you the following list of accounts and asks you to prepare a simple income statement using those accounts.

	Accounts ($000,000)
Depreciation	25
General and administrative expenses	22
Sales	345
Sales expenses	18
Cost of goods sold	155
Lease expense	4
Interest expense	3

a. Arrange the accounts into a well-labeled income statement. Make sure you label and solve for gross profit, operating profit, and net profit before taxes.
b. Using a 35% tax rate, calculate taxes paid and net profit after taxes.
c. Assuming a dividend of $1.10 per share with 4.25 million shares outstanding, calculate EPS and additions to retained earnings.

E2–2 Explain why the income statement can also be called a "profit and loss statement." What exactly does the word "balance" mean in the title of the balance sheet? Why do we balance the two halves?

E2–3 Cooper Industries, Inc., began 2006 with retained earnings of $25.32 million. During the year it paid four quarterly dividends of $0.35 per share to 2.75 million common stockholders. Preferred stockholders, holding 500,000 shares, were paid two semiannual dividends of $0.75 per share. The firm had a net profit after taxes of $5.15 million. Prepare the statement of retained earnings for the year ended December 31, 2006.

E2–4 Bluestone Metals, Inc., is a metal fabrication firm which manufactures prefabricated metal parts for customers in a variety of industries. The firm's motto is "If you need it, we can make it." The CEO of Bluestone recently held a board meeting during which he extolled the virtues of the corporation. The company, he stated confidently, had the capability to build any product and could do so using a lean manufacturing model. The firm would soon be profitable, claimed the CEO, because the company used state of the art technology to build a variety of products while keeping inventory levels low. As a business press reporter, you have calculated some ratios to analyze the financial health of the firm. Bluestone's current ratios and quick ratios for the past six years are shown in the table on the facing page.

	2001	2002	2003	2004	2005	2006
Current ratio	1.2	1.4	1.3	1.6	1.8	2.2
Quick ratio	1.1	1.3	1.2	0.8	0.6	0.4

What do you think of the CEO's claim that the firm is lean and soon to be profitable? (*Hint:* Is there a possible warning sign in the relationship between the two ratios?)

E2–5 If we know that a firm has a net profit margin of 4.5%, total asset turnover of 0.72, and an equity multiplier of 1.43, what is its ROE? What is the advantage to using the DuPont system to calculate ROE over the direct calculation of earnings available for common stockholders ÷ common stock equity?

PROBLEMS

P2–1 **Reviewing basic financial statements** The income statement for the year ended December 31, 2006, the balance sheets for December 31, 2006 and 2005, and the statement of retained earnings for the year ended December 31, 2006, for Technica, Inc., are given below and on page 76. Briefly discuss the form and informational content of each of these statements.

Technica, Inc.
Income Statement
for the Year Ended December 31, 2006

Sales revenue		$600,000
Less: Cost of goods sold		460,000
Gross profits		$140,000
Less: Operating expenses		
General and administrative expenses	$30,000	
Depreciation expense	30,000	
Total operating expense		60,000
Operating profits		$ 80,000
Less: Interest expense		10,000
Net profits before taxes		$ 70,000
Less: Taxes		27,100
Earnings available for common stockholders		$ 42,900
Earnings per share (EPS)		$2.15

Technica, Inc.
Balance Sheets

Assets	December 31 2006	December 31 2005
Cash	$ 15,000	$ 16,000
Marketable securities	7,200	8,000
Accounts receivable	34,100	42,200
Inventories	82,000	50,000
Total current assets	$138,300	$116,200
Land and buildings	$150,000	$150,000
Machinery and equipment	200,000	190,000
Furniture and fixtures	54,000	50,000
Other	11,000	10,000
Total gross fixed assets	$415,000	$400,000
Less: Accumulated depreciation	145,000	115,000
Net fixed assets	$270,000	$285,000
Total assets	$408,300	$401,200
Liabilities and Stockholders' Equity		
Accounts payable	$ 57,000	$ 49,000
Notes payable	13,000	16,000
Accruals	5,000	6,000
Total current liabilities	$ 75,000	$ 71,000
Long-term debt	$150,000	$160,000
Stockholders' equity		
Common stock equity (shares outstanding: 19,500 in 2006 and 20,000 in 2005)	$110,200	$120,000
Retained earnings	73,100	50,200
Total stockholders' equity	$183,300	$170,200
Total liabilities and stockholders' equity	$408,300	$401,200

Technica, Inc.
Statement of Retained Earnings
for the Year Ended December 31, 2006

Retained earnings balance (January 1, 2006)	$50,200
Plus: Net profits after taxes (for 2006)	42,900
Less: Cash dividends (paid during 2006)	20,000
Retained earnings balance (December 31, 2006)	$73,100

P2–2 **Financial statement account identification** Mark each of the accounts listed in the table on the facing page as follows:

    a. In column (1), indicate in which statement—income statement (IS) or balance sheet (BS)—the account belongs.

b. In column (2), indicate whether the account is a current asset (CA), current liability (CL), expense (E), fixed asset (FA), long-term debt (LTD), revenue (R), or stockholders' equity (SE).

Account name	(1) Statement	(2) Type of account
Accounts payable	BS	____
Accounts receivable	BS	____
Accruals	BS	____
Accumulated depreciation	BS	____
Administrative expense	IS	____
Buildings	BS	____
Cash	BS	____
Common stock (at par)	BS	____
Cost of goods sold	IS	____
Depreciation	IS	____
Equipment	BS	____
General expense	IS	____
Interest expense	IS	____
Inventories	IS	____
Land	BS	____
Long-term debts	BS	____
Machinery	BS	____
Marketable securities	BS	____
Notes payable	BS	____
Operating expense	IS	____
Paid-in capital in excess of par	BS	____
Preferred stock	BS	____
Preferred stock dividends	IS	____
Retained earnings	BS	____
Sales revenue	IS	____
Selling expense	IS	____
Taxes	IS	____
Vehicles	BS	____

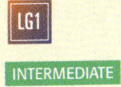

P2–3 **Income statement preparation** On December 31, 2006, Cathy Chen, a self-employed certified public accountant (CPA), completed her first full year in business. During the year, she billed $360,000 for her accounting services. She had two employees: a bookkeeper and a clerical assistant. In addition to her *monthly* salary of $8,000, Ms. Chen paid *annual* salaries of $48,000 and $36,000 to the bookkeeper and the clerical assistant, respectively. Employment taxes and benefit costs for Ms. Chen and her employees totaled $34,600 for the year. Expenses for office supplies, including postage, totaled $10,400 for the year. In addition, Ms. Chen spent $17,000 during the year on tax-deductible travel and entertainment associated with client visits and new business development. Lease payments for the office space rented (a tax-deductible expense) were $2,700 *per month*. Depreciation expense on the office furniture and fixtures was $15,600 for the year. During the year, Ms. Chen paid interest of $15,000 on the $120,000 borrowed to start the business. She paid an average tax rate of 30 percent during 2006.

a. Prepare an income statement for Cathy Chen, CPA, for the year ended December 31, 2006.
b. Evaluate her 2006 financial performance.

P2–4 **Calculation of EPS and retained earnings** Philagem, Inc., ended 2006 with a net profit *before* taxes of $218,000. The company is subject to a 40% tax rate and must pay $32,000 in preferred stock dividends before distributing any earnings on the 85,000 shares of common stock currently outstanding.

a. Calculate Philagem's 2006 earnings per share (EPS).
b. If the firm paid common stock dividends of $0.80 per share, how many dollars would go to retained earnings?

P2–5 **Balance sheet preparation** Use the *appropriate items* from the following list to prepare in good form Owen Davis Company's balance sheet at December 31, 2006.

Item	Value ($000) at December 31, 2006	Item	Value ($000) at December 31, 2006
Accounts payable	$ 220	Inventories	$ 375
Accounts receivable	450	Land	100
Accruals	55	Long-term debts	420
Accumulated depreciation	265	Machinery	420
Buildings	225	Marketable securities	75
Cash	215	Notes payable	475
Common stock (at par)	90	Paid-in capital in excess	
Cost of goods sold	2,500	of par	360
Depreciation expense	45	Preferred stock	100
Equipment	140	Retained earnings	210
Furniture and fixtures	170	Sales revenue	3,600
General expense	320	Vehicles	25

P2–6 **Initial sale price of common stock** Beck Corporation has one issue of preferred stock and one issue of common stock outstanding. Given Beck's stockholders' equity account that follows, determine the original price per share at which the firm sold its single issue of common stock.

Stockholders' Equity ($000)	
Preferred stock	$ 125
Common stock ($0.75 par, 300,000 shares outstanding)	225
Paid-in capital in excess of par on common stock	2,625
Retained earnings	900
Total stockholders' equity	$3,875

CHAPTER 2   Financial Statements and Analysis

P2–7 Statement of retained earnings Hayes Enterprises began 2006 with a retained earnings balance of $928,000. During 2006, the firm earned $377,000 after taxes. From this amount, preferred stockholders were paid $47,000 in dividends. At year-end 2006, the firm's retained earnings totaled $1,048,000. The firm had 140,000 shares of common stock outstanding during 2006.
a. Prepare a statement of retained earnings for the year ended December 31, 2006, for Hayes Enterprises. (*Note:* Be sure to calculate and include the amount of cash dividends paid in 2006.)
b. Calculate the firm's 2006 earnings per share (EPS).
c. How large a per-share cash dividend did the firm pay on common stock during 2006?

P2–8 Ratio comparisons Robert Arias recently inherited a stock portfolio from his uncle. Wishing to learn more about the companies in which he is now invested, Robert performs a ratio analysis on each one and decides to compare them to each other. Some of his ratios are listed below.

Ratio	Island Electric Utility	Burger Heaven	Fink Software	Roland Motors
Current ratio	1.10	1.3	6.8	4.5
Quick ratio	0.90	0.82	5.2	3.7
Debt ratio	0.68	0.46	0	0.35
Net profit margin	6.2%	14.3%	28.5%	8.4%

Assuming that his uncle was a wise investor who assembled the portfolio with care, Robert finds the wide differences in these ratios confusing. Help him out.
a. What problems might Robert encounter in comparing these companies to one another on the basis of their ratios?
b. Why might the current and quick ratios for the electric utility and the fast-food stock be so much lower than the same ratios for the other companies?
c. Why might it be all right for the electric utility to carry a large amount of debt, but not the software company?
d. Why wouldn't investors invest all of their money in software companies instead of in less profitable companies? (Focus on risk and return.)

P2–9 Liquidity management Bauman Company's total current assets, total current liabilities, and inventory for each of the past 4 years follow:

Item	2003	2004	2005	2006
Total current assets	$16,950	$21,900	$22,500	$27,000
Total current liabilities	9,000	12,600	12,600	17,400
Inventory	6,000	6,900	6,900	7,200

a. Calculate the firm's current and quick ratios for each year. Compare the resulting time series for these measures of liquidity.
b. Comment on the firm's liquidity over the 2003–2006 period.

c. If you were told that Bauman Company's inventory turnover for each year in the 2003–2006 period and the industry averages were as follows, would this information support or conflict with your evaluation in part **b**? Why?

Inventory turnover	2003	2004	2005	2006
Bauman Company	6.3	6.8	7.0	6.4
Industry average	10.6	11.2	10.8	11.0

P2–10 Inventory management Wilkins Manufacturing has annual sales of $4 million and a gross profit margin of 40%. Its *end-of-quarter inventories* are

Quarter	Inventory
1	$ 400,000
2	800,000
3	1,200,000
4	200,000

a. Find the average quarterly inventory and use it to calculate the firm's inventory turnover and the average age of inventory.
b. Assuming that the company is in an industry with an average inventory turnover of 2.0, how would you evaluate the activity of Wilkins' inventory?

P2–11 Accounts receivable management An evaluation of the books of Blair Supply, which follows, gives the end-of-year accounts receivable balance, which is believed to consist of amounts originating in the months indicated. The company had annual sales of $2.4 million. The firm extends 30-day credit terms.
a. Use the year-end total to evaluate the firm's collection system.

Month of origin	Amounts receivable
July	$ 3,875
August	2,000
September	34,025
October	15,100
November	52,000
December	193,000
Year-end accounts receivable	$300,000

b. If 70% of the firm's sales occur between July and December, would this affect the validity of your conclusion in part **a**? Explain.

P2–12 Debt analysis Springfield Bank is evaluating Creek Enterprises, which has requested a $4,000,000 loan, to assess the firm's financial leverage and financial risk. On the basis of the debt ratios for Creek, along with the industry averages and Creek's recent financial statements (on the facing page), evaluate and recommend appropriate action on the loan request.

Creek Enterprises
Income Statement
for the Year Ended December 31, 2006

Sales revenue		$30,000,000
Less: Cost of goods sold		21,000,000
Gross profits		$ 9,000,000
Less: Operating expenses		
Selling expense	$3,000,000	
General and administrative expenses	1,800,000	
Lease expense	200,000	
Depreciation expense	1,000,000	
Total operating expense		6,000,000
Operating profits		$ 3,000,000
Less: Interest expense		1,000,000
Net profits before taxes		$ 2,000,000
Less: Taxes (rate = 40%)		800,000
Net profits after taxes		$ 1,200,000
Less: Preferred stock dividends		100,000
Earnings available for common stockholders		$ 1,100,000

Creek Enterprises
Balance Sheet
December 31, 2006

Assets		Liabilities and Stockholders' Equity	
Current assets		Current liabilities	
Cash	$ 1,000,000	Accounts payable	$ 8,000,000
Marketable securities	3,000,000	Notes payable	8,000,000
Accounts receivable	12,000,000	Accruals	500,000
Inventories	7,500,000	Total current liabilities	$16,500,000
Total current assets	$23,500,000	Long-term debt (includes financial leases)[b]	$20,000,000
Gross fixed assets (at cost)[a]		Stockholders' equity	
Land and buildings	$11,000,000	Preferred stock (25,000 shares,	
Machinery and equipment	20,500,000	$4 dividend)	$ 2,500,000
Furniture and fixtures	8,000,000	Common stock (1 million shares at $5 par)	5,000,000
Gross fixed assets	$39,500,000	Paid-in capital in excess of par value	4,000,000
Less: Accumulated depreciation	13,000,000	Retained earnings	2,000,000
Net fixed assets	$26,500,000	Total stockholders' equity	$13,500,000
Total assets	$50,000,000	Total liabilities and stockholders' equity	$50,000,000

[a]The firm has a 4-year financial lease requiring annual beginning-of-year payments of $200,000. Three years of the lease have yet to run.
[b]Required annual principal payments are $800,000.

Industry averages

Debt ratio	0.51
Times interest earned ratio	7.30
Fixed-payment coverage ratio	1.85

P2–13 **Common-size statement analysis** A common-size income statement for Creek Enterprises' 2005 operations follows. Using the firm's 2006 income statement presented in Problem 2–12, develop the 2006 common-size income statement and compare it to the 2005 statement. Which areas require further analysis and investigation?

Creek Enterprises
Common-Size Income Statement
for the Year Ended December 31, 2005

Sales revenue ($35,000,000)		100.0%
Less: Cost of goods sold		65.9
Gross profits		34.1%
Less: Operating expenses		
Selling expense	12.7%	
General and administrative expenses	6.3	
Lease expense	0.6	
Depreciation expense	3.6	
Total operating expense		23.2
Operating profits		10.9%
Less: Interest expense		1.5
Net profits before taxes		9.4%
Less: Taxes (rate = 40%)		3.8
Net profits after taxes		5.6%
Less: Preferred stock dividends		0.1
Earnings available for common stockholders		5.5%

P2–14 **Ratio proficiency** McDougal Printing, Inc., had sales totaling $40,000,000 in fiscal year 2006. Some ratios for the company are listed below. Use this information to determine the dollar values of various income statement and balance sheet accounts as requested.

McDougal Printing, Inc.
Year Ended December 31, 2006

Sales	$40,000,000
Gross profit margin	80%
Operating profit margin	35%
Net profit margin	8%
Return on total assets	16%
Return on common equity	20%
Total asset turnover	2
Average collection period	62.2 days

Calculate values for the following:
a. Gross profits
b. Cost of goods sold
c. Operating profits
d. Operating expenses
e. Earnings available for common stockholders
f. Total assets
g. Total common stock equity
h. Accounts receivable

P2–15 Cross-sectional ratio analysis Use the financial statements below and on page 84 for Fox Manufacturing Company for the year ended December 31, 2006, along with the industry average ratios also given in what follows, to:
a. Prepare and interpret a complete ratio analysis of the firm's 2006 operations.
b. Summarize your findings and make recommendations.

Fox Manufacturing Company
Income Statement
for the Year Ended December 31, 2006

Sales revenue		$600,000
Less: Cost of goods sold		460,000
Gross profits		$140,000
Less: Operating expenses		
General and administrative expenses	$30,000	
Depreciation expense	30,000	
Total operating expense		60,000
Operating profits		$ 80,000
Less: Interest expense		10,000
Net profits before taxes		$ 70,000
Less: Taxes		27,100
Net profits after taxes (earnings available for common stockholders)		$ 42,900
Earnings per share (EPS)		$2.15

Fox Manufacturing Company
Balance Sheet
December 31, 2006

Assets	
Cash	$ 15,000
Marketable securities	7,200
Accounts receivable	34,100
Inventories	82,000
Total current assets	$138,300
Net fixed assets	270,000
Total assets	$408,300
Liabilities and Stockholders' Equity	
Accounts payable	$ 57,000
Notes payable	13,000
Accruals	5,000
Total current liabilities	$ 75,000
Long-term debt	$150,000
Stockholders' equity	
Common stock equity (20,000 shares outstanding)	$110,200
Retained earnings	73,100
Total stockholders' equity	$183,300
Total liabilities and stockholders' equity	$408,300

Ratio	Industry average, 2006
Current ratio	2.35
Quick ratio	0.87
Inventory turnover[a]	4.55
Average collection period[a]	35.8 days
Total asset turnover	1.09
Debt ratio	0.300
Times interest earned ratio	12.3
Gross profit margin	0.202
Operating profit margin	0.135
Net profit margin	0.091
Return on total assets (ROA)	0.099
Return on common equity (ROE)	0.167
Earnings per share (EPS)	$3.10

[a]Based on a 365-day year and on end-of-year figures.

P2–16 Financial statement analysis The financial statements for Zach Industries for the year ended December 31, 2006, are presented below.

Zach Industries
Income Statement
for the Year Ended December 31, 2006

Sales revenue	$160,000
Less: Cost of goods sold	106,000
Gross profits	$ 54,000
Less: Operating expenses	
Selling expense	$ 16,000
General and administrative expenses	10,000
Lease expense	1,000
Depreciation expense	10,000
Total operating expense	$ 37,000
Operating profits	$ 17,000
Less: Interest expense	6,100
Net profits before taxes	$ 10,900
Less: Taxes	4,360
Net profits after taxes	$ 6,540

Zach Industries
Balance Sheet
December 31, 2006

Assets

Cash	$ 500
Marketable securities	1,000
Accounts receivable	25,000
Inventories	45,500
Total current assets	$ 72,000
Land	$ 26,000
Buildings and equipment	90,000
Less: Accumulated depreciation	38,000
Net fixed assets	$ 78,000
Total assets	$150,000

Liabilities and Stockholders' Equity

Accounts payable	$ 22,000
Notes payable	47,000
Total current liabilities	$ 69,000
Long-term debt	$ 22,950
Common stock[a]	$ 31,500
Retained earnings	$ 26,550
Total liabilities and stockholders' equity	$150,000

[a]The firm's 3,000 outstanding shares of common stock closed 2006 at a price of $25 per share.

a. Use the preceding financial statements to complete the following table. Assume that the industry averages given in the table are applicable for both 2005 and 2006.

Ratio	Industry average	Actual 2005	Actual 2006
Current ratio	1.80	1.84	_____
Quick ratio	0.70	0.78	_____
Inventory turnover[a]	2.50	2.59	_____
Average collection period[a]	37.5 days	36.5 days	_____
Debt ratio	65%	67%	_____
Times interest earned ratio	3.8	4.0	_____
Gross profit margin	38%	40%	_____
Net profit margin	3.5%	3.6%	_____
Return on total assets	4.0%	4.0%	_____
Return on common equity	9.5%	8.0%	_____
Market/book ratio	1.1	1.2	_____

[a]Based on a 365-day year and on end-of-year figures.

b. Analyze Zach Industries' financial condition as it is related to (1) liquidity, (2) activity, (3) debt, (4) profitability, and (5) market. Summarize the company's overall financial condition.

P2–17 **DuPont system of analysis** Use the following ratio information for Johnson International and the industry averages for Johnson's line of business to:
a. Construct the DuPont system of analysis for both Johnson and the industry.
b. Evaluate Johnson (and the industry) over the 3-year period.
c. Indicate in which areas Johnson requires further analysis. Why?

	2004	2005	2006
Johnson			
Financial leverage multiplier	1.75	1.75	1.85
Net profit margin	0.059	0.058	0.049
Total asset turnover	2.11	2.18	2.34
Industry Averages			
Financial leverage multiplier	1.67	1.69	1.64
Net profit margin	0.054	0.047	0.041
Total asset turnover	2.05	2.13	2.15

P2–18 **ETHICS PROBLEM** Do some reading in periodicals and/or on the Internet to find out more about the Sarbanes-Oxley Act's provisions for companies. Select one of those provisions, and indicate why you think financial statements will be more trustworthy if company financial executives implement this provision of SOX.

CHAPTER 2 CASE

Assessing Martin Manufacturing's Current Financial Position

Terri Spiro, an experienced budget analyst at Martin Manufacturing Company, has been charged with assessing the firm's financial performance during 2006 and its financial position at year-end 2006. To complete this assignment, she gathered the firm's 2006 financial statements (below and on the facing page). In addition, Terri obtained the firm's ratio values for 2004 and 2005, along with the 2006 industry average ratios (also applicable to 2004 and 2005). These are presented in the table on page 88.

Martin Manufacturing Company
Income Statement
for the Year Ended December 31, 2006

Sales revenue		$5,075,000
Less: Cost of goods sold		3,704,000
Gross profits		$1,371,000
Less: Operating expenses		
Selling expense	$650,000	
General and administrative expenses	416,000	
Depreciation expense	152,000	
Total operating expense		1,218,000
Operating profits		$ 153,000
Less: Interest expense		93,000
Net profits before taxes		$ 60,000
Less: Taxes (rate = 40%)		24,000
Net profits after taxes		$ 36,000
Less: Preferred stock dividends		3,000
Earnings available for common stockholders		$ 33,000
Earnings per share (EPS)		$0.33

Martin Manufacturing Company
Balance Sheets

	December 31	
Assets	2006	2005
Current assets		
Cash	$ 25,000	$ 24,100
Accounts receivable	805,556	763,900
Inventories	700,625	763,445
Total current assets	$1,531,181	$1,551,445
Gross fixed assets (at cost)	$2,093,819	$1,691,707
Less: Accumulated depreciation	500,000	348,000
Net fixed assets	$1,593,819	$1,343,707
Total assets	$3,125,000	$2,895,152
Liabilities and Stockholders' Equity		
Current liabilities		
Accounts payable	$ 230,000	$ 400,500
Notes payable	311,000	370,000
Accruals	75,000	100,902
Total current liabilities	$ 616,000	$ 871,402
Long-term debt	$1,165,250	$ 700,000
Total liabilities	$1,781,250	$1,571,402
Stockholders' equity		
Preferred stock (2,500 shares, $1.20 dividend)	$ 50,000	$ 50,000
Common stock (100,000 shares at $4 par)[a]	400,000	400,000
Paid-in capital in excess of par value	593,750	593,750
Retained earnings	300,000	280,000
Total stockholders' equity	$1,343,750	$1,323,750
Total liabilities and stockholders' equity	$3,125,000	$2,895,152

[a] The firm's 100,000 outstanding shares of common stock closed 2006 at a price of $11.38 per share.

Note: Historical and industry average ratios appear at the top of page 88.

Martin Manufacturing Company
Historical and Industry Average Ratios

Ratio	Actual 2004	Actual 2005	Actual 2006	Industry average 2006
Current ratio	1.7	1.8	_____	1.5
Quick ratio	1.0	0.9	_____	1.2
Inventory turnover (times)	5.2	5.0	_____	10.2
Average collection period	50.7 days	55.8 days	_____	46 days
Total asset turnover (times)	1.5	1.5	_____	2.0
Debt ratio	45.8%	54.3%	_____	24.5%
Times interest earned ratio	2.2	1.9	_____	2.5
Gross profit margin	27.5%	28.0%	_____	26.0%
Net profit margin	1.1%	1.0%	_____	1.2%
Return on total assets (ROA)	1.7%	1.5%	_____	2.4%
Return on common equity (ROE)	3.1%	3.3%	_____	3.2%
Price/earnings (P/E) ratio	33.5	38.7	_____	43.4
Market/book (M/B) ratio	1.0	1.1	_____	1.2

TO DO

a. Calculate the firm's 2006 financial ratios, and then fill in the preceding table. (Assume a 365-day year.)
b. Analyze the firm's current financial position from both a cross-sectional and a time-series viewpoint. Break your analysis into evaluations of the firm's liquidity, activity, debt, profitability, and market.
c. Summarize the firm's overall financial position on the basis of your findings in part **b**.

SPREADSHEET EXERCISE

The income statement and balance sheet are the basic reports that a firm constructs for use by management and for distribution to stockholders, regulatory bodies, and the general public. They are the primary sources of historical financial information about the firm. Dayton Products, Inc., is a moderate-sized manufacturer. The company's management has asked you to perform a detailed financial statement analysis of the firm.

The income statement data for the years ending December 31, 2006 and 2005, respectively, are presented in the table at the top of the facing page. (*Note:* Purchases of inventory during 2006 amounted to $109,865.)

You also have the following balance sheet information as of December 31, 2006 and 2005, respectively.

Annual Income Statement
(Values in millions)

	For the year ended	
	December 31, 2006	December 31, 2005
Sales	$178,909.00	$187,510.00
Cost of goods sold	?	111,631.00
Selling, general, and administrative expenses	12,356.00	12,900.00
Other tax expense	33,572.00	33,377.00
Depreciation and amortization	12,103.00	7,944.00
Other income (add to EBIT to arrive at EBT)	3,147.00	3,323.00
Interest expense	398	293
Income tax rate (average)	35.324%	37.945%
Dividends paid per share	$1.47	$0.91
Basic EPS from total operations	$1.71	$2.25

Annual Balance Sheet
(Values in millions)

	December 31, 2006	December, 31, 2005
Cash and equivalents	$ 7,229.00	$ 6,547.00
Receivables	21,163.00	19,549.00
Inventories	8,068.00	7,904.00
Other current assets	1,831.00	1,681.00
Property, plant, and equipment, gross	204,960.00	187,519.00
Accumulated depreciation and depletion	110,020.00	97,917.00
Other noncurrent assets	19,413.00	17,891.00
Accounts payable	$ 13,792.00	$ 22,862.00
Short-term debt payable	4,093.00	3,703.00
Other current liabilities	15,290.00	3,549.00
Long-term debt payable	6,655.00	7,099.00
Deferred income taxes	16,484.00	16,359.00
Other noncurrent liabilities	21,733.00	16,441.00
Retained earnings	$ 74,597.00	$ 73,161.00
Total common shares outstanding	6.7 billion	6.8 billion

TO DO

a. Create a spreadsheet similar to the spreadsheet in Table 2.1 (which can be viewed at www.aw-bc.com/gitman) to model the following:
  (1) A multiple-step comparative income statement for Dayton, Inc., for the periods ending December 31, 2006 and 2005. You must calculate the cost of goods sold for the year 2006.

(2) A common-size income statement for Dayton, Inc., covering the years 2006 and 2005.
b. Create a spreadsheet similar to the spreadsheet in Table 2.2 (which can be viewed at www.aw-bc.com/gitman) to model the following:
(1) A detailed, comparative balance sheet for Dayton, Inc., for the years ended December 31, 2006 and 2005.
(2) A common-size balance sheet for Dayton, Inc., covering the years 2006 and 2005.
c. Create a spreadsheet similar to the spreadsheet in Table 2.8 (which can be viewed at www.aw-bc.com/gitman) to perform the following analysis:
(1) Create a table that reflects both 2006 and 2005 operating ratios for Dayton, Inc., segmented into (a) liquidity, (b) activity, (c) debt, (d) profitability, and (e) market. Assume that the current market price for the stock is $90.
(2) Compare the 2006 ratios to the 2005 ratios. Indicate whether the results "outperformed the prior year" or "underperformed relative to the prior year."

WEB EXERCISE

For this assignment, you will need a Web-based search engine such as Google.

TO DO

a. Enter the term "stock market" as a search keyword. Scan the results for the New York Stock Exchange and Nasdaq home sites. Compare and contrast the two stock markets' home pages.
b. Return to your search engine and search for "financial markets." Report on your findings, including a synopsis of a free site that you feel had very usable financial market news and analysis. This site should be used as a source of information in future assignments, so spend some time looking for a good site.

Remember to check the book's Web site at

www.aw-bc.com/gitman

for additional resources, including additional Web exercises.

Chapter 3

Cash Flow and Financial Planning

LEARNING GOALS

LG1 Understand tax depreciation procedures and the effect of depreciation on the firm's cash flows.

LG2 Discuss the firm's statement of cash flows, operating cash flow, and free cash flow.

LG3 Understand the financial planning process, including long-term (strategic) financial plans and short-term (operating) financial plans.

LG4 Discuss the cash-planning process and the preparation, evaluation, and use of the cash budget.

LG5 Explain the simplified procedures used to prepare and evaluate the pro forma income statement and the pro forma balance sheet.

LG6 Evaluate the simplified approaches to pro forma financial statement preparation and the common uses of pro forma statements.

Across the Disciplines Why This Chapter Matters to You

Accounting: You need to understand how depreciation is used for both tax and financial reporting purposes; how to develop the statement of cash flows; the primary focus on cash flows, rather than accruals, in financial decision making; and how pro forma financial statements are used within the firm.

Information systems: You need to understand the data that must be kept to record depreciation for tax and financial reporting; the information needs for strategic and operating plans; and what data are needed as inputs for preparing cash plans and profit plans.

Management: You need to understand the difference between strategic and operating plans, and the role of each; the importance of focusing on the firm's cash flows; and how use of pro forma statements can head off trouble for the firm.

Marketing: You need to understand the central role that marketing plays in formulating the firm's long-term, strategic plans, and the importance of the sales forecast as the key input for both cash planning and profit planning.

Operations: You need to understand how depreciation affects the value of the firm's plant assets; how the results of operations are captured in the statement of cash flows; that operations provide key inputs into the firm's short-term financial plans; and the distinction between fixed and variable operating costs.

Cash flow is the primary focus of financial management. The goal is twofold: to meet the firm's financial obligations and to generate positive cash flow for its owners. Financial planning focuses on the firm's cash and profits—both of which are key elements of continued financial success, and even survival. This chapter outlines how the firm analyzes its cash flows, including the effects of depreciation and the roles of operating and free cash flows, and how it uses cash budgets and pro forma statements in the financial planning process.

  ## Analyzing the Firm's Cash Flow

Cash flow, the lifeblood of the firm, is the primary focus of the financial manager both in managing day-to-day finances and in planning and making strategic decisions focused on creating shareholder value. We therefore place major emphasis on estimating and analyzing the cash flows associated with the major financial decisions discussed and demonstrated throughout this book.

An important factor affecting a firm's cash flow is depreciation (and any other noncash charges). From an accounting perspective, a firm's cash flows can be summarized in the statement of cash flows, which was described in Chapter 2. From a strict financial perspective, firms often focus on both *operating cash flow*, which is used in managerial decision making, and *free cash flow*, which is closely watched by participants in the capital market. We begin our analysis of cash flow by considering the key aspects of depreciation, which is closely related to the firm's cash flow.

Depreciation

depreciation
The systematic charging of a portion of the costs of fixed assets against annual revenues over time.

Business firms are permitted for tax and financial reporting purposes to charge a portion of the costs of fixed assets systematically against annual revenues. This allocation of historical cost over time is called **depreciation**. For tax purposes, the depreciation of business assets is regulated by the Internal Revenue Code. Because the objectives of financial reporting sometimes differ from those of tax legislation, firms often use different depreciation methods for financial reporting than those required for tax purposes. Tax laws are used to accomplish economic goals such as providing incentives for business investment in certain types of assets, whereas the objectives of financial reporting are, of course, quite different. Keeping two different sets of records for these two different purposes is legal.

modified accelerated cost recovery system (MACRS)
System used to determine the depreciation of assets for tax purposes.

Depreciation for tax purposes is determined by using the **modified accelerated cost recovery system (MACRS)**; a variety of depreciation methods are available for financial reporting purposes. Before we discuss the methods of depreciating an asset, you must understand the depreciable value of an asset and the depreciable life of an asset.

Depreciable Value of an Asset

Under the basic MACRS procedures, the depreciable value of an asset (the amount to be depreciated) is its *full* cost, including outlays for installation.[1] No adjustment is required for expected salvage value.

---

1. Land values are *not* depreciable. Therefore, to determine the depreciable value of real estate, the value of the land is subtracted from the cost of real estate. In other words, only buildings and other improvements are depreciable.

EXAMPLE

Baker Corporation acquired a new machine at a cost of $38,000, with installation costs of $2,000. Regardless of its expected salvage value, the depreciable value of the machine is $40,000: $38,000 cost + $2,000 installation cost. ■

Depreciable Life of an Asset

depreciable life
Time period over which an asset is depreciated.

The time period over which an asset is depreciated—its **depreciable life**—can significantly affect the pattern of cash flows. The shorter the depreciable life, the more quickly the cash flow created by the depreciation write-off will be received. Given the financial manager's preference for faster receipt of cash flows, a shorter depreciable life is preferred to a longer one. However, the firm must abide by certain Internal Revenue Service (IRS) requirements for determining depreciable life. These MACRS standards, which apply to both new and used assets, require the taxpayer to use as an asset's depreciable life the appropriate MACRS **recovery period**.[2] There are six MACRS recovery periods—3, 5, 7, 10, 15, and 20 years—excluding real estate. It is customary to refer to the property classes, in accordance with their recovery periods, as 3-, 5-, 7-, 10-, 15-, and 20-year property. The first four property classes—those routinely used by business—are defined in Table 3.1.

recovery period
The appropriate depreciable life of a particular asset as determined by MACRS.

Depreciation Methods

For *financial reporting purposes*, a variety of depreciation methods (straight-line, double-declining balance, and sum-of-the-years'-digits[3]) can be used. For *tax purposes*, using MACRS recovery periods, assets in the first four property classes are depreciated by the double-declining balance (200 percent) method, using the half-year convention and switching to straight-line when advantageous. Although tables of depreciation percentages are not provided by law, the *approximate percentages* (rounded to the nearest whole percent) written off each year for the first four property classes are shown in Table 3.2 (see page 94). Rather than using the percentages in the table, the firm can either use straight-line depreciation over the asset's recovery period with the half-year convention or use the alternative depreciation system. For purposes of this text, we will use the MACRS depreciation percentages, because they generally provide for the fastest write-off and therefore the best cash flow effects for the profitable firm.

TABLE 3.1	First Four Property Classes Under MACRS
Property class (recovery period)	Definition
3 years	Research equipment and certain special tools
5 years	Computers, typewriters, copiers, duplicating equipment, cars, light-duty trucks, qualified technological equipment, and similar assets
7 years	Office furniture, fixtures, most manufacturing equipment, railroad track, and single-purpose agricultural and horticultural structures
10 years	Equipment used in petroleum refining or in the manufacture of tobacco products and certain food products

---

2. An exception occurs in the case of assets depreciated under the *alternative depreciation system*. For convenience, in this text we ignore the depreciation of assets under this system.

3. For a review of these depreciation methods as well as other aspects of financial reporting, see any recently published financial accounting text.

TABLE 3.2 Rounded Depreciation Percentages by Recovery Year Using MACRS for First Four Property Classes

Recovery year	Percentage by recovery year[a]			
	3 years	5 years	7 years	10 years
1	33%	20%	14%	10%
2	45	32	25	18
3	15	19	18	14
4	7	12	12	12
5		12	9	9
6		5	9	8
7			9	7
8			4	6
9				6
10				6
11				4
Totals	100%	100%	100%	100%

[a]These percentages have been rounded to the nearest whole percent to simplify calculations while retaining realism. To calculate the *actual* depreciation for tax purposes, be sure to apply the actual unrounded percentages or directly apply double-declining balance (200%) depreciation using the half-year convention.

Because MACRS requires use of the half-year convention, assets are assumed to be acquired in the middle of the year, and therefore only one-half of the first year's depreciation is recovered in the first year. As a result, the final half-year of depreciation is recovered in the year immediately following the asset's stated recovery period. In Table 3.2, the depreciation percentages for an n-year class asset are given for $n + 1$ years. For example, a 5-year asset is depreciated over 6 recovery years. The application of the tax depreciation percentages given in Table 3.2 can be demonstrated by a simple example.

EXAMPLE Baker Corporation acquired, for an installed cost of $40,000, a machine having a recovery period of 5 years. Using the applicable percentages from Table 3.2, Baker calculates the depreciation in each year as follows:

Year	Cost (1)	Percentages (from Table 3.2) (2)	Depreciation [(1) × (2)] (3)
1	$40,000	20%	$ 8,000
2	40,000	32	12,800
3	40,000	19	7,600
4	40,000	12	4,800
5	40,000	12	4,800
6	40,000	5	2,000
Totals		100%	$40,000

Column 3 shows that the full cost of the asset is written off over 6 recovery years.

Because financial managers focus primarily on cash flows, *only tax depreciation methods will be utilized throughout this textbook.*

Developing the Statement of Cash Flows

The *statement of cash flows*, introduced in Chapter 2, summarizes the firm's cash flow over a given period of time. Before discussing the statement and its interpretation, we will review the cash flow through the firm and the classification of inflows and outflows of cash.

The Firm's Cash Flows

Figure 3.1 illustrates the firm's cash flows. Note that marketable securities are considered the same as cash because of their highly liquid nature. Both cash and

Hint In finance, cash is king. Income statement profits are good, but they don't pay the bills, nor do asset owners accept them in place of cash.

FIGURE 3.1 Cash Flows
The firm's cash flows

operating flows
Cash flows directly related to sale and production of the firm's products and services.

investment flows
Cash flows associated with purchase and sale of both fixed assets and business interests.

financing flows
Cash flows that result from debt and equity financing transactions; include incurrence and repayment of debt, cash inflow from the sale of stock, and cash outflows to pay cash dividends or repurchase stock.

marketable securities represent a reservoir of liquidity that is *increased by cash inflows* and *decreased by cash outflows*. Also note that the firm's cash flows can be divided into (1) operating flows, (2) investment flows, and (3) financing flows. The **operating flows** are cash inflows and outflows directly related to the sale and production of the firm's products and services. **Investment flows** are cash flows associated with the purchase and sale of both fixed assets and business interests. Clearly, purchase transactions would result in cash outflows, whereas sales transactions would generate cash inflows. The **financing flows** result from debt and equity financing transactions. Incurring (or repaying) either short-term or long-term debt would result in a corresponding cash inflow (or outflow). Similarly, the sale of stock would result in a cash inflow; the payment of cash dividends or repurchase of stock would result in a financing outflow. In combination, the firm's operating, investment, and financing cash flows during a given period affect the firm's cash and marketable securities balances.

Classifying Inflows and Outflows of Cash

The statement of cash flows, in effect, summarizes the inflows and outflows of cash during a given period. Table 3.3 classifies the basic inflows (sources) and outflows (uses) of cash. For example, if a firm's accounts payable increased by $1,000 during the year, the change would be an *inflow of cash*. If the firm's inventory increased by $2,500, the change would be an *outflow of cash*.

A few additional points can be made with respect to the classification scheme in Table 3.3:

1. A *decrease* in an asset, such as the firm's cash balance, is an *inflow of cash*, because cash that has been tied up in the asset is released and can be used for some other purpose, such as repaying a loan. On the other hand, an *increase* in the firm's cash balance is an *outflow of cash*, because additional cash is being tied up in the firm's cash balance.

   The classification of decreases and increases in a firm's cash balance is difficult for many to grasp. To clarify, imagine that you store all your cash in a bucket. Your cash balance is represented by the amount of cash in the bucket. When you need cash, you withdraw it from the bucket, which *decreases your cash balance and provides an inflow* of cash to you. Conversely, when you have excess cash, you deposit it in the bucket, which *increases your cash balance and represents an outflow* of cash from you. Focus on the movement of funds *in and out of your pocket*: Clearly, a decrease in cash (from the bucket) is an inflow (to your pocket); an increase in cash (in the bucket) is an outflow (from your pocket).

TABLE 3.3 The Inflows and Outflows of Cash

Inflows (sources)	Outflows (uses)
Decrease in any asset	Increase in any asset
Increase in any liability	Decrease in any liability
Net profits after taxes	Net loss
Depreciation and other noncash charges	Dividends paid
Sale of stock	Repurchase or retirement of stock

noncash charge
An expense that is deducted on the income statement but does not involve the actual outlay of cash during the period; includes depreciation, amortization, and depletion.

2. Depreciation (like amortization and depletion) is a **noncash charge**—an expense that is deducted on the income statement but does not involve the actual outlay of cash during the period. Because it shields the firm from taxes by lowering taxable income, the noncash charge is considered a cash inflow. From a strict accounting perspective, adding depreciation back to the firm's net profits after taxes provides an estimate of cash flow from operations[4]:

Cash flow from operations =
  Net profits after taxes + Depreciation and other noncash charges   (3.1)

Note that a firm can have a *net loss* (negative net profits after taxes) and still have positive cash flow from operations when depreciation (and other noncash charges) during the period is greater than the net loss. In the statement of cash flows, net profits after taxes (or net losses) and depreciation (and other noncash charges) are therefore treated as separate entries.

3. We will refine Equation 3.1 in the next section and apply the revised equation (Equation 3.4) in Chapter 8 to estimate the relevant operating cash inflows associated with a firm's present and proposed fixed-asset investments.

4. Because depreciation is treated as a separate cash inflow, only *gross* rather than *net* changes in fixed assets appear on the statement of cash flows. This treatment avoids the potential double counting of depreciation.

5. Direct entries of changes in retained earnings are not included on the statement of cash flows. Instead, entries for items that affect retained earnings appear as net profits or losses after taxes and dividends paid.

Preparing the Statement of Cash Flows

The statement of cash flows for a given period is developed using the income statement for the period, along with the beginning- and end-of-period balance sheets. The income statement for the year ended December 31, 2006, and the December 31 balance sheets for 2005 and 2006 for Baker Corporation are given in Tables 3.4 (see page 98) and 3.5 (see page 99), respectively. The statement of cash flows for the year ended December 31, 2006, for Baker Corporation is presented in Table 3.6 (see page 100). Note that all cash inflows as well as net profits after taxes and depreciation are treated as positive values. All cash outflows, any losses, and dividends paid are treated as negative values. The items in each category—operating, investment, and financing—are totaled, and the three totals are added to get the "Net increase (decrease) in cash and marketable securities" for the period. As a check, this value should reconcile with the actual change in cash and marketable securities for the year, which is obtained from the beginning- and end-of-period balance sheets.

Interpreting the Statement

The statement of cash flows allows the financial manager and other interested parties to analyze the firm's cash flow. The manager should pay special attention both to the major categories of cash flow and to the individual items of cash inflow and outflow, to assess whether any developments have occurred that are contrary to the company's financial policies. In addition, the statement can be

---
4. This equation is merely an estimate because it is based on the assumption that the firm's accounts receivable, inventory, accounts payable, and accruals remain unchanged during the period. Generally, these account balances will change over the period.

TABLE 3.4 Baker Corporation Income Statement ($000) for the Year Ended December 31, 2006

Sales revenue	$1,700
Less: Cost of goods sold	1,000
Gross profits	$ 700
Less: Operating expenses	
Selling expense	$ 70
General and administrative expenses	120
Lease expense[a]	40
Depreciation expense	100
Total operating expense	$ 330
Earnings before interest and taxes (EBIT)	$ 370
Less: Interest expense	70
Net profits before taxes	$ 300
Less: Taxes (rate = 40%)	120
Net profits after taxes	$ 180
Less: Preferred stock dividends	10
Earnings available for common stockholders	$ 170
Earnings per share (EPS)[b]	$1.70

[a]Lease expense is shown here as a separate item rather than included as interest expense as specified by the FASB for financial reporting purposes. The approach used here is consistent with tax reporting rather than financial reporting procedures.

[b]Calculated by dividing the earnings available for common stockholders by the number of shares of common stock outstanding ($170,000 ÷ 100,000 shares = $1.70 per share).

used to evaluate progress toward projected goals or to isolate inefficiencies. For example, increases in accounts receivable or inventories resulting in major cash outflows may signal credit or inventory problems, respectively. The financial manager also can prepare a statement of cash flows developed from projected financial statements. This approach can be used to determine whether planned actions are desirable in view of the resulting cash flows.

Because *an understanding of the basic financial principles presented throughout this text is absolutely essential to the effective interpretation of the statement of cash flows*, detailed interpretation of the statement is not included here.

Operating Cash Flow

operating cash flow (OCF)
The cash flow a firm generates from its normal operations; calculated as *net operating profits after taxes (NOPAT)* + depreciation.

A firm's **operating cash flow** (OCF) is the cash flow it generates from its normal operations—producing and selling its output of goods or services. A variety of definitions of OCF can be found in the financial literature. Equation 3.1 introduced the simple accounting definition of cash flow from operations. Here we refine this definition to estimate cash flows more accurately. Unlike the earlier definition, this one excludes interest and taxes to enable us to focus on the true cash flow resulting from operations without regard to interest expense and taxes.

TABLE 3.5 Baker Corporation Balance Sheets ($000)

	December 31	
Assets	2006	2005
Current assets		
Cash	$ 400	$ 300
Marketable securities	600	200
Accounts receivable	400	500
Inventories	600	900
Total current assets	$2,000	$1,900
Gross fixed assets (at cost)		
Land and buildings	$1,200	$1,050
Machinery and equipment	850	800
Furniture and fixtures	300	220
Vehicles	100	80
Other (includes certain leases)	50	50
Total gross fixed assets (at cost)	$2,500	$2,200
Less: Accumulated depreciation	1,300	1,200
Net fixed assets	$1,200	$1,000
Total assets	$3,200	$2,900
Liabilities and Stockholders' Equity		
Current liabilities		
Accounts payable	$ 700	$ 500
Notes payable	600	700
Accruals	100	200
Total current liabilities	$1,400	$1,400
Long-term debt	$ 600	$ 400
Total liabilities	$2,000	$1,800
Stockholders' equity		
Preferred stock	$ 100	$ 100
Common stock—$1.20 par, 100,000 shares outstanding in 2006 and 2005	120	120
Paid-in capital in excess of par on common stock	380	380
Retained earnings	600	500
Total stockholders' equity	$1,200	$1,100
Total liabilities and stockholders' equity	$3,200	$2,900

net operating profits after taxes (NOPAT)
A firm's earnings before interest and after taxes, EBIT × (1 − T).

The first step is to calculate **net operating profits after taxes** (**NOPAT**), which represent the firm's earnings before interest and after taxes. Letting T equal the applicable corporate tax rate, NOPAT is calculated as follows:

$$\text{NOPAT} = \text{EBIT} \times (1 - T) \qquad (3.2)$$

To convert NOPAT to operating cash flow (OCF), we merely add back depreciation:

$$\text{OCF} = \text{NOPAT} + \text{Depreciation} \qquad (3.3)$$

TABLE 3.6	Baker Corporation Statement of Cash Flows ($000) for the Year Ended December 31, 2006		
Cash Flow from Operating Activities			
Net profits after taxes		$180	
Depreciation		100	
Decrease in accounts receivable		100	
Decrease in inventories		300	
Increase in accounts payable		200	
Decrease in accruals		(100)[a]	
Cash provided by operating activities			$780
Cash Flow from Investment Activities			
Increase in gross fixed assets		($300)	
Changes in business interests		0	
Cash provided by investment activities			(300)
Cash Flow from Financing Activities			
Decrease in notes payable		($100)	
Increase in long-term debts		200	
Changes in stockholders' equity[b]		0	
Dividends paid		(80)	
Cash provided by financing activities			20
Net increase in cash and marketable securities			$500

[a]As is customary, parentheses are used to denote a negative number, which in this case is a cash outflow.

[b]Retained earnings are excluded here, because their change is actually reflected in the combination of the "Net profits after taxes" and "Dividends paid" entries.

We can substitute the expression for NOPAT from Equation 3.2 into Equation 3.3 to get a single equation for OCF:

$$OCF = [EBIT \times (1 - T)] + \text{Depreciation} \qquad (3.4)$$

EXAMPLE Substituting the values for Baker Corporation from its income statement (Table 3.4) into Equation 3.4, we get

$$OCF = [\$370 \times (1.00 - 0.40)] + \$100 = \$222 + \$100 = \$322$$

During 2006, Baker Corporation generated $322,000 of cash flow from producing and selling its output. Therefore, we can conclude that Baker's operations are generating positive cash flows.

Comparing Equations 3.1 and 3.4 reveals the key difference between the accounting and finance definitions of operating cash flow: The finance definition excludes interest—a financing cost—as an operating cash flow, whereas the accounting definition includes it as an operating flow. In the unlikely case that a firm has no interest expense, the accounting definition (Equation 3.1) and the finance definition (Equation 3.4) of operating cash flow would be the same.

Free Cash Flow

free cash flow (FCF)
The amount of cash flow available to investors (creditors and owners) after the firm has met all operating needs and paid for investments in net fixed assets and net current assets.

The firm's **free cash flow (FCF)** represents the amount of cash flow available to investors—the providers of debt (creditors) and equity (owners)—after the firm has met all operating needs and paid for investments in net fixed assets and net current assets. It represents the summation of the net amount of cash flow available to creditors and owners during the period. Free cash flow can be defined as follows:

$$\text{FCF} = \text{OCF} - \text{Net fixed asset investment (NFAI)} \\ - \text{Net current asset investment (NCAI)} \quad (3.5)$$

The *net fixed asset investment* (NFAI) can be calculated as shown here:

$$\text{NFAI} = \text{Change in net fixed assets} + \text{Depreciation} \quad (3.6)$$

EXAMPLE

Using the Baker Corporation's balance sheets in Table 3.5, we see that its change in net fixed assets between 2005 and 2006 was +$200 ($1,200 in 2006 − $1,000 in 2005). Substituting this value and the $100 of depreciation for 2006 into Equation 3.6, we get Baker's net fixed asset investment (NFAI) for 2006:

$$\text{NFAI} = \$200 + \$100 = \$300$$

Baker Corporation therefore invested a net $300,000 in fixed assets during 2006. This amount would, of course, represent a net cash outflow to acquire fixed assets during 2006.

Looking at Equation 3.6, we can see that if the depreciation during a year is less than the *decrease* during that year in net fixed assets, the NFAI would be negative. A negative NFAI represents a net cash *inflow* attributable to the fact that the firm sold more assets than it acquired during the year.

The *net current asset investment* (NCAI) represents the net investment made by the firm in its current (operating) assets. "Net" refers to the difference between current assets and the sum of accounts payable and accruals. Notes payable are not included in the NCAI calculation because they represent a negotiated creditor claim on the firm's free cash flow. Equation 3.7 shows the NCAI calculation.

$$\text{NCAI} = \text{Change in current assets} - \\ \text{Change in (accounts payable} + \text{accruals)} \quad (3.7)$$

EXAMPLE

Looking at the Baker Corporation's balance sheets for 2005 and 2006 in Table 3.5, we see that the change in current assets between 2005 and 2006 is +$100 ($2,000 in 2006 − $1,900 in 2005). The difference between Baker's accounts payable plus accruals of $800 in 2006 ($700 in accounts payable + $100 in accruals) and of $700 in 2005 ($500 in accounts payable + $200 in accruals) is +$100 ($800 in 2006 − $700 in 2005). Substituting into Equation 3.7 the change in current assets and the change in the sum of accounts payable plus accruals for Baker Corporation, we get its 2006 NCAI:

$$\text{NCAI} = \$100 - \$100 = \$0$$

This means that during 2006 Baker Corporation made no investment ($0) in its current assets net of accounts payable and accruals.

Now we can substitute Baker Corporation's 2006 operating cash flow (OCF) of $322, its net fixed asset investment (NFAI) of $300, and its net current asset investment (NCAI) of $0 into Equation 3.5 to find its free cash flow (FCF):

$$FCF = \$322 - \$300 - \$0 = \$22$$

We can see that during 2006 Baker generated $22,000 of free cash flow, which it can use to pay its investors—creditors (payment of interest) and owners (payment of dividends). Thus, the firm generated adequate cash flow to cover all of its operating costs and investments and had free cash flow available to pay investors.

Further analysis of free cash flow is beyond the scope of this initial introduction to cash flow. Clearly, cash flow is the lifeblood of the firm. We next consider various aspects of financial planning for cash flow and profit.

Review Questions

3–1 Briefly describe the first four *modified accelerated cost recovery system (MACRS)* property classes and recovery periods. Explain how the depreciation percentages are determined by using the MACRS recovery periods.

3–2 Describe the overall cash flow through the firm in terms of operating flows, investments flows, and financing flows.

3–3 Explain why a decrease in cash is classified as a *cash inflow (source)* and why an increase in cash is classified as a *cash outflow (use)* in preparing the statement of cash flows.

3–4 Why is depreciation (as well as amortization and depletion) considered a *noncash charge?* How do accountants estimate *cash flow from operations?*

3–5 Describe the general format of the statement of cash flows. How are cash inflows differentiated from cash outflows on this statement?

3–6 What is the difference between the accounting and finance definitions of *operating cash flow?* Under what circumstances are they the same?

3–7 From a strict financial perspective, define and differentiate between a firm's *operating cash flow (OCF)* and its *free cash flow (FCF).*

The Financial Planning Process

Financial planning is an important aspect of the firm's operations because it provides road maps for guiding, coordinating, and controlling the firm's actions to achieve its objectives. Two key aspects of the financial planning process are *cash planning* and *profit planning.* Cash planning involves preparation of the firm's cash budget. Profit planning involves preparation of pro forma statements. Both the cash budget and the pro forma statements are useful for internal financial planning; they also are routinely required by existing and prospective lenders.

The **financial planning process** begins with long-term, or *strategic,* financial plans. These, in turn, guide the formulation of short-term, or *operating,* plans and budgets. Generally, the short-term plans and budgets implement the firm's

financial planning process
Planning that begins with long-term, or *strategic,* financial plans that in turn guide the formulation of short-term, or *operating,* plans and budgets.

long-term strategic objectives. Although the remainder of this chapter places primary emphasis on short-term financial plans and budgets, a few preliminary comments on long-term financial plans are in order.

Long-Term (Strategic) Financial Plans

long-term (strategic) financial plans
Lay out a company's planned financial actions and the anticipated impact of those actions over periods ranging from 2 to 10 years.

Long-term (strategic) financial plans lay out a company's planned financial actions and the anticipated impact of those actions over periods ranging from 2 to 10 years. Five-year strategic plans, which are revised as significant new information becomes available, are common. Generally, firms that are subject to high degrees of operating uncertainty, relatively short production cycles, or both, tend to use shorter planning horizons.

Long-term financial plans are part of an integrated strategy that, along with production and marketing plans, guides the firm toward strategic goals. Those long-term plans consider proposed outlays for fixed assets, research and development activities, marketing and product development actions, capital structure, and major sources of financing. Also included would be termination of existing projects, product lines, or lines of business; repayment or retirement of outstanding debts; and any planned acquisitions. Such plans tend to be supported by a series of annual budgets and profit plans.

Hint Preparation of the annual budget is an important part of the firm's planning process that involves all managers. It represents a tedious but important management activity.

Short-Term (Operating) Financial Plans

short-term (operating) financial plans
Specify short-term financial actions and the anticipated impact of those actions.

Short-term (operating) financial plans specify short-term financial actions and the anticipated impact of those actions. These plans most often cover a 1- to 2-year period. Key inputs include the sales forecast and various forms of operating and financial data. Key outputs include a number of operating budgets, the cash budget, and pro forma financial statements. The entire short-term financial planning process is outlined in Figure 3.2. Here we ignore operating budgets, which

FIGURE 3.2

Short-Term Financial Planning
The short-term (operating) financial planning process

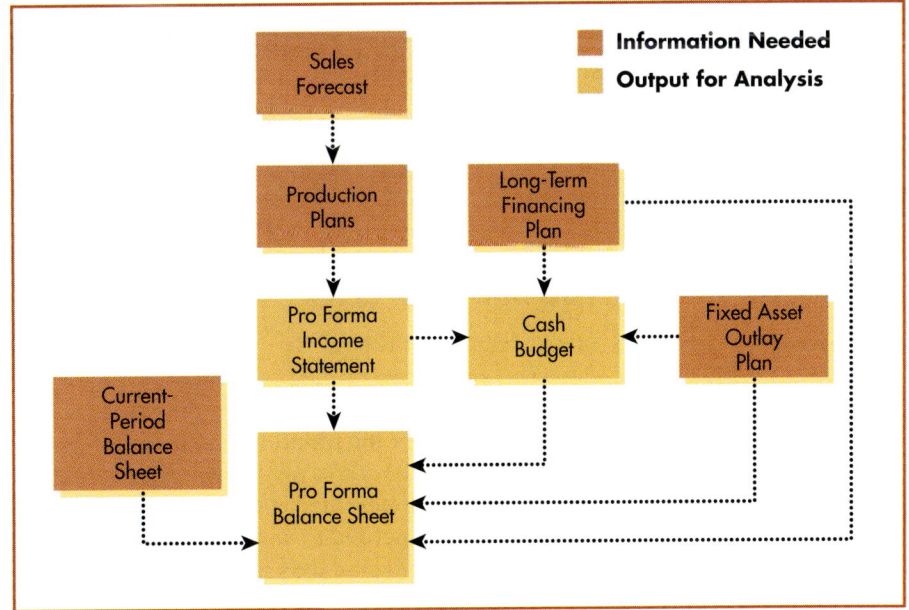

focus on the accounting aspects of short-term business plans, and instead focus solely on cash and profit planning from the financial manager's perspective.

Short-term financial planning begins with the sales forecast. From it, production plans are developed that take into account lead (preparation) times and include estimates of the required raw materials. Using the production plans, the firm can estimate direct labor requirements, factory overhead outlays, and operating expenses. Once these estimates have been made, the firm's pro forma income statement and cash budget can be prepared. With the basic inputs (pro forma income statement, cash budget, fixed asset outlay plan, long-term financing plan, and current-period balance sheet), the pro forma balance sheet can finally be developed.

Throughout the remainder of this chapter, we will concentrate on the key outputs of the short-term financial planning process: the cash budget, the pro forma income statement, and the pro forma balance sheet.

Hint Excel spreadsheets are widely used to streamline the process of preparing and evaluating these short-term financial planning statements.

Review Questions

3–8 What is the *financial planning process*? Contrast *long-term (strategic) financial plans* and *short-term (operating) financial plans*.

3–9 Which three statements result as part of the short-term (operating) financial planning process?

Cash Planning: Cash Budgets

cash budget (cash forecast)
A statement of the firm's planned inflows and outflows of cash that is used to estimate its short-term cash requirements.

The **cash budget,** or **cash forecast,** is a statement of the firm's planned inflows and outflows of cash. It is used by the firm to estimate its short-term cash requirements, with particular attention being paid to planning for surplus cash and for cash shortages.

Typically, the cash budget is designed to cover a 1-year period, divided into smaller time intervals. The number and type of intervals depend on the nature of the business. The more seasonal and uncertain a firm's cash flows, the greater the number of intervals. Because many firms are confronted with a seasonal cash flow pattern, the cash budget is quite often presented on a monthly basis. Firms with stable patterns of cash flow may use quarterly or annual time intervals.

The Sales Forecast

sales forecast
The prediction of the firm's sales over a given period, based on external and/or internal data; used as the key input to the short-term financial planning process.

The key input to the short-term financial planning process is the firm's **sales forecast.** This prediction of the firm's sales over a given period is ordinarily prepared by the marketing department. On the basis of the sales forecast, the financial manager estimates the monthly cash flows that will result from projected sales receipts and from outlays related to production, inventory, and sales. The manager also determines the level of fixed assets required and the amount of financing, if any, needed to support the forecast level of sales and production. In practice, obtaining good data is the most difficult aspect of forecasting. The sales forecast may be based on an analysis of external data, internal data, or a combination of the two.

An **external forecast** is based on the relationships observed between the firm's sales and certain key external economic indicators such as the gross domestic product (GDP), new housing starts, consumer confidence, and disposable personal income. Forecasts containing these indicators are readily available. Because the firm's sales are often closely related to some aspect of overall national economic activity, a forecast of economic activity should provide insight into future sales.

Internal forecasts are based on a buildup, or consensus, of sales forecasts through the firm's own sales channels. Typically, the firm's salespeople in the field are asked to estimate how many units of each type of product they expect to sell in the coming year. These forecasts are collected and totaled by the sales manager, who may adjust the figures using knowledge of specific markets or of the salesperson's forecasting ability. Finally, adjustments may be made for additional internal factors, such as production capabilities.

Firms generally use a combination of external and internal forecast data to make the final sales forecast. The internal data provide insight into sales expectations, and the external data provide a means of adjusting these expectations to take into account general economic factors. The nature of the firm's product also often affects the mix and types of forecasting methods used.

external forecast
A sales forecast based on the relationships observed between the firm's sales and certain key external economic indicators.

internal forecast
A sales forecast based on a buildup, or consensus, of sales forecasts through the firm's own sales channels.

Hint The firm needs to spend a great deal of time and effort to make the sales forecast as precise as possible. An "after-the-fact" analysis of the prior year's forecast can help the firm determine which approach or combination of approaches will give it the most accurate forecasts.

Preparing the Cash Budget

The general format of the cash budget is presented in Table 3.7. We will discuss each of its components individually. In addition, the *In Practice* box on page 106 discusses some real-world aspects of cash forecasting.

Cash Receipts

Cash receipts include all of a firm's inflows of cash during a given financial period. The most common components of cash receipts are cash sales, collections of accounts receivable, and other cash receipts.

cash receipts
All of a firm's inflows of cash during a given financial period.

TABLE 3.7 The General Format of the Cash Budget

	Jan.	Feb.	...	Nov.	Dec.
Cash receipts	$XXX	$XXG		$XXM	$XXT
Less: Cash disbursements	XXA	XXH	...	XXN	XXU
Net cash flow	$XXB	$XXI		$XXO	$XXV
Add: Beginning cash	XXC	XXD	XXJ	XXP	XXQ
Ending cash	$XXD	$XXJ		$XXQ	$XXW
Less: Minimum cash balance	XXE	XXK	...	XXR	XXY
Required total financing		$XXL		$XXS	
Excess cash balance	$XXF				$XXZ

In Practice FOCUS ON PRACTICE

CASH FORECASTS: EASIER SAID THAN DONE

Given the importance of cash to sound financial management, it is surprising how many companies ignore the cash forecasting process. Three reasons for this omission come up most often: Cash forecasts are always wrong; they are hard to do; and managers don't see the benefits of these forecasts unless the company is already in the midst of a cash crunch. In addition, each company has its own methodology for cash forecasting. If the firm's cash inflows and outflows don't form a pattern that managers can graph, it's tough to develop successful forecasts.

Yet the reasons to forecast cash are equally compelling: Cash forecasts allow the firm to plan for adequate liquidity, enable a company to minimize its borrowing costs or maximize its investment income, and help financial executives manage currency exposures more effectively. In times of tight credit, lenders expect borrowers to monitor cash carefully and will favor a company that prepares good cash forecasts. When cash needs and forecasted cash positions don't match, financial managers can plan to borrow funds to close the gap.

According to a 2003 survey conducted by Visa USA, fewer than 10 percent of corporate treasurers, CFOs, and controllers believe that their current cash flow and cash management processes are very efficient. In a separate survey conducted by GTNews and sponsored by REL Consultancy Group, 75 percent of multinational corporations admitted to having little or no confidence in the accuracy of their own cash flow forecasts. Poor internal communication was blamed for cash flow forecasting errors by more than half of the respondents. Poor sales projections and collection policies were noted by almost half of the treasurers responding to the survey, who cited problems in pricing, billing, and logistics that led to poor cash collections from customers.

Many companies are using technology to demystify cash forecasts and increase forecast accuracy. Software can apply statistical techniques, graph historical data, or build models based on each customer's payment patterns. It can also tap corporate databases for the firm's purchases, payment information, and shipments to customers. Even so, installing new and powerful budgeting and planning software is not the final answer to predicting cash flows. The next—and often difficult—step is getting the workforce to abandon their old methods, spreadsheets, or even pencil-and-paper forecasts and to utilize the new technology.

Sources: Adapted from Richard H. Gamble, "Cash Forecast: Cloudy But Clearing," *Business Finance* (May 2001), downloaded from www.businessfinancemag.com; and from Laurie Brannen, "Cash Forecasting Gets Short Shrift" and "The Trouble with Cash Management," downloaded from www.businessfinancemag.com on July 1, 2004.

■ How might cash flow forecasts vary among the marketing, sales, and finance departments within a large corporation?

EXAMPLE Coulson Industries, a defense contractor, is developing a cash budget for October, November, and December. Coulson's sales in August and September were $100,000 and $200,000, respectively. Sales of $400,000, $300,000, and $200,000 have been forecast for October, November, and December, respectively. Historically, 20% of the firm's sales have been for cash, 50% have generated accounts receivable collected after 1 month, and the remaining 30% have generated accounts receivable collected after 2 months. Bad-debt expenses (uncollectible accounts) have been negligible.[5] In December, the firm will receive a $30,000 dividend from stock in a subsidiary. The schedule of expected cash receipts for the company is presented in Table 3.8. It contains the following items:

---

5. Normally, it would be expected that the collection percentages would total slightly less than 100%, because some of the accounts receivable would be uncollectible. In this example, the sum of the collection percentages is 100% (20% + 50% + 30%), which reflects the fact that all sales are assumed to be collected.

TABLE 3.8 — A Schedule of Projected Cash Receipts for Coulson Industries ($000)

	Aug.	Sept.	Oct.	Nov.	Dec.
Forecast sales	$100	$200	$400	$300	$200
Cash sales (0.20)	$20	$40	$ 80	$ 60	$ 40
Collections of A/R:					
Lagged 1 month (0.50)		50	100	200	150
Lagged 2 months (0.30)			30	60	120
Other cash receipts					30
Total cash receipts			$210	$320	$340

Forecast sales This initial entry is *merely informational*. It is provided as an aid in calculating other sales-related items.

Cash sales The cash sales shown for each month represent 20% of the total sales forecast for that month.

Collections of A/R These entries represent the collection of accounts receivable (A/R) resulting from sales in earlier months.

Lagged 1 month These figures represent sales made in the preceding month that generated accounts receivable collected in the current month. Because 50% of the current month's sales are collected 1 month later, the collections of A/R with a 1-month lag shown for September represent 50% of the sales in August, collections for October represent 50% of September sales, and so on.

Lagged 2 months These figures represent sales made 2 months earlier that generated accounts receivable collected in the current month. Because 30% of sales are collected 2 months later, the collections with a 2-month lag shown for October represent 30% of the sales in August, and so on.

Other cash receipts These are cash receipts expected from sources other than sales. Interest received, dividends received, proceeds from the sale of equipment, stock and bond sale proceeds, and lease receipts may show up here. For Coulson Industries, the only other cash receipt is the $30,000 dividend due in December.

Total cash receipts This figure represents the total of all the cash receipts listed for each month. For Coulson Industries, we are concerned only with October, November, and December, as shown in Table 3.8.

Cash Disbursements

cash disbursements
All outlays of cash by the firm during a given financial period.

Cash disbursements include all outlays of cash by the firm during a given financial period. The most common cash disbursements are

- Cash purchases
- Payments of accounts payable
- Rent (and lease) payments
- Wages and salaries
- Tax payments
- Fixed-asset outlays
- Interest payments
- Cash dividend payments
- Principal payments (loans)
- Repurchases or retirements of stock

It is important to recognize that *depreciation and other noncash charges are NOT included in the cash budget,* because they merely represent a scheduled write-off of an earlier cash outflow. The impact of depreciation, as we noted earlier, is reflected in the reduced cash outflow for tax payments.

EXAMPLE

Coulson Industries has gathered the following data needed for the preparation of a cash disbursements schedule for October, November, and December.

Purchases The firm's purchases represent 70% of sales. Of this amount, 10% is paid in cash, 70% is paid in the month immediately following the month of purchase, and the remaining 20% is paid 2 months following the month of purchase.[6]

Rent payments Rent of $5,000 will be paid each month.

Wages and salaries Fixed salary cost for the year is $96,000, or $8,000 per month. In addition, wages are estimated as 10% of monthly sales.

Tax payments Taxes of $25,000 must be paid in December.

Fixed-asset outlays New machinery costing $130,000 will be purchased and paid for in November.

Interest payments An interest payment of $10,000 is due in December.

Cash dividend payments Cash dividends of $20,000 will be paid in October.

Principal payments (loans) A $20,000 principal payment is due in December.

Repurchases or retirements of stock No repurchase or retirement of stock is expected between October and December.

The firm's cash disbursements schedule, using the preceding data, is shown in Table 3.9. Some items in the table are explained in greater detail below.

Purchases This entry is *merely informational.* The figures represent 70% of the forecast sales for each month. They have been included to facilitate calculation of the cash purchases and related payments.

Cash purchases The cash purchases for each month represent 10% of the month's purchases.

Payments of A/P These entries represent the payment of accounts payable (A/P) resulting from purchases in earlier months.

  Lagged 1 month These figures represent purchases made in the preceding month that are paid for in the current month. Because 70% of the firm's purchases are paid for 1 month later, the payments with a 1-month lag shown for September represent 70% of the August purchases, payments for October represent 70% of September purchases, and so on.

  Lagged 2 months These figures represent purchases made 2 months earlier that are paid for in the current month. Because 20% of the firm's pur-

---

6. Unlike the collection percentages for sales, the total of the payment percentages should equal 100%, because it is expected that the firm will pay off all of its accounts payable.

TABLE 3.9 A Schedule of Projected Cash Disbursements for Coulson Industries ($000)

	Aug.	Sept.	Oct.	Nov.	Dec.
Purchases (0.70 × sales)	$70	$140	$280	$210	$140
Cash purchases (0.10)	$7	$14	$ 28	$ 21	$ 14
Payments of A/P:					
Lagged 1 month (0.70)		49	98	196	147
Lagged 2 months (0.20)			14	28	56
Rent payments			5	5	5
Wages and salaries			48	38	28
Tax payments					25
Fixed-asset outlays				130	
Interest payments					10
Cash dividend payments			20		
Principal payments					20
Total cash disbursements			$213	$418	$305

chases are paid for 2 months later, the payments with a 2-month lag for October represent 20% of the August purchases, and so on.

Wages and salaries These amounts were obtained by adding $8,000 to 10% of the *sales* in each month. The $8,000 represents the salary component; the rest represents wages.

The remaining items on the cash disbursements schedule are self-explanatory. ∎

Net Cash Flow, Ending Cash, Financing, and Excess Cash

Look back at the general-format cash budget in Table 3.7. We have inputs for the first two entries, and we now continue calculating the firm's cash needs. The firm's **net cash flow** is found by subtracting the cash disbursements from cash receipts in each period. Then we add beginning cash to the firm's net cash flow to determine the **ending cash** for each period. Finally, we subtract the desired minimum cash balance from ending cash to find the **required total financing** or the **excess cash balance**. If the ending cash is less than the minimum cash balance, *financing* is required. Such financing is typically viewed as short-term and is therefore represented by notes payable. If the ending cash is greater than the minimum cash balance, *excess cash* exists. Any excess cash is assumed to be invested in a liquid, short-term, interest-paying vehicle—that is, in marketable securities.

net cash flow The mathematical difference between the firm's cash receipts and its cash disbursements in each period.

ending cash The sum of the firm's beginning cash and its net cash flow for the period.

required total financing Amount of funds needed by the firm if the ending cash for the period is less than the desired minimum cash balance; typically represented by notes payable.

excess cash balance The (excess) amount available for investment by the firm if the period's ending cash is greater than the desired minimum cash balance; assumed to be invested in marketable securities.

EXAMPLE

Table 3.10 (see page 110) presents Coulson Industries' cash budget, based on the data already developed. At the end of September, Coulson's cash balance was $50,000, and its notes payable and marketable securities equaled $0. The company wishes to maintain, as a reserve for unexpected needs, a minimum cash balance of $25,000.

TABLE 3.10 A Cash Budget for Coulson Industries ($000)

	Oct.	Nov.	Dec.
Total cash receipts[a]	$210	$320	$340
Less: Total cash disbursements[b]	213	418	305
Net cash flow	($ 3)	($ 98)	$ 35
Add: Beginning cash	50	47	(51)
Ending cash	$ 47	($ 51)	($ 16)
Less: Minimum cash balance	25	25	25
Required total financing (notes payable)[c]	—	$ 76	$ 41
Excess cash balance (marketable securities)[d]	$ 22	—	—

[a]From Table 3.8.
[b]From Table 3.9.
[c]Values are placed in this line when the ending cash is less than the desired minimum cash balance. These amounts are typically financed short-term and therefore are represented by notes payable.
[d]Values are placed in this line when the ending cash is greater than the desired minimum cash balance. These amounts are typically assumed to be invested short-term and therefore are represented by marketable securities.

For Coulson Industries to maintain its required $25,000 ending cash balance, it will need total borrowing of $76,000 in November and $41,000 in December. In October the firm will have an excess cash balance of $22,000, which can be held in an interest-earning marketable security. The required total financing figures in the cash budget refer to *how much will be owed at the end of the month;* they do *not* represent the monthly changes in borrowing.

The monthly changes in borrowing and in excess cash can be found by further analyzing the cash budget. In October the $50,000 beginning cash, which becomes $47,000 after the $3,000 net cash outflow, results in a $22,000 excess cash balance once the $25,000 minimum cash is deducted. In November the $76,000 of required total financing resulted from the $98,000 net cash outflow less the $22,000 of excess cash from October. The $41,000 of required total financing in December resulted from reducing November's $76,000 of required total financing by the $35,000 of net cash inflow during December. Summarizing, the *financial activities for each month* would be as follows:

October: **Invest the $22,000** excess cash balance in marketable securities.

November: Liquidate the $22,000 of marketable securities and **borrow $76,000** (notes payable).

December: **Repay $35,000** of notes payable to leave $41,000 of outstanding required total financing.

Evaluating the Cash Budget

The cash budget indicates whether a cash shortage or surplus is expected in each of the months covered by the forecast. Each month's figure is based on the internally imposed requirement of a minimum cash balance and *represents the total balance at the end of the month.*

Hint Not only is the cash budget a great tool to let management know when it has cash shortages or excesses, but it may be a document required by potential creditors. It communicates to them what the money will be used for, and how and when their loans will be repaid.

At the end of each of the 3 months, Coulson expects the following balances in cash, marketable securities, and notes payable:

Account	End-of-month balance ($000)		
	Oct.	Nov.	Dec.
Cash	$25	$25	$25
Marketable securities	22	0	0
Notes payable	0	76	41

Note that the firm is assumed first to liquidate its marketable securities to meet deficits and then to borrow with notes payable if additional financing is needed. As a result, it will not have marketable securities and notes payable on its books at the same time.

Because it may be necessary to borrow up to $76,000 for the 3-month period, the financial manager should be certain that some arrangement is made to ensure the availability of these funds.

Hint Because of the uncertainty of the ending cash values, the financial manager will usually seek to borrow more than the maximum financing indicated in the cash budget.

Coping with Uncertainty in the Cash Budget

Aside from careful estimation of cash budget inputs, there are two ways of coping with the uncertainty of the cash budget.[7] One is to prepare several cash budgets—based on pessimistic, most likely, and optimistic forecasts. From this range of cash flows, the financial manager can determine the amount of financing necessary to cover the most adverse situation. The use of several cash budgets, based on differing assumptions, also should give the financial manager a sense of the riskiness of the various alternatives. This *sensitivity analysis,* or "what if" approach, is often used to analyze cash flows under a variety of circumstances. Clearly the use of electronic spreadsheets simplifies the process of performing sensitivity analysis.

EXAMPLE Table 3.11 (see page 112) presents the summary of Coulson Industries' cash budget prepared for each month of concern using pessimistic, most likely, and optimistic estimates of total cash receipts and disbursements. The most likely estimate is based on the expected outcomes presented earlier.

During October, Coulson will, at worst, need a maximum of $15,000 of financing and, at best, will have a $62,000 excess cash balance. During November, its financing requirement will be between $0 and $185,000, or it could experience an excess cash balance of $5,000. The December projections show maximum borrowing of $190,000 with a possible excess cash balance of $107,000. By considering the extreme values in the pessimistic and optimistic outcomes, Coulson Industries should be better able to plan its cash requirements. For the 3-month period, the peak borrowing requirement under the worst circumstances would be $190,000, which happens to be considerably greater than the most likely estimate of $76,000 for this period. ■

---

7. The term *uncertainty* is used here to refer to the variability of the cash flow outcomes that may actually occur.

TABLE 3.11 A Sensitivity Analysis of Coulson Industries' Cash Budget ($000)

	October			November			December		
	Pessi-mistic	Most likely	Opti-mistic	Pessi-mistic	Most likely	Opti-mistic	Pessi-mistic	Most likely	Opti-mistic
Total cash receipts	$160	$210	$285	$210	$320	$410	$275	$340	$422
Less: Total cash disbursements	200	213	248	380	418	467	280	305	320
Net cash flow	($40)	($3)	$37	($170)	($98)	($57)	($5)	$35	$102
Add: Beginning cash	50	50	50	10	47	87	(160)	(51)	30
Ending cash	$10	$47	$87	($160)	($51)	$30	($165)	($16)	$132
Less: Minimum cash balance	25	25	25	25	25	25	25	25	25
Required total financing	$15	—	—	$185	$76	—	$190	$41	—
Excess cash balance	—	$22	$62	—	—	$5	—	—	$107

A second and much more sophisticated way of coping with uncertainty in the cash budget is *simulation* (discussed in Chapter 9). By simulating the occurrence of sales and other uncertain events, the firm can develop a probability distribution of its ending cash flows for each month. The financial decision maker can then use the probability distribution to determine the amount of financing needed to protect the firm adequately against a cash shortage.

Review Questions

3–10 What is the purpose of the *cash budget*? What role does the sales forecast play in its preparation?

3–11 Briefly describe the basic format of the cash budget.

3–12 How can the two "bottom lines" of the cash budget be used to determine the firm's short-term borrowing and investment requirements?

3–13 What is the cause of uncertainty in the cash budget, and what two techniques can be used to cope with this uncertainty?

Profit Planning: Pro Forma Statements

pro forma statements
Projected, or forecast, income statements and balance sheets.

Whereas cash planning focuses on forecasting cash flows, *profit planning* relies on accrual concepts to project the firm's profit and overall financial position. Shareholders, creditors, and the firm's management pay close attention to the **pro forma statements**, which are projected, or forecast, income statements and balance sheets. The basic steps in the short-term financial planning process were shown in the flow diagram of Figure 3.2. The approaches for estimating the pro forma statements are all based on the belief that the financial relationships reflected in the firm's past financial statements will not change in the coming period. The commonly used simplified approaches are presented in subsequent discussions.

Two inputs are required for preparing pro forma statements: (1) financial statements for the preceding year and (2) the sales forecast for the coming year. A variety of assumptions must also be made. The company that we will use to illustrate the simplified approaches to pro forma preparation is Vectra Manufacturing, which manufactures and sells one product. It has two basic product models—X and Y—which are produced by the same process but require different amounts of raw material and labor.

Hint A key point in understanding pro forma statements is that they reflect the goals and objectives of the firm for the planning period. For these goals and objectives to be achieved, operational plans will have to be developed. Financial plans can be realized only if the correct actions are implemented.

Preceding Year's Financial Statements

The income statement for the firm's 2006 operations is given in Table 3.12. It indicates that Vectra had sales of $100,000, total cost of goods sold of $80,000, net profits before taxes of $9,000, and net profits after taxes of $7,650. The firm paid $4,000 in cash dividends, leaving $3,650 to be transferred to retained earnings. The firm's balance sheet for 2006 is given in Table 3.13 (see page 114).

Sales Forecast

Just as for the cash budget, the key input for pro forma statements is the sales forecast. Vectra Manufacturing's sales forecast for the coming year (2007), based on both external and internal data, is presented in Table 3.14 (see page 114). The

TABLE 3.12 Vectra Manufacturing's Income Statement for the Year Ended December 31, 2006

Sales revenue		
Model X (1,000 units at $20/unit)	$20,000	
Model Y (2,000 units at $40/unit)	80,000	
Total sales		$100,000
Less: Cost of goods sold		
Labor	$28,500	
Material A	8,000	
Material B	5,500	
Overhead	38,000	
Total cost of goods sold		80,000
Gross profits		$ 20,000
Less: Operating expenses		10,000
Operating profits		$ 10,000
Less: Interest expense		1,000
Net profits before taxes		$ 9,000
Less: Taxes (0.15 × $9,000)		1,350
Net profits after taxes		$ 7,650
Less: Common stock dividends		4,000
To retained earnings		$ 3,650

TABLE 3.13 Vectra Manufacturing's Balance Sheet, December 31, 2006

Assets		Liabilities and Stockholders' Equity	
Cash	$ 6,000	Accounts payable	$ 7,000
Marketable securities	4,000	Taxes payable	300
Accounts receivable	13,000	Notes payable	8,300
Inventories	16,000	Other current liabilities	3,400
Total current assets	$39,000	Total current liabilities	$19,000
Net fixed assets	$51,000	Long-term debt	$18,000
Total assets	$90,000	Stockholders' equity	
		Common stock	$30,000
		Retained earnings	$23,000
		Total liabilities and stockholders' equity	$90,000

TABLE 3.14 2007 Sales Forecast for Vectra Manufacturing

Unit sales	
Model X	1,500
Model Y	1,950
Dollar sales	
Model X ($25/unit)	$ 37,500
Model Y ($50/unit)	97,500
Total	$135,000

unit sale prices of the products reflect an increase from $20 to $25 for model X and from $40 to $50 for model Y. These increases are necessary to cover anticipated increases in costs.

Review Question

3–14 What is the purpose of *pro forma statements*? What inputs are required for preparing them using the simplified approaches?

Preparing the Pro Forma Income Statement

percent-of-sales method
A simple method for developing the pro forma income statement; it forecasts sales and then expresses the various income statement items as percentages of projected sales.

A simple method for developing a pro forma income statement is the **percent-of-sales method**. It forecasts sales and then expresses the various income statement items as percentages of projected sales. The percentages used are likely to be the percentages of sales for those items in the previous year. By using dollar values taken from Vectra's 2006 income statement (Table 3.12), we find that these percentages are

$$\frac{\text{Cost of goods sold}}{\text{Sales}} = \frac{\$80,000}{\$100,000} = 80.0\%$$

$$\frac{\text{Operating expenses}}{\text{Sales}} = \frac{\$10,000}{\$100,000} = 10.0\%$$

$$\frac{\text{Interest expense}}{\text{Sales}} = \frac{\$1,000}{\$100,000} = 1.0\%$$

Applying these percentages to the firm's forecast sales of $135,000 (developed in Table 3.14), we get the 2007 pro forma income statement shown in Table 3.15. We have assumed that Vectra will pay $4,000 in common stock dividends, so the expected contribution to retained earnings is $6,327. This represents a considerable increase over $3,650 in the preceding year (see Table 3.12).

Considering Types of Costs and Expenses

The technique that is used to prepare the pro forma income statement in Table 3.15 assumes that all the firm's costs and expenses are *variable*. That is, we assumed that for a given percentage increase in sales, the same percentage increase in cost of goods sold, operating expenses, and interest expense would result. For example, as Vectra's sales increased by 35 percent (from $100,000 in 2006 to $135,000 projected for 2007), we assumed that its costs of goods sold also increased by 35 percent (from $80,000 in 2006 to $108,000 in 2007). On the basis of this assumption, the firm's net profits before taxes also increased by 35 percent (from $9,000 in 2006 to $12,150 projected for 2007).

This approach implies that the firm will not receive the benefits that result from fixed costs when sales are increasing.[8] Clearly, though, if the firm has fixed

TABLE 3.15 A Pro Forma Income Statement, Using the Percent-of-Sales Method, for Vectra Manufacturing for the Year Ended December 31, 2007

Sales revenue	$135,000
Less: Cost of goods sold (0.80)	108,000
Gross profits	$ 27,000
Less: Operating expenses (0.10)	13,500
Operating profits	$ 13,500
Less: Interest expense (0.01)	1,350
Net profits before taxes	$ 12,150
Less: Taxes (0.15 × $12,150)	1,823
Net profits after taxes	$ 10,327
Less: Common stock dividends	4,000
To retained earnings	$ 6,327

---

8. The potential returns as well as risks resulting from use of fixed (operating and financial) costs to create "leverage" are discussed in Chapter 11. The key point to recognize here is that when the firm's revenue is *increasing*, fixed costs can magnify returns.

costs, these costs do not change when sales increase; the result is increased profits. But by remaining unchanged when sales decline, these costs tend to lower profits. Therefore, the use of past cost and expense ratios generally *tends to understate profits when sales are increasing.* (Likewise, it *tends to overstate profits when sales are decreasing.*) The best way to adjust for the presence of fixed costs when preparing a pro forma income statement is to break the firm's historical costs and expenses into *fixed* and *variable* components.

EXAMPLE Vectra Manufacturing's 2006 actual and 2007 pro forma income statements, broken into fixed and variable cost and expense components, follow:

Vectra Manufacturing Income Statements

	2006 Actual	2007 Pro forma
Sales revenue	$100,000	$135,000
Less: Cost of good sold		
Fixed cost	40,000	40,000
Variable cost (0.40 × sales)	40,000	54,000
Gross profits	$ 20,000	$ 41,000
Less: Operating expenses		
Fixed expense	5,000	5,000
Variable expense (0.05 × sales)	5,000	6,750
Operating profits	$ 10,000	$ 29,250
Less: Interest expense (all fixed)	1,000	1,000
Net profits before taxes	$ 9,000	$ 28,250
Less: Taxes (0.15 × net profits before taxes)	1,350	4,238
Net profits after taxes	$ 7,650	$ 24,012

Breaking Vectra's costs and expenses into fixed and variable components provides a more accurate projection of its pro forma profit. By assuming that *all* costs are variable (as shown in Table 3.15), we find that projected net profits before taxes would continue to equal 9 percent of sales (in 2006, $9,000 net profits before taxes ÷ $100,000 sales). Therefore, the 2007 net profits before taxes would have been $12,150 (0.09 × $135,000 projected sales) instead of the $28,250 obtained by using the firm's fixed-cost–variable-cost breakdown. ■

Clearly, when using a simplified approach to prepare a pro forma income statement, we should break down costs and expenses into fixed and variable components.

Review Questions

3–15 How is the *percent-of-sales method* used to prepare pro forma income statements?

3–16 Why does the presence of fixed costs cause the percent-of-sales method of pro forma income statement preparation to fail? What is a better method?

Preparing the Pro Forma Balance Sheet

judgmental approach
A simplified approach for preparing the pro forma balance sheet under which the values of certain balance sheet accounts are estimated, some as a percentage of sales and others by management assumption, and the firm's external financing is used as a balancing, or "plug," figure.

A number of simplified approaches are available for preparing the pro forma balance sheet. One involves estimating all balance sheet accounts as a strict percentage of sales. A better and more popular approach is the **judgmental approach**,[9] under which the values of certain balance sheet accounts are estimated, some as a percentage of sales and others by management assumption, and the firm's external financing is used as a balancing, or "plug," figure. To apply the judgmental approach to prepare Vectra Manufacturing's 2007 pro forma balance sheet, a number of assumptions must be made about levels of various balance sheet accounts:

1. A minimum cash balance of $6,000 is desired.
2. Marketable securities are assumed to remain unchanged from their current level of $4,000.
3. Accounts receivable on average represent about 45 days of sales. Because Vectra's annual sales are projected to be $135,000, accounts receivable should average $16,875 (1/8 × $135,000). (Forty-five days expressed fractionally is about one-eighth of a year: 45/365 ≈ 1/8.)
4. The ending inventory should remain at a level of about $16,000, of which 25 percent (approximately $4,000) should be raw materials and the remaining 75 percent (approximately $12,000) should consist of finished goods.
5. A new machine costing $20,000 will be purchased. Total depreciation for the year is $8,000. Adding the $20,000 acquisition to the existing net fixed assets of $51,000 and subtracting the depreciation of $8,000 yields net fixed assets of $63,000.
6. Purchases are expected to represent approximately 30% of annual sales, which in this case is approximately $40,500 (0.30 × $135,000). The firm estimates that it can take 73 days on average to satisfy its accounts payable. Thus accounts payable should equal one-fifth (73 days ÷ 365 days) of the firm's purchases, or $8,100 (1/5 × $40,500).
7. Taxes payable are expected to equal one-fourth of the current year's tax liability, which equals $455 (one-fourth of the tax liability of $1,823 shown in the pro forma income statement in Table 3.15).
8. Notes payable are assumed to remain unchanged from their current level of $8,300.
9. No change in other current liabilities is expected. They remain at the level of the previous year: $3,400.
10. The firm's long-term debt and its common stock are expected to remain unchanged at $18,000 and $30,000, respectively; no issues, retirements, or repurchases of bonds or stocks are planned.

---

9. The judgmental approach represents an improved version of the *percent-of-sales approach* to pro forma balance sheet preparation. Because the judgmental approach requires only slightly more information and should yield better estimates than the somewhat naive percent-of-sales approach, it is presented here.

11. Retained earnings will increase from the beginning level of $23,000 (from the balance sheet dated December 31, 2006, in Table 3.13) to $29,327. The increase of $6,327 represents the amount of retained earnings calculated in the year-end 2007 pro forma income statement in Table 3.15.

A 2007 pro forma balance sheet for Vectra Manufacturing based on these assumptions is presented in Table 3.16. A **"plug" figure**—called the **external financing required**—of $8,293 is needed to bring the statement into balance. This means that the firm will have to obtain about $8,293 of additional external financing to support the increased sales level of $135,000 for 2007.

A *positive* value for "external financing required," like that shown in Table 3.16, means that, based on its plans, the firm will not generate enough internal financing to support its forecast growth in assets. To support the forecast level of operation, the firm must raise funds externally by using debt and/or equity financing or by reducing dividends. Once the form of financing is determined, the pro forma balance sheet is modified to replace "external financing required" with the planned increases in the debt and/or equity accounts.

A *negative* value for "external financing required" indicates that, based on its plans, the firm will generate more financing internally than it needs to support its forecast growth in assets. In this case, funds are available for use in repaying debt, repurchasing stock, or increasing dividends. Once the specific actions are determined, "external financing required" is replaced in the pro forma balance sheet with the planned reductions in the debt and/or equity accounts. Obviously, besides being used to prepare the pro forma balance sheet, the judgmental approach is frequently used specifically to estimate the firm's financing requirements.

external financing required ("plug" figure)
Under the judgmental approach for developing a pro forma balance sheet, the amount of external financing needed to bring the statement into balance. It can be either a positive or a negative value.

TABLE 3.16 A Pro Forma Balance Sheet, Using the Judgmental Approach, for Vectra Manufacturing (December 31, 2007)

Assets			Liabilities and Stockholders' Equity	
Cash		$ 6,000	Accounts payable	$ 8,100
Marketable securities		4,000	Taxes payable	455
Accounts receivable		16,875	Notes payable	8,300
Inventories			Other current liabilities	3,400
Raw materials	$ 4,000		Total current liabilities	$ 20,255
Finished goods	12,000		Long-term debt	$ 18,000
Total inventory		16,000	Stockholders' equity	
Total current assets		$ 42,875	Common stock	$ 30,000
Net fixed assets		$ 63,000	Retained earnings	$ 29,327
Total assets		$105,875	Total	$ 97,582
			External financing required[a]	$ 8,293
			Total liabilities and stockholders' equity	$105,875

[a]The amount of external financing needed to force the firm's balance sheet to balance. Because of the nature of the judgmental approach, the balance sheet is not expected to balance without some type of adjustment.

Review Questions

3–17 Describe the *judgmental approach* for simplified preparation of the pro forma balance sheet.

3–18 What is the significance of the "plug" figure, *external financing required*? Differentiate between strategies associated with positive values and with negative values for external financing required.

Evaluation of Pro Forma Statements

It is difficult to forecast the many variables involved in preparing pro forma statements. As a result, investors, lenders, and managers frequently use the techniques presented in this chapter to make rough estimates of pro forma financial statements. However, it is important to recognize the basic weaknesses of these simplified approaches. The weaknesses lie in two assumptions: (1) that the firm's past financial condition is an accurate indicator of its future, and (2) that certain variables (such as cash, accounts receivable, and inventories) can be forced to take on certain "desired" values. These assumptions cannot be justified solely on the basis of their ability to simplify the calculations involved. However, despite their weaknesses, the simplified approaches to pro forma statement preparation are likely to remain popular because of their relative simplicity. The widespread use of spreadsheets is certainly helping to streamline the financial planning process.

However pro forma statements are prepared, analysts must understand how to use them to make financial decisions. Both financial managers and lenders can use pro forma statements to analyze the firm's inflows and outflows of cash, as well as its liquidity, activity, debt, profitability, and market value. Various ratios can be calculated from the pro forma income statement and balance sheet to evaluate performance. Cash inflows and outflows can be evaluated by preparing a pro forma statement of cash flows. After analyzing the pro forma statements, the financial manager can take steps to adjust planned operations to achieve short-term financial goals. For example, if projected profits on the pro forma income statement are too low, a variety of pricing and/or cost-cutting actions might be initiated. If the projected level of accounts receivable on the pro forma balance sheet is too high, changes in credit or collection policy may be called for. Pro forma statements are therefore of great importance in solidifying the firm's financial plans for the coming year.

Review Questions

3–19 What are the two basic weaknesses of the simplified approaches to preparing pro forma statements?

3–20 What is the financial manager's objective in evaluating pro forma statements?

Summary

FOCUS ON VALUE

Cash flow, the lifeblood of the firm, is a key determinant of the value of the firm. The financial manager must plan and manage—create, allocate, conserve, and monitor—the firm's cash flow. The goal is to ensure the firm's solvency by meeting financial obligations in a timely manner and to generate positive cash flow for the firm's owners. Both the magnitude and the risk of the cash flows generated on behalf of the owners determine the firm's value.

To carry out the responsibility **to create value for owners,** the financial manager uses tools such as cash budgets and pro forma financial statements as part of the process of generating positive cash flow. Good financial plans should result in large free cash flows that fully satisfy creditor claims and produce positive cash flows on behalf of owners. Clearly, the financial manager must use deliberate and careful planning and management of the firm's cash flows to achieve the firm's goal of maximizing share price.

REVIEW OF LEARNING GOALS

LG1 **Understand tax depreciation procedures and the effect of depreciation on the firm's cash flows.** Depreciation is an important factor affecting a firm's cash flow. The depreciable value of an asset and its depreciable life are determined by using the modified accelerated cost recovery system (MACRS) standards in the federal tax code. MACRS groups assets (excluding real estate) into six property classes based on length of recovery period—3, 5, 7, 10, 15, and 20 years—and can be applied over the appropriate period by using a schedule of yearly depreciation percentages for each period.

LG2 **Discuss the firm's statement of cash flows, operating cash flow, and free cash flow.** The statement of cash flows is divided into operating, investment, and financing flows. It reconciles changes in the firm's cash flows with changes in cash and marketable securities for the period. Interpreting the statement of cash flows requires an understanding of basic financial principles and involves both the major categories of cash flow and the individual items of cash inflow and outflow. From a strict financial point of view, a firm's operating cash flow is defined to exclude interest; the simpler accounting view does not make this exclusion. Of greater importance is a firm's free cash flow, which is the amount of cash flow available to creditors and owners.

LG3 **Understand the financial planning process, including long-term (strategic) financial plans and short-term (operating) financial plans.** The two key aspects of the financial planning process are cash planning and profit planning. Cash planning involves the cash budget or cash forecast. Profit planning relies on the pro forma income statement and balance sheet. Long-term (strategic) financial plans act as a guide for preparing short-term (operating) financial plans. Long-term plans tend to cover periods ranging from 2 to 10 years and are updated periodically. Short-term plans most often cover a 1- to 2-year period.

LG4 **Discuss the cash-planning process and the preparation, evaluation, and use of the cash budget.** The cash-planning process uses the cash budget, based on a sales forecast, to estimate short-term cash surpluses and shortages. The cash budget is typically prepared for a 1-year period divided into months. It nets cash receipts and disbursements for each period to calculate net cash flow. Ending cash is estimated by adding beginning cash to the net cash flow. By subtracting the desired minimum cash balance from the ending cash, the firm can determine required total financing or the excess cash balance. To cope with uncertainty in the cash budget, sensitivity analysis or simulation can be used. A firm must also consider its pattern of daily cash receipts and cash disbursements.

Explain the simplified procedures used to prepare and evaluate the pro forma income statement and the pro forma balance sheet. A pro forma income statement can be developed by calculating past percentage relationships between certain cost and expense items and the firm's sales and then applying these percentages to forecasts. Because this approach implies that all costs and expenses are variable, it tends to understate profits when sales are increasing and to overstate profits when sales are decreasing. This problem can be avoided by breaking down costs and expenses into fixed and variable components. In this case, the fixed components remain unchanged from the most recent year, and the variable costs and expenses are forecast on a percent-of-sales basis.

Under the judgmental approach, the values of certain balance sheet accounts are estimated, some as a percentage of sales and others by management assumption, and the firm's external financing is used as a balancing, or "plug," figure. A positive value for "external financing required" means that the firm will not generate enough internal financing to support its forecast growth in assets and will have to raise funds externally or reduce dividends. A negative value for "external financing required" indicates that the firm will generate more financing internally than it needs to support its forecast growth in assets and funds will be available for use in repaying debt, repurchasing stock, or increasing dividends.

Evaluate the simplified approaches to pro forma financial statement preparation and the common uses of pro forma statements. Simplified approaches for preparing pro forma statements assume that the firm's past financial condition is an accurate indicator of the future. Pro forma statements are commonly used to forecast and analyze the firm's level of profitability and overall financial performance so that adjustments can be made to planned operations to achieve short-term financial goals.

SELF-TEST PROBLEMS (SOLUTIONS IN APPENDIX B)

ST3–1 **Depreciation and cash flow** A firm expects to have earnings before interest and taxes (EBIT) of $160,000 in each of the next 6 years. It pays annual interest of $15,000. The firm is considering the purchase of an asset that costs $140,000, requires $10,000 in installation cost, and has a recovery period of 5 years. It will be the firm's only asset, and the asset's depreciation is already reflected in its EBIT estimates.
  a. Calculate the annual depreciation for the asset purchase using the MACRS depreciation percentages in Table 3.2 on page 94.
  b. Calculate the annual operating cash flows for each of the 6 years, using both the accounting and the finance definitions of *operating cash flow*. Assume that the firm is subject to a 40% ordinary tax rate.
  c. Suppose the firm's net fixed assets, current assets, accounts payable, and accruals had the values given at the top of page 122 at the start and end of the final year (year 6). Calculate the firm's free cash flow (FCF) for that year.

Account	Year 6 Start	Year 6 End
Net fixed assets	$ 7,500	$ 0
Current assets	90,000	110,000
Accounts payable	40,000	45,000
Accruals	8,000	7,000

  d. Compare and discuss the significance of each value calculated in parts b and c.

ST3–2 **Cash budget and pro forma balance sheet inputs** Jane McDonald, a financial analyst for Carroll Company, has prepared the following sales and cash disbursement estimates for the period February–June of the current year.

Month	Sales	Cash disbursements
February	$500	$400
March	600	300
April	400	600
May	200	500
June	200	200

McDonald notes that historically, 30% of sales have been for cash. Of *credit sales,* 70% are collected 1 month after the sale, and the remaining 30% are collected 2 months after the sale. The firm wishes to maintain a minimum ending balance in its cash account of $25. Balances above this amount would be invested in short-term government securities (marketable securities), whereas any deficits would be financed through short-term bank borrowing (notes payable). The beginning cash balance at April 1 is $115.
  a. Prepare a cash budget for April, May, and June.
  b. How much financing, if any, at a maximum would Carroll Company require to meet its obligations during this 3-month period?
  c. A pro forma balance sheet dated at the end of June is to be prepared from the information presented. Give the size of each of the following: cash, notes payable, marketable securities, and accounts receivable.

ST3–3 **Pro forma income statement** Euro Designs, Inc., expects sales during 2007 to rise from the 2006 level of $3.5 million to $3.9 million. Because of a scheduled large loan payment, the interest expense in 2007 is expected to drop to $325,000. The firm plans to increase its cash dividend payments during 2007 to $320,000. The company's year-end 2006 income statement is at the top of the facing page.
  a. Use the *percent-of-sales method* to prepare a 2007 pro forma income statement for Euro Designs, Inc.
  b. Explain why the statement may underestimate the company's actual 2007 pro forma income.

Euro Designs, Inc.
Income Statement
for the Year Ended December 31, 2006

Sales revenue	$3,500,000
Less: Cost of goods sold	1,925,000
Gross profits	$1,575,000
Less: Operating expenses	420,000
Operating profits	$1,155,000
Less: Interest expense	400,000
Net profits before taxes	$ 755,000
Less: Taxes (rate = 40%)	302,000
Net profits after taxes	$ 453,000
Less: Cash dividends	250,000
To retained earnings	$ 203,000

WARM-UP EXERCISES

LG1 **E3–1** The installed cost of a new computerized controller was $65,000. Calculate the depreciation schedule by year assuming a recovery period of 5 years and using the appropriate MACRS depreciation percentages given in Table 3.2 on page 94.

LG2 **E3–2** Classify the following changes in each of the accounts as either an *outflow* or an *inflow* of cash. During the year (a) marketable securities increased, (b) land and buildings decreased, (c) accounts payable increased, (d) vehicles decreased, (e) accounts receivable increased, and (f) dividends were paid.

LG2 **E3–3** Determine the *operating cash flow (OCF)* for Kleczka, Inc., based on the following data. (All values are in thousands of dollars.) During the year the firm had sales of $2,500, cost of goods sold totaled $1,800, operating expenses totaled $300, and depreciation expenses were $200. The firm is in the 35% tax bracket.

LG2 **E3–4** During the year, Xero, Inc., experienced an increase in net fixed assets of $300,000 and had depreciation of $200,000. It also experienced an increase in current assets of $150,000 and an increase in accounts payable of $75,000. If operating cash flow (OCF) for the year was $700,000, calculate the firm's *free cash flow (FCF)* for the year.

LG5 **E3–5** Rimier Corp. forecasts sales of $650,000 for 2007. Assume the firm has fixed costs of $250,000 and variable costs amounting to 35% of sales. Operating expenses are estimated to include fixed costs of $28,000 and a variable portion equal to 7.5% of sales. Interest expenses for the coming year are estimated to be $20,000. Estimate Rimier's net profits before taxes for 2007.

PROBLEMS

P3–1 Depreciation On March 20, 2006, Norton Systems acquired two new assets. Asset A was research equipment costing $17,000 and having a 3-year recovery period. Asset B was duplicating equipment having an installed cost of $45,000 and a 5-year recovery period. Using the MACRS depreciation percentages in Table 3.2 on page 94, prepare a depreciation schedule for each of these assets.

P3–2 Accounting cash flow A firm had earnings after taxes of $50,000 in 2006. Depreciation charges were $28,000, and a $2,000 charge for amortization of a bond discount was incurred. What was the firm's accounting *cash flow from operations* (see Equation 3.1) during 2006?

P3–3 Depreciation and accounting cash flow A firm in the third year of depreciating its only asset, which originally cost $180,000 and has a 5-year MACRS recovery period, has gathered the following data relative to the current year's operations.

Accruals	$ 15,000
Current assets	120,000
Interest expense	15,000
Sales revenue	400,000
Inventory	70,000
Total costs before depreciation, interest, and taxes	290,000
Tax rate on ordinary income	40%

a. Use the *relevant data* to determine the accounting *cash flow from operations* (see Equation 3.1) for the current year.
b. Explain the impact that depreciation, as well as any other noncash charges, has on a firm's cash flows.

P3–4 Classifying inflows and outflows of cash Classify each of the following items as an inflow (I) or an outflow (O) of cash, or as neither (N).

Item	Change ($)	Item	Change ($)
Cash	+100	Accounts receivable	−700
Accounts payable	−1,000	Net profits	+600
Notes payable	+500	Depreciation	+100
Long-term debt	−2,000	Repurchase of stock	+600
Inventory	+200	Cash dividends	+800
Fixed assets	+400	Sale of stock	+1,000

P3–5 Finding operating and free cash flows Consider the balance sheets and selected data from the income statement at the top of the facing page for Keith Corporation.

Keith Corporation
Balance Sheets

	December 31	
Assets	2006	2005
Cash	$ 1,500	$ 1,000
Marketable securities	1,800	1,200
Accounts receivable	2,000	1,800
Inventories	2,900	2,800
Total current assets	$ 8,200	$ 6,800
Gross fixed assets	$29,500	$28,100
Less: Accumulated depreciation	14,700	13,100
Net fixed assets	$14,800	$15,000
Total assets	$23,000	$21,800
Liabilities and Stockholders' Equity		
Accounts payable	$ 1,600	$ 1,500
Notes payable	2,800	2,200
Accruals	200	300
Total current liabilities	$ 4,600	$ 4,000
Long-term debt	$ 5,000	$ 5,000
Common stock	$10,000	$10,000
Retained earnings	3,400	2,800
Total stockholders' equity	$13,400	$12,800
Total liabilities and stockholders' equity	$23,000	$21,800

Income Statement Data (2006)

Depreciation expense	$1,600
Earnings before interest and taxes (EBIT)	2,700
Interest expense	367
Net profits after taxes	1,400
Tax rate	40%

a. Calculate the firm's accounting *cash flow from operations* for the year ended December 31, 2006, using Equation 3.1.
b. Calculate the firm's *net operating profit after taxes (NOPAT)* for the year ended December 31, 2006, using Equation 3.2.
c. Calculate the firm's *operating cash flow* (OCF) for the year ended December 31, 2006, using Equation 3.3.
d. Calculate the firm's *free cash flow* (FCF) for the year ended December 31, 2006, using Equation 3.5.
e. Interpret, compare, and contrast your cash flow estimates in parts **a, c,** and **d**.

P3–6 **Cash receipts** A firm has actual sales of $65,000 in April and $60,000 in May. It expects sales of $70,000 in June and $100,000 in July and in August. Assuming that sales are the only source of cash inflows and that half of them are for cash and the remainder are collected evenly over the following 2 months, what are the firm's expected cash receipts for June, July, and August?

P3–7 **Cash disbursements schedule** Maris Brothers, Inc., needs a cash disbursement schedule for the months of April, May, and June. Use the format of Table 3.9 and the following information in its preparation.

Sales: February = $500,000; March = $500,000; April = $560,000; May = $610,000; June = $650,000; July = $650,000

Purchases: Purchases are calculated as 60% of the next month's sales, 10% of purchases are made in cash, 50% of purchases are paid for 1 month after purchase, and the remaining 40% of purchases are paid for 2 months after purchase.

Rent: The firm pays rent of $8,000 per month.

Wages and salaries: Base wage and salary costs are fixed at $6,000 per month plus a variable cost of 7% of the current month's sales.

Taxes: A tax payment of $54,500 is due in June.

Fixed asset outlays: New equipment costing $75,000 will be bought and paid for in April.

Interest payments: An interest payment of $30,000 is due in June.

Cash dividends: Dividends of $12,500 will be paid in April.

Principal repayments and retirements: No principal repayments or retirements are due during these months.

P3–8 **Cash budget—Basic** Grenoble Enterprises had sales of $50,000 in March and $60,000 in April. Forecast sales for May, June, and July are $70,000, $80,000, and $100,000, respectively. The firm has a cash balance of $5,000 on May 1 and wishes to maintain a minimum cash balance of $5,000. Given the following data, prepare and interpret a cash budget for the months of May, June, and July.
(1) The firm makes 20% of sales for cash, 60% are collected in the next month, and the remaining 20% are collected in the second month following sale.
(2) The firm receives other income of $2,000 per month.
(3) The firm's actual or expected purchases, all made for cash, are $50,000, $70,000, and $80,000 for the months of May through July, respectively.
(4) Rent is $3,000 per month.
(5) Wages and salaries are 10% of the previous month's sales.
(6) Cash dividends of $3,000 will be paid in June.

(7) Payment of principal and interest of $4,000 is due in June.
(8) A cash purchase of equipment costing $6,000 is scheduled in July.
(9) Taxes of $6,000 are due in June.

P3–9 **Cash budget—Advanced** The actual sales and purchases for Xenocore, Inc., for September and October 2006, along with its forecast sales and purchases for the period November 2006 through April 2007, follow.

Year	Month	Sales	Purchases
2006	September	$210,000	$120,000
2006	October	250,000	150,000
2006	November	170,000	140,000
2006	December	160,000	100,000
2007	January	140,000	80,000
2007	February	180,000	110,000
2007	March	200,000	100,000
2007	April	250,000	90,000

The firm makes 20% of all sales for cash and collects on 40% of its sales in each of the 2 months following the sale. Other cash inflows are expected to be $12,000 in September and April, $15,000 in January and March, and $27,000 in February. The firm pays cash for 10% of its purchases. It pays for 50% of its purchases in the following month and for 40% of its purchases 2 months later.

Wages and salaries amount to 20% of the preceding month's sales. Rent of $20,000 per month must be paid. Interest payments of $10,000 are due in January and April. A principal payment of $30,000 is also due in April. The firm expects to pay cash dividends of $20,000 in January and April. Taxes of $80,000 are due in April. The firm also intends to make a $25,000 cash purchase of fixed assets in December.

a. Assuming that the firm has a cash balance of $22,000 at the beginning of November, determine the end-of-month cash balances for each month, November through April.
b. Assuming that the firm wishes to maintain a $15,000 minimum cash balance, determine the required total financing or excess cash balance for each month, November through April.
c. If the firm were requesting a line of credit to cover needed financing for the period November to April, how large would this line have to be? Explain your answer.

P3–10 **Cash flow concepts** Johnsfield & Co. will be undertaking the following financial transactions in the next planning period. For each transaction represented in the table at the top of page 128, check the statement or statements that will be affected immediately.

Transaction	Cash budget	Statement Pro forma income statement	Pro forma balance sheet
Cash sale			
Credit sale			
Accounts receivable are collected			
Asset with 5-year life is purchased			
Depreciation is taken			
Amortization of goodwill is taken			
Sale of common stock			
Retirement of outstanding bonds			
Fire insurance premium is paid for the next 3 years			

P3–11 **Multiple cash budgets—Sensitivity analysis** Brownstein, Inc., expects sales of $100,000 during each of the next 3 months. It will make monthly purchases of $60,000 during this time. Wages and salaries are $10,000 per month plus 5% of sales. Brownstein expects to make a tax payment of $20,000 in the next month and a $15,000 purchase of fixed assets in the second month and to receive $8,000 in cash from the sale of an asset in the third month. All sales and purchases are for cash. Beginning cash and the minimum cash balance are assumed to be zero.
a. Construct a cash budget for the next 3 months.
b. Brownstein is unsure of the sales levels, but all other figures are certain. If the most pessimistic sales figure is $80,000 per month and the most optimistic is $120,000 per month, what are the monthly minimum and maximum ending cash balances that the firm can expect for each of the 1-month periods?
c. Briefly discuss how the financial manager can use the data in parts a and b to plan for financing needs.

P3–12 **Pro forma income statement** The marketing department of Metroline Manufacturing estimates that its sales in 2007 will be $1.5 million. Interest expense is expected to remain unchanged at $35,000, and the firm plans to pay $70,000 in cash dividends during 2007. Metroline Manufacturing's income statement for the year ended December 31, 2006, is given at the top of the facing page, along with a breakdown of the firm's cost of goods sold and operating expenses into their fixed and variable components.
a. Use the *percent-of-sales method* to prepare a pro forma income statement for the year ended December 31, 2007.
b. Use *fixed and variable cost data* to develop a pro forma income statement for the year ended December 31, 2007.
c. Compare and contrast the statements developed in parts a and b. Which statement probably provides the better estimate of 2007 income? Explain why.

<table>
<tr><td colspan="2">Metroline Manufacturing
Income Statement
for the Year Ended December 31, 2006</td></tr>
<tr><td>Sales revenue</td><td>$1,400,000</td></tr>
<tr><td>Less: Cost of goods sold</td><td>910,000</td></tr>
<tr><td>Gross profits</td><td>$ 490,000</td></tr>
<tr><td>Less: Operating expenses</td><td>120,000</td></tr>
<tr><td>Operating profits</td><td>$ 370,000</td></tr>
<tr><td>Less: Interest expense</td><td>35,000</td></tr>
<tr><td>Net profits before taxes</td><td>$ 335,000</td></tr>
<tr><td>Less: Taxes (rate = 40%)</td><td>134,000</td></tr>
<tr><td>Net profits after taxes</td><td>$ 201,000</td></tr>
<tr><td>Less: Cash dividends</td><td>66,000</td></tr>
<tr><td>To retained earnings</td><td>$ 135,000</td></tr>
</table>

<table>
<tr><td colspan="2">Metroline Manufacturing
Breakdown of Costs and Expenses
into Fixed and Variable Components
for the Year Ended December 31, 2006</td></tr>
<tr><td colspan="2">Cost of goods sold</td></tr>
<tr><td>Fixed cost</td><td>$210,000</td></tr>
<tr><td>Variable cost</td><td>700,000</td></tr>
<tr><td>Total cost</td><td>$910,000</td></tr>
<tr><td colspan="2">Operating expenses</td></tr>
<tr><td>Fixed expenses</td><td>$ 36,000</td></tr>
<tr><td>Variable expenses</td><td>84,000</td></tr>
<tr><td>Total expenses</td><td>$120,000</td></tr>
</table>

P3–13 Pro forma balance sheet—Basic Leonard Industries wishes to prepare a pro forma balance sheet for December 31, 2007. The firm expects 2007 sales to total $3,000,000. The following information has been gathered.
(1) A minimum cash balance of $50,000 is desired.
(2) Marketable securities are expected to remain unchanged.
(3) Accounts receivable represent 10% of sales.
(4) Inventories represent 12% of sales.
(5) A new machine costing $90,000 will be acquired during 2007. Total depreciation for the year will be $32,000.
(6) Accounts payable represent 14% of sales.
(7) Accruals, other current liabilities, long-term debt, and common stock are expected to remain unchanged.
(8) The firm's net profit margin is 4%, and it expects to pay out $70,000 in cash dividends during 2007.
(9) The December 31, 2006, balance sheet is below.

<table>
<tr><td colspan="4">Leonard Industries
Balance Sheet
December 31, 2006</td></tr>
<tr><td colspan="2">Assets</td><td colspan="2">Liabilities and Stockholders' Equity</td></tr>
<tr><td>Cash</td><td>$ 45,000</td><td>Accounts payable</td><td>$ 395,000</td></tr>
<tr><td>Marketable securities</td><td>15,000</td><td>Accruals</td><td>60,000</td></tr>
<tr><td>Accounts receivable</td><td>255,000</td><td>Other current liabilities</td><td>30,000</td></tr>
<tr><td>Inventories</td><td>340,000</td><td>Total current liabilities</td><td>$ 485,000</td></tr>
<tr><td>Total current assets</td><td>$ 655,000</td><td>Long-term debt</td><td>$ 350,000</td></tr>
<tr><td>Net fixed assets</td><td>$ 600,000</td><td>Common stock</td><td>$ 200,000</td></tr>
<tr><td>Total assets</td><td>$1,255,000</td><td>Retained earnings</td><td>$ 220,000</td></tr>
<tr><td></td><td></td><td>Total liabilities and stockholders' equity</td><td>$1,255,000</td></tr>
</table>

a. Use the *judgmental approach* to prepare a pro forma balance sheet dated December 31, 2007, for Leonard Industries.
b. How much, if any, additional financing will Leonard Industries require in 2007? Discuss.
c. Could Leonard Industries adjust its planned 2007 dividend to avoid the situation described in part **b**? Explain how.

P3–14 **Pro forma balance sheet** Peabody & Peabody has 2006 sales of $10 million. It wishes to analyze expected performance and financing needs for 2008—2 years ahead. Given the following information, respond to parts **a** and **b**.
  (1) The percents of sales for items that vary directly with sales are as follows:
      Accounts receivable, 12%
      Inventory, 18%
      Accounts payable, 14%
      Net profit margin, 3%
  (2) Marketable securities and other current liabilities are expected to remain unchanged.
  (3) A minimum cash balance of $480,000 is desired.
  (4) A new machine costing $650,000 will be acquired in 2007, and equipment costing $850,000 will be purchased in 2008. Total depreciation in 2007 is forecast as $290,000, and in 2008 $390,000 of depreciation will be taken.
  (5) Accruals are expected to rise to $500,000 by the end of 2008.
  (6) No sale or retirement of long-term debt is expected.
  (7) No sale or repurchase of common stock is expected.
  (8) The dividend payout of 50% of net profits is expected to continue.
  (9) Sales are expected to be $11 million in 2007 and $12 million in 2008.
  (10) The December 31, 2006, balance sheet is given below.

Peabody & Peabody
Balance Sheet
December 31, 2006
($000)

Assets		Liabilities and Stockholders' Equity	
Cash	$ 400	Accounts payable	$1,400
Marketable securities	200	Accruals	400
Accounts receivable	1,200	Other current liabilities	80
Inventories	1,800	Total current liabilities	$1,880
Total current assets	$3,600	Long-term debt	$2,000
Net fixed assets	$4,000	Common equity	$3,720
Total assets	$7,600	Total liabilities and stockholders' equity	$7,600

a. Prepare a pro forma balance sheet dated December 31, 2008.
b. Discuss the financing changes suggested by the statement prepared in part **a**.

P3–15 Integrative—Pro forma statements Red Queen Restaurants wishes to prepare financial plans. Use the financial statements given below and the other information provided in what follows to prepare the financial plans.

Red Queen Restaurants
Income Statement for the
Year Ended December 31, 2006

Sales revenue	$800,000
Less: Cost of goods sold	600,000
Gross profits	$200,000
Less: Operating expenses	100,000
Net profits before taxes	$100,000
Less: Taxes (rate = 40%)	40,000
Net profits after taxes	$ 60,000
Less: Cash dividends	20,000
To retained earnings	$ 40,000

Red Queen Restaurants
Balance Sheet
December 31, 2006

Assets		Liabilities and Stockholders' Equity	
Cash	$ 32,000	Accounts payable	$100,000
Marketable securities	18,000	Taxes payable	20,000
Accounts receivable	150,000	Other current liabilities	5,000
Inventories	100,000	Total current liabilities	$125,000
Total current assets	$300,000	Long-term debt	$200,000
Net fixed assets	$350,000	Common stock	$150,000
Total assets	$650,000	Retained earnings	$175,000
		Total liabilities and stockholders' equity	$650,000

The following financial data are also available:
(1) The firm has estimated that its sales for 2007 will be $900,000.
(2) The firm expects to pay $35,000 in cash dividends in 2007.
(3) The firm wishes to maintain a minimum cash balance of $30,000.
(4) Accounts receivable represent approximately 18% of annual sales.
(5) The firm's ending inventory will change directly with changes in sales in 2007.
(6) A new machine costing $42,000 will be purchased in 2007. Total depreciation for 2007 will be $17,000.
(7) Accounts payable will change directly in response to changes in sales in 2007.
(8) Taxes payable will equal one-fourth of the tax liability on the pro forma income statement.
(9) Marketable securities, other current liabilities, long-term debt, and common stock will remain unchanged.

a. Prepare a pro forma income statement for the year ended December 31, 2007, using the *percent-of-sales method*.
b. Prepare a pro forma balance sheet dated December 31, 2007, using the *judgmental approach*.
c. Analyze these statements, and discuss the resulting *external financing required*.

P3–16 **ETHICS PROBLEM** The SEC is trying to get companies to notify the investment community more quickly when a "material change" will affect their forthcoming financial results. In what sense might a financial manager be seen as "more ethical" if he or she follows this directive and issues a press release indicating that sales will not be as high as previously anticipated?

CHAPTER 3 CASE

Preparing Martin Manufacturing's 2007 Pro Forma Financial Statements

To improve its competitive position, Martin Manufacturing is planning to implement a major equipment modernization program. Included will be replacement and modernization of key manufacturing equipment at a cost of $400,000 in 2007. The planned program is expected to lower the variable cost per unit of finished product. Terri Spiro, an experienced budget analyst, has been charged with preparing a forecast of the firm's 2007 financial position, assuming replacement and modernization of manufacturing equipment. She plans to use the 2006 financial statements presented on pages 86 and 87, along with the key projected financial data summarized in the following table.

Martin Manufacturing Company
Key Projected Financial Data (2007)

Data item	Value
Sales revenue	$6,500,000
Minimum cash balance	$25,000
Inventory turnover (times)	7.0
Average collection period	50 days
Fixed-asset purchases	$400,000
Total dividend payments (preferred and common)	$20,000
Depreciation expense	$185,000
Interest expense	$97,000
Accounts payable increase	20%
Accruals and long-term debt	Unchanged
Notes payable, preferred and common stock	Unchanged

TO DO

a. Use the historical and projected financial data provided to prepare a pro forma income statement for the year ended December 31, 2007. (*Hint:* Use the *percent-of-sales method* to estimate all values *except* depreciation expense and interest expense, which have been estimated by management and included in the table.)

b. Use the projected financial data along with relevant data from the pro forma income statement prepared in part **a** to prepare the pro forma balance sheet at December 31, 2007. (*Hint:* Use the *judgmental approach*.)
c. Will Martin Manufacturing Company need to obtain *external financing* to fund the proposed equipment modernization program? Explain.

SPREADSHEET EXERCISE

You have been assigned the task of putting together a statement for the ACME Company that shows its expected inflows and outflows of cash over the months of July 2007 through December 2007.

You have been given the following data for ACME Company:

1. Expected gross sales for May through December are $300,000, $400,000, $450,000, $400,000, $425,000, $400,000, $435,000, and $400,000, respectively.
2. 12% of the sales in any given month are collected during that month. The firm offers its customers a cash discount for early payment of their accounts and as a result factors a 3% discount into the current month's sales collection.
3. 75% of the sales in any given month are collected during the following month after the sale.
4. 13% of the sales in any given month are collected during the second month following the sale.
5. The expected purchases of raw materials in any given month are based on 80% of the expected sales during the following month.
6. The firm pays 100% of its current month's raw materials purchases in the following month.
7. Wages and salaries are paid on a monthly basis and are based on 6% of the current month's expected sales.
8. Monthly lease payments are 2% of the current month's expected sales.
9. The monthly advertising expense amounts to 3% of sales.
10. R&D expenditures are expected to be allocated to August, September, and October at the rate of 12% of sales in those months.
11. During December a prepayment of insurance for the following year will be made in the amount of $24,000.
12. During the months of July through December, the firm expects to have miscellaneous expenditures of $15,000, $20,000, $25,000, $30,000, $35,000, and $40,000, respectively.
13. Taxes will be paid in September in the amount of $40,000 and in December in the amount of $45,000.
14. Property, plant, and equipment expenditures of $180,000 are expected in September.
15. The beginning cash balance in July is $15,000.
16. The target cash balance is $15,000.
17. The firm can invest its surplus cash and earn a 6% annual return.

TO DO

a. Prepare a cash budget for July 2007 through December 2007 by creating a combined spreadsheet that incorporates spreadsheets similar to those in Tables 3.8, 3.9, and 3.10. Divide your spreadsheet into three sections:
   (1) Collections from sales and payments to purchase inventory
   (2) Operating expenditures over the time period
   (3) Cash budget covering the period of July through December

   The cash budget should reflect the following:
   (1) Beginning and ending monthly cash balances
   (2) The month(s) in which there will be a cash shortage
   (3) The month(s) in which there will be a cash surplus
   (4) The cumulative cash shortage and/or cash surplus

b. Based on your analysis, briefly describe the outlook for this company over the next six months. Discuss its specific obligations and the funds available to meet them. What could the firm do in the case of a cash shortage? (Where could it get the money?) What should the firm do if it has a cash surplus?

WEB EXERCISE

Taxation is forever a part of our lives. This is true of individuals as well as of corporations. This exercise looks at some tax-related issues for corporations.

TO DO

a. Visit the IRS's Web site at www.irs.gov/index.html. Go to Tax Stats. Here the IRS provides information in various forms regarding tax filing. View Tax Stats at a Glance. Look for information dealing with corporate income taxes. There has been serious debate in the past about eliminating the corporate income tax due to its high compliance costs relative to the amount of revenue raised by the tax. Concerns have also been raised regarding the double taxation of dividends. Because dividends are paid with after-tax dollars, eliminating the corporate income tax would eliminate the double taxation. Citing data contained on this page, discuss the merits of reducing or eliminating corporate income taxation. Would you advocate raising the ceiling so that only the largest corporations, as measured by assets, are taxed?

b. Use the link for Statistics by Topic to look up Corporate Tax Statistics. Find and describe the changes in relative importance of S-corporations as compared with total corporate filings. This information can be found under S-Corporations and then as a publication dated 2004, Selected Returns and Forms, Table #22. Within the same table, information is broken down across eight categories. Compare the relative numbers of returns filed.

Remember to check the book's Web site at

www.aw-bc.com/gitman

for additional resources, including additional Web exercises.

Part 2

Important Financial Concepts

Chapter 4
Time Value of Money

Chapter 5
Risk and Return

Chapter 6
Interest Rates and Bond Valuation

Chapter 7
Stock Valuation

Chapter 4

Time Value of Money

LEARNING GOALS

LG1 Discuss the role of time value in finance, the use of computational tools, and the basic patterns of cash flow.

LG2 Understand the concepts of future value and present value, their calculation for single amounts, and the relationship between them.

LG3 Find the future value and the present value of an ordinary annuity, and find the present value of a perpetuity.

LG4 Calculate both the future value and the present value of a mixed stream of cash flows.

LG5 Understand the effect that compounding interest more frequently than annually has on future value and on the effective annual rate of interest.

LG6 Describe the procedures involved in (1) determining deposits needed to accumulate a future sum, (2) loan amortization, (3) finding interest or growth rates, and (4) finding an unknown number of periods.

Across the Disciplines Why This Chapter Matters to You

Accounting: You need to understand time-value-of-money calculations to account for certain transactions such as loan amortization, lease payments, and bond interest rates.

Information systems: You need to understand time-value-of-money calculations to design systems that accurately measure and value the firm's cash flows.

Management: You need to understand time-value-of-money calculations so that you can manage cash receipts and disbursements in a way that will enable the firm to receive the greatest value from its cash flows.

Marketing: You need to understand time value of money because funding for new programs and products must be justified financially using time-value-of-money techniques.

Operations: You need to understand time value of money because the value of investments in new equipment, in new processes, and in inventory will be affected by the time value of money.

Because we view the firm as a going concern, we assess the decisions of its financial managers, and ultimately the value of the firm itself, in light of its cash flows. The opportunity to earn interest on the firm's funds makes the timing of its cash flows important, because a dollar received in the future is not the same as a dollar received today. Thus, money has a time value, which affects everyone—individuals, businesses, and government. In this chapter we explore the concepts related to the time value of money.

The Role of Time Value in Finance

Financial managers and investors are always confronted with opportunities to earn positive rates of return on their funds, whether through investment in attractive projects or in interest-bearing securities or deposits. Therefore, the timing of cash outflows and inflows has important economic consequences, which financial managers explicitly recognize as the *time value of money*. Time value is based on the belief that a dollar today is worth more than a dollar that will be received at some future date. We begin our study of time value in finance by considering the two views of time value—future value and present value, the computational tools used to streamline time value calculations, and the basic patterns of cash flow.

Hint The time value of money is one of the most important concepts in finance. Money that the firm has in its possession today is more valuable than money in the future because the money it now has can be invested and earn positive returns.

Future Value Versus Present Value

Financial values and decisions can be assessed by using either future value or present value techniques. Although these techniques will result in the same decisions, they view the decision differently. Future value techniques typically measure cash flows at the *end* of a project's life. Present value techniques measure cash flows at the *start* of a project's life (time zero). *Future value* is cash you will receive at a given future date, and *present value* is just like cash in hand today.

A **time line** can be used to depict the cash flows associated with a given investment. It is a horizontal line on which time zero appears at the leftmost end and future periods are marked from left to right. A time line covering five periods (in this case, years) is given in Figure 4.1. The cash flows occurring at time zero and at the end of each year are shown above the line; the negative values represent *cash outflows* ($10,000 at time zero) and the positive values represent *cash inflows* ($3,000 inflow at the end of year 1, $5,000 inflow at the end of year 2, and so on).

time line
A horizontal line on which time zero appears at the leftmost end and future periods are marked from left to right; can be used to depict investment cash flows.

FIGURE 4.1

Time Line
Time line depicting an investment's cash flows

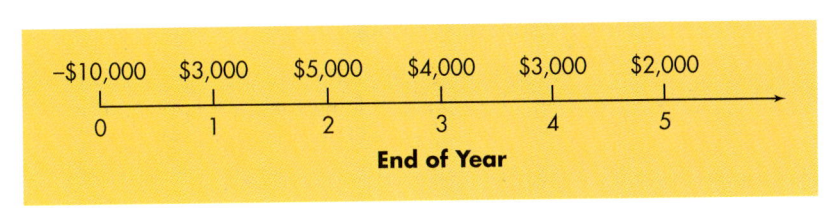

FIGURE 4.2

Compounding and Discounting
Time line showing compounding to find future value and discounting to find present value

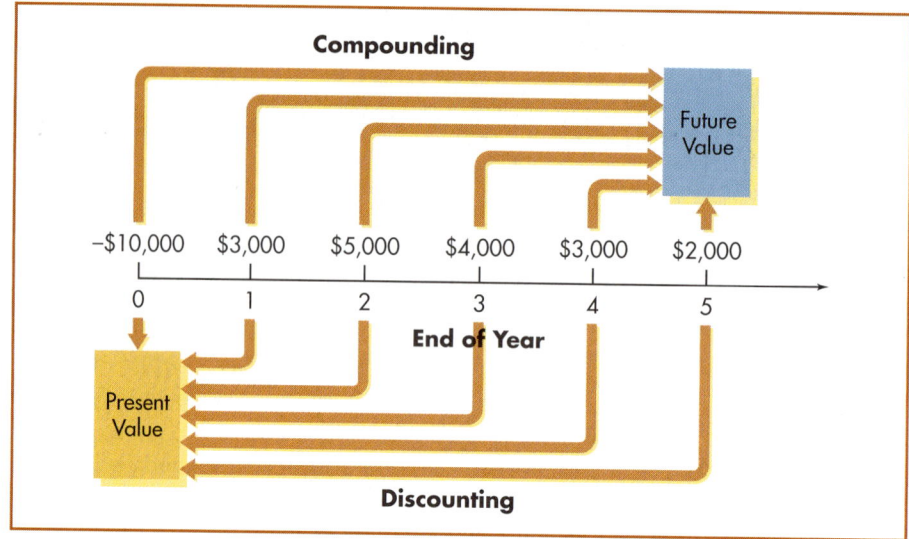

Because money has a time value, all of the cash flows associated with an investment, such as those in Figure 4.1, must be measured at the same point in time. Typically, that point is either the end or the beginning of the investment's life. The future value technique uses *compounding* to find the *future value* of each cash flow at the end of the investment's life and then sums these values to find the investment's future value. This approach is depicted above the time line in Figure 4.2. The figure shows that the future value of each cash flow is measured at the end of the investment's 5-year life. Alternatively, the present value technique uses *discounting* to find the *present value* of each cash flow at time zero and then sums these values to find the investment's value today. Application of this approach is depicted below the time line in Figure 4.2.

The meaning and mechanics of compounding to find future value and of discounting to find present value are covered in this chapter. Although future value and present value result in the same decisions, *financial managers—because they make decisions at time zero—tend to rely primarily on present value techniques.*

Computational Tools

Time-consuming calculations are often involved in finding future and present values. Although you should understand the concepts and mathematics underlying these calculations, the application of time value techniques can be streamlined. We focus on the use of financial tables, hand-held financial calculators, and electronic spreadsheets as aids in computation.

Financial Tables

Financial tables include various future and present value interest factors that simplify time value calculations. The values shown in these tables are easily developed from formulas, with various degrees of rounding. The tables are typically indexed by the interest rate (in columns) and the number of periods (in rows). Figure 4.3 shows this general layout. The interest factor at a 20 percent interest rate for 10 years would be found at the intersection of the 20% column and the 10-period row, as shown by the dark blue box. A full set of the four basic financial tables is

FIGURE 4.3

Financial Tables
Layout and use of a financial table

Period	1%	2%	...	10%	...	20%	...	50%
1			...		...		...	
2			...		...		...	
3			...		...		...	
⋮	⋮	⋮	...	⋮	...	⋮	...	⋮
→10	...	...	...	...	...	x.xxx	...	...
⋮	⋮	⋮	...	⋮	...	⋮	...	⋮
20			...		...		...	
⋮	⋮	⋮	...	⋮	...	⋮	...	⋮
50			...		...		...	

included in Appendix A at the end of the book. These tables are described more fully later in the chapter.

Financial Calculators

Financial calculators also can be used for time value computations. Generally, *financial calculators* include numerous preprogrammed financial routines. This chapter and those that follow show the keystrokes for calculating interest factors and making other financial computations. For convenience, we use the important financial keys, labeled in a fashion consistent with most major financial calculators.

We focus primarily on the keys pictured and defined in Figure 4.4. We typically use four of the first five keys shown in the left column, along with the compute (**CPT**) key. One of the four keys represents the unknown value being calculated. (Occasionally, all five of the keys are used, with one representing the unknown value.) The keystrokes on some of the more sophisticated calculators are menu-driven: After you select the appropriate routine, the calculator prompts you to input each value; on these calculators, a compute key is not needed to obtain a solution. Regardless, any calculator with the basic future and present value functions can be used in lieu of financial tables. See Appendix A for keystrokes for some of the more popular calculators. The keystrokes for other financial calculators are explained in the reference guides that accompany them.

Once you understand the basic underlying concepts, you probably will want to use a calculator to streamline routine financial calculations. With a little

FIGURE 4.4

Calculator Keys
Important financial keys on the typical calculator

N — Number of periods
I — Interest rate per period
PV — Present value
PMT — Amount of payment (used only for annuities)
FV — Future value
CPT — Compute key used to initiate financial calculation once all values are input

practice, you can increase both the speed and the accuracy of your financial computations. Note that because of a calculator's greater precision, slight differences are likely to exist between values calculated by using financial tables and those found with a financial calculator. Remember that *conceptual understanding of the material is the objective.* An ability to solve problems with the aid of a calculator does not necessarily reflect such an understanding, so don't just settle for answers. Work with the material until you are sure you also understand the concepts.

Electronic Spreadsheets

Hint Anyone familiar with an electronic spreadsheet, such as Excel, realizes that most of the time-value-of-money calculations can be performed expeditiously by using the special functions contained in the spreadsheet.

Like financial calculators, electronic spreadsheets have built-in routines that simplify time value calculations. We provide in the text a number of spreadsheet solutions that identify the cell entries for calculating time values. The value for each variable is entered in a cell in the spreadsheet, and the calculation is programmed using an equation that links the individual cells. If values of the variables are changed, the solution automatically changes as a result of the equation linking the cells. In the spreadsheet solutions in this book, the equation that determines the calculation is shown at the bottom of the spreadsheet.

Spreadsheets are the nearest thing we have to a universal business language. The ability to use electronic spreadsheets has become a prime skill for today's managers.

Basic Patterns of Cash Flow

The cash flow—both inflows and outflows—of a firm can be described by its general pattern. It can be defined as a single amount, an annuity, or a mixed stream.

Single amount: A lump-sum amount either currently held or expected at some future date. Examples include $1,000 today and $650 to be received at the end of 10 years.

Annuity: A level periodic stream of cash flow. For our purposes, we'll work primarily with *annual* cash flows. Examples include either paying out or receiving $800 at the end of each of the next 7 years.

Mixed stream: A stream of cash flow that is *not* an annuity; a stream of unequal periodic cash flows that reflect no particular pattern. Examples include the following two cash flow streams A and B.

	Mixed cash flow stream	
End of year	A	B
1	$ 100	−$ 50
2	800	100
3	1,200	80
4	1,200	− 60
5	1,400	
6	300	

Note that neither cash flow stream has equal, periodic cash flows and that A is a 6-year mixed stream and B is a 4-year mixed stream.

In the next three sections of this chapter, we develop the concepts and techniques for finding future and present values of single amounts, annuities, and mixed streams, respectively. Detailed demonstrations of these cash flow patterns are included.

Review Questions

4–1 What is the difference between *future value* and *present value*? Which approach is generally preferred by financial managers? Why?

4–2 Define and differentiate among the three basic patterns of cash flow: (1) a single amount, (2) an annuity, and (3) a mixed stream.

Single Amounts

Imagine that at age 25 you began making annual purchases of $2,000 of an investment that earns a guaranteed 5 percent annually. At the end of 40 years, at age 65, you would have invested a total of $80,000 (40 years × $2,000 per year). Assuming that all funds remain invested, how much would you have accumulated at the end of the fortieth year? $100,000? $150,000? $200,000? No, your $80,000 would have grown to $242,000! Why? Because the time value of money allowed your investments to generate returns that built on each other over the 40 years.

The most basic future value and present value concepts and computations concern single amounts, either present or future amounts. We begin by considering the future value of present amounts. Then we will use the underlying concepts to determine the present value of future amounts. You will see that although future value is more intuitively appealing, present value is more useful in financial decision making.

Future Value of a Single Amount

We often need to find the value at some future date of a given amount of money placed on deposit today. For example, if you deposit $500 today into an account that pays 5 percent annual interest, how much would you have in the account at the end of exactly 10 years? **Future value** is the value at a given future date of a present amount placed on deposit today and earning interest at a specified rate. It depends on the rate of interest earned and the length of time a given amount is left on deposit. Here we explore the future value of a single amount.

future value
The value at a given future date of a present amount placed on deposit today and earning interest at a specified rate. Found by applying *compound interest* over a specified period of time.

compound interest
Interest that is earned on a given deposit and has become part of the *principal* at the end of a specified period.

principal
The amount of money on which interest is paid.

The Concept of Future Value

We speak of **compound interest** to indicate that the amount of interest earned on a given deposit has become part of the principal at the end of a specified period. The term **principal** refers to the amount of money on which the interest is paid. Annual compounding is the most common type.

The *future value* of a present amount is found by applying *compound interest* over a specified period of time. Savings institutions advertise compound interest returns at a rate of x percent, or x percent interest, compounded annually, semi-annually, quarterly, monthly, weekly, daily, or even continuously. The concept of future value with annual compounding can be illustrated by a simple example.

EXAMPLE If Fred Moreno places $100 in a savings account paying 8% interest compounded annually, at the end of 1 year he will have $108 in the account—the initial principal of $100 plus 8% ($8) in interest. The future value at the end of the first year is calculated by using Equation 4.1:

$$\text{Future value at end of year } 1 = \$100 \times (1 + 0.08) = \$108 \quad (4.1)$$

If Fred were to leave this money in the account for another year, he would be paid interest at the rate of 8% on the new principal of $108. At the end of this second year there would be $116.64 in the account. This amount would represent the principal at the beginning of year 2 ($108) plus 8% of the $108 ($8.64) in interest. The future value at the end of the second year is calculated by using Equation 4.2:

$$\text{Future value at end of year } 2 = \$108 \times (1 + 0.08) \quad (4.2)$$
$$= \$116.64$$

Substituting the expression between the equals signs in Equation 4.1 for the $108 figure in Equation 4.2 gives us Equation 4.3:

$$\text{Future value at end of year } 2 = \$100 \times (1 + 0.08) \times (1 + 0.08) \quad (4.3)$$
$$= \$100 \times (1 + 0.08)^2$$
$$= \$116.64$$

The equations in the preceding example lead to a more general formula for calculating future value.

The Equation for Future Value

The basic relationship in Equation 4.3 can be generalized to find the future value after any number of periods. We use the following notation for the various inputs:

FV_n = future value at the end of period n
PV = initial principal, or present value
i = annual rate of interest paid. (*Note:* On financial calculators, I is typically used to represent this rate.)
n = number of periods (typically years) that the money is left on deposit

The general equation for the future value at the end of period n is

$$FV_n = PV \times (1 + i)^n \quad (4.4)$$

A simple example will illustrate how to apply Equation 4.4.

EXAMPLE Jane Farber places $800 in a savings account paying 6% interest compounded annually. She wants to know how much money will be in the account at the end of 5 years. Substituting $PV = \$800$, $i = 0.06$, and $n = 5$ into Equation 4.4 gives the amount at the end of year 5.

$$FV_5 = \$800 \times (1 + 0.06)^5 = \$800 \times (1.338) = \$1,070.40$$

This analysis can be depicted on a time line as follows:

Time line for future value of a single amount ($800 initial principal, earning 6%, at the end of 5 years)

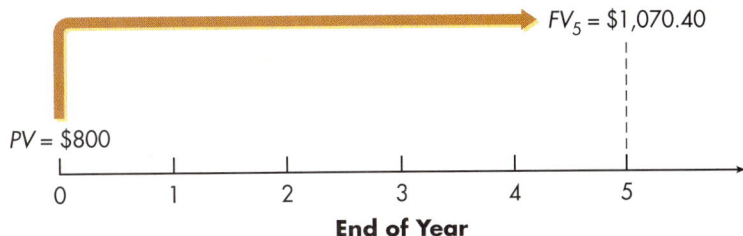

Using Computational Tools to Find Future Value

Solving the equation in the preceding example involves raising 1.06 to the fifth power. Using a future value interest table, a financial calculator, or an electronic spreadsheet greatly simplifies the calculation. A table that provides values for $(1+i)^n$ in Equation 4.4 is included near the back of the book in Appendix Table A–1.[1] The value in each cell of the table is called the **future value interest factor**. This factor is the multiplier used to calculate, at a specified interest rate, the future value of a present amount as of a given time. The future value interest factor for an initial principal of $1 compounded at i percent for n periods is referred to as $FVIF_{i,n}$.

future value interest factor The multiplier used to calculate, at a specified interest rate, the future value of a present amount as of a given time.

$$\text{Future value interest factor} = FVIF_{i,n} = (1+i)^n \quad (4.5)$$

By finding the intersection of the annual interest rate, i, and the appropriate periods, n, you will find the future value interest factor that is relevant to a particular problem.[2] Using $FVIF_{i,n}$ as the appropriate factor, we can rewrite the general equation for future value (Equation 4.4) as follows:

$$FV_n = PV \times (FVIF_{i,n}) \quad (4.6)$$

This expression indicates that to find the future value at the end of period n of an initial deposit, we have merely to multiply the initial deposit, PV, by the appropriate future value interest factor.[3]

EXAMPLE

In the preceding example, Jane Farber placed $800 in her savings account at 6% interest compounded annually and wishes to find out how much will be in the account at the end of 5 years.

Table Use The future value interest factor for an initial principal of $1 on deposit for 5 years at 6% interest compounded annually, $FVIF_{6\%, 5yrs}$, found in Table A–1, is 1.338. Using Equation 4.6, $800 \times 1.338 = \$1,070.40$. Therefore, the future value of Jane's deposit at the end of year 5 will be $1,070.40.

---

1. This table is commonly referred to as a "compound interest table" or a "table of the future value of one dollar." As long as you understand the source of the table values, the various names attached to it should not create confusion, because you can always make a trial calculation of a value for one factor as a check.

2. Although we commonly deal with years rather than periods, financial tables are frequently presented in terms of periods to provide maximum flexibility.

3. Occasionally, you may want to estimate roughly how long a given sum must earn at a given annual rate to double the amount. The *Rule of 72* is used to make this estimate; dividing the annual rate of interest into 72 results in the approximate number of periods it will take to double one's money at the given rate. For example, to double one's money at a 10% annual rate of interest will take about 7.2 years ($72 \div 10 = 7.2$). Looking at Table A–1, we can see that the future value interest factor for 10% and 7 years is slightly less than 2 (1.949); this approximation therefore appears to be reasonably accurate.

Calculator Use[4] The financial calculator can be used to calculate the future value directly.[5] First punch in $800 and depress **PV**; next punch in 5 and depress **N**; then punch in 6 and depress **I** (which is equivalent to "*i*" in our notation)[6]; finally, to calculate the future value, depress **CPT** and then **FV**. The future value of $1,070.58 should appear on the calculator display as shown at the left. On many calculators, this value will be preceded by a minus sign (−1,070.58). *If a minus sign appears on your calculator, ignore it here as well as in all other "Calculator Use" illustrations in this text.*[7]

Because the calculator is more accurate than the future value factors, which have been rounded to the nearest 0.001, a slight difference—in this case, $0.18—will frequently exist between the values found by these alternative methods. Clearly, the improved accuracy and ease of calculation tend to favor the use of the calculator. (*Note:* In future examples of calculator use, we will use only a display similar to that shown at the left. If you need a reminder of the procedures involved, go back and review the preceding paragraph.)

Spreadsheet Use The future value of the single amount also can be calculated as shown on the following Excel spreadsheet.

	A	B
1	**FUTURE VALUE OF A SINGLE AMOUNT**	
2	Present value	$800
3	Interest rate, pct per year compounded annually	6%
4	Number of years	5
5	Future value	$1,070.58

Entry in Cell B5 is =FV(B3,B4,0,−B2,0).
The minus sign appears before B2 because the present value is an outflow (i.e., a deposit made by Jane Farber).

A Graphical View of Future Value

Remember that we measure future value at the *end* of the given period. Figure 4.5 illustrates the relationship among various interest rates, the number of periods interest is earned, and the future value of one dollar. The figure shows that (1) the higher the interest rate, the higher the future value, and (2) the longer the period of time, the higher the future value. Note that for an interest rate of 0 percent, the future value always equals the present value ($1.00). But for any interest rate greater than zero, the future value is greater than the present value of $1.00.

---

4. Many calculators allow the user to set the number of payments per year. Most of these calculators are preset for monthly payments—12 payments per year. Because we work primarily with annual payments—one payment per year—it is important to *be sure that your calculator is set for one payment per year.* And although most calculators are preset to recognize that all payments occur at the end of the period, it is important to *make sure that your calculator is correctly set on the END mode.* Consult the reference guide that accompanies your calculator for instructions for setting these values.

5. To avoid including previous data in current calculations, *always clear all registers of your calculator before inputting values and making each computation.*

6. The known values *can be punched into the calculator in any order;* the order specified in this as well as other demonstrations of calculator use included in this text merely reflects convenience and personal preference.

7. The calculator differentiates inflows from outflows by preceding the outflows with a negative sign. For example, in the problem just demonstrated, the $800 present value (PV), because it was keyed as a positive number (800), is considered an inflow or deposit. Therefore, the calculated future value (FV) of −1,070.58 is preceded by a minus sign to show that it is the resulting outflow or withdrawal. Had the $800 present value been keyed in as a negative number (−800), the future value of $1,070.58 would have been displayed as a positive number (1,070.58). Simply stated, *the cash flows—present value (PV) and future value (FV)—will have opposite signs.*

FIGURE 4.5

Future Value Relationship
Interest rates, time periods, and future value of one dollar

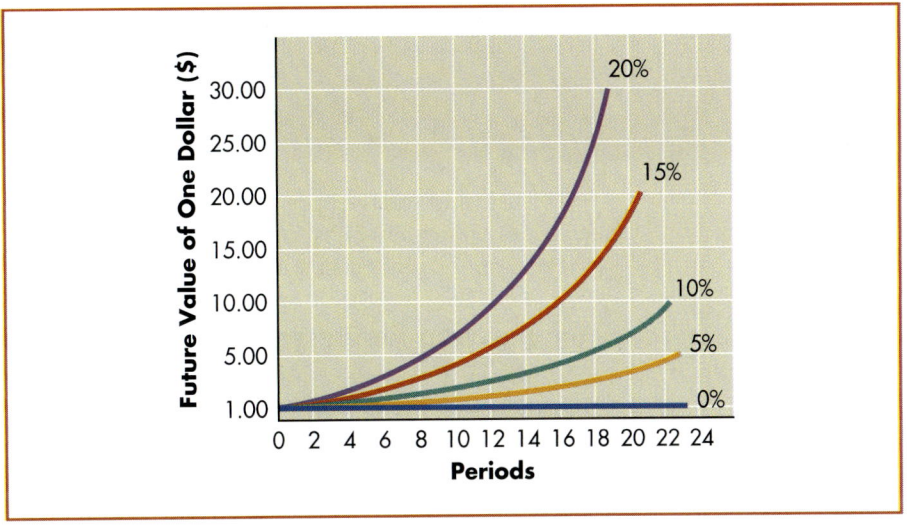

Present Value of a Single Amount

It is often useful to determine the value today of a future amount of money. For example, how much would I have to deposit today into an account paying 7 percent annual interest to accumulate $3,000 at the end of 5 years? **Present value** is the current dollar value of a future amount—the amount of money that would have to be invested today at a given interest rate over a specified period to equal the future amount. Present value depends largely on the investment opportunities and the point in time at which the amount is to be received. This section explores the present value of a single amount.

present value
The current dollar value of a future amount—the amount of money that would have to be invested today at a given interest rate over a specified period to equal the future amount.

The Concept of Present Value

discounting cash flows
The process of finding present values; the inverse of compounding interest.

The process of finding present values is often referred to as **discounting cash flows**. It is concerned with answering the following question: If I can earn i percent on my money, what is the most I would be willing to pay now for an opportunity to receive FV_n dollars n periods from today?

This process is actually the inverse of compounding interest. Instead of finding the future value of present dollars invested at a given rate, discounting determines the present value of a future amount, assuming an opportunity to earn a certain return on the money. This annual rate of return is variously referred to as the *discount rate, required return, cost of capital,* and *opportunity cost*. These terms will be used interchangeably in this text.

EXAMPLE

Paul Shorter has an opportunity to receive $300 one year from now. If he can earn 6% on his investments in the normal course of events, what is the most he should pay now for this opportunity? To answer this question, Paul must determine how many dollars he would have to invest at 6% today to have $300 one year from now. Letting PV equal this unknown amount and using the same notation as in the future value discussion, we have

$$PV \times (1 + 0.06) = \$300 \tag{4.7}$$

Solving Equation 4.7 for PV gives us Equation 4.8:

$$PV = \frac{\$300}{(1 + 0.06)} \qquad (4.8)$$
$$= \$283.02$$

The value today ("present value") of $300 received one year from today, given an opportunity cost of 6%, is $283.02. That is, investing $283.02 today at the 6% opportunity cost would result in $300 at the end of one year. ∎

The Equation for Present Value

The present value of a future amount can be found mathematically by solving Equation 4.4 for PV. In other words, the present value, PV, of some future amount, FV_n, to be received n periods from now, assuming an opportunity cost of i, is calculated as follows:

$$PV = \frac{FV_n}{(1 + i)^n} = FV_n \times \left[\frac{1}{(1 + i)^n}\right] \qquad (4.9)$$

Note the similarity between this general equation for present value and the equation in the preceding example (Equation 4.8). Let's use this equation in an example.

EXAMPLE Pam Valenti wishes to find the present value of $1,700 that will be received 8 years from now. Pam's opportunity cost is 8%. Substituting $FV_8 = \$1,700$, $n = 8$, and $i = 0.08$ into Equation 4.9 yields Equation 4.10:

$$PV = \frac{\$1,700}{(1 + 0.08)^8} = \frac{\$1,700}{1.851} = \$918.42 \qquad (4.10)$$

The following time line shows this analysis.

Time line for present value of a single amount ($1,700 future amount, discounted at 8%, from the end of 8 years)

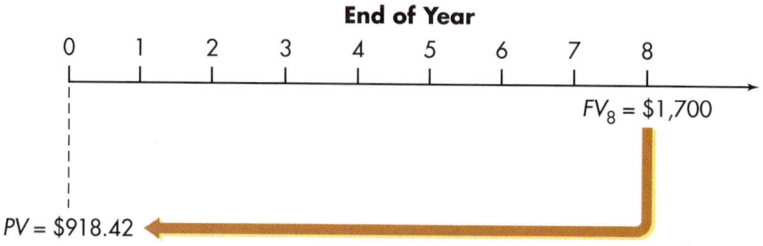

Using Computational Tools to Find Present Value

present value interest factor
The multiplier used to calculate, at a specified discount rate, the present value of an amount to be received in a future period.

The present value calculation can be simplified by using a **present value interest factor**. This factor is the multiplier used to calculate, at a specified discount rate, the present value of an amount to be received in a future period. The present value interest factor for the present value of $1 discounted at i percent for n periods is referred to as $PVIF_{i,n}$.

$$\text{Present value interest factor} = PVIF_{i,n} = \frac{1}{(1 + i)^n} \qquad (4.11)$$

Appendix Table A–2 presents present value interest factors for $1. By letting $PVIF_{i,n}$ represent the appropriate factor, we can rewrite the general equation for present value (Equation 4.9) as follows:

$$PV = FV_n \times (PVIF_{i,n}) \tag{4.12}$$

This expression indicates that to find the present value of an amount to be received in a future period, n, we have merely to multiply the future amount, FV_n, by the appropriate present value interest factor.

EXAMPLE

As noted, Pam Valenti wishes to find the present value of $1,700 to be received 8 years from now, assuming an 8% opportunity cost.

Table Use The present value interest factor for 8% and 8 years, $PVIF_{8\%, 8\,yrs}$, found in Table A–2, is 0.540. Using Equation 4.12, $1,700 \times 0.540 = $918. The present value of the $1,700 Pam expects to receive in 8 years is $918.

Calculator Use Using the calculator's financial functions and the inputs shown at the left, you should find the present value to be $918.46. The value obtained with the calculator is more accurate than the values found using the equation or the table, although for the purposes of this text, these differences are insignificant.

Spreadsheet Use The present value of the single future amount also can be calculated as shown on the following Excel spreadsheet.

	A	B
1	PRESENT VALUE OF A SINGLE AMOUNT	
2	Future value	$1,700
3	Interest rate, pct per year compounded annually	8%
4	Number of years	8
5	Present value	$918.46

Entry in Cell B5 is =-PV(B3,B4,0,B2).
The minus sign appears before PV to change
the present value to a positive amount.

A Graphical View of Present Value

Remember that present value calculations assume that the future values are measured at the *end* of the given period. The relationships among the factors in a present value calculation are illustrated in Figure 4.6 (see page 148). The figure clearly shows that, everything else being equal, (1) the higher the discount rate, the lower the present value, and (2) the longer the period of time, the lower the present value. Also note that given a discount rate of 0 percent, the present value always equals the future value ($1.00). But for any discount rate greater than zero, the present value is less than the future value of $1.00.

Comparing Present Value and Future Value

We will close this section with some important observations about present values. One is that the expression for the present value interest factor for i percent and n periods, $1/(1 + i)^n$, is the *inverse* of the future value interest factor for i percent and n periods, $(1 + i)^n$. You can confirm this very simply: Divide a present value interest

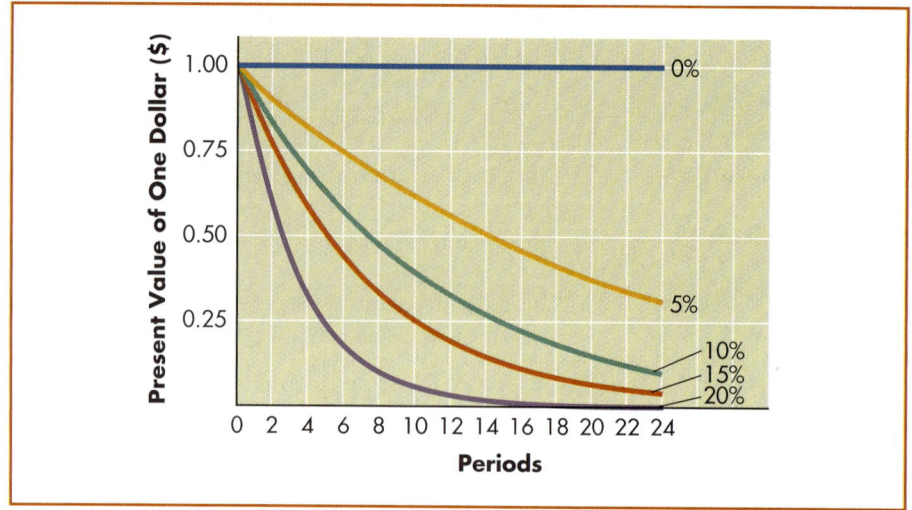

FIGURE 4.6

Present Value Relationship
Discount rates, time periods, and present value of one dollar

factor for *i* percent and *n* periods, $PVIF_{i,n}$, given in Table A–2, into 1.0, and compare the resulting value to the future value interest factor given in Table A–1 for *i* percent and *n* periods, $FVIF_{i,n}$. The two values should be equivalent.

Second, because of the relationship between present value interest factors and future value interest factors, we can find the present value interest factors given a table of future value interest factors, and vice versa. For example, the future value interest factor (from Table A–1) for 10 percent and 5 periods is 1.611. Dividing this value into 1.0 yields 0.621, which is the present value interest factor (given in Table A–2) for 10 percent and 5 periods.

Review Questions

4–3 How is the *compounding process* related to the payment of interest on savings? What is the general equation for future value?

4–4 What effect would a *decrease* in the interest rate have on the future value of a deposit? What effect would an *increase* in the holding period have on future value?

4–5 What is meant by "the present value of a future amount"? What is the general equation for present value?

4–6 What effect does *increasing* the required return have on the present value of a future amount? Why?

4–7 How are present value and future value calculations related?

LG3 Annuities

How much will you have at the end of 5 years if your employer withholds and invests $1,000 of your year-end bonus at the end of *each* of the next 5 years, guaranteeing you a 9 percent annual rate of return? How much would you pay today, given that you can earn 7 percent on low-risk investments, to receive a guaranteed $3,000 at the end of *each* of the next 20 years? To answer these ques-

annuity
A stream of equal periodic cash flows, over a specified time period. These cash flows can be *inflows* of returns earned on investments or *outflows* of funds invested to earn future returns.

ordinary annuity
An annuity for which the cash flow occurs at the *end* of each period.

annuity due
An annuity for which the cash flow occurs at the *beginning* of each period.

tions, you need to understand the application of the time value of money to *annuities*.

An **annuity** is a stream of equal periodic cash flows, over a specified time period. These cash flows are usually annual but can occur at other intervals, such as monthly (rent, car payments). The cash flows in an annuity can be *inflows* (the $3,000 received at the end of each of the next 20 years) or *outflows* (the $1,000 invested at the end of each of the next 5 years).

Types of Annuities

There are two basic types of annuities. For an **ordinary annuity**, the cash flow occurs at the *end* of each period. For an **annuity due,**, the cash flow occurs at the *beginning* of each period.

EXAMPLE

Fran Abrams is choosing which of two annuities to receive. Both are 5-year, $1,000 annuities; annuity A is an ordinary annuity, and annuity B is an annuity due. To better understand the difference between these annuities, she has listed their cash flows in Table 4.1. Note that the amount of each annuity totals $5,000. The two annuities differ in the timing of their cash flows: The cash flows are received sooner with the annuity due than with the ordinary annuity.

Although the cash flows of both annuities in Table 4.1 total $5,000, the annuity due would have a higher future value than the ordinary annuity, because each of its five annual cash flows can earn interest for one year more than each of the ordinary annuity's cash flows. In general, as will be demonstrated later in this chapter, *both the future value and the present value of an annuity due are always greater than the future value and the present value, respectively, of an otherwise identical ordinary annuity.*

Because ordinary annuities are more frequently used in finance, *unless otherwise specified, the term* annuity *is intended throughout this book to refer to ordinary annuities.* Discussions of annuities in this book concentrate on ordinary annuities. For discussion and computation of annuities due, see the book's Web site at www.aw-bc.com/gitman.

TABLE 4.1 **Comparison of Ordinary Annuity and Annuity Due Cash Flows ($1,000, 5 Years)**

	Annual cash flows	
End of year[a]	Annuity A (*ordinary*)	Annuity B (*annuity due*)
0	$ 0	$1,000
1	1,000	1,000
2	1,000	1,000
3	1,000	1,000
4	1,000	1,000
5	1,000	0
Totals	$5,000	$5,000

[a]The ends of years 0, 1, 2, 3, and 4 are equivalent to the beginnings of years 1, 2, 3, 4, and 5, respectively.

Finding the Future Value of an Ordinary Annuity

The calculations required to find the future value of an ordinary annuity are illustrated in the following example.

EXAMPLE

Fran Abrams wishes to determine how much money she will have at the end of 5 years if she chooses annuity A, the ordinary annuity. It represents deposits of $1,000 annually, at the *end of each* of the next 5 years, into a savings account paying 7% annual interest. This situation is depicted on the following time line:

Time line for future value of an ordinary annuity ($1,000 end-of-year deposit, earning 7%, at the end of 5 years)

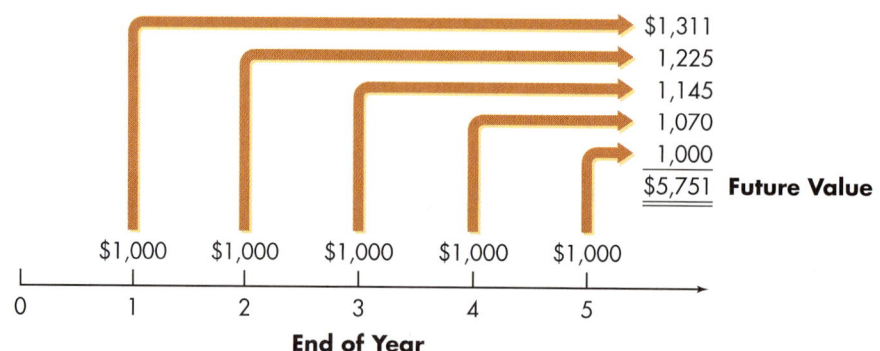

As the figure shows, at the end of year 5, Fran will have $5,751 in her account. Note that because the deposits are made at the end of the year, the first deposit will earn interest for 4 years, the second for 3 years, and so on. ∎

Using Computational Tools to Find the Future Value of an Ordinary Annuity

Annuity calculations can be simplified by using an interest table, a financial calculator, or an electronic spreadsheet. A table for the future value of a $1 *ordinary annuity* is given in Appendix Table A–3. The factors in the table are derived by summing the future value interest factors for the appropriate number of years. For example, the factor for the annuity in the preceding example is the sum of the factors for the five years (years 4 through 0): $1.311 + 1.225 + 1.145 + 1.070 + 1.000 = 5.751$. Because the deposits occur at the end of each year, they will earn interest from the end of the year in which each occurs to the end of year 5. Therefore, the first deposit earns interest for 4 years (end of year 1 through end of year 5), and the last deposit earns interest for zero years. The future value interest factor for zero years at any interest rate, $FVIF_{i,0}$, is 1.000, as we have noted. The formula for the **future value interest factor for an ordinary annuity** when interest is compounded annually at i percent for n periods, $FVIFA_{i,n}$, is[8]

future value interest factor for an ordinary annuity
The multiplier used to calculate the future value of an *ordinary annuity* at a specified interest rate over a given period of time.

$$FVIFA_{i,n} = \sum_{t=1}^{n}(1+i)^{t-1} \qquad (4.13)$$

---

8. A mathematical expression that can be applied to calculate the future value interest factor for an ordinary annuity more efficiently is

$$FVIFA_{i,n} = \frac{1}{i} \times [(1+i)^n - 1] \qquad (4.13a)$$

The use of this expression is especially attractive in the absence of the appropriate financial tables and of any financial calculator or electronic spreadsheet.

This factor is the multiplier used to calculate the future value of an *ordinary annuity* at a specified interest rate over a given period of time.

Using FVA_n for the future value of an *n*-year annuity, PMT for the amount to be deposited annually at the *end* of each year, and $FVIFA_{i,n}$ for the appropriate *future value interest factor for a one-dollar ordinary annuity compounded at i percent for n years*, we can express the relationship among these variables alternatively as

$$FVA_n = PMT \times (FVIFA_{i,n}) \tag{4.14}$$

The following example illustrates this calculation using a table, a calculator, and a spreadsheet.

EXAMPLE

As noted earlier, Fran Abrams wishes to find the future value (FVA_n) at the end of 5 years (*n*) of an annual *end-of-year deposit* of $1,000 ($PMT$) into an account paying 7% annual interest (*i*) during the next 5 years.

Table Use The future value interest factor for an ordinary 5-year annuity at 7% ($FVIFA_{7\%,5yrs}$), found in Table A–3, is 5.751. Using Equation 4.14, the $1,000 deposit × 5.751 results in a future value for the annuity of $5,751.

Calculator Use Using the calculator inputs shown at the left, you will find the future value of the ordinary annuity to be $5,750.74, a slightly more precise answer than that found using the table.

Spreadsheet Use The future value of the ordinary annuity also can be calculated as shown on the following Excel spreadsheet.

	A	B
1	FUTURE VALUE OF AN ORDINARY ANNUITY	
2	Annual payment	$1,000
3	Annual rate of interest, compounded annually	7%
4	Number of years	5
5	Future value of an ordinary annuity	$5,750.74

Entry in Cell B5 is =FV(B3,B4,−B2).
The minus sign appears before B2 because the annual payment is a cash outflow.

Finding the Present Value of an Ordinary Annuity

Quite often in finance, there is a need to find the present value of a *stream* of cash flows to be received in future periods. An annuity is, of course, a stream of equal periodic cash flows. (We'll explore the case of mixed streams of cash flows in a later section.) The method for finding the present value of an ordinary annuity is similar to the method just discussed. There are long and short methods for making this calculation.

EXAMPLE

Braden Company, a small producer of plastic toys, wants to determine the most it should pay to purchase a particular ordinary annuity. The annuity consists of cash flows of $700 at the end of each year for 5 years. The firm requires the annuity to provide a minimum return of 8%. This situation is depicted on the time line at the top page 152.

Time line for present value of an ordinary annuity ($700 end-of-year cash flows, discounted at 8%, over 5 years)

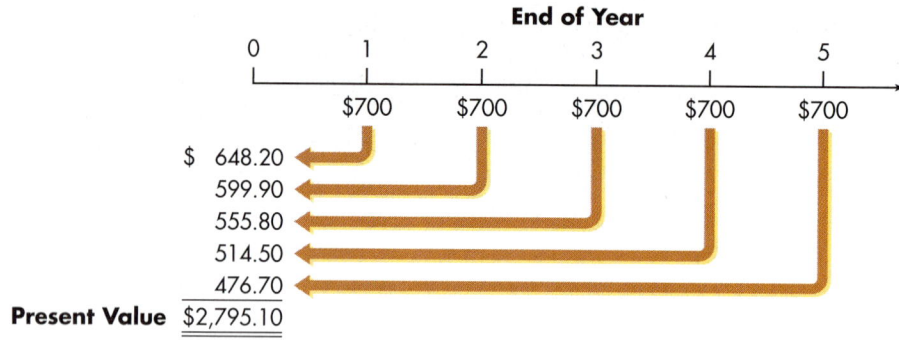

Table 4.2 shows the long method for finding the present value of the annuity. This method involves finding the present value of each payment and summing them. This procedure yields a present value of $2,795.10.

Using Computational Tools to Find the Present Value of an Ordinary Annuity

present value interest factor for an ordinary annuity The multiplier used to calculate the present value of an *ordinary annuity* at a specified discount rate over a given period of time.

Annuity calculations can be simplified by using an interest table for the present value of an annuity, a financial calculator, or an electronic spreadsheet. The values for the present value of a $1 ordinary annuity are given in Appendix Table A–4. The factors in the table are derived by summing the present value interest factors (in Table A–2) for the appropriate number of years at the given discount rate. The formula for the **present value interest factor for an ordinary annuity** with cash flows that are discounted at i percent for n periods, $PVIFA_{i,n}$, is[9]

$$PVIFA_{i,n} = \sum_{t=1}^{n} \frac{1}{(1+i)^t} \qquad (4.15)$$

TABLE 4.2 The Long Method for Finding the Present Value of an Ordinary Annuity

Year (n)	Cash flow (1)	$PVIF_{8\%,n}$[a] (2)	Present value [(1) × (2)] (3)
1	$700	0.926	$ 648.20
2	700	0.857	599.90
3	700	0.794	555.80
4	700	0.735	514.50
5	700	0.681	476.70
		Present value of annuity	$2,795.10

[a] Present value interest factors at 8% are from Table A–2.

---

[9]. A mathematical expression that can be applied to calculate the present value interest factor for an ordinary annuity more efficiently is

$$PVIFA_{i,n} = \frac{1}{i} \times \left[1 - \frac{1}{(1+i)^n}\right] \qquad (4.15a)$$

The use of this expression is especially attractive in the absence of the appropriate financial tables and of any financial calculator or an electronic spreadsheet.

This factor is the multiplier used to calculate the present value of an *ordinary annuity* at a specified discount rate over a given period of time.

By letting PVA_n equal the present value of an *n*-year *ordinary annuity*, letting PMT equal the amount to be received annually at the *end* of each year, and letting $PVIFA_{i,n}$ represent the appropriate *present value interest factor for a one-dollar ordinary annuity discounted at* i *percent for* n *years*, we can express the relationship among these variables as

$$PVA_n = PMT \times (PVIFA_{i,n}) \quad (4.16)$$

The following example illustrates this calculation using a table, a calculator, and a spreadsheet.

EXAMPLE

Braden Company, as we have noted, wants to find the present value of a 5-year ordinary annuity of $700, assuming an 8% opportunity cost.

Table Use The present value interest factor for an ordinary annuity at 8% for 5 years ($PVIFA_{8\%,5yrs}$), found in Table A–4, is 3.993. If we use Equation 4.16, $700 annuity × 3.993 results in a present value of $2,795.10.

Calculator Use Using the calculator's inputs shown at the left, you will find the present value of the ordinary annuity to be $2,794.90. The value obtained with the calculator is more accurate than those found using the equation or the table.

Spreadsheet Use The present value of the ordinary annuity also can be calculated as shown on the following Excel spreadsheet.

	A	B
1	PRESENT VALUE OF AN ORDINARY ANNUITY	
2	Annual payment	$700
3	Annual rate of interest, compounded annually	8%
4	Number of years	5
5	Present value of an ordinary annuity	$2,794.90

Entry in Cell B5 is =PV(B3,B4,–B2).
The minus sign appears before B2 because the annual payment is a cash outflow.

Finding the Present Value of a Perpetuity

perpetuity
An annuity with an infinite life, providing continual annual cash flow.

A **perpetuity** is an annuity with an infinite life—in other words, an annuity that never stops providing its holder with a cash flow at the end of each year (for example, the right to receive $500 at the end of each year forever).

It is sometimes necessary to find the present value of a perpetuity. The present value interest factor for a perpetuity discounted at the rate *i* is

$$PVIFA_{i,\infty} = \frac{1}{i} \quad (4.17)$$

As the equation shows, the appropriate factor, $PVIFA_{i,\infty}$, is found simply by dividing the discount rate, *i* (stated as a decimal), into 1. The validity of this method can be seen by looking at the factors in Table A–4 for 8, 10, 20, and 40 percent: As the number of periods (typically years) approaches 50, these factors approach the values calculated using Equation 4.17: $1 \div 0.08 = 12.50$; $1 \div 0.10 = 10.00$; $1 \div 0.20 = 5.00$; and $1 \div 0.40 = 2.50$.

EXAMPLE

Ross Clark wishes to endow a chair in finance at his alma mater. The university indicated that it requires $200,000 per year to support the chair, and the endowment would earn 10% per year. To determine the amount Ross must give the university to fund the chair, we must determine the present value of a $200,000 perpetuity discounted at 10%. The appropriate present value interest factor can be found by dividing 1 by 0.10, as noted in Equation 4.17. Substituting the resulting factor, $PVIFA_{10\%,\infty} = 10$, and the amount of the perpetuity, $PMT = \$200,000$, into Equation 4.16 results in a present value of $2,000,000 for the perpetuity. In other words, to generate $200,000 every year for an indefinite period requires $2,000,000 today if Ross Clark's alma mater can earn 10% on its investments. If the university earns 10% interest annually on the $2,000,000, it can withdraw $200,000 per year indefinitely without touching the initial $2,000,000, which would never be drawn upon.

Review Questions

4–8 What is the difference between an *ordinary annuity* and an *annuity due*? Which always has greater future value and present value for identical annuities and interest rates? Why?

4–9 What are the most efficient ways to calculate the present value of an ordinary annuity? What is the relationship between the *PVIF* and *PVIFA* interest factors given in Tables A–2 and A–4, respectively?

4–10 What is a *perpetuity*? How can the present value interest factor for such a stream of cash flows be determined?

Mixed Streams

mixed stream
A stream of unequal periodic cash flows that reflect no particular pattern.

Two basic types of cash flow streams are possible: the annuity and the mixed stream. Whereas an *annuity* is a pattern of equal periodic cash flows, a **mixed stream** is a stream of unequal periodic cash flows that reflect no particular pattern. Financial managers frequently need to evaluate opportunities that are expected to provide mixed streams of cash flows. Here we consider both the future value and the present value of mixed streams.

Future Value of a Mixed Stream

Determining the future value of a mixed stream of cash flows is straightforward. We determine the future value of each cash flow at the specified future date and then add all the individual future values to find the total future value.

EXAMPLE

Shrell Industries, a cabinet manufacturer, expects to receive the following mixed stream of cash flows over the next 5 years from one of its small customers.

End of year	Cash flow
1	$11,500
2	14,000
3	12,900
4	16,000
5	18,000

If Shrell expects to earn 8% on its investments, how much will it accumulate by the end of year 5 if it immediately invests these cash flows when they are received? This situation is depicted on the following time line:

Time line for future value of a mixed stream (end-of-year cash flows, compounded at 8% to the end of year 5)

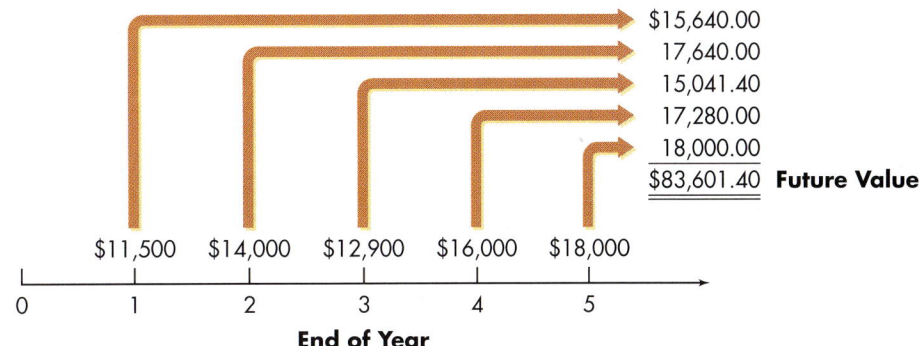

Table Use To solve this problem, we determine the future value of each cash flow compounded at 8% for the appropriate number of years. Note that the first cash flow of $11,500, received at the end of year 1, will earn interest for 4 years (end of year 1 through end of year 5); the second cash flow of $14,000, received at the end of year 2, will earn interest for 3 years (end of year 2 through end of year 5); and so on. The sum of the individual end-of-year-5 future values is the future value of the mixed cash flow stream. The future value interest factors required are those shown in Table A–1. Table 4.3 (see page 156) presents the calculations needed to find the future value of the cash flow stream, which turns out to be $83,601.40.

Calculator Use You can use your calculator to find the future value of each individual cash flow, as demonstrated earlier (page 144), and then sum the future values, to get the future value of the stream. Unfortunately, unless you can program your calculator, most calculators lack a function that would allow you to input *all of the cash flows*, specify the interest rate, and directly calculate the future value of the entire cash flow stream. Had you used your calculator to find the individual cash flow future values and then summed them, the future value of Shrell Industries' cash flow stream at the end of year 5 would have been $83,608.15, a more precise value than the one obtained by using a financial table.

TABLE 4.3 Future Value of a Mixed Stream of Cash Flows

Year	Cash flow (1)	Number of years earning interest (n) (2)	$FVIF_{8\%,n}$[a] (3)	Future value [(1) × (3)] (4)
1	$11,500	5 − 1 = 4	1.360	$15,640.00
2	14,000	5 − 2 = 3	1.260	17,640.00
3	12,900	5 − 3 = 2	1.166	15,041.40
4	16,000	5 − 4 = 1	1.080	17,280.00
5	18,000	5 − 5 = 0	1.000[b]	18,000.00
			Future value of mixed stream	$83,601.40

[a]Future value interest factors at 8% are from Table A–1.
[b]The future value of the end-of-year-5 deposit at the end of year 5 is its present value because it earns interest for zero years and $(1 + 0.08)^0 = 1.000$.

Spreadsheet Use The future value of the mixed stream also can be calculated as shown on the following Excel spreadsheet.

	A	B
1	FUTURE VALUE OF A MIXED STREAM	
2	Interest rate, pct/year	8%
3	Year	Year-End Cash Flow
4	1	$11,500
5	2	$14,000
6	3	$12,900
7	4	$16,000
8	5	$18,000
9	Future value	$83,608.15

Entry in Cell B9 is
=−FV(B2,A8,0,NPV(B2,B4:B8)).
The minus sign appears before FV to convert the future value to a positive amount.

If Shrell Industries invests at 8% interest the cash flows received from its customer over the next 5 years, the company will accumulate about $83,600 by the end of year 5.

Present Value of a Mixed Stream

Finding the present value of a mixed stream of cash flows is similar to finding the future value of a mixed stream. We determine the present value of each future amount and then add all the individual present values together to find the total present value.

EXAMPLE

Frey Company, a shoe manufacturer, has been offered an opportunity to receive the following mixed stream of cash flows over the next 5 years:

End of year	Cash flow
1	$400
2	800
3	500
4	400
5	300

If the firm must earn at least 9% on its investments, what is the most it should pay for this opportunity? This situation is depicted on the following time line:

Time line for present value of a mixed stream (end-of-year cash flows, discounted at 9% over the corresponding number of years)

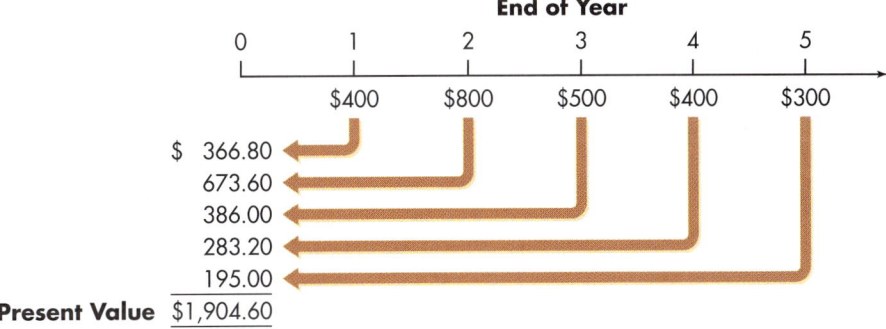

Table Use To solve this problem, determine the present value of each cash flow discounted at 9% for the appropriate number of years. The sum of these individual values is the present value of the total stream. The present value interest factors required are those shown in Table A–2. Table 4.4 presents the calculations needed to find the present value of the cash flow stream, which turns out to be $1,904.60.

TABLE 4.4 Present Value of a Mixed Stream of Cash Flows

Year (n)	Cash flow (1)	$PVIF_{9\%,n}$[a] (2)	Present value [(1) × (2)] (3)
1	$400	0.917	$ 366.80
2	800	0.842	673.60
3	500	0.772	386.00
4	400	0.708	283.20
5	300	0.650	195.00
		Present value of mixed stream	$1,904.60

[a]Present value interest factors at 9% are from Table A–2.

Calculator Use You can use a calculator to find the present value of each individual cash flow, as demonstrated earlier (page 147), and then sum the present values, to get the present value of the stream. However, most financial calculators have a function that allows you to punch in *all cash flows*, specify the discount rate, and then directly calculate the present value of the entire cash flow stream. Because calculators provide solutions more precise than those based on rounded table factors, the present value of Frey Company's cash flow stream found using a calculator is $1,904.76, which is close to the $1,904.60 value calculated before.

Spreadsheet Use The present value of the mixed stream of future cash flows also can be calculated as shown on the following Excel spreadsheet.

	A	B
1	PRESENT VALUE OF A MIXED STREAM OF CASH FLOWS	
2	Interest Rate, pct/year	9%
3	Year	Year-End Cash Flow
4	1	$400
5	2	$800
6	3	$500
7	4	$400
8	5	$300
9	Present value	$1,904.76
	Entry in Cell B9 is =NPV(B2,B4:B8).	

Paying about $1,905 would provide exactly a 9% return. Frey should pay no more than that amount for the opportunity to receive these cash flows.

Review Question

4–11 How is the future value of a mixed stream of cash flows calculated? How is the present value of a mixed stream of cash flows calculated?

Compounding Interest More Frequently Than Annually

Interest is often compounded more frequently than once a year. Savings institutions compound interest semiannually, quarterly, monthly, weekly, daily, or even continuously. This section discusses various issues and techniques related to these more frequent compounding intervals.

Semiannual Compounding

semiannual compounding
Compounding of interest over two periods within the year.

Semiannual compounding of interest involves two compounding periods within the year. Instead of the stated interest rate being paid once a year, one-half of the stated interest rate is paid twice a year.

TABLE 4.5 The Future Value from Investing $100 at 8% Interest Compounded Semiannually Over 24 Months (2 Years)

Period	Beginning principal (1)	Future value interest factor (2)	Future value at end of period [(1) × (2)] (3)
6 months	$100.00	1.04	$104.00
12 months	104.00	1.04	108.16
18 months	108.16	1.04	112.49
24 months	112.49	1.04	116.99

EXAMPLE Fred Moreno has decided to invest $100 in a savings account paying 8% interest *compounded semiannually.* If he leaves his money in the account for 24 months (2 years), he will be paid 4% interest compounded over four periods, each of which is 6 months long. Table 4.5 uses interest factors to show that at the end of 12 months (1 year) with 8% semiannual compounding, Fred will have $108.16; at the end of 24 months (2 years), he will have $116.99.

Quarterly Compounding

quarterly compounding
Compounding of interest over four periods within the year.

Quarterly compounding of interest involves four compounding periods within the year. One-fourth of the stated interest rate is paid four times a year.

EXAMPLE Fred Moreno has found an institution that will pay him 8% interest *compounded quarterly.* If he leaves his money in this account for 24 months (2 years), he will be paid 2% interest compounded over eight periods, each of which is 3 months long. Table 4.6 uses interest factors to show the amount Fred will have at the end of each period. At the end of 12 months (1 year), with 8% quarterly compounding, Fred will have $108.24; at the end of 24 months (2 years), he will have $117.17.

TABLE 4.6 The Future Value from Investing $100 at 8% Interest Compounded Quarterly Over 24 Months (2 Years)

Period	Beginning principal (1)	Future value interest factor (2)	Future value at end of period [(1) × (2)] (3)
3 months	$100.00	1.02	$102.00
6 months	102.00	1.02	104.04
9 months	104.04	1.02	106.12
12 months	106.12	1.02	108.24
15 months	108.24	1.02	110.41
18 months	110.40	1.02	112.62
21 months	112.61	1.02	114.87
24 months	114.86	1.02	117.17

TABLE 4.7 The Future Value at the End of Years 1 and 2 from Investing $100 at 8% Interest, Given Various Compounding Periods

End of year	Compounding period		
	Annual	Semiannual	Quarterly
1	$108.00	$108.16	$108.24
2	116.64	116.99	117.17

Table 4.7 compares values for Fred Moreno's $100 at the end of years 1 and 2 given annual, semiannual, and quarterly compounding periods at the 8 percent rate. As shown, *the more frequently interest is compounded, the greater the amount of money accumulated.* This is true for *any interest rate* for *any period of time.*

A General Equation for Compounding More Frequently Than Annually

The interest-factor formula for annual compounding (Equation 4.5) can be rewritten for use when compounding takes place more frequently. If m equals the number of times per year interest is compounded, the interest-factor formula for annual compounding can be rewritten as

$$FVIF_{i,n} = \left(1 + \frac{i}{m}\right)^{m \times n} \quad (4.18)$$

The basic equation for future value (Equation 4.4) can now be rewritten as

$$FV_n = PV \times \left(1 + \frac{i}{m}\right)^{m \times n} \quad (4.19)$$

If $m = 1$, Equation 4.19 reduces to Equation 4.4. Thus, if interest is compounded annually (once a year), Equation 4.19 will provide the same result as Equation 4.4. The general use of Equation 4.19 can be illustrated with a simple example.

EXAMPLE

The preceding examples calculated the amount that Fred Moreno would have at the end of 2 years if he deposited $100 at 8% interest compounded semiannually and compounded quarterly. For semiannual compounding, m would equal 2 in Equation 4.19; for quarterly compounding, m would equal 4. Substituting the appropriate values for semiannual and quarterly compounding into Equation 4.19, we find that

1. *For semiannual compounding:*

$$FV_2 = \$100 \times \left(1 + \frac{0.08}{2}\right)^{2 \times 2} = \$100 \times (1 + 0.04)^4 = \$116.99$$

2. *For quarterly compounding:*

$$FV_2 = \$100 \times \left(1 + \frac{0.08}{4}\right)^{4\times 2} = \$100 \times (1 + 0.02)^8 = \$117.17$$

These results agree with the values for FV_2 in Tables 4.5 and 4.6.

If the interest were compounded monthly, weekly, or daily, m would equal 12, 52, or 365, respectively.

Using Computational Tools for Compounding More Frequently Than Annually

We can use the future value interest factors for one dollar, given in Table A–1, when interest is compounded m times each year. Instead of indexing the table for i percent and n years, as we do when interest is compounded annually, we index it for $(i \div m)$ percent and $(m \times n)$ periods. However, the table is less useful, because it includes only selected rates for a limited number of periods. Instead, a financial calculator or an electronic spreadsheet is typically required.

EXAMPLE

Fred Moreno wished to find the future value of $100 invested at 8% interest compounded both semiannually and quarterly for 2 years. The number of compounding periods m, the interest rate $(i \div m)$, and the number of periods $(m \times n)$ used in each case, along with the future value interest factor, are as follows:

Compounding period	m	Interest rate $(i \div m)$	Periods $(m \times n)$	Future value interest factor from Table A–1
Semiannual	2	8% ÷ 2 = 4%	2 × 2 = 4	1.170
Quarterly	4	8% ÷ 4 = 2%	4 × 2 = 8	1.172

Table Use Multiplying each of the future value interest factors by the initial $100 deposit results in a value of $117.00 (1.170 × $100) for semiannual compounding and a value of $117.20 (1.172 × $100) for quarterly compounding.

Calculator Use If the calculator were used for the semiannual compounding calculation, the number of periods would be 4 and the interest rate would be 4%. The future value of $116.99 will appear on the calculator display as shown at the top left.

For the quarterly compounding case, the number of periods would be 8 and the interest rate would be 2%. The future value of $117.17 will appear on the calculator display as shown in the second display at the left.

Spreadsheet Use The future value of the single amount with semiannual and quarterly compounding also can be calculated as shown on the Excel spreadsheet on page 162.

	A	B
1	FUTURE VALUE OF A SINGLE AMOUNT WITH SEMIANNUAL AND QUARTERLY COMPOUNDING	
2	Present value	$100
3	Interest rate, pct per year compounded semiannually	8%
4	Number of years	2
5	Future value with semiannual compounding	$116.99
6	Present value	$100
7	Interest rate, pct per year compounded quarterly	8%
8	Number of years	2
9	Future value with quarterly compounding	$117.17

Entry in Cell B5 is =FV(B3/2,B4*2,0,−B2,0).
Entry in Cell B9 is =FV(B7/4,B8*4,0,−B2,0).
The minus sign appears before B2 because the present value is a cash outflow (i.e., a deposit made by Fred Moreno).

Comparing the calculator, table, and spreadsheet values, we can see that the calculator and spreadsheet values agree with the values in Table 4.7 but are more precise because the table factors have been rounded.

Continuous Compounding

continuous compounding
Compounding of interest an infinite number of times per year at intervals of microseconds.

In the extreme case, interest can be compounded continuously. **Continuous compounding** involves compounding over every microsecond—the smallest time period imaginable. In this case, m in Equation 4.18 would approach infinity. Through the use of calculus, we know that as m approaches infinity, the interest-factor equation becomes

$$FVIF_{i,n} \text{ (continuous compounding)} = e^{i \times n} \qquad (4.20)$$

where e is the exponential function,[10] which has a value of 2.7183. The future value for continuous compounding is therefore

$$FV_n \text{ (continuous compounding)} = PV \times (e^{i \times n}) \qquad (4.21)$$

EXAMPLE To find the value at the end of 2 years ($n = 2$) of Fred Moreno's $100 deposit ($PV = \$100$) in an account paying 8% annual interest ($i = 0.08$) compounded continuously, we can substitute into Equation 4.21:

$$FV_2 \text{ (continuous compounding)} = \$100 \times e^{0.08 \times 2}$$
$$= \$100 \times 2.7183^{0.16}$$
$$= \$100 \times 1.1735 = \$117.35$$

Calculator Use To find this value using the calculator, you need first to find the value of $e^{0.16}$ by punching in 0.16 and then pressing **2nd** and then e^x to get 1.1735. Next multiply this value by $100 to get the future value of $117.35 as shown at the left. (*Note:* On some calculators, you may not have to press **2nd** before pressing e^x.)

---

10. Most calculators have the exponential function, typically noted by e^x, built into them. The use of this key is especially helpful in calculating future value when interest is compounded continuously.

CHAPTER 4   Time Value of Money   163

Spreadsheet Use   The future value of the single amount with continuous compounding of Fred's deposit also can be calculated as shown on the following Excel spreadsheet.

	A	B
1	FUTURE VALUE OF A SINGLE AMOUNT WITH CONTINUOUS COMPOUNDING	
2	Present value	$100
3	Annual rate of interest, compounded continuously	8%
4	Number of years	2
5	Future value with continuous compounding	$117.35
Entry in Cell B5 is =B2*EXP(B3*B4).		

The future value with continuous compounding therefore equals $117.35. As expected, the continuously compounded value is larger than the future value of interest compounded semiannually ($116.99) or quarterly ($117.17). Continuous compounding results in the largest future value that would result from compounding interest more frequently than annually at a given rate over a stated period of time.

Nominal and Effective Annual Rates of Interest

Both businesses and investors need to make objective comparisons of loan costs or investment returns over different compounding periods. To put interest rates on a common basis, so as to allow comparison, we distinguish between nominal and effective annual rates. The **nominal, or stated, annual rate** is the contractual annual rate of interest charged by a lender or promised by a borrower. The **effective, or true, annual rate (EAR)** is the annual rate of interest actually paid or earned. The effective annual rate reflects the effects of compounding frequency, whereas the nominal annual rate does not.

Using the notation introduced earlier, we can calculate the effective annual rate, EAR, by substituting values for the nominal annual rate, i, and the compounding frequency, m, into Equation 4.22:

$$EAR = \left(1 + \frac{i}{m}\right)^m - 1 \qquad (4.22)$$

We can apply this equation using data from preceding examples.

nominal (stated) annual rate
Contractual annual rate of interest charged by a lender or promised by a borrower.

effective (true) annual rate (EAR)
The annual rate of interest actually paid or earned.

EXAMPLE   Fred Moreno wishes to find the effective annual rate associated with an 8% nominal annual rate ($i = 0.08$) when interest is compounded (1) annually ($m = 1$); (2) semiannually ($m = 2$); and (3) quarterly ($m = 4$). Substituting these values into Equation 4.22, we get

1. *For annual compounding:*

$$EAR = \left(1 + \frac{0.08}{1}\right)^1 - 1 = (1 + 0.08)^1 - 1 = 1 + 0.08 - 1 = 0.08 = 8\%$$

2. *For semiannual compounding:*

$$EAR = \left(1 + \frac{0.08}{2}\right)^2 - 1 = (1 + 0.04)^2 - 1 = 1.0816 - 1 = 0.0816 = 8.16\%$$

3. *For quarterly compounding:*

$$EAR = \left(1 + \frac{0.08}{4}\right)^4 - 1 = (1 + 0.02)^4 - 1 = 1.0824 - 1 = 0.0824 = 8.24\%$$

These values demonstrate two important points: The first is that nominal and effective annual rates are equivalent for annual compounding. The second is that the effective annual rate increases with increasing compounding frequency, up to a limit that occurs with *continuous compounding*.[11]

For an EAR example related to the "payday loan" business, with discussion of the ethical issues involved, see the *In Practice* box on the facing page.

At the consumer level, "truth-in-lending laws" require disclosure on credit card and loan agreements of the **annual percentage rate (APR)**. The APR is the *nominal annual rate* found by multiplying the periodic rate by the number of periods in one year. For example, a bank credit card that charges 1½ percent per month (the periodic rate) would have an APR of 18 percent (1.5% per month × 12 months per year).

"Truth-in-savings laws," on the other hand, require banks to quote the **annual percentage yield (APY)** on their savings products. The APY is the *effective annual rate* a savings product pays. For example, a savings account that pays 0.5 percent per month would have an APY of 6.17 percent [$(1.005)^{12} - 1$].

Quoting loan interest rates at their lower nominal annual rate (the APR) and savings interest rates at the higher effective annual rate (the APY) offers two advantages: It tends to standardize disclosure to consumers, and it enables financial institutions to quote the most attractive interest rates: low loan rates and high savings rates.

annual percentage rate (APR)
The *nominal annual rate* of interest, found by multiplying the periodic rate by the number of periods in one year, that must be disclosed to consumers on credit cards and loans as a result of "truth-in-lending laws."

annual percentage yield (APY)
The *effective annual rate* of interest that must be disclosed to consumers by banks on their savings products as a result of "truth-in-savings laws."

Review Questions

4–12 What effect does compounding interest more frequently than annually have on (a) future value and (b) the *effective annual rate (EAR)*? Why?

4–13 How does the future value of a deposit subject to continuous compounding compare to the value obtained by annual compounding?

4–14 Differentiate between a *nominal annual rate* and an *effective annual rate (EAR)*. Define *annual percentage rate (APR)* and *annual percentage yield (APY)*.

---

11. The effective annual rate for this extreme case can be found by using the following equation:

$$EAR \text{ (continuous compounding)} = e^i - 1 \qquad (4.22a)$$

For the 8% nominal annual rate ($i = 0.08$), substitution into Equation 4.22a results in an effective annual rate of

$$e^{0.08} - 1 = 1.0833 - 1 = 0.0833 = 8.33\%$$

in the case of continuous compounding. This is the highest effective annual rate attainable with an 8% nominal rate.

In Practice FOCUS ON ETHICS

HOW FAIR IS "CHECK INTO CASH"?

"Charge whatever price the market will bear" sounds like a recipe for maximizing profits. Are there ethical constraints? The "check into cash" or "payday loan" business provides a fascinating ethical case example.

Living "from paycheck to paycheck" is difficult enough, but a few consumers cannot manage even that. These consumers sometimes turn to the payday loan shop. There, the lender will advance you $93 today so you will not have to wait for your $100 paycheck in two weeks. You can simply endorse your check and repay the lender two weeks from now. What, though, is the effective (true) annual rate of interest on such a loan?

Equation 4.22 gives us the answer. First, let's calculate the interest rate for the two-week period. We determine the amount of interest by subtracting the amount advanced from the amount paid back: $100 − $93 = $7. Then, we calculate the interest rate for the two-week period (equivalent to i/m in Equation 4.22) by dividing the interest amount by the amount borrowed: $i/m = \$7/\$93 = 0.075269$, or 7.53%.

Maybe 7.53 percent is a small price to pay for getting cash today—after all, credit cards may charge 18 to 21 percent per year. However, that 7.53 percent is not the nominal (stated) annual rate. There are 26.07 (m in Equation 4.22) of these two-week (14-day) periods per year (365/14). Now we can calculate the *EAR* using Equation 4.22: $EAR = (1 + 0.0753)^{26.07} − 1 = 563.71\%$.

Gulp. Double-gulp. Why would anyone borrow at these astronomical rates? Payday loan shops are not classified as banks, so they fall outside the state usury laws that prohibit super-high consumer loan interest rates. Most consumers are likely unaware of the true interest rate.

The ethical standard that is germane here is that of *fairness*. Ethicist Jeffrey Seglin of Emerson College notes that "legal" does not equate to "ethical," and managers must consider the ethical impact of decisions on all constituencies, including customers. Behaving ethically includes avoiding deception.

Some might counter that common needs are being met here, and payday loan shops are just a case of "buyer beware." However, ethics includes three classes of fairness represented in this market offer:* freedom from misrepresentation, equal processing power (consumers need to have a basic competency level to process information without making mental errors), and equal bargaining power (which means neither party is richer than the other, constituting the basis for states' interest rate ceilings). An example to emulate here might be that of National Automobile Dealers Association (NADA), which rewrote its code of ethics to make it more exact and comprehensive, asking dealers throughout the United States to endorse it.

■ A payday loan shop will advance you $95 today so you will not have to wait a week to get your $100 paycheck. You will repay $100 on the day on which you get your paycheck. What is the EAR of this advance?

*Shefrin and Statman identify seven classes of fairness, based on the entitlements they provide, in their monograph, *Ethics, Fairness, Efficiency, and Financial Markets* (Research Foundation of the Institute of Chartered Financial Analysts; 1992). These are freedom from coercion, freedom from misrepresentation, equal information, equal processing power, freedom from impulse, efficient prices, and equal bargaining power.

Special Applications of Time Value

Future value and present value techniques have a number of important applications in finance. We'll study four of them in this section: (1) determining deposits needed to accumulate a future sum, (2) loan amortization, (3) finding interest or growth rates, and (4) finding an unknown number of periods.

Determining Deposits Needed to Accumulate a Future Sum

Suppose you want to buy a house 5 years from now, and you estimate that an initial down payment of $30,000 will be required at that time. To accumulate the $30,000, you will wish to make equal annual end-of-year deposits into an account paying annual interest of 6 percent. The solution to this problem is closely related to the process of finding the future value of an annuity. You must determine what size annuity will result in a single amount equal to $30,000 at the end of year 5.

Earlier in the chapter we found the future value of an n-year ordinary annuity, FVA_n, by multiplying the annual deposit, PMT, by the appropriate interest factor, $FVIFA_{i,n}$. The relationship of the three variables was defined by Equation 4.14, which is repeated here as Equation 4.23:

$$FVA_n = PMT \times (FVIFA_{i,n}) \qquad (4.23)$$

We can find the annual deposit required to accumulate FVA_n dollars by solving Equation 4.23 for PMT. Isolating PMT on the left side of the equation gives us

$$PMT = \frac{FVA_n}{FVIFA_{i,n}} \qquad (4.24)$$

Once this is done, we have only to substitute the known values of FVA_n and $FVIFA_{i,n}$ into the right side of the equation to find the annual deposit required.

EXAMPLE

As just stated, you want to determine the equal annual end-of-year deposits required to accumulate $30,000 at the end of 5 years, given an interest rate of 6%.

Table Use Table A–3 indicates that the future value interest factor for an ordinary annuity at 6% for 5 years ($FVIFA_{6\%,5yrs}$) is 5.637. Substituting $FVA_5 = \$30,000$ and $FVIFA_{6\%,5yrs} = 5.637$ into Equation 4.24 yields an annual required deposit, PMT, of $5,321.98. Thus, if $5,321.98 is deposited at the end of each year for 5 years at 6% interest, there will be $30,000 in the account at the end of the 5 years.

Calculator Use Using the calculator inputs shown at the left, you will find the annual deposit amount to be $5,321.89. Note that this value, except for a slight rounding difference, agrees with the value found by using Table A–3.

Spreadsheet Use The annual deposit needed to accumulate the future sum also can be calculated as shown on the following Excel spreadsheet.

	A	B
1	ANNUAL DEPOSIT NEEDED TO ACCUMULATE A FUTURE SUM	
2	Future value	$30,000
3	Number of years	5
4	Annual rate of interest	6%
5	Annual deposit	$5,321.89

Entry in Cell B5 is =–PMT(B4,B3,0,B2). The minus sign appears before PMT because the annual deposits are cash outflows.

Calculator inputs:
- Input 30000, Function FV
- Input 5, Function N
- Input 6, Function I
- CPT
- PMT
- Solution: 5,321.89

Loan Amortization

loan amortization
The determination of the equal periodic loan payments necessary to provide a lender with a specified interest return and to repay the loan principal over a specified period.

loan amortization schedule
A schedule of equal payments to repay a loan. It shows the allocation of each loan payment to interest and principal.

The term **loan amortization** refers to the determination of equal periodic loan payments. These payments provide a lender with a specified interest return and repay the loan principal over a specified period. The loan amortization process involves finding the future payments, over the term of the loan, whose present value at the loan interest rate equals the amount of initial principal borrowed. Lenders use a **loan amortization schedule** to determine these payment amounts and the allocation of each payment to interest and principal. In the case of home mortgages, these tables are used to find the equal *monthly* payments necessary to *amortize*, or pay off, the mortgage at a specified interest rate over a 15- to 30-year period.

Amortizing a loan actually involves creating an annuity out of a present amount. For example, say you borrow $6,000 at 10 percent and agree to make equal annual end-of-year payments over 4 years. To find the size of the payments, the lender determines the amount of a 4-year annuity discounted at 10 percent that has a present value of $6,000. This process is actually the inverse of finding the present value of an annuity.

Earlier in the chapter, we found the present value, PVA_n, of an n-year annuity by multiplying the annual amount, PMT, by the present value interest factor for an annuity, $PVIFA_{i,n}$. This relationship, which was originally expressed as Equation 4.16, is repeated here as Equation 4.25:

$$PVA_n = PMT \times (PVIFA_{i,n}) \qquad (4.25)$$

To find the equal annual payment required to pay off, or amortize, the loan, PVA_n, over a certain number of years at a specified interest rate, we need to solve Equation 4.25 for PMT. Isolating PMT on the left side of the equation gives us

$$PMT = \frac{PVA_n}{PVIFA_{i,n}} \qquad (4.26)$$

Once this is done, we have only to substitute the known values into the righthand side of the equation to find the annual payment required.

EXAMPLE

As just stated, you want to determine the equal annual end-of-year payments necessary to amortize fully a $6,000, 10% loan over 4 years.

Table Use Table A–4 indicates that the present value interest factor for an annuity corresponding to 10% and 4 years ($PVIFA_{10\%, 4yrs}$) is 3.170. Substituting $PVA_4 = \$6,000$ and $PVIFA_{10\%, 4yrs} = 3.170$ into Equation 4.26 and solving for PMT yield an annual loan payment of $1,892.74. Thus, to repay the interest and principal on a $6,000, 10%, 4-year loan, equal annual end-of-year payments of $1,892.74 are necessary.

Calculator Use Using the calculator inputs shown at the left, you will find the annual payment amount to be $1,892.82. Except for a slight rounding difference, this value agrees with the table solution.

The allocation of each loan payment to interest and principal can be seen in columns 3 and 4 of the *loan amortization schedule* in Table 4.8 at the top of page 169. The portion of each payment that represents interest (column 3) declines over the repayment period, and the portion going to principal repayment (column 4) increases. This pattern is typical of amortized loans; as the principal is reduced, the interest component declines, leaving a larger portion of each subsequent loan payment to repay principal.

Spreadsheet Use The annual payment to repay the loan also can be calculated as shown on the first Excel spreadsheet. The amortization schedule allocating each loan payment to interest and principal can be calculated precisely as shown on the second spreadsheet.

	A	B
1	ANNUAL PAYMENT TO REPAY A LOAN	
2	Loan principal (present value)	$6,000
3	Annual rate of interest	10%
4	Number of years	4
5	Annual payment	$1,892.82

Entry in Cell B5 is =−PMT(B3,B4,B2).
The minus sign appears before PMT because the annual payments are cash outflows.

	A	B	C	D	E
1		LOAN AMORTIZATION SCHEDULE			
2		Data: Loan principal		$6,000	
3		Annual rate of interest		10%	
4		Number of years		4	
5		Annual Payments			
6	Year	Total	To Interest	To Principal	Year-End Principal
7	0				$ 6,000.00
8	1	$1,892.82	$600.00	$1,292.82	4,707.18
9	2	$1,892.82	$470.72	$1,422.11	3,285.07
10	3	$1,892.82	$328.51	$1,564.32	1,720.75
11	4	$1,892.82	$172.07	$1,720.75	0.00

Key Cell Entries
Cell B8: =−PMT(D3,D4,D2), copy to B9:B11
Cell C8: =−CUMIPMT(D3,D4,D2,A8,A8,0), copy to C9:C11
Cell D8: =−CUMPRINC(D3,D4,D2,A8,A8,0), copy to D9:D11
Cell E8: =E7−D8, copy to E9:E11
The minus signs appear before the entries in Cells B8, C8, and D8 because these are cash outflows.

Finding Interest or Growth Rates

It is often necessary to calculate the compound annual interest or *growth rate* (that is, the annual rate of change in values) of a series of cash flows. Examples include finding the interest rate on a loan, the rate of growth in sales, and the rate of growth in earnings. In doing this, we can use either future value or present value interest factors. The use of present value interest factors is described in this section. The simplest situation is one in which a person wishes to find the rate of interest or growth in a *series of cash flows*.[12]

---

12. Because the calculations required for finding interest rates and growth rates, given the series of cash flows, are the same, this section refers to the calculations as those required to find interest *or* growth rates.

TABLE 4.8 Loan Amortization Schedule ($6,000 Principal, 10% Interest, 4-Year Repayment Period)

End of year	Beginning-of-year principal (1)	Loan payment (2)	Payments Interest $[0.10 \times (1)]$ (3)	Principal $[(2) - (3)]$ (4)	End-of-year principal $[(1) - (4)]$ (5)
1	$6,000.00	$1,892.74	$600.00	$1,292.74	$4,707.26
2	4,707.26	1,892.74	470.73	1,422.01	3,285.25
3	3,285.25	1,892.74	328.53	1,564.21	1,721.04
4	1,721.04	1,892.74	172.10	1,720.64	—[a]

[a]Because of rounding, a slight difference ($0.40) exists between the beginning-of-year-4 principal (in column 1) and the year-4 principal payment (in column 4).

EXAMPLE

Ray Noble wishes to find the rate of interest or growth reflected in the stream of cash flows he received from a real estate investment over the period 2002 through 2006. The following table lists those cash flows:

Year	Cash flow
2006	$1,520 } 4
2005	1,440 } 3
2004	1,370 } 2
2003	1,300 } 1
2002	1,250

By using the first year (2002) as a base year, we see that interest has been earned (or growth experienced) for 4 years.

Table Use The first step in finding the interest or growth rate is to divide the amount received in the earliest year (PV) by the amount received in the latest year (FV_n). Looking back at Equation 4.12, we see that this results in the present value interest factor for a *single amount* for 4 years, $PVIF_{i,4yrs}$, which is 0.822 ($1,250 ÷ $1,520). The interest rate in Table A–2 associated with the factor closest to 0.822 for 4 years is the interest or growth rate of Ray's cash flows. In the row for year 4 in Table A–2, the factor for 5 percent is 0.823—almost exactly the 0.822 value. Therefore, the interest or growth rate of the given cash flows is approximately (to the nearest whole percent) 5%.[13]

Calculator Use Using the calculator, we treat the earliest value as a present value, PV, and the latest value as a future value, FV_n. (*Note:* Most calculators require *either* the PV or the FV value to be input as a negative number to calculate an unknown interest or growth rate. That approach is used here.) Using the inputs shown at the left, you will find the interest or growth rate to be 5.01%, which is consistent with, but more precise than, the value found using Table A–2.

13. To obtain more precise estimates of interest or growth rates, *interpolation*—a mathematical technique for estimating unknown intermediate values—can be applied. For information on how to interpolate a more precise answer in this example, see the book's home page at www.aw-bc.com/gitman.

Spreadsheet Use The interest or growth rate for the series of cash flows also can be calculated as shown on the following Excel spreadsheet.

	A	B
1	INTEREST OR GROWTH RATE – SERIES OF CASH FLOWS	
2	Year	Cash Flow
3	2006	$1,520
4	2005	$1,440
5	2004	$1,370
6	2003	$1,300
7	2002	$1,250
8	Annual growth rate	5.01%

Entry in Cell B8 is =RATE((A3–A7),0,B7,B3,0). The expression A3–A7 in the entry calculates the number of years of growth. The minus sign appears before B3 because the investment in 2006 is treated as a cash outflow.

Another type of interest-rate problem involves finding the interest rate associated with an *annuity*, or equal-payment loan.

EXAMPLE Jan Jacobs can borrow $2,000 to be repaid in equal annual end-of-year amounts of $514.14 for the next 5 years. She wants to find the interest rate on this loan.

Table Use Substituting $PVA_5 = \$2,000$ and $PMT = \$514.14$ into Equation 4.25 and rearranging the equation to solve for $PVIFA_{i,5yrs}$, we get

$$PVIFA_{i,5yrs} = \frac{PVA_5}{PMT} = \frac{\$2,000}{\$514.14} = 3.890 \qquad (4.27)$$

The interest rate for 5 years associated with the annuity factor closest to 3.890 in Table A–4 is 9%. Therefore, the interest rate on the loan is approximately (to the nearest whole percent) 9%.

Calculator Use (*Note:* Most calculators require *either* the *PMT* or the *PV* value to be input as a negative number to calculate an unknown interest rate on an equal-payment loan. That approach is used here.) Using the inputs shown at the left, you will find the interest rate to be 9.00%, which is consistent with the value found using Table A–4.

Spreadsheet Use The interest or growth rate for the annuity also can be calculated as shown on the following Excel spreadsheet.

	A	B
1	INTEREST OR GROWTH RATE – ANNUITY	
2	Present value (loan principal)	$2,000
3	Number of years	5
4	Annual payment	$514.14
5	Annual interest rate	9.00%

Entry in Cell B5 is =RATE(B3,B4,–B2). The minus sign appears before B2 because the loan principal is treated as a cash outflow.

Finding an Unknown Number of Periods

Sometimes it is necessary to calculate the number of time periods needed to generate a given amount of cash flow from an initial amount. Here we briefly consider this calculation for both single amounts and annuities. This simplest case is when a person wishes to determine the number of periods, n, it will take for an initial deposit, PV, to grow to a specified future amount, FV_n, given a stated interest rate, i.

EXAMPLE Ann Bates wishes to determine the number of years it will take for her initial $1,000 deposit, earning 8% annual interest, to grow to equal $2,500. Simply stated, at an 8% annual rate of interest, how many years, n, will it take for Ann's $1,000, PV, to grow to $2,500, FV_n?

Table Use In a manner similar to our approach for finding an unknown interest or growth rate in a series of cash flows, we begin by dividing the amount deposited in the earliest year by the amount received in the latest year. This results in the present value interest factor for 8% and n years, $PVIF_{8\%,n}$, which is 0.400 ($1,000 ÷ $2,500). The number of years (periods) in Table A–2 associated with the factor closest to 0.400 for an 8% interest rate is the number of years required for $1,000 to grow to $2,500 at 8%. In the 8% column of Table A–2, the factor for 12 years is 0.397—almost exactly the 0.400 value. Therefore, the number of years necessary for the $1,000 to grow to a future value of $2,500 at 8% is approximately (to the nearest year) 12.

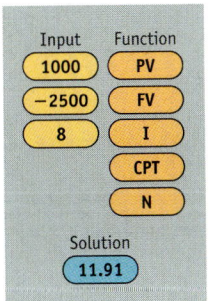

Calculator Use Using the calculator, we treat the initial value as the present value, PV, and the latest value as the future value, FV_n. (*Note:* Most calculators require *either* the PV or the FV value to be input as a negative number to calculate an unknown number of periods. That approach is used here.) Using the inputs shown at the left, we find the number of periods to be 11.91 years, which is consistent with, but more precise than, the value found using Table A–2.

Spreadsheet Use The number of years for the present value to grow to a specified future value also can be calculated as shown on the following Excel spreadsheet.

	A	B
1	YEARS FOR A PRESENT VALUE TO GROW TO A SPECIFIED FUTURE VALUE	
2	Present value (deposit)	$1,000
3	Annual rate of interest, compounded annually	8%
4	Future value	$2,500
5	Number of years	11.91

Entry in Cell B5 is =NPER(B3,0,B2,−B4).
The minus sign appears before B4 because
the future value is treated as a cash outflow.

Another type of number-of-periods problem involves finding the number of periods associated with an *annuity*. Occasionally we wish to find the unknown life, n, of an annuity, PMT, that is intended to achieve a specific objective, such as repaying a loan of a given amount, PVA_n, with a stated interest rate, i.

EXAMPLE

Bill Smart can borrow $25,000 at an 11% annual interest rate; equal, annual, end-of-year payments of $4,800 are required. He wishes to determine how long it will take to fully repay the loan. In other words, he wishes to determine how many years, n, it will take to repay the $25,000, 11% loan, PVA_n, if the payments of $4,800, PMT, are made at the end of each year.

Table Use Substituting $PVA_n = \$25,000$ and $PMT = \$4,800$ into Equation 4.25 and rearranging the equation to solve $PVIFA_{11\%,n}$, we get

$$PVIFA_{11\%,n} = \frac{PVA_n}{PMT} = \frac{\$25,000}{\$4,800} = 5.208 \qquad (4.28)$$

The number of periods for an 11% interest rate associated with the annuity factor closest to 5.208 in Table A–4 is 8 years. Therefore, the number of periods necessary to repay the loan fully is approximately (to the nearest year) 8 years.

Calculator Use (*Note:* Most calculators require *either* the *PV* or the *PMT* value to be input as a negative number to calculate an unknown number of periods. That approach is used here.) Using the inputs shown at the left, you will find the number of periods to be 8.15 years, which is consistent with the value found using Table A–4.

Spreadsheet Use The number of years to pay off the loan also can be calculated as shown on the following Excel spreadsheet.

	A	B
1	YEARS TO PAY OFF A LOAN	
2	Annual payment	$4,800
3	Annual rate of interest, compounded annually	11%
4	Present value (loan principal)	$25,000
5	Number of years to pay off the loan	8.15

Entry in Cell B5 is =NPER(B3,–B2,B4). The minus sign appears before B2 because the payments are treated as cash outflows.

Review Questions

4–15 How can you determine the size of the equal, annual, end-of-period deposits necessary to accumulate a certain future sum at the end of a specified future period at a given annual interest rate?

4–16 Describe the procedure used to amortize a loan into a series of equal periodic payments.

4–17 Which present value interest factors would be used to find (**a**) the growth rate associated with a series of cash flows and (**b**) the interest rate associated with an equal-payment loan?

4–18 How can you determine the unknown number of periods when you know the present and future values—single amount or annuity—and the applicable rate of interest?

Summary

FOCUS ON VALUE

Time value of money is an important tool that financial managers and other market participants use to assess the effects of proposed actions. Because firms have long lives and their important decisions affect their long-term cash flows, the effective application of time-value-of-money techniques is extremely important. Time value techniques enable financial managers to evaluate cash flows occurring at different times so as to combine, compare, and evaluate them and link them to the firm's **overall goal of share price maximization.** It will become clear in Chapters 6 and 7 that the application of time value techniques is a key part of the value determination process. Using them, we can measure the firm's value and evaluate the effects that various events and decisions might have on it. Clearly, an understanding of time-value-of-money techniques and an ability to apply them are needed to make intelligent value-creating decisions.

REVIEW OF LEARNING GOALS

Key definitions, formulas, and equations for this chapter are summarized in Table 4.9 (see page 174).

LG1 **Discuss the role of time value in finance, the use of computational tools, and the basic patterns of cash flow.** Financial managers and investors use time-value-of-money techniques when assessing the value of expected cash flow streams. Alternatives can be assessed by either compounding to find future value or discounting to find present value. Financial managers rely primarily on present value techniques. Financial tables, financial calculators, and electronic spreadsheets can streamline the application of time value techniques. The cash flow of a firm can be described by its pattern—single amount, annuity, or mixed stream.

LG2 **Understand the concepts of future value and present value, their calculation for single amounts, and the relationship between them.** Future value (FV) relies on compound interest to measure future amounts: The initial principal or deposit in one period, along with the interest earned on it, becomes the beginning principal of the following period.

The present value (PV) of a future amount is the amount of money today that is equivalent to the given future amount, considering the return that can be earned. Present value is the inverse of future value.

LG3 **Find the future value and the present value of an ordinary annuity, and find the present value of a perpetuity.** An annuity is a pattern of equal periodic cash flows. For an ordinary annuity, the cash flows occur at the end of the period. For an annuity due, cash flows occur at the beginning of the period.

The future value of an ordinary annuity can be found by using the future value interest factor for an annuity. The present value of an ordinary annuity can be found by using the present value interest factor for an annuity. The present value of a perpetuity—an infinite-lived annuity—is found using 1 divided by the discount rate to represent the present value interest factor.

LG4 **Calculate both the future value and the present value of a mixed stream of cash flows.** A mixed stream of cash flows is a stream

TABLE 4.9 Summary of Key Definitions, Formulas, and Equations for Time Value of Money

Definitions of variables

e = exponential function = 2.7183
EAR = effective annual rate
FV_n = future value or amount at the end of period n
FVA_n = future value of an n-year annuity
i = annual rate of interest
m = number of times per year interest is compounded
n = number of periods—typically years—over which money earns a return
PMT = amount deposited or received annually at the end of each year
PV = initial principal or present value
PVA_n = present value of an n-year annuity
t = period number index

Interest factor formulas

Future value of a single amount with annual compounding:

$$FVIF_{i,n} = (1+i)^n \qquad \text{[Equation 4.5; factors in Table A–1]}$$

Present value of a single amount:

$$PVIF_{i,n} = \frac{1}{(1+i)^n} \qquad \text{[Equation 4.11; factors in Table A–2]}$$

Future value of an ordinary annuity:

$$FVIFA_{i,n} = \sum_{t=1}^{n} (1+i)^{t-1} \qquad \text{[Equation 4.13; factors in Table A–3]}$$

Present value of an ordinary annuity:

$$PVIFA_{i,n} = \sum_{t=1}^{n} \frac{1}{(1+i)^t} \qquad \text{[Equation 4.15; factors in Table A–4]}$$

Present value of a perpetuity:

$$PVIFA_{i,\infty} = \frac{1}{i} \qquad \text{[Equation 4.17]}$$

Future value with compounding more frequently than annually:

$$FVIF_{i,n} = \left(1 + \frac{i}{m}\right)^{m \times n} \qquad \text{[Equation 4.18]}$$

For continuous compounding, $m = \infty$:

$$FVIF_{i,n} \text{ (continuous compounding)} = e^{i \times n} \qquad \text{[Equation 4.20]}$$

To find the effective annual rate:

$$EAR = \left(1 + \frac{i}{m}\right)^m - 1 \qquad \text{[Equation 4.22]}$$

Basic equations

Future value (single amount): $FV_n = PV \times (FVIF_{i,n})$ [Equation 4.6]
Present value (single amount): $PV = FV_n \times (PVIF_{i,n})$ [Equation 4.12]
Future value (annuity): $FVA_n = PMT \times (FVIFA_{i,n})$ [Equation 4.14]
Present value (annuity): $PVA_n = PMT \times (PVIFA_{i,n})$ [Equation 4.16]

of unequal periodic cash flows that reflect no particular pattern. The future value of a mixed stream of cash flows is the sum of the future values of each individual cash flow. Similarly, the present value of a mixed stream of cash flows is the sum of the present values of the individual cash flows.

LG5 **Understand the effect that compounding interest more frequently than annually has on future value and on the effective annual rate of interest.** Interest can be compounded at intervals ranging from annually to daily, and even continuously. The more often interest is compounded, the larger the future amount that will be accumulated, and the higher the effective, or true, annual rate (EAR).

The annual percentage rate (APR)—a nominal annual rate—is quoted on credit cards and loans. The annual percentage yield (APY)—an effective annual rate—is quoted on savings products.

LG6 **Describe the procedures involved in (1) determining deposits needed to accumulate a future sum, (2) loan amortization, (3) finding interest or growth rates, and (4) finding an unknown number of periods.** (1) The periodic deposit to accumulate a given future sum can be found by solving the equation for the future value of an annuity for the annual payment. (2) A loan can be amortized into equal periodic payments by solving the equation for the present value of an annuity for the periodic payment. (3) Interest or growth rates can be estimated by finding the unknown interest rate in the equation for the present value of a single amount or an annuity. (4) An unknown number of periods can be estimated by finding the unknown number of periods in the equation for the present value of a single amount or an annuity.

SELF-TEST PROBLEMS (SOLUTIONS IN APPENDIX B)

  ST4–1 **Future values for various compounding frequencies** Delia Martin has $10,000 that she can deposit in any of three savings accounts for a 3-year period. Bank A compounds interest on an annual basis, bank B compounds interest twice each year, and bank C compounds interest each quarter. All three banks have a stated annual interest rate of 4%.
  a. What amount would Ms. Martin have at the end of the third year, leaving all interest paid on deposit, in each bank?
  b. What *effective annual rate* (EAR) would she earn in each of the banks?
  c. On the basis of your findings in parts **a** and **b**, which bank should Ms. Martin deal with? Why?
  d. If a fourth bank (bank D), also with a 4% stated interest rate, compounds interest continuously, how much would Ms. Martin have at the end of the third year? Does this alternative change your recommendation in part **c**? Explain why or why not.

 ST4–2 **Future values of annuities** Ramesh Abdul wishes to choose the better of two equally costly cash flow streams: annuity X and annuity Y. Annuity X provides a cash inflow of $9,000 at the end of each of the next 6 years. Annuity Y provides a cash inflow of $10,000 at the end of each of the next 6 years. Assume that Ramesh can earn 15% on annuity X and 11% on annuity Y.

a. On a purely subjective basis, which annuity do you think is more attractive? Why?
b. Find the future value at the end of year 6, FVA_6, for both annuity X and annuity Y.
c. Use your finding in part **b** to indicate which annuity is more attractive. Compare your finding to your subjective response in part **a**.

   ST4–3 Present values of single amounts and streams You have a choice of accepting either of two 5-year cash flow streams or single amounts. One cash flow stream is an ordinary annuity, and the other is a mixed stream. You may accept alternative A or B—either as a cash flow stream or as a single amount. Given the cash flow stream and single amounts associated with each (see the following table), and assuming a 9% opportunity cost, which alternative (A or B) and in which form (cash flow stream or single amount) would you prefer?

	Cash flow stream	
End of year	Alternative A	Alternative B
1	$700	$1,100
2	700	900
3	700	700
4	700	500
5	700	300
	Single amount	
At time zero	$2,825	$2,800

 ST4–4 Deposits needed to accumulate a future sum Judi Janson wishes to accumulate $8,000 by the end of 5 years by making equal, annual, end-of-year deposits over the next 5 years. If Judi can earn 7% on her investments, how much must she deposit at the *end of each year* to meet this goal?

WARM-UP EXERCISES

 E4–1 Assume a firm makes a $2,500 deposit into its money market account. If this account is currently paying 0.7%, (yes, that's right, less than 1%!), what will the account balance be after 1 year?

  E4–2 If Bob and Judy combine their savings of $1,260 and $975, respectively, and deposit this amount into an account that pays 2% annual interest, compounded monthly, what will the account balance be after 4 years?

 E4–3 Gabrielle just won $2.5 million in the state lottery. She is given the option of receiving a total of $1.3 million now or she can elect to be paid $100,000 at the end of each of the next 25 years. If Gabrielle can earn 5% annually on her investments, from a strict economic point of view which option should she take?

E4–4 Your firm has the option of making an investment in new software that will cost $130,000 today and is estimated to provide the end-of-year savings shown in the following table over its 5-year life:

Year	Savings estimate
1	$35,000
2	50,000
3	45,000
4	25,000
5	15,000

Should the firm make this investment if it requires a minimum annual return of 9% on all investments?

E4–5 Joseph is a friend of yours. He has plenty of money but little financial sense. He received a gift of $12,000 for his recent graduation and is looking for a bank in which to deposit the funds. Partners' Savings Bank offers an account with an annual interest rate of 3% compounded semiannually, while Selwyn's offers an account with a 2.75% annual interest rate compounded monthly. Calculate the value of the two accounts at the end of one year and recommend to Joseph which account he should choose.

E4–6 Jack and Jill have just had their first child. If college is expected to cost $150,000 per year in 18 years, how much should the couple begin depositing annually at the end of each year to accumulate enough funds to pay the first year's tuition at the beginning of the 19th year? Assume that they can earn a 6% annual rate of return on their investment.

Problems

P4–1 **Using a time line** The financial manager at Starbuck Industries is considering an investment that requires an initial outlay of $25,000 and is expected to result in cash inflows of $3,000 at the end of year 1, $6,000 at the end of years 2 and 3, $10,000 at the end of year 4, $8,000 at the end of year 5, and $7,000 at the end of year 6.
  a. Draw and label a time line depicting the cash flows associated with Starbuck Industries' proposed investment.
  b. Use arrows to demonstrate, on the time line in part **a**, how compounding to find future value can be used to measure all cash flows at the end of year 6.
  c. Use arrows to demonstrate, on the time line in part **b**, how discounting to find present value can be used to measure all cash flows at time zero.
  d. Which of the approaches—future value or present value—do financial managers rely on most often for decision making? Why?

P4–2 **Future value calculation** *Without referring to tables or to the preprogrammed function on your financial calculator,* use the basic formula for future value along with the given interest rate, *i*, and the number of periods, *n*, to calculate the future value interest factor in each of the cases shown in the following table. Compare the calculated value to the value in Appendix Table A–1.

Case	Interest rate, i	Number of periods, n
A	12%	2
B	6	3
C	9	2
D	3	4

P4–3 **Future value tables** Use the future value interest factors in Appendix Table A–1 in each of the cases shown in the following table to estimate, to the nearest year, how long it would take an initial deposit, assuming no withdrawals,
a. To double.
b. To quadruple.

Case	Interest rate
A	7%
B	40
C	20
D	10

P4–4 **Future values** For each of the cases shown in the following table, calculate the future value of the single cash flow deposited today that will be available at the end of the deposit period if the interest is compounded annually at the rate specified over the given period.

Case	Single cash flow	Interest rate	Deposit period (years)
A	$ 200	5%	20
B	4,500	8	7
C	10,000	9	10
D	25,000	10	12
E	37,000	11	5
F	40,000	12	9

P4–5 **Time value** You have $1,500 to invest today at 7% interest compounded annually.
a. Find how much you will have accumulated in the account at the end of (1) 3 years, (2) 6 years, and (3) 9 years.
b. Use your findings in part **a** to calculate the amount of interest earned in (1) the first 3 years (years 1 to 3), (2) the second 3 years (years 4 to 6), and (3) the third 3 years (years 7 to 9).
c. Compare and contrast your findings in part **b**. Explain why the amount of interest earned increases in each succeeding 3-year period.

CHAPTER 4   Time Value of Money   179

P4–6 **Time value** As part of your financial planning, you wish to purchase a new car exactly 5 years from today. The car you wish to purchase costs $14,000 today, and your research indicates that its price will increase by 2% to 4% per year over the next 5 years.
a. Estimate the price of the car at the end of 5 years if inflation is (1) 2% per year and (2) 4% per year.
b. How much more expensive will the car be if the rate of inflation is 4% rather than 2%?

P4–7 **Time value** You can deposit $10,000 into an account paying 9% annual interest either today or exactly 10 years from today. How much better off will you be at the end of 40 years if you decide to make the initial deposit today rather than 10 years from today?

P4–8 **Single-payment loan repayment** A person borrows $200 to be repaid in 8 years with 14% annually compounded interest. The loan may be repaid at the end of any earlier year with no prepayment penalty.
a. What amount will be due if the loan is repaid at the end of year 1?
b. What is the repayment at the end of year 4?
c. What amount is due at the end of the eighth year?

P4–9 **Present value calculation** Without referring to tables or to the preprogrammed function on your financial calculator, use the basic formula for present value, along with the given opportunity cost, i, and the number of periods, n, to calculate the present value interest factor in each of the cases shown in the accompanying table. Compare the calculated value to the table value.

Case	Opportunity cost, i	Number of periods, n
A	2%	4
B	10	2
C	5	3
D	13	2

P4–10 **Present values** For each of the cases shown in the following table, calculate the present value of the cash flow, discounting at the rate given and assuming that the cash flow is received at the end of the period noted.

Case	Single cash flow	Discount rate	End of period (years)
A	$ 7,000	12%	4
B	28,000	8	20
C	10,000	14	12
D	150,000	11	6
E	45,000	20	8

P4–11 **Present value concept** Answer each of the following questions.
  a. What single investment made today, earning 12% annual interest, will be worth $6,000 at the end of 6 years?
  b. What is the present value of $6,000 to be received at the end of 6 years if the discount rate is 12%?
  c. What is the most you would pay today for a promise to repay you $6,000 at the end of 6 years if your opportunity cost is 12%?
  d. Compare, contrast, and discuss your findings in parts a through c.

P4–12 **Time value** Jim Nance has been offered a future payment of $500 three years from today. If his opportunity cost is 7% compounded annually, what value should he place on this opportunity today? What is the most he should pay to purchase this payment today?

P4–13 **Time value** An Iowa state savings bond can be converted to $100 at maturity 6 years from purchase. If the state bonds are to be competitive with U.S. savings bonds, which pay 8% annual interest (compounded annually), at what price must the state sell its bonds? Assume no cash payments on savings bonds prior to redemption.

P4–14 **Time value and discount rates** You just won a lottery that promises to pay you $1,000,000 exactly 10 years from today. Because the $1,000,000 payment is guaranteed by the state in which you live, opportunities exist to sell the claim today for an immediate single cash payment.
  a. What is the least you will sell your claim for if you can earn the following rates of return on similar-risk investments during the 10-year period?
     (1) 6%
     (2) 9%
     (3) 12%
  b. Rework part a under the assumption that the $1,000,000 payment will be received in 15 rather than 10 years.
  c. On the basis of your findings in parts a and b, discuss the effect of both the size of the rate of return and the time until receipt of payment on the present value of a future sum.

P4–15 **Time value comparisons of single amounts** In exchange for a $20,000 payment today, a well-known company will allow you to choose one of the alternatives shown in the following table. Your opportunity cost is 11%.

Alternative	Single amount
A	$28,500 at end of 3 years
B	$54,000 at end of 9 years
C	$160,000 at end of 20 years

  a. Find the value today of each alternative.
  b. Are all the alternatives acceptable—that is, worth $20,000 today?
  c. Which alternative, if any, will you take?

P4–16 **Cash flow investment decision** Tom Alexander has an opportunity to purchase any of the investments shown in the following table. The purchase price, the amount of the single cash inflow, and its year of receipt are given for each investment. Which purchase recommendations would you make, assuming that Tom can earn 10% on his investments?

Investment	Price	Single cash inflow	Year of receipt
A	$18,000	$30,000	5
B	600	3,000	20
C	3,500	10,000	10
D	1,000	15,000	40

P4–17 **Future value of an annuity** For each case in the accompanying table, calculate the future value of the annuity at the end of the deposit period, assuming that the annuity cash flows occur at the end of each year.

Case	Amount of annuity	Interest rate	Deposit period (years)
A	$ 2,500	8%	10
B	500	12	6
C	30,000	20	5
D	11,500	9	8
E	6,000	14	30

P4–18 **Present value of an annuity** For each case in the accompanying table, calculate the present value of the annuity, assuming that the annuity cash flows occur at the end of each year.

Case	Amount of annuity	Interest rate	Period (years)
A	$ 12,000	7%	3
B	55,000	12	15
C	700	20	9
D	140,000	5	7
E	22,500	10	5

P4–19 **Retirement planning** Hal Thomas, a 25-year-old college graduate, wishes to retire at age 65. To supplement other sources of retirement income, he can deposit $2,000 each year into a tax-deferred individual retirement arrangement (IRA). The IRA will be invested to earn an annual return of 10%, which is assumed to be attainable over the next 40 years.
  a. If Hal makes annual end-of-year $2,000 deposits into the IRA, how much will he have accumulated by the end of his sixty-fifth year?
  b. If Hal decides to wait until age 35 to begin making annual end-of-year $2,000 deposits into the IRA, how much will he have accumulated by the end of his sixty-fifth year?

c. Using your findings in parts **a** and **b**, discuss the impact of delaying making deposits into the IRA for 10 years (age 25 to age 35) on the amount accumulated by the end of Hal's sixty-fifth year.

P4–20 **Value of a retirement annuity** An insurance agent is trying to sell you an immediate-retirement annuity, which for a single amount paid today will provide you with $12,000 at the end of each year for the next 25 years. You currently earn 9% on low-risk investments comparable to the retirement annuity. Ignoring taxes, what is the most you would pay for this annuity?

P4–21 **Funding your retirement** You plan to retire in exactly 20 years. Your goal is to create a fund that will allow you to receive $20,000 at the end of each year for the 30 years between retirement and death (a psychic told you would die exactly 30 years after you retire). You know that you will be able to earn 11% per year during the 30-year retirement period.
a. How large a fund will you need *when you retire* in 20 years to provide the 30-year, $20,000 retirement annuity?
b. How much will you need *today* as a single amount to provide the fund calculated in part **a** if you earn only 9% per year during the 20 years preceding retirement?
c. What effect would an increase in the rate you can earn both during and prior to retirement have on the values found in parts **a** and **b**? Explain.

P4–22 **Value of an annuity versus a single amount** Assume that you just won the state lottery. Your prize can be taken either in the form of $40,000 at the end of each of the next 25 years (i.e., $1,000,000 over 25 years) or as a single amount of $500,000 paid immediately.
a. If you expect to be able to earn 5% annually on your investments over the next 25 years, ignoring taxes and other considerations, which alternative should you take? Why?
b. Would your decision in part **a** change if you could earn 7% rather than 5% on your investments over the next 25 years? Why?
c. On a strictly economic basis, at approximately what earnings rate would you be indifferent between the two plans?

P4–23 **Perpetuities** Consider the data in the following table.

Perpetuity	Annual amount	Discount rate
A	$ 20,000	8%
B	100,000	10
C	3,000	6
D	60,000	5

Determine, for each of the perpetuities:
a. The appropriate present value interest factor.
b. The present value.

P4–24 **Creating an endowment** Upon completion of her introductory finance course, Marla Lee was so pleased with the amount of useful and interesting knowledge she gained that she convinced her parents, who were wealthy alumni of the uni-

versity she was attending, to create an endowment. The endowment is to allow three needy students to take the introductory finance course each year in perpetuity. The guaranteed annual cost of tuition and books for the course is $600 per student. The endowment will be created by making a single payment to the university. The university expects to earn exactly 6% per year on these funds.
a. How large an initial single payment must Marla's parents make to the university to fund the endowment?
b. What amount would be needed to fund the endowment if the university could earn 9% rather than 6% per year on the funds?

P4–25 **Value of a mixed stream** For each of the mixed streams of cash flows shown in the following table, determine the future value at the end of the final year if deposits are made at the *beginning of each year* into an account paying annual interest of 12%, assuming that no withdrawals are made during the period.

	Cash flow stream		
Year	A	B	C
1	$ 900	$30,000	$1,200
2	1,000	25,000	1,200
3	1,200	20,000	1,000
4		10,000	1,900
5		5,000	

P4–26 **Value of a single amount versus a mixed stream** Gina Vitale has just contracted to sell a small parcel of land that she inherited a few years ago. The buyer is willing to pay $24,000 at the closing of the transaction or will pay the amounts shown in the following table at the *beginning* of each of the next 5 years. Because Gina doesn't really need the money today, she plans to let it accumulate in an account that earns 7% annual interest. Given her desire to buy a house at the end of 5 years after closing on the sale of the lot, she decides to choose the payment alternative—either the $24,000 single amount or the mixed stream of payments in the following table—that provides the higher future value at the end of 5 years.

Mixed stream	
Beginning of year	Cash flow
1	$ 2,000
2	4,000
3	6,000
4	8,000
5	10,000

a. What is the future value of the single amount at the end of year 5?
b. What is the future value of the mixed stream at the end of year 5?
c. On the basis of your findings in parts **a** and **b**, which alternative should Gina take?
d. If Gina could earn 10% rather than 7% on the funds, would your recommendation in part **c** change? Explain.

P4–27 **Value of mixed streams** Find the present value of the streams of cash flows shown in the following table. Assume that the firm's opportunity cost is 12%.

A		B		C	
Year	Cash flow	Year	Cash flow	Year	Cash flow
1	−$2,000	1	$10,000	1–5	$10,000/yr
2	3,000	2–5	5,000/yr	6–10	8,000/yr
3	4,000	6	7,000		
4	6,000				
5	8,000				

P4–28 **Present value—Mixed streams** Consider the mixed streams of cash flows shown in the following table.

	Cash flow stream	
Year	A	B
1	$ 50,000	$ 10,000
2	40,000	20,000
3	30,000	30,000
4	20,000	40,000
5	10,000	50,000
Totals	$150,000	$150,000

a. Find the present value of each stream using a 15% discount rate.
b. Compare the calculated present values and discuss them in light of the fact that the undiscounted cash flows total $150,000 in each case.

P4–29 **Value of a mixed stream** Harte Systems, Inc., a maker of electronic surveillance equipment, is considering selling to a well-known hardware chain the rights to market its home security system. The proposed deal calls for the hardware chain to pay Harte $30,000 and $25,000 at the end of years 1 and 2 and to make annual year-end payments of $15,000 in years 3 through 9. A final payment to Harte of $10,000 would be due at the end of year 10.
a. Lay out on a time line the cash flows involved in the offer.
b. If Harte applies a required rate of return of 12% to them, what is the present value of this series of payments?
c. A second company has offered Harte an immediate one-time payment of $100,000 for the rights to market the home security system. Which offer should Harte accept?

P4–30 **Funding budget shortfalls** As part of your personal budgeting process, you have determined that in each of the next 5 years you will have budget shortfalls. In other words, you will need the amounts shown in the table (at the top of the facing page) at the end of the given year to balance your budget—that is, to make inflows equal outflows. You expect to be able to earn 8% on your investments during the next 5 years and wish to fund the budget shortfalls over the next 5 years with a single amount.

End of year	Budget shortfall
1	$ 5,000
2	4,000
3	6,000
4	10,000
5	3,000

a. How large must the single deposit today into an account paying 8% annual interest be to provide for full coverage of the anticipated budget shortfalls?
b. What effect would an increase in your earnings rate have on the amount calculated in part a? Explain.

P4–31 **Relationship between future value and present value—Mixed stream** Using *only* the information in the accompanying table, answer the questions that follow.

Year (t)	Cash flow	Future value interest factor at 5% ($FVIF_{5\%,n}$)
1	$ 800	1.050
2	900	1.102
3	1,000	1.158
4	1,500	1.216
5	2,000	1.276

a. Determine the *present value* of the mixed stream of cash flows using a 5% discount rate.
b. How much would you be willing to pay for an opportunity to buy this stream, assuming that you can at best earn 5% on your investments?
c. What effect, if any, would a 7% rather than a 5% opportunity cost have on your analysis? (Explain verbally.)

P4–32 **Changing compounding frequency** Using annual, semiannual, and quarterly compounding periods, for each of the following, (1) calculate the future value if $5,000 is deposited initially, and (2) determine the *effective annual rate* (EAR).
a. At 12% annual interest for 5 years.
b. At 16% annual interest for 6 years.
c. At 20% annual interest for 10 years.

P4–33 **Compounding frequency, time value, and effective annual rates** For each of the cases in the table near the top of page 186:
a. Calculate the future value at the end of the specified deposit period.
b. Determine the *effective annual rate, EAR*.

c. Compare the nominal annual rate, i, to the effective annual rate, EAR. What relationship exists between compounding frequency and the nominal and effective annual rates?

Case	Amount of initial deposit	Nominal annual rate, i	Compounding frequency, m (times/year)	Deposit period (years)
A	$ 2,500	6%	2	5
B	50,000	12	6	3
C	1,000	5	1	10
D	20,000	16	4	6

P4–34 **Continuous compounding** For each of the cases in the following table, find the future value at the end of the deposit period, assuming that interest is compounded continuously at the given nominal annual rate.

Case	Amount of initial deposit	Nominal annual rate, i	Deposit period (years), n
A	$1,000	9%	2
B	600	10	10
C	4,000	8	7
D	2,500	12	4

P4–35 **Compounding frequency and time value** You plan to invest $2,000 in an individual retirement arrangement (IRA) today at a *nominal annual rate* of 8%, which is expected to apply to all future years.
   a. How much will you have in the account at the end of 10 years if interest is compounded (1) annually? (2) semiannually? (3) daily (assume a 365-day year)? (4) continuously?
   b. What is the *effective annual rate, EAR*, for each compounding period in part a?
   c. How much greater will your IRA balance be at the end of 10 years if interest is compounded continuously rather than annually?
   d. How does the compounding frequency affect the future value and effective annual rate for a given deposit? Explain in terms of your findings in parts a through c.

P4–36 **Comparing compounding periods** René Levin wishes to determine the future value at the end of 2 years of a $15,000 deposit made today into an account paying a nominal annual rate of 12%.
   a. Find the future value of René's deposit, assuming that interest is compounded (1) annually, (2) quarterly, (3) monthly, and (4) continuously.
   b. Compare your findings in part a, and use them to demonstrate the relationship between compounding frequency and future value.
   c. What is the maximum future value obtainable given the $15,000 deposit, the 2-year time period, and the 12% nominal annual rate? Use your findings in part a to explain.

P4–37 Annuities and compounding Janet Boyle intends to deposit $300 per year in a credit union for the next 10 years, and the credit union pays an annual interest rate of 8%.
  a. Determine the future value that Janet will have at the end of 10 years, given that end-of-period deposits are made and no interest is withdrawn, if
    (1) $300 is deposited annually and the credit union pays interest annually.
    (2) $150 is deposited semiannually and the credit union pays interest semiannually.
    (3) $75 is deposited quarterly and the credit union pays interest quarterly.
  b. Use your finding in part **a** to discuss the effect of more frequent deposits and compounding of interest on the future value of an annuity.

P4–38 Deposits to accumulate future sums For each of the cases shown in the following table, determine the amount of the equal, annual, end-of-year deposits necessary to accumulate the given sum at the end of the specified period, assuming the stated annual interest rate.

Case	Sum to be accumulated	Accumulation period (years)	Interest rate
A	$ 5,000	3	12%
B	100,000	20	7
C	30,000	8	10
D	15,000	12	8

P4–39 Creating a retirement fund To supplement your planned retirement in exactly 42 years, you estimate that you need to accumulate $220,000 by the end of 42 years from today. You plan to make equal, annual, end-of-year deposits into an account paying 8% annual interest.
  a. How large must the annual deposits be to create the $220,000 fund by the end of 42 years?
  b. If you can afford to deposit only $600 per year into the account, how much will you have accumulated by the end of the forty-second year?

P4–40 Accumulating a growing future sum A retirement home at Deer Trail Estates now costs $185,000. Inflation is expected to cause this price to increase at 6% per year over the 20 years before C. L. Donovan retires. How large an equal, annual, end-of-year deposit must be made each year into an account paying an annual interest rate of 10% for Donovan to have the cash needed to purchase a home at retirement?

P4–41 Deposits to create a perpetuity You have decided to endow your favorite university with a scholarship. It is expected to cost $6,000 per year to attend the university into perpetuity. You expect to give the university the endowment in 10 years and will accumulate it by making annual (end-of-year) deposits into an account. The rate of interest is expected to be 10% for all future time periods.
  a. How large must the endowment be?
  b. How much must you deposit at the end of each of the next 10 years to accumulate the required amount?

P4–42 **Loan payment** Determine the equal, annual, end-of-year payment required each year over the life of the loans shown in the following table to repay them fully during the stated term of the loan.

Loan	Principal	Interest rate	Term of loan (years)
A	$12,000	8%	3
B	60,000	12	10
C	75,000	10	30
D	4,000	15	5

P4–43 **Loan amortization schedule** Joan Messineo borrowed $15,000 at a 14% annual rate of interest to be repaid over 3 years. The loan is amortized into three equal, annual, end-of-year payments.
a. Calculate the annual, end-of-year loan payment.
b. Prepare a loan amortization schedule showing the interest and principal breakdown of each of the three loan payments.
c. Explain why the interest portion of each payment declines with the passage of time.

P4–44 **Loan interest deductions** Liz Rogers just closed a $10,000 business loan that is to be repaid in three equal, annual, end-of-year payments. The interest rate on the loan is 13%. As part of her firm's detailed financial planning, Liz wishes to determine the annual interest deduction attributable to the loan. (Because it is a business loan, the interest portion of each loan payment is tax-deductible to the business.)
a. Determine the firm's annual loan payment.
b. Prepare an amortization schedule for the loan.
c. How much interest expense will Liz's firm have in *each* of the next 3 years as a result of this loan?

P4–45 **Monthly loan payments** Tim Smith is shopping for a used car. He has found one priced at $4,500. The dealer has told Tim that if he can come up with a down payment of $500, the dealer will finance the balance of the price at a 12% annual rate over 2 years (24 months).
a. Assuming that Tim accepts the dealer's offer, what will his *monthly* (end-of-month) payment amount be?
b. Use a financial calculator or Equation 4.15a (found in footnote 9) to help you figure out what Tim's *monthly* payment would be if the dealer were willing to finance the balance of the car price at a 9% annual rate.

P4–46 **Growth rates** You are given the series of cash flows shown in the table at the top of the facing page.
a. Calculate the compound annual growth rate associated with each cash flow stream.
b. If year-1 values represent initial deposits in a savings account paying annual interest, what is the annual rate of interest earned on each account?
c. Compare and discuss the growth rate and interest rate found in parts **a** and **b**, respectively.

Year	Cash flows		
	A	B	C
1	$500	$1,500	$2,500
2	560	1,550	2,600
3	640	1,610	2,650
4	720	1,680	2,650
5	800	1,760	2,800
6		1,850	2,850
7		1,950	2,900
8		2,060	
9		2,170	
10		2,280	

P4–47 **Rate of return** Rishi Singh has $1,500 to invest. His investment counselor suggests an investment that pays no stated interest but will return $2,000 at the end of 3 years.
  a. What annual rate of return will Rishi earn with this investment?
  b. Rishi is considering another investment, of equal risk, that earns an annual return of 8%. Which investment should he make, and why?

P4–48 **Rate of return and investment choice** Clare Jaccard has $5,000 to invest. Because she is only 25 years old, she is not concerned about the length of the investment's life. What she is sensitive to is the rate of return she will earn on the investment. With the help of her financial advisor, Clare has isolated four equally risky investments, each providing a single amount at the end of its life, as shown in the following table. All of the investments require an initial $5,000 payment.

Investment	Single amount	Investment life (years)
A	$ 8,400	6
B	15,900	15
C	7,600	4
D	13,000	10

  a. Calculate, to the nearest 1%, the rate of return on each of the four investments available to Clare.
  b. Which investment would you recommend to Clare, given her goal of maximizing the rate of return?

P4–49 **Rate of return—Annuity** What is the rate of return on an investment of $10,606 if the company will receive $2,000 each year for the next 10 years?

P4–50 **Choosing the best annuity** Raina Herzig wishes to choose the best of four immediate-retirement annuities available to her. In each case, in exchange for paying a single premium today, she will receive equal, annual, end-of-year cash benefits for a specified number of years. She considers the annuities to be equally risky and is not concerned about their differing lives. Her decision will be based solely on the rate of return she will earn on each annuity. The key terms of the four annuities are shown in the following table.

Annuity	Premium paid today	Annual benefit	Life (years)
A	$30,000	$3,100	20
B	25,000	3,900	10
C	40,000	4,200	15
D	35,000	4,000	12

a. Calculate to the nearest 1% the rate of return on each of the four annuities Raina is considering.
b. Given Raina's stated decision criterion, which annuity would you recommend?

P4–51 **Interest rate for an annuity** Anna Waldheim was seriously injured in an industrial accident. She sued the responsible parties and was awarded a judgment of $2,000,000. Today, she and her attorney are attending a settlement conference with the defendants. The defendants have made an initial offer of $156,000 per year for 25 years. Anna plans to counteroffer at $255,000 per year for 25 years. Both the offer and the counteroffer have a present value of $2,000,000, the amount of the judgment. Both assume payments at the end of each year.
a. What interest rate assumption have the defendants used in their offer (rounded to the nearest whole percent)?
b. What interest rate assumption have Anna and her lawyer used in their counteroffer (rounded to the nearest whole percent)?
c. Anna is willing to settle for an annuity that carries an interest rate assumption of 9%. What annual payment would be acceptable to her?

P4–52 **Loan rates of interest** John Flemming has been shopping for a loan to finance the purchase of a used car. He has found three possibilities that seem attractive and wishes to select the one with the lowest interest rate. The information available with respect to each of the three $5,000 loans is shown in the following table.

Loan	Principal	Annual payment	Term (years)
A	$5,000	$1,352.81	5
B	5,000	1,543.21	4
C	5,000	2,010.45	3

a. Determine the interest rate associated with each of the loans.
b. Which loan should John take?

P4–53 **Number of years to equal future amount** For each of the cases presented in the table at the top of the facing page, determine the number of years it will take for the initial deposit to grow to equal the future amount at the given interest rate.

Case	Initial deposit	Future amount	Interest rate
A	$ 300	$ 1,000	7%
B	12,000	15,000	5
C	9,000	20,000	10
D	100	500	9
E	7,500	30,000	15

P4–54 **Time to accumulate a given sum** Manuel Rios wishes to determine how long it will take an initial deposit of $10,000 to double.
   a. If Manuel earns 10% annual interest on the deposit, how long will it take for him to double his money?
   b. How long will it take if he earns only 7% annual interest?
   c. How long will it take if he can earn 12% annual interest?
   d. Reviewing your findings in parts **a, b,** and **c,** indicate what relationship exists between the interest rate and the amount of time it will take Manuel to double his money.

P4–55 **Number of years to provide a given return** In each of the following cases, determine the number of years that the given annual *end-of-year* cash flow must continue to provide the given rate of return on the given initial amount.

Case	Initial amount	Annual cash flow	Rate of return
A	$ 1,000	$ 250	11%
B	150,000	30,000	15
C	80,000	10,000	10
D	600	275	9
E	17,000	3,500	6

P4–56 **Time to repay installment loan** Mia Salto wishes to determine how long it will take to repay a loan with initial proceeds of $14,000 where annual *end-of-year* installment payments of $2,450 are required.
   a. If Mia can borrow at a 12% annual rate of interest, how long will it take for her to repay the loan fully?
   b. How long will it take if she can borrow at a 9% annual rate?
   c. How long will it take if she has to pay 15% annual interest?
   d. Reviewing your answers in parts **a, b,** and **c,** describe the general relationship between the interest rate and the amount of time it will take Mia to repay the loan fully.

P4–57 **ETHICS PROBLEM** A manager at a "check into cash" business (see *In Practice* box on page 165) defends his business practice as simply "charging what the market will bear." "After all," says the manager, "we don't force people to come in the door." How would you respond to this ethical defense of the payday-advance business?

Chapter 4 Case

Funding Jill Moran's Retirement Annuity

Sunrise Industries wishes to accumulate funds to provide a retirement annuity for its vice president of research, Jill Moran. Ms. Moran, by contract, will retire at the end of exactly 12 years. Upon retirement, she is entitled to receive an annual end-of-year payment of $42,000 for exactly 20 years. If she dies prior to the end of the 20-year period, the annual payments will pass to her heirs. During the 12-year "accumulation period" Sunrise wishes to fund the annuity by making equal, annual, end-of-year deposits into an account earning 9% interest. Once the 20-year "distribution period" begins, Sunrise plans to move the accumulated monies into an account earning a guaranteed 12% per year. At the end of the distribution period, the account balance will equal zero. Note that the first deposit will be made at the end of year 1 and that the first distribution payment will be received at the end of year 13.

TO DO

a. Draw a time line depicting all of the cash flows associated with Sunrise's view of the retirement annuity.
b. How large a sum must Sunrise accumulate by the end of year 12 to provide the 20-year, $42,000 annuity?
c. How large must Sunrise's equal, annual, end-of-year deposits into the account be over the 12-year accumulation period to fund fully Ms. Moran's retirement annuity?
d. How much would Sunrise have to deposit annually during the accumulation period if it could earn 10% rather than 9% during the accumulation period?
e. How much would Sunrise have to deposit annually during the accumulation period if Ms. Moran's retirement annuity were a perpetuity and all other terms were the same as initially described?

Spreadsheet Exercise

At the end of 2005, Uma Corporation was considering undertaking a major long-term project in an effort to remain competitive in its industry. The production and sales departments determined the potential annual cash flow savings that could accrue to the firm if it acts soon. Specifically, they estimate that a mixed stream of future cash flow savings will occur at the end of the years 2006 through 2011. The years 2012 through 2016 will see consecutive and equal cash flow savings at the end of each year. The firm estimates that its discount rate over the first 6 years will be 7%. The expected discount rate over the years 2012 through 2016 will be 11%.

The project managers will find the project acceptable if it results in present cash flow savings of at least $860,000. The cash flow savings data at the top of the facing page are supplied to the finance department for analysis:

End of year	Cash flow savings
2006	$110,000
2007	120,000
2008	130,000
2009	150,000
2010	160,000
2011	150,000
2012	90,000
2013	90,000
2014	90,000
2015	90,000
2016	90,000

TO DO

Create a spreadsheet similar to Tables 4.2 and 4.4 (or to one that can be viewed at www.aw-bc.com/gitman), and then answer the following questions:

a. Determine the value (at the beginning of 2006) of the future cash flow savings expected to be generated by this project.
b. Based solely on the one criterion set by management, should the firm undertake this specific project? Explain.
c. What is the "interest rate risk," and how might it influence the recommendation made in part **b**? Explain.

WEB EXERCISE

Mortgage interest rates vary daily. Over a period of time, mortgage interest rates have followed definite trends based on federal interest rate policies and economic conditions. Historical interest rate information is available on the Web.

TO DO

a. For this Web exercise, direct your Internet browser to www.mbaa.org/, the home page of the Mortgage Bankers Association. View the current mortgage interest rates listed on the right side of the screen. Now direct your browser to the Mortgage and Market Data link at the top of the page, highlighting Interest rates. This page contains data for mortgage rates over the past decades. Study and comment on the levels of interest rates over the recent past. The Freddie Mac Average Rate for 30-Year Fixed Rate Mortgages, 1971—present (Monthly) link is a good place to start. How do interest rates recently—in the past year, for example—compare with those that prevailed during the 1970s, 1980s, and 1990s? Do you see any trends in the level of interest rates?

One way to perform this analysis would be to graph the monthly data. While this can be accomplished by hand, the use of a graphing tool such as that found in Excel would facilitate the process. Here graphing the entire series in one graph is feasible, but dividing the data into three or more graphs along decade lines should make the analysis clearer.

b. A second set of data can be found at the Federal Reserve System's Web site. Point your browser to www.federalreserve.gov/. Go to the Economic and Research Data link on the left side of the page. Next, go to the Statistics: Releases and Historical Data link at the top of the page. At this page, look at G.13 Selected Interest Rates, choosing Historical Data. Now scan about one-third of the way down the page, under U.S. Government Securities, Treasury constant maturities, 10-year, and highlight monthly frequency. (The Web address to access these data directly is www.federalreserve.gov/releases/h15/data/m/tcm10y.txt.) This data set goes back to April 1953. (The data shown are actually yields, not interest rates. This topic will be covered in Chapter 6, but for now you can treat the yield as an interest rate.) Compare the trend in the U.S. government 10-year rates and your earlier analysis of mortgage rates. Because mortgage data went back only to 1971, begin your comparison there. Nevertheless, you should look closely at today's rates and the rates that prevailed in the late 1950s and early 1960s. Graphs are required for a complete comparison of the two series.

Remember to check the book's Web site at

www.aw-bc.com/gitman

for additional resources, including additional Web exercises.

Chapter 5

Risk and Return

LEARNING GOALS

LG1 Understand the meaning and fundamentals of risk, return, and risk aversion.

LG2 Describe procedures for assessing and measuring the risk of a single asset.

LG3 Discuss risk measurement for a single asset using the standard deviation and coefficient of variation.

LG4 Understand the risk and return characteristics of a portfolio in terms of correlation and diversification, and the impact of international assets on a portfolio.

LG5 Review the two types of risk and the derivation and role of beta in measuring the relevant risk of both an individual security and a portfolio.

LG6 Explain the capital asset pricing model (CAPM) and its relationship to the security market line (SML).

Across the Disciplines Why This Chapter Matters to You

Accounting: You need to understand the relationship between risk and return because of the effect that riskier projects will have on the firm's annual net income and on your efforts to stabilize reported net income.

Information systems: You need to understand how to do sensitivity and correlation analyses to build decision packages that help management analyze the risk and return of various business opportunities.

Management: You need to understand the relationship between risk and return, and how to measure that relationship to evaluate data that come from finance personnel and translate those data into decisions that increase the value of the firm.

Marketing: You need to understand that although higher-risk projects may produce higher returns, they may not be the best choice for the firm if they produce an erratic earnings pattern and fail to optimize the value of the firm.

Operations: You need to understand why investments in plant, equipment, and systems need to be evaluated in light of their impact on the firm's risk and return, which together will affect the firm's value.

The concept that return should increase if risk increases is fundamental to modern management and finance. This relationship is regularly observed in the financial markets, and important clarification of it has led to Nobel prizes. In this chapter we discuss these two key factors in finance—risk and return—and introduce some quantitative tools and techniques used to measure risk and return for individual assets and for groups of assets.

Risk and Return Fundamentals

To maximize share price, the financial manager must learn to assess two key determinants: risk and return. Each financial decision presents certain risk and return characteristics, and the unique combination of these characteristics has an impact on share price. Risk can be viewed as it is related either to a single asset or to a **portfolio**—a collection, or group, of assets. We will look at both, beginning with the risk of a single asset. First, though, it is important to introduce some fundamental ideas about risk, return, and risk preferences.

portfolio
A collection, or group, of assets.

Risk Defined

risk
The chance of financial loss or, more formally, the *variability of returns associated with a given asset.*

In the most basic sense, **risk** is the chance of financial loss. Assets having greater chances of loss are viewed as more risky than those with lesser chances of loss. More formally, the term *risk* is used interchangeably with *uncertainty* to refer to the *variability of returns associated with a given asset.* A $1,000 government bond that guarantees its holder $5 interest after 30 days has no risk, because there is no variability associated with the return. A $1,000 investment in a firm's common stock, which over the same 30 days may earn anywhere from $0 to $10, is very risky because of the high variability of its return. The more nearly certain the return from an asset, the less variability and therefore the less risk.

Some risks directly affect both financial managers and shareholders. Table 5.1 briefly describes the common sources of risk that affect both firms and their shareholders. As you can see, business risk and financial risk are more firm-specific and therefore are of greatest interest to financial managers. Interest rate, liquidity, and market risks are more shareholder-specific and therefore are of greatest interest to stockholders. Event, exchange rate, purchasing-power, and tax risk directly affect both firms and shareholders. A number of these risks are discussed in more detail later in this text. Clearly, both financial managers and shareholders must assess these and other risks as they make investment decisions.

Return Defined

return
The total gain or loss experienced on an investment over a given period of time; calculated by dividing the asset's cash distributions during the period, plus change in value, by its beginning-of-period investment value.

Obviously, if we are going to assess risk on the basis of variability of return, we need to be certain we know what *return* is and how to measure it. The **return** is the total gain or loss experienced on an investment over a given period of time. It is commonly measured as cash distributions during the period plus the change in value, expressed as a percentage of the beginning-of-period investment value. The

TABLE 5.1	Popular Sources of Risk Affecting Financial Managers and Shareholders
Source of risk	Description
Firm-Specific Risks	
Business risk	The chance that the firm will be unable to cover its operating costs. Level is driven by the firm's revenue stability and the structure of its operating costs (fixed versus variable).
Financial risk	The chance that the firm will be unable to cover its financial obligations. Level is driven by the predictability of the firm's operating cash flows and its fixed-cost financial obligations.
Shareholder-Specific Risks	
Interest rate risk	The chance that changes in interest rates will adversely affect the value of an investment. Most investments lose value when the interest rate rises and increase in value when it falls.
Liquidity risk	The chance that an investment cannot be easily liquidated at a reasonable price. Liquidity is significantly affected by the size and depth of the market in which an investment is customarily traded.
Market risk	The chance that the value of an investment will decline because of market factors that are independent of the investment (such as economic, political, and social events). In general, the more a given investment's value responds to the market, the greater its risk; the less it responds, the smaller its risk.
Firm and Shareholder Risks	
Event risk	The chance that a totally unexpected event will have a significant effect on the value of the firm or a specific investment. These infrequent events, such as government-mandated withdrawal of a popular prescription drug, typically affect only a small group of firms or investments.
Exchange rate risk	The exposure of future expected cash flows to fluctuations in the currency exchange rate. The greater the chance of undesirable exchange rate fluctuations, the greater the risk of the cash flows and therefore the lower the value of the firm or investment.
Purchasing-power risk	The chance that changing price levels caused by inflation or deflation in the economy will adversely affect the firm's or investment's cash flows and value. Typically, firms or investments with cash flows that move with general price levels have a low purchasing-power risk, and those with cash flows that do not move with general price levels have a high purchasing-power risk.
Tax risk	The chance that unfavorable changes in tax laws will occur. Firms and investments with values that are sensitive to tax law changes are more risky.

expression for calculating the rate of return earned on any asset over period t, k_t, is commonly defined as

$$k_t = \frac{C_t + P_t - P_{t-1}}{P_{t-1}} \tag{5.1}$$

where

k_t = actual, expected, or required rate of return during period t

C_t = cash (flow) received from the asset investment in the time period $t-1$ to t

P_t = price (value) of asset at time t

P_{t-1} = price (value) of asset at time $t-1$

198   PART 2   Important Financial Concepts

The return, k_t, reflects the combined effect of cash flow, C_t, and changes in value, $P_t - P_{t-1}$, over period t.

Equation 5.1 is used to determine the rate of return over a time period as short as 1 day or as long as 10 years or more. However, in most cases, t is 1 year, and k therefore represents an annual rate of return.

EXAMPLE

Robin's Gameroom, a high-traffic video arcade, wishes to determine the return on two of its video machines, Conqueror and Demolition. Conqueror was purchased 1 year ago for $20,000 and currently has a market value of $21,500. During the year, it generated $800 of after-tax cash receipts. Demolition was purchased 4 years ago; its value in the year just completed declined from $12,000 to $11,800. During the year, it generated $1,700 of after-tax cash receipts. Substituting into Equation 5.1, we can calculate the annual rate of return, k, for each video machine.

Conqueror (C):
$$k_C = \frac{\$800 + \$21,500 - \$20,000}{\$20,000} = \frac{\$2,300}{\$20,000} = \underline{\underline{11.5\%}}$$

Demolition (D):
$$k_D = \frac{\$1,700 + \$11,800 - \$12,000}{\$12,000} = \frac{\$1,500}{\$12,000} = \underline{\underline{12.5\%}}$$

Although the market value of Demolition declined during the year, its cash flow caused it to earn a higher rate of return than Conqueror earned during the same period. Clearly, the combined impact of cash flow and changes in value, as measured by the rate of return, is important. ■

Historical Returns

Investment returns vary both over time and between different types of investments. By averaging historical returns over a long period of time, it becomes possible to eliminate the impact of market and other types of risk. This enables the financial decision maker to focus on the differences in return that are attributable primarily to the types of investment. Table 5.2 shows the average annual rates of return for a number of popular security investments (and inflation) over the 78-year period January 1, 1926, through December 31, 2003. Each rate represents the average annual rate of return an investor would have realized had he or she purchased the investment on January 1, 1926, and sold it on December 31, 2003. You can see that significant differences exist between the average annual rates of return realized on the various types of stocks, bonds, and bills shown. Later in this chapter, we will see how these differences in return can be linked to differences in the risk of each of these investments.

Risk Aversion

risk-averse
The attitude toward risk in which an increased return would be required for an increase in risk.

Financial managers generally seek to avoid risk. Most managers are **risk-averse**; for a given increase in risk, they require an increase in return. This attitude is believed consistent with that of the owners for whom the firm is being managed.

TABLE 5.2	Historical Returns for Selected Security Investments (1926–2003)
Investment	Average annual return
Large-company stocks	12.4%
Small-company stocks	17.5
Long-term corporate bonds	6.2
Long-term government bonds	5.8
U.S. Treasury bills	3.8
Inflation	3.1%

Source: *Stocks, Bonds, Bills, and Inflation, 2004 Yearbook* (Chicago: Ibbotson Associates, Inc., 2004).

Managers generally tend to be conservative rather than aggressive when accepting risk for their firm. Accordingly, a *risk-averse financial manager requiring higher returns for greater risk is assumed throughout this text.*

Review Questions

5–1 What is *risk* in the context of financial decision making?
5–2 Define *return*, and describe how to find the rate of return on an investment.
5–3 Describe the attitude toward return of a *risk-averse* financial manager.

  # Risk of a Single Asset

The concept of risk can be developed by first considering a single asset held in isolation. We can look at expected-return behaviors to assess risk, and statistics can be used to measure it.

Risk Assessment

Sensitivity analysis and probability distributions can be used to assess the general level of risk embodied in a given asset.

Sensitivity Analysis

sensitivity analysis
An approach for assessing risk that uses several possible-return estimates to obtain a sense of the variability among outcomes.

range
A measure of an asset's risk, which is found by subtracting the pessimistic (worst) outcome from the optimistic (best) outcome.

Sensitivity analysis uses several possible-return estimates to obtain a sense of the variability among outcomes. One common method involves making pessimistic (worst), most likely (expected), and optimistic (best) estimates of the returns associated with a given asset. In this case, the asset's risk can be measured by the range of returns. The **range** is found by subtracting the pessimistic outcome from the optimistic outcome. The greater the range, the more variability, or risk, the asset is said to have.

TABLE 5.3	Assets A and B	
	Asset A	Asset B
Initial investment	$10,000	$10,000
Annual rate of return		
Pessimistic	13%	7%
Most likely	15%	15%
Optimistic	17%	23%
Range	4%	16%

EXAMPLE

Norman Company, a custom golf equipment manufacturer, wants to choose the better of two investments, A and B. Each requires an initial outlay of $10,000, and each has a *most likely* annual rate of return of 15%. Management has made *pessimistic* and *optimistic* estimates of the returns associated with each. The three estimates for each asset, along with its range, are given in Table 5.3. Asset A appears to be less risky than asset B; its range of 4% (17% − 13%) is less than the range of 16% (23% − 7%) for asset B. The risk-averse decision maker would prefer asset A over asset B, because A offers the same most likely return as B (15%) with lower risk (smaller range). ■

Although the use of sensitivity analysis and the range is rather crude, it does give the decision maker a feel for the behavior of returns, which can be used to estimate the risk involved.

Probability Distributions

Probability distributions provide a more quantitative insight into an asset's risk. The **probability** of a given outcome is its *chance* of occurring. An outcome with an 80 percent probability of occurrence would be expected to occur 8 out of 10 times. An outcome with a probability of 100 percent is certain to occur. Outcomes with a probability of zero will never occur.

probability
The *chance* that a given outcome will occur.

EXAMPLE

Norman Company's past estimates indicate that the probabilities of the pessimistic, most likely, and optimistic outcomes are 25%, 50%, and 25%, respectively. Note that the sum of these probabilities must equal 100%; that is, they must be based on all the alternatives considered. ■

probability distribution
A model that relates probabilities to the associated outcomes.

bar chart
The simplest type of probability distribution; shows only a limited number of outcomes and associated probabilities for a given event.

continuous probability distribution
A probability distribution showing all the possible outcomes and associated probabilities for a given event.

A **probability distribution** is a model that relates probabilities to the associated outcomes. The simplest type of probability distribution is the **bar chart**, which shows only a limited number of outcome–probability coordinates. The bar charts for Norman Company's assets A and B are shown in Figure 5.1. Although both assets have the same most likely return, the range of return is much greater, or more dispersed, for asset B than for asset A—16 percent versus 4 percent.

If we knew all the possible outcomes and associated probabilities, we could develop a **continuous probability distribution**. This type of distribution can be thought of as a bar chart for a very large number of outcomes. Figure 5.2 presents continuous probability distributions for assets A and B. Note that although assets A and B have the same most likely return (15 percent), the distribution of returns for asset B has much greater *dispersion* than the distribution for asset A. Clearly, asset B is more risky than asset A.

FIGURE 5.1
Bar Charts
Bar charts for asset A's and asset B's returns

Risk Measurement

In addition to considering its *range*, the risk of an asset can be measured quantitatively by using statistics. Here we consider two statistics—the standard deviation and the coefficient of variation—that can be used to measure the variability of asset returns.

standard deviation (σ_k)
The most common statistical indicator of an asset's risk; it measures the dispersion around the *expected value*.

expected value of a return ($\bar{k}$)
The most likely return on a given asset.

Standard Deviation

The most common statistical indicator of an asset's risk is the **standard deviation**, σ_k, which measures the dispersion around the *expected value*. The **expected value of a return**, $\bar{k}$, is the most likely return on an asset. It is calculated as follows:[1]

$$\bar{k} = \sum_{j=1}^{n} k_j \times Pr_j \tag{5.2}$$

FIGURE 5.2
Continuous Probability Distributions
Continuous probability distributions for asset A's and asset B's returns

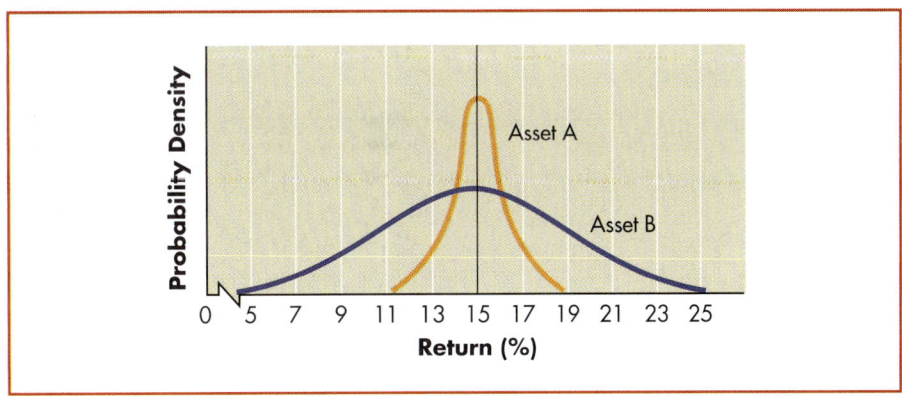

---

1. The formula for finding the expected value of return, $\bar{k}$, when all of the outcomes, k_j, are known *and* their related probabilities are assumed to be equal, is a simple arithmetic average:

$$\bar{k} = \frac{\sum_{j=1}^{n} k_j}{n} \tag{5.2a}$$

where *n* is the number of observations. Equation 5.2 is emphasized in this chapter because returns and related probabilities are often available.

TABLE 5.4 Expected Values of Returns for Assets A and B

Possible outcomes	Probability (1)	Returns (2)	Weighted value [(1) × (2)] (3)
Asset A			
Pessimistic	.25	13%	3.25%
Most likely	.50	15	7.50
Optimistic	.25	17	4.25
Total	1.00	Expected return	15.00%
Asset B			
Pessimistic	.25	7%	1.75%
Most likely	.50	15	7.50
Optimistic	.25	23	5.75
Total	1.00	Expected return	15.00%

where

k_j = return for the jth outcome

Pr_j = probability of occurrence of the jth outcome

n = number of outcomes considered

EXAMPLE The expected values of returns for Norman Company's assets A and B are presented in Table 5.4. Column 1 gives the Pr_j's and column 2 gives the k_j's. In each case n equals 3. The expected value for each asset's return is 15%.

The expression for the *standard deviation of returns*, σ_k, is[2]

$$\sigma_k = \sqrt{\sum_{j=1}^{n}(k_j - \bar{k})^2 \times Pr_j} \qquad (5.3)$$

In general, the higher the standard deviation, the greater the risk.

EXAMPLE Table 5.5 presents the standard deviations for Norman Company's assets A and B, based on the earlier data. The standard deviation for asset A is 1.41%, and the standard deviation for asset B is 5.66%. The higher risk of asset B is clearly reflected in its higher standard deviation.

Historical Returns and Risk We can now use the standard deviation as a measure of risk to assess the historical (1926–2003) investment return data in Table 5.2. Table 5.6 (see page 204) repeats the historical returns in column 1 and

---

2. The formula that is commonly used to find the standard deviation of returns, σ_k, in a situation in which *all* outcomes are known *and* their related probabilities are assumed equal, is

$$\sigma_k = \sqrt{\frac{\sum_{j=1}^{n}(k_j - \bar{k})^2}{n - 1}} \qquad (5.3a)$$

where n is the number of observations. Equation 5.3 is emphasized in this chapter because returns and related probabilities are often available.

TABLE 5.5 The Calculation of the Standard Deviation of the Returns for Assets A and B[a]

j	k_j	$\bar{k}$	$k_j - \bar{k}$	$(k_j - \bar{k})^2$	Pr_j	$(k_j - \bar{k})^2 \times Pr_j$
			Asset A			
1	13%	15%	−2%	4%	.25	1%
2	15	15	0	0	.50	0
3	17	15	2	4	.25	1

$$\sum_{j=1}^{3}(k_j - \bar{k})^2 \times Pr_j = 2\%$$

$$\sigma_{k_A} = \sqrt{\sum_{j=1}^{n}(k_j - \bar{k})^2 \times Pr_j} = \sqrt{2\%} = \underline{\underline{1.41\%}}$$

j	k_j	$\bar{k}$	$k_j - \bar{k}$	$(k_j - \bar{k})^2$	Pr_j	$(k_j - \bar{k})^2 \times Pr_j$
			Asset B			
1	7%	15%	−8%	64%	.25	16%
2	15	15	0	0	.50	0
3	23	15	8	64	.25	16

$$\sum_{j=1}^{k}(k_j - \bar{k})^2 \times Pr_j = 32\%$$

$$\sigma_{k_B} = \sqrt{\sum_{j=1}^{3}(k_j - \bar{k})^2 \times Pr_j} = \sqrt{32\%} = \underline{\underline{5.66\%}}$$

[a]Calculations in this table are made in percentage form rather than decimal form—e.g., 13% rather than 0.13. As a result, some of the intermediate computations may appear to be inconsistent with those that would result from using decimal form. Regardless, the resulting standard deviations are correct and identical to those that would result from using decimal rather than percentage form.

shows the standard deviations associated with each of them in column 2. A close relationship can be seen between the investment returns and the standard deviations: Investments with higher returns have higher standard deviations. Because higher standard deviations are associated with greater risk, the historical data confirm the existence of a positive relationship between risk and return. That relationship reflects *risk aversion* by market participants, who require higher returns as compensation for greater risk. The historical data in columns 1 and 2 of Table 5.6 clearly show that during the 1926–2003 period, investors were rewarded with higher returns on higher-risk investments.

Coefficient of Variation

coefficient of variation (CV)
A measure of relative dispersion that is useful in comparing the risks of assets with differing expected returns.

The **coefficient of variation,** *CV,* is a measure of relative dispersion that is useful in comparing the risks of assets with differing expected returns. Equation 5.4 gives the expression for the coefficient of variation:

$$CV = \frac{\sigma_k}{\bar{k}} \tag{5.4}$$

The higher the coefficient of variation, the greater the risk and therefore the higher the expected return. This relationship can be seen by comparing the coefficients of variation in column 3 of Table 5.6, which shows historical 1926–2003 investment

TABLE 5.6 Historical Returns, Standard Deviations, and Coefficients of Variation for Selected Security Investments (1926–2003)

Investment	Average annual return (1)	Standard deviation (2)	Coefficient of variation[a] (3)
Large-company stocks	12.4%	20.4%	1.65
Small-company stocks	17.5	33.3	1.90
Long-term corporate bonds	6.2	8.6	1.39
Long-term government bonds	5.8	9.4	1.62
U.S. Treasury bills	3.8	3.1	0.82
Inflation	3.1%	4.3%	1.39

[a]Calculated by dividing the standard deviation in column 2 by the average annual return in column 1.
Source: *Stocks, Bonds, Bills, and Inflation, 2004 Yearbook* (Chicago: Ibbotson Associates, Inc., 2004).

data, with the average annual returns in column 1. As with the standard deviations in column 2, higher returns are associated with higher coefficients of variation.

EXAMPLE

When the standard deviations (from Table 5.5) and the expected returns (from Table 5.4) for assets A and B are substituted into Equation 5.4, the coefficients of variation for A and B are 0.094 (1.41% ÷ 15%) and 0.377 (5.66% ÷ 15%), respectively. Asset B has the higher coefficient of variation and is therefore more risky than asset A—which we already know from the standard deviation. (Because both assets have the same expected return, the coefficient of variation has not provided any new information.)

The real utility of the coefficient of variation comes in comparing the risks of assets that have *different* expected returns.

EXAMPLE

A firm wants to select the less risky of two alternative assets—C and D. The expected return, standard deviation, and coefficient of variation for each of these assets' returns are

Statistics	Asset C	Asset D
(1) Expected return	12%	20%
(2) Standard deviation	9%[a]	10%
(3) Coefficient of variation [(2) ÷ (1)]	0.75	0.50[a]

[a]Preferred asset using the given risk measure.

Judging solely on the basis of their standard deviations, the firm would prefer asset C, which has a lower standard deviation than asset D (9% versus 10%). However, management would be making a serious error in choosing asset C over asset D, because the dispersion—the risk—of the asset, as reflected in the coefficient of variation, is lower for D (0.50) than for C (0.75). Clearly, using the coefficient of variation to compare asset risk is effective because it also considers the relative size, or expected return, of the assets.

Review Questions

5–4 Explain how the *range* is used in sensitivity analysis.
5–5 What does a plot of the *probability distribution* of outcomes show a decision maker about an asset's risk?
5–6 What relationship exists between the size of the *standard deviation* and the degree of asset risk?
5–7 When is the *coefficient of variation* preferred over the standard deviation for comparing asset risk?

efficient portfolio
A portfolio that maximizes return for a given level of risk or minimizes risk for a given level of return.

Risk of a Portfolio

In real-world situations, the risk of any single investment would not be viewed independently of other assets. (We did so for teaching purposes.) New investments must be considered in light of their impact on the risk and return of the *portfolio* of assets. The financial manager's goal is to create an **efficient portfolio**, one that maximizes return for a given level of risk or minimizes risk for a given level of return. We therefore need a way to measure the return and the standard deviation of a portfolio of assets. Once we can do that, we will look at the statistical concept of *correlation*, which underlies the process of diversification that is used to develop an efficient portfolio.

correlation
A statistical measure of the relationship between any two series of numbers representing data of any kind.

positively correlated
Describes two series that move in the same direction.

negatively correlated
Describes two series that move in opposite directions.

correlation coefficient
A measure of the degree of correlation between two series.

perfectly positively correlated
Describes two *positively correlated* series that have a *correlation coefficient* of +1.

perfectly negatively correlated
Describes two *negatively correlated* series that have a *correlation coefficient* of −1.

Correlation

Correlation is a statistical measure of the relationship between any two series of numbers. The numbers may represent data of any kind, from returns to test scores. If two series move in the same direction, they are **positively correlated**. If the series move in opposite directions, they are **negatively correlated**.

The degree of correlation is measured by the **correlation coefficient**, which ranges from +1 for **perfectly positively correlated** series to −1 for **perfectly negatively correlated** series. These two extremes are depicted for series M and N in Figure 5.3. The perfectly positively correlated series move exactly together; the perfectly negatively correlated series move in exactly opposite directions.

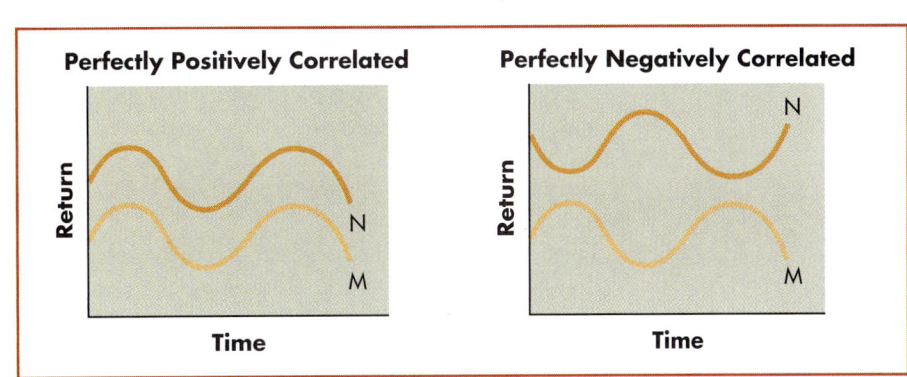

FIGURE 5.3

Correlations
The correlation between series M and series N

FIGURE 5.4

Diversification
Combining negatively correlated assets to reduce, or diversify, risk

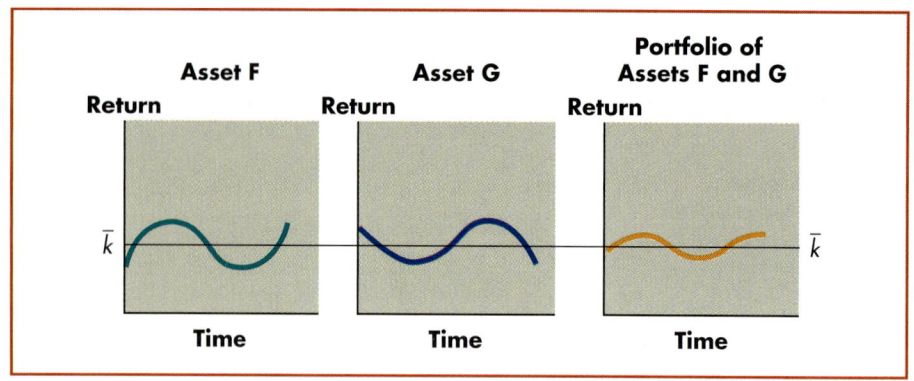

Diversification

The concept of correlation is essential to developing an efficient portfolio. To reduce overall risk, it is best to *diversify* by combining, or adding to the portfolio, assets that have a negative (or a low positive) correlation. Combining negatively correlated assets can reduce the overall variability of returns. Figure 5.4 shows that a portfolio containing the negatively correlated assets F and G, both of which have the same expected return, $\bar{k}$, also has that same return $\bar{k}$ but has less risk (variability) than either of the individual assets. Even if assets are not negatively correlated, the lower the positive correlation between them, the lower the resulting risk.

Some assets are **uncorrelated**—that is, there is no interaction between their returns. Combining uncorrelated assets can reduce risk, not so effectively as combining negatively correlated assets, but more effectively than combining positively correlated assets. The correlation coefficient for uncorrelated assets is close to zero and acts as the midpoint between perfect positive and perfect negative correlation.

The creation of a portfolio that combines two assets with perfectly positively correlated returns results in overall portfolio risk that at minimum equals that of the least risky asset and at maximum equals that of the most risky asset. However, a portfolio combining two assets with less than perfectly positive correlation *can* reduce total risk to a level below that of either of the components, which in certain situations may be zero. For example, assume that you manufacture machine tools. The business is very *cyclical*, with high sales when the economy is expanding and low sales during a recession. If you acquired another machine-tool company, with sales positively correlated with those of your firm, the combined sales would still be cyclical and risk would remain the same. Alternatively, however, you could acquire a sewing machine manufacturer, whose sales are *countercyclical*. It typically has low sales during economic expansion and high sales during recession (when consumers are more likely to make their own clothes). Combination with the sewing machine manufacturer, which has negatively correlated sales, should reduce risk.

uncorrelated
Describes two series that lack any interaction and therefore have a *correlation coefficient* close to zero.

EXAMPLE

Table 5.7 presents the forecasted returns from three different assets—X, Y, and Z—over the next 5 years, along with their expected values and standard deviations. Each of the assets has an expected value of return of 12% and a standard deviation of 3.16%. The assets therefore have equal return and equal risk. The

TABLE 5.7 Forecasted Returns, Expected Values, and Standard Deviations for Assets X, Y, and Z and Portfolios XY and XZ

	Assets			Portfolios	
				XY[a]	XZ[b]
Year	X	Y	Z	(50% X + 50% Y)	(50% X + 50% Z)
2007	8%	16%	8%	12%	8%
2008	10	14	10	12	10
2009	12	12	12	12	12
2010	14	10	14	12	14
2011	16	8	16	12	16
Statistics:[c]					
Expected value	12%	12%	12%	12%	12%
Standard deviation[d]	3.16%	3.16%	3.16%	0%	3.16%

[a]Portfolio XY, which consists of 50% of asset X and 50% of asset Y, illustrates *perfect negative correlation* because these two return streams behave in completely opposite fashion over the 5-year period. Its return values are calculated as shown in the following table.

	Forecasted return			
	Asset X	Asset Y	Portfolio return calculation[a]	Expected portfolio return, k_p
Year	(1)	(2)	(3)	(4)
2007	8%	16%	$(.50 \times 8\%) + (.50 \times 16\%) =$	12%
2008	10	14	$(.50 \times 10\%) + (.50 \times 14\%) =$	12
2009	12	12	$(.50 \times 12\%) + (.50 \times 12\%) =$	12
2010	14	10	$(.50 \times 14\%) + (.50 \times 10\%) =$	12
2011	16	8	$(.50 \times 16\%) + (.50 \times 8\%) =$	12

[b]Portfolio XZ, which consists of 50% of asset X and 50% of asset Z, illustrates *perfect positive correlation* because these two return streams behave identically over the 5-year period. Its return values are calculated using the same method demonstrated in note *a* above for portfolio XY.

[c]Because the probabilities associated with the returns are not given, the general equation, Equation 5.2a in footnote 1, is used to calculate expected values as demonstrated below for portfolio XY.

$$\bar{k}_{xy} = \frac{12\% + 12\% + 12\% + 12\% + 12\%}{5} = \frac{60\%}{5} = \underline{\underline{12\%}}$$

The same formula is applied to find the expected value of return for assets X, Y, and Z, and portfolio XZ.

[d]Because the probabilities associated with the returns are not given, the general equation, Equation 5.3a in footnote 2, is used to calculate the standard deviations as demonstrated below for portfolio XY.

$$\sigma_{k_{xy}} = \sqrt{\frac{(12\% - 12\%)^2 + (12\% - 12\%)^2 + (12\% - 12\%)^2 + (12\% - 12\%)^2 + (12\% - 12\%)^2}{5 - 1}}$$

$$= \sqrt{\frac{0\% + 0\% + 0\% + 0\% + 0\%}{4}} = \sqrt{\frac{0}{4}}\% = \underline{\underline{0\%}}$$

The same formula is applied to find the standard deviation of returns for assets X, Y, and Z, and portfolio XZ.

return patterns of assets X and Y are perfectly negatively correlated. They move in exactly opposite directions over time. The returns of assets X and Z are perfectly positively correlated. They move in precisely the same direction. (*Note:* The returns for X and Z are identical.)[3]

Portfolio XY Portfolio XY (shown in Table 5.7) is created by combining equal portions of assets X and Y, the perfectly negatively correlated assets.[4] The risk in this portfolio, as reflected by its standard deviation, is reduced to 0%, whereas the expected return remains at 12%. Because both assets have the same expected return values, are combined in equal parts, and are perfectly negatively correlated, the combination results in the complete elimination of risk. Whenever assets are perfectly negatively correlated, an optimal combination (similar to the 50–50 mix in the case of assets X and Y) exists for which the resulting standard deviation will equal 0.

Portfolio XZ Portfolio XZ (shown in Table 5.7) is created by combining equal portions of assets X and Z, the perfectly positively correlated assets. The risk in this portfolio, as reflected by its standard deviation, is unaffected by this combination. Risk remains at 3.16%, and the expected return value remains at 12%. Whenever perfectly positively correlated assets such as X and Y are combined, the standard deviation of the resulting portfolio cannot be reduced *below that of the least risky asset*; the maximum portfolio standard deviation will be that of the riskiest asset. Because assets X and Z have the same standard deviation, the minimum and maximum standard deviations are the same (3.16%), which is the only value that can be taken on by a combination of these assets. This result can be attributed to the unlikely situation that X and Z are identical assets.

Correlation, Diversification, Risk, and Return

Hint Remember, low correlation between two series of numbers is less positive and more negative—indicating greater dissimilarity of behavior of the two series.

In general, the lower the correlation between asset returns, the greater the potential diversification of risk. (This should be clear from the behaviors illustrated in Table 5.7.) For each pair of assets, there is a combination that will result in the lowest risk (standard deviation) possible. How much risk can be reduced by this combination depends on the degree of correlation. Many potential combinations (assuming divisibility) could be made, but only one combination of the infinite number of possibilities will minimize risk.

Three possible correlations—perfect positive, uncorrelated, and perfect negative—illustrate the effect of correlation on the diversification of risk and return. Table 5.8 summarizes the impact of correlation on the range of return and risk for various two-asset portfolio combinations. The table shows that as we move from perfect positive correlation to uncorrelated assets to perfect negative correlation, the ability to reduce risk is improved. Note that in no case will a portfolio of assets be riskier than the riskiest asset included in the portfolio. Further discussion of these relationships is included at the text's Web site (www.aw-bc.com/gitman).

---

3. Identical return streams are used in this example to permit clear illustration of the concepts, but it is *not* necessary for return streams to be identical for them to be perfectly positively correlated. Any return streams that move (i.e., vary) exactly together—regardless of the relative magnitude of the returns—are perfectly positively correlated.

4. For illustrative purposes it has been assumed that each of the assets—X, Y, and Z—can be divided up and combined with other assets to create portfolios. This assumption is made only to permit clear illustration of the concepts. The assets are not actually divisible.

TABLE 5.8	Correlation, Return, and Risk for Various Two-Asset Portfolio Combinations	
Correlation coefficient	Range of return	Range of risk
+1 (perfect positive)	Between returns of two assets held in isolation	Between risk of two assets held in isolation
0 (uncorrelated)	Between returns of two assets held in isolation	Between risk of most risky asset and an amount less than risk of least risky asset but greater than 0
−1 (perfect negative)	Between returns of two assets held in isolation	Between risk of most risky asset and 0

International Diversification

The ultimate example of portfolio diversification involves including foreign assets in a portfolio. The inclusion of assets from countries with business cycles that are not highly correlated with the U.S. business cycle reduces the portfolio's responsiveness to market movements and to foreign currency fluctuations.

Returns from International Diversification

Over long periods, returns from internationally diversified portfolios tend to be superior to those of purely domestic ones. This is particularly so if the U.S. economy is performing relatively poorly and the dollar is depreciating in value against most foreign currencies. At such times, the dollar returns to U.S. investors on a portfolio of foreign assets can be very attractive. However, over any single short or intermediate period, international diversification can yield subpar returns, particularly during periods when the dollar is appreciating in value relative to other currencies. When the U.S. currency gains in value, the dollar value of a foreign-currency-denominated portfolio of assets declines. Even if this portfolio yields a satisfactory return in local currency, the return to U.S. investors will be reduced when translated into dollars. Subpar local currency portfolio returns, coupled with an appreciating dollar, can yield truly dismal dollar returns to U.S. investors.

Overall, though, the logic of international portfolio diversification assumes that these fluctuations in currency values and relative performance will average out over long periods. Compared to similar, purely domestic portfolios, an internationally diversified portfolio will tend to yield a comparable return at a lower level of risk.

Risks of International Diversification

political risk
Risk that arises from the possibility that a host government will take actions harmful to foreign investors or that political turmoil in a country will endanger investments there.

U.S. investors should also be aware of the potential dangers of international investing. In addition to the risk induced by currency fluctuations, several other financial risks are unique to international investing. Most important is **political risk**, which arises from the possibility that a host government will take actions harmful to foreign investors or that political turmoil in a country will endanger investments there. Political risks are particularly acute in developing countries,

In Practice GLOBAL FOCUS

AN INTERNATIONAL FLAVOR TO RISK REDUCTION

What do the Dodge Caravan, Kit Kat chocolate bars, aspirin, and Fox TV have in common? While they may be products with which you are familiar, all are products of non-U.S. corporations. The Dodge Caravan is a product of **DaimlerChrysler**, a German company. Kit Kat bars are a product of Swiss company **Nestlé**. Aspirin is produced by **Bayer AG**, a German company, and Fox TV is part of **News Corp**, an Australian company. Just as Americans use many products and services created by companies headquartered in foreign countries, so many U.S. corporations seek to expand internationally. The result is a more globally integrated economy.

One method of reducing investment risk is diversification. Allocating a portion of one's portfolio to non-U.S. equities has historically provided better risk-adjusted returns than a portfolio consisting solely of U.S. assets. As you have learned in this chapter, the benefit of diversification between two assets is enhanced if the two asset classes are not highly correlated, and it is largest when two asset classes are perfectly negatively correlated.

From the mid-1990s through 2000, when the technology bubble burst, international and U.S. markets moved more closely together than usual. The increased correlation between the U.S. asset and international asset classes caused some to question the wisdom of international diversification. Compounding the issue was the effect that the poor performance of international markets had in a diversified portfolio during the heady days of the bull market in the late 1990s. Although investors are often willing to accept less risk in the form of less volatility of their portfolios, it is not as easy to recognize the benefits of diversification when the diversified portfolio lags behind a pure U.S. equity portfolio.

In terms of pure risk-adjusted reward, diversification does work. It is safe to say that international markets and U.S. markets will never be entirely perfectly correlated. The easiest way to diversify a portfolio is to include an international or global mutual fund in an investment portfolio. The professional portfolio managers have more experience in navigating the international markets than does the average investor.

■ *International mutual funds do not include any domestic assets whereas global mutual funds include both foreign and domestic assets. How might this difference affect their correlation with U.S. equity mutual funds?*

---

where unstable or ideologically motivated governments may attempt to block return of profits by foreign investors or even seize (nationalize) their assets in the host country. An example of political risk was the heightened concern during 2003–2004 that Operation Enduring Freedom would damage oil production facilities in Iraq and cause a worldwide oil shortage and higher gas prices. This concern was indeed validated by the rapid rise in fuel prices that began early in 2004 and continued throughout the year.

Even where governments do not impose exchange controls or seize assets, international investors may suffer if a shortage of hard currency prevents payment of dividends or interest to foreigners. When governments are forced to allocate scarce foreign exchange, they rarely give top priority to the interests of foreign investors. Instead, hard-currency reserves are typically used to pay for necessary imports such as food, medicine, and industrial materials and to pay interest on the government's debt. Because most of the debt of developing countries is held by banks rather than individuals, foreign investors are often badly harmed when a country experiences political or economic problems.

For more discussion of reducing risk through international diversification, see the *In Practice* box above.

Review Questions

5–8 Why must assets be evaluated in a portfolio context? What is an *efficient portfolio*?

5–9 Why is the *correlation* between asset returns important? How does diversification allow risky assets to be combined so that the risk of the portfolio is less than the risk of the individual assets in it?

5–10 How does international diversification enhance risk reduction? When might international diversification result in subpar returns? What are *political risks,* and how do they affect international diversification?

Risk and Return: The Capital Asset Pricing Model (CAPM)

The most important aspect of risk is the *overall risk* of the firm as viewed by investors in the marketplace. Overall risk significantly affects investment opportunities and—even more important—the owners' wealth. The basic theory that links risk and return for all assets is the **capital asset pricing model (CAPM)**.[5] We will use CAPM to understand the basic risk–return tradeoffs involved in all types of financial decisions.

capital asset pricing model (CAPM)
The basic theory that links risk and return for all assets.

Types of Risk

To understand the basic types of risk, consider what happens to the risk of a portfolio consisting of a single security (asset), to which we add securities randomly selected from, say, the population of all actively traded securities. Using the standard deviation of return, σ_{k_p}, to measure the total portfolio risk, Figure 5.5 (see page 212) depicts the behavior of the total portfolio risk (y axis) as more securities are added (x axis). With the addition of securities, the total portfolio risk declines, as a result of the effects of diversification, and tends to approach a lower limit. Research has shown that, on average, most of the risk-reduction benefits of diversification can be gained by forming portfolios containing 15 to 20 randomly selected securities.

The **total risk** of a security can be viewed as consisting of two parts:

$$\text{Total security risk} = \text{Nondiversifiable risk} + \text{Diversifiable risk} \qquad (5.5)$$

total risk
The combination of a security's *nondiversifiable risk* and *diversifiable risk*.

diversifiable risk
The portion of an asset's risk that is attributable to firm-specific, random causes; can be eliminated through diversification. Also called *unsystematic risk*.

nondiversifiable risk
The relevant portion of an asset's risk attributable to market factors that affect all firms; cannot be eliminated through diversification. Also called *systematic risk*.

Diversifiable risk (sometimes called *unsystematic risk*) represents the portion of an asset's risk that is associated with random causes that can be eliminated through diversification. It is attributable to firm-specific events, such as strikes, lawsuits, regulatory actions, and loss of a key account. **Nondiversifiable risk** (also called *systematic risk*) is attributable to market factors that affect all firms; it

---

[5]. The initial development of this theory is generally attributed to William F. Sharpe, "Capital Asset Prices: A Theory of Market Equilibrium Under Conditions of Risk," *Journal of Finance* 19 (September 1964), pp. 425–442, and John Lintner, "The Valuation of Risk Assets and the Selection of Risky Investments in Stock Portfolios and Capital Budgets," *Review of Economics and Statistics* 47 (February 1965), pp. 13–37. A number of authors subsequently advanced, refined, and tested this now widely accepted theory.

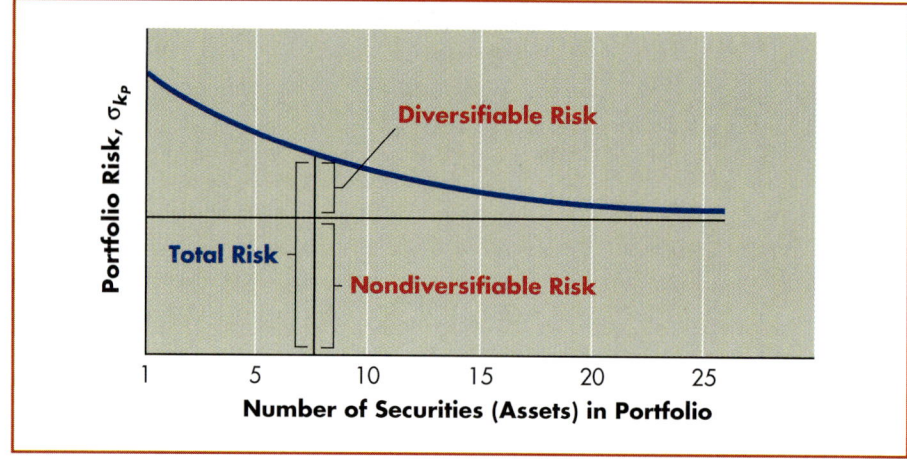

FIGURE 5.5

Risk Reduction
Portfolio risk and diversification

cannot be eliminated through diversification. (It is the shareholder-specific *market risk* described in Table 5.1.) Factors such as war, inflation, international incidents, and political events account for nondiversifiable risk.

Because any investor can create a portfolio of assets that will eliminate virtually all diversifiable risk, *the only relevant risk is nondiversifiable risk*. Any investor or firm therefore must be concerned solely with nondiversifiable risk. The measurement of nondiversifiable risk is thus of primary importance in selecting assets with the most desired risk–return characteristics.

The Model: CAPM

The capital asset pricing model (CAPM) links nondiversifiable risk and return for all assets. We will discuss the model in five sections. The first deals with the beta coefficient, which is a measure of nondiversifiable risk. The second section presents an equation of the model itself, and the third graphically describes the relationship between risk and return. The fourth section discusses the effects of changes in inflationary expectations and risk aversion on the relationship between risk and return. The final section offers some comments on the CAPM.

Beta Coefficient

beta coefficient (*b*)
A relative measure of nondiversifiable risk. An *index* of the degree of movement of an asset's return in response to a change in the *market return*.

market return
The return on the market portfolio of all traded securities.

The **beta coefficient**, *b*, is a relative measure of nondiversifiable risk. It is an *index* of the degree of movement of an asset's return in response to a change in the *market return*. An asset's historical returns are used in finding the asset's beta coefficient. The **market return** is the return on the market portfolio of all traded securities. The *Standard & Poor's 500 Stock Composite Index* or some similar stock index is commonly used as the market return. Betas for actively traded stocks can be obtained from a variety of sources, but you should understand how they are derived and interpreted and how they are applied to portfolios.

Deriving Beta from Return Data An asset's historical returns are used in finding the asset's beta coefficient. Figure 5.6 plots the relationship between the returns of two assets—R and S—and the market return. Note that the horizontal (*x*) axis measures the historical market returns and that the vertical (*y*) axis meas-

FIGURE 5.6

Beta Derivation[a]

Graphical derivation of beta for assets R and S

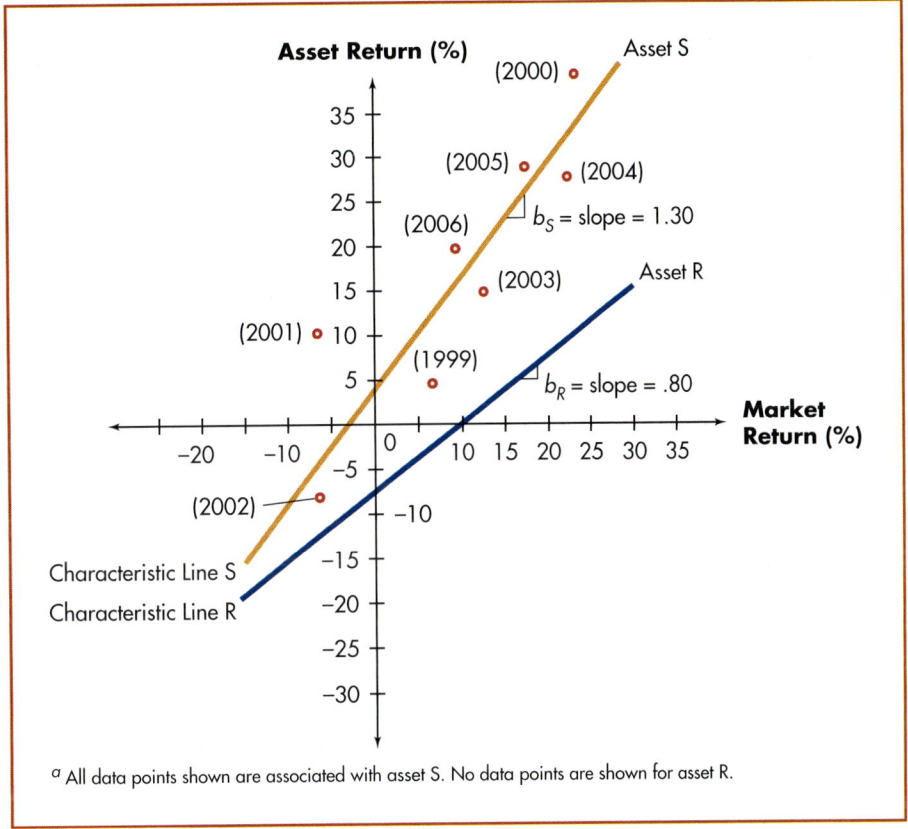

[a] All data points shown are associated with asset S. No data points are shown for asset R.

ures the individual asset's historical returns. The first step in deriving beta involves plotting the coordinates for the market return and asset returns from various points in time. Such annual "market return–asset return" coordinates are shown *for asset S only* for the years 1999 through 2006. For example, in 2006, asset S's return was 20 percent when the market return was 10 percent. By use of statistical techniques, the "characteristic line" that best explains the relationship between the asset return and the market return coordinates is fit to the data points. The slope of this line is *beta*. The beta for asset R is about .80 and that for asset S is about 1.30. Asset S's higher beta (steeper characteristic line slope) indicates that its return is more responsive to changing market returns. *Therefore asset S is more risky than asset R.*

Interpreting Betas The beta coefficient for the market is considered to be equal to 1.0. All other betas are viewed in relation to this value. Asset betas may be positive or negative, but positive betas are the norm. The majority of beta coefficients fall between .5 and 2.0. The return of a stock that is half as responsive as the market ($b = .5$) is expected to change by 1/2 percent for each 1 percent change in the return of the market portfolio. A stock that is twice as responsive as the market ($b = 2.0$) is expected to experience a 2 percent change in its return for each 1 percent change in the return of the market portfolio. Table 5.9 (see page 214) provides various beta values and their interpretations. Beta coefficients for actively traded stocks can be obtained from published sources such as *Value Line*

Hint Remember that published betas are calculated using historical data. When investors use beta for decision making, they should recognize that past performance relative to the market average may not accurately predict future performance.

TABLE 5.9 Selected Beta Coefficients and Their Interpretations

Beta	Comment	Interpretation
2.0	Move in same direction as market	Twice as responsive as the market
1.0		Same response as the market
.5		Only half as responsive as the market
0		Unaffected by market movement
−.5	Move in opposite direction to market	Only half as responsive as the market
−1.0		Same response as the market
−2.0		Twice as responsive as the market

Investment Survey, via the Internet, or through brokerage firms. Betas for some selected stocks are given in Table 5.10.

Portfolio Betas The beta of a portfolio can be easily estimated by using the betas of the individual assets it includes. Letting w_j represent the proportion of the portfolio's total dollar value represented by asset j, and letting b_j equal the beta of asset j, we can use Equation 5.6 to find the portfolio beta, b_p:

$$b_p = (w_1 \times b_1) + (w_2 \times b_2) + \cdots + (w_n \times b_n) = \sum_{j=1}^{n} w_j \times b_j \quad (5.6)$$

Hint Mutual fund managers are key users of the portfolio beta and return concepts. They are continually evaluating what would happen to the fund's beta and return if the securities of a particular firm were added to or deleted from the fund's portfolio.

Of course, $\sum_{j=1}^{n} w_j = 1$, which means that 100 percent of the portfolio's assets must be included in this computation.

Portfolio betas are interpreted in the same way as the betas of individual assets. They indicate the degree of responsiveness of the *portfolio's* return to changes in the market return. For example, when the market return increases by 10 percent, a portfolio with a beta of .75 will experience a 7.5 percent increase in

TABLE 5.10 Beta Coefficients for Selected Stocks (October 22, 2004)

Stock	Beta	Stock	Beta
Amazon.com	1.55	JP Morgan Chase & Co.	1.50
Anheuser-Busch	.60	Merrill Lynch & Co.	1.55
DaimlerChrysler AG	1.20	Microsoft	1.10
Disney	1.30	Nike, Inc.	.90
eBay	1.40	PepsiCo, Inc.	.65
ExxonMobil Corp.	.80	Qualcomm	1.15
Gap (The), Inc.	1.35	Sempra Energy	.90
General Electric	1.30	Wal-Mart Stores	.95
Intel	1.35	Xerox	1.45
Int'l Business Machines	1.05	Yahoo! Inc.	1.80

Source: Value Line Investment Survey (New York: Value Line Publishing, October 22, 2004).

its return (.75 × 10%); a portfolio with a beta of 1.25 will experience a 12.5 percent increase in its return (1.25 × 10%). Clearly, a portfolio containing mostly low-beta assets will have a low beta, and one containing mostly high-beta assets will have a high beta.

EXAMPLE

The Austin Fund, a large investment company, wishes to assess the risk of two portfolios it is considering assembling—V and W. Both portfolios contain five assets, with the proportions and betas shown in Table 5.11. The betas for the two portfolios, b_v and b_w, can be calculated by substituting data from the table into Equation 5.6:

$$b_v = (.10 \times 1.65) + (.30 \times 1.00) + (.20 \times 1.30) + (.20 \times 1.10) + (.20 \times 1.25)$$
$$= .165 + .300 + .260 + .220 + .250 = 1.195 \approx \underline{\underline{1.20}}$$

$$b_w = (.10 \times .80) + (.10 \times 1.00) + (.20 \times .65) + (.10 \times .75) + (.50 \times 1.05)$$
$$= .080 + .100 + .130 + .075 + .525 = \underline{\underline{.91}}$$

Portfolio V's beta is about 1.20, and portfolio W's is .91. These values make sense, because portfolio V contains relatively high-beta assets, and portfolio W contains relatively low-beta assets. Clearly, portfolio V's returns are more responsive to changes in market returns and are therefore more risky than portfolio W's. ■

The Equation

Using the beta coefficient to measure nondiversifiable risk, the *capital asset pricing model (CAPM)* is given in Equation 5.7:

$$k_j = R_F + [b_j \times (k_m - R_F)] \tag{5.7}$$

where

k_j = required return on asset j

R_F = risk-free rate of return, commonly measured by the return on a U.S. Treasury bill

b_j = beta coefficient or index of nondiversifiable risk for asset j

k_m = market return; return on the market portfolio of assets

TABLE 5.11 Austin Fund's Portfolios V and W

	Portfolio V		Portfolio W	
Asset	Proportion	Beta	Proportion	Beta
1	.10	1.65	.10	.80
2	.30	1.00	.10	1.00
3	.20	1.30	.20	.65
4	.20	1.10	.10	.75
5	.20	1.25	.50	1.05
Totals	1.00		1.00	

risk-free rate of return, (R_F)
The required return on a *risk-free asset*, typically a 3-month U.S. Treasury bill.

U.S. Treasury bills (T-bills)
Short-term IOUs issued by the U.S. Treasury; considered the *risk-free asset*.

The CAPM can be divided into two parts: (1) the **risk-free rate of return, R_F**, which is the required return on a *risk-free asset*, typically a 3-month **U.S. Treasury bill** (T-bill), a short-term IOU issued by the U.S. Treasury, and (2) the *risk premium*. These are, respectively, the two elements on either side of the plus sign in Equation 5.7. The $(k_m - R_F)$ portion of the risk premium is called the *market risk premium*, because it represents the premium the investor must receive for taking the average amount of risk associated with holding the market portfolio of assets.[6]

Historical Risk Premiums Using the historical return data for selected security investments for the 1926–2003 period shown in Table 5.2, we can calculate the risk premiums for each investment category. The calculation (consistent with Equation 5.7) involves merely subtracting the historical U.S. Treasury bill's average return from the historical average return for a given investment:

Investment	Risk premium[a]
Large-company stocks	12.4% − 3.8% = 8.6%
Small company stocks	17.5 − 3.8 = 13.7
Long-term corporate bonds	6.2 − 3.8 = 2.4
Long-term government bonds	5.8 − 3.8 = 2.0
U.S. Treasury bills	3.8 − 3.8 = 0.0

[a]Return values obtained from Table 5.2.

Reviewing the risk premiums calculated above, we can see that the risk premium is highest for small-company stocks, followed by large-company stocks, long-term corporate bonds, and long-term government bonds. This outcome makes sense intuitively because small-company stocks are riskier than large-company stocks, which are riskier than long-term corporate bonds (equity is riskier than debt investment). Long-term corporate bonds are riskier than long-term government bonds (because the government is less likely to renege on debt). And of course, U.S. Treasury bills, because of their lack of default risk and their very short maturity, are virtually risk-free, as indicated by their lack of any risk premium.

EXAMPLE

Benjamin Corporation, a growing computer software developer, wishes to determine the required return on an asset Z, which has a beta of 1.5. The risk-free rate of return is 7%; the return on the market portfolio of assets is 11%. Substituting $b_Z = 1.5$, $R_F = 7\%$, and $k_m = 11\%$ into the capital asset pricing model given in Equation 5.7 yields a required return of

$$k_Z = 7\% + [1.5 \times (11\% - 7\%)] = 7\% + 6\% = \underline{\underline{13\%}}$$

---

6. Although CAPM has been widely accepted, a broader theory, *arbitrage pricing theory (APT)*, first described by Stephen A. Ross, "The Arbitrage Theory of Capital Asset Pricing," *Journal of Economic Theory* (December 1976), pp. 341–360, has received a great deal of attention in the financial literature. The theory suggests that the risk premium on securities may be better explained by a number of factors underlying and in place of the market return used in CAPM. The CAPM in effect can be viewed as being derived from APT. Although testing of APT confirms the importance of the market return, it has thus far failed to identify other risk factors clearly. As a result of this failure, as well as APT's lack of practical acceptance and usage, we concentrate our attention here on CAPM.

The market risk premium of 4% (11% − 7%), when adjusted for the asset's index of risk (beta) of 1.5, results in a risk premium of 6% (1.5 × 4%). That risk premium, when added to the 7% risk-free rate, results in a 13% required return. ■

Other things being equal, *the higher the beta, the higher the required return, and the lower the beta, the lower the required return.*

The Graph: The Security Market Line (SML)

security market line (SML)
The depiction of the *capital asset pricing model (CAPM)* as a graph that reflects the required return in the marketplace for each level of nondiversifiable risk (beta).

When the capital asset pricing model (Equation 5.7) is depicted graphically, it is called the **security market line (SML)**. The SML will, in fact, be a straight line. It reflects the required return in the marketplace for each level of nondiversifiable risk (beta). In the graph, risk as measured by beta, b, is plotted on the x axis, and required returns, k, are plotted on the y axis. The risk–return tradeoff is clearly represented by the SML.

EXAMPLE

In the preceding example for Benjamin Corporation, the risk-free rate, R_F, was 7%, and the market return, k_m, was 11%. The SML can be plotted by using the two sets of coordinates for the betas associated with R_F and k_m, b_{R_F} and b_m (that is, $b_{R_F} = 0$,[7] $R_F = 7\%$; and $b_m = 1.0$, $k_m = 11\%$). Figure 5.7 presents the resulting security market line. As traditionally shown, the security market line in Figure 5.7 depicts the required return associated with all positive betas. The market risk premium of 4% (k_m of 11% − R_F of 7%) has been highlighted. For a beta for asset Z, b_Z, of 1.5, its corresponding required return, k_Z, is 13%. Also shown in

FIGURE 5.7

Security Market Line
Security market line (SML) with Benjamin Corporation's asset Z data shown

---

7. Because R_F is the rate of return on a risk-free asset, the beta associated with the risk-free asset, b_{R_F}, would equal 0. The zero beta on the risk-free asset reflects not only its absence of risk but also that the asset's return is unaffected by movements in the market return.

the figure is asset Z's risk premium of 6% (k_Z of 13% − R_F of 7%). It should be clear that for assets with betas greater than 1, the risk premium is greater than that for the market; for assets with betas less than 1, the risk premium is less than that for the market.

Some Comments on CAPM

The capital asset pricing model generally relies on historical data. The betas may or may not actually reflect the *future* variability of returns. Therefore, the required returns specified by the model can be viewed only as rough approximations. Users of betas commonly make subjective adjustments to the historically determined betas to reflect their expectations of the future.

The CAPM was developed to explain the behavior of security prices and provide a mechanism whereby investors could assess the impact of a proposed security investment on their portfolio's overall risk and return. It is based on an assumed **efficient market** with the following characteristics: many small investors, all having the same information and expectations with respect to securities; no restrictions on investment, no taxes, and no transaction costs; and rational investors, who view securities similarly and are risk-averse, preferring higher returns and lower risk.

Although the perfect world of the efficient market appears to be unrealistic, studies have provided support for the existence of the expectational relationship described by CAPM in active markets such as the New York Stock Exchange.[8] In the case of real corporate assets, such as plant and equipment, research thus far has failed to prove the general applicability of CAPM because of indivisibility, relatively large size, limited number of transactions, and absence of an efficient market for such assets.

Despite the limitations of CAPM, it provides a useful conceptual framework for evaluating and linking risk and return. An awareness of this tradeoff and an attempt to consider risk as well as return in financial decision making should help financial managers achieve their goals.

efficient market
A market with the following characteristics: many small investors, all having the same information and expectations with respect to securities; no restrictions on investment, no taxes, and no transaction costs; and rational investors, who view securities similarly and are risk-averse, preferring higher returns and lower risk.

Review Questions

5–11 How are total risk, nondiversifiable risk, and diversifiable risk related? Why is nondiversifiable risk the *only relevant risk*?

5–12 What risk does *beta* measure? How can you find the beta of a portfolio?

5–13 Explain the meaning of each variable in the *capital asset pricing model (CAPM)* equation. What is the *security market line (SML)*?

5–14 Why do financial managers have some difficulty applying CAPM in financial decision making? Generally, what benefit does CAPM provide them?

---

8. A study by Eugene F. Fama and Kenneth R. French, "The Cross-Section of Expected Stock Returns," *Journal of Finance* 47 (June 1992), pp. 427–465, raised serious questions about the validity of CAPM. The study failed to find a significant relationship between the *historical* betas and *historical* returns on over 2,000 stocks during 1963–1990. In other words, it found that the magnitude of a stock's *historical* beta had no relationship to the level of its *historical* return. Although Fama and French's study continues to receive attention, CAPM has not been abandoned because its rejection as a *historical* model fails to discredit its validity as an *expectational* model. Therefore, in spite of this challenge, CAPM continues to be viewed as a logical and useful framework—both conceptually and operationally—for linking *expected* nondiversifiable risk and return.

Summary

FOCUS ON VALUE

A firm's risk and expected return directly affect its share price. As we shall see in Chapter 7, risk and return are the two key determinants of the firm's value. It is therefore the financial manager's responsibility to assess carefully the risk and return of all major decisions so as to ensure that the expected returns justify the level of risk being introduced.

The way the financial manager can expect to achieve **the firm's goal of increasing its share price** (and thereby benefiting its owners) is to take only those actions that earn returns at least commensurate with their risk. Clearly, financial managers need to recognize, measure, and evaluate risk–return tradeoffs to ensure that their decisions contribute to the creation of value for owners.

REVIEW OF LEARNING GOALS

Key definitions and formulas for this chapter are summarized in Table 5.12 (see page 220).

LG1 **Understand the meaning and fundamentals of risk, return, and risk aversion.** Risk is the chance of loss or, more formally, the variability of returns. A number of sources of firm-specific and shareholder-specific risks exist. Return is any cash distributions plus the change in value expressed as a percentage of the initial value. Investment returns vary both over time and between different types of investments. Most financial decision makers are risk-averse. They require higher expected returns as compensation for taking greater risk.

LG2 **Describe procedures for assessing and measuring the risk of a single asset.** The risk of a single asset is measured in much the same way as the risk of a portfolio of assets. Sensitivity analysis and probability distributions can be used to assess risk. Probability distributions, both bar charts and continuous distributions, can be used to assess an asset's general level of risk.

LG3 **Discuss risk measurement for a single asset using the standard deviation and coefficient of variation.** In addition to the range, which is the optimistic (best) outcome minus the pessimistic (worst) outcome, the standard deviation and the coefficient of variation can be used to measure risk quantitatively. The standard deviation measures the dispersion around an asset's expected value, and the coefficeint of variation uses the standard deviation to measure dispersion on a relative basis.

LG4 **Understand the risk and return characteristics of a portfolio in terms of correlation and diversification, and the impact of international assets on a portfolio.** The financial manager's goal is to create an efficient portfolio that maximizes return for a given level of risk. The risk of a portfolio of assets may be reduced by diversification—combining assets with low correlation to reduce the risk of the portfolio. Correlation, the statistical relationship between asset returns, affects diversification. The more negative (or less positive) the correlation, the greater the risk-reducing benefits of diversification.

International diversification can be used to reduce a portfolio's risk further. Foreign assets have the risk of currency fluctuation and political risks.

LG5 **Review the two types of risk and the derivation and role of beta in measuring the relevant risk of both an individual security and a portfolio.** The total risk of a security consists of nondiversifiable and diversifiable risk. Diversifiable risk can be eliminated through diversification. Nondiversifiable risk is the only relevant risk.

TABLE 5.12 Summary of Key Definitions and Formulas for Risk and Return

Definitions of variables

- b_j = beta coefficient or index of nondiversifiable risk for asset j
- b_p = portfolio beta
- C_t = cash received from the asset investment in the time period $t-1$ to t
- CV = coefficient of variation
- $\bar{k}$ = expected value of a return
- k_j = return for the jth outcome; return on asset j; required return on asset j
- k_m = market return; the return on the market portfolio of assets
- k_t = actual, expected, or required rate of return during period t
- n = number of outcomes considered
- P_t = price (value) of asset at time t
- P_{t-1} = price (value) of asset at time $t-1$
- Pr_j = probability of occurrence of the jth outcome
- R_F = risk-free rate of return
- σ_k = standard deviation of returns
- w_j = proportion of total portfolio dollar value represented by asset j

Risk and return formulas

Rate of return during period t:

$$k_t = \frac{C_t + P_t - P_{t-1}}{P_{t-1}} \qquad \text{[Equation 5.1]}$$

Expected value of a return:
For probabilistic data:

$$\bar{k} = \sum_{j=1}^{n} k_j \times Pr_j \qquad \text{[Equation 5.2]}$$

General formula:

$$\bar{k} = \frac{\sum_{j=1}^{n} k_j}{n} \qquad \text{[Equation 5.2a]}$$

Standard deviation of return:
For probabilistic data:

$$\sigma_k = \sqrt{\sum_{j=1}^{n} (k_j - \bar{k})^2 \times Pr_j} \qquad \text{[Equation 5.3]}$$

General formula:

$$\sigma_k = \sqrt{\frac{\sum_{j=1}^{n} (k_j - \bar{k})^2}{n-1}} \qquad \text{[Equation 5.3a]}$$

Coefficient of variation:

$$CV = \frac{\sigma_k}{\bar{k}} \qquad \text{[Equation 5.4]}$$

Total security risk = Nondiversifiable risk + Diversifiable risk [Equation 5.5]

Portfolio beta:

$$b_p = \sum_{j=1}^{n} w_j \times b_j \qquad \text{[Equation 5.6]}$$

Capital asset pricing model (CAPM):

$$k_j = R_F + [b_j \times (k_m - R_F)] \qquad \text{[Equation 5.7]}$$

Nondiversifiable risk is measured by the beta coefficient, which is a relative measure of the relationship between an asset's return and the market return. Beta is derived by finding the slope of the "characteristic line" that best explains the historical relationship between the asset's return and the market return. The beta of a portfolio is a weighted average of the betas of the individual assets that it includes.

 Explain the capital asset pricing model (CAPM) and its relationship to the security market line (SML). The capital asset pricing model (CAPM) uses beta to relate an asset's risk relative to the market to the asset's required return. The graphical depiction of CAPM is the security market line (SML). Although it has some shortcomings, CAPM provides a useful conceptual framework for evaluating and linking risk and return.

SELF-TEST PROBLEMS (SOLUTIONS IN APPENDIX B)

  ST5–1 Portfolio analysis You have been asked for your advice in selecting a portfolio of assets and have been given the following data:

	Expected return		
Year	Asset A	Asset B	Asset C
2007	12%	16%	12%
2008	14	14	14
2009	16	12	16

No probabilities have been supplied. You have been told that you can create two portfolios—one consisting of assets A and B and the other consisting of assets A and C—by investing equal proportions (50%) in each of the two component assets.
a. What is the expected return for each asset over the 3-year period?
b. What is the standard deviation for each asset's return?
c. What is the expected return for each of the two portfolios?
d. How would you characterize the correlations of returns of the two assets making up each of the two portfolios identified in part c?
e. What is the standard deviation for each portfolio?
f. Which portfolio do you recommend? Why?

ST5–2 Beta and CAPM Currently under consideration is a project with a beta, b, of 1.50. At this time, the risk-free rate of return, R_F, is 7%, and the return on the market portfolio of assets, k_m, is 10%. The project is actually *expected* to earn an annual rate of return of 11%.
a. If the return on the market portfolio were to increase by 10%, what would you expect to happen to the project's *required return*? What if the market return were to decline by 10%?
b. Use the capital asset pricing model (CAPM) to find the *required return* on this investment.
c. On the basis of your calculation in part b, would you recommend this investment? Why or why not?
d. Assume that as a result of investors becoming less risk-averse, the market return drops by 1% to 9%. What impact would this change have on your responses in parts b and c?

WARM-UP EXERCISES

LG1 **E5–1** An analyst predicted last year that the stock of Logistics, Inc., would offer a total return of at least 10% in the coming year. At the beginning of the year, the firm had a stock market value of $10 million. At the end of the year, it had a market value of $12 million even though it experienced a loss, or negative net income, of $2.5 million. Did the analyst's prediction prove correct? Explain using the values for total annual return.

LG2 **E5–2** Four analysts cover the stock of Fluorine Chemical. One forecasts a 5% return for the coming year. A second expects the return to be negative 5%. A third predicts a 10% return. A fourth expects a 3% return in the coming year. You are relatively confident that the return will be positive but not large, so you arbitrarily assign probabilities of being correct of 35%, 5%, 20%, and 40%, respectively, to the analysts' forecasts. Given these probabilities, what is Fluorine Chemical's *expected return* for the coming year?

LG3 **E5–3** The expected annual returns are 15% for investment 1 and 12% for investment 2. The standard deviation of the first investment's return is 10%; the second investment's return has a standard deviation of 5%. Which investment is less risky based solely on *standard deviation*? Which investment is less risky based on *coefficient of variation*? Which is a better measure given that the expected returns of the two investments are not the same?

LG4 **E5–4** Your portfolio has three asset classes. U.S. government T-bills account for 45% of the portfolio, large-company stocks constitute another 40%, and small-company stocks make up the remaining 15%. If the expected returns are 3.8% for the T-bills, 12.4% for the large-company stocks, and 17.5% for the small-company stocks, what is the expected return of the portfolio?

LG5 **E5–5** You wish to calculate the risk level of your portfolio based on its beta. The five stocks in the portfolio with their respective weights and betas are as follows:

Stock	Portfolio weight	Beta
Alpha	20%	1.15
Centauri	10	.85
Zen	15	1.6
Wren	20	1.35
Yukos	35	1.85

Calculate the beta of your portfolio.

LG5 **LG6** **E5–6** a. Calculate the required rate of return for an asset that has a beta of 1.8, given a risk-free rate of 5% and a market return of 10%.
b. If investors have become more risk-averse due to recent geopolitical events, and the market return rises to 13%, what is the required rate of return for the same asset?

c. Use your findings in part **a.** to graph the initial *security market line (SML)*, and then use your findings in part **b.** to graph (on the same set of axes) the shift in the SML.
d. Compare and discuss the differences in the two SMLs plotted in part **c.**

PROBLEMS

BASIC

P5–1 **Rate of return** Douglas Keel, a financial analyst for Orange Industries, wishes to estimate the rate of return for two similar-risk investments, X and Y. Douglas's research indicates that the immediate past returns will serve as reasonable estimates of future returns. A year earlier, investment X had a market value of $20,000; investment Y had a market value of $55,000. During the year, investment X generated cash flow of $1,500 and investment Y generated cash flow of $6,800. The current market values of investments X and Y are $21,000 and $55,000, respectively.
 a. Calculate the expected rate of return on investments X and Y using the most recent year's data.
 b. Assuming that the two investments are equally risky, which one should Douglas recommend? Why?

BASIC

P5–2 **Return calculations** For each of the investments shown in the following table, calculate the rate of return earned over the unspecified time period.

Investment	Cash flow during period	Beginning-of-period value	End-of-period value
A	−$ 100	$ 800	$ 1,100
B	15,000	120,000	118,000
C	7,000	45,000	48,000
D	80	600	500
E	1,500	12,500	12,400

INTERMEDIATE

P5–3 **Risk aversion** Sharon Smith, the financial manager for Barnett Corporation, wishes to evaluate three prospective investments: X, Y, and Z. Currently, the firm earns 12% on its investments, which have a risk index of 6%. The expected return and expected risk of the investments are shown below. If Sharon Smith is *risk-averse*, which investment, if any, would she select? Why?

Investment	Expected return	Expected risk index
X	14%	7%
Y	12	8
Z	10	9

P5–4 Risk analysis Solar Designs is considering an investment in an expanded product line. Two possible types of expansion are being considered. After investigating the possible outcomes, the company made the estimates shown in the following table:

	Expansion A	Expansion B
Initial investment	$12,000	$12,000
Annual rate of return		
Pessimistic	16%	10%
Most likely	20%	20%
Optimistic	24%	30%

a. Determine the *range* of the rates of return for each of the two projects.
b. Which project is less risky? Why?
c. If you were making the investment decision, which one would you choose? Why? What does this imply about your feelings toward risk?
d. Assume that expansion B's most likely outcome is 21% per year and that all other facts remain the same. Does this change your answer to part **c**? Why?

P5–5 Risk and probability Micro-Pub, Inc., is considering the purchase of one of two microfilm cameras, R and S. Both should provide benefits over a 10-year period, and each requires an initial investment of $4,000. Management has constructed the following table of estimates of rates of return and probabilities for pessimistic, most likely, and optimistic results.

	Camera R		Camera S	
	Amount	Probability	Amount	Probability
Initial investment	$4,000	1.00	$4,000	1.00
Annual rate of return				
Pessimistic	20%	.25	15%	.20
Most likely	25%	.50	25%	.55
Optimistic	30%	.25	35%	.25

a. Determine the *range* for the rate of return for each of the two cameras.
b. Determine the *expected value* of return for each camera.
c. Purchase of which camera is riskier? Why?

P5–6 Bar charts and risk Swan's Sportswear is considering bringing out a line of designer jeans. Currently, it is negotiating with two different well-known designers. Because of the highly competitive nature of the industry, the two lines of jeans have been given code names. After market research, the firm has established the expectations shown in the table at the top of the facing page about the annual rates of return:

		Annual rate of return	
Market acceptance	Probability	Line J	Line K
Very poor	.05	.0075	.010
Poor	.15	.0125	.025
Average	.60	.0850	.080
Good	.15	.1475	.135
Excellent	.05	.1625	.150

Use the table to:
a. Construct a bar chart for each line's annual rate of return.
b. Calculate the *expected value* of return for each line.
c. Evaluate the relative riskiness for each jean line's rate of return using the bar charts.

P5–7 Coefficient of variation Metal Manufacturing has isolated four alternatives for meeting its need for increased production capacity. The data gathered relative to each of these alternatives are summarized in the following table:

Alternative	Expected return	Standard deviation of return
A	20%	7.0%
B	22	9.5
C	19	6.0
D	16	5.5

a. Calculate the *coefficient of variation* for each alternative.
b. If the firm wishes to minimize risk, which alternative do you recommend? Why?

P5–8 Assessing return and risk Swift Manufacturing must choose between two asset purchases. The annual rate of return and the related probabilities given in the following table summarize the firm's analysis to this point.

Project 257		Project 432	
Rate of return	Probability	Rate of return	Probability
−10%	.01	10%	.05
10	.04	15	.10
20	.05	20	.10
30	.10	25	.15
40	.15	30	.20
45	.30	35	.15
50	.15	40	.10
60	.10	45	.10
70	.05	50	.05
80	.04		
100	.01		

a. For each project, compute:
   (1) The range of possible rates of return.
   (2) The expected value of return.
   (3) The standard deviation of the returns.
   (4) The coefficient of variation of the returns.
b. Construct a bar chart of each distribution of rates of return.
c. Which project would you consider less risky? Why?

P5–9 **Integrative—Expected return, standard deviation, and coefficient of variation** Three assets—F, G, and H—are currently being considered by Perth Industries. The probability distributions of expected returns for these assets are shown in the following table:

	Asset F		Asset G		Asset H	
j	Pr_j	Return, k_j	Pr_j	Return, k_j	Pr_j	Return, k_j
1	.10	40%	.40	35%	.10	40%
2	.20	10	.30	10	.20	20
3	.40	0	.30	−20	.40	10
4	.20	−5			.20	0
5	.10	−10			.10	−20

a. Calculate the expected value of return, $\bar{k}$, for each of the three assets. Which provides the largest expected return?
b. Calculate the standard deviation, σ_k, for each of the three assets' returns. Which appears to have the greatest risk?
c. Calculate the coefficient of variation, CV, for each of the three assets' returns. Which appears to have the greatest *relative* risk?

P5–10 **Portfolio return and standard deviation** Jamie Wong is considering building a portfolio containing two assets, L and M. Asset L will represent 40% of the dollar value of the portfolio, and asset M will account for the other 60%. The expected returns over the next 6 years, 2007–2012, for each of these assets, are shown in the following table:

	Expected return	
Year	Asset L	Asset M
2007	14%	20%
2008	14	18
2009	16	16
2010	17	14
2011	17	12
2012	19	10

a. Calculate the expected portfolio return, k_p, for *each* of the 6 years.
b. Calculate the expected value of portfolio returns, $\bar{k}_p$, over the 6-year period.

c. Calculate the standard deviation of expected portfolio returns, σ_{k_p}, over the 6-year period.
d. How would you characterize the correlation of returns of the two assets L and M?
e. Discuss any benefits of diversification achieved through creation of the portfolio.

P5–11 **Portfolio analysis** You have been given the return data shown in the first table on three assets—F, G, and H—over the period 2007–2010.

	Expected return		
Year	Asset F	Asset G	Asset H
2007	16%	17%	14%
2008	17	16	15
2009	18	15	16
2010	19	14	17

Using these assets, you have isolated the three investment alternatives shown in the following table:

Alternative	Investment
1	100% of asset F
2	50% of asset F and 50% of asset G
3	50% of asset F and 50% of asset H

a. Calculate the expected return over the 4-year period for each of the three alternatives.
b. Calculate the standard deviation of returns over the 4-year period for each of the three alternatives.
c. Use your findings in parts a and b to calculate the coefficient of variation for each of the three alternatives.
d. On the basis of your findings, which of the three investment alternatives do you recommend? Why?

P5–12 **Correlation, risk, and return** Matt Peters wishes to evaluate the risk and return behaviors associated with various combinations of assets V and W under three assumed degrees of correlation: perfect positive, uncorrelated, and perfect negative. The expected return and risk values calculated for each of the assets are shown in the following table.

Asset	Expected return, $\bar{k}$	Risk (standard deviation), σ_k
V	8%	5%
W	13	10

a. If the returns of assets V and W are *perfectly positively correlated* (correlation coefficient = +1), describe the *range* of (1) expected return and (2) risk associated with all possible portfolio combinations.
b. If the returns of assets V and W are *uncorrelated* (correlation coefficient = 0), describe the *approximate range* of (1) expected return and (2) risk associated with all possible portfolio combinations.
c. If the returns of assets V and W are *perfectly negatively correlated* (correlation coefficient = −1), describe the *range* of (1) expected return and (2) risk associated with all possible portfolio combinations.

P5–13 **Total, nondiversifiable, and diversifiable risk** David Talbot randomly selected securities from all those listed on the New York Stock Exchange for his portfolio. He began with a single security and added securities one by one until a total of 20 securities were held in the portfolio. After each security was added, David calculated the portfolio standard deviation, σ_{k_p}. The calculated values are shown in the following table.

Number of securities	Portfolio risk, σ_{k_p}	Number of securities	Portfolio risk, σ_{k_p}
1	14.50%	11	7.00%
2	13.30	12	6.80
3	12.20	13	6.70
4	11.20	14	6.65
5	10.30	15	6.60
6	9.50	16	6.56
7	8.80	17	6.52
8	8.20	18	6.50
9	7.70	19	6.48
10	7.30	20	6.47

a. On a set of "number of securities in portfolio (*x* axis)–portfolio risk (*y* axis)" axes, plot the portfolio risk data given in the preceding table.
b. Divide the total portfolio risk in the graph into its *nondiversifiable* and *diversifiable* risk components and label each of these on the graph.
c. Describe which of the two risk components is the *relevant risk*, and explain why it is relevant. How much of this risk exists in David Talbot's portfolio?

P5–14 **Graphical derivation of beta** A firm wishes to estimate graphically the betas for two assets, A and B. It has gathered the return data shown in the table at the top of the facing page for the market portfolio and for both assets over the last 10 years, 1997–2006.
a. On a set of "market return (*x* axis)–asset return (*y* axis)" axes, use the data given to draw the characteristic line for asset A and for asset B.
b. Use the characteristic lines from part **a** to estimate the betas for assets A and B.
c. Use the betas found in part **b** to comment on the relative risks of assets A and B.

| | Actual return | | |
Year	Market portfolio	Asset A	Asset B
1997	6%	11%	16%
1998	2	8	11
1999	−13	−4	−10
2000	−4	3	3
2001	−8	0	−3
2002	16	19	30
2003	10	14	22
2004	15	18	29
2005	8	12	19
2006	13	17	26

P5–15 Interpreting beta A firm wishes to assess the impact of changes in the market return on an asset that has a beta of 1.20.
  a. If the market return increased by 15%, what impact would this change be expected to have on the asset's return?
  b. If the market return decreased by 8%, what impact would this change be expected to have on the asset's return?
  c. If the market return did not change, what impact, if any, would be expected on the asset's return?
  d. Would this asset be considered more or less risky than the market? Explain.

P5–16 Betas Answer the following questions for assets A to D shown in the following table.

Asset	Beta
A	.50
B	1.60
C	−.20
D	.90

  a. What impact would a *10% increase* in the market return be expected to have on each asset's return?
  b. What impact would a *10% decrease* in the market return be expected to have on each asset's return?
  c. If you were certain that the market return would *increase* in the near future, which asset would you prefer? Why?
  d. If you were certain that the market return would *decrease* in the near future, which asset would you prefer? Why?

P5–17 Betas and risk rankings Stock A has a beta of .80, stock B has a beta of 1.40, and stock C has a beta of −.30.
  a. Rank these stocks from the most risky to the least risky.
  b. If the return on the market portfolio increased by 12%, what change would you expect in the return for each of the stocks?

c. If the return on the market portfolio decreased by 5%, what change would you expect in the return for each of the stocks?
d. If you felt that the stock market was getting ready to experience a significant decline, which stock would you probably add to your portfolio? Why?
e. If you anticipated a major stock market rally, which stock would you add to your portfolio? Why?

P5–18 **Portfolio betas** Rose Berry is attempting to evaluate two possible portfolios, which consist of the same five assets held in different proportions. She is particularly interested in using beta to compare the risks of the portfolios, so she has gathered the data shown in the following table.

		Portfolio weights	
Asset	Asset beta	Portfolio A	Portfolio B
1	1.30	10%	30%
2	.70	30	10
3	1.25	10	20
4	1.10	10	20
5	.90	40	20
Totals		100%	100%

a. Calculate the betas for portfolios A and B.
b. Compare the risks of these portfolios to the market as well as to each other. Which portfolio is more risky?

P5–19 **Capital asset pricing model (CAPM)** For each of the cases shown in the following table, use the capital asset pricing model to find the required return.

Case	Risk-free rate, R_F	Market return, k_m	Beta, b
A	5%	8%	1.30
B	8	13	.90
C	9	12	−.20
D	10	15	1.00
E	6	10	.60

P5–20 **Beta coefficients and the capital asset pricing model** Katherine Wilson is wondering how much risk she must undertake to generate an acceptable return on her portfolio. The risk-free return currently is 5%. The return on the average stock (market return) is 16%. Use the CAPM to calculate the beta coefficient associated with each of the following portfolio returns.
a. 10%
b. 15%
c. 18%
d. 20%

e. Katherine is risk-averse. What is the highest return she can expect if she is unwilling to take more than an average risk?

P5–21 **Manipulating CAPM** Use the basic equation for the capital asset pricing model (CAPM) to work each of the following problems.
a. Find the *required return* for an asset with a beta of .90 when the risk-free rate and market return are 8% and 12%, respectively.
b. Find the *risk-free rate* for a firm with a required return of 15% and a beta of 1.25 when the market return is 14%.
c. Find the *market return* for an asset with a required return of 16% and a beta of 1.10 when the risk-free rate is 9%.
d. Find the *beta* for an asset with a required return of 15% when the risk-free rate and market return are 10% and 12.5%, respectively.

P5–22 **Security market line (SML)** Assume that the risk-free rate, R_F, is currently 9% and that the market return, k_m, is currently 13%.
a. Draw the security market line (SML) on a set of "nondiversifiable risk (x axis)–required return (y axis)" axes.
b. Calculate and label the *market risk premium* on the axes in part a.
c. Given the previous data, calculate the required return on asset A having a beta of .80 and asset B having a beta of 1.30.
d. Draw in the betas and required returns from part c for assets A and B on the axes in part a. Label the *risk premium* associated with each of these assets, and discuss them.

P5–23 **Integrative—Risk, return, and CAPM** Wolff Enterprises must consider several investment projects, A through E, using the capital asset pricing model (CAPM) and its graphical representation, the security market line (SML). Relevant information is presented in the following table.

Item	Rate of return	Beta, b
Risk-free asset	9%	0
Market portfolio	14	1.00
Project A	—	1.50
Project B	—	.75
Project C	—	2.00
Project D	—	0
Project E	—	−.5

a. Calculate (1) the required rate of return and (2) the risk premium for each project, given its level of nondiversifiable risk.
b. Use your findings in part a to draw the security market line (required return relative to nondiversifiable risk).
c. Discuss the relative nondiversifiable risk of projects A through E.

P5–24 **ETHICS PROBLEM** Integrity, especially honesty, is trait number one for being hired as a CFO in corporate America today. How might you assess a job candidate's honesty if you were interviewing a potential CFO candidate?

CHAPTER 5 CASE

Analyzing Risk and Return on Chargers Products' Investments

Junior Sayou, a financial analyst for Chargers Products, a manufacturer of stadium benches, must evaluate the risk and return of two assets, X and Y. The firm is considering adding these assets to its diversified asset portfolio. To assess the return and risk of each asset, Junior gathered data on the annual cash flow and beginning- and end-of-year values of each asset over the immediately preceding 10 years, 1997–2006. These data are summarized in the table below. Junior's investigation suggests that both assets, on average, will tend to perform in the future just as they have during the past 10 years. He therefore believes that the expected annual return can be estimated by finding the average annual return for each asset over the past 10 years.

Return Data for Assets X and Y, 1997–2006

	Asset X			Asset Y		
		Value			Value	
Year	Cash flow	Beginning	Ending	Cash flow	Beginning	Ending
1997	$1,000	$20,000	$22,000	$1,500	$20,000	$20,000
1998	1,500	22,000	21,000	1,600	20,000	20,000
1999	1,400	21,000	24,000	1,700	20,000	21,000
2000	1,700	24,000	22,000	1,800	21,000	21,000
2001	1,900	22,000	23,000	1,900	21,000	22,000
2002	1,600	23,000	26,000	2,000	22,000	23,000
2003	1,700	26,000	25,000	2,100	23,000	23,000
2004	2,000	25,000	24,000	2,200	23,000	24,000
2005	2,100	24,000	27,000	2,300	24,000	25,000
2006	2,200	27,000	30,000	2,400	25,000	25,000

Junior believes that each asset's risk can be assessed in two ways: in isolation and as part of the firm's diversified portfolio of assets. The risk of the assets in isolation can be found by using the standard deviation and coefficient of variation of returns over the past 10 years. The capital asset pricing model (CAPM) can be used to assess the asset's risk as part of the firm's portfolio of assets. Applying some sophisticated quantitative techniques, Junior estimated betas for assets X and Y of 1.60 and 1.10, respectively. In addition, he found that the risk-free rate is currently 7% and that the market return is 10%.

TO DO

a. Calculate the annual rate of return for each asset in *each* of the 10 preceding years, and use those values to find the average annual return for each asset over the 10-year period.

b. Use the returns calculated in part **a** to find (1) the standard deviation and (2) the coefficient of variation of the returns for each asset over the 10-year period 1997–2006.

c. Use your findings in parts **a** and **b** to evaluate and discuss the return and risk associated with each asset. Which asset appears to be preferable? Explain.
d. Use the CAPM to find the required return for each asset. Compare this value with the average annual returns calculated in part **a**.
e. Compare and contrast your findings in parts **c** and **d**. What recommendations would you give Junior with regard to investing in either of the two assets? Explain to Junior why he is better off using beta rather than the standard deviation and coefficient of variation to assess the risk of each asset.

SPREADSHEET EXERCISE

Jane is considering investing in three different stocks or creating three distinct two-stock portfolios. Jane considers herself to be a rather conservative investor. She is able to obtain forecasted returns for the three securities for the years 2007 through 2013. The data are as follows:

Year	Stock A	Stock B	Stock C
2007	10%	10%	12%
2008	13	11	14
2009	15	8	10
2010	14	12	11
2011	16	10	9
2012	14	15	9
2013	12	15	10

In any of the possible two-stock portfolios, the weight of each stock in the portfolio will be 50%. The three possible portfolio combinations are AB, AC, and BC.

TO DO

Create a spreadsheet similar to Table 5.7 (or the spreadsheets that can be viewed at www.aw-bc.com/gitman) to answer the following:

a. Calculate the expected return for each individual stock.
b. Calculate the standard deviation for each individual stock.
c. Calculate the expected returns for portfolios AB, AC, and BC.
d. Calculate the standard deviations for portfolios AB, AC, and BC.
e. Would you recommend that Jane invest in the single stock A or the portfolio consisting of stocks A and B? Explain your answer from a risk–return viewpoint.
f. Would you recommend that Jane invest in the single stock B or the portfolio consisting of stocks B and C? Explain your answer from a risk–return viewpoint.

WEB EXERCISE

One risk mentioned in the text is inflation risk. We have looked previously at interest rates on mortgages and yields on 10-year U.S. Treasury bonds. Here we will look at inflation rates in the United States over the past decades.

TO DO

Point your browser to the Bureau of Labor Statistics' home page at www.bls.gov/. Inflation and Consumer Spending is the first heading; under it you will find the link for the consumer price index (CPI). Here you can find information and data covering this most-familiar consumer inflation measure.

a. After acclimating yourself with this page and the general information on the CPI, go to Get Detailed CPI Statistics and highlight All Urban Consumers (Current Series). Select the first box, US All Items. At the bottom of the page, click "Retrieve Data." The table that is retrieved produces the index numbers with the time period of 1982–1984 = 100. You will need to convert this index into a percentage change at an annual rate. Choose More Formatting Options at the top of the page. On the next page, you will highlight the box for 12 months percent change. You also will change the data range to 1953 to the present. Now retrieve data again.

   At this point, you should have two tables, with the new one appearing at the bottom. Find the annual column that calculates the inflation rate for each year over the past 5 decades. Note the pattern of annual inflation rates. Compare it to the pattern exhibited in the 10-year Treasury bonds and the mortgage rate data from Chapter 4. While this is an annual series and you are comparing it to monthly data, you should still be able to discern a pattern between rising and falling rates of interest over time, as exhibited both in the 10-year series and the 30-year mortgage rate series, and rates of inflation, as measured by the CPI series.

b. Return to the CPI series, and look for any trends in the monthly rates that foretold the rising or falling rates shown in the annual column. For example, look at the 1972–1974 period. Rates of inflation at the annual level appear to have risen almost without warning from 3.2% to 6.2% to 11% over the 3 years. However, if you look at the monthly rates for the 3 years, you will see the increasing trend more clearly. Interest rates and yields would not be set only once a year with solely annual data. Instead, changes are incorporated minute by minute. A monthly frequency is better than an annual review and does capture much of any changing trend(s).

Remember to check the book's Web site at

www.aw-bc.com/gitman

for additional resources, including additional Web exercises.

Chapter 6

Interest Rates and Bond Valuation

LEARNING GOALS

LG1 Describe interest rate fundamentals, the term structure of interest rates, and risk premiums.

LG2 Review the legal aspects of bond financing and bond cost.

LG3 Discuss the general features, quotations, ratings, popular types, and international issues of corporate bonds.

LG4 Understand the key inputs and basic model used in the valuation process.

LG5 Apply the basic valuation model to bonds and describe the impact of required return and time to maturity on bond values.

LG6 Explain yield to maturity (YTM), its calculation, and the procedure used to value bonds that pay interest semiannually.

Across the Disciplines Why This Chapter Matters to You

Accounting: You need to understand interest rates and the various types of bonds to be able to account properly for amortization of bond premiums and discounts and for bond purchases and retirements.

Information systems: You need to understand the data that you will need to track in bond amortization schedules and bond valuation.

Management: You need to understand the behavior of interest rates and how they will affect the types of funds the firm can raise and the timing and cost of bond issues and retirements.

Marketing: You need to understand how the interest rate level and the firm's ability to issue bonds may affect the availability of financing for marketing research projects and new-product development.

Operations: You need to understand how the interest rate level may affect the firm's ability to raise funds to maintain and grow the firm's production capacity.

The interactions of suppliers and demanders of funds in the financial markets affect interest rates. The interest rates (returns) required by suppliers of funds also depend on the perceived risk of an asset. In this chapter, we apply the concepts of risk and return in a process called valuation. This chapter discusses interest rates, describes the key aspects of corporate bonds, and demonstrates the valuation process for the easiest financial asset to value, bonds.

Interest Rates and Required Returns

As noted in Chapter 1, financial institutions and markets create the mechanism through which funds flow between savers (funds suppliers) and investors (funds demanders). The level of funds flow between suppliers and demanders can significantly affect economic growth. Growth results from the interaction of a variety of economic factors (such as the money supply, trade balances, and economic policies) that affect the cost of money—the interest rate or required return.

The interest rate level acts as a regulating device that controls the flow of funds between suppliers and demanders. The *Board of Governors of the Federal Reserve System* regularly assesses economic conditions and, when necessary, initiates actions to raise or lower interest rates to control inflation and economic growth. Generally, the lower the interest rate, the greater the funds flow and therefore the greater the economic growth; the higher the interest rate, the lower the funds flow and economic growth.

Interest Rate Fundamentals

interest rate
The compensation paid by the borrower of funds to the lender; from the borrower's point of view, the cost of borrowing funds.

required return
The cost of funds obtained by selling an ownership interest; it reflects the funds supplier's level of expected return.

liquidity preferences
General preferences of investors for shorter-term securities.

real rate of interest
The rate that creates an equilibrium between the supply of savings and the demand for investment funds in a perfect world, without inflation, where funds suppliers and demanders are indifferent to the term of loans or investments and have no *liquidity preference*, and where all outcomes are certain.

The **interest rate** or required return represents the cost of money. It is the compensation that a demander of funds must pay a supplier. When funds are lent, the cost of borrowing the funds is the interest rate. When funds are obtained by selling an ownership interest—as in the sale of stock—the cost to the issuer (demander) is commonly called the **required return,** which reflects the funds supplier's level of expected return. In both cases the supplier is compensated for providing funds. Ignoring risk factors, the cost of funds results from the *real rate of interest* adjusted for inflationary expectations and **liquidity preferences**—general preferences of investors for shorter-term securities.

The Real Rate of Interest

Assume a *perfect world* in which there is no inflation and in which funds suppliers and demanders are indifferent to the term of loans or investments because they have no *liquidity preference* and all outcomes are certain.[1] At any given point in time in that perfect world, there would be one cost of money—the **real rate of interest.** The real rate of interest creates an equilibrium between the supply of savings and the demand for investment funds. It represents the most basic cost of money. The real rate of interest in the United States is assumed to be stable and

---

1. These assumptions are made to describe the most basic interest rate, the *real rate of interest*. Subsequent discussions relax these assumptions to develop the broader concept of the interest rate and required return.

FIGURE 6.1

Supply–Demand Relationship
Supply of savings and demand for investment funds

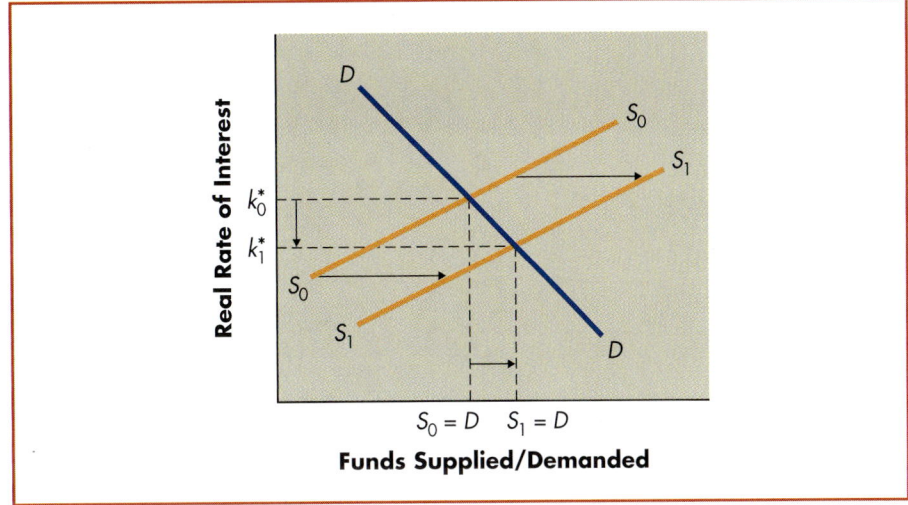

equal to around 1 percent.[2] This supply–demand relationship is shown in Figure 6.1 by the supply function (labeled S_0) and the demand function (labeled D). An equilibrium between the supply of funds and the demand for funds ($S_0 = D$) occurs at a rate of interest k_0^*, the real rate of interest.

Clearly, the real rate of interest changes with changing economic conditions, tastes, and preferences. A trade surplus could result in an increased supply of funds, causing the supply function in Figure 6.1 to shift to, say, S_1. This could result in a lower real rate of interest, k_1^*, at equilibrium ($S_1 = D$). Likewise, a change in tax laws or other factors could affect the demand for funds, causing the real rate of interest to rise or fall to a new equilibrium level.

Inflation and the Cost of Money

Ignoring risk factors, the cost of funds—the interest rate or rquired return—is closely tied to inflationary expectations. This can be demonstrated by using the **risk-free rate of interest, R_F,** which was defined in Chapter 5 as the required return on the risk-free asset. The risk-free asset is typically considered to be a 3-month *U.S. Treasury bill* (*T-bill*), which is a short-term IOU issued regularly by the U.S. Treasury.

Figure 6.2 (see page 238) illustrates the annual movement of the rate of inflation and the risk-free rate of return during the period 1978–2004. During this period the two rates tended to move in a similar fashion. Between 1978 and the early 1980s, inflation and interest rates were quite high, peaking at over 13 percent in 1980–1981. Since 1981 these rates have declined to levels generally below those in 1978. Note that during 2003 and 2004 the annual rate of inflation actually exceeded the average 3-month Treasury bill rate. The data in Figure 6.2 clearly illustrate the significant impact of inflation on the nominal rate of interest for the risk-free asset.

risk-free rate of interest, R_F
The required return on a risk-free asset, typically a 3-month U.S. Treasury bill (T-bill).

---

2. Data in *Stocks, Bonds, Bills and Inflation, 2004 Yearbook* (Chicago: Ibbotson Associates, Inc., 2004), show that over the period 1926–2003, U.S. Treasury bills provided an average annual real rate of return of about 0.70 percent. Because of certain major economic events that occurred during the 1926–2003 period, many economists believe that the real rate of interest during recent years has been about 1 percent.

FIGURE 6.2

Impact of Inflation
Relationship between annual rate of inflation and 3-month U.S. Treasury bill average annual returns, 1978–2004

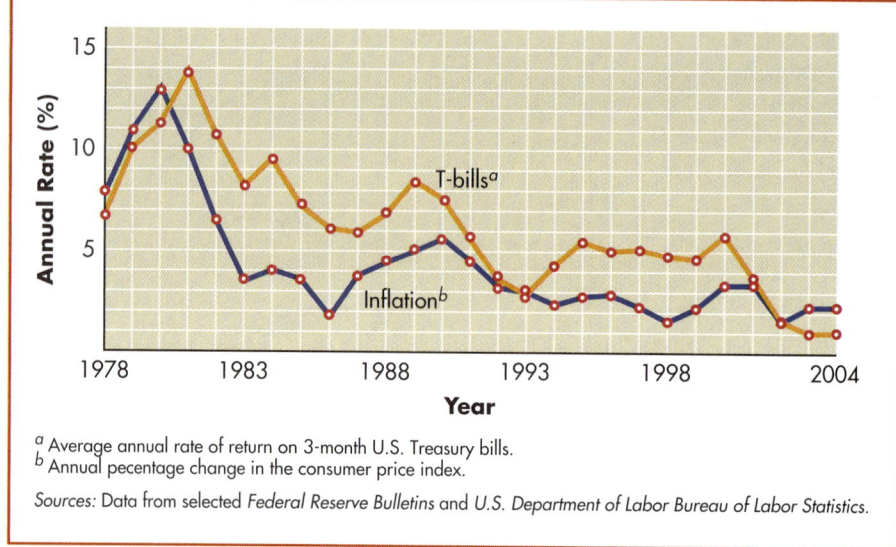

a Average annual rate of return on 3-month U.S. Treasury bills.
b Annual pecentage change in the consumer price index.

Sources: Data from selected *Federal Reserve Bulletins* and *U.S. Department of Labor Bureau of Labor Statistics.*

term structure of interest rates
The relationship between the interest rate or rate of return and the time to maturity.

yield to maturity
Annual rate of return earned on a debt security purchased on a given day and held to maturity.

yield curve
A graph of the relationship between the debt's remaining time to maturity (*x* axis) and its yield to maturity (*y* axis); it shows the yield to maturity for debts of equal quality and different maturities. Graphically depicts the *term structure of interest rates.*

inverted yield curve
A *downward-sloping* yield curve that indicates generally cheaper long-term borrowing costs than short-term borrowing costs.

normal yield curve
An *upward-sloping* yield curve that indicates generally cheaper short-term borrowing costs than long-term borrowing costs.

flat yield curve
A yield curve that reflects relatively similar borrowing costs for both short- and longer-term loans.

Term Structure of Interest Rates

For any class of similar-risk securities, the **term structure of interest rates** relates the interest rate or rate of return to the time to maturity. For convenience we will use Treasury securities as an example, but other classes could include securities that have similar overall quality or risk. The riskless nature of Treasury securities also provides a laboratory in which to develop the term structure.

Yield Curves

A debt security's **yield to maturity** (discussed later in this chapter) represents the annual rate of return earned on a debt security purchased on a given day and held to maturity. At any point in time, the relationship between the debt's remaining time to maturity and its yield to maturity is represented by the **yield curve.** The yield curve shows the yield to maturity for debts of equal quality and different maturities; it is a graphical depiction of the *term structure of interest rates.* Figure 6.3 shows three yield curves for all U.S. Treasury securities: one at May 22, 1981, a second at September 29, 1989, and a third at May 17, 2004.

Note that both the position and the shape of the yield curves change over time. The yield curve of May 22, 1981, indicates that short-term interest rates at that time were above longer-term rates. This curve is described as *downward-sloping,* reflecting long-term borrowing costs generally cheaper than short-term borrowing costs. Historically, the downward-sloping yield curve, which is often called an **inverted yield curve,** has been the exception. More frequently, yield curves similar to that of May 17, 2004, have existed. These *upward-sloping* or **normal yield curves** indicate that short-term borrowing costs are below long-term borrowing costs. Sometimes, a **flat yield curve,** similar to that of September 29, 1989, exists. It reflects relatively similar borrowing costs for both short- and longer-term loans.

The shape of the yield curve may affect the firm's financing decisions. A financial manager who faces a downward-sloping yield curve is likely to rely

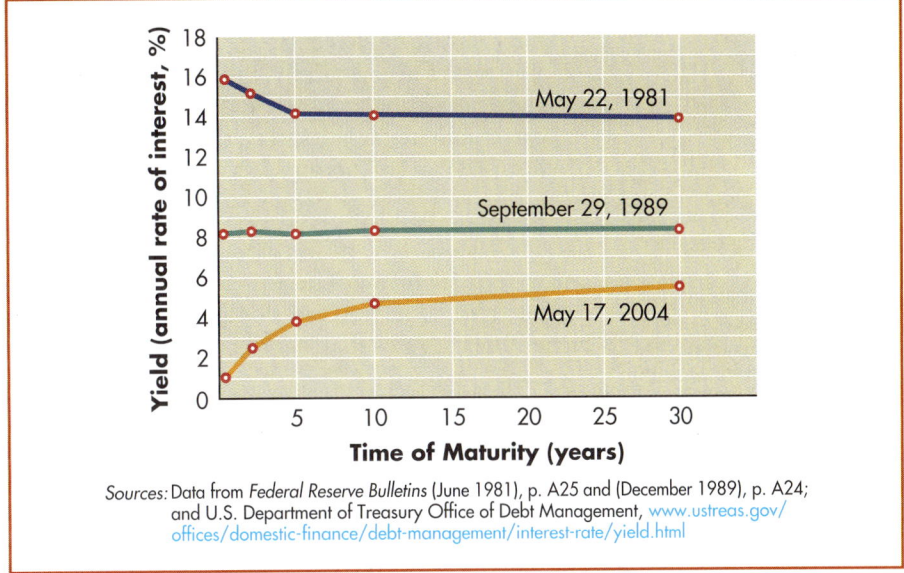

FIGURE 6.3

Treasury Yield Curves
Yield curves for U.S. Treasury securities: May 22, 1981; September 29, 1989; and May 17, 2004

more heavily on cheaper, long-term financing; when the yield curve is upward-sloping, the manager is more likely to use cheaper, short-term financing. Although a variety of other factors influence the choice of loan maturity, the shape of the yield curve provides useful insights into future interest rate expectations.

Theories of Term Structure

Three theories are frequently cited to explain the general shape of the yield curve: the expectations theory, the liquidity preference theory, and the market segmentation theory.

expectations theory
The theory that the yield curve reflects investor expectations about future interest rates and inflation; an increasing inflation expectation results in an upward-sloping yield curve, and a decreasing inflation expectation results in a downward-sloping yield curve.

Expectations Theory One theory of the term structure of interest rates, the **expectations theory,** suggests that the yield curve reflects investor expectations about future interest rates and inflation. Higher future rates of expected inflation will result in higher long-term interest rates; the opposite occurs with lower future rates. This widely accepted explanation of the term structure can be applied to the securities of any issuer.

Generally, under the expectations theory, an increasing inflation expectation results in an upward-sloping yield curve; a decreasing inflation expectation results in a downward-sloping yield curve; and a stable inflation expectation results in a flat yield curve. Although, as we'll see, other theories exist, the observed strong relationship between inflation and interest rates (see Figure 6.2) supports this widely accepted theory.

liquidity preference theory
Theory suggesting that for any given issuer, long-term interest rates tend to be higher than short-term rates because (1) lower liquidity and higher responsiveness to general interest rate movements of longer-term securities exists and (2) borrower willingness to pay a higher rate for long-term financing cause the yield curve to be upward-sloping.

Liquidity Preference Theory The tendency for yield curves to be upward-sloping can be further explained by the **liquidity preference theory.** This theory holds that for a given issuer, such as the U.S. Treasury, long-term rates tend to be higher than short-term rates. This belief is based on two behavioral facts:

1. Investors perceive less risk in short-term securities than in longer-term securities and are therefore willing to accept lower yields on them. The reason is

that shorter-term securities are more liquid and less responsive to general interest rate movements.³

2. Borrowers are generally willing to pay a higher rate for long-term than for short-term financing. By locking in funds for a longer period of time, they can eliminate the potential adverse consequences of having to roll over short-term debt at unknown costs to obtain long-term financing.

Investors (lenders) tend to require a premium for tying up funds for longer periods, whereas borrowers are generally willing to pay a premium to obtain longer-term financing. These preferences of lenders and borrowers cause the yield curve to tend to be upward-sloping. Simply stated, longer maturities tend to have higher interest rates than shorter maturities.

Market Segmentation Theory The **market segmentation theory** suggests that the market for loans is segmented on the basis of maturity and that the supply of and demand for loans within each segment determine its prevailing interest rate. In other words, the equilibrium between suppliers and demanders of short-term funds, such as seasonal business loans, would determine prevailing short-term interest rates, and the equilibrium between suppliers and demanders of long-term funds, such as real estate loans, would determine prevailing long-term interest rates. The slope of the yield curve would be determined by the general relationship between the prevailing rates in each market segment. Simply stated, low rates in the short-term segment and high rates in the long-term segment cause the yield curve to be upward-sloping. The opposite occurs for high short-term rates and low long-term rates.

All three theories of term structure have merit. From them we can conclude that at any time, the slope of the yield curve is affected by (1) inflationary expectations, (2) liquidity preferences, and (3) the comparative equilibrium of supply and demand in the short- and long-term market segments. Upward-sloping yield curves result from higher future inflation expectations, lender preferences for shorter-maturity loans, and greater supply of short-term loans than of long-term loans relative to demand. The opposite behaviors would result in a downward-sloping yield curve. At any time, the interaction of these three forces determines the prevailing slope of the yield curve.

market segmentation theory
Theory suggesting that the market for loans is segmented on the basis of maturity and that the supply of and demand for loans within each segment determine its prevailing interest rate; the slope of the yield curve is determined by the general relationship between the prevailing rates in each market segment.

Hint An upward-sloping yield curve will result if the supply outstrips the demand for short-term loans, thereby resulting in relatively low short-term rates at a time when long-term rates are high because the demand for long-term loans is far above their supply.

Risk Premiums: Issuer and Issue Characteristics

So far we have considered only risk-free U.S. Treasury securities. We now add the element of risk, in order to assess what effect it has on the cost of funds. The amount by which the interest rate or required return exceeds the risk-free rate of interest, R_F, is a security's **risk premium.** The risk premium varies with specific issuer and issue characteristics; it causes similar-maturity securities to have differing rates of interest.

risk premium
The amount by which the interest rate or required return on a security exceeds the risk-free rate of interest R_F; it varies with specific issuer and issue characteristics.

---

3. Later in this chapter we demonstrate that debt instruments with longer maturities are more sensitive to changing market interest rates. For a given change in market rates, the price or value of longer-term debts will be more significantly changed (up or down) than the price or value of debts with shorter maturities.

TABLE 6.1	Debt-Specific Issuer- and Issue-Related Risk Premium Components
Component	Description
Default risk	The possibility that the issuer of debt will not pay the contractual interest or principal as scheduled. The greater the uncertainty as to the borrower's ability to meet these payments, the greater the risk premium. High bond ratings reflect low default risk, and low bond ratings reflect high default risk.
Maturity risk	The fact that the longer the maturity, the more the value of a security will change in response to a given change in interest rates. If interest rates on otherwise similar-risk securities suddenly rise as a result of a change in the money supply, the prices of long-term bonds will decline by more than the prices of short-term bonds, and vice versa.[a]
Contractual provision risk	Conditions that are often included in a debt agreement or a stock issue. Some of these reduce risk, whereas others may increase risk. For example, a provision allowing a bond issuer to retire its bonds prior to their maturity under favorable terms increases the bond's risk.

[a] A detailed discussion of the effects of interest rates on the price or value of bonds and other fixed-income securities is presented later in this chapter.

The risk premium consists of a number of issuer- and issue-related components, including business risk, financial risk, interest rate risk, liquidity risk, and tax risk, which were defined in Table 5.1 on page 197, and the purely debt-specific risks—default risk, maturity risk, and contractual provision risk, briefly defined in Table 6.1. In general, the highest risk premiums and therefore the highest returns result from securities issued by firms with a high risk of default and from long-term maturities that have unfavorable contractual provisions.

Review Questions

6–1 What is the *real rate of interest?* Differentiate it from the *risk-free rate of interest* for a 3-month U.S. Treasury bill.

6–2 What is the *term structure of interest rates,* and how is it related to the *yield curve?*

6–3 For a given class of similar-risk securities, what does each of the following yield curves reflect about interest rates: (**a**) downward-sloping; (**b**) upward-sloping; and (**c**) flat? Which form has been historically dominant?

6–4 Briefly describe the following theories of the general shape of the yield curve: (**a**) expectations theory; (**b**) liquidity preference theory; and (**c**) market segmentation theory.

6–5 List and briefly describe the potential issuer- and issue-related risk components that are embodied in the risk premium. Which are the purely debt-specific risks?

Corporate Bonds

A **corporate bond** is a long-term debt instrument indicating that a corporation has borrowed a certain amount of money and promises to repay it in the future under clearly defined terms. Most bonds are issued with maturities of 10 to 30 years and with a par value, or face value, of $1,000. The **coupon interest rate** on a bond represents the percentage of the bond's par value that will be paid annually, typically in two equal semiannual payments, as interest. The bondholders, who are the lenders, are promised the semiannual interest payments and, at maturity, repayment of the principal amount.

corporate bond
A long-term debt instrument indicating that a corporation has borrowed a certain amount of money and promises to repay it in the future under clearly defined terms.

coupon interest rate
The percentage of a bond's par value that will be paid annually, typically in two equal semiannual payments, as interest.

Legal Aspects of Corporate Bonds

Certain legal arrangements are required to protect purchasers of bonds. Bondholders are protected primarily through the indenture and the trustee.

Bond Indenture

A **bond indenture** is a legal document that specifies both the rights of the bondholders and the duties of the issuing corporation. Included in the indenture are descriptions of the amount and timing of all interest and principal payments, various standard and restrictive provisions, and, frequently, sinking-fund requirements and security interest provisions.

bond indenture
A legal document that specifies both the rights of the bondholders and the duties of the issuing corporation.

Standard Provisions The **standard debt provisions** in the bond indenture specify certain record-keeping and general business practices that the bond issuer must follow. Standard debt provisions do not normally place a burden on a financially sound business.

The borrower commonly must (1) *maintain satisfactory accounting records* in accordance with generally accepted accounting principles (GAAP); (2) periodically *supply audited financial statements*; (3) *pay taxes and other liabilities when due*; and (4) *maintain all facilities in good working order*.

standard debt provisions
Provisions in a *bond indenture* specifying certain record-keeping and general business practices that the bond issuer must follow; normally, they do not place a burden on a financially sound business.

Restrictive Provisions Bond indentures also normally include certain **restrictive covenants**, which place operating and financial constraints on the borrower. These provisions help protect the bondholder against increases in borrower risk. Without them, the borrower could increase the firm's risk but not have to pay increased interest to compensate for the increased risk.

The most common restrictive covenants do the following:

1. Require a *minimum level of liquidity*, to ensure against loan default.
2. *Prohibit the sale of accounts receivable* to generate cash. Selling receivables could cause a long-run cash shortage if proceeds were used to meet current obligations.
3. Impose *fixed-asset restrictions*. The borrower must maintain a specified level of fixed assets to guarantee its ability to repay the bonds.
4. *Constrain subsequent borrowing*. Additional long-term debt may be prohibited, or additional borrowing may be *subordinated* to the original loan. **Subordination** means that subsequent creditors agree to wait until all claims of the *senior debt* are satisfied.

restrictive covenants
Provisions in a *bond indenture* that place operating and financial constraints on the borrower.

subordination
In a bond indenture, the stipulation that subsequent creditors agree to wait until all claims of the *senior debt* are satisfied.

5. *Limit the firm's annual cash dividend payments* to a specified percentage or amount.

Other restrictive covenants are sometimes included in bond indentures.

The violation of any standard or restrictive provision by the borrower gives the bondholders the right to demand immediate repayment of the debt. Generally, bondholders evaluate any violation to determine whether it jeopardizes the loan. They may then decide to demand immediate repayment, continue the loan, or alter the terms of the bond indenture.

Sinking-Fund Requirements Another common restrictive provision is a **sinking-fund requirement.** Its objective is to provide for the systematic retirement of bonds prior to their maturity. To carry out this requirement, the corporation makes semiannual or annual payments that are used to retire bonds by purchasing them in the marketplace.

sinking-fund requirement
A restrictive provision often included in a bond indenture, providing for the systematic retirement of bonds prior to their maturity.

Security Interest The bond indenture identifies any collateral pledged against the bond and specifies how it is to be maintained. The protection of bond collateral is crucial to guarantee the safety of a bond issue.

Trustee

trustee
A paid individual, corporation, or commercial bank trust department that acts as the third party to a *bond indenture* and can take specified actions on behalf of the bondholders if the terms of the indenture are violated.

A **trustee** is a third party to a *bond indenture*. The trustee can be an individual, a corporation, or (most often) a commercial bank trust department. The trustee is paid to act as a "watchdog" on behalf of the bondholders and can take specified actions on behalf of the bondholders if the terms of the indenture are violated.

Cost of Bonds to the Issuer

The cost of bond financing is generally greater than the issuer would have to pay for short-term borrowing. The major factors that affect the cost, which is the rate of interest paid by the bond issuer, are the bond's maturity, the size of the offering, the issuer's risk, and the basic cost of money.

Impact of Bond Maturity on Bond Cost

Generally, as we noted earlier, long-term debt pays higher interest rates than short-term debt. In a practical sense, the longer the maturity of a bond, the less accuracy there is in predicting future interest rates, and therefore the greater the bondholders' risk of giving up an opportunity to lend money at a higher rate. In addition, the longer the term, the greater the chance that the issuer might default.

Impact of Offering Size on Bond Cost

The size of the bond offering also affects the interest cost of borrowing, but in an inverse manner: Bond flotation and administration costs per dollar borrowed are likely to decrease with increasing offering size. On the other hand, the risk to the bondholders may increase, because larger offerings result in greater risk of default.

Impact of Issuer's Risk

The greater the issuer's *default risk*, the higher the interest rate. Some of this risk can be reduced through inclusion of appropriate restrictive provisions in the bond indenture. Clearly, bondholders must be compensated with higher returns for taking greater risk. Frequently, bond buyers rely on bond ratings (discussed later) to determine the issuer's overall risk.

Impact of the Cost of Money

The cost of money in the capital market is the basis for determining a bond's coupon interest rate. Generally, the rate on U.S. Treasury securities of equal maturity is used as the lowest-risk cost of money. To that basic rate is added a *risk premium* (as described earlier in this chapter) that reflects the factors mentioned above (maturity, offering size, and issuer's risk).

General Features of a Bond Issue

Three features sometimes included in a corporate bond issue are a conversion feature, a call feature, and stock purchase warrants. These features provide the issuer or the purchaser with certain opportunities for replacing or retiring the bond or supplementing it with some type of equity issue.

Convertible bonds offer a **conversion feature** that allows bondholders to change each bond into a stated number of shares of common stock. Bondholders convert their bonds into stock only when the market price of the stock is such that conversion will provide a profit for the bondholder. Inclusion of the conversion feature by the issuer lowers the interest cost and provides for automatic conversion of the bonds to stock if future stock prices appreciate noticeably.

The **call feature** is included in nearly all corporate bond issues. It gives the issuer the opportunity to repurchase bonds prior to maturity. The **call price** is the stated price at which bonds may be repurchased prior to maturity. Sometimes the call feature can be exercised only during a certain period. As a rule, the call price exceeds the par value of a bond by an amount equal to 1 year's interest. For example, a $1,000 bond with a 10 percent coupon interest rate would be callable for around $1,100 [$1,000 + (10% × $1,000)]. The amount by which the call price exceeds the bond's par value is commonly referred to as the **call premium.** This premium compensates bondholders for having the bond called away from them; to the issuer, it is the cost of calling the bonds.

The call feature enables an issuer to call an outstanding bond when interest rates fall and issue a new bond at a lower interest rate. When interest rates rise, the call privilege will not be exercised, except possibly to meet *sinking-fund requirements*. Of course, to sell a callable bond in the first place, the issuer must pay a higher interest rate than on noncallable bonds of equal risk, to compensate bondholders for the risk of having the bonds called away from them.

Bonds occasionally have stock purchase warrants attached as "sweeteners" to make them more attractive to prospective buyers. **Stock purchase warrants** are instruments that give their holders the right to purchase a certain number of shares of the issuer's common stock at a specified price over a certain period of time. Their inclusion typically enables the issuer to pay a slightly lower coupon interest rate than would otherwise be required.

---

conversion feature
A feature of *convertible bonds* that allows bondholders to change each bond into a stated number of shares of common stock.

call feature
A feature included in nearly all corporate bond issues that gives the issuer the opportunity to repurchase bonds at a stated *call price* prior to maturity.

call price
The stated price at which a bond may be repurchased, by use of a *call feature,* prior to maturity.

call premium
The amount by which a bond's *call price* exceeds its par value.

stock purchase warrants
Instruments that give their holders the right to purchase a certain number of shares of the issuer's common stock at a specified price over a certain period of time. Occasionally attached to bonds as "sweeteners."

Interpreting Bond Quotations

The financial manager needs to stay abreast of the market values of the firm's outstanding securities, whether they are traded on an organized exchange, over the counter, or in international markets. Similarly, existing and prospective investors in the firm's securities need to monitor the prices of the securities they own because these prices represent the current value of their investment. Information on bonds, stocks, and other securities is contained in **quotations,** which include current price data along with statistics on recent price behavior. Security price quotations are readily available for actively traded bonds and stocks. The most up-to-date "quotes" can be obtained electronically, via a personal computer. Price information is available from stockbrokers and is widely published in news media. Popular sources of daily security price quotations include financial newspapers, such as the *Wall Street Journal* and *Investor's Business Daily,* and the business sections of daily general newspapers. Here we focus on bond quotations; stock quotations are reviewed in Chapter 7.

Figure 6.4 includes an excerpt from the "Forty most active fixed-coupon corporate bonds" quotations reported in the *Wall Street Journal* for transactions through the close of trading on Tuesday, May 18, 2004. We will look at the corporate bonds quotation for General Motors (GM), which is highlighted in Figure 6.4. The first column following the company name gives the bond's coupon interest rate (7.200%), and the next column gives the bond's maturity date (January 15, 2011). This information allows investors to differentiate between

quotations
Information on bonds, stocks, and other securities, including current price data and statistics on recent price behavior.

FIGURE 6.4

Bond Quotations
Selected bond quotations for May 18, 2004

Corporate Bonds
Tuesday, May 18, 2004
Forty most active fixed-coupon corporate bonds

COMPANY (TICKER)	COUPON	MATURITY	LAST PRICE	LAST YIELD	*EST SPREAD	UST†	EST $ VOL (000's)
General Motors (GM)	8.375	Jul 15, 2033	102.655	8.134	268	30	334,869
Ford Motor Credit (F)	7.000	Oct 01, 2013	100.002	6.998	227	10	229,101
Altria Group (MO)	7.000	Nov 04, 2013	100.019	6.992	226	10	166,186
General Motors Acceptance (GMAC)	6.875	Sep 15, 2011	101.623	6.590	185	10	164,077
Liberty Media (L)	3.500	Sep 25, 2006	99.865	3.559	104	2	124,704
General Motors Acceptance (GMAC)	7.750	Jan 19, 2010	108.318	5.993	214	5	120,744
Wyeth (WYE)	5.500	Feb 01, 2014	96.782	5.939	121	10	116,133
Ford Motor Credit (F)	7.375	Oct 28, 2009	105.747	6.115	227	5	111,809
General Motors Acceptance (GMAC)	6.875	Aug 28, 2012	100.781	6.748	201	10	107,817
Credit Suisse First Boston (USA) (CRDSUI)	6.500	Jan 15, 2012	107.043	5.364	64	10	106,127
Medtronic (MDT)-c	1.250	Sep 15, 2021	102.797	0.220	n.a.	n.a.	100,167
Sprint Capital (FON)	6.125	Nov 15, 2008	105.336	4.788	95	5	98,221
Citigroup (C)	6.000	Oct 31, 2033	94.007	6.454	101	30	80,490
General Motors (GM)	7.200	Jan 15, 2011	103.143	6.606	187	10	76,419
Goldman Sachs Group (GS)	5.150	Jan 15, 2014	95.140	5.814	108	10	74,871
General Motors Acceptance (GMAC)	5.850	Jan 14, 2009	100.876	5.631	179	5	70,711
Sprint Capital (FON)	7.625	Jan 30, 2011	110.421	5.726	100	10	69,156
Credit Suisse First Boston (USA) (CRDSUI)	6.125	Nov 15, 2011	104.639	5.364	63	10	68,727
Ford Motor Credit (F)	6.875	Feb 01, 2006	105.160	3.701	117	2	65,011
General Motors Acceptance (GMAC)	6.125	Aug 28, 2007	104.390	4.659	154	3	64,253
Ford Motor (F)	7.450	Jul 16, 2031	93.146	8.075	263	30	63,092
General Motors Acceptance (GMAC)	7.250	Mar 02, 2011	104.135	6.484	175	10	60,122
General Motors Acceptance (GMAC)	4.500	Jul 15, 2006	101.384	3.821	130	2	59,458
Alcoa (AA)	5.375	Jan 15, 2013	100.291	5.331	61	10	57,850
Lehman Brothers Holdings (LEH)	4.800	Mar 13, 2014	92.543	5.806	107	10	55,211
CIT Group (CIT)	3.375	Apr 01, 2009	94.357	4.686	81	5	54,721
General Motors Acceptance (GMAC)	6.125	Sep 15, 2006	104.711	3.973	145	2	53,886
Verizon Global Funding (VZ)	7.375	Sep 01, 2012	112.386	5.491	76	10	51,828
Bank of America (BAC)	6.625	Jun 15, 2004	100.367	1.085	n.a.	n.a.	51,718
Wisconsin Public Service (WPS)	4.875	Dec 01, 2012	97.930	5.178	44	10	51,628

Source: *Wall Street Journal,* May 19, 2004, p. C12.

the various bonds issued by a corporation. Note that on the day of this quote, GM had two bonds listed (the other one is the first one listed in the quote).

The next column, labeled "Last Price," gives the last price at which the bond traded on May 18, 2004. Although most corporate bonds are issued with a *par*, or *face*, *value* of $1,000, *all bonds are quoted as a percentage of par*. A $1,000-par-value bond quoted at 92.543 is priced at $925.43 (92.543% × $1,000). Corporate bonds are quoted in dollars and cents. Thus GM's last price of 103.143 for the day was $1,031.43—that is, 103.143% × $1,000.

The next column, labeled "Last Yield," represents the bond's *yield*, or *compound annual rate of return*. For the GM bond, this yield is 6.606%. The last yield assumes that the bond is purchased on the given day at the "Last Price" and held to the stated "Maturity" date.

The fifth column gives the "Est(imated) Spread" in *basis points* (100 basis points is one percentage point) over a U.S. Treasury security of similar maturity. The maturity of the Treasury issue used to find the estimated spread is given in the next column. For the GM bond, its spread above a 10-year U.S. Treasury issue is 187 basis points (1.87%).

The final column in the bond quote gives the dollar value (in $000) of the bond traded on the given day. GM's "Est(imated) $ Vol(ume)" on May 18, 2004, was $76,419,000.

Bond Ratings

Independent agencies such as Moody's and Standard & Poor's assess the riskiness of publicly traded bond issues. These agencies derive their ratings by using financial ratio and cash flow analyses to assess the likely payment of bond interest and principal. Table 6.2 summarizes these ratings. For discussion of ethical issues related to the bond-rating agencies, see the *In Practice* box on the facing page.

Hint Note that Moody's has 9 major ratings; Standard & Poor's has 10.

TABLE 6.2 Moody's and Standard & Poor's Bond Ratings[a]

Moody's	Interpretation	Standard & Poor's	Interpretation
Aaa	Prime quality	AAA	Bank investment quality
Aa	High grade	AA	
A	Upper medium grade	A	
Baa	Medium grade	BBB	
Ba	Lower medium grade or speculative	BB	Speculative
		B	
B	Speculative		
Caa	From very speculative	CCC	
Ca	to near or in default	CC	
C	Lowest grade	C	Income bond
		D	In default

[a]Some ratings may be modified to show relative standing within a major rating category; for example, Moody's uses numerical modifiers (1, 2, 3), whereas Standard & Poor's uses plus (+) and minus (−) signs.

Sources: Moody's Investors Service, Inc. and Standard & Poor's Corporation.

In Practice FOCUS ON ETHICS

CAN WE TRUST THE BOND RATERS?

Most investors have neither the time nor the expertise to do their own credit appraisals for potential bond investments, but assessing default risk still requires an evaluation of creditworthiness. Enter credit rating agencies, which offer a way to receive a third-party credit appraisal. But how reliable are their ratings? At least two of these agencies reportedly had "investment grade" ratings on Enron just a few weeks before its financial meltdown. Similar oversights occurred in the cases of WorldCom and Italian corporate giant Parmalat. The rating agencies, which are registered and approved by the SEC, command significant market power, but they have recently come under fire for questionable ethics in two areas: conflict of interest and timeliness of rating changes.

Most bond ratings are paid for by the bond issuer as a way to broaden the market appeal of its bonds. Companies want to be rated because the market for publicly traded unrated issues is much smaller and relatively illiquid. The lower a bond's rating, the higher the perceived default risk, and the higher the interest rate required by bond investors. A conflict of interest may arise because it is not in the best interest of the rater to downgrade the bonds of the corporate customer paying for the rating. A Senate Governmental Affairs Committee found that raters should have asked more and better questions in the raters' private discussions with companies such as Enron and Xerox.

The Sarbanes-Oxley Act enacted in 2002 dictated that the SEC conduct a review of credit-rating agencies. When the SEC asked for comments from the corporate community, the Association for Financial Professionals (AFP) conducted a survey of its membership of treasury and finance professionals. The survey responses were clear: Even though the raters say they serve the interests of debt investors first and foremost, only 22 percent of respondents believed that investors' interests are favored. In addition, of the respondents whose companies have rated debt, only 40 percent believed that changes in their companies' ratings are made on a timely basis. More than 70 percent of the finance professionals agreed that the SEC should evaluate registration of the credit agencies periodically.

One rating agency responded to these charges by asserting that it must balance investor and corporate issuer interests. Investors want faster rating changes, but corporate issuers want slower and more deliberate adjustments to ratings. The fact remains that it is the investors' interests that should be kept primary in the ratings process, however. Doing risk–return analysis in the bond markets depends on having trustworthy, accurate, timely information. No doubt the increased scrutiny from the SEC, regardless of any registration process that might or might not be added in the future, will add to the value of the ratings received by the investing public.

Sources: Association for Financial Professionals, "Rating Agencies Survey: Accuracy, Timeliness, and Regulation," November 2002, www.afponline.org/pub/pdf/ratings_survey.pdf.(Accessed June 14, 2004); and Lisa Yoon, "Downgrade Possible? SEC Looking at Credit Raters," June 9, 2003, www.cfo.com (Accessed June 13, 2004).

■ Which of the AFP's findings would present the most serious ethics problems for the raters?

Normally an inverse relationship exists between the quality of a bond and the rate of return that it must provide bondholders: High-quality (high-rated) bonds provide lower returns than lower-quality (low-rated) bonds. This reflects the lender's risk–return trade-off. When considering bond financing, the financial manager must be concerned with the expected ratings of the bond issue, because these ratings affect salability and cost.

Popular Types of Bonds

Bonds can be classified in a variety of ways. Here we break them into traditional bonds (the basic types that have been around for years) and contemporary bonds (newer, more innovative types). The traditional types of bonds are summarized in

TABLE 6.3 Characteristics and Priority of Lender's Claim of Traditional Types of Bonds

Bond type	Characteristics	Priority of lender's claim
Unsecured Bonds		
Debentures	Unsecured bonds that only creditworthy firms can issue. Convertible bonds are normally debentures.	Claims are the same as those of any general creditor. May have other unsecured bonds subordinated to them.
Subordinated debentures	Claims are not satisfied until those of the creditors holding certain (senior) debts have been fully satisfied.	Claim is that of a general creditor but not as good as a senior debt claim.
Income bonds	Payment of interest is required only when earnings are available. Commonly issued in reorganization of a failing firm.	Claim is that of a general creditor. Are not in default when interest payments are missed, because they are contingent only on earnings being available.
Secured Bonds		
Mortgage bonds	Secured by real estate or buildings.	Claim is on proceeds from sale of mortgaged assets; if not fully satisfied, the lender becomes a general creditor. The *first-mortgage* claim must be fully satisfied before distribution of proceeds to *second-mortgage* holders, and so on. A number of mortgages can be issued against the same collateral.
Collateral trust bonds	Secured by stock and (or) bonds that are owned by the issuer. Collateral value is generally 25% to 35% greater than bond value.	Claim is on proceeds from stock and (or) bond collateral; if not fully satisfied, the lender becomes a general creditor.
Equipment trust certificates	Used to finance "rolling stock"—airplanes, trucks, boats, railroad cars. A trustee buys such an asset with funds raised through the sale of trust certificates and then leases it to the firm, which, after making the final scheduled lease payment, receives title to the asset. A type of leasing.	Claim is on proceeds from the sale of the asset; if proceeds do not satisfy outstanding debt, trust certificate lenders become general creditors.

debentures
subordinated debentures
income bonds
mortgage bonds
collateral trust bonds
equipment trust certificates
See Table 6.3 above.

zero- (or low-) coupon bonds
junk bonds
floating-rate bonds
extendible notes
putable bonds
See Table 6.4 on page 249.

terms of their key characteristics and priority of lender's claim in Table 6.3. Note that the first three types—**debentures, subordinated debentures,** and **income bonds**—are unsecured, whereas the last three—**mortgage bonds, collateral trust bonds,** and **equipment trust certificates**—are secured.

Table 6.4 describes the key characteristics of five contemporary types of bonds: **zero- (or low-) coupon bonds, junk bonds, floating-rate bonds, extendible notes,** and **putable bonds.** These bonds can be either unsecured or secured. Changing capital market conditions and investor preferences have spurred further innovations in bond financing in recent years and will probably continue to do so.

International Bond Issues

Companies and governments borrow internationally by issuing bonds in two principal financial markets: the Eurobond market and the foreign bond market. Both give borrowers the opportunity to obtain large amounts of long-term

TABLE 6.4	Characteristics of Contemporary Types of Bonds
Bond type	Characteristics[a]
Zero- (or low-) coupon bonds	Issued with no (zero) or a very low coupon (stated interest) rate and sold at a large discount from par. A significant portion (or all) of the investor's return comes from gain in value (i.e., par value minus purchase price). Generally callable at par value. Because the issuer can annually deduct the current year's interest accrual without having to pay the interest until the bond matures (or is called), its cash flow each year is increased by the amount of the tax shield provided by the interest deduction.
Junk bonds	Debt rated Ba or lower by Moody's or BB or lower by Standard & Poor's. Commonly used during the 1980s by rapidly growing firms to obtain growth capital, most often as a way to finance mergers and takeovers. High-risk bonds with high yields—often yielding 2% to 3% more than the best-quality corporate debt.
Floating-rate bonds	Stated interest rate is adjusted periodically within stated limits in response to changes in specified money market or capital market rates. Popular when future inflation and interest rates are uncertain. Tend to sell at close to par because of the automatic adjustment to changing market conditions. Some issues provide for annual redemption at par at the option of the bondholder.
Extendible notes	Short maturities, typically 1 to 5 years, that can be renewed for a similar period at the option of holders. Similar to a floating-rate bond. An issue might be a series of 3-year renewable notes over a period of 15 years; every 3 years, the notes could be extended for another 3 years, at a new rate competitive with market interest rates at the time of renewal.
Putable bonds	Bonds that can be redeemed at par (typically, $1,000) at the option of their holder either at specific dates after the date of issue and every 1 to 5 years thereafter or when and if the firm takes specified actions, such as being acquired, acquiring another company, or issuing a large amount of additional debt. In return for its conferring the right to "put the bond" at specified times or when the firm takes certain actions, the bond's yield is lower than that of a nonputable bond.

[a]The claims of lenders (i.e., bondholders) against issuers of each of these types of bonds vary, depending on the bonds' other features. Each of these bonds can be unsecured or secured.

debt financing quickly, in the currency of their choice and with flexible repayment terms.

A **Eurobond** is issued by an international borrower and sold to investors in countries with currencies other than the currency in which the bond is denominated. An example is a dollar-denominated bond issued by a U.S. corporation and sold to Belgian investors. From the founding of the Eurobond market in the 1960s until the mid-1980s, "blue chip" U.S. corporations were the largest single class of Eurobond issuers. Some of these companies were able to borrow in this market at interest rates below those the U.S. government paid on Treasury bonds. As the market matured, issuers became able to choose the currency in which they borrowed, and European and Japanese borrowers rose to prominence. In more recent years, the Eurobond market has become much more balanced in terms of the mix of borrowers, total issue volume, and currency of denomination.

Eurobond
A bond issued by an international borrower and sold to investors in countries with currencies other than the currency in which the bond is denominated.

foreign bond
A bond issued in a host country's financial market, in the host country's currency, by a foreign borrower.

In contrast, a **foreign bond** is issued in a host country's financial market, in the host country's currency, by a foreign borrower. A Swiss-franc–denominated bond issued in Switzerland by a U.S. company is an example of a foreign bond. The three largest foreign-bond markets are Japan, Switzerland, and the United States.

Review Questions

6–6 What are typical maturities, denominations, and interest payments of a corporate bond? What mechanisms protect bondholders?

6–7 Differentiate between *standard debt provisions* and *restrictive covenants* included in a bond indenture. What are the consequences of violation of them by the bond issuer?

6–8 How is the cost of bond financing typically related to the cost of short-term borrowing? In addition to a bond's maturity, what other major factors affect its cost to the issuer?

6–9 What is a *conversion feature?* A *call feature?* *Stock purchase warrants?*

6–10 What information is found in a bond *quotation?* How are bonds rated, and why?

6–11 Compare the basic characteristics of *Eurobonds* and *foreign bonds.*

Valuation Fundamentals

valuation
The process that links risk and return to determine the worth of an asset.

Valuation is the process that links risk and return to determine the worth of an asset. It is a relatively simple process that can be applied to *expected* streams of benefits from bonds, stocks, income properties, oil wells, and so on. To determine an asset's worth at a given point in time, a financial manager uses the time-value-of-money techniques presented in Chapter 4 and the concepts of risk and return developed in Chapter 5.

Key Inputs

There are three key inputs to the valuation process: (1) cash flows (returns), (2) timing, and (3) a measure of risk, which determines the required return. Each is described below.

Cash Flows (Returns)

The value of any asset depends on the cash flow(s) it is *expected* to provide over the ownership period. To have value, an asset does not have to provide an annual cash flow; it can provide an intermittent cash flow or even a single cash flow over the period.

EXAMPLE Celia Sargent, financial analyst for Groton Corporation, a diversified holding company, wishes to estimate the value of three of its assets: common stock in Michaels Enterprises, an interest in an oil well, and an original painting by a well-known artist. Her cash flow estimates for each are as follows:

Stock in Michaels Enterprises Expect to receive cash dividends of $300 per year indefinitely.

Oil well *Expect* to receive cash flow of $2,000 at the end of year 1, $4,000 at the end of year 2, and $10,000 at the end of year 4, when the well is to be sold.

Original painting *Expect* to be able to sell the painting in 5 years for $85,000.

With these cash flow estimates, Celia has taken the first step toward placing a value on each of the assets.

Timing

In addition to making cash flow estimates, we must know the timing of the cash flows.[4] For example, Celia expects the cash flows of $2,000, $4,000, and $10,000 for the oil well to occur at the ends of years 1, 2, and 4, respectively. The combination of the cash flow and its timing fully defines the return expected from the asset.

Risk and Required Return

Hint The required rate of return is the result of investors being risk-averse. For the risk-averse investor to purchase a given asset, the investor *must expect* at least enough return to compensate for the asset's perceived risk.

The level of risk associated with a given cash flow can significantly affect its value. In general, the greater the risk of (or the less certain) a cash flow, the lower its value. Greater risk can be incorporated into a valuation analysis by using a higher required return or discount rate. As in the previous chapter, the higher the risk, the greater the required return, and the lower the risk, the less the required return.

EXAMPLE

Let's return to Celia Sargent's task of placing a value on Groton Corporation's original painting and consider two scenarios.

Scenario 1—Certainty A major art gallery has contracted to buy the painting for $85,000 at the end of 5 years. Because this is considered a certain situation, Celia views this asset as "money in the bank." She thus would use the prevailing risk-free rate of 9% as the required return when calculating the value of the painting.

Scenario 2—High Risk The values of original paintings by this artist have fluctuated widely over the past 10 years. Although Celia expects to be able to get $85,000 for the painting, she realizes that its sale price in 5 years could range between $30,000 and $140,000. Because of the high uncertainty surrounding the painting's value, Celia believes that a 15% required return is appropriate.

These two estimates of the appropriate required return illustrate how this rate captures risk. The often subjective nature of such estimates is also clear.

The Basic Valuation Model

Simply stated, the value of any asset is *the present value of all future cash flows it is expected to provide over the relevant time period*. The time period can be any length, even infinity. The value of an asset is therefore determined by discounting the expected cash flows back to their present value, using the required return commensurate with the asset's risk as the appropriate discount rate. Utilizing the

---

4. Although cash flows can occur at any time during a year, for computational convenience as well as custom, we will assume they occur at the *end of the year* unless otherwise noted.

TABLE 6.5 Valuation of Groton Corporation's Assets by Celia Sargent

Asset	Cash flow, CF		Appropriate required return	Valuation[a]
Michaels Enterprises stock[b]	$300/year indefinitely		12%	$V_0 = \$300 \times (PVIFA_{12\%,\infty})$ $= \$300 \times \dfrac{1}{0.12} = \underline{\underline{\$2,500}}$
Oil well[c]	Year (t) 1 2 3 4	CF_t $\$\ 2,000$ $4,000$ 0 $10,000$	20%	$V_0 = [\$2,000 \times (PVIF_{20\%,1})]$ $\quad + [\$4,000 \times (PVIF_{20\%,2})]$ $\quad + [\$0 \times (PVIF_{20\%,3})]$ $\quad + [\$10,000 \times (PVIF_{20\%,4})]$ $= [\$2,000 \times (0.833)]$ $\quad + [\$4,000 \times (0.694)]$ $\quad + [\$0 \times (0.579)]$ $\quad + [\$10,000 \times (0.482)]$ $= \$1,666 + \$2,776$ $\quad + \$0 + \$4,820$ $= \underline{\underline{\$9,262}}$
Original painting[d]	$85,000 at end of year 5		15%	$V_0 = \$85,000 \times (PVIF_{15\%,5})$ $= \$85,000 \times (0.497)$ $= \underline{\underline{\$42,245}}$

[a] Based on *PVIF* interest factors from Table A–2. If calculated using a calculator, the values of the oil well and original painting would have been $9,266.98 and $42,260.03, respectively.
[b] This is a perpetuity (infinite-lived annuity), and therefore the present value interest factor given in Equation 4.19 is applied.
[c] This is a mixed stream of cash flows and therefore requires a number of *PVIF*s, as noted.
[d] This is a single-amount cash flow and therefore requires a single *PVIF*.

present value techniques explained in Chapter 4, we can express the value of any asset at time zero, V_0, as

$$V_0 = \frac{CF_1}{(1+k)^1} + \frac{CF_2}{(1+k)^2} + \cdots + \frac{CF_n}{(1+k)^n} \quad (6.1)$$

where

V_0 = value of the asset at time zero
CF_t = cash flow *expected* at the end of year t
k = appropriate required return (discount rate)
n = relevant time period

Using present value interest factor notation, $PVIF_{k,n}$ from Chapter 4, Equation 6.1 can be rewritten as

$$V_0 = [CF_1 \times (PVIF_{k,1})] + [CF_2 \times (PVIF_{k,2})] + \cdots + [CF_n \times (PVIF_{k,n})] \quad (6.2)$$

We can use Equation 6.2 to determine the value of any asset.

EXAMPLE Celia Sargent used Equation 6.2 to calculate the value of each asset (using present value interest factors from Table A–2), as shown in Table 6.5. Michaels Enterprises stock has a value of $2,500, the oil well's value is $9,262, and the original painting has a value of $42,245. Note that regardless of the pattern of the expected cash flow from an asset, the basic valuation equation can be used to determine its value.

Review Questions

6–12 Why is it important for financial managers to understand the valuation process?

6–13 What are the three key inputs to the valuation process?

6–14 Does the valuation process apply only to assets that provide an annual cash flow? Explain.

6–15 Define and specify the general equation for the value of any asset, V_0.

Bond Valuation

The basic valuation equation can be customized for use in valuing specific securities: bonds, common stock, and preferred stock. Bond valuation is described in this chapter, and valuation of common stock and preferred stock is discussed in Chapter 7.

Bond Fundamentals

Hint A bondholder receives two cash flows from a bond if it is held to maturity—interest and the bond's face value. For valuation purposes, the interest is an annuity and the face value is a single payment received at a specified future date.

As noted earlier in this chapter, *bonds* are long-term debt instruments used by business and government to raise large sums of money, typically from a diverse group of lenders. Most corporate bonds pay interest *semiannually* (every 6 months) at a stated *coupon interest rate*, have an initial *maturity* of 10 to 30 years, and have a *par value*, or *face value*, of $1,000 that must be repaid at maturity.

EXAMPLE Mills Company, a large defense contractor, on January 1, 2007, issued a 10% coupon interest rate, 10-year bond with a $1,000 par value that pays interest semiannually. Investors who buy this bond receive the contractual right to two cash flows: (1) $100 annual interest (10% coupon interest rate × $1,000 par value) distributed as $50 (1/2 × $100) at the end of each 6 months, and (2) the $1,000 par value at the end of the tenth year.

We will use data for Mills's bond issue to look at basic bond valuation.

Basic Bond Valuation

The value of a bond is the present value of the payments its issuer is contractually obligated to make, from the current time until it matures. The basic model for the value, B_0, of a bond is given by Equation 6.3:

$$B_0 = I \times \left[\sum_{t=1}^{n} \frac{1}{(1 + k_d)^t} \right] + M \times \left[\frac{1}{(1 + k_d)^n} \right] \quad (6.3)$$

$$= I \times (PVIFA_{k_d,n}) + M \times (PVIF_{k_d,n}) \quad (6.3a)$$

where

B_0 = value of the bond at time zero
I = *annual* interest paid in dollars[5]
n = number of years to maturity
M = par value in dollars
k_d = required return on a bond

We can calculate bond value using Equation 6.3a and the appropriate financial tables (Tables A–2 and A–4) or by using a financial calculator.

EXAMPLE

Assuming that interest on the Mills Company bond issue is paid annually and that the required return is equal to the bond's coupon interest rate, $I = \$100$, $k_d = 10\%$, $M = \$1,000$, and $n = 10$ years.

The computations involved in finding the bond value are depicted graphically on the following time line.

Time line for bond valuation (Mills Company's 10% coupon interest rate, 10-year maturity, $1,000 par, January 1, 2007, issue paying annual interest; required return = 10%)

Table Use Substituting the values noted above into Equation 6.3a yields

$$B_0 = \$100 \times (PVIFA_{10\%,10\text{yrs}}) + \$1,000 \times (PVIF_{10\%,10\text{yrs}})$$
$$= \$100 \times (6.145) + \$1,000 \times (0.386)$$
$$= \$614.50 + \$386.00 = \underline{\$1,000.50}$$

The bond therefore has a value of approximately $1,000.[6]

Calculator Use Using the Mills Company's inputs shown at the left, you should find the bond value to be exactly $1,000. Note that *the calculated bond value is equal to its par value; this will always be the case when the required return is equal to the coupon interest rate.*

---

5. The payment of annual rather than semiannual bond interest is assumed throughout the following discussion. This assumption simplifies the calculations involved, while maintaining the conceptual accuracy of the valuation procedures presented.

6. Note that a slight rounding error ($0.50) results here from the use of the table factors, which are rounded to the nearest thousandth.

Spreadsheet Use   The value of the Mills Company bond also can be calculated as shown in the following Excel spreadsheet. (For another spreadsheet model that computes the value of the Mills Company bond, see the book's Web site, www.aw-bc.com/gitman, Chapter 6.)

	A	B
1	BOND VALUE, ANNUAL INTEREST, REQUIRED RETURN = COUPON INTEREST RATE	
2	Annual interest payment	$100
3	Coupon interest rate	10%
4	Number of years to maturity	10
5	Par value	$1,000
6	Bond value	$1,000.00

Entry in Cell B6 is
(B2 * (1-(1/(1+B3)^B4))/B3) + (B6 * (1/(1+B3)^B4))

The expression 1-(1/(1+B3)^B4))/B3) calculates the Present Value Interest Factor for an Annuity.
The expression 1/(1+B3)^B4 calculates the Present Value Interest Factor for a Single Amount

Bond Value Behavior

In practice, the value of a bond in the marketplace is rarely equal to its par value. In bond quotations (see Figure 6.4 on page 245), the last prices of bonds often differ from their par values of 100 (100 percent of par). Some bonds are valued below par (quoted below 100), and others are valued above par (quoted above 100). A variety of forces in the economy, as well as the passage of time, tend to affect value. Although these external forces are in no way controlled by bond issuers or investors, it is useful to understand the impact that required return and time to maturity have on bond value.

Required Returns and Bond Values

Whenever the required return on a bond differs from the bond's coupon interest rate, the bond's value will differ from its par value. The required return is likely to differ from the coupon interest rate because either (1) economic conditions have changed, causing a shift in the basic cost of long-term funds, or (2) the firm's risk has changed. Increases in the basic cost of long-term funds or in risk will raise the required return; decreases in the cost of funds or in risk will lower the required return.

Regardless of the exact cause, what is important is the relationship between the required return and the coupon interest rate: When the required return is greater than the coupon interest rate, the bond value, B_0, will be less than its par value, M. In this case, the bond is said to sell at a **discount**, which will equal $M - B_0$. When the required return falls below the coupon interest rate, the bond value will be greater than par. In this situation, the bond is said to sell at a **premium**, which will equal $B_0 - M$.

discount
The amount by which a bond sells at a value that is less than its par value.

premium
The amount by which a bond sells at a value that is greater than its par value.

EXAMPLE   The preceding example showed that when the required return equaled the coupon interest rate, the bond's value equaled its $1,000 par value. If for the same bond the required return were to rise or fall, its value would be found as follows (using Equation 6.3a):

TABLE 6.6	Bond Values for Various Required Returns (Mills Company's 10% Coupon Interest Rate, 10-Year Maturity, $1,000 Par, January 1, 2007, Issue Paying Annual Interest)		
Required return, k_d		Bond value, B_0	Status
12%		$ 887.00	Discount
10		1,000.00	Par value
8		1,134.00	Premium

Table Use

Required Return = 12%

$B_0 = \$100 \times (PVIFA_{12\%, 10yrs}) + \$1,000 \times (PVIF_{12\%, 10yrs})$

$= \underline{\$887.00}$

Required Return = 8%

$B_0 = \$100 \times (PVIFA_{8\%, 10yrs}) + \$1,000 \times (PVIF_{8\%, 10yrs})$

$= \underline{\$1,134.00}$

Calculator Use   Using the inputs shown at the left for the two different required returns, you will find the value of the bond to be below or above par. At a 12% required return, the bond would sell at a *discount* of $113.00 ($1,000 par value − $887.00 value). At the 8% required return, the bond would sell for a *premium* of about $134.00 ($1,134.00 value − $1,000 par value). The results of this and earlier calculations for Mills Company's bond values are summarized in Table 6.6 and graphically depicted in Figure 6.5. The inverse relationship between bond value and required return is clearly shown in the figure.

Spreadsheet Use   The values for the Mills Company bond at required returns of 12% and 8% also can be calculated as shown in the following Excel spreadsheet. (See the book's Web site, www.aw-bc.com/gitman, Chapter 6, for another spreadsheet model that computes the values of the Mills Company bond at a discount and a premium.)

	A	B	C
1	BOND VALUE, ANNUAL INTEREST, REQUIRED RETURN NOT EQUAL TO COUPON INTEREST RATE		
2	Annual interest payment	$100	$100
3	Coupon interest rate	10%	10%
4	Required return	12%	8%
5	Number of years to maturity	10	10
6	Par value	$1,000	$1,000
7	Bond value	$887.00	$1,134.20

Entry in Cell B7, a **bond discount**, is
(B2*(1-(1/(1+B4)^B5))/B4) + (B6*(1/(1+B4)^B5))
The expression 1-(1/(1+B4)^B5))/B4 calculates the Present Value Interest Factor for an Annuity.
The expression 1/(1+B4)^B5 calculates the Present Value Interest Factor for a Single Amount.

Entry in Cell C7, a **bond premium**, is
(C2*(1-(1/(1+C4)^C5))/C4) + (C6*(1/(1+C4)^C5))
The expression 1-(1/(1+C4)^C5))/C4 calculates the Present Value Interest Factor for an Annuity.
The expression 1/(1+C4)^C5 calculates the Present Value Interest Factor for a Single Amount.

FIGURE 6.5

Bond Values and Required Returns

Bond values and required returns (Mills Company's 10% coupon interest rate, 10-year maturity, $1,000 par, January 1, 2007, issue paying annual interest)

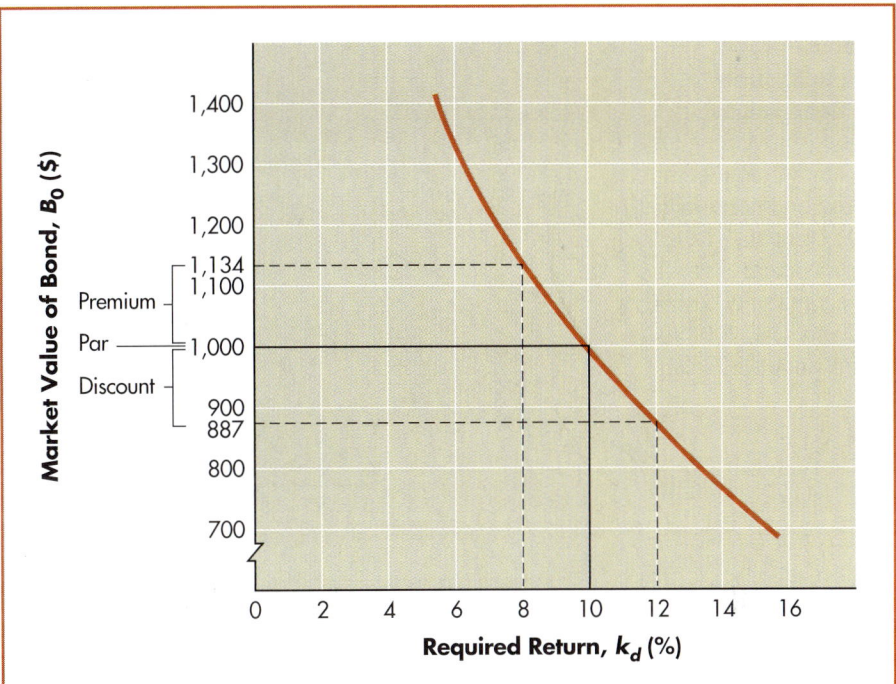

Time to Maturity and Bond Values

Whenever the required return is different from the coupon interest rate, the amount of time to maturity affects bond value. An additional factor is whether required returns are constant or change over the life of the bond.

Constant Required Returns When the required return is different from the coupon interest rate and is assumed to be *constant until maturity*, the value of the bond will approach its par value as the passage of time moves the bond's value closer to maturity. (Of course, when the required return *equals* the coupon interest rate, the bond's value will remain at par until it matures.)

EXAMPLE

Figure 6.6 (see page 258) depicts the behavior of the bond values calculated earlier and presented in Table 6.6 for Mills Company's 10% coupon interest rate bond paying annual interest and having 10 years to maturity. Each of the three required returns—12%, 10%, and 8%—is assumed to remain constant over the 10 years to the bond's maturity. The bond's value at both 12% and 8% approaches and ultimately equals the bond's $1,000 par value at its maturity, as the discount (at 12%) or premium (at 8%) declines with the passage of time. ■

Changing Required Returns The chance that interest rates will change and thereby change the required return and bond value is called **interest rate risk**. (This was described as a shareholder-specific risk in Chapter 5, Table 5.1.) Bondholders are typically more concerned with rising interest rates because a rise in interest rates, and therefore in the required return, causes a decrease in bond value. The shorter the amount of time until a bond's maturity, the less responsive its market value to a given change in the required return. In other words, *short maturities have less interest rate risk than long maturities* when all other features

interest rate risk
The chance that interest rates will change and thereby change the required return and bond value. Rising rates, which result in decreasing bond values, are of greatest concern.

FIGURE 6.6

Time to Maturity and Bond Values

Relationship among time to maturity, required returns, and bond values (Mills Company's 10% coupon interest rate, 10-year maturity, $1,000 par, January 1, 2007, issue paying annual interest)

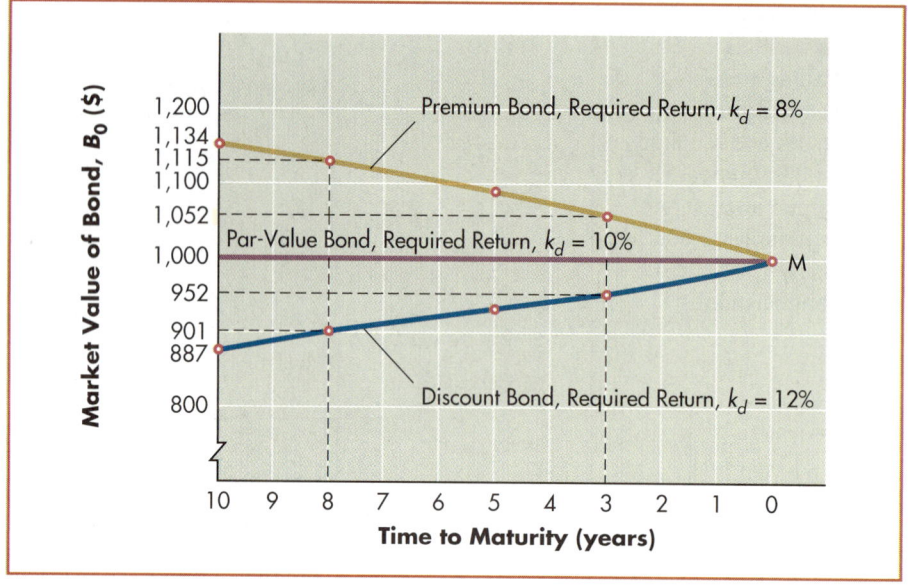

(coupon interest rate, par value, and interest payment frequency) are the same. This is because of the mathematics of time value; the present values of short-term cash flows change far less than the present values of longer-term cash flows in response to a given change in the discount rate (required return).

EXAMPLE The effect of changing required returns on bonds with differing maturities can be illustrated by using Mills Company's bond and Figure 6.6. If the required return rises from 10% to 12% when the bond has 8 years to maturity (see the dashed line at 8 years), the bond's value decreases from $1,000 to $901—a 9.9% decrease. If the same change in required return had occurred with only 3 years to maturity (see the dashed line at 3 years), the bond's value would have dropped to just $952—only a 4.8% decrease. Similar types of responses can be seen for the change in bond value associated with decreases in required returns. The shorter the time to maturity, the less the impact on bond value caused by a given change in the required return.

Yield to Maturity (YTM)

yield to maturity (YTM)
The rate of return that investors earn if they buy a bond at a specific price and hold it until maturity. (Assumes that the issuer makes all scheduled interest and principal payments as promised.)

When investors evaluate bonds, they commonly consider **yield to maturity (YTM)**. This is the rate of return that investors earn if they buy the bond at a specific price and hold it until maturity. (The measure assumes, of course, that the issuer makes all scheduled interest and principal payments as promised.) The yield to maturity on a bond with a current price equal to its par value (that is, $B_0 = M$) will always equal the coupon interest rate. When the bond value differs from par, the yield to maturity will differ from the coupon interest rate.

Assuming that interest is paid annually, the yield to maturity on a bond can be found by solving Equation 6.3 for k_d. In other words, the current value, the annual interest, the par value, and the years to maturity are known, and the required return must be found. The required return is the bond's yield to maturity. The YTM can be found by trial and error, by using a financial calculator, or by using an Excel spreadsheet. The calculator provides accurate YTM values with minimum effort.

EXAMPLE

The Mills Company bond, which currently sells for $1,080, has a 10% coupon interest rate and $1,000 par value, pays interest annually, and has 10 years to maturity. Because $B_0 = \$1{,}080$, $I = \$100$ $(0.10 \times \$1{,}000)$, $M = \$1{,}000$, and $n = 10$ years, substituting into Equation 6.3a yields

$$\$1{,}080 = \$100 \times (PVIFA_{k_d, 10\text{yrs}}) + \$1{,}000 \times (PVIF_{k_d, 10\text{yrs}})$$

Our objective is to solve the equation for k_d, the YTM.

Trial and Error Because we know that a required return, k_d, of 10% (which equals the bond's 10% coupon interest rate) would result in a value of $1,000, the discount rate that would result in $1,080 must be less than 10%. (Remember that the lower the discount rate, the higher the present value, and the higher the discount rate, the lower the present value.) Trying 9%, we get

$$\$100 \times (PVIFA_{9\%, 10\text{yrs}}) + \$1{,}000 \times (PVIF_{9\%, 10\text{yrs}})$$
$$= \$100 \times (6.418) + \$1{,}000 \times (0.422)$$
$$= \$641.80 + \$422.00$$
$$= \$1{,}063.80$$

Because the 9% rate is not quite low enough to bring the value up to $1,080, we next try 8% and get

$$\$100 \times (PVIFA_{8\%, 10\text{yrs}}) + \$1{,}000 \times (PVIF_{8\%, 10\text{yrs}})$$
$$= \$100 \times (6.710) + \$1{,}000 \times (0.463)$$
$$= \$671.00 + \$463.00$$
$$= \$1{,}134.00$$

Because the value at the 8% rate is higher than $1,080 and the value at the 9% rate is lower than $1,080, the bond's yield to maturity must be between 8% and 9%. Because the $1,063.80 is closer to $1,080, the YTM to the nearest whole percent is 9%. (By using *interpolation*, we could eventually find the more precise YTM value to be 8.77%.)[7]

Calculator Use [*Note:* Most calculators require *either* the present value (B_0 in this case) or the future values (I and M in this case) to be input as negative numbers to calculate yield to maturity. That approach is employed here.] Using the inputs shown at the left, you should find the YTM to be 8.766%.

Spreadsheet Use The yield to maturity of the 10% coupon rate Mills Company bond also can be calculated as shown in the Excel spreadsheet on page 260. (See the book's Web site, www.aw-bc.com/gitman, Chapter 6, for another spreadsheet model that computes the yield to maturity of the Mills Company bond.)

---

7. For information on how to interpolate to get a more precise answer, see the book's home page at www.aw-bc.com/gitman.

	A	B
1	YIELD TO MATURITY, ANNUAL INTEREST	
2	Annual interest payment	$100
3	Coupon interest rate	10%
4	Number of years to maturity	10
5	Par value	$1,000
6	Current bond price	$1,080
7	Yield to maturity	8.77%
8	Trial and error method:	
9	Choose various required rates and place them in Cell A14	
10	The spreadsheet will recalculate each time. Continue the process	
11	until the value of the bond equals the current price of the bond	
12	(in this example, it is $1,080).	
13		
14	8.77%	
15	Payments PVIFA PVIF	PV
16	$100 6.4831	$ 648
17	$1,000 0.4314	$ 431
18	Bond Value	$ 1,080

Semiannual Interest and Bond Values

The procedure used to value bonds paying interest semiannually is similar to that shown in Chapter 4 for compounding interest more frequently than annually, except that here we need to find present value instead of future value. It involves

1. Converting annual interest, I, to semiannual interest by dividing I by 2.
2. Converting the number of years to maturity, n, to the number of 6-month periods to maturity by multiplying n by 2.
3. Converting the required stated (rather than effective) annual return for similar-risk bonds that also pay semiannual interest from an annual rate, k_d, to a semiannual rate by dividing k_d by 2.

Substituting these three changes into Equation 6.3 yields

$$B_0 = \frac{I}{2} \times \left[\sum_{t=1}^{2n} \frac{1}{\left(1 + \frac{k_d}{2}\right)^t}\right] + M \times \left[\frac{1}{\left(1 + \frac{k_d}{2}\right)^{2n}}\right] \quad (6.4)$$

$$= \frac{I}{2} \times (PVIFA_{k_d/2,2n}) + M \times (PVIF_{k_d/2,2n}) \quad (6.4a)$$

EXAMPLE Assuming that the Mills Company bond pays interest semiannually and that the required stated annual return, k_d, is 12% for similar-risk bonds that also pay semiannual interest, substituting these values into Equation 6.4a yields

$$B_0 = \frac{\$100}{2} \times (PVIFA_{12\%/2, 2 \times 10yrs}) + \$1,000 \times (PVIF_{12\%/2, 2 \times 10yrs})$$

Table Use

$$B_0 = \$50 \times (PVIFA_{6\%,20periods}) + \$1,000 \times (PVIF_{6\%,20periods})$$
$$= \$50 \times (11.470) + \$1,000 \times (0.312) = \underline{\$885.50}$$

Calculator Use In using a calculator to find bond value when interest is paid semiannually, we must double the number of periods and divide both the required stated annual return and the annual interest by 2. For the Mills Company bond, we would use 20 periods (2 × 10 years), a required return of 6% (12% ÷ 2), and an interest payment of $50 ($100 ÷ 2). Using these inputs, you should find the bond value with semiannual interest to be $885.30, as shown at the left. Note that this value is more precise than the value calculated using the rounded financial-table factors.

Spreadsheet Use The value of the Mills Company bond paying semiannual interest at a required return of 12% also can be calculated as shown in the following Excel spreadsheet. (See the book's Web site, www.aw-bc.com/gitman, Chapter 6, for another spreadsheet model that computes the value of the Mills Company bond paying semiannual interest.)

	A	B
1	BOND VALUE, SEMIANNUAL INTEREST	
2	Annual interest payment	$100
3	Stated annual return	12%
4	Number of years to maturity	10
5	Par value	$1,000
6	Bond value	$885.30

Entry in Cell B6 is
B2/2*(1-(1/(1+B3/2)^(2*B4)))/(B3/2) + (B5*(1/(1+B3/2)^(2*B4)))
The expression 1-(1/(1+B3/2)^(2*B4))/(B3/2) calculates the Present Value Interest Factor for an Annuity (semiannual interest).
The expression 1/(1+B3/2)^(2*B4) calculates the Present Value Interest Factor for a Single Amount (semiannual interest).

Comparing this result with the $887.00 value found earlier for annual compounding (see Table 6.6 on page 256), we can see that the bond's value is lower when semiannual interest is paid. *This will always occur when the bond sells at a discount.* For bonds selling at a premium, the opposite will occur: The value with semiannual interest will be greater than with annual interest.

Review Questions

6–16 What basic procedure is used to value a bond that pays annual interest? Semiannual interest?

6–17 What relationship between the required return and the coupon interest rate will cause a bond to sell at a *discount*? At a *premium*? At its *par value*?

6–18 If the required return on a bond differs from its coupon interest rate, describe the behavior of the bond value over time as the bond moves toward maturity.

6–19 As a risk-averse investor, would you prefer bonds with short or long periods until maturity? Why?

6–20 What is a bond's *yield to maturity* (*YTM*)? Briefly describe the trial-and-error approach, the use of a financial calculator, and the use of an Excel spreadsheet for finding YTM.

Summary

FOCUS ON VALUE

Interest rates and required returns embody the real cost of money, inflationary expectations, and issuer and issue risk. They reflect the level of return required by market participants as compensation for the risk perceived in a specific security or asset investment. Because these returns are affected by economic expectations, they vary as a function of time, typically rising for longer-term maturities or transactions. The yield curve reflects such market expectations at any point in time.

The value of an asset can be found by calculating the present value of its expected cash flows, using the required return as the discount rate. Bonds are the easiest financial assets to value, because both the amounts and the timing of their cash flows are contractual and therefore known with certainty. The financial manager needs to understand how to apply valuation techniques to bonds, stocks, and tangible assets (as will be demonstrated in the following chapters) to make decisions that are consistent with the firm's **share price maximization goal.**

REVIEW OF LEARNING GOALS

Key definitions and formulas for this chapter are summarized in Table 6.7.

LG1 **Describe interest rate fundamentals, the term structure of interest rates, and risk premiums.** The flow of funds between savers and investors is regulated by the interest rate or required return. In a perfect, inflation-free, certain world there would be one cost of money—the real rate of interest.

For any class of similar-risk securities, the term structure of interest rates reflects the relationship between the interest rate or rate of return and the time to maturity. Yield curves can be downward-sloping (inverted), upward-sloping (normal), or flat. The expectations theory, liquidity preference theory, and market segmentation theory are cited to explain the shape of the yield curve. Risk premiums for non-Treasury debt issues result from business risk, financial risk, interest rate risk, liquidity risk, tax risk, default risk, maturity risk, and contractual provision risk.

LG2 **Review the legal aspects of bond financing and bond cost.** Corporate bonds are long-term debt instruments indicating that a corporation has borrowed an amount that it promises to repay in the future under clearly defined terms. Most bonds are issued with maturities of 10 to 30 years and a par value of $1,000. The bond indenture, enforced by a trustee, states all conditions of the bond issue. It contains both standard debt provisions and restrictive covenants, which may include a sinking-fund requirement and/or a security interest. The cost of a bond to an issuer depends on its maturity, offering size, and issuer risk and on the basic cost of money.

TABLE 6.7 Summary of Key Valuation Definitions and Formulas for Any Asset and for Bonds

Definitions of variables

B_0 = bond value
CF_t = cash flow *expected* at the end of year t
I = annual interest on a bond
k = appropriate required return (discount rate)
k_d = required return on a bond
M = par, or face, value of a bond
n = relevant time period, or number of years to maturity
V_0 = value of the asset at time zero

Valuation formulas

Value of any asset:

$$V_0 = \frac{CF_1}{(1+k)^1} + \frac{CF_2}{(1+k)^2} + \cdots + \frac{CF_n}{(1+k)^n} \quad \text{[Equation 6.1]}$$

$$= [CF_1 \times (PVIF_{k,1})] + [CF_2 \times (PVIF_{k,2})] + \cdots + [CF_n \times (PVIF_{k,n})] \quad \text{[Equation 6.2]}$$

Bond value:

$$B_0 = I \times \left[\sum_{t=1}^{n} \frac{1}{(1+k_d)^t}\right] + M \times \left[\frac{1}{(1+k_d)^n}\right] \quad \text{[Equation 6.3]}$$

$$= I \times (PVIFA_{k_d,n}) + M \times (PVIF_{k_d,n}) \quad \text{[Equation 6.3a]}$$

LG3 Discuss the general features, quotations, ratings, popular types, and international issues of corporate bonds. A bond issue may include a conversion feature, a call feature, or stock purchase warrants. Bond quotations provide information such as current price, yield, and volume data. Bond ratings by independent agencies indicate the risk of a bond issue. Various types of traditional and contemporary bonds are available. Eurobonds and foreign bonds enable established creditworthy companies and governments to borrow large amounts internationally.

LG4 Understand the key inputs and basic model used in the valuation process. Key inputs to the valuation process include cash flows (returns), timing, and risk and the required return. The value of any asset is equal to the present value of all future cash flows it is *expected* to provide over the relevant time period.

LG5 Apply the basic valuation model to bonds and describe the impact of required return and time to maturity on bond values. The value of a bond is the present value of its interest payments plus the present value of its par value. The discount rate used to determine bond value is the required return, which may differ from the bond's coupon interest rate. A bond can sell at a discount, at par, or at a premium, depending on whether the required return is greater than, equal to, or less than its coupon interest rate. The amount of time to maturity affects bond values. The value of a bond will approach its par value as the bond moves closer to maturity. The chance that interest rates will change and thereby change the required return and bond value is called interest rate risk. The shorter the amount of time until a bond's maturity, the less responsive its market value to a given change in the required return.

Explain yield to maturity (YTM), its calculation, and the procedure used to value bonds that pay interest semiannually. Yield to maturity is the rate of return investors earn if they buy a bond at a specific price and hold it until maturity. YTM can be calculated by trial and error, by using a financial calculator, or by using an Excel spreadsheet. Bonds that pay interest semiannually are valued by using the same procedure used to value bonds paying annual interest, except that the interest payments are one-half of the annual interest payments, the number of periods is twice the number of years to maturity, and the required return is one-half of the stated annual required return on similar-risk bonds.

SELF-TEST PROBLEMS (SOLUTIONS IN APPENDIX B)

  ST6–1 Bond valuation Lahey Industries has outstanding a $1,000 par-value bond with an 8% coupon interest rate. The bond has 12 years remaining to its maturity date.
   a. If interest is paid *annually,* find the value of the bond when the required return is (1) 7%, (2) 8%, and (3) 10%.
   b. Indicate for each case in part **a** whether the bond is selling at a discount, at a premium, or at its par value.
   c. Using the 10% required return, find the bond's value when interest is paid *semiannually.*

 ST6–2 Yield to maturity Elliot Enterprises' bonds currently sell for $1,150, have an 11% coupon interest rate and a $1,000 par value, pay interest *annually,* and have 18 years to maturity.
   a. Calculate the bonds' *yield to maturity (YTM).*
   b. Compare the YTM calculated in part **a** to the bonds' coupon interest rate, and use a comparison of the bonds' current price and their par value to explain this difference.

WARM-UP EXERCISES

 E6–1 The yields for Treasuries with differing maturities on a recent day were as shown in the following table:

Maturity	Yield
3 months	1.41%
6 months	1.71
2 years	2.68
3 years	3.01
5 years	3.7
10 years	4.51
30 years	5.25

Use the information above to construct a *yield curve* for this date.

E6–2 Recently, the annual inflation rate measured by the Consumer Price Index (CPI) was forecast to be 3.3%. How could a T-bill have had a negative real rate of return over the same period? How could it have had a zero real rate of return? What minimum rate of return must the T-bill have earned to meet your requirement of a 2% real rate of return? (*Hint:* Assume the T-bill rate is the sum of the real rate of return and the forecast annual inflation rate.)

E6–3 You have two assets and must calculate their values today based on their different payment streams and appropriate required returns. Asset 1 has a required return of 15% and will produce a stream of $500 at the end of each year indefinitely. Asset 2 has a required return of 10% and will produce an end-of-year cash flow of $1,200 in the first year, $1,500 in the second year, and $850 in its third and final year.

E6–4 A bond with 5 years to maturity and a coupon rate of 6% has a face value of $20,000. Interest is paid annually. If you required a return of 8% on this bond, what is the value of this bond to you?

E6–5 Assume a 5-year Treasury bond has a coupon rate of 4.5%.
  a. Give examples of required rates of return that would make the bond sell at a discount, at a premium, and at par.
  b. If this bond's par value is $10,000, calculate the differing values for this bond given the required rates you chose in part **a**.

Problems

P6–1 **Yield curve** A firm wishing to evaluate interest rate behavior has gathered yield data on five U.S. Treasury securities, each having a different maturity and all measured at the same point in time. The summarized data follow.

U.S. Treasury security	Time to maturity	Yield
A	1 year	12.6%
B	10 years	11.2
C	6 months	13.0
D	20 years	11.0
E	5 years	11.4

  a. Draw the yield curve associated with these data.
  b. Describe the resulting yield curve in part **a**, and explain the general expectations embodied in it.

P6–2 **Term structure of interest rates** The yield data for a number of highest-quality corporate bonds existed at each of the three points in time noted in the table at the top of page 266.

| | Yield | | |
Time to maturity (years)	5 years ago	2 years ago	Today
1	9.1%	14.6%	9.3%
3	9.2	12.8	9.8
5	9.3	12.2	10.9
10	9.5	10.9	12.6
15	9.4	10.7	12.7
20	9.3	10.5	12.9
30	9.4	10.5	13.5

a. On the same set of axes, draw the yield curve at each of the three given times.
b. Label each curve in part **a** with its general shape (downward-sloping, upward-sloping, flat).
c. Describe the general inflationary and interest rate expectation existing at each of the three times.

P6–3 **Risk-free rate and risk premiums** The real rate of interest is currently 3%; the inflation expectation and risk premiums for a number of securities follow.

Security	Inflation expectation premium	Risk premium
A	6%	3%
B	9	2
C	8	2
D	5	4
E	11	1

a. Find the risk-free rate of interest, R_F, that is applicable to each security.
b. Although not noted, what factor must be the cause of the differing risk-free rates found in part **a**?
c. Find the nominal rate of interest for each security.

P6–4 **Risk premiums** Eleanor Burns is attempting to find the nominal rate of interest for each of two securities—A and B—issued by different firms at the same point in time. She has gathered the following data:

Characteristic	Security A	Security B
Time to maturity	3 years	15 years
Inflation expectation premium	9.0%	7.0%
Risk premium for:		
Liquidity risk	1.0%	1.0%
Default risk	1.0%	2.0%
Maturity risk	0.5%	1.5%
Other risk	0.5%	1.5%

a. If the real rate of interest is currently 2%, find the risk-free rate of interest applicable to each security.
b. Find the total risk premium attributable to each security's issuer and issue characteristics.
c. Calculate the nominal rate of interest for each security. Compare and discuss your findings.

P6–5 **Bond interest payments before and after taxes** Charter Corp. has issued 2,500 debentures with a total principal value of $2,500,000. The bonds have a coupon interest rate of 7%.
a. What dollar amount of interest per bond can an investor expect to receive each year from Charter?
b. What is Charter's total interest expense per year associated with this bond issue?
c. Assuming that Charter is in a 35% corporate tax bracket, what is the company's net after-tax interest cost associated with this bond issue?

P6–6 **Bond quotation** Assume that the following quote for the Financial Management Corporation's $1,000-par-value bond was found in the Wednesday, November 8, issue of the *Wall Street Journal*.

Financial Management (FM)   5.700   May 15, 2013   97.708   6.034   129   10   47,807

Given this information, answer the following questions.
a. On what day did the trading activity occur?
b. What was the last price at which the bond traded on November 7?
c. When does the bond mature?
d. What dollar value of these bonds was traded on the day quoted?
e. What is the bond's coupon interest rate?
f. What is the bond's *yield?* Explain what this value represents.
g. What was this bond's spread over a similar-maturity U.S. Treasury issue? What maturity Treasury issue is used in this comparison?

P6–7 **Valuation fundamentals** Imagine that you are trying to evaluate the economics of purchasing an automobile. You expect the car to provide annual after-tax cash benefits of $1,200 at the end of each year, and assume that you can sell the car for after-tax proceeds of $5,000 at the end of the planned 5-year ownership period. All funds for purchasing the car will be drawn from your savings, which are currently earning 6% after taxes.
a. Identify the cash flows, their timing, and the required return applicable to valuing the car.
b. What is the maximum price you would be willing to pay to acquire the car? Explain.

P6–8 **Valuation of assets** Using the information provided in the table at the top of page 268, find the value of each asset.

Asset	Cash flow End of year	Amount	Appropriate required return
A	1	$ 5,000	18%
	2	5,000	
	3	5,000	
B	1 through ∞	$ 300	15%
C	1	$ 0	16%
	2	0	
	3	0	
	4	0	
	5	35,000	
D	1 through 5	$ 1,500	12%
	6	8,500	
E	1	$ 2,000	14%
	2	3,000	
	3	5,000	
	4	7,000	
	5	4,000	
	6	1,000	

P6–9 Asset valuation and risk Laura Drake wishes to estimate the value of an asset expected to provide cash inflows of $3,000 per year at the end of years 1 through 4 and $15,000 at the end of year 5. Her research indicates that she must earn 10% on low-risk assets, 15% on average-risk assets, and 22% on high-risk assets.
a. Determine what is the most Laura should pay for the asset if it is classified as (1) low-risk, (2) average-risk, and (3) high-risk.
b. Suppose Laura is unable to assess the risk of the asset and wants to be certain she's making a good deal. On the basis of your findings in part **a,** what is the most she should pay? Why?
c. All else being the same, what effect does increasing risk have on the value of an asset? Explain in light of your findings in part **a.**

P6–10 Basic bond valuation Complex Systems has an outstanding issue of $1,000-par-value bonds with a 12% coupon interest rate. The issue pays interest *annually* and has 16 years remaining to its maturity date.
a. If bonds of similar risk are currently earning a 10% rate of return, how much should the Complex Systems bond sell for today?
b. Describe the *two* possible reasons why similar-risk bonds are currently earning a return below the coupon interest rate on the Complex Systems bond.
c. If the required return were at 12% instead of 10%, what would the current value of Complex Systems' bond be? Contrast this finding with your findings in part **a** and discuss.

P6–11 **Bond valuation—Annual interest** Calculate the value of each of the bonds shown in the following table, all of which pay interest *annually*.

Bond	Par value	Coupon interest rate	Years to maturity	Required return
A	$1,000	14%	20	12%
B	1,000	8	16	8
C	100	10	8	13
D	500	16	13	18
E	1,000	12	10	10

P6–12 **Bond value and changing required returns** Midland Utilities has outstanding a bond issue that will mature to its $1,000 par value in 12 years. The bond has a coupon interest rate of 11% and pays interest *annually*.
a. Find the value of the bond if the required return is (1) 11%, (2) 15%, and (3) 8%.
b. Plot your findings in part a on a set of "required return (x axis)–market value of bond (y axis)" axes.
c. Use your findings in parts a and b to discuss the relationship between the coupon interest rate on a bond and the required return and the market value of the bond relative to its par value.
d. What *two* possible reasons could cause the required return to differ from the coupon interest rate?

P6–13 **Bond value and time—Constant required returns** Pecos Manufacturing has just issued a 15-year, 12% coupon interest rate, $1,000-par bond that pays interest *annually*. The required return is currently 14%, and the company is certain it will remain at 14% until the bond matures in 15 years.
a. Assuming that the required return does remain at 14% until maturity, find the value of the bond with (1) 15 years, (2) 12 years, (3) 9 years, (4) 6 years, (5) 3 years, and (6) 1 year to maturity.
b. Plot your findings on a set of "time to maturity (x axis)–market value of bond (y axis)" axes constructed similarly to Figure 6.6 on page 258.
c. All else remaining the same, when the required return differs from the coupon interest rate and is assumed to be constant to maturity, what happens to the bond value as time moves toward maturity? Explain in light of the graph in part b.

P6–14 **Bond value and time—Changing required returns** Lynn Parsons is considering investing in either of two outstanding bonds. The bonds both have $1,000 par values and 11% coupon interest rates and pay *annual* interest. Bond A has exactly 5 years to maturity, and bond B has 15 years to maturity.
a. Calculate the value of bond A if the required return is (1) 8%, (2) 11%, and (3) 14%.
b. Calculate the value of bond B if the required return is (1) 8%, (2) 11%, and (3) 14%.

c. From your findings in parts **a** and **b**, complete the following table, and discuss the relationship between time to maturity and changing required returns.

Required return	Value of bond A	Value of bond B
8%	?	?
11	?	?
14	?	?

d. If Lynn wanted to minimize *interest rate risk*, which bond should she purchase? Why?

P6–15 **Yield to maturity** The relationship between a bond's yield to maturity and coupon interest rate can be used to predict its pricing level. For each of the bonds listed, state whether the price of the bond will be at a premium to par, at par, or at a discount to par.

Bond	Coupon interest rate	Yield to maturity	Price
A	6%	10%	Discount
B	8	8	Par
C	9	7	Premium
D	7	9	Discount
E	12	10	Premium

P6–16 **Yield to maturity** The Salem Company bond currently sells for $955, has a 12% coupon interest rate and a $1,000 par value, pays interest *annually,* and has 15 years to maturity.
a. Calculate the *yield to maturity* (YTM) on this bond.
b. Explain the relationship that exists between the coupon interest rate and yield to maturity and the par value and market value of a bond.

P6–17 **Yield to maturity** Each of the bonds shown in the following table pays interest *annually*.

Bond	Par value	Coupon interest rate	Years to maturity	Current value
A	$1,000	9%	8	$ 820
B	1,000	12	16	1,000
C	500	12	12	560
D	1,000	15	10	1,120
E	1,000	5	3	900

a. Calculate the *yield to maturity* (YTM) for each bond.
b. What relationship exists between the coupon interest rate and yield to maturity and the par value and market value of a bond? Explain.

P6–18 **Bond valuation—Semiannual interest** Find the value of a bond maturing in 6 years, with a $1,000 par value and a coupon interest rate of 10% (5% paid semiannually) if the required return on similar-risk bonds is 14% annual interest (7% paid semiannually).

P6–19 **Bond valuation—Semiannual interest** Calculate the value of each of the bonds shown in the following table, all of which pay interest *semiannually*.

Bond	Par value	Coupon interest rate	Years to maturity	Required stated annual return
A	$1,000	10%	12	8%
B	1,000	12	20	12
C	500	12	5	14
D	1,000	14	10	10
E	100	6	4	14

P6–20 **Bond valuation—Quarterly interest** Calculate the value of a $5,000-par-value bond paying quarterly interest at an annual coupon interest rate of 10% and having 10 years until maturity if the required return on similar-risk bonds is currently a 12% annual rate paid *quarterly*.

P6–21 **ETHICS PROBLEM** Bond rating agencies have invested significant sums of money in an effort to determine which quantitative and nonquantitative factors best predict bond defaults. Furthermore, some of the raters invest time and money to legally meet privately with corporate personnel to get nonpublic information that is used in assigning the issue's bond rating. Does this approach provide an acceptable defense against the ethics charges that are being made against bond raters, as described in the *In Practice* box on page 247?

CHAPTER 6 CASE

Evaluating Annie Hegg's Proposed Investment in Atilier Industries Bonds

Annie Hegg has been considering investing in the bonds of Atilier Industries. The bonds were issued 5 years ago at their $1,000 par value and have exactly 25 years remaining until they mature. They have an 8% coupon interest rate, are convertible into 50 shares of common stock, and can be called any time at $1,080. The bond is rated Aa by Moody's. Atilier Industries, a manufacturer of sporting goods, recently acquired a small athletic-wear company that was in financial distress. As a result of the acquisition, Moody's and other rating agencies are considering a rating change for Atilier bonds. Recent economic data suggest that expected inflation, currently at 5% annually, is likely to increase to a 6% annual rate.

Annie remains interested in the Atilier bond but is concerned about inflation, a potential rating change, and maturity risk. To get a feel for the potential impact of these factors on the bond value, she decided to apply the valuation techniques she learned in her finance course.

TO DO

a. If the price of the common stock into which the bond is convertible rises to $30 per share after 5 years and the issuer calls the bonds at $1,080, should Annie let the bond be called away from her or should she convert it into common stock?

b. For each of the following required returns, calculate the bond's value, assuming annual interest. Indicate whether the bond will sell at a discount, at a premium, or at par value.
   (1) Required return is 6%.
   (2) Required return is 8%.
   (3) Required return is 10%.

c. Repeat the calculations in part **b**, assuming that interest is paid *semiannually* and that the semiannual required returns are one-half of those shown. Compare and discuss differences between the bond values for each required return calculated here and in part **b** under the annual versus semiannual payment assumptions.

d. If Annie strongly believes that expected inflation will rise by 1% during the next few months, what is the most she should pay for the bond, assuming annual interest?

e. If the Atilier bonds are downrated by Moody's from Aa to A, and if such a rating change will result in an increase in the required return from 8% to 8.75%, what impact will this have on the bond value, assuming annual interest?

f. If Annie buys the bond today at its $1,000 par value and holds it for exactly 3 years, at which time the required return is 7%, how much of a gain or loss will she experience in the value of the bond (ignoring interest already received and assuming annual interest)?

g. Rework part **f**, assuming that Annie holds the bond for 10 years and sells it when the required return is 7%. Compare your finding to that in part **f**, and comment on the bond's *maturity risk*.

h. Assume that Annie buys the bond at its last price of 98.380 and holds it until maturity. What will her *yield to maturity* (*YTM*) be, assuming annual interest?

i. After evaluating all of the issues raised above, what recommendation would you give Annie with regard to her proposed investment in the Atilier Industries bonds?

SPREADSHEET EXERCISE

CSM Corporation has a bond issue outstanding at the end of 2006. The bond has 15 years remaining to maturity and carries a coupon interest rate of 6%. Interest on the bond is compounded on a semiannual basis. The par value of the CSM bond is $1,000 and it is currently selling for $874.42.

TO DO

Create a spreadsheet similar to the spreadsheets for yield to maturity and semi-annual interest that can be viewed at www.aw-bc.com/gitman, to model the following:

a. Using the trial and error method, determine the *annual* required rate of return (k_d). Find one interest rate that results in a bond value greater than the current bond price, and then find another rate that results in a bond value lower than the current bond price.
b. What is the time to maturity (n)?
c. What is the semiannual coupon payment (pmt)?
d. What is the semiannual required rate of return ($k_d/2$)?

WEB EXERCISE

Although several Web sites offer bond quotes, a particularly user-friendly site is the bond page at Yahoo! Finance (bonds.yahoo.com/). One very useful page is the composite bond rates page.

TO DO

a. From the home page, direct your browser to Bonds and highlight Rates. This page will give you a screen with both Treasury yields and corporate yields, allowing the risk premium to be estimated directly from this page. The top of this page shows the latest yield curve for Treasuries. Note the pattern of the curve as discussed in your text.
b. Next, a table for Treasuries shows the yields for all maturities. This table gives yields for the specified day, the day before, one week earlier, and one month earlier. Note the changes in yield over this period.
c. The next table gives similar information for municipal securities. Note the difference in yields between Treasuries and munis (municipal bonds). The difference is driven in part by taxation issues.
d. The final table gives the information on corporates.
   (1) Note the differences between the Treasuries and the corporate bonds.
   (2) Note the shape of the yield curve as discussed in the chapter.
   (3) Note the changes in yield over this period.

> **Remember to check the book's Web site at**
> www.aw-bc.com/gitman
> **for additional resources, including additional Web exercises.**

Chapter 7

Stock Valuation

LEARNING GOALS

LG1 Differentiate between debt and equity capital.

LG2 Discuss the rights, characteristics, and features of both common and preferred stock.

LG3 Describe the process of issuing common stock, including venture capital, going public, and the investment banker, and interpreting stock quotations.

LG4 Understand the concept of market efficiency and basic common stock valuation using the zero-growth and constant-growth models.

LG5 Discuss the free cash flow valuation model and the book value, liquidation value, and price/earnings (P/E) multiples approaches.

LG6 Explain the relationships among financial decisions, return, risk, and the firm's value.

Across the Disciplines Why This Chapter Matters to You

Accounting: You need to understand the difference between debt and equity in terms of tax treatment; the ownership claims of capital providers, including venture capitalists and stockholders; and why book value per share is not a sophisticated basis for common stock valuation.

Information systems: You need to understand the procedures used to issue common stock; the sources and types of information that affect stock value; and how such information can be used in stock valuation models to link proposed actions to share price.

Management: You need to understand the difference between debt and equity capital; the rights and claims of stockholders; the process of raising funds from venture capitalists and through initial public offerings; and the various stock valuation models used to value the firm's common stock.

Marketing: You need to understand that the firm's ideas for products and services will greatly affect the willingness of venture capitalists and stockholders to contribute capital to the firm and that a perceived increase in risk as a result of new projects may negatively affect the firm's stock value.

Operations: You need to understand that the amount of capital the firm has to invest in plant assets and inventory will depend on the evaluations of venture capitalists and would-be investors; the better the prospects look for growth, the more money the firm will have for operations.

Owning corporate stock is a popular investment activity. Each weekday, the news media report on the movements of stock prices in the financial markets. The price of each share of a firm's common stock is driven by the cash flows (dividends) owners expect to receive from owning the stock and the perceived riskiness of those forecasted cash flows. This chapter describes the key aspects of corporate stock and continues our discussion of the valuation process—this time, of the valuation of stock.

Differences Between Debt and Equity Capital

capital
The long-term funds of a firm; all items on the right-hand side of the firm's balance sheet, *excluding current liabilities*.

debt capital
All long-term borrowing incurred by a firm, including bonds.

equity capital
The long-term funds provided by the firm's owners, the stockholders.

The term **capital** denotes the long-term funds of a firm. All items on the right-hand side of the firm's balance sheet, *excluding current liabilities*, are sources of capital. **Debt capital** includes all long-term borrowing incurred by a firm, including bonds, which were discussed in Chapter 6. **Equity capital** consists of long-term funds provided by the firm's owners, the stockholders. A firm can obtain equity capital either *internally*, by retaining earnings rather than paying them out as dividends to its stockholders, or *externally*, by selling common or preferred stock. The key differences between debt and equity capital are summarized in Table 7.1 and discussed below.

Voice in Management

Unlike creditors (lenders), holders of equity capital (common and preferred stockholders) are owners of the firm. Holders of common stock have voting rights that permit them to select the firm's directors and to vote on special issues. In contrast, debtholders and preferred stockholders may receive voting privileges only when the firm has violated its stated contractual obligations to them.

Claims on Income and Assets

Holders of equity have claims on both income and assets that are secondary to the claims of creditors. Their *claims on income* cannot be paid until the claims of all creditors (including both interest and scheduled principal payments) have

TABLE 7.1 Key Differences Between Debt and Equity Capital

	Type of capital	
Characteristic	Debt	Equity
Voice in management[a]	No	Yes
Claims on income and assets	Senior to equity	Subordinate to debt
Maturity	Stated	None
Tax treatment	Interest deduction	No deduction

[a]In the event that the issuer violates its stated contractual obligations to them, debtholders and preferred stockholders *may* receive a voice in management; otherwise, only common stockholders have voting rights.

been satisfied. After satisfying these claims, the firm's board of directors decides whether to distribute dividends to the owners.

The equity holders' *claims on assets* also are secondary to the claims of creditors. If the firm fails, its assets are sold, and the proceeds are distributed in this order: employees and customers, the government, creditors, and (finally) equity holders. Because equity holders are the last to receive any distribution of assets, they expect greater returns from dividends and/or increases in stock price.

As is explained in Chapter 10, the costs of equity financing are generally higher than debt costs. One reason is that the suppliers of equity capital take more risks because of their subordinate claims on income and assets. Despite being more costly, equity capital is necessary for a firm to grow. All corporations must initially be financed with some common stock equity.

Maturity

Unlike debt, equity capital is a *permanent form* of financing for the firm. It does not "mature" so repayment is not required. Because equity is liquidated only during bankruptcy proceedings, stockholders must recognize that although a ready market may exist for their shares, the price that can be realized may fluctuate. This fluctuation of the market price of equity makes the overall returns to a firm's stockholders even more risky.

Tax Treatment

Interest payments to debtholders are treated as tax-deductible expenses by the issuing firm, whereas dividend payments to a firm's common and preferred stockholders are not tax-deductible. The tax deductibility of interest lowers the corporation's cost of debt financing, further causing it to be lower than the cost of equity financing.

Review Question

7–1 What are the key differences between *debt capital* and *equity capital*?

  ## Common and Preferred Stock

A firm can obtain equity, or ownership, capital by selling either common or preferred stock. All corporations initially issue common stock to raise equity capital. Some of these firms later issue either additional common stock or preferred stock to raise more equity capital. Although both common and preferred stock are forms of equity capital, preferred stock has some similarities to debt capital that significantly differentiate it from common stock. Here we first consider the rights, characteristics, and features of both common and preferred stock and then describe the process of issuing common stock, including the use of venture capital.

Common Stock

The true owners of business firms are the common stockholders. Common stockholders are sometimes referred to as *residual owners* because they receive what is left—the residual—after all other claims on the firm's income and assets have been satisfied. They are assured of only one thing: that they cannot lose any more than they have invested in the firm. As a result of this generally uncertain position, common stockholders expect to be compensated with adequate dividends and, ultimately, capital gains.

Ownership

privately owned (stock)
All common stock of a firm owned by a single individual.

closely owned (stock)
All common stock of a firm owned by a small group of investors (such as a family).

publicly owned (stock)
Common stock of a firm owned by a broad group of unrelated individual or institutional investors.

The common stock of a firm can be **privately owned** by a single individual, **closely owned** by a small group of investors (such as a family), or **publicly owned** by a broad group of unrelated individual or institutional investors. Typically, small corporations are privately or closely owned; if their shares are traded, this trading occurs infrequently and in small amounts. Large corporations, which are emphasized in the following discussions, are publicly owned, and their shares are generally actively traded on the major securities exchanges described in Chapter 1.

Par Value

par value (stock)
A relatively useless value for a stock established for legal purposes in the firm's corporate charter.

Unlike bonds, which always have a par value, common stock may be sold with or without a par value. The **par value** of a common stock is a relatively useless value established for legal purposes in the firm's corporate charter. It is generally quite low, about $1.

Firms often issue stock with no par value, in which case they may assign the stock a value or record it on the books at the price at which it is sold. A low par value may be advantageous in states where certain corporate taxes are based on the par value of stock; if a stock has no par value, the tax may be based on an arbitrarily determined per-share figure.

Preemptive Rights

preemptive right
Allows common stockholders to maintain their *proportionate* ownership in the corporation when new shares are issued.

dilution of ownership
Occurs when a new stock issue results in each present shareholder having a claim on a *smaller* part of the firm's earnings than previously.

rights
Financial instruments that allow stockholders to purchase additional shares at a price below the market price, in direct proportion to their number of owned shares.

The **preemptive right** allows common stockholders to maintain their *proportionate* ownership in the corporation when new shares are issued. It allows existing shareholders to maintain voting control and protects them against the dilution of their ownership. **Dilution of ownership** usually results in the dilution of earnings, because each present shareholder has a claim on a *smaller* part of the firm's earnings than previously.

In a *rights offering*, the firm grants **rights** to its shareholders. These financial instruments allow stockholders to purchase additional shares at a price below the market price, in direct proportion to their number of owned shares. Rights are used primarily by smaller corporations whose shares are either *closely owned* or *publicly owned* and not actively traded. In these situations, rights are an important financing tool without which shareholders would run the risk of losing their proportionate control of the corporation.

From the firm's viewpoint, the use of rights offerings to raise new equity capital may be less costly and may generate more interest than a public offering of stock. An example may help to clarify the use of rights.

> **EXAMPLE**

Dominic Company, a regional advertising firm, currently has 100,000 shares of common stock outstanding and is contemplating a rights offering of an additional 10,000 shares. Each existing shareholder will receive one right per share, and each right will entitle the shareholder to purchase one-tenth of a share of new common stock (10,000 ÷ 100,000), so 10 rights will be required to purchase one share of the stock. The holder of 1,000 shares (1 percent) of the outstanding common stock will receive 1,000 rights, each permitting the purchase of one-tenth of a share of new common stock, for a total of 100 new shares. If the shareholder exercises the rights, he or she will end up with a total of 1,100 shares of common stock, or 1 percent of the total number of shares then outstanding (110,000). Thus, the shareholder maintains the same proportion of ownership he or she had prior to the rights offering. ■

authorized shares
The number of shares of common stock that a firm's corporate charter allows it to issue.

outstanding shares
The number of shares of common stock held by the public.

treasury stock
The number of shares of outstanding stock that have been repurchased by the firm.

issued shares
The number of shares of common stock that have been put into circulation; the sum of outstanding shares and treasury stock.

Authorized, Outstanding, and Issued Shares

A firm's corporate charter indicates how many **authorized shares** it can issue. The firm cannot sell more shares than the charter authorizes without obtaining approval through a shareholder vote. To avoid later having to amend the charter, firms generally attempt to authorize more shares than they initially plan to issue.

Authorized shares become **outstanding shares** when they are held by the public. If the *firm* repurchases any of its outstanding shares, these shares are recorded as **treasury stock** and are no longer considered to be outstanding shares. **Issued shares** are the shares of common stock that have been put into circulation; they represent the sum of outstanding shares and treasury stock.

> **EXAMPLE**

Golden Enterprises, a producer of medical pumps, has the following stockholders' equity account on December 31:

Stockholders' Equity	
Common stock—$0.80 par value:	
Authorized 35,000,000 shares; issued 15,000,000 shares	$ 12,000,000
Paid-in capital in excess of par	63,000,000
Retained earnings	31,000,000
	$106,000,000
Less: Cost of treasury stock (1,000,000 shares)	4,000,000
Total stockholders' equity	$102,000,000

How many shares of additional common stock can Golden sell without gaining approval from its shareholders? The firm has 35 million authorized shares, 15 million issued shares, and 1 million shares of treasury stock. Thus 14 million shares are outstanding (15 million issued shares − 1 million shares of treasury stock), and Golden can issue 21 million additional shares (35 million authorized shares − 14 million outstanding shares) without seeking shareholder approval. This total includes the treasury shares currently held, which the firm can reissue to the public without obtaining shareholder approval. ■

Voting Rights

Generally, each share of common stock entitles its holder to one vote in the election of directors and on special issues. Votes are generally assignable and may be cast at the annual stockholders' meeting.

In recent years, many firms have issued two or more classes of common stock; they differ mainly in having unequal voting rights. A firm can use different classes of stock as a defense against a *hostile takeover* in which an outside group, without management support, tries to gain voting control of the firm by buying its shares in the marketplace. **Supervoting shares** of stock give each owner multiple votes. When supervoting shares are issued to "insiders," an outside group, whose shares have only one vote each typically cannot obtain enough votes to gain control of the firm. At other times, a class of **nonvoting common stock** is issued when the firm wishes to raise capital through the sale of common stock but does not want to give up its voting control.

When different classes of common stock are issued on the basis of unequal voting rights, class A common is typically—but not universally—designated as nonvoting, and class B common has voting rights. Generally, higher classes of shares (class A, for example) are given preference in the distribution of earnings (dividends) and assets; lower-class shares, in exchange, receive voting rights. Treasury stock, which is held within the corporation, generally *does not* have voting rights, *does not* earn dividends, and *does not* have a claim on assets in liquidation.

Because most small stockholders do not attend the annual meeting to vote, they may sign a **proxy statement** transferring their votes to another party. The solicitation of proxies from shareholders is closely controlled by the Securities and Exchange Commission to ensure that proxies are not being solicited on the basis of false or misleading information. Existing management generally receives the stockholders' proxies, because it is able to solicit them at company expense.

Occasionally, when the firm is widely owned, outsiders may wage a **proxy battle** to unseat the existing management and gain control. To win a corporate election, votes from a majority of the shares voted are required. However, the odds of a nonmanagement group winning a proxy battle are generally slim.

supervoting shares
Stock that carries with it multiple votes per share rather than the single vote per share typically given on regular shares of common stock.

nonvoting common stock
Common stock that carries no voting rights; issued when the firm wishes to raise capital through the sale of common stock but does not want to give up its voting control.

proxy statement
A statement transferring the votes of a stockholder to another party.

proxy battle
The attempt by a nonmanagement group to gain control of the management of a firm by soliciting a sufficient number of proxy votes.

Dividends

The payment of dividends to the firm's shareholders is at the discretion of the corporation's board of directors. Most corporations pay dividends quarterly. Dividends may be paid in cash, stock, or merchandise. Cash dividends are the most common, merchandise dividends the least.

Common stockholders are not promised a dividend, but they come to expect certain payments on the basis of the historical dividend pattern of the firm. Before dividends are paid to common stockholders, the claims of the government, all creditors, and preferred stockholders must be satisfied. Since passage of the *Jobs and Growth Tax Relief Reconciliation Act of 2003*, many firms have begun to pay larger dividends to shareholders, who are subject to a maximum tax rate of 15 percent on dividends rather than the maximum tax rate of 39 percent in effect prior to passage of the act. Because of the importance of the dividend decision to the growth and valuation of the firm, dividends are discussed in greater detail in Chapter 12.

International Stock Issues

Although the international market for common stock is not as large as the international market for bonds, cross-border issuance and trading of common stock have increased dramatically in the past 25 years.

Some corporations *issue stock in foreign markets*. For example, the stock of General Electric trades in Frankfurt, London, Paris, and Tokyo; the stocks of Time Warner and Microsoft trade in Frankfurt and London; and the stock of McDonalds trades in Frankfurt, London, and Paris. The London, Frankfurt, and Tokyo markets are the most popular. Issuing stock internationally broadens the ownership base and helps a company to integrate itself into the local business scene. A listing on a foreign stock exchange both increases local business press coverage and serves as effective corporate advertising. Having locally traded stock can also facilitate corporate acquisitions, because shares can be used as an acceptable method of payment.

Foreign corporations have also discovered the benefits of trading their stock in the United States. The disclosure and reporting requirements mandated by the U.S. Securities and Exchange Commission have historically discouraged all but the largest foreign firms from directly listing their shares on the New York Stock Exchange or the American Stock Exchange. For example, in 1993, Daimler-Benz (now DaimlerChrysler) became the first large German company to be listed on the NYSE.

American depositary receipts (ADRs)
Claims issued by U.S. banks representing ownership of shares of a foreign company's stock held on deposit by the U.S. bank in the foreign market and issued in dollars to U.S. investors.

As an alternative, most foreign companies choose to tap the U.S. market through **American depositary receipts (ADRs)**. These are claims issued by U.S. banks representing ownership of shares of a foreign company's stock held on deposit by the U.S. bank in the foreign market. Because ADRs are issued, in dollars, by a U.S. bank to U.S. investors, they are subject to U.S. securities laws. At the same time, they give investors the opportunity to diversify their portfolios internationally.

Preferred Stock

Preferred stock gives its holders certain privileges that make them senior to common stockholders. Preferred stockholders are promised a fixed periodic dividend, which is stated either as a percentage or as a dollar amount. How the dividend is specified depends on whether the preferred stock has a *par value*, which, as in common stock, is a relatively useless stated value established for legal purposes. **Par-value preferred stock** has a stated face value, and its annual dividend is specified as a percentage of this value. **No-par preferred stock** has no stated face value, but its annual dividend is stated in dollars. Preferred stock is most often issued by public utilities, by acquiring firms in merger transactions, and by firms that are experiencing losses and need additional financing.

par-value preferred stock
Preferred stock with a stated face value that is used with the specified dividend percentage to determine the annual dollar dividend.

no-par preferred stock
Preferred stock with no stated face value but with a stated annual dollar dividend.

Basic Rights of Preferred Stockholders

The basic rights of preferred stockholders are somewhat more favorable than the rights of common stockholders. Preferred stock is often considered *quasi-debt* because, much like interest on debt, it specifies a fixed periodic payment (dividend). Of course, as ownership, preferred stock is unlike debt in that it has no maturity date. Because they have a fixed claim on the firm's income that takes precedence over the claim of common stockholders, preferred stockholders are exposed to less risk. They are consequently *not normally given a voting right*.

Preferred stockholders have *preference over common stockholders in the distribution of earnings*. If the stated preferred stock dividend is "passed" (not paid) by the board of directors, the payment of dividends to common stockholders is prohibited. It is this preference in dividend distribution that makes common stockholders the true risk takers.

Preferred stockholders are also usually given *preference over common stockholders in the liquidation of assets* in a legally bankrupt firm, although they must "stand in line" behind creditors. The amount of the claim of preferred stockholders in liquidation is normally equal to the par or stated value of the preferred stock.

Features of Preferred Stock

A number of features are generally included as part of a preferred stock issue. These features, along with the stock's par value, the amount of dividend payments, the dividend payment dates, and any restrictive covenants, are specified in an agreement similar to a *bond indenture*.

Restrictive Covenants The restrictive covenants in a preferred stock issue are aimed at ensuring the firm's continued existence and regular payment of the dividend. These covenants include provisions about passing dividends, the sale of senior securities, mergers, sales of assets, minimum liquidity requirements, and repurchases of common stock. The violation of preferred stock covenants usually permits preferred stockholders either to obtain representation on the firm's board of directors or to force the retirement of their stock at or above its par or stated value.

cumulative (preferred stock)
Preferred stock for which all passed (unpaid) dividends in arrears, along with the current dividend, must be paid before dividends can be paid to common stockholders.

noncumulative (preferred stock)
Preferred stock for which passed (unpaid) dividends do not accumulate.

Cumulation Most preferred stock is **cumulative** with respect to any dividends passed. That is, all dividends in arrears, along with the current dividend, must be paid before dividends can be paid to common stockholders. If preferred stock is **noncumulative**, passed (unpaid) dividends do not accumulate. In this case, only the current dividend must be paid before dividends can be paid to common stockholders. Because the common stockholders can receive dividends only after the dividend claims of preferred stockholders have been satisfied, it is in the firm's best interest to pay preferred dividends when they are due.[1]

> **EXAMPLE**
>
> Utley Corporation, a manufacturer of specialty automobiles, currently has outstanding an issue of $6 preferred stock on which quarterly dividends of $1.50 are to be paid. Because of a cash shortage, the last two quarterly dividends were passed. The directors of the company have been receiving a large number of complaints from common stockholders, who have, of course, not received any dividends in the past two quarters either. If the preferred stock is *cumulative*, the company will have to pay its preferred stockholders $4.50 per share ($3.00 of dividends in arrears plus the current $1.50 dividend) prior to paying dividends to its common stockholders. If the preferred stock is *noncumulative,* the firm must pay only the current $1.50 dividend to its preferred stockholders prior to paying dividends to its common stockholders.

---

1. Most preferred stock is cumulative, because it is difficult to sell noncumulative stock. Common stockholders obviously prefer issuance of noncumulative preferred stock, because it does not place them in quite so risky a position. But it is often in the best interest of the firm to sell cumulative preferred stock because of its lower cost.

Other Features Preferred stock is generally *callable*—the issuer can retire outstanding stock within a certain period of time at a specified price. The call option generally cannot be exercised until after a specified date. The call price is normally set above the initial issuance price, but it may decrease as time passes. Making preferred stock callable provides the issuer with a way to bring the fixed-payment commitment of the preferred issue to an end if conditions in the financial markets make it desirable to do so.

Preferred stock quite often contains a **conversion feature** that allows *holders of convertible preferred stock* to change each share into a stated number of shares of common stock. Sometimes the number of shares of common stock that the preferred stock can be exchanged for changes according to a prespecified formula.

conversion feature (preferred stock)
A feature of *convertible preferred stock* that allows holders to change each share into a stated number of shares of common stock.

Issuing Common Stock

Because of the high risk associated with a business startup, a firm's initial financing typically comes from its founders in the form of a common stock investment. Until the founders have made an equity investment, it is highly unlikely that others will contribute either equity or debt capital. Early-stage investors in the firm's equity, as well as lenders who provide debt capital, want to be assured that they are taking no more risk than the founding owner(s). In addition, they want confirmation that the founders are confident enough in their vision for the firm that they are willing to risk their own money.

The initial nonfounder financing for business startups with attractive growth prospects comes from private equity investors. Then, as the firm establishes the viability of its product or service offering and begins to generate revenues, cash flow, and profits, it will often "go public" by issuing shares of common stock to a much broader group of investors.

Before we consider the initial *public* sales of equity, let's review some of the key aspects of early-stage equity financing in firms that have attractive growth prospects.

Venture Capital

The initial external equity financing privately raised by firms, typically early-stage firms with attractive growth prospects, is called **venture capital**. Those who provide venture capital are known as **venture capitalists** (**VCs**). They typically are formal business entities that maintain strong oversight over the firms they invest in and that have clearly defined exit strategies. Less visible early-stage investors called **angel capitalists** (or **angels**) tend to be investors who do not actually operate as a business; they are often wealthy individual investors who are willing to invest in promising early-stage companies in exchange for a portion of the firm's equity. Although angels play a major role in early-stage equity financing, we will focus on VCs because of their more formal structure and greater public visibility.

venture capital
Privately raised external equity capital used to fund early-stage firms with attractive growth prospects.

venture capitalists (VCs)
Providers of venture capital; typically, formal businesses that maintain strong oversight over the firms they invest in and that have clearly defined exit strategies.

angel capitalists (angels)
Wealthy individual investors who do not operate as a business but invest in promising early-stage companies in exchange for a portion of the firm's equity.

Organization and Investment Stages Institutional venture capital investors tend to be organized in one of four basic ways, as described in Table 7.2. The *VC limited partnership* is by far the dominant structure. These funds have as their sole objective to earn high returns, rather than to obtain access to the companies in order to sell or buy other products or services.

TABLE 7.2 Organization of Institutional Venture Capital Investors

Organization	Description
Small business investment companies (SBICs)	Corporations chartered by the federal government that can borrow at attractive rates from the U.S. Treasury and use the funds to make venture capital investments in private companies.
Financial VC funds	Subsidiaries of financial institutions, particularly banks, set up to help young firms grow and, it is hoped, become major customers of the institution.
Corporate VC funds	Firms, sometimes subsidiaries, established by nonfinancial firms, typically to gain access to new technologies that the corporation can access to further its own growth.
VC limited partnerships	Limited partnerships organized by professional VC firms, which serve as the general partner and organize, invest, and manage the partnership using the limited partners' funds; the professional VCs ultimately liquidate the partnership and distribute the proceeds to all partners.

VCs can invest in early-stage companies, later-stage companies, or buyouts and acquisitions. Generally, about 40 to 50 percent of VC investments are devoted to early-stage companies (for startup funding and expansion) and a similar percentage to later-stage companies (for marketing, production expansion, and preparation for public offering); the remaining 5 to 10 percent are devoted to the buyout or acquisition of other companies. Generally, VCs look for compound annual rates of return ranging from 20 to 50 percent or more, depending on both the development stage and the attributes of each company. Earlier-stage investments tend to demand higher returns than later-stage investments because of the higher risk associated with the earlier stages of a firm's growth.

Deal Structure and Pricing Regardless of the development stage, venture capital investments are made under a legal contract that clearly allocates responsibilities and ownership interests between existing owners (founders) and the VC fund or limited partnership. The terms of the agreement will depend on numerous factors related to the founders; the business structure, stage of development, and outlook; and other market and timing issues. The specific financial terms will, of course, depend on the value of the enterprise, the amount of funding, and the perceived risk. To control the VC's risk, various covenants are included in the agreement, and the actual funding may be pegged to the achievement of measurable *milestones*. The VC will negotiate numerous other provisions into the contract, both to ensure the firm's success and to control its risk exposure. The contract will have an explicit exit strategy for the VC that may be tied both to measurable milestones and to time.

Each VC investment is unique. The amount of equity to which the VC is entitled will depend on the value of the firm, the terms of the contract, the exit terms, and the minimum compound annual rate of return required by the VC on its investment. The transaction will be structured to provide the VC with a high rate of return that is consistent with the typically high risk of such transactions. The exit strategy of most VC investments is to take the firm public through an initial public offering.

Going Public

When a firm wishes to sell its stock in the primary market, it has three alternatives. It can make (1) a *public offering,* in which it offers its shares for sale to the general public; (2) a *rights offering,* in which new shares are sold to existing stockholders; or (3) a *private placement,* in which the firm sells new securities directly to an investor or group of investors. Here we focus on public offerings, particularly the **initial public offering (IPO),** which is the first public sale of a firm's stock. IPOs are typically made by small, rapidly growing companies that either require additional capital to continue expanding or have met a milestone for going public that was established in a contract signed earlier in order to obtain VC funding.

initial public offering (IPO)
The first public sale of a firm's stock.

To go public, the firm must first obtain the approval of its current shareholders, the investors who own its privately issued stock. Next, the company's auditors and lawyers must certify that all documents for the company are legitimate. The company then finds an investment bank willing to *underwrite* the offering. This underwriter is responsible for promoting the stock and facilitating the sale of the company's IPO shares. The underwriter often brings in other investment banking firms as participants. We'll discuss the role of the investment banker in more detail in the next section.

The company files a registration statement with the SEC. One portion of the registration statement is called the **prospectus.** It describes the key aspects of the issue, the issuer, and its management and financial position. During the waiting period between the statement's filing and its approval, prospective investors can receive a preliminary prospectus. This preliminary version is called a **red herring,** because a notice printed in red on the front cover indicates the tentative nature of the offer. The cover of the preliminary prospectus describing the 2004 stock issue of Genworth Financial, Inc., is shown in Figure 7.1. Note the red herring printed vertically on its left edge.

prospectus
A portion of a security registration statement that describes the key aspects of the issue, the issuer, and its management and financial position.

red herring
A preliminary prospectus made available to prospective investors during the waiting period between the registration statement's filing with the SEC and its approval.

After the SEC approves the registration statement, the investment community can begin analyzing the company's prospects. However, from the time it files until at least one month after the IPO is complete, the company must observe a *quiet period,* during which there are restrictions on what company officials may say about the company. The purpose of the quiet period is to make sure that all potential investors have access to the same information about the company—the information presented in the preliminary prospectus—and not to any unpublished data that might give them an unfair advantage.

The investment bankers and company executives promote the company's stock offering through a *road show,* a series of presentations to potential investors around the country and sometimes overseas. In addition to providing investors with information about the new issue, road show sessions help the investment bankers gauge the demand for the offering and set an expected pricing range. After the underwriter sets terms and prices the issue, the SEC must approve the offering.

investment banker
Financial intermediary that specializes in selling new security issues and advising firms with regard to major financial transactions.

The Investment Banker's Role

underwriting
The role of the *investment banker* in bearing the risk of reselling, at a profit, the securities purchased from an issuing corporation at an agreed-on price.

Most public offerings are made with the assistance of an **investment banker.** The investment banker is a financial intermediary (such as Salomon Brothers or Goldman, Sachs) that specializes in selling new security issues and advising firms with regard to major financial transactions. The main activity of the investment banker is **underwriting.** This process involves purchasing the security issue from

FIGURE 7.1

Cover of a Preliminary Prospectus for a Stock Issue

Some of the key factors related to the 2004 common stock issue by Genworth Financial, Inc., are summarized on the cover of the prospectus. The type printed vertically on the left edge is normally red, which explains its name "red herring." (*Source:* Genworth Financial, Inc., April 28, 2004, p. 1.)

underwriting syndicate
A group formed by an investment banker to share the financial risk associated with *underwriting* new securities.

selling group
A large number of brokerage firms that join the originating investment banker(s); each accepts responsibility for selling a certain portion of a new security issue on a commission basis.

the issuing corporation at an agreed-on price and bearing the risk of reselling it to the public at a profit. The investment banker also provides the issuer with advice about pricing and other important aspects of the issue.

In the case of very large security issues, the investment banker brings in other bankers as partners to form an **underwriting syndicate**. The syndicate shares the financial risk associated with buying the entire issue from the issuer and reselling the new securities to the public. The originating investment banker and the syndicate members put together a **selling group**, normally made up of themselves and a large number of brokerage firms. Each member of the selling group accepts the responsibility for selling a certain portion of the issue and is paid a commission on the securities it sells. The selling process for a large security issue is depicted in Figure 7.2 (see page 286).

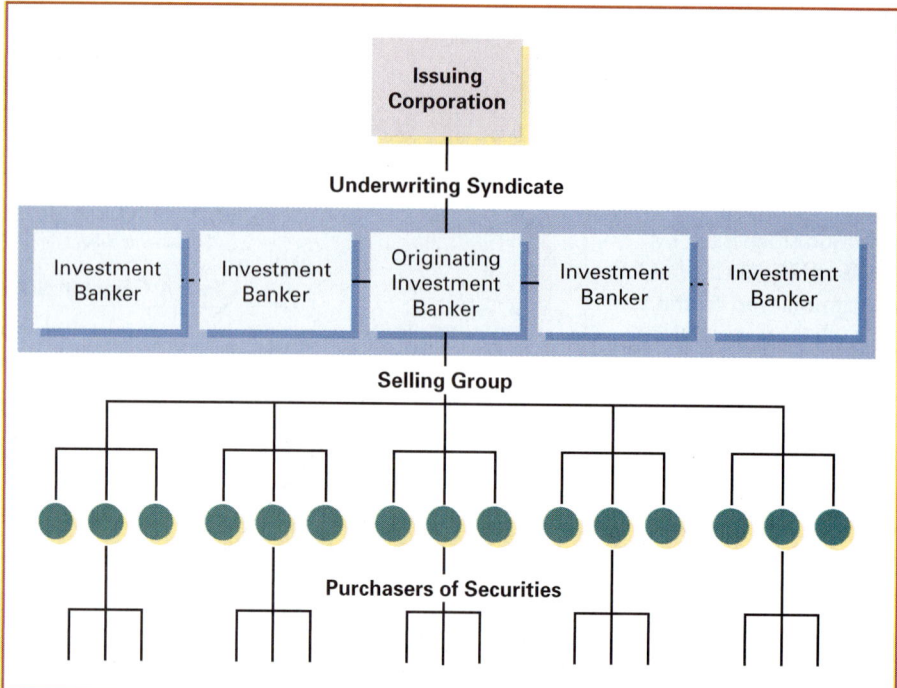

FIGURE 7.2

The Selling Process for a Large Security Issue
The investment banker hired by the issuing corporation may form an underwriting syndicate. The underwriting syndicate buys the entire security issue from the issuing corporation at an agreed-on price. The underwriter then has the opportunity (and bears the risk) of reselling the issue to the public at a profit. Both the originating investment banker and the other syndicate members put together a selling group to sell the issue on a commission basis to investors.

Compensation for underwriting and selling services typically comes in the form of a discount on the sale price of the securities. For example, an investment banker may pay the issuing firm $24 per share for stock that will be sold for $26 per share. The investment banker may then sell the shares to members of the selling group for $25.25 per share. In this case, the original investment banker earns $1.25 per share ($25.25 sale price − $24 purchase price). The members of the selling group earn 75 cents for each share they sell ($26 sale price − $25.25 purchase price). Although some primary security offerings are directly placed by the issuer, the majority of new issues are sold through public offering via the mechanism just described.

Interpreting Stock Quotations

The financial manager needs to stay abreast of the market values of the firm's outstanding stock, whether it is traded on an organized exchange, over the counter, or in international markets. Similarly, existing and prospective stockholders need to monitor the prices of the securities they own because these prices represent the current value of their investments. Price *quotations,* which include current price data along with statistics on recent price behavior, are readily available for actively traded stocks. The most up-to-date "quotes" can be obtained electronically, via a personal computer. Price information is available from stockbrokers and is widely published in news media. Popular sources of daily security price quotations include financial newspapers, such as the *Wall Street Journal* and *Investor's Business Daily,* and the business sections of daily general newspapers.

Figure 7.3 includes an excerpt from the NYSE quotations, reported in the *Wall Street Journal* of May 19, 2004, for transactions through the close of trad-

FIGURE 7.3

Stock Quotations
Selected stock quotations for May 18, 2004

YTD % CHG	52-WEEK HI	52-WEEK LO	STOCK (SYM)	DIV	YLD %	PE	VOL 100S	CLOSE	NET CHG	
-8.6	29	18	MasoniteIntl MHM	...	...	12	159	24.37	-0.17	
10.4	26.90	10.80	MasseyEngy MEE	.16	.7	dd	10453	22.97	0.67	
-72.3	16.50	3.15	MasTec MTZ	...	...	dd	2991	4.10	-0.01	
5.3	23.34	15.74	Matav MTA	2.05e	10.4	...	140	19.70	0.83	
-10.8	13.09	8.38	MaterlSci MSC	.01e	.1	dd	1109	9.02	0.21	
-6.0	15.80	8.32	MatsuElec MC	.12e	.9	...	1004	13.10	0.38	
-11.3	22.33	16.74	Mattel MAT	.40f	2.3	15	17320	17.10	0.12	
10.4	27.99	14.29	♦MavrckTube MVK	...	...	17	5765	21.25	0.29	
-12.6	41.24	23.90	Maximus MMS	...	...	20	304	34.19	0.28	
-38.6	15.38	6.09	Maxtor MXO	...	...	20	13340	6.82	0.05	
-0.9	36.48	20.02	MayDeptStrs MAY	.97	3.4	21	19416	28.82	0.43	
-10.0	32.21	21.06	Maytag MYG	.72	2.9	16	8786	25.07	0.18	
1.7	74.38	55.58	McClatchy A MNI	.48f	.7	21	464	69.95	0.75	
↓ 17.6	34.85	25.13	McCrmkCo Vtg MKCV	.56	1.6	...	1	35.10	0.90	
↓ 17.5	35.38	25.12	McCrmkCo MKC	.56	1.6	23	6527	35.38	0.27	
-41.8	12.56	3.70	McDermInt MDR	...	...	dd	9512	6.95	-0.12	
3.9	29.98	16.58	McDonalds MCD	.40f	1.6	20	35174	25.79	-0.08	← McDonalds
10.3	81.34	58.60	McGrawH MHP	1.20	1.6	22	6055	77.12	0.56	
4.5	37.14	27.01	McKesson MCK	.24	.7	15	17423	33.61	-0.13	
-30.4	20	10.35	McMoRanExpl MMR	.63e	4.8	dd	731	13.05	-0.30	
24.3	5.86	2.75	♦MdwbrkInsGp MIG	...	...	15	1934	5.26	-0.04	
-12.5	30.19	23.50	MeadWVaco MWV	.92	3.5	77	6065	26.03	0.18	
8.2	39.25	20.20	MedcoHlthSol MHS n	...	...	23	10822	36.77	0.32	
4.6	72.48	53.67	MediaGen A MEG	.80	1.2	23	547	68.10	0.15	
↓ -48.2	12.31	5.79	MedStaffNtwk MRN	...	...	dd	1029	5.67	-0.13	
20.0	45.26	26.03	MedicisPhrm MRX s	.10	.2	cc	8099	42.79	-0.28	
1.0	52.92	42.90	Medtronic MDT	.29	.6	32	44221	49.10	-0.20	
-12.6	34.13	25.30	MellonFnl MEL	.72f	2.6	15	15806	28.08	0.41	
-4.3	31.25	17.20	MensWearhs MW	...	...	18	2632	23.93	0.69	
25.4	33.12	18.66	MentorCp MNT	.60	2.0	27	2642	30.18	0.38	
1.4	60.10	40.57	Merck MRK	1.48	3.2	16	37488	46.85	0.21	
4.6	53.40	42.05	♦MercuryGen MCY	1.48f	3.0	13	634	48.70	0.18	
5.5	53.47	41.59	Meredith MDP	.48	.9	26	771	51.49	0.33	
-18.1	15.72	8.95	♦MeridnGld MDG	...	...	31	6926	11.96	0.38	

Source: *Wall Street Journal,* May 19, 2004, p. C6.

Hint Preferred stock quotations are listed separately and include only four data items: dividend, dividend yield, closing price, and change in closing price from the previous day.

ing on Tuesday, May 18, 2004. We'll look at the quotations for the common stock of McDonalds, highlighted in the figure. The quotations show that stock prices are quoted in dollars and cents.

The first column gives the percent change in the stock's closing price for the calendar year to date. You can see that McDonalds' price has increased 3.9 percent (+3.9) since the start of 2004. The next two columns, labeled "HI" and "LO," show the highest and lowest prices at which the stock sold during the preceding 52 weeks. McDonalds common stock, for example, traded between $16.58 and $29.98 during the 52-week period that ended May 18, 2004. Listed to the right of the company's name is its *stock symbol*; McDonalds goes by "MCD." The figure listed right after the stock symbol under "DIV" is the annual cash dividend paid on each share of stock. The dividend for McDonalds was $0.40 per share. The next item, labeled "YLD%," is the *dividend yield*, which is found by dividing the stated dividend by the closing share price. The dividend yield for McDonalds is 1.6 percent (0.40 ÷ 25.79 = 0.0155 = 1.6%).

The *price/earnings (P/E) ratio*, labeled "PE," is next. It is calculated by dividing the closing market price by the firm's most recent annual earnings per share (EPS). The price/earnings (P/E) ratio, as noted in Chapter 2, measures the amount investors are willing to pay for each dollar of the firm's earnings. McDonalds' P/E ratio was 20—the stock was trading at 20 times its earnings. The P/E ratio is believed to reflect investor expectations concerning the firm's future prospects: Higher P/E ratios reflect investor optimism and confidence; lower P/E ratios reflect investor pessimism and concern.

The daily volume, labeled "VOL 100s," follows the P/E ratio. Here the day's sales are quoted in lots of 100 shares. The value 35174 for McDonalds indicates that 3,517,400 shares of its common stock were traded on May 18, 2004. The next column, labeled "CLOSE," contains the closing (last) price at which the stock sold on the given day. The value for McDonalds was $25.79. The final column, "NET CHG," indicates the change in the closing price from that on the prior trading day. McDonalds closed down $0.08 from May 17, 2004, which means the closing price on that day was $25.87.

Similar quotations systems are used for stocks that trade on other exchanges such as the American Stock Exchange (AMEX) and for the over-the-counter (OTC) exchange's Nasdaq National Market Issues. Also note that when a stock (or bond) issue is not traded on a given day, it generally is not quoted in the financial and business press.

Review Questions

7-2 What risks do common stockholders take that other suppliers of long-term capital do not?

7-3 How does a *rights offering* protect a firm's stockholders against the *dilution of ownership*?

7-4 Explain the relationships among authorized shares, outstanding shares, treasury stock, and issued shares.

7-5 What are the advantages to both U.S.-based and foreign corporations of issuing stock outside their home markets? What are *American depositary receipts (ADRs)*?

7-6 What claims do preferred stockholders have with respect to distribution of earnings (dividends) and assets?

7-7 Explain the *cumulative feature* of preferred stock. What is the purpose of a *call feature* in a preferred stock issue?

7-8 What is the difference between a *venture capitalist* (VC) and an *angel capitalist* (angel)?

7-9 Into what bodies are institutional VCs most commonly organized? How are their deals structured and priced?

7-10 What general procedures must a private firm follow to go public via an *initial public offering* (IPO)?

7-11 What role does an *investment banker* play in a public offering? Explain the sequence of events in the issuing of stock.

7-12 Describe the key items of information included in a stock *quotation*. What information does the stock's *price/earnings (P/E) ratio* provide?

Common Stock Valuation

Common stockholders expect to be rewarded through periodic cash dividends and an increasing—or at least nondeclining—share value. Like current owners, prospective owners and security analysts frequently estimate the firm's value.

In Practice: FOCUS ON ETHICS

DO INVESTORS NOW REQUIRE A "CREDIBILITY PREMIUM"?

Possibly following the "moral" advice of actor Michael Douglas in the movie *Wall Street* that "Greed is good," numerous public companies have published inaccurate and misleading financial reports in recent years. Stock brokerages further muddied the investment information waters by overrating the prospects of companies whose securities they helped bring to the market. These ethical lapses have serious implications for investors and for the value of the stocks they hold.

A March 2004 survey of finance executives by *CFO* magazine asked these managers to put themselves in the role of investing their own money. Their responses were highly revealing: A mere 27 percent would feel "very confident" that they were getting high-quality and complete information from public companies (with 65 percent feeling somewhat confident and 8 percent feeling not confident). Lynn Turner, former SEC chief accountant, believes stock investors lost $100 billion over the past 6 years due to restatements of financial reports. Warren Buffett said it best: "Situational ethics has reared its ugly head."

Information put out by securities analysts working for stock brokerages has been equally flawed—or worse. According to *Kiplinger's Magazine,* N.Y. state attorney general Eliot Spitzer levied a $1.4 billion fine on ten Wall Street firms, documenting ratings that were routinely inflated, bribes to other firms' analysts to get them to write glowing reports, and pressure on individual analysts to reverse negative ratings.

Why should the analyst doing valuation care about the public attitude? Because when people don't trust the numbers, they price assets to reflect both a risk premium (for business and financial risks) and what Robert Arnott calls "a credibility premium." As a result, stock prices are lower than they should be, and honest companies may get penalized along with the dishonest ones. The good news is that the heightened scrutiny and Sarbanes-Oxley Act are having a positive effect: 77 percent of CFOs surveyed said that the new law makes it easier for them to resist pressure to misstate financials. Many corporate executives are hopeful that investor confidence will be restored as a result.

Sources: Fred Frailey, "How About Real Remorse?" *Kiplinger's,* July 2003; Andy Serwer, "Dirty Rotten Numbers," *Fortune,* February 18, 2002.

■ *If you were a professor in a business school, what might you tell students about the effects of dishonesty and greed?*

Investors purchase the stock when they believe that it is *undervalued*—when its true value is greater than its market price. They sell the stock when they feel that it is *overvalued*—when its market price is greater than its true value. As the *In Practice* box above discusses, some investors include a "credibility premium" in their valuation, to offset overly optimistic financial reports.

In this section, we will describe specific stock valuation techniques. First, though, we will look at the concept of an efficient market, which questions whether the prices of actively traded stocks can differ from their true values.

Market Efficiency

Hint Be sure to clarify in your own mind the difference between the required return and the expected return. *Required return* is what an investor *has to have* to invest in a specific asset, and *expected return* is the return an investor *thinks he or she will get* if the asset is purchased.

Economically rational buyers and sellers use their assessment of an asset's risk and return to determine its value. To a buyer, the asset's value represents the maximum price that he or she would pay to acquire it; a seller views the asset's value as a minimum sale price. In competitive markets with many active participants, such as the New York Stock Exchange, the interactions of many buyers and sellers result in an equilibrium price—the *market value*—for each security. This price reflects the collective actions that buyers and sellers take on the basis of all available information. Buyers and sellers are assumed to digest new information immediately as it becomes available and, through their purchase and sale activities, to create a new market equilibrium price quickly.

The Efficient-Market Hypothesis

As noted in Chapter 1, active markets such as the New York Stock Exchange are *efficient*—they are made up of many rational investors who react quickly and objectively to new information. The **efficient-market hypothesis (EMH)**, which is the basic theory describing the behavior of such a "perfect" market, specifically states that

1. Securities are typically in equilibrium, which means that they are fairly priced and that their expected returns equal their required returns.
2. At any point in time, security prices fully reflect all public information available about the firm and its securities,[2] and these prices react swiftly to new information.
3. Because stocks are fully and fairly priced, investors need not waste their time trying to find and capitalize on mispriced (undervalued or overvalued) securities.

efficient-market hypothesis (EMH)
Theory describing the behavior of an assumed "perfect" market in which (1) securities are typically in equilibrium, (2) security prices fully reflect all public information available and react swiftly to new information, and, (3) because stocks are fully and fairly priced, investors need not waste time looking for mispriced securities.

Not all market participants are believers in the efficient-market hypothesis. Some feel that it is worthwhile to search for undervalued or overvalued securities and to trade them to profit from market inefficiencies. Others argue that it is mere luck that would allow market participants to anticipate new information correctly and as a result earn *excess returns*—that is, actual returns greater than required returns. They believe it is unlikely that market participants can *over the long run* earn excess returns. Contrary to this belief, some well-known investors such as Warren Buffett and Peter Lynch *have* over the long run consistently earned excess returns on their portfolios. It is unclear whether their success is the result of their superior ability to anticipate new information or of some form of market inefficiency.

The Behavioral Finance Challenge

Although considerable evidence supports the concept of market efficiency, a growing body of academic evidence has begun to cast doubt on the validity of this notion. The research documents various *anomalies*—deviations from accepted beliefs—in stock returns. A number of academics as well as practitioners have also recognized that emotions and other subjective factors play a role in investment decisions.

behavioral finance
A growing body of research that focuses on investor behavior and its impact on investment decisions and stock prices. Advocates are commonly referred to as "behaviorists."

This focus on investor behavior has resulted in a significant body of research, which is collectively referred to as **behavioral finance.** Advocates of behavioral finance are commonly referred to as "behaviorists." One notable event that acknowledged the importance of the field of behavioral finance was the awarding

---

2. Those market participants who have nonpublic—*inside*—information may have an unfair advantage that enables them to earn an excess return. Since the mid-1980s disclosure of the insider-trading activities of a number of well-known financiers and investors, major national attention has been focused on the "problem" of insider trading and its resolution. Clearly, those who trade securities on the basis of inside information have an unfair and illegal advantage. Empirical research has confirmed that those with inside information do indeed have an opportunity to earn an excess return. Here we ignore this possibility, given its illegality and the fact that enhanced surveillance and enforcement by the securities industry and the government have in recent years (it appears) significantly reduced insider trading. We, in effect, assume that all relevant information is public and that therefore the market is efficient.

of the 2002 Nobel Prize in economics to Daniel Kahneman for his work in integrating insights from psychology and economics. Ongoing research into the psychological factors that can affect investor behavior and the resulting effects on stock prices will likely result in growing acceptance of behavioral finance.

Throughout this text we ignore both disbelievers and behaviorists and continue to assume market efficiency. This means that *the terms "expected return" and "required return" are used interchangeably,* because they should be equal in an efficient market. This also means that stock prices accurately reflect true value based on risk and return. In other words, we will operate under the assumption that the market price at any point in time is the best estimate of value. We're now ready to look closely at the mechanics of common stock valuation.

The Basic Common Stock Valuation Equation

Like the value of a bond, which we discussed in Chapter 6, *the value of a share of common stock is equal to the present value of all future cash flows (dividends) that it is expected to provide over an infinite time horizon.* Although a stockholder can earn capital gains by selling stock at a price above that originally paid, what is really sold is the right to all future dividends. What about stocks that are not expected to pay dividends in the foreseeable future? Such stocks have a value attributable to a distant dividend expected to result from sale of the company or liquidation of its assets. Therefore, *from a valuation viewpoint, only dividends are relevant.*

By redefining terms, the basic valuation model in Equation 6.1 can be specified for common stock, as given in Equation 7.1:

$$P_0 = \frac{D_1}{(1+k_s)^1} + \frac{D_2}{(1+k_s)^2} + \cdots + \frac{D_\infty}{(1+k_s)^\infty} \qquad (7.1)$$

where

P_0 = value of common stock

D_t = per-share dividend *expected* at the end of year t

k_s = required return on common stock

The equation can be simplified somewhat by redefining each year's dividend, D_t, in terms of anticipated growth. We will demonstrate two models here: zero-growth and constant-growth. A third model—variable-growth—will be defined and a detailed explanation is at the book's Web site (www.aw-bc.com/gitman).

Zero-Growth Model

zero-growth model
An approach to dividend valuation that assumes a constant, nongrowing dividend stream.

The simplest approach to dividend valuation, the **zero-growth model,** assumes a constant, nongrowing dividend stream. In terms of the notation already introduced,

$$D_1 = D_2 = \cdots = D_\infty$$

When we let D_1 represent the amount of the annual dividend, Equation 7.1 under zero growth reduces to

$$P_0 = D_1 \times \sum_{t=1}^{\infty} \frac{1}{(1+k_s)^t} = D_1 \times (PVIFA_{k_s,\infty}) = D_1 \times \frac{1}{k_s} = \frac{D_1}{k_s} \qquad (7.2)$$

The equation shows that with zero growth, the value of a share of stock would equal the present value of a perpetuity of D_1 dollars discounted at a rate k_s. (Perpetuities were introduced in Chapter 4; see Equation 4.17 and the related discussion.)

EXAMPLE The dividend of Denham Company, an established textile producer, is expected to remain constant at $3 per share indefinitely. If the required return on its stock is 15%, the stock's value is $20 ($3 ÷ 0.15) per share.

Preferred Stock Valuation Because preferred stock typically provides its holders with a fixed annual dividend over its assumed infinite life, *Equation 7.2 can be used to find the value of preferred stock.* The value of preferred stock can be estimated by substituting the stated dividend on the preferred stock for D_1 and the required return for k_s in Equation 7.2. For example, a preferred stock paying a $5 stated annual dividend and having a required return of 13 percent would have a value of $38.46 ($5 ÷ 0.13) per share.

Constant-Growth Model

constant-growth model
A widely cited dividend valuation approach that assumes that dividends will grow at a constant rate, but a rate that is less than the required return.

The most widely cited dividend valuation approach, the **constant-growth model**, assumes that dividends will grow at a constant rate, but a rate that is less than the required return. (The assumption that the constant rate of growth, g, is less than the required return, k_s, is a necessary mathematical condition for deriving this model.) By letting D_0 represent the most recent dividend, we can rewrite Equation 7.1 as follows:

$$P_0 = \frac{D_0 \times (1 + g)^1}{(1 + k_s)^1} + \frac{D_0 \times (1 + g)^2}{(1 + k_s)^2} + \cdots + \frac{D_0 \times (1 + g)^\infty}{(1 + k_s)^\infty} \quad (7.3)$$

If we simplify Equation 7.3, it can be rewritten as[3]

$$P_0 = \frac{D_1}{k_s - g} \quad (7.4)$$

Gordon model
A common name for the *constant-growth model* that is widely cited in dividend valuation.

The constant-growth model in Equation 7.4 is commonly called the **Gordon model**. An example will show how it works.

---

[3]. For the interested reader, the calculations necessary to derive Equation 7.4 from Equation 7.3 follow. The first step is to multiply each side of Equation 7.3 by $(1 + k_s)/(1 + g)$ and subtract Equation 7.3 from the resulting expression. This yields

$$\frac{P_0 \times (1 + k_s)}{1 + g} - P_0 = D_0 - \frac{D_0 \times (1 + g)^\infty}{(1 + k_s)^\infty} \quad (1)$$

Because k_s is assumed to be greater than g, the second term on the right side of Equation 1 should be zero. Thus

$$P_0 \times \left(\frac{1 + k_s}{1 + g} - 1\right) = D_0 \quad (2)$$

Equation 2 is simplified as follows:

$$P_0 \times \left[\frac{(1 + k_s) - (1 + g)}{1 + g}\right] = D_0 \quad (3)$$

$$P_0 \times (k_s - g) = D_0 \times (1 + g) \quad (4)$$

$$P_0 = \frac{D_1}{k_s - g} \quad (5)$$

Equation 5 equals Equation 7.4.

EXAMPLE

Lamar Company, a small cosmetics company, from 2001 through 2006 paid the following per-share dividends:

Year	Dividend per share
2006	$1.40
2005	1.29
2004	1.20
2003	1.12
2002	1.05
2001	1.00

We assume that the historical compound annual growth rate of dividends is an accurate estimate of the future constant annual rate of dividend growth, g. Using Appendix Table A–2 or a financial calculator, we find that the historical compound annual growth rate of Lamar Company dividends equals 7%.[4] The company estimates that its dividend in 2007, D_1, will equal $1.50. The required return, k_s, is assumed to be 15%. By substituting these values into Equation 7.4, we find the value of the stock to be

$$P_0 = \frac{\$1.50}{0.15 - 0.07} = \frac{\$1.50}{0.08} = \underline{\$18.75} \text{ per share}$$

Assuming that the values of D_1, k_s, and g are accurately estimated, Lamar Company's stock value is $18.75 per share.

Variable-Growth Model

variable-growth model
A dividend valuation approach that allows for a change in the dividend growth rate.

The zero- and constant-growth common stock models do not allow for any shift in expected growth rates. Because future growth rates might shift up or down in response to changing expectations, it is useful to consider a **variable-growth model** that allows for a change in the dividend growth rate. For an explanation of how the variable-growth model can be used to determine the value of a share of stock, see the book's Web site at www.aw-bc.com/gitman.

---

4. The technique involves solving the following equation for g:

$$D_{2006} = D_{2001} \times (1 + g)^5$$

$$\frac{D_{2001}}{D_{2006}} = \frac{1}{(1+g)^5} = PVIF_{g,5}$$

To do so, we can use financial tables or a financial calculator.

Two basic steps can be followed using the present value table. First, dividing the earliest dividend ($D_{2001} = \$1.00$) by the most recent dividend ($D_{2006} = \$1.40$) yields a factor for the present value of one dollar, $PVIF$, of 0.714 ($1.00 ÷ $1.40). Although six dividends are shown, *they reflect only 5 years of growth*. (The number of years of growth can also be found by subtracting the earliest year from the most recent year—that is, 2006 − 2001 = *5 years of growth*.) By looking across the Appendix Table A–2 at the $PVIF$ for 5 years, we find that the factor closest to 0.714 occurs at 7% (0.713). Therefore, the growth rate of the dividends, rounded to the nearest whole percent, is 7%.

Alternatively, a financial calculator can be used. (*Note:* Most calculators require *either* the PV or FV value to be input as a negative number to calculate an unknown interest or growth rate. That approach is used here.) Using the inputs shown at the left, you should find the growth rate to be 6.96%, which we round to 7%.

An electronic spreadsheet could also be used to make this computation. Given space considerations, we have forgone that computational aid here.

Free Cash Flow Valuation Model

As an alternative to the dividend valuation models presented above, a firm's value can be estimated by using its projected *free cash flows* (FCFs). This approach is appealing when one is valuing firms that have no dividend history or are startups or when one is valuing an operating unit or division of a larger public company. Although dividend valuation models are widely used and accepted, in these situations it is preferable to use a more general free cash flow valuation model.

The **free cash flow valuation model** is based on the same basic premise as dividend valuation models: The value of a share of common stock is the present value of all future cash flows it is expected to provide over an infinite time horizon. However, in the free cash flow valuation model, instead of valuing the firm's expected dividends, we value the firm's expected *free cash flows*, defined in Equation 3.5 (on page 101). They represent the amount of cash flow available to investors—the providers of debt (creditors) and equity (owners)—after all other obligations have been met.

The free cash flow valuation model estimates the value of the entire company by finding the present value of its expected free cash flows discounted at its *weighted average cost of capital*, which is its expected average future cost of funds over the long run (see Chapter 10), as specified in Equation 7.5.

free cash flow valuation model
A model that determines the value of an entire company as the present value of its expected *free cash flows* discounted at the firm's *weighted average cost of capital*, which is its expected average future cost of funds over the long run.

$$V_C = \frac{FCF_1}{(1 + k_a)^1} + \frac{FCF_2}{(1 + k_a)^2} + \cdots + \frac{FCF_\infty}{(1 + k_a)^\infty} \quad (7.5)$$

where

V_C = value of the entire company
FCF_t = free cash flow *expected* at the end of year t
k_a = the firm's weighted average cost of capital

Note the similarity between Equations 7.5 and 7.1, the general stock valuation equation.

Because the value of the entire company, V_C, is the market value of the entire enterprise (that is, of all assets), to find common stock value, V_S, we must subtract the market value of all of the firm's debt, V_D, and the market value of preferred stock, V_P, from V_C.

$$V_S = V_C - V_D - V_P \quad (7.6)$$

Because it is difficult to forecast a firm's free cash flow, specific annual cash flows are typically forecast for only about 5 years, beyond which a constant growth rate is assumed. Here we assume that the first 5 years of free cash flows are explicitly forecast and that a constant rate of free cash flow growth occurs beyond the end of year 5 to infinity. This model is methodologically similar to the variable-growth model presented earlier. Its application is best demonstrated with an example.

EXAMPLE Dewhurst, Inc., wishes to determine the value of its stock by using the free cash flow valuation model. To apply the model, the firm's CFO developed the data given in Table 7.3. Application of the model can be performed in four steps.

Step 1 Calculate the present value of the free cash flow occurring from the end of 2012 to infinity, measured at the beginning of 2012 (that is, at the end

TABLE 7.3 Dewhurst, Inc.'s Data for Free Cash Flow Valuation Model

Year (t)	Free cash flow $(FCF_t)^a$	Other data
2007	$400,000	Growth rate of FCF, beyond 2011 to infinity, $g_{FCF} = 3\%$
2008	450,000	Weighted average cost of capital, $k_a = 9\%$
2009	520,000	Market value of all debt, $V_D = \$3,100,000$
2010	560,000	Market value of preferred stock, $V_P = \$800,000$
2011	600,000	Number of shares of common stock outstanding = 300,000

^{a}Developed using Equations 3.4 and 3.5 (on pages 100 and 101).

of 2011). Because a constant rate of growth in FCF is forecast beyond 2011, we can use the constant-growth dividend valuation model (Equation 7.4) to calculate the value of the free cash flows from the end of 2012 to infinity.

$$\text{Value of } FCF_{2012 \to \infty} = \frac{FCF_{2012}}{k_a - g_{FCF}}$$

$$= \frac{\$600,000 \times (1 + 0.03)}{0.09 - 0.03}$$

$$= \frac{\$618,000}{0.06} = \underline{\$10,300,000}$$

Note that to calculate the FCF in 2012, we had to increase the 2011 FCF value of $600,000 by the 3% FCF growth rate, g_{FCF}.

Step 2 Add the present value of the FCF from 2012 to infinity, which is measured at the end of 2011, to the 2011 FCF value to get the total FCF in 2011.

Total $FCF_{2011} = \$600,000 + \$10,300,000 = \$10,900,000$

Step 3 Find the sum of the present values of the FCFs for 2007 through 2011 to determine the value of the entire company, V_C. This calculation is shown in Table 7.4 (see page 296), using present value interest factors, $PVIFs$, from Appendix Table A-2.

Step 4 Calculate the value of the common stock using Equation 7.6. Substituting the value of the entire company, V_C, calculated in Step 3, and the market values of debt, V_D, and preferred stock, V_P, given in Table 7.3, yields the value of the common stock, V_S:

$V_S = \$8,628,620 - \$3,100,000 - \$800,000 = \underline{\$4,728,620}$

The value of Dewhurst's common stock is therefore estimated to be $4,728,620. By dividing this total by the 300,000 shares of common stock that the firm has outstanding, we get a common stock value of *$15.76 per share* ($4,728,620 ÷ 300,000).

TABLE 7.4 Calculation of the Value of the Entire Company for Dewhurst, Inc.

Year (t)	FCF_t (1)	$PVIF_{9\%,t}$ (2)	Present value of FCF_t [(1) × (2)] (3)
2007	$ 400,000	0.917	$ 366,800
2008	450,000	0.842	378,900
2009	520,000	0.772	401,440
2010	560,000	0.708	396,480
2011	10,900,000^a	0.650	7,085,000
		Value of entire company, $V_C =$	$8,628,620

^{a}This amount is the sum of the FCF_{2011} of $600,000 from Table 7.3 and the $10,300,000 value of the $FCF_{2012 \to \infty}$ calculated in Step 1.

It should now be clear that the free cash flow valuation model is consistent with the dividend valuation models presented earlier. The appeal of this approach is its focus on the free cash flow estimates rather than on forecast dividends, which are far more difficult to estimate, given that they are paid at the discretion of the firm's board. The more general nature of the free cash flow model is responsible for its growing popularity, particularly with CFOs and other financial managers.

Other Approaches to Common Stock Valuation

Many other approaches to common stock valuation exist. The more popular approaches include book value, liquidation value, and some type of price/earnings multiple.

Book Value

book value per share
The amount per share of common stock that would be received if all of the firm's assets were *sold for their exact book (accounting) value* and the proceeds remaining after paying all liabilities (including preferred stock) were divided among the common stockholders.

Book value per share is simply the amount per share of common stock that would be received if all of the firm's assets were *sold for their exact book (accounting) value* and the proceeds remaining after paying all liabilities (including preferred stock) were divided among the common stockholders. This method lacks sophistication and can be criticized on the basis of its reliance on historical balance sheet data. It ignores the firm's expected earnings potential and generally lacks any true relationship to the firm's value in the marketplace. Let us look at an example.

EXAMPLE At year-end 2006, Lamar Company's balance sheet shows total assets of $6 million, total liabilities (including preferred stock) of $4.5 million, and 100,000 shares of common stock outstanding. Its book value per share therefore would be

$$\frac{\$6,000,000 - \$4,500,000}{100,000 \text{ shares}} = \underline{\underline{\$15}} \text{ per share}$$

Because this value assumes that assets could be sold for their book value, it may not represent the minimum price at which shares are valued in the marketplace.

As a matter of fact, although most stocks sell above book value, it is not unusual to find stocks selling below book value when investors believe either that assets are overvalued or that the firm's liabilities are understated.

Liquidation Value

liquidation value per share
The *actual amount* per share of common stock that would be received if all of the firm's assets were *sold for their market value,* liabilities (including preferred stock) were paid, and any remaining money were divided among the common stockholders.

Liquidation value per share is the *actual amount* per share of common stock that would be received if all of the firm's assets were *sold for their market value,* liabilities (including preferred stock) were paid, and any remaining money were divided among the common stockholders.[5] This measure is more realistic than book value—because it is based on the current market value of the firm's assets—but it still fails to consider the earning power of those assets. An example will illustrate.

EXAMPLE

Lamar Company found upon investigation that it could obtain only $5.25 million if it sold its assets today. The firm's liquidation value per share therefore would be

$$\frac{\$5,250,000 - \$4,500,000}{100,000 \text{ shares}} = \underline{\underline{\$7.50}} \text{ per share}$$

Ignoring liquidation expenses, this amount would be the firm's minimum value.

Price/Earnings (P/E) Multiples

The *price/earnings (P/E) ratio,* introduced in Chapter 2, reflects the amount investors are willing to pay for each dollar of earnings. The average P/E ratio in a particular industry can be used as the guide to a firm's value—if it is assumed that investors value the earnings of that firm in the same way they do the "average" firm in the industry. The **price/earnings multiple approach** is a popular technique used to estimate the firm's share value; it is calculated by multiplying the firm's expected earnings per share (EPS) by the average price/earnings (P/E) ratio for the industry. The average P/E ratio for the industry can be obtained from a source such as *Standard & Poor's Industrial Ratios.*

price/earnings multiple approach
A popular technique used to estimate the firm's share value; calculated by multiplying the firm's expected earnings per share (EPS) by the average price/earnings (P/E) ratio for the industry.

The use of P/E multiples is especially helpful in valuing firms that are not publicly traded, whereas market price quotations can be used to value publicly traded firms. In any case, the price/earnings multiple approach is considered superior to the use of book or liquidation values because it considers *expected* earnings. An example will demonstrate the use of price/earnings multiples.

EXAMPLE

Lamar Company is expected to earn $2.60 per share next year (2007). This expectation is based on an analysis of the firm's historical earnings trend and of expected economic and industry conditions. The average price/earnings (P/E) ratio for firms in the same industry is 7. Multiplying Lamar's expected earnings per share (EPS) of $2.60 by this ratio gives us a value for the firm's shares of $18.20, assuming that investors will continue to value the average firm at 7 times its earnings.

So how much is Lamar Company's stock worth? That's a trick question—there's no one right answer. It is important to recognize that the answer depends on the assumptions made and the techniques used. Professional securities analysts

---

5. In the event of liquidation, creditors' claims must be satisfied first, then those of the preferred stockholders. Anything left goes to common stockholders.

typically use a variety of models and techniques to value stocks. For example, an analyst might use the constant-growth model, liquidation value, and price/earnings (P/E) multiples to estimate the worth of a given stock. If the analyst feels comfortable with his or her estimates, the stock would be valued at no more than the largest estimate. Of course, should the firm's estimated liquidation value per share exceed its "going concern" value per share, estimated by using one of the valuation models (zero-, constant-, or variable-growth or free cash flow) or the P/E multiple approach, the firm would be viewed as being "worth more dead than alive." In such an event, the firm would lack sufficient earning power to justify its existence and should probably be liquidated.

Hint From an investor's perspective, the stock in this situation would be an attractive investment only if it could be purchased at a price below its liquidation value—which in an efficient market could never occur.

Review Questions

7–13 What does the *efficient-market hypothesis (EMH)* say about (**a**) securities prices, (**b**) their reaction to new information, and (**c**) investor opportunities to profit? What is the *behavioral finance* challenge to this hypothesis?

7–14 Describe, compare, and contrast the following common stock dividend valuation models: (**a**) zero-growth and (**b**) constant-growth.

7–15 Describe the *free cash flow valuation model* and explain how it differs from the dividend valuation models. What is the appeal of this model?

7–16 Explain each of the three other approaches to common stock valuation: (**a**) book value, (**b**) liquidation value, and (**c**) price/earnings (P/E) multiples. Which of these is considered the best?

Decision Making and Common Stock Value

Valuation equations measure the stock value at a point in time based on expected return and risk. Any decisions of the financial manager that affect these variables can cause the value of the firm to change. Figure 7.4 depicts the relationship among financial decisions, return, risk, and stock value.

Changes in Expected Return

Assuming that economic conditions remain stable, any management action that would cause current and prospective stockholders to raise their dividend expectations should increase the firm's value. In Equation 7.4, we can see that P_0 will

FIGURE 7.4

Decision Making and Stock Value
Financial decisions, return, risk, and stock value

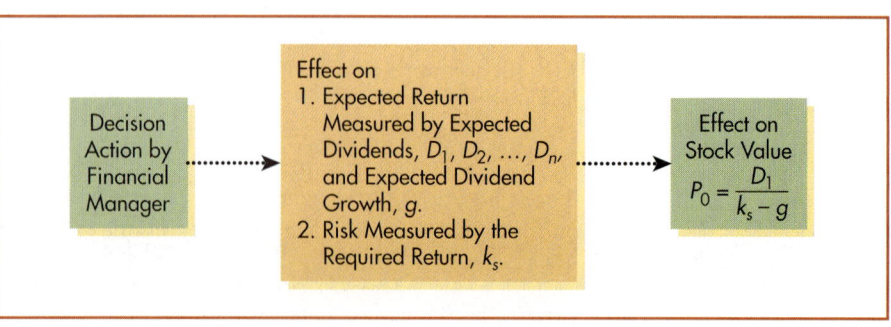

increase for any increase in D_1 or g. Any action of the financial manager that will increase the level of expected returns without changing risk (the required return) should be undertaken, because it will positively affect owners' wealth.

EXAMPLE

Using the constant-growth model, we found Lamar Company to have a share value of $18.75. On the following day, the firm announced a major technological breakthrough that would revolutionize its industry. Current and prospective stockholders would not be expected to adjust their required return of 15%, but they would expect that future dividends will increase. Specifically, they expect that although the dividend next year, D_1, will remain at $1.50, the expected rate of growth thereafter will increase from 7% to 9%. If we substitute $D_1 = \$1.50$, $k_s = 0.15$, and $g = 0.09$ into Equation 7.4, the resulting share value is $25 [\$1.50 \div (0.15 - 0.09)]$. The increased value therefore resulted from the higher expected future dividends reflected in the increase in the growth rate.

Changes in Risk

Although k_s is defined as the required return, we know from Chapter 5 that it is directly related to the nondiversifiable risk, which can be measured by beta. The *capital asset pricing model (CAPM)* given in Equation 5.7 is restated here as Equation 7.7:

$$k_s = R_F + [b \times (k_m - R_F)] \tag{7.7}$$

With the risk-free rate, R_F, and the market return, k_m, held constant, the required return, k_s, depends directly on beta. Any action taken by the financial manager that increases risk (beta) will also increase the required return. In Equation 7.4, we can see that with everything else constant, an increase in the required return, k_s, will reduce share value, P_0. Likewise, a decrease in the required return will increase share value. Thus any action of the financial manager that increases risk contributes to a reduction in value, and any action that decreases risk contributes to an increase in value.

EXAMPLE

Assume that Lamar Company's 15% required return resulted from a risk-free rate of 9%, a market return of 13%, and a beta of 1.50. Substituting into the capital asset pricing model, Equation 7.7, we get a required return, k_s, of 15%:

$$k_s = 9\% + [1.50 \times (13\% - 9\%)] = \underline{\underline{15}}\%$$

With this return, the firm's share value was calculated in an earlier example (on page 293) to be $18.75.

Now imagine that the financial manager makes a decision that, without changing expected dividends, causes the firm's beta to increase to 1.75. Assuming that R_F and k_m remain at 9% and 13%, respectively, the required return will increase to 16% ($9\% + [1.75 \times (13\% - 9\%)]$) to compensate stockholders for the increased risk. Substituting $D_1 = \$1.50$, $k_s = 0.16$, and $g = 0.07$ into the valuation equation, Equation 7.4, results in a share value of $16.67 [\$1.50 \div (0.16 - 0.07)]$. As expected, raising the required return, without any corresponding increase in expected return, causes the firm's stock value to decline. Clearly, the financial manager's action was not in the owners' best interest.

Combined Effect

A financial decision rarely affects return and risk independently; most decisions affect both factors. In terms of the measures presented, with an increase in risk (b), one would expect an increase in return (D_1 or g, or both), assuming that R_F and k_m remain unchanged. The net effect on value depends on the size of the changes in these variables.

EXAMPLE

If we assume that the two changes illustrated for Lamar Company in the preceding examples occur simultaneously, key variable values would be $D_1 = \$1.50$, $k_s = 0.16$, and $g = 0.09$. Substituting into the valuation model, we obtain a share price of $21.43 [$1.50 \div (0.16 - 0.09)]$. The net result of the decision, which increased return (g, from 7% to 9%) as well as risk (b, from 1.50 to 1.75 and therefore k_s from 15% to 16%), is positive: The share price increased from $18.75 to $21.43. The decision appears to be in the best interest of the firm's owners, because it increases their wealth.

Review Questions

7–17 Explain the linkages among financial decisions, return, risk, and stock value.

7–18 Assuming that all other variables remain unchanged, what impact would *each* of the following have on stock price? (a) The firm's beta increases. (b) The firm's required return decreases. (c) The dividend expected next year decreases. (d) The rate of growth in dividends is expected to increase.

SUMMARY

FOCUS ON VALUE

The price of each share of a firm's common stock is the value of each ownership interest. Although common stockholders typically have voting rights, which indirectly give them a say in management, their only significant right is their claim on the residual cash flows of the firm. This claim is subordinate to those of vendors, employees, customers, lenders, the government (for taxes), and preferred stockholders. The value of the common stockholders' claim is embodied in the cash flows they are entitled to receive from now to infinity. The present value of those expected cash flows is the firm's share value.

To determine this present value, forecast cash flows are discounted at a rate that reflects their risk. Riskier cash flows are discounted at higher rates, resulting in lower present values than less risky expected cash flows, which are discounted at lower rates. The value of the firm's common stock is therefore driven by its expected cash flows (returns) and risk (certainty of the expected cash flows).

In pursuing the firm's goal of **maximizing the stock price,** the financial manager must carefully consider the balance of return and risk associated with each proposal and must undertake only those actions that create value for owners—that is, increase share price. By focusing on value creation and by managing and monitoring the firm's cash flows and risk, the financial manager should be able to achieve the firm's goal of share price maximization.

REVIEW OF LEARNING GOALS

Key definitions and formulas for this chapter are summarized in Table 7.5 (see page 302).

LG1 **Differentiate between debt and equity capital.** Holders of equity capital (common and preferred stock) are owners of the firm. Typically, only common stockholders have a voice in management. Equity holders' claims on income and assets are secondary to creditors' claims, there is no maturity date, and dividends paid to stockholders are not tax-deductible, as is interest paid to debtholders.

LG2 **Discuss the rights, characteristics, and features of both common and preferred stock.** The common stock of a firm can be privately owned, closely owned, or publicly owned. It can be sold with or without a par value. Preemptive rights allow common stockholders to avoid dilution of ownership when new shares are issued. Not all shares authorized in the corporate charter are outstanding. If a firm has treasury stock, it will have issued more shares than are outstanding. Some firms have two or more classes of common stock that differ mainly in having unequal voting rights. Proxies transfer voting rights from one party to another. The decision to pay dividends to common stockholders is made by the firm's board of directors. Firms can issue stock in foreign markets. The stock of many foreign corporations is traded in the form of American depositary receipts (ADRs) in U.S. markets.

Preferred stockholders have preference over common stockholders with respect to the distribution of earnings and assets. They do not normally have voting privileges. Preferred stock issues may have certain restrictive covenants, cumulative dividends, a call feature, and a conversion feature.

LG3 **Describe the process of issuing common stock, including venture capital, going public, and the investment banker, and interpreting stock quotations.** The initial nonfounder financing for business startups with attractive growth prospects typically comes from private equity investors. These investors can be either angel capitalists or venture capitalists (VCs). VCs usually invest in both early-stage and later-stage companies that they hope to take public so as to cash out their investments.

The first public issue of a firm's stock is called an initial public offering (IPO). The company selects an investment banker to advise it and to sell the securities. The lead investment banker may form a selling syndicate with other investment bankers. The IPO process includes getting SEC approval, promoting the offering to investors, and pricing the issue.

Stock quotations provide information on calendar-year change in price, 52-week high and low, dividend, dividend yield, P/E ratio, volume, closing price, and net price change from the prior trading day.

LG4 **Understand the concept of market efficiency and basic common stock valuation using the zero-growth and constant-growth models.** Market efficiency assumes that the quick reactions of rational investors to new information cause the market value of common stock to adjust upward or downward quickly. The efficient-market hypothesis (EMH) suggests that securities are fairly priced, that they reflect fully all publicly available information, and that investors should therefore not waste time trying to find and capitalize on mispriced securities. Behavioral finance advocates challenge this hypothesis by arguing that emotion and other factors play a role in investment decisions.

The value of a share of common stock is the present value of all future dividends it is expected to provide over an infinite time horizon. Two dividend growth models—zero-growth and constant-growth—can be considered in common stock valuation. The most widely cited model is the constant-growth model. (A third model, the variable-growth model, allows for a change in the dividend growth rate.)

TABLE 7.5 Summary of Key Valuation Definitions and Formulas for Common Stock

Definitions of variables

D_t = per-share dividend *expected* at the end of year t
FCF_t = free cash flow *expected* at the end of year t
g = constant rate of growth in dividends
k_a = weighted average cost of capital
k_s = required return on common stock
P_0 = value of common stock
V_C = value of the entire company
V_D = market value of all the firm's debt
V_P = market value of preferred stock
V_S = value of common stock

Valuation formulas

Basic stock value:

$$P_0 = \frac{D_1}{(1+k_s)^1} + \frac{D_2}{(1+k_s)^2} + \cdots + \frac{D_\infty}{(1+k_s)^\infty} \qquad \text{[Equation 7.1]}$$

Common stock value:
  Zero-growth:

$$P_0 = \frac{D_1}{k_s} \quad \text{(also used to value preferred stock)} \qquad \text{[Equation 7.2]}$$

  Constant-growth:

$$P_0 = \frac{D_1}{k_s - g} \qquad \text{[Equation 7.4]}$$

  Variable-growth: See the book's Web site.
  FCF value of entire company:

$$V_C = \frac{FCF_1}{(1+k_a)^1} + \frac{FCF_2}{(1+k_a)^2} + \cdots + \frac{FCF_\infty}{(1+k_a)^\infty} \qquad \text{[Equation 7.5]}$$

FCF common stock value:

$$V_S = V_C - V_D - V_P \qquad \text{[Equation 7.6]}$$

LG5 Discuss the free cash flow valuation model and the book value, liquidation value, and price/earnings (P/E) multiples approaches. The free cash flow valuation model values startups, firms that have no dividend history, or operating units of a larger public company. The model finds the value of the entire company by discounting the firm's expected free cash flow at its weighted average cost of capital. The common stock value is found by subtracting the market values of the firm's debt and preferred stock from the value of the entire company.

Book value per share is the amount per share of common stock that would be received if all of the firm's assets were *sold for their exact book (accounting) value* and the proceeds remaining after paying all liabilities (including preferred stock) were divided among the common stockholders. Liquidation value per share is the *actual amount per share of common stock that would be received if all of the firm's assets were sold for their market value*, liabilities (including preferred stock) were paid, and the remaining money were divided among the common stockholders. The price/earnings (P/E) multiples approach estimates stock value by multiplying the firm's expected earnings per share (EPS) by the average price/earnings (P/E) ratio for the industry.

 Explain the relationships among financial decisions, return, risk, and the firm's value. In a stable economy, any action of the financial manager that increases the level of expected return without changing risk should increase share value; any action that reduces the level of expected return without changing risk should reduce share value. Similarly, any action that increases risk (required return) will reduce share value; any action that reduces risk will increase share value. An assessment of the combined effect of return and risk on stock value must be part of the financial decision-making process.

SELF-TEST PROBLEMS (SOLUTIONS IN APPENDIX B)

ST7-1 Common stock valuation Perry Motors' common stock currently pays an annual dividend of $1.80 per share. The required return on the common stock is 12%. Estimate the value of the common stock under each of the following assumptions about the dividend.
   a. Dividends are expected to grow at an annual rate of 0% to infinity.
   b. Dividends are expected to grow at a constant annual rate of 5% to infinity.

ST7-2 Free cash flow valuation Erwin Footwear wishes to assess the value of its Active Shoe Division. This division has debt with a market value of $12,500,000 and no preferred stock. Its weighted average cost of capital is 10%. The Active Shoe Division's estimated free cash flow each year from 2007 through 2010 is given in the following table. Beyond 2010 to infinity, the firm expects its free cash flow to grow at 4% annually.

Year (t)	Free cash flow (FCF_t)
2007	$ 800,000
2008	1,200,000
2009	1,400,000
2010	1,500,000

   a. Use the *free cash flow valuation model* to estimate the value of Erwin's entire Active Shoe Division.
   b. Use your finding in part **a** along with the data provided above to find this division's common stock value.
   c. If the Active Shoe Division as a public company will have 500,000 shares outstanding, use your finding in part **b** to calculate its value per share.

WARM-UP EXERCISES

E7-1 A balance sheet balances assets with their sources of debt and equity financing. If a corporation has assets equal to $5.2 million and a debt ratio of 75.0%, how much debt does the corporation have on its books?

E7–2 Angina, Inc., has 5 million shares outstanding. The firm is considering issuing an additional 1 million shares. After selling these shares at their $20 per share offering price and netting 95% of the sale proceeds, the firm is obligated by an earlier agreement to sell an additional 250,000 shares at 90% of the offering price. In total, how much cash will the firm net from these stock sales?

E7–3 Figurate Industries has 750,000 shares of cumulative preferred stock outstanding. It has passed the last three quarterly dividends of $2.50 per share and now wishes to distribute a total of $12 million to its shareholders. If Figurate has 3 million shares of common stock outstanding, how large a per-share common stock dividend will it be able to pay?

E7–4 Today the common stock of Gresham Technology closed at $24.60 per share, down $0.35 from yesterday. If the company has 4.6 million shares outstanding and annual earnings of $11.2 million, what is its P/E ratio today? What was its P/E ratio yesterday?

E7–5 Stacker Weight Loss currently pays an annual year-end dividend of $1.20 per share. It plans to increase this dividend by 5% next year and maintain it at the new level for the foreseeable future. If the required return on this firm's stock is 8%, what is the value of Stacker's stock?

E7–6 Brash Corporation initiated a new corporate strategy that fixes its annual dividend at $2.25 per share. Currently the risk-free rate is 4.5%, and Brash has a beta of 1.8. If the market return is 10.5%, what is the value of Brash's stock?

PROBLEMS

P7–1 **Authorized and available shares** Aspin Corporation's charter authorizes issuance of 2,000,000 shares of common stock. Currently, 1,400,000 shares are outstanding and 100,000 shares are being held as treasury stock. The firm wishes to raise $48,000,000 for a plant expansion. Discussions with its investment bankers indicate that the sale of new common stock will net the firm $60 per share.
   a. What is the maximum number of new shares of common stock that the firm can sell without receiving further authorization from shareholders?
   b. Judging on the basis of the data given and your finding in part **a**, will the firm be able to raise the needed funds without receiving further authorization?
   c. What must the firm do to obtain authorization to issue more than the number of shares found in part **a**?

P7–2 **Preferred dividends** Slater Lamp Manufacturing has an outstanding issue of preferred stock with an $80 par value and an 11% annual dividend.
   a. What is the annual dollar dividend? If it is paid quarterly, how much will be paid each quarter?
   b. If the preferred stock is *noncumulative* and the board of directors has passed the preferred dividend for the last 3 quarters, how much must be paid to preferred stockholders before dividends are paid to common stockholders?

c. If the preferred stock is *cumulative* and the board of directors has passed the preferred dividend for the last 3 quarters, how much must be paid to preferred stockholders before dividends are paid to common stockholders?

P7–3 **Preferred dividends** In each case in the table below, how many dollars of preferred dividends per share must be paid to preferred stockholders before common stock dividends are paid?

Case	Type	Par value	Dividend per share per period	Periods of dividends passed
A	Cumulative	$ 80	$ 5	2
B	Noncumulative	110	8%	3
C	Noncumulative	100	$11	1
D	Cumulative	60	8.5%	4
E	Cumulative	90	9%	0

P7–4 **Convertible preferred stock** Valerian Corp. convertible preferred stock has a fixed conversion ratio of 5 common shares per 1 share of preferred stock. The preferred stock pays a dividend of $10.00 per share per year. The common stock currently sells for $20.00 per share and pays a dividend of $1.00 per share per year.
   a. Judging on the basis of the conversion ratio and the price of the common shares, what is the current conversion value of each preferred share?
   b. If the preferred shares are selling at $96.00 each, should an investor convert the preferred shares to common shares?
   c. What factors might cause an investor not to convert from preferred to common stock?

P7–5 **Stock quotation** Assume that the following quote for the Advanced Business Machines stock (traded on the NYSE) was found in the Thursday, December 14, issue of the *Wall Street Journal*.

+3.2 84.13 51.25 AdvBusMach ABM 1.32 1.6 23 12432 81.75 +1.63

Given this information, answer the following questions:
   a. On what day did the trading activity occur?
   b. At what price did the stock sell at the end of the day on Wednesday, December 13?
   c. What percentage change has occurred in the stock's closing price since the beginning of the calendar year?
   d. What is the firm's price/earnings ratio? What does it indicate?
   e. What is the last price at which the stock traded on the day quoted?
   f. How large a dividend is expected in the current year?
   g. What are the highest and the lowest price at which the stock traded during the latest 52-week period?
   h. How many shares of stock were traded on the day quoted?
   i. How much, if any, of a change in stock price took place between the day quoted and the day before? At what price did the stock close on the day before?

P7–6 **Common stock valuation—Zero growth** Scotto Manufacturing is a mature firm in the machine tool component industry. The firm's most recent common stock dividend was $2.40 per share. Because of its maturity as well as its stable sales and earnings, the firm's management feels that dividends will remain at the current level for the foreseeable future.
a. If the required return is 12%, what will be the value of Scotto's common stock?
b. If the firm's risk as perceived by market participants suddenly increases, causing the required return to rise to 20%, what will be the common stock value?
c. Judging on the basis of your findings in parts a and b, what impact does risk have on value? Explain.

P7–7 **Common stock value—Zero growth** Kelsey Drums, Inc., is a well-established supplier of fine percussion instruments to orchestras all over the United States. The company's class A common stock has paid a dividend of $5.00 per share per year for the last 15 years. Management expects to continue to pay at that rate for the foreseeable future. Sally Talbot purchased 100 shares of Kelsey class A common 10 years ago at a time when the required rate of return for the stock was 16%. She wants to sell her shares today. The current required rate of return for the stock is 12%. How much capital gain or loss will Sally have on her shares?

P7–8 **Preferred stock valuation** Jones Design wishes to estimate the value of its outstanding preferred stock. The preferred issue has an $80 par value and pays an annual dividend of $6.40 per share. Similar-risk preferred stocks are currently earning a 9.3% annual rate of return.
a. What is the market value of the outstanding preferred stock?
b. If an investor purchases the preferred stock at the value calculated in part a, how much does she gain or lose per share if she sells the stock when the required return on similar-risk preferreds has risen to 10.5%? Explain.

P7–9 **Common stock value—Constant growth** Use the constant-growth model (Gordon model) to find the value of each firm shown in the following table.

Firm	Dividend expected next year	Dividend growth rate	Required return
A	$1.20	8%	13%
B	4.00	5	15
C	0.65	10	14
D	6.00	8	9
E	2.25	8	20

P7–10 **Common stock value—Constant growth** McCracken Roofing, Inc., common stock paid a dividend of $1.20 per share last year. The company expects earnings and dividends to grow at a rate of 5% per year for the foreseeable future.
a. What required rate of return for this stock would result in a price per share of $28?
b. If McCracken expects both earnings and dividends to grow at an annual rate of 10%, what required rate of return would result in a price per share of $28?

P7–11 Common stock value—Constant growth Elk County Telephone has paid the dividends shown in the following table over the past 6 years.

Year	Dividend per share
2006	$2.87
2005	2.76
2004	2.60
2003	2.46
2002	2.37
2001	2.25

The firm's dividend per share next year is expected to be $3.02.
a. If you can earn 13% on similar-risk investments, what is the most you would be willing to pay per share?
b. If you can earn only 10% on similar-risk investments, what is the most you would be willing to pay per share?
c. Compare and contrast your findings in parts **a** and **b**, and discuss the impact of changing risk on share value.

P7–12 Common stock value—Both growth models You are evaluating the potential purchase of a small business currently generating $42,500 of after-tax cash flow ($D_0 = \$42,500$). On the basis of a review of similar-risk investment opportunities, you must earn an 18% rate of return on the proposed purchase. Because you are relatively uncertain about future cash flows, you decide to estimate the firm's value using two possible assumptions about the growth rate of cash flows.
a. What is the firm's value if cash flows are expected to grow at an annual rate of 0% from now to infinity?
b. What is the firm's value if cash flows are expected to grow at a constant annual rate of 7% from now to infinity?

P7–13 Free cash flow valuation Nabor Industries is considering going public but is unsure of a fair offering price for the company. Before hiring an investment banker to assist in making the public offering, managers at Nabor have decided to make their own estimate of the firm's common stock value. The firm's CFO has gathered data for performing the valuation using the free cash flow valuation model.

The firm's weighted average cost of capital is 11%, and it has $1,500,000 of debt at market value and $400,000 of preferred stock at its assumed market value. The estimated free cash flows over the next 5 years, 2007 through 2011, are given below. Beyond 2011 to infinity, the firm expects its free cash flow to grow by 3% annually.

Year (t)	Free cash flow (FCF_t)
2007	$200,000
2008	250,000
2009	310,000
2010	350,000
2011	390,000

a. Estimate the value of Nabor Industries' entire company by using the *free cash flow valuation model.*
b. Use your finding in part **a**, along with the data provided above, to find Nabor Industries' common stock value.
c. If the firm plans to issue 200,000 shares of common stock, what is its estimated value per share?

P7–14 **Using the free cash flow valuation model to price an IPO** Assume that you have an opportunity to buy the stock of CoolTech, Inc., an IPO being offered for $12.50 per share. Although you are very much interested in owning the company, you are concerned about whether it is fairly priced. To determine the value of the shares, you have decided to apply the free cash flow valuation model to the firm's financial data that you've developed from a variety of data sources. The key values you have compiled are summarized in the following table.

Free cash flow		
Year (*t*)	FCF_t	Other data
2007	$ 700,000	Growth rate of FCF, beyond 2010 to infinity = 2%
2008	800,000	Weighted average cost of capital = 8%
2009	950,000	Market value of all debt = $2,700,000
2010	1,100,000	Market value of preferred stock = $1,000,000
		Number of shares of common stock outstanding = 1,100,000

a. Use the *free cash flow valuation model* to estimate CoolTech's common stock value per share.
b. Judging on the basis of your finding in part **a** and the stock's offering price, should you buy the stock?
c. Upon further analysis, you find that the growth rate in FCF beyond 2010 will be 3% rather than 2%. What effect would this finding have on your responses in parts **a** and **b**?

P7–15 **Book and liquidation value** The balance sheet for Gallinas Industries is as follows.

Gallinas Industries
Balance Sheet
December 31

Assets		Liabilities and Stockholders' Equity	
Cash	$ 40,000	Accounts payable	$100,000
Marketable securities	60,000	Notes payable	30,000
Accounts receivable	120,000	Accrued wages	30,000
Inventories	160,000	Total current liabilities	$160,000
Total current assets	$380,000	Long-term debt	$180,000
Land and buildings (net)	$150,000	Preferred stock	$ 80,000
Machinery and equipment	250,000	Common stock (10,000 shares)	360,000
Total fixed assets (net)	$400,000	Total liabilities and stockholders' equity	$780,000
Total assets	$780,000		

Additional information with respect to the firm is available:
(1) Preferred stock can be liquidated at book value.
(2) Accounts receivable and inventories can be liquidated at 90% of book value.
(3) The firm has 10,000 shares of common stock outstanding.
(4) All interest and dividends are currently paid up.
(5) Land and buildings can be liquidated at 130% of book value.
(6) Machinery and equipment can be liquidated at 70% of book value.
(7) Cash and marketable securities can be liquidated at book value.

Given this information, answer the following:
a. What is Gallinas Industries' book value per share?
b. What is its liquidation value per share?
c. Compare, contrast, and discuss the values found in parts a and b.

P7–16 **Valuation with price/earnings multiples** For each of the firms shown in the following table, use the data given to estimate its common stock value employing price/earnings (P/E) multiples.

Firm	Expected EPS	Price/earnings multiple
A	$3.00	6.2
B	4.50	10.0
C	1.80	12.6
D	2.40	8.9
E	5.10	15.0

P7–17 **Management action and stock value** REH Corporation's most recent dividend was $3 per share, its expected annual rate of dividend growth is 5%, and the required return is now 15%. A variety of proposals are being considered by management to redirect the firm's activities. Determine the impact on share price for each of the following proposed actions, and indicate the best alternative.
a. Do nothing, which will leave the key financial variables unchanged.
b. Invest in a new machine that will increase the dividend growth rate to 6% and lower the required return to 14%.
c. Eliminate an unprofitable product line, which will increase the dividend growth rate to 7% and raise the required return to 17%.
d. Merge with another firm, which will reduce the growth rate to 4% and raise the required return to 16%.
e. Acquire a subsidiary operation from another manufacturer. The acquisition should increase the dividend growth rate to 8% and increase the required return to 17%.

P7–18 **Integrative—Valuation and CAPM formulas** Given the following information for the stock of Foster Company, calculate its beta.

Current price per share of common	$50.00
Expected dividend per share next year	$ 3.00
Constant annual dividend growth rate	9%
Risk-free rate of return	7%
Return on market portfolio	10%

P7–19 **Integrative—Risk and valuation** Giant Enterprises has a beta of 1.20, the risk-free rate of return is currently 10%, and the market return is 14%. The company, which plans to pay a dividend of $2.60 per share in the coming year, anticipates that its future dividends will increase at an annual rate consistent with that experienced over the 2000–2006 period, when the following dividends were paid:

Year	Dividend per share
2006	$2.45
2005	2.28
2004	2.10
2003	1.95
2002	1.82
2001	1.80
2000	1.73

a. Use the capital asset pricing model (CAPM) to determine the required return on Giant's stock.
b. Using the constant-growth model and your finding in part **a**, estimate the value of Giant's stock.
c. Explain what effect, if any, a decrease in beta would have on the value of Giant's stock.

P7–20 **Integrative—Valuation and CAPM** Hamlin Steel Company wishes to determine the value of Craft Foundry, a firm that it is considering acquiring for cash. Hamlin wishes to use the capital asset pricing model (CAPM) to determine the applicable discount rate to use as an input to the constant-growth valuation model. Craft's stock is not publicly traded. After studying the betas of firms similar to Craft that are publicly traded, Hamlin believes that an appropriate beta for Craft's stock would be 1.25. The risk-free rate is currently 9%, and the market return is 13%. Craft's dividend per share for each of the past 6 years is shown in the following table.

Year	Dividend per share
2006	$3.44
2005	3.28
2004	3.15
2003	2.90
2002	2.75
2001	2.45

a. Given that Craft is expected to pay a dividend of $3.68 next year, determine the maximum cash price that Hamlin should pay for each share of Craft.
b. Discuss the use of the CAPM for estimating the value of common stock, and describe the effect on the resulting value of Craft of:

(1) A decrease in its dividend growth rate of 2% from that exhibited over the 2001–2006 period.
(2) A decrease in its beta to 1.

P7–21 **ETHICS PROBLEM** Melissa is trying to value Generic Utility, Inc.'s stock, which is clearly not growing at all. Generic declared and paid a $5 dividend last year. The required rate of return for utility stocks is 11%, but Melissa is unsure about the financial reporting integrity of Generic's finance team. She decides to add an extra 1% "credibility" risk premium to the required return as part of her valuation analysis.
a. What is the value of Generic's stock, assuming that the financials are trustworthy?
b. What is the value of Generic's stock, assuming that Melissa includes the extra 1% "credibility" risk premium?
c. What is the difference between the values found in parts **a** and **b,** and how might one interpret that difference?

CHAPTER 7 CASE

Assessing the Impact of Suarez Manufacturing's Proposed Risky Investment on Its Stock Value

Early in 2007, Inez Marcus, the chief financial officer for Suarez Manufacturing, was given the task of assessing the impact of a proposed risky investment on the firm's stock value. To perform the necessary analysis, Inez gathered the following information on the firm's stock.

During the immediate past 5 years (2002–2006), the annual dividends paid on the firm's common stock were as follows:

Year	Dividend per share
2006	$1.90
2005	1.70
2004	1.55
2003	1.40
2002	1.30

The firm expects that without the proposed investment, the dividend in 2007 will be $2.09 per share and the historical annual rate of growth (rounded to the nearest whole percent) will continue in the future. Currently, the required return on the common stock is 14%. Inez's research indicates that if the proposed investment is undertaken, the 2007 dividend will rise to $2.15 per share and the annual rate of dividend growth will increase to 13%. As a result of the increased risk associated with the proposed risky investment, the required return on the common stock is expected to increase by 2% to an annual rate of 16%.

Armed with the preceding information, Inez must now assess the impact of the proposed risky investment on the market value of Suarez's stock. To simplify her calculations, she plans to round the historical growth rate in common stock dividends to the nearest whole percent.

TO DO

a. Find the *current* value per share of Suarez Manufacturing's common stock.
b. Find the value of Suarez's common stock in the event that it *undertakes the proposed risky investment* and assuming that the dividend growth rate stays at 13% forever. Compare this value to that found in part **a**. What effect would the proposed investment have on the firm's stockholders? Explain.
c. On the basis of your findings in part **b**, do the stockholders win or lose as a result of undertaking the proposed risky investment? Should the firm do it? Why?

SPREADSHEET EXERCISE

You are interested in purchasing the common stock of Azure Corporation. The firm recently paid a dividend of $3 per share. It expects its earnings—and hence its dividends—to grow at a rate of 7% for the foreseeable future. Currently, similar-risk stocks have required returns of 10%.

TO DO

Set up spreadsheets to do the following calculations.

a. Given the data above, calculate the present value of this security. Use the constant-growth model (Equation 7.4) to find the stock value.
b. One year later, your broker offers to sell you additional shares of Azure at $73. The most recent dividend paid was $3.21, and the expected growth rate for earnings remains at 7%. To determine the required rate of return, you decide to use the capital asset pricing model (CAPM). The risk-free rate, R_F, is currently 5.25%; the market return, k_m, is 11.55%; and the stock's beta, b_{Azure}, is 1.07. Substitute the appropriate values into the CAPM (Equation 5.7) to determine the firm's current required return, k_{Azure}.
c. Applying Equation 7.4, determine the value of the stock using the new dividend and required return from part **b**.
d. Given your calculation in part **c**, would you buy the additional shares from your broker at $73 per share? Explain.
e. Given your calculation in part **c**, would you sell your old shares for $73? Explain.

WEB EXERCISE

Stock market investing has become increasingly popular. Many Web sites provide detailed information relating to the topics covered in this chapter.

TO DO

Go to moneycentral.msn.com/investor/home.asp, the Web site jointly hosted by CNBC and MSN. Investigate this site and report your findings. Look up current quotations for three stocks in which you are interested and report the specifics of the quotes. They should include the following information:

a. Information on price, including the current price, recent changes in the price, and the high and low over the past 52 weeks.
b. Information on valuation, by reporting the P/E ratio, market capitalization, earnings per share, and dividend yield.
c. Other topics of interest, including trading volume.

Remember to check the book's Web site at

www.aw-bc.com/gitman

for additional resources, including additional Web exercises.

Part 3

Long-Term Investment Decisions

Chapter
8
Capital Budgeting Cash Flows

Chapter
9
Capital Budgeting Techniques: Certainty and Risk

Chapter 8

Capital Budgeting Cash Flows

LEARNING GOALS

LG1 Understand the key motives for capital expenditure and the steps in the capital budgeting process.

LG2 Define basic capital budgeting terminology.

LG3 Discuss relevant cash flows, expansion versus replacement decisions, sunk costs and opportunity costs, and international capital budgeting.

LG4 Calculate the initial investment associated with a proposed capital expenditure.

LG5 Find the relevant operating cash inflows associated with a proposed capital expenditure.

LG6 Determine the terminal cash flow associated with a proposed capital expenditure.

Across the Disciplines   Why This Chapter Matters to You

Accounting: You need to understand capital budgeting cash flows to provide revenue, cost, depreciation, and tax data for use both in monitoring existing projects and in developing cash flows for proposed projects.

Information systems: You need to understand capital budgeting cash flows to maintain and facilitate the retrieval of cash flow data for both completed and existing projects.

Management: You need to understand capital budgeting cash flows so that you will understand which cash flows are relevant in making decisions about proposals for acquiring additional production facilities, for new products, and for the expansion of existing product lines.

Marketing: You need to understand capital budgeting cash flows so that you can make revenue and cost estimates for proposals for new marketing programs, for new products, and for the expansion of existing product lines.

Operations: You need to understand capital budgeting cash flows so that you can make revenue and cost estimates for proposals for the acquisition of new equipment and production facilities.

The Capital Budgeting Decision Process

Long-term investments represent sizable outlays of funds that commit a firm to some course of action. Consequently, the firm needs procedures to analyze and properly select its long-term investments. It must be able to measure cash flows and apply appropriate decision techniques. As time passes, fixed assets may become obsolete or may require an overhaul; at these points, too, financial decisions may be required. **Capital budgeting** is the process of evaluating and selecting long-term investments that are consistent with the firm's goal of maximizing owner wealth. Firms typically make a variety of long-term investments, but the most common for the manufacturing firm is in *fixed assets*, which include property (land), plant, and equipment. These assets, often referred to as *earning assets*, generally provide the basis for the firm's earning power and value.

Because firms treat capital budgeting (investment) and financing decisions *separately*, Chapters 8 and 9 concentrate on fixed-asset acquisition without regard to the specific method of financing used. We begin by discussing the motives for capital expenditure.

capital budgeting
The process of evaluating and selecting long-term investments that are consistent with the firm's goal of maximizing owner wealth.

Motives for Capital Expenditure

A **capital expenditure** is an outlay of funds by the firm that is expected to produce benefits over a period of time *greater than* 1 year. An **operating expenditure** is an outlay resulting in benefits received *within* 1 year. Fixed-asset outlays are capital expenditures, but not all capital expenditures are classified as fixed assets. A $60,000 outlay for a new machine with a usable life of 15 years is a capital expenditure that would appear as a fixed asset on the firm's balance sheet. A $60,000 outlay for an advertising campaign that is expected to produce benefits over a long period is also a capital expenditure, but would rarely be shown as a fixed asset.

Capital expenditures are made for many reasons. The basic motives for capital expenditures are to expand, replace, or renew fixed assets or to obtain some other, less tangible benefit over a long period. Table 8.1 (see page 318) briefly describes the key motives for making capital expenditures.

capital expenditure
An outlay of funds by the firm that is expected to produce benefits over a period of time *greater than* 1 year.

operating expenditure
An outlay of funds by the firm resulting in benefits received *within* 1 year.

Steps in the Process

The **capital budgeting process** consists of five distinct but interrelated steps.

1. *Proposal generation.* Proposals are made at all levels within a business organization and are reviewed by finance personnel. Proposals that require large outlays are more carefully scrutinized than less costly ones.

capital budgeting process
Five distinct but interrelated steps: *proposal generation, review and analysis, decision making, implementation,* and *follow-up.*

TABLE 8.1	Key Motives for Making Capital Expenditures
Motive	Description
Expansion	The most common motive for a capital expenditure is to expand the level of operations—usually through acquisition of fixed assets. A growing firm often needs to acquire new fixed assets rapidly, as in the purchase of property and plant facilities.
Replacement	As a firm's growth slows and it reaches maturity, most capital expenditures will be made to replace or renew obsolete or worn-out assets. Each time a machine requires a major repair, the outlay for the repair should be compared to the outlay to replace the machine and the benefits of replacement.
Renewal	Renewal, an alternative to replacement, may involve rebuilding, overhauling, or retrofitting an existing fixed asset. For example, an existing drill press could be renewed by replacing its motor and adding a computer control system, or a physical facility could be renewed by rewiring and adding air conditioning. To improve efficiency, both replacement and renewal of existing machinery may be suitable solutions.
Other purposes	Some capital expenditures do not result in the acquisition or transformation of tangible fixed assets. Instead, they involve a long-term commitment of funds in expectation of a future return. These expenditures include outlays for advertising campaigns, research and development, management consulting, and new products.

2. *Review and analysis.* Formal review and analysis is performed to assess the appropriateness of proposals and evaluate their economic viability. Once the analysis is complete, a summary report is submitted to decision makers.
3. *Decision making.* Firms typically delegate capital expenditure decision making on the basis of dollar limits. Generally, the board of directors must authorize expenditures beyond a certain amount. Often plant managers are given authority to make decisions necessary to keep the production line moving.
4. *Implementation.* Following approval, expenditures are made and projects implemented. Expenditures for a large project often occur in phases.
5. *Follow-up.* Results are monitored, and actual costs and benefits are compared with those that were expected. Action may be required if actual outcomes differ from projected ones.

Each step in the process is important. Review and analysis and decision making (Steps 2 and 3) consume the majority of time and effort, however. Follow-up (Step 5) is an important but often ignored step aimed at allowing the firm to improve the accuracy of its cash flow estimates continuously. Because of their fundamental importance, this and the following chapters give primary consideration to review and analysis and to decision making.

Basic Terminology

Before we develop the concepts, techniques, and practices related to the capital budgeting process, we need to explain some basic terminology. In addition, we will present some key assumptions that are used to simplify the discussion in the remainder of this chapter and in Chapter 9.

Independent Versus Mutually Exclusive Projects

The two most common types of projects are (1) independent projects and (2) mutually exclusive projects. **Independent projects** are those whose cash flows are unrelated or independent of one another; the acceptance of one *does not eliminate* the others from further consideration. **Mutually exclusive projects** are those that have the same function and therefore compete with one another. The acceptance of one *eliminates* from further consideration all other projects that serve a similar function. For example, a firm in need of increased production capacity could obtain it by (1) expanding its plant, (2) acquiring another company, or (3) contracting with another company for production. Clearly, accepting any one option eliminates the need for either of the others.

independent projects
Projects whose cash flows are unrelated or independent of one another; the acceptance of one *does not eliminate* the others from further consideration.

mutually exclusive projects
Projects that compete with one another, so that the acceptance of one *eliminates* from further consideration all other projects that serve a similar function.

Unlimited Funds Versus Capital Rationing

The availability of funds for capital expenditures affects the firm's decisions. If a firm has **unlimited funds** for investment, making capital budgeting decisions is quite simple: All independent projects that will provide an acceptable return can be accepted. Typically, though, firms operate under **capital rationing** instead. This means that they have only a fixed number of dollars available for capital expenditures and that numerous projects will compete for these dollars. Procedures for dealing with capital rationing are presented in Chapter 9. The discussions that follow here and in the following chapter assume unlimited funds.

unlimited funds
The financial situation in which a firm is able to accept all independent projects that provide an acceptable return.

capital rationing
The financial situation in which a firm has only a fixed number of dollars available for capital expenditures, and numerous projects compete for these dollars.

Accept–Reject Versus Ranking Approaches

Two basic approaches to capital budgeting decisions are available. The **accept–reject approach** involves evaluating capital expenditure proposals to determine whether they meet the firm's minimum acceptance criterion. This approach can be used when the firm has unlimited funds, as a preliminary step when evaluating mutually exclusive projects, or in a situation in which capital must be rationed. In these cases, only acceptable projects should be considered.

The second method, the **ranking approach,** involves ranking projects on the basis of some predetermined measure, such as the rate of return. The project with the highest return is ranked first, and the project with the lowest return is ranked last. Only acceptable projects should be ranked. Ranking is useful in selecting the "best" of a group of mutually exclusive projects and in evaluating projects with a view to capital rationing.

accept–reject approach
The evaluation of capital expenditure proposals to determine whether they meet the firm's minimum acceptance criterion.

ranking approach
The ranking of capital expenditure projects on the basis of some predetermined measure, such as the rate of return.

Conventional Versus Nonconventional Cash Flow Patterns

Cash flow patterns associated with capital investment projects can be classified as *conventional* or *nonconventional*. A **conventional cash flow pattern** consists of an initial outflow followed only by a series of inflows. For example, a firm may spend $10,000 today and as a result expect to receive equal annual cash inflows (an annuity) of $2,000 each year for the next 8 years, as depicted on the timeline in Figure 8.1 (see page 320).[1] A conventional cash flow pattern that provides a mixed stream of cash inflows is depicted in Figure 8.3 on page 322.

conventional cash flow pattern
An initial outflow followed only by a series of inflows.

---

1. Arrows rather than plus or minus signs are frequently used on time lines to distinguish between cash inflows and cash outflows. Upward-pointing arrows represent cash inflows (positive cash flows), and downward-pointing arrows represent cash outflows (negative cash flows).

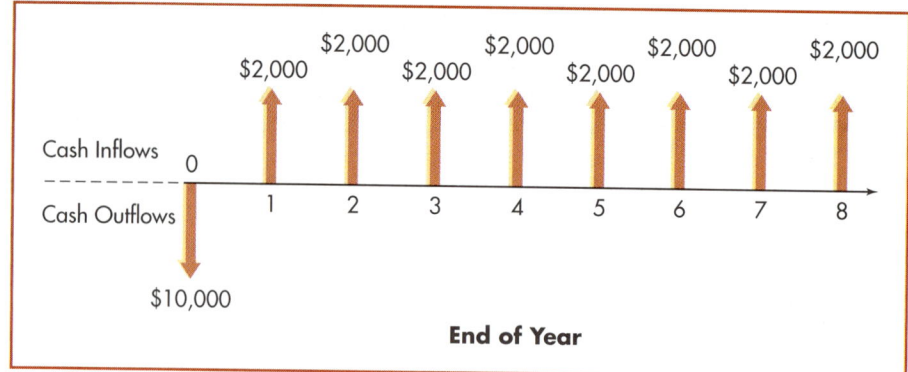

FIGURE 8.1

Conventional Cash Flow
Time line for a conventional cash flow pattern

nonconventional cash flow pattern
An initial outflow followed by a series of inflows *and* outflows.

A **nonconventional cash flow pattern** is one in which an initial outflow is followed by a series of inflows *and* outflows. For example, the purchase of a machine may require an initial cash outflow of $20,000 and may generate cash inflows of $5,000 each year for 4 years. In the fifth year after purchase, an outflow of $8,000 may be required to overhaul the machine, after which it generates inflows of $5,000 each year for 5 more years. This nonconventional pattern is illustrated on the time line in Figure 8.2.

Difficulties often arise in evaluating projects with nonconventional patterns of cash flow. *The discussions in the remainder of this chapter and in Chapter 9 are therefore limited to the evaluation of conventional cash flow patterns.*

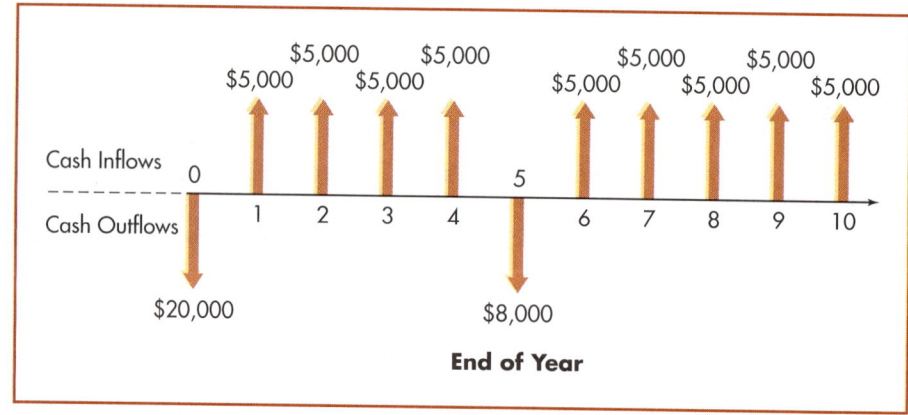

FIGURE 8.2

Nonconventional Cash Flow
Time line for a nonconventional cash flow pattern

Review Questions

8–1 What is *capital budgeting*? Do all capital expenditures involve fixed assets? Explain.

8–2 What are the key motives for making capital expenditures? Discuss, compare, and contrast them.

8–3 What are the five steps involved in the capital budgeting process?

8–4 Differentiate between the members of each of the following pairs of capital budgeting terms: (a) independent versus mutually exclusive projects; (b) unlimited funds versus capital rationing; (c) accept–reject versus ranking approaches; and (d) conventional versus nonconventional cash flow patterns.

The Relevant Cash Flows

relevant cash flows
The *incremental cash outflow (investment) and resulting subsequent inflows* associated with a proposed capital expenditure.

incremental cash flows
The *additional* cash flows—outflows or inflows—expected to result from a proposed capital expenditure.

To evaluate capital expenditure alternatives, the firm must determine the **relevant cash flows.** These are the *incremental cash outflow (investment) and resulting subsequent inflows.* The **incremental cash flows** represent the *additional* cash flows—outflows or inflows—expected to result from a proposed capital expenditure. As noted in Chapter 3, cash flows rather than accounting figures are used, because cash flows directly affect the firm's ability to pay bills and purchase assets. The *In Practice* box below takes a look at the accuracy of cash flow estimates in practice.

The remainder of this chapter is devoted to the procedures for measuring the relevant cash flows associated with proposed capital expenditures.

In Practice FOCUS ON ETHICS

HOW ACCURATE ARE CASH FLOWS?

The process of capital budgeting based on calculating various decision measures from projected cash flows has been a part of the investment decision process for more than 40 years. This procedure for evaluating investment opportunities works well when cash flows can be estimated with certainty, but in real-world corporate practice many investment decisions involve a high degree of uncertainty.

Because estimates of the cash flows from an investment project involve making assumptions about the future, they may be subject to considerable error. The problem becomes more complicated as the period of time under consideration becomes longer and when the project is unique in nature with no comparables. Other complications may arise involving accounting for additional (extraordinary) cash flows beyond the project's operating cash flows—for example, the cost of litigation, compliance with tougher environmental standards, or the costs of disposal or recycling of an asset at the completion of the project.

Examples of how cash flow estimates may differ from reality can readily be found. When financial analysts tried several years ago to value Internet startup companies with little or no revenues, negative earnings and operating cash flows, and no history of performance, they encountered many difficulties in forecasting most of the relevant financial information. For example, in the case of online retailer **Amazon.com,** according to forecasts made in early 2000, analysts expected revenues of $5.6 billion in 2001, $9.8 billion in 2002, and $14.7 billion in 2003. These projections proved to be completely off the mark, as the actual revenues were $3.1 billion, $3.9 billion, and $5.2 billion, respectively, when revenue growth slowed considerably as a result of the bursting of the Internet bubble and subsequent recession. Estimates of free cash flow proved equally wrong. In fact, Amazon.com started generating positive cash flows 4 years earlier than forecast, despite the fact that revenues were about only 40 percent of those predicted.

The preceding example indicates how crucial calculations of cash flows from the project are for capital budgeting decisions. Consequently, capital budgeting decisions can only be as accurate as cash flow projections. The temptation to "shade" cash flow projections in an effort to "make the numbers work," especially when projected benefits are inaccurate in some way, can exist. Financial managers need to take a hard look at cash flow projections, to be sure that they are realistic and based on more than just wishful thinking.

Source: Aswath Damodaran, "The Dark Side of Valuations: Firms with No Earnings, No History, and No Comparables. Can Amazon.com Be Valued?" *Stern School of Business,* NYU, March 2000.

■ As a company manager, should you focus on net income rather than cash flows? If so, why?

Major Cash Flow Components

The cash flows of any project having the *conventional pattern* can include three basic components: (1) an initial investment, (2) operating cash inflows, and (3) terminal cash flow. All projects—whether for expansion, replacement, renewal, or some other purpose—have the first two components. Some, however, lack the final component, terminal cash flow.

Figure 8.3 depicts on a time line the cash flows for a project. The **initial investment** for the proposed project is $50,000. This is the relevant cash outflow at time zero. The **operating cash inflows,** which are the incremental after-tax cash inflows resulting from implementation of the project during its life, gradually increase from $4,000 in its first year to $10,000 in its tenth and final year. The **terminal cash flow** is the after-tax nonoperating cash flow occurring in the final year of the project. It is usually attributable to liquidation of the project. In this case it is $25,000, received at the end of the project's 10-year life. Note that the terminal cash flow does *not* include the $10,000 operating cash inflow for year 10.

initial investment
The relevant cash outflow for a proposed project at time zero.

operating cash inflows
The incremental after-tax cash inflows resulting from implementation of a project during its life.

terminal cash flow
The after-tax nonoperating cash flow occurring in the final year of a project. It is usually attributable to liquidation of the project.

Expansion Versus Replacement Decisions

Developing relevant cash flow estimates is most straightforward in the case of *expansion decisions*. In this case, the initial investment, operating cash inflows, and terminal cash flow are merely the after-tax cash outflow and inflows associated with the proposed capital expenditure.

Identifying relevant cash flows for *replacement decisions* is more complicated, because the firm must identify the *incremental* cash outflow and inflows that would result from the proposed replacement. The initial investment in the case of replacement is the difference between the initial investment needed to

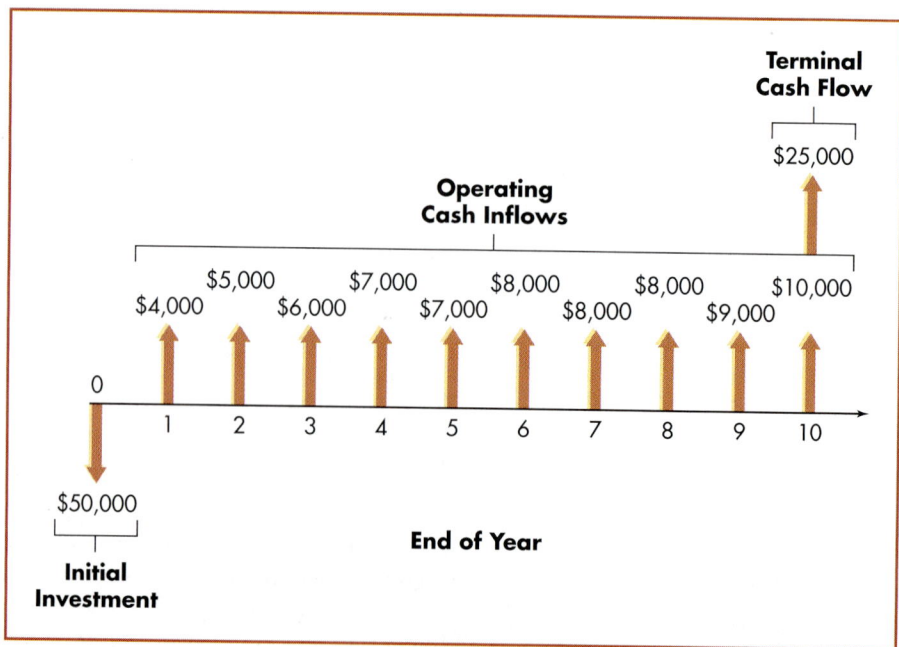

FIGURE 8.3

Cash Flow Components
Time line for major cash flow components

FIGURE 8.4

Relevant Cash Flows for Replacement Decisions
Calculation of the three components of relevant cash flow for a replacement decision

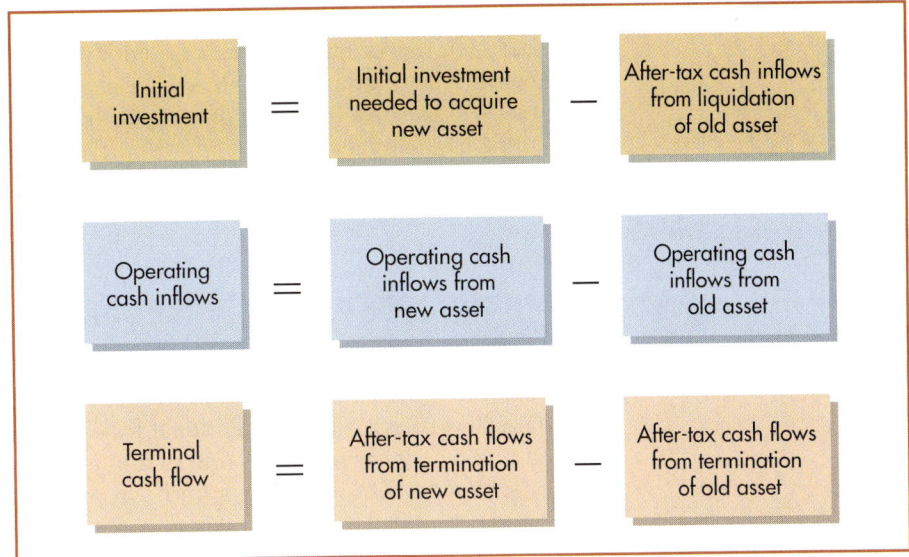

acquire the new asset and any after-tax cash inflows expected from liquidation of the old asset. The operating cash inflows are the difference between the operating cash inflows from the new asset and those from the old asset. The terminal cash flow is the difference between the after-tax cash flows expected upon termination of the new and the old assets. These relationships are shown in Figure 8.4.

Actually, all capital budgeting decisions can be viewed as replacement decisions. Expansion decisions are merely replacement decisions in which all cash flows from the old asset are zero. In light of this fact, this chapter focuses primarily on replacement decisions.

Sunk Costs and Opportunity Costs

When estimating the relevant cash flows associated with a proposed capital expenditure, the firm must recognize any sunk costs and opportunity costs. These costs are easy to mishandle or ignore, particularly when determining a project's incremental cash flows. **Sunk costs** are cash outlays that have already been made (past outlays) and therefore have no effect on the cash flows relevant to the current decision. As a result, *sunk costs should not be included in a project's incremental cash flows.*

Opportunity costs are cash flows that could be realized from the best alternative use of an owned asset. They therefore represent cash flows that *will not be realized* as a result of employing that asset in the proposed project. Because of this, any *opportunity costs should be included as cash outflows when one is determining a project's incremental cash flows.*

sunk costs
Cash outlays that have already been made (past outlays) and therefore have no effect on the cash flows relevant to a current decision.

opportunity costs
Cash flows that could be realized from the best alternative use of an owned asset.

EXAMPLE

Jankow Equipment is considering renewing its drill press X12, which it purchased 3 years earlier for $237,000, by retrofitting it with the computerized control system from an obsolete piece of equipment it owns. The obsolete equipment could be sold today for a high bid of $42,000, but without its computerized control system, it would be worth nothing. Jankow is in the process of estimating the labor and materials costs of retrofitting the system to drill press X12 and the

Hint Sunk costs and opportunity costs are concepts you must fully understand. Funds already spent are irrelevant to future decisions, but the returns given up so that an existing asset can be used in a given project *are* considered a relevant cost.

benefits expected from the retrofit. The $237,000 cost of drill press X12 is a *sunk cost* because it represents an earlier cash outlay. It *would not be included* as a cash outflow when determining the cash flows relevant to the retrofit decision. Although Jankow owns the obsolete piece of equipment, the proposed use of its computerized control system represents an *opportunity cost* of $42,000—the highest price at which it could be sold today. This opportunity cost *would be included* as a cash outflow associated with using the computerized control system.

International Capital Budgeting and Long-Term Investments

Although the same basic capital budgeting principles are used for domestic and international projects, several additional factors must be addressed in evaluating foreign investment opportunities. International capital budgeting differs from the domestic version because (1) cash outflows and inflows occur in a foreign currency, and (2) foreign investments entail potentially significant political risk. Both of these risks can be minimized through careful planning.

Companies face both long-term and short-term *currency risks* related to both the invested capital and the cash flows resulting from it. Long-term currency risk can be minimized by financing the foreign investment at least partly in the local capital markets rather than with dollar-denominated capital from the parent company. This step ensures that the project's revenues, operating costs, and financing costs will be in the local currency. Likewise, the dollar value of short-term, local-currency cash flows can be protected by using special securities and strategies such as futures, forwards, and options market instruments.

Political risks can be minimized by using both operating and financial strategies. For example, by structuring the investment as a joint venture and selecting a well-connected local partner, the U.S. company can minimize the risk of its operations being seized or harassed. Companies also can protect themselves from having their investment returns blocked by local governments by structuring the financing of such investments as debt rather than as equity. Debt-service payments are legally enforceable claims, whereas equity returns (such as dividends) are not. Even if local courts do not support the claims of the U.S. company, the company can threaten to pursue its case in U.S. courts.

In spite of the preceding difficulties, **foreign direct investment,** which involves the transfer of capital, managerial, and technical assets to a foreign country, has surged in recent years. This is evident in the growing market values of foreign assets owned by U.S.-based companies and of foreign direct investment in the United States, particularly by British, Canadian, Dutch, German, and Japanese companies. Furthermore, foreign direct investment by U.S. companies seems to be accelerating.

foreign direct investment The transfer of capital, managerial, and technical assets to a foreign country.

Review Questions

8–5 Why is it important to evaluate capital budgeting projects on the basis of *incremental cash flows?*

8–6 What three components of cash flow may exist for a given project? How can expansion decisions be treated as replacement decisions? Explain.

8–7 What effect do *sunk costs* and *opportunity costs* have on a project's incremental cash flows?

8–8 How can *currency risk* and *political risk* be minimized when one is making *foreign direct investment?*

Finding the Initial Investment

The term *initial investment* as used here refers to the relevant cash outflows to be considered when evaluating a prospective capital expenditure. Because our discussion of capital budgeting is concerned only with investments that exhibit conventional cash flows, the initial investment occurs at *time zero*—the time at which the expenditure is made. The initial investment is calculated by subtracting all cash inflows occurring at time zero from all cash outflows occurring at time zero.

The basic format for determining the initial investment is given in Table 8.2. The cash flows that must be considered when determining the initial investment associated with a capital expenditure are the installed cost of the new asset, the after-tax proceeds (if any) from the sale of an old asset, and the change (if any) in net working capital. Note that if there are no installation costs and the firm is not replacing an existing asset, then the purchase price of the asset, adjusted for any change in net working capital, is equal to the initial investment.

Installed Cost of New Asset

cost of new asset
The net outflow necessary to acquire a new asset.

installation costs
Any added costs that are necessary to place an asset into operation.

installed cost of new asset
The *cost of new asset* plus its *installation costs;* equals the asset's depreciable value.

As shown in Table 8.2, the installed cost of the new asset is found by adding the cost of the new asset to its installation costs. The **cost of new asset** is the net outflow that its acquisition requires. Usually, we are concerned with the acquisition of a fixed asset for which a definite purchase price is paid. **Installation costs** are any added costs that are necessary to place an asset into operation. The Internal Revenue Service (IRS) requires the firm to add installation costs to the purchase price of an asset to determine its depreciable value, which is expensed over a period of years. The **installed cost of new asset**, calculated by adding the *cost of new asset* to its *installation costs*, equals its depreciable value.

TABLE 8.2	The Basic Format for Determining Initial Investment

Installed cost of new asset =
    Cost of new asset
    + Installation costs
− After-tax proceeds from sale of old asset =
    Proceeds from sale of old asset
    ∓ Tax on sale of old asset
± Change in net working capital
Initial investment

After-Tax Proceeds from Sale of Old Asset

after-tax proceeds from sale of old asset
The difference between the old asset's sale proceeds and any applicable taxes or tax refunds related to its sale.

proceeds from sale of old asset
The cash inflows, net of any *removal* or *cleanup costs*, resulting from the sale of an existing asset.

tax on sale of old asset
Tax that depends on the relationship between the old asset's sale price and *book value*, and on existing government tax rules.

Table 8.2 shows that the **after-tax proceeds from sale of old asset** decrease the firm's initial investment in the new asset. These proceeds are the difference between the old asset's sale proceeds and any applicable taxes or tax refunds related to its sale. The **proceeds from sale of old asset** are the net cash inflows it provides. This amount is net of any costs incurred in the process of removing the asset. Included in these *removal costs* are *cleanup costs*, such as those related to removal and disposal of chemical and nuclear wastes. These costs may not be trivial.

The proceeds from the sale of an old asset are normally subject to some type of tax.[2] This **tax on sale of old asset** depends on the relationship between its sale price and *book value*, and on existing government tax rules.

Book Value

book value
The strict accounting value of an asset, calculated by subtracting its accumulated depreciation from its installed cost.

The **book value** of an asset is its strict accounting value. It can be calculated by using the following equation:

$$\text{Book value} = \text{Installed cost of asset} - \text{Accumulated depreciation} \quad (8.1)$$

> **EXAMPLE**
>
> Hudson Industries, a small electronics company, 2 years ago acquired a machine tool with an installed cost of $100,000. The asset was being depreciated under MACRS using a 5-year recovery period.[3] Table 3.2 (on page 94) shows that under MACRS for a 5-year recovery period, 20% and 32% of the installed cost would be depreciated in years 1 and 2, respectively. In other words, 52% (20% + 32%) of the $100,000 cost, or $52,000 (0.52 × $100,000), would represent the accumulated depreciation at the end of year 2. Substituting into Equation 8.1, we get
>
> $$\text{Book value} = \$100{,}000 - \$52{,}000 = \underline{\underline{\$48{,}000}}$$
>
> The book value of Hudson's asset at the end of year 2 is therefore $48,000. ∎

Basic Tax Rules

Three potential tax situations can occur when an asset is sold. These situations depend on the relationship between the asset's sale price and its book value. The two key forms of taxable income and their associated tax treatments are defined and summarized in Table 8.3. The assumed tax rates used throughout this text are noted in the final column. There are three possible tax situations. The asset may be sold (1) for more than its book value, (2) for its book value, or (3) for less than its book value. An example will illustrate.

> **EXAMPLE**
>
> The old asset purchased 2 years ago for $100,000 by Hudson Industries has a current book value of $48,000. What will happen if the firm now decides to sell the asset and replace it? The tax consequences depend on the sale price. Figure 8.5

---

2. A brief discussion of the tax treatment of ordinary and capital gains income was presented in Chapter 1. Because corporate capital gains and ordinary income are taxed at the same rate, for convenience, we do not differ between them in the following discussions.

3. For a review of MACRS, see Chapter 3. Under current tax law, most manufacturing equipment has a 7-year recovery period, as noted in Table 3.1. Using this recovery period results in 8 years of depreciation, which unnecessarily complicates examples and problems. To simplify, *manufacturing equipment is treated as a 5-year asset in this and the following chapters.*

TABLE 8.3 Tax Treatment on Sales of Assets

Form of taxable income	Definition	Tax treatment	Assumed tax rate
Gain on sale of asset	Portion of the sale price that is *greater than* book value.	All gains above book value are taxed as ordinary income.	40%
Loss on sale of asset	Amount by which sale price is *less than* book value.	If the asset is depreciable and used in business, loss is deducted from ordinary income.	40% of loss is a tax savings
		If the asset is *not* depreciable or is *not* used in business, loss is deductible only against capital gains.	40% of loss is a tax savings

depicts the taxable income resulting from four possible sale prices in light of the asset's initial purchase price of $100,000 and its current book value of $48,000. The taxable consequences of each of these sale prices are described below.

The sale of the asset for more than its book value If Hudson sells the old asset for $110,000, it realizes a gain of $62,000 ($110,000 − $48,000). Technically this gain is made up of two parts—a capital gain and **recaptured depreciation**, which is the portion of the sale price that is above book value and below the initial purchase price. For Hudson, the capital gain is $10,000 ($110,000 sale

recaptured depreciation
The portion of an asset's sale price that is above its book value and below its initial purchase price.

FIGURE 8.5 Taxable Income from Sale of Asset
Taxable income from sale of asset at various sale prices for Hudson Industries

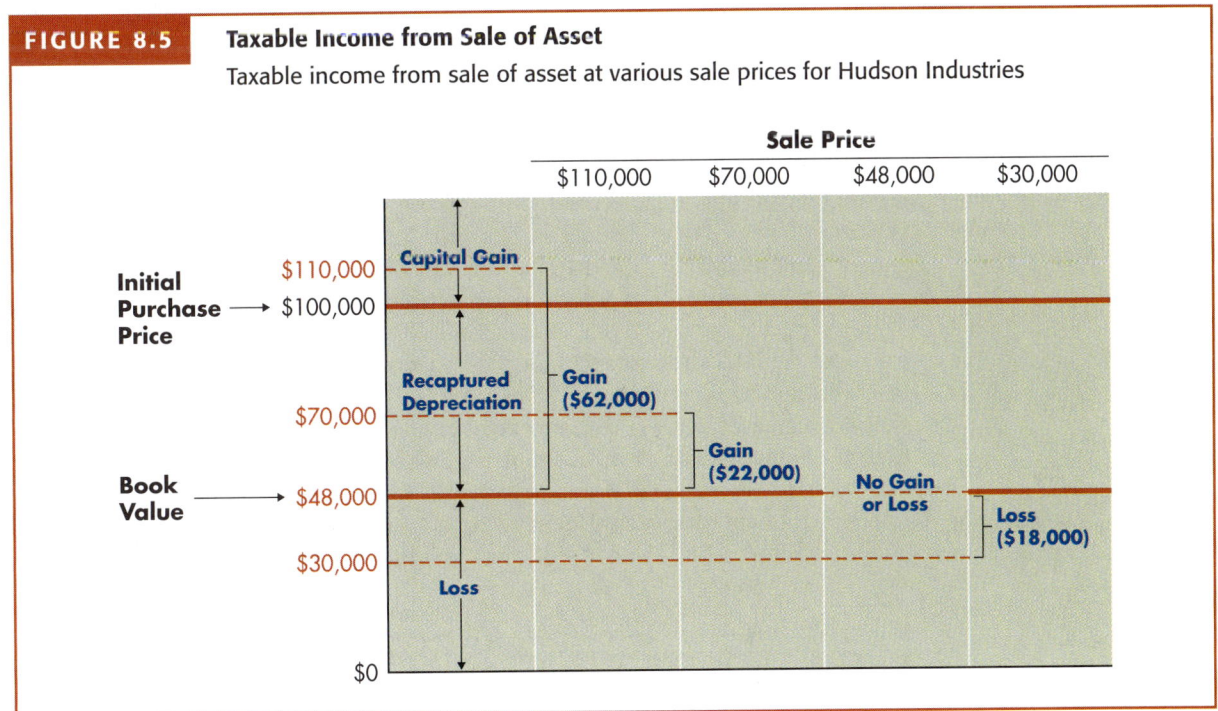

price − $100,000 initial purchase price); recaptured depreciation is $52,000 (the $100,000 initial purchase price − $48,000 book value).[4]

Both the $10,000 capital gain and the $52,000 recaptured depreciation are shown under the $110,000 sale price in Figure 8.5. The total gain above book value of $62,000 is taxed as ordinary income at the 40% rate, resulting in taxes of $24,800 (0.40 × $62,000). These taxes should be used in calculating the initial investment in the new asset, using the format in Table 8.2. In effect, the taxes raise the amount of the firm's initial investment in the new asset by reducing the proceeds from the sale of the old asset.

If Hudson instead sells the old asset for $70,000, it experiences a gain above book value (in the form of *recaptured depreciation*) of $22,000 ($70,000 − $48,000), as shown under the $70,000 sale price in Figure 8.5. This gain is taxed as ordinary income. Because the firm is assumed to be in the 40% tax bracket, the taxes on the $22,000 gain are $8,800 (0.40 × $22,000). This amount in taxes should be used in calculating the initial investment in the new asset.

The sale of the asset for its book value If the asset is sold for $48,000, its book value, the firm breaks even. There is no gain or loss, as shown under the $48,000 sale price in Figure 8.5. Because *no tax results from selling an asset for its book value*, there is no tax effect on the initial investment in the new asset.

The sale of the asset for less than its book value If Hudson sells the asset for $30,000, it experiences a loss of $18,000 ($48,000 − $30,000), as shown under the $30,000 sale price in Figure 8.5. If this is a depreciable asset used in the business, the loss may be used to offset ordinary operating income. If the asset is *not* depreciable or is *not* used in the business, the loss can be used only to offset capital gains. In either case, the loss will save the firm $7,200 (0.40 × $18,000) in taxes. And, if current operating earnings or capital gains are not sufficient to offset the loss, the firm may be able to apply these losses to prior or future years' taxes.[5]

Change in Net Working Capital

net working capital
The amount by which a firm's current assets exceed its current liabilities.

Net working capital is the amount by which a firm's current assets exceed its current liabilities. This topic is treated in depth in Chapter 13, but at this point it is important to note that changes in net working capital often accompany capital expenditure decisions. If a firm acquires new machinery to expand its level of operations, it will experience an increase in levels of cash, accounts receivable, inventories, accounts payable, and accruals. These increases result from the need for more cash to support expanded operations, more accounts receivable and inventories to support increased sales, and more accounts payable and accruals to support increased outlays made to meet expanded product demand. As noted in Chapter 3, increases in cash, accounts receivable, and inventories are *outflows of cash*, whereas increases in accounts payable and accruals are *inflows of cash*.

change in net working capital
The difference between a change in current assets and a change in current liabilities.

The difference between the change in current assets and the change in current liabilities is the **change in net working capital**. Generally, current assets increase

---

4. Although the current tax law requires corporate capital gains to be treated as ordinary income, the structure for corporate capital gains is retained under the law to facilitate a rate differential in the likely event of future tax revisions. For clarity and convenience, this distinction is *not* made throughout the text discussions.

5. The tax law provides detailed procedures for using *tax loss carrybacks/carryforwards*. Application of such procedures to capital budgeting is beyond the scope of this text, and they are therefore ignored in subsequent discussions.

by more than current liabilities, resulting in an increased investment in net working capital. This increased investment is treated as an initial outflow. If the change in net working capital were negative, it would be shown as an initial inflow. The change in net working capital—regardless of whether it is an increase or a decrease—*is not taxable* because it merely involves a net buildup or net reduction of current accounts.

EXAMPLE

Danson Company, a metal products manufacturer, is contemplating expanding its operations. Financial analysts expect that the changes in current accounts summarized in Table 8.4 will occur and will be maintained over the life of the expansion. Current assets are expected to increase by $22,000, and current liabilities are expected to increase by $9,000, resulting in a $13,000 increase in net working capital. In this case, the increase will represent an increased net working capital investment and will be treated as a cash outflow in calculating the initial investment.

Calculating the Initial Investment

A variety of tax and other considerations enter into the initial investment calculation. The following example illustrates calculation of the initial investment according to the format in Table 8.2.

EXAMPLE

Powell Corporation, a large, diversified manufacturer of aircraft components, is trying to determine the initial investment required to replace an old machine with a new, more sophisticated model. The proposed machine's purchase price is $380,000, and an additional $20,000 will be necessary to install it. It will be depreciated under MACRS using a 5-year recovery period. The present (old) machine was purchased 3 years ago at a cost of $240,000 and was being depreciated under MACRS using a 5-year recovery period. The firm has found a buyer willing to pay $280,000 for the present machine and to remove it at the buyer's expense. The firm expects that a $35,000 increase in current assets and an $18,000 increase in current liabilities will accompany the replacement; these changes will result in a $17,000 ($35,000 − $18,000) *increase* in net working capital. The firm pays taxes at a rate of 40%.

TABLE 8.4 Calculation of Change in Net Working Capital for Danson Company

Current account	Change in balance	
Cash	+$ 4,000	
Accounts receivable	+ 10,000	
Inventories	+ 8,000	
(1) Current assets		+$22,000
Accounts payable	+$ 7,000	
Accruals	+ 2,000	
(2) Current liabilities		+ 9,000
Change in net working capital [(1) − (2)]		+$13,000

The only component of the initial investment calculation that is difficult to obtain is taxes. The book value of the present machine can be found by using the depreciation percentages from Table 3.2 (on page 94) of 20%, 32%, and 19% for years 1, 2, and 3, respectively. The resulting *book value is $69,600* ($240,000 − [(0.20 + 0.32 + 0.19) × $240,000]). A *gain* of $210,400 ($280,000 − $69,600) is realized on the sale. The total taxes on the gain are $84,160 (0.40 × $210,400). Substituting these amounts into the format in Table 8.2 results in an initial investment of $221,160, which represents the net cash outflow required at time zero.

Installed cost of proposed machine		
Cost of proposed machine	$380,000	
+ Installation costs	20,000	
Total installed cost—proposed (depreciable value)		$400,000
− After-tax proceeds from sale of present machine		
Proceeds from sale of present machine	$280,000	
− Tax on sale of present machine	84,160	
Total after-tax proceeds—present		195,840
+ Change in net working capital		17,000
Initial investment		**$221,160**

Review Questions

8–9 Explain how each of the following inputs is used to calculate the *initial investment*: **(a)** cost of new asset, **(b)** installation costs, **(c)** proceeds from sale of old asset, **(d)** tax on sale of old asset, and **(e)** change in net working capital.

8–10 How is the *book value* of an asset calculated? What are the two key forms of taxable income?

8–11 What three tax situations may result from the sale of an asset that is being replaced?

8–12 Referring to the basic format for calculating initial investment, explain how a firm would determine the *depreciable value* of the new asset.

Finding the Operating Cash Inflows

The benefits expected from a capital expenditure or "project" are embodied in its *operating cash inflows*, which are *incremental after-tax cash inflows*. In this section we use the income statement format to develop clear definitions of the terms *after-tax, cash inflows,* and *incremental*.

Interpreting the Term *After-Tax*

Benefits expected to result from proposed capital expenditures must be measured on an *after-tax basis,* because the firm will not have the use of any benefits until it has satisfied the government's tax claims. These claims depend on the firm's taxable income, so deducting taxes *before* making comparisons between proposed investments is necessary for consistency when evaluating capital expenditure alternatives.

Interpreting the Term *Cash Inflows*

All benefits expected from a proposed project must be measured on a *cash flow basis*. Cash inflows represent dollars that can be spent, not merely "accounting profits." A simple accounting technique for converting after-tax net profits into operating cash inflows was given in Equation 3.1 on page 97. The basic calculation requires adding depreciation and any other *noncash charges* (amortization and depletion) deducted as expenses on the firm's income statement back to net profits after taxes. Because depreciation is commonly found on income statements, it is the only noncash charge we consider.

EXAMPLE

Powell Corporation's estimates of its revenue and expenses (excluding depreciation and interest), with and without the proposed new machine described in the preceding example, are given in Table 8.5. Note that both the expected usable life of the proposed machine and the remaining usable life of the present machine are 5 years. The amount to be depreciated with the proposed machine is calculated by summing the purchase price of $380,000 and the installation costs of $20,000. The proposed machine is to be depreciated under MACRS using a 5-year recovery period.[6] The resulting depreciation on this machine for each of the 6 years, as well as the remaining 3 years of depreciation (years 4, 5, and 6) on the present machine, are calculated in Table 8.6 (see page 332).[7]

The *operating cash inflows* each year can be calculated by using the income statement format shown in Table 8.7 (see page 333). Note that we exclude interest because we are focusing purely on the "investment decision." The interest is relevant to the "financing decision," which is separately considered. Because we

TABLE 8.5 Powell Corporation's Revenue and Expenses (Excluding Depreciation and Interest) for Proposed and Present Machines

	With proposed machine			With present machine	
Year	Revenue (1)	Expenses (excl. depr. and int.) (2)	Year	Revenue (1)	Expenses (excl. depr. and int.) (2)
1	$2,520,000	$2,300,000	1	$2,200,000	$1,990,000
2	2,520,000	2,300,000	2	2,300,000	2,110,000
3	2,520,000	2,300,000	3	2,400,000	2,230,000
4	2,520,000	2,300,000	4	2,400,000	2,250,000
5	2,520,000	2,300,000	5	2,250,000	2,120,000

---

6. As noted in Chapter 3, it takes $n + 1$ years to depreciate an n-year class asset under current tax law. Therefore, MACRS percentages are given for each of 6 years for use in depreciating an asset with a 5-year recovery period.

7. It is important to recognize that although both machines will provide 5 years of use, the proposed new machine will be depreciated over the 6-year period, whereas the present machine, as noted in the preceding example, has been depreciated over 3 years and therefore has remaining only its final 3 years (years 4, 5, and 6) of depreciation (12%, 12%, and 5%, respectively, under MACRS).

TABLE 8.6   Depreciation Expense for Proposed and Present Machines for Powell Corporation

Year	Cost (1)	Applicable MACRS depreciation percentages (from Table 3.2) (2)	Depreciation [(1) × (2)] (3)
With proposed machine			
1	$400,000	20%	$ 80,000
2	400,000	32	128,000
3	400,000	19	76,000
4	400,000	12	48,000
5	400,000	12	48,000
6	400,000	5	20,000
Totals		100%	$400,000
With present machine			
1	$240,000	12% (year-4 depreciation)	$28,800
2	240,000	12 (year-5 depreciation)	28,800
3	240,000	5 (year-6 depreciation)	12,000
4	Because the present machine is at the end of the third year of its cost recovery at the time the analysis is performed, it has only the final 3 years of depreciation (as noted above) still applicable.		0
5			0
6			0
Total			$69,600[a]

[a] The total $69,600 represents the book value of the present machine at the end of the third year, as calculated in the preceding example.

exclude interest expense, "earnings before interest and taxes (EBIT)" is equivalent to "net profits before taxes," and the calculation of "operating cash inflow" in Table 8.7 is equivalent to "operating cash flow (OCF)" (defined in Equation 3.4, on page 100). Simply stated, the income statement format calculates OCF.

Substituting the data from Tables 8.5 and 8.6 into this format and assuming a 40% tax rate, we get Table 8.8. It demonstrates the calculation of operating cash inflows for each year for both the proposed and the present machine. Because the proposed machine is depreciated over 6 years, the analysis must be performed over the 6-year period to capture fully the tax effect of its year-6 depreciation. The resulting operating cash inflows are shown in the final row of Table 8.8 for each machine. The $8,000 year-6 operating cash inflow for the proposed machine results solely from the tax benefit of its year-6 depreciation deduction. ■

Interpreting the Term *Incremental*

The final step in estimating the operating cash inflows for a proposed replacement project is to calculate the *incremental (relevant)* cash inflows. Incremental operating cash inflows are needed, because our concern is *only* with the change in operating cash inflows that result from the proposed project. Clearly, if this were an expansion project, the project's cash flows would be the incremental cash flows.

TABLE 8.7 Calculation of Operating Cash Inflows Using the Income Statement Format

Revenue
− Expenses (excluding depreciation and interest)
Earnings before depreciation, interest, and taxes (EBDIT)
− Depreciation
Earnings before interest and taxes (EBIT)
− Taxes (rate = T)
Net operating profit after taxes [NOPAT = EBIT × (1 − T)]
+ Depreciation
Operating cash inflows (same as OCF in Equation 3.4)

TABLE 8.8 Calculation of Operating Cash Inflows for Powell Corporation's Proposed and Present Machines

	Year 1	Year 2	Year 3	Year 4	Year 5	Year 6
With proposed machine						
Revenue[a]	$2,520,000	$2,520,000	$2,520,000	$2,520,000	$2,520,000	$ 0
− Expenses (excl. depr. and int.)[b]	2,300,000	2,300,000	2,300,000	2,300,000	2,300,000	0
Earnings before depr., int., and taxes	$ 220,000	$ 220,000	$ 220,000	$ 220,000	$ 220,000	$ 0
− Depreciation[c]	80,000	128,000	76,000	48,000	48,000	20,000
Earnings before interest and taxes	$ 140,000	$ 92,000	$ 144,000	$ 172,000	$ 172,000	−$20,000
− Taxes (rate, T = 40%)	56,000	36,800	57,600	68,800	68,800	− 8,000
Net operating profit after taxes	$ 84,000	$ 55,200	$ 86,400	$ 103,200	$ 103,200	−$12,000
+ Depreciation[c]	80,000	128,000	76,000	48,000	48,000	20,000
Operating cash inflows	$ 164,000	$ 183,200	$ 162,400	$ 151,200	$ 151,200	$ 8,000
With present machine						
Revenue[a]	$2,200,000	$2,300,000	$2,400,000	$2,400,000	$2,250,000	$ 0
− Expenses (excl. depr. and int.)[b]	1,990,000	2,110,000	2,230,000	2,250,000	2,120,000	0
Earnings before depr., int., and taxes	$ 210,000	$ 190,000	$ 170,000	$ 150,000	$ 130,000	$ 0
− Depreciation[c]	28,800	28,800	12,000	0	0	0
Earnings before interest and taxes	$ 181,200	$ 161,200	$ 158,000	$ 150,000	$ 130,000	$ 0
− Taxes (rate, T = 40%)	72,480	64,480	63,200	60,000	52,000	0
Net operating profit after taxes	$ 108,720	$ 96,720	$ 94,800	$ 90,000	$ 78,000	$ 0
+ Depreciation[c]	28,800	28,800	12,000	0	0	0
Operating cash inflows	$ 137,520	$ 125,520	$ 106,800	$ 90,000	$ 78,000	$ 0

[a]From column 1 of Table 8.5.
[b]From column 2 of Table 8.5.
[c]From column 3 of Table 8.6.

TABLE 8.9 Incremental (Relevant) Operating Cash Inflows for Powell Corporation

	Operating cash inflows		
Year	Proposed machine[a] (1)	Present machine[a] (2)	Incremental (relevant) [(1) − (2)] (3)
1	$164,000	$137,520	$26,480
2	183,200	125,520	57,680
3	162,400	106,800	55,600
4	151,200	90,000	61,200
5	151,200	78,000	73,200
6	8,000	0	8,000

[a]From final row for respective machine in Table 8.8.

EXAMPLE Table 8.9 demonstrates the calculation of Powell Corporation's *incremental (relevant) operating cash inflows* for each year. The estimates of operating cash inflows developed in Table 8.8 are given in columns 1 and 2. Column 2 values represent the amount of operating cash inflows that Powell Corporation will receive if it does not replace the present machine. If the proposed machine replaces the present machine, the firm's operating cash inflows for each year will be those shown in column 1. Subtracting the present machine's operating cash inflows from the proposed machine's operating cash inflows, we get the incremental operating cash inflows for each year, shown in column 3. These cash flows represent the amounts by which each respective year's cash inflows will increase as a result of the replacement. For example, in year 1, Powell Corporation's cash inflows would increase by $26,480 if the proposed project were undertaken. Clearly, these are the relevant inflows to be considered when evaluating the benefits of making a capital expenditure for the proposed machine. ■

Review Questions

8–13 How does depreciation enter into the calculation of operating cash inflows? How does the income statement format in Table 8.7 relate to Equation 3.4 (on page 100) for finding operating cash flow (OCF)?

8–14 How are the *incremental (relevant) operating cash inflows* that are associated with a replacement decision calculated?

LG6 Finding the Terminal Cash Flow

Terminal cash flow is the cash flow resulting from termination and liquidation of a project at the end of its economic life. It represents the after-tax cash flow, exclusive of operating cash inflows, that occurs in the final year of the project.

> **TABLE 8.10** **The Basic Format for Determining Terminal Cash Flow**
>
> After-tax proceeds from sale of new asset =
>   Proceeds from sale of new asset
>   ∓ Tax on sale of new asset
> − After-tax proceeds from sale of old asset =
>   Proceeds from sale of old asset
>   ∓ Tax on sale of old asset
> ± Change in net working capital
> Terminal cash flow

When it applies, this flow can significantly affect the capital expenditure decision. Terminal cash flow can be calculated for replacement projects by using the basic format presented in Table 8.10.

Proceeds from Sale of Assets

The proceeds from sale of the new and the old asset, often called "salvage value," represent the amount *net of any removal or cleanup costs* expected upon termination of the project. For replacement projects, proceeds from both the new asset and the old asset must be considered. For expansion and renewal types of capital expenditures, the proceeds from the old asset are zero. Of course, it is not unusual for the value of an asset to be zero at the termination of a project.

Taxes on Sale of Assets

Earlier we calculated the tax on sale of old asset (as part of finding the initial investment). Similarly, taxes must be considered on the terminal sale of both the new and the old asset for replacement projects and on only the new asset in other cases. The tax calculations apply whenever an asset is sold for a value different from its book value. If the net proceeds from the sale are expected to exceed book value, a tax payment shown as an *outflow* (deduction from sale proceeds) will occur. When the net proceeds from the sale are less than book value, a tax rebate shown as a cash *inflow* (addition to sale proceeds) will result. For assets sold to net exactly book value, no taxes will be due.

Change in Net Working Capital

When we calculated the initial investment, we took into account any change in net working capital that is attributable to the new asset. Now, when we calculate the terminal cash flow, the change in net working capital represents the reversion of any initial net working capital investment. Most often, this will show up as a cash inflow due to the reduction in net working capital; with termination of the project, the need for the increased net working capital investment is assumed to end. Because the net working capital investment is in no way consumed, the amount recovered at termination will equal the amount shown in the calculation of the initial investment. Tax considerations are not involved.

Calculating the terminal cash flow involves the same procedures as those used to find the initial investment. In the following example, the terminal cash flow is calculated for a replacement decision.

EXAMPLE

Continuing with the Powell Corporation example, assume that the firm expects to be able to liquidate the new machine at the end of its 5-year usable life to net $50,000 after paying removal and cleanup costs. The old machine can be liquidated at the end of the 5 years to net $10,000. The firm expects to recover its $17,000 net working capital investment upon termination of the project. The firm pays taxes at a rate of 40%.

From the analysis of the operating cash inflows presented earlier, we can see that the proposed (new) machine will have a book value of $20,000 (equal to the year-6 depreciation) at the end of 5 years. The present (old) machine will be fully depreciated and therefore have a book value of zero at the end of the 5 years. Because the sale price of $50,000 for the proposed (new) machine is below its initial installed cost of $400,000 but greater than its book value of $20,000, taxes will have to be paid only on the recaptured depreciation of $30,000 ($50,000 sale proceeds − $20,000 book value). Applying the ordinary tax rate of 40% to this $30,000 results in a tax of $12,000 (0.40 × $30,000) on the sale of the proposed machine. Its after-tax sale proceeds would therefore equal $38,000 ($50,000 sale proceeds − $12,000 taxes). Because the present machine would net $10,000 at termination, which is less than its original purchase price of $240,000 and above its book value of zero, it would experience a taxable gain of $10,000 ($10,000 sale price − $0 book value). Applying the 40% tax rate to the $10,000 gain, the firm will have to pay a tax of $4,000 (0.40 × $10,000) on the sale of the present machine at the end of year 5. Its after-tax sale proceeds from the present machine would therefore equal $6,000 ($10,000 sale price − $4,000 taxes). Substituting the appropriate values into the format in Table 8.10 results in the terminal cash inflow of $49,000.

After-tax proceeds from sale of proposed machine		
Proceeds from sale of proposed machine	$50,000	
− Tax on sale of proposed machine	12,000	
Total after-tax proceeds—proposed		$38,000
− After-tax proceeds from sale of present machine		
Proceeds from sale of present machine	$10,000	
− Tax on sale of present machine	4,000	
Total after-tax proceeds—present		6,000
+ Change in net working capital		17,000
Terminal cash flow		$49,000

Review Question

8–15 Explain how the *terminal cash flow* is calculated for replacement projects.

Summarizing the Relevant Cash Flows

Hint Capital expenditures are critical to a firm's success, and these funds are usually limited. Because of this, the process of determining cash flows should be finely tuned so that it is both objective and realistic.

The initial investment, operating cash inflows, and terminal cash flow together represent a project's *relevant cash flows*. These cash flows can be viewed as the incremental after-tax cash flows attributable to the proposed project. They represent, in a cash flow sense, how much better or worse off the firm will be if it chooses to implement the proposal.

EXAMPLE

The relevant cash flows for Powell Corporation's proposed replacement expenditure can be shown graphically, on a time line. Note that because the new asset is assumed to be sold at the end of its 5-year usable life, the year-6 incremental operating cash inflow calculated in Table 8.9 has no relevance; the terminal cash flow effectively replaces this value in the analysis. As the following time line shows, the relevant cash flows follow a *conventional cash flow pattern*.

Time line for Powell Corporation's relevant cash flows with the proposed machine

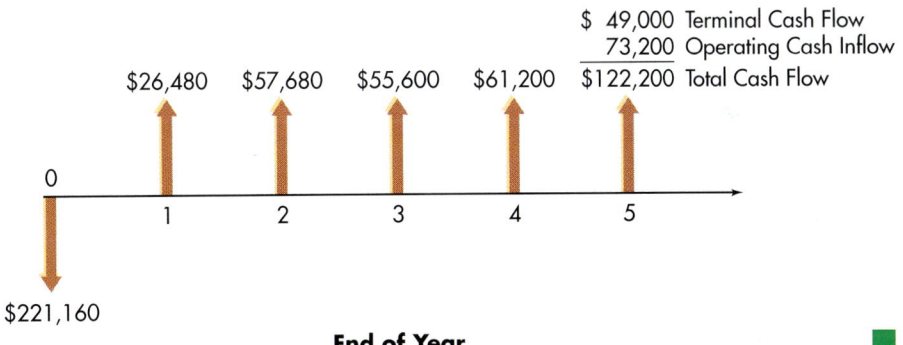

Techniques for analyzing conventional cash flow patterns to determine whether to undertake a proposed capital investment are discussed in Chapter 9.

Review Question

8–16 Diagram and describe the three components of the relevant cash flows for a capital budgeting project.

SUMMARY

FOCUS ON VALUE

A key responsibility of financial managers is to review and analyze proposed investment decisions to make sure that only those that contribute positively to the value of the firm are undertaken. Utilizing a variety of tools and techniques, financial managers estimate the cash flows that a proposed investment will generate and then apply appropriate decision techniques to assess the investment's impact on the firm's value. The most difficult and important aspect of this capital budgeting process is developing good estimates of the relevant cash flows.

The relevant cash flows are the incremental after-tax cash flows resulting from a proposed investment. These estimates represent the cash flow benefits that are likely to accrue to the firm as a result of implementing the investment. By applying to the cash flows decision techniques that capture the time value of money and risk factors, the financial manager can estimate how the investment will affect the firm's share price. Clearly, only those investments that can be expected to increase the stock price should be undertaken. Consistent application of capital budgeting procedures to proposed long-term investments should therefore allow the firm to **maximize its stock price**.

REVIEW OF LEARNING GOALS

LG1 **Understand the key motives for capital expenditure and the steps in the capital budgeting process.** Capital budgeting is the process used to evaluate and select capital expenditures. Capital expenditures are long-term investments made to expand, replace, or renew fixed assets or to obtain some less tangible benefit. The capital budgeting process includes five distinct but interrelated steps: proposal generation, review and analysis, decision making, implementation, and follow-up.

LG2 **Define basic capital budgeting terminology.** Capital expenditure proposals may be independent or mutually exclusive. Typically, firms have only limited funds for capital investments and must ration them among projects. Two basic capital budgeting approaches are the accept–reject approach and the ranking approach. Conventional cash flow patterns consist of an initial outflow followed by a series of inflows; any other pattern is nonconventional.

LG3 **Discuss relevant cash flows, expansion versus replacement decisions, sunk costs and opportunity costs, and international capital budgeting.** The relevant cash flows for capital budgeting decisions are the initial investment, the operating cash inflows, and the terminal cash flow. For replacement decisions, these flows are the difference between the cash flows of the new asset and the old asset. Expansion decisions are viewed as replacement decisions in which all cash flows from the old asset are zero. When estimating relevant cash flows, ignore sunk costs and include opportunity costs as cash outflows. In international capital budgeting, currency risks and political risks can be minimized through careful planning.

LG4 **Calculate the initial investment associated with a proposed capital expenditure.** The initial investment is the initial outflow required, taking into account the installed cost of the new asset, the after-tax proceeds from the sale of the old asset, and any change in net working capital. The initial investment is reduced by finding the after-tax proceeds from sale of the old asset. The book value of an asset is used to determine the taxes owed as a result of its sale. Either of two forms of taxable income—a gain or a loss—can result from sale of an asset. The form of taxable income that applies depends on whether the asset is sold for (1) more than book value, (2) book value, or (3) less than book value. The change in net working capital is the difference between the change in current assets and the change in current liabilities expected to accompany a given capital expenditure.

LG5 **Find the relevant operating cash inflows associated with a proposed capital expenditure.** The operating cash inflows are the incremental after-tax cash inflows expected to result from a project. The income statement format involves adding depreciation back to net operating profit after taxes and gives the operating cash inflows, which are the same as operating cash flows (OCF), associated with the proposed and present projects. The relevant (incremental) cash inflows for a replacement project are the difference between the operating cash inflows of the proposed project and those of the present project.

LG6 **Determine the terminal cash flow associated with a proposed capital expenditure.** The terminal cash flow represents the after-tax cash flow (exclusive of operating cash inflows) that is expected from liquidation of a project. It is calculated for replacement projects by finding the difference between the after-tax proceeds from sale of the new and the old asset at termination and then adjusting this difference for any change in net working capital. Sale price and depreciation data are used to find the taxes and the after-tax sale proceeds on the new and old assets. The change in net working capital typically represents the reversion of any initial net working capital investment.

SELF-TEST PROBLEMS (SOLUTIONS IN APPENDIX B)

ST8–1 **Book value, taxes, and initial investment** Irvin Enterprises is considering the purchase of a new piece of equipment to replace the current equipment. The new equipment costs $75,000 and requires $5,000 in installation costs. It will be depreciated under MACRS using a 5-year recovery period. The old piece of equipment was purchased 4 years ago for an installed cost of $50,000; it was being depreciated under MACRS using a 5-year recovery period. The old equipment can be sold today for $55,000 net of any removal or cleanup costs. As a result of the proposed replacement, the firm's investment in net working capital is expected to increase by $15,000. The firm pays taxes at a rate of 40%. (Table 3.2 on page 94 contains the applicable MACRS depreciation percentages.)
  a. Calculate the book value of the old piece of equipment.
  b. Determine the taxes, if any, attributable to the sale of the old equipment.
  c. Find the *initial investment* associated with the proposed equipment replacement.

ST8–2 **Determining relevant cash flows** A machine currently in use was originally purchased 2 years ago for $40,000. The machine is being depreciated under MACRS using a 5-year recovery period; it has 3 years of usable life remaining. The current machine can be sold today to net $42,000 after removal and cleanup costs. A new machine, using a 3-year MACRS recovery period, can be purchased at a price of $140,000. It requires $10,000 to install and has a 3-year usable life. If the new machine is acquired, the investment in accounts receivable will be expected to rise by $10,000, the inventory investment will increase by $25,000, and accounts payable will increase by $15,000. *Earnings before depreciation, interest, and taxes* are expected to be $70,000 for each of the next 3 years with the old machine and to be $120,000 in the first year and $130,000 in the second and third years with the new machine. At the end of 3 years, the market value of the old machine will equal zero, but the new machine could be sold to net $35,000 before taxes. The firm is subject to a 40% tax rate. (Table 3.2 on page 94 contains the applicable MACRS depreciation percentages.)
  a. Determine the *initial investment* associated with the proposed replacement decision.
  b. Calculate the *incremental operating cash inflows* for years 1 to 4 associated with the proposed replacement. (*Note:* Only depreciation cash flows must be considered in year 4.)
  c. Calculate the *terminal cash flow* associated with the proposed replacement decision. (*Note:* This is at the end of year 3.)
  d. Depict on a time line the relevant cash flows found in parts **a, b,** and **c** that are associated with the proposed replacement decision, assuming that it is terminated at the end of year 3.

WARM-UP EXERCISES

E8–1 If Halley Industries reimburses employees who earn master's degrees and who agree to remain with the firm for an additional 3 years, should the expense of the tuition reimbursement be categorized as an operating expenditure or a capital expenditure?

E8–2 Canvas Reproductions, Inc., is considering two mutually exclusive investments. Project A requires an initial outlay of $20,000 and has expected cash inflows of $5,000 for each of the next 5 years. Project B requires an initial outlay of $25,000 and has expected cash inflows of $6,500 for each of the following 5 years. Use a simple rate of return measure to determine which project the company should choose.

E8–3 Iridium Corp. has spent $3.5 billion over the past decade developing a satellite-based telecommunication system. It is currently trying to decide whether to spend an additional $350 million on the project. The firm expects that this outlay will finish the project and will generate cash inflow of $15 million per year over the next 5 years. A competitor has offered $450 million for the satellites already in orbit. Classify the firm's outlays as *sunk costs* or *opportunity costs*, and specify the *relevant cash flows*.

E8–4 A few years ago, Largo Industries implemented an inventory auditing system at an installed cost of $175,000. Since then, it has taken depreciation deductions totalling $124,250. What is the system's current *book value*? If Largo sold the system for $110,000, how much *recaptured depreciation* would result?

E8–5 Bryson Sciences is planning to purchase a high-powered microscopy machine for $55,000 and incur an additional $7,500 in installation costs. It is replacing similar microscopy equipment that can be sold to net $35,000, resulting in taxes from a gain on the sale of $11,250. Because of this transaction, current assets will increase by $6,000 and current liabilities will increase by $4,000. Calculate the *initial investment* in the high-powered microscopy machine.

PROBLEMS

BASIC

P8–1 Classification of expenditures Given the following list of outlays, indicate whether each is normally considered a *capital* or an *operating* expenditure. Explain your answers.
  a. An initial lease payment of $5,000 for electronic point-of-sale cash register systems.
  b. An outlay of $20,000 to purchase patent rights from an inventor.
  c. An outlay of $80,000 for a major research and development program.
  d. An $80,000 investment in a portfolio of marketable securities.
  e. A $300 outlay for an office machine.
  f. An outlay of $2,000 for a new machine tool.
  g. An outlay of $240,000 for a new building.
  h. An outlay of $1,000 for a marketing research report.

P8–2 **Basic terminology** A firm is considering the following three separate situations.

Situation A Build either a small office building or a convenience store on a parcel of land located in a high-traffic area. Adequate funding is available, and both projects are known to be acceptable. The office building requires an initial investment of $620,000 and is expected to provide operating cash inflows of $40,000 per year for 20 years. The convenience store is expected to cost $500,000 and to provide a growing stream of operating cash inflows over its 20-year life. The initial operating cash inflow is $20,000, and it will increase by 5% each year.

Situation B Replace a machine with a new one that requires a $60,000 initial investment and will provide operating cash inflows of $10,000 per year for the first 5 years. At the end of year 5, a machine overhaul costing $20,000 will be required. After it is completed, expected operating cash inflows will be $10,000 in year 6; $7,000 in year 7; $4,000 in year 8; and $1,000 in year 9, at the end of which the machine will be scrapped.

Situation C Invest in any or all of the four machines whose relevant cash flows are given in the following table. The firm has $500,000 budgeted to fund these machines, all of which are known to be acceptable. The initial investment for each machine is $250,000.

	Operating cash inflows			
Year	Machine 1	Machine 2	Machine 3	Machine 4
1	$ 50,000	$70,000	$65,000	$90,000
2	70,000	70,000	65,000	80,000
3	90,000	70,000	80,000	70,000
4	− 30,000	70,000	80,000	60,000
5	100,000	70,000	− 20,000	50,000

For each situation, indicate:
a. Whether the projects involved are independent or mutually exclusive.
b. Whether the availability of funds is unlimited or capital rationing exists.
c. Whether accept–reject or ranking decisions are required.
d. Whether each project's cash flows are conventional or nonconventional.

P8–3 **Relevant cash flow pattern fundamentals** For each of the following projects, determine the *relevant cash flows*, classify the cash flow pattern, and depict the cash flows on a time line.
  a. A project that requires an initial investment of $120,000 and will generate annual operating cash inflows of $25,000 for the next 18 years. In each of the 18 years, maintenance of the project will require a $5,000 cash outflow.
  b. A new machine with an installed cost of $85,000. Sale of the old machine will yield $30,000 after taxes. Operating cash inflows generated by the replacement will exceed the operating cash inflows of the old machine by $20,000 in each year of a 6-year period. At the end of year 6, liquidation of the new machine will yield $20,000 after taxes, which is $10,000 greater than the after-tax proceeds expected from the old machine had it been retained and liquidated at the end of year 6.

c. An asset that requires an initial investment of $2 million and will yield annual operating cash inflows of $300,000 for each of the next 10 years. Operating cash outlays will be $20,000 for each year except year 6, when an overhaul requiring an additional cash outlay of $500,000 will be required. The asset's liquidation value at the end of year 10 is expected to be zero.

P8–4 **Expansion versus replacement cash flows** Edison Systems has estimated the cash flows over the 5-year lives for two projects, A and B. These cash flows are summarized in the table below.

	Project A	Project B
Initial investment	$40,000	$12,000[a]
Year	Operating cash inflows	
1	$10,000	$ 6,000
2	12,000	6,000
3	14,000	6,000
4	16,000	6,000
5	10,000	6,000

[a]After-tax cash inflow expected from liquidation.

a. If project A were actually a *replacement* for project B and if the $12,000 initial investment shown for project B were the after-tax cash inflow expected from liquidating it, what would be the *relevant cash flows* for this replacement decision?
b. How can an *expansion decision* such as project A be viewed as a special form of a replacement decision? Explain.

P8–5 **Sunk costs and opportunity costs** Covol Industries is developing the relevant cash flows associated with the proposed replacement of an existing machine tool with a new, technologically advanced one. Given the following costs related to the proposed project, explain whether each would be treated as a *sunk cost* or an *opportunity cost* in developing the relevant cash flows associated with the proposed replacement decision.
a. Covol would be able to use the same tooling, which had a book value of $40,000, on the new machine tool as it had used on the old one.
b. Covol would be able to use its existing computer system to develop programs for operating the new machine tool. The old machine tool did not require these programs. Although the firm's computer has excess capacity available, the capacity could be leased to another firm for an annual fee of $17,000.
c. Covol would have to obtain additional floor space to accommodate the larger new machine tool. The space that would be used is currently being leased to another company for $10,000 per year.
d. Covol would use a small storage facility to store the increased output of the new machine tool. The storage facility was built by Covol 3 years earlier at a cost of $120,000. Because of its unique configuration and location, it is currently of no use to either Covol or any other firm.
e. Covol would retain an existing overhead crane, which it had planned to sell for its $180,000 market value. Although the crane was not needed with the

old machine tool, it would be used to position raw materials on the new machine tool.

P8–6 **Book value** Find the book value for each of the assets shown in the following table, assuming that MACRS depreciation is being used. (*Note:* See Table 3.2 on page 94 for the applicable depreciation percentages.)

Asset	Installed cost	Recovery period (years)	Elapsed time since purchase (years)
A	$ 950,000	5	3
B	40,000	3	1
C	96,000	5	4
D	350,000	5	1
E	1,500,000	7	5

P8–7 **Book value and taxes on sale of assets** Troy Industries purchased a new machine 3 years ago for $80,000. It is being depreciated under MACRS with a 5-year recovery period using the percentages given in Table 3.2 on page 94. Assume a 40% tax rate.
a. What is the *book value* of the machine?
b. Calculate the firm's tax liability if it sold the machine for each of the following amounts: $100,000; $56,000; $23,200; and $15,000.

P8–8 **Tax calculations** For each of the following cases, determine the total taxes resulting from the transaction. Assume a 40% tax rate. The asset was purchased 2 years ago for $200,000 and is being depreciated under MACRS using a 5-year recovery period. (See Table 3.2 on page 94 for the applicable depreciation percentages.)
a. The asset is sold for $220,000.
b. The asset is sold for $150,000.
c. The asset is sold for $96,000.
d. The asset is sold for $80,000.

P8–9 **Change in net working capital calculation** Samuels Manufacturing is considering the purchase of a new machine to replace one it believes is obsolete. The firm has total current assets of $920,000 and total current liabilities of $640,000. As a result of the proposed replacement, the following *changes* are anticipated in the levels of the current asset and current liability accounts noted.

Account	Change
Accruals	+ $ 40,000
Marketable securities	0
Inventories	− 10,000
Accounts payable	+ 90,000
Notes payable	0
Accounts receivable	+ 150,000
Cash	+ 15,000

a. Using the information given, calculate the change, if any, in net working capital that is expected to result from the proposed replacement action.
b. Explain why a change in these current accounts would be relevant in determining the initial investment for the proposed capital expenditure.
c. Would the change in net working capital enter into any of the other cash flow components that make up the relevant cash flows? Explain.

P8–10 **Calculating initial investment** Vastine Medical, Inc., is considering replacing its existing computer system, which was purchased 2 years ago at a cost of $325,000. The system can be sold today for $200,000. It is being depreciated using MACRS and a 5-year recovery period (see Table 3.2, page 94). A new computer system will cost $500,000 to purchase and install. Replacement of the computer system would not involve any change in net working capital. Assume a 40% tax rate.
a. Calculate the *book value* of the existing computer system.
b. Calculate the after-tax proceeds of its sale for $200,000.
c. Calculate the *initial investment* associated with the replacement project.

P8–11 **Initial investment—Basic calculation** Cushing Corporation is considering the purchase of a new grading machine to replace the existing one. The existing machine was purchased 3 years ago at an installed cost of $20,000; it was being depreciated under MACRS using a 5-year recovery period. (See Table 3.2 on page 94 for the applicable depreciation percentages.) The existing machine is expected to have a usable life of at least 5 more years. The new machine costs $35,000 and requires $5,000 in installation costs; it will be depreciated using a 5-year recovery period under MACRS. The existing machine can currently be sold for $25,000 without incurring any removal or cleanup costs. The firm is subject to a 40% tax rate. Calculate the *initial investment* associated with the proposed purchase of a new grading machine.

P8–12 **Initial investment at various sale prices** Edwards Manufacturing Company (EMC) is considering replacing one machine with another. The old machine was purchased 3 years ago for an installed cost of $10,000. The firm is depreciating the machine under MACRS, using a 5-year recovery period. (See Table 3.2 on page 94 for the applicable depreciation percentages.) The new machine costs $24,000 and requires $2,000 in installation costs. The firm is subject to a 40% tax rate. In each of the following cases, calculate the *initial investment* for the replacement.
a. EMC sells the old machine for $11,000.
b. EMC sells the old machine for $7,000.
c. EMC sells the old machine for $2,900.
d. EMC sells the old machine for $1,500.

P8–13 **Depreciation** A firm is evaluating the acquisition of an asset that costs $64,000 and requires $4,000 in installation costs. If the firm depreciates the asset under MACRS, using a 5-year recovery period (see Table 3.2 on page 94 for the applicable depreciation percentages), determine the depreciation charge for each year.

P8–14 **Incremental operating cash inflows** A firm is considering renewing its equipment to meet increased demand for its product. The cost of equipment modifications is $1.9 million plus $100,000 in installation costs. The firm will depreciate the equipment modifications under MACRS, using a 5-year recovery period. (See Table 3.2 on page 94 for the applicable depreciation percentages.) Additional sales revenue from the renewal should amount to $1.2 million per year, and additional operating expenses and other costs (excluding depreciation and interest) will amount to 40% of the additional sales. The firm is subject to a tax rate of 40%. (*Note:* Answer the following questions for each of the next 6 *years.*)

a. What incremental earnings before depreciation, interest, and taxes will result from the renewal?
b. What incremental net operating profits after taxes will result from the renewal?
c. What *incremental operating cash inflows* will result from the renewal?

P8–15 **Incremental operating cash inflows—Expense reduction** Miller Corporation is considering replacing a machine. The replacement will reduce operating expenses (that is, increase earnings before depreciation, interest, and taxes) by $16,000 per year for each of the 5 years the new machine is expected to last. Although the old machine has zero book value, it can be used for 5 more years. The depreciable value of the new machine is $48,000. The firm will depreciate the machine under MACRS using a 5-year recovery period (see Table 3.2 on page 94 for the applicable depreciation percentages) and is subject to a 40% tax rate. Estimate the *incremental operating cash inflows* generated by the replacement. (*Note:* Be sure to consider the depreciation in year 6.)

P8–16 **Incremental operating cash inflows** Strong Tool Company has been considering purchasing a new lathe to replace a fully depreciated lathe that will last 5 more years. The new lathe is expected to have a 5-year life and depreciation charges of $2,000 in year 1; $3,200 in year 2; $1,900 in year 3; $1,200 in both year 4 and year 5; and $500 in year 6. The firm estimates the revenues and expenses (excluding depreciation and interest) for the new and the old lathes to be as shown in the following table. The firm is subject to a 40% tax rate.

	New lathe		Old lathe	
Year	Revenue	Expenses (excl. depr. and int.)	Revenue	Expenses (excl. depr. and int.)
1	$40,000	$30,000	$35,000	$25,000
2	41,000	30,000	35,000	25,000
3	42,000	30,000	35,000	25,000
4	43,000	30,000	35,000	25,000
5	44,000	30,000	35,000	25,000

a. Calculate the *operating cash inflows* associated with each lathe. (*Note:* Be sure to consider the depreciation in year 6.)

b. Calculate the *incremental (relevant) operating cash inflows* resulting from the proposed lathe replacement.
c. Depict on a time line the incremental operating cash inflows calculated in part **b**.

P8–17 **Terminal cash flow—Various lives and sale prices** Looner Industries is currently analyzing the purchase of a new machine that costs $160,000 and requires $20,000 in installation costs. Purchase of this machine is expected to result in an increase in net working capital of $30,000 to support the expanded level of operations. The firm plans to depreciate the machine under MACRS using a 5-year recovery period (see Table 3.2 on page 94 for the applicable depreciation percentages) and expects to sell the machine to net $10,000 before taxes at the end of its usable life. The firm is subject to a 40% tax rate.
a. Calculate the *terminal cash flow* for a usable life of (1) 3 years, (2) 5 years, and (3) 7 years.
b. Discuss the effect of usable life on terminal cash flows using your findings in part **a**.
c. Assuming a 5-year usable life, calculate the terminal cash flow if the machine were sold to net (1) $9,000 or (2) $170,000 (before taxes) at the end of 5 years.
d. Discuss the effect of sale price on terminal cash flow using your findings in part **c**.

P8–18 **Terminal cash flow—Replacement decision** Russell Industries is considering replacing a fully depreciated machine that has a remaining useful life of 10 years with a newer, more sophisticated machine. The new machine will cost $200,000 and will require $30,000 in installation costs. It will be depreciated under MACRS using a 5-year recovery period (see Table 3.2 on page 94 for the applicable depreciation percentages). A $25,000 increase in net working capital will be required to support the new machine. The firm's managers plan to evaluate the potential replacement over a 4-year period. They estimate that the old machine could be sold at the end of 4 years to net $15,000 before taxes; the new machine at the end of 4 years will be worth $75,000 before taxes. Calculate the *terminal cash flow* at the end of year 4 that is relevant to the proposed purchase of the new machine. The firm is subject to a 40% tax rate.

P8–19 **Relevant cash flows for a marketing campaign** Marcus Tube, a manufacturer of high-quality aluminum tubing, has maintained stable sales and profits over the past 10 years. Although the market for aluminum tubing has been expanding by 3% per year, Marcus has been unsuccessful in sharing this growth. To increase its sales, the firm is considering an aggressive marketing campaign that centers on regularly running ads in all relevant trade journals and exhibiting products at all major regional and national trade shows. The campaign is expected to require an *annual* tax-deductible expenditure of $150,000 over the next 5 years. Sales revenue, as shown in the income statement for 2006 (top of facing page), totaled $20,000,000. If the proposed marketing campaign is not initiated, sales are expected to remain at this level in each of the next 5 years, 2007–2011. With the marketing campaign, sales are expected to rise to the levels shown in the accompanying table for each of the next 5 years; cost of goods sold is expected to remain at 80% of sales; general and administrative expense (exclusive of any marketing campaign outlays) is expected to remain at 10% of sales; and annual depreciation expense is expected to remain at $500,000. Assuming a 40% tax rate, find the *relevant cash flows* over the next 5 years associated with the proposed marketing campaign.

Marcus Tube
Income Statement
for the Year Ended December 31, 2006

Sales revenue		$20,000,000
Less: Cost of goods sold (80%)		16,000,000
Gross profits		$ 4,000,000
Less: Operating expenses		
General and administrative expense (10%)	$2,000,000	
Depreciation expense	500,000	
Total operating expense		2,500,000
Earnings before interest and taxes		$ 1,500,000
Less: Taxes (rate = 40%)		600,000
Net operating profit after taxes		$ 900,000

Marcus Tube
Sales Forecast

Year	Sales revenue
2007	$20,500,000
2008	21,000,000
2009	21,500,000
2010	22,500,000
2011	23,500,000

P8–20 **Relevant cash flows—No terminal value** Central Laundry and Cleaners is considering replacing an existing piece of machinery with a more sophisticated machine. The old machine was purchased 3 years ago at a cost of $50,000, and this amount was being depreciated under MACRS using a 5-year recovery period. The machine has 5 years of usable life remaining. The new machine that is being considered costs $76,000 and requires $4,000 in installation costs. The new machine would be depreciated under MACRS using a 5-year recovery period. The firm can currently sell the old machine for $55,000 without incurring any removal or cleanup costs. The firm is subject to a tax rate of 40%. The revenues and expenses (excluding depreciation and interest) associated with the new and the old machines for the next 5 years are given in the table below. (Table 3.2 on page 94 contains the applicable MACRS depreciation percentages.)

| | New machine | | Old machine | |
Year	Revenue	Expenses (excl. depr. and int.)	Revenue	Expenses (excl. depr. and int.)
1	$750,000	$720,000	$674,000	$660,000
2	750,000	720,000	676,000	660,000
3	750,000	720,000	680,000	660,000
4	750,000	720,000	678,000	660,000
5	750,000	720,000	674,000	660,000

a. Calculate the *initial investment* associated with replacement of the old machine by the new one.

b. Determine the *incremental operating cash inflows* associated with the proposed replacement. (*Note:* Be sure to consider the depreciation in year 6.)
c. Depict on a time line the *relevant cash flows* found in parts a and b associated with the proposed replacement decision.

P8–21 **Integrative—Determining relevant cash flows** Lombard Company is contemplating the purchase of a new high-speed widget grinder to replace the existing grinder. The existing grinder was purchased 2 years ago at an installed cost of $60,000; it was being depreciated under MACRS using a 5-year recovery period. The existing grinder is expected to have a usable life of 5 more years. The new grinder costs $105,000 and requires $5,000 in installation costs; it has a 5-year usable life and would be depreciated under MACRS using a 5-year recovery period. Lombard can currently sell the existing grinder for $70,000 without incurring any removal or cleanup costs. To support the increased business resulting from purchase of the new grinder, accounts receivable would increase by $40,000, inventories by $30,000, and accounts payable by $58,000. At the end of 5 years, the existing grinder is expected to have a market value of zero; the new grinder would be sold to net $29,000 after removal and cleanup costs and before taxes. The firm is subject a 40% tax rate. The estimated *earnings before depreciation, interest, and taxes* over the 5 years for both the new and the existing grinder are shown in the following table. (Table 3.2 on page 94 contains the applicable MACRS depreciation percentages.)

	Earnings before depreciation, interest, and taxes	
Year	New grinder	Existing grinder
1	$43,000	$26,000
2	43,000	24,000
3	43,000	22,000
4	43,000	20,000
5	43,000	18,000

a. Calculate the *initial investment* associated with the replacement of the existing grinder by the new one.
b. Determine the *incremental operating cash inflows* associated with the proposed grinder replacement. (*Note:* Be sure to consider the depreciation in year 6.)
c. Determine the *terminal cash flow* expected at the end of year 5 from the proposed grinder replacement.
d. Depict on a time line the *relevant cash flows* associated with the proposed grinder replacement decision.

P8–22 **ETHICS PROBLEM** According to academic research, capital budgeting cash flow projections are used rarely in practice by small firms, which often use accounting projections instead. What is the most likely explanation of this behavior?

CHAPTER 8 CASE

Developing Relevant Cash Flows for Clark Upholstery Company's Machine Renewal or Replacement Decision

Bo Humphries, chief financial officer of Clark Upholstery Company, expects the firm's *net operating profit after taxes* for the next 5 years to be as shown in the following table.

Year	Net operating profit after taxes
1	$100,000
2	150,000
3	200,000
4	250,000
5	320,000

Bo is beginning to develop the relevant cash flows needed to analyze whether to renew or replace Clark's *only* depreciable asset, a machine that originally cost $30,000, has a current book value of zero, and can now be sold for $20,000. (*Note:* Because the firm's only depreciable asset is fully depreciated—its book value is zero—its expected operating cash inflows equal its net operating profit after taxes.) He estimates that at the end of 5 years, the existing machine can be sold to net $2,000 before taxes. Bo plans to use the following information to develop the relevant cash flows for each of the alternatives.

Alternative 1 Renew the existing machine at a total depreciable cost of $90,000. The renewed machine would have a 5-year usable life and would be depreciated under MACRS using a 5-year recovery period. Renewing the machine would result in the following projected revenues and expenses (excluding depreciation and interest):

Year	Revenue	Expenses (excl. depr. and int.)
1	$1,000,000	$801,500
2	1,175,000	884,200
3	1,300,000	918,100
4	1,425,000	943,100
5	1,550,000	968,100

The renewed machine would result in an increased investment in net working capital of $15,000. At the end of 5 years, the machine could be sold to net $8,000 before taxes.

Alternative 2 Replace the existing machine with a new machine that costs $100,000 and requires installation costs of $10,000. The new machine would have a 5-year usable life and would be depreciated under MACRS using a 5-year recovery period. The firm's projected revenues and expenses (excluding depreciation and interest), if it acquires the machine, would be as follows:

Year	Revenue	Expenses (excl. depr. and int.)
1	$1,000,000	$764,500
2	1,175,000	839,800
3	1,300,000	914,900
4	1,425,000	989,900
5	1,550,000	998,900

The new machine would result in an increased investment in net working capital of $22,000. At the end of 5 years, the new machine could be sold to net $25,000 before taxes.

The firm is subject to a 40% tax rate. As noted, the company uses MACRS depreciation. (See Table 3.2 on page 94 for the applicable depreciation percentages.)

TO DO

a. Calculate the *initial investment* associated with each of Clark Upholstery's alternatives.
b. Calculate the *incremental operating cash inflows* associated with each of Clark's alternatives. (*Note:* Be sure to consider the depreciation in year 6.)
c. Calculate the *terminal cash flow* at the end of year 5 associated with each of Clark's alternatives.
d. Use your findings in parts **a, b,** and **c** to depict on a time line the *relevant cash flows* associated with each of Clark Upholstery's alternatives.
e. Solely on the basis of your comparison of their relevant cash flows, which alternative appears to be better? Why?

SPREADSHEET EXERCISE

Damon Corporation, a sports equipment manufacturer, has a machine currently in use that was originally purchased 3 years ago for $120,000. The firm depreciates the machine under MACRS using a 5-year recovery period. Once removal and cleanup costs are taken into consideration, the expected net selling price for the present machine will be $70,000.

Damon can buy a new machine for a net price of $160,000 (including installation costs of $15,000). The proposed machine will be depreciated under a 5-year MACRS period. If the firm acquires the new machine, its working capital needs will change—accounts receivable will increase $15,000, inventory will increase $19,000, and accounts payable will increase $16,000.

Earnings before depreciation, interest, and taxes (EBDIT) for the present machine are expected to be $95,000 for each of the successive 5 years. For the proposed machine, the expected EBDIT for each of the next 5 years are $105,000, $110,000, $120,000, $120,000, and $120,000, respectively. The corporate tax

b. Calculate the *incremental (relevant) operating cash inflows* resulting from the proposed lathe replacement.
c. Depict on a time line the incremental operating cash inflows calculated in part **b**.

P8–17 **Terminal cash flow—Various lives and sale prices** Looner Industries is currently analyzing the purchase of a new machine that costs $160,000 and requires $20,000 in installation costs. Purchase of this machine is expected to result in an increase in net working capital of $30,000 to support the expanded level of operations. The firm plans to depreciate the machine under MACRS using a 5-year recovery period (see Table 3.2 on page 94 for the applicable depreciation percentages) and expects to sell the machine to net $10,000 before taxes at the end of its usable life. The firm is subject to a 40% tax rate.
a. Calculate the *terminal cash flow* for a usable life of (1) 3 years, (2) 5 years, and (3) 7 years.
b. Discuss the effect of usable life on terminal cash flows using your findings in part **a**.
c. Assuming a 5-year usable life, calculate the terminal cash flow if the machine were sold to net (1) $9,000 or (2) $170,000 (before taxes) at the end of 5 years.
d. Discuss the effect of sale price on terminal cash flow using your findings in part **c**.

P8–18 **Terminal cash flow—Replacement decision** Russell Industries is considering replacing a fully depreciated machine that has a remaining useful life of 10 years with a newer, more sophisticated machine. The new machine will cost $200,000 and will require $30,000 in installation costs. It will be depreciated under MACRS using a 5-year recovery period (see Table 3.2 on page 94 for the applicable depreciation percentages). A $25,000 increase in net working capital will be required to support the new machine. The firm's managers plan to evaluate the potential replacement over a 4-year period. They estimate that the old machine could be sold at the end of 4 years to net $15,000 before taxes; the new machine at the end of 4 years will be worth $75,000 before taxes. Calculate the *terminal cash flow* at the end of year 4 that is relevant to the proposed purchase of the new machine. The firm is subject to a 40% tax rate.

P8–19 **Relevant cash flows for a marketing campaign** Marcus Tube, a manufacturer of high-quality aluminum tubing, has maintained stable sales and profits over the past 10 years. Although the market for aluminum tubing has been expanding by 3% per year, Marcus has been unsuccessful in sharing this growth. To increase its sales, the firm is considering an aggressive marketing campaign that centers on regularly running ads in all relevant trade journals and exhibiting products at all major regional and national trade shows. The campaign is expected to require an *annual* tax-deductible expenditure of $150,000 over the next 5 years. Sales revenue, as shown in the income statement for 2006 (top of facing page), totaled $20,000,000. If the proposed marketing campaign is not initiated, sales are expected to remain at this level in each of the next 5 years, 2007–2011. With the marketing campaign, sales are expected to rise to the

P8–14 **Incremental operating cash inflows** A firm is considering renewing its equipment to meet increased demand for its product. The cost of equipment modifications is $1.9 million plus $100,000 in installation costs. The firm will depreciate the equipment modifications under MACRS, using a 5-year recovery period. (See Table 3.2 on page 94 for the applicable depreciation percentages.) Additional sales revenue from the renewal should amount to $1.2 million per year, and additional operating expenses and other costs (excluding depreciation and interest) will amount to 40% of the additional sales. The firm is subject to a tax rate of 40%. (*Note:* Answer the following questions for each of the next 6 *years*.)
  a. What incremental earnings before depreciation, interest, and taxes will result from the renewal?
  b. What incremental net operating profits after taxes will result from the renewal?
  c. What *incremental operating cash inflows* will result from the renewal?

P8–15 **Incremental operating cash inflows—Expense reduction** Miller Corporation is considering replacing a machine. The replacement will reduce operating expenses (that is, increase earnings before depreciation, interest, and taxes) by $16,000 per year for each of the 5 years the new machine is expected to last. Although the old machine has zero book value, it can be used for 5 more years. The depreciable value of the new machine is $48,000. The firm will depreciate the machine under MACRS using a 5-year recovery period (see Table 3.2 on page 94 for the applicable depreciation percentages) and is subject to a 40% tax rate. Estimate the *incremental operating cash inflows* generated by the replacement. (*Note:* Be sure to consider the depreciation in year 6.)

P8–16 **Incremental operating cash inflows** Strong Tool Company has been considering purchasing a new lathe to replace a fully depreciated lathe that will last 5 more years. The new lathe is expected to have a 5-year life and depreciation charges of $2,000 in year 1; $3,200 in year 2; $1,900 in year 3; $1,200 in both year 4 and year 5; and $500 in year 6. The firm estimates the revenues and expenses (excluding depreciation and interest) for the new and the old lathes to be as shown in the following table. The firm is subject to a 40% tax rate.

	New lathe		Old lathe	
Year	Revenue	Expenses (excl. depr. and int.)	Revenue	Expenses (excl. depr. and int.)
1	$40,000	$30,000	$35,000	$25,000
2	41,000	30,000	35,000	25,000
3	42,000	30,000	35,000	25,000
4	43,000	30,000	35,000	25,000
5	44,000	30,000	35,000	25,000

  a. Calculate the *operating cash inflows* associated with each lathe. (*Note:* Be sure to consider the depreciation in year 6.)

rate (T) for the firm is 40%. (Table 3.2 on page 94 contains the applicable MACRS depreciation percentages.)

Damon expects to be able to liquidate the proposed machine at the end of its 5-year usable life for $24,000 (after paying removal and cleanup costs). The present machine is expected to net $8,000 upon liquidation at the end of the same period. Damon expects to recover its net working capital investment upon termination of the project. The firm is subject to a tax rate of 40%.

TO DO

Create a spreadsheet similar to Tables 8.2, 8.6, 8.8, and 8.10 (or the spreadsheets that can be viewed at www.aw-bc.com/gitman), to answer the following:

a. Create a spreadsheet to calculate the *initial investment*.
b. Create a spreadsheet to prepare a *depreciation schedule* for both the proposed and the present machine. Both machines are depreciated using a 5-year MACRS. Remember, the present machine has only 3 years of depreciation remaining.
c. Create a spreadsheet to calculate the *operating cash inflows* for Damon Corporation for both the proposed and the present machine.
d. Create a spreadsheet to calculate the *terminal cash flow* associated with the project.

WEB EXERCISE

For this exercise, you are to go to a Web site of your choosing where you can investigate the recent past of two corporations (also of your own choosing). You will need access to annual reports for the two firms so that you can assess their levels of capital expenditures.

TO DO

a. For each corporation, report the amount of capital spending. Go back 3 years and compare the levels within each firm. Has the amount been roughly constant, or were there big fluctuations? Describe the purposes of the capital expenditures made by each firm.
b. Compare the level of capital spending across the two firms. Are they greatly different, particularly in comparison to their relative sizes?

Remember to check the book's Web site at

www.aw-bc.com/gitman

for additional resources, including additional Web exercises.

Chapter 9

Capital Budgeting Techniques: Certainty and Risk

LEARNING GOALS

LG1 Calculate, interpret, and evaluate the payback period.

LG2 Apply net present value (NPV) and internal rate of return (IRR) to relevant cash flows to choose acceptable capital expenditures.

LG3 Use net present value profiles to compare the NPV and IRR techniques in light of conflicting rankings.

LG4 Discuss two additional considerations in capital budgeting—recognizing real options and choosing projects under capital rationing.

LG5 Recognize sensitivity analysis and scenario analysis, decision trees, and simulation as behavioral approaches for dealing with project risk, and the unique risks that multinational companies face.

LG6 Understand the calculation and practical aspects of risk-adjusted discount rates (RADRs).

Across the Disciplines **Why This Chapter Matters to You**

Accounting: You need to understand capital budgeting techniques to develop good estimates of the relevant cash flows associated with a proposed capital expenditure and to appreciate how risk may affect the variability of cash flows.

Information systems: You need to understand capital budgeting techniques, including how risk is measured in those techniques, to design decision modules that help reduce the amount of work required in analyzing proposed capital expenditures.

Management: You need to understand capital budgeting techniques to correctly analyze the relevant cash flows of proposed projects and decide whether to accept or reject them; the role of real options; selecting projects when capital must be rationed; and behavioral and risk-adjustment approaches for dealing with risk, including international risk.

Marketing: You need to understand capital budgeting techniques to grasp how proposals for new products and expansion of existing product lines will be evaluated by the firm's decision makers and how risk of proposed projects is treated in capital budgeting.

Operations: You need to understand capital budgeting techniques to know how proposals for the acquisition of new equipment and plants will be evaluated by the firm's decision makers, especially when capital must be rationed.

Firms use the relevant cash flows to make decisions about proposed capital expenditures. These decisions can be expressed in the form of project acceptance or rejection or of project rankings. A number of techniques are used in such decision making, some more sophisticated than others. These techniques are the topic of this chapter, wherein we describe the assumptions on which capital budgeting techniques are based, show how they are used in both certain and risky situations, and evaluate their strengths and weaknesses.

Capital Budgeting Techniques

When firms have developed relevant cash flows, as demonstrated in Chapter 8, they analyze them to assess whether a project is acceptable or to rank projects. A number of techniques are available for performing such analyses. The preferred approaches integrate time value procedures, risk and return considerations, and valuation concepts to select capital expenditures that are consistent with the firm's goal of maximizing owners' wealth. This section and the following one focus on the use of these techniques in an environment of certainty. Later in the chapter we will look at capital budgeting under uncertain circumstances.

Bennett Company's Relevant Cash Flows

We will use one basic problem to illustrate all the techniques described in this chapter. The problem concerns Bennett Company, a medium-sized metal fabricator that is currently contemplating two projects: Project A requires an initial investment of $42,000; project B requires an initial investment of $45,000. The projected relevant cash flows for the two projects are presented in Table 9.1 and depicted on the time lines in Figure 9.1 (see page 354).[1] The projects exhibit

Hint Remember that the initial investment is an *outflow* occurring at time zero.

TABLE 9.1 Capital Expenditure Data for Bennett Company

	Project A	Project B
Initial investment	$42,000	$45,000
Year	Operating cash inflows	
1	$14,000	$28,000
2	14,000	12,000
3	14,000	10,000
4	14,000	10,000
5	14,000	10,000

---

1. For simplification, these 5-year-lived projects with 5 years of cash inflows are used throughout this chapter. Projects with usable lives equal to the number of years of cash inflows are also included in the end-of-chapter problems. Recall from Chapter 8 that under current tax law, MACRS depreciation results in $n + 1$ years of depreciation for an n-year class asset. This means that projects will commonly have at least 1 year of cash flow beyond their recovery period. In actual practice, the usable lives of projects (and the associated cash inflows) may differ significantly from their depreciable lives. Generally, under MACRS, usable lives are longer than depreciable lives.

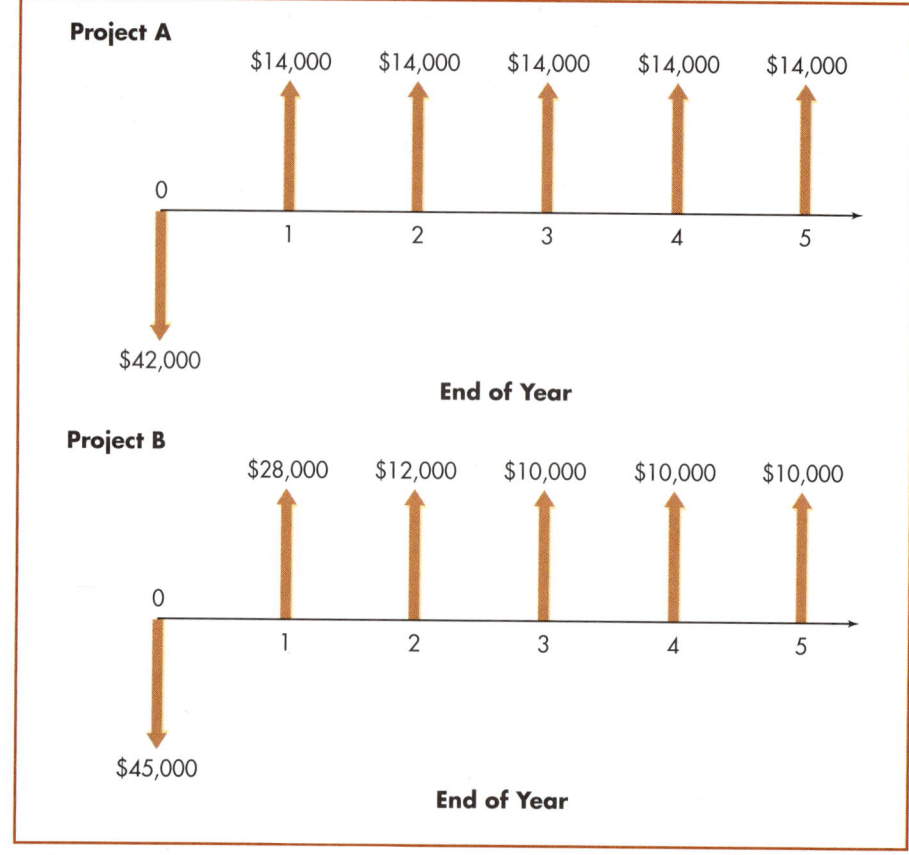

FIGURE 9.1

Bennett Company's Projects A and B
Time lines depicting the conventional cash flows of projects A and B

conventional cash flow patterns, which are assumed throughout the text. In addition, we initially assume that all projects' cash flows have the same level of risk, that projects being compared have equal usable lives, and that the firm has unlimited funds. Because very few decisions are actually made under such conditions, some of these simplifying assumptions are relaxed in later sections of the chapter.

Here we begin with a look at the three most popular capital budgeting techniques: payback period, net present value, and internal rate of return.[2]

Payback Period

payback period
The amount of time required for a firm to recover its initial investment in a project, as calculated from *cash inflows.*

Payback periods are commonly used to evaluate proposed investments. The **payback period** is the amount of time required for the firm to recover its initial investment in a project, as calculated from *cash inflows.* In the case of an *annuity,* the payback period can be found by dividing the initial investment by the annual cash inflow. For a *mixed stream* of cash inflows, the yearly cash inflows must be

---

2. Two other, closely related techniques that are sometimes used to evaluate capital budgeting projects are the *average (or accounting) rate of return (ARR)* and the *profitability index (PI).* The ARR is an unsophisticated technique that is calculated by dividing a project's average profits after taxes by its average investment. Because it fails to consider cash flows and the time value of money, it is ignored here. The PI, sometimes called the *benefit–cost ratio,* is calculated by dividing the present value of cash inflows by the initial investment. This technique, which does consider the time value of money, is sometimes used as a starting point in the selection of projects under capital rationing; the more popular NPV and IRR methods are discussed here.

accumulated until the initial investment is recovered. Although popular, the payback period is generally viewed as an *unsophisticated capital budgeting technique,* because it does not *explicitly* consider the time value of money.

The Decision Criteria

When the payback period is used to make accept–reject decisions, the following decision criteria apply.

- If the payback period is *less than* the maximum acceptable payback period, *accept* the project.
- If the payback period is *greater than* the maximum acceptable payback period, *reject* the project.

The length of the maximum acceptable payback period is determined by management. This value is set *subjectively* on the basis of a number of factors, including the type of project (expansion, replacement, renewal), the perceived risk of the project, and the perceived relationship between the payback period and the share value. It is simply a value that management feels, on average, will result in value-creating investment decisions.

EXAMPLE

We can calculate the payback period for Bennett Company's projects A and B using the data in Table 9.1. *For project A, which is an annuity, the payback period is 3.0 years ($42,000 initial investment ÷ $14,000 annual cash inflow).* Because project B generates a mixed stream of cash inflows, the calculation of its payback period is not as clear-cut. In year 1, the firm will recover $28,000 of its $45,000 initial investment. By the end of year 2, $40,000 ($28,000 from year 1 + $12,000 from year 2) will have been recovered. At the end of year 3, $50,000 will have been recovered. Only 50% of the year-3 cash inflow of $10,000 is needed to complete the payback of the initial $45,000. *The payback period for project B is therefore 2.5 years (2 years + 50% of year 3).*

If Bennett's maximum acceptable payback period were 2.75 years, project A would be rejected and project B would be accepted. If the maximum payback were 2.25 years, both projects would be rejected. If the projects were being ranked, B would be preferred over A, because it has a shorter payback period.

Pros and Cons of Payback Periods

Hint In *all three* of the decision methods presented in this text, the relevant data are *after-tax cash flows.* Accounting profit is used only to help determine the after-tax cash flow.

Hint The payback period indicates to firms taking on projects of high risk how quickly they can recover their investment. In addition, it tells firms with limited sources of capital how quickly the funds invested in a given project will become available for future projects.

The payback period is widely used by large firms to evaluate small projects and by small firms to evaluate most projects. Its popularity results from its computational simplicity and intuitive appeal. It is also appealing in that it considers cash flows rather than accounting profits. By measuring how quickly the firm recovers its initial investment, the payback period also gives *implicit* consideration to the timing of cash flows and therefore to the time value of money. Because it can be viewed as a measure of *risk exposure,* many firms use the payback period as a decision criterion or as a supplement to other decision techniques. The longer the firm must wait to recover its invested funds, the greater the possibility of a calamity. Therefore, the shorter the payback period, the lower the firm's exposure to such risk.

The major weakness of the payback period is that the appropriate payback period is merely a subjectively determined number. It cannot be specified in light of the wealth maximization goal because it is not based on discounting cash flows

TABLE 9.2 Relevant Cash Flows and Payback Periods for DeYarman Enterprises' Projects

	Project Gold	Project Silver
Initial investment	$50,000	$50,000
Year	Operating cash inflows	
1	$ 5,000	$40,000
2	5,000	2,000
3	40,000	8,000
4	10,000	10,000
5	10,000	10,000
Payback period	3 years	3 years

to determine whether they add to the firm's value. Instead, the appropriate payback period is simply the maximum acceptable period of time over which management decides that a project's cash flows must break even (that is, just equal the initial investment).

A second weakness is that this approach fails to take *fully* into account the time factor in the value of money.[3] This weakness can be illustrated by an example.

EXAMPLE

DeYarman Enterprises, a small medical appliance manufacturer, is considering two mutually exclusive projects, which it has named projects Gold and Silver. The firm uses only the payback period to choose projects. The relevant cash flows and payback period for each project are given in Table 9.2. Both projects have 3-year payback periods, which would suggest that they are equally desirable. But comparison of the pattern of cash inflows over the first 3 years shows that more of the $50,000 initial investment in project Silver is recovered sooner than is recovered for project Gold. For example, in year 1, $40,000 of the $50,000 invested in project Silver is recovered, whereas only $5,000 of the $50,000 investment in project Gold is recovered. Given the time value of money, project Silver would clearly be preferred over project Gold, in spite of the fact that both have identical 3-year payback periods. The payback approach does not fully account for the time value of money, which, if recognized, would cause project Silver to be preferred over project Gold. ■

A third weakness of payback is its failure to recognize cash flows that occur *after* the payback period.

EXAMPLE

Rashid Company, a software developer, has two investment opportunities, X and Y. Data for X and Y are given in Table 9.3. The payback period for project X is 2 years; for project Y it is 3 years. Strict adherence to the payback approach suggests that project X is preferable to project Y. However, if we look beyond the payback period, we see that project X returns only an additional $1,200 ($1,000

---

[3]. To consider differences in timing explicitly in applying the payback method, the *present value payback period* is sometimes used. It is found by first calculating the present value of the cash inflows at the appropriate discount rate and then finding the payback period by using the present value of the cash inflows.

TABLE 9.3 Calculation of the Payback Period for Rashid Company's Two Alternative Investment Projects

	Project X	Project Y
Initial investment	$10,000	$10,000
Year	\multicolumn{2}{c}{Operating cash inflows}	
1	$5,000	$3,000
2	5,000	4,000
3	1,000	3,000
4	100	4,000
5	100	3,000
Payback period	2 years	3 years

in year 3 + $100 in year 4 + $100 in year 5), whereas project Y returns an additional $7,000 ($4,000 in year 4 + $3,000 in year 5). On the basis of this information, project Y appears preferable to X. The payback approach ignored the cash inflows occurring after the end of the payback period.[4]

Net Present Value (NPV)

Because *net present value (NPV)* gives explicit consideration to the time value of money, it is considered a *sophisticated capital budgeting technique*. All such techniques in one way or another discount the firm's cash flows at a specified rate. This rate—often called the *discount rate, required return, cost of capital,* or *opportunity cost*—is the minimum return that must be earned on a project to leave the firm's market value unchanged. In this chapter, we take this rate as a "given." In Chapter 10 we will explore how it is determined.

net present value (NPV)
A sophisticated capital budgeting technique; found by subtracting a project's initial investment from the present value of its cash inflows discounted at a rate equal to the firm's cost of capital.

The **net present value (NPV)** is found by subtracting a project's initial investment (CF_0) from the present value of its cash inflows (CF_t) discounted at a rate equal to the firm's cost of capital (k).

NPV = Present value of cash inflows − Initial investment

$$\text{NPV} = \sum_{t=1}^{n} \frac{CF_t}{(1+k)^t} - CF_0 \tag{9.1}$$

$$= \sum_{t=1}^{n} (CF_t \times PVIF_{k,t}) - CF_0 \tag{9.1a}$$

When NPV is used, both inflows and outflows are measured in terms of present dollars. Because we are dealing only with investments that have *conventional cash flow patterns,* the initial investment is automatically stated in terms of

---

[4]. To get around this weakness, some analysts add a desired dollar return to the initial investment and then calculate the payback period for the increased amount. For example, if the analyst wished to pay back the initial investment plus 20% for projects X and Y in Table 9.3, the amount to be recovered would be $12,000 [$10,000 + (0.20 × $10,000)]. For project X, the payback period would be infinite because the $12,000 would never be recovered; for project Y, the payback period would be 3.5 years [3 years + ($2,000 ÷ $4,000) years]. Clearly, project Y would be preferred.

today's dollars. If it were not, the present value of a project would be found by subtracting the present value of outflows from the present value of inflows.

The Decision Criteria

When NPV is used to make accept–reject decisions, the decision criteria are as follows:

- If the NPV is *greater than* $0, *accept* the project.
- If the NPV is *less than* $0, *reject* the project.

If the NPV is greater than $0, the firm will earn a return greater than its cost of capital. Such action should increase the market value of the firm, and therefore the wealth of its owners by an amount equal to the NPV.

EXAMPLE We can illustrate the net present value (NPV) approach by using the Bennett Company data presented in Table 9.1. If the firm has a 10% cost of capital, the net present values for projects A (an annuity) and B (a mixed stream) can be calculated as shown on the time lines in Figure 9.2. These calculations result in net

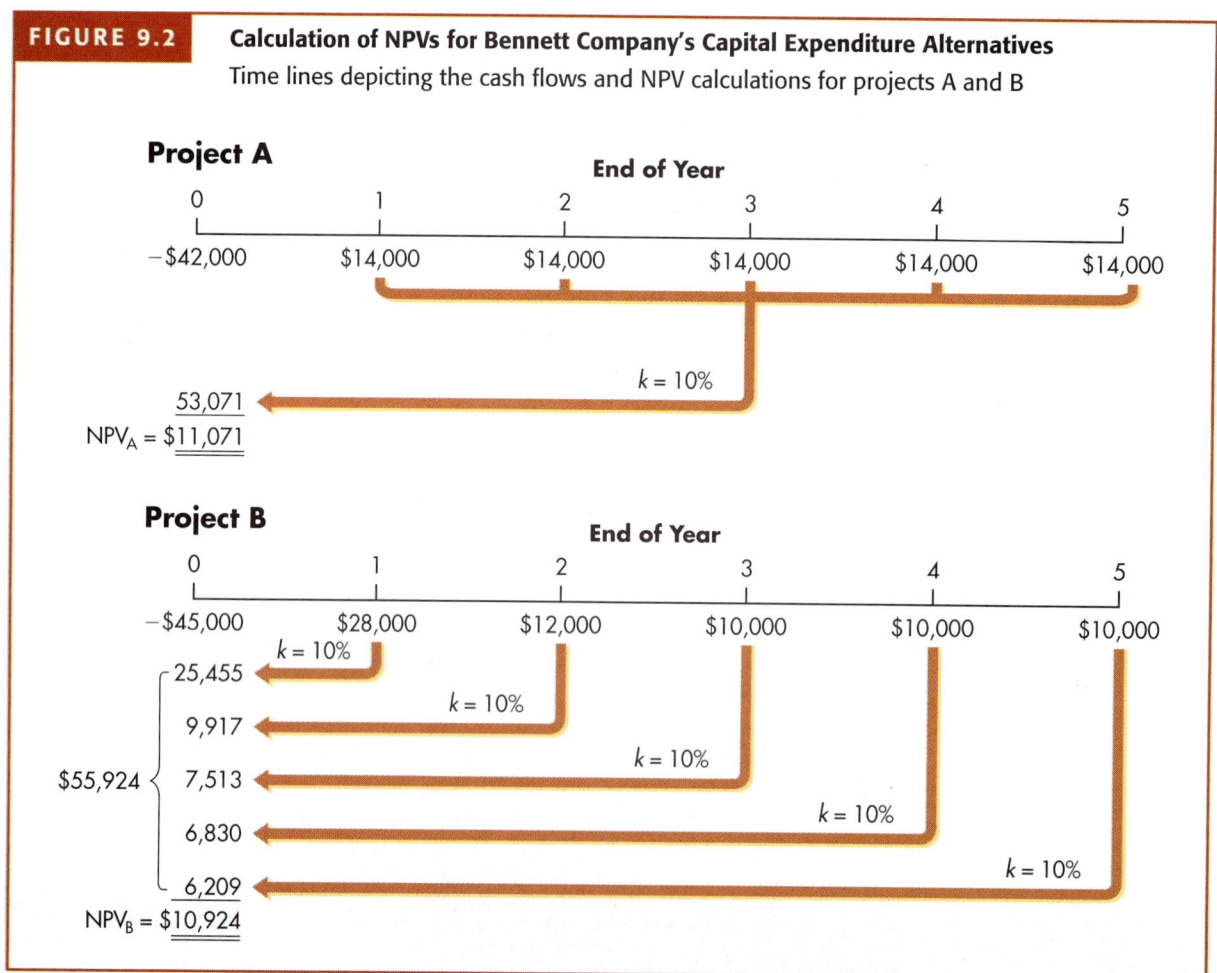

FIGURE 9.2 Calculation of NPVs for Bennett Company's Capital Expenditure Alternatives
Time lines depicting the cash flows and NPV calculations for projects A and B

Project A

Project B

present values for projects A and B of $11,071 and $10,924, respectively. Both projects are acceptable, because the net present value of each is greater than $0. If the projects were being ranked, however, project A would be considered superior to B, because it has a higher net present value than that of B ($11,071 versus $10,924).

Calculator Use The preprogrammed NPV function in a financial calculator can be used to simplify the NPV calculation. The keystrokes for project A—the annuity—typically are as shown at left. Note that because project A is an annuity, only its first cash inflow, $CF_1 = 14000$, is input, followed by its frequency, $N = 5$.

The keystrokes for project B—the mixed stream—are as shown at left. Because the last three cash inflows for project B are the same ($CF_3 = CF_4 = CF_5 = 10000$), after inputting the first of these cash inflows, CF_3, we merely input its frequency, $N = 3$.

The calculated NPVs for projects A and B of $11,071 and $10,924, respectively, agree with the NPVs cited above.

Spreadsheet Use The NPVs can be calculated as shown on the following Excel spreadsheet.

	A	B	C
1	DETERMINING THE NET PRESENT VALUE		
2	Firm's cost of capital		10%
3		Year-End Cash Flow	
4	Year	Project A	Project B
5	0	$ (42,000)	$ (45,000)
6	1	$ 14,000	$ 28,000
7	2	$ 14,000	$ 12,000
8	3	$ 14,000	$ 10,000
9	4	$ 14,000	$ 10,000
10	5	$ 14,000	$ 10,000
11	NPV	$ 11,071	$ 10,924
12	Choice of project		Project A

Entry in Cell B11 is
=NPV(C2,B6:B10)+B5
Copy the entry in Cell B11 to Cell C11.
Entry in Cell C12 is IF(B11>C11,B4,C4).

Internal Rate of Return (IRR)

internal rate of return (IRR)
A sophisticated capital budgeting technique; the discount rate that equates the NPV of an investment opportunity with $0 (because the present value of cash inflows equals the initial investment); it is the compound annual rate of return that the firm will earn if it invests in the project and receives the given cash inflows.

The *internal rate of return (IRR)* is probably the most widely used *sophisticated capital budgeting technique*. However, it is considerably more difficult than NPV to calculate by hand. The **internal rate of return (IRR)** is the discount rate that equates the NPV of an investment opportunity with $0 (because the present value of cash inflows equals the initial investment). It is the compound annual rate of return that the firm will earn if it invests in the project and receives the given cash inflows. Mathematically, the IRR is the value of k in Equation 9.1 that causes NPV to equal $0.

$$\$0 = \sum_{t=1}^{n} \frac{CF_t}{(1 + IRR)^t} - CF_0 \qquad (9.2)$$

$$\sum_{t=1}^{n} \frac{CF_t}{(1 + IRR)^t} = CF_0 \qquad (9.2a)$$

The Decision Criteria

When IRR is used to make accept–reject decisions, the decision criteria are as follows:

- If the IRR is *greater than* the cost of capital, *accept* the project.
- If the IRR is *less than* the cost of capital, *reject* the project.

These criteria guarantee that the firm will earn at least its required return. Such an outcome should increase the market value of the firm and therefore the wealth of its owners.

Calculating the IRR

The actual calculation by hand of the IRR from Equation 9.2a is no easy chore. It involves a complex trial-and-error search technique that logically tries different discount rates until one is found that causes the project's present value of cash inflows to just equal its initial investment (or NPV to equal $0). Details of this technique are described and demonstrated on this text's Web site: www.aw-bc.com/gitman. Fortunately, many financial calculators have a preprogrammed IRR function that can be used to simplify the IRR calculation. With these calculators, you merely punch in all cash flows just as if to calculate NPV and then depress IRR to find the internal rate of return. Computer software, including spreadsheets, is also available for simplifying these calculations. All NPV and IRR values presented in this and subsequent chapters are obtained by using these functions on a popular financial calculator.

EXAMPLE

We can demonstrate the internal rate of return (IRR) approach using the Bennett Company data presented in Table 9.1. Figure 9.3 uses time lines to depict the framework for finding the IRRs for Bennett's projects A and B, both of which have conventional cash flow patterns. It can be seen in the figure that the IRR is the unknown discount rate that causes the NPV just to equal $0.

Calculator Use To find the IRR using the preprogrammed function in a financial calculator, the keystrokes for each project are the same as those shown on page 359 for the NPV calculation, except that the last two NPV keystrokes (punching **I** and then **NPV**) are replaced by a single **IRR** keystroke.

Comparing the IRRs of projects A and B given in Figure 9.3 to Bennett Company's 10% cost of capital, we can see that both projects are acceptable because

$$IRR_A = 19.9\% > 10.0\% \text{ cost of capital}$$
$$IRR_B = 21.7\% > 10.0\% \text{ cost of capital}$$

Comparing the two projects' IRRs, we would prefer project B over project A because $IRR_B = 21.7\% > IRR_A = 19.9\%$. If these projects are mutually exclusive, the IRR decision technique would recommend project B.

CHAPTER 9 Capital Budgeting Techniques: Certainty and Risk

FIGURE 9.3 **Calculation of IRRs for Bennett Company's Capital Expenditure Alternatives**
Time lines depicting the cash flows and IRR calculations for projects A and B

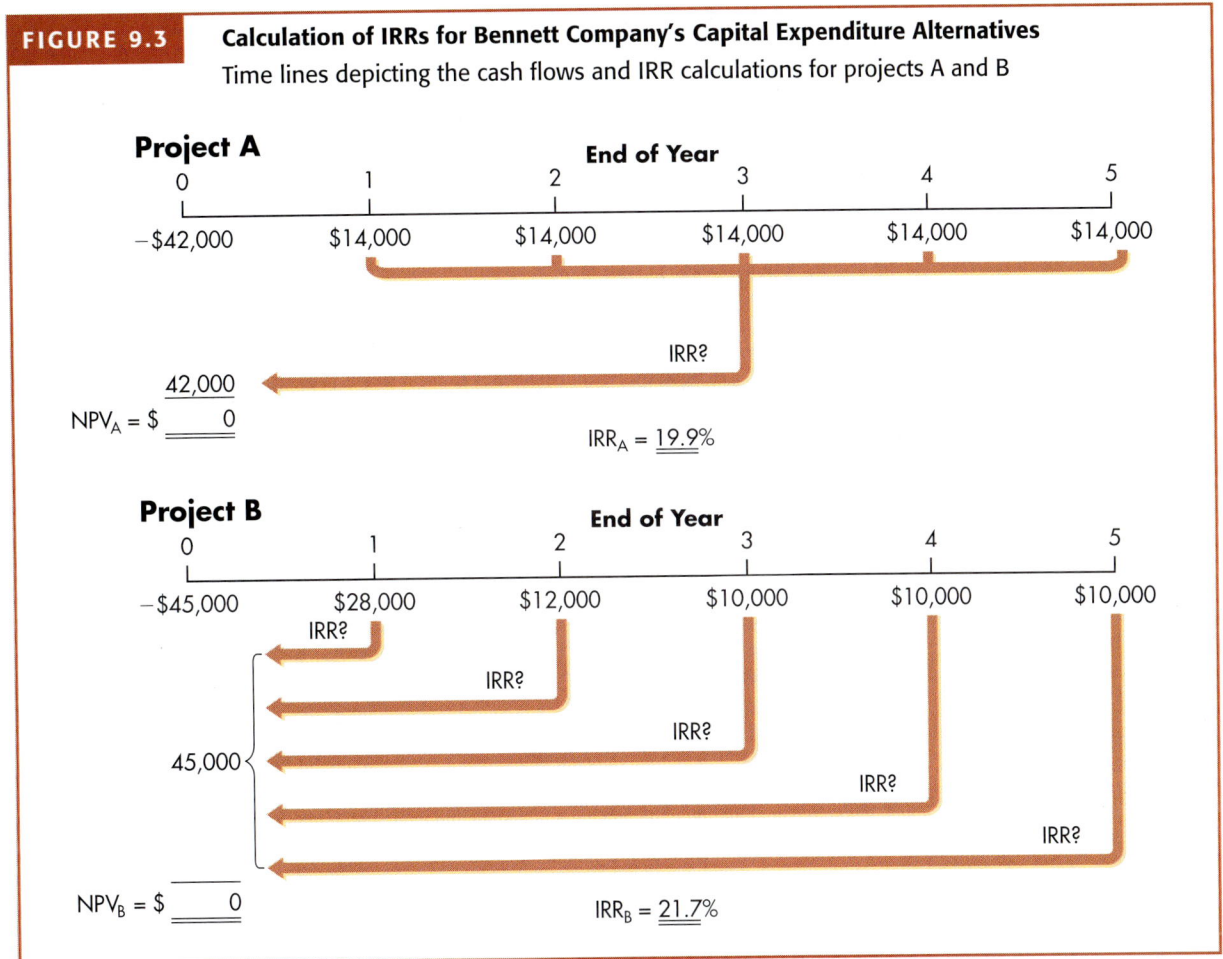

Spreadsheet Use The internal rate of return also can be calculated as shown on the following Excel spreadsheet.

	A	B	C
1	\multicolumn{3}{c}{DETERMINING THE INTERNAL RATE OF RETURN}	
2		\multicolumn{2}{c}{Year-End Cash Flow}	
3	Year	Project A	Project B
4	0	$ (42,000)	$ (45,000)
5	1	$ 14,000	$ 28,000
6	2	$ 14,000	$ 12,000
7	3	$ 14,000	$ 10,000
8	4	$ 14,000	$ 10,000
9	5	$ 14,000	$ 10,000
10	IRR	19.9%	21.7%
11	\multicolumn{2}{c}{Choice of Project}	Project B

Entry in Cell B10 is =IRR(B4:B9).
Copy the entry in Cell B10 to Cell C10.
Entry in Cell C11 is =IF(B10>C10,B3,C3).

It is interesting to note in the preceding example that the IRR suggests that project B, which has an IRR of 21.7%, is preferable to project A, which has an IRR of 19.9%. This conflicts with the NPV rankings obtained in an earlier example. Such conflicts are not unusual. *There is no guarantee that NPV and IRR will rank projects in the same order. However, both methods should reach the same conclusion about the acceptability or nonacceptability of projects.*

Review Questions

9-1 What is the *payback period*? How is it calculated? What weaknesses are commonly associated with the use of the payback period to evaluate a proposed investment?

9-2 How is the *net present value (NPV)* calculated for a project with a *conventional cash flow pattern*? What are the acceptance criteria for NPV?

9-3 What is the *internal rate of return (IRR)* on an investment? How is it determined? What are the acceptance criteria for IRR?

Comparing NPV and IRR Techniques

To understand the differences between the NPV and IRR techniques and decision makers' preferences in their use, we need to look at net present value profiles, conflicting rankings, and the question of which approach is better.

Net Present Value Profiles

net present value profile
Graph that depicts a project's NPVs for various discount rates.

Projects can be compared graphically by constructing **net present value profiles** that depict the project's NPVs for various discount rates. These profiles are useful in evaluating and comparing projects, especially when conflicting rankings exist. They are best demonstrated via an example.

EXAMPLE To prepare net present value profiles for Bennett Company's two projects, A and B, the first step is to develop a number of "discount rate–net present value" coordinates. Three coordinates can be easily obtained for each project; they are at discount rates of 0%, 10% (the cost of capital, k), and the IRR. The net present value at a 0% discount rate is found by merely adding all the cash inflows and subtracting the initial investment. Using the data in Table 9.1 and Figure 9.1, we get

For project A:

($14,000 + $14,000 + $14,000 + $14,000 + $14,000) − $42,000 = $28,000

For project B:

($28,000 + $12,000 + $10,000 + $10,000 + $10,000) − $45,000 = $25,000

The net present values for projects A and B at the 10% cost of capital are $11,071 and $10,924, respectively (from Figure 9.2). Because the IRR is the discount rate for which net present value equals zero, the IRRs (from Figure 9.3) of

TABLE 9.4 Discount Rate–NPV Coordinates for Projects A and B

Discount rate	Net present value Project A	Net present value Project B
0 %	$28,000	$25,000
10	11,071	10,924
19.9	0	—
21.7	—	0

19.9% for project A and 21.7% for project B result in $0 NPVs. The three sets of coordinates for each of the projects are summarized in Table 9.4.

Plotting the data from Table 9.4 results in the net present value profiles for projects A and B shown in Figure 9.4. The figure indicates that for any discount rate less than approximately 10.7%, the NPV for project A is greater than the NPV for project B. Beyond this point, the NPV for project B is greater. Because the net present value profiles for projects A and B cross at a positive NPV that occurs at a discount rate (10.7%), which is higher than the firm's cost of capital (10.0%), the IRRs for the projects result in conflicting rankings with their NPVs.

Conflicting Rankings

Ranking is an important consideration when projects are mutually exclusive or when capital rationing is necessary. When projects are mutually exclusive, ranking enables the firm to determine which project is best from a financial standpoint. When capital rationing is necessary, ranking projects will provide a logical starting point for determining which group of projects to accept. As we'll see, **conflicting rankings** using NPV and IRR result from *differences in the magnitude and timing of cash flows.*

The underlying cause of conflicting rankings is different implicit assumptions about the *reinvestment* of **intermediate cash inflows**—cash inflows received prior to the termination of a project. NPV assumes that intermediate cash inflows are

conflicting rankings
Conflicts in the ranking given a project by NPV and IRR, resulting from *differences in the magnitude and timing of cash flows.*

intermediate cash inflows
Cash inflows received prior to the termination of a project.

FIGURE 9.4
NPV Profiles
Net present value profiles for Bennett Company's projects A and B

TABLE 9.5 Preferences Associated with Extreme Discount Rates and Dissimilar Cash Inflow Patterns

Discount rate	Cash inflow pattern	
	Lower early-year cash inflows	Higher early-year cash inflows
Low	Preferred	Not preferred
High	Not preferred	Preferred

reinvested at the cost of capital, whereas IRR assumes that intermediate cash inflows are invested at a rate equal to the project's IRR.[5]

In general, projects with similar-size investments and lower cash inflows in the early years tend to be preferred at lower discount rates. Projects that have higher cash inflows in the early years tend to be preferred at higher discount rates. Why? Because at high discount rates, later-year cash inflows tend to be severely penalized in present value terms. For example, at a high discount rate, say 20 percent, the present value of $1 received at the end of 5 years is about 40 cents, whereas for $1 received at the end of 15 years it is less than 7 cents. Clearly, at high discount rates a project's early-year cash inflows count most in terms of its NPV. Table 9.5 summarizes the preferences associated with extreme discount rates and dissimilar cash inflow patterns.

EXAMPLE

Bennett Company's projects A and B were found to have conflicting rankings at the firm's 10% cost of capital (as depicted in Figure 9.4). If we review each project's cash inflow pattern as presented in Table 9.1 and Figure 9.1, we see that although the projects require similar initial investments, they have dissimilar cash inflow patterns. Table 9.5 indicates that project B, which has higher early-year cash inflows than project A, would be preferred over project A at higher discount rates. Figure 9.4 shows that this is in fact the case. At any discount rate in excess of 10.7%, project B's NPV surpasses that of project A. Clearly, the magnitude and timing of the projects' cash inflows do affect their rankings.

Which Approach Is Better?

Many companies use both the NPV and IRR techniques because current technology makes them easy to calculate. But it is difficult to choose one approach over the other, because the theoretical and practical strengths of the approaches differ. Clearly, it is wise to view NPV and IRR techniques in each of these dimensions.

---

5. To eliminate the reinvestment rate assumption of the IRR, some practitioners calculate the *modified internal rate of return (MIRR)*. The MIRR is found by converting each operating cash inflow to its future value measured at the end of the project's life and then summing the future values of all inflows to get the project's *terminal value*. Each future value is found by using the cost of capital, thereby eliminating the reinvestment rate criticism of the traditional IRR. The MIRR represents the discount rate that causes the terminal value just to equal the initial investment. Because it uses the cost of capital as the reinvestment rate, the MIRR is generally viewed as a better measure of a project's true profitability than the IRR. Although this technique is frequently used in commercial real estate valuation and is a preprogrammed function on some financial calculators, its failure to resolve the issue of conflicting rankings and its theoretical inferiority to NPV have resulted in the MIRR receiving only limited attention and acceptance in the financial literature. For a thorough analysis of the arguments surrounding IRR and MIRR, see D. Anthony Plath and William F. Kennedy, "Teaching Return-Based Measures of Project Evaluation," *Financial Practice and Education* (Spring/Summer 1994), pp. 77–86.

Theoretical View

On a purely theoretical basis, NPV is the better approach to capital budgeting as a result of several factors. Most important is that the use of NPV implicitly assumes that any intermediate cash inflows generated by an investment are *reinvested at the firm's cost of capital*. The use of IRR assumes *reinvestment at the often high rate specified by the IRR*. Because the cost of capital tends to be a reasonable estimate of the rate at which the firm could *actually reinvest* intermediate cash inflows, the use of NPV, with its more conservative and realistic reinvestment rate, is in theory preferable.

In addition, certain mathematical properties may cause a project with a *nonconventional cash flow pattern* to have **multiple IRRs**—more than one IRR. Mathematically, the maximum number of *real* roots to an equation is equal to its number of sign changes. Take an equation like $x^2 - 5x + 6 = 0$, which has two sign changes in its coefficients—from positive ($+x^2$) to negative ($-5x$) and then from negative ($-5x$) to positive ($+6$). If we factor the equation (remember factoring from high school math?), we get $(x - 2) \times (x - 3)$, which means that x can equal either 2 or 3—there are two correct values for x. Substitute them back into the equation, and you'll see that both values work.

This same outcome can occur when finding the IRR for projects with nonconventional cash flows, because they have more than one sign change. Clearly, when multiple IRRs occur for nonconventional cash flows, the analyst faces the time-consuming need to interpret their meanings so as to evaluate the project. The fact that such a challenge does not exist when using NPV enhances its theoretical superiority.

multiple IRRs
More than one IRR resulting from a capital budgeting project with a *nonconventional cash flow pattern;* the maximum number of IRRs for a project is equal to the number of sign changes in its cash flows.

Practical View

Evidence suggests that in spite of the theoretical superiority of NPV, *financial managers prefer to use IRR*.[6] The preference for IRR is due to the general disposition of businesspeople toward *rates of return* rather than actual *dollar returns*. Because interest rates, profitability, and so on are most often expressed as annual rates of return, the use of IRR makes sense to financial decision makers. They tend to find NPV less intuitive because it does not measure benefits *relative to the amount invested*. Because a variety of techniques are available for avoiding the pitfalls of the IRR, its widespread use does not imply a lack of sophistication on the part of financial decision makers. Clearly, corporate financial analysts are responsible for identifying and resolving problems with the IRR before the decision makers use it as a decision technique.

Review Questions

9–4 Do the net present value (NPV) and internal rate of return (IRR) always agree with respect to accept–reject decisions? With respect to ranking decisions? Explain.

---

6. For example, see John R. Graham and Campbell R. Harvey, "The Theory and Practice of Corporate Finance: Evidence from the Field," *Journal of Financial Economics* (May/June 2001), pp. 187–243; Harold Bierman, Jr., "Capital Budgeting in 1992: A Survey," *Financial Management* (Autumn 1993), p. 24; and Lawrence J. Gitman and Charles E. Maxwell, "A Longitudinal Comparison of Capital Budgeting Techniques Used by Major U.S. Firms: 1986 versus 1976," *Journal of Applied Business Research* (Fall 1987), pp. 41–50, for discussions of evidence with respect to capital budgeting decision-making practices in major U.S. firms.

9–5 How is a *net present value profile* used to compare projects? What causes conflicts in the ranking of projects via net present value and internal rate of return?

9–6 Does the assumption concerning the reinvestment of intermediate cash inflow tend to favor NPV or IRR? In practice, which technique is preferred and why?

Additional Considerations: Real Options and Capital Rationing

Two important issues that often confront the financial manager when making capital budgeting decisions are (1) the potential real options embedded in capital projects, and (2) the availability of only limited funding for acceptable projects. Here we briefly consider each of these situations.

Recognizing Real Options

The procedures described in Chapter 8 and thus far in this chapter suggest that to make capital budgeting decisions, we must (1) estimate relevant cash flows and (2) apply an appropriate decision technique such as NPV or IRR to those cash flows. Although this traditional procedure is believed to yield good decisions, a more *strategic approach* to these decisions has emerged in recent years. This more modern view considers any **real options**—opportunities that are embedded in capital projects ("real," rather than financial, asset investments) that enable managers to alter their cash flows and risk in a way that affects project acceptability (NPV). Because these opportunities are more likely to exist in, and be more important to, large "strategic" capital budgeting projects, they are sometimes called *strategic options*.

real options
Opportunities that are embedded in capital projects that enable managers to alter their cash flows and risk in a way that affects project acceptability (NPV). Also called *strategic options*.

Some of the more common types of real options—abandonment, flexibility, growth, and timing—are briefly described in Table 9.6. It should be clear from their descriptions that each of these types of options could be embedded in a capital budgeting decision and that explicit recognition of them would probably alter the cash flow and risk of a project and change its NPV.

By explicitly recognizing these options when making capital budgeting decisions, managers can make improved, more strategic decisions that consider in advance the economic impact of certain contingent actions on project cash flow and risk. The explicit recognition of real options embedded in capital budgeting projects will cause the project's *strategic NPV* to differ from its *traditional NPV* as indicated by Equation 9.3.

$$NPV_{strategic} = NPV_{traditional} + \text{Value of real options} \qquad (9.3)$$

Application of this relationship is illustrated in the following example.

EXAMPLE Assume that a strategic analysis of Bennett Company's projects A and B (see cash flows and NPVs in Figure 9.2) finds no real options embedded in project A and two real options embedded in project B. The two real options in project B are as follows: (1) The project would have, during the first two years, some downtime

TABLE 9.6 Major Types of Real Options

Option type	Description
Abandonment option	The option to abandon or terminate a project prior to the end of its planned life. This option allows management to avoid or minimize losses on projects that turn bad. Explicitly recognizing the abandonment option when evaluating a project often increases its NPV.
Flexibility option	The option to incorporate flexibility into the firm's operations, particularly production. It generally includes the opportunity to design the production process to accept multiple inputs, use flexible production technology to create a variety of outputs by reconfiguring the same plant and equipment, and purchase and retain excess capacity in capital-intensive industries subject to wide swings in output demand and long lead time in building new capacity from scratch. Recognition of this option embedded in a capital expenditure should increase the NPV of the project.
Growth option	The option to develop follow-on projects, expand markets, expand or retool plants, and so on, that would not be possible without implementation of the project that is being evaluated. If a project being considered has the measurable potential to open new doors if successful, then recognition of the cash flows from such opportunities should be included in the initial decision process. Growth opportunities embedded in a project often increase the NPV of the project in which they are embedded.
Timing option	The option to determine when various actions with respect to a given project are taken. This option recognizes the firm's opportunity to delay acceptance of a project for one or more periods, to accelerate or slow the process of implementing a project in response to new information, or to shut down a project temporarily in response to changing product market conditions or competition. As in the case of the other types of options, the explicit recognition of timing opportunities can improve the NPV of a project that fails to recognize this option in an investment decision.

that would result in unused production capacity that could be used to perform contract manufacturing for another firm, and (2) the project's computerized control system could, with some modification, control two other machines, thereby reducing labor cost, without affecting operation of the new project.

Bennett's management estimated the NPV of the contract manufacturing over the 2 years following implementation of project B to be $1,500 and the NPV of the computer control sharing to be $2,000. Management felt there was a 60% chance that the contract manufacturing option would be exercised and only a 30% chance that the computer control sharing option would be exercised. The combined value of these two real options would be the sum of their expected values.

$$\text{Value of real options for project B} = (0.60 \times \$1,500) + (0.30 \times \$2,000)$$
$$= \$900 + \$600 = \$1,500$$

Substituting the $1,500 real options value along with the traditional NPV of $10,924 for project B (from Figure 9.2) into Equation 9.3, we get the strategic NPV for project B.

$$\text{NPV}_{\text{strategic}} = \$10,924 + \$1,500 = \underline{\$12,424}$$

Bennett Company's project B therefore has a strategic NPV of $12,424, which is above its traditional NPV and now exceeds project A's NPV of $11,071. Clearly, recognition of project B's real options improved its NPV (from $10,924 to $12,424) and causes it to be preferred over project A (NPV of $12,424 for B > NPV of $11,071 for A), which has no real options embedded in it.

It is important to realize that the recognition of attractive real options when determining NPV could cause an otherwise unacceptable project ($NPV_{traditional} < \$0$) to become acceptable ($NPV_{strategic} > \$0$). The failure to recognize the value of real options could therefore cause management to reject projects that are acceptable. Although doing so requires more strategic thinking and analysis, it is important for the financial manager to identify and incorporate real options in the NPV process. The procedures for doing this efficiently are emerging, and the use of the strategic NPV that incorporates real options is expected to become more commonplace in the future.

Choosing Projects under Capital Rationing

Hint Because everyone in the firm knows that long-term funds are rationed and they want a portion of them, there is *intense competition* for those funds. This competition increases the need for the firm to be objective and proficient in its analysis. Knowing how to use the techniques discussed in this chapter to justify your needs will help you get your share of the available long-term funds.

Firms commonly operate under *capital rationing*—they have more acceptable independent projects than they can fund. *In theory,* capital rationing should not exist. Firms should accept all projects that have positive NPVs (or IRRs > the cost of capital). However, *in practice,* most firms operate under capital rationing. Generally, firms attempt to isolate and select the best acceptable projects subject to a capital expenditure budget set by management. Research has found that management internally imposes capital expenditure constraints to avoid what it deems to be "excessive" levels of new financing, particularly debt. Although failing to fund all acceptable independent projects is theoretically inconsistent with the goal of maximizing owner wealth, here we will discuss capital rationing procedures because they are widely used in practice.

The objective of *capital rationing* is to select the group of projects that provides the *highest overall net present value* and does not require more dollars than are budgeted. As a prerequisite to capital rationing, the best of any mutually exclusive projects must be chosen and placed in the group of independent projects. Two basic approaches to project selection under capital rationing are discussed here.

Internal Rate of Return Approach

internal rate of return approach
An approach to capital rationing that involves graphing project IRRs in descending order against the total dollar investment to determine the group of acceptable projects.

investment opportunities schedule (IOS)
The graph that plots project IRRs in descending order against the total dollar investment.

The **internal rate of return approach** involves graphing project IRRs in descending order against the total dollar investment. This graph, which is discussed in more detail in Chapter 10, is called the **investment opportunities schedule (IOS)**. By drawing the cost-of-capital line and then imposing a budget constraint, the financial manager can determine the group of acceptable projects. The problem with this technique is that it does not guarantee the maximum dollar return to the firm. It merely provides a satisfactory solution to capital-rationing problems.

EXAMPLE

Tate Company, a fast-growing plastics company, is confronted with six projects competing for its fixed budget of $250,000. The initial investment and IRR for each project are as follows:

Project	Initial investment	IRR
A	$ 80,000	12%
B	70,000	20
C	100,000	16
D	40,000	8
E	60,000	15
F	110,000	11

The firm has a cost of capital of 10%. Figure 9.5 presents the IOS that results from ranking the six projects in descending order on the basis of their IRRs. According to the schedule, only projects B, C, and E should be accepted. Together they will absorb $230,000 of the $250,000 budget. Projects A and F are acceptable but cannot be chosen because of the budget constraint. Project D is not worthy of consideration; its IRR is less than the firm's 10% cost of capital.

The drawback of this approach is that there is no guarantee that the acceptance of projects B, C, and E will maximize *total dollar returns* and therefore owners' wealth.

Net Present Value Approach

net present value approach
An approach to capital rationing that is based on the use of present values to determine the group of projects that will maximize owners' wealth.

The **net present value approach** is based on the use of present values to determine the group of projects that will maximize owners' wealth. It is implemented by ranking projects on the basis of IRRs and then evaluating the present value of the benefits from each potential project to determine *the combination of projects with the highest overall present value.* This is the same as maximizing net present value, because the entire budget is viewed as the total initial investment. Any portion of the firm's budget that is not used does not increase the firm's value. At best, the unused money can be invested in marketable securities or returned to the owners in the form of cash dividends. In either case, the wealth of the owners is not likely to be enhanced.

FIGURE 9.5

Investment Opportunities Schedule
Investment opportunities schedule (IOS) for Tate Company projects

TABLE 9.7	Rankings for Tate Company Projects			
Project	Initial investment	IRR	Present value of inflows at 10%	
B	$ 70,000	20%	$112,000	
C	100,000	16	145,000	
E	60,000	15	79,000	
A	80,000	12	100,000	
F	110,000	11	126,500	
D	40,000	8	36,000	Cutoff point (IRR<10%)

EXAMPLE

The group of projects described in the preceding example is ranked in Table 9.7 on the basis of IRRs. The present value of the cash inflows associated with the projects is also included in the table. Projects B, C, and E, which together require $230,000, yield a present value of $336,000. However, if projects B, C, and A were implemented, the total budget of $250,000 would be used, and the present value of the cash inflows would be $357,000. This is greater than the return expected from selecting the projects on the basis of the highest IRRs. Implementing B, C, and A is preferable, because they maximize the present value for the given budget. *The firm's objective is to use its budget to generate the highest present value of inflows.* Assuming that any unused portion of the budget does not gain or lose money, the total NPV for projects B, C, and E would be $106,000 ($336,000 − $230,000), whereas the total NPV for projects B, C, and A would be $107,000 ($357,000 − $250,000). Selection of projects B, C, and A will therefore maximize NPV. ∎

Review Questions

9–7 What are *real options*? What are some major types of real options?

9–8 What is the difference between the *strategic NPV* and the *traditional NPV*? Do they always result in the same accept–reject decisions?

9–9 What is *capital rationing*? In theory, should capital rationing exist? Why does it frequently occur in practice?

9–10 Compare and contrast the *internal rate of return approach* and the *net present value approach* to capital rationing. Which is better? Why?

Behavioral Approaches for Dealing with Risk

risk (in capital budgeting)
The chance that a project will prove unacceptable or, more formally, the degree of variability of cash flows.

In the context of capital budgeting, the term **risk** refers to the chance that a project will prove unacceptable—that is, NPV < $0 or IRR < cost of capital. More formally, risk in capital budgeting is the degree of variability of cash flows. Projects with a small chance of acceptability and a broad range of expected cash flows are more risky than projects that have a high chance of acceptability and a narrow range of expected cash flows.

In the conventional capital budgeting projects assumed here, risk stems almost entirely from *cash inflows,* because the initial investment is generally known with relative certainty. These inflows, of course, derive from a number of variables related to revenues, expenditures, and taxes. Examples include the level of sales, the cost of raw materials, labor rates, utility costs, and tax rates. We will concentrate on the risk in the cash inflows, but remember that this risk actually results from the interaction of these underlying variables.

Behavioral approaches can be used to get a "feel" for the level of project risk, whereas other approaches explicitly recognize project risk. Here we present a few behavioral approaches for dealing with risk in capital budgeting: sensitivity and scenario analysis, decision trees, and simulation. In addition, we discuss some international risk considerations.

Sensitivity and Scenario Analysis

Two approaches for dealing with project risk to capture the variability of cash inflows and NPVs are sensitivity analysis and scenario analysis. As noted in Chapter 5, *sensitivity analysis* is a behavioral approach that uses several possible values for a given variable, such as cash inflows, to assess that variable's impact on the firm's return, measured here by NPV. This technique is often useful in getting a feel for the variability of return in response to changes in a key variable. In capital budgeting, one of the most common sensitivity approaches is to estimate the NPVs associated with pessimistic (worst), most likely (expected), and optimistic (best) estimates of cash inflow. The *range* can be determined by subtracting the pessimistic-outcome NPV from the optimistic-outcome NPV.

EXAMPLE

Treadwell Tire Company, a tire retailer with a 10% cost of capital, is considering investing in either of two mutually exclusive projects, A or B. Each requires a $10,000 initial investment, and both are expected to provide equal annual cash inflows over their 15-year lives. The firm's financial manager made pessimistic, most likely, and optimistic estimates of the cash inflows for each project. The cash inflow estimates and resulting NPVs in each case are summarized in Table 9.8 (see page 372). Comparing the ranges of cash inflows ($1,000 for project A and $4,000 for B) and, more important, the ranges of NPVs ($7,606 for project A and $30,424 for B) makes it clear that project A is less risky than project B. Given that both projects have the same most likely NPV of $5,212, the assumed risk-averse decision maker will take project A because it has less risk (smaller NPV range) and no possibility of loss (all NPVs > $0). ■

scenario analysis
A behavioral approach that evaluates the impact on the firm's return of simultaneous changes in *a number of variables.*

Scenario analysis is a behavioral approach similar to sensitivity analysis but broader in scope. It evaluates the impact on the firm's return of simultaneous changes in *a number of variables,* such as cash inflows, cash outflows, and the cost of capital. For example, the firm could evaluate the impact of both high inflation (scenario 1) and low inflation (scenario 2) on a project's NPV. Each scenario will affect the firm's cash inflows, cash outflows, and cost of capital, thereby resulting in different levels of NPV. The decision maker can use these NPV estimates to assess the risk involved with respect to the level of inflation. The widespread availability of computers and spreadsheets has greatly enhanced the use of both scenario and sensitivity analysis.

TABLE 9.8 Sensitivity Analysis of Treadwell's Projects A and B

	Project A	Project B
Initial investment	$10,000	$10,000
Annual cash inflows		
Outcome		
Pessimistic	$1,500	$ 0
Most likely	2,000	2,000
Optimistic	2,500	4,000
Range	$1,000	$ 4,000
Net present values[a]		
Outcome		
Pessimistic	$1,409	−$10,000
Most likely	5,212	5,212
Optimistic	9,015	20,424
Range	$7,606	$30,424

[a] These values were calculated by using the corresponding annual cash inflows. A 10% cost of capital and a 15-year life for the annual cash inflows were used.

Decision Trees

decision trees
A behavioral approach that uses diagrams to map the various investment decision alternatives and payoffs, along with their probabilities of occurrence.

Decision trees are a behavioral approach that uses diagrams to map the various investment decision alternatives and payoffs, along with their probabilities of occurrence. Their name derives from their resemblance to the branches of a tree (see Figure 9.6). Decision trees rely on estimates of the probabilities associated with the outcomes (payoffs) of competing courses of action. The payoffs of each course of action are weighted by the associated probability; the weighted payoffs are summed; and the expected value of each course of action is then determined. The alternative that provides the highest expected value is preferred.

EXAMPLE

Convoy, Inc., a manufacturer of picture frames, wishes to choose between two equally risky projects, I and J. To make this decision, Convoy's management has gathered the necessary data, which are depicted in the decision tree in Figure 9.6. Project I requires an initial investment of $120,000; a resulting expected present value of cash inflows of $130,000 is shown in column 4. Project I's expected net present value, which is calculated below the decision tree, is therefore $10,000. The expected net present value of project J is determined in a similar fashion. Project J is preferred because it offers a higher NPV—$15,000.

Simulation

simulation
A statistics-based behavioral approach that applies predetermined probability distributions and random numbers to estimate risky outcomes.

Simulation is a statistics-based behavioral approach that applies predetermined probability distributions and random numbers to estimate risky outcomes. By tying the various cash flow components together in a mathematical model and repeating the process numerous times, the financial manager can develop a probability distribution of project returns.

FIGURE 9.6

Decision Tree for NPV
Decision Tree for Convoy, Inc.'s choice between projects I and J

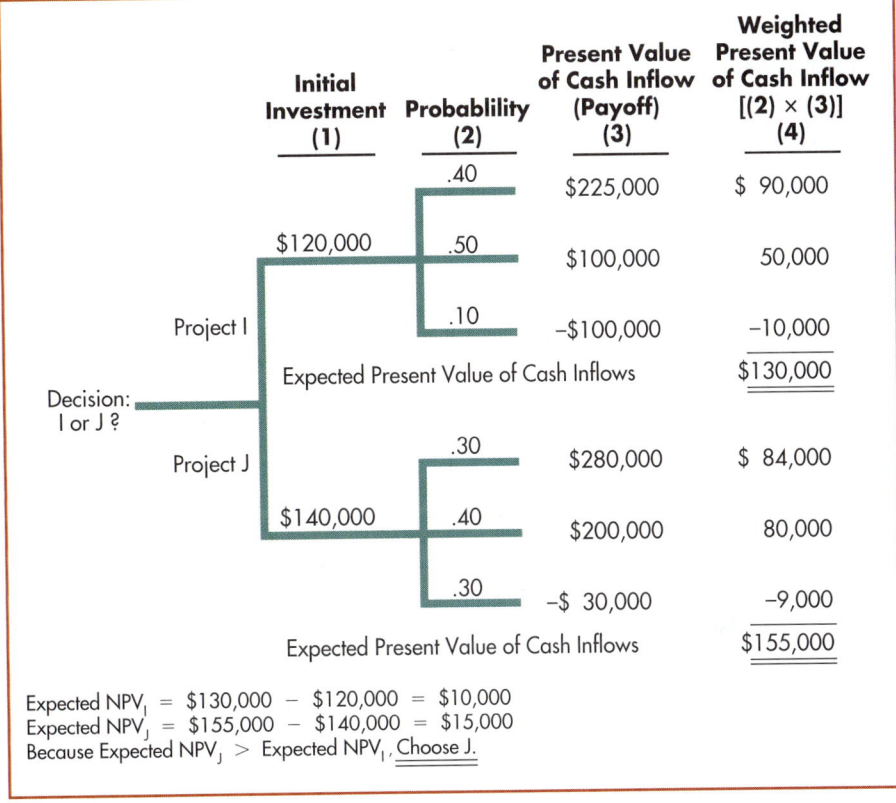

Figure 9.7 (see page 374) presents a flowchart of the simulation of the net present value of a project. The process of generating random numbers and using the probability distributions for cash inflows and cash outflows enables the financial manager to determine values for each of these variables. Substituting these values into the mathematical model results in an NPV. By repeating this process perhaps a thousand times, managers can create a probability distribution of net present values.

Although only gross cash inflows and cash outflows are simulated in Figure 9.7, more sophisticated simulations using individual inflow and outflow components, such as sales volume, sale price, raw material cost, labor cost, maintenance expense, and so on, are quite common. From the distribution of returns, the decision maker can determine not only the expected value of the return but also the probability of achieving or surpassing a given return. The use of computers has made the simulation approach feasible.

The output of simulation provides an excellent basis for decision making, because it enables the decision maker to view a continuum of risk–return trade-offs rather than a single-point estimate.

Hint These behavioral approaches may seem a bit imprecise to one who has not used them. But repeated use and an "after-the-fact" review of previous analyses improve the accuracy of the users.

International Risk Considerations

Although the basic techniques of capital budgeting are the same for multinational companies (MNCs) as for purely domestic firms, firms that operate in several countries face risks that are unique to the international arena. Two types of risk are particularly important: exchange rate risk and political risk.

FIGURE 9.7

NPV Simulation
Flowchart of a net present value simulation

exchange rate risk
The danger that an unexpected change in the exchange rate between the dollar and the currency in which a project's cash flows are denominated will reduce the market value of that project's cash flow.

Exchange rate risk reflects the danger that an unexpected change in the exchange rate between the dollar and the currency in which a project's cash flows are denominated will reduce the market value of that project's cash flow. The dollar value of future cash inflows can be dramatically altered if the local currency depreciates against the dollar. In the short term, specific cash flows can be hedged by using financial instruments such as currency futures and options. Long-term exchange rate risk can best be minimized by financing the project, in whole or in part, in local currency.

Political risk is much harder to protect against. Once a foreign project is accepted, the foreign government can block the return of profits, seize the firm's assets, or otherwise interfere with a project's operation. The inability to manage political risk after the fact makes it even more important that managers account for political risks before making an investment. They can do so either by adjusting a project's expected cash inflows to account for the probability of political interference or by using risk-adjusted discount rates (discussed later in this chapter) in capital budgeting formulas. In general, it is much better to adjust individual project cash flows for political risk subjectively than to use a blanket adjustment for all projects.

In addition to unique risks that MNCs must face, several other special issues are relevant only for international capital budgeting. One of these special issues is *taxes*. Because only after-tax cash flows are relevant for capital budgeting, financial managers must carefully account for taxes paid to foreign governments on profits earned within their borders. They must also assess the impact of these tax payments on the parent company's U.S. tax liability.

Another special issue in international capital budgeting is *transfer pricing*. Much of the international trade involving MNCs is, in reality, simply the shipment of goods and services from one of a parent company's subsidiaries to another subsidiary located abroad. The parent company therefore has great discretion in setting **transfer prices,** the prices that subsidiaries charge each other for the goods and services traded between them. The widespread use of transfer pricing in international trade makes capital budgeting in MNCs very difficult unless the transfer prices that are used accurately reflect actual costs and incremental cash flows.

Finally, MNCs often must approach international capital projects from a *strategic point of view,* rather than from a strictly financial perspective. For example, an MNC may feel compelled to invest in a country to ensure continued access, even if the project itself may not have a positive net present value. This motivation was important for Japanese automakers that set up assembly plants in the United States in the early 1980s. For much the same reason, U.S. investment in Europe surged during the years before the market integration of the European Community in 1992. MNCs often invest in production facilities in the home country of major rivals to deny these competitors an uncontested home market. MNCs also may feel compelled to invest in certain industries or countries to achieve a broad corporate objective such as completing a product line or diversifying raw material sources, even when the project's cash flows may not be sufficiently profitable.

transfer prices
Prices that subsidiaries charge each other for the goods and services traded between them.

Review Questions

9–11 Define *risk* in terms of the cash inflows from a capital budgeting project. Briefly describe and compare the following behavioral approaches, explaining how each can be used to deal with project risk: (a) sensitivity analysis, (b) scenario analysis, (c) decision trees, and (d) simulation.

9–12 Briefly explain how the following items affect the capital budgeting decisions of multinational companies: (a) exchange rate risk; (b) political risk; (c) tax law differences; (d) transfer pricing; and (e) a strategic rather than a strict financial viewpoint.

Risk-Adjusted Discount Rates

The approaches for dealing with risk that have been presented so far enable the financial manager to get a "feel" for project risk. Unfortunately, they do not explicitly recognize project risk. We will now illustrate the most popular risk-adjustment technique that employs the net present value (NPV) decision method.[7] The NPV decision rule of accepting only those projects with NPVs > $0 will continue to hold. Close examination of the basic equation for NPV, Equation 9.1,

---

[7]. The IRR could just as well have been used, but because NPV is theoretically preferable, it is used instead.

should make it clear that because the initial investment (CF_0) is known with certainty, a project's risk is embodied in the present value of its cash inflows:

$$\sum_{t=1}^{n} \frac{CF_t}{(1+k)^t}$$

Two opportunities to adjust the present value of cash inflows for risk exist: (1) The cash inflows (CF_t) can be adjusted, or (2) the discount rate (k) can be adjusted. Adjusting the cash inflows is highly subjective, so here we describe the more popular process of adjusting the discount rate. In addition, we consider the practical aspects of the risk-adjusted discount rate.

Determining Risk-Adjusted Discount Rates (RADRs)

A popular approach for risk adjustment involves the use of risk-adjusted discount rates (RADRs). This approach uses Equation 9.1 but employs a risk-adjusted discount rate, as noted in the following expression:

$$\text{NPV} = \sum_{t=1}^{n} \frac{CF_t}{(1+RADR)^t} - CF_0 \qquad (9.4)$$

risk-adjusted discount rate (RADR)
The rate of return that must be earned on a given project to compensate the firm's owners adequately—that is, to maintain or improve the firm's share price.

The **risk-adjusted discount rate (RADR)** is the rate of return that must be earned on a given project to compensate the firm's owners adequately—that is, to maintain or improve the firm's share price. The higher the risk of a project, the higher the RADR, and therefore the lower the net present value for a given stream of cash inflows. The logic underlying the use of RADRs is closely linked to the capital asset pricing model (CAPM) developed in Chapter 5.

Because the CAPM is based on an assumed efficient market, which does *not* exist for real corporate (nonfinancial) assets such as plant and equipment, the CAPM is not directly applicable in making capital budgeting decisions. Financial managers therefore assess the *total risk* of a project and use it to determine the risk-adjusted discount rate (RADR), which can be used in Equation 9.4 to find the NPV.

To avoid damaging its market value, the firm must use the correct discount rate to evaluate a project. If a firm discounts a risky project's cash inflows at too low a rate and accepts the project, the firm's market price may drop as investors recognize that the firm itself has become more risky. Conversely, if the firm discounts a project's cash inflows at too high a rate, it will reject acceptable projects. Eventually the firm's market price may drop, because investors who believe that the firm is being overly conservative will sell their stock, putting downward pressure on the firm's market value. The *In Practice* box on the facing page describes a case in which failure to correctly evaluate risk turned out *well* for one company.

Unfortunately, there is no formal mechanism for linking *total project risk* to the level of required return. As a result, most firms subjectively determine the RADR by adjusting their existing required return. They adjust it up or down depending on whether the proposed project is more or less risky, respectively, than the average risk of the firm. This CAPM-type of approach provides a "rough estimate" of the project risk and required return because both the project risk measure and the linkage between risk and required return are estimates.

In Practice **FOCUS ON ETHICS**

WARREN BUFFETT VERSUS CALIFORNIA EARTHQUAKE AUTHORITY

Risk is an inherent component of business decisions. Risk may involve uncertainty concerning the project's future cash flows, political and exchange rate risks, inflation, and other variables affecting the net present value of the investment decision.

Another kind of risk may involve large volatility of cash flows, especially when potential gains from the project are quite small. Examples include the pricing of catastrophic insurance. Such projects require that insurers have deep pockets, and they usually command substantial risk premiums. To help diversify such catastrophic risk, the investment banker **Morgan Stanley** was asked to help the **California Earthquake Authority (CEA)**. This public agency was created to insure California homeowners when most insurance companies left the state after the devastating Northridge earthquake of 1994.

The plan created by the CEA provided that, in the event of an earthquake, the first $4 billion of losses would be covered by contributions from participating insurance companies and premiums collected from policyholders. Reinsurance would then absorb the losses from $4 billion to $6 billion. The next $1 billion of losses would be covered by a line of credit to be repaid with proceeds from a bond offering. An additional $1.5 billion of risk would be underwritten in the capital markets. In case of devastating losses, $2 billion more would be paid by the participating insurance companies.

The CEA limited the insurance coverage to homeowners in an effort to keep insurance companies in a state where insurers have suffered huge losses because of fires, earthquakes, and mud slides. To raise additional funds and spread the risk, Morgan Stanley offered a plan to underwrite $1.5 billion of catastrophe (CAT) bonds to big institutional investors. Bondholders would earn 10 percent interest payments for four years, but if any earthquake were to cause more than $7 billion in losses to the state, bondholders could lose their principal. The California earthquake bonds were never issued, however, because a unit of Warren Buffet's **Berkshire Hathaway** stepped in at the last moment.

Berkshire Hathaway offered to reinsure the $1.5 billion of risk originally slated for the capital markets. The company was to receive almost $148 million per year in premiums for 4 years, an average premium rate of about 14 percent per year. (This was 40 percent more than what the capital markets were charging.) The probability that $1.5 billion in insurance would be needed was estimated by an independent consulting firm to be 1.27 percent per year. Had the proper capital budgeting techniques been implemented, the annual premiums should have been $19 million per year, and even less with discounted cash flows. (The original deal was later scaled back by a factor of 0.7 due to the fact that only 70 percent of eligible participants decided to buy insurance.) Nevertheless, "Berkshire got a pretty sweet deal," commented Mark Broido, marketing director of a Silicon Valley catastrophe risk management firm.

Source: Carolyn T. Geer and Ashlea Ebeling, "A Quack in the China Shop," *Forbes*, (October 20, 1997).

■ *Clearly, it is a public good for homeowners to have access to insurance against catastrophic loss. Do you think Berkshire Hathaway got an "excess return" on the deal, or was its success merely an example of the workings of market forces?*

EXAMPLE

Bennett Company wishes to use the risk-adjusted discount rate approach to determine, according to NPV, whether to implement project A or project B. In addition to the data presented earlier, Bennett's management after much analysis assigned "risk indexes" of 1.6 to project A and 1.0 to project B. The risk index is merely a numerical scale used to classify project risk: Higher index values are assigned to higher-risk projects, and vice versa. The CAPM-type relationship used by the firm to link risk (measured by the risk index) and the required return (RADR) is shown in the table on page 378.

	Risk index	Required return (RADR)
	0.0	6% (risk-free rate, R_F)
	0.2	7
	0.4	8
	0.6	9
	0.8	10
Project B →	1.0	11
	1.2	12
	1.4	13
Project A →	1.6	14
	1.8	16
	2.0	18

Because project A is riskier than project B, its RADR of 14% is greater than project B's 11%. The net present value of each project, calculated using its RADR, is found as shown on the time lines in Figure 9.8. The results clearly show

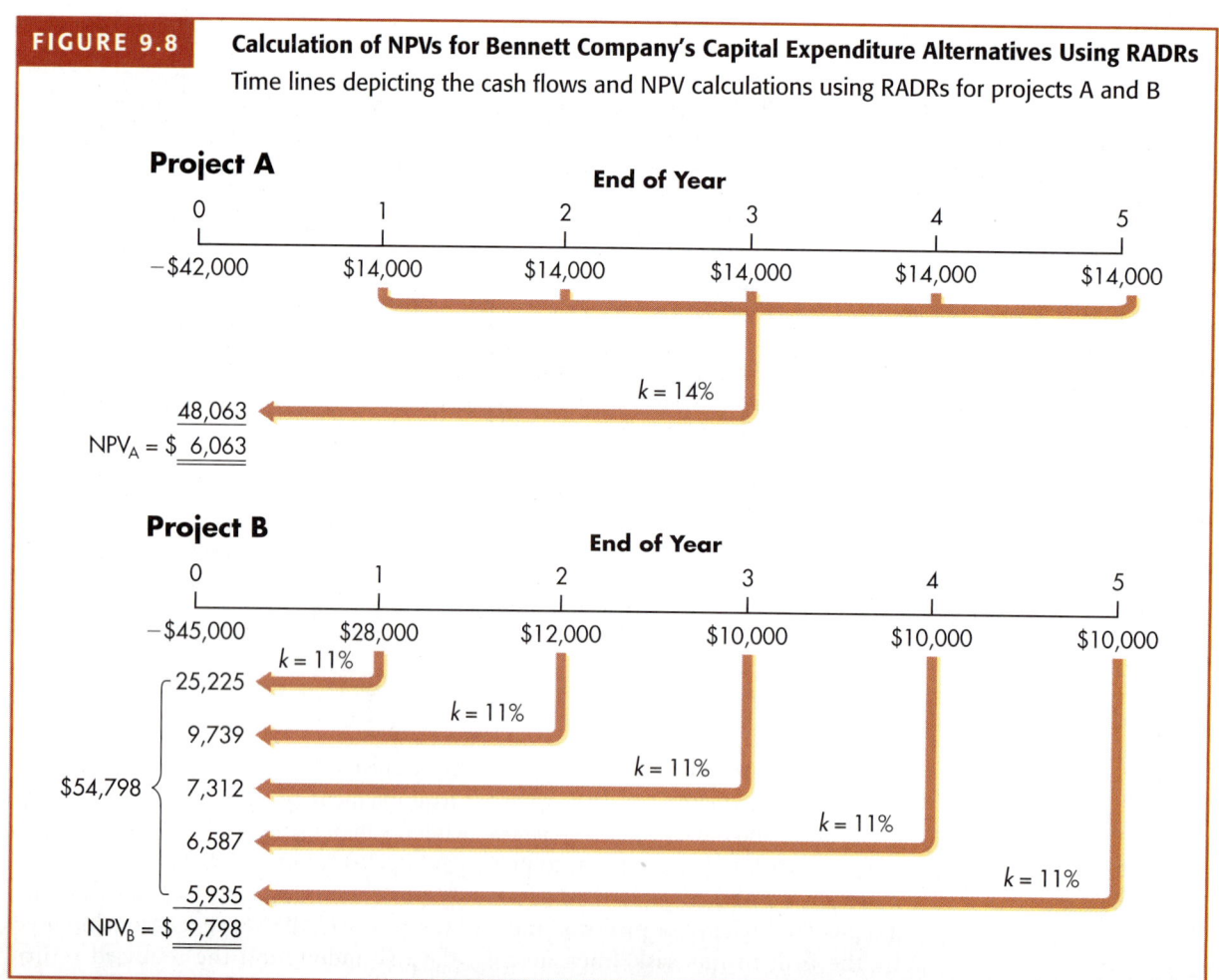

FIGURE 9.8 Calculation of NPVs for Bennett Company's Capital Expenditure Alternatives Using RADRs
Time lines depicting the cash flows and NPV calculations using RADRs for projects A and B

Note: When we use the risk indexes of 1.6 and 1.0 for projects A and B, respectively, along with the table above, a risk-adjusted discount rate (RADR) of 14% results for project A and a RADR of 11% results for project B.

Project A

Project B

that project B is preferable, because its risk-adjusted NPV of $9,798 is greater than the $6,063 risk-adjusted NPV for project A. As reflected by the NPVs in Figure 9.2, if the discount rates were not adjusted for risk, project A would be preferred to project B.

Calculator Use We can again use the preprogrammed NPV function in a financial calculator to simplify the NPV calculation. The keystrokes for project A—the annuity—typically are as shown at the left. The keystrokes for project B—the mixed stream—are also shown at the left. The calculated NPVs for projects A and B of $6,063 and $9,798, respectively, agree with those shown in Figure 9.8.

Spreadsheet Use Analysis of projects using risk-adjusted discount rates (RADRs) also can be performed as shown on the following Excel spreadsheet.

	A	B	C	D
1	ANALYSIS OF PROJECTS USING RISK-ADJUSTED DISCOUNT RATES			
2	Year	Cash Inflow	Present Value	Formulas for Calculated Values in Column C
3	Project A			
4	1–5	$ 14,000	$48,063	–PV(C7,5,B4,0)
5	Initial Investment		$42,000	
6	Net Present Value		$ 6,063	C4–C5
7	Required Return (RADR)		14%	
8	Project B			
9	1	$ 28,000	$25,225	–PV(C17,A9,0,B9,0)
10	2	12,000	9,739	–PV(C17,A10,0,B10,0)
11	3	10,000	7,312	–PV(C17,A11,0,B11,0)
12	4	10,000	6,587	–PV(C17,A12,0,B12,0)
13	5	10,000	5,935	–PV(C17,A13,0,B13,0)
14	Present value		$54,798	SUM(C9:C13) or NPV(C17,B9:B13)
15	Initial Investment		$45,000	
16	Net Present Value		$ 9,798	C14–C15
17	Required Return (RADR)		11%	
18	Choice of project		B	IF(C6>=C16,"A","B")

The minus signs appear before the entries in Cells C4 and C9:C13 to convert the results to positive values.

The usefulness of risk-adjusted discount rates should now be clear. The real difficulty lies in estimating project risk and linking it to the required return (RADR).

RADRs in Practice

In spite of the appeal of total risk, *RADRs are often used in practice*. Their popularity stems from two facts: (1) They are consistent with the general disposition of financial decision makers toward rates of return, and (2) they are easily estimated and applied. The first reason is clearly a matter of personal preference, but the second is based on the computational convenience and well-developed procedures involved in the use of RADRs.

Hint The use of risk classes is consistent with the concept that risk-averse investors require a greater return for greater risks. To increase shareholders' wealth—and hence warrant acceptance—risky projects must earn greater returns.

In practice, firms often establish a number of *risk classes,* with an RADR assigned to each. Each project is then subjectively placed in the appropriate risk class, and the corresponding RADR is used to evaluate it. This is sometimes done

TABLE 9.9 Bennett Company's Risk Classes and RADRs

Risk class	Description	Risk-adjusted discount rate, RADR
I	*Below-average risk:* Projects with low risk. Typically involve routine replacement without renewal of existing activities.	8%
II	*Average risk:* Projects similar to those currently implemented. Typically involve replacement or renewal of existing activities.	10%[a]
III	*Above-average risk:* Projects with higher than normal, but not excessive, risk. Typically involve expansion of existing or similar activities.	14%
IV	*Highest risk:* Projects with very high risk. Typically involve expansion into new or unfamiliar activities.	20%

[a]This RADR is actually the firm's cost of capital, which is discussed in detail in Chapter 10. It represents the firm's required return on its existing portfolio of projects, which is assumed to be unchanged with acceptance of the "average risk" project.

on a division-by-division basis, in which case each division has its own set of risk classes and associated RADRs, similar to those for Bennett Company in Table 9.9. The use of *divisional costs of capital* and associated risk classes enables a large multidivisional firm to incorporate differing levels of divisional risk into the capital budgeting process and still recognize differences in the levels of individual project risk.

EXAMPLE

Assume that the management of Bennett Company decided to use risk classes to analyze projects and so placed each project in one of four risk classes according to its perceived risk. The classes ranged from I for the lowest-risk projects to IV for the highest-risk projects. Associated with each class was an RADR appropriate to the level of risk of projects in the class, as given in Table 9.9. Bennett classified as lower-risk those projects that tend to involve routine replacement or renewal activities; higher-risk projects involve expansion, often into new or unfamiliar activities.

The financial manager of Bennett has assigned project A to class III and project B to class II. The cash flows for project A would be evaluated using a 14% RADR, and project B's would be evaluated using a 10% RADR.[8] The NPV of project A at 14% was calculated in Figure 9.8 to be $6,063, and the NPV for project B at a 10% RADR was shown in Figure 9.2 to be $10,924. Clearly, with RADRs based on the use of risk classes, project B is preferred over project A. As noted earlier, this result is contrary to the preferences shown in Figure 9.2, where differing risks of projects A and B were not taken into account.

Review Questions

9–13 Describe the logic involved in using *risk-adjusted discount rates (RADRs)*. How is this approach related to the *capital asset pricing model (CAPM)?*

9–14 How are *risk classes* often used to apply RADRs?

---

8. Note that the 10% RADR for project B using the risk classes in Table 9.9 differs from the 11% RADR used in the preceding example for project B. This difference is attributable to the less precise nature of the use of risk classes.

Summary

FOCUS ON VALUE

After estimating the relevant cash flows, the financial manager must apply appropriate decision techniques to assess whether the project creates value for shareholders. Net present value (NPV) and internal rate of return (IRR) are the generally preferred capital budgeting techniques. Both use the cost of capital as the required return needed to compensate shareholders for undertaking projects with the same risk as that of the firm. Both indicate whether a proposed investment creates or destroys shareholder value. NPV is the theoretically preferred approach, but IRR is preferred in practice because of its intuitive appeal.

Procedures for explicitly recognizing real options embedded in capital projects and procedures for selecting projects under capital rationing enable the financial manager to refine the capital budgeting process further. Not all capital budgeting projects have the same level of risk as the firm's existing portfolio of projects. The financial manager must therefore adjust projects for differences in risk when evaluating their acceptability. Risk-adjusted discount rates (RADRs) provide a mechanism for adjusting the discount rate so that it is consistent with the risk–return preferences of market participants and thereby with accepting only value-creating projects. These techniques should enable the financial manager to make capital budgeting decisions that are consistent with the firm's goal of **maximizing stock price**.

REVIEW OF LEARNING GOALS

Key formulas and decision criteria for this chapter are summarized in Table 9.10 (see page 382).

LG1 **Calculate, interpret, and evaluate the payback period.** The payback period is the amount of time required for the firm to recover its initial investment, as calculated from cash inflows. Shorter payback periods are preferred. The payback period is relatively easy to calculate, has simple intuitive appeal, considers cash flows, and measures risk exposure. Its weaknesses include lack of linkage to the wealth maximization goal, failure to consider time value explicitly, and the fact that it ignores cash flows that occur after the payback period.

LG2 **Apply net present value (NPV) and internal rate of return (IRR) to relevant cash flows to choose acceptable capital expenditures.** Sophisticated capital budgeting techniques use the cost of capital to consider the time factor in the value of money. NPV measures the amount of value created by a given project; only positive NPV projects are acceptable. IRR is the compound annual rate of return that the firm will earn by investing in a project and receiving the given cash inflows. Both NPV and IRR yield the same accept–reject decisions, but often provide conflicting rankings.

LG3 **Use net present value profiles to compare the NPV and IRR techniques in light of conflicting rankings.** A net present value profile graphs projects' NPVs for various discount rates. NPV profiles are useful for comparing projects, especially when NPV and IRR rankings conflict. On a purely theoretical basis, NPV is preferred over IRR because NPV assumes the more conservative reinvestment rate and does not exhibit the mathematical problem of multiple IRRs that often occurs when IRRs are calculated for nonconventional cash flows. In practice, the IRR is more commonly used because it is consistent with the general preference of businesspeople for rates of return.

LG4 **Discuss two additional considerations in capital budgeting—recognizing real options and choosing projects under capital rationing.** By

TABLE 9.10 Summary of Key Formulas/Definitions and Decision Criteria for Capital Budgeting Techniques

Technique	Formula/definition	Decision criteria
Payback period[a]	*For annuity:* $$\frac{\text{Initial investment}}{\text{Annual cash inflow}}$$ *For mixed stream:* Calculate cumulative cash inflows on year-to-year basis until the initial investment is recovered.	*Accept* if < maximum acceptable payback period. *Reject* if > maximum acceptable payback period.
Net present value (NPV)[b]	Present value of cash inflows − Initial investment.	*Accept* if > $0. *Reject* if < $0.
Internal rate of return (IRR)[b]	The discount rate that causes $NPV = \$0$ (present value of cash inflows equals the initial investment).	*Accept* if > the cost of capital. *Reject* if < the cost of capital.

[a]Unsophisticated technique, because it does not give explicit consideration to the time value of money.
[b]Sophisticated technique, because it gives explicit consideration to the time value of money.

explicitly recognizing real options—opportunities that are embedded in capital projects and that allow managers to alter their cash flow and risk in a way that affects project acceptability (NPV)—the financial manager can find a project's strategic NPV. Some of the more common types of real options are abandonment, flexibility, growth, and timing options. The strategic NPV improves the quality of the capital budgeting decision.

Capital rationing commonly occurs in practice. Its objective is to select from all acceptable projects the group that provides the highest overall net present value and does not require more dollars than are budgeted. The two basic approaches for choosing projects under capital rationing are the internal rate of return approach and the net present value approach. The NPV approach better achieves the objective of using the budget to generate the highest present value of cash inflows.

LG5 **Recognize sensitivity analysis and scenario analysis, decision trees, and simulation as behavioral approaches for dealing with project risk, and the unique risks that multinational companies face.** Risk in capital budgeting is concerned with either the chance that a project will prove unacceptable or, more formally, the degree of variability of cash flows. Sensitivity analysis and scenario analysis are two behavioral approaches for capturing the variability of cash inflows and NPVs. A decision tree is a behavioral approach for dealing with risk that relies on estimates of probabilities associated with the outcomes of competing courses of action to determine the expected values used to select a preferred action. Simulation is a statistics-based behavioral approach that results in a probability distribution of project returns.

Although the basic capital budgeting techniques are the same for multinational and purely domestic companies, firms that operate in several countries must also deal with exchange rate and political risks, tax law differences, transfer pricing, and strategic issues.

LG6 **Understand the calculation and practical aspects of risk-adjusted discount rates (RADRs).** The risk-adjusted discount rate (RADR) uses a market-based adjustment of the discount rate to calculate NPV. The RADR is closely linked to CAPM, but because real corporate assets are generally not traded in an efficient market, the CAPM cannot be applied directly to capital budgeting. RADRs are commonly used in practice because decision makers prefer rates of return and find them easy to estimate and apply.

Self-Test Problems (Solutions in Appendix B)

   ST9–1 **All techniques with NPV profile—Mutually exclusive projects** Fitch Industries is in the process of choosing the better of two equal-risk, mutually exclusive capital expenditure projects—M and N. The relevant cash flows for each project are shown in the following table. The firm's cost of capital is 14%.

	Project M	Project N
Initial investment (CF_0)	$28,500	$27,000
Year (t)	Cash inflows (CF_t)	
1	$10,000	$11,000
2	10,000	10,000
3	10,000	9,000
4	10,000	8,000

a. Calculate each project's *payback period*.
b. Calculate the *net present value (NPV)* for each project.
c. Calculate the *internal rate of return (IRR)* for each project.
d. Summarize the preferences dictated by each measure you calculated, and indicate which project you would recommend. Explain why.
e. Draw the *net present value profiles* for these projects on the same set of axes, and explain the circumstances under which a conflict in rankings might exist.

ST9–2 **Risk-adjusted discount rates** CBA Company is considering two mutually exclusive projects, A and B. The following table shows the CAPM-type relationship between a risk index and the required return (RADR) applicable to CBA Company.

Risk index	Required return (RADR)
0.0	7.0% (risk-free rate, R_F)
0.2	8.0
0.4	9.0
0.6	10.0
0.8	11.0
1.0	12.0
1.2	13.0
1.4	14.0
1.6	15.0
1.8	16.0
2.0	17.0

Project data are shown as follows:

	Project A	Project B
Initial investment (CF_0)	$15,000	$20,000
Project life	3 years	3 years
Annual cash inflow (CF)	$7,000	$10,000
Risk index	0.4	1.8

a. Ignoring any differences in risk and assuming that the firm's cost of capital is 10%, calculate the *net present value (NPV)* of each project.
b. Use NPV to evaluate the projects, using *risk-adjusted discount rates (RADRs)* to account for risk.
c. Compare, contrast, and explain your findings in parts **a** and **b**.

WARM-UP EXERCISES

E9–1 Elysian Fields, Inc., uses a maximum payback period of 6 years, and currently must choose between two mutually exclusive projects. Project Hydrogen requires an initial outlay of $25,000; project Helium requires an initial outlay of $35,000. Using the expected cash inflows given for each project in the following table, calculate each project's *payback period*. Which project meets Elysian's standards?

	Expected cash inflows	
Year	Hydrogen	Helium
1	$6,000	$7,000
2	6,000	7,000
3	8,000	8,000
4	4,000	5,000
5	3,500	5,000
6	2,000	4,000

E9–2 Herky Foods is considering acquisition of a new wrapping machine. The initial investment is estimated at $1.25 million, and the machine will have a 5-year life with no salvage value. Using a 6% discount rate, determine the *net present value (NPV)* of the machine given its expected operating cash inflows shown in the table at the right. Based on the project's NPV, should Herky make this investment?

Year	Cash inflow
1	$400,000
2	375,000
3	300,000
4	350,000
5	200,000

E9–3 Billabong Tech uses the *internal rate of return (IRR)* to select projects. Calculate the IRR for each of the following projects and recommend the best project based on this measure. Project T-Shirt requires an initial investment of $15,000 and generates cash inflows of $8,000 per year for 4 years. Project Board Shorts requires an initial investment of $25,000 and produces cash inflows of $12,000 per year for 5 years.

E9–4 Cooper Electronics uses *NPV profiles* to visually evaluate competing projects. Key data for the two projects under consideration is given in the following table. Using these data, graph, on the same set of axes, the NPV profiles for each project using discount rates of 0%, 8%, and the IRR.

	Terra	Firma
Initial investment	$30,000	$25,000
Year	Operating cash inflows	
1	$ 7,000	$ 6,000
2	10,000	9,000
3	12,000	9,000
4	10,000	8,000

E9–5 Longchamps Electric is faced with a capital budget of $150,000 for the coming year. It is considering six investment projects and has a cost of capital of 7%. The six projects are listed below, along with their initial investments and their IRRs. Using the data given, prepare an *investment opportunities schedule (IOS)*. Which projects does the IOS suggest should be funded? Does this group of projects maximize NPV? Explain.

Project	Initial investment	IRR
1	$75,000	8%
2	40,000	10
3	35,000	7
4	50,000	11
5	45,000	9
6	20,000	6

E9–6 Like most firms in its industry, Yeastime Bakeries uses a subjective risk assessment tool of its own design. The tool is a simple index by which projects are ranked by level of perceived risk on a scale of 0–10. The scale is recreated below.

Risk	Required Return
0	4.0% (current risk-free rate)
1	4.5
2	5.0
3	5.5
4	6.0
5	6.5 (current IRR)
6	7.0
7	7.5
8	8.0
9	8.5
10	9.0

The firm is analyzing two projects based on their RADRs. Project Sourdough requires an initial investment of $12,500 and is assigned a risk index of 6.0. Project Greek Salad requires an initial investment of $7,500 and is assigned a risk index of 8.0. The two projects have 7-year lives. Sourdough is projected to generate cash inflows of $5,500 per year. Greek Salad is projected to generate cash inflows of $4,000 per year. Use each project's RADR to select the best project.

PROBLEMS

BASIC

P9–1 Payback period Lee Corporation is considering a capital expenditure that requires an initial investment of $42,000 and returns after-tax cash inflows of $7,000 per year for 10 years. The firm has a maximum acceptable payback period of 8 years.
a. Determine the *payback period* for this project.
b. Should the company accept the project? Why or why not?

INTERMEDIATE

P9–2 Payback comparisons Dallas Tool has a 5-year maximum acceptable payback period. The firm is considering the purchase of a new machine and must choose between two alternative ones. The first machine requires an initial investment of $14,000 and generates annual after-tax cash inflows of $3,000 for each of the next 7 years. The second machine requires an initial investment of $21,000 and provides an annual cash inflow after taxes of $4,000 for 20 years.
a. Determine the *payback period* for each machine.
b. Comment on the acceptability of the machines, assuming that they are independent projects.
c. Which machine should the firm accept? Why?
d. Do the machines in this problem illustrate any of the weaknesses of using payback? Discuss.

BASIC

P9–3 NPV Calculate the *net present value (NPV)* for the following 20-year projects. Comment on the acceptability of each. Assume that the firm has an opportunity cost of 14%.
a. Initial investment is $10,000; cash inflows are $2,000 per year.
b. Initial investment is $25,000; cash inflows are $3,000 per year.
c. Initial investment is $30,000; cash inflows are $5,000 per year.

BASIC

P9–4 NPV for varying costs of capital Cheryl's Beauty Aids is evaluating a new fragrance-mixing machine. The machine requires an initial investment of $24,000 and will generate after-tax cash inflows of $5,000 per year for 8 years. For each of the costs of capital listed, (1) calculate the *net present value (NPV)*, (2) indicate whether to accept or reject the machine, and (3) explain your decision.
a. The cost of capital is 10%.
b. The cost of capital is 12%.
c. The cost of capital is 14%.

INTERMEDIATE

P9–5 Net present value—Independent projects Using a 14% cost of capital, calculate the *net present value* for each of the independent projects shown in the table at the top of the facing page, and indicate whether each is acceptable.

	Project A	Project B	Project C	Project D	Project E
Initial investment (CF_0)	$26,000	$500,000	$170,000	$950,000	$80,000
Year (t)			Cash inflows (CF_t)		
1	$4,000	$100,000	$20,000	$230,000	$ 0
2	4,000	120,000	19,000	230,000	0
3	4,000	140,000	18,000	230,000	0
4	4,000	160,000	17,000	230,000	20,000
5	4,000	180,000	16,000	230,000	30,000
6	4,000	200,000	15,000	230,000	0
7	4,000		14,000	230,000	50,000
8	4,000		13,000	230,000	60,000
9	4,000		12,000		70,000
10	4,000		11,000		

P9–6 **NPV and maximum return** A firm can purchase a fixed asset for a $13,000 initial investment. The asset generates an annual after-tax cash inflow of $4,000 for 4 years.
a. Determine the *net present value (NPV)* of the asset, assuming that the firm has a 10% cost of capital. Is the project acceptable?
b. Determine the maximum required rate of return (closest whole-percentage rate) that the firm can have and still accept the asset. Discuss this finding in light of your response in part a.

P9–7 **NPV—Mutually exclusive projects** Jackson Enterprises is considering the replacement of one of its old drill presses. Three alternative replacement presses are under consideration. The relevant cash flows associated with each are shown in the following table. The firm's cost of capital is 15%.

	Press A	Press B	Press C
Initial investment (CF_0)	$85,000	$60,000	$130,000
Year (t)		Cash inflows (CF_t)	
1	$18,000	$12,000	$50,000
2	18,000	14,000	30,000
3	18,000	16,000	20,000
4	18,000	18,000	20,000
5	18,000	20,000	20,000
6	18,000	25,000	30,000
7	18,000	—	40,000
8	18,000	—	50,000

a. Calculate the *net present value (NPV)* of each press.
b. Using NPV, evaluate the acceptability of each press.
c. Rank the presses from best to worst using NPV.

P9–8 **Payback and NPV** McAllister Products has three projects under consideration. The cash flows for each project are shown in the following table. The firm has a 16% cost of capital.

	Project A	Project B	Project C
Initial investment (CF_0)	$40,000	$40,000	$40,000
Year (t)	Cash inflows (CF_t)		
1	$13,000	$ 7,000	$19,000
2	13,000	10,000	16,000
3	13,000	13,000	13,000
4	13,000	16,000	10,000
5	13,000	19,000	7,000

a. Calculate each project's *payback period*. Which project is preferred according to this method?
b. Calculate each project's *net present value (NPV)*. Which project is preferred according to this method?
c. Comment on your findings in parts **a** and **b**, and recommend the best project. Explain your recommendation.

P9–9 **Internal rate of return** For each of the projects shown in the following table, calculate the *internal rate of return (IRR)*. Then indicate, for each project, the maximum cost of capital that the firm could have and still find the IRR acceptable.

	Project A	Project B	Project C	Project D
Initial investment (CF_0)	$90,000	$490,000	$20,000	$240,000
Year (t)	Cash inflows (CF_t)			
1	$20,000	$150,000	$7,500	$120,000
2	25,000	150,000	7,500	100,000
3	30,000	150,000	7,500	80,000
4	35,000	150,000	7,500	60,000
5	40,000	—	7,500	—

P9–10 **IRR—Mutually exclusive projects** Paulus Corporation is attempting to choose the better of two mutually exclusive projects for expanding the firm's warehouse capacity. The relevant cash flows for the projects are shown in the table at the top of the facing page. The firm's cost of capital is 15%.
a. Calculate the IRR to the nearest whole percent for each of the projects.
b. Assess the acceptability of each project on the basis of the IRRs found in part **a**.
c. Which project, on this basis, is preferred?

	Project X	Project Y
Initial investment (CF_0)	$500,000	$325,000
Year (t)	Cash inflows (CF_t)	
1	$100,000	$140,000
2	120,000	120,000
3	150,000	95,000
4	190,000	70,000
5	250,000	50,000

P9–11 **IRR, investment life, and cash inflows** Cincinnati Machine Tool (CMT) accepts projects earning more than the firm's 15% cost of capital. CMT is currently considering a 10-year project that provides annual cash inflows of $10,000 and requires an initial investment of $61,450. (*Note:* All amounts are after taxes.)
a. Determine the IRR of this project. Is it acceptable?
b. Assuming that the cash inflows continue to be $10,000 per year, how many *additional years* would the flows have to continue to make the project acceptable (that is, to make it have an IRR of 15%)?
c. With the given life, initial investment, and cost of capital, what is the minimum annual cash inflow that the firm should accept?

P9–12 **NPV and IRR** Lilo Manufacturing has prepared the following estimates for a long-term project it is considering. The initial investment is $18,250, and the project is expected to yield after-tax cash inflows of $4,000 per year for 7 years. The firm has a 10% cost of capital.
a. Determine the *net present value (NPV)* for the project.
b. Determine the *internal rate of return (IRR)* for the project.
c. Would you recommend that the firm accept or reject the project? Explain your answer.

P9–13 **Payback, NPV, and IRR** Bruce Reed Enterprises is attempting to evaluate the feasibility of investing $95,000 in a piece of equipment that has a 5-year life. The firm has estimated the *cash inflows* associated with the proposal as shown in the following table. The firm has a 12% cost of capital.

Year (t)	Cash inflows (CF_t)
1	$20,000
2	25,000
3	30,000
4	35,000
5	40,000

a. Calculate the *payback period* for the proposed investment.
b. Calculate the *net present value (NPV)* for the proposed investment.

c. Calculate the *internal rate of return (IRR)*, rounded to the nearest whole percent, for the proposed investment.
d. Evaluate the acceptability of the proposed investment using NPV and IRR. What recommendation would you make relative to implementation of the project? Why?

P9–14 **NPV, IRR, and NPV profiles** Candor Enterprises is considering two mutually exclusive projects. The firm, which has a 12% cost of capital, has estimated its cash flows as shown in the following table.

	Project A	Project B
Initial investment (CF_0)	$130,000	$85,000
Year (t)	Cash inflows (CF_t)	
1	$25,000	$40,000
2	35,000	35,000
3	45,000	30,000
4	50,000	10,000
5	55,000	5,000

a. Calculate the NPV of each project, and assess its acceptability.
b. Calculate the IRR for each project, and assess its acceptability.
c. Draw the *NPV profiles* for both projects on the same set of axes.
d. Evaluate and discuss the rankings of the two projects on the basis of your findings in parts **a**, **b**, and **c**.
e. Explain your findings in part **d** in light of the pattern of cash inflows associated with each project.

P9–15 **All techniques—Decision among mutually exclusive investments** Easi Chair Company is attempting to select the best of three mutually exclusive projects. The initial investment and after-tax cash inflows associated with these projects are shown in the following table.

Cash flows	Project A	Project B	Project C
Initial investment (CF_0)	$60,000	$100,000	$110,000
Cash inflows (CF_t), $t = 1$ to 5	$20,000	$31,500	$32,500

a. Calculate the *payback period* for each project.
b. Calculate the *net present value (NPV)* of each project, assuming that the firm has a cost of capital equal to 13%.
c. Calculate the *internal rate of return (IRR)* for each project.
d. Draw the *net present value profiles* for both projects on the same set of axes, and discuss any conflict in ranking that may exist between NPV and IRR.
e. Summarize the preferences dictated by each measure, and indicate which project you would recommend. Explain why.

P9–16 **All techniques with NPV profile—Mutually exclusive projects** Projects A and B, of equal risk, are alternatives for expanding Rosa Company's capacity. The firm's cost of capital is 13%. The cash flows for each project are shown in the following table.

	Project A	Project B
Initial investment (CF_0)	$80,000	$50,000
Year (t)	Cash inflows (CF_t)	
1	$15,000	$15,000
2	20,000	15,000
3	25,000	15,000
4	30,000	15,000
5	35,000	15,000

a. Calculate each project's *payback period*.
b. Calculate the *net present value (NPV)* for each project.
c. Calculate the *internal rate of return (IRR)* for each project.
d. Draw the *net present value profiles* for both projects on the same set of axes, and discuss any conflict in ranking that may exist between NPV and IRR.
e. Summarize the preferences dictated by each measure, and indicate which project you would recommend. Explain why.

P9–17 **Integrative—Complete investment decision** Hot Springs Press is considering the purchase of a new printing press. The total installed cost of the press is $2.2 million. This outlay would be partially offset by the sale of an existing press. The old press has zero book value, cost $1 million 10 years ago, and can be sold currently for $1.2 million before taxes. As a result of acquisition of the new press, sales in each of the next 5 years are expected to be $1.6 million higher than with the existing press, but product costs (excluding depreciation) will represent 50% of sales. The new press will not affect the firm's net working capital requirements. The new press will be depreciated under MACRS using a 5-year recovery period (see Table 3.2 on page 94). The firm is subject to a 40% tax rate. Hot Springs' cost of capital is 11%. (*Note:* Assume that both the old and the new press will have terminal values of $0 at the end of year 6.)
a. Determine the *initial investment* required by the new press.
b. Determine the *operating cash inflows* attributable to the new press. (*Note:* Be sure to consider the depreciation in year 6.)
c. Determine the *payback period*.
d. Determine the *net present value (NPV)* and the *internal rate of return (IRR)* related to the proposed new press.
e. Make a recommendation to accept or reject the new press, and justify your answer.

P9–18 **Integrative—Investment decision** Holliday Manufacturing is considering the replacement of an existing machine. The new machine costs $1.2 million and requires installation costs of $150,000. The existing machine can be sold currently for $185,000 before taxes. It is 2 years old, cost $800,000 new, and has a $384,000 book value and a remaining useful life of 5 years. It was being depreciated under MACRS using a 5-year recovery period (see Table 3.2 on page 94) and therefore has the final 4 years of depreciation remaining. If it is held for 5 more years, the machine's market value at the end of year 5 will be $0. Over its 5-year life, the new machine should reduce operating costs by $350,000 per year. The new machine will be depreciated under MACRS using a 5-year recovery period (see Table 3.2 on page 94). The new machine can be sold for $200,000 net of removal and cleanup costs at the end of 5 years. An increased investment in net working capital of $25,000 will be needed to support operations if the new machine is acquired. Assume that the firm has adequate operating income against which to deduct any loss experienced on the sale of the existing machine. The firm has a 9% cost of capital and is subject to a 40% tax rate.

a. Develop the *relevant cash flows* needed to analyze the proposed replacement.
b. Determine the *net present value (NPV)* of the proposal.
c. Determine the *internal rate of return (IRR)* of the proposal.
d. Make a recommendation to accept or reject the replacement proposal, and justify your answer.
e. What is the highest cost of capital that the firm could have and still accept the proposal? Explain.

P9–19 **Real options and the strategic NPV** Jenny Rene, the CFO of Asor Products, Inc., has just completed an evaluation of a proposed capital expenditure for equipment that would expand the firm's manufacturing capacity. Using the traditional NPV methodology, she found the project unacceptable because

$$NPV_{traditional} = -\$1{,}700 < \$0$$

Before recommending rejection of the proposed project, she has decided to assess whether there might be real options embedded in the firm's cash flows. Her evaluation uncovered three options:

> Option 1: *Abandonment*—The project could be abandoned at the end of 3 years, resulting in an addition to NPV of $1,200.
>
> Option 2: *Expansion*—If the projected outcomes occurred, an opportunity to expand the firm's product offerings further would become available at the end of 4 years. Exercise of this option is estimated to add $3,000 to the project's NPV.
>
> Option 3: *Delay*—Certain phases of the proposed project could be delayed if market and competitive conditions caused the firm's forecast revenues to develop more slowly than planned. Such a delay in implementation at that point has a NPV of $10,000.

Jenny estimated that there was a 25% chance that the abandonment option would need to be exercised, a 30% chance that the expansion option would be exercised, and only a 10% chance that the implementation of certain phases of the project would have to be delayed.

a. Use the information provided to calculate the strategic NPV, $NPV_{strategic}$, for Asor Products' proposed equipment expenditure.

b. Judging on the basis of your findings in part **a**, what action should Jenny recommend to management with regard to the proposed equipment expenditure?
c. In general, how does this problem demonstrate the importance of considering real options when making capital budgeting decisions?

P9–20 **Capital rationing—IRR and NPV approaches** Bromley and Sons is attempting to select the best of a group of independent projects competing for the firm's fixed capital budget of $4.5 million. The firm recognizes that any unused portion of this budget will earn less than its 15% cost of capital, thereby resulting in a present value of inflows that is less than the initial investment. The firm has summarized, in the following table, the key data to be used in selecting the best group of projects.

Project	Initial investment	IRR	Present value of inflows at 15%
A	$5,000,000	17%	$5,400,000
B	800,000	18	1,100,000
C	2,000,000	19	2,300,000
D	1,500,000	16	1,600,000
E	800,000	22	900,000
F	2,500,000	23	3,000,000
G	1,200,000	20	1,300,000

a. Use the *internal rate of return (IRR) approach* to select the best group of projects.
b. Use the *net present value (NPV) approach* to select the best group of projects.
c. Compare, contrast, and discuss your findings in parts **a** and **b**.
d. Which projects should the firm implement? Why?

P9–21 **Capital rationing—NPV approach** A firm with a 13% cost of capital must select the optimal group of projects from those shown in the following table, given its capital budget of $1 million.

Project	Initial investment	NPV at 13% cost of capital
A	$300,000	$ 84,000
B	200,000	10,000
C	100,000	25,000
D	900,000	90,000
E	500,000	70,000
F	100,000	50,000
G	800,000	160,000

a. Calculate the *present value of cash inflows* associated with each project.
b. Select the optimal group of projects, keeping in mind that unused funds are costly.

P9–22 **Basic sensitivity analysis** Renaissance Pharmaceutical is in the process of evaluating two mutually exclusive additions to its processing capacity. The firm's financial analysts have developed pessimistic, most likely, and optimistic estimates of the annual cash inflows associated with each project. These estimates are shown in the following table.

	Project A	Project B
Initial investment (CF_0)	$8,000	$8,000
Outcome	Annual cash inflows (CF)	
Pessimistic	$ 200	$ 900
Most likely	1,000	1,000
Optimistic	1,800	1,100

a. Determine the *range* of annual cash inflows for each of the two projects.
b. Assume that the firm's cost of capital is 10% and that both projects have 20-year lives. Construct a table similar to this for the NPVs for each project. Include the *range* of NPVs for each project.
c. Do parts **a** and **b** provide consistent views of the two projects? Explain.
d. Which project do you recommend? Why?

P9–23 **Sensitivity analysis** James Secretarial Services is considering the purchase of one of two new personal computers, P and Q. Both are expected to provide benefits over a 10-year period, and each has a required investment of $3,000. The firm uses a 10% cost of capital. Management has constructed the following table of estimates of annual cash inflows for pessimistic, most likely, and optimistic results.

	Computer P	Computer Q
Initial investment (CF_0)	$3,000	$3,000
Outcome	Annual cash inflows (CF)	
Pessimistic	$ 500	$ 400
Most likely	750	750
Optimistic	1,000	1,200

a. Determine the *range* of annual cash inflows for each of the two computers.
b. Construct a table similar to this for the NPVs associated with each outcome for both computers.
c. Find the *range* of NPVs, and subjectively compare the risks associated with purchasing these computers.

P9–24 **Decision trees** The Ouija Board-Games Company can bring out one of two new games this season. The *Signs Away* game has a higher initial cost but also a higher expected return. *Monopolistic Competition,* the alternative, has a slightly lower initial cost but also a lower expected return. The present values and probabilities associated with each game are listed in the following table.

Games	Initial investment	Present value of cash inflows	Probabilities
Signs Away	$140,000		1.00
		$320,000	.30
		220,000	.50
		− 80,000	.20
Monopolistic Competition	$120,000		1.00
		$260,000	.20
		200,000	.45
		− 50,000	.35

a. Construct a *decision tree* to analyze the games.
b. Which game do you recommend (following a decision-tree analysis)?
c. Has your analysis captured the differences in the risks associated with these games? Explain.

P9–25 **Simulation** Wales Castings has compiled the following information on a capital expenditure proposal:
(1) The projected cash *inflows* are normally distributed with a mean of $36,000 and a standard deviation of $9,000.
(2) The projected cash *outflows* are normally distributed with a mean of $30,000 and a standard deviation of $6,000.
(3) The firm has an 11% cost of capital.
(4) The probability distributions of cash inflows and cash outflows are not expected to change over the project's 10-year life.

a. Describe how the foregoing data can be used to develop a simulation model for finding the net present value of the project.
b. Discuss the advantages of using a simulation to evaluate the proposed project.

P9–26 **Risk-adjusted discount rates—Basic** Country Wallpapers is considering investing in one of three mutually exclusive projects, E, F, and G. The firm's cost of capital, k, is 15%, and the risk-free rate, R_F, is 10%. The firm has gathered the following basic cash flow and risk index data for each project.

	Project (j)		
	E	F	G
Initial investment (CF_0)	$15,000	$11,000	$19,000
Year (t)	Cash inflows (CF_t)		
1	$ 6,000	$ 6,000	$ 4,000
2	6,000	4,000	6,000
3	6,000	5,000	8,000
4	6,000	2,000	12,000
Risk index (RI_j)	1.80	1.00	0.60

a. Find the *net present value (NPV)* of each project using the firm's cost of capital. Which project is preferred in this situation?
b. The firm uses the following equation to determine the risk-adjusted discount rate, $RADR_j$, for each project j:

$$RADR_j = R_F + [RI_j \times (k - R_F)]$$

where

R_F = risk-free rate of return
RI_j = risk index for project j
k = cost of capital

Substitute each project's risk index into this equation to determine its RADR.
c. Use the RADR for each project to determine its *risk-adjusted NPV*. Which project is preferable in this situation?
d. Compare and discuss your findings in parts **a** and **c**. Which project do you recommend that the firm accept?

P9–27 **Risk-adjusted discount rates—Tabular** After a careful evaluation of investment alternatives and opportunities, Joely Company has developed a CAPM-type relationship linking a risk index to the required return (RADR), as shown in the following table.

Risk index	Required return (RADR)
0.0	7.0% (risk-free rate, R_F)
0.2	8.0
0.4	9.0
0.6	10.0
0.8	11.0
1.0	12.0
1.2	13.0
1.4	14.0
1.6	15.0
1.8	16.0
2.0	17.0

The firm is considering two mutually exclusive projects, A and B. Following are the data the firm has been able to gather about the projects.

	Project A	Project B
Initial investment (CF_0)	$20,000	$30,000
Project life	5 years	5 years
Annual cash inflow (CF)	$7,000	$10,000
Risk index	0.2	1.4

All the firm's cash inflows have already been adjusted for taxes.
a. Evaluate the projects using *risk-adjusted discount rates*.
b. Discuss your findings in part **a**, and recommend the preferred project.

P9–28 **Risk classes and RADR** Attila Industries is attempting to select the best of three mutually exclusive projects, X, Y, and Z. Although all the projects have 5-year lives, they possess differing degrees of risk. Project X is in class V, the highest-risk class; project Y is in class II, the below-average-risk class; and project Z is in class III, the average-risk class. The basic cash flow data for each project and the risk classes and risk-adjusted discount rates (RADRs) used by the firm are shown in the following tables.

	Project X	Project Y	Project Z
Initial investment (CF_0)	$180,000	$235,000	$310,000
Year (t)	Cash inflows (CF_t)		
1	$80,000	$50,000	$90,000
2	70,000	60,000	90,000
3	60,000	70,000	90,000
4	60,000	80,000	90,000
5	60,000	90,000	90,000

Risk Classes and RADRs

Risk Class	Description	Risk-adjusted discount rate (RADR)
I	Lowest risk	10%
II	Below-average risk	13
III	Average risk	15
IV	Above-average risk	19
V	Highest risk	22

a. Find the *risk-adjusted NPV* for each project.
b. Which project, if any, would you recommend that the firm undertake?

P9–29 **ETHICS PROBLEM** Based on historical data, an investor estimates that one in twenty similar investment projects is a complete failure. In light of this finding, how large a business insurance premium needs to be added to the cost of capital in order for the firm to stay in business?

CHAPTER 9 CASE

Making Norwich Tool's Lathe Investment Decision

Norwich Tool, a large machine shop, is considering replacing one of its lathes with either of two new lathes—lathe A or lathe B. Lathe A is a highly automated, computer-controlled lathe; lathe B is a less expensive lathe that uses standard technology. To analyze these alternatives, Mario Jackson, a financial analyst, prepared estimates of the initial investment and incremental (relevant) cash inflows associated with each lathe. These are shown in the following table.

	Lathe A	Lathe B
Initial investment (CF_0)	$660,000	$360,000
Year (t)	Cash inflows (CF_t)	
1	$128,000	$ 88,000
2	182,000	120,000
3	166,000	96,000
4	168,000	86,000
5	450,000	207,000

Note that Mario plans to analyze both lathes over a 5-year period. At the end of that time, the lathes would be sold, thus accounting for the large fifth-year cash inflows.

One of Mario's dilemmas centered on the risk of the two lathes. He believes that although the two lathes are equally risky, lathe A has a much higher chance of breakdown and repair because of its sophisticated and not fully proven solid-state electronic technology. Mario is unable to quantify this possibility effectively, so he decides to apply the firm's 13% cost of capital when analyzing the lathes. Norwich Tool requires all projects to have a maximum payback period of 4.0 years.

TO DO

a. Use the *payback period* to assess the acceptability and relative ranking of each lathe.
b. Assuming equal risk, use the following sophisticated capital budgeting techniques to assess the acceptability and relative ranking of each lathe:
   (1) Net present value (NPV).
   (2) Internal rate of return (IRR).
c. Summarize the preferences indicated by the techniques used in parts a and b, and indicate which lathe you recommend, if either, (1) if the firm has unlimited funds and (2) if the firm has capital rationing.
d. Repeat part b assuming that Mario decides that because of its greater risk, lathe A's cash inflows should be evaluated by using a 15% cost of capital.
e. What effect, if any, does recognition of lathe A's greater risk in part d have on your recommendation in part c?

SPREADSHEET EXERCISE

The Drillago Company is involved in searching for locations in which to drill for oil. The firm's current project requires an initial investment of $15 million and has an estimated life of 10 years. The expected future cash inflows for the project are shown in the table at the top of the facing page.

Year	Cash inflows
1	$ 600,000
2	1,000,000
3	1,000,000
4	2,000,000
5	3,000,000
6	3,500,000
7	4,000,000
8	6,000,000
9	8,000,000
10	12,000,000

The firm's current cost of capital is 13%.

TO DO

Create a spreadsheet to answer the following:

a. Calculate the project's *net present value (NPV)*. Is the project acceptable under the NPV technique? Explain.
b. Calculate the project's *internal rate of return (IRR)*. Is the project acceptable under the IRR technique? Explain.
c. In this case, did the two methods produce the same results? Generally, is there a preference between the NPV and IRR techniques? Explain.
d. Calculate the *payback period* for the project. If the firm usually accepts projects that have payback periods between 1 and 7 years, is this project acceptable?

WEB EXERCISE

Many Web sites offer financial calculators and tutorials with varying degrees of detail. In this exercise, you will evaluate a Web site in terms of its focus on NPV and IRR.

TO DO

a. Direct your browser to www.investopedia.com/default.asp. The best way to begin is to search for NPV in this Web site's dedicated search engine. Follow the links to the definition and then tutorials. Next, do the same for IRR.
b. Summarize how each topic was handled on this Web site, and compare and contrast how this site handled these topics relative to how this textbook covers the same material. What aspects of the Web site did you like, and why? What didn't you like?

> **Remember to check the book's Web site at**
> www.aw-bc.com/gitman
> **for additional resources, including additional Web exercises.**

Part 4

Long-Term Financial Decisions

Chapter
10
The Cost of Capital

Chapter
11
Leverage and Capital Structure

Chapter
12
Dividend Policy

Chapter 10

The Cost of Capital

LEARNING GOALS

LG1 Understand the key assumptions, the basic concept, and the specific sources of capital associated with the cost of capital.

LG2 Determine the cost of long-term debt and the cost of preferred stock.

LG3 Calculate the cost of common stock equity and convert it into the cost of retained earnings and the cost of new issues of common stock.

LG4 Calculate the weighted average cost of capital (WACC) and discuss alternative weighting schemes and economic value added (EVA®).

LG5 Describe the procedures used to determine break points and the weighted marginal cost of capital (WMCC).

LG6 Explain the weighted marginal cost of capital (WMCC) and its use with the investment opportunities schedule (IOS) to make financing/investment decisions.

Across the Disciplines   Why This Chapter Matters to You

Accounting: You need to understand the various sources of capital and how their costs are calculated to provide the data necessary to determine the firm's overall cost of capital.

Information systems: You need to understand the various sources of capital and how their costs are calculated to develop systems that will estimate the costs of those sources of capital, as well as the overall cost of capital.

Management: You need to understand the cost of capital to select long-term investments after assessing their acceptability and relative rankings.

Marketing: You need to understand the firm's cost of capital because proposed projects must earn returns in excess of it to be acceptable.

Operations: You need to understand the firm's cost of capital to assess the economic viability of investments in plant and equipment needed to improve or grow the firm's capacity.

The cost of capital is used to select capital investments that increase shareholder value. In applying the net present value and internal rate of return techniques in Chapter 9, we simply assumed a reasonable cost of capital. Now we will demonstrate how the cost of capital is calculated. This chapter considers the costs of long-term debt, preferred stock, common stock, and retained earnings and shows how to combine them to determine the cost of capital and related measures that the firm will use in making long-term financing/investment decisions.

An Overview of the Cost of Capital

cost of capital
The rate of return that a firm must earn on the projects in which it invests to maintain its market value and attract funds.

The **cost of capital** is the rate of return that a firm must earn on the projects in which it invests to maintain the market value of its stock. It can also be thought of as the rate of return required by the market suppliers of capital to attract their funds to the firm. If risk is held constant, projects with a rate of return above the cost of capital will increase the value of the firm, and projects with a rate of return below the cost of capital will decrease the value of the firm.

The cost of capital is an extremely important financial concept. It acts as a major link between the firm's long-term investment decisions (discussed in Part 3) and the wealth of the owners as determined by investors in the marketplace. It is, in effect, the "magic number" that is used to decide whether a proposed corporate investment will increase or decrease the firm's stock price. Clearly, only those investments that are expected to increase stock price (NPV > $0, or IRR > cost of capital) would be recommended. Because of its key role in financial decision making, the importance of the cost of capital cannot be overemphasized.

Some Key Assumptions

business risk
The risk to the firm of being unable to cover operating costs.

financial risk
The risk to the firm of being unable to cover required financial obligations (interest, lease payments, preferred stock dividends).

Hint Because of the positive relationship between risk and return, a firm's financing cost (cost of capital) will change if the acceptance of a project changes the firm's business or financial risk. The cost of capital can therefore be more easily measured by assuming that new projects do not change these risks.

The cost of capital is a dynamic concept affected by a variety of economic and firm-specific factors. To isolate the basic structure of the cost of capital, we make some key assumptions relative to risk and taxes:

1. **Business risk**—the risk to the firm of being unable to cover operating costs—*is assumed to be unchanged.* This assumption means that the firm's acceptance of a given project does not affect its ability to meet operating costs.
2. **Financial risk**—the risk to the firm of being unable to cover required financial obligations (interest, lease payments, preferred stock dividends)—*is assumed to be unchanged.* This assumption means that projects are financed in such a way that the firm's ability to meet required financing costs is unchanged. For an example of the catastrophic effect that inability to manage financial risk had on one company, WorldCom, see the *In Practice* box on page 404.
3. **After-tax costs are considered relevant.** In other words, *the cost of capital is measured on an after-tax basis.* This assumption is consistent with the after-tax framework used to make capital budgeting decisions.

In Practice: FOCUS ON ETHICS

CREATIVE ACCOUNTING AND COST OF CAPITAL AT WORLDCOM

Cost of capital is the minimum rate of return on invested funds that a firm must earn in order to stay in business. However, this widely accepted definition of cost of capital was not what some executives at **WorldCom** had in mind when they embarked on the $11 billion accounting fraud that brought the $185 billion telecommunications giant to its knees in the summer of 2002.

The spectacular implosion of WorldCom has been by far the largest fraud and the biggest bankruptcy in corporate history. In the complaint filed in November 2002, the Securities and Exchange Commission alleged that several accounting executives at WorldCom from early 1999 until the spring of 2002 fraudulently manipulated its financial results by improperly reducing its operating expenses.

Many of the improper accounting entries were related to fees WorldCom paid to third-party telecommunication carriers to maintain sufficient network capacity. Anticipating fast growth in telecommunications services due to the expansion of the Internet, WorldCom entered into a number of long-term lease agreements with various third-party carriers to have the right to access their networks. Many of these leases required WorldCom to make fixed monthly payments to the contracted company over the full term of the lease, regardless of whether WorldCom used all or only some of the capacity of the leased networks. These fees were properly recorded as operating expenses and reported as operating expenses on WorldCom's income statement.

However, these fixed payments became an increasingly large percentage of company revenues, cutting into operating margins and resulting in a decline in WorldCom's net income. Company management, including the CFO David Sullivan, knew that this decline in income could fail to meet the expectations of Wall Street analysts and result in a substantial decline of WorldCom's stock price.

Under increasing pressure from the management, accountants at WorldCom concealed the true magnitude of the lease costs: first, by improperly reducing loss reserves held against these costs, and then, after exhausting all reserves, by booking lease fees as capital expenditures. Accounting rules require that operating expenses are reported on a company's income statement and subtracted from revenues in the period in which the expense is incurred or paid, thus affecting net income. Capital expenditures, on the other hand, are reported as capital assets on a company's balance sheet.

As a result of accounting gimmicks, WorldCom falsely portrayed itself as a profitable business and concealed the large losses it suffered. Because it kept its investment-grade credit rating, WorldCom was able to borrow large amounts of money at relatively low interest rates in the months preceding bankruptcy.

The SEC first estimated that fraudulent accounting at WorldCom resulted in inflating the pretax earnings by $3.8 billion during five quarters. More recent estimates indicate that accounting fraud was closer to $11 billion. By concealing its dire financial situation, the company, for a while, created the illusion of solvency, by which it lowered its cost of financing.

Source: SEC Amended Complaint Against Worldcom—Litigation Release: www.sec.gov/litigation/litreleases/lr17829.htm

■ *How did "creative accounting" at WorldCom affect its cost of capital?*

The Basic Concept

The cost of capital is estimated at a given point in time. It reflects the *expected average future cost of funds over the long run*. Although firms typically raise money in lumps, the cost of capital should reflect the interrelatedness of financing activities. For example, if a firm raises funds with debt (borrowing) today, it is likely that some form of equity, such as common stock, will have to be used

target capital structure
The desired optimal mix of debt and equity financing that most firms attempt to maintain.

the next time it needs funds. Most firms attempt to maintain a desired optimal mix of debt and equity financing. This mix is commonly called a **target capital structure**—a topic that will be addressed in Chapter 11. Here, it is sufficient to say that although firms raise money in lumps, they tend toward some desired *mix of financing*.

To capture the interrelatedness of financing assuming the presence of a target capital structure, we need to look at the *overall cost of capital* rather than the cost of the specific source of funds used to finance a given expenditure.

EXAMPLE

A firm is *currently* faced with an investment opportunity. Assume the following:

Best project available today

$$\text{Cost} = \$100{,}000$$
$$\text{Life} = 20 \text{ years}$$
$$\text{IRR} = 7\%$$

Cost of least-cost financing source available

$$\text{Debt} = 6\%$$

Because it can earn 7% on the investment of funds costing only 6%, the firm undertakes the opportunity. Imagine that *1 week later* a new investment opportunity is available:

Best project available 1 week later

$$\text{Cost} = \$100{,}000$$
$$\text{Life} = 20 \text{ years}$$
$$\text{IRR} = 12\%$$

Cost of least-cost financing source available

$$\text{Equity} = 14\%$$

In this instance, the firm rejects the opportunity, because the 14% financing cost is greater than the 12% expected return.

Were the firm's actions in the best interests of its owners? No; it accepted a project yielding a 7% return and rejected one with a 12% return. Clearly, there should be a better way, and there is: The firm can use a combined cost, which over the long run will yield better decisions. By weighting the cost of each source of financing by its *target proportion* in the firm's capital structure, the firm can obtain a *weighted average cost* that reflects the interrelationship of financing decisions. Assuming that a 50–50 mix of debt and equity is targeted, the weighted average cost here would be 10% [(0.50 × 6% debt) + (0.50 × 14% equity)]. With this cost, the first opportunity would have been rejected (7% IRR < 10% weighted average cost), and the second would have been accepted (12% IRR > 10% weighted average cost). Such an outcome would clearly be more desirable. ■

Specific Sources of Capital

This chapter focuses on finding the costs of specific sources of capital and combining them to determine the weighted average cost of capital. Our concern is only with the *long-term* sources of funds available to a business firm, because these sources supply the permanent financing. Long-term financing supports the firm's fixed-asset investments.[1] We assume throughout the chapter that such investments are selected by using appropriate capital budgeting techniques.

There are four basic sources of long-term funds for the business firm: long-term debt, preferred stock, common stock, and retained earnings. The right-hand side of the balance sheet below can be used to illustrate these sources:

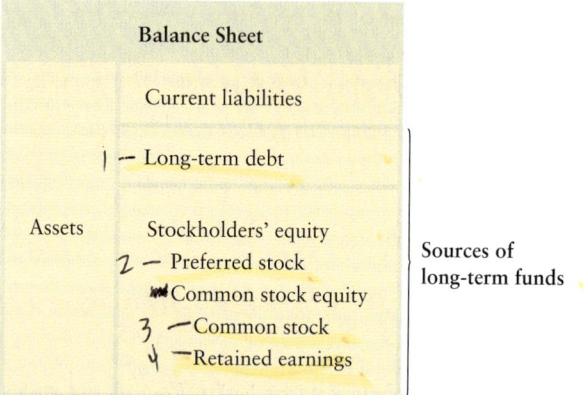

Although not every firm will use all of these methods of financing, each firm is expected to have funds from some of these sources in its capital structure.

The *specific cost* of each source of financing is the *after-tax* cost of obtaining the financing *today*, not the historically based cost reflected by the existing financing on the firm's books. Techniques for determining the specific cost of each source of long-term funds are presented on the following pages. Although these techniques tend to develop precisely calculated values, the resulting values are at best *rough approximations* because of the numerous assumptions and forecasts that underlie them. Although we round calculated costs to the nearest 0.1 percent throughout this chapter, it is not unusual for practicing financial managers to use costs rounded to the nearest 1 percent because these values are merely estimates.

Review Questions

10-1 What is the *cost of capital*? What role does it play in long-term investment decisions?

10-2 Why do we assume that *business risk* and *financial risk* are unchanged when evaluating the cost of capital? Discuss the implications of these assumptions on the acceptance and financing of new projects.

10-3 Why is the cost of capital measured on an *after-tax basis*? Why is use of a weighted average cost of capital rather than the cost of the specific source of funds recommended?

10-4 You have just been told, "Because we are going to finance this project with debt, its required rate of return must exceed the cost of debt." Do you agree or disagree? Explain.

---

1. The role of both long-term and short-term financing in supporting both fixed- and current-asset investments is addressed in Chapter 13. Suffice it to say that long-term funds are at minimum used to finance fixed assets.

The Cost of Long-Term Debt

cost of long-term debt, k_i
The after-tax cost today of raising long-term funds through borrowing.

The **cost of long-term debt**, k_i, is the after-tax cost today of raising long-term funds through borrowing. For convenience, we typically assume that the funds are raised through the sale of bonds. In addition, as we did in Chapter 6, we assume that the bonds pay *annual* (rather than *semiannual*) interest.

Net Proceeds

net proceeds
Funds actually received from the sale of a security.

flotation costs
The total costs of issuing and selling a security.

Most corporate long-term debts are incurred through the sale of bonds. The **net proceeds** from the sale of a bond, or any security, are the funds that are actually received from the sale. **Flotation costs**—the total costs of issuing and selling a security—reduce the net proceeds from the sale. These costs apply to all public offerings of securities—debt, preferred stock, and common stock. They include two components: (1) *underwriting costs*—compensation earned by investment bankers for selling the security, and (2) *administrative costs*—issuer expenses such as legal, accounting, printing, and other expenses.

EXAMPLE

Duchess Corporation, a major hardware manufacturer, is contemplating selling $10 million worth of 20-year, 9% coupon (stated *annual* interest rate) bonds, each with a par value of $1,000. Because similar-risk bonds earn returns greater than 9%, the firm must sell the bonds for $980 to compensate for the lower coupon interest rate. The flotation costs are 2% of the par value of the bond ($0.02 \times \$1,000$), or $20. The *net proceeds* to the firm from the sale of each bond are therefore $960 ($980 − $20).

Before-Tax Cost of Debt

The before-tax cost of debt, k_d, for a bond can be obtained in any of three ways: quotation, calculation, or approximation.

Using Cost Quotations

Hint From the issuer's perspective, the IRR on a bond's cash flows is its *cost to maturity*; from the investor's perspective, the IRR on a bond's cash flows is its *yield to maturity* (YTM), as explained in Chapter 6. These two measures are conceptually similar, although their point of view is different.

When the net proceeds from sale of a bond equal its par value, the before-tax cost just equals the coupon interest rate. For example, a bond with a 10 percent coupon interest rate that nets proceeds equal to the bond's $1,000 par value would have a before-tax cost, k_d, of 10 percent.

A second quotation that is sometimes used is the *yield to maturity* (YTM) on a similar-risk bond[2] (see Chapter 6). For example, if a similar-risk bond has a YTM of 9.7 percent, this value can be used as the before-tax cost of debt, k_d.

Calculating the Cost

This approach finds the before-tax cost of debt by calculating the *internal rate of return* (IRR) on the bond cash flows. From the issuer's point of view, this value is the *cost to maturity* of the cash flows associated with the debt. The cost to maturity can be calculated by using a trial-and-error technique[3], a financial calculator,

---

2. Generally, the yield to maturity of bonds with a similar "rating" is used. Bond ratings, which are published by independent agencies, were discussed in Chapter 6.

3. The trial-and-error technique is presented at the book's Web site www.aw-bc.com/gitman.

or an electronic spreadsheet. It represents the annual before-tax percentage cost of the debt.

EXAMPLE

In the preceding example, the net proceeds of a $1,000, 9% coupon interest rate, 20-year bond were found to be $960. The calculation of the annual cost is quite simple. The cash flow pattern is exactly the opposite of a conventional pattern; it consists of an initial inflow (the net proceeds) followed by a series of annual outlays (the interest payments). In the final year, when the debt is retired, an outlay representing the repayment of the principal also occurs. The cash flows associated with Duchess Corporation's bond issue are as follows:

End of year(s)	Cash flow
0	$ 960
1–20	−$ 90
20	−$1,000

The initial $960 inflow is followed by annual interest outflows of $90 (9% coupon interest rate × $1,000 par value) over the 20-year life of the bond. In year 20, an outflow of $1,000 (the repayment of the principal) occurs. We can determine the cost of debt by finding the IRR, which is the discount rate that equates the present value of the outflows to the initial inflow.

Calculator Use [Note: Most calculators require either the present (net proceeds) or the future (annual interest payments and repayment of principal) values to be input as negative numbers when we calculate cost to maturity. That approach is used here.] Using the calculator and the inputs shown at the left, you should find the before-tax cost (cost to maturity) to be 9.452%.

Spreadsheet Use The before-tax cost of debt on the Duchess Corporation bond also can be calculated as shown in the Excel spreadsheet starting below and continued at the top of the facing page.

	A	B	C	D
1	FINDING THE IRR ON A 20-YEAR BOND			
2	Net Proceeds from sale of bond	$960		
3	(coupon payment)	$90		
4	Years to maturity	20		
5	Par value (principal)	$1,000		
6	Before taxes	9.452%		
7				
8	Trial and Error method:			
9	Choose various required rates and place them in Cell C12			
10	The spreadsheet will recalculate each time. Continue the process until			
11	the sum of the NPV (Cell D36) is $0			
12			9.452%	
13	End of Year(s)	Cash Flow	PVIF	PV
14	0	$ 960	1.0000	$ 960
15	1	$ (90)	0.9136	(82)

Input: 20 N, 960 PV, −90 PMT, −1000 FV, CPT I
Solution: 9.452

16	2	$	(90)	0.8347	(75)
17	3	$	(90)	0.7627	(69)
18	4	$	(90)	0.6968	(63)
19	5	$	(90)	0.6366	(57)
20	6	$	(90)	0.5816	(52)
21	7	$	(90)	0.5314	(48)
22	8	$	(90)	0.4855	(44)
23	9	$	(90)	0.4436	(40)
24	10	$	(90)	0.4053	(36)
25	11	$	(90)	0.3703	(33)
26	12	$	(90)	0.3383	(30)
27	13	$	(90)	0.3091	(28)
28	14	$	(90)	0.2824	(25)
29	15	$	(90)	0.2580	(23)
30	16	$	(90)	0.2357	(21)
31	17	$	(90)	0.2154	(19)
32	18	$	(90)	0.1968	(18)
33	19	$	(90)	0.1798	(16)
34	20	$	(90)	0.1643	(15)
35	20	$	(1,000)	0.1643	(16.4)
36	(The rate of 9.452% equates the NPV to zero)			$	(0)

Approximating the Cost

The before-tax cost of debt, k_d, for a bond with a $1,000 par value can be approximated by using the following equation:

$$k_d = \frac{I + \frac{\$1{,}000 - N_d}{n}}{\frac{N_d + \$1{,}000}{2}} \tag{10.1}$$

where

I = annual interest in dollars
N_d = net proceeds from the sale of debt (bond)
n = number of years to the bond's maturity

EXAMPLE Substituting the appropriate values from the Duchess Corporation example into the approximation formula given in Equation 10.1, we get

$$k_d = \frac{\$90 + \frac{\$1{,}000 - \$960}{20}}{\frac{\$960 + \$1{,}000}{2}} = \frac{\$90 + \$2}{\$980}$$

$$= \frac{\$92}{\$980} = \underline{\underline{9.4\%}}$$

This approximate before-tax cost of debt is close to the 9.452% value calculated precisely in the preceding example.

After-Tax Cost of Debt

As indicated earlier, the *specific cost* of financing must be stated on an after-tax basis. Because interest on debt is tax deductible, it reduces the firm's taxable income. The after-tax cost of debt, k_i, can be found by multiplying the before-tax cost, k_d, by 1 minus the tax rate, T, as stated in the following equation:

$$k_i = k_d \times (1 - T) \tag{10.2}$$

EXAMPLE Duchess Corporation has a 40% tax rate. Using the 9.4% before-tax debt cost calculated above, and applying Equation 10.2, we find an after-tax cost of debt of 5.6% [9.4% × (1 − 0.40)]. Typically, the cost of long-term debt is less than the cost of any of the alternative forms of long-term financing, primarily because of the tax deductibility of interest.

Review Questions

10–5 What are the *net proceeds* from the sale of a bond? What are *flotation costs* and how do they affect a bond's net proceeds?

10–6 What three methods can be used to find the before-tax cost of debt?

10–7 How is the before-tax cost of debt converted into the after-tax cost?

The Cost of Preferred Stock

Preferred stock represents a special type of ownership interest in the firm. It gives preferred stockholders the right to receive their *stated* dividends before any earnings can be distributed to common stockholders. Because preferred stock is a form of ownership, the proceeds from its sale are expected to be held for an infinite period of time. The key characteristics of preferred stock were described in Chapter 7. However, the one aspect of preferred stock that requires review is dividends.

Preferred Stock Dividends

Most preferred stock dividends are stated as a *dollar amount:* "x dollars per year." When dividends are stated this way, the stock is often referred to as "x-dollar preferred stock." Thus a "$4 preferred stock" is expected to pay preferred stockholders $4 in dividends each year on each share of preferred stock owned.

Sometimes preferred stock dividends are stated as an *annual percentage rate*. This rate represents the percentage of the stock's par, or face, value that equals the annual dividend. For instance, an 8 percent preferred stock with a $50 par value would be expected to pay an annual dividend of $4 per share (0.08 × $50 par = $4). Before the cost of preferred stock is calculated, any dividends stated as percentages should be converted to annual dollar dividends.

Calculating the Cost of Preferred Stock

cost of preferred stock, k_p
The ratio of the preferred stock dividend to the firm's net proceeds from the sale of preferred stock; calculated by dividing the annual dividend, D_p, by the net proceeds from the sale of the preferred stock, N_p.

The **cost of preferred stock**, k_p, is the ratio of the preferred stock dividend to the firm's net proceeds from the sale of the preferred stock. The net proceeds represents the amount of money to be received minus any flotation costs. Equation 10.3 gives the cost of preferred stock, k_p, in terms of the annual dollar dividend, D_p, and the net proceeds from the sale of the stock, N_p:

$$k_p = \frac{D_p}{N_p} \qquad k_p = \frac{8.70}{82} = 10.6\% \qquad (10.3)$$

Because preferred stock dividends are paid out of the firm's *after-tax* cash flows, a tax adjustment is not required.

EXAMPLE

Duchess Corporation is contemplating issuance of a 10% preferred stock that is expected to sell for its $87-per-share par value. The cost of issuing and selling the stock is expected to be $5 per share. The first step in finding the cost of the stock is to calculate the dollar amount of the annual preferred dividend, which is $8.70 (0.10 × $87). The net proceeds per share from the proposed sale of stock equals the sale price minus the flotation costs ($87 − $5 = $82). Substituting the annual dividend, D_p, of $8.70 and the net proceeds, N_p, of $82 into Equation 10.3 gives the cost of preferred stock, 10.6% ($8.70 ÷ $82). ■

The cost of Duchess's preferred stock (10.6%) is much greater than the cost of its long-term debt (5.6%). This difference exists primarily because the cost of long-term debt (the interest) is tax deductible.

Review Question

10–8 How would you calculate the cost of preferred stock?

The Cost of Common Stock

The *cost of common stock* is the return required on the stock by investors in the marketplace. There are two forms of common stock financing: (1) retained earnings and (2) new issues of common stock. As a first step in finding each of these costs, we must estimate the cost of common stock equity.

Finding the Cost of Common Stock Equity

cost of common stock equity, k_s
The rate at which investors discount the expected dividends of the firm to determine its share value.

The **cost of common stock equity**, k_s, is the rate at which investors discount the expected dividends of the firm to determine its share value. Two techniques are used to measure the cost of common stock equity. One relies on the constant-growth valuation model, the other on the capital asset pricing model (CAPM).

Using the Constant-Growth Valuation (Gordon) Model

constant-growth valuation (Gordon) model
Assumes that the value of a share of stock equals the present value of all future dividends (assumed to grow at a constant rate) that it is expected to provide over an infinite time horizon.

In Chapter 7 we found the value of a share of stock to be equal to the present value of all future dividends, which in one model were assumed to grow at a constant annual rate over an infinite time horizon. This is the **constant-growth valuation model**, also known as the **Gordon model**. The key expression derived for this model was presented as Equation 7.4 and is restated here:

$$P_0 = \frac{D_1}{k_s - g} \quad (10.4)$$

where

P_0 = value of common stock
D_1 = per-share dividend *expected* at the end of year 1
k_s = required return on common stock
g = constant rate of growth in dividends

Solving Equation 10.4 for k_s results in the following expression for the *cost of common stock equity*:

$$k_s = \frac{D_1}{P_0} + g \quad (10.5)$$

Equation 10.5 indicates that the cost of common stock equity can be found by dividing the dividend expected at the end of year 1 by the current price of the stock and adding the expected growth rate. Because common stock dividends are paid from *after-tax* income, no tax adjustment is required.

EXAMPLE

Duchess Corporation wishes to determine its cost of common stock equity, k_s. The market price, P_0, of its common stock is $50 per share. The firm expects to pay a dividend, D_1, of $4 at the end of the coming year, 2007. The dividends paid on the outstanding stock over the past 6 years (2001–2006) were as follows:

Year	Dividend
2006	$3.80
2005	3.62
2004	3.47
2003	3.33
2002	3.12
2001	2.97

Using the table for the present value interest factors, *PVIF* (Table A–2), or a financial calculator or electronic spreadsheet in conjunction with the technique described for finding growth rates in Chapter 4, we can calculate the annual growth rate of dividends, g. It turns out to be approximately 5% (more precisely, it is 5.05%). Substituting $D_1 = \$4$, $P_0 = \$50$, and $g = 5\%$ into Equation 10.5 yields the cost of common stock equity:

$$k_s = \frac{\$4}{\$50} + 0.05 = 0.08 + 0.05 = 0.130, \text{ or } \underline{\underline{13.0\%}}$$

The 13.0% cost of common stock equity represents the return required by *existing* shareholders on their investment. If the actual return is less than that, shareholders are likely to begin selling their stock.

Using the Capital Asset Pricing Model (CAPM)

capital asset pricing model (CAPM)
Describes the relationship between the required return, k_s, and the nondiversifiable risk of the firm as measured by the beta coefficient, b.

Recall from Chapter 5 that the **capital asset pricing model (CAPM)** describes the relationship between the required return, k_s, and the nondiversifiable risk of the firm as measured by the beta coefficient, b. The basic CAPM is

$$k_s = R_F + [b \times (k_m - R_F)] \tag{10.6}$$

where

R_F = risk-free rate of return

k_m = market return; return on the market portfolio of assets

Using CAPM indicates that the cost of common stock equity is the return required by investors as compensation for the firm's nondiversifiable risk, measured by beta.

EXAMPLE

Duchess Corporation now wishes to calculate its cost of common stock equity, k_s, by using the capital asset pricing model. The firm's investment advisors and its own analyses indicate that the risk-free rate, R_F, equals 7%; the firm's beta, b, equals 1.5; and the market return, k_m, equals 11%. Substituting these values into Equation 10.6, the company estimates the cost of common stock equity, k_s, to be

$$k_s = 7.0\% + [1.5 \times (11.0\% - 7.0\%)] = 7.0\% + 6.0\% = \underline{13.0\%}$$

The 13.0% cost of common stock equity represents the required return of investors in Duchess Corporation common stock. It is the same as that found by using the constant-growth valuation model.

The Cost of Retained Earnings

cost of retained earnings, k_r
The same as the cost of an *equivalent fully subscribed issue of additional common stock*, which is equal to the cost of common stock equity, k_s.

As you know, dividends are paid out of a firm's earnings. Their payment, made in cash to common stockholders, reduces the firm's retained earnings. Suppose a firm needs common stock equity financing of a certain amount. It has two choices relative to retained earnings: It can issue additional common stock in that amount and still pay dividends to stockholders out of retained earnings, or it can increase common stock equity by retaining the earnings (not paying the cash dividends) in the needed amount. In a strict accounting sense, the retention of earnings increases common stock equity in the same way that the sale of additional shares of common stock does. Thus the **cost of retained earnings, k_r**, to the firm is the same as the cost of an *equivalent fully subscribed issue of additional common stock*. Stockholders find the firm's retention of earnings acceptable only if they expect that it will earn at least their required return on the reinvested funds.

Hint Using retained earnings as a major source of financing for capital expenditures does not give away control of the firm and does not dilute present earnings per share, as would occur if new common stock were issued. However, the firm must effectively manage retained earnings to produce profits that increase future retained earnings.

Viewing retained earnings as a fully subscribed issue of additional common stock, we can set the firm's cost of retained earnings, k_r, equal to the cost of common stock equity as given by Equations 10.5 and 10.6.[4]

$$k_r = k_s \tag{10.7}$$

---

4. Technically, if a stockholder received dividends and wished to invest them in additional shares of the firm's stock, he or she would first have to pay personal taxes at capital gains rates on the dividends and then pay brokerage fees before acquiring additional shares. By using pt as the average stockholder's capital gains tax rate and bf as the average brokerage fees stated as a percentage, we can specify the cost of retained earnings, k_r, as $k_r = k_s \times (1 - pt) \times (1 - bf)$. Because of the difficulty in estimating pt and bf, only the simpler definition of k_r given in Equation 10.7 is used here.

It is not necessary to adjust the cost of retained earnings for flotation costs, because by retaining earnings, the firm "raises" equity capital without incurring these costs.

EXAMPLE

The cost of retained earnings for Duchess Corporation was actually calculated in the preceding examples: It is equal to the cost of common stock equity. Thus k_r equals 13.0%. As we will show in the next section, the cost of retained earnings is always lower than the cost of a new issue of common stock, because it entails no flotation costs.

The Cost of New Issues of Common Stock

cost of a new issue of common stock, k_n
The cost of common stock, net of underpricing and associated flotation costs.

underpriced
Stock sold at a price below its current market price, P_0.

Our purpose in finding the firm's overall cost of capital is to determine the after-tax cost of *new* funds required for financing projects. The **cost of a new issue of common stock, k_n**, is determined by calculating the cost of common stock, net of underpricing and associated flotation costs. Normally, for a new issue to sell, it has to be **underpriced**—sold at a price below its current market price, P_0.

Firms underprice new issues for a variety of reasons. First, when the market is in equilibrium (that is, the demand for shares equals the supply of shares), additional demand for shares can be achieved only at a lower price. Second, when additional shares are issued, each share's percentage of ownership in the firm is diluted, thereby justifying a lower share value. Finally, many investors view the issuance of additional shares as a signal that management is using common stock equity financing because it believes that the shares are currently overpriced. Recognizing this information, they will buy shares only at a price below the current market price. Clearly, these and other factors necessitate underpricing of new offerings of common stock. Flotation costs paid for issuing and selling the new issue will further reduce proceeds.

We can use the constant-growth valuation model expression for the cost of existing common stock, k_s, as a starting point. If we let N_n represent the net proceeds from the sale of new common stock after subtracting underpricing and flotation costs, the cost of the new issue, k_n, can be expressed as follows:

$$k_n = \frac{D_1}{N_n} + g \qquad (10.8)$$

The net proceeds from sale of new common stock, N_n, will be less than the current market price, P_0. Therefore, the cost of new issues, k_n, will always be greater than the cost of existing issues, k_s, which is equal to the cost of retained earnings, k_r. *The cost of new common stock is normally greater than any other long-term financing cost.* Because common stock dividends are paid from after-tax cash flows, no tax adjustment is required.

EXAMPLE

In the constant-growth valuation example, we found Duchess Corporation's cost of common stock equity, k_s, to be 13%, using the following values: an expected dividend, D_1, of $4; a current market price, P_0, of $50; and an expected growth rate of dividends, g, of 5%.

To determine its cost of *new* common stock, k_n, Duchess Corporation has estimated that on the average, new shares can be sold for $47. The $3-per-share underpricing is due to the competitive nature of the market. A second cost associated with a new issue is flotation costs of $2.50 per share that would be paid to issue and sell the new shares. The total underpricing and flotation costs per share are therefore expected to be $5.50.

Subtracting the $5.50-per-share underpricing and flotation cost from the current $50 share price results in expected net proceeds of $44.50 per share ($50.00 − $5.50). Substituting $D_1 = \$4$, $N_n = \$44.50$, and $g = 5\%$ into Equation 10.8 results in a cost of new common stock, k_n, as follows:

$$k_n = \frac{\$4.00}{\$44.50} + 0.05 = 0.09 + 0.05 = 0.140, \text{ or } \underline{\underline{14.0\%}}$$

Duchess Corporation's cost of new common stock is therefore 14.0%. This is the value to be used in subsequent calculations of the firm's overall cost of capital. ■

Review Questions

10–9 What premise about share value underlies the constant-growth valuation (Gordon) model that is used to measure the cost of common stock equity, k_s?

10–10 Why is the cost of financing a project with retained earnings less than the cost of financing it with a new issue of common stock?

The Weighted Average Cost of Capital

Now that we have calculated the cost of specific sources of financing, we can determine the overall cost of capital. As noted earlier, the **weighted average cost of capital (WACC)**, k_a, reflects the expected average future cost of funds over the long run. It is found by weighting the cost of each specific type of capital by its proportion in the firm's capital structure.

weighted average cost of capital (WACC), k_a
Reflects the expected average future cost of funds over the long run; found by weighting the cost of each specific type of capital by its proportion in the firm's capital structure.

Calculating the Weighted Average Cost of Capital (WACC)

Calculating the weighted average cost of capital (WACC) is straightforward: Multiply the specific cost of each form of financing by its proportion in the firm's capital structure and sum the weighted values. As an equation, the weighted average cost of capital, k_a, can be specified as follows:

$$k_a = (w_i \times k_i) + (w_p \times k_p) + (w_s \times k_{r \text{ or } n}) \tag{10.9}$$

where

w_i = proportion of long-term debt in capital structure
w_p = proportion of preferred stock in capital structure
w_s = proportion of common stock equity in capital structure
$w_i + w_p + w_s = 1.0$

Three important points should be noted in Equation 10.9:

1. For computational convenience, it is best to convert the weights into decimal form and leave the specific costs in percentage terms.
2. *The sum of the weights must equal 1.0.* Simply stated, all capital structure components must be accounted for.

3. The firm's common stock equity weight, w_s, is multiplied by either the cost of retained earnings, k_r, or the cost of new common stock, k_n. Which cost is used depends on whether the firm's common stock equity will be financed using retained earnings, k_r, or new common stock, k_n.

EXAMPLE

In earlier examples, we found the costs of the various types of capital for Duchess Corporation to be as follows:

$$\text{Cost of debt, } k_i = 5.6\%$$
$$\text{Cost of preferred stock, } k_p = 10.6\%$$
$$\text{Cost of retained earnings, } k_r = 13.0\%$$
$$\text{Cost of new common stock, } k_n = 14.0\%$$

The company uses the following weights in calculating its weighted average cost of capital:

Source of capital	Weight
Long-term debt	40%
Preferred stock	10
Common stock equity	50
Total	100%

Because the firm expects to have a sizable amount of retained earnings available ($300,000), it plans to use its cost of retained earnings, k_r, as the cost of common stock equity. Duchess Corporation's weighted average cost of capital is calculated in Table 10.1. The resulting weighted average cost of capital for Duchess is 9.8%. Assuming an unchanged risk level, the firm should accept all projects that will earn a return greater than 9.8%.

Weighting Schemes

Weights can be calculated on the basis of either *book value* or *market value* and using either *historical* or *target* proportions.

Hint For computational convenience, the financing proportion weights are listed in decimal form in column 1 and the specific costs are shown in percentage terms in column 2.

TABLE 10.1 Calculation of the Weighted Average Cost of Capital for Duchess Corporation

Source of capital	Weight (1)	Cost (2)	Weighted cost [(1) × (2)] (3)
Long-term debt	0.40	5.6%	2.2%
Preferred stock	0.10	10.6	1.1
Common stock equity	0.50	13.0	6.5
Totals	1.00		9.8%

Weighted average cost of capital = 9.8%

Book Value Versus Market Value

book value weights
Weights that use accounting values to measure the proportion of each type of capital in the firm's financial structure.

market value weights
Weights that use market values to measure the proportion of each type of capital in the firm's financial structure.

Book value weights use accounting values to measure the proportion of each type of capital in the firm's financial structure. **Market value weights** measure the proportion of each type of capital at its market value. Market value weights are appealing, because the market values of securities closely approximate the actual dollars to be received from their sale. Moreover, because the costs of the various types of capital are calculated by using prevailing market prices, it seems reasonable to use market value weights. In addition, the long-term investment cash flows to which the cost of capital is applied are estimated in terms of current as well as future market values. *Market value weights are clearly preferred over book value weights.*

Historical Versus Target

historical weights
Either book or market value weights based on *actual* capital structure proportions.

target weights
Either book or market value weights based on *desired* capital structure proportions.

Historical weights can be either book or market value weights based on *actual* capital structure proportions. For example, past or current book value proportions would constitute a form of historical weighting, as would past or current market value proportions. Such a weighting scheme would therefore be based on real—rather than desired—proportions.

Target weights, which can also be based on either book or market values, reflect the firm's *desired* capital structure proportions. Firms using target weights establish such proportions on the basis of the "optimal" capital structure they wish to achieve. (The development of these proportions and the optimal structure are discussed in detail in Chapter 11.)

When one considers the somewhat approximate nature of the calculation of weighted average cost of capital, the choice of weights may not be critical. However, from a strictly theoretical point of view, the *preferred weighting scheme is target market value proportions*, and these are assumed throughout this chapter.

Economic Value Added (EVA®)

economic value added (EVA®)
A popular measure used by many firms to determine whether an investment contributes positively to the owners' wealth; calculated as the difference between an investment's *net operating profit after taxes (NOPAT)* and the cost of the funds used to finance the investment, which is found by multiplying the dollar amount of the funds used to finance the investment by the firm's weighted average cost of capital (WACC).

Economic value added (EVA®) is a popular measure used by firms to determine whether an investment—proposed or existing—contributes positively to the owners' wealth. The application of EVA® requires use of the firm's weighted average cost of capital (WACC). EVA® is calculated as the difference between an investment's *net operating profit after taxes (NOPAT)* and the cost of the funds used to finance the investment. The cost of funds is found by multiplying the dollar amount of the funds used to finance the investment by the firm's WACC. Investments with positive EVA®s increase shareholder value; those with negative EVA®s reduce shareholder value. Clearly, only those investments with positive EVA®s are desirable. For example, the EVA® of an investment of $3.75 million by a firm with a WACC of 10 percent in a project expected to generate NOPAT of $410,000 would be $35,000 [$410,000 − (0.10 × $3,750,000)]. Because this EVA® is positive, the proposed investment is expected to increase owner wealth and is therefore acceptable.

EVA®-type models are used by many well-known corporations, including Coca-Cola, Reynolds Metals, Siemens, and Tenneco. Despite the operational simplicity of EVA®-type models, we continue to focus on the theoretically more sound NPV approach introduced in Chapter 9.

Review Questions

10–11 What is the *weighted average cost of capital (WACC)*, and how is it calculated?

10–12 Describe the logic underlying the use of *target capital structure weights*, and compare and contrast this approach with the use of *historical weights*. What is the preferred weighting scheme?

10–13 What is *economic value added (EVA®)*? How is the *weighted average cost of capital (WACC)* used in calculating EVA®?

  ## The Marginal Cost and Investment Decisions

The firm's weighted average cost of capital is a key input to the investment decision-making process. As demonstrated earlier in the chapter, the firm should make only those investments for which the expected return is greater than the weighted average cost of capital. Of course, at any given time, the firm's financing costs and investment returns will be affected by the volume of financing and investment undertaken. The *weighted marginal cost of capital* and the *investment opportunities schedule* are mechanisms whereby financing and investment decisions can be made simultaneously.

The Weighted Marginal Cost of Capital (WMCC)

The weighted average cost of capital may vary over time, depending on the volume of financing that the firm plans to raise. *As the volume of financing increases, the costs of the various types of financing will increase, raising the firm's weighted average cost of capital.* Therefore, it is useful to calculate the **weighted marginal cost of capital (WMCC)**, which is simply the firm's weighted average cost of capital (WACC) associated with its *next dollar* of total new financing. This marginal cost is relevant to current decisions.

The costs of the financing components (debt, preferred stock, and common stock) rise as larger amounts are raised. Suppliers of funds require greater returns in the form of interest, dividends, or growth as compensation for the increased risk introduced by larger volumes of *new* financing. The WMCC is therefore an increasing function of the level of total new financing.

Another factor that causes the weighted average cost of capital to increase is the use of common stock equity financing. New financing provided by common stock equity will be provided by retaining earnings until this supply is exhausted and then will be obtained through new common stock financing. Because retained earnings are a less expensive form of common stock equity financing than the sale of new common stock, the weighted average cost of capital will rise with the addition of new common stock.

Finding Break Points

To calculate the WMCC, we must calculate **break points**, which reflect the level of *total* new financing at which the cost of one of the financing components rises. The following general equation can be used to find break points:

weighted marginal cost of capital (WMCC)
The firm's weighted average cost of capital (WACC) associated with its *next dollar* of total new financing.

break point
The level of *total* new financing at which the cost of one of the financing components rises, thereby causing an upward shift in the *weighted marginal cost of capital (WMCC)*.

$$BP_j = \frac{AF_j}{w_j} \qquad (10.10)$$

where

BP_j = break point for financing source j
AF_j = amount of funds available from financing source j at a given cost
w_j = capital structure weight (stated in decimal form) for financing source j

EXAMPLE

When Duchess Corporation exhausts its $300,000 of available retained earnings (at $k_r = 13.0\%$), it must use the more expensive new common stock financing (at $k_n = 14.0\%$) to meet its common stock equity needs. In addition, the firm expects that it can borrow only $400,000 of debt at the 5.6% cost; additional debt will have an after-tax cost (k_i) of 8.4%. Two break points therefore exist: (1) when the $300,000 of retained earnings costing 13.0% is exhausted, and (2) when the $400,000 of long-term debt costing 5.6% is exhausted.

The break points can be found by substituting these values and the corresponding capital structure weights given earlier into Equation 10.10. We get the dollar amounts of *total* new financing at which the costs of the given financing sources rise:

$$BP_{\text{common equity}} = \frac{\$300,000}{0.50} = \$600,000 \quad \text{[50\% equity]}$$

$$BP_{\text{long-term debt}} = \frac{\$400,000}{0.40} = \$1,000,000 \quad \text{[40\% debt]}$$ ■

Calculating the WMCC

Once the break points have been determined, the next step is to calculate the weighted average cost of capital over the range of total new financing between break points. First, we find the WACC for a level of total new financing between zero and the first break point. Next, we find the WACC for a level of total new financing between the first and second break points, and so on. By definition, for each of the ranges of total new financing between break points, certain component capital costs (such as debt or common equity) will increase. This will cause the weighted average cost of capital to increase to a higher level than that over the preceding range.

Together, these data can be used to prepare a **weighted marginal cost of capital (WMCC) schedule**. This graph relates the firm's weighted average cost of capital to the level of total new financing.

weighted marginal cost of capital (WMCC) schedule
Graph that relates the firm's weighted average cost of capital to the level of total new financing.

EXAMPLE

Table 10.2 (see page 420) summarizes the calculation of the WACC for Duchess Corporation over the three ranges of total new financing created by the two break points—$600,000 and $1,000,000. Comparing the costs in column 3 of the table for each of the three ranges, we can see that the costs in the first range ($0 to $600,000) are those calculated in earlier examples and used in Table 10.1. The second range ($600,000 to $1,000,000) reflects the increase in the common stock equity cost to 14.0%. In the final range, the increase in the long-term debt cost to 8.4% is introduced.

TABLE 10.2 Weighted Average Cost of Capital for Ranges of Total New Financing for Duchess Corporation

Range of total new financing	Source of capital (1)	Weight (2)	Cost (3)	Weighted cost [(2) × (3)] (4)
$0 to $600,000	Debt	.40	5.6%	2.2%
	Preferred	.10	10.6	1.1
	Common	.50	13.0	6.5
			Weighted average cost of capital	9.8%
$600,000 to $1,000,000	Debt	.40	5.6%	2.2%
	Preferred	.10	10.6	1.1
	Common	.50	14.0	7.0
			Weighted average cost of capital	10.3%
$1,000,000 and above	Debt	.40	8.4%	3.4%
	Preferred	.10	10.6	1.1
	Common	.50	14.0	7.0
			Weighted average cost of capital	11.5%

The weighted average costs of capital (WACC) for the three ranges are summarized in the table shown at the bottom of Figure 10.1. These data describe the weighted marginal cost of capital (WMCC), which increases as levels of total new financing increase. Figure 10.1 presents the WMCC schedule. Again, it is clear that the WMCC is an increasing function of the amount of total new financing raised.

FIGURE 10.1
WMCC Schedule
Weighted marginal cost of capital (WMCC) schedule for Duchess Corporation

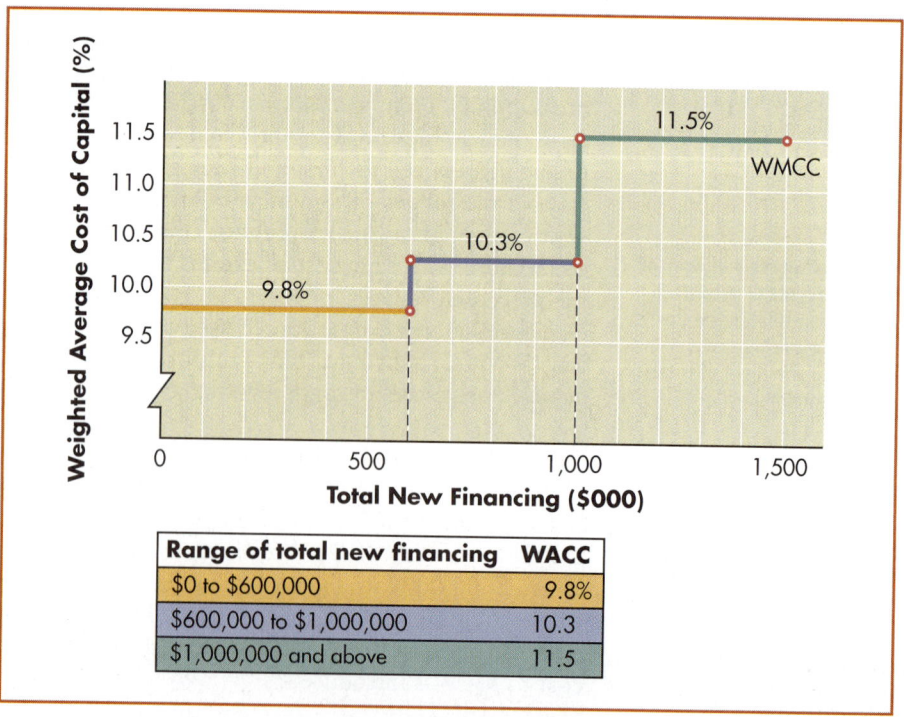

Range of total new financing	WACC
$0 to $600,000	9.8%
$600,000 to $1,000,000	10.3
$1,000,000 and above	11.5

The Investment Opportunities Schedule (IOS)

At any given time, a firm has certain investment opportunities available to it. These opportunities differ with respect to the size of investment, risk, and return.[5] The firm's **investment opportunities schedule (IOS)** is a ranking of investment possibilities from best (highest return) to worst (lowest return). Generally, the first project selected will have the highest return, the next project the second highest, and so on. The return on investments will *decrease* as the firm accepts additional projects.

investment opportunities schedule (IOS)
A ranking of investment possibilities from best (highest return) to worst (lowest return).

EXAMPLE

Column 1 of Table 10.3 shows Duchess Corporation's current investment opportunities schedule (IOS) listing the investment possibilities from best (highest return) to worst (lowest return). Column 2 of the table shows the initial investment required by each project. Column 3 shows the cumulative total invested funds necessary to finance all projects better than and including the corresponding investment opportunity. Plotting the project returns against the cumulative investment (column 1 against column 3) results in the firm's investment opportunities schedule (IOS). A graph of the IOS for Duchess Corporation is given in Figure 10.2 (see page 422).

Using the WMCC and IOS to Make Financing/Investment Decisions

As long as a project's internal rate of return is greater than the weighted marginal cost of new financing, the firm should accept the project.[6] The return will decrease with the acceptance of more projects, and the weighted marginal cost of capital will increase because greater amounts of financing will be required. The

TABLE 10.3 Investment Opportunities Schedule (IOS) for Duchess Corporation

Investment opportunity	Internal rate of return (IRR) (1)	Initial investment (2)	Cumulative investment[a] (3)
A	15.0%	$100,000	$ 100,000
B	14.5	200,000	300,000
C	14.0	400,000	700,000
D	13.0	100,000	800,000
E	12.0	300,000	1,100,000
F	11.0	200,000	1,300,000
G	10.0	100,000	1,400,000

[a]The cumulative investment represents the total amount invested in projects with higher returns plus the investment required for the corresponding investment opportunity.

---

5. Because the calculated weighted average cost of capital does not apply to risk-changing investments, we assume that all opportunities have equal risk similar to the firm's risk.

6. Although net present value could be used to make these decisions, the internal rate of return is used here because of the ease of comparison it offers.

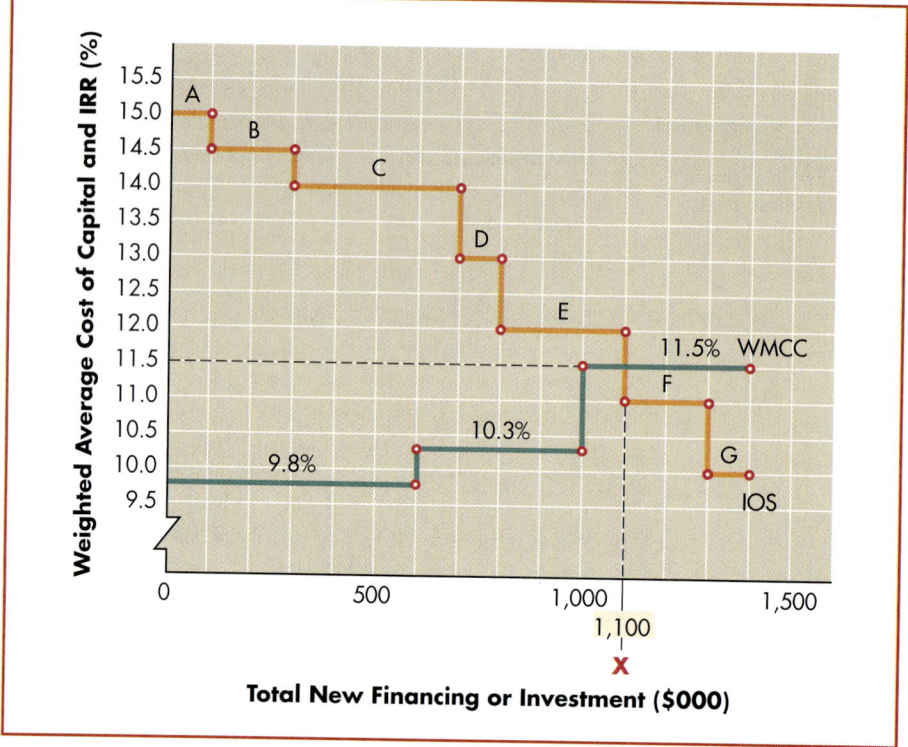

FIGURE 10.2

IOS and WMCC Schedules
Using the IOS and WMCC to select projects for Duchess Corporation

decision rule therefore would be: *Accept projects up to the point at which the marginal return on an investment equals its weighted marginal cost of capital.* Beyond that point, its investment return will be less than its capital cost.

This approach is consistent with the maximization of net present value (NPV) for conventional projects for two reasons: (1) The NPV is positive as long as the IRR exceeds the weighted average cost of capital, k_a. (2) The larger the difference between the IRR and k_a, the larger the resulting NPV. Therefore, the acceptance of projects beginning with those that have the greatest positive difference between IRR and k_a, down to the point at which IRR just equals k_a, should result in the maximum total NPV for all independent projects accepted. Such an outcome is completely consistent with the firm's goal of maximizing owner wealth.

EXAMPLE Figure 10.2 shows Duchess Corporation's WMCC schedule and IOS on the same set of axes. By raising $1,100,000 of new financing and investing these funds in projects A, B, C, D, and E, the firm should maximize the wealth of its owners, because these projects result in the maximum total net present value. Note that the 12.0% return on the last dollar invested (in project E) *exceeds* its 11.5% weighted average cost. Investment in project F is not feasible, because its 11.0% return is *less than* the 11.5% cost of funds available for investment. ■

The firm's optimal capital budget of $1,100,000 is marked with an X in Figure 10.2. At that point, the IRR equals the weighted average cost of capital, and the firm's size as well as its shareholder value will be optimized. In a sense, the size of the firm is determined by the market—the availability of and returns on investment opportunities, and the availability and cost of financing.

In practice, most firms operate under *capital rationing*. That is, management imposes constraints that keep the capital expenditure budget below optimal (where IRR = k_a). Because of this, a gap frequently exists between the theoretically optimal capital budget and the firm's actual level of financing/investment.

Review Questions

10–14 What is the *weighted marginal cost of capital (WMCC)*? What does the *WMCC schedule* represent? Why does this schedule increase?

10–15 What is the *investment opportunities schedule (IOS)*? Is it typically depicted as an increasing or a decreasing function? Why?

10–16 How can the WMCC schedule and the IOS be used to find the level of financing/investment that maximizes owner wealth? Why do many firms finance/invest at a level below this optimum?

SUMMARY

FOCUS ON VALUE

The cost of capital is an extremely important rate of return used by the firm in the long-term decision process, particularly in capital budgeting decisions. It is the expected average future cost to the firm of funds over the long run. Because the cost of capital is the pivotal rate of return used in the investment decision process, its accuracy can significantly affect the quality of these decisions.

Even with good estimates of project cash flows, the application of NPV and IRR decision techniques, and adequate consideration of project risk, a poorly estimated cost of capital can result in the destruction of shareholder value. Underestimation of the cost of capital can result in the mistaken acceptance of poor projects, whereas overestimation can cause good projects to be rejected. In either situation, the firm's action could be detrimental to the firm's value. By applying the techniques presented in this chapter to estimate the firm's cost of capital, the financial manager will improve the likelihood that the firm's long-term decisions will be consistent with the firm's overall goal of **maximizing stock price (owner wealth).**

REVIEW OF LEARNING GOALS

Key definitions and formulas for this chapter are summarized in Table 10.4 (see page 424).

LG1 **Understand the key assumptions, the basic concept, and the specific sources of capital associated with the cost of capital.** The cost of capital is the rate of return that a firm must earn on its investments to maintain its market value and attract needed funds. It is affected by business and financial risks, and is measured on an after-tax basis. A weighted average cost of capital should be used to find the expected average future cost of funds over the long run. The specific costs of the basic sources of capital (long-term debt, preferred stock, retained earnings, and common stock) can be calculated individually.

TABLE 10.4 Summary of Key Definitions and Formulas for Cost of Capital

Definitions of variables

AF_j = amount of funds available from financing source j at a given cost
b = beta coefficient or measure of nondiversifiable risk
BP_j = break point for financing source j
D_1 = per-share dividend *expected* at the end of year 1
D_p = annual preferred stock dividend (in dollars)
g = constant rate of growth in dividends
I = annual interest in dollars
k_a = weighted average cost of capital
k_d = before-tax cost of debt
k_i = after-tax cost of debt
k_m = required return on the market portfolio
k_n = cost of a new issue of common stock
k_p = cost of preferred stock
k_r = cost of retained earnings
k_s = required return on common stock
n = number of years to the bond's maturity
N_d = net proceeds from the sale of debt (bond)
N_n = net proceeds from the sale of new common stock
N_p = net proceeds from the sale of preferred stock
P_0 = value of common stock
R_F = risk-free rate of return
T = firm's tax rate
w_i = proportion of long-term debt in capital structure
w_j = capital structure proportion (historical or target, stated in decimal form) for financing source j
w_p = proportion of preferred stock in capital structure
w_s = proportion of common stock equity in capital structure

Cost of capital formulas

Before-tax cost of debt (approximation):

$$k_d = \frac{I + \frac{\$1{,}000 - N_d}{n}}{\frac{N_d + \$1{,}000}{2}}$$ [Equation 10.1]

After-tax cost of debt: $k_i = k_d \times (1 - T)$ [Equation 10.2]

Cost of preferred stock: $k_p = \frac{D_p}{N_p}$ [Equation 10.3]

Cost of common stock equity:

Using constant-growth valuation model: $k_s = \frac{D_1}{P_0} + g$ [Equation 10.5]

Using CAPM: $k_s = R_F + [b \times (k_m - R_F)]$ [Equation 10.6]

Cost of retained earnings: $k_r = k_s$ [Equation 10.7]

Cost of new issues of common stock: $k_n = \frac{D_1}{N_n} + g$ [Equation 10.8]

Weighted average cost of capital (WACC): $k_a = (w_i \times k_i) + (w_p \times k_p) + (w_s \times k_{r \text{ or } n})$ [Equation 10.9]

Break point: $BP_j = \frac{AF_j}{w_j}$ [Equation 10.10]

LG2 **Determine the cost of long-term debt and the cost of preferred stock.** The cost of long-term debt is the after-tax cost today of raising long-term funds through borrowing. Cost quotations, calculation, or an approximation can be used to find the before-tax cost of debt, which must then be tax-adjusted. The cost of preferred stock is the ratio of the preferred stock dividend to the firm's net proceeds from the sale of preferred stock.

LG3 **Calculate the cost of common stock equity and convert it into the cost of retained earnings and the cost of new issues of common stock.** The cost of common stock equity can be calculated by using the constant-growth valuation (Gordon) model or the CAPM. The cost of retained earnings is equal to the cost of common stock equity. An adjustment in the cost of common stock equity to reflect underpricing and flotation costs is necessary to find the cost of new issues of common stock.

LG4 **Calculate the weighted average cost of capital (WACC) and discuss alternative weighting schemes and economic value added (EVA®).** The firm's WACC reflects the expected average future cost of funds over the long run. It combines the costs of specific types of capital after weighting each of them by its proportion. The theoretically preferred approach uses target weights based on market values. Economic value added (EVA®) is a popular measure that uses the WACC to determine whether a proposed investment is expected to make a positive contribution to the owners' wealth.

LG5 **Describe the procedures used to determine break points and the weighted marginal cost of capital (WMCC).** As total new financing increases, the costs of the various types of financing will increase, raising the firm's WACC. The WMCC is the firm's WACC associated with its next dollar of total new financing. Break points represent the level of total new financing at which the cost of one of the financing components rises, causing an upward shift in the WMCC. The WMCC schedule relates the WACC to each level of total new financing.

LG6 **Explain the weighted marginal cost of capital (WMCC) and its use with the investment opportunities schedule (IOS) to make financing/investment decisions.** The IOS ranks currently available investments from best to worst. It is used with the WMCC to find the level of financing/investment that maximizes owner wealth. The firm accepts projects up to the point at which the marginal return on its investment equals its weighted marginal cost of capital.

SELF-TEST PROBLEM (SOLUTION IN APPENDIX B)

ST10–1 **Specific costs, WACC, WMCC, and IOS** Humble Manufacturing is interested in measuring its overall cost of capital. The firm is in the 40% tax bracket. Current investigation has gathered the following data:

Debt The firm can raise an unlimited amount of debt by selling $1,000-par-value, 10% coupon interest rate, 10-year bonds on which *annual interest* payments will be made. To sell the issue, an average discount of $30 per bond must be given. The firm must also pay flotation costs of $20 per bond.

Preferred stock The firm can sell 11% (annual dividend) preferred stock at its $100-per-share par value. The cost of issuing and selling the preferred stock is expected to be $4 per share. An unlimited amount of preferred stock can be sold under these terms.

Common stock The firm's common stock is currently selling for $80 per share. The firm expects to pay cash dividends of $6 per share next year. The firm's dividends have been growing at an annual rate of 6%, and this rate is expected to continue in the future. The stock will have to be underpriced by $4 per share, and flotation costs are expected to amount to $4 per share. The firm can sell an unlimited amount of new common stock under these terms.

Retained earnings The firm expects to have $225,000 of retained earnings available in the coming year. Once these retained earnings are exhausted, the firm will use new common stock as the form of common stock equity financing.

a. Calculate the specific cost of each source of financing. (Round to the nearest 0.1%.)
b. The firm uses the weights shown in the following table, which are based on target capital structure proportions, to calculate its weighted average cost of capital. (Round to the nearest 0.1%.)

Source of capital	Weight
Long-term debt	40%
Preferred stock	15
Common stock equity	45
Total	100%

   (1) Calculate the single *break point* associated with the firm's financial situation. (*Hint:* This point results from the exhaustion of the firm's retained earnings.)
   (2) Calculate the weighted average cost of capital associated with total new financing *below* the break point calculated in part (1).
   (3) Calculate the weighted average cost of capital associated with total new financing *above* the break point calculated in part (1).

c. Using the results of part b along with the information shown in the following table on the available investment opportunities, draw the firm's weighted marginal cost of capital (WMCC) schedule and investment opportunities schedule (IOS) on the same set of axes (total new financing or investment on the x axis and weighted average cost of capital and IRR on the y axis).

Investment opportunity	Internal rate of return (IRR)	Initial investment
A	11.2%	$100,000
B	9.7	500,000
C	12.9	150,000
D	16.5	200,000
E	11.8	450,000
F	10.1	600,000
G	10.5	300,000

d. Which, if any, of the available investments do you recommend that the firm accept? Explain your answer. How much total new financing is required?

WARM-UP EXERCISES

E10–1 Weekend Warriors, Inc., has 35% debt and 65% equity in its capital structure. The firm's estimated cost of debt is 8% and its estimated cost of equity is 13%. Determine the firm's *weighted average cost of capital (WACC)*.

E10–2 A firm raises capital by selling $20,000 worth of debt with flotation costs equal to 2% of its par value. If the debt matures in 10 years and has a coupon interest rate of 8%, what is the bond's IRR?

E10–3 Your firm, People's Consulting Group, has been asked to consult on a potential preferred stock offering by Brave New World. This 15% preferred stock issue would be sold at its par value of $35 per share. Flotation costs would total $3 per share. Calculate Brave New World's *cost of preferred stock*.

E10–4 Duke Energy has been paying dividends steadily for 20 years. During that time, dividends have grown at a compound annual rate of 7%. If Duke Energy's current stock price is $78 and the firm plans to pay a dividend of $6.50 next year, what is Duke's *cost of common stock equity*?

E10–5 Oxy Corporation uses debt, preferred stock, and common stock to raise capital. The firm's capital structure targets the following proportions: debt, 55%; preferred stock, 10%; and common stock, 35%. If the cost of debt is 6.7%, preferred stock costs 9.2%, and common stock costs 10.6%, what is Oxy's *weighted average cost of capital (WACC)*?

Problems

P10–1 Concept of cost of capital Wren Manufacturing is in the process of analyzing its investment decision-making procedures. The two projects evaluated by the firm during the past month were projects 263 and 264. The basic variables surrounding each project analysis, using the IRR decision technique, and the resulting decision actions are summarized in the following table.

Basic variables	Project 263	Project 264
Cost	$64,000	$58,000
Life	15 years	15 years
IRR	8%	15%
Least-cost financing		
Source	Debt	Equity
Cost (after-tax)	7%	16%
Decision		
Action	Accept	Reject
Reason	8% IRR > 7% cost	15% IRR < 16% cost

a. Evaluate the firm's decision-making procedures, and explain why the acceptance of project 263 and rejection of project 264 may not be in the owners' best interest.
b. If the firm maintains a capital structure containing 40% debt and 60% equity, find its weighted average cost using the data in the table.
c. If the firm had used the weighted average cost calculated in part **b**, what actions would have been indicated relative to projects 263 and 264?
d. Compare and contrast the firm's actions with your findings in part **c**. Which decision method seems more appropriate? Explain why.

P10–2 **Cost of debt using both methods** Currently, Warren Industries can sell 15-year, $1,000-par-value bonds paying *annual interest* at a 12% coupon rate. As a result of current interest rates, the bonds can be sold for $1,010 each; flotation costs of $30 per bond will be incurred in this process. The firm is in the 40% tax bracket.
a. Find the net proceeds from sale of the bond, N_d.
b. Show the cash flows from the firm's point of view over the maturity of the bond.
c. Use the *IRR approach* to calculate the before-tax and after-tax costs of debt.
d. Use the *approximation formula* to estimate the before-tax and after-tax costs of debt.
e. Compare and contrast the costs of debt calculated in parts c and d. Which approach do you prefer? Why?

P10–3 **Cost of debt using the approximation formula** For each of the following $1,000-par-value bonds, assuming *annual interest* payment and a 40% tax rate, calculate the *after-tax* cost to maturity using the *approximation formula*.

Bond	Life	Underwriting fee	Discount (−) or premium (+)	Coupon interest rate
A	20 years	$25	−$20	9%
B	16	40	+ 10	10
C	15	30	− 15	12
D	25	15	Par	9
E	22	20	− 60	11

P10–4 **Cost of preferred stock** Taylor Systems has just issued preferred stock. The stock has a 12% annual dividend and a $100 par value and was sold at $97.50 per share. In addition, flotation costs of $2.50 per share must be paid.
a. Calculate the *cost of the preferred stock*.
b. If the firm sells the preferred stock with a 10% annual dividend and nets $90.00 after flotation costs, what is its cost?

P10–5 **Cost of preferred stock** Determine the cost for each of the following preferred stocks.

Preferred stock	Par value	Sale price	Flotation cost	Annual dividend
A	$100	$101	$9.00	11%
B	40	38	$3.50	8%
C	35	37	$4.00	$5.00
D	30	26	5% of par	$3.00
E	20	20	$2.50	9%

P10–6 **Cost of common stock equity—CAPM** J&M Corporation common stock has a beta, b, of 1.2. The risk-free rate is 6%, and the market return is 11%.
a. Determine the risk premium on J&M common stock.
b. Determine the required return that J&M common stock should provide.
c. Determine J&M's *cost of common stock equity* using the CAPM.

P10–7 **Cost of common stock equity** Ross Textiles wishes to measure its cost of common stock equity. The firm's stock is currently selling for $57.50. The firm expects to pay a $3.40 dividend at the end of the year (2007). The dividends for the past 5 years are shown in the following table.

Year	Dividend
2006	$3.10
2005	2.92
2004	2.60
2003	2.30
2002	2.12

After underpricing and flotation costs, the firm expects to net $52 per share on a new issue.

a. Determine the growth rate of dividends.
b. Determine the net proceeds, N_n, that the firm will actually receive.
c. Using the constant-growth valuation model, determine the *cost of retained earnings*, k_r.
d. Using the constant-growth valuation model, determine the *cost of new common stock*, k_n.

P10–8 **Retained earnings versus new common stock** Using the data for each firm shown in the following table, calculate the *cost of retained earnings* and the *cost of new common stock* using the constant-growth valuation model.

Firm	Current market price per share	Dividend growth rate	Projected dividend per share next year	Underpricing per share	Flotation cost per share
A	$50.00	8%	$2.25	$2.00	$1.00
B	20.00	4	1.00	0.50	1.50
C	42.50	6	2.00	1.00	2.00
D	19.00	2	2.10	1.30	1.70

P10–9 **WACC—Book weights** Ridge Tool has on its books the amounts and specific (after-tax) costs shown in the following table for each source of capital.

Source of capital	Book value	Specific cost
Long-term debt	$700,000	5.3%
Preferred stock	50,000	12.0
Common stock equity	650,000	16.0

a. Calculate the firm's weighted average cost of capital using book value weights.
b. Explain how the firm can use this cost in the investment decision-making process.

P10–10 WACC—Book weights and market weights Webster Company has compiled the information shown in the following table.

Source of capital	Book value	Market value	After-tax cost
Long-term debt	$4,000,000	$3,840,000	6.0%
Preferred stock	40,000	60,000	13.0
Common stock equity	1,060,000	3,000,000	17.0
Totals	$5,100,000	$6,900,000	

a. Calculate the weighted average cost of capital using *book value weights*.
b. Calculate the weighted average cost of capital using *market value weights*.
c. Compare the answers obtained in parts **a** and **b**. Explain the differences.

P10–11 WACC and target weights After careful analysis, Dexter Brothers has determined that its optimal capital structure is composed of the sources and target market value weights shown in the following table.

Source of capital	Target market value weight
Long-term debt	30%
Preferred stock	15
Common stock equity	55
Total	100%

The cost of debt is estimated to be 7.2%; the cost of preferred stock is estimated to be 13.5%; the cost of retained earnings is estimated to be 16.0%; and the cost of new common stock is estimated to be 18.0%. All of these are after-tax rates. The company's debt represents 25%, the preferred stock represents 10%, and the common stock equity represents 65% of total capital on the basis of the market values of the three components. The company expects to have a significant amount of retained earnings available and does not expect to sell any new common stock.

a. Calculate the weighted average cost of capital on the basis of *historical market value weights*.
b. Calculate the weighted average cost of capital on the basis of *target market value weights*.
c. Compare the answers obtained in parts **a** and **b**. Explain the differences.

P10–12 Calculation of specific costs, WACC, and WMCC Dillon Labs has asked its financial manager to measure the cost of each specific type of capital as well as the weighted average cost of capital. The weighted average cost is to be measured by using the following weights: 40% long-term debt, 10% preferred stock, and 50% common stock equity (retained earnings, new common stock, or both). The firm's tax rate is 40%.

Debt The firm can sell for $980 a 10-year, $1,000-par-value bond paying *annual interest* at a 10% coupon rate. A flotation cost of 3% of the par value is required in addition to the discount of $20 per bond.

Preferred stock Eight percent (annual dividend) preferred stock having a par value of $100 can be sold for $65. An additional fee of $2 per share must be paid to the underwriters.

Common stock The firm's common stock is currently selling for $50 per share. The dividend expected to be paid at the end of the coming year (2007) is $4. Its dividend payments, which have been approximately 60% of earnings per share in each of the past 5 years, were as shown in the following table.

Year	Dividend
2006	$3.75
2005	3.50
2004	3.30
2003	3.15
2002	2.85

It is expected that to attract buyers, new common stock must be underpriced $5 per share, and the firm must also pay $3 per share in flotation costs. Dividend payments are expected to continue at 60% of earnings.

a. Calculate the specific cost of each source of financing. (Assume that $k_r = k_s$.)
b. If earnings available to common shareholders are expected to be $7 million, what is the *break point* associated with the exhaustion of retained earnings?
c. Determine the weighted average cost of capital between zero and the break point calculated in part **b**.
d. Determine the weighted average cost of capital just beyond the break point calculated in part **b**.

P10–13 **Calculation of specific costs, WACC, and WMCC** Lang Enterprises is interested in measuring its overall cost of capital. Current investigation has gathered the following data. The firm is in the 40% tax bracket.

Debt The firm can raise an unlimited amount of debt by selling $1,000-par-value, 8% coupon interest rate, 20-year bonds on which *annual interest* payments will be made. To sell the issue, an average discount of $30 per bond would have to be given. The firm also must pay flotation costs of $30 per bond.

Preferred stock The firm can sell 8% preferred stock at its $95-per-share par value. The cost of issuing and selling the preferred stock is expected to be $5 per share. An unlimited amount of preferred stock can be sold under these terms.

Common stock The firm's common stock is currently selling for $90 per share. The firm expects to pay cash dividends of $7 per share next year. The firm's dividends have been growing at an annual rate of 6%, and this growth is expected to continue into the future. The stock must be underpriced by $7 per share, and flotation costs are expected to amount to $5 per share. The firm can sell an unlimited amount of new common stock under these terms.

Retained earnings When measuring this cost, the firm does not concern itself with the tax bracket or brokerage fees of owners. It expects to have available $100,000 of retained earnings in the coming year; once these retained earnings are exhausted, the firm will use new common stock as the form of common stock equity financing.

a. Calculate the specific cost of each source of financing. (Round answers to the nearest 0.1%.)

Source of capital	Weight
Long-term debt	30%
Preferred stock	20
Common stock equity	50
Total	100%

b. The firm's capital structure weights used in calculating its weighted average cost of capital are shown in the table above. (Round answer to the nearest 0.1%.)
   (1) Calculate the single *break point* associated with the firm's financial situation. (*Hint:* This point results from exhaustion of the firm's retained earnings.)
   (2) Calculate the weighted average cost of capital associated with total new financing below the break point calculated in part (1).
   (3) Calculate the weighted average cost of capital associated with total new financing above the break point calculated in part (1).

P10–14 **Integrative—WACC, WMCC, and IOS** Cartwell Products has compiled the data shown in the following table for the current costs of its three basic sources of capital—long-term debt, preferred stock, and common stock equity—for various ranges of new financing.

Source of capital	Range of new financing	After-tax cost
Long-term debt	$0 to $320,000	6%
	$320,000 and above	8
Preferred stock	$0 and above	17%
Common stock equity	$0 to $200,000	20%
	$200,000 and above	24

The company's capital structure weights used in calculating its weighted average cost of capital are shown in the following table.

Source of capital	Weight
Long-term debt	40%
Preferred stock	20
Common stock equity	40
Total	100%

a. Determine the *break points* and ranges of *total* new financing associated with each source of capital.

b. Using the data developed in part **a**, determine the break points (levels of *total* new financing) at which the firm's weighted average cost of capital will change.
c. Calculate the weighted average cost of capital for each range of total new financing found in part **b**. (*Hint:* There are three ranges.)
d. Using the results of part **c**, along with the following information on the available investment opportunities, draw the firm's weighted marginal cost of capital (WMCC) schedule and investment opportunities schedule (IOS) on the same set of axes (total new financing or investment on the x axis and weighted average cost of capital and IRR on the y axis).

Investment opportunity	Internal rate of return (IRR)	Initial investment
A	19%	$200,000
B	15	300,000
C	22	100,000
D	14	600,000
E	23	200,000
F	13	100,000
G	21	300,000
H	17	100,000
I	16	400,000

e. Which, if any, of the available investments do you recommend that the firm accept? Explain your answer.

P10–15 **ETHICS PROBLEM** Why did the implosion of the communication giant WorldCom happen so rapidly despite its large size—assets estimated to be close to $105 billion and stockholders' equity of $58 billion—reported just a few months before the bankruptcy?

CHAPTER 10 CASE   Making Star Products' Financing/Investment Decision

Star Products Company is a growing manufacturer of automobile accessories whose stock is actively traded on the over-the-counter (OTC) exchange. During 2006, the Dallas-based company experienced sharp increases in both sales and earnings. Because of this recent growth, Melissa Jen, the company's treasurer, wants to make sure that available funds are being used to their fullest. Management policy is to maintain the current capital structure proportions of 30% long-term debt, 10% preferred stock, and 60% common stock equity for at least the next 3 years. The firm is in the 40% tax bracket.

Star's division and product managers have presented several competing investment opportunities to Jen. However, because funds are limited, choices of which projects to accept must be made. The investment opportunities schedule (IOS) is shown in the table at the top of page 434.

Investment Opportunities Schedule (IOS) for Star Products Company

Investment opportunity	Internal rate of return (IRR)	Initial investment
A	15%	$400,000
B	22	200,000
C	25	700,000
D	23	400,000
E	17	500,000
F	19	600,000
G	14	500,000

To estimate the firm's weighted average cost of capital (WACC), Jen contacted a leading investment banking firm, which provided the financing cost data shown in the following table.

Financing Cost Data Star Products Company

Long-term debt: The firm can raise $450,000 of additional debt by selling 15-year, $1,000-par-value, 9% coupon interest rate bonds that pay *annual interest*. It expects to net $960 per bond after flotation costs. Any debt in excess of $450,000 will have a before-tax cost, k_d, of 13%.

Preferred stock: Preferred stock, regardless of the amount sold, can be issued with a $70 par value and a 14% annual dividend rate and will net $65 per share after flotation costs.

Common stock equity: The firm expects dividends and earnings per share to be $0.96 and $3.20, respectively, in 2007 and to continue to grow at a constant rate of 11% per year. The firm's stock currently sells for $12 per share. Star expects to have $1,500,000 of retained earnings available in the coming year. Once the retained earnings have been exhausted, the firm can raise additional funds by selling new common stock, netting $9 per share after underpricing and flotation costs.

TO DO

a. Calculate the cost of each source of financing, as specified:
   (1) Long-term debt, first $450,000.
   (2) Long-term debt, greater than $450,000.
   (3) Preferred stock, all amounts.
   (4) Common stock equity, first $1,500,000.
   (5) Common stock equity, greater than $1,500,000.
b. Find the *break points* associated with each source of capital, and use them to specify each of the ranges of total new financing over which the firm's weighted average cost of capital (WACC) remains constant.
c. Calculate the weighted average cost of capital (WACC) over each of the ranges of total new financing specified in part **b**.
d. Using your findings in part **c** along with the investment opportunities schedule (IOS), draw the firm's weighted marginal cost of capital (WMCC)

and IOS on the same set of axes (total new financing or investment on the *x* axis and weighted average cost of capital and IRR on the *y* axis).

e. Which, if any, of the available investments would you recommend that the firm accept? Explain your answer.

SPREADSHEET EXERCISE

Nova Corporation is interested in measuring the cost of each specific type of capital as well as the weighted average cost of capital. Historically, the firm has raised capital in the following manner:

Source of capital	Weight
Long-term debt	35%
Preferred stock	12
Common stock equity	53

The tax rate of the firm is currently 40%. The needed financial information and data are as follows:

Debt Nova can raise an unlimited amount of debt by selling $1,000-par-value, 6.5% coupon interest rate, 10-year bonds on which *annual interest payments* will be made. To sell the issue, an average discount of $20 per bond needs to be given. There is an associated flotation cost of 2% of par value.

Preferred stock An unlimited amount of preferred stock can be sold under the following terms: The security has a par value of $100 per share, the annual dividend rate is 6% of the par value, and the floatation cost is expected to be $4 per share. The preferred stock is expected to sell for $102 before cost considerations.

Common stock The current price of Nova's common stock is $35 per share. The cash dividend is expected to be $3.25 per share next year. The firm's dividends have grown at an annual rate of 5%, and it is expected that the dividend will continue at this rate for the foreseeable future. The flotation costs are expected to be approximately $2 per share. Nova can sell an unlimited amount of new common stock under these terms.

Retained earnings The firm expects to have available $100,000 of retained earnings in the coming year. Once these retained earnings are exhausted, the firm will use new common stock as the form of common stock equity financing. (*Note:* When measuring this cost, the firm does not concern itself with the tax bracket or brokerage fees of owners.)

TO DO

Create a spreadsheet to answer the following questions:

a. Calculate the specific cost of *each source of financing*. (Round answers to the nearest 0.1%.)

b. Calculate the single *break point* associated with the firm's financial situation. This point results from exhaustion of the firm's retained earnings.

c. Calculate the *weighted average cost of capital (WACC)* associated with total financing *below* the break point calculated in part **b**.
d. Calculate the *weighted average cost of capital (WACC)* associated with total financing *above* the break point calculated in part **b**.

WEB EXERCISE

This chapter uses the cost of capital to introduce the topic of long-term financial decisions. The place to begin any of this analysis is the applicable rate of interest. In that vein, we will again review different market rates of interest.

TO DO

a. Point your browser to www.bankrate.com/brm/default.asp. This Web site provides a myriad of current interest rates for all types of financing decisions. Your assignment is simply to wade through the information and retrieve the recent rates for several types of borrowing. Report the recent rates across as many types of loans as you can find.
b. Describe the recent trend you observe in rates.

Remember to check the book's Web site at

www.aw-bc.com/gitman

for additional resources, including additional Web exercises.

Chapter 11

Leverage and Capital Structure

LEARNING GOALS

LG1 Discuss leverage, capital structure, break-even analysis, the operating breakeven point, and the effect of changing costs on it.

LG2 Understand operating, financial, and total leverage and the relationships among them.

LG3 Describe the types of capital, external assessment of capital structure, the capital structure of non-U.S. firms, and capital structure theory.

LG4 Explain the optimal capital structure using a graphical view of the firm's cost-of-capital functions and a zero-growth valuation model.

LG5 Discuss the EBIT–EPS approach to capital structure.

LG6 Review the return and risk of alternative capital structures, their linkage to market value, and other important considerations related to capital structure.

Across the Disciplines Why This Chapter Matters to You

Accounting: You need to understand how to calculate and analyze operating and financial leverage and to be familiar with the tax and earnings effects of various capital structures.

Information systems: You need to understand the types of capital and what capital structure is, because you will provide much of the information needed in management's determination of the best capital structure for the firm.

Management: You need to understand leverage so that you can control risk and magnify returns for the firm's owners and to understand capital structure theory so that you can make decisions about the firm's optimal capital structure.

Marketing: You need to understand breakeven analysis, which you will use in pricing and product feasibility decisions.

Operations: You need to understand the impact of fixed and variable operating costs on the firm's breakeven point and its operating leverage, because these costs will have a major impact on the firm's risk and return.

everage involves the use of fixed costs to magnify returns. Its use in the capital structure of the firm has the potential to increase its return and risk. Leverage and capital structure are closely related concepts that are linked to capital budgeting decisions through the cost of capital. These concepts can be used to minimize the firm's cost of capital and maximize its owners' wealth. This chapter discusses leverage and capital-structure concepts and techniques and how the firm can use them to create the best capital structure.

Leverage

leverage
Results from the use of fixed-cost assets or funds to magnify returns to the firm's owners.

capital structure
The mix of long-term debt and equity maintained by the firm.

Leverage results from the use of fixed-cost assets or funds to magnify returns to the firm's owners. Generally, increases in leverage result in increased return and risk, whereas decreases in leverage result in decreased return and risk. The amount of leverage in the firm's **capital structure**—the mix of long-term debt and equity maintained by the firm—can significantly affect its value by affecting return and risk. Unlike some causes of risk, management has almost complete control over the risk introduced through the use of leverage. Because of its effect on value, the financial manager must understand how to measure and evaluate leverage, particularly when making capital structure decisions.

The three basic types of leverage can best be defined with reference to the firm's income statement, as shown in the general income statement format in Table 11.1.

- *Operating leverage* is concerned with the relationship between the firm's sales revenue and its earnings before interest and taxes, or EBIT. (EBIT is a descriptive label for *operating profits*.)

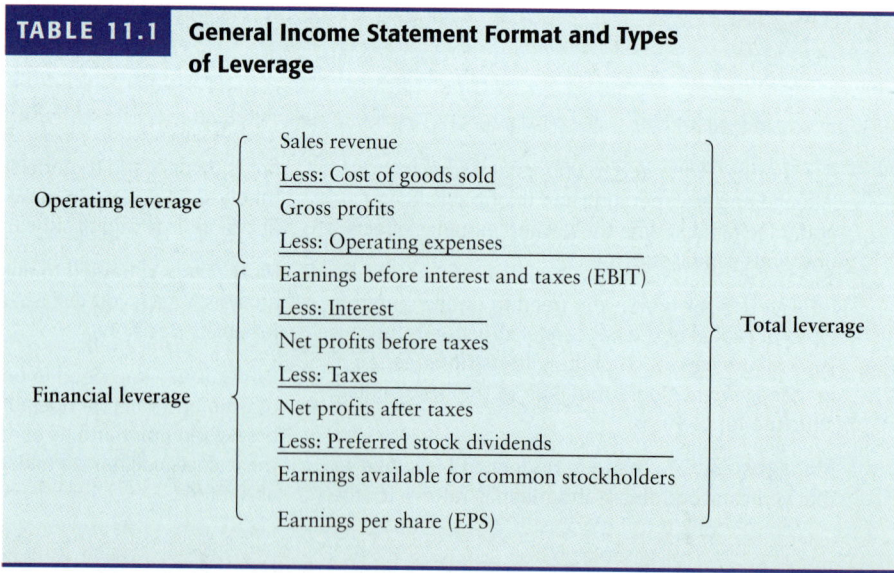

TABLE 11.1 General Income Statement Format and Types of Leverage

- *Financial leverage* is concerned with the relationship between the firm's EBIT and its common stock earnings per share (EPS).
- *Total leverage* is concerned with the relationship between the firm's sales revenue and EPS.

We will examine the three types of leverage concepts in detail in sections that follow. First, though, we will look at breakeven analysis, which lays the foundation for leverage concepts by demonstrating the effects of fixed costs on the firm's operations.

Breakeven Analysis

breakeven analysis
Indicates the level of operations necessary to cover all costs and the profitability associated with various levels of sales.

operating breakeven point
The level of sales necessary to cover all *operating costs;* the point at which EBIT = $0.

Breakeven analysis, sometimes called *cost-volume-profit analysis,* is used by the firm (1) to determine the level of operations necessary to cover all costs and (2) to evaluate the profitability associated with various levels of sales. The firm's **operating breakeven point** is the level of sales necessary to cover all *operating costs.* At that point, earnings before interest and taxes equals $0.[1]

The first step in finding the operating breakeven point is to divide the cost of goods sold and operating expenses into fixed and variable operating costs. *Fixed costs* are a function of time, not sales volume, and are typically contractual; rent, for example, is a fixed cost. *Variable costs* vary directly with sales and are a function of volume, not time; shipping costs, for example, are a variable cost.[2]

The Algebraic Approach

Using the following variables, we can recast the operating portion of the firm's income statement given in Table 11.1 into the algebraic representation shown in Table 11.2.

P = sale price per unit

Q = sales quantity in units

FC = fixed *operating* cost per period

VC = variable *operating* cost per unit

TABLE 11.2 Operating Leverage, Costs, and Breakeven Analysis

	Item	Algebraic representation
Operating leverage	Sales revenue	$(P \times Q)$
	Less: Fixed operating costs	$- FC$
	Less: Variable operating costs	$- (VC \times Q)$
	Earnings before interest and taxes	EBIT

---

1. Quite often, the breakeven point is calculated so that it represents the point at which *all costs*—both operating *and financial*—are covered. Our concern in this chapter is not with this overall breakeven point.

2. Some costs, commonly called *semifixed* or *semivariable,* are partly fixed and partly variable. An example is sales commissions that are fixed for a certain volume of sales and then increase to higher levels for higher volumes. For convenience and clarity, we assume that all costs can be classified as either fixed or variable.

Rewriting the algebraic calculations in Table 11.2 as a formula for earnings before interest and taxes yields Equation 11.1:

$$\text{EBIT} = (P \times Q) - FC - (VC \times Q) \qquad (11.1)$$

Simplifying Equation 11.1 yields

$$\text{EBIT} = Q \times (P - VC) - FC \qquad (11.2)$$

As noted above, the operating breakeven point is the level of sales at which all fixed and variable *operating costs* are covered—the level at which EBIT equals $0. Setting EBIT equal to $0 and solving Equation 11.2 for Q yield

$$Q = \frac{FC}{P - VC} \qquad (11.3)$$

Q is the firm's operating breakeven point.

EXAMPLE Assume that Cheryl's Posters, a small poster retailer, has fixed operating costs of $2,500, its sale price per unit (poster) is $10, and its variable operating cost per unit is $5. Applying Equation 11.3 to these data yields

$$Q = \frac{\$2,500}{\$10 - \$5} = \frac{\$2,500}{\$5} = 500 \text{ units}$$

At sales of 500 units, the firm's EBIT should just equal $0. The firm will have positive EBIT for sales greater than 500 units and negative EBIT, or a loss, for sales less than 500 units. We can confirm this by substituting values above and below 500 units, along with the other values given, into Equation 11.1.

The Graphical Approach

Figure 11.1 presents in graphical form the breakeven analysis of the data in the preceding example. The firm's operating breakeven point is the point at which its *total operating cost*—the sum of its fixed and variable operating costs—equals sales revenue. At this point, EBIT equals $0. The figure shows that for sales *below* 500 units, total operating cost exceeds sales revenue, and EBIT is less than $0 (a loss). For sales *above* the breakeven point of 500 units, sales revenue exceeds total operating cost, and EBIT is greater than $0.

Changing Costs and the Operating Breakeven Point

A firm's operating breakeven point is sensitive to a number of variables: fixed operating cost (FC), the sale price per unit (P), and the variable operating cost per unit (VC). The effects of increases or decreases in these variables can be readily seen by referring to Equation 11.3. The sensitivity of the breakeven sales volume (Q) to an *increase* in each of these variables is summarized in Table 11.3. As might be expected, an increase in cost (FC or VC) tends to increase the operating breakeven point, whereas an increase in the sale price per unit (P) decreases the operating breakeven point.

EXAMPLE Assume that Cheryl's Posters wishes to evaluate the impact of several options: (1) increasing fixed operating costs to $3,000, (2) increasing the sale price per unit to $12.50, (3) increasing the variable operating cost per unit to $7.50, and

FIGURE 11.1

Breakeven Analysis
Graphical operating breakeven analysis

(4) simultaneously implementing all three of these changes. Substituting the appropriate data into Equation 11.3 yields the following results:

(1) Operating breakeven point = $\dfrac{\$3{,}000}{\$10 - \$5} = 600$ units

(2) Operating breakeven point = $\dfrac{\$2{,}500}{\$12.50 - \$5} = 333\tfrac{1}{3}$ units

(3) Operating breakeven point = $\dfrac{\$2{,}500}{\$10 - \$7.50} = 1{,}000$ units

(4) Operating breakeven point = $\dfrac{\$3{,}000}{\$12.50 - \$7.50} = 600$ units

TABLE 11.3 Sensitivity of Operating Breakeven Point to Increases in Key Breakeven Variables

Increase in variable	Effect on operating breakeven point
Fixed operating cost *(FC)*	Increase
Sale price per unit *(P)*	Decrease
Variable operating cost per unit *(VC)*	Increase

Note: Decreases in each of the variables shown would have the opposite effect from their effect on operating breakeven point.

Comparing the resulting operating breakeven points to the initial value of 500 units, we can see that the cost increases (actions 1 and 3) raise the breakeven point, whereas the revenue increase (action 2) lowers the breakeven point. The combined effect of increasing all three variables (action 4) also results in an increased operating breakeven point.

We now turn our attention to the three types of leverage. It is important to recognize that the demonstrations of leverage that follow are conceptual in nature and that the measures presented are *not* routinely used by financial managers for decision-making purposes.

Operating Leverage

operating leverage
The potential use of *fixed operating costs* to magnify the effects of changes in sales on the firm's earnings before interest and taxes.

Operating leverage results from the existence of *fixed operating costs* in the firm's income stream. Using the structure presented in Table 11.2, we can define **operating leverage** as the potential use of *fixed operating costs* to magnify the effects of changes in sales on the firm's earnings before interest and taxes.

EXAMPLE

Using the data for Cheryl's Posters (sale price, $P = \$10$ per unit; variable operating cost, $VC = \$5$ per unit; fixed operating cost, $FC = \$2,500$), Figure 11.2 presents the operating breakeven graph originally shown in Figure 11.1. The additional notations on the graph indicate that as the firm's sales increase from 1,000 to 1,500 units (Q_1 to Q_2), its EBIT increases from \$2,500 to \$5,000 ($EBIT_1$ to $EBIT_2$). In other words, a 50% increase in sales (1,000 to 1,500 units)

FIGURE 11.2

Operating Leverage
Breakeven analysis and operating leverage

TABLE 11.4 The EBIT for Various Sales Levels

	Case 2		Case 1
	−50% ←	→	+50%
Sales (in units)	500	1,000	1,500
Sales revenue[a]	$5,000	$10,000	$15,000
Less: Variable operating costs[b]	2,500	5,000	7,500
Less: Fixed operating costs	2,500	2,500	2,500
Earnings before interest and taxes (EBIT)	$ 0	$ 2,500	$ 5,000
	−100% ←	→	+100%

[a]Sales revenue = $10/unit × sales in units.
[b]Variable operating costs = $5/unit × sales in units.

results in a 100% increase in EBIT ($2,500 to $5,000). Table 11.4 includes the data for Figure 11.2 as well as relevant data for a 500-unit sales level. We can illustrate two cases using the 1,000-unit sales level as a reference point.

Case 1 A 50% *increase* in sales (from 1,000 to 1,500 units) results in a 100% *increase* in earnings before interest and taxes (from $2,500 to $5,000).

Case 2 A 50% *decrease* in sales (from 1,000 to 500 units) results in a 100% *decrease* in earnings before interest and taxes (from $2,500 to $0).

From the preceding example, we see that operating leverage works in *both directions*. When a firm has fixed operating costs, operating leverage is present. An increase in sales results in a more-than-proportional increase in EBIT; a decrease in sales results in a more-than-proportional decrease in EBIT.

Measuring the Degree of Operating Leverage (DOL)

degree of operating leverage (DOL)
The numerical measure of the firm's operating leverage.

The **degree of operating leverage (DOL)** is the numerical measure of the firm's operating leverage. It can be derived using the following equation:[3]

$$\text{DOL} = \frac{\text{Percentage change in EBIT}}{\text{Percentage change in sales}} \quad (11.4)$$

Whenever the percentage change in EBIT resulting from a given percentage change in sales is greater than the percentage change in sales, operating leverage exists. This means that as long as DOL is greater than 1, there is operating leverage.

---

3. The degree of operating leverage also depends on the base level of sales used as a point of reference. The closer the base sales level used is to the operating breakeven point, the greater the operating leverage. *Comparison of the degree of operating leverage of two firms is valid only when the same base level of sales is used for both firms.*

EXAMPLE

Applying Equation 11.4 to cases 1 and 2 in Table 11.4 yields the following results:[4]

$$\text{Case 1:} \quad \frac{+100\%}{+50\%} = 2.0$$

$$\text{Case 2:} \quad \frac{-100\%}{-50\%} = 2.0$$

Because the result is greater than 1, operating leverage exists. For a given base level of sales, the higher the value resulting from applying Equation 11.4, the greater the degree of operating leverage. ■

A more direct formula for calculating the degree of operating leverage at a base sales level, Q, is shown in Equation 11.5.

$$\text{DOL at base sales level } Q = \frac{Q \times (P - VC)}{Q \times (P - VC) - FC} \quad (11.5)$$

EXAMPLE

Substituting $Q = 1{,}000$, $P = \$10$, $VC = \$5$, and $FC = \$2{,}500$ into Equation 11.5 yields the following result:

$$\text{DOL at 1,000 units} = \frac{1{,}000 \times (\$10 - \$5)}{1{,}000 \times (\$10 - \$5) - \$2{,}500} = \frac{\$5{,}000}{\$2{,}500} = 2.0$$

The use of the formula results in the same value for DOL (2.0) as that found by using Table 11.4 and Equation 11.4.[5] ■

See the *In Practice* box on the facing page for discussion of operating leverage at software maker Adobe.

Fixed Costs and Operating Leverage

Changes in fixed operating costs affect operating leverage significantly. Firms sometimes can incur fixed operating costs rather than variable operating costs and at other times may be able to substitute one type of cost for the other. For example, a firm could make fixed-dollar lease payments rather than payments equal to a specified percentage of sales. Or it could compensate sales representatives with a fixed salary and bonus rather than on a pure percent-of-sales commission basis. The effects of changes in fixed operating costs on operating leverage can best be illustrated by continuing our example.

---

4. Because the concept of leverage is *linear*, positive and negative changes of equal magnitude will always result in equal degrees of leverage when the same base sales level is used as a point of reference. This relationship holds for all types of leverage discussed in this chapter.

5. When total revenue in dollars from sales—instead of unit sales—is available, the following equation, in which TR = total revenue in dollars at a base level of sales and TVC = total variable operating costs in dollars, can be used:

$$\text{DOL at base dollar sales } TR = \frac{TR - TVC}{TR - TVC - FC}$$

This formula is especially useful for finding the DOL for multiproduct firms. It should be clear that because in the case of a single-product firm, $TR = P \times Q$ and $TVC = VC \times Q$, substitution of these values into Equation 11.5 results in the equation given here.

In Practice FOCUS ON PRACTICE

ADOBE'S OPERATING LEVERAGE

Adobe Systems, the second largest PC software company in the United States, dominates the markets for graphic design, imaging, dynamic media, and authoring-tool software. Web site designers prefer its Photoshop and Illustrator software applications, and Adobe's Acrobat software has become a standard for sharing documents online.

Despite a sales slowdown in 2001–2002, the company continued to meet its earnings targets. Its ability to manage discretionary expenses helped to keep its bottom line strong. As a software company, Adobe has an additional advantage: *operating leverage,* the use of fixed operating costs to magnify the effects of changes in sales on earnings before interest and taxes (EBIT).

Adobe and its peers in the software industry incur the bulk of their costs early in a product's life cycle, during the research and development (R&D) and initial marketing stages. The up-front development costs are fixed, regardless of how many copies of a program the company sells, and subsequent production costs are practically zero. The economies of scale are huge. Indeed, once a company sells enough copies to cover its fixed costs, incremental dollars go primarily to profit.

As demonstrated in the table below, operating leverage magnified the *increase* in Adobe's EBIT in 2000 and 2003 while magnifying the *decrease* in EBIT in 2001 and 2002. A 2.8 percent drop in 2001 sales resulted in an EBIT reduction of 7.3 percent. In 2002, an additional drop in sales of 5.3 percent resulted in a 24.1 percent decrease in EBIT. In 2003, a modest increase in sales—just over 11 percent—turned into a 32 percent increase in EBIT. Because the company has no long-term debt in its capital structure, its total leverage is derived only from fixed operating costs.

(It's important to remember that this example represents only 4 years of data and that Adobe's degree of operating leverage may change in the future.)

The table below demonstrates the impact of operating leverage on Adobe Systems in fiscal years (FYs) 2000–2003.

Sources: Adapted from Zeke Ashton, "The Software Advantage," *Motley Fool* (March 31, 2000); and "Operating Leverage Helps Adobe," *Motley Fool* (March 16, 2001), both downloaded from www.motley.fool.com; updated using data from Adobe's 2003 Annual Report.

■ What events might have accelerated the degree of operating leverage for Adobe in 2002?

Item	FY1999	FY2000	FY2001	FY2002	FY2003
Sales revenue (millions)	$1,015	$1,266	$1,230	$1,165	$1,295
EBIT (millions)	$260	$408	$378	$287	$379
(1) Percent change in sales		24.7%	−2.8%	−5.3%	11.2%
(2) Percent change in EBIT		56.9%	−7.3%	−24.1%	32.0%
DOL [(2) ÷ (1)]		2.3	2.6	4.5	2.6

EXAMPLE

Assume that Cheryl's Posters exchanges a portion of its variable operating costs for fixed operating costs by eliminating sales commissions and increasing sales salaries. This exchange results in a reduction in the variable operating cost per unit from $5 to $4.50 and an increase in the fixed operating costs from $2,500 to $3,000. Table 11.5 (see page 446) presents an analysis like that in Table 11.4, but using the new costs. Although the EBIT of $2,500 at the 1,000-unit sales level is the same as before the shift in operating cost structure, Table 11.5 shows that the firm has increased its operating leverage by shifting to greater fixed operating costs.

TABLE 11.5   Operating Leverage and Increased Fixed Costs

	Case 2		Case 1
	−50% ←		→ +50%
Sales (in units)	500	1,000	1,500
Sales revenue[a]	$5,000	$10,000	$15,000
Less: Variable operating costs[b]	2,250	4,500	6,750
Less: Fixed operating costs	3,000	3,000	3,000
Earnings before interest and taxes (EBIT)	−$ 250	$ 2,500	$ 5,250
	−110% ←		→ +110%

[a] Sales revenue was calculated as indicated in Table 11.4.
[b] Variable operating costs = $4.50/unit × sales in units.

With the substitution of the appropriate values into Equation 11.5, the degree of operating leverage at the 1,000-unit base level of sales becomes

$$\text{DOL at 1,000 units} = \frac{1{,}000 \times (\$10 - \$4.50)}{1{,}000 \times (\$10 - \$4.50) - \$3{,}000} = \frac{\$5{,}500}{\$2{,}500} = 2.2$$

Comparing this value to the DOL of 2.0 before the shift to more fixed costs makes it is clear that the higher the firm's fixed operating costs relative to variable operating costs, the greater the degree of operating leverage. ■

Financial Leverage

Financial leverage results from the presence of *fixed financial costs* in the firm's income stream. Using the framework in Table 11.1, we can define **financial leverage** as the potential use of *fixed financial costs* to magnify the effects of changes in earnings before interest and taxes on the firm's earnings per share. The two fixed financial costs that may be found on the firm's income statement are (1) interest on debt and (2) preferred stock dividends. These charges must be paid regardless of the amount of EBIT available to pay them.[6]

financial leverage
The potential use of *fixed financial costs* to magnify the effects of changes in earnings before interest and taxes on the firm's earnings per share.

EXAMPLE   Chen Foods, a small Asian food company, expects EBIT of $10,000 in the current year. It has a $20,000 bond with a 10% (annual) coupon rate of interest and an issue of 600 shares of $4 (annual dividend per share) preferred stock outstanding. It also has 1,000 shares of common stock outstanding. The annual interest on the bond issue is $2,000 (0.10 × $20,000). The annual dividends on the preferred

---

[6]. As noted in Chapter 7, although preferred stock dividends can be "passed" (not paid) at the option of the firm's directors, it is generally believed that payment of such dividends is necessary. *This text treats the preferred stock dividend as a contractual obligation, not only to be paid as a fixed amount, but also to be paid as scheduled.* Although failure to pay preferred dividends cannot force the firm into bankruptcy, it increases the common stockholders' risk because they cannot be paid dividends until the claims of preferred stockholders are satisfied.

TABLE 11.6 The EPS for Various EBIT Levels[a]

	Case 2		Case 1
	−40%		+40%
EBIT	$6,000	$10,000	$14,000
Less: Interest (I)	2,000	2,000	2,000
Net profits before taxes	$4,000	$ 8,000	$12,000
Less: Taxes (T = 0.40)	1,600	3,200	4,800
Net profits after taxes	$2,400	$ 4,800	$ 7,200
Less: Preferred stock dividends (PD)	2,400	2,400	2,400
Earnings available for common (EAC)	$ 0	$ 2,400	$ 4,800
Earnings per share (EPS)	$\frac{\$0}{1,000} = \$0$	$\frac{\$2,400}{1,000} = \$2.40$	$\frac{\$4,800}{1,000} = \$4.80$
	−100%		+100%

[a]As noted in Chapter 1, for accounting and tax purposes, interest is a *tax-deductible expense,* whereas dividends must be paid from after-tax cash flows.

stock are $2,400 ($4.00/share × 600 shares). Table 11.6 presents the EPS corresponding to levels of EBIT of $6,000, $10,000, and $14,000, assuming that the firm is in the 40% tax bracket. Two situations are shown:

Case 1   A 40% *increase* in EBIT (from $10,000 to $14,000) results in a 100% *increase* in earnings per share (from $2.40 to $4.80).

Case 2   A 40% *decrease* in EBIT (from $10,000 to $6,000) results in a 100% *decrease* in earnings per share (from $2.40 to $0).

The effect of financial leverage is such that an increase in the firm's EBIT results in a more-than-proportional increase in the firm's earnings per share, whereas a decrease in the firm's EBIT results in a more-than-proportional decrease in EPS.

Measuring the Degree of Financial Leverage (DFL)

degree of financial leverage (DFL)
The numerical measure of the firm's financial leverage.

The **degree of financial leverage (DFL)** is the numerical measure of the firm's financial leverage. Computing it is much like computing the degree of operating leverage. The following equation presents one approach for obtaining the DFL.[7]

$$\text{DFL} = \frac{\text{Percentage change in EPS}}{\text{Percentage change in EBIT}} \tag{11.6}$$

Whenever the percentage change in EPS resulting from a given percentage change in EBIT is greater than the percentage change in EBIT, financial leverage exists. This means that whenever DFL is greater than 1, there is financial leverage.

---

7. This approach is valid only when the same base level of EBIT is used to calculate and compare these values. In other words, *the base level of EBIT must be held constant to compare the financial leverage associated with different levels of fixed financial costs.*

EXAMPLE

Applying Equation 11.6 to cases 1 and 2 in Table 11.6 yields

$$\text{Case 1: } \frac{+100\%}{+40\%} = 2.5$$

$$\text{Case 2: } \frac{-100\%}{-40\%} = 2.5$$

In both cases, the quotient is greater than 1, so financial leverage exists. The higher this value, the greater the degree of financial leverage. ■

A more direct formula for calculating the degree of financial leverage at a base level of EBIT is given by Equation 11.7, where the notation from Table 11.6 is used. Note that in the denominator, the term $1/(1 - T)$ converts the after-tax preferred stock dividend to a before-tax amount for consistency with the other terms in the equation.

$$\text{DFL at base level EBIT} = \frac{\text{EBIT}}{\text{EBIT} - I - \left(PD \times \frac{1}{1-T}\right)} \quad (11.7)$$

EXAMPLE

Substituting EBIT = $10,000, I = $2,000, PD = $2,400, and the tax rate (T = 0.40) into Equation 11.7 yields the following result:

$$\text{DFL at } \$10{,}000 \text{ EBIT} = \frac{\$10{,}000}{\$10{,}000 - \$2{,}000 - \left(\$2{,}400 \times \frac{1}{1 - 0.40}\right)}$$

$$= \frac{\$10{,}000}{\$4{,}000} = 2.5 \quad \blacksquare$$

Note that the formula given in Equation 11.7 provides a more direct method for calculating the degree of financial leverage than the approach illustrated using Table 11.6 and Equation 11.6.

Total Leverage

We also can assess the combined effect of operating and financial leverage on the firm's risk by using a framework similar to that used to develop the individual concepts of leverage. This combined effect, or **total leverage**, can be defined as the potential use of *fixed costs, both operating and financial,* to magnify the effects of changes in sales on the firm's earnings per share. Total leverage can therefore be viewed as the *total impact of the fixed costs* in the firm's operating and financial structure.

total leverage
The potential use of *fixed costs, both operating and financial,* to magnify the effects of changes in sales on the firm's earnings per share.

EXAMPLE

Cables Inc., a computer cable manufacturer, expects sales of 20,000 units at $5 per unit in the coming year and must meet the following obligations: variable operating costs of $2 per unit, fixed operating costs of $10,000, interest of $20,000, and preferred stock dividends of $12,000. The firm is in the 40% tax bracket and has 5,000 shares of common stock outstanding. Table 11.7 presents

TABLE 11.7 The Total Leverage Effect

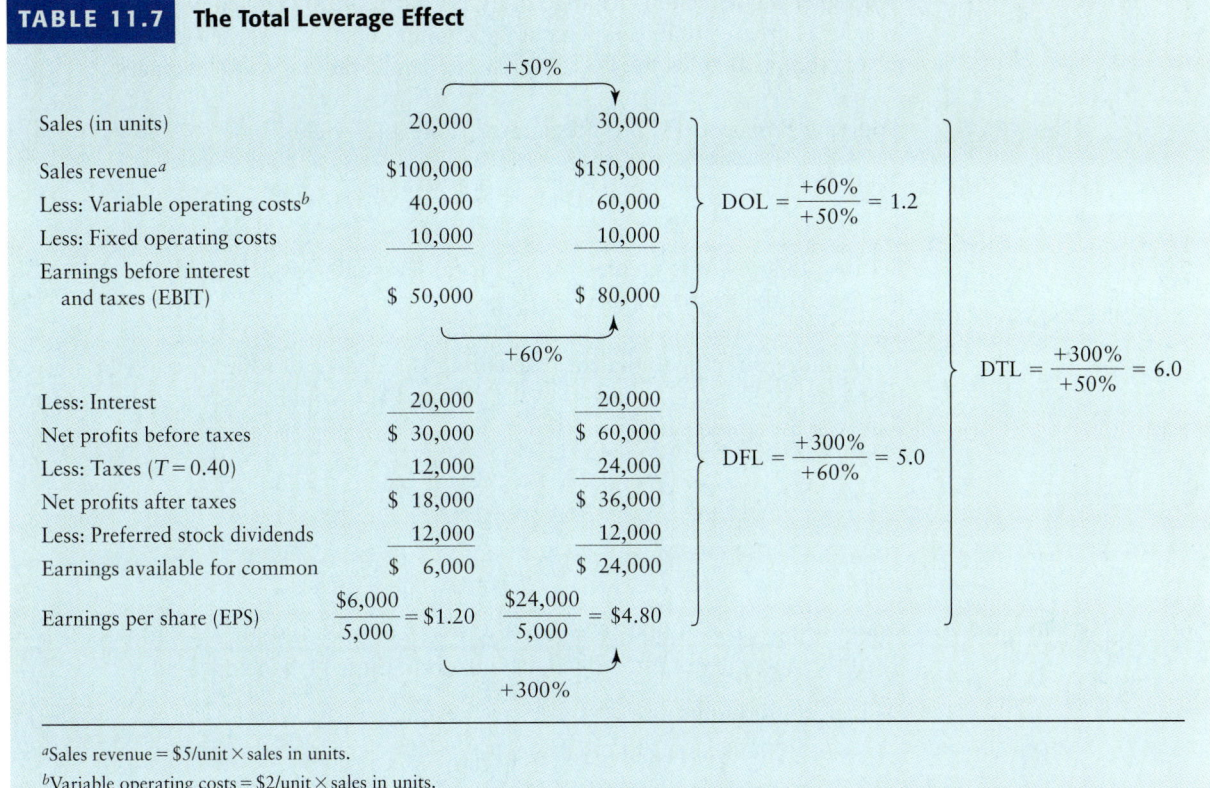

^aSales revenue = $5/unit × sales in units.
^bVariable operating costs = $2/unit × sales in units.

the levels of earnings per share associated with the expected sales of 20,000 units and with sales of 30,000 units.

The table illustrates that as a result of a 50% increase in sales (from 20,000 to 30,000 units), the firm would experience a 300% increase in earnings per share (from $1.20 to $4.80). Although it is not shown in the table, a 50% decrease in sales would, conversely, result in a 300% decrease in earnings per share. The linear nature of the leverage relationship accounts for the fact that sales changes of equal magnitude in opposite directions result in EPS changes of equal magnitude in the corresponding direction. At this point, it should be clear that whenever a firm has fixed costs—operating or financial—in its structure, total leverage will exist.

Measuring the Degree of Total Leverage (DTL)

degree of total leverage (DTL)
The numerical measure of the firm's total leverage.

The **degree of total leverage (DTL)** is the numerical measure of the firm's total leverage. It can be computed much as operating and financial leverage are computed. The following equation presents one approach for measuring DTL:[8]

$$\text{DTL} = \frac{\text{Percentage change in EPS}}{\text{Percentage change in sales}} \qquad (11.8)$$

---

8. This approach is valid only when the same base level of sales is used to calculate and compare these values. In other words, *the base level of sales must be held constant if we are to compare the total leverage associated with different levels of fixed costs.*

Whenever the percentage change in EPS resulting from a given percentage change in sales is greater than the percentage change in sales, total leverage exists. This means that as long as the DTL is greater than 1, there is total leverage.

EXAMPLE

Applying Equation 11.8 to the data in Table 11.7 yields

$$\text{DTL} = \frac{+300\%}{+50\%} = 6.0$$

Because this result is greater than 1, total leverage exists. The higher the value, the greater the degree of total leverage.

A more direct formula for calculating the degree of total leverage at a given base level of sales, Q, is given by Equation 11.9, which uses the same notation that was presented earlier:

$$\text{DTL at base sales level } Q = \frac{Q \times (P - VC)}{Q \times (P - VC) - FC - I - \left(PD \times \dfrac{1}{1 - T}\right)} \quad (11.9)$$

EXAMPLE

Substituting $Q = 20{,}000$, $P = \$5$, $VC = \$2$, $FC = \$10{,}000$, $I = \$20{,}000$, $PD = \$12{,}000$, and the tax rate ($T = 0.40$) into Equation 11.9 yields

DTL at 20,000 units

$$= \frac{20{,}000 \times (\$5 - \$2)}{20{,}000 \times (\$5 - \$2) - \$10{,}000 - \$20{,}000 - \left(\$12{,}000 \times \dfrac{1}{1 - 0.40}\right)}$$

$$= \frac{\$60{,}000}{\$10{,}000} = 6.0$$

Clearly, the formula used in Equation 11.9 provides a more direct method for calculating the degree of total leverage than the approach illustrated using Table 11.7 and Equation 11.8.

The Relationship of Operating, Financial, and Total Leverage

Total leverage reflects the *combined impact* of operating and financial leverage on the firm. High operating leverage and high financial leverage will cause total leverage to be high. The opposite will also be true. The relationship between operating leverage and financial leverage is *multiplicative* rather than *additive*. The relationship between the degree of total leverage (DTL) and the degrees of operating leverage (DOL) and financial leverage (DFL) is given by Equation 11.10.

$$\text{DTL} = \text{DOL} \times \text{DFL} \quad (11.10)$$

EXAMPLE

Substituting the values calculated for DOL and DFL, shown on the right-hand side of Table 11.7, into Equation 11.10 yields

$$\text{DTL} = 1.2 \times 5.0 = 6.0$$

The resulting degree of total leverage is the same value that we calculated directly in the preceding examples.

Review Questions

11–1 What is meant by the term *leverage*? How are operating leverage, financial leverage, and total leverage related to the income statement?

11–2 What is the *operating breakeven point*? How do changes in fixed operating costs, the sale price per unit, and the variable operating cost per unit affect it?

11–3 What is *operating leverage*? What causes it? How is the *degree of operating leverage (DOL)* measured?

11–4 What is *financial leverage*? What causes it? How is the *degree of financial leverage (DFL)* measured?

11–5 What is the general relationship among operating leverage, financial leverage, and the total leverage of the firm? Do these types of leverage complement one another? Why or why not?

The Firm's Capital Structure

Capital structure is one of the most complex areas of financial decision making because of its interrelationship with other financial decision variables.[9] Poor capital structure decisions can result in a high cost of capital, thereby lowering the NPVs of projects and making more of them unacceptable. Effective capital structure decisions can lower the cost of capital, resulting in higher NPVs and more acceptable projects—and thereby increasing the value of the firm. This section links together many of the concepts presented in Chapters 4, 5, 6, 7, and 10 and the discussion of leverage in this chapter.

Types of Capital

All of the items on the right-hand side of the firm's balance sheet, excluding current liabilities, are sources of capital. The following simplified balance sheet illustrates the basic breakdown of total capital into its two components, *debt capital* and *equity capital*.

---

9. Of course, although capital structure is financially important, it—like many business decisions—is generally not so important as the firm's products or services. In a practical sense, a firm can probably more readily increase its value by improving quality and reducing costs than by fine-tuning its capital structure.

The various types and characteristics of *corporate bonds,* a major source of *debt capital,* were discussed in detail in Chapter 6. The cost of debt is lower than the cost of other forms of financing. Lenders demand relatively lower returns because they take the least risk of any long-term contributors of capital: (1) They have a higher priority of claim against any earnings or assets available for payment. (2) They can exert far greater legal pressure against the company to make payment than can owners of preferred or common stock. (3) The tax deductibility of interest payments lowers the debt cost to the firm substantially.

Unlike debt capital, which must be repaid at some future date, *equity capital* is expected to remain in the firm for an indefinite period of time. The two basic sources of equity capital are (1) preferred stock and (2) common stock equity, which includes common stock and retained earnings. Common stock is typically the most expensive form of equity, followed by retained earnings and then preferred stock. Our concern here is the relationship between debt and equity capital. Key differences between these two types of capital, relative to voice in management, claims on income and assets, maturity, and tax treatment, were summarized in Chapter 7, Table 7.1. Because of equity's secondary position relative to debt, suppliers of equity capital take greater risk than suppliers of debt capital and therefore must be compensated with higher expected returns.

External Assessment of Capital Structure

We saw earlier that *financial leverage* results from the use of fixed-cost financing, such as debt and preferred stock, to magnify return and risk. The amount of leverage in the firm's capital structure can affect its value by affecting return and risk. Those outside the firm can make a rough assessment of capital structure by using measures found in the firm's financial statements. Some of these important debt ratios were presented in Chapter 2. For example, a direct measure of the degree of indebtedness is the *debt ratio.* The higher this ratio, the greater the relative amount of debt (or financial leverage) in the firm's capital structure. Measures of the firm's ability to meet contractual payments associated with debt include the *times interest earned ratio* and the *fixed-payment coverage ratio.* These ratios provide indirect information on financial leverage. Generally, the smaller these ratios, the greater the firm's financial leverage and the less able it is to meet payments as they come due.

The level of debt (financial leverage) that is acceptable for one industry or line of business can be highly risky in another, because different industries and lines of business have different operating characteristics. Table 11.8 presents the debt and times interest earned ratios for selected industries and lines of business. Significant industry differences can be seen in these data. Differences in debt positions are also likely to exist *within* an industry or line of business.

Capital Structure of Non-U.S. Firms

In general, non-U.S. companies have much higher degrees of indebtedness than their U.S. counterparts. Most of the reasons for this are related to the fact that U.S. capital markets have played a greater role in corporate financing than has been the case in other countries. In most European countries and especially in Japan and other Pacific Rim nations, large commercial banks are more actively

TABLE 11.8	Debt Ratios for Selected Industries and Lines of Business (Fiscal Years Ended 4/1/02 Through 3/31/03)	
Industry or line of business	Debt ratio	Times interest earned ratio
Manufacturing industries		
Books	75.1%	3.4
Dairy products	73.8	4.1
Electronic computers	59.2	2.1
Iron and steel forgings	70.0	1.9
Machine tools, metal cutting types	65.4	1.3
Wines and distilled alcoholic beverages	65.7	4.8
Women's and girls' dresses	66.0	4.2
Wholesaling industries		
Furniture	67.2	2.3
General groceries	68.3	3.5
Men's and boys' clothing	63.0	4.4
Retailing industries		
Department stores	57.6	4.4
New car dealers	80.1	3.0
Supermarkets and grocery stores	75.6	2.9
Service industries		
Advertising agencies	87.9	4.3
General automotive repair	75.8	2.6
Insurance agencies and brokerages	85.1	4.8
Offices of Certified Public Accountants	70.4	7.2

Source: RMA Annual Statement Studies, 2003–2004 (fiscal years ended 4/1/02 through 3/31/03) (Philadelphia: Risk Management Association, 2003). Copyright © 2003 by Risk Management Association.

Note: The Risk Management Association recommends that these ratios be regarded only as general guidelines and not as absolute industry norms. No claim is made as to the representativeness of these figures.

involved in the financing of corporate activity than has been true in the United States. Furthermore, in many of these countries, banks are allowed to make large equity investments in nonfinancial corporations—a practice that is prohibited for U.S. banks. Finally, tight ownership among founding-family, institutional, and even public investors in Europe and Asia enables owners to understand the firm's financial condition better, resulting in their willingness to tolerate a higher degree of indebtedness.

On the other hand, similarities do exist between U.S. corporations and corporations in other countries. First, the same industry patterns of capital structure tend to be found all around the world. For example, in nearly all countries, pharmaceutical and other high-growth industrial firms tend to have lower debt ratios than do steel companies, airlines, and electric utility companies. Second, the capital structures of the largest U.S.-based multinational companies, which have access to many different capital markets around the world, typically resemble the capital structures of multinational companies from other countries more than they resemble those of smaller U.S. companies. Finally, the worldwide trend is away from reliance on banks for corporate financing and toward greater reliance on security issuance. Over time, the differences in the capital structures of U.S. and non-U.S. firms will probably lessen.

Capital Structure Theory

Scholarly research suggests that there is an optimal capital structure range. *It is not yet possible to provide financial managers with a specified methodology for use in determining a firm's optimal capital structure.* Nevertheless, financial theory does offer help in understanding how a firm's chosen financing mix affects the firm's value.

In 1958, Franco Modigliani and Merton H. Miller[10] (commonly known as "M and M") demonstrated algebraically that, assuming perfect markets,[11] the capital structure that a firm chooses does not affect its value. Many researchers, including M and M, have examined the effects of less restrictive assumptions on the relationship between capital structure and the firm's value. The result is a *theoretical* optimal capital structure based on balancing the benefits and costs of debt financing. The major benefit of debt financing is the tax shield, which allows interest payments to be deducted in calculating taxable income. The costs of debt financing result from (1) the increased probability of bankruptcy caused by debt obligations, (2) the *agency costs* of the lender's constraining the firm's actions, and (3) the costs associated with managers having more information about the firm's prospects than do investors.

Tax Benefits

Allowing firms to deduct interest payments on debt when calculating taxable income reduces the amount of the firm's earnings paid in taxes, thereby making more earnings available for bondholders and stockholders. The deductibility of interest means the cost of debt, k_i, to the firm is subsidized by the government. Letting k_d equal the before-tax cost of debt and letting T equal the tax rate, from Chapter 10 (Equation 10.2), we have $k_i = k_d \times (1 - T)$.

Probability of Bankruptcy

The chance that a firm will become bankrupt because of an inability to meet its obligations as they come due depends largely on its level of both business risk and financial risk.

Business Risk In Chapter 10, we defined *business risk* as the risk to the firm of being unable to cover its operating costs. In general, the greater the firm's *operating leverage*—the use of fixed operating costs—the higher its business risk. Although operating leverage is an important factor affecting business risk, two other factors—revenue stability and cost stability—also affect it.

---

10. Franco Modigliani and Merton H. Miller, "The Cost of Capital, Corporation Finance, and the Theory of Investment," *American Economic Review* (June 1958), pp. 261–297.

11. Perfect-market assumptions include (1) no taxes, (2) no brokerage or flotation costs for securities, (3) symmetrical information—investors and managers have the same information about the firm's investment prospects, and (4) investor ability to borrow at the same rate as corporations.

Revenue stability reflects the relative variability of the firm's sales revenues. Firms with reasonably stable levels of demand and with products that have stable prices have stable revenues. The result is low levels of business risk. Firms with highly volatile product demand and prices have unstable revenues that result in high levels of business risk.

Cost stability reflects the relative predictability of input prices such as those for labor and materials. The more predictable and stable these input prices are, the lower the business risk; the less predictable and stable they are, the higher the business risk.

Business risk varies among firms, regardless of their lines of business, and is not affected by capital structure decisions. The level of business risk must be taken as a "given." The higher a firm's business risk, the more cautious the firm must be in establishing its capital structure. Firms with high business risk therefore tend toward less highly leveraged capital structures; firms with low business risk tend toward more highly leveraged capital structures. We will hold business risk constant throughout the discussions that follow.

Financial Risk The firm's capital structure directly affects its *financial risk*, which is the risk to the firm of being unable to cover required financial obligations. The penalty for not meeting financial obligations is bankruptcy. The more fixed-cost financing—debt (including financial leases) and preferred stock—a firm has in its capital structure, the greater its financial leverage and risk. Financial risk depends on the capital structure decision made by the management, and that decision is affected by the business risk the firm faces. The *total risk* of a firm—business and financial risk combined—determines its probability of bankruptcy.

> **Hint** The cash flows to investors from bonds are less risky than the dividends from preferred stock, which are ess risky than dividends from common stock. Only with bonds is the issuer contractually obligated to pay the scheduled interest, and the amounts due to bondholders and preferred stockholders are usually fixed. Therefore, the required return for bonds is generally lower than that for preferred stock, which is lower than that for common stock.

Agency Costs Imposed by Lenders

As noted in Chapter 1, the managers of firms typically act as *agents* of the owners (stockholders). The owners give the managers the authority to manage the firm for the owners' benefit. The *agency problem* created by this relationship extends not only to the relationship between owners and managers but also to the relationship between owners and lenders.

When a lender provides funds to a firm, the interest rate charged is based on the lender's assessment of the firm's risk. The lender–borrower relationship, therefore, depends on the lender's expectations for the firm's subsequent behavior. The borrowing rates are locked in when the loans are negotiated. After obtaining a loan at a certain rate, the firm could increase its risk by investing in risky projects or by incurring additional debt. Such action could weaken the lender's position in terms of its claim on the cash flow of the firm. From another point of view, if these risky investment strategies paid off, the stockholders would benefit. Because payment obligations to the lender remain unchanged, the excess cash flows generated by a positive outcome from the riskier action would enhance the value of the firm to its owners. In other words, if the risky investments pay off, the owners receive all the benefits; if the risky investments do not pay off, the lenders share in the costs.

Clearly, an incentive exists for the managers acting on behalf of the stockholders to "take advantage" of lenders. To avoid this situation, lenders impose certain monitoring techniques on borrowers, who as a result incur *agency costs*. The most obvious strategy is to deny subsequent loan requests or to increase the cost of future loans to the firm. Because this strategy is an after-the-fact approach, other controls must be included in the loan agreement. Lenders typically protect themselves by including provisions that limit the firm's ability to alter significantly its business and financial risk. These loan provisions tend to center on issues such as the minimum level of liquidity, asset acquisitions, executive salaries, and dividend payments.

Hint Typical loan provisions included in corporate bonds are discussed in Chapter 6.

By including appropriate provisions in the loan agreement, the lender can control the firm's risk and thus protect itself against the adverse consequences of this agency problem. Of course, in exchange for incurring agency costs by agreeing to the operating and financial constraints placed on it by the loan provisions, the firm should benefit by obtaining funds at a reasonable cost.

Asymmetric Information

Two surveys examined capital structure decisions.[12] Financial executives were asked which of two major criteria determined their financing decisions: (1) maintaining a *target capital structure* or (2) following a hierarchy of financing. This hierarchy, called a **pecking order,** begins with retained earnings, which is followed by debt financing and finally external equity financing. Respondents from 31 percent of *Fortune* 500 firms and from 11 percent of the (smaller) 500 largest over-the-counter firms answered target capital structure. Respondents from 69 percent of the *Fortune* 500 firms and 89 percent of the 500 largest OTC firms chose the pecking order.

pecking order
A hierarchy of financing that begins with retained earnings, which is followed by debt financing and finally external equity financing.

At first glance, on the basis of financial theory, this choice appears to be inconsistent with wealth maximization goals, but Stewart Myers has explained how "asymmetric information" could account for the pecking order financing preferences of financial managers.[13] **Asymmetric information** results when managers of a firm have more information about operations and future prospects than do investors. Assuming that managers make decisions with the goal of maximizing the wealth of existing stockholders, then asymmetric information can affect the capital structure decisions that managers make.

asymmetric information
The situation in which managers of a firm have more information about operations and future prospects than do investors.

Suppose, for example, that management has found a valuable investment that will require additional financing. Management believes that the prospects for the firm's future are very good and that the market, as indicated by the firm's current stock price, does not fully appreciate the firm's value. In this case, it would be advantageous to current stockholders if management raised the required funds using debt rather than issuing new stock. Using debt to raise funds is frequently viewed as a **signal** that reflects management's view of the firm's stock value. Debt financing is a *positive signal* suggesting that management believes that the stock is "undervalued" and therefore a bargain. When the firm's positive future outlook becomes known to the market, the increased value will be fully captured by existing owners, rather than having to be shared with new stockholders.

signal
A financing action by management that is believed to reflect its view of the firm's stock value; generally, debt financing is viewed as a *positive signal* that management believes the stock is "undervalued," and a stock issue is viewed as a *negative signal* that management believes the stock is "overvalued."

If, however, the outlook for the firm is poor, management may believe that the firm's stock is "overvalued." In that case, it would be in the best interest of

---

12. The results of the survey of *Fortune* 500 firms are reported in J. Michael Pinegar and Lisa Wilbricht, "What Managers Think of Capital Structure Theory: A Survey," *Financial Management* (Winter 1989), pp. 82–91, and the results of a similar survey of the 500 largest OTC firms are reported in Linda C. Hittle, Kamal Haddad, and Lawrence J. Gitman, "Over-the-Counter Firms, Asymmetric Information, and Financing Preferences," *Review of Financial Economics* (Fall 1992), pp. 81–92.

13. Stewart C. Myers, "The Capital Structure Puzzle," *Journal of Finance* (July 1984), pp. 575–592.

existing stockholders for the firm to issue new stock. Therefore, investors often interpret the announcement of a stock issue as a *negative signal*—bad news concerning the firm's prospects—and the stock price declines. This decrease in stock value, along with high underwriting costs for stock issues (compared to debt issues), make new stock financing very expensive. When the negative future outlook becomes known to the market, the decreased value is shared with new stockholders, rather than being fully captured by existing owners.

Because conditions of asymmetric information exist from time to time, firms should maintain some reserve borrowing capacity by keeping debt levels low. This reserve allows the firm to take advantage of good investment opportunities without having to sell stock at a low value and thus send signals that unduly influence the stock price.

The Optimal Capital Structure

What, then, *is* the optimal capital structure, even if it exists (so far) only in theory? To provide some insight into an answer, we will examine some basic financial relationships. It is generally believed that *the value of the firm is maximized when the cost of capital is minimized.* By using a modification of the simple zero-growth valuation model (see Equation 7.2 in Chapter 7), we can define the value of the firm, V, by Equation 11.11.

$$V = \frac{EBIT \times (1 - T)}{k_a} = \frac{NOPAT}{k_a} \qquad (11.11)$$

where

$EBIT$ = earnings before interest and taxes

T = tax rate

$NOPAT$ = net operating profits after taxes, which (as noted in Chapters 3 and 8) is the after-tax operating earnings available to the debt and equity holders, $EBIT \times (1 - T)$

k_a = weighted average cost of capital

Clearly, if we assume that NOPAT (and therefore EBIT) is constant, the value of the firm, V, is maximized by minimizing the weighted average cost of capital, k_a.

Cost Functions

Figure 11.3(a) (see page 458) plots three cost functions—the cost of debt, the cost of equity, and the weighted average cost of capital (WACC)—as a function of financial leverage measured by the debt ratio (debt to total assets). The *cost of debt*, k_i, remains low because of the tax shield, but it slowly increases as leverage increases, to compensate lenders for increasing risk. The *cost of equity*, k_s, is above the cost of debt. It increases as financial leverage increases, but it generally increases more rapidly than the cost of debt. The cost of equity rises because the stockholders require a higher return as leverage increases, to compensate for the higher degree of financial risk.

FIGURE 11.3

Cost Functions and Value
Capital costs and the optimal capital structure

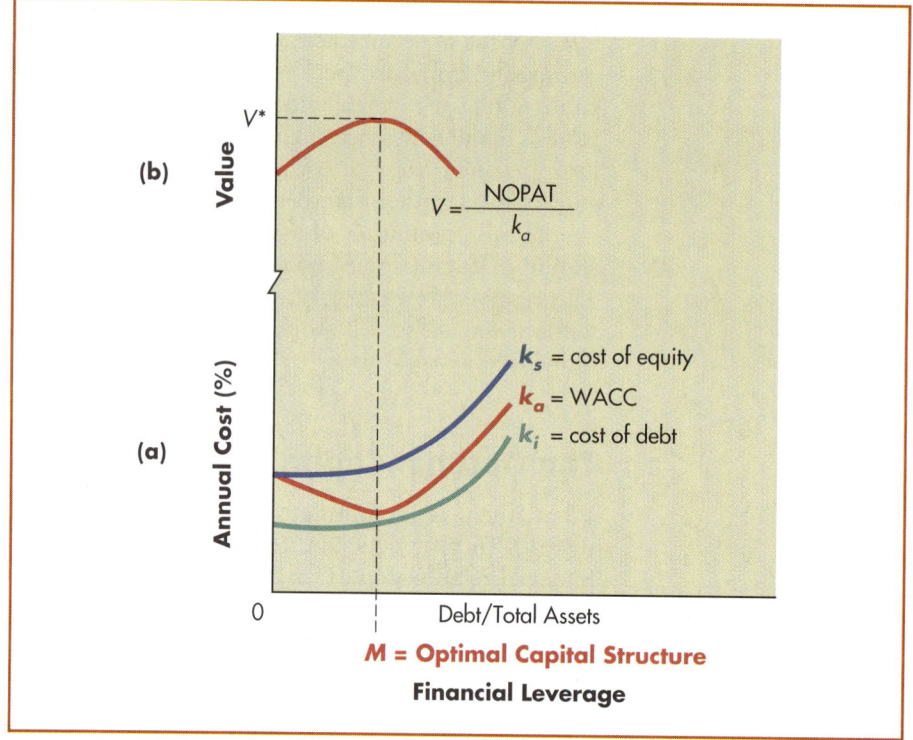

The *weighted average cost of capital*, k_a (WACC) results from a weighted average of the firm's debt and equity capital costs. At a debt ratio of zero, the firm is 100 percent equity-financed. As debt is substituted for equity and as the debt ratio increases, the WACC declines because the debt cost is less than the equity cost ($k_i < k_s$). As the debt ratio continues to increase, the increased debt and equity costs eventually cause the WACC to rise (after point M in Figure 11.3(a)). This behavior results in a U-shaped, or saucer-shaped, weighted average cost-of-capital function, k_a.

A Graphical View of the Optimal Structure

optimal capital structure
The capital structure at which the weighted average cost of capital is minimized, thereby maximizing the firm's value.

Because the maximization of value, V, is achieved when the overall cost of capital, k_a, is at a minimum (see Equation 11.11), the **optimal capital structure** is that at which the weighted average cost of capital, k_a, is minimized. In Figure 11.3(a), point M represents the *minimum weighted average cost of capital*—the point of optimal financial leverage and hence of optimal capital structure for the firm. Figure 11.3(b) plots the value of the firm that results from substitution of k_a in Figure 11.3(a) for various levels of financial leverage into the zero-growth valuation model in Equation 11.11. As shown in Figure 11.3(b), at the optimal capital structure, point M, the value of the firm is maximized at V^*.

Generally, the lower the firm's weighted average cost of capital, the greater the difference between the return on a project and the WACC, and therefore the greater the owners' return. Simply stated, minimizing the weighted average cost of capital allows management to undertake a larger number of profitable projects, thereby further increasing the value of the firm.

Review Questions

11–6 What is a firm's *capital structure*? What ratios assess the degree of financial leverage in a firm's capital structure?

11–7 In what ways are the capital structures of U.S. and non-U.S. firms different? How are they similar?

11–8 What is the major benefit of debt financing? How does it affect the firm's cost of debt?

11–9 What are *business risk* and *financial risk*? How does each of them influence the firm's capital structure decisions?

11–10 Briefly describe the *agency problem* that exists between owners and lenders. How do lenders cause firms to incur *agency costs* to resolve this problem?

11–11 How does *asymmetric information* affect the firm's capital structure decisions? How do the firm's financing actions give investors *signals* that reflect management's view of stock value?

11–12 How do the cost of debt, the cost of equity, and the weighted average cost of capital (WACC) behave as the firm's financial leverage increases from zero? Where is the *optimal capital structure*? What is its relationship to the firm's value at that point?

The EBIT–EPS Approach to Capital Structure

It should be clear from earlier chapters that the goal of the financial manager is to maximize owner wealth—that is, the firm's stock price. One of the widely followed variables affecting the firm's stock price is its earnings, which represents the returns earned on behalf of owners. In spite of the fact that focusing on earnings ignores risk—the other key variable affecting the firm's stock price—earnings per share (EPS) can be conveniently used to analyze alternative capital structures. The **EBIT–EPS approach** to capital structure involves selecting the capital structure that maximizes EPS over the expected range of earnings before interest and taxes (EBIT).

EBIT–EPS approach
An approach for selecting the capital structure that maximizes earnings per share (EPS) over the expected range of earnings before interest and taxes (EBIT).

Presenting a Financing Plan Graphically

To analyze the effects of a firm's capital structure on the owners' returns, we consider the relationship between earnings before interest and taxes (EBIT) and earnings per share (EPS). A constant level of EBIT—constant *business risk*—is assumed, to isolate the effect on returns of the financing costs associated with alternative capital structures. EPS is used to measure the owners' returns, which are expected to be closely related to share price.

The Data Required

To graph a financing plan, we need to know at least two EBIT–EPS coordinates. The approach for obtaining coordinates can be illustrated by an example.

EXAMPLE

The current capital structure of JSG Company, a soft-drink manufacturer, is as shown in the following table. Note that JSG's capital structure currently contains only common stock equity; the firm has no debt or preferred stock. If (for convenience) we assume the firm has no current liabilities, its debt ratio (total liabilities ÷ total assets) is currently 0% ($0 ÷ $500,000); it therefore has *zero* financial leverage. Assume the firm is in the 40% tax bracket.

Current capital structure	
Long-term debt	$ 0
Common stock equity ($25,000 shares @ $20)	500,000
Total capital (assets)	$500,000

EBIT–EPS coordinates for JSG's current capital structure can be found by assuming two EBIT values and calculating the EPS associated with them.[14] Because the EBIT–EPS graph is a straight line, any two EBIT values can be used to find coordinates. Here we arbitrarily use values of $100,000 and $200,000.

EBIT (assumed)	$100,000	$200,000
− Interest (rate × $0 debt)	0	0
Net profits before taxes	$100,000	$200,000
− Taxes (T = 0.40)	40,000	80,000
Net profits after taxes	$ 60,000	$120,000
EPS	$60,000 / 25,000 sh. = $2.40	$120,000 / 25,000 sh. = $4.80

The two EBIT-EPS coordinates resulting from these calculations are (1) $100,000 EBIT and $2.40 EPS and (2) $200,000 EBIT and $4.80 EPS. ■

Plotting the Data

The EBIT–EPS coordinates for JSG's current zero-leverage (debt ratio = 0%) situation can be plotted on a set of EBIT–EPS axes, as shown in Figure 11.4. The figure shows the level of EPS expected for each level of EBIT. For levels of EBIT below the *x*-axis intercept, a loss (negative EPS) results. Each of the *x*-axis intercepts is a **financial breakeven point**, the level of EBIT necessary to just cover all *fixed financial costs* (EPS = $0).

financial breakeven point
The level of EBIT necessary to just cover all *fixed financial costs;* the level of EBIT for which EPS = $0.

---

14. A convenient method for finding one EBIT–EPS coordinate is to calculate the *financial breakeven point*, the level of EBIT for which the firm's EPS just equals $0. It is the level of EBIT needed just to cover all fixed financial costs—annual interest (*I*) and preferred stock dividends (*PD*). The equation for the financial breakeven point is

$$\text{Financial breakeven point} = I + \frac{PD}{1-T}$$

where *T* is the tax rate. It can be seen that when *PD* = $0, the financial breakeven point is equal to *I*, the annual interest payment.

FIGURE 11.4

Graphic Presentation of a Financing Plan
JSG Company's zero-leverage financing plan

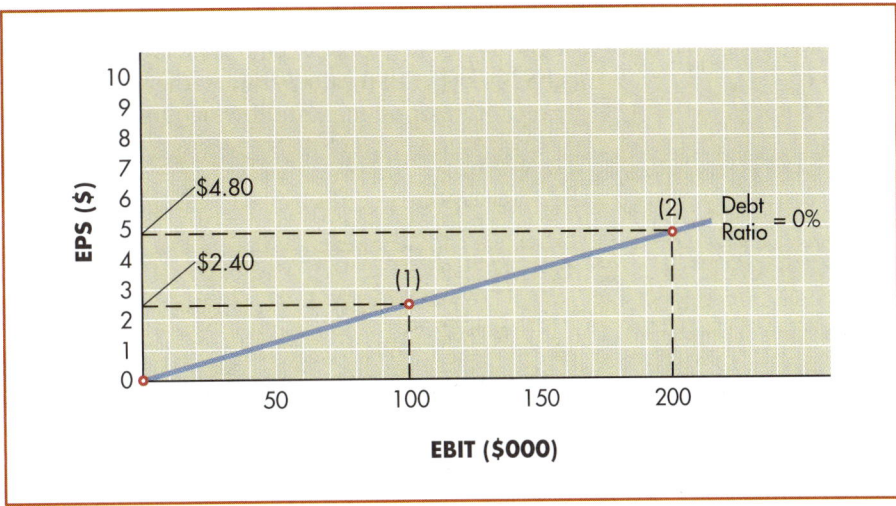

Comparing Alternative Capital Structures

We can compare alternative capital structures by graphing financing plans as shown in Figure 11.4. The following example illustrates this procedure.

EXAMPLE

JSG Company, whose current zero-leverage capital structure was described above, is contemplating shifting its capital structure to either of two leveraged positions. To maintain its $500,000 of total capital, JSG's capital structure will be shifted to greater leverage by issuing debt and using the proceeds to retire an equivalent amount of common stock. The two alternative capital structures result in debt ratios of 30% and 60%, respectively. The basic information on the current and two alternative capital structures is summarized in Table 11.9.

TABLE 11.9 Basic Information on JSG Company's Current and Alternative Capital Structures

Capital structure debt ratio (1)	Total assets[a] (2)	Debt [(1) × (2)] (3)	Equity [(2) − (3)] (4)	Interest rate on debt[b] (5)	Annual interest [(3) × (5)] (6)	Shares of common stock outstanding [(4) ÷ $20][c] (7)
0% (current)	$500,000	$ 0	$500,000	0 %	$ 0	25,000
30	500,000	150,000	350,000	10	15,000	17,500
60	500,000	300,000	200,000	16.5	49,500	10,000

[a]Because for convenience the firm is assumed to have no current liabilities, total assets equals total capital of $500,000.

[b]The interest rate on all debt increases with increases in the debt ratio due to the greater leverage and risk associated with higher debt ratios.

[c]The $20 value represents the book value of common stock equity.

Using the data in Table 11.9, we can calculate the coordinates needed to plot the 30% and 60% debt capital structures. For convenience, using the $100,000 and $200,000 EBIT values used earlier to plot the current capital structure, we get the information in the following table.

	Capital structure			
	30% Debt ratio		60% Debt ratio	
EBIT (assumed)	$100,000	$200,000	$100,000	$200,000
− Interest (Table 11.9)	15,000	15,000	49,500	49,500
Net profits before taxes	$ 85,000	$185,000	$ 50,500	$150,500
− Taxes ($T = 0.40$)	34,000	74,000	20,200	60,200
Net profits after taxes	$ 51,000	$111,000	$ 30,300	$ 90,300
EPS	$\frac{\$51{,}000}{17{,}500 \text{ sh.}} = \$2.91$	$\frac{\$111{,}000}{17{,}500 \text{ sh.}} = \$6.34$	$\frac{\$30{,}300}{10{,}000 \text{ sh.}} = \$3.03$	$\frac{\$90{,}300}{10{,}000 \text{ sh.}} = \$9.03$

The two sets of EBIT–EPS coordinates developed in the preceding table, along with those developed for the current zero-leverage capital structure, are summarized and plotted on the EBIT–EPS axes in Figure 11.5. This figure shows that *each* capital structure is superior to the others in terms of maximizing EPS over certain ranges of EBIT: The zero-leverage capital structure (debt ratio = 0%) is superior to either of the other capital structures for levels of EBIT between $0 and $50,000. Between $50,000 and $95,000 of EBIT, the capital structure associated with a debt ratio of 30% is preferred. And at a level of EBIT above $95,500, the 60% debt ratio capital structure provides the highest earnings per share.[15] ■

Considering Risk in EBIT–EPS Analysis

When interpreting EBIT–EPS analysis, it is important to consider the risk of each capital structure alternative. Graphically, the risk of each capital structure can be viewed in light of two measures: (1) the *financial breakeven point* (EBIT-axis intercept) and (2) the *degree of financial leverage* reflected in the slope of the capital structure line: *The higher the financial breakeven point and the steeper the slope of the capital structure line, the greater the financial risk.*

Further assessment of risk can be performed by using ratios. As financial leverage (measured by the debt ratio) increases, we expect a corresponding decline in the firm's ability to make scheduled interest payments (measured by the times interest earned ratio).

EXAMPLE

Reviewing the three capital structures plotted for JSG Company in Figure 11.5, we can see that as the debt ratio increases, so does the financial risk of each alternative. Both the financial breakeven point and the slope of the capital structure lines increase with increasing debt ratios. If we use the $100,000 EBIT value, for example, the times interest earned ratio (EBIT ÷ interest) for the zero-leverage

---

15. An algebraic technique can be used to find the *indifference points* between the capital structure alternatives. Due to its relative complexity, this technique is not presented. Instead, emphasis is given here to the visual estimation of these points from the graph.

FIGURE 11.5

EBIT–EPS Approach
A comparison of selected capital structures for JSG Company

capital structure is infinity ($100,000 ÷ $0); for the 30% debt case, it is 6.67 ($100,000 ÷ $15,000); and for the 60% debt case, it is 2.02 ($100,000 ÷ $49,500). Because lower times interest earned ratios reflect higher risk, these ratios support the conclusion that the risk of the capital structures increases with increasing financial leverage. The capital structure for a debt ratio of 60% is riskier than that for a debt ratio of 30%, which in turn is riskier than the capital structure for a debt ratio of 0%.

The Basic Shortcoming of EBIT–EPS Analysis

The most important point to recognize when using EBIT–EPS analysis is that this technique tends to concentrate on *maximizing earnings* rather than maximizing owner wealth as reflected in the firm's stock price. The use of an EPS-maximizing approach generally ignores risk. If investors did not require risk premiums (additional returns) as the firm increased the proportion of debt in its capital structure, a strategy involving maximizing EPS would also maximize stock price. But because risk premiums increase with increases in financial leverage, the maximization of EPS *does not* ensure owner wealth maximization. To select the best capital structure, both return (EPS) and risk (via the required return, k_s) must be integrated into a valuation framework consistent with the capital structure theory presented earlier.

Review Question

11–13 Explain the *EBIT–EPS approach* to capital structure. Include in your explanation a graph indicating the *financial breakeven point;* label the axes. Is this approach consistent with maximizing owners' wealth?

Choosing the Optimal Capital Structure

A wealth maximization framework for use in making capital structure decisions should include the two key factors of return and risk. This section describes the procedures for linking to market value the return and risk associated with alternative capital structures.

Linkage

To determine the firm's value under alternative capital structures, the firm must find the level of return that must be earned to compensate owners for the risk being incurred. Such a framework is consistent with the overall valuation framework developed in Chapters 6 and 7 and applied to capital budgeting decisions in Chapter 9.

The required return associated with a given level of financial risk can be estimated in a number of ways. Theoretically, the preferred approach would be first to estimate the beta associated with each alternative capital structure and then to use the CAPM framework presented in Equation 5.7 to calculate the required return, k_s. A more operational approach involves linking the financial risk associated with each capital structure alternative directly to the required return. Such an approach is similar to the CAPM-type approach demonstrated in Chapter 9 for linking project risk and required return (RADR). Here it involves estimating the required return associated with each level of financial risk, as measured by a statistic such as the coefficient of variation of EPS. Regardless of the approach used, one would expect the required return to increase as the financial risk increases.

EXAMPLE Expanding the JSG Company example presented earlier, we assume that the firm is attempting to choose the best of seven alternative capital structures—debt ratios of 0%, 10%, 20%, 30%, 40%, 50%, and 60%. For each of these structures the firm estimated the (1) EPS, (2) coefficient of variation of EPS, and (3) required return, k_s. These values are shown in columns 1 through 3 of Table 11.10. Note that EPS (in column 1) is maximized at a 50% debt ratio though the risk of EPS measured by its coefficient of variation (in column 2) is constantly increasing. As expected, the estimated required return of owners, k_s (in column 3), increases with

TABLE 11.10 Calculation of Share Value Estimates Associated with Alternative Capital Structures for JSG Company

Capital structure debt ratio	Expected EPS (1)	Estimated coefficient of variation of EPS (2)	Estimated required return, k_s (3)	Estimated share value [(1) ÷ (3)] (4)
0%	$2.40	0.71	.115	$20.87
10	2.55	0.74	.117	21.79
20	2.72	0.78	.121	22.48
30	2.91	0.83	.125	23.28
40	3.12	0.91	.140	22.29
50	3.18	1.07	.165	19.27
60	3.03	1.40	.190	15.95

increasing risk, as measured by the coefficient of variation of EPS (in column 2). Simply stated, for higher degrees of financial leverage—debt ratios—owners require higher rates of return.

Estimating Value

The value of the firm associated with alternative capital structures can be estimated by using one of the standard valuation models. If, for simplicity, we assume that all earnings are paid out as dividends, we can use a zero-growth valuation model such as that developed in Chapter 7. The model, originally stated in Equation 7.2, is restated here with EPS substituted for dividends (because in each year the dividends would equal EPS):

$$P_0 = \frac{\text{EPS}}{k_s} \quad (11.12)$$

By substituting the expected level of EPS and the associated required return, k_s, into Equation 11.12, we can estimate the per share value of the firm, P_0.

EXAMPLE We can now estimate the value of JSG Company's stock under each of the alternative capital structures. Substituting the expected EPS (column 1 of Table 11.10) and the required returns, k_s (column 3 of Table 11.10), into Equation 11.12 for each of the capital structures, we obtain the share values given in column 4 of the table. Plotting the resulting share values against the associated debt ratios, as shown in Figure 11.6 on page 466, clearly illustrates that the maximum share value occurs at the capital structure associated with a debt ratio of 30%.

Maximizing Value Versus Maximizing EPS

Throughout this text, the goal of the financial manager has been specified as maximizing owner wealth, not profit. Although some relationship exists between expected profit and value, there is no reason to believe that profit-maximizing

FIGURE 11.6

Estimating Value
Estimated share value and EPS for alternative capital structures for JSG Company

strategies necessarily result in wealth maximization. It is therefore the wealth of the owners as reflected in the estimated share value that should serve as the criterion for selecting the best capital structure. A final look at JSG Company will highlight this point.

EXAMPLE

Further analysis of Figure 11.6 clearly shows that although the firm's profits (EPS) are maximized at a debt ratio of 50%, share value is maximized at a 30% debt ratio. Therefore, the preferred capital structure would be the 30% debt ratio. The two approaches provide different conclusions because EPS maximization does not consider risk.

Some Other Important Considerations

Because there is really no practical way to calculate the optimal capital structure, any quantitative analysis of capital structure must be tempered with other important considerations. Some of the more important additional factors involved in capital structure decisions are summarized in Table 11.11.

Review Questions

11–14 Why do *maximizing EPS* and *maximizing value* not necessarily lead to the same conclusion about the optimal capital structure?

11–15 What important factors in addition to quantitative factors should a firm consider when it is making a capital structure decision?

TABLE 11.11 Important Factors to Consider in Making Capital Structure Decisions

Concern	Factor	Description
Business risk	Revenue stability	Firms that have stable and predictable revenues can more safely undertake highly leveraged capital structures than can firms with volatile patterns of sales revenue. Firms with growing sales tend to benefit from added debt; they can reap the positive benefits of financial leverage, magnifying the effect of these increases.
	Cash flow	When considering a new capital structure, the firm must focus on its ability to generate the cash flows necessary to meet obligations. Cash forecasts reflecting an ability to service debts (and preferred stock) must support any shift in capital structure.
Agency costs	Contractual obligations	A firm may be contractually constrained with respect to the type of funds that it can raise (e.g., might be prohibited from selling additional debt except when such debt is made subordinate to existing debt). Contractual constraints on the sale of additional stock, as well as on the ability to distribute dividends on stock, might also exist.
	Management preferences	Occasionally, a firm will impose an internal constraint on the use of debt to limit risk exposure to a level acceptable to management. Because of risk aversion, management constrains the firm's capital structure at a level that may or may not be optimum.
	Control	A management group concerned about control may prefer to issue debt rather than (voting) common stock. Under favorable market conditions, a firm that wanted to sell equity could make a *preemptive offering* or issue *nonvoting shares* (see Chapter 7), allowing each shareholder to maintain proportionate ownership. Generally, only in closely held firms or firms threatened by takeover does control become a major concern in the capital structure decision.
Asymmetric information	External risk assessment	The firm's ability to raise funds quickly and at favorable rates depends on the external risk assessments of lenders and bond raters. The firm must therefore consider the impact of capital structure decisions both on share value and on published financial statements from which lenders and raters assess the firm's risk.
	Timing	At times when the general level of interest rates is low, debt financing might be more attractive; when interest rates are high, the sale of stock may be more appealing. Sometimes both debt and equity capital become unavailable at reasonable terms. General economic conditions—especially those of the capital market—can thus significantly affect capital structure decisions.

SUMMARY

FOCUS ON VALUE

The amount of leverage (fixed-cost assets or funds) employed by a firm directly affects its risk, return, and share value. Generally, higher leverage raises risk and return, and lower leverage reduces risk and return. Operating leverage is concerned with the level of fixed operating costs; financial leverage focuses on fixed financial costs, particularly interest on debt and any preferred stock dividends. The firm's financial leverage is determined by its capital structure. Because of its fixed interest payments, the more debt a firm employs relative to its equity, the greater its financial leverage.

The value of the firm is clearly affected by its degree of operating leverage and by the composition of its capital structure. The financial manager must therefore carefully consider the types of operating and financial costs it incurs, recognizing that with greater fixed costs comes higher risk. Major decisions with regard to both operating cost structure and capital structure must therefore focus on their impact on the firm's value. Only those leverage and capital structure decisions that are consistent with the firm's goal of **maximizing its stock price** should be implemented.

REVIEW OF LEARNING GOALS

LG1 **Discuss leverage, capital structure, breakeven analysis, the operating breakeven point, and the effect of changing costs on it.** Leverage results from the use of fixed costs to magnify returns to a firm's owners. Capital structure, the firm's mix of long-term debt and equity, affects leverage and therefore the firm's value. Breakeven analysis measures the level of sales necessary to cover total operating costs. The operating breakeven point may be calculated algebraically, by dividing fixed operating costs by the difference between the sale price per unit and variable operating cost per unit, or it may be determined graphically. The operating breakeven point increases with increased fixed and variable operating costs and decreases with an increase in sale price, and vice versa.

LG2 **Understand operating, financial, and total leverage and the relationships among them.** Operating leverage is the use of fixed operating costs by the firm to magnify the effects of changes in sales on EBIT. The higher the fixed operating costs, the greater the operating leverage. Financial leverage is the use of fixed financial costs by the firm to magnify the effects of changes in EBIT on EPS. The higher the fixed financial costs, the greater the financial leverage. The total leverage of the firm is the use of fixed costs—both operating and financial—to magnify the effects of changes in sales on EPS.

LG3 **Describe the types of capital, external assessment of capital structure, the capital structure of non-U.S. firms, and capital structure theory.** Debt capital and equity capital make up a firm's capital structure. Capital structure can be externally assessed by using financial ratios—debt ratio, times interest earned ratio, and fixed-payment coverage ratio. Non-U.S. companies tend to have much higher degrees of indebtedness than do their U.S. counterparts, primarily because U.S. capital markets are much more developed.

Research suggests that there is an optimal capital structure that balances the firm's benefits and costs of debt financing. The major benefit of debt financing is the tax shield. The costs of debt financing include the probability of bankruptcy; agency costs imposed by lenders; and asymmetric information, which typically causes firms to raise funds in a pecking order so as to send positive signals to the market and thereby enhance shareholder wealth.

LG4 **Explain the optimal capital structure using a graphical view of the firm's cost-of-capital functions and a zero-growth valuation model.** The zero-growth valuation model defines the firm's value as its net operating profits after taxes (NOPAT), or after-tax EBIT, divided by its weighted average cost of capital. Assuming that NOPAT is constant, the value of the firm is maximized by minimizing its weighted average cost of capital (WACC). The optimal capital structure is the one that minimizes the WACC. Graphically, the firm's WACC exhibits a U-shape, whose minimum value defines the optimal capital structure that maximizes owner wealth.

Discuss the EBIT–EPS approach to capital structure. The EBIT–EPS approach evaluates capital structures in light of the returns they provide the firm's owners and their degree of financial risk. Under the EBIT–EPS approach, the preferred capital structure is the one that is expected to provide maximum EPS over the firm's expected range of EBIT. Graphically, this approach reflects risk in terms of the financial breakeven point and the slope of the capital structure line. The major shortcoming of EBIT–EPS analysis is that it concentrates on maximizing earnings (returns) rather than owners' wealth, which considers risk as well as return.

 Review the return and risk of alternative capital structures, their linkage to market value, and other important considerations related to capital structure. The best capital structure can be selected by using a valuation model to link return and risk factors. The preferred capital structure is the one that results in the highest estimated share value, not the highest EPS. Other important nonquantitative factors must also be considered when making capital structure decisions.

SELF-TEST PROBLEMS (SOLUTIONS IN APPENDIX B)

ST11–1 **Breakeven point and all forms of leverage** TOR most recently sold 100,000 units at $7.50 each; its variable operating costs are $3.00 per unit, and its fixed operating costs are $250,000. Annual interest charges total $80,000, and the firm has 8,000 shares of $5 (annual dividend) preferred stock outstanding. It currently has 20,000 shares of common stock outstanding. Assume that the firm is subject to a 40% tax rate.
  a. At what level of sales (in units) would the firm break even on operations (that is, EBIT = $0)?
  b. Calculate the firm's *earnings per share (EPS)* in tabular form at (1) the current level of sales and (2) a 120,000-unit sales level.
  c. Using the current *$750,000 level of sales as a base*, calculate the firm's degree of operating leverage (DOL).
  d. Using the EBIT *associated with the $750,000 level of sales as a base*, calculate the firm's degree of financial leverage (DFL).
  e. Use the degree of total leverage (DTL) concept to determine the effect (in percentage terms) of a 50% increase in TOR's sales *from the $750,000 base level* on its earnings per share.

 ST11–2 **EBIT–EPS analysis** Newlin Electronics is considering additional financing of $10,000. It currently has $50,000 of 12% (annual interest) bonds and 10,000 shares of common stock outstanding. The firm can obtain the financing through a 12% (annual interest) bond issue or through the sale of 1,000 shares of common stock. The firm has a 40% tax rate.
  a. Calculate two EBIT–EPS coordinates for each plan by selecting any two EBIT values and finding their associated EPS values.
  b. Plot the two financing plans on a set of EBIT–EPS axes.
  c. On the basis of your graph in part **b**, at what level of EBIT does the bond plan become superior to the stock plan?

ST11–3 Optimal capital structure Hawaiian Macadamia Nut Company has collected the following data with respect to its capital structure, expected earnings per share, and required return.

Capital structure debt ratio	Expected earnings per share	Required return, k_s
0%	$3.12	13%
10	3.90	15
20	4.80	16
30	5.44	17
40	5.51	19
50	5.00	20
60	4.40	22

a. Compute the *estimated share value* associated with each of the capital structures, using the simplified method described in this chapter (see Equation 11.12). (*Hint:* Be sure to convert required returns to decimal form.)
b. Determine the optimal capital structure on the basis of (1) maximization of expected earnings per share and (2) maximization of share value.
c. Which capital structure do you recommend? Why?

WARM-UP EXERCISES

E11–1 Canvas Reproductions has fixed operating costs of $12,500, variable operating costs of $10 per unit, and sells its paintings for $25 each. At what level of unit sales will the company break even in terms of EBIT?

E11–2 The Great Fish Taco Corporation currently has fixed operating costs of $15,000, sells its pre-made tacos for $6 per box, and incurs variable operating costs of $2.50 per box. If the firm has a potential investment that would simultaneously raise its fixed costs to $16,500 and allow it to charge a per-box sale price of $6.50 due to better-textured tacos, what will the impact be on its operating breakeven point in boxes?

E11–3 Chico's has sales of 15,000 units at a price of $20 per unit. The firm incurs fixed operating costs of $30,000 and variable operating costs of $12 per unit. What is Chico's *degree of operating leverage (DOL)* at a base level of sales of 15,000 units?

E11–4 Parker Investments has EBIT of $20,000, interest expense of $3,000, and preferred dividends of $4,000. If it pays taxes at a rate of 38%, what is Parker's *degree of financial leverage (DFL)* at a base level of EBIT of $20,000?

E11–5 Cobalt Industries had sales of 150,000 units at a price of $10 per unit. It faced fixed operating costs of $250,000 and variable operating costs of $5 per unit. The company is subject to a tax rate of 38% and has a weighted average cost of capital of 8.5%. Calculate Cobalt's *net operating profits after taxes (NOPAT)*, and use it to estimate the value of the firm.

PROBLEMS

P11–1 **Breakeven point—Algebraic** Kate Rowland wishes to estimate the number of flower arrangements she must sell at $24.95 to break even. She has estimated fixed operating costs of $12,350 per year and variable operating costs of $15.45 per arrangement. How many flower arrangements must Kate sell to break even on operating costs?

P11–2 **Breakeven comparisons—Algebraic** Given the price and cost data shown in the accompanying table for each of the three firms, F, G, and H, answer the following questions.

Firm	F	G	H
Sale price per unit	$ 18.00	$ 21.00	$ 30.00
Variable operating cost per unit	6.75	13.50	12.00
Fixed operating cost	45,000	30,000	90,000

a. What is the *operating breakeven point* in units for each firm?
b. How would you rank these firms in terms of their risk?

P11–3 **Breakeven point—Algebraic and graphical** Fine Leather Enterprises sells its single product for $129.00 per unit. The firm's fixed operating costs are $473,000 annually, and its variable operating costs are $86.00 per unit.
a. Find the firm's *operating breakeven point* in units.
b. Label the *x* axis "Sales (units)" and the *y* axis "Costs/Revenues ($)," and then graph the firm's sales revenue, total operating cost, and fixed operating cost functions on these axes. In addition, label the operating breakeven point and the areas of loss and profit (EBIT).

P11–4 **Breakeven analysis** Barry Carter is considering opening a music store. He wants to estimate the number of CDs he must sell to break even. The CDs will be sold for $13.98 each, variable operating costs are $10.48 per CD, and annual fixed operating costs are $73,500.
a. Find the *operating breakeven point* in number of CDs.
b. Calculate the total operating costs at the breakeven volume found in part **a**.
c. If Barry estimates that at a minimum he can sell 2,000 CDs *per month*, should he go into the music business?
d. How much EBIT will Barry realize if he sells the minimum 2,000 CDs per month noted in part **c**?

P11–5 **Breakeven point—Changing costs/revenues** JWG Company publishes *Creative Crosswords*. Last year the book of puzzles sold for $10 with variable operating cost per book of $8 and fixed operating costs of $40,000. How many books must JWG sell this year to achieve the breakeven point for the stated operating costs, given the following different circumstances?
a. All figures remain the same as for last year.
b. Fixed operating costs increase to $44,000; all other figures remain the same.

c. The selling price increases to $10.50; all costs remain the same as for last year.
d. Variable operating cost per book increases to $8.50; all other figures remain the same.
e. What conclusions about the operating breakeven point can be drawn from your answers?

P11–6 **EBIT sensitivity** Stewart Industries sells its finished product for $9 per unit. Its fixed operating costs are $20,000, and the variable operating cost per unit is $5.
a. Calculate the firm's earnings before interest and taxes (EBIT) for sales of 10,000 units.
b. Calculate the firm's EBIT for sales of 8,000 and 12,000 units, respectively.
c. Calculate the percentage changes in sales (from the 10,000-unit base level) and associated percentage changes in EBIT for the shifts in sales indicated in part b.
d. On the basis of your findings in part c, comment on the sensitivity of changes in EBIT in response to changes in sales.

P11–7 **Degree of operating leverage** Grey Products has fixed operating costs of $380,000, variable operating costs of $16 per unit, and a selling price of $63.50 per unit.
a. Calculate the *operating breakeven point* in units.
b. Calculate the firm's EBIT at 9,000, 10,000, and 11,000 units, respectively.
c. With 10,000 units as a base, what are the percentage changes in units sold and EBIT as sales move from the base to the other sales levels used in part b?
d. Use the percentages computed in part c to determine the degree of operating leverage (DOL).
e. Use the formula for degree of operating leverage to determine the DOL at 10,000 units.

P11–8 **Degree of operating leverage—Graphical** Levin Corporation has fixed operating costs of $72,000, variable operating costs of $6.75 per unit, and a selling price of $9.75 per unit.
a. Calculate the *operating breakeven point* in units.
b. Compute the degree of operating leverage (DOL) for the following unit sales levels: 25,000, 30,000, 40,000. Use the formula given in the chapter.
c. Graph the DOL figures that you computed in part b (on the *y* axis) against sales levels (on the *x* axis).
d. Compute the degree of operating leverage at 24,000 units; add this point to your graph.
e. What principle do your graph and figures illustrate?

P11–9 **EPS calculations** Southland Industries has $60,000 of 16% (annual interest) bonds outstanding, 1,500 shares of preferred stock paying an annual dividend of $5 per share, and 4,000 shares of common stock outstanding. Assuming that the firm has a 40% tax rate, compute earnings per share (EPS) for the following levels of EBIT:
a. $24,600
b. $30,600
c. $35,000

P11-10 **Degree of financial leverage** Northwestern Savings and Loan has a current capital structure consisting of $250,000 of 16% (annual interest) debt and 2,000 shares of common stock. The firm pays taxes at the rate of 40%.
a. Using EBIT values of $80,000 and $120,000, determine the associated earnings per share (EPS).
b. Using $80,000 of EBIT as a base, calculate the degree of financial leverage (DFL).
c. Rework parts **a** and **b** assuming that the firm has $100,000 of 16% (annual interest) debt and 3,000 shares of common stock.

P11-11 **DFL and graphical display of financing plans** Wells and Associates has EBIT of $67,500. Interest costs are $22,500, and the firm has 15,000 shares of common stock outstanding. Assume a 40% tax rate.
a. Use the degree of financial leverage (DFL) formula to calculate the DFL for the firm.
b. Using a set of EBIT–EPS axes, plot Wells and Associates' financing plan.
c. If the firm also has 1,000 shares of preferred stock paying a $6.00 annual dividend per share, what is the DFL?
d. Plot the financing plan, including the 1,000 shares of $6.00 preferred stock, on the axes used in part **b**.
e. Briefly discuss the graph of the two financing plans.

P11-12 **Integrative—Multiple leverage measures** Play-More Toys produces inflatable beach balls, selling 400,000 balls per year. Each ball produced has a variable operating cost of $0.84 and sells for $1.00. Fixed operating costs are $28,000. The firm has annual interest charges of $6,000, preferred dividends of $2,000, and a 40% tax rate.
a. Calculate the *operating breakeven point* in units.
b. Use the degree of operating leverage (DOL) formula to calculate DOL.
c. Use the degree of financial leverage (DFL) formula to calculate DFL.
d. Use the degree of total leverage (DTL) formula to calculate DTL. Compare this to the product of DOL and DFL calculated in parts **b** and **c**.

P11-13 **Integrative—Leverage and risk** Firm R has sales of 100,000 units at $2.00 per unit, variable operating costs of $1.70 per unit, and fixed operating costs of $6,000. Interest is $10,000 per year. Firm W has sales of 100,000 units at $2.50 per unit, variable operating costs of $1.00 per unit, and fixed operating costs of $62,500. Interest is $17,500 per year. Assume that both firms are in the 40% tax bracket.
a. Compute the degree of operating, financial, and total leverage for firm R.
b. Compute the degree of operating, financial, and total leverage for firm W.
c. Compare the relative risks of the two firms.
d. Discuss the principles of leverage that your answers illustrate.

P11-14 **Various capital structures** Charter Enterprises currently has $1 million in total assets and is totally equity-financed. It is contemplating a change in its capital structure. Compute the amount of debt and equity that would be outstanding if the firm were to shift to each of the following debt ratios: 10%, 20%, 30%, 40%, 50%, 60%, and 90%. (*Note:* The amount of total assets would not change.) Is there a limit to the debt ratio's value?

474   PART 4   Long-Term Financial Decisions

P11–15 EBIT–EPS and capital structure   Data-Check is considering two capital structures. The key information is shown in the following table. Assume a 40% tax rate.

Source of capital	Structure A	Structure B
Long-term debt	$100,000 at 16% coupon rate	$200,000 at 17% coupon rate
Common stock	4,000 shares	2,000 shares

a. Calculate two *EBIT–EPS coordinates* for each of the structures by selecting any two EBIT values and finding their associated EPS values.
b. Plot the two capital structures on a set of EBIT–EPS axes.
c. Indicate over what EBIT range, if any, each structure is preferred.
d. Discuss the leverage and risk aspects of each structure.
e. If the firm is fairly certain that its EBIT will exceed $75,000, which structure would you recommend? Why?

P11–16 EBIT–EPS and preferred stock   Litho-Print is considering two possible capital structures, A and B, shown in the following table. Assume a 40% tax rate.

Source of capital	Structure A	Structure B
Long-term debt	$75,000 at 16% coupon rate	$50,000 at 15% coupon rate
Preferred stock	$10,000 with an 18% annual dividend	$15,000 with an 18% annual dividend
Common stock	8,000 shares	10,000 shares

a. Calculate two *EBIT–EPS coordinates* for each of the structures by selecting any two EBIT values and finding their associated EPS values.
b. Graph the two capital structures on the same set of EBIT–EPS axes.
c. Discuss the leverage and risk associated with each of the structures.
d. Over what range of EBIT is each structure preferred?
e. Which structure do you recommend if the firm expects its EBIT to be $35,000? Explain.

P11–17 Optimal capital structure   Nelson Corporation has collected the following data associated with four possible capital structures.

Capital structure debt ratio	Expected EPS	Estimated coefficient of variation of EPS
0%	$1.92	.4743
20	2.25	.5060
40	2.72	.5581
60	3.54	.6432

The firm's research indicates that the marketplace assigns the following required returns to risky earnings per share.

Coefficient of variation of EPS	Estimated required return, k_s
0.43	15%
0.47	16
0.51	17
0.56	18
0.60	22
0.64	24

a. Find the required return associated with each of the four capital structures.
b. Compute the estimated share value associated with each of the four capital structures using the simplified method described in this chapter (see Equation 11.12). (*Hint:* Be sure to convert required returns to decimal form.)
c. Determine the optimal capital structure based on (1) maximization of expected EPS and (2) maximization of share value.
d. Construct a graph (similiar to Figure 11.6) showing the relationships in part c.
e. Which capital structure do you recommend? Why?

P11–18 **Integrative—Optimal capital structure** Triple D Corporation wishes to analyze five possible capital structures—0%, 15%, 30%, 45%, and 60% debt ratios. The firm's total assets of $1 million are assumed to be constant. Its common stock has a book value of $25 per share, and the firm is in the 40% tax bracket. The following additional data have been gathered for use in analyzing the five capital structures under consideration.

Capital structure debt ratio	Interest rate on debt, k_d	Expected EPS	Required return, k_s
0%	0.0%	$3.60	10.0%
15	8.0	4.03	10.5
30	10.0	4.50	11.6
45	13.0	4.95	14.0
60	17.0	5.18	20.0

a. Calculate the amount of debt, the amount of equity, and the number of shares of common stock outstanding for each of the capital structures being considered.
b. Calculate the annual interest on the debt under each of the capital structures being considered. (*Note:* The interest rate given is applicable to *all* debt associated with the corresponding debt ratio.)
c. Calculate the EPS associated with $150,000 and $250,000 of EBIT for each of the five capital structures being considered.
d. Using the EBIT–EPS data developed in part c, plot the capital structures on the same set of EBIT–EPS axes, and discuss the ranges over which each is preferred. What is the major problem with the use of this approach?
e. Using the valuation model given in Equation 11.12 and the appropriate data, estimate the share value for each of the capital structures being considered. (*Hint:* Be sure to convert required returns to decimal form.)
f. Construct a graph similar to Figure 11.6 showing the relationships between the debt ratio (*x* axis) and expected EPS (*y* axis) and share value (*y* axis).

g. Referring to the graph in part f: Which structure is preferred if the goal is to *maximize EPS?* Which structure is preferred if the goal is to *maximize share value?* Which capital structure do you recommend? Explain.

P11–19 **ETHICS PROBLEM** "Information asymmetry lies at the heart of the ethical dilemma that managers, stockholders, and bondholders confront when companies initiate management buyouts or swap debt for equity." Comment on this statement. What steps might a board of directors take to ensure that the company's actions are ethical to all parties?

CHAPTER 11 CASE

Evaluating McGraw Industries' Capital Structure

McGraw Industries, an established producer of printing equipment, expects its sales to remain flat for the next 3 to 5 years because of both a weak economic outlook and an expectation of little new printing technology development over that period. On the basis of this scenario, the firm's management has been instructed by its board to institute programs that will allow it to operate more efficiently, earn higher profits, and, most important, maximize share value.

In this regard, the firm's chief financial officer (CFO), Ron Lewis, has been charged with evaluating the firm's capital structure. Lewis believes that the current capital structure, which contains 10% debt and 90% equity, may lack adequate financial leverage. To evaluate the firm's capital structure, Lewis has gathered the data summarized in the following table on the current capital structure (10% debt ratio) and two alternative capital structures—A (30% debt ratio) and B (50% debt ratio)—that he would like to consider.

Source of capital	Capital structure[a]		
	Current (10% debt)	A (30% debt)	B (50% debt)
Long-term debt	$1,000,000	$3,000,000	$5,000,000
Coupon interest rate[b]	9%	10%	12%
Common stock	100,000 shares	70,000 shares	40,000 shares
Required return on equity, k_s[c]	12%	13%	18%

[a]These structures are based on maintaining the firm's current level of $10,000,000 of total financing.
[b]Interest rate applicable to *all* debt.
[c]Market-based return for the given level of risk.

Lewis expects the firm's earnings before interest and taxes (EBIT) to remain at its current level of $1,200,000. The firm has a 40% tax rate.

TO DO

a. Use the current level of EBIT to calculate the times interest earned ratio for each capital structure. Evaluate the current and two alternative capital structures using the times interest earned and debt ratios.

b. Prepare a single EBIT–EPS graph showing the current and two alternative capital structures.
c. On the basis of the graph in part **b,** which capital structure will maximize McGraw's earnings per share (EPS) at its expected level of EBIT of $1,200,000? Why might this *not* be the best capital structure?
d. Using the zero-growth valuation model given in Equation 11.12, find the market value of McGraw's equity under each of the three capital structures at the $1,200,000 level of expected EBIT.
e. On the basis of your findings in parts **c** and **d,** which capital structure would you recommend? Why?

SPREADSHEET EXERCISE

Starstruck Company would like to determine its optimal capital structure. Several of its managers believe that the best method is to rely on the estimated earnings per share (EPS) of the firm, because they feel that profits and stock price are closely related. The financial managers have suggested another method that depends on the estimated required returns of the firm. The following financial data are available.

Capital structure debt ratio	Estimated EPS	Estimated required return
0%	$1.75	11.40%
10	1.90	11.80
20	2.25	12.50
30	2.55	13.25
40	3.18	18.00
50	3.06	19.00
60	3.10	25.00

TO DO

a. Based upon the given financial data, create a spreadsheet to calculate the estimated share values associated with the seven alternative capital structures. Refer to Table 11.10 in the text (or view it at www.aw-bc.com/gitman).
b. Use Excel to graph the relationship between capital structure and the estimated EPS of the firm. What is the optimal debt ratio? Refer to Figure 11.6 in the text (or view it at www.aw-bc.com/gitman).
c. Use Excel to graph the relationship between capital structure and the estimated share value of the firm. What is the optimal debt ratio? Refer to Figure 11.6 in the text (or view it at www.aw-bc.com/gitman).
d. Do both methods lead to the same *optimal capital structure?* Which method do you favor? Explain.
e. What is the major difference between the EPS and required return methods?

Web Exercise

In this assignment, you will revisit the Web sites with which you have become familiar in your previous work. Your goal is to use the tools of leverage analysis to describe a publicly traded firm.

TO DO

a. Go to a company Web site of your own choosing. Find the firm's EBIT and EPS for the last two periods and graph this information.
b. Connect the dots on your graph in part **a** and make statements about the value of the firm.
c. Discuss the capital structure of your chosen firm. What has happened recently to your firm's debt ratio?

> **Remember to check the book's Web site at**
> **www.aw-bc.com/gitman**
> **for additional resources, including additional Web exercises.**

Chapter 12

Dividend Policy

LEARNING GOALS

LG1 Understand cash dividend payment procedures, the tax treatment of dividends, and the role of dividend reinvestment plans.

LG2 Describe the residual theory of dividends and the key arguments with regard to dividend irrelevance and relevance.

LG3 Discuss the key factors involved in establishing a dividend policy.

LG4 Review and evaluate the three basic types of dividend policies.

LG5 Evaluate stock dividends from accounting, shareholder, and company points of view.

LG6 Explain stock splits and stock repurchases and the firm's motivation for undertaking each of them.

Across the Disciplines Why This Chapter Matters to You

Accounting: You need to understand the types of dividends and payment procedures for them because you will need to record and report the declaration and payment of dividends; you also will provide the financial data that management must have to make dividend decisions.

Information systems: You need to understand types of dividends, payment procedures, and the financial data that the firm must have to make and implement dividend decisions.

Management: To make appropriate dividend decisions for the firm, you need to understand types of dividends, the factors that affect dividend policy, types of dividend policies, and arguments about the relevance of dividends.

Marketing: You need to understand factors affecting dividend policy because you may want to argue that the firm would be better off retaining funds for use in new marketing programs or products, rather than paying them out as dividends.

Operations: You need to understand factors affecting dividend policy because you may find that the firm's dividend policy imposes limitations on planned replacement, modernization, or expansion projects.

Dividends represent a source of cash flow to stockholders and provide information about the firm's performance. Some stockholders expect to receive dividends. Others are content to see an increase in stock price and no dividends. The firm's dividend policy depends on various factors. This chapter considers whether dividends matter to stockholders and explains the key factors in dividend policy, basic types of dividend policies, and alternative forms of dividends.

Dividend Fundamentals

Expected cash dividends are the key return variable from which owners and investors determine share value. They represent a source of cash flow to stockholders and provide information about the firm's current and future performance. Because **retained earnings,** earnings not distributed to owners as dividends, are a form of *internal* financing, the dividend decision can significantly affect the firm's *external* financing requirements. In other words, if the firm needs financing, the larger the cash dividend paid, the greater the amount of financing that must be raised externally through borrowing or through the sale of common or preferred stock. (Remember that although dividends are charged to retained earnings, they are actually paid out of cash.) The first thing to know about cash dividends is the procedures for paying them.

retained earnings
Earnings not distributed to owners as dividends; a form of *internal* financing.

Cash Dividend Payment Procedures

Whether and in what amount to pay cash dividends to corporate stockholders is decided by the firm's board of directors at quarterly or semiannual meetings. The past period's financial performance and future outlook, as well as recent dividends paid, are key inputs to the dividend decision. The payment date of the cash dividend, if one is declared, must also be established.

Amount of Dividends

Whether dividends should be paid, and if so, in what amount, are important decisions that depend primarily on the firm's dividend policy. Most firms have a set policy with respect to the periodic dividend, but the firm's directors can change this amount, largely on the basis of significant increases or decreases in earnings.

Relevant Dates

date of record (dividends)
Set by the firm's directors, the date on which all persons whose names are recorded as stockholders receive a declared dividend at a specified future time.

ex dividend
Period, beginning 2 *business days* prior to the date of record, during which a stock is sold without the right to receive the current dividend.

If the directors of the firm declare a dividend, they also typically issue a statement indicating the dividend decision, the record date, and the payment date. This statement is generally quoted in the *Wall Street Journal* and other financial news media.

Record Date All persons whose names are recorded as stockholders on the **date of record** set by the directors receive a declared dividend at a specified future time. These stockholders are often referred to as *holders of record*.

Because of the time needed to make bookkeeping entries when a stock is traded, the stock begins selling **ex dividend** 2 *business days* prior to the date of record. Purchasers of a stock selling ex dividend do not receive the current dividend. A simple way to determine the first day on which the stock sells ex dividend is to subtract 2 days from the date of record; if a weekend intervenes, subtract 4 days. Ignoring general market fluctuations, the stock's price is expected to drop by the amount of the declared dividend on the ex dividend date.

Payment Date The **payment date,** also set by the directors, is the actual date on which the firm mails the dividend payment to the holders of record. It is generally a few weeks after the record date. An example will clarify the various dates and the accounting effects.

payment date
Set by the firm's directors, the actual date on which the firm mails the dividend payment to the holders of record.

EXAMPLE

At the quarterly dividend meeting of Rudolf Company, a distributor of office products, held on June 10, the directors declared an $0.80-per-share cash dividend for holders of record on Friday, July 2. The firm had 100,000 shares of common stock outstanding. The payment date for the dividend was Monday, August 2. A time line depicting the key dates relative to the Rudolf Company's dividend is given in Figure 12.1. Before the dividend was declared, the key accounts of the firm were as follows:

Cash $200,000   Dividends payable $ 0
                   Retained earnings   1,000,000

When the dividend was announced by the directors, $80,000 of the retained earnings ($0.80 per share × 100,000 shares) was transferred to the dividends payable account. The key accounts thus became

Cash $200,000   Dividends payable $ 80,000
                   Retained earnings   920,000

Rudolf Company's stock began selling ex dividend 2 *business days* prior to the date of record, which was Wednesday, June 30. This date was found by subtracting 2 days from the July 2 date of record. Purchasers of Rudolf's stock on Tuesday, June 29 or earlier received the rights to the dividends; those who purchased the stock on or after June 30 did not. Assuming a stable market, Rudolf's stock price was expected to drop by approximately $0.80 per share when it began selling ex dividend on June 30. On August 2 the firm mailed dividend

FIGURE 12.1

Dividend Payment Time Line
Time line for the announcement and payment of a cash dividend for Rudolf Company

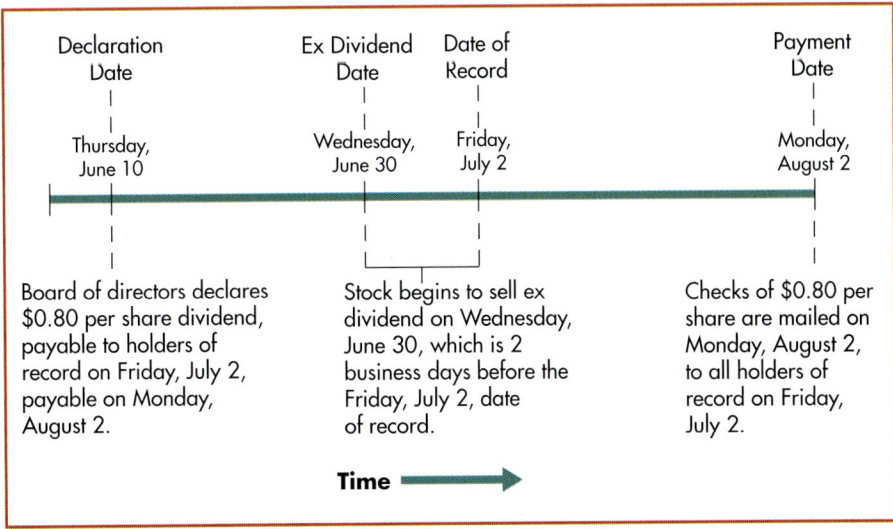

checks to the holders of record as of July 2. This produced the following balances in the key accounts of the firm:

Cash	$120,000	Dividends payable	$ 0
		Retained earnings	920,000

The net effect of declaring and paying the dividend was to reduce the firm's total assets (and stockholders' equity) by $80,000.

Tax Treatment of Dividends

The *Jobs and Growth Tax Relief Reconciliation Act of 2003* significantly changed the tax treatment of corporate dividends for most taxpayers. Prior to passage of the 2003 law, dividends received by investors were taxed as ordinary income at rates as high as 35 percent. The 2003 act reduced the tax rate on corporate dividends for most taxpayers to the tax rate applicable to capital gains, which is a maximum rate of 15 percent. This change significantly diminishes the degree of "double taxation" of dividends that results from the corporation first being taxed on its income and then the investor who receives the dividend also being taxed on it.

Immediately after passage of the act in 2003, many firms either initiated or increased dividends paid to their stockholders. Clearly, the fact that the after-tax cash flow to dividend recipients is much greater at the lower applicable tax rate has resulted in noticeably higher dividend payouts by corporations today than prior to passage of the 2003 legislation. The reduction in the degree of double taxation is expected to continue to result in higher dividend payouts and an increase in the appeal of common stocks to investors, particularly those in need of income rather than capital gains.

Dividend Reinvestment Plans

dividend reinvestment plans (DRIPs)
Plans that enable stockholders to use dividends received on the firm's stock to acquire additional shares—even fractional shares—at little or no transaction cost.

Today many firms offer **dividend reinvestment plans (DRIPs)**, which enable stockholders to use dividends received on the firm's stock to acquire additional shares—even fractional shares—at little or no transaction cost. Some companies even allow investors to make their *initial purchases* of the firm's stock directly from the company without going through a broker. With DRIPs, plan participants typically can acquire shares at about 5 percent below the prevailing market price. From its point of view, the firm can issue new shares to participants more economically, avoiding the underpricing and flotation costs that would accompany the public sale of new shares. Clearly, the existence of a DRIP may enhance the market appeal of a firm's shares.

Review Questions

12–1 Who are *holders of record*? When does a stock sell *ex dividend*?
12–2 What effect did the *Jobs and Growth Tax Relief Reconciliation Act of 2003* have on the taxation of corporate dividends? On corporate dividend payouts?

12–3 What benefit is available to participants in a *dividend reinvestment plan?* How might the firm benefit?

The Relevance of Dividend Policy

Numerous theories and empirical findings concerning dividend policy have been reported in the financial literature. Although this research provides some interesting insights about dividend policy, capital budgeting and capital structure decisions are generally considered far more important than dividend decisions. In other words, good investment and financing decisions should not be sacrificed for a dividend policy of questionable importance.

A number of key questions have yet to be resolved: Does dividend policy matter? What effect does dividend policy have on share price? Is there a model that can be used to evaluate alternative dividend policies in view of share value? Here we begin by describing the residual theory of dividends, which is used as a backdrop for discussion of the key arguments in support of dividend irrelevance and then those in support of dividend relevance.

The Residual Theory of Dividends

residual theory of dividends
A school of thought that suggests that the dividend paid by a firm should be viewed as a *residual*—the amount left over after all acceptable investment opportunities have been undertaken.

The **residual theory of dividends** is a school of thought that suggests that the dividend paid by a firm should be viewed as a *residual*—the amount left over after all acceptable investment opportunities have been undertaken. Using this approach, the firm would treat the dividend decision in three steps, as follows:

Step 1 Determine its optimal level of capital expenditures, which would be the level generated by the point of intersection of the investment opportunities schedule (IOS) and weighted marginal cost of capital (WMCC) schedule (see Chapter 10).

Step 2 Using the optimal capital structure proportions (see Chapter 11), estimate the total amount of equity financing needed to support the expenditures generated in Step 1.

Step 3 Because the cost of retained earnings, k_r, is less than the cost of new common stock, k_n, use retained earnings to meet the equity requirement determined in Step 2. If retained earnings are inadequate to meet this need, sell new common stock. If the available retained earnings are in excess of this need, distribute the surplus amount—the residual—as dividends.

According to this approach, as long as the firm's equity need exceeds the amount of retained earnings, no cash dividend is paid. The argument for this approach is that it is sound management to be certain that the company has the money it needs to compete effectively. This view of dividends suggests that the required return of investors, k_s, is *not* influenced by the firm's dividend policy—a premise that in turn implies that dividend policy is irrelevant.

FIGURE 12.2

WMCC and IOSs
WMCC and IOSs for Overbrook Industries

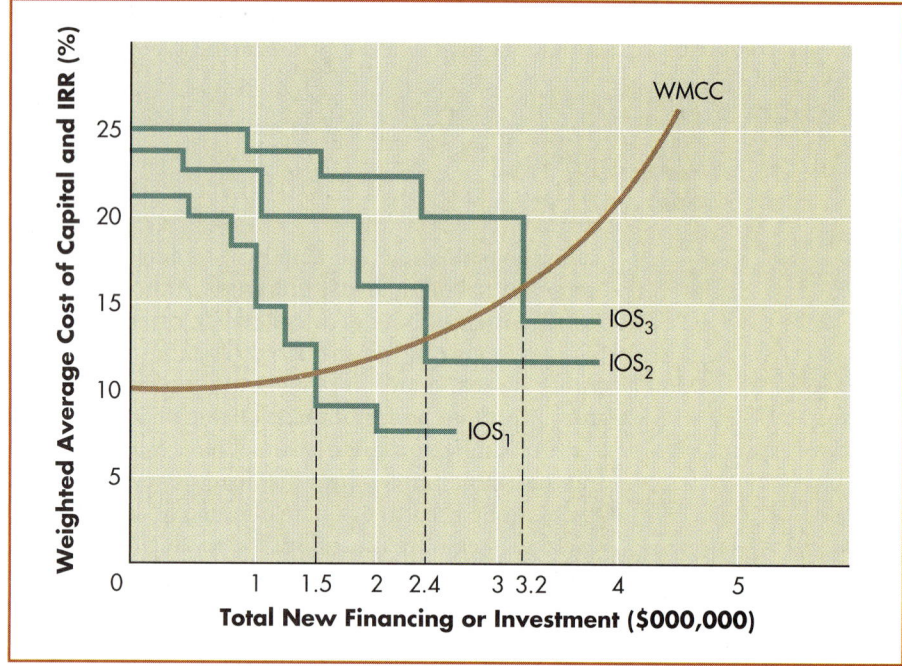

EXAMPLE

Overbrook Industries, a manufacturer of canoes and other small watercraft, has available from the current period's operations $1.8 million that can be retained or paid out in dividends. The firm's optimal capital structure is at a debt ratio of 30%, which represents 30% debt and 70% equity. Figure 12.2 depicts the firm's weighted marginal cost of capital (WMCC) schedule along with three investment opportunities schedules. For each IOS, the level of total new financing or investment determined by the point of intersection of the IOS and the WMCC has been noted. For IOS_1, it is $1.5 million, for IOS_2 $2.4 million, and for IOS_3 $3.2 million. Although only one IOS will exist in practice, it is useful to look at the possible dividend decisions generated by applying the residual theory in each of the three cases. Table 12.1 summarizes this analysis.

TABLE 12.1 Applying the Residual Theory of Dividends to Overbrook Industries for Each of Three IOSs (Shown in Figure 12.2)

	Investment opportunities schedules		
Item	IOS_1	IOS_2	IOS_3
(1) New financing or investment (Fig. 12.2)	$1,500,000	$2,400,000	$3,200,000
(2) Retained earnings available (given)	$1,800,000	$1,800,000	$1,800,000
(3) Equity needed [70% × (1)]	1,050,000	1,680,000	2,240,000
(4) Dividends [(2) − (3)]	$ 750,000	$ 120,000	$ 0[a]
(5) Dividend payout ratio [(4) ÷ (2)]	41.7%	6.7%	0%

[a]In this case, additional new common stock in the amount of $440,000 ($2,240,000 needed − $1,800,000 available) would have to be sold; no dividends would be paid.

Table 12.1 shows that if IOS_1 exists, the firm will pay out $750,000 in dividends, because only $1,050,000 of the $1,800,000 of available earnings is needed. A 41.7% payout ratio results. For IOS_2, dividends of $120,000 (a payout ratio of 6.7%) result. Should IOS_3 exist, the firm would pay no dividends (a 0% payout ratio), because its retained earnings of $1,800,000 would be less than the $2,240,000 of equity needed. In this case, the firm would have to obtain additional new common stock financing to meet the new requirements generated by the intersection of the IOS_3 and WMCC. Depending on which IOS exists, the firm's dividend would in effect be the residual, if any, remaining after all acceptable investments had been financed.

Arguments for Dividend Irrelevance

The residual theory of dividends implies that if the firm cannot invest its earnings to earn a return (IRR) that is in excess of cost (WMCC), it should distribute the earnings by paying dividends to stockholders. This approach suggests that dividends represent an earnings residual rather than an active decision variable that affects the firm's value. Such a view is consistent with the **dividend irrelevance theory** put forth by Merton H. Miller and Franco Modigliani (M and M).[1] They argue that the firm's value is determined solely by the earning power and risk of its assets (investments) and that the manner in which it splits its earnings stream between dividends and internally retained (and reinvested) funds does not affect this value. M and M's theory suggests that in a perfect world (certainty, no taxes, no transactions costs, and no other market imperfections), the value of the firm is unaffected by the distribution of dividends.

However, studies have shown that large changes in dividends do affect share price. Increases in dividends result in increased share price, and decreases in dividends result in decreased share price. In response, M and M argue that these effects are attributable not to the dividend itself but rather to the **informational content** of dividends with respect to future earnings. Investors view a change in dividends, up or down, as a *signal* that management expects future earnings to change in the same direction. An increase in dividends is viewed as a *positive signal*, and investors bid up the share price; a decrease in dividends is a *negative signal* that causes a decrease in share price as investors sell their shares.

M and M further argue that a **clientele effect** exists: A firm attracts shareholders whose preferences for the payment and stability of dividends correspond to the firm's actual payment pattern and stability of dividends. Investors who desire stable dividends as a source of income hold the stock of firms that pay about the same dividend amount each period. Investors who prefer to earn capital gains are more attracted to growing firms that reinvest a large portion of their earnings, favoring growth over a stable pattern of dividends. Because the shareholders get what they expect, M and M argue, the value of their firm's stock is unaffected by dividend policy.

The views of M and M and other proponents of dividend irrelevance are consistent with the residual theory, which focuses on making the best investment decisions to maximize share value. The proponents of dividend irrelevance

dividend irrelevance theory
Miller and Modigliani's theory that in a perfect world, the firm's value is determined solely by the earning power and risk of its assets (investments) and that the manner in which it splits its earnings stream between dividends and internally retained (and reinvested) funds does not affect this value.

informational content
The information provided by the dividends of a firm with respect to future earnings, which causes owners to bid up or down the price of the firm's stock.

clientele effect
The argument that a firm attracts shareholders whose preferences for the payment and stability of dividends correspond to the firm's actual payment pattern and stability of dividends.

---

1. Merton H. Miller and Franco Modigliani, "Dividend Policy, Growth and the Valuation of Shares," *Journal of Business* 34 (October 1961), pp. 411–433.

conclude that because dividends are irrelevant to a firm's value, the firm does not need to have a dividend policy. Although many research studies have been performed to validate or refute the dividend irrelevance theory, none has been successful in providing irrefutable evidence.

Arguments for Dividend Relevance

dividend relevance theory
The theory, advanced by Gordon and Lintner, that there is a direct relationship between a firm's dividend policy and its market value.

bird-in-the-hand argument
The belief, in support of *dividend relevance theory,* that investors see current dividends as less risky than future dividends or capital gains.

The key argument in support of **dividend relevance theory** is attributed to Myron J. Gordon and John Lintner,[2] who suggest that there is, in fact, a direct relationship between the firm's dividend policy and its market value. Fundamental to this proposition is their **bird-in-the-hand argument,** which suggests that investors see current dividends as less risky than future dividends or capital gains. "A bird in the hand is worth two in the bush." Gordon and Lintner argue that current dividend payments reduce investor uncertainty, causing investors to discount the firm's earnings at a lower rate and, all else being equal, to place a higher value on the firm's stock. Conversely, if dividends are reduced or are not paid, investor uncertainty will increase, raising the required return and lowering the stock's value.

Although many other arguments related to dividend relevance have been put forward, *empirical studies fail to provide conclusive evidence in support of the intuitively appealing dividend relevance argument*. In practice, however, the actions of both financial managers and stockholders tend to support the belief that dividend policy does affect stock value.[3]

Because we focus on the day-to-day behavior of firms, the remainder of this chapter is consistent with the belief that *dividends are relevant*—that each firm must develop a dividend policy that fulfills the goals of its owners and maximizes their wealth as reflected in the firm's share price.

Review Questions

12–4 Does following the *residual theory of dividends* lead to a stable dividend? Is this approach consistent with dividend relevance?

12–5 Contrast the basic arguments about dividend policy advanced by Miller and Modigliani (M and M) and by Gordon and Lintner.

Factors Affecting Dividend Policy

dividend policy
The firm's plan of action to be followed whenever a dividend decision is made.

The firm's **dividend policy** represents a plan of action to be followed whenever the dividend decision is made. Firms develop policies consistent with their goals. Before we review some of the popular types of dividend policies, we discuss the

---

2. Myron J. Gordon, "Optimal Investment and Financing Policy," *Journal of Finance* 18 (May 1963), pp. 264–272, and John Lintner, "Dividends, Earnings, Leverage, Stock Prices, and the Supply of Capital to Corporations," *Review of Economics and Statistics* 44 (August 1962), pp. 243–269.

3. A common exception is small firms, because they frequently treat dividends as a residual remaining after all acceptable investments have been initiated. Small firms follow this course of action because they usually do not have ready access to capital markets. The use of retained earnings therefore is a key source of financing for growth, which is generally an important goal of a small firm.

factors that are considered in establishing a dividend policy. These include legal constraints, contractual constraints, internal constraints, the firm's growth prospects, owner considerations, and market considerations.

Legal Constraints

Most states prohibit corporations from paying out as cash dividends any portion of the firm's "legal capital," which is typically measured by the par value of common stock. Other states define legal capital to include not only the par value of the common stock, but also any paid-in capital in excess of par. These *capital impairment restrictions* are generally established to provide a sufficient equity base to protect creditors' claims. An example will clarify the differing definitions of capital.

EXAMPLE

The stockholders' equity account of Miller Flour Company, a large grain processor, is presented in the following table.

Miller Flour Company Stockholders' Equity	
Common stock at par	$100,000
Paid-in capital in excess of par	200,000
Retained earnings	140,000
Total stockholders' equity	$440,000

In states where the firm's legal capital is defined as the par value of its common stock, the firm could pay out $340,000 ($200,000 + $140,000) in cash dividends without impairing its capital. In states where the firm's legal capital includes all paid-in capital, the firm could pay out only $140,000 in cash dividends.

An earnings requirement limiting the amount of dividends is sometimes imposed. With this restriction, the firm cannot pay more in cash dividends than the sum of its most recent and past retained earnings. However, *the firm is not prohibited from paying more in dividends than its current earnings*.[4]

EXAMPLE

Assume that Miller Flour Company, from the preceding example, in the year just ended has $30,000 in earnings available for common stock dividends. As the preceding table indicates, the firm has past retained earnings of $140,000. Thus it can legally pay dividends of up to $170,000.

If a firm has overdue liabilities or is legally insolvent or bankrupt, most states prohibit its payment of cash dividends. In addition, the Internal Revenue Service prohibits firms from accumulating earnings to reduce the owners' taxes. If the IRS can determine that a firm has accumulated an excess of earnings to allow

---

4. A firm that has an operating loss in the current period can still pay cash dividends as long as sufficient retained earnings against which to charge the dividend are available and, of course, as long as it has the cash with which to make the payments.

excess earnings accumulation tax
The tax the IRS levies on retained earnings above $250,000 for most businesses when it determines that the firm has accumulated an excess of earnings to allow owners to delay paying ordinary income taxes on dividends received.

owners to delay paying ordinary income taxes on dividends received, it may levy an **excess earnings accumulation tax** on any retained earnings above $250,000 for most businesses.

Contractual Constraints

Often the firm's ability to pay cash dividends is constrained by restrictive provisions in a loan agreement. Generally, these constraints prohibit the payment of cash dividends until a certain level of earnings has been achieved, or they may limit dividends to a certain dollar amount or percentage of earnings. Constraints on dividends help to protect creditors from losses due to the firm's insolvency.

Internal Constraints

The firm's ability to pay cash dividends is generally constrained by the amount of liquid assets (cash and marketable securities) available. Although it is possible for a firm to borrow funds to pay dividends, lenders are generally reluctant to make such loans because they produce no tangible or operating benefits that will help the firm repay the loan.

EXAMPLE

Miller Flour Company's stockholders' equity account presented earlier indicates that if the firm's legal capital is defined as all paid-in capital, the firm can pay $140,000 in dividends. If the firm has total liquid assets of $50,000 ($20,000 in cash plus marketable securities worth $30,000) and $35,000 of this is needed for operations, the maximum cash dividend the firm can pay is $15,000 ($50,000 − $35,000).

Growth Prospects

Hint Firms that grow very rapidly, such as high-tech firms, cannot afford to pay dividends. Their stockholders are influenced by the possibility of exceptionally higher share price and dividend levels in the future.

The firm's financial requirements are directly related to how much it expects to grow and what assets it will need to acquire. It must evaluate its profitability and risk to develop insight into its ability to raise capital externally. In addition, the firm must determine the cost and speed with which it can obtain financing. Generally, a large, mature firm has adequate access to new capital, whereas a rapidly growing firm may not have sufficient funds available to support its acceptable projects. A growth firm is likely to have to depend heavily on internal financing through retained earnings, so it is likely to pay out only a very small percentage of its earnings as dividends. A more established firm is in a better position to pay out a large proportion of its earnings, particularly if it has ready sources of financing.

It sometimes is difficult to determine how much cash to retain for growth prospects (or other uses), as the *In Practice* box on the facing page demonstrates.

Owner Considerations

The firm must establish a policy that has a favorable effect on the wealth of the *majority* of owners. One consideration is the *tax status of a firm's owners*. If a firm has a large percentage of wealthy stockholders who have sizable incomes, it

In Practice: FOCUS ON ETHICS

WERE FORD MANAGERS HOARDING CASH?

When managers don't pay dividends or pay only minimal dividends, they open themselves up to the charge that they are hoarding cash unnecessarily. Shareholders may believe this practice is unethical if they are convinced that managers are simply playing it safe in an effort to protect their jobs or to keep from having to answer to external funding sources.

According to Morgan Stanley, in midyear 2004 nonfinancial firms in the S&P 500 were holding 10 percent of their assets in cash—a figure twice that of just 5 years earlier, and the highest level in at least 20 years. Some of these companies sell products in stagnant markets and cannot point to future asset funding requirements to justify their cash buildup. "Empire building" behavior, such as hoarding cash, reminds us once again that shareholder wealth maximization has to be ethically constrained.

One example of how difficult it can be to decide how much cash to hold involves **Ford Motor Company**. In 1999, when Jacques Nasser became CEO, Ford's cash and securities totaled *$14 billion more than its entire debt.* Nasser had plans for the accumulated cash: He not only invested chunks of it when acquiring **Volvo** and **Land Rover**, but also initiated a combined $5.7 billion cash dividend and share repurchase. Wall Street securities analysts praised Ford for returning excess cash to shareholders, and the stock price went up 2 percent when shareholders heard about the dividend and repurchase.

However, Nasser may have gone too far—or maybe his timing was just bad. In 2001, Ford had to spend $3.5 billion to replace faulty tires on some of its SUVs. Not only did Ford have to cut its normal quarterly dividend, but its debt was also downgraded because investment bankers decided Ford was now in a "cash crisis." In March 2003, Moody's and Standard & Poor's rated Ford bonds barely above junk levels. Had it not been for banks' commitment to make credit available to Ford upon demand and the company's access to the asset-backed securities market (in which it could sell securities backed by receivables), the debt would have fallen into the junk-bond category.

The *Wall St. Journal* stated that in hindsight, Ford management had been wise to hoard cash against hard times, and investors were unwise to clamor for bigger payouts of cash to shareholders. Since 2001, Ford has built its cash and equivalents to $15.6 billion, and its cash and investments position is back up to $32 billion (as of midyear 2004)—although about $4 billion of that is reserved for near-term pension obligations. Its dividend yield is now 2.7 percent, versus 3.7 percent for the auto industry as a whole.

Caution and prudence are virtues—and these virtues provide ethical justification for managers accused of putting self-interest ahead of shareholder interests. As Ford's case demonstrates, it is probably wisest to give the benefit of the doubt to managers.

Sources: Bernard Condon, "Sitting Pretty," *Forbes* (July 1, 2004), www.forbes.com/business/2004/07/01/cs_bc_0701cashrich.html (accessed July 30, 2004); and Moody's press release (March 7, 2003).

■ *Summarize the arguments against holding large cash positions. Which do you find most convincing? Why?*

---

may decide to pay out a *lower* percentage of its earnings to allow the owners to delay the payment of taxes until they sell the stock. Because cash dividends are taxed at the same rate as capital gains (as a result of the 2003 Tax Act), this strategy benefits owners through the tax deferral rather than as a result of a lower tax rate. Lower-income shareholders, however, who need dividend income, will prefer a *higher* payout of earnings.

A second consideration is the *owners' investment opportunities*. A firm should not retain funds for investment in projects yielding lower returns than the owners could obtain from external investments of equal risk. If it appears that the owners have better opportunities externally, the firm should pay out a higher percentage of its earnings. If the firm's investment opportunities are at least as good as similar-risk external investments, a lower payout is justifiable.

A final consideration is the *potential dilution of ownership*. If a firm pays out a high percentage of earnings, new equity capital will have to be raised with common stock. The result of a new stock issue may be dilution of both control and earnings for the existing owners. By paying out a low percentage of its earnings, the firm can minimize the possibility of such dilution.

Market Considerations

An awareness of the market's probable response to certain types of policies is also helpful in formulating dividend policy. Stockholders are believed to value a *fixed or increasing level of dividends* as opposed to a fluctuating pattern of dividends. This belief is supported by the research of John Lintner, who found that corporate managers are averse to changing the dollar amount of dividends in response to changes in earnings, particularly when earnings decline.[5] In addition, stockholders are believed to value a policy of *continuous dividend payment*. Because regularly paying a fixed or increasing dividend eliminates uncertainty about the frequency and magnitude of dividends, the returns of the firm are likely to be discounted at a lower rate. This should result in an increase in the market value of the stock and therefore an increase in the owners' wealth.

A final market consideration is *informational content*. As noted earlier, shareholders often view a dividend payment as a *signal* of the firm's future success. A stable and continuous dividend is a *positive signal*, conveying the firm's good financial health. Shareholders are likely to interpret a passed dividend payment due to a loss or to very low earnings as a *negative signal*. The nonpayment of the dividend creates uncertainty about the future, which is likely to result in lower stock value. Owners and investors generally construe a dividend payment during a period of losses as an indication that the loss is merely temporary.

Hint The risk–return concept also applies to the firm's dividend policy. A firm that lets its dividends fluctuate from period to period will be viewed as risky, and investors will require a higher rate of return, which will increase the firm's cost of capital.

Review Question

12–6 What are the six factors that affect *dividend policy?* Briefly describe each of them.

Types of Dividend Policies

The firm's dividend policy must be formulated with two basic objectives in mind: providing for sufficient financing and maximizing the wealth of the firm's owners. Three of the more commonly used dividend policies are described in the following sections. A particular firm's cash dividend policy may incorporate elements of each.

---

5. John Lintner, "Distribution of Income of Corporations Among Dividends, Retained Earnings, and Taxes," *American Economic Review* 46 (May 1956), pp. 97–113.

Constant-Payout-Ratio Dividend Policy

dividend payout ratio
Indicates the percentage of each dollar earned that is distributed to the owners in the form of cash. It is calculated by dividing the firm's cash dividend per share by its earnings per share.

constant-payout-ratio dividend policy
A dividend policy based on the payment of a certain percentage of earnings to owners in each dividend period.

One type of dividend policy involves use of a constant payout ratio. The **dividend payout ratio** indicates the percentage of each dollar earned that is distributed to the owners in the form of cash. It is calculated by dividing the firm's cash dividend per share by its earnings per share. With a **constant-payout-ratio dividend policy,** the firm establishes that a certain percentage of earnings is paid to owners in each dividend period.

The problem with this policy is that if the firm's earnings drop or if a loss occurs in a given period, the dividends may be low or even nonexistent. Because dividends are often considered an indicator of the firm's future condition and status, the firm's stock price may be adversely affected.

EXAMPLE

Peachtree Industries, a miner of potassium, has a policy of paying out 40% of earnings in cash dividends. In periods when a loss occurs, the firm's policy is to pay no cash dividends. Data on Peachtree's earnings, dividends, and average stock prices for the past 6 years follow.

Year	Earnings/share	Dividends/share	Average price/share
2006	−$0.50	$0.00	$42.00
2005	3.00	1.20	52.00
2004	1.75	0.70	48.00
2003	−1.50	0.00	38.00
2002	2.00	0.80	46.00
2001	4.50	1.80	50.00

Dividends increased in 2004 and in 2005 but decreased in the other years. In years of decreasing dividends, the firm's stock price dropped; when dividends increased, the price of the stock increased. Peachtree's sporadic dividend payments appear to make its owners uncertain about the returns they can expect.

Although some firms use a constant-payout-ratio dividend policy, it is *not* recommended.

Hint Regulated utilities in low-growth areas can use a constant-payout-ratio dividend policy. Their capital requirements are usually low and their earnings are more stable than those of most firms.

Regular Dividend Policy

regular dividend policy
A dividend policy based on the payment of a fixed-dollar dividend in each period.

The **regular dividend policy** is based on the payment of a fixed-dollar dividend in each period. This policy provides the owners with generally positive information, thereby minimizing their uncertainty. Often, firms that use this policy increase the regular dividend once a *proven* increase in earnings has occurred. Under this policy, dividends are almost never decreased.

EXAMPLE

The dividend policy of Woodward Laboratories, a producer of a popular artificial sweetener, is to pay annual dividends of $1.00 per share until per-share earnings have exceeded $4.00 for three consecutive years. At that point, the annual dividend is raised to $1.50 per share, and a new earnings plateau is established. The firm does not anticipate decreasing its dividend unless its liquidity is in jeopardy.

Data for Woodward's earnings, dividends, and average stock prices for the past 12 years follow.

Year	Earnings/share	Dividends/share	Average price/share
2006	$4.50	$1.50	$47.50
2005	3.90	1.50	46.50
2004	4.60	1.50	45.00
2003	4.20	1.00	43.00
2002	5.00	1.00	42.00
2001	2.00	1.00	38.50
2000	6.00	1.00	38.00
1999	3.00	1.00	36.00
1998	0.75	1.00	33.00
1997	0.50	1.00	33.00
1996	2.70	1.00	33.50
1995	2.85	1.00	35.00

Whatever the level of earnings, Woodward Laboratories paid dividends of $1.00 per share through 2003. In 2004, the dividend increased to $1.50 per share because earnings in excess of $4.00 per share had been achieved for 3 years. In 2004, the firm also had to establish a new earnings plateau for further dividend increases. Woodward Laboratories' average price per share exhibited a stable, increasing behavior in spite of a somewhat volatile pattern of earnings.

target dividend-payout ratio
A dividend policy under which the firm attempts to pay out a certain *percentage* of earnings as a stated dollar dividend and adjusts that dividend toward a target payout as proven earnings increases occur.

Often a regular dividend policy is built around a **target dividend-payout ratio**. Under this policy, the firm attempts to pay out a certain *percentage* of earnings, but rather than let dividends fluctuate, it pays a stated dollar dividend and adjusts that dividend toward the target payout as proven earnings increases occur. For instance, Woodward Laboratories appears to have a target payout ratio of around 35 percent. The payout was about 35 percent ($1.00 ÷ $2.85) when the dividend policy was set in 1995, and when the dividend was raised to $1.50 in 2004, the payout ratio was about 33 percent ($1.50 ÷ $4.60).

Low-Regular-and-Extra Dividend Policy

low-regular-and-extra dividend policy
A dividend policy based on paying a low regular dividend, supplemented by an additional dividend when earnings are higher than normal in a given period.

extra dividend
An additional dividend optionally paid by the firm if earnings are higher than normal in a given period.

Some firms establish a **low-regular-and-extra dividend policy,** paying a low regular dividend, supplemented by an additional dividend when earnings are higher than normal in a given period. By calling the additional dividend an **extra dividend,** the firm avoids giving shareholders false hopes. This policy is especially common among companies that experience cyclical shifts in earnings.

By establishing a low regular dividend that is paid each period, the firm gives investors the stable income necessary to build confidence in the firm, and the extra dividend permits them to share in the earnings from an especially good period. Firms using this policy must raise the level of the regular dividend once proven increases in earnings have been achieved. The extra dividend should not be a regular event; otherwise, it becomes meaningless. The use of a target dividend-payout ratio in establishing the regular dividend level is advisable.

Review Question

12–7 Describe a constant-payout-ratio dividend policy, a regular dividend policy, and a low-regular-and-extra dividend policy. What are the effects of these policies?

Other Forms of Dividends

Dividends can be paid in forms other than cash. Here we discuss two other methods of paying dividends—stock dividends and stock repurchases—as well as a closely related topic, stock splits.

Stock Dividends

stock dividend
The payment, to existing owners, of a dividend in the form of stock.

A **stock dividend** is the payment, to existing owners, of a dividend in the form of stock. Often firms pay stock dividends as a replacement for or a supplement to cash dividends. Although stock dividends do not have a real value, stockholders may perceive them to represent something they did not have before.

Accounting Aspects

In an accounting sense, the payment of a stock dividend is a shifting of funds between stockholders' equity accounts rather than an outflow of funds. When a firm declares a stock dividend, the procedures for announcement and distribution are the same as those described earlier for a cash dividend. The accounting entries associated with the payment of a stock dividend vary depending on its size. A **small (ordinary) stock dividend** is a stock dividend that represents less than 20 to 25 percent of the common stock outstanding when the dividend is declared. Small stock dividends are most common.

small (ordinary) stock dividend
A stock dividend representing less than 20 to 25 percent of the common stock outstanding when the dividend is declared.

EXAMPLE The current stockholders' equity on the balance sheet of Garrison Corporation, a distributor of prefabricated cabinets, is as shown in the following accounts.

Preferred stock	$ 300,000
Common stock (100,000 shares at $4 par)	400,000
Paid-in capital in excess of par	600,000
Retained earnings	700,000
Total stockholders' equity	$2,000,000

Garrison, which has 100,000 shares outstanding, declares a 10% stock dividend when the market price of its stock is $15 per share. Because 10,000 new shares (10% of 100,000) are issued at the prevailing market price of $15 per share, $150,000 ($15 per share × 10,000 shares) is shifted from retained earnings to the common stock and paid-in capital accounts. A total of $40,000 ($4 par × 10,000 shares) is added to common stock, and the remaining $110,000

[($15 − $4) × 10,000 shares] is added to the paid-in capital in excess of par. The resulting account balances are as follows:

Preferred stock	$ 300,000
Common stock (110,000 shares at $4 par)	440,000
Paid-in capital in excess of par	710,000
Retained earnings	550,000
Total stockholders' equity	$2,000,000

The firm's total stockholders' equity has not changed; funds have merely been *shifted* among stockholders' equity accounts.

The Shareholder's Viewpoint

The shareholder receiving a stock dividend typically receives nothing of value. After the dividend is paid, the per-share value of the shareholder's stock decreases in proportion to the dividend in such a way that the market value of his or her total holdings in the firm remains unchanged. The shareholder's proportion of ownership in the firm also remains the same, and *as long as the firm's earnings remain unchanged,* so does his or her share of total earnings. (However, if the firm's earnings and cash dividends increase when the stock dividend is issued, an increase in share value is likely to result.)

EXAMPLE Ms. X owned 10,000 shares of Garrison Corporation's stock. The company's most recent earnings were $220,000, and earnings are not expected to change in the near future. Before the stock dividend, Ms. X owned 10% (10,000 shares ÷ 100,000 shares) of the firm's stock, which was selling for $15 per share. Earnings per share were $2.20 ($220,000 ÷ 100,000 shares). Because Ms. X owned 10,000 shares, her earnings were $22,000 ($2.20 per share × 10,000 shares). After receiving the 10% stock dividend, Ms. X has 11,000 shares, which again is 10% of the ownership (11,000 shares ÷ 110,000 shares). The market price of the stock can be expected to drop to $13.64 per share [$15 × (1.00 ÷ 1.10)], which means that the market value of Ms. X's holdings is $150,000 (11,000 shares × $13.64 per share). This is the same as the initial value of her holdings (10,000 shares × $15 per share). The future earnings per share drops to $2 ($220,000 ÷ 110,000 shares) because the same $220,000 in earnings must now be divided among 110,000 shares. Because Ms. X still owns 10% of the stock, her share of total earnings is still $22,000 ($2 per share × 11,000 shares).

In summary, if the firm's earnings remain constant and total cash dividends do not increase, a stock dividend results in a lower per-share market value for the firm's stock.

The Company's Viewpoint

Stock dividends are more costly to issue than cash dividends, but certain advantages may outweigh these costs. Firms find the stock dividend to be a way to give owners something without having to use cash. Generally, when a firm needs to preserve cash to finance rapid growth, a stock dividend is used. When the stockholders recognize that the firm is reinvesting the cash flow so as to maximize future earnings, the market value of the firm should at least remain unchanged. However, if the stock dividend is paid so that cash can be retained to satisfy past-due bills, a decline in market value may result.

Stock Splits

stock split
A method commonly used to lower the market price of a firm's stock by increasing the number of shares belonging to each shareholder.

Although not a type of dividend, *stock splits* have an effect on a firm's share price similar to that of stock dividends. A **stock split** is a method commonly used to lower the market price of a firm's stock by increasing the number of shares belonging to each shareholder. In a 2-for-1 split, for example, two new shares are exchanged for each old share, with each new share being worth half the value of each old share. A stock split has no effect on the firm's capital structure.

Quite often, a firm believes that its stock is priced too high and that lowering the market price will enhance trading activity. Stock splits are often made prior to issuing additional stock to enhance that stock's marketability and stimulate market activity. It is not unusual for a stock split to cause a slight increase in the market value of the stock, attributable to its informational content and to the fact that *total* dividends paid commonly increase slightly after a split.

EXAMPLE

Delphi Company, a forest products concern, had 200,000 shares of $2-par-value common stock and no preferred stock outstanding. Because the stock is selling at a high market price, the firm has declared a 2-for-1 stock split. The total before- and after-split stockholders' equity is shown in the following table.

Before split	
Common stock (200,000 shares at $2 par)	$ 400,000
Paid-in capital in excess of par	4,000,000
Retained earnings	2,000,000
Total stockholders' equity	$6,400,000
After 2-for-1 split	
Common stock (400,000 shares at $1 par)	$ 400,000
Paid-in capital in excess of par	4,000,000
Retained earnings	2,000,000
Total stockholders' equity	$6,400,000

The insignificant effect of the stock split on the firm's books is obvious.

reverse stock split
A method used to raise the market price of a firm's stock by exchanging a certain number of outstanding shares for one new share.

Stock can be split in any way desired. Sometimes a **reverse stock split** is made: A certain number of outstanding shares are exchanged for one new share. For example, in a 1-for-3 split, one new share is exchanged for three old shares. Reverse stock splits are initiated to raise the market price of a firm's stock when it is selling at too low a price to appear respectable.[6]

---

6. If a firm's stock is selling at a low price—possibly less than a few dollars—many investors are hesitant to purchase it because they believe it is "cheap." These somewhat unsophisticated investors correlate cheapness and quality, and they feel that a low-priced stock is a low-quality investment. A reverse stock split raises the stock price and increases per-share earnings.

Stock Repurchases

stock repurchase
The repurchase by the firm of outstanding common stock in the marketplace; desired effects of stock repurchases are that they either enhance shareholder value or help to discourage an unfriendly takeover.

In recent years, firms have increased their repurchasing of outstanding common stock in the marketplace. The practical motives for **stock repurchases** include obtaining shares to be used in acquisitions, having shares available for employee stock option plans, and retiring shares. The recent increase in frequency and importance of stock repurchases is due to the fact that they either enhance shareholder value or help to discourage an unfriendly takeover. Stock repurchases enhance shareholder value by (1) reducing the number of shares outstanding and thereby raising earnings per share, (2) sending a *positive signal* to investors in the marketplace that management believes that the stock is undervalued, and (3) providing a temporary floor for the stock price, which may have been declining. The use of repurchases to discourage unfriendly takeovers is predicated on the belief that a corporate raider is less likely to gain control of the firm if there are fewer publicly traded shares available. Here we focus on retiring shares through repurchase, because this motive for repurchase is similar to the payment of cash dividends.

Stock Repurchases Viewed as a Cash Dividend

When common stock is repurchased for retirement, the underlying motive is to distribute excess cash to the owners. Generally, as long as earnings remain constant, the repurchase reduces the number of outstanding shares, raising the earnings per share and therefore the market price per share. In addition, an owner tax deferral benefit may result. The repurchase of common stock results in a type of *reverse dilution,* because the EPS and the market price of stock are increased by reducing the number of shares outstanding. The net effect of the repurchase is similar to the payment of a cash dividend.

EXAMPLE

Benton Company, a national sportswear chain, has released the following financial data:

Earnings available for common stockholders	$1,000,000
Number of shares of common stock outstanding	400,000
Earnings per share ($1,000,000 ÷ 400,000)	$2.50
Market price per share	$50
Price/earnings (P/E) ratio ($50 ÷ $2.50)	20

The firm wants to use $800,000 of its earnings either to pay cash dividends or to repurchase shares. If the firm paid cash dividends, the amount of the dividend would be $2 per share ($800,000 ÷ 400,000 shares). If the firm paid $52 per share to repurchase stock, it could repurchase approximately 15,385 shares ($800,000 ÷ $52 per share). As a result of this repurchase, 384,615 shares (400,000 shares − 15,385 shares) of common stock would remain outstanding. Earnings per share (EPS) would rise to $2.60 ($1,000,000 ÷ 384,615). If the stock still sold at 20 times earnings (P/E = 20), its market price could be estimated by multiplying the new EPS by this P/E ratio (the *price/earnings multiple approach* presented in Chapter 7). The price would therefore rise to $52 per share ($2.60 × 20). In both cases, the stockholders would receive $2 per share: a $2 cash dividend in the dividend case or a $2 increase in share price ($50 per share to $52 per share) in the repurchase case.

Besides the advantage of an increase in per-share earnings, an owner tax deferral benefit results. Although the owners would have to pay capital gains taxes in either case (the $2 dividend or the $2 increase in market value), the dividend tax would be paid in the current year. In contrast, the tax on the gain from the repurchase would effectively be deferred until the stock is sold. Clearly, the repurchase provides the stockholder with the opportunity to defer taxes. The IRS is alleged to monitor firms that regularly repurchase stock and levies a penalty when it believes repurchases have been deliberately made to delay the payment of taxes by stockholders.

Accounting Entries

The accounting entries that result when common stock is repurchased are a reduction in cash and the establishment of a contra capital account called "treasury stock," which is shown as a deduction from stockholders' equity. The label *treasury stock* is used on the balance sheet to indicate the presence of repurchased shares.

The Repurchase Process

When a company intends to repurchase a block of outstanding shares, it should make shareholders aware of its intentions. Specifically, it should advise them of the purpose of the repurchase (acquisition, stock options, retirement) and the disposition (if any) planned for the repurchased shares (traded for shares of another firm, distribution to executives, or held in the treasury).

Three basic methods of repurchase are commonly used. One is to purchase shares on the *open market*. This places upward pressure on the price of shares if the number of shares being repurchased is reasonably large in comparison with the total number outstanding. The second method is through tender offers. A **tender offer** is a formal offer to purchase a given number of shares of a firm's stock at a specified price. The price at which a tender offer is made is set above the current market price to attract sellers. If the number of shares desired cannot be repurchased through the tender offer, open-market purchases can be used to obtain the additional shares. Tender offers are preferred when large numbers of shares are repurchased, because the company's intentions are clearly stated and each stockholder has an opportunity to sell shares at the tendered price. A third method that is sometimes used involves the purchase, on a *negotiated basis*, of a large block of shares from one or more major stockholders. Again, in this case, the firm has to state its intentions and make certain that the purchase price is fair and equitable in view of the interests and opportunities of the remaining shareholders.

tender offer
A formal offer to purchase a given number of shares of a firm's stock at a specified price.

Review Questions

12–8 Why do firms issue *stock dividends?* Comment on the following statement: "I have a stock that promises to pay a 20 percent stock dividend every year, and therefore it guarantees that I will break even in 5 years."

12–9 Compare a *stock split* with a *stock dividend*.

12–10 What is the logic behind *repurchasing shares* of common stock to distribute excess cash to the firm's owners?

Summary

FOCUS ON VALUE

Cash dividends are the cash flows that a firm distributes to its common stockholders. A share of common stock gives its owner the right to receive all future dividends. The present value of all those future dividends expected over a firm's assumed infinite life determines the firm's stock value.

Dividends not only represent cash flows to shareholders but also contain useful information with regard to the firm's current and future performance. Such information affects the shareholders' perception of the firm's risk. A firm can also pay stock dividends, initiate stock splits, or repurchase stock. All of these dividend-related actions can affect the firm's risk, return, and value as a result of their cash flows and informational content.

Although the theory with regard to the relevance of dividends is still evolving, the behavior of most firms and stockholders suggests that dividend policy affects share prices. It is therefore believed to be important for the financial manager to develop and implement a dividend policy that is consistent with the firm's goal of **maximizing stock price**.

REVIEW OF LEARNING GOALS

LG1 **Understand cash dividend payment procedures, the tax treatment of dividends, and the role of dividend reinvestment plans.** The cash dividend decision is normally made and declared by the board of directors, which establishes the record and payment dates. Generally, the larger the dividend charged to retained earnings and paid in cash, the greater the amount of financing that must be raised externally. As a result of the Jobs and Growth Tax Relief Reconciliation Act of 2003, most taxpayers pay taxes on corporate dividends at a maximum rate of 15 percent. Some firms offer dividend reinvestment plans that allow stockholders to acquire shares in lieu of cash dividends.

LG2 **Describe the residual theory of dividends and the key arguments with regard to dividend irrelevance and relevance.** The residual theory suggests that dividends should be viewed as the earnings left after all acceptable investment opportunities have been undertaken.

Miller and Modigliani argue in favor of dividend irrelevance, using a perfect world wherein information content and clientele effects exist.

Gordon and Lintner advance the theory of dividend relevance, basing their argument on the uncertainty-reducing effect of dividends, supported by their bird-in-the-hand argument. Empirical studies fail to provide clear support of dividend relevance. Even so, the actions of financial managers and stockholders tend to support the belief that dividend policy does affect stock value.

LG3 **Discuss the key factors involved in establishing a dividend policy.** A firm's dividend policy should provide for sufficient financing and maximize stockholders' wealth. Dividend policy is affected by legal, contractual, and internal constraints; by growth prospects; and by owner and market considerations. Legal constraints prohibit corporations from paying out as cash dividends any portion of the firm's "legal capital." Nor can firms with overdue liabilities and legally insolvent or bankrupt firms pay cash dividends. Contractual constraints result from restrictive provisions in the firm's loan agreements. Internal constraints result from a firm's limited availability of excess cash. Growth prospects affect the relative importance of retaining earnings rather than paying them out in dividends. The tax status of owners, the owners' investment opportunities, and the potential dilution of ownership are important owner considerations. Finally, market considerations are related to the stockholders' preference for the continuous payment of fixed or increasing streams of dividends and the perceived informational content of dividends.

Review and evaluate the three basic types of dividend policies. With a constant-payout-ratio dividend policy, the firm pays a fixed percentage of earnings to the owners each period; dividends move up and down with earnings, and no dividend is paid when a loss occurs. Under a regular dividend policy, the firm pays a fixed-dollar dividend each period; it increases the amount of dividends only after a proven increase in earnings. The low-regular-and-extra dividend policy is similar to the regular dividend policy, except that it pays an extra dividend when the firm's earnings are higher than normal. The regular and the low-regular-and-extra dividend policies are generally preferred because they reduce uncertainty.

Evaluate stock dividends from accounting, shareholder, and company points of view. Firms may pay stock dividends as a replacement for or supplement to cash dividends. The payment of stock dividends involves a shifting of funds between capital accounts rather than an outflow of funds. Stock dividends do not change the market value of stockholders' holdings, proportion of ownership, or share of total earnings. However, stock dividends may satisfy owners and enable the firm to preserve its market value without having to use cash.

Explain stock splits and stock repurchases and the firm's motivation for undertaking each of them. Stock splits are used to enhance trading activity of a firm's shares by lowering or raising their market price. A stock split merely involves accounting adjustments; it has no effect on the firm's cash or on its capital structure.

Stock repurchases can be made in lieu of cash dividend payments to retire outstanding shares. They reduce the number of outstanding shares, thereby increasing earnings per share and the market price per share. They also defer the tax payments of stockholders.

SELF-TEST PROBLEM (SOLUTION IN APPENDIX B)

ST12–1 **Stock repurchase** The Off-Shore Steel Company has earnings available for common stockholders of $2 million and has 500,000 shares of common stock outstanding at $60 per share. The firm is currently contemplating the payment of $2 per share in cash dividends.
  a. Calculate the firm's current earnings per share (EPS) and price/earnings (P/E) ratio.
  b. If the firm can repurchase stock at $62 per share, how many shares can be purchased in lieu of making the proposed cash dividend payment?
  c. How much will the EPS be after the proposed repurchase? Why?
  d. If the stock sells at the old P/E ratio, what will the market price be after repurchase?
  e. Compare and contrast the earnings per share before and after the proposed repurchase.
  f. Compare and contrast the stockholders' position under the dividend and repurchase alternatives.

WARM-UP EXERCISES

E12–1 Stephanie's Cafes, Inc. has declared a dividend of $1.30 per share for shareholders of record on Tuesday, May 2. The firm has 200,000 shares outstanding and will pay the dividend on May 24. How much cash will be needed to pay the dividend? When will the stock begin selling *ex dividend*?

E12–2 Chancellor Industries has retained earnings available of $1.2 million. The firm plans to make two investments that require financing of $950,000 and $1.75 million, respectively. Chancellor uses a target capital structure with 60% debt and 40% equity. Apply the *residual theory* to determine what dividends, if any, can be paid out, and calculate the resulting *dividend payout ratio*.

E12–3 Ashkenazi Companies has the following stockholders' equity account:

Common stock (350,000 shares at $3 par)	$1,050,000
Paid-in capital in excess of par	2,500,000
Retained earnings	750,000
Total stockholders' equity	$4,300,000

Assuming that state laws define legal capital solely as the par value of common stock, how much of a per-share dividend can Ashkenazi pay? If legal capital were more broadly defined to include all paid-in capital, how much of a per-share dividend can Ashkenazi pay?

E12–4 The board of Kopi Industries is considering a new dividend policy that would set dividends at 60% of earnings. The recent past has witnessed earnings per share (EPS) and dividends paid per share as follows:

Year	EPS	Dividend/share
2003	$1.75	$0.95
2004	1.95	1.20
2005	2.05	1.25
2006	2.25	1.30

Based on Kopi's historical dividend payout ratio, discuss whether a *constant payout ratio* of 60% would benefit shareholders.

E12–5 The current stockholders' equity account for Hilo Farms is as follows:

Common stock (50,000 shares at $3 par)	$150,000
Paid-in capital in excess of par	250,000
Retained earnings	450,000
Total stockholders' equity	$850,000

Hilo has announced plans to issue an additional 5,000 shares of common stock as part of its stock dividend plan. The current market price of Hilo's common stock is $20 per share. Show how the proposed *stock dividend* would affect the stockholders' equity account.

Problems

P12–1 **Dividend payment procedures** At the quarterly dividend meeting, Wood Shoes declared a cash dividend of $1.10 per share for holders of record on Monday, July 10. The firm has 300,000 shares of common stock outstanding and has set a payment date of July 31. Prior to the dividend declaration, the firm's key accounts were as follows:

Cash	$500,000	Dividends payable	$ 0
		Retained earnings	2,500,000

a. Show the entries after the meeting adjourned.
b. When is the *ex dividend* date?
c. What values would the key accounts have after the July 31 payment date?
d. What effect, if any, will the dividend have on the firm's total assets?
e. Ignoring general market fluctuations, what effect, if any, will the dividend have on the firm's stock price on the ex dividend date?

P12–2 **Dividend payment** Kathy Snow wishes to purchase shares of Countdown Computing, Inc. The company's board of directors has declared a cash dividend of $0.80 to be paid to holders of record on Wednesday, May 12.
a. What is the last day that Kathy can purchase the stock (trade date) and still receive the dividend?
b. What day does this stock begin trading "ex dividend"?
c. What change, if any, would you expect in the price per share when the stock begins trading on the ex dividend day?
d. If Kathy held the stock for less than one quarter and then sold it for $39 per share, would she achieve a higher investment return by (1) buying the stock *prior to* the ex dividend date at $35 per share and collecting the $0.80 dividend, or (2) buying it *on* the ex dividend date at $34.20 per share but not receiving the dividend?

P12–3 **Residual dividend policy** As president of Young's of California, a large clothing chain, you have just received a letter from a major stockholder. The stockholder asks about the company's dividend policy. In fact, the stockholder has asked you to estimate the amount of the dividend that you are likely to pay next year. You have not yet collected all the information about the expected dividend payment, but you do know the following:
(1) The company follows a residual dividend policy.
(2) The total capital budget for next year is likely to be one of three amounts, depending on the results of capital budgeting studies that are currently under way. The capital expenditure amounts are $2 million, $3 million, and $4 million.
(3) The forecasted level of potential retained earnings next year is $2 million.
(4) The target or optimal capital structure is a debt ratio of 40%.

You have decided to respond by sending the stockholder the best information available to you.
a. Describe a *residual dividend policy*.
b. Compute the amount of the dividend (or the amount of new common stock needed) and the dividend payout ratio for each of the three capital expenditure amounts.

c. Compare, contrast, and discuss the amount of dividends (calculated in part **b**) associated with each of the three capital expenditure amounts.

P12–4 **Dividend constraints** The Howe Company's stockholders' equity account is as follows:

Common stock (400,000 shares at $4 par)	$1,600,000
Paid-in capital in excess of par	1,000,000
Retained earnings	1,900,000
Total stockholders' equity	$4,500,000

The earnings available for common stockholders from this period's operations are $100,000, which have been included as part of the $1.9 million retained earnings.

a. What is the maximum dividend per share that the firm can pay? (Assume that legal capital includes *all* paid-in capital.)
b. If the firm has $160,000 in cash, what is the largest per-share dividend it can pay without borrowing?
c. Indicate the accounts and changes, if any, that will result if the firm pays the dividends indicated in parts **a** and **b**.
d. Indicate the effects of an $80,000 cash dividend on stockholders' equity.

P12–5 **Dividend constraints** A firm has $800,000 in paid-in capital, retained earnings of $40,000 (including the current year's earnings), and 25,000 shares of common stock outstanding. In the current year, it has $29,000 of earnings available for the common stockholders.

a. What is the most the firm can pay in cash dividends to each common stockholder? (Assume that legal capital includes *all* paid-in capital.)
b. What effect would a cash dividend of $0.80 per share have on the firm's balance sheet entries?
c. If the firm cannot raise any new funds from external sources, what do you consider the key constraint with respect to the magnitude of the firm's dividend payments? Why?

P12–6 **Alternative dividend policies** Over the last 10 years, a firm has had the earnings per share shown in the following table.

Year	Earnings per share
2006	$4.00
2005	3.80
2004	3.20
2003	2.80
2002	3.20
2001	2.40
2000	1.20
1999	1.80
1998	−0.50
1997	0.25

a. If the firm's dividend policy were based on a *constant payout ratio* of 40% for all years with positive earnings and 0% otherwise, what would be the annual dividend for each year?
b. If the firm had a dividend payout of $1.00 per share, increasing by $0.10 per share whenever the dividend payout fell below 50% for two consecutive years, what annual dividend would the firm pay each year?
c. If the firm's policy were to pay $0.50 per share each period except when earnings per share exceed $3.00, when an extra dividend equal to 80% of earnings beyond $3.00 would be paid, what annual dividend would the firm pay each year?
d. Discuss the pros and cons of each dividend policy described in parts **a** through **c**.

P12–7 **Alternative dividend policies** Given the earnings per share over the period 1999–2006 shown in the following table, determine the annual dividend per share under each of the policies set forth in parts **a** through **d**.

Year	Earnings per share
2006	$1.40
2005	1.56
2004	1.20
2003	– 0.85
2002	1.05
2001	0.60
2000	1.00
1999	0.44

a. Pay out 50% of earnings in all years with positive earnings.
b. Pay $0.50 per share and increase to $0.60 per share whenever earnings per share rise above $0.90 per share for two consecutive years.
c. Pay $0.50 per share except when earnings exceed $1.00 per share, in which case pay an extra dividend of 60% of earnings above $1.00 per share.
d. Combine the policies described in parts **b** and **c**. When the dividend is raised (in part **b**), raise the excess dividend base (in part **c**) from $1.00 to $1.10 per share.
e. Compare and contrast each of the dividend policies described in parts **a** through **d**.

P12–8 **Stock dividend—Firm** Columbia Paper has the following stockholders' equity account. The firm's common stock has a current market price of $30 per share.

Preferred stock	$100,000
Common stock (10,000 shares at $2 par)	20,000
Paid-in capital in excess of par	280,000
Retained earnings	100,000
Total stockholders' equity	$500,000

a. Show the effects on Columbia of a 5% stock dividend.
b. Show the effects of (1) a 10% and (2) a 20% stock dividend.

c. In light of your answers to parts **a** and **b**, discuss the effects of stock dividends on stockholders' equity.

P12–9 **Cash versus stock dividend** Milwaukee Tool has the following stockholders' equity account. The firm's common stock currently sells for $4 per share.

Preferred stock	$ 100,000
Common stock (400,000 shares at $1 par)	400,000
Paid-in capital in excess of par	200,000
Retained earnings	320,000
Total stockholders' equity	$1,020,000

a. Show the effects on the firm of a *cash* dividend of $0.01, $0.05, $0.10, and $0.20 per share.
b. Show the effects on the firm of a 1%, 5%, 10%, and 20% *stock* dividend.
c. Compare the effects in parts **a** and **b**. What are the significant differences between the two methods of paying dividends?

P12–10 **Stock dividend—Investor** Sarah Warren currently holds 400 shares of Nutri-Foods. The firm has 40,000 shares outstanding. The firm most recently had earnings available for common stockholders of $80,000, and its stock has been selling for $22 per share. The firm intends to retain its earnings and pay a 10% stock dividend.
a. How much does the firm currently earn per share?
b. What proportion of the firm does Warren currently own?
c. What proportion of the firm will Warren own after the stock dividend? Explain your answer.
d. At what market price would you expect the stock to sell after the stock dividend?
e. Discuss what effect, if any, the payment of stock dividends will have on Warren's share of the ownership and earnings of Nutri-Foods.

P12–11 **Stock dividend—Investor** Security Data Company has outstanding 50,000 shares of common stock currently selling at $40 per share. The firm most recently had earnings available for common stockholders of $120,000, but it has decided to retain these funds and is considering either a 5% or a 10% stock dividend in lieu of a cash dividend.
a. Determine the firm's current earnings per share.
b. If Sam Waller currently owns 500 shares of the firm's stock, determine his proportion of ownership currently and under each of the proposed stock dividend plans. Explain your findings.
c. Calculate and explain the market price per share under each of the stock dividend plans.
d. For each of the proposed stock dividends, calculate the earnings per share after payment of the stock dividend.
e. What is the value of Waller's holdings under each of the plans? Explain.
f. Should Waller have any preference with respect to the proposed stock dividends? Why or why not?

P12–12 Stock split—Firm Growth Industries' current stockholders' equity account is as follows:

Preferred stock	$ 400,000
Common stock (600,000 shares at $3 par)	1,800,000
Paid-in capital in excess of par	200,000
Retained earnings	800,000
Total stockholders' equity	$3,200,000

a. Indicate the change, if any, expected if the firm declares a 2-for-1 stock split.
b. Indicate the change, if any, expected if the firm declares a 1-for-1½ *reverse* stock split.
c. Indicate the change, if any, expected if the firm declares a 3-for-1 stock split.
d. Indicate the change, if any, expected if the firm declares a 6-for-1 stock split.
e. Indicate the change, if any, expected if the firm declares a 1-for-4 *reverse* stock split.

P12–13 Stock split versus stock dividend—Firm Mammoth Corporation is considering a 3-for-2 stock split. It currently has the stockholders' equity position shown. The current stock price is $120 per share. The most recent period's earnings available for common stock is included in retained earnings.

Preferred stock	$ 1,000,000
Common stock (100,000 shares at $3 par)	300,000
Paid-in capital in excess of par	1,700,000
Retained earnings	10,000,000
Total stockholders' equity	$13,000,000

a. What effects on Mammoth would result from the *stock split*?
b. What change in stock price would you expect to result from the stock split?
c. What is the maximum cash dividend per share that the firm could pay on common stock before and after the stock split? (Assume that legal capital includes *all* paid-in capital.)
d. Contrast your answers to parts **a** through **c** with the circumstances surrounding a 50% *stock dividend*.
e. Explain the differences between stock splits and stock dividends.

P12–14 Stock repurchase The following financial data on the Bond Recording Company are available:

Earnings available for common stockholders	$800,000
Number of shares of common stock outstanding	400,000
Earnings per share ($800,000 ÷ 400,000)	$2
Market price per share	$20
Price/earnings (P/E) ratio ($20 ÷ $2)	10

The firm is currently considering whether it should use $400,000 of its earnings to pay cash dividends of $1 per share or to repurchase stock at $21 per share.

a. Approximately how many shares of stock can the firm repurchase at the $21-per-share price, using the funds that would have gone to pay the cash dividend?
b. Calculate the EPS after the repurchase. Explain your calculations.
c. If the stock still sells at 10 times earnings, what will the market price be after the repurchase?
d. Compare the pre- and post-repurchase earnings per share.
e. Compare and contrast the stockholders' positions under the dividend and repurchase alternatives. What are the tax implications under each alternative?

P12–15 **ETHICS PROBLEM** Look back at the *In Practice* box on page 489. Ford could lose an estimated $5 billion per year during an economic downturn. Based on this, how long could it survive, given its midyear-2004 liquidity position? Is that enough liquidity? Too much? Not enough? Justify your answer, commenting on its ethical implications.

CHAPTER 12 CASE

Establishing General Access Company's Dividend Policy and Initial Dividend

General Access Company (GAC) is a fast-growing Internet access provider that initially went public in early 2000. Its revenue growth and profitability have steadily risen since the firm's inception in late 1998. GAC's growth has been financed through the initial common stock offering, the sale of bonds in 2003, and the retention of all earnings. Because of its rapid growth in revenue and profits, with only short-term earnings declines, GAC's common stockholders have been content to let the firm reinvest earnings as part of its plan to expand capacity to meet the growing demand for its services. This strategy has benefited most stockholders in terms of stock splits and capital gains. Since the company's initial public offering in 2000, GAC's stock twice has been split 2-for-1. In terms of total growth, the market price of GAC's stock, after adjustment for stock splits, has increased by 800% during the 7-year period 2000–2006.

Because GAC's rapid growth is beginning to slow, the firm's CEO, Marilyn McNeely, believes that its shares are becoming less attractive to investors. McNeely has had discussions with her CFO, Bobby Joe Rook, who believes that the firm must begin to pay cash dividends. He argues that many investors value regular dividends and that by beginning to pay them, GAC would increase the demand—and therefore the price—for its shares. McNeely decided that at the next board meeting she would propose that the firm begin to pay dividends on a regular basis.

McNeely realized that if the board approved her recommendation, it would have to (1) establish a dividend policy and (2) set the amount of the initial annual dividend. She had Rook prepare a summary of the firm's annual EPS. It is given in the table at the top of the facing page.

Year	EPS
2006	$3.70
2005	4.10
2004	3.90
2003	3.30
2002	2.20
2001	0.83
2000	0.55

Rook indicated that he expects EPS to remain within 10% (plus or minus) of the most recent (2006) value during the next 3 years. His most likely estimate is an annual increase of about 5%.

After much discussion, McNeely and Rook agreed that she would recommend to the board one of the following types of dividend policies:

1. Constant-payout-ratio dividend policy
2. Regular dividend policy
3. Low-regular-and-extra dividend policy

McNeely realizes that her dividend proposal would significantly affect future financing opportunities and costs and the firm's share price. She also knows that she must be sure that her proposal is complete and that it fully educates the board with regard to the long-term implications of each policy.

TO DO

a. Analyze each of the three dividend policies in light of GAC's financial position.
b. Which dividend policy would you recommend? Justify your recommendation.
c. What are the key factors to consider when setting the amount of a firm's initial annual dividend?
d. How should Ms. McNeely go about deciding what initial annual dividend she will recommend to the board?
e. In view of your dividend policy recommendation in part b, how large an initial dividend would you recommend? Justify your recommendation.

SPREADSHEET EXERCISE

One way to lower the market price of a firm's stock is via a stock split. Rock-O Corporation finds itself in a different situation: Its stock has been selling at relatively low prices. To increase the market price of the stock, the company chooses to use a *reverse stock split* of 2-for-3.

The company currently has 700,000 common shares outstanding and no preferred stock. The common stock carries a par value of $1. At this time, the paid-in capital in excess of par is $7,000,000, and the firm's retained earnings is $3,500,000.

TO DO

Create a spreadsheet to determine the following:

a. The stockholders' equity section of the balance sheet *before* the reverse stock split.
b. The stockholders' equity section of the balance sheet *after* the reverse stock split.

WEB EXERCISE

Dividends have consequences for both firms and shareholders. This assignment combines an investigation of both the dividend payment history of several firms and the increasing availability of *dividend reinvestment plans (DRIPs)* for shareholders.

TO DO

a. Begin by investigating the dividend policies of several firms. Report concisely on the pattern exhibited in the recent history of dividend payments for each firm.
b. Point your browser to www.dripcentral.com/. This Web site is a good source of information about DRIP plans for various firms. Begin by reading about DRIP basics, and then report on the various firms and programs described at this Web site.

Remember to check the book's Web site at
www.aw-bc.com/gitman
for additional resources, including additional Web exercises.

Part 5

Short-Term Financial Decisions

Chapter 13
Working Capital and Current Assets Management

Chapter 14
Current Liabilities Management

Chapter 13

Working Capital and Current Assets Management

LEARNING GOALS

LG1 Understand short-term financial management, net working capital, and the related tradeoff between profitability and risk.

LG2 Describe the cash conversion cycle, its funding requirements, and the key strategies for managing it.

LG3 Discuss inventory management: differing views, common techniques, and international concerns.

LG4 Explain the credit selection process and the quantitative procedure for evaluating changes in credit standards.

LG5 Review the procedures for quantitatively considering cash discount changes, other aspects of credit terms, and credit monitoring.

LG6 Understand the management of receipts and disbursements, including float, speeding up collections, slowing down payments, cash concentration, zero-balance accounts, and investing in marketable securities.

Across the Disciplines Why This Chapter Matters to You

Accounting: You need to understand the cash conversion cycle and the management of inventory, accounts receivable, and receipts and disbursements of cash.

Information systems: You need to understand the cash conversion cycle, inventory, accounts receivable, and receipts and disbursements of cash to design financial information systems that facilitate effective short-term financial management.

Management: You need to understand the management of working capital so that you can efficiently manage current assets and decide whether to finance the firm's funds requirements aggressively or conservatively.

Marketing: You need to understand credit selection and monitoring because sales will be affected by the availability of credit to purchasers; sales will also be affected by inventory management.

Operations: You need to understand the cash conversion cycle because you will be responsible for reducing the cycle through the efficient management of production, inventory, and costs.

CHAPTER 13 Working Capital and Current Assets Management

An important consideration for all firms is the ability to finance the transition from cash to inventories to receivables and back to cash. Various strategies exist for managing current assets in order to reduce the amount of financing needed to support this cycle. In addition to managing cash, firms also must manage the accounts that typically represent the firm's largest investment in current assets—inventories and accounts receivable. This chapter looks at the management of these various aspects of the firm's current assets.

Net Working Capital Fundamentals

The firm's balance sheet provides information about the structure of the firm's investments on the one hand and the structure of its financing sources on the other hand. The structures chosen should consistently lead to the maximization of the value of the owners' investment in the firm.

Important components of the firm's financial structure include the level of investment in current assets and the extent of current liability financing. In U.S. manufacturing firms, current assets account for about 40 percent of total assets; current liabilities represent about 26 percent of total financing. Therefore, it should not be surprising to learn that **short-term financial management**—managing current assets and current liabilities—is one of the financial manager's most important and time-consuming activities. A study of *Fortune* 1000 firms found that more than one-third of financial management time is spent managing current assets and about one-fourth of financial management time is spent managing current liabilities.

short-term financial management
Management of current assets and current liabilities.

The goal of short-term financial management is to manage each of the firm's current assets (inventory, accounts receivable, cash, and marketable securities) and current liabilities (accounts payable, accruals, and notes payable) to achieve a balance between profitability and risk that contributes positively to the firm's value. This chapter does not discuss the optimal level of current assets and current liabilities that a firm should have. That issue is unresolved in the financial literature. Here we first use net working capital to consider the basic relationship between current assets and current liabilities and then use the cash conversion cycle to consider the key aspects of current asset management. In the following chapter, we consider current liability management.

Net Working Capital

working capital
Current assets, which represent the portion of investment that circulates from one form to another in the ordinary conduct of business.

Current assets, commonly called **working capital,** represent the portion of investment that circulates from one form to another in the ordinary conduct of business. This idea embraces the recurring transition from cash to inventories to receivables and back to cash. As cash substitutes, *marketable securities* are considered part of working capital.

Current liabilities represent the firm's short-term financing, because they include all debts of the firm that come due (must be paid) in 1 year or less. These debts usually include amounts owed to suppliers (accounts payable), employees and governments (accruals), and banks (notes payable), among others.

net working capital
The difference between the firm's current assets and its current liabilities; can be *positive* or *negative*.

As noted in Chapter 8, **net working capital** is commonly defined as the difference between the firm's current assets and its current liabilities. When the current assets exceed the current liabilities, the firm has *positive net working capital*. When current assets are less than current liabilities, the firm has *negative net working capital*.

The conversion of current assets from inventory to receivables to cash provides the cash used to pay the current liabilities. The cash outlays for current liabilities are relatively predictable. When an obligation is incurred, the firm generally knows when the corresponding payment will be due. What is difficult to predict are the cash inflows—the conversion of the current assets to more liquid forms. The more predictable its cash inflows, the less net working capital a firm needs. Because most firms are unable to match cash inflows to outflows with certainty, current assets that more than cover outflows for current liabilities are usually necessary. In general, the greater the margin by which a firm's current assets cover its current liabilities, the better able it will be to pay its bills as they come due.

Hint Stated differently, some portion of current assets is usually held to provide liquidity in case it is unexpectedly needed.

The Tradeoff Between Profitability and Risk

profitability
The relationship between revenues and costs generated by using the firm's assets—both current and fixed—in productive activities.

risk (of technical insolvency)
The probability that a firm will be unable to pay its bills as they come due.

technically insolvent
Describes a firm that is unable to pay its bills as they come due.

A tradeoff exists between a firm's profitability and its risk. **Profitability,** in this context, is the relationship between revenues and costs generated by using the firm's assets—both current and fixed—in productive activities. A firm's profits can be increased by (1) increasing revenues or (2) decreasing costs. **Risk,** in the context of short-term financial management, is the probability that a firm will be unable to pay its bills as they come due. A firm that cannot pay its bills as they come due is said to be **technically insolvent.** It is generally assumed that the greater the firm's net working capital, the lower its risk. In other words, the more net working capital, the more liquid the firm and therefore the lower its risk of becoming technically insolvent. Using these definitions of profitability and risk, we can demonstrate the tradeoff between them by considering changes in current assets and current liabilities separately.

Changes in Current Assets

How changing the level of the firm's current assets affects its profitability–risk tradeoff can be demonstrated using the ratio of current assets to total assets. This ratio indicates the *percentage of total assets* that is current. For purposes of illustration, we will assume that the level of total assets remains unchanged.[1] The effects on both profitability and risk of an increase or decrease in this ratio are summarized in the upper portion of Table 13.1. When the ratio increases—that is, when current assets increase—profitability decreases. Why? Because current assets are less profitable than fixed assets. Fixed assets are more profitable because they add more value to the product than that provided by current assets. Without fixed assets, the firm could not produce the product.

The risk effect, however, decreases as the ratio of current assets to total assets increases. The increase in current assets increases net working capital, thereby reducing the risk of technical insolvency. In addition, as you go down the asset

Hint It is generally easier to turn receivables into the more liquid asset cash than it is to turn inventory into cash. As we will learn in Chapter 14, the firm can sell its receivables for cash. Often inventory is sold on credit and is therefore converted to a receivable before it becomes cash.

---

[1] To isolate the effect of changing asset and financing mixes on the firm's profitability and risk, we assume the level of total assets to be *constant* in this and the following discussion.

TABLE 13.1	Effects of Changing Ratios on Profits and Risk		
Ratio	Change in ratio	Effect on profit	Effect on risk
Current assets / Total assets	Increase	Decrease	Decrease
	Decrease	Increase	Increase
Current liabilities / Total assets	Increase	Increase	Increase
	Decrease	Decrease	Decrease

side of the balance sheet, the risk associated with the assets increases: Investment in cash and marketable securities is less risky than investment in accounts receivable, inventories, and fixed assets. Accounts receivable investment is less risky than investment in inventories and fixed assets. Investment in inventories is less risky than investment in fixed assets. The nearer an asset is to cash, the less risky it is. The opposite effects on profit and risk result from a decrease in the ratio of current assets to total assets.

Changes in Current Liabilities

How changing the level of the firm's current liabilities affects its profitability–risk tradeoff can be demonstrated by using the ratio of current liabilities to total assets. This ratio indicates the percentage of total assets that has been financed with current liabilities. Again, assuming that total assets remain unchanged, the effects on both profitability and risk of an increase or decrease in the ratio are summarized in the lower portion of Table 13.1. When the ratio increases, profitability increases. Why? Because the firm uses more of the less expensive current liabilities financing and less long-term financing. Current liabilities are less expensive because only notes payable, which represent about 20 percent of the typical manufacturer's current liabilities, have a cost. The other current liabilities are basically debts on which the firm pays no charge or interest. However, when the ratio of current liabilities to total assets increases, the risk of technical insolvency also increases, because the increase in current liabilities in turn decreases net working capital. The opposite effects on profit and risk result from a decrease in the ratio of current liabilities to total assets.

Review Questions

13–1 Why is *short-term financial management* one of the most important and time-consuming activities of the financial manager? What is *net working capital*?

13–2 What is the relationship between the predictability of a firm's cash inflows and its required level of net working capital? How are net working capital, liquidity, and *risk of technical insolvency* related?

13–3 Why does an increase in the ratio of current to total assets decrease both profits and risk as measured by net working capital? How do changes in the ratio of current liabilities to total assets affect profitability and risk?

The Cash Conversion Cycle

Central to short-term financial management is an understanding of the firm's cash conversion cycle.[2] This cycle frames discussion of the management of the firm's current assets in this chapter and that of the management of current liabilities in Chapter 14. Here, we begin by demonstrating the calculation and application of the cash conversion cycle.

Calculating the Cash Conversion Cycle

operating cycle (OC)
The time from the beginning of the production process to the collection of cash from the sale of the finished product.

A firm's **operating cycle (OC)** is the time from the beginning of the production process to collection of cash from the sale of the finished product. The operating cycle encompasses two major short-term asset categories: inventory and accounts receivable. It is measured in elapsed time by summing the *average age of inventory (AAI)* and the *average collection period (ACP)*.

$$OC = AAI + ACP \qquad (13.1)$$

Hint A firm can lower its working capital if it can speed up its operating cycle. For example, if a firm accepts bank credit (like a Visa card), it will receive cash sooner after the sale is transacted than if it has to wait until the customer pays its accounts receivable.

However, the process of producing and selling a product also includes the purchase of production inputs (raw materials) on account, which results in accounts payable. Accounts payable reduce the number of days a firm's resources are tied up in the operating cycle. The time it takes to pay the accounts payable, measured in days, is the *average payment period (APP)*. The operating cycle less the average payment period is referred to as the **cash conversion cycle (CCC)**. It represents the amount of time the firm's resources are tied up. The formula for the cash conversion cycle is

cash conversion cycle (CCC)
The amount of time a firm's resources are tied up; calculated by subtracting the average payment period from the *operating cycle*.

$$CCC = OC - APP \qquad (13.2)$$

Substituting the relationship in Equation 13.1 into Equation 13.2, we can see that the cash conversion cycle has three main components, as shown in Equation 13.3: (1) average age of the inventory, (2) average collection period, and (3) average payment period.

$$CCC = AAI + ACP - APP \qquad (13.3)$$

Clearly, if a firm changes any of these time periods, it changes the amount of resources tied up in the day-to-day operation of the firm.

EXAMPLE

MAX Company, a producer of paper dinnerware, has annual sales of $10 million, a cost of goods sold of 75% of sales, and purchases that are 65% of cost of goods sold. MAX has an average age of inventory (AAI) of 60 days, an average collection period (ACP) of 40 days, and an average payment period (APP) of 35 days. Thus the cash conversion cycle for MAX is 65 days (60 + 40 − 35). Figure 13.1 presents MAX Company's cash conversion cycle as a time line.

---

2. The conceptual model that is used in this section to demonstrate basic short-term financial management strategies was developed by Lawrence J. Gitman in "Estimating Corporate Liquidity Requirements: A Simplified Approach," *The Financial Review* (1974), pp. 79–88, and refined and operationalized by Lawrence J. Gitman and Kanwal S. Sachdeva in "A Framework for Estimating and Analyzing the Required Working Capital Investment," *Review of Business and Economic Research* (Spring 1982), pp. 35–44.

FIGURE 13.1

Time Line for MAX Company's Cash Conversion Cycle

MAX Company's operating cycle is 100 days, and its cash conversion cycle is 65 days

The resources MAX has invested in this cash conversion cycle (assuming a 365-day year) are

Inventory	= ($10,000,000 × 0.75) × (60/365)	= $1,232,877
+ Accounts receivable	= (10,000,000 × 40/365)	= 1,095,890
− Accounts payable	= (10,000,000 × 0.75 × 0.65) × (35/365) =	467,466
	= Resources invested	= $1,861,301

Changes in any of the time periods will change the resources tied up in operations. For example, if MAX could reduce the average collection period on its accounts receivable by 5 days, it would shorten the cash conversion time line and thus reduce the amount of resources MAX has invested in operations. For MAX, a 5-day reduction in the average collection period would reduce the resources invested in the cash conversion cycle by $136,986 [$10,000,000 × (5/365)]. ∎

Funding Requirements of the Cash Conversion Cycle

We can use the cash conversion cycle as a basis for discussing how the firm funds its required investment in operating assets. We first differentiate between permanent and seasonal funding needs and then describe aggressive and conservative seasonal funding strategies.

Permanent Versus Seasonal Funding Needs

permanent funding requirement
A constant investment in operating assets resulting from constant sales over time.

If the firm's sales are constant, then its investment in operating assets should also be constant, and the firm will have only a **permanent funding requirement.** If the firm's sales are cyclic, then its investment in operating assets will vary over time

seasonal funding requirement
An investment in operating assets that varies over time as a result of cyclic sales.

with its sales cycles, and the firm will have **seasonal funding requirements** in addition to the permanent funding required for its minimum investment in operating assets.

> **EXAMPLE**
>
> Nicholson Company holds, on average, $50,000 in cash and marketable securities, $1,250,000 in inventory, and $750,000 in accounts receivable. Nicholson's business is very stable over time, so its operating assets can be viewed as permanent. In addition, Nicholson's accounts payable of $425,000 are stable over time. Thus Nicholson has a permanent investment in operating assets of $1,625,000 ($50,000 + $1,250,0000 + $750,000 − $425,000). That amount would also equal its permanent funding requirement.
>
> In contrast, Semper Pump Company, which produces bicycle pumps, has seasonal funding needs. Semper has seasonal sales, with its peak sales being driven by the summertime purchases of bicycle pumps. Semper holds, at minimum, $25,000 in cash and marketable securities, $100,000 in inventory, and $60,000 in accounts receivable. At peak times, Semper's inventory increases to $750,000, and its accounts receivable increase to $400,000. To capture production efficiencies, Semper produces pumps at a constant rate throughout the year. Thus accounts payable remain at $50,000 throughout the year. Accordingly, Semper has a permanent funding requirement for its minimum level of operating assets of $135,000 ($25,000 + $100,000 + $60,000 − $50,000) and peak seasonal funding requirements (in excess of its permanent need) of $990,000 [($25,000 + $750,000 + $400,000 − $50,000) − $135,000]. Semper's total funding requirements for operating assets vary from a minimum of $135,000 (permanent) to a seasonal peak of $1,125,000 ($135,000 + $990,000). Figure 13.2 depicts these needs over time.

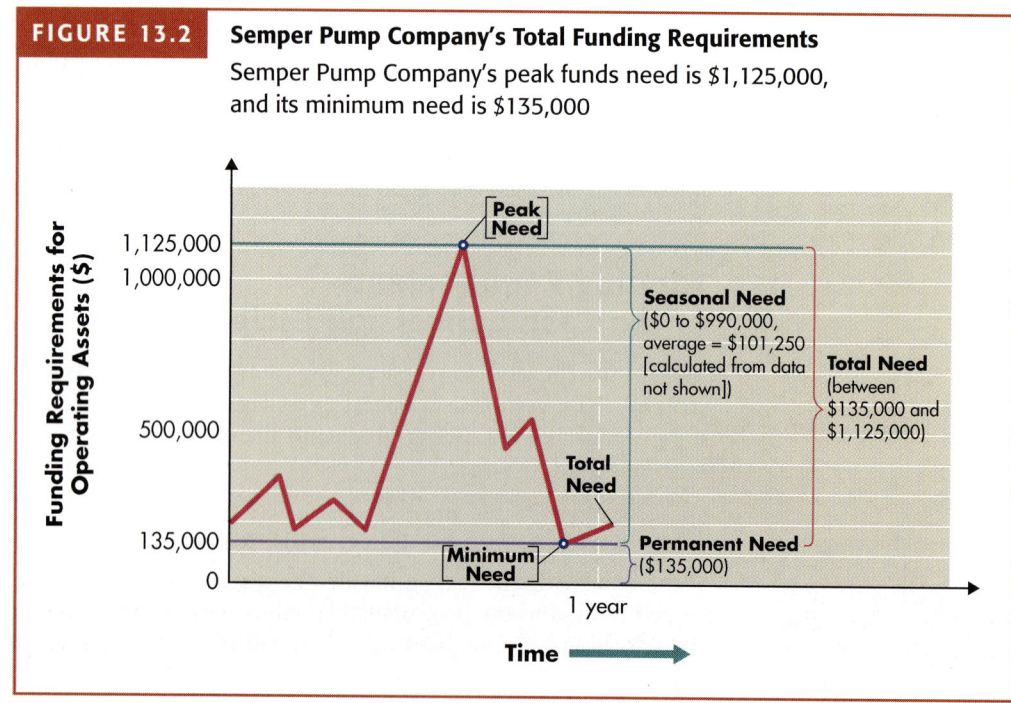

FIGURE 13.2 **Semper Pump Company's Total Funding Requirements**
Semper Pump Company's peak funds need is $1,125,000, and its minimum need is $135,000

Aggressive Versus Conservative Seasonal Funding Strategies

aggressive funding strategy
A funding strategy under which the firm funds its seasonal requirements with short-term debt and its permanent requirements with long-term debt.

conservative funding strategy
A funding strategy under which the firm funds both its seasonal and its permanent requirements with long-term debt.

Short-term funds are typically less expensive than long-term funds. (The yield curve is typically upward-sloping.) However, long-term funds allow the firm to lock in its cost of funds over a period of time and thus avoid the risk of increases in short-term interest rates. Also, long-term funding ensures that the required funds are available to the firm when needed. Short-term funding exposes the firm to the risk that it may not be able to obtain the funds needed to cover its seasonal peaks. Under an **aggressive funding strategy**, the firm funds its seasonal requirements with short-term debt and its permanent requirements with long-term debt. Under a **conservative funding strategy**, the firm funds both its seasonal and its permanent requirements with long-term debt.

EXAMPLE

Semper Pump Company has a permanent funding requirement of $135,000 in operating assets and seasonal funding requirements that vary between $0 and $990,000 and average $101,250 (calculated from data not shown). If Semper can borrow short-term funds at 6.25% and long-term funds at 8%, and if it can earn 5% on the investment of any surplus balances, then the annual cost of an aggressive strategy for seasonal funding will be

$$
\begin{array}{lrrr}
\text{Cost of short-term financing} & = 0.0625 \times & \$101{,}250 = & \$\ 6{,}328.13 \\
+ \text{ Cost of long-term financing} & = 0.0800 \times & 135{,}000 = & 10{,}800.00 \\
- \text{ Earnings on surplus balances}^3 & = 0.0500 \times & 0 = & 0 \\
\text{Total cost of aggressive strategy} & & & \underline{\$17{,}128.13}
\end{array}
$$

Alternatively, Semper can choose a conservative strategy, under which surplus cash balances are fully invested. (In Figure 13.2, this surplus will be the difference between the peak need of $1,125,000 and the total need, which varies between $135,000 and $1,125,000 during the year.) The cost of the conservative strategy will be

$$
\begin{array}{lrrr}
\text{Cost of short-term financing} & = 0.0625 \times \$ & 0 = & \$\ \ \ \ \ \ \ \ 0 \\
+ \text{ Cost of long-term financing} & = 0.0800 \times & 1{,}125{,}000 = & 90{,}000.00 \\
- \text{ Earnings on surplus balances}^4 & = 0.0500 \times & 888{,}750 = & 44{,}437.50 \\
\text{Total cost of conservative strategy} & & & \underline{\$45{,}562.50}
\end{array}
$$

It is clear from these calculations that for Semper, the aggressive strategy is far less expensive than the conservative strategy. However, it is equally clear that Semper has substantial peak-season operating-asset needs and that it must have adequate funding available to meet the peak needs and ensure ongoing operations.

Clearly, the aggressive strategy's heavy reliance on short-term financing makes it riskier than the conservative strategy because of interest rate swings and possible difficulties in obtaining needed short-term financing quickly when seasonal peaks

---

3. Because under this strategy the amount of financing exactly equals the estimated funding need, no surplus balances exist.

4. The average surplus balance would be calculated by subtracting the sum of the permanent need ($135,000) and the average seasonal need ($101,250) from the seasonal peak need ($1,125,000) to get $888,750 ($1,125,000 − $135,000 − $101,250). This represents the surplus amount of financing that on average could be invested in short-term vehicles that earn a 5% annual return.

occur. The conservative strategy avoids these risks through the locked-in interest rate and long-term financing, but it is more costly because of the negative spread between the earnings rate on surplus funds (5% in the example) and the cost of the long-term funds that create the surplus (8% in the example). Where the firm operates, between the extremes of the aggressive and conservative seasonal funding strategies, depends on management's disposition toward risk and the strength of its banking relationships.

Strategies for Managing the Cash Conversion Cycle

A positive cash conversion cycle, as we saw for MAX Company in the earlier example, means the firm must use negotiated liabilities (such as bank loans) to support its operating assets. Negotiated liabilities carry an explicit cost, so the firm benefits by minimizing their use in supporting operating assets. Simply stated, the goal is to *minimize the length of the cash conversion cycle,* which minimizes negotiated liabilities. This goal can be realized through application of the following strategies:

1. *Turn over inventory as quickly as possible* without stockouts that result in lost sales.
2. *Collect accounts receivable as quickly as possible* without losing sales from high-pressure collection techniques.
3. *Manage mail, processing, and clearing time* to reduce them when collecting from customers and to increase them when paying suppliers.
4. *Pay accounts payable as slowly as possible* without damaging the firm's credit rating.

Techniques for implementing these four strategies are the focus of the remainder of this chapter and the following chapter.

Review Questions

13–4 What is the difference between the firm's *operating cycle* and its *cash conversion cycle?*

13–5 Why is it helpful to divide the funding needs of a seasonal business into its permanent and seasonal funding requirements when developing a funding strategy?

13–6 What are the benefits, costs, and risks of an *aggressive funding strategy* and of a *conservative funding strategy?* Under which strategy is the borrowing often in excess of the actual need?

13–7 Why is it important for a firm to minimize the length of its cash conversion cycle?

Inventory Management

The first component of the cash conversion cycle is the average age of inventory. The objective for managing inventory, as noted earlier, is to turn over inventory as quickly as possible without losing sales from stockouts. The financial manager tends to act as an advisor or "watchdog" in matters concerning inventory; he or she does not have direct control over inventory but does provide input to the inventory management process.

Differing Viewpoints About Inventory Level

Differing viewpoints about appropriate inventory levels commonly exist among a firm's finance, marketing, manufacturing, and purchasing managers. Each views inventory levels in light of his or her own objectives. The *financial manager's* general disposition toward inventory levels is to keep them low, to ensure that the firm's money is not being unwisely invested in excess resources. The *marketing manager*, on the other hand, would like to have large inventories of the firm's finished products. This would ensure that all orders could be filled quickly, eliminating the need for backorders due to stockouts.

The *manufacturing manager's* major responsibility is to implement the production plan so that it results in the desired amount of finished goods of acceptable quality at a low cost. In fulfilling this role, the manufacturing manager would keep raw materials inventories high to avoid production delays. He or she also would favor large production runs for the sake of lower unit production costs, which would result in high finished goods inventories.

The *purchasing manager* is concerned solely with the raw materials inventories. He or she must have on hand, in the correct quantities at the desired times and at a favorable price, whatever raw materials are required by production. Without proper control, in an effort to get quantity discounts or in anticipation of rising prices or a shortage of certain materials, the purchasing manager may purchase larger quantities of resources than are actually needed at the time.

Common Techniques for Managing Inventory

Numerous techniques are available for effectively managing the firm's inventory. Here we briefly consider four commonly used techniques.

The ABC System

ABC inventory system
Inventory management technique that divides inventory into three groups—A, B, and C, in descending order of importance and level of monitoring, on the basis of the dollar investment in each.

A firm using the **ABC inventory system** divides its inventory into three groups: A, B, and C. The A group includes those items with the largest dollar investment. Typically, this group consists of 20 percent of the firm's inventory items but 80 percent of its investment in inventory. The B group consists of items that account for the next largest investment in inventory. The C group consists of a large number of items that require a relatively small investment.

two-bin method
Unsophisticated inventory-monitoring technique that is typically applied to C group items and involves reordering inventory when one of two bins is empty.

The inventory group of each item determines the item's level of monitoring. The A group items receive the most intense monitoring because of the high dollar investment. Typically, A group items are tracked on a perpetual inventory system that allows daily verification of each item's inventory level. B group items are frequently controlled through periodic, perhaps weekly, checking of their levels. C group items are monitored with unsophisticated techniques, such as the two-bin method. With the **two-bin method,** the item is stored in two bins. As an item is needed, inventory is removed from the first bin. When that bin is empty, an order is placed to refill the first bin while inventory is drawn from the second bin. The second bin is used until empty, and so on.

The large dollar investment in A and B group items suggests the need for a better method of inventory management than the ABC system. The EOQ model, discussed next, is an appropriate model for the management of A and B group items.

The Economic Order Quantity (EOQ) Model

One of the most common techniques for determining the optimal order size for inventory items is the **economic order quantity (EOQ) model**. The EOQ model considers various costs of inventory and then determines what order size minimizes total inventory cost. EOQ assumes that the relevant costs of inventory can be divided into *order costs* and *carrying costs*. (The model excludes the actual cost of the inventory item.) Each of them has certain key components and characteristics.

Order costs include the fixed clerical costs of placing and receiving orders: the cost of writing a purchase order, of processing the resulting paperwork, and of receiving an order and checking it against the invoice. Order costs are stated in dollars per order.

Carrying costs are the variable costs per unit of holding an item of inventory for a specific period of time. Carrying costs include storage costs, insurance costs, the costs of deterioration and obsolescence, and the opportunity or financial cost of having funds invested in inventory. These costs are stated in dollars per unit per period.

Order costs decrease as the size of the order increases. Carrying costs, however, increase with increases in the order size. The EOQ model analyzes the tradeoff between order costs and carrying costs to determine the *order quantity that minimizes the total inventory cost*.

Mathematical Development of EOQ A formula can be developed for determining the firm's EOQ for a given inventory item, where

S = usage in units per period
O = order cost per order
C = carrying cost per unit per period
Q = order quantity in units

The first step is to derive the cost functions for order cost and carrying cost. The order cost can be expressed as the product of the cost per order and the number of orders. Because the number of orders equals the usage during the period divided by the order quantity (S/Q), the order cost can be expressed as follows:

$$\text{Order cost} = O \times S/Q \tag{13.4}$$

The carrying cost is defined as the cost of carrying a unit of inventory per period multiplied by the firm's average inventory. The average inventory is the order quantity divided by 2 ($Q/2$), because inventory is assumed to be depleted at a constant rate. Thus carrying cost can be expressed as follows:

$$\text{Carrying cost} = C \times Q/2 \tag{13.5}$$

The firm's **total cost of inventory** is found by summing the order cost and the carrying cost. Thus the total cost function is

$$\text{Total cost} = (O \times S/Q) + (C \times Q/2) \tag{13.6}$$

Because the EOQ is defined as the order quantity that minimizes the total cost function, we must solve the total cost function for the EOQ. The resulting equation is

$$\text{EOQ} = \sqrt{\frac{2 \times S \times O}{C}} \quad (13.7)$$

Although the EOQ model has weaknesses, it is certainly better than subjective decision making. Despite the fact that the use of the EOQ model is outside the control of the financial manager, the financial manager must be aware of its utility and must provide certain inputs, specifically with respect to inventory carrying costs.

Reorder Point Once the firm has determined its economic order quantity, it must determine when to place an order. The **reorder point** reflects the firm's daily usage of the inventory item and the number of days needed to place and receive an order. Assuming that inventory is used at a constant rate, the formula for the reorder point is

$$\text{Reorder point} = \text{Days of lead time} \times \text{Daily usage} \quad (13.8)$$

For example, if a firm knows it takes 3 days to place and receive an order, and if it uses 15 units per day of the inventory item, then the reorder point is 45 units of inventory (3 days × 15 units/day). Thus, as soon as the item's inventory level falls to the reorder point (45 units, in this case) an order will be placed at the item's EOQ. If the estimates of lead time and usage are correct, then the order will arrive exactly as the inventory level reaches zero. However, lead times and usage rates are not precise, so most firms hold **safety stock** (extra inventory) to prevent stockouts of important items.

> **Hint** The EOQ calculation helps management minimize the total cost of inventory. Lowering order costs will cause an increase in carrying costs and may increase total cost. Likewise, a decrease in total cost may result from reduced carrying costs. The goal, facilitated by using the EOQ calculation, is to lower total cost.

reorder point
The point at which to reorder inventory, expressed as days of lead time × daily usage.

safety stock
Extra inventory that is held to prevent stockouts of important items.

EXAMPLE MAX Company has an A group inventory item that is vital to the production process. This item costs $1,500, and MAX uses 1,100 units of the item per year. MAX wants to determine its optimal order strategy for the item. To calculate the EOQ, we need the following inputs:

$$\text{Order cost per order} = \$150$$
$$\text{Carrying cost per unit per year} = \$200$$

Substituting into Equation 13.7, we get

$$\text{EOQ} = \sqrt{\frac{2 \times 1,100 \times \$150}{\$200}} \approx \underline{\underline{41}} \text{ units}$$

The reorder point for MAX depends on the number of days MAX operates per year. Assuming that MAX operates 250 days per year and uses 1,100 units of this item, its daily usage is 4.4 units (1,100 ÷ 250). If its lead time is 2 days and MAX wants to maintain a safety stock of 4 units, the reorder point for this item is 12.8 units [(2 × 4.4) + 4]. However, orders are made only in whole units, so the order is placed when the inventory falls to 13 units. ■

The firm's goal for inventory is to turn it over as quickly as possible without stockouts. Inventory turnover is best calculated by dividing cost of goods sold by average inventory. The EOQ model determines the optimal order size and, indirectly, through the assumption of constant usage, the average inventory. Thus the EOQ model determines the firm's optimal inventory turnover rate, given the firm's specific costs of inventory.

Just-in-Time (JIT) System

The **just-in-time (JIT) system** is used to minimize inventory investment. The philosophy is that materials should arrive at exactly the time they are needed for production. Ideally, the firm would have only work-in-process inventory. Because its objective is to minimize inventory investment, a JIT system uses no (or very little) safety stock. Extensive coordination among the firm's employees, its suppliers, and shipping companies must exist to ensure that material inputs arrive on time. Failure of materials to arrive on time results in a shutdown of the production line until the materials arrive. Likewise, a JIT system requires high-quality parts from suppliers. When quality problems arise, production must be stopped until the problems are resolved.

The goal of the JIT system is manufacturing efficiency. It uses inventory as a tool for attaining efficiency by emphasizing quality of the materials used and their timely delivery. When JIT is working properly, it forces process inefficiencies to surface.

Knowing the level of inventory is, of course, an important part of any inventory management system. As described in the *In Practice* box on the facng page, radio frequency identification technology may be the "next new thing" in improving inventory and supply chain management.

Computerized Systems for Resource Control

Today a number of systems are available for controlling inventory and other resources. One of the most basic is the **materials requirement planning (MRP) system.** It is used to determine what materials to order and when to order them. MRP applies EOQ concepts to determine how much to order. Using a computer, MRP simulates each product's bill of materials, inventory status, and manufacturing process. The *bill of materials* is simply a list of all parts and materials that go into making the finished product. For a given production plan, the computer simulates material requirements by comparing production needs to available inventory balances. On the basis of the time it takes for a product that is in process to move through the various production stages and the lead time to get materials, the MRP system determines when orders should be placed for various items on the bill of materials. The objective of this system is to lower the firm's inventory investment without impairing production. If the firm's opportunity cost of capital for investments of equal risk is 15 percent, every dollar of investment released from inventory will increase before-tax profits by $0.15.

A popular extension of MRP is **manufacturing resource planning II (MRP II)**, which integrates data from numerous areas such as finance, accounting, marketing, engineering, and manufacturing using a sophisticated computer system. This system generates production plans as well as numerous financial and management reports. In essence, it models the firm's processes so that the effects of changes in one area of operations on other areas can be assessed and monitored. For example, the MRP II system would allow the firm to assess the effect of an increase in labor costs on sales and profits.

Whereas MRP and MRP II tend to focus on internal operations, **enterprise resource planning (ERP)** systems expand the focus to the external environment

---

just-in-time (JIT) system
Inventory management technique that minimizes inventory investment by having materials arrive at exactly the time they are needed for production.

materials requirement planning (MRP) system
Inventory management technique that applies EOQ concepts and a computer to compare production needs to available inventory balances and determine when orders should be placed for various items on a product's *bill of materials*.

manufacturing resource planning II (MRP II)
A sophisticated computerized system that integrates data from numerous areas such as finance, accounting, marketing, engineering, and manufacturing and generates production plans as well as numerous financial and management reports.

enterprise resource planning (ERP)
A computerized system that electronically integrates external information about the firm's suppliers and customers with the firm's departmental data so that information on all available resources—human and material—can be instantly obtained in a fashion that eliminates production delays and controls costs.

In Practice FOCUS ON PRACTICE

RFID: THE WAVE OF THE FUTURE

Wal-Mart Stores, Inc., the world's #1 retailer, has more than 4,800 stores, including some 1,475 discount stores, 1,750 combination discount and grocery stores, and 540 warehouse stores. With 2003 sales of $256 billion, Wal-Mart is able to exert tremendous pressure on its suppliers. So when Wal-Mart announced in April 2004 that it was beginning a pilot program to test *radio frequency identification (RFID)* technology to improve its inventory and supply chain management, suppliers and competitors alike sat up and took notice.

Radio frequency identification is not new technology—it's been around since the 1940s. Anyone unlocking a car door using a keyless remote or using a tollbooth transponder is already using RFID. In their inventory control capacity, passive RFID chips with small antennae are attached to cases and pallets. A tag reader activates the chip, and its unique product identifier code is transmitted back to an inventory control system.

One of the first companies to introduce bar codes in the early 1980s, Wal-Mart plans to require its top 100 suppliers to put RFID tags on shipping crates and pallets by January 2005, with the next 200 largest suppliers using the technology by January 2006. Wal-Mart's goal is to have all of its 86,000-plus suppliers on board using electronic product codes (EPC) with RFID technology.

Several hurdles must be dealt with before full implementation can be achieved. Currently, capacity for manufacturing the new chips is insufficient to produce chips in the quantity needed for full implementation of Wal-Mart's plans. Wal-Mart's move is expected to require nearly 1 billion RFID tags. **Texas Instruments,** a producer of RFID tags, has shipped a total of 200 million RFID tags to date. With the expected increase in demand for more chips, Texas Instruments is considering a potential investment in a new production facility to increase its RFID manufacturing capacity. Such a facility would cost more than $1 billion. A second issue is per-chip cost. Each chip currently sells for 30 to 50 cents; Wal-Mart has requested a price of 5 cents per tag. With a substantial increase in demand for chips, it expects economies of scale to push the price down.

Initially, Wal-Mart plans to use RFID technology to improve its inventory management. One of the company's measures of efficiency is inventory growth at a rate of less than half of sales growth. For 2003, Wal-Mart's inventories grew at 9.1 percent while sales increased 11.6 percent. Using RFID technology, Wal-Mart will attempt to improve this number and reduce its net working capital requirements.

Sources: Wal-Mart press releases, www.walmartstores.com (accessed August 25, 2004); and Jaikumar Vijayan and Bob Brewin, "Wal-Mart's Plan Poses Challenges for Chip Makers" (June 16, 2003), www.computerworld.com (accessed August 25, 2004).

■ *What problem might occur with the full implementation of RFID technology in retail industries? Specifically, consider the amount of data that might be collected.*

---

by including information about suppliers and customers. ERP electronically integrates all of a firm's departments so that, for example, production can call up sales information and immediately know how much must be produced to fill customer orders. Because all available resources—human and material—are known, the system can eliminate production delays and control costs. ERP systems automatically note changes, such as a supplier's inability to meet a scheduled delivery date, so that necessary adjustments can be made.

International Inventory Management

International inventory management is typically much more complicated for exporters in general, and for multinational companies in particular, than for purely domestic firms. The production and manufacturing economies of scale that might be expected from selling products globally may prove elusive if products must be tailored for individual local markets, as very frequently happens, or if actual production takes place in factories around the world. When raw materials, intermediate goods, or finished products must be transported over long distances—particularly by ocean shipping—there will inevitably be more delays, confusion, damage, theft, and other difficulties than occur in a one-country operation. The international inventory manager therefore puts a premium on flexibility. He or she is usually less concerned about ordering the economically optimal quantity of inventory than about making sure that sufficient quantities of inventory are delivered where they are needed, when they are needed, and in a condition to be used as planned.

Review Questions

13–8 What are likely to be the viewpoints of each of the following managers about the levels of the various types of inventory: finance, marketing, manufacturing, and purchasing? Why is inventory an investment?

13–9 Briefly describe each of the following techniques for managing inventory: ABC system, economic order quantity (EOQ) model, just-in-time (JIT) system, and computerized systems for resource control—MRP, MRP II, and ERP.

13–10 What factors make managing inventory more difficult for exporters and multinational companies?

Accounts Receivable Management

The second component of the cash conversion cycle is the average collection period. This period is the average length of time from a sale on credit until the payment becomes usable funds for the firm. The average collection period has two parts. The first part is the time from the sale until the customer mails the payment. The second part is the time from when the payment is mailed until the firm has the collected funds in its bank account. The first part of the average collection period involves managing the credit available to the firm's customers, and the second part involves collecting and processing payments. This section of the chapter discusses the firm's accounts receivable credit management.

Hint Some small businesses resolve these problems by selling their accounts receivable to a third party at a discount. Though expensive, this strategy overcomes the problem of not having adequate personnel. It also creates a buffer between the small business and those customers who need a little prodding to stay current.

The objective for managing accounts receivable is to collect accounts receivable as quickly as possible without losing sales from high-pressure collection techniques. Accomplishing this goal encompasses three topics: (1) credit selection and standards, (2) credit terms, and (3) credit monitoring.

Credit Selection and Standards

credit standards
The firm's minimum requirements for extending credit to a customer.

Credit selection involves application of techniques for determining which customers should receive credit. This process involves evaluating the customer's creditworthiness and comparing it to the firm's **credit standards,** its minimum requirements for extending credit to a customer.

CHAPTER 13 Working Capital and Current Assets Management

Five C's of Credit

five C's of credit
The five key dimensions—character, capacity, capital, collateral, and conditions—used by credit analysts to provide a framework for in-depth credit analysis.

One popular credit selection technique is the **five C's of credit**, which provides a framework for in-depth credit analysis. Because of the time and expense involved, this credit selection method is used for large-dollar credit requests. The five C's are

1. *Character:* The applicant's record of meeting past obligations.
2. *Capacity:* The applicant's ability to repay the requested credit, as judged in terms of financial statement analysis focused on cash flows available to repay debt obligations.
3. *Capital:* The applicant's debt relative to equity.
4. *Collateral:* The amount of assets the applicant has available for use in securing the credit. The larger the amount of available assets, the greater the chance that a firm will recover funds if the applicant defaults.
5. *Conditions:* Current general and industry-specific economic conditions, and any unique conditions surrounding a specific transaction.

Hint Computers are widely used to aid in the credit decision process. Data on each customer's payment patterns are maintained and can be called forth to evaluate requests for renewed or additional credit.

Analysis via the five C's of credit does not yield a specific accept/reject decision, so its use requires an analyst experienced in reviewing and granting credit requests. Application of this framework tends to ensure that the firm's credit customers will pay, without being pressured, within the stated credit terms.

Credit Scoring

credit scoring
A credit selection method commonly used with high-volume/small-dollar credit requests; relies on a credit score determined by applying statistically derived weights to a credit applicant's scores on key financial and credit characteristics.

Credit scoring is a method of credit selection that is commonly used with high-volume/small-dollar credit requests. **Credit scoring** applies statistically derived weights to a credit applicant's scores on key financial and credit characteristics to predict whether he or she will pay the requested credit in a timely fashion. Simply stated, the procedure results in a score that measures the applicant's overall credit strength, and the score is used to make the accept/reject decision for granting the applicant credit. Credit scoring is most commonly used by large credit card operations, such as those of banks, oil companies, and department stores. The purpose of credit scoring is to make a relatively informed credit decision quickly and inexpensively, recognizing that the cost of a single bad scoring decision is small. However, if bad debts from scoring decisions increase, then the scoring system must be reevaluated. For a demonstration of credit scoring, including use of a spreadsheet for that purpose, see the book's Web site at www.aw-bc.com/gitman.

Changing Credit Standards

Hint Relaxing the credit standards and/or credit terms will increase the risk of the firm, but it may also increase the return to the firm. Bad debts and the average collection period will both increase with more lenient credit standards and/or credit terms, but the increased revenue may produce profits that exceed these costs.

The firm sometimes will contemplate changing its credit standards in an effort to improve its returns and create greater value for its owners. To demonstrate, consider the following changes and effects on profits expected to result from the *relaxation* of credit standards.

Effects of Relaxation of Credit Standards		
Variable	Direction of change	Effect on profits
Sales volume	Increase	Positive
Investment in accounts receivable	Increase	Negative
Bad-debt expenses	Increase	Negative

If credit standards were tightened, the opposite effects would be expected.

EXAMPLE

Dodd Tool, a manufacturer of lathe tools, is currently selling a product for $10 per unit. Sales (all on credit) for last year were 60,000 units. The variable cost per unit is $6. The firm's total fixed costs are $120,000.

The firm is currently contemplating a *relaxation of credit standards* that is expected to result in the following: a 5% increase in unit sales to 63,000 units; an increase in the average collection period from 30 days (the current level) to 45 days; an increase in bad-debt expenses from 1% of sales (the current level) to 2%. The firm's required return on equal-risk investments, which is the opportunity cost of tying up funds in accounts receivable, is 15%.

To determine whether to relax its credit standards, Dodd Tool must calculate its effect on the firm's additional profit contribution from sales, the cost of the marginal investment in accounts receivable, and the cost of marginal bad debts.

Additional Profit Contribution from Sales Because fixed costs are "sunk" and therefore are unaffected by a change in the sales level, the only cost relevant to a change in sales is variable costs. Sales are expected to increase by 5%, or 3,000 units. The profit contribution per unit will equal the difference between the sale price per unit ($10) and the variable cost per unit ($6). The profit contribution per unit therefore will be $4. The total additional profit contribution from sales will be $12,000 (3,000 units × $4 per unit).

Cost of the Marginal Investment in Accounts Receivable To determine the cost of the marginal investment in accounts receivable, Dodd must find the difference between the cost of carrying receivables under the two credit standards. Because its concern is only with the out-of-pocket costs, *the relevant cost is the variable cost*. The average investment in accounts receivable can be calculated by using the following formula:

$$\frac{\text{Average investment}}{\text{in accounts receivable}} = \frac{\text{Total variable cost of annual sales}}{\text{Turnover of accounts receivable}} \quad (13.9)$$

where

$$\text{Turnover of accounts receivable} = \frac{365}{\text{Average collection period}}$$

The total variable cost of annual sales under the present and proposed plans can be found as follows, using the variable cost per unit of $6.

Total variable cost of annual sales

Under present plan: ($6 × 60,000 units) = $360,000
Under proposed plan: ($6 × 63,000 units) = $378,000

The turnover of accounts receivable is the number of times each year that the firm's accounts receivable are actually turned into cash. It is found by dividing the average collection period into 365 (the number of days assumed in a year).

Turnover of accounts receivable

Under present plan: $\frac{365}{30} = 12.2$

Under proposed plan: $\frac{365}{45} = 8.1$

By substituting the cost and turnover data just calculated into Equation 13.9 for each case, we get the following average investments in accounts receivable:

Average investment in accounts receivable

$$\text{Under present plan:} \quad \frac{\$360{,}000}{12.2} = \$29{,}508$$

$$\text{Under proposed plan:} \quad \frac{\$378{,}000}{8.1} = \$46{,}667$$

The marginal investment in accounts receivable and its cost are calculated as follows:

Cost of marginal investment in accounts receivable

Average investment under proposed plan	$46,667
− Average investment under present plan	29,508
Marginal investment in accounts receivable	$17,159
× Required return on investment	0.15
Cost of marginal investment in A/R	$ 2,574

The resulting value of $2,574 is considered a cost because it represents the maximum amount that could have been earned on the $17,159 had it been placed in the best equal-risk investment alternative available at the firm's required return on investment of 15%.

Cost of Marginal Bad Debts The cost of marginal bad debts is found by taking the difference between the levels of bad debts before and after the proposed relaxation of credit standards.

Cost of marginal bad debts

Under proposed plan:	(0.02 × $10/unit × 63,000 units)	= $12,600
Under present plan:	(0.01 × $10/unit × 60,000 units)	= 6,000
Cost of marginal bad debts		$ 6,600

Note that the bad-debt costs are calculated by using the sale price per unit ($10) to deduct not just the true loss of variable cost ($6) that results when a customer fails to pay its account, but also the profit contribution per unit (in this case $4) that is included in the "additional profit contribution from sales." Thus the resulting cost of marginal bad debts is $6,600.

Making the Credit Standard Decision To decide whether to relax its credit standards, the firm must compare the additional profit contribution from sales to the added costs of the marginal investment in accounts receivable and marginal bad debts. If the additional profit contribution is greater than marginal costs, credit standards should be relaxed.

EXAMPLE The results and key calculations related to Dodd Tool's decision whether to relax its credit standards are summarized in Table 13.2 (on page 528). The net addition to total profits resulting from such an action will be $2,826 per year. Therefore, the firm *should* relax its credit standards as proposed.

TABLE 13.2   The Effects on Dodd Tool of a Relaxation of Credit Standards

Additional profit contribution from sales [3,000 units × ($10 − $6)]		$12,000
Cost of marginal investment in A/R[a]		
Average investment under proposed plan:		
$\dfrac{\$6 \times 63{,}000}{8.1} = \dfrac{\$378{,}000}{8.1}$	$46,667	
Average investment under present plan:		
$\dfrac{\$6 \times 60{,}000}{12.2} = \dfrac{\$360{,}000}{12.2}$	29,508	
Marginal investment in A/R	$17,159	
Cost of marginal investment in A/R (0.15 × $17,159)		($ 2,574)
Cost of marginal bad debts		
Bad debts under proposed plan (0.02 × $10 × 63,000)	$12,600	
Bad debts under present plan (0.01 × $10 × 60,000)	6,000	
Cost of marginal bad debts		($ 6,600)
Net profit from implementation of proposed plan		$ 2,826

[a]The denominators 8.1 and 12.2 in the calculation of the average investment in accounts receivable under the proposed and present plans are the accounts receivable turnovers for each of these plans (365/45 = 8.1 and 365/30 = 12.2).

The procedure described here for evaluating a proposed change in credit standards is also commonly used to evaluate other changes in the management of accounts receivable. If Dodd Tool had been contemplating tightening its credit standards, for example, the cost would have been a reduction in the profit contribution from sales, and the return would have been from reductions in the cost of the investment in accounts receivable and in the cost of bad debts. Another application of this procedure is demonstrated later in the chapter.

Managing International Credit

Credit management is difficult enough for managers of purely domestic companies, and these tasks become much more complex for companies that operate internationally. This is partly because (as we have seen before) international operations typically expose a firm to *exchange rate risk*. It is also due to the dangers and delays involved in shipping goods long distances and in having to cross at least two international borders.

Exports of finished goods are usually priced in the currency of the importer's local market; most commodities, on the other hand, are priced in dollars. Therefore, a U.S. company that sells a product in Japan, for example, would have to price that product in Japanese yen and extend credit to a Japanese wholesaler in the local currency (yen). If the yen *depreciates* against the dollar before the U.S. exporter collects on its account receivable, the U.S. company experiences an exchange rate loss; the yen collected are worth fewer dollars than expected at the time the sale was made. Of course, the dollar could just as easily depreciate against the yen, yielding an exchange rate gain to the U.S. exporter. Most companies fear the loss more than they welcome the gain.

For a major currency such as the Japanese yen, the exporter can *hedge* against this risk by using the currency futures, forward, or options markets, but it is costly to do so, particularly for relatively small amounts. If the exporter is selling to a customer in a developing country—where 40 percent of U.S. exports are now sold—there will probably be no effective instrument available for protecting against exchange rate risk at any price. This risk may be further magnified because credit standards may be much lower (and acceptable collection techniques much different) in developing countries than in the United States. Although it may seem tempting just "not to bother" with exporting, U.S. companies no longer can concede foreign markets to international rivals. These export sales, if carefully monitored and (where possible) effectively hedged against exchange rate risk, often prove to be very profitable.

Credit Terms

credit terms
The terms of sale for customers who have been extended credit by the firm.

cash discount
A percentage deduction from the purchase price; available to the credit customer who pays its account within a specified time.

Credit terms are the terms of sale for customers who have been extended credit by the firm. Terms of *net 30* mean the customer has 30 days from the beginning of the credit period (typically *end of month* or *date of invoice*) to pay the full invoice amount. Some firms offer **cash discounts,** percentage deductions from the purchase price for paying within a specified time. For example, terms of *2/10 net 30* mean the customer can take a 2 percent discount from the invoice amount if the payment is made within 10 days of the beginning of the credit period or can pay the full amount of the invoice within 30 days.

A firm's regular credit terms are strongly influenced by the firm's business. For example, a firm selling perishable items will have very short credit terms, because its items have little long-term collateral value; a firm in a seasonal business may tailor its terms to fit the industry cycles. A firm wants its regular credit terms to conform to its industry's standards. If its terms are more restrictive than its competitors', it will lose business; if its terms are less restrictive than its competitors', it will attract poor-quality customers that probably could not pay under the standard industry terms. The bottom line is that a firm should compete on the basis of quality and price of its product and service offerings, not its credit terms. Accordingly, the firm's regular credit terms should match the industry standards, but individual customer terms should reflect the riskiness of the customer.

Cash Discount

Including a cash discount in the credit terms is a popular way to achieve the goal of speeding up collections without putting pressure on customers. The cash discount provides an incentive for customers to pay sooner. By speeding collections, the discount decreases the firm's investment in accounts receivable (which is the objective), but it also decreases the per-unit profit. Additionally, initiating a cash discount should reduce bad debts because customers will pay sooner, and it should increase sales volume because customers who take the discount pay a lower price for the product. Accordingly, firms that consider offering a cash discount must perform a benefit–cost analysis to determine whether extending a cash discount is profitable.

EXAMPLE

MAX Company has an average collection period of 40 days (turnover = 365/40 = 9.1). In accordance with the firm's credit terms of net 30, this period is divided into 32 days until the customers place their payments in the mail (not everyone pays within 30 days) and 8 days to receive, process, and collect payments once they are mailed. MAX is considering initiating a cash discount by changing its credit terms from net 30 to 2/10 net 30. The firm expects this change to reduce the amount of time until the payments are placed in the mail, resulting in an average collection period of 25 days (turnover = 365/25 = 14.6).

As noted earlier in the EOQ example (on page 521), MAX has a raw material with current annual usage of 1,100 units. Each finished product produced requires 1 unit of this raw material at a variable cost of $1,500 per unit, incurs another $800 of variable cost in the production process, and sells for $3,000 on terms of net 30. Variable costs therefore total $2,300 ($1,500 + $800). MAX estimates that 80% of its customers will take the 2% discount and that offering the discount will increase sales of the finished product by 50 units (from 1,100 to 1,150 units) per year but will not alter its bad-debt percentage. MAX's opportunity cost of funds invested in accounts receivable is 14%. Should MAX offer the proposed cash discount? An analysis similar to that demonstrated earlier for the credit standard decision, presented in Table 13.3, shows a net loss from the cash discount of $6,640. Thus *MAX should not initiate the proposed cash discount.* However, other discounts may be advantageous.

cash discount period
The number of days after the beginning of the credit period during which the cash discount is available.

Cash Discount Period

The **cash discount period,** the number of days after the beginning of the credit period during which the cash discount is available, can be changed by the finan-

TABLE 13.3 Analysis of Initiating a Cash Discount for MAX Company

Additional profit contribution from sales [50 units × ($3,000 − $2,300)]		$35,000
Cost of marginal investment in A/R[a]		
Average investment presently (without discount): $\dfrac{\$2,300 \times 1,100 \text{ units}}{9.1} = \dfrac{\$2,530,000}{9.1}$	$278,022	
Average investment with proposed cash discount:[b] $\dfrac{\$2,300 \times 1,150 \text{ units}}{14.6} = \dfrac{\$2,645,000}{14.6}$	181,164	
Reduction in accounts receivable investment	$ 96,858	
Cost savings from reduced investments in accounts receivable (0.14 × $96,858)[c]		$13,560
Cost of cash discount (0.02 × 0.80 × 1,150 × $3,000)		($55,200)
Net profit from initiation of proposed cash discount		($ 6,640)

[a]In analyzing the investment in accounts receivable, we use the variable cost of the product sold ($1,500 raw materials cost + $800 production cost = $2,300 per unit variable cost) instead of the sale price, because the variable cost is a better indicator of the firm's investment.
[b]The average investment in accounts receivable with the proposed cash discount is estimated to be tied up for an average of 25 days instead of the 40 days under the original terms.
[c]MAX's opportunity cost of funds is 14%.

cial manager. The net effect of changes in this period is difficult to analyze because of the nature of the forces involved. For example, if a firm were to increase its cash discount period by 10 days (for example, changing its credit terms from 2/10 net 30 to 2/20 net 30), the following changes would be expected to occur: (1) Sales would increase, positively affecting profit. (2) Bad-debt expenses would decrease, positively affecting profit. (3) The profit per unit would decrease as a result of more people taking the discount, negatively affecting profit. The difficulty for the financial manager lies in assessing what impact an increase in the cash discount period would have on the firm's investment in accounts receivable. This investment will decrease because of non–discount takers now paying earlier. However, the investment in accounts receivable will increase for two reasons: (1) Discount takers will still get the discount but will pay later, and (2) new customers attracted by the new policy will result in new accounts receivable. If the firm were to decrease the cash discount period, the effects would be the opposite of those just described.

Credit Period

credit period
The number of days after the beginning of the credit period until full payment of the account is due.

Changes in the **credit period,** the number of days after the beginning of the credit period until full payment of the account is due, also affect a firm's profitability. For example, increasing a firm's credit period from net 30 days to net 45 days should increase sales, positively affecting profit. But both the investment in accounts receivable and bad-debt expenses would also increase, negatively affecting profit. The increased investment in accounts receivable would result from both more sales and generally slower pay, on average, as a result of the longer credit period. The increase in bad-debt expenses results from the fact that the longer the credit period, the more time available for a firm to fail, making it unable to pay its accounts payable. A decrease in the length of the credit period is likely to have the opposite effects. Note that the variables affected by an increase in the credit period behave in the same way they would have if the credit standards had been relaxed, as demonstrated earlier in Table 13.2.

Credit Monitoring

credit monitoring
The ongoing review of a firm's accounts receivable to determine whether customers are paying according to the stated credit terms.

The final issue a firm should consider in its accounts receivable management is credit monitoring. **Credit monitoring** is an ongoing review of the firm's accounts receivable to determine whether customers are paying according to the stated credit terms. If they are not paying in a timely manner, credit monitoring will alert the firm to the problem. Slow payments are costly to a firm because they lengthen the average collection period and thus increase the firm's investment in accounts receivable. Two frequently used techniques for credit monitoring are average collection period and aging of accounts receivable. In addition, a number of popular collection techniques are used by firms.

Average Collection Period

The *average collection period* is the second component of the cash conversion cycle. As noted in Chapter 2, it is the average number of days that credit sales are outstanding. The average collection period has two components: (1) the time from sale until the customer places the payment in the mail and (2) the time to receive, process, and collect the payment once it has been mailed by the customer. The formula for finding the average collection period is

$$\text{Average collection period} = \frac{\text{Accounts receivable}}{\text{Average sales per day}} \qquad (13.10)$$

Assuming receipt, processing, and collection time is constant, the average collection period tells the firm, on average, when its customers pay their accounts.

Knowing its average collection period enables the firm to determine whether there is a general problem with accounts receivable. For example, a firm that has credit terms of net 30 would expect its average collection period (minus receipt, processing, and collection time) to equal about 30 days. If the actual collection period is significantly greater than 30 days, the firm has reason to review its credit operations. If the firm's average collection period is increasing over time, it has cause for concern about its accounts receivable management. A first step in analyzing an accounts receivable problem is to "age" the accounts receivable. By this process the firm can determine whether the problem exists in its accounts receivable in general or is attributable to a few specific accounts.

Aging of Accounts Receivable

aging schedule
A credit-monitoring technique that breaks down accounts receivable into groups on the basis of their time of origin; it shows the percentages of the total accounts receivable balance that have been outstanding for specified periods of time.

An **aging schedule** breaks down accounts receivable into groups on the basis of their time of origin. The breakdown is typically made on a month-by-month basis, going back 3 or 4 months. The resulting schedule indicates the percentages of the total accounts receivable balance that have been outstanding for specified periods of time. The purpose of the aging schedule is to enable the firm to pinpoint problems. The form and evaluation of an aging schedule can be illustrated with a simple example.

EXAMPLE

The accounts receivable balance on the books of Dodd Tool on December 31, 2006, was $200,000. The firm extends net 30-day credit terms to its customers. To gain insight into the firm's relatively lengthy—51.3-day—average collection period, Dodd prepared the following aging schedule.

Age of account	Balance outstanding	Percentage of total balance outstanding
0–30 days	$ 80,000	40%
31–60 days	36,000	18
61–90 days	52,000	26
91–120 days	26,000	13
Over 120 days	6,000	3%
Totals at 12/31/06	$200,000	100%

Because Dodd extends 30-day credit terms to its customers, its customers have 30 days after the end of the month of sale to remit payment. Therefore the 40% of the balance outstanding with an age of 0–30 days is *current*. The balances outstanding for 31–60 days, 61–90 days, 91–120 days, and over 120 days are *overdue*.

Reviewing the aging schedule we see that 40% of the accounts are current (age < 30 days) and the remaining 60% are overdue (age > 30 days). Eighteen

TABLE 13.4	Popular Collection Techniques
Technique[a]	Brief description
Letters	After a certain number of days, the firm sends a polite letter reminding the customer of the overdue account. If the account is not paid within a certain period after this letter has been sent, a second, more demanding letter is sent.
Telephone calls	If letters prove unsuccessful, a telephone call may be made to the customer to request immediate payment. If the customer has a reasonable excuse, arrangements may be made to extend the payment period. A call from the seller's attorney may be used.
Personal visits	This technique is much more common at the consumer credit level, but it may also be effectively employed by industrial suppliers. Sending a local salesperson or a collection person to confront the customer can be very effective. Payment may be made on the spot.
Collection agencies	A firm can turn uncollectible accounts over to a collection agency or an attorney for collection. The fees for this service are typically quite high; the firm may receive less than 50 cents on the dollar from accounts collected in this way.
Legal action	Legal action is the most stringent step, an alternative to the use of a collection agency. Not only is direct legal action expensive, but it may force the debtor into bankruptcy without guaranteeing the ultimate receipt of the overdue amount.

[a] The techniques are listed in the order in which they are typically followed in the collection process.

percent of the balance outstanding is 1–30 days overdue, 26% is 31–60 days overdue, 13% is 61–90 days overdue, and 3% is more than 90 days overdue. Although the collections seem generally slow, a noticeable irregularity in these data is the high percentage of the balance outstanding that is 31–60 days overdue (ages of 61–90 days). Clearly, a problem must have occurred 61–90 days ago. Investigation may find that the problem can be attributed to the hiring of a new credit manager, the acceptance of a new account that made a large credit purchase but has not yet paid for it, or ineffective collection policy. When these types of discrepancies are found in the aging schedule, the analyst should determine, evaluate, and remedy its cause.

Popular Collection Techniques

A number of collection techniques, ranging from letters to legal action, are employed. As an account becomes more and more overdue, the collection effort becomes more personal and more intense. In Table 13.4 the popular collection techniques are listed, and briefly described, in the order typically followed in the collection process.

Review Questions

13–11 What is the role of the *five C's of credit* in the credit selection activity?

13–12 Explain why *credit scoring* is typically applied to consumer credit decisions rather than to mercantile credit decisions.

13–13 What are the basic tradeoffs in a *tightening* of credit standards?

13–14 Why are the risks involved in international credit management more complex than those associated with purely domestic credit sales?

13–15 Why do a firm's regular credit terms typically conform to those of its industry?

13–16 Why should a firm actively monitor the accounts receivable of its credit customers? How are the *average collection period* and an *aging schedule* used for credit monitoring?

Management of Receipts and Disbursements

Hint The financial manager of a small business must have a very strong relationship with a commercial banker. Because the small firm cannot afford to hire someone strictly as a manager of receipts and disbursements, the financial manager, who is probably a generalist, needs to rely on the expertise of the commercial banker for the firm's most cost-effective means of managing cash.

As discussed in the previous section, the average collection period (the second component of the cash conversion cycle) has two parts: (1) the time from sale until the customer mails the payment and (2) the receipt, processing, and collection time. The third component of the cash conversion cycle, the average payment period, also has two parts: (1) the time from purchase of goods on account until the firm mails its payment and (2) the receipt, processing, and collection time required by the firm's suppliers. The receipt, processing, and collection time for the firm, both from its customers and to its suppliers, is the focus of receipts and disbursements management.

Float

float
Funds that have been sent by the payer but are not yet usable funds to the payee.

mail float
The time delay between when payment is placed in the mail and when it is received.

processing float
The time between receipt of a payment and its deposit into the firm's account.

clearing float
The time between deposit of a payment and when spendable funds become available to the firm.

Float refers to funds that have been sent by the payer but are not yet usable funds to the payee. Float is important in the cash conversion cycle because its presence lengthens both the firm's average collection period and its average payment period. However, the goal of the firm should be to shorten its average collection period and lengthen its average payment period. Both can be accomplished by managing float.

Float has three component parts:

1. **Mail float** is the time delay between when payment is placed in the mail and when it is received.
2. **Processing float** is the time between receipt of the payment and its deposit into the firm's account.
3. **Clearing float** is the time between deposit of the payment and when spendable funds become available to the firm. This component of float is attributable to the time required for a check to clear the banking system.

Some popular techniques for managing the component parts of float to speed up collections and slow down payments are described here.

Speeding Up Collections

Hint One method of accelerating the collection of accounts receivable is to let someone else do the financing for you, such as by using bank credit cards or selling accounts receivable to a third party at a discount. Another method is to change the credit terms: Increase the cash discount and shorten the required payment period.

Speeding up collections reduces customer *collection float* time and thus reduces the firm's average collection period, which reduces the investment the firm must make in its cash conversion cycle. In our earlier examples, MAX Company had annual sales of $10 million and 8 days of total collection float (receipt, processing, and collection time). If MAX can reduce its float time by 3 days, it will reduce its investment in the cash conversion cycle by $82,192 [$10,000,000 × (3/365)].

A popular technique for speeding up collections is a lockbox system. A **lockbox system** works as follows: Instead of mailing payments to the company, customers mail payments to a post office box. The firm's bank empties the post office box regularly, processes each payment, and deposits the payments in the firm's account. Deposit slips, along with payment enclosures, are sent (or transmitted electronically) to the firm by the bank so that the firm can properly credit customers' accounts. Lockboxes are geographically dispersed to match the locations of the firm's customers. A lockbox system affects all three components of float. Lockboxes reduce mail time and often clearing time by being near the firm's customers. Lockboxes reduce processing time to nearly zero because the bank deposits payments before the firm processes them. Obviously a lockbox system reduces collection float time, but not without a cost; therefore, a firm must perform an economic analysis to determine whether to implement a lockbox system.

Lockbox systems are commonly used by large firms whose customers are geographically dispersed. However, a firm does not have to be large to benefit from a lockbox. Smaller firms can also benefit from a lockbox system. The benefit to small firms often comes primarily from transferring the processing of payments to the bank.

> **lockbox system**
> A collection procedure in which customers mail payments to a post office box that is emptied regularly by the firm's bank, which processes the payments and deposits them in the firm's account. This system speeds up collection time by reducing processing time as well as mail and clearing time.

Slowing Down Payments

Float is also a component of the firm's average payment period. In this case, the float is in the favor of the firm. The firm may benefit by increasing all three of the components of its *payment float*. One popular technique for increasing payment float is **controlled disbursing**, which involves the strategic use of mailing points and bank accounts to lengthen mail float and clearing float, respectively. This approach should be used carefully, though, because longer payment periods may strain supplier relations.

In summary, a reasonable overall policy for float management is (1) to collect payments as quickly as possible, because once the payment is in the mail, the funds belong to the firm, and (2) to delay making payment to suppliers, because once the payment is mailed, the funds belong to the supplier.

> **controlled disbursing**
> The strategic use of mailing points and bank accounts to lengthen mail float and clearing float, respectively.
>
> **Hint** Data on clearing times among banks located in various cities can be developed by the firm itself. They also can be obtained from a major bank's cash management service department or purchased from a firm that sells such information.

Cash Concentration

Cash concentration is the process used by the firm to bring lockbox and other deposits together into one bank, often called the *concentration bank*. Cash concentration has three main advantages. First, it creates a large pool of funds for use in making short-term cash investments. Because there is a fixed-cost component in the transaction cost associated with such investments, investing a single pool of funds reduces the firm's transaction costs. The larger investment pool also allows the firm to choose from a greater variety of short-term investment

> **cash concentration**
> The process used by the firm to bring lockbox and other deposits together into one bank, often called the *concentration bank*.

vehicles. Second, concentrating the firm's cash in one account improves the tracking and internal control of the firm's cash. Third, having one concentration bank enables the firm to implement payment strategies that reduce idle cash balances.

There are a variety of mechanisms for transferring cash from the lockbox bank and other collecting banks to the concentration bank. One mechanism is a **depository transfer check (DTC)**, which is an unsigned check drawn on one of the firm's bank accounts and deposited in another. For cash concentration, a DTC is drawn on each lockbox or other collecting bank account and deposited in the concentration bank account. Once the DTC has cleared the bank on which it is drawn (which may take several days), the transfer of funds is completed. Most firms currently provide deposit information by telephone to the concentration bank, which then prepares and deposits into its account the DTC drawn on the lockbox or other collecting bank account.

A second mechanism is an **ACH (automated clearinghouse) transfer,** which is a preauthorized electronic withdrawal from the payer's account. A computerized clearing facility (called the *automated clearinghouse,* or *ACH*) makes a paperless transfer of funds between the payer and payee banks. An ACH settles accounts among participating banks. Individual accounts are settled by respective bank balance adjustments. ACH transfers clear in one day. For cash concentration, an ACH transfer is made from each lockbox bank or other collecting bank to the concentration bank. An ACH transfer can be thought of as an electronic DTC, but because the ACH transfer clears in one day, it provides benefits over a DTC; however, both banks in the ACH transfer must be members of the clearinghouse.

A third cash concentration mechanism is a **wire transfer.** A wire transfer is an electronic communication that, via bookkeeping entries, removes funds from the payer's bank and deposits them in the payee's bank. Wire transfers can eliminate mail and clearing float and may reduce processing float as well. For cash concentration, the firm moves funds using a wire transfer from each lockbox or other collecting account to its concentration account. Wire transfers are a substitute for DTC and ACH transfers, but they are more expensive.

It is clear that the firm must balance the costs and benefits of concentrating cash to determine the type and timing of transfers from its lockbox and other collecting accounts to its concentration account. The transfer mechanism selected should be the one that is most profitable. (The profit per period of any transfer mechanism equals earnings on the increased availability of funds minus the cost of the transfer system.)

Zero-Balance Accounts

Zero-balance accounts (ZBAs) are disbursement accounts that always have an end-of-day balance of zero. The purpose is to eliminate nonearning cash balances in corporate checking accounts. A ZBA works well as a disbursement account under a cash concentration system.

ZBAs work as follows: Once all of a given day's checks are presented for payment from the firm's ZBA, the bank notifies the firm of the total amount of checks, and the firm transfers funds into the account to cover the amount of that day's checks. This leaves an end-of-day balance of $0 (zero dollars). The ZBA enables the firm to keep all of its operating cash in an interest-earning account, thereby eliminating idle cash balances. Thus a firm that used a ZBA in conjunction with a cash concentration system would need two accounts. The firm would concentrate its cash from the lockboxes and other collecting banks into an interest-earning account and would write checks against its ZBA. The firm would cover the exact dollar amount of checks presented against the ZBA with transfers from the interest-earning account, leaving the end-of-day balance in the ZBA at $0.

A ZBA is a disbursement management tool. As we discussed earlier, the firm would prefer to maximize its payment float. However, some cash managers feel that actively attempting to increase float time on payments is unethical. A ZBA enables the firm to maximize the use of float on each check without altering the float time of payments to its suppliers. Keeping all the firm's cash in an interest-earning account enables the firm to maximize earnings on its cash balances by capturing the full float time on each check it writes.

Investing in Marketable Securities

Marketable securities are short-term, interest-earning, money market instruments that can easily be converted into cash.[5] Marketable securities are classified as part of the firm's liquid assets. The firm uses them to earn a return on temporarily idle funds. To be truly marketable, a security must have (1) a ready market so as to minimize the amount of time required to convert it into cash, and (2) safety of principal, which means that it experiences little or no loss in value over time.

The securities that are most commonly held as part of the firm's marketable-securities portfolio are divided into two groups: (1) government issues, which have relatively low yields as a consequence of their low risk, and (2) nongovernment issues, which have slightly higher yields than government issues with similar maturities because of the slightly higher risk associated with them. Table 13.5 (on page 538) summarizes the key features and recent (November 17, 2004) yields for popular marketable securities.

Review Questions

13–17 What is *float* and what are its three components?

13–18 What are the firm's objectives with regard to *collection float* and to *payment float*?

13–19 What are the three main advantages of cash concentration?

13–20 What are three mechanisms of cash concentration? What is the objective of using a *zero-balance account (ZBA)* in a cash concentration system?

13–21 What two characteristics make a security marketable? Why are the yields on nongovernment marketable securities generally higher than the yields on government issues with similar maturities?

---

5. As explained in Chapter 1, the *money market* results from a financial relationship between the suppliers and demanders of short-term funds, that is, marketable securities.

TABLE 13.5 Features and Recent Yields on Popular Marketable Securities[a]

Security	Issuer	Description	Initial maturity	Risk and return	Yield on Nov. 17, 2004[b]
Government Issues					
Treasury bills	U.S. Treasury	Issued weekly at auction; sold at a discount; strong secondary market	91 and 182 days	Lowest, virtually risk-free	2.08%
Treasury notes	U.S. Treasury	Stated interest rate; interest paid semiannually; strong secondary market	1 to 10 years	Low, but slightly higher than U.S. Treasury bills	2.14%
Federal agency issues	Agencies of federal government	Not an obligation of U.S. Treasury; strong secondary market	9 months to 30 years	Slightly higher than U.S. Treasury issues	2.11%[c]
Nongovernment Issues					
Negotiable certificates of deposit (CDs)	Commercial banks	Represent specific cash deposits in commercial banks; amounts and maturities tailored to investor needs; large denominations; good secondary market	1 month to 3 years	Higher than U.S. Treasury issues and comparable to commercial paper	2.28%
Commercial paper	Corporation with a high credit standing	Unsecured note of issuer; large denominations	3 to 270 days	Higher than U.S. Treasury issues and comparable to negotiable CDs	2.25%
Banker's acceptances	Banks	Results from a bank guarantee of a business transaction; sold at discount from maturity value	30 to 180 days	About the same as negotiable CDs and commercial paper but higher than U.S. Treasury issues	2.26%
Eurodollar deposits	Foreign banks	Deposits of currency not native to the country in which the bank is located; large denominations; active secondary market	1 day to 3 years	High, due to less regulation of despository banks and some foreign exchange risk	2.27%
Money market mutual funds	Professional portfolio management companies	Professionally managed portfolios of marketable securities; provide instant liquidity	None—depends on wishes of investor	Vary, but generally higher than U.S. Treasury issues and comparable to negotiable CDs and commercial paper	1.14%[d]
Repurchase agreements	Bank or security dealer	Bank or security dealer sells specific securities to firm and agrees to repurchase them at a specific price and time	Customized to purchaser's needs	Generally slightly below that associated with the outright purchase of the security	—

[a]The prime rate of interest at this time was 5.00%.
[b]Yields obtained for 3-month maturities of each security.
[c]Federal National Mortgage Association (Fannie Mae) issue with 3 months to maturity is used here.
[d]The Dryfus Money Market Fund with an average maturity of 42 days is used here in the absence of any average-yield data. Comparatively low money market mutual fund yields occur when interest rates are relatively low, as was the case in late 2004.
Source: Wall Street Journal, November 18, 2004, pp. C14, C15, and C17.

Summary

FOCUS ON VALUE

It is important for a firm to maintain a reasonable level of net working capital. To do so, it must balance the high profit and high risk associated with low levels of current assets and high levels of current liabilities against the low profit and low risk that result from high levels of current assets and low levels of current liabilities. A strategy that achieves a reasonable balance between profits and liquidity should positively contribute to the firm's value.

Similarly, the firm should manage its cash conversion cycle by turning inventory quickly; collecting accounts receivable quickly; managing mail, processing, and clearing time; and paying accounts payable slowly. These strategies should enable the firm to manage its current accounts efficiently and to minimize the amount of resources invested in operating assets.

The financial manager can manage inventory, accounts receivable, and cash receipts to minimize the firm's operating cycle investment, thereby reducing the amount of resources needed to support its business. Employing these strategies, and managing accounts payable and cash disbursements so as to shorten the cash conversion cycle, should minimize the negotiated liabilities needed to support the firm's resource requirements. Active management of the firm's working capital and current assets should positively contribute to the firm's goal of **maximizing its stock price**.

REVIEW OF LEARNING GOALS

LG1 Understand short-term financial management, net working capital, and the related tradeoff between profitability and risk. Short-term financial management focuses on managing each of the firm's current assets (inventory, accounts receivable, cash, and marketable securities) and current liabilities (accounts payable, accruals, and notes payable) in a manner that positively contributes to the firm's value. Net working capital is the difference between current assets and current liabilities. Risk, in the context of short-term financial decisions, is the probability that a firm will be unable to pay its bills as they come due. Assuming a constant level of total assets, the higher a firm's ratio of current assets to total assets, the less profitable the firm, and the less risky it is. The converse is also true. With constant total assets, the higher a firm's ratio of current liabilities to total assets, the more profitable and the more risky the firm is. The converse of this statement is also true.

LG2 Describe the cash conversion cycle, its funding requirements, and the key strategies for managing it. The cash conversion cycle has three components: (1) average age of inventory, (2) average collection period, and (3) average payment period. The length of the cash conversion cycle determines the amount of time resources are tied up in the firm's day-to-day operations. The firm's investment in short-term assets often consists of both permanent and seasonal funding requirements. The seasonal requirements can be financed using either an aggressive (low-cost, high-risk) financing strategy or a conservative (high-cost, low-risk) financing strategy. The firm's funding decision for its cash conversion cycle ultimately depends on management's disposition toward risk and the strength of the firm's banking relationships. To minimize its reliance on negotiated liabilities, the financial manager seeks to (1) turn over inventory as quickly as possible, (2) collect accounts receivable as quickly as possible, (3) manage mail, processing, and clearing time, and (4) pay accounts payable as slowly as possible. Use of these strategies should minimize the length of the cash conversion cycle.

LG3 **Discuss inventory management: differing views, common techniques, and international concerns.** The viewpoints of marketing, manufacturing, and purchasing managers about the appropriate levels of inventory tend to cause higher inventories than those deemed appropriate by the financial manager. Four commonly used techniques for effectively managing inventory to keep its level low are (1) the ABC system, (2) the economic order quantity (EOQ) model, (3) the just-in-time (JIT) system, and (4) computerized systems for resource control—MRP, MRP II, and ERP. International inventory managers place greater emphasis on making sure that sufficient quantities of inventory are delivered where and when needed, and in the right condition, than on ordering the economically optimal quantities.

LG4 **Explain the credit selection process and the quantitative procedure for evaluating changes in credit standards.** Credit selection techniques determine which customers' creditworthiness is consistent with the firm's credit standards. Two popular credit selection techniques are the five C's of credit and credit scoring. Changes in credit standards can be evaluated mathematically by assessing the effects of a proposed change on profits from sales, the cost of accounts receivable investment, and bad-debt costs.

LG5 **Review the procedures for quantitatively considering cash discount changes, other aspects of credit terms, and credit monitoring.** Changes in credit terms—the cash discount, the cash discount period, and the credit period—can be quantified similarly to changes in credit standards. Credit monitoring, the ongoing review of accounts receivable, frequently involves use of the average collection period and an aging schedule. A number of popular collection techniques are used by firms.

LG6 **Understand the management of receipts and disbursements, including float, speeding up collections, slowing down payments, cash concentration, zero-balance accounts, and investing in marketable securities.** Float refers to funds that have been sent by the payer but are not yet usable funds to the payee. The components of float are mail time, processing time, and clearing time. Float occurs in both the average collection period and the average payment period. One technique for speeding up collections to reduce collection float is a lockbox system. A popular technique for slowing payments to increase payment float is controlled disbursing.

The goal for managing operating cash is to balance the opportunity cost of nonearning balances against the transaction cost of temporary investments. Firms commonly use depository transfer checks (DTCs), ACH transfers, and wire transfers to transfer lockbox receipts to their concentration banks quickly. Zero-balance accounts (ZBAs) can be used to eliminate nonearning cash balances in corporate checking accounts. Marketable securities are short-term, interest-earning, money market instruments used by the firm to earn a return on temporarily idle funds. They may be government or nongovernment issues.

SELF-TEST PROBLEMS (SOLUTIONS IN APPENDIX B)

ST13–1 Cash conversion cycle Hurkin Manufacturing Company pays accounts payable on the tenth day after purchase. The average collection period is 30 days, and the average age of inventory is 40 days. The firm currently has annual sales of about $18 million. The firm is considering a plan that would stretch its accounts payable by 20 days. If the firm pays 12% per year for its resource investment, what annual savings can it realize by this plan? Assume no difference in the investment per dollar of sales in inventory, receivables, and payables; no discount for early payment of accounts payable; and a 365-day year.

ST13-2 **EOQ analysis** Thompson Paint Company uses 60,000 gallons of pigment per year. The cost of ordering pigment is $200 per order, and the cost of carrying the pigment in inventory is $1 per gallon per year. The firm uses pigment at a constant rate every day throughout the year.
   a. Calculate the EOQ.
   b. Assuming that it takes 20 days to receive an order once it has been placed, determine the reorder point in terms of gallons of pigment. (*Note:* Use a 365-day year.)

ST13-3 **Relaxing credit standards** Regency Rug Repair Company is trying to decide whether it should relax its credit standards. The firm repairs 72,000 rugs per year at an average price of $32 each. Bad-debt expenses are 1% of sales, the average collection period is 40 days, and the variable cost per unit is $28. Regency expects that if it does relax its credit standards, the average collection period will increase to 48 days and that bad debts will increase to 1½% of sales. Sales will increase by 4,000 repairs per year. If the firm has a required rate of return on equal-risk investments of 14%, what recommendation would you give the firm? Use your analysis to justify your answer. (*Note:* Use a 365-day year.)

WARM-UP EXERCISES

E13-1 Sharam Industries has a 120-day *operating cycle*. If its average age of inventory is 50 days, how long is its average collection period? If its average payment period is 30 days, what is its *cash conversion cycle*? Place all of this information on a time line similar to Figure 13.1 on page 515.

E13-2 Icy Treats, Inc., is a seasonal business that sells frozen desserts. At the peak of its summer selling season the firm has $35,000 in cash, $125,000 in inventory, $70,000 in accounts receivable, and $65,000 in accounts payable. During the slow winter period the firm holds $10,000 in cash, $55,000 in inventory, $40,000 in accounts receivable, and $35,000 in accounts payable. Calculate Icy Treats' minimum and peak funding requirements.

E13-3 Mama Leone's Frozen Pizzas uses 50,000 units of cheese per year. Each unit costs $2.50. The ordering cost for the cheese is $250 per order, and its carrying cost is $0.50 per unit per year. Calculate the firm's *economic order quantity (EOQ)* for the cheese. Mama Leone's operates 250 days per year and maintains a minimum inventory level of 2 days' worth of cheese. If the lead time to receive orders of cheese is 3 days, calculate the *reorder point*.

E13-4 Forrester Fashions has annual credit sales of 250,000 units with an average collection period of 70 days. The company has a per-unit variable cost of $20 and a per-unit sale price of $30. Bad debts currently are 5% of sales. The firm estimates that a proposed relaxation of credit standards would not affect its 70-day average collection period, but would increase bad debts to 7.5% of sales, which would increase to 300,000 units per year. Forrester requires a 12% return on investments. Show all necessary calculations required to evaluate Forrester's proposed relaxation of credit standards.

E13–5 Klein's Tools is considering offering a cash discount to speed up the collection of accounts receivable. Currently the firm has an average collection period of 65 days, annual sales are 35,000 units, the per-unit sale price is $40, and the per-unit variable cost is $29. A 2% cash discount is being considered. Klein's Tools estimates that 80% of its customers will take the 2% discount. If sales are expected to rise to 37,000 units per year and the firm has a 15% required rate of return, what minimum average collection period is required to approve the cash discount plan?

PROBLEMS

 P13–1 **Cash conversion cycle** American Products is concerned about managing cash efficiently. On the average, inventories have an age of 90 days, and accounts receivable are collected in 60 days. Accounts payable are paid approximately 30 days after they arise. The firm has annual sales of about $30 million. Assume there is no difference in the investment per dollar of sales in inventory, receivables, and payables; and a 365-day year.
  a. Calculate the firm's *operating cycle*.
  b. Calculate the firm's *cash conversion cycle*.
  c. Calculate the amount of resources needed to support the firm's cash conversion cycle.
  d. Discuss how management might be able to reduce the cash conversion cycle.

 P13–2 **Changing cash conversion cycle** Camp Manufacturing turns over its inventory 8 times each year, has an average payment period of 35 days, and has an average collection period of 60 days. The firm's annual sales are $3.5 million. Assume there is no difference in the investment per dollar of sales in inventory, receivables, and payables; and a 365-day year.
  a. Calculate the firm's *operating cycle* and *cash conversion cycle*.
  b. Calculate the firm's daily cash operating expenditure. How much in resources must be invested to support its cash conversion cycle?
  c. If the firm pays 14% for these resources, by how much would it increase its annual profits by *favorably* changing its current cash conversion cycle by 20 days?

 P13–3 **Multiple changes in cash conversion cycle** Garrett Industries turns over its inventory 6 times each year; it has an average collection period of 45 days and an average payment period of 30 days. The firm's annual sales are $3 million. Assume there is no difference in the investment per dollar of sales in inventory, receivables, and payables; and a 365-day year.
  a. Calculate the firm's *cash conversion cycle,* its daily cash operating expenditure, and the amount of resources needed to support its cash conversion cycle.
  b. Find the firm's cash conversion cycle and resource investment requirement if it makes the following changes simultaneously.
    (1) Shortens the average age of inventory by 5 days.
    (2) Speeds the collection of accounts receivable by an average of 10 days.
    (3) Extends the average payment period by 10 days.

c. If the firm pays 13% for its resource investment, by how much, if anything, could it increase its annual profit as a result of the changes in part **b**?
d. If the annual cost of achieving the profit in part **c** is $35,000, what action would you recommend to the firm? Why?

P13–4 **Aggressive versus conservative seasonal funding strategy** Dynabase Tool has forecast its total funds requirements for the coming year as shown in the following table.

Month	Amount	Month	Amount
January	$2,000,000	July	$12,000,000
February	2,000,000	August	14,000,000
March	2,000,000	September	9,000,000
April	4,000,000	October	5,000,000
May	6,000,000	November	4,000,000
June	9,000,000	December	3,000,000

a. Divide the firm's monthly funds requirement into (1) a *permanent* component and (2) a *seasonal* component, and find the monthly average for each of these components.
b. Describe the amount of long-term and short-term financing used to meet the total funds requirement under (1) an *aggressive funding strategy* and (2) a *conservative funding strategy*. Assume that under the aggressive strategy, long-term funds finance permanent needs and short-term funds are used to finance seasonal needs.
c. Assuming that short-term funds cost 12% annually and that the cost of long-term funds is 17% annually, use the averages found in part **a** to calculate the total cost of each of the strategies described in part **b**.
d. Discuss the profitability–risk tradeoffs associated with the aggressive strategy and those associated with the conservative strategy.

P13–5 **EOQ analysis** Tiger Corporation purchases 1,200,000 units per year of one component. The fixed cost per order is $25. The annual carrying cost of the item is 27% of its $2 cost.
a. Determine the EOQ under the following conditions: (1) no changes, (2) order cost of zero, and (3) carrying cost of zero.
b. What do your answers illustrate about the EOQ model? Explain.

P13–6 **EOQ, reorder point, and safety stock** Alexis Company uses 800 units of a product per year on a continuous basis. The product has a fixed cost of $50 per order, and its carrying cost is $2 per unit per year. It takes 5 days to receive a shipment after an order is placed, and the firm wishes to hold 10 days' usage in inventory as a safety stock.
a. Calculate the EOQ.
b. Determine the average level of inventory. *(Note:* Use a 365-day year to calculate daily usage.)
c. Determine the *reorder point*.

d. Indicate which of the following variables change if the firm does not hold the safety stock: (1) order cost, (2) carrying cost, (3) total inventory cost, (4) reorder point, (5) economic order quantity. Explain.

P13–7 **Accounts receivable changes without bad debts** Tara's Textiles currently has credit sales of $360 million per year and an average collection period of 60 days. Assume that the price of Tara's products is $60 per unit and that the variable costs are $55 per unit. The firm is considering an accounts receivable change that will result in a 20% increase in sales and a 20% increase in the average collection period. No change in bad debts is expected. The firm's equal-risk opportunity cost on its investment in accounts receivable is 14%. (*Note:* Use a 365-day year.)
  a. Calculate the *additional profit contribution from new sales* that the firm will realize if it makes the proposed change.
  b. What *marginal investment in accounts receivable* will result?
  c. Calculate the *cost of the marginal investment in accounts receivable*.
  d. Should the firm implement the proposed change? What other information would be helpful in your analysis?

P13–8 **Accounts receivable changes with bad debts** A firm is evaluating an accounts receivable change that would increase bad debts from 2% to 4% of sales. Sales are currently 50,000 units, the selling price is $20 per unit, and the variable cost per unit is $15. As a result of the proposed change, sales are forecast to increase to 60,000 units.
  a. What are bad debts in dollars currently and under the proposed change?
  b. Calculate the *cost of the marginal bad debts* to the firm.
  c. Ignoring the additional profit contribution from increased sales, if the proposed change saves $3,500 and causes no change in the average investment in accounts receivable, would you recommend it? Explain.
  d. Considering *all* changes in costs and benefits, would you recommend the proposed change? Explain.
  e. Compare and discuss your answers in parts c and d.

P13–9 **Relaxation of credit standards** Lewis Enterprises is considering relaxing its credit standards to increase its currently sagging sales. As a result of the proposed relaxation, sales are expected to increase by 10% from 10,000 to 11,000 units during the coming year; the average collection period is expected to increase from 45 to 60 days; and bad debts are expected to increase from 1% to 3% of sales. The sale price per unit is $40, and the variable cost per unit is $31. The firm's required return on equal-risk investments is 25%. Evaluate the proposed relaxation, and make a recommendation to the firm. (*Note:* Assume a 365-day year.)

P13–10 **Initiating a cash discount** Gardner Company currently makes all sales on credit and offers no cash discount. The firm is considering offering a 2% cash discount for payment within 15 days. The firm's current average collection period is 60 days, sales are 40,000 units, selling price is $45 per unit, and variable cost per unit is $36. The firm expects that the change in credit terms will result in an increase in sales to 42,000 units, that 70% of the sales will take the discount, and that the average collection period will fall to 30 days. If the firm's required rate of return on equal-risk investments is 25%, should the proposed discount be offered? (*Note:* Assume a 365-day year.)

P13–11 **Shortening the credit period** A firm is contemplating *shortening* its credit period from 40 to 30 days and believes that as a result of this change, its average collection period will decline from 45 to 36 days. Bad-debt expenses are expected to decrease from 1.5% to 1% of sales. The firm is currently selling 12,000 units but believes that as a result of the proposed change, sales will decline to 10,000 units. The sale price per unit is $56, and the variable cost per unit is $45. The firm has a required return on equal-risk investments of 25%. Evaluate this decision, and make a recommendation to the firm. (*Note:* Assume a 365-day year.)

P13–12 **Lengthening the credit period** Parker Tool is considering lengthening its credit period from 30 to 60 days. All customers will continue to pay on the net date. The firm currently bills $450,000 for sales and has $345,000 in variable costs. The change in credit terms is expected to increase sales to $510,000. Bad-debt expenses will increase from 1% to 1.5% of sales. The firm has a required rate of return on equal-risk investments of 20%. (*Note:* Assume a 365-day year.)
 a. What *additional profit contribution from sales* will be realized from the proposed change?
 b. What is the *cost of the marginal investment in accounts receivable*?
 c. What is the *cost of the marginal bad debts*?
 d. Do you recommend this change in credit terms? Why or why not?

P13–13 **Float** Simon Corporation has daily cash receipts of $65,000. A recent analysis of its collections indicated that customers' payments were in the mail an average of 2.5 days. Once received, the payments are processed in 1.5 days. After payments are deposited, it takes an average of 3 days for these receipts to clear the banking system.
 a. How much *collection float (in days)* does the firm currently have?
 b. If the firm's opportunity cost is 11%, would it be economically advisable for the firm to pay an annual fee of $16,500 to reduce collection float by 3 days? Explain why or why not.

P13–14 **Lockbox system** Eagle Industries feels that a lockbox system can shorten its accounts receivable collection period by 3 days. Credit sales are $3,240,000 per year, billed on a continuous basis. The firm has other equally risky investments with a return of 15%. The cost of the lockbox system is $9,000 per year. (*Note:* Assume a 365-day year.)
 a. What amount of cash will be made available for other uses under the lockbox system?
 b. What net benefit (cost) will the firm realize if it adopts the lockbox system? Should it adopt the proposed lockbox system?

P13–15 **Zero-balance account** Union Company is considering establishment of a zero-balance account. The firm currently maintains an average balance of $420,000 in its disbursement account. As compensation to the bank for maintaining the zero-balance account, the firm will have to pay a monthly fee of $1,000 and maintain a $300,000 non–interest-earning deposit in the bank. The firm currently has no other deposits in the bank. Evaluate the proposed zero-balance account, and make a recommendation to the firm, assuming that it has a 12% opportunity cost.

P13–16 ETHICS PROBLEM Controlled disbursing is defined as an information product—that is, the bank on which the company's checks are drawn provides an early-morning notification of the total dollar amount of checks that will clear the account that day. Based on that notification, the company may then fund the account for that amount by the close of business that afternoon. How might controlled disbursing still be viewed as a form of "remote disbursing," and therefore be considered unethical?

CHAPTER 13 CASE

Assessing Roche Publishing Company's Cash Management Efficiency

Lisa Pinto, vice president of finance at Roche Publishing Company, a rapidly growing publisher of college texts, is concerned about the firm's high level of short-term resource investment. She believes that the firm can improve the management of its cash and, as a result, reduce this investment. In this regard, she charged Arlene Bessenoff, the treasurer, with assessing the firm's cash management efficiency. Arlene decided to begin her investigation by studying the firm's operating and cash conversion cycles.

Arlene found that Roche's average payment period was 25 days. She consulted industry data, which showed that the average payment period for the industry was 40 days. Investigation of three similar publishing companies revealed that their average payment period was also 40 days. She estimated the annual cost of achieving a 40-day payment period to be $53,000.

Next, Arlene studied the production cycle and inventory policies. The average age of inventory was 120 days. She determined that the industry standard as reported in a survey done by *Publishing World*, the trade association journal, was 85 days. She estimated the annual cost of achieving an 85-day average age of inventory to be $150,000.

Further analysis showed Arlene that the firm's average collection period was 60 days. The industry average, derived from the trade association data and information on three similar publishing companies, was found to be 42 days—30% lower than Roche's. Arlene estimated that if Roche initiated a 2% cash discount for payment within 10 days of the beginning of the credit period, the firm's average collection period would drop from 60 days to the 42-day industry average. She also expected the following to occur as a result of the discount: Annual sales would increase from $13,750,000 to $15,000,000; bad debts would remain unchanged; and the 2% cash discount would be applied to 75% of the firm's sales. The firm's variable costs equal 80% of sales.

Roche Publishing Company is currently spending $12,000,000 per year on its operating-cycle investment, but it expects that initiating a cash discount will increase its operating-cycle investment to $13,100,000 per year. (*Note:* The operating-cycle investment per dollar of inventory, receivables, and payables is assumed to be the same.) Arlene's concern was whether the firm's cash management was as efficient as it could be. Arlene knew that the company paid 12% annual interest for its resource investment and therefore viewed this value as the firm's required return. For this reason, she was concerned about the resource investment cost resulting from any inefficiencies in the management of Roche's cash conversion cycle. (*Note:* Assume a 365-day year.)

TO DO

a. Assuming a constant rate for purchases, production, and sales throughout the year, what are Roche's existing *operating cycle (OC)*, *cash conversion cycle (CCC)*, and *resource investment* need?
b. If Roche can optimize operations according to industry standards, what would its *operating cycle (OC)*, *cash conversion cycle (CCC)*, and *resource investment* need be under these more efficient conditions?
c. In terms of resource investment requirements, what is the annual cost of Roche's operational inefficiency?
d. Evaluate whether Roche's strategy for speeding its collection of accounts receivable would be acceptable. What annual net profit or loss would result from implementation of the cash discount?
e. Use your finding in part **d,** along with the payables and inventory costs given, to determine the total annual cost the firm would incur to achieve the industry level of operational efficiency.
f. Judging on the basis of your findings in parts **c** and **e,** should the firm incur the annual cost to achieve the industry level of operational efficiency? Explain why or why not.

SPREADSHEET EXERCISE

The current balance in accounts receivable for Eboy Corporation is $443,000. This level was achieved with annual (365 days) credit sales of $3,544,000. The firm offers its customers credit terms of *net 30*. However, in an effort to help its cash flow position and to follow the actions of its rivals, the firm is considering changing its credit terms from net 30 to *2/10 net 30*. The objective is to speed up the receivable collections and thereby improve the firm's cash flows. Eboy would like to increase its accounts receivable turnover to 12.0.

The firm works with a raw material whose current annual usage is 1,450 units. Each finished product requires 1 unit of this raw material at a variable cost of $2,600 per unit and sells for $4,200 on terms of net 30. It is estimated that 70% of the firm's customers will take the 2% cash discount and that with the discount, sales of the finished product will increase by 50 units per year. The firm's opportunity cost of funds invested in accounts receivable is 12.5%

In analyzing the investment in accounts receivable, use the variable cost of the product sold instead of the sale price, because the variable cost is a better indicator of the firm's investment.

TO DO

Create a spreadsheet similar to Table 13.3 (or to one that can be viewed at www.aw-bc.com/gitman) to analyze whether the firm should initiate the proposed cash discount. What is your advice? Make sure you calculate the following:

a. Additional profit contribution from sales.
b. Average investment in accounts receivable at present (without cash discount).
c. Average investment in accounts receivable with the proposed cash discount.

d. Reduction in investment in accounts receivable.
e. Cost savings from reduced investment in accounts receivable.
f. Cost of the cash discount.
g. Net profit (loss) from initiation of the proposed cash discount.

WEB EXERCISE

As this chapter points out, cash management is not only important, but it is also challenging. Many small businesses simply do not have the managerial expertise needed to properly manage working capital and current assets. As a result of this knowledge vacuum, many banks have stepped in to offer small business services.

TO DO

Point your browser to www.bankofamerica.com/, the home page for the Bank of America (BoA). Click on the small business tab and investigate the types of services BoA offers. Report on those services offered by BoA and how they relate to the topics covered in this chapter.

Remember to check the book's Web site at

www.aw-bc.com/gitman

for additional resources, including additional Web exercises.

Chapter 14

Current Liabilities Management

LEARNING GOALS

LG1 Review accounts payable, the key components of credit terms, and the procedures for analyzing those terms.

LG2 Understand the effects of stretching accounts payable on their cost, and the use of accruals.

LG3 Describe interest rates and the basic types of unsecured bank sources of short-term loans.

LG4 Discuss the basic features of commercial paper and the key aspects of international short-term loans.

LG5 Explain the characteristics of secured short-term loans and the use of accounts receivable as short-term-loan collateral.

LG6 Describe the various ways in which inventory can be used as short-term-loan collateral.

Across the Disciplines Why This Chapter Matters to You

Accounting: You need to understand how to analyze supplier credit terms to decide whether the firm should take or give up cash discounts; you also need to understand the various types of short-term loans, both unsecured and secured, that you will be required to record and report.

Information systems: You need to understand what data the firm will need to process accounts payable, track accruals, and meet bank loans and other short-term debt obligations in a timely manner.

Management: You need to know the sources of short-term loans so that if short-term financing is needed, you will understand its availability and cost.

Marketing: You need to understand how accounts receivable and inventory can be used as loan collateral; the procedures used by the firm to secure short-term loans with such collateral could affect customer relationships.

Operations: You need to understand the use of accounts payable as a form of short-term financing and the effect on one's suppliers of stretching payables; you also need to understand the process by which a firm uses inventory as collateral.

Accounts payable and accruals represent forms of spontaneous financing for the firm. The longer the firm can hold the cash intended for paying those accounts, the longer it can use those funds for its own purposes. Firms typically, though, must arrange for short-term loans to even out seasonal cash flows or to cover unexpected outlays. This chapter looks at various aspects of current liabilities management—spontaneous liabilities and how best to manage them, and both unsecured and secured sources of short-term loans.

Spontaneous Liabilities

spontaneous liabilities
Financing that arises from the normal course of business; the two major short-term sources of such liabilities are accounts payable and accruals.

Spontaneous liabilities arise from the normal course of business. The two major spontaneous sources of short-term financing are accounts payable and accruals. As the firm's sales increase, accounts payable increase in response to the increased purchases necessary to produce at higher levels. Also in response to increasing sales, the firm's accruals increase as wages and taxes rise because of greater labor requirements and the increased taxes on the firm's increased earnings. There is normally no explicit cost attached to either of these current liabilities, although they do have certain implicit costs. In addition, both are forms of **unsecured short-term financing**—short-term financing obtained without pledging specific assets as collateral. The firm should take advantage of these "interest-free" sources of unsecured short-term financing whenever possible.

unsecured short-term financing
Short-term financing obtained without pledging specific assets as collateral.

Accounts Payable Management

Hint An account payable of a purchaser is an account receivable on the supplier's books. Chapter 13 highlighted the key strategies and considerations involved in extending credit to customers.

Accounts payable are the major source of unsecured short-term financing for business firms. They result from transactions in which merchandise is purchased but no formal note is signed to show the purchaser's liability to the seller. The purchaser in effect agrees to pay the supplier the amount required in accordance with credit terms normally stated on the supplier's invoice. The discussion of accounts payable here is presented from the viewpoint of the purchaser.

Role in the Cash Conversion Cycle

The average payment period is the final component of the *cash conversion cycle* introduced in Chapter 13. The average payment period has two parts: (1) the time from the purchase of raw materials until the firm mails the payment and (2) payment float time (the time it takes after the firm mails its payment until the supplier has withdrawn spendable funds from the firm's account). In the preceding chapter, we discussed issues related to payment float time. Here we discuss the management by the firm of the time that elapses between its purchase of raw materials and its mailing payment to the supplier. This activity is **accounts payable management.**

accounts payable management
Management by the firm of the time that elapses between its purchase of raw materials and its mailing payment to the supplier.

 The firm's goal is to pay as slowly as possible without damaging its credit rating. This means that accounts should be paid on the last day possible, given the supplier's stated credit terms. For example, if the terms are net 30, then the account should be paid 30 days from the *beginning of the credit period*, which is typically either the *date of invoice* or the *end of the month* (*EOM*) in which the purchase was made. This allows for the maximum use of an interest-free loan from the supplier and will not damage the firm's credit rating (because the account is paid within the stated credit terms).

> **EXAMPLE**
>
> In the demonstration of the cash conversion cycle in Chapter 13 (see pages 514–515), MAX Company had an average payment period of 35 days (consisting of 30 days until payment was mailed and 5 days of payment float), which resulted in average accounts payable of $467,466. Thus the daily accounts payable generated by MAX totaled $13,356 ($467,466/35). If MAX were to mail its payments in 35 days instead of 30 days, its accounts payable would increase by $66,780 (5 × $13,356). As a result, MAX's cash conversion cycle would decrease by 5 days, and the firm would reduce its investment in operations by $66,780. Clearly, if this action did not damage MAX's credit rating, it would be in the company's best interest.

Analyzing Credit Terms

The credit terms that a firm is offered by its suppliers enable it to delay payments for its purchases. Because the supplier's cost of having its money tied up in merchandise after it is sold is probably reflected in the purchase price, the purchaser is already indirectly paying for this benefit. The purchaser should therefore carefully analyze credit terms to determine the best trade credit strategy. If a firm is extended credit terms that include a cash discount, it has two options—to take the cash discount or to give it up.

Taking the Cash Discount If a firm intends to take a cash discount, it should pay on the last day of the discount period. There is no cost associated with taking a cash discount.

> **EXAMPLE**
>
> Lawrence Industries, operator of a small chain of video stores, purchased $1,000 worth of merchandise on February 27 from a supplier extending terms of 2/10 net 30 EOM. If the firm takes the cash discount, it must pay $980 [$1,000 − (0.02 × $1,000)] by March 10, thereby saving $20.

Giving Up the Cash Discount If the firm chooses to give up the cash discount, it should pay on the final day of the credit period. There is an implicit cost associated with giving up a cash discount. The **cost of giving up a cash discount** is the implied rate of interest paid to delay payment of an account payable for an additional number of days. In other words, the amount is the interest being paid by the firm to keep its money for a number of days. This cost can be illustrated by a simple example. The example assumes that payment will be made on the last possible day (either the final day of the cash discount period or the final day of the credit period).

cost of giving up a cash discount
The implied rate of interest paid to delay payment of an account payable for an additional number of days.

> **EXAMPLE**
>
> In the preceding example, we saw that Lawrence Industries could take the cash discount on its February 27 purchase by paying $980 on March 10. If Lawrence gives up the cash discount, payment can be made on March 30. To keep its money for an extra 20 days, the firm must give up an opportunity to pay $980 for its $1,000 purchase. In other words, it will cost the firm $20 to delay payment for 20 days. Figure 14.1 (on page 552) shows the payment options that are open to the company.

FIGURE 14.1

Payment Options
Payment options for Lawrence Industries

To calculate the cost of giving up the cash discount, the *true purchase price* must be viewed as the *discounted cost of the merchandise*, which is $980 for Lawrence Industries. The annual percentage cost of giving up the cash discount can be calculated using Equation 14.1:

$$\text{Cost of giving up cash discount} = \frac{CD}{100\% - CD} \times \frac{365}{N} \quad (14.1)$$

where

CD = stated cash discount in percentage terms

N = number of days that payment can be delayed by giving up the cash discount

Substituting the values for CD (2%) and N (20 days) into Equation 14.1 results in an annualized cost of giving up the cash discount of 37.24% [(2% ÷ 98%) × (365 ÷ 20)]. A 365-day year is assumed.

A simple way to *approximate* the cost of giving up a cash discount is to use the stated cash discount percentage, CD, in place of the first term of Equation 14.1:

$$\text{Approximate cost of giving up cash discount} = CD \times \frac{365}{N} \quad (14.2)$$

The smaller the cash discount, the closer the approximation to the actual cost of giving it up. Using this approximation, the cost of giving up the cash discount for Lawrence Industries is 36.5% [2% × (365 ÷ 20)]. ■

Using the Cost of Giving Up a Cash Discount in Decision Making The financial manager must determine whether it is advisable to take a cash discount. Financial managers must remember that taking cash discounts may represent an important source of additional profitability.

EXAMPLE Mason Products, a large building-supply company, has four possible suppliers, each offering different credit terms. Otherwise, their products and services are identical. Table 14.1 presents the credit terms offered by suppliers A, B, C, and D

TABLE 14.1 Cash Discounts and Associated Costs for Mason Products

Supplier	Credit terms	Approximate cost of giving up a cash discount
A	2/10 net 30 EOM	36.5%
B	1/10 net 55 EOM	8.1
C	3/20 net 70 EOM	21.9
D	4/10 net 60 EOM	29.2

and the cost of giving up the cash discounts in each transaction. The approximation method of calculating the cost of giving up a cash discount (Equation 14.2) has been used. The cost of giving up the cash discount from supplier A is 36.5%; from supplier B, 8.1%; from supplier C, 21.9%; and from supplier D, 29.2%.

If the firm needs short-term funds, which it can borrow from its bank at an interest rate of 13%, and if each of the suppliers is viewed *separately,* which (if any) of the suppliers' cash discounts will the firm give up? In dealing with supplier A, the firm takes the cash discount, because the cost of giving it up is 36.5%, and then borrows the funds it requires from its bank at 13% interest. With supplier B, the firm would do better to give up the cash discount, because the cost of this action is less than the cost of borrowing money from the bank (8.1% versus 13%). With either supplier C or supplier D, the firm should take the cash discount, because in both cases the cost of giving up the discount is greater than the 13% cost of borrowing from the bank.

The example shows that the cost of giving up a cash discount is relevant when one is evaluating a single supplier's credit terms in light of certain *bank borrowing costs*. However, other factors relative to payment strategies may also need to be considered. For example, some firms, particularly small firms and poorly managed firms, routinely give up *all* discounts because they either lack alternative sources of unsecured short-term financing or fail to recognize the implicit costs of their actions.

Effects of Stretching Accounts Payable

stretching accounts payable
Paying bills as late as possible without damaging the firm's credit rating.

A strategy that is often employed by a firm is **stretching accounts payable**—that is, paying bills as late as possible without damaging its credit rating. Such a strategy can reduce the cost of giving up a cash discount.

EXAMPLE

Lawrence Industries was extended credit terms of 2/10 net 30 EOM. The cost of giving up the cash discount, assuming payment on the last day of the credit period, was found to be approximately 36.5% [$2\% \times (365 \div 20)$]. If the firm were able to stretch its account payable to 70 days without damaging its credit rating, the cost of giving up the cash discount would be only 12.2% [$2\% \times (365 \div 60)$]. Stretching accounts payable reduces the implicit cost of giving up a cash discount.

Although stretching accounts payable may be financially attractive, it raises an important ethical issue: It may cause the firm to violate the agreement it

In Practice FOCUS ON ETHICS

AMAZON STAYS ETHICAL TO AVOID BITING THE HANDS THAT FEED IT

Top managers in a tiny central Ohio company fret but say nothing publicly as a giant retailer routinely waits 120 days to pay its invoices marked "due in 30 days." The credit manager keeps quiet, partly because the company depends on this key account for survival, and partly because "stretching payables" is the most widespread unethical practice in corporate America.

E-tailer **Amazon.com,** despite its size and marketing success, pays its suppliers *on time* amidst intense pressures on it to become profitable. In a change of strategy, Amazon emphasizes profitability over growth. CFO Warren Jensen, describing the critical role that working capital management plays in the quest for profits, was quoted in *CFO* magazine as saying, "This isn't about trying to string our vendors out." Amazon has negative net working capital (current liabilities exceed current assets), but has chosen to employ just-in-time inventory delivery from book publishers—rather than delayed payments—as the route to reduce its need for short-term bank loans. The bonus associated with Amazon's payables policy is the likelihood that suppliers will work with the company should its cash position temporarily drop below that needed to cover payables.

In economic downturns, companies face even greater temptation to delay payments, and many choose to do so. Warns Stephen Payne of REL Consultancy Group, that practice "can bite you in the rear end" if suppliers detect it and jack up prices to counter the effect. After all, the buyer's average payment period represents its suppliers' average collection periods.

Stretching payables is unethical for two reasons. First, the buyer is violating the terms of its trade credit agreement. Second, the buyer is, in effect, doing additional borrowing from its suppliers without their knowledge or authorization. "Everybody's doing it" is never an adequate defense for trying to add to shareholder wealth through such blatantly unethical behavior. Shareholder wealth maximization is once again seen to be subject to ethical constraints.

■ If stretching accounts payable is such a common business practice in the United States, does that prove that it is ethical? Would a company's stock price drop if it suddenly started paying its bills on time?

entered into with its supplier when it purchased merchandise. Clearly, a supplier would not look kindly on a customer who regularly and purposely postponed paying for purchases. The *In Practice* box above discusses the ethics of stretching payables.

Accruals

accruals
Liabilities for services received for which payment has yet to be made.

The second spontaneous source of short-term business financing is accruals. **Accruals** are liabilities for services received for which payment has yet to be made. The most common items accrued by a firm are wages and taxes. Because taxes are payments to the government, their accrual cannot be manipulated by the firm. However, the accrual of wages can be manipulated to some extent. This is accomplished by delaying payment of wages, thereby receiving an interest-free loan from employees who are paid sometime after they have performed the work. The pay period for employees who earn an hourly rate is often governed by union regulations or by state or federal law. However, in other cases, the frequency of payment is at the discretion of the company's management.

EXAMPLE

Tenney Company, a large janitorial service company, currently pays its employees at the end of each work week. The weekly payroll totals $400,000. If the firm were to extend the pay period so as to pay its employees 1 week later throughout an entire year, the employees would in effect be lending the firm $400,000 for a year. If the firm could earn 10% annually on invested funds, such a strategy would be worth $40,000 per year ($0.10 \times \$400,000$).

Review Questions

14–1 What are the two major sources of spontaneous short-term financing for a firm? How do their balances behave relative to the firm's sales?

14–2 Is there a cost associated with *taking a cash discount*? Is there any cost associated with *giving up a cash discount*? How do short-term borrowing costs affect the cash discount decision?

14–3 What is "stretching accounts payable"? What effect does this action have on the cost of giving up a cash discount?

Unsecured Sources of Short-Term Loans

Businesses obtain unsecured short-term loans from two major sources, banks and commercial paper. Unlike the spontaneous sources of unsecured short-term financing, bank loans and commercial paper are negotiated and result from actions taken by the firm's financial manager. Bank loans are more popular, because they are available to firms of all sizes; commercial paper tends to be available only to large firms. In addition, international loans can be used to finance international transactions.

Bank Loans

Banks are a major source of unsecured short-term loans to businesses. The major type of loan made by banks to businesses is the **short-term, self-liquidating loan.** These loans are intended merely to carry the firm through seasonal peaks in financing needs that are due primarily to buildups of inventory and accounts receivable. As inventories and receivables are converted into cash, the funds needed to retire these loans are generated. In other words, the use to which the borrowed money is put provides the mechanism through which the loan is repaid—hence the term *self-liquidating*. Banks lend unsecured, short-term funds in three basic ways: through single-payment notes, lines of credit, and revolving credit agreements. Before we look at these types of loans, we consider loan interest rates.

short-term, self-liquidating loan
An unsecured short-term loan in which the use to which the borrowed money is put provides the mechanism through which the loan is repaid.

prime rate of interest (prime rate)
The lowest rate of interest charged by leading banks on business loans to their most important business borrowers.

Loan Interest Rates

The interest rate on a bank loan can be a fixed or a floating rate, typically based on the prime rate of interest. The **prime rate of interest (prime rate)** is the lowest rate of interest charged by leading banks on business loans to their most important business borrowers.[1] The prime rate fluctuates with changing supply-and-demand relationships for short-term funds.[2] Banks generally determine the rate to be charged to various borrowers by adding a premium to the prime rate to adjust it for the borrower's "riskiness." The premium may amount to 4 percent or more, although most unsecured short-term loans carry premiums of less than 2 percent.

Fixed- and Floating-Rate Loans Loans can have either fixed or floating interest rates. On a **fixed-rate loan**, the rate of interest is determined at a set increment above the prime rate on the date of the loan and remains unvarying at that fixed rate until maturity. On a **floating-rate loan**, the increment above the prime rate is initially established, and the rate of interest is allowed to "float," or vary, above prime *as the prime rate varies* until maturity. Generally, the increment above the prime rate will be *lower* on a floating-rate loan than on a fixed-rate loan of equivalent risk, because the lender bears less risk with a floating-rate loan. As a result of the volatile nature of the prime rate during recent years, today *most short-term business loans are floating-rate loans.*

fixed-rate loan
A loan with a rate of interest that is determined at a set increment above the prime rate and at which it remains fixed until maturity.

floating-rate loan
A loan with a rate of interest initially set at an increment above the prime rate and allowed to "float," or vary, above prime *as the prime rate varies* until maturity.

Method of Computing Interest Once the *nominal (or stated) annual rate* is established, the method of computing interest is determined. Interest can be paid either when a loan matures or in advance. If interest is paid *at maturity*, the *effective (or true) annual rate*—the actual rate of interest paid—for an assumed 1-year period[3] is equal to

$$\frac{\text{Interest}}{\text{Amount borrowed}} \tag{14.3}$$

Most bank loans to businesses require the interest payment at maturity.

When interest is paid *in advance*, it is deducted from the loan so that the borrower actually receives less money than is requested. Loans on which interest is paid in advance are called **discount loans.** The *effective annual rate for a discount loan*, assuming a 1-year period, is calculated as

discount loans
Loans on which interest is paid in advance by being deducted from the amount borrowed.

$$\frac{\text{Interest}}{\text{Amount borrowed} - \text{Interest}} \tag{14.4}$$

Paying interest in advance raises the effective annual rate above the stated annual rate.

EXAMPLE Wooster Company, a manufacturer of athletic apparel, wants to borrow $10,000 at a stated annual rate of 10% interest for 1 year. If the interest on the loan is paid at maturity, the firm will pay $1,000 (0.10 × $10,000) for the use of the $10,000

---

1. A trend away from using the prime rate as a benchmark has begun in the United States in response to various borrower lawsuits against banks. Some banks now use the term *base rate* or *reference rate* rather than *prime rate* for pricing corporate and other loans. In fact, the use of the *London Interbank Offered Rate* (*LIBOR*) is gaining momentum as a base lending rate in the United States.

2. During the past 25 years, the prime rate has varied from a record high of 21.5% (December 1980) to a low of 4.00% (July 2003 through June 2004). Since January 2001, it has fluctuated in the range from a high of 9.50% to a low of 4.00%.

3. Effective annual rates (EARs) for loans with maturities of less than 1 year can be found by using the technique presented in Chapter 4 for finding EARs when interest is compounded more frequently than annually. See Equation 4.22.

for the year. Substituting into Equation 14.3 reveals that the effective annual rate is therefore

$$\frac{\$1{,}000}{\$10{,}000} = 10.0\%$$

If the money is borrowed at the same *stated* annual rate for 1 year but interest is paid in advance, the firm still pays $1,000 in interest, but it receives only $9,000 ($10,000 − $1,000). Substituting into Equation 14.4, the effective annual rate in this case is

$$\frac{\$1{,}000}{\$10{,}000 - \$1{,}000} = \frac{\$1{,}000}{\$9{,}000} = 11.1\%$$

Paying interest in advance thus makes the effective annual rate (11.1%) greater than the stated annual rate (10.0%).

Single-Payment Notes

single-payment note
A short-term, one-time loan made to a borrower who needs funds for a specific purpose for a short period.

A **single-payment note** can be obtained from a commercial bank by a creditworthy business borrower. This type of loan is usually a one-time loan made to a borrower who needs funds for a specific purpose for a short period. The resulting instrument is a *note*, signed by the borrower, that states the terms of the loan, including the length of the loan and the interest rate. This type of short-term note generally has a maturity of 30 days to 9 months or more. The interest charged is usually tied in some way to the prime rate of interest.

EXAMPLE

Gordon Manufacturing, a producer of rotary mower blades, recently borrowed $100,000 from each of two banks—bank A and bank B. The loans were incurred on the same day, when the prime rate of interest was 6%. Each loan involved a 90-day note with interest to be paid at the end of 90 days. The interest rate was set at 1½% above the prime rate on bank A's *fixed-rate note*. Over the 90-day period, the rate of interest on this note will remain at 7½% (6% prime rate + 1½% increment) regardless of fluctuations in the prime rate. The total interest cost on this loan is $1,849 [$100,000 × (7½% × 90/365)]. The effective 90-day rate on this loan is 1.85% ($1,849/$100,000).

Assuming that the loan from bank A is rolled over each 90 days throughout the year under the same terms and circumstances, its effective *annual* interest rate is found by using Equation 4.22. Because the loan costs 1.85% for 90 days, it is necessary to compound (1 + 0.0185) for 4.06 periods in the year (that is, 365/90) and then subtract 1:

$$\text{Effective annual rate} = (1 + 0.0185)^{4.06} - 1$$
$$= 1.0773 - 1 = 0.0773 = \underline{\underline{7.73\%}}$$

The effective annual rate of interest on the fixed-rate, 90-day note is 7.73%.

Bank B set the interest rate at 1% above the prime rate on its *floating-rate note*. The rate charged over the 90 days will vary directly with the prime rate. Initially, the rate will be 7% (6% + 1%), but when the prime rate changes, so will the rate of interest on the note. For instance, if after 30 days the prime rate rises to 6.5%, and after another 30 days it drops to 6.25%, the firm will be paying 0.575% for the first 30 days (7% × 30/365), 0.616% for the next 30 days (7.5% × 30/365), and 0.596% for the last 30 days (7.25% × 30/365). Its total interest cost will be $1,787 [$100,000 × (0.575% + 0.616% + 0.596%)], resulting in an effective 90-day rate of 1.79% ($1,787/$100,000).

Again, assuming the loan is rolled over each 90 days throughout the year under the same terms and circumstances, its effective *annual* rate is 7.46%:

$$\text{Effective annual rate} = (1 + 0.01787)^{4.06} - 1$$
$$= 1.0746 - 1 = 0.0746 = \underline{7.46\%}$$

Clearly, in this case the floating-rate loan would have been less expensive than the fixed-rate loan because of its generally lower effective annual rate.

Lines of Credit

A **line of credit** is an agreement between a commercial bank and a business specifying the amount of unsecured short-term borrowing the bank will make available to the firm over a given period of time. It is similar to the agreement under which issuers of bank credit cards, such as MasterCard, Visa, and Discover, extend preapproved credit to cardholders. A line-of-credit agreement is typically made for a period of 1 year and often places certain constraints on the borrower. It is *not a guaranteed loan* but indicates that if the bank has sufficient funds available, it will allow the borrower to owe it *up to* a certain amount of money. The amount of a line of credit is the *maximum amount the firm can owe the bank* at any point in time.

When applying for a line of credit, the borrower may be required to submit such documents as its cash budget, its pro forma income statement, its pro forma balance sheet, and its recent financial statements. If the bank finds the customer acceptable, the line of credit will be extended. The major attraction of a line of credit from the bank's point of view is that it eliminates the need to examine the creditworthiness of a customer each time it borrows money within the year.

Interest Rates The interest rate on a line of credit is normally stated as a floating rate—the *prime rate plus a premium*. If the prime rate changes, the interest rate charged on new *as well as outstanding* borrowing automatically changes. The amount a borrower is charged in excess of the prime rate depends on its creditworthiness. The more creditworthy the borrower, the lower the premium (interest increment) above prime, and vice versa.

Operating-Change Restrictions In a line-of-credit agreement, a bank may impose **operating-change restrictions,** which give it the right to revoke the line if any major changes occur in the firm's financial condition or operations. The firm is usually required to submit up-to-date, and preferably audited, financial statements for periodic review. In addition, the bank typically needs to be informed of shifts in key managerial personnel or in the firm's operations before changes take place. Such changes may affect the future success and debt-paying ability of the firm and thus could alter its credit status. If the bank does not agree with the proposed changes and the firm makes them anyway, the bank has the right to revoke the line of credit.

Compensating Balances To ensure that the borrower will be a "good customer," many short-term unsecured bank loans—single-payment notes and lines of

compensating balance
A required checking account balance equal to a certain percentage of the amount borrowed from a bank under a line-of-credit or revolving credit agreement.

credit—require the borrower to maintain, in a checking account, a **compensating balance** equal to a certain percentage of the amount borrowed. Compensating balances of 10 to 20 percent are frequently required. A compensating balance not only forces the borrower to be a good customer of the bank but may also raise the interest cost to the borrower.

EXAMPLE

Hint Sometimes the compensating balance is stated as a percentage of the amount of the line of credit. In other cases, it is linked to both the amount borrowed and the amount of the line of credit.

Estrada Graphics, a graphic design firm, has borrowed $1 million under a line-of-credit agreement. It must pay a stated interest rate of 10% and maintain, in its checking account, a compensating balance equal to 20% of the amount borrowed, or $200,000. Thus it actually receives the use of only $800,000. To use that amount for a year, the firm pays interest of $100,000 (0.10 × $1,000,000). The effective annual rate on the funds is therefore 12.5% ($100,000 ÷ $800,000), 2.5% more than the stated rate of 10%.

If the firm normally maintains a balance of $200,000 or more in its checking account, the effective annual rate equals the stated annual rate of 10% because none of the $1 million borrowed is needed to satisfy the compensating-balance requirement. If the firm normally maintains a $100,000 balance in its checking account, only an additional $100,000 will have to be tied up, leaving it with $900,000 of usable funds. The effective annual rate in this case would be 11.1% ($100,000 ÷ $900,000). Thus a compensating balance raises the cost of borrowing *only if* it is larger than the firm's normal cash balance. ■

Annual Cleanups To ensure that money lent under a line-of-credit agreement is actually being used to finance seasonal needs, many banks require an **annual cleanup.** This means that the borrower must have a loan balance of zero—that is, owe the bank nothing—for a certain number of days during the year. Insisting that the borrower carry a zero loan balance for a certain period ensures that short-term loans do not turn into long-term loans.

annual cleanup
The requirement that for a certain number of days during the year borrowers under a line of credit carry a zero loan balance (that is, owe the bank nothing).

All the characteristics of a line-of-credit agreement are negotiable to some extent. Today, banks bid competitively to attract large, well-known firms. A prospective borrower should attempt to negotiate a line of credit with the most favorable interest rate, for an optimal amount of funds, and with a minimum of restrictions. Borrowers today frequently pay fees to lenders instead of maintaining deposit balances as compensation for loans and other services. The lender attempts to get a good return with maximum safety. Negotiations should produce a line of credit that is suitable to both borrower and lender.

Revolving Credit Agreements

revolving credit agreement
A line of credit *guaranteed* to a borrower by a commercial bank regardless of the scarcity of money.

commitment fee
The fee that is normally charged on a *revolving credit agreement;* it often applies to the *average unused portion* of the borrower's credit line.

A **revolving credit agreement** is nothing more than a *guaranteed line of credit.* It is guaranteed in the sense that the commercial bank assures the borrower that a specified amount of funds will be made available regardless of the scarcity of money. The interest rate and other requirements are similar to those for a line of credit. It is not uncommon for a revolving credit agreement to be for a period greater than 1 year. Because the bank guarantees the availability of funds, a **commitment fee** is normally charged on a revolving credit agreement. This fee often applies to the average unused balance of the borrower's credit line. It is normally about 0.5 percent of the *average unused portion* of the line.

EXAMPLE

REH Company, a major real estate developer, has a $2 million revolving credit agreement with its bank. Its average borrowing under the agreement for the past year was $1.5 million. The bank charges a commitment fee of 0.5%. Because the average unused portion of the committed funds was $500,000 ($2 million − $1.5 million), the commitment fee for the year was $2,500 (0.005 × $500,000). Of course, REH also had to pay interest on the actual $1.5 million borrowed under the agreement. Assuming that $112,500 interest was paid on the $1.5 million borrowed, the effective cost of the agreement was 7.67% [($112,500 + $2,500)/$1,500,000]. Although more expensive than a line of credit, a revolving credit agreement can be less risky from the borrower's viewpoint, because the availability of funds is guaranteed.

Commercial Paper

commercial paper
A form of financing consisting of short-term, unsecured promissory notes issued by firms with a high credit standing.

Commercial paper is a form of financing that consists of short-term, unsecured promissory notes issued by firms with a high credit standing. Generally, only quite large firms of unquestionable financial soundness are able to issue commercial paper. Most commercial paper issues have maturities ranging from 3 to 270 days. Although there is no set denomination, such financing is generally issued in multiples of $100,000 or more. A large portion of the commercial paper today is issued by finance companies; manufacturing firms account for a smaller portion of this type of financing. Businesses often purchase commercial paper, which they hold as marketable securities, to provide an interest-earning reserve of liquidity.

Interest on Commercial Paper

Commercial paper is sold at a discount from its *par*, or *face, value*. The interest paid by the issuer of commercial paper is determined by the size of the discount and the length of time to maturity. The actual interest earned by the purchaser is determined by certain calculations, illustrated by the following example.

EXAMPLE

Bertram Corporation, a large shipbuilder, has just issued $1 million worth of commercial paper that has a 90-day maturity and sells for $990,000. At the end of 90 days, the purchaser of this paper will receive $1 million for its $990,000 investment. The interest paid on the financing is therefore $10,000 on a principal of $990,000. The effective 90-day rate on the paper is 1.01% ($10,000/$990,000). Assuming that the paper is rolled over each 90 days throughout the year (that is, 365/90 = 4.06 times per year), the effective annual rate for Bertram's commercial paper, found by using Equation 4.22, is 4.16% $[(1 + 0.0101)^{4.06} - 1]$.

An interesting characteristic of commercial paper is that its interest cost is *normally* 2 to 4 percent below the prime rate. In other words, firms are able to raise funds more cheaply by selling commercial paper than by borrowing from a commercial bank. The reason is that many suppliers of short-term funds do not have the option, as banks do, of making low-risk business loans at the prime rate. They can invest safely only in marketable securities such as Treasury bills and commercial paper. The yields on these marketable securities on November 17, 2004, when the prime rate of interest was 5.00 percent, were about 2.08 percent for 3-month Treasury bills and about 2.25 percent for 3-month commercial paper.

Hint Commercial paper is directly placed with investors by the issuer or is sold by dealers in commercial paper. Most of it is purchased by other businesses and financial institutions.

Although the stated interest cost of borrowing through the sale of commercial paper is normally lower than the prime rate, the *overall cost* of commercial paper may not be less than that of a bank loan. Additional costs include the fees paid by most issuers to obtain the bank line of credit used to back the paper, fees paid to obtain third-party ratings used to make the paper more salable, and flotation costs. In addition, even if it is slightly more expensive to borrow from a commercial bank, it may at times be advisable to do so to establish a good working relationship with a bank. This strategy ensures that when money is tight, funds can be obtained promptly and at a reasonable interest rate.

International Loans

In some ways, arranging short-term financing for international trade is no different from financing purely domestic operations. In both cases, producers must finance production and inventory and then continue to finance accounts receivable before collecting any cash payments from sales. In other ways, however, the short-term financing of international sales and purchases is fundamentally different from that of strictly domestic trade.

International Transactions

The important difference between international and domestic transactions is that payments are often made or received in a foreign currency. Not only must a U.S. company pay the costs of doing business in the foreign exchange market, but it also is exposed to *exchange rate risk*. A U.S.-based company that exports goods and has accounts receivable denominated in a foreign currency faces the risk that the U.S. dollar will appreciate in value relative to the foreign currency. The risk to a U.S. importer with foreign-currency-denominated accounts payable is that the dollar will depreciate. Although *exchange rate risk* can often be *hedged* by using currency forward, futures, or options markets, doing so is costly and is not possible for all foreign currencies.

Typical international transactions are large in size and have long maturity dates. Therefore, companies that are involved in international trade generally have to finance larger dollar amounts for longer time periods than companies that operate domestically. Furthermore, because foreign companies are rarely well known in the United States, some financial institutions are reluctant to lend to U.S. exporters or importers, particularly smaller firms.

Financing International Trade

Several specialized techniques have evolved for financing international trade. Perhaps the most important financing vehicle is the **letter of credit**, a letter written by a company's bank to the company's foreign supplier, stating that the bank guarantees payment of an invoiced amount if all the underlying agreements are met. The letter of credit essentially substitutes the bank's reputation and creditworthiness for that of its commercial customer. A U.S. exporter is more willing to sell goods to a foreign buyer if the transaction is covered by a letter of credit issued by a well-known bank in the buyer's home country.

Firms that do business in foreign countries on an ongoing basis often finance their operations, at least in part, in the local market. A company that has an assembly plant in Mexico, for example, might choose to finance its purchases of

letter of credit
A letter written by a company's bank to the company's foreign supplier, stating that the bank guarantees payment of an invoiced amount if all the underlying agreements are met.

Mexican goods and services with peso funds borrowed from a Mexican bank. This not only minimizes exchange rate risk but also improves the company's business ties to the host community. Multinational companies, however, sometimes finance their international transactions through dollar-denominated loans from international banks. The *Eurocurrency loan markets* allow creditworthy borrowers to obtain financing on very attractive terms.

Transactions Between Subsidiaries

Much international trade involves transactions between corporate subsidiaries. A U.S. company might, for example, manufacture one part in an Asian plant and another part in the United States, assemble the product in Brazil, and sell it in Europe. The shipment of goods back and forth between subsidiaries creates accounts receivable and accounts payable, but the parent company has considerable discretion about how and when payments are made. In particular, the parent can minimize foreign exchange fees and other transaction costs by "netting" what affiliates owe each other and paying only the net amount due, rather than having both subsidiaries pay each other the gross amounts due.

Review Questions

14-4 How is the *prime rate of interest* relevant to the cost of short-term bank borrowing? What is a *floating-rate loan*?

14-5 How does the *effective annual rate* differ between a loan requiring interest payments *at maturity* and another, similar loan requiring interest *in advance*?

14-6 What are the basic terms and characteristics of a *single-payment note*? How is the *effective annual rate* on such a note found?

14-7 What is a *line of credit*? Describe each of the following features that are often included in these agreements: (a) operating-change restrictions; (b) compensating balance; and (c) annual cleanup.

14-8 What is a *revolving credit agreement*? How does this arrangement differ from the line-of-credit agreement? What is a *commitment fee*?

14-9 How is *commercial paper* used to raise short-term funds? Who can issue commercial paper? Who buys commercial paper?

14-10 What is the important difference between international and domestic transactions? How is a *letter of credit* used in financing international trade transactions? How is "netting" used in transactions between subsidiaries?

Secured Sources of Short-Term Loans

secured short-term financing
Short-term financing (loan) that has specific assets pledged as collateral.

When a firm has exhausted its sources of unsecured short-term financing, it may be able to obtain additional short-term loans on a secured basis. **Secured short-term financing** has specific assets pledged as collateral. The *collateral* commonly takes the form of an asset, such as accounts receivable or inventory. The lender

security agreement
The agreement between the borrower and the lender that specifies the collateral held against a secured loan.

obtains a security interest in the collateral through the execution of a **security agreement** with the borrower that specifies the collateral held against the loan. In addition, the terms of the loan against which the security is held form part of the security agreement. They specify the conditions required for the security interest to be removed, along with the interest rate on the loan, repayment dates, and other loan provisions. A copy of the security agreement is filed in a public office within the state—typically, a county or state court. Filing provides subsequent lenders with information about which assets of a prospective borrower are unavailable for use as collateral. The filing requirement protects the lender by legally establishing the lender's security interest.

Characteristics of Secured Short-Term Loans

Although many people believe that holding collateral as security reduces the risk of a loan, lenders do not usually view loans in this way. Lenders recognize that holding collateral can reduce losses if the borrower defaults, but *the presence of collateral has no impact on the risk of default.* A lender requires collateral to ensure recovery of some portion of the loan in the event of default. What the lender wants above all, however, is to be repaid as scheduled. In general, lenders prefer to make less risky loans at lower rates of interest than to be in a position in which they must liquidate collateral.

Collateral and Terms

Lenders of secured short-term funds prefer collateral that has a duration closely matched to the term of the loan. Current assets—accounts receivable and inventory—are the most desirable short-term-loan collateral, because they can normally be converted into cash much sooner than fixed assets. Thus the short-term lender of secured funds generally accepts only liquid current assets as collateral.

percentage advance
The percentage of the book value of the collateral that constitutes the principal of a secured loan.

Typically, the lender determines the desirable **percentage advance** to make against the collateral. This percentage advance constitutes the principal of the secured loan and is normally between 30 and 100 percent of the book value of the collateral. It varies according to the type and liquidity of collateral.

Hint Remember that firms typically borrow on a secured basis only after exhausting less costly, unsecured sources of short-term funds.

The interest rate that is charged on secured short-term loans is typically *higher* than the rate on unsecured short-term loans. Lenders do not normally consider secured loans less risky than unsecured loans. In addition, negotiating and administering secured loans is more troublesome for the lender than negotiating and administering unsecured loans. The lender therefore normally requires added compensation in the form of a service charge, a higher interest rate, or both.

Institutions Extending Secured Short-Term Loans

commercial finance companies
Lending institutions that make *only* secured loans—both short-term and long-term—to businesses.

The primary sources of secured short-term loans to businesses are commercial banks and commercial finance companies. Both institutions deal in short-term loans secured primarily by accounts receivable and inventory. The operations of commercial banks have already been described. **Commercial finance companies** are lending institutions that make *only* secured loans—both short-term and long-term—to businesses. Unlike banks, finance companies are not permitted to hold deposits.

Only when its unsecured and secured short-term borrowing power from the commercial bank is exhausted will a borrower turn to the commercial finance company for additional secured borrowing. Because the finance company generally ends up with higher-risk borrowers, its interest charges on secured short-term loans are usually higher than those of commercial banks. The leading U.S. commercial finance companies include The CIT Group and GE Corporate Financial Services.

The Use of Accounts Receivable as Collateral

Two commonly used means of obtaining short-term financing with accounts receivable are *pledging accounts receivable* and *factoring accounts receivable*. Actually, only a pledge of accounts receivable creates a secured short-term loan; factoring really entails the *sale* of accounts receivable at a discount. Although factoring is not actually a form of secured short-term borrowing, it does involve the use of accounts receivable to obtain needed short-term funds.

Pledging Accounts Receivable

A **pledge of accounts receivable** is often used to secure a short-term loan. Because accounts receivable are normally quite liquid, they are an attractive form of short-term-loan collateral.

pledge of accounts receivable
The use of a firm's accounts receivable as security, or collateral, to obtain a short-term loan.

The Pledging Process When a firm requests a loan against accounts receivable, the lender first evaluates the firm's accounts receivable to determine their desirability as collateral. The lender makes a list of the acceptable accounts, along with the billing dates and amounts. If the borrowing firm requests a loan for a fixed amount, the lender needs to select only enough accounts to secure the funds requested. If the borrower wants the maximum loan available, the lender evaluates all the accounts to select the maximum amount of acceptable collateral.

After selecting the acceptable accounts, the lender normally adjusts the dollar value of these accounts for expected returns on sales and other allowances. If a customer whose account has been pledged returns merchandise or receives some type of allowance, such as a cash discount for early payment, the amount of the collateral is automatically reduced. For protection from such occurrences, the lender normally reduces the value of the acceptable collateral by a fixed percentage.

Next, the percentage to be advanced against the collateral must be determined. The lender evaluates the quality of the acceptable receivables and the expected cost of their liquidation. This percentage represents the principal of the loan and typically ranges between 50 and 90 percent of the face value of acceptable accounts receivable. To protect its interest in the collateral, the lender files a **lien,** which is a publicly disclosed legal claim on the collateral. For an example of the complete pledging process, see the book's Web site at www.aw-bc.com/gitman.

lien
A publicly disclosed legal claim on loan collateral.

nonnotification basis
The basis on which a borrower, having pledged an account receivable, continues to collect the account payments without notifying the account customer.

Notification Pledges of accounts receivable are normally made on a **nonnotification basis,** meaning that a customer whose account has been pledged as collateral is not notified. Under the nonnotification arrangement, the borrower still collects the pledged account receivable, and the lender trusts the borrower to remit these payments as they are received. If a pledge of accounts receivable is

CHAPTER 14   Current Liabilities Management   565

made on a **notification basis,** the customer is notified to remit payment directly to the lender.

Pledging Cost   The stated cost of a pledge of accounts receivable is normally 2 to 5 percent above the prime rate. In addition to the stated interest rate, a service charge of up to 3 percent may be levied by the lender to cover its administrative costs. Clearly, pledges of accounts receivable are a high-cost source of short-term financing.

Factoring Accounts Receivable

Factoring accounts receivable involves selling them outright, at a discount, to a financial institution. A **factor** is a financial institution that specializes in purchasing accounts receivable from businesses. Some commercial banks and commercial finance companies also factor accounts receivable. Although it is not the same as obtaining a short-term loan, factoring accounts receivable is similar to borrowing with accounts receivable as collateral.

Factoring Agreement   A factoring agreement normally states the exact conditions and procedures for the purchase of an account. The factor, like a lender against a pledge of accounts receivable, chooses accounts for purchase, selecting only those that appear to be acceptable credit risks. Where factoring is to be on a continuing basis, the factor will actually make the firm's credit decisions, because this will guarantee the acceptability of accounts.[4] Factoring is normally done on a *notification basis,* and the factor receives payment of the account directly from the customer. In addition, most sales of accounts receivable to a factor are made on a **nonrecourse basis.** This means that the factor agrees to accept all credit risks. Thus, if a purchased account turns out to be uncollectible, the factor must absorb the loss.

Typically, the factor is not required to pay the firm until the account is collected or until the last day of the credit period, whichever occurs first. The factor sets up an account similar to a bank deposit account for each customer. As payment is received or as due dates arrive, the factor deposits money into the seller's account, from which the seller is free to make withdrawals as needed.

In many cases, if the firm leaves the money in the account, a *surplus* will exist on which the factor will pay interest. In other instances, the factor may make *advances* to the firm against uncollected accounts that are not yet due. These advances represent a negative balance in the firm's account, on which interest is charged.

Factoring Cost   Factoring costs include commissions, interest levied on advances, and interest earned on surpluses. The factor deposits in the firm's account the book value of the collected or due accounts purchased by the factor, less the commissions. The commissions are typically stated as a 1 to 3 percent

notification basis
The basis on which an account customer whose account has been pledged (or factored) is notified to remit payment directly to the lender (or factor).

factoring accounts receivable
The outright sale of accounts receivable at a discount to a *factor* or other financial institution.

factor
A financial institution that specializes in purchasing accounts receivable from businesses.

nonrecourse basis
The basis on which accounts receivable are sold to a factor with the understanding that the factor accepts all credit risks on the purchased accounts.

---

4. The use of credit cards such as MasterCard, Visa, and Discover by consumers has some similarity to factoring, because the vendor that accepts the card is reimbursed at a discount for purchases made with the card. The difference between factoring and credit cards is that cards are nothing more than a line of credit extended by the issuer, which charges the vendors a fee for accepting the cards. In factoring, the factor does not analyze credit until after the sale has been made; in many cases (except when factoring is done on a continuing basis), the initial credit decision is the responsibility of the vendor, not the factor that purchases the account.

discount from the book value of factored accounts receivable. The *interest levied on advances* is generally 2 to 4 percent above the prime rate. It is levied on the actual amount advanced. The *interest paid on surpluses* is generally between 0.2 and 0.5 percent per month. An example of the factoring process is included on the book's Web site at www.aw-bc.com/gitman.

Although its costs may seem high, factoring has certain advantages that make it attractive to many firms. One is the ability it gives the firm to *turn accounts receivable immediately into cash* without having to worry about repayment. Another advantage of factoring is that it ensures a *known pattern of cash flows.* In addition, if factoring is undertaken on a continuing basis, the firm *can eliminate its credit and collection departments.*

The Use of Inventory as Collateral

Inventory is generally second to accounts receivable in desirability as short-term loan collateral. Inventory normally has a market value that is greater than its book value, which is used to establish its value as collateral. A lender whose loan is secured with inventory will probably be able to sell that inventory for at least book value if the borrower defaults on its obligations.

The most important characteristic of inventory being evaluated as loan collateral is *marketability,* which must be considered in light of its physical properties. A warehouse of *perishable* items, such as fresh peaches, may be quite marketable, but if the cost of storing and selling the peaches is high, they may not be desirable collateral. *Specialized items,* such as moon-roving vehicles, are not desirable collateral either, because finding a buyer for them could be difficult. When evaluating inventory as possible loan collateral, the lender looks for items with very stable market prices that have ready markets and that lack undesirable physical properties.

Floating Inventory Liens

floating inventory lien
A secured short-term loan against inventory under which the lender's claim is on the borrower's inventory in general.

A lender may be willing to secure a loan under a **floating inventory lien,** which is a claim on inventory in general. This arrangement is most attractive when the firm has a stable level of inventory that consists of a diversified group of relatively inexpensive merchandise. Inventories of items such as auto tires, screws and bolts, and shoes are candidates for floating-lien loans. Because it is difficult for a lender to verify the presence of the inventory, the lender generally advances less than 50 percent of the book value of the average inventory. The interest charge on a floating lien is 3 to 5 percent above the prime rate. Commercial banks often require floating liens as extra security on what would otherwise be an unsecured loan. Floating-lien inventory loans may also be available from commercial finance companies. An example of a floating lien is included on the book's Web site at www.aw-bc.com/gitman.

Trust Receipt Inventory Loans

trust receipt inventory loan
A secured short-term loan against inventory under which the lender advances 80 to 100 percent of the cost of the borrower's relatively expensive inventory items in exchange for the borrower's promise to repay the lender, with accrued interest, immediately after the sale of each item of collateral.

A **trust receipt inventory loan** often can be made against relatively expensive automotive, consumer durable, and industrial goods that can be identified by serial number. Under this agreement, the borrower keeps the inventory, and the lender may advance 80 to 100 percent of its cost. The lender files a *lien* on all the items financed. The borrower is free to sell the merchandise but is *trusted* to remit the amount lent, along with accrued interest, to the lender immediately after the sale. The lender then releases the lien on the item. The lender makes periodic checks of the borrower's inventory to make sure that the required amount of collateral remains in the hands of the borrower. The interest charge to the borrower is normally 2 percent or more above the prime rate.

Trust receipt loans are often made by manufacturers' wholly owned financing subsidiaries, known as *captive finance companies,* to their customers. Captive finance companies are especially popular in industries that manufacture consumer durable goods, because they provide the manufacturer with a useful sales tool. For example, General Motors Acceptance Corporation (GMAC), the financing subsidiary of General Motors, grants these types of loans to its dealers. Trust receipt loans are also available through commercial banks and commercial finance companies.

Warehouse Receipt Loans

warehouse receipt loan
A secured short-term loan against inventory under which the lender receives control of the pledged inventory collateral, which is stored by a designated warehousing company on the lender's behalf.

A **warehouse receipt loan** is an arrangement whereby the lender, which may be a commercial bank or commercial finance company, receives control of the pledged inventory collateral, which is stored by a designated agent on the lender's behalf. After selecting acceptable collateral, the lender hires a warehousing company to act as its agent and take possession of the inventory.

Two types of warehousing arrangements are possible. A *terminal warehouse* is a central warehouse that is used to store the merchandise of various customers. The lender normally uses such a warehouse when the inventory is easily transported and can be delivered to the warehouse relatively inexpensively. Under a *field warehouse* arrangement, the lender hires a field warehousing company to set up a warehouse on the borrower's premises or to lease part of the borrower's warehouse to store the pledged collateral. Regardless of which type of warehouse is used, the warehousing company places a guard over the inventory. Only on written approval of the lender can any portion of the secured inventory be released by the warehousing company.

The actual lending agreement specifically states the requirements for the release of inventory. As in the case of other secured loans, the lender accepts only collateral that is believed to be readily marketable and advances only a portion—generally 75 to 90 percent—of the collateral's value. The specific costs of warehouse receipt loans are generally higher than those of any other secured lending arrangements because of the need to hire and pay a warehousing company to guard and supervise the collateral. The basic interest charged on warehouse receipt loans is higher than that charged on unsecured loans, generally ranging from 3 to 5 percent above the prime rate. In addition to the interest charge, the borrower must absorb the costs of warehousing by paying the warehouse fee, which is generally between 1 and 3 percent of the amount of the loan. The borrower is normally also required to pay the insurance costs on the warehoused merchandise. An example of the procedures and costs of a warehouse receipt loan is included on the book's Web site at www.aw-bc.com/gitman.

Review Questions

14–11 Are secured short-term loans viewed as more risky or less risky than unsecured short-term loans? Why?

14–12 In general, what interest rates and fees are levied on secured short-term loans? Why are these rates generally *higher* than the rates on unsecured short-term loans?

14–13 Describe and compare the basic features of the following methods of using *accounts receivable* to obtain short-term financing: (a) pledging accounts receivable, and (b) factoring accounts receivable. Be sure to mention the institutions that offer each of them.

14–14 For the following methods of using *inventory* as short-term loan collateral, describe the basic features of each, and compare their use: (a) floating lien; (b) trust receipt loan; and (c) warehouse receipt loan.

SUMMARY

FOCUS ON VALUE

Current liabilities represent an important and generally inexpensive source of financing for a firm. The level of short-term (current liabilities) financing employed by a firm affects its profitability and risk. Accounts payable are an inexpensive, spontaneous source of short-term financing. They should be paid as late as possible without damaging the firm's credit rating. This strategy will shorten the firm's cash conversion cycle and reduce its investment in operations. If vendors offer cash discounts, the firm must consider the economics of giving up versus taking the discount. Accruals, another spontaneous liability, should be maximized because they represent free financing. Notes payable, which represent negotiated short-term financing, can be obtained from banks on an unsecured basis. They should be obtained at the lowest cost under the best possible terms. Large, well-known firms can obtain unsecured short-term financing through the sale of commercial paper. On a secured basis, the firm can obtain loans from banks or commercial finance companies, using either accounts receivable or inventory as collateral.

The financial manager must obtain the right quantity and form of current liabilities financing so as to provide the lowest-cost funds with the least risk. Such a strategy should positively contribute to the firm's goal of **maximizing the stock price.**

REVIEW OF LEARNING GOALS

Key features of short-term financing sources are summarized in Table 14.2 on pages 569–570.

LG1 **Review accounts payable, the key components of credit terms, and the procedures for analyzing those terms.** The major spontaneous source of short-term financing is accounts payable, which result from credit purchases of merchandise. They are the primary source of short-term funds. Credit terms may differ with respect to the credit period, cash discount, cash discount period, and beginning of the credit period. Cash discounts should be given up only when a firm in need of short-term funds must pay an interest rate on borrowing that is greater than the cost of giving up the cash discount.

LG2 **Understand the effects of stretching accounts payable on their cost, and the use of accruals.** Stretching accounts payable can lower the cost of

TABLE 14.2 Summary of Key Features of Common Sources of Short-Term Financing

Type of short-term financing	Source	Cost or conditions	Characteristics
I. Spontaneous liabilities			
Accounts payable	Suppliers of merchandise	No stated cost except when a cash discount is offered for early payment.	Credit extended on open account for 0 to 120 days. The largest source of short-term financing.
Accruals	Employees and government	Free.	Result because wages (employees) and taxes (government) are paid at discrete points in time after the service has been rendered. Hard to manipulate this source of financing.
II. Unsecured sources of short-term loans			
Bank sources			
(1) Single-payment notes	Commercial banks	Prime plus 0% to 4% risk premium—fixed or floating rate.	A single-payment loan used to meet a funds shortage expected to last only a short period of time.
(2) Lines of credit	Commercial banks	Prime plus 0% to 4% risk premium—fixed or floating rate. Often must maintain 10% to 20% compensating balance and clean up the line annually.	A prearranged borrowing limit under which funds, if available, will be lent to allow the borrower to meet seasonal needs.
(3) Revolving credit agreements	Commercial banks	Prime plus 0% to 4% risk premium—fixed or floating rate. Often must maintain 10% to 20% compensating balance and pay a commitment fee of approximately 0.5% of the average unused balance.	A line-of-credit agreement under which the availability of funds is guaranteed. Often for a period greater than 1 year.
Commercial paper	Business firms—both nonfinancial and financial	Generally 2% to 4% below the prime rate of interest.	A short-term, unsecured promissory note issued by the most financially sound firms.

(continued)

TABLE 14.2 Summary of Key Features of Common Sources of Short-Term Financing (continued)

Type of short-term financing	Source	Cost or conditions	Characteristics
III. Secured sources of short-term loans			
Accounts receivable collateral			
(1) Pledging	Commercial banks and commercial finance companies	2% to 5% above prime plus up to 3% in fees. Advance 50% to 90% of collateral value.	Selected accounts receivable are used as collateral. The borrower is trusted to remit to the lender on collection of pledged accounts. Done on a nonnotification basis.
(2) Factoring	Factors, commercial banks, and commercial finance companies	1% to 3% discount from face value of factored accounts. Interest of 2% to 4% above prime levied on advances. Interest between 0.2% and 0.5% per month earned on surplus balances left with factor.	Selected accounts are sold—generally without recourse—at a discount. All credit risks go with the accounts. Factor will lend (make advances) against uncollected accounts that are not yet due. Factor will also pay interest on surplus balances. Typically done on a notification basis.
Inventory collateral			
(1) Floating liens	Commercial banks and commercial finance companies	3% to 5% above prime. Advance less than 50% of collateral value.	A loan against inventory in general. Made when firm has stable inventory of a variety of inexpensive items.
(2) Trust receipts	Manufacturers' captive financing subsidiaries, commercial banks, and commercial finance companies	2% or more above prime. Advance 80% to 100% of cost of collateral.	Loan against relatively expensive automotive, consumer durable, and industrial goods that can be identified by serial number. Collateral remains in possession of the borrower, who is trusted to remit proceeds to the lender upon its sale.
(3) Warehouse receipts	Commercial banks and commercial finance companies	3% to 5% above prime plus a 1% to 3% warehouse fee. Advance 75% to 90% of collateral value.	Inventory used as collateral is placed under control of the lender either through a terminal warehouse or through a field warehouse. A third party—a warehousing company—guards the inventory for the lender. Inventory is released only on written approval of the lender.

giving up a cash discount. Accruals, which result primarily from wage and tax obligations, are virtually free.

LG3 **Describe interest rates and the basic types of unsecured bank sources of short-term loans.** Banks are the major source of unsecured short-term loans to businesses. The interest rate on these loans is tied to the prime rate of interest by a risk premium and may be fixed or floating. It should be evaluated by using the effective annual rate. Whether interest is paid when the loan matures or in advance affects the rate. Bank loans may take the form of a single-payment note, a line of credit, or a revolving credit agreement.

LG4 **Discuss the basic features of commercial paper and the key aspects of international short-term loans.** Commercial paper is an unsecured IOU issued by firms with a high credit standing. International sales and purchases expose firms to exchange rate risk. Such transactions are larger and of longer maturity than domestic transactions, and they can be financed by using a letter of credit, by borrowing in the local market, or through dollar-denominated loans from international banks. On transactions between subsidiaries, "netting" can be used to minimize foreign exchange fees and other transaction costs.

LG5 **Explain the characteristics of secured short-term loans and the use of accounts receivable as short-term-loan collateral.** Secured short-term loans are those for which the lender requires collateral—typically, current assets such as accounts receivable or inventory. Only a percentage of the book value of acceptable collateral is advanced by the lender. These loans are more expensive than unsecured loans. Commercial banks and commercial finance companies make secured short-term loans. Both pledging and factoring involve the use of accounts receivable to obtain needed short-term funds.

LG6 **Describe the various ways in which inventory can be used as short-term-loan collateral.** Inventory can be used as short-term-loan collateral under a floating lien, a trust receipt arrangement, or a warehouse receipt loan.

SELF-TEST PROBLEM (SOLUTION IN APPENDIX B)

   ST14–1 Cash discount decisions The credit terms for each of three suppliers are shown in the following table. (*Note:* Assume a 365-day year.)

Supplier	Credit terms
X	1/10 net 55 EOM
Y	2/10 net 30 EOM
Z	2/20 net 60 EOM

a. Determine the *approximate* cost of giving up the cash discount from each supplier.
b. Assuming that the firm needs short-term financing, indicate whether it would be better to give up the cash discount or take the discount and borrow from a bank at 15% annual interest. Evaluate each supplier *separately* using your findings in part **a**.
c. What impact, if any, would the fact that the firm could stretch its accounts payable (net period only) by 20 days from supplier Z have on your answer in part **b** relative to this supplier?

WARM-UP EXERCISES

E14–1 Lyman Nurseries purchased seeds costing $25,000 with terms of 3/15 net 30 EOM on January 12. How much will the firm pay if it takes the cash discount? What is the *approximate cost of giving up the cash discount,* using the simplified formula?

E14–2 Cleaner's, Inc., is switching to paying employees every two weeks rather than weekly and will therefore "skip" 1 week's pay. The firm has 25 employees who work a 60-hour week and earn an average wage of $12.50 per hour. Using a 10% rate of interest, how much will this change save the firm annually?

E14–3 Jasmine Scents has been given two competing offers for short-term financing. Both offers are for borrowing $15,000 for 1 year. The first offer is a *discount loan* at a stated interest rate of 8%; the second offer is for interest to be paid *at maturity* at a stated interest rate of 9%. Calculate the *effective annual rates* for each loan and indicate which loan offers the best terms.

E14–4 Jackson Industries has borrowed $125,000 under a line-of-credit agreement. While the company normally maintains a checking account balance of $15,000 in the lending bank, this credit line requires a 20% compensating balance. The stated interest rate on the borrowed funds is 10%. What is the *effective annual rate of interest* on the line of credit?

E14–5 Horizon Telecom sold $300,000 worth of 120-day commercial paper for $298,000. What is the dollar amount of interest paid on the commercial paper? What is the *effective 120-day rate* on the paper?

PROBLEMS

P14–1 **Payment dates** Determine when a firm must pay for purchases made and invoices dated on November 25 under each of the following credit terms.
a. net 30 date of invoice
b. net 30 EOM
c. net 45 date of invoice
d. net 60 EOM

P14–2 **Cost of giving up cash discounts** Determine the *cost of giving up cash discounts* under each of the following terms of sale. (*Note:* Assume a 365-day year.)
a. 2/10 net 30
b. 1/10 net 30
c. 2/10 net 45
d. 3/10 net 45
e. 1/10 net 60
f. 3/10 net 30
g. 4/10 net 180

P14–3 **Credit terms** Purchases made on credit are due in full by the end of the billing period. Many firms extend a discount for payment made in the first part of the billing period. The original invoice contains a type of "short-hand" notation that explains the credit terms that apply. (*Note:* Assume a 365-day year.)

a. Write the short-hand expression of credit terms for each of the following.

Cash discount	Cash discount period	Credit period	Beginning of credit period
1%	15 days	45 days	date of invoice
2	10	30	end of month
2	7	28	date of invoice
1	10	60	end of month

b. For each of the sets of credit terms in part **a**, calculate the number of days until full payment is due for invoices dated March 12.
c. For each of the sets of credit terms, calculate the *cost of giving up the cash discount*.
d. If the firm's cost of short-term financing is 8%, what would you recommend in regard to taking the discount or giving it up in each case?

P14–4 **Cash discount versus loan** Erica Stone works in an accounts payable department. She has attempted to convince her boss to take the discount on the 3/10 net 45 credit terms most suppliers offer, but her boss argues that giving up the 3% discount is less costly than a short-term loan at 14%. Prove to whoever is wrong that the other is correct. (*Note:* Assume a 365-day year.)

P14–5 **Cash discount decisions** Prairie Manufacturing has four possible suppliers, all of which offer different credit terms. Except for the differences in credit terms, their products and services are virtually identical. The credit terms offered by these suppliers are shown in the following table. (*Note:* Assume a 365-day year.)

Supplier	Credit terms
J	1/10 net 30 EOM
K	2/20 net 80 EOM
L	1/20 net 60 EOM
M	3/10 net 55 EOM

a. Calculate the *approximate cost of giving up the cash discount* from each supplier.
b. If the firm needs short-term funds, which are currently available from its commercial bank at 16%, and if each of the suppliers is viewed *separately*, which, if any, of the suppliers' cash discounts should the firm give up? Explain why.
c. What impact, if any, would the fact that the firm could stretch its accounts payable (net period only) by 30 days from supplier M have on your answer in part **b** relative to this supplier?

P14–6 **Changing payment cycle** Upon accepting the position of chief executive officer and chairman of Reeves Machinery, Frank Cheney changed the firm's weekly payday from Monday afternoon to the following Friday afternoon. The firm's weekly payroll was $10 million, and the cost of short-term funds was 13%. If the effect of this change was to delay check clearing by 1 week, what *annual* savings, if any, were realized?

P14–7 **Spontaneous sources of funds, accruals** When Tallman Haberdashery, Inc., merged with Meyers Men's Suits, Inc., Tallman's employees were switched from a weekly to a biweekly pay period. Tallman's weekly payroll amounted to $750,000. The cost of funds for the combined firms is 11%. What annual savings, if any, are realized by this change of pay period?

P14–8 **Cost of bank loan** Data Back-Up Systems has obtained a $10,000, 90-day bank loan at an annual interest rate of 15%, payable at maturity. (*Note:* Assume a 365-day year.)
   a. How much interest (in dollars) will the firm pay on the 90-day loan?
   b. Find the *effective 90-day rate* on the loan.
   c. Annualize your result in part **b** to find the *effective annual rate* for this loan, assuming that it is rolled over every 90 days throughout the year under the same terms and circumstances.

P14–9 **Effective annual rate** A financial institution made a $10,000, 1-year discount loan at 10% interest, requiring a compensating balance equal to 20% of the face value of the loan. Determine the *effective annual rate* associated with this loan. (*Note:* Assume that the firm currently maintains $0 on deposit in the financial institution.)

P14–10 **Compensating balances and effective annual rates** Lincoln Industries has a line of credit at Bank Two that requires it to pay 11% interest on its borrowing and to maintain a compensating balance equal to 15% of the amount borrowed. The firm has borrowed $800,000 during the year under the agreement. Calculate the *effective annual rate* on the firm's borrowing in each of the following circumstances:
   a. The firm normally maintains no deposit balances at Bank Two.
   b. The firm normally maintains $70,000 in deposit balances at Bank Two.
   c. The firm normally maintains $150,000 in deposit balances at Bank Two.
   d. Compare, contrast, and discuss your findings in parts **a**, **b**, and **c**.

P14–11 **Compensating balance versus discount loan** Weathers Catering Supply, Inc., needs to borrow $150,000 for 6 months. State Bank has offered to lend the funds at a 9% annual rate subject to a 10% compensating balance. (*Note:* Weathers currently maintains $0 on deposit in State Bank.) Frost Finance Co. has offered to lend the funds at a 9% annual rate with discount-loan terms. The principal of both loans would be payable at maturity as a single sum.
   a. Calculate the *effective annual rate of interest* on each loan.
   b. What could Weathers do that would reduce the effective annual rate on the State Bank loan?

P14–12 **Integrative—Comparison of loan terms** Cumberland Furniture wishes to establish a prearranged borrowing agreement with a local commercial bank. The bank's terms for a line of credit are 3.30% over the prime rate, and each year the borrowing must be reduced to zero for a 30-day period. For an equivalent revolving credit agreement, the rate is 2.80% over prime with a commitment fee of 0.50% on the average unused balance. With both loans, the required compensating balance is equal to 20% of the amount borrowed. (*Note:* Cumberland currently maintains $0 on deposit at the bank.) The prime rate is currently 8%. Both agreements have $4 million borrowing limits. The firm expects on average

to borrow $2 million during the year no matter which loan agreement it decides to use.
a. What is the *effective annual rate* under the line of credit?
b. What is the *effective annual rate* under the revolving credit agreement? (*Hint:* Compute the ratio of the dollars that the firm will pay in interest and commitment fees to the dollars that the firm will effectively have use of.)
c. If the firm does expect to borrow an average of half the amount available, which arrangement would you recommend for the borrower? Explain why.

P14–13 **Cost of commercial paper** Commercial paper is usually sold at a discount. Fan Corporation has just sold an issue of 90-day commercial paper with a face value of $1 million. The firm has received initial proceeds of $978,000. (*Note:* Assume a 365-day year.)
a. What *effective annual rate* will the firm pay for financing with commercial paper, assuming that it is rolled over every 90 days throughout the year?
b. If a brokerage fee of $9,612 was paid from the initial proceeds to an investment banker for selling the issue, what *effective annual rate* will the firm pay, assuming that the paper is rolled over every 90 days throughout the year?

P14–14 **Accounts receivable as collateral** Kansas City Castings (KCC) is attempting to obtain the maximum loan possible using accounts receivable as collateral. The firm extends net-30-day credit. The amounts that are owed KCC by its 12 credit customers, the average age of each account, and the customer's average payment period are as shown in the following table.

Customer	Account receivable	Average age of account	Average payment period of customer
A	$37,000	40 days	30 days
B	12,000	25	50
C	15,000	40	60
D	8,000	30	35
E	50,000	31	40
F	12,000	28	30
G	24,000	30	70
H	46,000	29	40
I	3,000	30	65
J	22,000	25	35
K	62,000	35	40
L	80,000	60	70

a. If the bank will accept all accounts that can be collected in 45 days or less as long as the customer has a history of paying within 45 days, which accounts will be acceptable? What is the total dollar amount of accounts receivable collateral? (*Note:* Accounts receivable that have an average age greater than the customer's average payment period are also excluded.)
b. In addition to the conditions in part **a**, the bank recognizes that 5% of credit sales will be lost to returns and allowances. Also, the bank will lend only 80% of the acceptable collateral (after adjusting for returns and allowances). What level of funds would be made available through this lending source?

P14–15 Accounts receivable as collateral Springer Products wishes to borrow $80,000 from a local bank using its accounts receivable to secure the loan. The bank's policy is to accept as collateral any accounts that are normally paid within 30 days of the end of the credit period, as long as the average age of the account is not greater than the customer's average payment period. Springer's accounts receivable, their average ages, and the average payment period for each customer are shown in the following table. The company extends terms of net 30 days.

Customer	Account receivable	Average age of account	Average payment period of customer
A	$20,000	10 days	40 days
B	6,000	40	35
C	22,000	62	50
D	11,000	68	65
E	2,000	14	30
F	12,000	38	50
G	27,000	55	60
H	19,000	20	35

a. Calculate the dollar amount of acceptable accounts receivable collateral held by Springer Products.
b. The bank reduces collateral by 10% for returns and allowances. What is the level of acceptable collateral under this condition?
c. The bank will advance 75% against the firm's acceptable collateral (after adjusting for returns and allowances). What amount can Springer borrow against these accounts?

P14–16 Accounts receivable as collateral, cost of borrowing Maximum Bank has analyzed the accounts receivable of Scientific Software, Inc. The bank has chosen eight accounts totaling $134,000 that it will accept as collateral. The bank's terms include a lending rate set at prime + 3% and a 2% commission charge. The prime rate currently is 8.5%.
a. The bank will adjust the accounts by 10% for returns and allowances. It then will lend up to 85% of the adjusted acceptable collateral. What is the maximum amount that the bank will lend to Scientific Software?
b. What is Scientific Software's *effective annual rate of interest* if it borrows $100,000 for 12 months? For 6 months? For 3 months? (*Note:* Assume a 365-day year and a prime rate that remains at 8.5% during the life of the loan.)

P14–17 Factoring Blair Finance factors the accounts of the Holder Company. All eight factored accounts are shown in the table at the top of the facing page, with the amount factored, the date due, and the status on May 30. Indicate the amounts that Blair should have remitted to Holder as of May 30 and the dates of those remittances. Assume that the factor's commission of 2% is deducted as part of determining the amount of the remittance.

Account	Amount	Date due	Status on May 30
A	$200,000	May 30	Collected May 15
B	90,000	May 30	Uncollected
C	110,000	May 30	Uncollected
D	85,000	June 15	Collected May 30
E	120,000	May 30	Collected May 27
F	180,000	June 15	Collected May 30
G	90,000	May 15	Uncollected
H	30,000	June 30	Collected May 30

P14–18 **Inventory financing** Raymond Manufacturing faces a liquidity crisis—it needs a loan of $100,000 for 1 month. Having no source of additional unsecured borrowing, the firm must find a secured short-term lender. The firm's accounts receivable are quite low, but its inventory is considered liquid and reasonably good collateral. The book value of the inventory is $300,000, of which $120,000 is finished goods. (*Note:* Assume a 365-day year.)

(1) City-Wide Bank will make a $100,000 *trust receipt* loan against the finished goods inventory. The annual interest rate on the loan is 12% on the outstanding loan balance plus a 0.25% administration fee levied against the $100,000 initial loan amount. Because it will be liquidated as inventory is sold, the average amount owed over the month is expected to be $75,000.

(2) Sun State Bank will lend $100,000 against a *floating lien* on the book value of inventory for the 1-month period at an annual interest rate of 13%.

(3) Citizens' Bank and Trust will lend $100,000 against a *warehouse receipt* on the finished goods inventory and charge 15% annual interest on the outstanding loan balance. A 0.5% warehousing fee will be levied against the average amount borrowed. Because the loan will be liquidated as inventory is sold, the average loan balance is expected to be $60,000.

a. Calculate the dollar cost of each of the proposed plans for obtaining an initial loan amount of $100,000.
b. Which plan do you recommend? Why?
c. If the firm had made a purchase of $100,000 for which it had been given terms of 2/10 net 30, would it increase the firm's profitability to give up the discount and not borrow as recommended in part **b**? Why or why not?

P14–19 **ETHICS PROBLEM** A group of angry shareholders has placed a corporate resolution before all shareholders at a company's annual stockholders' meeting. The resolution demands that the company *stretch its accounts payable*, because these shareholders have determined that all of the company's competitors do so, and the firm operates in a highly competitive industry. How could management at the annual stockholders' meeting defend the firm's practice of paying suppliers on time?

Chapter 14 Case

Selecting Kanton Company's Financing Strategy and Unsecured Short-Term Borrowing Arrangement

Morton Mercado, the CFO of Kanton Company, carefully developed the estimates of the firm's total funds requirements for the coming year. These are shown in the following table.

Month	Total funds	Month	Total funds
January	$1,000,000	July	$6,000,000
February	1,000,000	August	5,000,000
March	2,000,000	September	5,000,000
April	3,000,000	October	4,000,000
May	5,000,000	November	2,000,000
June	7,000,000	December	1,000,000

In addition, Morton expects short-term financing costs of about 10% and long-term financing costs of about 14% during that period. He developed the three possible financing strategies that follow:

Strategy 1—Aggressive: Finance seasonal needs with short-term funds and permanent needs with long-term funds.

Strategy 2—Conservative: Finance an amount equal to the peak need with long-term funds and use short-term funds only in an emergency.

Strategy 3—Tradeoff: Finance $3,000,000 with long-term funds and finance the remaining funds requirements with short-term funds.

Using the data on the firm's total funds requirements, Morton estimated the average annual short-term and long-term financing requirements for each strategy in the coming year, as shown in the following table.

	Average annual financing		
Type of financing	Strategy 1 (aggressive)	Strategy 2 (conservative)	Strategy 3 (tradeoff)
Short-term	$2,500,000	$ 0	$1,666,667
Long-term	1,000,000	7,000,000	3,000,000

To ensure that, along with spontaneous financing from accounts payable and accruals, adequate short-term financing will be available, Morton plans to establish an unsecured short-term borrowing arrangement with its local bank, Third National. The bank has offered either a line-of-credit agreement or a revolving credit agreement. Third National's terms for a line of credit are an interest rate of 2.50% above the prime rate, and the borrowing must be reduced to zero for a 30-day period during the year. On an equivalent revolving credit agreement, the interest rate would be 3.00% above prime with a commitment fee of 0.50% on the average unused balance. Under both loans, a compensating balance equal to 20% of the amount borrowed would be required. The prime rate is currently 7%.

Both the line-of-credit agreement and the revolving credit agreement would have borrowing limits of $1,000,000. For purposes of his analysis, Morton estimates that Kanton will borrow $600,000 on the average during the year, regardless of which financing strategy and loan arrangement it chooses. (*Note:* Assume a 365-day year.)

TO DO

a. Determine the total annual cost of each of the three possible financing strategies.
b. Assuming that the firm expects its current assets to total $4 million throughout the year, determine the average amount of net working capital under each financing strategy. (*Hint:* Current liabilities equal average short-term financing.)
c. Using the net working capital found in part **b** as a measure of risk, discuss the profitability–risk tradeoff associated with each financing strategy. Which strategy would you recommend to Morton Mercado for Kanton Company? Why?
d. Find the *effective annual rate* under:
   (1) The line-of-credit agreement.
   (2) The revolving credit agreement. (*Hint:* Find the ratio of the dollars that the firm will pay in interest and commitment fees to the dollars that the firm will effectively have use of.)
e. If the firm does expect to borrow an average of $600,000, which borrowing arrangement would you recommend to Kanton? Explain why.

SPREADSHEET EXERCISE

Your company is considering manufacturing carrying cases for the portable video game machines that are currently popular. It is decided to borrow $200,000 from each of two banks—First American and First Citizen. On the day that you visit both banks, the quoted prime interest rate is 7%. Each loan is similar in that each involves a 60-day note, with interest to be paid at the end of 60 days.

The interest rate was set at 2% above the prime rate on First American's *fixed-rate note*. Over the 60-day period, the rate of interest on this note will remain at the 2% premium over the prime rate regardless of fluctuations in the prime rate.

First Citizen sets its interest rate at 1.5% above the prime rate on its *floating-rate note*. The rate charged over the 60 days will vary directly with the prime rate.

TO DO

First, create a spreadsheet to calculate the following for the First American loan:

a. Calculate the total dollar interest cost on the loan. Assume a 365-day year.
b. Calculate the *effective 60-day rate* on the loan.
c. Assume that the loan is rolled over each 60 days throughout the year under identical conditions and terms. Calculate the *effective annual rate of interest* on the fixed-rate, 60-day First American note.

Next, create a spreadsheet to calculate the following for the First Citizen loan:

d. Calculate the initial interest rate.
e. If the prime rate immediately jumps to 7.5%, and after 30 days it drops to 7.25%, calculate the interest rate for the first 30 days and the second 30 days of the loan.
f. Calculate the total dollar interest cost.
g. Calculate the *effective 60-day rate of interest*.
h. Assume the loan is rolled over each 60 days throughout the year under the same conditions and terms. Calculate the *effective annual interest rate*.
i. Which loan would you choose, and why?

WEB EXERCISE

Many firms offer factoring services whereby firms can liquefy their accounts receivable, essentially selling them for cash.

TO DO

Point your browser to www.wfgfactor.com/index.php, the home page of Winston Financial Group, Inc. Your assignment is to explore this Web site and to report what services Winston offers and how the process of factoring works.

Remember to check the book's Web site at

www.aw-bc.com/gitman

for additional resources, including additional Web exercises.

Appendix A

Financial Tables

TABLE A–1 Future Value Interest Factors for One Dollar Compounded at i Percent for n Periods:

$$FVIF_{i,n} = (1 + i)^n$$

TABLE A–2 Present Value Interest Factors for One Dollar Discounted at i Percent for n Periods:

$$PVIF_{i,n} = \frac{1}{(1 + i)^n}$$

TABLE A–3 Future Value Interest Factors for a One-Dollar Ordinary Annuity Compounded at i Percent for n Periods:

$$FVIFA_{i,n} = \sum_{t=1}^{n} (1 + i)^{t-1}$$

TABLE A–4 Present Value Interest Factors for a One-Dollar Annuity Discounted at i Percent for n Periods:

$$PVIFA_{i,n} = \sum_{t=1}^{n} \frac{1}{(1 + i)^t}$$

APPENDIX A

TABLE A-1 Future Value Interest Factors for One Dollar Compounded at *i* Percent for *n* Periods: $FVIF_{i,n} = (1+i)^n$

Period	1%	2%	3%	4%	5%	6%	7%	8%	9%	10%	11%	12%	13%	14%	15%	16%	17%	18%	19%	20%
1	1.010	1.020	1.030	1.040	1.050	1.060	1.070	1.080	1.090	1.100	1.110	1.120	1.130	1.140	1.150	1.160	1.170	1.180	1.190	1.200
2	1.020	1.040	1.061	1.082	1.102	1.124	1.145	1.166	1.188	1.210	1.232	1.254	1.277	1.300	1.322	1.346	1.369	1.392	1.416	1.440
3	1.030	1.061	1.093	1.125	1.158	1.191	1.225	1.260	1.295	1.331	1.368	1.405	1.443	1.482	1.521	1.561	1.602	1.643	1.685	1.728
4	1.041	1.082	1.126	1.170	1.216	1.262	1.311	1.360	1.412	1.464	1.518	1.574	1.630	1.689	1.749	1.811	1.874	1.939	2.005	2.074
5	1.051	1.104	1.159	1.217	1.276	1.338	1.403	1.469	1.539	1.611	1.685	1.762	1.842	1.925	2.011	2.100	2.192	2.288	2.386	2.488
6	1.062	1.126	1.194	1.265	1.340	1.419	1.501	1.587	1.677	1.772	1.870	1.974	2.082	2.195	2.313	2.436	2.565	2.700	2.840	2.986
7	1.072	1.149	1.230	1.316	1.407	1.504	1.606	1.714	1.828	1.949	2.076	2.211	2.353	2.502	2.660	2.826	3.001	3.185	3.379	3.583
8	1.083	1.172	1.267	1.369	1.477	1.594	1.718	1.851	1.993	2.144	2.305	2.476	2.658	2.853	3.059	3.278	3.511	3.759	4.021	4.300
9	1.094	1.195	1.305	1.423	1.551	1.689	1.838	1.999	2.172	2.358	2.558	2.773	3.004	3.252	3.518	3.803	4.108	4.435	4.785	5.160
10	1.105	1.219	1.344	1.480	1.629	1.791	1.967	2.159	2.367	2.594	2.839	3.106	3.395	3.707	4.046	4.411	4.807	5.234	5.695	6.192
11	1.116	1.243	1.384	1.539	1.710	1.898	2.105	2.332	2.580	2.853	3.152	3.479	3.836	4.226	4.652	5.117	5.624	6.176	6.777	7.430
12	1.127	1.268	1.426	1.601	1.796	2.012	2.252	2.518	2.813	3.138	3.498	3.896	4.334	4.818	5.350	5.936	6.580	7.288	8.064	8.916
13	1.138	1.294	1.469	1.665	1.886	2.133	2.410	2.720	3.066	3.452	3.883	4.363	4.898	5.492	6.153	6.886	7.699	8.599	9.596	10.699
14	1.149	1.319	1.513	1.732	1.980	2.261	2.579	2.937	3.342	3.797	4.310	4.887	5.535	6.261	7.076	7.987	9.007	10.147	11.420	12.839
15	1.161	1.346	1.558	1.801	2.079	2.397	2.759	3.172	3.642	4.177	4.785	5.474	6.254	7.138	8.137	9.265	10.539	11.974	13.589	15.407
16	1.173	1.373	1.605	1.873	2.183	2.540	2.952	3.426	3.970	4.595	5.311	6.130	7.067	8.137	9.358	10.748	12.330	14.129	16.171	18.488
17	1.184	1.400	1.653	1.948	2.292	2.693	3.159	3.700	4.328	5.054	5.895	6.866	7.986	9.276	10.761	12.468	14.426	16.672	19.244	22.186
18	1.196	1.428	1.702	2.026	2.407	2.854	3.380	3.996	4.717	5.560	6.543	7.690	9.024	10.575	12.375	14.462	16.879	19.673	22.900	26.623
19	1.208	1.457	1.753	2.107	2.527	3.026	3.616	4.316	5.142	6.116	7.263	8.613	10.197	12.055	14.232	16.776	19.748	23.214	27.251	31.948
20	1.220	1.486	1.806	2.191	2.653	3.207	3.870	4.661	5.604	6.727	8.062	9.646	11.523	13.743	16.366	19.461	23.105	27.393	32.429	38.337
21	1.232	1.516	1.860	2.279	2.786	3.399	4.140	5.034	6.109	7.400	8.949	10.804	13.021	15.667	18.821	22.574	27.033	32.323	38.591	46.005
22	1.245	1.546	1.916	2.370	2.925	3.603	4.430	5.436	6.658	8.140	9.933	12.100	14.713	17.861	21.644	26.186	31.629	38.141	45.923	55.205
23	1.257	1.577	1.974	2.465	3.071	3.820	4.740	5.871	7.258	8.954	11.026	13.552	16.626	20.361	24.891	30.376	37.005	45.007	54.648	66.247
24	1.270	1.608	2.033	2.563	3.225	4.049	5.072	6.341	7.911	9.850	12.239	15.178	18.788	23.212	28.625	35.236	43.296	53.108	65.031	79.496
25	1.282	1.641	2.094	2.666	3.386	4.292	5.427	6.848	8.623	10.834	13.585	17.000	21.230	26.461	32.918	40.874	50.656	62.667	77.387	95.395
30	1.348	1.811	2.427	3.243	4.322	5.743	7.612	10.062	13.267	17.449	22.892	29.960	39.115	50.949	66.210	85.849	111.061	143.367	184.672	237.373
35	1.417	2.000	2.814	3.946	5.516	7.686	10.676	14.785	20.413	28.102	38.574	52.799	72.066	98.097	133.172	180.311	243.495	327.988	440.691	590.657
40	1.489	2.208	3.262	4.801	7.040	10.285	14.974	21.724	31.408	45.258	64.999	93.049	132.776	188.876	267.856	378.715	533.846	750.353	1051.642	1469.740
45	1.565	2.438	3.781	5.841	8.985	13.764	21.002	31.920	48.325	72.888	109.527	163.985	244.629	363.662	538.752	795.429	1170.425	1716.619	2509.583	3657.176
50	1.645	2.691	4.384	7.106	11.467	18.419	29.456	46.900	74.354	117.386	184.559	288.996	450.711	700.197	1083.619	1670.669	2566.080	3927.189	5988.730	9100.191

Using the Calculator to Compute the Future Value of a Single Amount

Before you begin, make sure to clear the memory, ensure that you are in the *end mode* and that your calculator is set for *one payment per year*, and set the number of decimal places that you want (usually two for dollar-related accuracy).

Sample Problem

You place $800 in a savings account at 6% compounded annually. What is your account balance at the end of 5 years?

Hewlett-Packard HP 12C, 17 BII, and 19 BII[a]

Input	Function
800	PV
5	N
6	I%YR
	FV

Solution[b]
1,070.58

---

[a] For the 12C, you would use the **n** key instead of the **N** key and use the **i** key instead of the **I%YR** key.
[b] The minus sign that precedes the solution should be ignored.

Financial Tables   A-3

TABLE A–1   (Continued)

Period	21%	22%	23%	24%	25%	26%	27%	28%	29%	30%	31%	32%	33%	34%	35%	40%	45%	50%
1	1.210	1.220	1.230	1.240	1.250	1.260	1.270	1.280	1.290	1.300	1.310	1.320	1.330	1.340	1.350	1.400	1.450	1.500
2	1.464	1.488	1.513	1.538	1.562	1.588	1.613	1.638	1.664	1.690	1.716	1.742	1.769	1.796	1.822	1.960	2.102	2.250
3	1.772	1.816	1.861	1.907	1.953	2.000	2.048	2.097	2.147	2.197	2.248	2.300	2.353	2.406	2.460	2.744	3.049	3.375
4	2.144	2.215	2.289	2.364	2.441	2.520	2.601	2.684	2.769	2.856	2.945	3.036	3.129	3.224	3.321	3.842	4.421	5.063
5	2.594	2.703	2.815	2.932	3.052	3.176	3.304	3.436	3.572	3.713	3.858	4.007	4.162	4.320	4.484	5.378	6.410	7.594
6	3.138	3.297	3.463	3.635	3.815	4.001	4.196	4.398	4.608	4.827	5.054	5.290	5.535	5.789	6.053	7.530	9.294	11.391
7	3.797	4.023	4.259	4.508	4.768	5.042	5.329	5.629	5.945	6.275	6.621	6.983	7.361	7.758	8.172	10.541	13.476	17.086
8	4.595	4.908	5.239	5.589	5.960	6.353	6.767	7.206	7.669	8.157	8.673	9.217	9.791	10.395	11.032	14.758	19.541	25.629
9	5.560	5.987	6.444	6.931	7.451	8.004	8.595	9.223	9.893	10.604	11.362	12.166	13.022	13.930	14.894	20.661	28.334	38.443
10	6.727	7.305	7.926	8.594	9.313	10.086	10.915	11.806	12.761	13.786	14.884	16.060	17.319	18.666	20.106	28.925	41.085	57.665
11	8.140	8.912	9.749	10.657	11.642	12.708	13.862	15.112	16.462	17.921	19.498	21.199	23.034	25.012	27.144	40.495	59.573	86.498
12	9.850	10.872	11.991	13.215	14.552	16.012	17.605	19.343	21.236	23.298	25.542	27.982	30.635	33.516	36.644	56.694	86.380	129.746
13	11.918	13.264	14.749	16.386	18.190	20.175	22.359	24.759	27.395	30.287	33.460	36.937	40.745	44.912	49.469	79.371	125.251	194.620
14	14.421	16.182	18.141	20.319	22.737	25.420	28.395	31.691	35.339	39.373	43.832	48.756	54.190	60.181	66.784	111.119	181.614	291.929
15	17.449	19.742	22.314	25.195	28.422	32.030	36.062	40.565	45.587	51.185	57.420	64.358	72.073	80.643	90.158	155.567	263.341	437.894
16	21.113	24.085	27.446	31.242	35.527	40.357	45.799	51.923	58.808	66.541	75.220	84.953	95.857	108.061	121.713	217.793	381.844	656.841
17	25.547	29.384	33.758	38.740	44.409	50.850	58.165	66.461	75.862	86.503	98.539	112.138	127.490	144.802	164.312	304.911	553.674	985.261
18	30.912	35.848	41.523	48.038	55.511	64.071	73.869	85.070	97.862	112.454	129.086	148.022	169.561	194.035	221.822	426.875	802.826	1477.892
19	37.404	43.735	51.073	59.567	69.389	80.730	93.813	108.890	126.242	146.190	169.102	195.389	225.517	260.006	299.459	597.625	1164.098	2216.838
20	45.258	53.357	62.820	73.863	86.736	101.720	119.143	139.379	162.852	190.047	221.523	257.913	299.937	348.408	404.270	836.674	1687.942	3325.257
21	54.762	65.095	77.268	91.591	108.420	128.167	151.312	178.405	210.079	247.061	290.196	340.446	398.916	466.867	545.764	1171.343	2447.515	4987.883
22	66.262	79.416	95.040	113.572	135.525	161.490	192.165	228.358	271.002	321.178	380.156	449.388	530.558	625.601	736.781	1639.878	3548.896	7481.824
23	80.178	96.887	116.899	140.829	169.407	203.477	244.050	292.298	349.592	417.531	498.004	593.192	705.642	838.305	994.653	2295.829	5145.898	11222.738
24	97.015	118.203	143.786	174.628	211.758	256.381	309.943	374.141	450.974	542.791	652.385	783.013	938.504	1123.328	1342.781	3214.158	7461.547	16834.109
25	117.388	144.207	176.857	216.539	264.698	323.040	393.628	478.901	581.756	705.627	854.623	1033.577	1248.210	1505.258	1812.754	4499.816	10819.242	25251.164
30	304.471	389.748	497.904	634.810	807.793	1025.904	1300.477	1645.488	2078.208	2619.936	3297.081	4142.008	5194.516	6503.285	8128.426	24201.043	69348.375	191751.000
35	789.716	1053.370	1401.749	1861.020	2465.189	3258.053	4296.547	5653.840	7423.988	9727.598	12719.918	16598.906	21617.363	28096.695	36448.051	130158.687	*	*
40	2048.309	2846.941	3946.340	5455.797	7523.156	10346.879	14195.051	19426.418	26520.723	36117.754	49072.621	66519.313	89962.188	121388.437	163433.875	700022.688	*	*
45	5312.758	7694.418	11110.121	15994.316	22958.844	32859.457	46897.973	66748.500	94739.937	134102.187	*	*	*	*	*	*	*	*
50	13779.844	20795.680	31278.301	46889.207	70064.812	104354.562	154942.687	229345.875	338440.000	497910.125	*	*	*	*	*	*	*	*

*Not shown because of space limitations.

[c]For the Texas Instruments BAII, you would use the `2nd` key instead of the `CPT` key; for the Texas Instruments BAII Plus, you would use the `I/Y` key instead of the `%i` key.

[d]If a minus sign precedes the solution, it should be ignored.

TABLE A–2 Present Value Interest Factors for One Dollar Discounted at i Percent for n Periods: $PVIF_{i,n} = \dfrac{1}{(1+i)^n}$

Period	1%	2%	3%	4%	5%	6%	7%	8%	9%	10%	11%	12%	13%	14%	15%	16%	17%	18%	19%	20%
1	.990	.980	.971	.962	.952	.943	.935	.926	.917	.909	.901	.893	.885	.877	.870	.862	.855	.847	.840	.833
2	.980	.961	.943	.925	.907	.890	.873	.857	.842	.826	.812	.797	.783	.769	.756	.743	.731	.718	.706	.694
3	.971	.942	.915	.889	.864	.840	.816	.794	.772	.751	.731	.712	.693	.675	.658	.641	.624	.609	.593	.579
4	.961	.924	.888	.855	.823	.792	.763	.735	.708	.683	.659	.636	.613	.592	.572	.552	.534	.516	.499	.482
5	.951	.906	.863	.822	.784	.747	.713	.681	.650	.621	.593	.567	.543	.519	.497	.476	.456	.437	.419	.402
6	.942	.888	.837	.790	.746	.705	.666	.630	.596	.564	.535	.507	.480	.456	.432	.410	.390	.370	.352	.335
7	.933	.871	.813	.760	.711	.665	.623	.583	.547	.513	.482	.452	.425	.400	.376	.354	.333	.314	.296	.279
8	.923	.853	.789	.731	.677	.627	.582	.540	.502	.467	.434	.404	.376	.351	.327	.305	.285	.266	.249	.233
9	.914	.837	.766	.703	.645	.592	.544	.500	.460	.424	.391	.361	.333	.308	.284	.263	.243	.225	.209	.194
10	.905	.820	.744	.676	.614	.558	.508	.463	.422	.386	.352	.322	.295	.270	.247	.227	.208	.191	.176	.162
11	.896	.804	.722	.650	.585	.527	.475	.429	.388	.350	.317	.287	.261	.237	.215	.195	.178	.162	.148	.135
12	.887	.789	.701	.625	.557	.497	.444	.397	.356	.319	.286	.257	.231	.208	.187	.168	.152	.137	.124	.112
13	.879	.773	.681	.601	.530	.469	.415	.368	.326	.290	.258	.229	.204	.182	.163	.145	.130	.116	.104	.093
14	.870	.758	.661	.577	.505	.442	.388	.340	.299	.263	.232	.205	.181	.160	.141	.125	.111	.099	.088	.078
15	.861	.743	.642	.555	.481	.417	.362	.315	.275	.239	.209	.183	.160	.140	.123	.108	.095	.084	.074	.065
16	.853	.728	.623	.534	.458	.394	.339	.292	.252	.218	.188	.163	.141	.123	.107	.093	.081	.071	.062	.054
17	.844	.714	.605	.513	.436	.371	.317	.270	.231	.198	.170	.146	.125	.108	.093	.080	.069	.060	.052	.045
18	.836	.700	.587	.494	.416	.350	.296	.250	.212	.180	.153	.130	.111	.095	.081	.069	.059	.051	.044	.038
19	.828	.686	.570	.475	.396	.331	.277	.232	.194	.164	.138	.116	.098	.083	.070	.060	.051	.043	.037	.031
20	.820	.673	.554	.456	.377	.312	.258	.215	.178	.149	.124	.104	.087	.073	.061	.051	.043	.037	.031	.026
21	.811	.660	.538	.439	.359	.294	.242	.199	.164	.135	.112	.093	.077	.064	.053	.044	.037	.031	.026	.022
22	.803	.647	.522	.422	.342	.278	.226	.184	.150	.123	.101	.083	.068	.056	.046	.038	.032	.026	.022	.018
23	.795	.634	.507	.406	.326	.262	.211	.170	.138	.112	.091	.074	.060	.049	.040	.033	.027	.022	.018	.015
24	.788	.622	.492	.390	.310	.247	.197	.158	.126	.102	.082	.066	.053	.043	.035	.028	.023	.019	.015	.013
25	.780	.610	.478	.375	.295	.233	.184	.146	.116	.092	.074	.059	.047	.038	.030	.024	.020	.016	.013	.010
30	.742	.552	.412	.308	.231	.174	.131	.099	.075	.057	.044	.033	.026	.020	.015	.012	.009	.007	.005	.004
35	.706	.500	.355	.253	.181	.130	.094	.068	.049	.036	.026	.019	.014	.010	.008	.006	.004	.003	.002	.002
40	.672	.453	.307	.208	.142	.097	.067	.046	.032	.022	.015	.011	.008	.005	.004	.003	.002	.001	.001	.001
45	.639	.410	.264	.171	.111	.073	.048	.031	.021	.014	.009	.006	.004	.003	.002	.001	.001	.001	*	*
50	.608	.372	.228	.141	.087	.054	.034	.021	.013	.009	.005	.003	.002	.001	.001	.001	*	*	*	*

*$PVIF$ is zero to three decimal places.

Using the Calculator to Compute the Present Value of a Single Amount

Hewlett-Packard HP 12C, 17 BII, and 19 BII[a]

Input	Function
1700	FV
8	N
8	I%YR
	PV

Solution[b]
918.46

Before you begin, make sure to clear the memory, ensure that you are in the *end mode* and that your calculator is set for *one payment per year*, and set the number of decimal places that you want (usually two for dollar-related accuracy).

Sample Problem

You want to know the present value of $1,700 to be received at the end of 8 years, assuming an 8% discount rate.

---

[a] For the 12C, you would use the (n) key instead of the (N) key and use the (i) key instead of the (I%YR) key.
[b] The minus sign that precedes the solution should be ignored.

Financial Tables A-5

TABLE A–2 (Continued)

Period	21%	22%	23%	24%	25%	26%	27%	28%	29%	30%	31%	32%	33%	34%	35%	40%	45%	50%
1	.826	.820	.813	.806	.800	.794	.787	.781	.775	.769	.763	.758	.752	.746	.741	.714	.690	.667
2	.683	.672	.661	.650	.640	.630	.620	.610	.601	.592	.583	.574	.565	.557	.549	.510	.476	.444
3	.564	.551	.537	.524	.512	.500	.488	.477	.466	.455	.445	.435	.425	.416	.406	.364	.328	.296
4	.467	.451	.437	.423	.410	.397	.384	.373	.361	.350	.340	.329	.320	.310	.301	.260	.226	.198
5	.386	.370	.355	.341	.328	.315	.303	.291	.280	.269	.259	.250	.240	.231	.223	.186	.156	.132
6	.319	.303	.289	.275	.262	.250	.238	.227	.217	.207	.198	.189	.181	.173	.165	.133	.108	.088
7	.263	.249	.235	.222	.210	.198	.188	.178	.168	.159	.151	.143	.136	.129	.122	.095	.074	.059
8	.218	.204	.191	.179	.168	.157	.148	.139	.130	.123	.115	.108	.102	.096	.091	.068	.051	.039
9	.180	.167	.155	.144	.134	.125	.116	.108	.101	.094	.088	.082	.077	.072	.067	.048	.035	.026
10	.149	.137	.126	.116	.107	.099	.092	.085	.078	.073	.067	.062	.058	.054	.050	.035	.024	.017
11	.123	.112	.103	.094	.086	.079	.072	.066	.061	.056	.051	.047	.043	.040	.037	.025	.017	.012
12	.102	.092	.083	.076	.069	.062	.057	.052	.047	.043	.039	.036	.033	.030	.027	.018	.012	.008
13	.084	.075	.068	.061	.055	.050	.045	.040	.037	.033	.030	.027	.025	.022	.020	.013	.008	.005
14	.069	.062	.055	.049	.044	.039	.035	.032	.028	.025	.023	.021	.018	.017	.015	.009	.006	.003
15	.057	.051	.045	.040	.035	.031	.028	.025	.022	.020	.017	.016	.014	.012	.011	.006	.004	.002
16	.047	.042	.036	.032	.028	.025	.022	.019	.017	.015	.013	.012	.010	.009	.008	.005	.003	.002
17	.039	.034	.030	.026	.023	.020	.017	.015	.013	.012	.010	.009	.008	.007	.006	.003	.002	.001
18	.032	.028	.024	.021	.018	.016	.014	.012	.010	.009	.008	.007	.006	.005	.005	.002	.001	.001
19	.027	.023	.020	.017	.014	.012	.011	.009	.008	.007	.006	.005	.004	.004	.003	.002	.001	*
20	.022	.019	.016	.014	.012	.010	.008	.007	.006	.005	.005	.004	.003	.003	.002	.001	.001	*
21	.018	.015	.013	.011	.009	.008	.007	.006	.005	.004	.003	.003	.003	.002	.002	.001	*	*
22	.015	.013	.011	.009	.007	.006	.005	.004	.004	.003	.003	.002	.002	.002	.001	.001	*	*
23	.012	.010	.009	.007	.006	.005	.004	.003	.003	.002	.002	.002	.001	.001	.001	*	*	*
24	.010	.008	.007	.006	.005	.004	.003	.003	.002	.002	.002	.001	.001	.001	.001	*	*	*
25	.009	.007	.006	.005	.004	.003	.003	.002	.002	.001	.001	.001	.001	.001	.001	*	*	*
30	.003	.003	.002	.002	.001	.001	.001	.001	*	*	*	*	*	*	*	*	*	*
35	.001	.001	.001	.001	*	*	*	*	*	*	*	*	*	*	*	*	*	*
40	*	*	*	*	*	*	*	*	*	*	*	*	*	*	*	*	*	*
45	*	*	*	*	*	*	*	*	*	*	*	*	*	*	*	*	*	*
50	*	*	*	*	*	*	*	*	*	*	*	*	*	*	*	*	*	*

*PVIF is zero to three decimal places.

Texas Instruments, BA-35, BAII, and BAII Plus[c]

Input	Function
1700	FV
8	N
8	%i
	CPT
	FV

Solution[d]
918.46

[c] For the Texas Instruments BAII, you would use the `2nd` key instead of the `CPT` key; for the Texas Instruments BAII Plus, you would use the `I/Y` key instead of the `%i` key.

[d] If a minus sign precedes the solution, it should be ignored.

APPENDIX A

TABLE A-3 Future Value Interest Factors for a One-Dollar Ordinary Annuity
Compounded at i Percent for n Periods: $FVIFA_{i,n} = \sum_{t=1}^{n}(1+i)^{t-1}$

Period	1%	2%	3%	4%	5%	6%	7%	8%	9%	10%	11%	12%	13%	14%	15%	16%	17%	18%	19%	20%
1	1.000	1.000	1.000	1.000	1.000	1.000	1.000	1.000	1.000	1.000	1.000	1.000	1.000	1.000	1.000	1.000	1.000	1.000	1.000	1.000
2	2.010	2.020	2.030	2.040	2.050	2.060	2.070	2.080	2.090	2.100	2.110	2.120	2.130	2.140	2.150	2.160	2.170	2.180	2.190	2.200
3	3.030	3.060	3.091	3.122	3.152	3.184	3.215	3.246	3.278	3.310	3.342	3.374	3.407	3.440	3.472	3.506	3.539	3.572	3.606	3.640
4	4.060	4.122	4.184	4.246	4.310	4.375	4.440	4.506	4.573	4.641	4.710	4.779	4.850	4.921	4.993	5.066	5.141	5.215	5.291	5.368
5	5.101	5.204	5.309	5.416	5.526	5.637	5.751	5.867	5.985	6.105	6.228	6.353	6.480	6.610	6.742	6.877	7.014	7.154	7.297	7.442
6	6.152	6.308	6.468	6.633	6.802	6.975	7.153	7.336	7.523	7.716	7.913	8.115	8.323	8.535	8.754	8.977	9.207	9.442	9.683	9.930
7	7.214	7.434	7.662	7.898	8.142	8.394	8.654	8.923	9.200	9.487	9.783	10.089	10.405	10.730	11.067	11.414	11.772	12.141	12.523	12.916
8	8.286	8.583	8.892	9.214	9.549	9.897	10.260	10.637	11.028	11.436	11.859	12.300	12.757	13.233	13.727	14.240	14.773	15.327	15.902	16.499
9	9.368	9.755	10.159	10.583	11.027	11.491	11.978	12.488	13.021	13.579	14.164	14.776	15.416	16.085	16.786	17.518	18.285	19.086	19.923	20.799
10	10.462	10.950	11.464	12.006	12.578	13.181	13.816	14.487	15.193	15.937	16.722	17.549	18.420	19.337	20.304	21.321	22.393	23.521	24.709	25.959
11	11.567	12.169	12.808	13.486	14.207	14.972	15.784	16.645	17.560	18.531	19.561	20.655	21.814	23.044	24.349	25.733	27.200	28.755	30.403	32.150
12	12.682	13.412	14.192	15.026	15.917	16.870	17.888	18.977	20.141	21.384	22.713	24.133	25.650	27.271	29.001	30.850	32.824	34.931	37.180	39.580
13	13.809	14.680	15.618	16.627	17.713	18.882	20.141	21.495	22.953	24.523	26.211	28.029	29.984	32.088	34.352	36.786	39.404	42.218	45.244	48.496
14	14.947	15.974	17.086	18.292	19.598	21.015	22.550	24.215	26.019	27.975	30.095	32.392	34.882	37.581	40.504	43.672	47.102	50.818	54.841	59.196
15	16.097	17.293	18.599	20.023	21.578	23.276	25.129	27.152	29.361	31.772	34.405	37.280	40.417	43.842	47.580	51.659	56.109	60.965	66.260	72.035
16	17.258	18.639	20.157	21.824	23.657	25.672	27.888	30.324	33.003	35.949	39.190	42.753	46.671	50.980	55.717	60.925	66.648	72.938	79.850	87.442
17	18.430	20.012	21.761	23.697	25.840	28.213	30.840	33.750	36.973	40.544	44.500	48.883	53.738	59.117	65.075	71.673	78.978	87.067	96.021	105.930
18	19.614	21.412	23.414	25.645	28.132	30.905	33.999	37.450	41.301	45.599	50.396	55.749	61.724	68.393	75.836	84.140	93.404	103.739	115.265	128.116
19	20.811	22.840	25.117	27.671	30.539	33.760	37.379	41.446	46.018	51.158	56.939	63.439	70.748	78.968	88.211	98.603	110.283	123.412	138.165	154.739
20	22.019	24.297	26.870	29.778	33.066	36.785	40.995	45.762	51.159	57.274	64.202	72.052	80.946	91.024	102.443	115.379	130.031	146.626	165.417	186.687
21	23.239	25.783	28.676	31.969	35.719	39.992	44.865	50.422	56.764	64.002	72.264	81.698	92.468	104.767	118.809	134.840	153.136	174.019	197.846	225.024
22	24.471	27.299	30.536	34.248	38.505	43.392	49.005	55.456	62.872	71.402	81.213	92.502	105.489	120.434	137.630	157.414	180.169	206.342	236.436	271.028
23	25.716	28.845	32.452	36.618	41.430	46.995	53.435	60.893	69.531	79.542	91.147	104.602	120.203	138.295	159.274	183.600	211.798	244.483	282.359	326.234
24	26.973	30.421	34.426	39.082	44.501	50.815	58.176	66.764	76.789	88.496	102.173	118.154	136.829	158.656	184.166	213.976	248.803	289.490	337.007	392.480
25	28.243	32.030	36.459	41.645	47.726	54.864	63.248	73.105	84.699	98.346	114.412	133.333	155.616	181.867	212.790	249.212	292.099	342.598	402.038	471.976
30	34.784	40.567	47.575	56.084	66.438	79.057	94.459	113.282	136.305	164.491	199.018	241.330	293.192	356.778	434.738	530.306	647.423	790.932	966.698	1181.865
35	41.659	49.994	60.461	73.651	90.318	111.432	138.234	172.314	215.705	271.018	341.583	431.658	546.663	693.552	881.152	1120.699	1426.448	1816.607	2314.173	2948.294
40	48.885	60.401	75.400	95.024	120.797	154.758	199.630	259.052	337.872	442.580	581.812	767.080	1013.667	1341.979	1779.048	2360.724	3134.412	4163.094	5529.711	7343.715
45	56.479	71.891	92.718	121.027	159.695	212.737	285.741	386.497	525.840	718.881	986.613	1358.208	1874.086	2590.464	3585.031	4965.191	6879.008	9531.258	13203.105	18280.914
50	64.461	84.577	112.794	152.664	209.341	290.325	406.516	573.756	815.051	1163.865	1668.723	2399.975	3459.344	4994.301	7217.488	10435.449	15088.805	21812.273	31514.492	45496.094

Using the Calculator to Compute the Future Value of an Ordinary Annuity

Hewlett-Packard HP 12C, 17 BII, and 19 BII[a]

Before you begin, make sure to clear the memory, ensure that you are in the *end mode* and that your calculator is set for *one payment per year*, and set the number of decimal places that you want (usually two for dollar-related accuracy).

Sample Problem

You want to know what the future value will be at the end of 5 years if you place five end-of-year deposits of $1,000 in an account paying 7% annually. What is your account balance at the end of 5 years?

[a] For the 12C, you would use the `n` key instead of the `N` key and use the `i` key instead of the `I%YR` key.
[b] The minus sign that precedes the solution should be ignored.

TABLE A-3 (Continued)

Period	21%	22%	23%	24%	25%	26%	27%	28%	29%	30%	31%	32%	33%	34%	35%	40%	45%	50%
1	1.000	1.000	1.000	1.000	1.000	1.000	1.000	1.000	1.000	1.000	1.000	1.000	1.000	1.000	1.000	1.000	1.000	1.000
2	2.210	2.220	2.230	2.240	2.250	2.260	2.270	2.280	2.290	2.300	2.310	2.320	2.330	2.340	2.350	2.400	2.450	2.500
3	3.674	3.708	3.743	3.778	3.813	3.848	3.883	3.918	3.954	3.990	4.026	4.062	4.099	4.136	4.172	4.360	4.552	4.750
4	5.446	5.524	5.604	5.684	5.766	5.848	5.931	6.016	6.101	6.187	6.274	6.362	6.452	6.542	6.633	7.104	7.601	8.125
5	7.589	7.740	7.893	8.048	8.207	8.368	8.533	8.700	8.870	9.043	9.219	9.398	9.581	9.766	9.954	10.946	12.022	13.188
6	10.183	10.442	10.708	10.980	11.259	11.544	11.837	12.136	12.442	12.756	13.077	13.406	13.742	14.086	14.438	16.324	18.431	20.781
7	13.321	13.740	14.171	14.615	15.073	15.546	16.032	16.534	17.051	17.583	18.131	18.696	19.277	19.876	20.492	23.853	27.725	32.172
8	17.119	17.762	18.430	19.123	19.842	20.588	21.361	22.163	22.995	23.858	24.752	25.678	26.638	27.633	28.664	34.395	41.202	49.258
9	21.714	22.670	23.669	24.712	25.802	26.940	28.129	29.369	30.664	32.015	33.425	34.895	36.429	38.028	39.696	49.152	60.743	74.887
10	27.274	28.657	30.113	31.643	33.253	34.945	36.723	38.592	40.556	42.619	44.786	47.062	49.451	51.958	54.590	69.813	89.077	113.330
11	34.001	35.962	38.039	40.238	42.566	45.030	47.639	50.398	53.318	56.405	59.670	63.121	66.769	70.624	74.696	98.739	130.161	170.995
12	42.141	44.873	47.787	50.895	54.208	57.738	61.501	65.510	69.780	74.326	79.167	84.320	89.803	95.636	101.840	139.234	189.734	257.493
13	51.991	55.745	59.778	64.109	68.760	73.750	79.106	84.853	91.016	97.624	104.709	112.302	120.438	129.152	138.484	195.928	276.114	387.239
14	63.909	69.009	74.528	80.496	86.949	93.925	101.465	109.611	118.411	127.912	138.169	149.239	161.183	174.063	187.953	275.299	401.365	581.858
15	78.330	85.191	92.669	100.815	109.687	119.346	129.860	141.302	153.750	167.285	182.001	197.996	215.373	234.245	254.737	386.418	582.980	873.788
16	95.779	104.933	114.983	126.010	138.109	151.375	165.922	181.867	199.337	218.470	239.421	262.354	287.446	314.888	344.895	541.985	846.321	1311.681
17	116.892	129.019	142.428	157.252	173.636	191.733	211.721	233.790	258.145	285.011	314.642	347.307	383.303	422.949	466.608	759.778	1228.165	1968.522
18	142.439	158.403	176.187	195.993	218.045	242.583	269.885	300.250	334.006	371.514	413.180	459.445	510.792	567.751	630.920	1064.689	1781.838	2953.783
19	173.351	194.251	217.710	244.031	273.556	306.654	343.754	385.321	431.868	483.968	542.266	607.467	680.354	761.786	852.741	1491.563	2584.665	4431.672
20	210.755	237.986	268.783	303.598	342.945	387.384	437.568	494.210	558.110	630.157	711.368	802.856	905.870	1021.792	1152.200	2089.188	3748.763	6648.508
21	256.013	291.343	331.603	377.461	429.681	489.104	556.710	633.589	720.962	820.204	932.891	1060.769	1205.807	1370.201	1556.470	2925.862	5436.703	9973.762
22	310.775	356.438	408.871	469.052	538.101	617.270	708.022	811.993	931.040	1067.265	1223.087	1401.215	1604.724	1837.068	2102.234	4097.203	7884.215	14961.645
23	377.038	435.854	503.911	582.624	673.626	778.760	900.187	1040.351	1202.042	1388.443	1603.243	1850.603	2135.282	2462.669	2839.014	5737.078	11433.109	22443.469
24	457.215	532.741	620.810	723.453	843.032	982.237	1144.237	1332.649	1551.634	1805.975	2101.247	2443.795	2840.924	3300.974	3833.667	8032.906	16579.008	33666.207
25	554.230	650.944	764.596	898.082	1054.791	1238.617	1454.180	1706.790	2002.608	2348.765	2753.631	3226.808	3779.428	4424.301	5176.445	11247.062	24040.555	50500.316
30	1445.111	1767.044	2160.459	2640.881	3227.172	3941.953	4812.891	5873.172	7162.785	8729.805	10632.543	12940.672	15737.945	19124.434	23221.258	60500.207	154105.313	383500.000
35	3755.814	4783.520	6090.227	7750.094	9856.746	12527.160	15909.480	20188.742	25596.512	32422.090	41028.887	51868.563	65504.199	82634.625	104134.500	325394.688	*	*
40	9749.141	12936.141	17153.691	22728.367	30088.621	39791.957	52570.707	69376.562	91447.375	120389.375	*	*	*	*	*	*	*	*
45	25294.223	34970.230	48300.660	66638.937	91831.312	126378.937	173692.875	238384.312	326686.375	447005.062	*	*	*	*	*	*	*	*

*Not shown because of space limitations.

Texas Instruments,
BA-35, BAII,
and BAII Plus[c]

Solution[d]
5,750.74

[c]For the Texas Instruments BAII, you would use the 2nd key instead of the CPT key; for the Texas Instruments BAII Plus, you would use the I/Y key instead of the %i key.
[d]If a minus sign precedes the solution, it should be ignored.

APPENDIX A

TABLE A-4 Present Value Interest Factors for a One-Dollar Annuity Discounted at i Percent for n Periods: $PVIFA_{i,n} = \sum_{t=1}^{n} \frac{1}{(1+i)^t}$

Period	1%	2%	3%	4%	5%	6%	7%	8%	9%	10%	11%	12%	13%	14%	15%	16%	17%	18%	19%	20%
1	.990	.980	.971	.962	.952	.943	.935	.926	.917	.909	.901	.893	.885	.877	.870	.862	.855	.847	.840	.833
2	1.970	1.942	1.913	1.886	1.859	1.833	1.808	1.783	1.759	1.736	1.713	1.690	1.668	1.647	1.626	1.605	1.585	1.566	1.547	1.528
3	2.941	2.884	2.829	2.775	2.723	2.673	2.624	2.577	2.531	2.487	2.444	2.402	2.361	2.322	2.283	2.246	2.210	2.174	2.140	2.106
4	3.902	3.808	3.717	3.630	3.546	3.465	3.387	3.312	3.240	3.170	3.102	3.037	2.974	2.914	2.855	2.798	2.743	2.690	2.639	2.589
5	4.853	4.713	4.580	4.452	4.329	4.212	4.100	3.993	3.890	3.791	3.696	3.605	3.517	3.433	3.352	3.274	3.199	3.127	3.058	2.991
6	5.795	5.601	5.417	5.242	5.076	4.917	4.767	4.623	4.486	4.355	4.231	4.111	3.998	3.889	3.784	3.685	3.589	3.498	3.410	3.326
7	6.728	6.472	6.230	6.002	5.786	5.582	5.389	5.206	5.033	4.868	4.712	4.564	4.423	4.288	4.160	4.039	3.922	3.812	3.706	3.605
8	7.652	7.326	7.020	6.733	6.463	6.210	5.971	5.747	5.535	5.335	5.146	4.968	4.799	4.639	4.487	4.344	4.207	4.078	3.954	3.837
9	8.566	8.162	7.786	7.435	7.108	6.802	6.515	6.247	5.995	5.759	5.537	5.328	5.132	4.946	4.772	4.607	4.451	4.303	4.163	4.031
10	9.471	8.983	8.530	8.111	7.722	7.360	7.024	6.710	6.418	6.145	5.889	5.650	5.426	5.216	5.019	4.833	4.659	4.494	4.339	4.192
11	10.368	9.787	9.253	8.760	8.306	7.887	7.499	7.139	6.805	6.495	6.207	5.938	5.687	5.453	5.234	5.029	4.836	4.656	4.486	4.327
12	11.255	10.575	9.954	9.385	8.863	8.384	7.943	7.536	7.161	6.814	6.492	6.194	5.918	5.660	5.421	5.197	4.988	4.793	4.611	4.439
13	12.134	11.348	10.635	9.986	9.394	8.853	8.358	7.904	7.487	7.103	6.750	6.424	6.122	5.842	5.583	5.342	5.118	4.910	4.715	4.533
14	13.004	12.106	11.296	10.563	9.899	9.295	8.745	8.244	7.786	7.367	6.982	6.628	6.302	6.002	5.724	5.468	5.229	5.008	4.802	4.611
15	13.865	12.849	11.938	11.118	10.380	9.712	9.108	8.560	8.061	7.606	7.191	6.811	6.462	6.142	5.847	5.575	5.324	5.092	4.876	4.675
16	14.718	13.578	12.561	11.652	10.838	10.106	9.447	8.851	8.313	7.824	7.379	6.974	6.604	6.265	5.954	5.668	5.405	5.162	4.938	4.730
17	15.562	14.292	13.166	12.166	11.274	10.477	9.763	9.122	8.544	8.022	7.549	7.120	6.729	6.373	6.047	5.749	5.475	5.222	4.990	4.775
18	16.398	14.992	13.754	12.659	11.690	10.828	10.059	9.372	8.756	8.201	7.702	7.250	6.840	6.467	6.128	5.818	5.534	5.273	5.033	4.812
19	17.226	15.679	14.324	13.134	12.085	11.158	10.336	9.604	8.950	8.365	7.839	7.366	6.938	6.550	6.198	5.877	5.584	5.316	5.070	4.843
20	18.046	16.352	14.878	13.590	12.462	11.470	10.594	9.818	9.129	8.514	7.963	7.469	7.025	6.623	6.259	5.929	5.628	5.353	5.101	4.870
21	18.857	17.011	15.415	14.029	12.821	11.764	10.836	10.017	9.292	8.649	8.075	7.562	7.102	6.687	6.312	5.973	5.665	5.384	5.127	4.891
22	19.661	17.658	15.937	14.451	13.163	12.042	11.061	10.201	9.442	8.772	8.176	7.645	7.170	6.743	6.359	6.011	5.696	5.410	5.149	4.909
23	20.456	18.292	16.444	14.857	13.489	12.303	11.272	10.371	9.580	8.883	8.266	7.718	7.230	6.792	6.399	6.044	5.723	5.432	5.167	4.925
24	21.244	18.914	16.936	15.247	13.799	12.550	11.469	10.529	9.707	8.985	8.348	7.784	7.283	6.835	6.434	6.073	5.746	5.451	5.182	4.937
25	22.023	19.524	17.413	15.622	14.094	12.783	11.654	10.675	9.823	9.077	8.422	7.843	7.330	6.873	6.464	6.097	5.766	5.467	5.195	4.948
30	25.808	22.396	19.601	17.292	15.373	13.765	12.409	11.258	10.274	9.427	8.694	8.055	7.496	7.003	6.566	6.177	5.829	5.517	5.235	4.979
35	29.409	24.999	21.487	18.665	16.374	14.498	12.948	11.655	10.567	9.644	8.855	8.176	7.586	7.070	6.617	6.215	5.858	5.539	5.251	4.992
40	32.835	27.356	23.115	19.793	17.159	15.046	13.332	11.925	10.757	9.779	8.951	8.244	7.634	7.105	6.642	6.233	5.871	5.548	5.258	4.997
45	36.095	29.490	24.519	20.720	17.774	15.456	13.606	12.108	10.881	9.863	9.008	8.283	7.661	7.123	6.654	6.242	5.877	5.552	5.261	4.999
50	39.196	31.424	25.730	21.482	18.256	15.762	13.801	12.233	10.962	9.915	9.042	8.304	7.675	7.133	6.661	6.246	5.880	5.554	5.262	4.999

Using the Calculator to Compute the Present Value of an Annuity

Before you begin, make sure to clear the memory, ensure that you are in the *end mode* and that your calculator is set for *one payment per year,* and set the number of decimal places that you want (usually two for dollar-related accuracy).

Sample Problem

You want to know what the present value of an annuity of $700 received at the end of each year for 5 years, given a discount rate of 8%.

Hewlett-Packard HP 12C, 17 BII, and 19 BII[a]

Input	Function
700	PMT
5	N
8	I%YR
	PV

Solution[b]
2,794.90

---

[a] For the 12C, you would use the **n** key instead of the **N** key and use the **i** key instead of the **I%YR** key.
[b] The minus sign that precedes the solution should be ignored.

Financial Tables **A-9**

TABLE A–4 (Continued)

Period	21%	22%	23%	24%	25%	26%	27%	28%	29%	30%	31%	32%	33%	34%	35%	40%	45%	50%
1	.826	.820	.813	.806	.800	.794	.787	.781	.775	.769	.763	.758	.752	.746	.741	.714	.690	.667
2	1.509	1.492	1.474	1.457	1.440	1.424	1.407	1.392	1.376	1.361	1.346	1.331	1.317	1.303	1.289	1.224	1.165	1.111
3	2.074	2.042	2.011	1.981	1.952	1.923	1.896	1.868	1.842	1.816	1.791	1.766	1.742	1.719	1.696	1.589	1.493	1.407
4	2.540	2.494	2.448	2.404	2.362	2.320	2.280	2.241	2.203	2.166	2.130	2.096	2.062	2.029	1.997	1.849	1.720	1.605
5	2.926	2.864	2.803	2.745	2.689	2.635	2.583	2.532	2.483	2.436	2.390	2.345	2.302	2.260	2.220	2.035	1.876	1.737
6	3.245	3.167	3.092	3.020	2.951	2.885	2.821	2.759	2.700	2.643	2.588	2.534	2.483	2.433	2.385	2.168	1.983	1.824
7	3.508	3.416	3.327	3.242	3.161	3.083	3.009	2.937	2.868	2.802	2.739	2.677	2.619	2.562	2.508	2.263	2.057	1.883
8	3.726	3.619	3.518	3.421	3.329	3.241	3.156	3.076	2.999	2.925	2.854	2.786	2.721	2.658	2.598	2.331	2.109	1.922
9	3.905	3.786	3.673	3.566	3.463	3.366	3.273	3.184	3.100	3.019	2.942	2.868	2.798	2.730	2.665	2.379	2.144	1.948
10	4.054	3.923	3.799	3.682	3.570	3.465	3.364	3.269	3.178	3.092	3.009	2.930	2.855	2.784	2.715	2.414	2.168	1.965
11	4.177	4.035	3.902	3.776	3.656	3.544	3.437	3.335	3.239	3.147	3.060	2.978	2.899	2.824	2.752	2.438	2.185	1.977
12	4.278	4.127	3.985	3.851	3.725	3.606	3.493	3.387	3.286	3.190	3.100	3.013	2.931	2.853	2.779	2.456	2.196	1.985
13	4.362	4.203	4.053	3.912	3.780	3.656	3.538	3.427	3.322	3.223	3.129	3.040	2.956	2.876	2.799	2.469	2.204	1.990
14	4.432	4.265	4.108	3.962	3.824	3.695	3.573	3.459	3.351	3.249	3.152	3.061	2.974	2.892	2.814	2.478	2.210	1.993
15	4.489	4.315	4.153	4.001	3.859	3.726	3.601	3.483	3.373	3.268	3.170	3.076	2.988	2.905	2.825	2.484	2.214	1.995
16	4.536	4.357	4.189	4.033	3.887	3.751	3.623	3.503	3.390	3.283	3.183	3.088	2.999	2.914	2.834	2.489	2.216	1.997
17	4.576	4.391	4.219	4.059	3.910	3.771	3.640	3.518	3.403	3.295	3.193	3.097	3.007	2.921	2.840	2.492	2.218	1.998
18	4.608	4.419	4.243	4.080	3.928	3.786	3.654	3.529	3.413	3.304	3.201	3.104	3.012	2.926	2.844	2.494	2.219	1.999
19	4.635	4.442	4.263	4.097	3.942	3.799	3.664	3.539	3.421	3.311	3.207	3.109	3.017	2.930	2.848	2.496	2.220	1.999
20	4.657	4.460	4.279	4.110	3.954	3.808	3.673	3.546	3.427	3.316	3.211	3.113	3.020	2.933	2.850	2.497	2.221	1.999
21	4.675	4.476	4.292	4.121	3.963	3.816	3.679	3.551	3.432	3.320	3.215	3.116	3.023	2.935	2.852	2.498	2.221	2.000
22	4.690	4.488	4.302	4.130	3.970	3.822	3.684	3.556	3.436	3.323	3.217	3.118	3.025	2.936	2.853	2.498	2.222	2.000
23	4.703	4.499	4.311	4.137	3.976	3.827	3.689	3.559	3.438	3.325	3.219	3.120	3.026	2.938	2.854	2.499	2.222	2.000
24	4.713	4.507	4.318	4.143	3.981	3.831	3.692	3.562	3.441	3.327	3.221	3.121	3.027	2.939	2.855	2.499	2.222	2.000
25	4.721	4.514	4.323	4.147	3.985	3.834	3.694	3.564	3.442	3.329	3.222	3.122	3.028	2.939	2.856	2.499	2.222	2.000
30	4.746	4.534	4.339	4.160	3.995	3.842	3.701	3.569	3.447	3.332	3.225	3.124	3.030	2.941	2.857	2.500	2.222	2.000
35	4.756	4.541	4.345	4.164	3.998	3.845	3.703	3.571	3.448	3.333	3.226	3.125	3.030	2.941	2.857	2.500	2.222	2.000
40	4.760	4.544	4.347	4.166	3.999	3.846	3.703	3.571	3.448	3.333	3.226	3.125	3.030	2.941	2.857	2.500	2.222	2.000
45	4.761	4.545	4.347	4.166	4.000	3.846	3.704	3.571	3.448	3.333	3.226	3.125	3.030	2.941	2.857	2.500	2.222	2.000
50	4.762	4.545	4.348	4.167	4.000	3.846	3.704	3.571	3.448	3.333	3.226	3.125	3.030	2.941	2.857	2.500	2.222	2.000

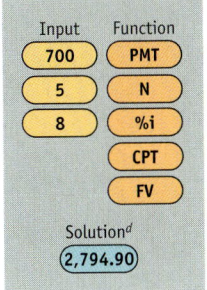

[c]For the Texas Instruments BAII, you would use the **2nd** key instead of the **CPT** key; for the Texas Instruments BAII Plus, you would use the **I/Y** key instead of the **%i** key.

[d]If a minus sign precedes the solution, it should be ignored.

Appendix B

Solutions to Self-Test Problems

Chapter 1

ST1–1 a. Capital gains = $180,000 sale price − $150,000 original purchase price = $30,000

b. Total taxable income = $280,000 operating earnings + $30,000 capital gain = $310,000

c. Firm's tax liability:

Using Table 1.3:

Total taxes due = $22,250 + [0.39 × ($310,000 − $100,000)]
= $22,250 + (0.39 × $210,000) = $22,250 + $81,900
= $104,150

d. Average tax rate = $\dfrac{\$104,150}{\$310,000}$ = 33.6%

Marginal tax rate = 39%

Chapter 2

ST2–1

Ratio	Too high	Too low
Current ratio = current assets/current liabilities	May indicate that the firm is holding excessive cash, accounts receivable, or inventory.	May indicate poor ability to satisfy short-term obligations.
Inventory turnover = CGS/inventory	May indicate lower level of inventory, which may cause stockouts and lost sales.	May indicate poor inventory management, excessive inventory, or obsolete inventory.
Times interest earned = earnings before interest and taxes/interest	✗	May indicate poor ability to pay contractual interest payments.
Gross profit margin = gross profits/sales	Indicates the low cost of merchandise sold relative to the sales price; may indicate noncompetitive pricing and potential lost sales.	Indicates the high cost of the merchandise sold relative to the sales price; may indicate either a low sales price or a high cost of goods sold.
Return on total assets = net profits after taxes/total assets	✗	Indicates ineffective management in generating profits with the available assets.
Price/earnings (P/E) ratio = market price per share of common stock/earnings per share	Investors may have an excessive degree of confidence in the firm's future and underestimate its risk.	Investors lack confidence in the firm's future outcomes and feel that the firm has an excessive level of risk.

ST2–2

O'Keefe Industries
Balance Sheet
December 31, 2006

Assets		Liabilities and Stockholders' Equity	
Cash	$ 32,720	Accounts payable	$ 120,000
Marketable securities	25,000	Notes payable	160,000[e]
Accounts receivable	197,280[a]	Accruals	20,000
Inventories	225,000[b]	Total current liabilities	$ 300,000[d]
Total current assets	$ 480,000	Long-term debt	$ 600,000[f]
Net fixed assets	$1,020,000[c]	Stockholders' equity	$ 600,000
Total assets	$1,500,000	Total liabilities and stockholders' equity	$1,500,000

[a] Average collection period (ACP) = 40 days
ACP = Accounts receivable/Average sales per day
40 = Accounts receivable/($1,800,000/365)
40 = Accounts receivable/$4,932
$197,280 = Accounts receivable

[b] Inventory turnover = 6.0
Inventory turnover = Cost of goods sold/Inventory
6.0 = [Sales × (1 − Gross profit margin)]/Inventory
6.0 = [$1,800,000 × (1 − 0.25)]/Inventory
$225,000 = Inventory

[c] Total asset turnover = 1.20
Total asset turnover = Sales/Total assets
1.20 = $1,800,000/Total assets
$1,500,000 = Total assets
Total assets = Current assets + Net fixed assets
$1,500,000 = $480,000 + Net fixed assets
$1,020,000 = Net fixed assets

[d] Current ratio = 1.60
Current ratio = Current assets/Current liabilities
1.60 = $480,000/Current liabilities
$300,000 = Current liabilities

[e] Notes payable = Total current liabilities − Accounts payable − Accruals
= $300,000 − $120,000 − $20,000
= $160,000

[f] Debt ratio = 0.60
Debt ratio = Total liabilities/Total assets
0.60 = Total liabilities/$1,500,000
$900,000 = Total liabilities

Total liabilities = Current liabilities + Long-term debt
$900,000 = $300,000 + Long-term debt
$600,000 = Long-term debt

Chapter 3

ST3–1 **a.** Depreciation schedule

Year	Cost[a] (1)	Percentages (from Table 3.2) (2)	Depreciation [(1) × (2)] (3)
1	$150,000	20%	$30,000
2	150,000	32	48,000
3	150,000	19	28,500
4	150,000	12	18,000
5	150,000	12	18,000
6	150,000	5	7,500
Totals		100%	$150,000

[a] $140,000 asset cost + $10,000 installation cost.

b. Accounting definition:

Year	EBIT (1)	Interest (2)	Net profits before taxes [(1) − (2)] (3)	Taxes [0.40 × (3)] (4)	Net profits after taxes [(3) − (4)] (5)	Depreciation (from part a, col. 3) (6)	Cash flows from operations [(5) + (6)] (7)
1	$160,000	$15,000	$145,000	$58,000	$87,000	$30,000	$117,000
2	160,000	15,000	145,000	58,000	87,000	48,000	135,000
3	160,000	15,000	145,000	58,000	87,000	28,500	115,500
4	160,000	15,000	145,000	58,000	87,000	18,000	105,000
5	160,000	15,000	145,000	58,000	87,000	18,000	105,000
6	160,000	15,000	145,000	58,000	87,000	7,500	94,500

Financial definition:

Year	EBIT (1)	NOPAT [(1) × (1 − 0.40)] (2)	Depreciation (3)	Operating cash flows [(2) + (3)] (4)
1	$160,000	$96,000	$30,000	$126,000
2	160,000	96,000	48,000	144,000
3	160,000	96,000	28,500	124,500
4	160,000	96,000	18,000	114,000
5	160,000	96,000	18,000	114,000
6	160,000	96,000	7,500	103,500

c. Change in net fixed assets in year 6 = $0 − $7,500 = −$7,500

   NFAI in year 6 = −$7,500 + $7,500 = $0

   Change in current assets in year 6 = $110,000 − $90,000 = $20,000

   Change in (Accounts payable + Accruals) in year 6 = ($45,000 + $7,000) − ($40,000 + $8,000) = $52,000 − $48,000 = $4,000

   NCAI in year 6 = $20,000 − $4,000 = $16,000

   For year 6

   FCF = OCF − NFAI − NCAI

   = $103,500* − $0 − $16,000 = $87,500

   *From part b financial definition, column 4 value for year 6.

d. In part b we can see that in each of the six years, the operating cash flow is greater when viewed from a financial perspective than when viewed from a strict accounting point of view. This difference results from the fact that the accounting definition includes interest as an operating flow, whereas the financial definition excludes it. This causes (in this case) each year's accounting flow to be $9,000 below the financial flow; $9,000 is equal to the after-tax cost of the $15,000 annual interest, $15,000 × (1 − 0.40). The free cash flow (FCF) calculated in part c for year 6 represents the cash flow available to investors—providers of debt and equity—after covering all operating needs and paying for net fixed asset investment (NFAI) and net current asset investment (NCAI) that occurred during the year.

ST3–2 a.

	Caroll Company Cash Budget April–June					Accounts receivable at end of June	
	February	March	April	May	June	July	August
Forecast sales	$500	$600	$400	$200	$200		
Cash sales (0.30)	$150	$180	$120	$ 60	$ 60		
Collections of A/R							
Lagged 1 month [(0.7 × 0.7) = 0.49]		245	294	196	98	$ 98	
Lagged 2 months [(0.3 × 0.7) = 0.21]			105	126	84	42	$42
						$140 + $42 = $182	
Total cash receipts			$519	$382	$242		
Less: Total cash disbursements			600	500	200		
Net cash flow			($ 81)	($118)	$ 42		
Add: Beginning cash			115	34	(84)		
Ending cash			$ 34	($ 84)	($ 42)		
Less: Minimum cash balance			25	25	25		
Required total financing (notes payable)			—	$109	$ 67		
Excess cash balance (marketable securities)			$ 9	—	—		

b. Caroll Company would need a maximum of $109 in financing over the 3-month period.

c.

Account	Amount	Source of amount
Cash	$ 25	Minimum cash balance—June
Notes payable	67	Required total financing—June
Marketable securities	0	Excess cash balance—June
Accounts receivable	182	Calculation at right of cash budget statement

ST3–3 a.

**Euro Designs, Inc.,
Pro Forma Income Statement
for the Year Ended December 31, 2007**

Sales revenue (given)	$3,900,000
Less: Cost of goods sold (0.55)^a	2,145,000
Gross profits	$1,755,000
Less: Operating expenses (0.12)^b	468,000
Operating profits	$1,287,000
Less: Interest expense (given)	325,000
Net profits before taxes	$ 962,000
Less: Taxes (0.40 × $962,000)	384,800
Net profits after taxes	$ 577,200
Less: Cash dividends (given)	320,000
To retained earnings	$ 257,200

^{a}From 2006: CGS/Sales = $1,925,000/$3,500,000 = 0.55.
^{b}From 2006: Oper. Exp./Sales = $420,000/$3,500,000 = 0.12.

b. The percent-of-sales method may underestimate actual 2007 pro forma income by assuming that all costs are variable. If the firm has fixed costs, which by definition would not increase with increasing sales, the 2007 pro forma income would probably be underestimated.

Chapter 4

ST4–1 a. *Bank A:*

$FV_3 = \$10,000 \times FVIF_{4\%/3yrs} = \$10,000 \times 1.125 = \underline{\$11,250}$

(Calculator solution = $11,248.64)

Bank B:

$FV_3 = \$10,000 \times FVIF_{4\%/2, 2 \times 3yrs} = \$10,000 \times FVIF_{2\%, 6yrs}$
$= \$10,000 \times 1.126 = \underline{\$11,260}$

(Calculator solution = $11,261.62)

Bank C:

$FV_3 = \$10,000 \times FVIF_{4\%/4, 4 \times 3yrs} = \$10,000 \times FVIF_{1\%, 12yrs}$
$= \$10,000 \times 1.127 = \underline{\$11,270}$

(Calculator solution = $11,268.25)

b. *Bank A:*

$$EAR = (1 + 4\%/1)^1 - 1 = (1 + 0.04)^1 - 1 = 1.04 - 1 = 0.04 = \underline{\underline{4\%}}$$

Bank B:

$$EAR = (1 + 4\%/2)^2 - 1 = (1 + 0.02)^2 - 1 = 1.0404 - 1 = 0.0404 = \underline{\underline{4.04\%}}$$

Bank C:

$$EAR = (1 + 4\%/4)^4 - 1 = (1 + 0.01)^4 - 1 = 1.0406 - 1 = 0.0406 = \underline{\underline{4.06\%}}$$

c. Ms. Martin should deal with Bank C: The quarterly compounding of interest at the given 4% rate results in the highest future value as a result of the corresponding highest effective annual rate.

d. *Bank D:*

$$FV_3 = \$10,000 \times FVIF_{4\%, 3yrs} \text{ (continuous compounding)}$$
$$= \$10,000 \times e^{0.04 \times 3} = \$10,000 \times e^{0.12}$$
$$= \$10,000 \times 1.127497$$
$$= \underline{\underline{\$11,274.97}}$$

This alternative is better than Bank C; it results in a higher future value because of the use of continuous compounding, which with otherwise identical cash flows always results in the highest future value of any compounding period.

ST4–2 a. On a purely subjective basis, annuity Y looks more attractive than annuity X because it provides $1,000 more each year than does annuity X. Of course, the fact that Ramesh can earn 15% on annuity X and only 11% on annuity Y will impact this decision.

b. *Annuity X:*

$$FVA_6 = \$9,000 \times FVIFA_{15\%, 6yrs}$$
$$= \$9,000 \times 8.754 = \underline{\underline{\$78,786.00}}$$

(Calculator solution = $78,783.65)

Annuity Y:

$$FVA_6 = \$10,000 \times FVIFA_{11\%, 6yrs}$$
$$= \$10,000 \times 7.913 = \underline{\underline{\$79,130.00}}$$

(Calculator solution = $79,128.60)

c. Annuity Y is more attractive, because its future value at the end of year 6, FVA_6, of $79,130.00 is greater than annuity X's end-of-year-6 future value, FVA_6, of $78,786.00. The subjective assessment in part a was correct. The benefit of receiving annuity Y's $1,000 larger cash inflows each year appears to have outweighed the fact that Ramesh will earn 15% annually on annuity X and only 11% annually on annuity Y.

ST4–3 *Alternative A:*

Cash flow stream:

$PVA_5 = \$700 \times PVIFA_{9\%, 5yrs}$
$= \$700 \times 3.890 = \underline{\underline{\$2,723}}$

(Calculator solution = $2,722.76)

Single amount: $\underline{\underline{\$2,825}}$

Alternative B:

Cash flow stream:

Year (n)	Cash flow (1)	$FVIF_{9\%, n}$ (2)	Present value [(1) × (2)] (3)
1	$1,100	0.917	$1,008.70
2	900	0.842	757.80
3	700	0.772	540.40
4	500	0.708	354.00
5	300	0.650	195.00
		Present value	$2,855.90

(Calculator solution = $2,856.41)

Single amount: $\underline{\underline{\$2,800}}$

Conclusion: Alternative B in the form of a cash flow stream is preferred because its present value of $2,855.90 is greater than the other three values.

ST4–4 $FVA_5 = \$8,000$; $FVIFA_{7\%, 5yrs} = 5.751$; $PMT = ?$

$FVA_n = PMT \times (FVIFA_{k,n})$ [Equation 4.14 or 4.23]

$\$8,000 = PMT \times 5.751$

$PMT = \$8,000/5.751 = \underline{\underline{\$1,391.06}}$

(Calculator solution = $1,391.13)

Judi should deposit $1,391.06 at the end of each of the 5 years to meet her goal of accumulating $8,000 at the end of the fifth year.

Chapter 5

ST5–1 a. Expected return, $\bar{k} = \dfrac{\Sigma \text{Returns}}{3}$ (*Equation 5.2a in footnote 1*)

$\bar{k}_A = \dfrac{12\% + 14\% + 16\%}{3} = \dfrac{42\%}{3} = \underline{\underline{14\%}}$

$\bar{k}_B = \dfrac{16\% + 14\% + 12\%}{3} = \dfrac{42\%}{3} = \underline{\underline{14\%}}$

$\bar{k}_C = \dfrac{12\% + 14\% + 16\%}{3} = \dfrac{42\%}{3} = \underline{\underline{14\%}}$

b. Standard deviation, $\sigma_k = \sqrt{\dfrac{\sum_{j=1}^{n}(k_j - \bar{k})^2}{n-1}}$ (Equation 5.3a in footnote 2)

$$\sigma_{k_A} = \sqrt{\dfrac{(12\% - 14\%)^2 + (14\% - 14\%)^2 + (16\% - 14\%)^2}{3-1}}$$

$$= \sqrt{\dfrac{4\% + 0\% + 4\%}{2}} = \sqrt{\dfrac{8\%}{2}} = \underline{\underline{2\%}}$$

$$\sigma_{k_B} = \sqrt{\dfrac{(16\% - 14\%)^2 + (14\% - 14\%)^2 + (12\% - 14\%)^2}{3-1}}$$

$$= \sqrt{\dfrac{4\% + 0\% + 4\%}{2}} = \sqrt{\dfrac{8\%}{2}} = \underline{\underline{2\%}}$$

$$\sigma_{k_C} = \sqrt{\dfrac{(12\% - 14\%)^2 + (14\% - 14\%)^2 + (16\% - 14\%)^2}{3-1}}$$

$$= \sqrt{\dfrac{4\% + 0\% + 4\%}{2}} = \sqrt{\dfrac{8\%}{2}} = \underline{\underline{2\%}}$$

c.

	Annual expected returns	
Year	Portfolio AB	Portfolio AC
2007	$(0.50 \times 12\%) + (0.50 \times 16\%) = 14\%$	$(0.50 \times 12\%) + (0.50 \times 12\%) = 12\%$
2008	$(0.50 \times 14\%) + (0.50 \times 14\%) = 14\%$	$(0.50 \times 14\%) + (0.50 \times 14\%) = 14\%$
2009	$(0.50 \times 16\%) + (0.50 \times 12\%) = 14\%$	$(0.50 \times 16\%) + (0.50 \times 16\%) = 16\%$

Over the 3-year period:

$$\bar{k}_{AB} = \dfrac{14\% + 14\% + 14\%}{3} = \dfrac{42\%}{3} = \underline{\underline{14\%}}$$

$$\bar{k}_{AC} = \dfrac{12\% + 14\% + 16\%}{3} = \dfrac{42\%}{3} = \underline{\underline{14\%}}$$

d. AB is perfectly negatively correlated.
AC is perfectly positively correlated.

e. Standard deviation of the portfolios

$$\sigma_{k_{AB}} = \sqrt{\dfrac{(14\% - 14\%)^2 + (14\% - 14\%)^2 + (14\% - 14\%)^2}{3-1}}$$

$$= \sqrt{\dfrac{(0\% + 0\% + 0\%)}{2}} = \sqrt{\dfrac{0\%}{2}} = \underline{\underline{0\%}}$$

$$\sigma_{k_{AC}} = \sqrt{\dfrac{(12\% - 14\%)^2 + (14\% - 14\%)^2 + (16\% - 14\%)^2}{3-1}}$$

$$= \sqrt{\dfrac{4\% + 0\% + 4\%}{2}} = \sqrt{\dfrac{8\%}{2}} = \underline{\underline{2\%}}$$

f. Portfolio AB is preferred, because it provides the same return (14%) as AC but with less risk [$(\sigma_{k_{AB}}=0\%)<(\sigma_{k_{AC}}=2\%)$].

ST5–2 a. When the market return increases by 10%, the project's required return would be expected to increase by 15% ($1.50 \times 10\%$). When the market return decreases by 10%, the project's required return would be expected to decrease by 15% [$1.50 \times (-10\%)$].

b. $k_j = R_F + [b_j \times (k_m - R_F)]$
$= 7\% + [1.50 \times (10\% - 7\%)]$
$= 7\% + 4.5\% = \underline{\underline{11.5\%}}$

c. No, the project should be rejected, because its *expected* return of 11% is less than the 11.5% return *required* from the project.

d. $k_j = 7\% + [1.50 \times (9\% - 7\%)]$
$= 7\% + 3\% = \underline{\underline{10\%}}$

The project would now be acceptable, because its *expected* return of 11% is now in excess of the *required* return, which has declined to 10% as a result of investors in the marketplace becoming less risk-averse.

Chapter 6

ST6–1 a. $B_0 = I \times (PVIFA_{k_d,n}) + M \times (PVIF_{k_d,n})$
$I = 0.08 \times \$1,000 = \$80$
$M = \$1,000$
$n = 12$ yrs
(1) $k_d = 7\%$
$B_0 = \$80 \times (PVIFA_{7\%,12yrs}) + \$1,000 \times (PVIF_{7\%,12yrs})$
$= (\$80 \times 7.943) + (\$1,000 \times 0.444)$
$= \$635.44 + \$444.00 = \underline{\underline{\$1,079.44}}$

(Calculator solution = $1,079.43)
(2) $k_d = 8\%$
$B_0 = \$80 \times (PVIFA_{8\%,12yrs}) + \$1,000 \times (PVIF_{8\%,12yrs})$
$= (\$80 \times 7.536) + (\$1,000 \times 0.397)$
$= \$602.88 + \$397.00 = \underline{\underline{\$999.88}}$

(Calculator solution = $1,000)
(3) $k_d = 10\%$
$B_0 = \$80 \times (PVIFA_{10\%,12yrs}) + \$1,000 \times (PVIF_{10\%,12yrs})$
$= (\$80 \times 6.814) + (\$1,000 \times 0.319)$
$= \$545.12 + \$319.00 = \underline{\underline{\$864.12}}$

(Calculator solution = $863.73)

b. (1) $k_d = 7\%$, $B_0 = \$1,079.44$; sells at a *premium*
(2) $k_d = 8\%$, $B_0 = \$999.88 \approx \$1,000.00$; sells at its *par value*
(3) $k_d = 10\%$, $B_0 = \$864.12$; sells at a *discount*

c. $B_0 = \dfrac{I}{2} \times (PVIFA_{k_d/2, 2n}) + M \times (PVIF_{k_d/2, 2n})$

$= \dfrac{\$80}{2} \times (PVIFA_{10\%/2, 2 \times 12\text{periods}}) + \$1,000 \times (PVIF_{10\%/2, 2 \times 12\text{periods}})$

$= \$40 \times (PVIFA_{5\%, 24\text{periods}}) + \$1,000 \times (PVIF_{5\%, 24\text{periods}})$

$= (\$40 \times 13.799) + (\$1,000 \times 0.310)$

$= \$551.96 + \$310.00 = \underline{\underline{\$861.96}}$

(Calculator solution = $862.01)

ST6–2 a. $B_0 = \$1,150$
$I = 0.11 \times \$1,000 = \$110$
$M = \$1,000$
$n = 18$ yrs

$\$1,150 = \$110 \times (PVIFA_{k_d, 18\text{yrs}}) + \$1,000 \times (PVIF_{k_d, 18\text{yrs}})$

Because if $k_d = 11\%$, $B_0 = \$1,000 = M$, try $k_d = 10\%$.

$B_0 = \$110 \times (PVIFA_{10\%, 18\text{yrs}}) + \$1,000 \times (PVIF_{10\%, 18\text{yrs}})$
$= (\$110 \times 8.201) + (\$1,000 \times 0.180)$
$= \$902.11 + \$180.00 = \$1,082.11$

Because $\$1,082.11 < \$1,150$, try $k_d = 9\%$.

$B_0 = \$110 \times (PVIFA_{9\%, 18\text{yrs}}) + \$1,000 \times (PVIF_{9\%, 18\text{yrs}})$
$= (\$110 \times 8.756) + (\$1,000 \times 0.212)$
$= \$963.16 + \$212.00 = \$1,175.16$

Because the $1,175.16 value at 9% is higher than $1,150, and the $1,082.11 value at 10% rate is lower than $1,150, the bond's yield to maturity must be between 9% and 10%. Because the $1,175.16 value is closer to $1,150, rounding to the nearest whole percent, the YTM is 9%. (By using interpolation, the more precise YTM value is 9.27%.)

(Calculator solution = 9.26%)

b. The calculated YTM of 9+% is below the bond's 11% coupon interest rate, because the bond's market value of $1,150 is above its $1,000 par value. Whenever a bond's market value is above its par value (it sells at a *premium*), its YTM will be below its coupon interest rate; when a bond sells at *par*, the YTM will equal its coupon interest rate; and when the bond sells for less than par (at a *discount*), its YTM will be greater than its coupon interest rate.

Chapter 7

ST7-1 $D_0 = \$1.80/\text{share}$
$k_s = 12\%$

a. *Zero growth:*
$$P_0 = \frac{D_1}{k_s} = \frac{D_1 = D_0 = \$1.80}{0.12} = \underline{\underline{\$15/\text{share}}}$$

b. *Constant growth, g = 5%:*
$D_1 = D_0 \times (1+g) = \$1.80 = (1+0.05) = \$1.89/\text{share}$
$$P_0 = \frac{D_1}{k_s - g} = \frac{\$1.89}{0.12 - 0.05} = \frac{\$1.89}{0.07} = \underline{\underline{\$27/\text{share}}}$$

ST7-2 a. **Step 1:** Present value of free cash flow from end of 2011 to infinity measured at the end of 2010.

$FCF_{2011} = \$1,500,000 \times (1+0.04) = \$1,560,000$

$$\text{Value of } FCF_{2011 \to \infty} = \frac{\$1,560,000}{0.10 - 0.04} = \frac{\$1,560,000}{0.06} = \underline{\underline{\$26,000,000}}$$

Step 2: Add the value found in Step 1 to the 2010 FCF.
Total $FCF_{2010} = \$1,500,000 + \$26,000,000 = \underline{\underline{\$27,500,000}}$

Step 3: Find the sum of the present values of the FCFs for 2007 through 2010 to determine company value, V_C.

Year (t)	FCF_t (1)	$PVIF_{10\%,t}$ (2)	Present value of FCF_t [(1) × (2)] (3)
2007	$ 800,000	0.909	$ 727,200
2008	1,200,000	0.826	991,200
2009	1,400,000	0.751	1,051,400
2010	27,500,000	0.683	18,782,500
		Value of entire company, V_C =	$21,552,300

(Calculator solution = $21,553,719)

b. Common Stock value, $V_S = V_C - V_D - V_P$
$V_C = \$21,552,300$ (calculated in part a)
$V_D = \$12,500,000$ (given)
$V_P = \$0$ (given)
$V_S = \$21,552,300 - \$12,500,000 - \$0 = \underline{\underline{\$9,052,300}}$
(Calculator solution = $9,053,719)

c. Price per share = $\dfrac{\$9,052,300}{500,000} = \underline{\underline{\$18.10/\text{share}}}$

(Calculator solution = $18.11/share)

Chapter 8

ST8–1 **a.** Book value = Installed cost − Accumulated depreciation
Installed cost = $50,000
Accumulated depreciation = $50,000 × (0.20 + 0.32 + 0.19 + 0.12)
   = $50,000 × 0.83 = $41,500
Book value = $50,000 − $41,500 = $8,500

b. Taxes on sale of old equipment:
Gain on sale = Sale price − Book value
   = $55,000 − $8,500 = $46,500
Taxes = 0.40 × $46,500 = $18,600

c. Initial investment:

Installed cost of new equipment		
Cost of new equipment	$75,000	
+ Installation costs	5,000	
Total installed cost—new		$80,000
− After-tax proceeds from sale of old equipment		
Proceeds from sale of old equipment	$55,000	
− Taxes on sale of old equipment	18,600	
Total after-tax proceeds—old		36,400
+ Change in net working capital		15,000
Initial investment		$58,600

ST8–2 **a.** Initial investment:

Installed cost of new machine		
Cost of new machine	$140,000	
+ Installation costs	10,000	
Total installed cost—new (depreciable value)		$150,000
− After-tax proceeds from sale of old machine		
Proceeds from sale of old machine	$ 42,000	
− Taxes on sale of old machine[1]	9,120	
Total after-tax proceeds—old		32,880
+ Change in net working capital[2]		20,000
Initial investment		$137,120

---

[1]Book value of old machine = $40,000 − [(0.20 + 0.32) × $40,000]
   = $40,000 − (0.52 × $40,000)
   = $40,000 − $20,800 = $19,200
Gain on sale = $42,000 − $19,200 = $22,800
Taxes = .40 × $22,800 = $9,120

[2]Change in net working capital = +$10,000 + $25,000 − $15,000
   = $35,000 − $15,000 = $20,000

b. Incremental operating cash inflows:

Calculation of Depreciation Expense

Year	Cost (1)	Applicable MACRS depreciation percentages (from Table 3.2) (2)	Depreciation [(1) × (2)] (3)
With new machine			
1	$150,000	33%	$ 49,500
2	150,000	45	67,500
3	150,000	15	22,500
4	150,000	7	10,500
		Totals 100%	$150,000
With old machine			
2	$ 40,000	19% (year-3 depreciation)	$ 7,600
2	40,000	12 (year-4 depreciation)	4,800
3	40,000	12 (year-5 depreciation)	4,800
4	40,000	5 (year-6 depreciation)	2,000
		Total	$19,200[a]

[a]The total of $19,200 represents the book value of the old machine at the end of the second year, which was calculated in part a.

Calculation of Operating Cash Inflows

	Year			
	1	2	3	4
With new machine				
Earnings before depr., int., and taxes[a]	$120,000	$130,000	$130,000	$ 0
− Depreciation[b]	49,500	67,500	22,500	10,500
Earnings before int. and taxes	$ 70,500	$ 62,500	$107,500	−$10,500
− Taxes (rate, T = 40%)	28,200	25,000	43,000	− 4,200
Net operating profit after taxes	$ 42,300	$ 37,500	$ 64,500	−$ 6,300
+ Depreciation[b]	49,500	67,500	22,500	10,500
Operating cash inflows	$ 91,800	$105,000	$ 87,000	$ 4,200
With old machine				
Earnings before depr., int., and taxes[a]	$ 70,000	$ 70,000	$ 70,000	$ 0
− Depreciation[c]	7,600	4,800	4,800	2,000
Earnings before int. and taxes	$ 62,400	$ 65,200	$ 65,200	−$ 2,000
− Taxes (rate, T = 40%)	24,960	26,080	26,080	− 800
Net operating profit after taxes	$ 37,440	$ 39,120	$ 39,120	−$ 1,200
+ Depreciation	7,600	4,800	4,800	2,000
Operating cash inflows	$ 45,040	$ 43,920	$ 43,920	$ 800

[a]Given in the problem.
[b]From column 3 of the preceding table, top.
[c]From column 3 of the preceding table, bottom.

Solutions to Self-Test Problems B-14

Calculation of Incremental Operating Cash Inflows

	Operating cash inflows		
Year	New machine[a] (1)	Old machine[a] (2)	Incremental (relevant) [(1) − (2)] (3)
1	$ 91,800	$45,040	$46,760
2	105,000	43,920	61,080
3	87,000	43,920	43,080
4	4,200	800	3,400

[a]From the final row for the respective machine in the preceding table.

c. Terminal cash flow (end of year 3):

After-tax proceeds from sale of new machine		
Proceeds from sale of new machine	$35,000	
Total after-tax proceeds—new[1]	9,800	
Total after-tax proceeds—new		$25,200
− After-tax proceeds from sale of old machine		
Proceeds from sale of old machine	$ 0	
− Tax on sale of old machine[2]	− 800	
Total after-tax proceeds—old		800
+ Change in net working capital		20,000
Terminal cash flow		$44,400

[1]Book value of new machine at end of year 3
$= \$150,000 - [(0.33 + 0.45 + 0.15) \times \$150,000] = \$150,000 - (0.93 \times \$150,000)$
$= \$150,000 - \$139,500 = \$10,500$
Tax on sale $= 0.40 \times (\$35,000 \text{ sale price} - \$10,500 \text{ book value})$
$= 0.40 \times \$24,500 = \underline{\$9,800}$

[2]Book value of old machine at end of year 3
$= \$40,000 - [(0.20 + 0.32 + 0.19 + 0.12 + 0.12) \times \$40,000] = \$40,000 - (0.95 \times \$40,000)$
$= \$40,000 - \$38,000 = \$2,000$

Tax on sale $= 0.40 \times (\$0 \text{ sale price} - \$2,000 \text{ book value})$
$= 0.40 \times (-\$2,500 = -\underline{\$800}$ (i.e., $800 tax saving)

d.

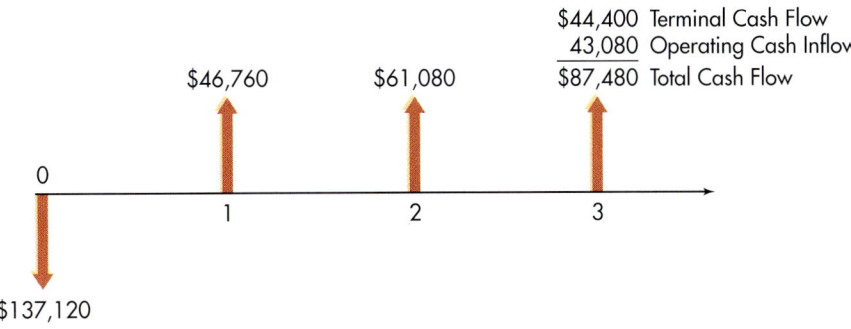

Chapter 9

ST9–1 a. Payback period:

Project M: $\dfrac{\$28,500}{\$10,000} = \underline{\underline{2.85}}$ years

Project N:

Year (t)	Cash inflows (CF_t)	Cumulative cash inflows
1	$11,000	$11,000
2	10,000	21,000 ←
3	9,000	30,000
4	8,000	38,000

$2 + \dfrac{\$27,000 - \$21,000}{\$9,000}$ years

$2 + \dfrac{\$6,000}{\$9,000}$ years = $\underline{\underline{2.67}}$ years

b. Net present value (NPV):

Project M: NPV = ($10,000 × $PVIFA_{14\%,4yrs}$) − $28,500
= ($10,000 × 2.914) − $28,500
= $29,140 − $28,500 = $\underline{\underline{\$640}}$

(Calculator solution = $637.12)

Project N:

Year (t)	Cash inflows (CF_t) (1)	$PVIF_{14\%,t}$ (2)	Present value at 14% [(1) ÷ (2)] (3)
1	$11,000	0.877	$ 9,647
2	10,000	0.769	7,690
3	9,000	0.675	6,075
4	8,000	0.592	4,736
		Present value of cash inflows	$28,148
		− Initial investment	27,000
		Net present value (NPV)	$ 1,148

(Calculator solution = $1,155.18)

Note: The year-4 incremental operating cash inflow of $3,400 is not directly included; it is instead reflected in the book values used to calculate the taxes on sale of the machines at the end of year 3 and is therefore part of the terminal cash flow.

c. Internal rate of return (IRR):

Project M: $\dfrac{\$28,500}{\$10,000} = 2.850$

$PVIFA_{IRR,4yrs} = 2.850$

From Table A–4:

$PVIFA_{15\%,4yrs} = 2.855$
$PVIFA_{16\%,4yrs} = 2.798$
IRR = 15% (2.850 is closest to 2.855)

(Calculator solution = 15.09%)

Project N:

Average annual cash inflow $= \dfrac{\$11,000 + \$10,000 + \$9,000 + \$8,000}{4}$

$= \dfrac{\$38,000}{4} = \$9,500$

$PVIFA_{k,4yrs} = \dfrac{\$27,000}{\$9,500} = 2.842$

$k \approx 15\%$

Try 16%, because there are more cash inflows in early years.

Year (t)	CF_t (1)	$PVIF_{16\%,t}$ (2)	Present value at 16% [(1) × (2)] (3)	$PVIF_{17\%,t}$ (4)	Present value at 17% [(1) × (4)] (5)
1	$11,000	0.862	$ 9,482	0.855	$ 9,405
2	10,000	0.743	7,430	0.731	7,310
3	9,000	0.641	5,769	0.624	5,616
4	8,000	0.552	4,416	0.534	4,272
		Present value of cash inflows	$27,097		$26,603
		− Initial investment	27,000		27,000
		NPV	$ 97		−$ 397

IRR = 16% (rounding to nearest whole percent)
(Calculator solution = 16.19%)

d.

	Project	
	M	N
Payback period	2.85 years	2.67 years[a]
NPV	$640	$1,148[a]
IRR	15%	16%[a]

[a]Preferred project.

Project N is recommended, because it has the shorter payback period and the higher NPV, which is greater than zero, and the larger IRR, which is greater than the 14% cost of capital.

e. Net present value profiles:

	Data	
	NPV	
Discount rate	Project M	Project N
0%	$11,500^a	$11,000^b
14	640	1,148
15	0	—
16	—	0

^{a}($10,000 + $10,000 + $10,000 + $10,000) − $28,500
= $40,000 − $28,500
= $11,500

^{b}($11,000 + $10,000 + $9,000 + $8,000) − $27,000
= $38,000 − $27,000
= $11,000

From the NPV profile that follows, it can be seen that if the firm has a cost of capital below approximately 6% (exact value is 5.75%), conflicting rankings of the projects would exist using the NPV and IRR decision techniques. Because the firm's cost of capital is 14%, it can be seen in part **d** that no conflict exists.

ST9–2 a. $NPV_A = (\$7,000 \times PVIFA_{10\%, 3yrs}) - \$15,000$
   $= (\$7,000 \times 2.487) - \$15,000$
   $= \$17,409 - \$15,000 = \underline{\$2,409}$

(Calculator solution = $2,407.96)

$$NPV_B = (\$10{,}000 \times PVIFA_{10\%,3yrs}) - \$20{,}000$$
$$= (\$10{,}000 - 2.487) - \$20{,}000$$
$$= \$24{,}870 - \$20{,}000 = \underline{\$4{,}870^*}$$

(Calculator solution = $4,868.52)

*Preferred project, because higher NPV.

b. From the CAPM-type relationship, the risk-adjusted discount rate ($RADR$) for project A, which has a risk index of 0.4, is 9%; for project B, with a risk index of 1.8, the $RADR$ is 16%.

$$NPV_A = (\$7{,}000 \times PVIFA_{9\%,3yrs}) - \$15{,}000$$
$$= (\$7{,}000 \times 2.531) - \$15{,}000$$
$$= \$17{,}717 - \$15{,}000 = \underline{\$2{,}717^*}$$

(Calculator solution = $2,719.06)

$$NPV_B = (\$10{,}000 \times PVIFA_{16\%,3yrs}) - \$20{,}000$$
$$= (\$10{,}000 \times 2.246) - \$20{,}000$$
$$= \$22{,}460 - \$20{,}000 = \underline{\$2{,}460}$$

(Calculator solution = $2,458.90)

*Preferred project, because higher NPV.

c. When the differences in risk were ignored in part **a**, project B was preferred over project A; but when the higher risk of project B is incorporated into the analysis using risk-adjusted discount rates in part **b**, *project A is preferred over project B*. Clearly, project A should be implemented.

Chapter 10

ST10–1 a. Cost of debt, k_i (using approximation formula)

$$k_d = \frac{I + \dfrac{\$1{,}000 - N_d}{n}}{\dfrac{N_d + \$1{,}000}{2}}$$

$I = 0.10 \times \$1{,}000 = \$100$
$N_d = \$1{,}000 - \$30 \text{ discount} - \$20 \text{ flotation cost} = \$950$
$n = 10$ years

$$k_d = \frac{\$100 + \dfrac{\$1{,}000 - \$950}{10}}{\dfrac{\$950 + \$1{,}000}{2}} = \frac{\$100 + \$5}{\$975} = 10.8\%$$

(Calculator solution = 10.8%)

$k_i = k_d \times (1 - T)$
$T = 0.40$
$k_i = 10.8\% \times (1 - 0.40) = \underline{6.5\%}$

Cost of preferred stock, k_p

$$k_p = \frac{D_p}{N_p}$$

$D_p = 0.11 \times \$100 = \$11$
$N_p = \$100 - \$4 \text{ flotation cost} = \$96$

$$k_p = \frac{\$11}{\$96} = \underline{\underline{11.5\%}}$$

Cost of retained earnings, k_r

$$k_r = k_s = \frac{D_1}{P_0} + g$$

$$= \frac{\$6}{\$80} + 6.0\% = 7.5\% + 6.0\% = \underline{\underline{13.5\%}}$$

Cost of new common stock, k_n

$$k_n = \frac{D_1}{N_n} + g$$

$D_1 = \$6$
$N_n = \$80 - \$4 \text{ underpricing} - \$4 \text{ flotation cost} = \$72$
$g = 6.0\%$

$$k_n = \frac{\$6}{\$72} + 6.0\% = 8.3\% + 6.0\% = \underline{\underline{14.3\%}}$$

b. (1) Break point, BP

$$BP_{\text{common equity}} = \frac{AF_{\text{common equity}}}{w_{\text{common equity}}}$$

$AF_{\text{common equity}} = \$225{,}000$
$w_{\text{common equity}} = 45\%$

$$BP_{\text{common equity}} = \frac{\$225{,}000}{0.45} = \$500{,}000$$

(2) WACC for total new financing $< \$500{,}000$

Source of capital	Weight (1)	Cost (2)	Weighted cost [(1) × (2)] (3)
Long-term debt	.40	6.5%	2.6%
Preferred stock	.15	11.5	1.7
Common stock equity	.45	13.5	6.1
Totals	1.00		10.4%

Weighted average cost of capital = 10.4%

(3) WACC for total new financing > $500,000

Source of capital	Weight (1)	Cost (2)	Weighted cost [(1) × (2)] (3)
Long-term debt	.40	6.5%	2.6%
Preferred stock	.15	11.5	1.7
Common stock equity	.45	14.3	6.4
Totals	1.00		10.7%

Weighted average cost of capital = 10.7%

c. IOS data for graph

Investment opportunity	Internal rate of return (IRR)	Initial investment	Cumulative investment
D	16.5%	$200,000	$ 200,000
C	12.9	150,000	350,000
E	11.8	450,000	800,000
A	11.2	100,000	900,000
G	10.5	300,000	1,200,000
F	10.1	600,000	1,800,000
B	9.7	500,000	2,300,000

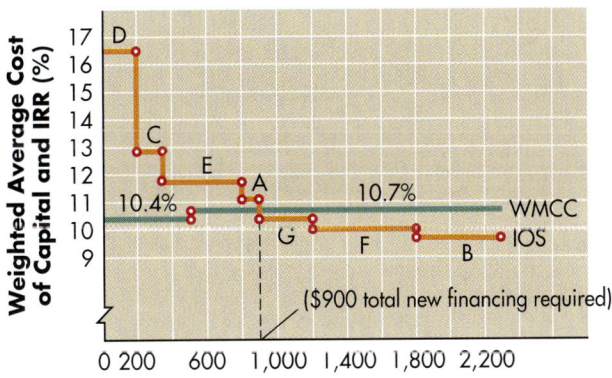

d. Projects D, C, E, and A should be accepted because their respective IRRs exceed the WMCC. They will require $900,000 of total new financing.

Chapter 11

ST11–1 a. $Q = \dfrac{FC}{P - VC}$

$= \dfrac{\$250{,}000}{\$7.50 - \$3.00} = \dfrac{\$250{,}000}{\$4.50} = \underline{\underline{55{,}556}}$ units

b.

	+20%	
Sales (in units)	100,000	120,000
Sales revenue (units × $7.50/unit)	$750,000	$900,000
Less: Variable operating costs (units × $3.00/unit)	300,000	360,000
Less: Fixed operating costs	250,000	250,000
Earnings before interest and taxes (EBIT)	$200,000	$290,000
	+45%	
Less: Interest	80,000	80,000
Net profits before taxes	$120,000	$210,000
Less: Taxes ($T = 0.40$)	48,000	84,000
Net profits after taxes	$ 72,000	$126,000
Less: Preferred dividends (8,000 shares × $5.00/share)	40,000	40,000
Earnings available for common	$132,000	$ 86,000
Earnings per share (EPS)	$32,000/20,000 = $1.60/share	$86,000/20,000 = $4.30/share
	+169%	

c. $\text{DOL} = \dfrac{\%\ \text{change in EBIT}}{\%\ \text{change in sales}} = \dfrac{+45\%}{+20\%} = \underline{\underline{2.25}}$

d. $\text{DFL} = \dfrac{\%\ \text{change in EPS}}{\%\ \text{change in EBIT}} = \dfrac{+169\%}{+45} = \underline{\underline{3.76}}$

e. $\text{DTL} = \text{DOL} \times \text{DFL}$

$= 2.25 \times 3.76 = \underline{\underline{8.46}}$

Using the other DTL formula:

$\text{DTL} = \dfrac{\%\ \text{change in EPS}}{\%\ \text{change in sales}}$

$8.46 = \dfrac{\%\ \text{change in EPS}}{+50\%}$

% change in EPS = $8.46 \times 0.50 = 4.23 = \underline{\underline{+423\%}}$

ST11–2

Data summary for alternative plans

Source of capital	Plan A (bond)	Plan B (stock)
Long-term debt	$60,000 at 12% annual interest	$50,000 at 12% annual interest
Annual interest =	0.12 = $60,000 = $7,200	0.12 × $50,000 = $6,000
Common stock	10,000 shares	11,000 shares

a.

	Plan A (bond)		Plan B (stock)	
EBIT[a]	$30,000	$40,000	$30,000	$40,000
Less: Interest	7,200	7,200	6,000	6,000
Net profits before taxes	$22,800	$32,800	$24,000	$34,000
Less: Taxes ($T = 0.40$)	9,120	13,120	9,600	13,600
Net profits after taxes	$13,680	$19,680	$14,400	$20,400
EPS (10,000 shares)	$1.37	$1.97		
(11,000 shares)			$1.31	$1.85

[a]Values were arbitrarily selected; other values could have been used.

	Coordinates	
	EBIT	
	$30,000	$40,000
Financing plan	Earnings per share (EPS)	
A (Bond)	$1.37	$1.97
B (Stock)	1.31	1.85

b.

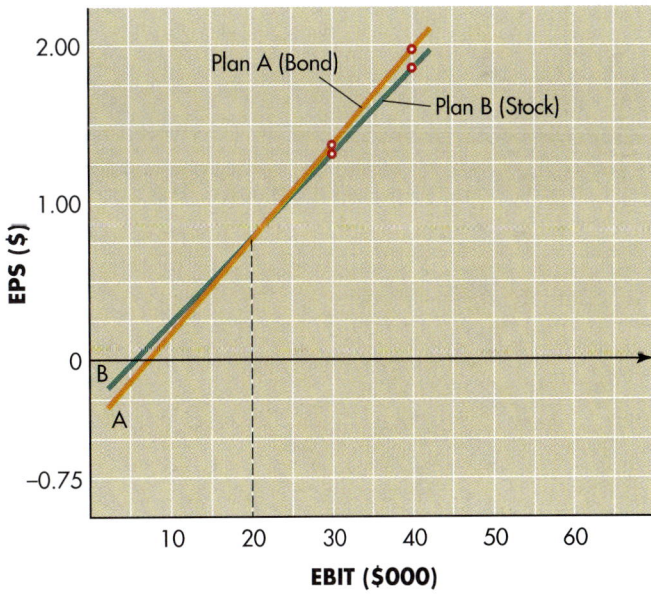

c. The bond plan (Plan A) becomes superior to the stock plan (Plan B) at *around $20,000* of EBIT, as represented by the dashed vertical line in the figure in part **b**. (*Note:* The actual point is $19,200, which can be determined algebraically by using a technique described in more advanced texts.)

ST11–3 a.

Capital structure debt ratio	Expected EPS (1)	Required return, k_s (2)	Estimated share value [(1) ÷ (2)] (3)
0%	$3.12	.13	$24.00
10	3.90	.15	26.00
20	4.80	.16	30.00
30	5.44	.17	32.00
40	5.51	.19	29.00
50	5.00	.20	25.00
60	4.40	.22	20.00

b. Using the table in part **a**:
   (1) Maximization of EPS: *40% debt ratio, EPS = $5.51/share* (see column 1).
   (2) Maximization of share value: *30% debt ratio, share value = $32.00* (see column 3).

c. Recommend *30% debt ratio*, because it results in the maximum share value and is therefore consistent with the firm's goal of owner wealth maximization.

Chapter 12

ST12–1 a. Earnings per share (EPS) = $\dfrac{\$2,000,000 \text{ earnings available}}{500,000 \text{ shares of common outstanding}}$

= $\underline{\underline{\$4.00/\text{share}}}$

Price/earnings (P/E) ratio = $\dfrac{\$60 \text{ market price}}{\$4.00 \text{ EPS}} = \underline{\underline{15}}$

b. Proposed dividends = 500,000 shares × $2 per share = $1,000,000

Shares that can be repurchased = $\dfrac{\$1,000,000}{\$62} = \underline{\underline{16{,}129 \text{ shares}}}$

c. *After proposed repurchase:*
Shares outstanding = 500,000 − 16,129 = 483,871

EPS = $\dfrac{\$2,000,000}{483,871} = \underline{\underline{\$4.13/\text{share}}}$

d. Market price = $4.13/share × 15 = $\underline{\underline{\$61.95/\text{share}}}$

e. The earnings per share (EPS) are higher after the repurchase, because there are fewer shares of stock outstanding (483,871 shares versus 500,000 shares) to divide up the firm's $2,000,000 of available earnings.

f. In both cases, the stockholders would receive $2 per share—a $2 cash dividend in the dividend case or an approximately $2 increase in share price ($60.00 per share to $61.95 per share) in the repurchase case. [*Note:* The difference of $0.05 per share ($2.00 − $1.95) difference is due to rounding.]

Chapter 13

ST13–1

Basic data

Time component	Current	Proposed
Average payment period (APP)	10 days	30 days
Average collection period (ACP)	30 days	30 days
Average age of inventory (AAI)	40 days	40 days

Cash conversion cycle (CCC) = AAI + ACP − APP

$\text{CCC}_{\text{current}}$ = 40 days + 30 days − 10 days = 60 days

$\text{CCC}_{\text{proposed}}$ = 40 days + 30 days − 30 days = 40 days

Reduction in CCC = 20 days

Annual operating cycle investment = $18,000,000

Daily expenditure = $18,000,000 ÷ 365 = $49,315

Reduction in resource investment = $49,315 × 20 days = $986,300

Annual profit increase = 0.12 × $986,300 = $118,356

ST13–2 a. *Data:*

S = 60,000 gallons
O = $200 per order
C = $1 per gallon per year

Calculation:

$$EOQ = \sqrt{\frac{2 \times S \times O}{C}}$$

$$= \sqrt{\frac{2 \times 60{,}000 \times \$200}{\$1}}$$

$$= \sqrt{24{,}000{,}000}$$

$$= \underline{4{,}899} \text{ gallons}$$

b. *Data:*

Lead time = 20 days
Daily usage = 60,000 gallons/365 days
= 164.38 gallons/day

Calculation:

Reorder point = lead time in days × daily usage
= 20 days × 164.38 gallons/day
= 3,287.6 gallons

ST13–3 Tabular Calculation of the Effects of Relaxing Credit Standards on Regency Rug Repair Company:

APPENDIX B

Additional profit contribution from sales	
[4,000 rugs × ($32 avg. sale price − $28 var. cost)]	$16,000
Cost of marginal investment in accounts receivable	
Average investment under proposed plan:	
$\dfrac{(\$28 \times 76{,}000 \text{ rugs})}{365/48} = \dfrac{\$2{,}128{,}000}{7.6}$ $\quad\$280{,}000$	
Average investment under present plan:	
$\dfrac{(\$28 \times 72{,}000 \text{ rugs})}{365/40} = \dfrac{\$2{,}016{,}000}{9.1}$ $\quad 221{,}538$	
Marginal investment in A/R $\quad\$58{,}462$	
Cost of marginal investment in A/R (0.14 × $58,462)	($8,185)
Cost of marginal bad debts	
Bad debts under proposed plan	
(0.015 × $32 × 76,000 rugs) $\quad\$36{,}480$	
Bad debts under present plan	
(0.010 × $32 × 72,000 rugs) $\quad 23{,}040$	
Cost of marginal bad debts	($13,440)
Net loss from implementation of proposed plan	($5,625)

Recommendation: Because a net loss of $5,625 is expected to result from relaxing credit standards, *the proposed plan should not be implemented.*

Chapter 14

ST14–1 **a.**

Supplier	Approximate cost of giving up cash discount
X	1% × [365/(55 − 10)] = 1% × 365/45 = 1% × 8 = **8.1%**
Y	2% × [365/(30 − 10)] = 2% × 365/20 = 2% × 18 = **36.5%**
Z	2% × [365/(60 − 20)] = 2% × 365/40 = 2% × 9 = **18.3%**

b.

Supplier	Recommendation
X	8.1% cost of giving up discount < 15% interest cost from bank; therefore, *give up discount.*
Y	36.5% cost of giving up discount > 15% interest cost from bank; therefore, *take discount and borrow from bank.*
Z	18.3% cost of giving up discount > 15% interest cost from bank; therefore, *take discount and borrow from bank.*

c. Stretching accounts payable for supplier Z would change the cost of giving up the cash discount to

$$2\% \times [365/[(60 + 20) - 20]] = 2\% \times 365/60 = 2\% \times 6.1 = \underline{12.2\%}$$

In this case, in light of the 15% interest cost from the bank, the recommended strategy in part **b** would be to *give up the discount,* because the 12.2% cost of giving up the discount would be less than the 15% interest cost from the bank.

Appendix C

Answers to Selected End-of-Chapter Problems

The following list of answers to selected problems and portions of problems is included to provide "check figures" for use in preparing detailed solutions to end-of-chapter problems requiring calculations. For problems that are relatively straightforward, the key answer is given; for more complex problems, answers to a number of parts of the problem are included. Detailed calculations are not shown—only the final and, in some cases, intermediate answers, which should help to confirm whether the correct solution is being developed. Answers to problems involving present and future value were solved by using the appropriate tables; calculator solutions are not given. For problems containing a variety of cases for which similar calculations are required, the answers for only one or two cases have been included. The only verbal answers included are simple yes-or-no or "choice of best alternative" responses; answers to problems requiring detailed explanations or discussions are not given

The problems and portions of problems for which answers have been included were selected randomly; therefore, there is no discernible pattern to the choice of problem answers given. The answers given are based on what are believed to be the most obvious and reasonable assumptions related to the given problem; in some cases, other reasonable assumptions could result in equally correct answers.

APPENDIX C

1–1 a. Ms. Harper has unlimited liability: $60,000
     c. Ms. Harper has limited liability
1–2 a. $160,000
     b. $150,000
1–5 a. $19,700
     b. $72,800
     c. 21.3%
1–8 e. Total tax liability: $206,400
1–9 a. Earnings after tax: $18,000
1–10 b. Asset X: $100
        Asset Y: $2,000
2–3 a. Net profit after tax: $38,500
2–4 a. Earnings per share: $1.162
2–6 Initial sale price: $9.50
2–7 b. Earnings per share: $2.36
     c. Cash dividend per share: $1.50
2–9 a.
     Current ratio   2003: 1.88   2005: 1.79
     Quick ratio   2003: 1.22   2005: 1.24
2–11 a. 45.62 days
2–12

	Creek	Industry
Debt ratio	0.73	0.51
Times interest earned	3.00	7.30

2–16 a.

	Actual 2006
Current ratio:	1.04
Average collection period:	57 days
Debt ratio:	61.3%
Net profit margin:	4.1%
Return on equity:	11.3%

2–17 a. 2006 Johnson ROE = 21.21%
                Industry ROE = 14.46%
3–5 b. $1,620
     c. $3,220
3–7

	April	May
	($000)	
Cash 1 month delay	168	183
Cash 2 months delay	120	134.4
Total disbursements	465.3	413.1

3–11 a. To retained earnings: $146,600
     b. To retained earnings: $157,400
3–12 a. Total assets: $1,383,000
        Total current liabilities: $510,000
        External funds required: $53,000
3–14 a. To retained earnings: $32,500
     c. $11,250
4–3 C: 3 years < n < 4 years
4–4 A: $530.60
     D: $78.450
4–6 a. (1) $15,456
4–10 B: $6,020
     D $80,250
4–17 a. (1) A: $36,217.50
        (2) A: $39,114.90

4–18 a. (1) C: $2,821.70
        (2) C: $3,386.04
4–21 b. $30,950.64
4–23 b. B: $1,000,000
        D: $1,200,000
4–25 a. A: $3,862.50
4–27 b. B: $26,039
4–30 a. $22,215
4–32 a.
        (1) Annual: $8,810
            Semiannual: $8,955
            Quarterly: $9,030
4–33 b. B: 12.6%
        D: 17.0%
4–38 B: $2,439.32
4–41 a. $60,000
     b. $3,764.82
4–42 A: $4,656.58
     B: $10,619.47
     C: $7,955.87
4–46 a. A: 12% < i < 13%
        Calculator solution 12.47%
        C: 2% < i < 3%
        Calculator solution 2.50%
4–48 a. B: 8% < i < 9%
        Calculator solution 8.02%
        D: 10% < i < 11%
        Calculator solution 10.03%
4–53 A: 17 < n < 18
        Calculator solution 17.79
     D: 18 < n < 19
        Calculator solution 18.68
5–1 a. X: 12.50%
        Y: 12.36%
5–2 A: 25%
5–4 a. A: 8%
        B: 20%
5–5 a. R: 10%
        S: 20%
     b. R: 25%
        S: 25.5%
5–8 a.
        (4) Project 257 CV: .368
            Project 432 CV: .354
5–9 a. F: 4%
     b. F: 13.38%
     c. F: 3.345
5–10 b. Portfolio return: 15.5%
     c. Standard deviation: 1.511%
5–15 a. 18% increase
     b. 9.6% decrease
     c. No change
5–19 A: 8.9%
     D: 15%

5–21	b. 10%			b.	@$100,000: $30,720
6–3	a. A: 9%				@$56,000: $13,120
	B: 12%		8–8	a.	Total tax: $49,600
6–5	b. $175,000			d.	Total tax: ($6,400)
	c. $113,750		8–11		Initial investment $22,680
6–7	b. $8,789.40		8–12	a.	Initial investment: $18,240
6–8	C: $16,660.00			c.	Initial investment: $23,100
	D: $9,717.00		8–14	c.	Cash inflow, Year 3: $584,000
6–10	a. $1,156.88		8–16	b.	Incremental cash flow, Year 3: $1,960
6–14	a. (1) $1,120.23		8–18		Terminal cash flow: $76,640
	(2) $1,000.00		9–2	a.	Machine 1: 4 years, 8 months
	(3) $896.63				Machine 2: 5 years, 3 months
6–17	a. A: approximate: 12.36%		9–3	a.	$3,246 Accept
	Calculator solution: 12.71%			b.	−$5,131 Reject
	C: approximate: 10.38%		9–4	a.	$2,675 Accept
	Calculator solution: 10.22%			c.	−$805 Reject
	E: approximate: 8.77%		9–8	a.	Project A: 3.08 years
	Calculator solution: 8.95%				Project C: 2.38 years
6–19	A: $1,152.35			b.	Project C: NPV $5,451
	C: $464.72		9–9	a.	Project A: 17%
	E: $76.11				Project D: 21%
7–1	b. 800,000 shares		9–12	a.	NPV = $1,222
7–3	A: $15.00			b.	IRR = 12%
	C: $11.00			c.	Accept
	D: $25.50		9–17	a.	Initial investment: $1,480,000
7–6	a. $20			b.	Year Cash Flow
	b. $12				1 $656,000
7–8	a. $68.82				2 761,600
	b. $60.95				3 647,200
7–9	A: $24.00				4 585,600
	B: $40.00				5 585,600
	E: $18.75				6 44,000
7–11	a. $37.75			c.	2.1 years
	b. $60.40			d.	NPV = $959,289
7–13	a. (1) $5,021,250				IRR = 35%
	(2) $5,411,250		9–19	a.	Value of real options: $2,200
	(3) $4,049,331				NPV$_{strategic}$: $500
	b. $2,191,331		9–22	a.	Range A: $1,600
	c. $10.96				Range B: $200
7–15	a. Book value: $36.00		9–23	b.	Project A:
	b. Liquidation value: $30.20				Pessimistic: $73
7–16	A: $18.60				Most likely: $1,609
	B: $45.00				Optimistic: $3,145
	E: $76.50		9–26	a.	Project E: $2,130; Project F: $1,678
8–1	a. Operating expenditure			c.	Project E: $834; Project F: $1,678
	d. Operating expenditure		9–28	a.	Project X: NPV = $14,960
	f. Capital expenditure				Project Y: NPV = $2,650
8–4	Year Relevant cash flow		10–2	a.	$980
	1 $4,000			d.	7.36% after tax
	2 $6,000		10–6	a.	6%
	4 $10,000			b.	12%
8–6	A: $275,500		10–7	d.	16.54%
	B: $26,800		10–11	a.	13.55%
8–7	a. $23,200			b.	12.985%

11–1 1,300

11–4 a. 21,000 CDs
b. $293,580
d. $10,500

11–7 a. 8,000 units
b. @ 10,000 units: $95,000

11–10 b. 2
c. 1.25

11–16 a. Structure A:
EBIT $30,000: EPS $1.125
Structure B:
EBIT $50,000: EPS 2.28

12–4 a. $4.75 per share
b. $0.40 per share

12–6 a. *Year $ Dividend*
1997   0.10
2001   0.96
2004   1.28
2006   1.60
c. *Year $ Dividend*
1997   0.50
2001   0.50
2004   0.66
2007   1.30

12–8 a. Common stock: $21,000
Paid in capital: $294,000
Retained earnings: $85,000

12–10 a. $2.00
d. $20.00 per share

12–12 a. 1,200,000 shares @ $1.50 par
d. 3,600,000 shares @ $0.50 par

12–14 a. 19,047 shares
b. $2.10

13–1 a. OC = 150 days
b. CCC = 120 days
c. $9,863,013.70

13–2 b. CCC = 70 days
c. $26,849

13–4 a. Average season requirement: $4,000,000

13–6 a. 200 units
b. 121.92 units
c. 32.88 units

13–9 Loss from implementation: $4,659

13–11 Loss from implementation: $11,972

13–13 a. 7 days
b. $21,450

14–2 a. 37.21%
b. 18.43%
c. 7.37%

14–6 $1,300,000

14–7 $82,500

14–9 14.29%

14–10 a. Effective rate: 12.94%
b. Effective rate: 11.73%

14–13 a. Effective 90-day rate: 2.25%
b. Effective annual rate: 13.89%

14–17   *Amount remitted*
A: $196,000
C: $107,800
F: $176,400
G: $ 88,200

Glossary

ABC inventory system Inventory management technique that divides inventory into three groups—A, B, and C, in descending order of importance and level of monitoring, on the basis of the dollar investment in each. (Chapter 13)

ability to service debts The ability of a firm to make the payments required on a scheduled basis over the life of a debt. (Chapter 2)

accept–reject approach The evaluation of capital expenditure proposals to determine whether they meet the firm's minimum acceptance criterion. (Chapter 8)

accounts payable management Management by the firm of the time that elapses between its purchase of raw materials and its mailing payment to the supplier. (Chapter 14)

accrual basis In preparation of financial statements, recognizes revenue at the time of sale and recognizes expenses when they are incurred. (Chapter 1)

accruals Liabilities for services received for which payment has yet to be made. (Chapter 14)

ACH (automated clearinghouse) transfer Preauthorized electronic withdrawal from the payer's account and deposit into the payee's account via a settlement among banks by the *automated clearinghouse,* or *ACH.* (Chapter 13)

activity ratios Measure the speed with which various accounts are converted into sales or cash—inflows or outflows. (Chapter 2)

after-tax proceeds from sale of old asset The difference between the old asset's sale proceeds and any applicable taxes or tax refunds related to its sale. (Chapter 8)

agency costs The costs borne by stockholders to maintain a *governance structure* that minimizes agency problems and contributes to the maximization of owner wealth. (Chapter 1)

agency problem The likelihood that managers may place personal goals ahead of corporate goals. (Chapter 1)

aggressive funding strategy A funding strategy under which the firm funds its seasonal requirements with short-term debt and its permanent requirements with long-term debt. (Chapter 13)

aging schedule A credit-monitoring technique that breaks down accounts receivable into groups on the basis of their time of origin; it shows the percentages of the total accounts receivable balance that have been outstanding for specified periods of time. (Chapter 13)

American depositary receipts (ADRs) Claims issued by U.S. banks representing ownership of shares of a foreign company's stock held on deposit by the U.S. bank in the foreign market and issued in dollars to U.S. investors. (Chapter 7)

angel capitalists (angels) Wealthy individual investors who do not operate as a business but invest in promising early-stage companies in exchange for a portion of the firm's equity. (Chapter 7)

annual cleanup The requirement that for a certain number of days during the year borrowers under a line of credit carry a zero loan balance (that is, owe the bank nothing). (Chapter 14)

annual percentage rate (APR) The *nominal annual rate* of interest, found by multiplying the periodic rate by the number of periods in one year, that must be disclosed to consumers on credit cards and loans as a result of "truth-in-lending laws." (Chapter 4)

annual percentage yield (APY) The *effective annual rate* of interest that must be disclosed to consumers by banks on their savings products as a result of "truth-in-savings laws." (Chapter 4)

annuity A stream of equal periodic cash flows, over a specified time period. These cash flows can be *inflows* of returns earned on investments or *outflows* of funds invested to earn future returns. (Chapter 4)

annuity due An annuity for which the cash flow occurs at the *beginning* of each period. (Chapter 4)

articles of partnership The written contract used to formally establish a business partnership. (Chapter 1)

asymmetric information The situation in which managers of a firm have more information about operations and future prospects than do investors. (Chapter 11)

authorized shares The number of shares of common stock that a firm's corporate charter allows it to issue. (Chapter 7)

average age of inventory Average number of days' sales in inventory. (Chapter 2)

average collection period The average amount of time needed to collect accounts receivable. (Chapter 2)

average payment period The average amount of time needed to pay accounts payable. (Chapter 2)

average tax rate A firm's taxes divided by its taxable income. (Chapter 1)

balance sheet Summary statement of the firm's financial position at a given point in time. (Chapter 2)

bar chart The simplest type of probability distribution; shows only a limited number of outcomes and associated probabilities for a given event. (Chapter 5)

behavioral finance A growing body of research that focuses on investor behavior and its impact on investment decisions and stock prices. Advocates are commonly referred to as "behaviorists." (Chapter 7)

benchmarking A type of *cross-sectional analysis* in which the firm's ratio values are compared to those of a key competitor or group of competitors that it wishes to emulate. (Chapter 2)

beta coefficient (*b*) A relative measure of nondiversifiable risk. An *index* of the degree of movement of an asset's return in response to a change in the *market return*. (Chapter 5)

bird-in-the-hand argument The belief, in support of *dividend relevance theory*, that investors see current dividends as less risky than future dividends or capital gains. (Chapter 12)

board of directors Group elected by the firm's stockholders and typically responsible for developing strategic goals and plans, setting general policy, guiding corporate affairs, approving major expenditures, and hiring/firing, compensating, and monitoring key officers and executives. (Chapter 1)

bond Long-term debt instrument used by business and government to raise large sums of money, generally from a diverse group of lenders. (Chapter 1)

bond indenture A legal document that specifies both the rights of the bondholders and the duties of the issuing corporation. (Chapter 6)

book value The strict accounting value of an asset, calculated by subtracting its accumulated depreciation from its installed cost. (Chapter 8)

book value per share The amount per share of common stock that would be received if all of the firm's assets were *sold for their exact book (accounting) value* and the proceeds remaining after paying all liabilities (including preferred stock) were divided among the common stockholders. (Chapter 7)

book value weights Weights that use accounting values to measure the proportion of each type of capital in the firm's financial structure. (Chapter 10)

breakeven analysis Indicates the level of operations necessary to cover all operating costs and the profitability associated with various levels of sales. (Chapter 11)

break point The level of *total* new financing at which the cost of one of the financing components rises, thereby causing an upward shift in the *weighted marginal cost of capital (WMCC)*. (Chapter 10)

business risk The risk to the firm of being unable to cover operating costs. (Chapter 10)

call feature A feature included in nearly all corporate bond issues that gives the issuer the opportunity to repurchase bonds at a stated *call price* prior to maturity. (Chapter 6)

call premium The amount by which a bond's *call price* exceeds its par value. (Chapter 6)

call price The stated price at which a bond may be repurchased, by use of a *call feature*, prior to maturity. (Chapter 6)

capital The long-term funds of a firm; all items on the right-hand side of the firm's balance sheet, *excluding current liabilities*. (Chapter 7)

capital asset pricing model (CAPM) The basic theory that links risk and return for all assets; describes the relationship between the required return, k_s, and the nondiversifiable risk of the firm as measured by the beta coefficient, *b*. (Chapters 5 and 10)

capital budgeting The process of evaluating and selecting long-term investments that are consistent with the firm's goal of maximizing owner wealth. (Chapter 8)

capital budgeting process Five distinct but interrelated steps: *proposal generation, review and analysis, decision making, implementation,* and *follow-up.* (Chapter 8)

capital expenditure An outlay of funds by the firm that is expected to produce benefits over a period of time *greater than* 1 year. (Chapter 8)

capital gain The amount by which the sale price of an asset exceeds the asset's initial purchase price. (Chapter 1)

capital market A market that enables suppliers and demanders of *long-term funds* to make transactions. (Chapter 1)

capital rationing The financial situation in which a firm has only a fixed number of dollars available for capital expenditures, and numerous projects compete for these dollars. (Chapter 8)

capital structure The mix of long-term debt and equity maintained by the firm. (Chapter 11)

carrying costs The variable costs per unit of holding an item in inventory for a specific period of time. (Chapter 13)

cash basis Recognizes revenues and expenses only with respect to actual inflows and outflows of cash. (Chapter 1)

cash bonuses Cash paid to management for achieving certain performance goals. (Chapter 1)

cash budget (cash forecast) A statement of the firm's planned inflows and outflows of cash that is used to estimate its short-term cash requirements. (Chapter 3)

cash concentration The process used by the firm to bring lockbox and other deposits together into one bank, often called the *concentration bank*. (Chapter 13)

cash conversion cycle (CCC) The amount of time a firm's resources are tied up; calculated by subtracting the average payment period from the *operating cycle*. (Chapter 13)

cash disbursements All outlays of cash by the firm during a given financial period. (Chapter 3)

cash discount A percentage deduction from the purchase price; available to the credit customer who pays its account within a specified time. (Chapter 13)

cash discount period The number of days after the beginning of the credit period during which the cash discount is available. (Chapter 13)

cash receipts All of a firm's inflows of cash during a given financial period. (Chapter 3)

change in net working capital The difference between a change in current assets and a change in current liabilities. (Chapter 8)

clearing float The time between deposit of a payment and when spendable funds become available to the firm. (Chapter 13)

clientele effect The argument that a firm attracts shareholders whose preferences for the payment and stability of dividends correspond to the payment pattern and stability of the firm itself. (Chapter 12)

closely owned (stock) All common stock of a firm owned by a small group of investors (such as a family). (Chapter 7)

coefficient of variation (CV) A measure of relative dispersion that is useful in comparing the risks of assets with differing expected returns. (Chapter 5)

collateral trust bonds See Table 6.3 (Chapter 6)

commercial finance companies Lending institutions that make *only* secured loans—both short-term and long-term—to businesses. (Chapter 14)

commercial paper A form of financing consisting of short-term, unsecured promissory notes issued by firms with a high credit standing. (Chapter 14)

commitment fee The fee that is normally charged on a *revolving credit agreement*; it often applies to the *average unused portion* of the borrower's credit line. (Chapter 14)

common stock The purest and most basic form of corporate ownership. (Chapter 1)

common-size income statement An income statement in which each item is expressed as a percentage of sales. (Chapter 2)

compensating balance A required checking account balance equal to a certain percentage of the amount borrowed from a bank under a line-of-credit or revolving credit agreement. (Chapter 14)

compound interest Interest that is earned on a given deposit and has become part of the *principal* at the end of a specified period. (Chapter 4)

conflicting rankings Conflicts in the ranking given a project by NPV and IRR, resulting from *differences in the magnitude and timing of cash flows*. (Chapter 9)

conservative funding strategy A funding strategy under which the firm funds both its seasonal and its permanent requirements with long-term debt. (Chapter 13)

constant-growth model A widely cited dividend valuation approach that assumes that dividends will grow at a constant rate, but a rate that is less than the required return. (Chapter 7)

constant-growth valuation (Gordon) model Assumes that the value of a share of stock equals the present value of all future dividends (assumed to grow at a constant rate) that it is expected to provide over an infinite time horizon. (Chapter 10)

constant-payout-ratio dividend policy A dividend policy based on the payment of a certain percentage of earnings to owners in each dividend period. (Chapter 12)

continuous compounding Compounding of interest an infinite number of times per year at intervals of microseconds. (Chapter 4)

continuous probability distribution A probability distribution showing all the possible outcomes and associated probabilities for a given event. (Chapter 5)

controlled disbursing The strategic use of mailing points and bank accounts to lengthen mail float and clearing float, respectively. (Chapter 13)

controller The firm's chief accountant, who is responsible for the firm's accounting activities, such as corporate accounting, tax management, financial accounting, and cost accounting. (Chapter 1)

conventional cash flow pattern An initial outflow followed only by a series of inflows. (Chapter 8)

conversion feature An option that is included as part of a bond or a preferred stock issue and allows its holder to change the security into a stated number of shares of common stock. (Chapter 6)

corporate bond A long-term debt instrument indicating that a corporation has borrowed a certain amount of money and promises to repay it in the future under clearly defined terms. (Chapter 6)

corporate governance The system used to direct and control a corporation. Defines the rights and responsibilities of key corporate participants, decision-making procedures, and how the firm will set, achieve, and monitor objectives. (Chapter 1)

corporation An artificial being created by law (often called a "legal entity"). (Chapter 1)

correlation A statistical measure of the relationship between any two series of numbers representing data of any kind. (Chapter 5)

correlation coefficient A measure of the degree of correlation between two series. (Chapter 5)

cost of capital The rate of return that a firm must earn on the projects in which it invests to maintain its market value and attract funds. (Chapter 10)

cost of common stock equity, k_s The rate at which investors discount the expected dividends of the firm to determine its share value. (Chapter 10)

cost of giving up a cash discount The implied rate of interest paid to delay payment of an account payable for an additional number of days. (Chapter 14)

cost of long-term debt, k_i The after-tax cost today of raising long-term funds through borrowing. (Chapter 10)

cost of new asset The net outflow necessary to acquire a new asset. (Chapter 8)

cost of a new issue of common stock, k_n The cost of common stock, net of underpricing and associated flotation costs. (Chapter 10)

cost of preferred stock, k_p The ratio of the preferred stock dividend to the firm's net proceeds from the sale of preferred stock; calculated by dividing the annual dividend, D_p, by the net proceeds from the sale of the preferred stock, N_p. (Chapter 10)

cost of retained earnings, k_r The same as the cost of an *equivalent fully subscribed issue of additional common stock*, which is equal to the cost of common stock equity, k_s. (Chapter 10)

coupon interest rate The percentage of a bond's par value that will be paid annually, typically in two equal semiannual payments, as interest. (Chapter 6)

coverage ratios Ratios that measure the firm's ability to pay certain fixed charges. (Chapter 2)

credit monitoring The ongoing review of a firm's accounts receivable to determine whether customers are paying according to the stated credit terms. (Chapter 13)

credit period The number of days after the beginning of the credit period until full payment of the account is due. (Chapter 13)

credit scoring A credit selection method commonly used with high-volume/small-dollar credit requests; relies on a credit score determined by applying statistically derived weights to a credit applicant's scores on key financial and credit characteristics. (Chapter 13)

credit standards The firm's minimum requirements for extending credit to a customer. (Chapter 13)

credit terms The terms of sale for customers who have been extended credit by the firm. (Chapter 13)

cross-sectional analysis Comparison of different firms' financial ratios at the same point in time; involves comparing the firm's ratios to those of other firms in its industry or to industry averages. (Chapter 2)

cumulative preferred stock Preferred stock for which all passed (unpaid) dividends in arrears, along with the current dividend, must be paid before dividends can be paid to common stockholders. (Chapter 7)

current assets Short-term assets, expected to be converted into cash within 1 year or less. (Chapter 2)

current liabilities Short-term liabilities, expected to be paid within 1 year or less. (Chapter 2)

current ratio A measure of liquidity calculated by dividing the firm's current assets by its current liabilities. (Chapter 2)

date of record (dividends) Set by the firm's directors, the date on which all persons whose names are recorded as stockholders receive a declared dividend at a specified future time. (Chapter 12)

debentures See Table 6.3 (Chapter 6)

debt capital All long-term borrowing incurred by a firm, including bonds. (Chapter 7)

debt ratio Measures the proportion of total assets financed by the firm's creditors. (Chapter 2)

decision trees A behavioral approach that uses diagrams to map the various investment decision alternatives and payoffs, along with their probabilities of occurrence. (Chapter 9)

degree of financial leverage (DFL) The numerical measure of the firm's financial leverage. (Chapter 11)

degree of indebtedness Measures the amount of debt relative to other significant balance sheet amounts. (Chapter 2)

degree of operating leverage (DOL) The numerical measure of the firm's operating leverage. (Chapter 11)

degree of total leverage (DTL) The numerical measure of the firm's total leverage. (Chapter 11)

depository transfer check (DTC) An unsigned check drawn on one of a firm's bank accounts and deposited in another. (Chapter 13)

depreciable life Time period over which an asset is depreciated. (Chapter 3)

depreciation The systematic charging of a portion of the costs of fixed assets against annual revenues over time. (Chapter 3)

dilution of ownership Occurs when a new stock issue results in each present shareholder having a claim on a *smaller* part of the firm's earnings than previously. (Chapter 7)

discount The amount by which a bond sells at a value that is less than its par value. (Chapter 6)

discount loans Loans on which interest is paid in advance by being deducted from the amount borrowed. (Chapter 14)

discounting cash flows The process of finding present values; the inverse of compounding interest. (Chapter 4)

diversifiable risk The portion of an asset's risk that is attributable to firm-specific, random causes; can be eliminated through diversification. Also called *unsystematic risk*. (Chapter 5)

dividend irrelevance theory Miller and Modigliani's theory that in a perfect world, the firm's value is determined solely by the earning power and risk of its assets (investments) and that the manner in which it splits its earnings stream between dividends and internally retained (and reinvested) funds does not affect this value. (Chapter 12)

dividend payout ratio Indicates the percentage of each dollar earned that is distributed to the owners in the form of cash. It is calculated by dividing the firm's cash dividend per share by its earnings per share. (Chapter 12)

dividend per share (DPS) The dollar amount of cash distributed during the period on behalf of each outstanding share of common stock. (Chapter 2)

dividend policy The firm's plan of action to be followed whenever a dividend decision is made. (Chapter 12)

dividend reinvestment plans (DRIPs) Plans that enable stockholders to use dividends received on the firm's stock to acquire additional shares—even fractional shares—at little or no transaction cost. (Chapter 12)

dividend relevance theory The theory, advanced by Gordon and Lintner, that there is a direct relationship between a firm's dividend policy and its market value. (Chapter 12)

dividends Periodic distributions of earnings to the stockholders of a firm. (Chapter 1)

double taxation Occurs when the already once-taxed earnings of a corporation are distributed as cash dividends to stockholders, who must pay taxes of up to a maximum rate of 15 percent on them. (Chapter 1)

DuPont formula Multiplies the firm's *net profit margin* by its *total asset turnover* to calculate the firm's *return on total assets (ROA)*. (Chapter 2)

DuPont system of analysis System used to dissect the firm's financial statements and to assess its financial condition. (Chapter 2)

earnings per share (EPS) The amount earned during the period on behalf of each outstanding share of common stock, calculated by dividing the period's total earnings available for the firm's common stockholders by the number of shares of common stock outstanding. (Chapter 1)

EBIT–EPS approach An approach for selecting the capital structure that maximizes earnings per share (EPS) over the expected range of earnings before interest and taxes (EBIT). (Chapter 11)

economic order quantity (EOQ) model Inventory management technique for determining an item's optimal order size, which is the size that minimizes the total of its *order costs* and *carrying costs*. (Chapter 13)

economic value added (EVA®) A popular measure used by many firms to determine whether an investment contributes positively to the owners' wealth; calculated as the difference between an investment's *net operating profit after taxes (NOPAT)* and the cost of funds used to finance the investment which is found by multiplying the dollar amount of funds used to finance the investment by the firm's weighted average cost of capital (WACC). (Chapter 10)

effective (true) annual rate (EAR) The annual rate of interest actually paid or earned. (Chapter 4)

efficient market A market that allocates funds to their most productive uses as a result of competition among wealth-maximizing investors that determines and publicizes prices that are believed to be close to their true value; a market with the following characteristics: many small investors, all having the same information and expectations with respect to securities; no restrictions on investment, no taxes, and no transaction costs; and rational investors, who view securities similarly and are risk-averse, preferring higher returns and lower risk. (Chapters 1 and 5)

efficient-market hypothesis (EMH) Theory describing the behavior of an assumed "perfect" market in which (1) securities are typically in equilibrium, (2) security prices fully reflect all public information available and react swiftly to new information, and, (3) because stocks are fully and fairly priced, investors need not waste time looking for mispriced securities. (Chapter 7)

efficient portfolio A portfolio that maximizes return for a given level of risk or minimizes risk for a given level of return. (Chapter 5)

ending cash The sum of the firm's beginning cash and its net cash flow for the period. (Chapter 3)

enterprise resource planning (ERP) A computerized system that electronically integrates external information about the firm's suppliers and customers with the firm's departmental data so that information on all available resources—human and material—can be instantly obtained in a fashion that eliminates production delays and controls costs. (Chapter 13)

equipment trust certificates See Table 6.3 (Chapter 6)

equity capital The long-term funds provided by the firm's owners, the stockholders. (Chapter 7)

ethics Standards of conduct or moral judgment. (Chapter 1)

Eurobond An *international bond* that is sold primarily in countries other than the country of the currency in which the issue is denominated. (Chapter 6)

Eurobond market The market in which corporations and governments typically issue bonds denominated in dollars and sell them to investors located outside the United States. (Chapter 1)

Eurocurrency market International equivalent of the domestic money market. (Chapter 1)

ex dividend Period, beginning 2 *business days* prior to the date of record, during which a stock is sold without the right to receive the current dividend. (Chapter 12)

excess cash balance The (excess) amount available for investment by the firm if the period's ending cash is greater than the desired minimum cash balance; assumed to be invested in marketable securities. (Chapter 3)

excess earnings accumulation tax The tax the IRS levies on retained earnings above $250,000 when it determines that the firm has accumulated an excess of earnings to allow owners to delay paying ordinary income taxes on dividends received. (Chapter 12)

exchange rate risk The danger that an unexpected change in the exchange rate between the dollar and the currency in which a project's cash flows are denominated will reduce the market value of that project's cash flow; the risk caused by varying exchange rates between two currencies. (Chapter 9)

expectations theory The theory that the yield curve reflects investor expectations about future interest rates and inflation; an increasing inflation expectation results in an upward-sloping yield curve, and a decreasing inflation expectation results in a downward-sloping yield curve. (Chapter 6)

expected value of a return ($\bar{k}$) The most likely return on a given asset. (Chapter 5)

extendible notes See Table 6.4 (Chapter 6)

external financing required ("plug" figure) Under the judgmental approach for developing a pro forma balance sheet, the amount of external financing needed to bring the statement into balance. It can be either a positive or a negative value. (Chapter 3)

external forecast A sales forecast based on the relationships observed between the firm's sales and certain key external economic indicators. (Chapter 3)

extra dividend An additional dividend optionally paid by the firm if earnings are higher than normal in a given period. (Chapter 12)

factor A financial institution that specializes in purchasing accounts receivable from businesses. (Chapter 14)

factoring accounts receivable The outright sale of accounts receivable at a discount to a *factor* or other financial institution. (Chapter 14)

federal funds Loan transactions between commercial banks in which the Federal Reserve banks become involved. (Chapter 1)

finance The art and science of managing money. (Chapter 1)

Financial Accounting Standards Board (FASB) Standard No. 52 Mandates that U.S.-based companies translate their foreign-currency-denominated assets and liabilities into dollars, for consolidation with the parent company's financial statements. (Chapter 2)

Financial Accounting Standards Board (FASB) The accounting profession's rule-setting body, which authorizes *generally accepted accounting principles (GAAP)*. (Chapter 2)

financial breakeven point The level of EBIT necessary to just cover all *fixed financial costs*; the level of EBIT for which EPS = $0. (Chapter 11)

financial institution An intermediary that channels the savings of individuals, businesses, and governments into loans or investments. (Chapter 1)

financial leverage multiplier (FLM) The ratio of the firm's total assets to its common stock equity. (Chapter 2)

financial leverage The potential use of *fixed financial costs* to magnify the effects of changes in earnings before interest and taxes on the firm's earnings per share. (Chapters 2 and 11)

financial manager Actively manages the financial affairs of any type of business, whether financial or nonfinancial, private or public, large or small, profit-seeking or not-for-profit. (Chapter 1)

financial markets Forums in which suppliers of funds and demanders of funds can transact business directly. (Chapter 1)

financial planning process Planning that begins with long-term, or *strategic,* financial plans that in turn guide the formulation of short-term, or *operating,* plans and budgets. (Chapter 3)

financial risk The risk to the firm of being unable to cover required financial obligations (interest, lease payments, preferred stock dividends). (Chapter 10)

financial services The part of finance concerned with the design and delivery of advice and financial products to individuals, business, and government. (Chapter 1)

financing flows Cash flows that result from debt and equity financing transactions; includes incurrence and repayment of debt, cash inflow from the sale of stock, and cash outflows to pay cash dividends or repurchase stock. (Chapter 3)

five C's of credit The five key dimensions—character, capacity, capital, collateral, and conditions—used by credit analysts to provide a framework for in-depth credit analysis. (Chapter 13)

fixed-payment coverage ratio Measures the firm's ability to meet all fixed-payment obligations. (Chapter 2)

fixed-rate loan A loan with a rate of interest that is determined at a set increment above the prime rate and at which it remains fixed until maturity. (Chapter 14)

flat yield curve A yield curve that reflects relatively similar borrowing costs for both short- and longer-term loans. (Chapter 6)

float Funds that have been sent by the payer but are not yet usable funds to the payee. (Chapter 13)

floating inventory lien A secured short-term loan against inventory under which the lender's claim is on the borrower's inventory in general. (Chapter 14)

floating-rate bonds See Table 6.4 (Chapter 6)

floating-rate loan A loan with a rate of interest initially set at an increment above the prime rate and allowed to "float," or vary, above prime *as the prime rate varies* until maturity. (Chapter 14)

flotation costs The total costs of issuing and selling a security. (Chapter 10)

foreign bond Bond that is issued by a foreign corporation or government and is denominated in the investor's home currency and sold in the investor's home market. (Chapters 1 and 6)

foreign direct investment (FDI) The transfer by a multinational firm of capital, managerial, and technical assets from its home country to a host country. (Chapter 8)

foreign exchange manager The manager responsible for monitoring and managing the firm's exposure to loss from currency fluctuations. (Chapter 1)

free cash flow (FCF) The amount of cash flow available to investors (creditors and owners) after the firm has met all operating needs and paid for investments in net fixed assets and net current assets. (Chapter 3)

free cash flow valuation model A model that determines the value of an entire company as the present value of its expected *free cash flows* discounted at the firm's *weighted average cost of capital,* which is its expected average future cost of funds over the long run. (Chapter 7)

future value The value at a given future date of a present amount placed on deposit today and earning interest at a specified rate. Found by applying *compound interest* over a specified period of time. (Chapter 4)

future value interest factor The multiplier used to calculate, at a specified interest rate, the future value of a present amount as of a given time. (Chapter 4)

future value interest factor for an ordinary annuity The multiplier used to calculate the future value of an *ordinary annuity* at a specified interest rate over a given period of time. (Chapter 4)

generally accepted accounting principles (GAAP) The practice and procedure guidelines used to prepare and maintain financial records and reports; authorized by the *Financial Accounting Standards Board (FASB).* (Chapter 2)

Gordon model A common name for the *constant-growth model* that is widely cited in dividend valuation. (Chapter 7)

gross profit margin Measures the percentage of each sales dollar remaining after the firm has paid for its goods. (Chapter 2)

historical weights Either book or market value weights based on *actual* capital structure proportions. (Chapter 10)

incentive plans Management compensation plans that tend to tie management compensation to share price; most popular incentive plan involves the grant of *stock options.* (Chapter 1)

income bonds See Table 6.3 (Chapter 6)

income statement Provides a financial summary of the firm's operating results during a specified period. (Chapter 2)

incremental cash flows The *additional* cash flows—outflows or inflows—expected to result from a proposed capital expenditure. (Chapter 8)

independent projects Projects whose cash flows are unrelated or independent of one another; the acceptance of one *does not eliminate* the others from further consideration. (Chapter 8)

individual investors Investors who buy relatively small quantities of shares in order to meet personal investment goals. (Chapter 1)

informational content The information provided by the dividends of a firm with respect to future earnings, which causes owners to bid up or down the price of the firm's stock. (Chapter 12)

initial investment The relevant cash outflow for a proposed project at time zero. (Chapter 8)

initial public offering (IPO) The first public sale of a firm's stock. (Chapter 7)

installation costs Any added costs that are necessary to place an asset into operation. (Chapter 8)

installed cost of new asset The cost of *a new asset* plus its *installation costs*; equals the asset's depreciable value. (Chapter 8)

institutional investors Investment professionals, such as insurance companies, mutual funds, and pension funds, that are paid to manage other people's money and that trade large quantities of securities. (Chapter 1)

intercorporate dividends Dividends received by one corporation on common and preferred stock held in other corporations. (Chapter 1)

interest rate The compensation paid by the borrower of funds to the lender; from the borrower's point of view, the cost of borrowing funds. (Chapter 6)

interest rate risk The chance that interest rates will change and thereby change the required return and bond value. Rising rates, which result in decreasing bond values, are of greatest concern. (Chapter 6)

intermediate cash inflows Cash inflows received prior to the termination of a project. (Chapter 9)

internal forecast A sales forecast based on a buildup, or consensus, of sales forecasts through the firm's own sales channels. (Chapter 3)

internal rate of return (IRR) A sophisticated capital budgeting technique; the discount rate that equates the NPV of an investment opportunity with $0 (because the present value of cash inflows equals the initial investment); it is the compound annual rate of return that the firm will earn if it invests in the project and receives the given cash inflows. (Chapter 9)

internal rate of return approach An approach to capital rationing that involves graphing project IRRs in descending order against the total dollar investment to determine the group of acceptable projects. (Chapter 9)

international equity market A market that allows corporations to sell blocks of shares to investors in a number of different countries simultaneously. (Chapter 1)

inventory turnover Measures the activity, or liquidity, of a firm's inventory. (Chapter 2)

inverted yield curve A *downward-sloping* yield curve that indicates generally cheaper long-term borrowing costs than short-term borrowing costs. (Chapter 6)

investment bankers Financial intermediaries who, in addition to their role in selling new security issues, can be hired by acquirers in mergers to find suitable target companies and assist in negotiations. (Chapter 7)

investment flows Cash flows associated with purchase and sale of both fixed assets and business interests. (Chapter 3)

investment opportunities schedule (IOS) A ranking of investment possibilities from best (highest return) to worst (lowest return); the graph that plots project IRRs in descending order against the total dollar investment. (Chapters 9 and 10)

issued shares The number of shares of common stock that have been put into circulation; the sum of outstanding shares and treasury stock. (Chapter 7)

judgmental approach A simplified approach for preparing the pro forma balance sheet under which the values of certain balance sheet accounts are estimated, some as a percentage of sales and others by management assumption, and the firm's external financing is used as a balancing, or "plug," figure. (Chapter 3)

junk bonds See Table 6.4 (Chapter 6)

just-in-time (JIT) system Inventory management technique that minimizes inventory investment by having materials arrive at exactly the time they are needed for production. (Chapter 13)

letter of credit A letter written by a company's bank to the company's foreign supplier, stating that the bank guarantees payment of an invoiced amount if all the underlying agreements are met. (Chapter 14)

letter to stockholders Typically, the first element of the annual stockholders' report and the primary communication from management. (Chapter 2)

leverage Results from the use of fixed-cost assets or funds to magnify returns to the firm's owners. (Chapter 11)

lien A publicly disclosed legal claim on collateral. (Chapter 14)

line of credit An agreement between a commercial bank and a business specifying the amount of unsecured short-term borrowing the bank will make available to the firm over a given period of time. (Chapter 14)

liquidation value per share The *actual amount* per share of common stock that would be received if all of the firm's assets were *sold for their market value*, liabilities (including preferred stock) were paid, and any remaining money were divided among the common stockholders. (Chapter 7)

liquidity A firm's ability to satisfy its short-term obligations *as they come due*. (Chapter 2)

liquidity preferences General preferences of investors for shorter-term securities. (Chapter 6)

liquidity preference theory Theory suggesting that for any given issuer, long-term interest rates tend to be higher than short-term rates because (1) lower liquidity and higher responsiveness to general interest rate movements of longer-term securities exist and (2) borrower willingness to pay a higher rate for long-term financing causes the yield curve to be upward-sloping. (Chapter 6)

loan amortization The determination of the equal periodic loan payments necessary to provide a lender with a specified interest return and to repay the loan principal over a specified period. (Chapter 4)

loan amortization schedule A schedule of equal payments to repay a loan. It shows the allocation of each loan payment to interest and principal. (Chapter 4)

lockbox system A collection procedure in which customers mail payments to a post office box that is emptied regularly by the firm's bank, who processes the payments and deposits them in the firm's account. This system speeds up collection time by reducing processing time as well as mail and clearing time. (Chapter 13)

London Interbank Offered Rate (LIBOR) The base rate that is used to price all Eurocurrency loans. (Chapter 1)

long-term debt Debts for which payment is not due in the current year. (Chapter 2)

long-term (strategic) financial plans Lay out a company's planned financial actions and the anticipated impact of those actions over periods ranging from 2 to 10 years. (Chapter 3)

low-regular-and-extra dividend policy A dividend policy based on paying a low regular dividend, supplemented by an additional dividend when earnings are higher than normal in a given period. (Chapter 12)

mail float The time delay between when payment is placed in the mail and when it is received. (Chapter 13)

managerial finance Concerns the duties of the *financial manager* in the business firm. (Chapter 1)

manufacturing resource planning II (MRP II) A sophisticated computerized system that integrates data from numerous areas such as finance, accounting, marketing, engineering, and manufacturing and generates production plans as well as numerous financial and management reports. (Chapter 13)

marginal cost-benefit analysis Economic principle that states that financial decisions should be made and actions taken only when the added benefits exceed the added costs. (Chapter 1)

marginal tax rate The rate at which *additional income* is taxed. (Chapter 1)

market/book (M/B) ratio Provides an assessment of how investors view the firm's performance. Firms expected to earn high returns relative to their risk typically sell at higher M/B multiples. (Chapter 2)

market ratios Relate a firm's market value, as measured by its current share price, to certain accounting values. (Chapter 2)

market return The return on the market portfolio of all traded securities. (Chapter 5)

market segmentation theory Theory suggesting that the market for loans is segmented on the basis of maturity and that the supply of and demand for loans within each segment determine its prevailing interest rate; the slope of the yield curve is determined by the general relationship between the prevailing rates in each market segment. (Chapter 6)

market value weights Weights that use market values to measure the proportion of each type of capital in the firm's financial structure. (Chapter 10)

marketable securities Short-term debt instruments, such as U.S. Treasury bills, commercial paper, and negotiable certificates of deposit issued by government, business, and financial institutions, respectively. (Chapter 1)

materials requirement planning (MRP) system Applies EOQ concepts to determine what materials to order and when to order them; simulates each product's bill of materials, inventory status, and manufacturing process. (Chapter 13)

mixed stream A stream of unequal periodic cash flows that reflect no particular pattern. (Chapter 4)

modified accelerated cost recovery system (MACRS) System used to determine the depreciation of assets for tax purposes. (Chapter 3)

modified DuPont formula Relates the firm's *return on total assets (ROA)* to its *return on common equity (ROE)* using the *financial leverage multiplier (FLM)*. (Chapter 2)

money market A financial relationship created between suppliers and demanders of *short-term funds*. (Chapter 1)

mortgage bonds See Table 6.3 (Chapter 6)

multiple IRRs More than one IRR resulting from a capital budgeting project with a *nonconventional cash flow pattern*; the maximum number of IRRs for a project is equal to the number of sign changes in its cash flows. (Chapter 9)

mutually exclusive projects Projects that compete with one another, so that the acceptance of one *eliminates* from further consideration all other projects that serve a similar function. (Chapter 8)

negatively correlated Describes two series that move in opposite directions. (Chapter 5)

net cash flow The mathematical difference between the firm's cash receipts and its cash disbursements in each period. (Chapter 3)

net operating profits after taxes (NOPAT) A firm's earnings before interest and after taxes, EBIT $\times (1 - T)$. (Chapter 3)

net present value (NPV) A sophisticated capital budgeting technique; found by subtracting a project's initial investment from the present value of its cash inflows discounted at a rate equal to the firm's cost of capital. (Chapter 9)

net present value approach An approach to capital rationing that is based on the use of present values to determine the group of projects that will maximize owners' wealth. (Chapter 9)

net present value profile Graph that depicts a project's NPV for various discount rates. (Chapter 9)

net proceeds Funds actually received from the sale of a security. (Chapter 10)

net profit margin Measures the percentage of each sales dollar remaining after all costs and expenses, *including* interest, taxes, and preferred stock dividends, have been deducted. (Chapter 2)

net working capital The amount by which a firm's current assets exceed its current liabilities; can be *positive* or *negative*. (Chapters 8 and 13)

nominal (stated) annual rate Contractual annual rate of interest charged by a lender or promised by a borrower. (Chapter 4)

noncash charge An expense that is deducted on the income statement but does not involve the actual outlay of cash during the period; includes depreciation, amortization, and depletion. (Chapter 3)

nonconventional cash flow pattern An initial outflow followed by a series of inflows *and* outflows. (Chapter 8)

noncumulative preferred stock Preferred stock for which passed (unpaid) dividends do not accumulate. (Chapter 7)

nondiversifiable risk The relevant portion of an asset's risk attributable to market factors that affect all firms; cannot be eliminated through diversification. Also called *systematic risk*. (Chapter 5)

nonnotification basis The basis on which a borrower, having pledged an account receivable, continues to collect the account payments without notifying the account customer. (Chapter 14)

nonrecourse basis The basis on which accounts receivable are sold to a factor with the understanding that the factor accepts all credit risks on the purchased accounts. (Chapter 14)

nonvoting common stock Common stock that carries no voting rights; issued when the firm wishes to raise capital through the sale of common stock but does not want to give up its voting control. (Chapter 7)

no-par preferred stock Preferred stock with no stated face value but with a stated annual dollar dividend. (Chapter 7)

normal yield curve An *upward-sloping* yield curve that indicates generally cheaper short-term borrowing costs than long-term borrowing costs. (Chapter 6)

notes to the financial statements Footnotes detailing information on the accounting policies, procedures, calculations, and transactions underlying entries in the financial statements. (Chapter 2)

notification basis The basis on which an account customer whose account has been pledged (or factored) is notified to remit payment directly to the lender (or factor). (Chapter 14)

operating breakeven point The level of sales necessary to cover all *operating costs*; the point at which EBIT = $0. (Chapter 11)

operating cash flow (OCF) The cash flow a firm generates from its normal operations; calculated as net operating profits after taxes (NOPAT) + depreciation. (Chapter 3)

operating cash inflows The incremental after-tax cash inflows resulting from implementation of a project during its life. (Chapter 8)

operating cycle (OC) The time from the beginning of the production process to the collection of cash from the sale of the finished product. (Chapter 13)

operating expenditure An outlay of funds by the firm resulting in benefits received *within* 1 year. (Chapter 8)

operating flows Cash flows directly related to sale and production of the firm's products and services. (Chapter 3)

operating leverage The potential use of *fixed operating costs* to magnify the effects of changes in sales on the firm's earnings before interest and taxes. (Chapter 11)

operating profit margin Measures the percentage of each sales dollar remaining after all costs and expenses *other than* interest, taxes, and preferred stock dividends are deducted; the "pure profits" earned on each sales dollar. (Chapter 2)

operating-change restrictions Contractual restrictions that a bank may impose on a firm's financial condition or operations as part of a line-of-credit agreement. (Chapter 14)

opportunity costs Cash flows that could be realized from the best alternative use of an owned asset. (Chapter 8)

optimal capital structure The capital structure at which the weighted average cost of capital is minimized, thereby maximizing the firm's value. (Chapter 11)

order costs The fixed clerical costs of placing and receiving an inventory order. (Chapter 13)

ordinary annuity An annuity for which the cash flow occurs at the *end* of each period. (Chapter 4)

ordinary income Income earned through the sale of a firm's goods or services. (Chapter 1)

organized securities exchanges Tangible organizations that act as *secondary markets* where outstanding securities are resold. (Chapter 1)

outstanding shares The number of shares of common stock held by the public. (Chapter 7)

over-the-counter (OTC) exchange An intangible market for the purchase and sale of securities not listed by the organized exchanges. (Chapter 1)

paid-in capital in excess of par The amount of proceeds in excess of the par value received from the original sale of common stock. (Chapter 2)

partnership A business owned by two or more people and operated for profit. (Chapter 1)

par value (stock) A relatively useless value for a stock established for legal purposes in the firm's corporate charter. (Chapter 7)

par-value preferred stock Preferred stock with a stated face value that is used with the specified dividend percentage to determine the annual dollar dividend. (Chapter 7)

payback period The amount of time required for a firm to recover its initial investment in a project, as calculated from *cash inflows*. (Chapter 9)

payment date Set by the firm's directors, the actual date on which the firm mails the dividend payment to the holders of record. (Chapter 12)

pecking order A hierarchy of financing that begins with retained earnings, which is followed by debt financing and finally external equity financing. (Chapter 11)

percentage advance The percent of the book value of the collateral that constitutes the principal of a secured loan. (Chapter 14)

percent-of-sales method A simple method for developing the pro forma income statement; it forecasts sales and then expresses the various income statement items as percentages of projected sales. (Chapter 3)

perfectly negatively correlated Describes two *negatively correlated* series that have a *correlation coefficient* of −1. (Chapter 5)

perfectly positively correlated Describes two *positively correlated* series that have a *correlation coefficient* of +1. (Chapter 5)

performance plans Plans that tie management compensation to measures such as EPS, growth in EPS, and other measures of return. *Performance shares* and/or *cash bonuses* are used as compensation under these plans. (Chapter 1)

performance shares Shares of stock given to management for meeting stated performance goals. (Chapter 1)

permanent funding requirement A constant investment in operating assets resulting from constant sales over time. (Chapter 13)

perpetuity An annuity with an infinite life, providing continual annual cash flow. (Chapter 4)

pledge of accounts receivable The use of a firm's accounts receivable as security, or collateral, to obtain a short-term loan. (Chapter 14)

political risk Risk that arises from the possibility that a host government will take actions harmful to foreign investors or that political turmoil in a country will endanger investments there. (Chapter 5)

portfolio A collection, or group, of assets. (Chapter 5)

positively correlated Describes two series that move in the same direction. (Chapter 5)

preemptive right Allows common stockholders to maintain their *proportionate* ownership in the corporation when new shares are issued. (Chapter 7)

preferred stock A special form of ownership having a fixed periodic dividend that must be paid prior to payment of any dividends to common stockholders. (Chapter 1)

premium The amount by which a bond sells at a value that is greater than its par value. (Chapter 6)

present value The current dollar value of a future amount—the amount of money that would have to be invested today at a given interest rate over a specified period to equal the future amount. (Chapter 4)

present value interest factor The multiplier used to calculate, at a specified discount rate, the present value of an amount to be received in a future period. (Chapter 4)

present value interest factor for an ordinary annuity The multiplier used to calculate the present value of an *ordinary annuity* at a specified discount rate over a given period of time. (Chapters 4 and 10)

president or chief executive officer (CEO) Corporate official responsible for managing the firm's day-to-day operations and carrying out the policies established by the *board of directors*. (Chapter 1)

price/earnings multiple approach A popular technique used to estimate the firm's share value; calculated by multiplying the firm's expected earnings per share (EPS) by the average price/earnings (P/E) ratio for the industry. (Chapter 7)

price/earnings (P/E) ratio Measures the amount that investors are willing to pay for each dollar of a firm's earnings; the higher the P/E ratio, the greater is investor confidence. (Chapter 2)

primary market Financial market in which securities are initially issued; the only market in which the issuer is directly involved in the transaction. (Chapter 1)

prime rate of interest (prime rate) The lowest rate of interest charged by leading banks on business loans to their most important business borrowers. (Chapter 14)

principal The amount of money on which interest is paid. (Chapter 4)

private placement The sale of a new security issue, typically bonds or preferred stock, directly to an investor or group of investors. (Chapter 1)

privately owned (stock) All common stock of a firm owned by a single individual. (Chapter 7)

pro forma statements Projected, or forecast, income statements and balance sheets. (Chapter 3)

probability The *chance* that a given outcome will occur. (Chapter 5)

probability distribution A model that relates probabilities to the associated outcomes. (Chapter 5)

proceeds from sale of old asset The cash inflows, net of any *removal* or *cleanup costs*, resulting from the sale of an existing asset. (Chapter 8)

processing float The time between receipt of a payment and its deposit into the firm's account. (Chapter 13)

profitability The relationship between revenues and costs generated by using the firm's assets—both current and fixed—in productive activities. (Chapter 13)

prospectus A portion of a security registration statement that describes the key aspects of the issue, the issuer, and its management and financial position. (Chapter 7)

proxy battle The attempt by a nonmanagement group to gain control of the management of a firm by soliciting a sufficient number of proxy votes. (Chapter 7)

proxy statement A statement transferring the votes of a stockholder to another party. (Chapter 7)

Public Company Accounting Oversight Board (PCAOB) A not-for-profit corporation established by the *Sarbanes-Oxley Act of 2002* to protect the interests of investors and further the public interest in the preparation of informative, fair, and independent audit reports. (Chapter 2)

public offering The nonexclusive sale of either bonds or stocks to the general public. (Chapter 1)

publicly owned (stock) Common stock of a firm owned by a broad group of unrelated individual or institutional investors. (Chapter 7)

putable bonds See Table 6.4 (Chapter 6)

quarterly compounding Compounding of interest over four periods within the year. (Chapter 4)

quick (acid-test) ratio A measure of liquidity calculated by dividing the firm's current assets minus inventory by its current liabilities. (Chapter 2)

quotations Information on bonds, stocks, and other securities, including current price data and statistics on recent price behavior. ((Chapter 6)

range A measure of an asset's risk, which is found by subtracting the pessimistic (worst) outcome from the optimistic (best) outcome. (Chapter 5)

ranking approach The ranking of capital expenditure projects on the basis of some predetermined measure, such as the rate of return. (Chapter 8)

ratio analysis Involves methods of calculating and interpreting financial ratios to analyze and monitor the firm's performance. (Chapter 2)

real options Opportunities that are embedded in capital projects that enable managers to alter their cash flows and risk in a way that affects project acceptability (NPV). Also called *strategic options*. (Chapter 9)

real rate of interest The rate that creates an equilibrium between the supply of savings and the demand for investment funds in a perfect world, without inflation, where funds suppliers and demanders are indifferent to the term of loans or investments and have no *liquidity preference*, and where all outcomes are certain. (Chapter 6)

recaptured depreciation The portion of an asset's sale price that is above its book value and below its initial purchase price. (Chapter 8)

recovery period The appropriate depreciable life of a particular asset as determined by MACRS. (Chapter 3)

red herring A preliminary prospectus made available to prospective investors during the waiting period between the registration statement's filing with the SEC and its approval. (Chapter 7)

regular dividend policy A dividend policy based on the payment of a fixed-dollar dividend in each period. (Chapter 12)

relevant cash flows The *incremental cash outflow (investment) and resulting subsequent inflows* associated with a proposed capital expenditure. (Chapter 8)

reorder point The point at which to reorder inventory, expressed as days of lead time × daily usage. (Chapter 13)

required return The cost of funds obtained by selling an ownership interest; it reflects the funds supplier's level of expected return. (Chapter 6)

required total financing Amount of funds needed by the firm if the ending cash for the period is less than the desired minimum cash balance; typically represented by notes payable. (Chapter 3)

residual theory of dividends A school of thought that suggests that the dividend paid by a firm should be viewed as a *residual*—the amount left over after all acceptable investment opportunities have been undertaken. (Chapter 12)

restrictive covenants Provisions in a *bond indenture* that place operating and financial constraints on the borrower. (Chapter 6)

retained earnings The cumulative total of all earnings, net of dividends, that have been retained and reinvested in the firm since its inception; earnings not distributed to owners as dividends—a form of *internal* financing. (Chapters 2 and 12)

return The total gain or loss experienced on an investment over a given period of time; calculated by dividing the asset's cash distributions during the period, plus change in value, by its beginning-of-period investment value. (Chapter 5)

return on common equity (ROE) Measures the return earned on the common stockholders' investment in the firm. (Chapter 2)

return on total assets (ROA) Measures the overall effectiveness of management in generating profits with its available assets; also called the *return on investment (ROI)*. (Chapter 2)

reverse stock split A method used to raise the market price of a firm's stock by exchanging a certain number of outstanding shares for one new share. (Chapter 12)

revolving credit agreement A line of credit *guaranteed* to a borrower by a commercial bank regardless of the scarcity of money. (Chapter 14)

rights Financial instruments that allow stockholders to purchase additional shares at a price below the market price, in direct proportion to their number of owned shares. (Chapter 7)

risk The chance of financial loss or, more formally, the *variability of returns associated with a given asset.* (Chapters 1 and 5)

risk (in capital budgeting) The chance that a project will prove unacceptable or, more formally, the degree of variability of cash flows. (Chapter 9)

risk (of technical insolvency) The probability that a firm will be unable to pay its bills as they come due. (Chapter 13)

risk premium The amount by which the interest rate or required return on a security exceeds the risk-free rate of interest, R_F; it varies with specific issuer and issue characteristics. (Chapter 6)

risk-adjusted discount rate (RADR) The rate of return that must be earned on a given project to compensate the firm's owners adequately—that is, to maintain or improve the firm's share price. (Chapter 9)

risk-averse The attitude toward risk in which an increased return would be required for an increase in risk. (Chapters 1 and 5)

risk-free rate of interest, R_F See *risk-free rate of return*. (Chapter 6)

risk-free rate of return, R_F The required return on a *risk-free asset*, typically a 3-month *U.S. Treasury bill*. (Chapter 5)

safety stock Extra inventory that is held to prevent stockouts of important items. (Chapter 13)

sales forecast The prediction of the firm's sales over a given period, based on external and/or internal data; used as the key input to the short-term financial planning process. (Chapter 3)

Sarbanes-Oxley Act of 2002 (SOX) An act aimed at eliminating corporate disclosure and conflict of interest problems. Contains provisions about corporate financial disclosures and the relationships among corporations, analysts, auditors, attorneys, directors, officers, and shareholders. (Chapter 1)

scenario analysis A behavioral approach that evaluates the impact on the firm's return of simultaneous changes in *a number of variables*. (Chapter 9)

seasonal funding requirement An investment in operating assets that varies over time as a result of cyclic sales. (Chapter 13)

secondary market Financial market in which preowned securities (those that are not new issues) are traded. (Chapter 1)

secured short-term financing Short-term financing (loan) that has specific assets pledged as collateral. (Chapter 14)

Securities and Exchange Commission (SEC) The federal regulatory body that governs the sale and listing of securities. (Chapter 2)

securities exchanges Organizations that provide the marketplace in which firms can raise funds through the sale of new securities and purchasers can resell securities. (Chapter 1)

security agreement The agreement between the borrower and the lender that specifies the collateral held against a secured loan. (Chapter 14)

security market line (SML) The depiction of the *capital asset pricing model* (*CAPM*) as a graph that reflects the required return in the marketplace for each level of nondiversifiable risk (beta). (Chapter 5)

selling group A large number of brokerage firms that join the originating investment banker(s); each accepts responsibility for selling a certain portion of a new security issue on a commission basis. (Chapter 7)

semiannual compounding Compounding of interest over two periods within the year. (Chapter 4)

sensitivity analysis An approach for assessing risk that uses several possible-return estimates to obtain a sense of the variability among outcomes. (Chapter 5)

short-term (operating) financial plans Specify short-term financial actions and the anticipated impact of those actions. (Chapter 3)

short-term financial management Management of current assets and current liabilities. (Chapter 13)

short-term, self-liquidating loan An unsecured short-term loan in which the use to which the borrowed money is put provides the mechanism through which the loan is repaid. (Chapter 14)

signal A financing action by management that is believed to reflect its view of the firm's stock value; generally, debt financing is viewed as a *positive signal* that management believes the stock is "undervalued," and a stock issue is viewed as a *negative signal* that management believes the stock is "overvalued." (Chapter 11)

simulation A statistics-based behavioral approach that applies predetermined probability distributions and random numbers to estimate risky outcomes. (Chapter 9)

single-payment note A short-term, one-time loan made to a borrower who needs funds for a specific purpose for a short period. (Chapter 14)

sinking-fund requirement A restrictive provision often included in a bond indenture, providing for the systematic retirement of bonds prior to their maturity. (Chapter 6)

small (ordinary) stock dividend A stock dividend representing less than 20 to 25 percent of the common stock outstanding when the dividend is declared. (Chapter 12)

sole proprietorship A business owned by one person and operated for his or her own profit. (Chapter 1)

spontaneous liabilities Financing that arises from the normal course of business; the two major short-term sources of such liabilities are accounts payable and accruals. (Chapter 14)

stakeholders Groups such as employees, customers, suppliers, creditors, owners, and others who have a direct economic link to the firm. (Chapter 1)

standard debt provisions Provisions in a *bond indenture* specifying certain record-keeping and general business practices that the bond issuer must follow; normally, they do not place a burden on a financially sound business. (Chapter 6)

standard deviation (σ_k) The most common statistical indicator of an asset's risk; it measures the dispersion around the *expected value*. (Chapter 5)

statement of cash flows Provides a summary of the firm's operating, investment, and financing cash flows and reconciles them with changes in its cash and marketable securities during the period. (Chapter 2)

statement of retained earnings Reconciles the net income earned during a given year, and any cash dividends paid, with the change in retained earnings between the start and the end of that year. An abbreviated form of the *statement of stockholders' equity*. (Chapter 2)

statement of stockholders' equity Shows all equity account transactions that occur during a given year. (Chapter 2)

stock dividend The payment, to existing owners, of a dividend in the form of stock. (Chapter 12)

stock options An incentive allowing managers to purchase stock at the market price set at the time of the grant. (Chapter 1)

stock purchase warrants Instruments that give their holders the right to purchase a certain number of shares of the issuer's common stock at a specified price over a certain period of time. Occasionally attached to bonds as "sweeteners." (Chapter 6)

stock repurchase The repurchase by the firm of outstanding common stock in the marketplace; desired effects of stock repurchases are that they either enhance shareholder value or help to discourage an unfriendly takeover. (Chapter 12)

stock split A method commonly used to lower the market price of a firm's stock by increasing the number of shares belonging to each shareholder. (Chapter 12)

stockholders The owners of a corporation, whose ownership, or *equity*, is evidenced by either common stock or preferred stock. (Chapter 1)

stockholders' report Annual report that publicly owned corporations must provide to stockholders; it summarizes and documents the firm's financial activities during the past year. (Chapter 2)

stretching accounts payable Paying bills as late as possible without damaging the firm's credit rating. (Chapter 14)

subordinated debentures See Table 6.3 (Chapter 6)

subordination In a bond indenture, the stipulation that subsequent creditors agree to wait until all claims of the *senior debt* are satisfied. (Chapter 6)

sunk costs Cash outlays that have already been made (past outlays) and therefore have no effect on the cash flows relevant to a current decision. (Chapter 8)

supervoting shares Stock that carries with it multiple votes per share rather than the single vote per share typically given on regular shares of common stock. (Chapter 7)

target capital structure The desired optimal mix of debt and equity financing that most firms attempt to maintain. (Chapter 10)

target dividend-payout ratio A dividend policy under which the firm attempts to pay out a certain *percentage* of earnings as a stated dollar dividend and adjusts that dividend toward a target payout as proven earnings increases occur. (Chapter 12)

target weights Either book or market value weights based on *desired* capital structure proportions. (Chapter 10)

tax on sale of old asset Tax that depends on the relationship among the old asset's sale price, initial purchase price, and *book value*, and on existing government tax rules. (Chapter 8)

technically insolvent Describes a firm that is unable to pay its bills as they come due. (Chapter 13)

tender offer A formal offer to purchase a given number of shares of a firm's stock at a specified price. (Chapter 12)

term structure of interest rates The relationship between the interest rate or rate of return and the time to maturity. (Chapter 6)

terminal cash flow The after-tax nonoperating cash flow occurring in the final year of a project. It is usually attributable to liquidation of the project. (Chapter 8)

time line A horizontal line on which time zero appears at the leftmost end and future periods are marked from left to right; can be used to depict investment cash flows. (Chapter 4)

times interest earned ratio Measures the firm's ability to make contractual interest payments; sometimes called the *interest coverage ratio*. (Chapter 2)

time-series analysis Evaluation of the firm's financial performance over time using financial ratio analysis. (Chapter 2)

total asset turnover Indicates the efficiency with which the firm uses its assets to generate sales. (Chapter 2)

total cost of inventory The sum of order costs and carrying costs of inventory. (Chapter 13)

total leverage The potential use of *fixed costs*, both *operating and financial*, to magnify the effects of changes in sales on the firm's earnings per share. (Chapter 11)

total risk The combination of a security's *nondiversifiable risk* and *diversifiable risk*. (Chapter 5)

transfer prices Prices that subsidiaries charge each other for the goods and services traded between them. (Chapter 9)

treasurer The firm's chief financial manager, who is responsible for the firm's financial activities, such as financial planning and fund raising, making capital expenditure decisions, and managing cash, credit, the pension fund, and foreign exchange. (Chapter 1)

treasury stock The number of shares of outstanding stock that have been repurchased by the firm. (Chapter 7)

trust receipt inventory loan A secured short-term loan against inventory under which the lender advances 80 to 100 percent of the cost of the borrower's relatively expensive inventory items in exchange for the borrower's promise to repay the lender, with accrued interest, immediately after the sale of each item of collateral. (Chapter 14)

trustee A paid individual, corporation, or commercial bank trust department that acts as the third party to a *bond indenture* and can take specified actions on behalf of the bondholders if the terms of the indenture are violated. (Chapter 6)

two-bin method Unsophisticated inventory-monitoring technique that is typically applied to C group items and involves reordering inventory when one of two bins is empty. (Chapter 13)

uncorrelated Describes two series that lack any interaction and therefore have a correlation coefficient close to zero. (Chapter 5)

U.S. Treasury bills (T-bills) Short-term IOUs issued by the U.S. Treasury; considered the *risk-free asset*. (Chapter 5)

underpriced Stock sold at a price below its current market price, P_0. (Chapter 10)

underwriting The role of the *investment banker* in bearing the risk of reselling, at a profit, the securities purchased from an issuing corporation at an agreed-on price. (Chapter 7)

underwriting syndicate A group formed by an investment banker to share the financial risk associated with *underwriting* new securities. (Chapter 7)

unlimited funds The financial situation in which a firm is able to accept all independent projects that provide an acceptable return. (Chapter 8)

unlimited liability The condition of a sole proprietorship (or general partnership) allowing the owner's total wealth to be taken to satisfy creditors. (Chapter 1)

unsecured short-term financing Short-term financing obtained without pledging specific assets as collateral. (Chapter 14)

valuation The process that links risk and return to determine the worth of an asset. (Chapter 6)

variable-growth model A dividend valuation approach that allows for a change in the dividend growth rate. (Chapter 7)

venture capital Privately raised external equity capital used to fund early-stage firms with attractive growth prospects. (Chapter 7)

venture capitalists (VCs) Providers of venture capital; typically, formal businesses that maintain strong oversight over the firms they invest in and that have clearly defined exit strategies. (Chapter 7)

warehouse receipt loan A secured short-term loan against inventory under which the lender receives control of the pledged inventory collateral, which is stored by a designated warehousing company on the lender's behalf. (Chapter 14)

weighted average cost of capital (WACC), k_a Reflects the expected average future cost of funds over the long run; found by weighting the cost of each specific type of capital by its proportion in the firm's capital structure. (Chapter 10)

weighted marginal cost of capital (WMCC) The firm's weighted average cost of capital (WACC) associated with its *next dollar* of total new financing. (Chapter 10)

weighted marginal cost of capital (WMCC) schedule Graph that relates the firm's weighted average cost of capital to the level of total new financing. (Chapter 10)

wire transfer An electronic communication that, via bookkeeping entries, removes funds from the payer's bank and deposits them in the payee's bank. (Chapter 13)

working capital Current assets, which represent the portion of investment that circulates from one form to another in the ordinary conduct of business. (Chapter 13)

yield curve A graph of the relationship between the debt's remaining time to maturity (x axis) and its yield to maturity (y axis); it shows the yield to maturity for debts of equal quality and different maturities. Graphically depicts the *term structure of interest rates*. (Chapter 6)

yield to maturity (YTM) The rate of return that investors earn if they buy a bond at a specific price and hold it until maturity. (Assumes that the issuer makes all scheduled interest and principal payments as promised.) (Chapter 6)

zero- (or low-) coupon bonds See Table 6.4 (Chapter 6)

zero-balance account (ZBA) A disbursement account that always has an end-of-day balance of zero because the firm deposits money to cover checks drawn on the account only as they are presented for payment each day. (Chapter 13)

zero-growth model An approach to dividend valuation that assumes a constant, nongrowing dividend stream. (Chapter 7)

Credits

Bold page numbers indicate location of feature.

16: From Robert A. Cooke, "Business Ethics: A Perspective," in *Arthur Andersen Cases on Business Ethics* (Chicago: Arthur Andersen, September 1991), pages 2 and 5. Copyright © 1991 Arthur Andersen. All rights reserved. Reprinted by permission.

49: Data from *Industry Norms and Key Business Ratios*. Dun & Bradstreet, Inc.

199: Data from *Stocks, Bonds, Bills, and Inflation, 2004 Yearbook* (Chicago: Ibbotson Associates, Inc., 2004).

204: Data from *Stocks, Bonds, Bills, and Inflation, 2004 Yearbook* (Chicago: Ibbotson Associates, Inc.), 2004.

214: Data from *Value Line Investment Survey* (New York: Value Line Publishing, March 8, 2002).

245: AP Wideworld Photos; Reprinted from *The Wall Street Journal,* May 19, 2004, p. C12.

287: Reprinted from *The Wall Street Journal,* May 19, 2004, p. C26.

Index

AAI. *See* Average age of inventory (AAI)
Abandonment option, 367
ABC inventory system, 519–520, 540
Ability to service debts, 57
Accept-reject approach, 319
Accept-reject decisions, 355, 358, 360
Accounting
   fraud, 404
   in bankruptcy, 404
Accounting entries, after common stock repurchase, 497
Accounting function, 2
Accounting records, 242
Accounting value, 296, 302
Accounts payable (A/P), 44, 518, 549
   in short-term financing, 568
   key short-term financing features of, 569–570
Accounts payable management, 550–553, **568**–**571**
Accounts payable payments, 108–109
Accounts receivable (A/R), 44. *See also* Factoring accounts receivable
   aging of, 532
   as collateral, 564–566, 571
   collections of, 105–106, 518
   key short-term financing features of, 569–570
   marginal investment in, 526
   pledging, 564–565, 571
   sale of, 242, 566
Accounts receivable (A/R) management, 524–534
Accounts receivable turnover, 526
Accrual basis, 10
Accruals, 44, 554, 568, 571
   key short-term financing features of, 569–570
Accumulated depreciation, 44
ACH. *See* Automated clearinghouse (ACH)
ACH transfer, 536, 540
Acid-test ratio, 52–53
ACP. *See* Average collection period (ACP)
Activity analysis, 65
Activity ratios, 53–56

Actual amount per share, 303
Actual capital structure proportions, 417
Additional common stock, equivalent fully subscribed issue of, 413
Administrative costs, 407
Adobe Systems, 445
ADRs. *See* American depositary receipts (ADRs)
Advances, interest levied on, 566
After-tax basis, 330
After-tax cost of debt, 410
After-tax costs, 406
After-tax proceeds from sale of old asset, 326–**328**
Agency, 17–19
Agency costs, 17–18, 454, 455
   lender-imposed, 455–456
Agency problem, 17–18, 455
Aggressive funding strategy, 517
Aging of accounts receivable, 532–533
Aging schedule, 532
Algebraic approach, to breakeven analysis, 439–440
Almanac of Business and Industrial Financial Ratios, 48
Alternative capital structures
   comparing, 461–462
   firm value and, 464
Amazon, payables policy of, 554
Amazon.com, 321
American depositary receipts (ADRs), 280, 301
American Express Co., 15, 25
American Stock Exchange (AMEX), 23, 280, 288
Amortization, 167–168
Analysis, sensitivity and correlation, 195. *See also* Activity analysis; Benefit-cost analysis; Breakeven analysis; Combined analysis; Complete ratio analysis; Correlation analyses; Cost-volume-profit analysis; Cross-sectional analysis; Debt analysis; DuPont system of analysis; EBIT–EPS analysis; Financial statements/analysis; Liquidity analysis; Marginal analysis; Market analysis; Net present value analysis; Profitability analysis; Ratio; ROI analysis; Scenario analysis; Sensitivity analysis; Time-series analysis
Angel capitalists (angels), 282. *See also* Venture capitalists (VCs)
Annual cleanup, 559
Annual interest, 407
Annual percentage rate (APR), 164, 410
Annual percentage yield (APY), 164
Annual rate of return, 145
Annuities, 149, 148–154. *See also* Ordinary annuity
   interest rate associated with, 170
   types of, 149
Annuity cash flow, 140
Annuity due, 149
   future and present value of, 149
A/P. *See* Accounts payable (A/P)
APP. *See* Average payment period (APP)
APR. *See* Annual percentage rate (APR)
APY. *See* Annual percentage yield (APY)
A/R. *See* Accounts receivable (A/R)
Articles of partnership, 4
Ask price, 24
Assets, 42. *See also* Earning assets; Portfolio correlation; Single asset
   book value of, 326
   claims on, 375–376
   current, 44
   depreciable life of, 92–93
   depreciable value of, 92
   high-beta, 215
   key valuation definitions and formulas for, 263
   liquidation of, 280
   low-beta, 215
   proceeds from sale of, 326–328, 335
   risk-free, 216
   uncorrelated, 206
   valuation of, 250–253, 263
   variability of returns associated with, 197
Association for Finance Professional (AFP), 247

I-1

I-2 INDEX

Associations, 7
Asymmetric information, 456–457
Auction process, 23
Audited financial statements, 51
Authorized shares, 278
Automated clearinghouse (ACH), 536. *See also* ACH transfer
Average age of inventory (AAI), 54, 536
Average collection period (ACP), 54–55, 514, 524–525, 531–532
Average payment period (APP), 55, 514
Average tax rate, 27

Bad debts, marginal, 527
Balance sheet, 42–45, 511
Bank borrowing costs, 553
Banker's acceptances, features and recent yields on, 538
Bank loans, 555–560, 571
Bankruptcy, probability of, 454–457
Banks, short-term loans from, 571. *See also* Bank loans
Bar chart, 200–201
Bayer, AG, 210
Before-tax cost of debt, 407–409
Behavioral finance, 290
Benchmarking, 48
Benefit-cost analysis, 529
Berkshire Hathaway, 25, 377
Beta coefficient, 212, 219–221. *See also* Portfolio beta coefficients
  interpreting, 213–214
  required return and, 217
Bid price, 24
Bill of materials, 522
Bird-in-the-hand argument, 486
Board of directors, 5
Board of Governors of the Federal Reserve System, 236
Boeing, 15
Bond amortization schedules, 235
Bond cost, 262
Bond financing, 262
  cost of, 243–244
Bond indenture, 242–243, 281
Bond issues
  general features of, 244
  international, 248–250
Bond maturity, impact on bond cost, 243
Bond offering size, impact on bond cost, 243
Bond quotations, interpreting, 245–246
Bond ratings, 246–247
Bonds, 22
  convertible, 244
  corporate, 242–250
  fundamentals of, 253
  issuer's default risk, 244
  key valuation definitions and formulas for, 263
  popular types of, 247–248

Bond valuation, 251–253
Bond values, 264
  behavior of, 255–258
  finding, 253–255
  required returns and, 255–258
  semiannual interest and, 260–261
  time to maturity and, 257–258
Book value, 326
  sale of asset and, 327–328
  per share, 296, 302
Book value weights, 417
Breakeven analysis, 437, 439–442, 468
Breakeven point, 468. *See also* Financial breakeven point; Operating breakeven point
Break points, 418, 425
  finding, 418–419
Buffett, Warren, 25, 290, 377
Business, finance and, 3–8. *See also* Cyclical business
Business loans, short-term, 555–556
Business Month, 48
Business organization, legal forms of, 4–7. *See also* Corporations; Firms
Business risk, 266, 403. *See also* Constant business risk; Risk
  constant, 459
  probability of bankruptcy and, 454–455
Business taxation, 2, 26–29, 32
Buy orders, 23

Calculator financial functions, 146–147
Calculator keys, 139
California Earthquake Authority (CEA), 377
Callable preferred stock, 282
Call feature, 244. *See also* Put option
Call premium, 244
Call price, 244
Capacity, as dimension of credit, 525
Capital, 275. *See also* Cash entries; Cost of capital; Funds; Money; Venture capital; Weighted average cost of capital (WACC); Weighted marginal cost of capital (WMCC)
  cost of specific sources of, 405–406
  as dimension of credit, 525
  sources of, 402
  types of, 451–452, 468–469
  weighted average cost of, 294
Capital asset pricing model (CAPM), 195, 211–218, 219–221, 299, **413**, 425. *See also* Security market line (SML)
  comments on, 218
  equation, 215–217
  sections of, 212–218
  using to find risk-adjusted discount rate (RADR), 376
Capital budgeting, 317
Capital budgeting cash flows, 316–351
Capital budgeting process, 317–318

Capital budgeting techniques, 321, 352–400
  key formulas, definitions, and decision criteria for, 382
Capital budgeting terminology, 318–320, 338
Capital expenditures, 317
  key motives for making, 318, 338
Capital expenditures managers, 7
Capital gains, 29
  taxation, 29
Capital impairment restrictions, 487
Capital markets, 2, 20, **22**–24, 31
Capital rationing, 319, 368
Capital structure(s), 437, 438, 451–459. *See also* Alternative capital structures; Capital structure theory; Optimal capital structure
  assessment of, 468–469
  of corporations, 422
  EBIT–EPS approach to, **459**–464
  external assessment of, 452
  of non-U.S. firms, 452–454
  optimal, 468
Capital structure decisions, factors to consider in, 465
Capital structure theory, 454, 469
CAPM. *See* Capital asset pricing model (CAPM)
Captive finance companies, 567
Career opportunities, 3
  in managerial finance, 7
Carrying costs, 520
Cash. *See* Capital; Ending cash; Excess cash; Funds; Money
Cash basis, 10
Cash bonuses, 18
Cash budgets, 104–112, 120–121
  evaluating, 110–111
  preparing, 105–110
  uncertainty in, 111–112
Cash concentration, 535–536
Cash conversion cycle (CCC), 510, 514–518, 539
  accounts payable and, 550–551
  funding requirements of, 515–518
  managing, 518
Cash disbursements, 107–109
Cash discount changes, 510
Cash discount period, 530–531
Cash discounts, 529–530, 540, 551–553
Cash dividend payments, 108, 480–482
Cash dividends, 498
  stock repurchases viewed as, 496–497
Cash flow, 91, 119. *See also* Cash flows; Conventional cash flow patterns; Free cash flow (FCF); Mixed stream cash flow; Net cash flow; Operating cash flow (OCF); Reinvestment; Single amount cash flow; Terminal cash flow
  analyzing, 92–102

basic patterns of, 140–141
present value and, 300
Cash flow basis, 331
Cash flow components, 322
Cash flow patterns, conventional versus nonconventional, 319–320
Cash flows, 10–11, 13, 262. *See also* Capital budgeting cash flows; Cash flow; Discounting cash flows; Incremental cash flows; Mixed streams; Relevant cash flows; Series of cash flows; Statement of cash flows
 cost to maturity of, 256
 expansion versus replacement, 322–323
 magnitude and timing of, 363
 mixed stream, 154–158
 relevant, 321–325
 summarizing relevant, 337
 valuation and, 250–251
Cash forecasts, 104–105, 106, 107
Cash hoarding, 489
Cash inflows, 96–97, 149 419. *See also* Cash flows; Incremental (relevant) cash inflows; Intermediate cash inflows; Mixed stream of cash inflows; Operating cash inflows; Relevant cash inflows
 interpreting, 331–332
Cash inflows/outflows, classifying, 96–97. *See also* Cash flows; Cash outflows; Incremental cash outflow and inflows
Cash managers, 7
Cash outflows, 95–96. *See also* Cash flows; Cash inflows; Cash inflows/outflows; Incremental cash outflow
Cash planning, 91, 102, 120
Cash purchases, 108
Cash receipts, 105–107
Cash sales, 105
CCC. *See* Cash conversion cycle (CCC)
CDs. *See* Certificates of deposit (CDs)
CEO. *See* Chief executive officer (CEO)
Certificates of deposit (CDs), features and recent yields on, 538
CFO. *See* Chief financial officer (CFO)
Change in net working capital, 328–329
Changing required returns, 257–258
Character, as dimension of credit, 525
Chicago Stock Exchange, 23
Chief executive officer (CEO), 6
 highest-paid, 18
Chief financial officer (CFO), 6, 8
Cleanup costs, 326, 335
Clearing float, 534
Clientele effect, 485
Closely owned shares, 277
Closely owned stock, 277
Coca-Cola, 25
Coefficient of variation (CV), 203–204

Collateral, 549, 563, 569
 accounts receivable as, 565–566, 571
 as dimension of credit, 525
 inventory as, 566–567
Collateral trust bonds, 248
Collection department, 566
Collection float time, 534
Collections, speeding up, 529, 534–535, 540
Collection techniques, 533, 540
Combined analysis, 50
Commercial finance companies, 563
Commercial paper, 549, 560–561, 568, 571
 features and recent yields on, 538
 key short-term financing features of, 569–570
Commitment fee, 559
Common-size income statements, 59
Common stock, 5, 22, 44, 274, 277–280, 301. *See also* Additional common stock
 cost of, 411–415
 cost of new issues of, 414–415
 issuing, 282–286
 key valuation definitions and formulas for, 302
 nonvoting, 279
 valuation of, 288–298
Common stock equity, cost of, 411–413, 425
Common stock equity weight, 415
Common stockholders, 277
Common stock repurchase, 496
Common stock value, decision making and, 298–300
Compensating balance, 559
Complete ratio analysis, 64–71
Compounding, 138, 158–160, 173
 continuous, 162–163
 quarterly, 159–160
 semiannual, 158–159
Compound interest, 141
Comptroller, 9. *See also* Controller
Computational tools, 138–140
 for compounding more frequently than annually, 161–162
 using to find future value, 143–144
 using to find future value of an ordinary annuity, 152–153
 using to find present value, 146–147
 using to find present value of an ordinary annuity, 150–151
Compute (CPT) key, 139
Computerized systems for resource control, 522–523
Concentration bank, 535
Conditions, as dimension of credit, 525
Conflicting rankings, 363–364
Conservative funding strategy, 517–518
Constant business risk, 459
Constant-growth model, 292–293, 301

Constant-growth valuation model, 412
Constant-payout-ratio dividend policy, 491
Constant required returns, 257
Continuous compounding, 162–163
 future value with, 163
Continuous dividend payment, 490
Continuous probability distribution, 200–201
Contractual provision risk, 241
Controlled disbursing, 535
Controller, 7, 9. *See also* Chief financial officer (CFO)
Conventional cash flow patterns, 319, 337, 354, 357
Conversion feature, 244
 of preferred stock, 282
Convertible bonds, 244
Convertible preferred stock, 282
Cooke, Robert A., 16
"cookie jar reserves," 47
"Cooking the Books," 47
Corporate bonds, 22, 242–250, 262, 452
 legal aspects of, 242–243
 long-term, 216
Corporate capital gains, 29
Corporate financing, 454
Corporate governance, 14–15
Corporate image, 2
Corporate tax rates, 26
Corporations, 4–6. *See also* Business organization; Firms; Limited liability corporations (LLCs); Publicly owned corporations; Small corporations
 capital budgeting by, 422, 423
 general organization of, 6
 strengths and weaknesses of, 5
Correlation, 205, 219
 effect on the diversification of risk and return, 207, 208–209
Correlation analyses, 195
Correlation coefficient, 205
Cost. *See also* Costs; Expenses
 of common stock, 411–415
 of common stock equity, 411–413
 of debt, 457
 of equity, 457
 of giving up a cash discount, 551, 552
 of goods sold, 41
 of least-cost financing source available, 405
 of long-term debt, 407–410
 of new assets, 325
 of new issues of common stock, 414–415
 of preferred stock, 410–411, 425
 of retained earnings, 413, 425
Cost estimates, 316, 457
Cost of capital, 145, 357, 402–436
 calculation of, 423, 425–426
 key formulas for, 424
 overview of, 403–406

Cost of money, impact on bond coupon interest rate, 243
Cost quotations, using, 407
Costs. *See also* Cost; Expenses
   effects of changing, 468
   sunk and opportunity, 323–324
   types of, 115–116
Cost stability, 454
Cost to maturity, 407
Cost-volume-profit analysis, 439
Countercyclical sales, 206
Coupon interest rate, 22, 242, 245–246, 253
Coverage ratios, 57–58
CPT key. *See* Compute (CPT) key
Credit, five C's of, 525, 540. *See also* International credit; Revolving credit agreements
Credit analyst/managers, 7
Credit department, 566
Credit lines, 558–559, 568
Credit management, 2
Credit monitoring, 531–533, 540
Credit period, 531
Credit scoring, 525
Credit selection, 510
Credit standard decision, 527
Credit standards, 524–529, 540
   changing, 525–528, 540
Credit terms, 529–531, 540
   analyzing, 551–553
Cross-sectional analysis, 48
Cumulative preferred stock, 281
Currency risks, 324
Current assets, 44, 563
   changes in, 512–513
Current liabilities, 44, 513, 568, 571
   changes in, 513
Current liabilities management, 549–571
Current ratio, 52
CV. *See* Coefficient of variation (CV)
Cyclical business, 206
Cyclical sales, 206

Daimler Chrysler, 210
Data plotting, 460
Date of invoice, 550
Date of record, 480
Dates, dividend-related, 480–481
Debentures, 248
Debt, 44, 72. *See also* Ability to service debts; Bad debts; Degree of indebtedness; Liabilities; Loans; Long-term debt; Marginal bad debts; Standard debt provisions; Tax benefits
   after-tax cost of, 410
   before-tax cost of, 407–409
   in capital structure, 438
   cost of long-term, 425
   equity capital versus, 301
   long-term, 44

   risk and, 56
   versus equity, 274
Debt analysis, 65
Debt capital, 451
   versus equity capital, **275**
Debt level, 452
Debt position of a firm, 56
Debt ratios, 56–59, 57, 452
Debt-service payments, 324
Debt-specific premium components, 241
Decision criteria, 352
   internal rate of return and, 360
   net present value and, 358–359
   payback period and, 355
Decision making, 11
   common stock value and, 298–300
   cost of giving up a cash discount in, 553
   giving up a cash discount and, 553
Decisions. *See also* Accept-reject decisions
   credit standard, 527–528
   expansion and replacement, 322–323
   financing/investment, 421–422
Decisions dividend, 479
Deductibility of interest, tax benefits of, 454
Default risk, 241, 244, 247
Degree of correlation, 205
Degree of financial leverage (DFL), 447–448, 462
Degree of indebtedness, 57
Degree of operating leverage (DOL), 443–444
Degree of total leverage (DTL), 449–450
Depository transfer check (DTC), 536, 540
Deposits, future sum accumulation and, 166
Depreciable life, 92–95, 120
Depreciable value of an asset, 120
Depreciation, 91, 92–95
   accumulated, 44
   cash budget and, 108
   cash flow and, 120
   recaptured, 327
Depreciation methods, 93–95
Desired capital structure proportions, 417
DFL. *See* Degree of financial leverage (DFL)
Dilution of ownership, 277
Disbursement management tool, 537
Disbursements, management of, 534–538, 540
Discount, 255
Discounting, 138, 300–301
Discounting cash flows, 145
Discount loans, 556
Discount rate, 145, 261, 357
   risk-adjusted, 375–380
"Discount rate-net present value" coordinates, 362–363
Diversifiable risk, 211

Diversification. *See also* International diversification
   international, 210
Diversification portfolio, 206–208
Dividend amounts, 480
Dividend income, 27–28
Dividend irrelevance, 498
   theory, 485
Dividend level, 490
Dividend payment, continuous, 490
Dividend payout ratio, 491
Dividend per share (DPS), 42, 62
Dividend policies, 479–508
   factors affecting, **486–490**
   fundamentals of, **480–483**
   relevance of, 483–486
   types of, 490–493, 499
Dividend reinvestment plans (DRIPs), 482, 498
Dividend relevance theory, arguments for, 486
Dividends, 5, 498. *See also* Residual theory of dividends
   evaluating, 498
   informational content of, 485
   preferred stock, 410
   reinvestment of, 498
   types of, 490–493
   relevance of, 291, 498
   residual theory of, 498
   stated, 410
Dividends stock, 279
Dividend yield, 287
Divisional costs of capital, 380
DOL. *See* Degree of operating leverage (DOL)
Dollar returns, versus rates of return, 365
Double taxation, 28
Double-declining balance depreciation, 94
Downward-sloping yield curve, 238, 239
DPS. *See* Dividend per share (DPS)
DRIPs. *See* Dividend reinvestment plans (DRIPs)
Dryfuss Money Market Fund, features and recent yields on, 538
DTC. *See* Depository transfer check (DTC)
DTL. *See* Degree of total leverage (DTL)
Dun & Bradstreet's Industry Norms and Key Business Ratios, 48
DuPont formula, 68
DuPont system of analysis, 64, 68–71, 72
   modified, 70

EAR. *See* Effective (true) annual rate (EAR) of interest
Earning assets, 317
Earnings. *See also* Profits; Return; Returns; Wages
   available for common stockholders, 41
   cyclical shifts in, 492
   distribution of, 281

increase in, 491
maximizing, 463
Earnings before interest and taxes (EBIT), 41, 58, 332, 438, 445, 459, 460, 462, 463, 468, 469. *See also* EBIT entries
growth of, 445
results, 447
sales and, 442
Earnings pattern, 195
Earnings per share (EPS), 12, 41, 62, 303, 468–469
Earnings requirement, 487
EBIT. *See* Earnings before interest and taxes (EBIT)
EBIT–EPS analysis
risk in, 462
shortcomings of, 463
EBIT–EPS approach, 459–464, 469–470
Economic order quantity (EOQ) model, 520–522, 540
Economic value added (EVA), 402, 417–418, 425
Effective (true) annual rate (EAR) of interest, 163–164, 165, 556, 557, 558
Efficiency, manufacturing, 522
Efficient-market hypothesis (EMH), 290
Efficient markets, 24, 218
Efficient portfolio, 205
Electronic spreadsheets, 140
Ending cash, 109
End of the month (EOM), 550
Enron Corporation, 15, 47, 247
Enterprise resource planning (ERP), 522–523
EOQ. *See* Economic order quantity (EOQ) model
EPS. *See* Earnings per share (EPS)
EPS maximization, versus value maximization, 465–466
Equipment trust certificates, 248
Equity, 42
in capital structure, 438
versus debt, 274
Equity capital, 451, 452
versus debt capital, 275, 301
Ethics, 2
role of, 15–16
share price and, 16
EU. *See* European Union (EU)
Eurobond market, 24
Eurobonds, 249
Eurocurrency loan markets, 562
Eurocurrency markets, 20, 22
Eurodollar deposits, features and recent yields on, 538
European Community, 375
EVA. *See* Economic value added (EVA)
Event risk, 197
Excel spreadsheet, 144, 147, 151, 153, 156, 158, 161–162, 163, 166, 168, 170, 171, 172, 379, 408–409

Excess cash, 109
Excess cash balance, 109
Excess earnings accumulation tax, 488
Excess returns, 290
Exchange rate risks, 197, 374, 528, 561,
Ex dividend, 480
Expansion decisions, 322–323, 338
as capital expenditure motive, 318
Expectations theory, 239
Expected earnings, 297
Expected return,
changes in, 298–299
share price and, 219
Expected value, 201–202
of a return, 201
Expenses. *See also* Cost; Costs
tax-deductible, 28–29
types of, 115–116
variable, 115
Exports, 528–529
Extendible notes, 248
External financing, 480
required, 118
External forecast, 105
Extra dividend, 492

Face value, 22, 252. *See also* Par value
Factor, 565
key short-term financing features of, 569–570
Factoring accounts receivable, 565–566, 568, 571
Factoring agreement, 565, 568, 571
Factoring costs, 565–566
FASB. *See* Financial Accounting Standards Board (FASB)
FCF. *See* Free cash flow (FCF)
FDI. *See* Foreign direct investment (FDI)
Federal agency issues, features and recent yields on, 538
Federal funds, 21
Federal National Mortgage Association (Fannie Mae), features and recent yields on, 538
Field warehouse, 567
Finance, 31
business and, 3–8
relationship to accounting, 10–11
relationship to economics, 9
role of time value in, 136, 137–141, 173
Finance function, 2, 31
organization of, 8–9
Finance personnel, 2
Financial Accounting Standards Board (FASB), 40.
Standard No. 52, 46, 72
Financial actions, 12
Financial analysts, 7
Financial breakeven point, 460, 464
Financial calculators, 139–140, 143, 158, 360
ANPV on, 399

Financial costs, fixed, 446
Financial data, collection and presentation of, 11
Financial institutions, 2, 19–26. *See also* Banks
key customers of, 19
major, 21
markets and, 31–32
Financial leverage, 56, 72, 439, 446, 452, 468
degree of, 462
relationship to operating and total leverage, 450
risk and, 452
Financial leverage multiplier (FLM), 70
Financial managers, 4, 519
functions of, 2, 11, 31
Financial markets, 19–26, 20
Financial news media, 480
Financial planning process, 91, 102–104
Financial principles, understanding, 98
Financial ratios, 48–52, 72
categories of, 51
Financial reporting, depreciation methods and, 93
Financial risk, 197, 403, 455
linking to required return, 464–465
probability of bankruptcy and, 455
Financial services, 3
Financial statements. *See also* International financial statements
audited, 51
key, 41–45
notes to, 45
preceding year's, 113–114
Financial statements/analysis, 39–101
Financial structure, 511
Financial tables, 138–139
Financial VC funds, 282–283
Financing, 109
common stock, 411
corporate, 454
costs of, 418
"excessive" levels of, 368
of international trade, 561, 562, 571
specific cost of, 410
unsecured short-term, 550, 571
Financing decisions, 331
using WMCC and IOS for, 421–422
Financing flows, 96
Financing mix, 405
Financing plan, graphical presentation of, 459–460
Firms. *See also* Business organization; Corporations; Non-U.S. firms
capital structure of, 95–97
cash flows of, 119–121
cost of capital calculation by, 422
debt position of, 56
goals of, 12–19, 30, 31, 219, 301, 370, 467, 498, 538–539, 568
liquidity of, 65, 72

organization of, 2
overall risk of, 211
profitability of, 65–66, 72
total risk of, 455
value of, 303, 457, 465
Firm-specific risks, 197
Five C's of credit, 525, 540
Fixed-asset outlays, 107
Fixed-asset restrictions, 242
Fixed assets, 44, 317
Fixed costs, 439, 448
   operating leverage and, 444–446
Fixed financial costs, 446, 460
Fixed operating costs, 440, 442
Fixed-payment coverage ratio, 58, 452
Fixed-rate loan, 556
Fixed-rate note, 556
Flat yield curve, 238
Flexibility option, 367
Float, 534, 540
Floating inventory lien, 566, 571
Floating liens
   key short-term financing features of, 569–570
Floating-rate bonds, 248
Floating-rate loan, 556
Floating-rate note, 557
Float management policy, 534
Flotation costs, 407
Ford Motor Company
   cash hoarding by, 489
Forecasts, internal and external, 105
Forecast sales, 104–105
Foreign bonds, 24, 250
Foreign bond valuation, 250–253
Foreign direct investment (FDI), 324
Foreign exchange managers, 7, 9
Foreign markets, stock in, 280
Free cash flow (FCF), 92, **101**–102, 120, 294–296, 302
Free cash flow valuation model, 294–296
FTC Quarterly Reports, 48
Funding needs, permanent versus seasonal, 515–516
Funding strategies, aggressive versus conservative, 517–518
Funds. *See also* Capital; Federal funds; Money
   flow of, 21
   long-term sources of, 405
   timing of, 12
Future sum, determining deposits needed to accumulate, 166
Future value, 136, 137–138, **141**–145, 173
   with continuous compounding, 163
   equation for, 142–143
   graphical view of, 144–145
   of a mixed stream, 154–156
   using computational tools to find, 143–144
   versus present value, 147–148
Future value interest factor, 143
   for an ordinary annuity, 150

Future value of an ordinary annuity, 150–151
   using computational tools to find, 150–151

GAAP. *See* Generally accepted accounting principles (GAAP)
GDP. *See* Gross domestic product (GDP)
Generally accepted accounting principles (GAAP), 40, 242
General Motors (GM), 245
General Motors Acceptance Corporation (GMAC), 567
General partnership, 4
Gillette, 25
Global Research Center, Shanghai, 245
GM. *See* General Motors (GM)
GMAC. *See* General Motors Acceptance Corporation (GMAC)
"Going public," 284, 301
Gordon model, 292, 412, 425
Gordon, Myron J., 486
Government issues, 537
   features and recent yields on, 537
Graphical approach, to breakeven analysis, 440
Gross domestic product (GDP), 105
Gross fixed assets, 44
Gross profit margin, 60
Gross profits, 41
Growth option, 367
Growth prospects, dividend policy and, 488
Growth rate, 168–170, 175
Guaranteed line of credit, 559–560

Hierarchy of financing, 456
High-beta assets, 215
Historical returns, 198
   risk and, 202–203
Historical risk premiums, 216–217
Historical weights, 417
Holders of common stock, voting rights of, 275, 279
Holders of record, 480
Hostile takeovers, 279

Incentive plans, 17
Income
   claims on, 275–276
   interest and dividend, 27–28
Income bonds, 248
Income statements, 39, 41–42
   common-size, 59–60
Incremental after-tax cash inflows, 330
Incremental cash flows, 321, 322
Incremental cash outflow, 321, 322
Incremental cash outflow and inflows, 322, 338–339
Incremental (relevant) cash inflows, 334
Independent projects, 319
Inflation, 51, 237
   impact of, 238
Inflation expectation premium (IP), 240

Inflow of cash, 108. *See also* Cash inflows; Cash inflows/outflows
Information, asymmetric, 456–457
Informational content, 485
Informational content of dividends, 485
Initial investment, 322, 338
   calculating, 329–330, 338
   finding, 325–330
Initial public offering (IPO), 284, 301
Initial stock purchases, 482
"inside directors," 5–6
Installation costs, 325
Installed cost of new asset, 325
Institutional venture capitalists, 282
Institutions, markets and, 20. *See also* Financial institutions
Intercorporate dividends, 28
Interest
   calculating, 165, 168–170, 556–557
   compounding, 136, 175
   compounding more frequently than annually, 161–162
   deductibility of, 454
Interest coverage ratio, 58
Interested parties, 48
Interest expense, 41
"Interest-free" sources of unsecured short-term financing, 550
Interest income, 27–28
Interest payments, 108
Interest payments to debtholders, tax treatment of, 276
Interest rate level, 235
Interest rate risk, 197, 257
Interest rates, 235–241, **237,** 262, 264, 555–557. *See also* Loan interest rates; Nominal (annual) rate of interest; Prime rate of interest (prime rate)
   required returns and, 236–241
   term structure of, 238–240
Intermediate cash inflows, 363
Internal constraints, on dividend policy, 488
Internal financing, 480
Internal forecasts, 105
Internal rate of return (IRR), 359–362, 407, 422–423
   calculating, 360–362
   evaluating, 381
   multiple, 365
   ranking via, 381
Internal rate of return approach, 359
Internal rate of return techniques, versus net present value techniques, 362–366
Internal Revenue Code, 92
Internal Revenue Service (IRS), 325, 487
International bond issues, 248–250
International capital budgeting, 324
International capital markets, 24
International credit, managing, 528–529
International diversification, 209–211
International equity market, 24

International financial statements, 46–47
International inventory management, 523–524
International loans, 561, 571
International risk considerations, 210, 373–375
International stock issues, 280
International trade, financing, 561–562, 571
Interpolation, 169, 259
Inventories, 44, 549
  as collateral, 566–568
  key short-term financing features of, 569–570
Inventory level, viewpoints about, 519
Inventory management, 510, 518–524, 540
  international, 523–524
  techniques for, 519–522, 540
Inventory turnover, 54, 518
Inverted yield curve, 238
Investment bankers, 284, 301
  role in public offerings, 284
Investment decisions, 331
  marginal cost and, 418–423
  using WMCC and IOS for, 421–422
Investment flows, 96
Investment opportunities, owners', 488–490
Investment opportunities schedule (IOS), 368, 369, 421, 483
  using to make financing/investment decisions, 421–422, 425
Investment possibilities, ranking of, 421
Investments
  in marketable securities, 537, 540
  individual, 14
  institutional, 14
  long-term, 324
Investor's Business Daily, 245, 286
IP. *See* Inflation expectation premium (IP); Inflation premium (IP)
IPO. *See* Initial public offering (IPO)
Iraq, 210
IRR. *See* Internal rate of return (IRR)
Irrelevance, of dividends, 498
IRR function, 360
IRS. *See* Internal Revenue Service (IRS)
Issued shares, 278
Issue-related premium components, 241
Issuer-related premium components, 241

JIT. *See* Just-in-time (JIT) system
Jobs and Growth Tax Relief Reconciliation Act of 2003, 279
Judgmental approach, 117
Junk bonds, 248, 249
Just-in-time (JIT) system, 522, 540

Kahneman, Daniel, 291
Key customers, of financial institutions, 19
Key financial statements, 41–45
KPMG, 15–16

Land Rover, 489
Legal capital, 487
Legal constraints, on dividend policy, 487
"Legal entity," 4–5
Lender-borrower relationship, 455
Lender-imposed agency costs, 455–456
Lernout & Hauspie Speech Products NV, 15–16
Letter of credit, 561
Letter to stockholders, 40
Leverage, 137, 438–451, 468. *See also* Financial leverage; Operating leverage
  total, 448–451
  types of, 438–439
Liabilities. *See also* Accounts payable (A/P); Debt
  current, 44
  spontaneous, 550–555
LIBOR. *See* London Interbank Offered Rate (LIBOR)
Lien, 564, 571
Limited liability, 5
Limited liability corporations (LLCs), 6–7
Limited liability partnerships (LLPs), 6–7
Limited partnerships (LPs), 6–7
Lines of credit, 558–559, 571
Linkage, of financial risk to required return, 464–465
Lintner, John, 486, 490
Liquidation value,
  per share, 397
Liquidity, 52, 72
Liquidity analysis, 65
Liquidity level, 242
Liquidity preferences, 236
Liquidity preference theory, 239
Liquidity ratios, 52–53
Liquidity risk, 197
LLCs. *See* Limited liability corporations (LLCs)
LLPs. *See* Limited liability partnerships (LLPs)
Loan amortization, 167–168, 175
Loan amortization schedule, 167, 168, 169
Loan collateral,
  marketability of, 566
Loan interest rates, 555–557
Loan payments, 108
Loans. *See also* Capital; Credit; Debt; International loans; Short-term loans
  fixed- and floating-rate, 556
  floating-lien inventory, 566
  trust receipt inventory, 566–567, 571
  warehouse receipt, 567, 571
Lockbox system, 535
London Interbank Offered Rate (LIBOR), 22
Long-term assets, 44
Long-term corporate bonds, 216
Long-term currency risk, 324
Long-term debt, 44
  cost of, 407–409, 423

Long-term funding, 22, 517
Long-term investments, 324
Long-term sources of funds, 405
Long-term (strategic) financial plans, 103, 120
Low-beta assets, 215
Low-coupon bonds, 248, 249
Low-regular-and-extra dividend policy, 492
LPs. *See* Limited partnerships (LPs)
Lynch, Peter, 290

MACRS. *See* Modified accelerated cost recovery system (MACRS)
MACRS property classes, 92
MACRS recovery periods, 93
Mail float, 534
Major shareholders, 17
Management compensation, 2
  current view of, 18
  structuring, 17
Management compensation plans, 18
Managerial finance, 2, 3–4, 8–11, 31
  role and environment of, 2–38
  study of, 7–8
Managers, 6, 519
Manufacturing efficiency, 522
Manufacturing manager, 519
Manufacturing resource planning II, (MRPII), 522
Marginal analysis, 9
Marginal bad debts, 527
Marginal cost, 418–423
Marginal investment, in accounts receivable, 527
Marginal tax rate, 27
Marketable securities, 21, 44, 511
  investing in, 537, 540
Market analysis, 68
Market/book (M/B) ratio, 63–64, 68
Market considerations, dividend policy and, 490
Market efficiency, 290, 301
Market forces, 17
Marketing, role of, 91
Marketing manager, 519
Market ratios, 63–64
Market return, 212
"Market return–asset return" coordinates, 213
Market risk, 197, 212
Market risk premium, 216
Markets, 2
  financial institutions and, 32
  institutions and, 20
Market segmentation theory, 240
Market value, 72, 289–290, 297, 301
Market value weights, 417
Materials requirement planning (MRP) system, 522–523, 540
Maturity, 253, 264. *See also* Time to maturity
  equity capital and, 275–276
  interest paid at, 556

Maturity risk, 241
M/B ratio. *See* Market/book (M/B) ratio
Members, 5
Merchandise, discounted cost of, 551
Miller, Merton H., 454, 596
Minimum weighted average cost of capital, 458
Mix, of financing, 405
Mixed stream cash flow, 140, 154–158. *See also* Cash flow
Mixed stream of cash inflows, 319, 354. *See also* Cash inflow
Mixed streams
  future value of, **154–156**, 173–175
  present value of, **156–158**, 173
MNCs. *See* Multinational companies (MNCs)
Modified accelerated cost recovery system (MACRS), 92, 120. *See also* MACRS entries
Modified DuPont Formula, 70
Modigliani, Franco, 454, 485
Money, 30–32. *See also* Capital; Funds; Time value of money
Money market, 2, 20–21
Money market instrument, issuing and purchasing, 21
Money market mutual funds, features and recent yields on, 538
Moody's bond ratings, 246
Morgan Stanley, 377
Mortgage bonds, 248
MRP system. *See* Materials requirement planning (MRP) system
MSN Money Central Investor, 23
Multinational companies(MNCs),473-475
Multiple IRRs, 365
Mutually exclusive projects, 319
Myers, Stewart, 456

Nasdaq National Market Issues, 288
Nasser, Jacques, 489
National Association of Securities Dealers Automated Quotation (Nasdaq) system, 24
NCAI. *See* Net current asset investment (NCAI)
Negative correlation, 205–206
Negative net working capital, 511
Negative signal, 457, 485, 490
Negotiable certificates of deposit (CDS), features and recent yields on, 538
Negotiated basis purchase, 497
Negotiated liabilities, 518
Net cash flow, 109
Net current asset investment (NCAI), 101–102
Net demanders of funds, 19
Net fixed asset investment (NFAI), 102
Net fixed assets, 44
Net loss, 97
Net operating profits after taxes (NOPAT), 99, 417, 457

Net present value (NPV), 357–359. *See also* NPV entries; Present value (PV)
  evaluating, 381
  highest overall, 368
Net present value analysis, 422
Net present value approach, 369–370
Net present value profiles, 362–363, 381
Net present value techniques, versus internal rate of return techniques, 363–366
Net proceeds, 407
Net profit margin, 61, 68
Net profits before taxes, 41, 332
Net suppliers, 19
Net working capital, 539
  change in, 328–329
  fundamentals of, 511–512
New information, market adjustment to, 289–290
New marketing programs, proposals for, 352
News Corp., 210
New York Stock Exchange (NYSE), 23, 289
NFAI. *See* Net fixed asset investment (NFAI)
Nominal annual rate, 163–164, 556
Nominal (stated) annual rate of interest, 163–164
Noncash charges, 97, 108, 331
Nonconventional cash flow pattern, 320, 365
Noncumulative preferred stock, 281
Nondiversifiable risk, 211–212, 217
Nongovernment issues, 537
  features and recent yields on, 538
Nonnotification basis, 564–565
Nonrecourse basis, 565
Non-U.S. firms, capital structure of, 452–454, 468
Nonvoting common stock, 279
No-par preferred stock, 280
Normal yield curves, 238
Notes
  to financial statements, 45–46
  single-payment, 557–558, 568, 571
Notes payable, 44, 568
Notification basis, 565
Notification basis factoring, 565
NPV. *See* Net present value (NPV)
NPV decision rule, 375–376
NPV function, 359
NPV simulation, 372–373
NYSE. *See* New York Stock Exchange (NYSE)

OC. *See* Operating cycle (OC)
OCF. *See* Operating cash flow (OCF)
Open-market purchases, 497
Operating breakeven point, 439–442, 468
Operating cash flow (OCF), 96, 98–100, 120, 332

Operating cash inflows, **322,** 338
  finding, 330–334, 338
Operating-change restrictions, 558
Operating costs, 437, 439
Operating cycle (OC), 514
Operating expenditure capital budgeting process, steps in, **317–318**
Operating expenses, 41
Operating financial plans, 103–104, 120
Operating flows, 96
Operating leverage, 438, 442–446, 468
  business risk and, 454–455
  fixed costs and, 444–446
  relationship to financial and total leverage, 450
Operating plans, 91, 102
Operating profit margin, 61
Operating profits, 41, 58, 438
Operation Enduring Freedom, 210
Opportunity costs, 145, 323, 357
Optimal capital structure, 417, 458, 457–459, 468
  choosing, 464–466
  determining, 454
  graphical view of, 458–459
Optimistic estimates of returns, 199
Options, 381–382
  types of, 367
Order costs, 520
Ordinary annuity, 149. *See also* Annuities
  future value interest factor for, 150–151
  future value of, 150–151, 173
  present value interest factor for, 152
  present value of, 151–153, 173
Ordinary income, 26–29
Ordinary stock dividend, 493
Organized securities exchanges, 23
OTC exchange. *See* Over-the-counter (OTC) exchange
Outflow of cash, 96–98. *See also* Cash inflows/outflows; Cash outflows
"outside directors," 5
Outstanding shares, 278
Over-the-counter (OTC) exchange, 23
Overall cost of capital, 405
Overall risk of a firm, 211
Overvalued stock, 290, 456
Owner considerations, dividend policy and, 488–490
Owners, tax status of, 488–490
Ownership, potential dilution of, 488–490
Owners' investment opportunities, 488–490
Owner wealth, maximizing, 13, 30, 31

Pacific Stock Exchange, 23
Paid-in capital in excess of par, 44
Par value, 22, 246, 253, **277,** 280, 560
Par-value preferred stock, 280
Parmalat, 247
Partnerships, 4
  strengths and weaknesses of, 5

Payables policy, 554
Payback periods, 354–357, 382
  pros and cons of, 355–357
Payment date, 481
Payment float, 535
Payments, slow, 531, **535**, 540
PDA. *See* Personal digital assistant (PDA)
Pecking order, 456
P/E multiple approach. *See* Price/earnings (P/E) multiple approach
Pension fund managers, 7
Pentagon, 15
P/E ratios. *See* Price/earnings (P/E) ratios
Percentage advance, 563
Percentage of total assets, 512
Percent-of-sales method, 114
Perfect negative correlation, 205
Perfect positive correlation, 205
Performance plans, 17
Performance shares, 18
Periods, finding an unknown number of, 171–172, 175
Permanent funding requirement, 515
Perpetuity, present value of, **153–154**, 173
Pessimistic estimates of returns, 200
Plant assets, investments in, 195
Pledge
  key short-term financing features of, 568
  of accounts receivable, 564–565, 571
"Plug" figure, 117
Point of view, strategic, 375
Political risks, 209, 324, 374
Portfolio, 196
  risk associated with, 205–211
  standard deviation of, 219
Portfolio beta coefficients, 212–215, 220–221
Portfolio correlation, 205
Portfolio diversification, 206–208
  international, 209–210
Positive correlation, 205–206
Positive net working capital, 512
Positive signal, 456, 485, 490, 496
Potential dilution of ownership, 490
Preceding year's financial statements, 113
Preemptive rights, 277, 301
Preferred stock, 23, 44, **277–278**, 301
  cost of, 410–411, 425
  valuation of, 292
Preferred stock dividends, 410
Preferred stockholders, basic rights of, 281
Premium, 255
  risk, 262
Premium components, debt-specific, 241
Present value (PV), **136**, **137–138**, 173. *See also* Net present value (NPV)
  cash flow and, 284–285
  equation for, 146
  graphical view of, 147
  of a mixed stream, 156–158
  of a perpetuity, finding, 153–154

of a single amount, **145–147**
  using computational tools to find, 146–147
  versus future value, 147–148
Present value interest factor, 146
  for an ordinary annuity, **152**
Present value of an ordinary annuity, 151–153
  using computational tools to find, 152–153
President or chief executive officer (CEO), 6
Price/earnings (P/E) multiple approach, **274**, **297**, 301, 496
Price/earnings (P/E) ratios, 63, **68**, 287–288, 297
Price quotations, 287
Primary market, 20, 24
Prime rate of interest (prime rate), 555
Prime rate plus a premium, 558
Principal, 141
Principal payments (loans), 108
Privately owned stock, 277
Private placement, 19, **20**, 284
Pro forma balance sheet, 117–119
  preparing, 117–118
Pro forma income statement, 91, 114
  preparing, 114–117
Pro forma statements, 112, 114
  evaluating, 119
Probability, defined, 200
Probability distributions, 200–201
Proceeds from sale of old asset, 326
Processing float, 534
Products, 274
Profitability, 72
  design for financial leverage, 446–448
Profitability analysis, 65
Profitability ratios, 59–63
Profitability-risk tradeoff, 512–513, 539
Profit contribution from sales, 526
Profit maximization, 12–13
Profit planning, 102, 112
Profits. *See also* Earnings
  sales and, 114–115
Project finance managers, 7
Project risk, estimates of, 376
Projects
  acceptability or nonacceptability of, 358
  total risk of, 376
  with highest overall present value, 369–370
Property classes, under MACRS, 93
Prospectus, 284, 285
Proxies, 279, 301
Proxy battle, 279
Proxy statement, 279
Public Company Accounting Oversight Board (PCAOB), 40
Publicly owned corporations, 40
Publicly owned shares, 277
Publicly owned stock, 277

Public offering, 20, 284
  investment banker role in, 284
Purchases, 108
Purchasing manager, 519
Purchasing-power risk, 197
Put option. *See also* Call feature
  role in fund raising, 513
Putable bonds, 248

Quarterly compounding, 159–160
  equation for, 161
Quick (acid-test) ratio, 52
Quiet period, 284
Quotations
  bond, **245–246**
  stock, 301

Radio frequency identification (RFID), 523
RADR. *See* Risk-adjusted discount rate (RADR)
Range, 199, 371
Ranking approach, 319
Rates of return, versus dollar returns, 364–365
Ratio analysis, 39, **48**, 72
  cautions for using, 50–51
  complete, 64–71
Ratio comparisons, 48–49
Ratios, 48
  summarizing, 64–71
Ratio value, interpretation of, 48–49
Real options
  attractive, 368
  recognizing, **366–370**
  types of, 367
Real rate of interest, 236–237
Recaptured depreciation, 327
Receipts, management of, 534–537, 540
Receivables. *See* Accounts receivable (A/R)
Record date, 480
Recovery period, 93
Red herring, 284
Regular dividend policy, 491–492
Regular partnership, 4
Reinvestment
  of dividends, 498
  of intermediate cash inflows, 363
Reinvestment plans, dividend, 482. *See also* Dividend reinvestment plans (DRIPs)
Relative values, 48
Relaxation of credit standards, 525
Relevance of dividends, 498
Relevant cash flows, 321–325
  summarizing, 337, 338
Relevant cash inflows, 334, 338
Relevant cost, 526
Removal costs, 326, 335
Renewal decisions, as capital expenditure motive, 318
Rent payments, 108
Reorder point, 521

Replacement decisions, 322–323, 338
  as capital expenditure motive, 318
Repurchase agreements, features
  and recent yields on, 538
Repurchases, of stocks, 499
Required returns, 145, **236**–241, 262,
  263, 290, 357
  bond values and, 255–257
  constant and changing, 257–258
  linking financial risk to, 464–465
  valuation and, 251
Required total financing, 109
Residual owners, 277
Residual theory of dividends,
  483–485, 498
Resource control, computerized systems
  for, 522–523
Restrictive covenants, 242, 281
Retained earnings, 44, 480
  cost of, 413–414, 425
Return, 219. *See also* Capital asset pricing
  model (CAPM); Historical returns;
  Required returns; Returns
  defined, **196**–198
  from international diversification,
   209–210
  fundamentals of, 196–199
  key definitions and formulas for, 220
Return data, deriving beta coefficient
  from, 212–213
Return on common equity (ROE), 62, 70
Return on investment (ROI), 62
Return on total assets (ROA), 62, 68, 70
Returns. *See also* Return
  pessimistic and optimistic estimates
   of, 199
  valuation and, 250–251
Revenue estimates, 316
Revenue stability, 455
Reverse dilution, 496
Reverse stock split, 495
Revolving credit agreements, 559
  key short-term financing features of,
   569–570
Rights
  stockholder, 301
  shareholder, **277**
Rights offering, 277, 284
Risk, **13,** 219, 377. *See also* Business risk;
  Capital asset pricing model (CAPM);
  Constant business risk; Default
  risk; Diversifiable risk; EBIT–EPS
  analysis; Exchange rate risks;
  International risk considerations;
  Nondiversifiable risk; Overall risk
  of a firm; Political risks; Shareholder-
  specific risks
  behavioral approaches for dealing with,
   370–375
  in capital budgeting, 352–399, **370**
  cash flow and, 300–301
  changes in, 299
  coefficient of variation and, 203–204

debt and, 56
defined, 196
diversification and, 208
in EBIT–EPS analysis, 462–463
financial leverage and, 438
firm-specific, 197
fundamentals of, 196–199
historical returns and, 202–203
of international diversification, 209–211
key definitions and formulas for, 220
of a portfolio, 205–211
return and, 197–198
shareholder-specific, 197
share price and, 219
of a single asset, 199–205
of technical insolvency, 512
types of, 197, 211–212
valuation and, 251
Risk-adjusted discount rate (RADR),
  376–379, 464
  applying, 376–379
  popularity of, 379
Risk assessment, 199–200
Risk-averse attitude, **198**
Risk-averse stockholders, 13
Risk aversion, 198–199, 203, 219
Risk considerations, international,
  373–375
Risk exposure, 355
Risk-free assets, 216
Risk-free rate of interest, R_f, **237**
Risk-free rate of return, 216
"Risk index," 377–378
Risk measurement, 201–205
Risk premiums, 216, **240**–241, 244–262
  historical, 216
Risk-profitability tradeoff, 512–513, 539
Risk–return relationship, 195
RMA Annual Statement Studies, 48
ROA. *See* Return on total assets (ROA)
Road show, 284
ROE. *See* Return on common equity (ROE)
ROI. *See* Return on investment (ROI)

Safety stock, 521
Salaries, 108
Sale price per unit, 440–441
Sales
  countercyclical, 206
  cyclical, 206
  profit contribution from, 115, 526
Sales forecast, 104, 112–113
Salomon Brothers, 284
Salvage value, 335
Sarbanes-Oxley Act (SOX) 15, 16, 31,
  40, 47
SBICs. *See* Small business investment
  companies (SBICs)
Scenario analysis, 371
Seasonal funding requirements, 516
SEC. *See* Securities and Exchange
  Commission (SEC)
Secondary market, 20, 23, 24

Secured loans, short-term, 563, 571.
  See also Short-term loans
Secured short-term loans, institutions
  extending, 562–563, 571
Securities. *See also* Security issue features
  and recent yields on popular, 538
  total risk of, 211
**Securities and Exchange Commission
  (SEC), 18, 40,** 247, 279, 404
Securities exchanges, 23, 24
  role of, 24–25
Security agreement, 563
Security interest, 243
Security issue, selling process for, 286.
  See also Securities
Security market line (SML), 195, **217,** 221
Self-liquidating loan, 555
Selling group, 285
Sell orders, 23
Semiannual compounding, 158–159
  equation for, 160
Semiannual interest, bond values and,
  260–261
Sensitivity analysis, 111, 195, **199**–200,
  371–372
Series of cash flows, rate of interest
  in, 168
Services, 274
Shareholder rights, 277–278
Shareholder-specific market risk, 212
Shareholder-specific risks, 197
Shareholder wealth
  creating, 24
  maximizing, 13
Share price
  determinants of, 13
  ethics and, 16
  expected return and, 219
  risk and, 219
Share price maximization, 14
  time value of money and, 173
Short-term business loans, 556
Short-term financial management, 510,
  511, 539
Short-term financing, 568, 692
  sources of, 571
Short-term funds, 20–21, 517
Short-term loans
  institutions extending, 564, 571
  secured sources of, 562–567
  sources of, 549
  unsecured sources of, 555–562, 571
Short-term note, 557
Short-term (operating) financial plans,
  103–104, 120
Short-term, self-liquidating loan, 555
Signal, 456, 485, 490
Simulation, 112, 372–373
Single amount
  future value of, 141–145
  present value of, 145–147
Single amount cash flow, 141–148
Single asset, risk of, 199–205, 219

INDEX I-11

Single-payment notes, 577–558, 571
    key short-term financing features of, 569–570
Sinking-fund requirements, 243
Small business investment companies (SBICs), 283
Small corporations, 4
Small (ordinary) stock dividend, 493
SML. *See* Security market line (SML)
"Social responsibility," 14
Sole proprietorships, 4
    strengths and weaknesses of, 5
Sophisticated capital budgeting technique, 357, 359
Spontaneous liabilities, 550
    key short-term financing features of, 569–570
Spreadsheets, 140
Stakeholder focus, 14
Stakeholders, 13
Standard & Poor's bond ratings, 246
Standard & Poor's 500 Stock Composite Index, 212
Standard & Poor's Industrial Ratios, 297
Standard debt provisions, 242
Standard deviation, 201–203
    of returns, 202
Stated annual rate, 556
Stated dividends, 410
Statement of cash flows, 39, 45, 91
    developing, 95–98
    interpreting, 97–98
    preparing, 97
Statement of retained earnings, 45
Statement of stockholders' equity, 40, 45
Statistics, risk of an asset and, 199–205. *See also* Probability
Stock, 26. *See also* Cost of common stock; Cost of preferred stock
    common and preferred, 276–288
    underpriced, 414
    undervalued and overvalued, 456
Stock buybacks, 496
Stock dividends, 279, 493–495
    company viewpoint on, 494–495
    shareholder viewpoint on, 494
Stockholders, 5
    dividends for, 498
    preferred, 280–281
    rights of, 301
Stockholders' equity, 45
Stockholders' report, 39, 40–47, 72
Stock issues, international, 280
"Stock markets," 23
Stock options, 17
Stock ownership, 277
Stock price, maximizing, 300, 468, 498, 539, 568
Stock purchase warrants, 244
Stock quotations, 301
    interpreting, 286–288
Stock repurchases, 496–497, 499
Stock repurchases/retirements, 108

Stock splits, 495, 499
Stock symbol, 287
Stock valuation, 274–313
Stock valuation equation, 291–293
Straight-line depreciation, 93
Strategic approach, 366
Strategic financial plans, 102, 120
Strategic options, 366
Strategic plans, 91
Strategic point of view, 375
Stream of cash flows, present value of, 151–153
Stretching accounts payable, 549, 553–554, 568–569
Subordinated debentures, 248
Subordination, 242
Subsidiaries
    transactions between, 562
Sum-of-the-years'-digits depreciation, 93
Sullivan, David, 404
Sunk costs, 323
Supervoting shares, 279
Supplier credit terms, 549
Supply and demand, 24–25, 236–237
Surpluses, interest paid on, 565
Systematic risk, 211

Takeovers. *See also* Hostile takeovers
    threat of, 17
Target capital structure, 405, 456
Target dividend-payout ratio, 492
Target proportion, 405
Target weights, 417
Taxation
    business, 2, 32
Tax benefits, of deductibility of interest, 454
Tax-deductible expenses, 28–29
Tax depreciation methods, 93–95, 120
Taxes
    corporate, 5, 26
    excess earnings accumulation, 487
    multinational companies and, 374–375
    on dividends, 482
    on sale of assets, 335
    on sale of old asset, 326
Tax laws, 92
Tax payments, 107, 108
Tax rate schedule, corporate, 26
Tax risk, 197
Tax rules, for asset sales, 326–328
Tax status, owner's, 488–490
Tax treatments, on asset sales, 327
Technical insolvency, 512
Tender offers, 497
Term structure
    of interest rates, 238–240
    theories of, 239–240
Terminal cash flow, 322, 334–336, 338–339
    calculating, 336
Terminal warehouse, 567
Time deposits, 22

Time line, 137
    for bond valuation, 254
    for future value of an ordinary annuity, 150
    for future value of a single amount, 143
    for present value of an annuity, 152
    for present value of a single amount, 146
Time periods, finding an unknown number of, 171–172
Time-series analysis, 50
Times interest earned ratio, 58, 452
Time to maturity, bond values and, 257–258
Time value of money, 136–194
    in finance, 137–141, 173
    key definitions, formulas, and equations for, 174
    share price maximization and, 173
    special applications of, 165–172
Time zero, 325
Timing option, 367
    valuation and, 251
Total asset turnover, 65, 68
Total balance, 110
Total cash receipts, 107
Total cost of inventory, 520
Total dollar returns, 369
Total impact of the fixed costs, 448
Total leverage, 439, 448–451
    relationship to operating and financial leverage, 450
Total new financing, 418
Total operating cost, 440
Total risk, 211
    of a firm, 455
Transactions
    between subsidiaries, 562
    international, 561, 571
Transfer pricing, 375
Translation method, 47
Treasurer, 6, 8
Treasury bills (T-bills), features and recent yields on, 538. *See also* U.S. Treasury bills (T-bills)
Treasury notes, features and recent yields on, 538
Treasury stock, 278, 497
Treasury yield curves, 238
Trial-and-error technique, 407
Triple taxation, 28
True annual rate, 556
Trust receipt inventory loan, 566–567, 571
Trust receipts, key short-term financing features of, 569–570
Trustee, 243
"Truth-in-savings laws," 164
Two-bin method, 519
2/10 net 30, 529, 531
Tyco Capital, 47

Uncorrelated assets, 206
Underpriced stock, **414**

Undervalued stock, 289, 456
Underwriting, 284
Underwriting costs, 407
Underwriting syndicate, 285
U.S. Treasury bills (T-bills), 216, 238
 features and recent yields on, 538
Unlimited funds, 319
Unlimited liability, 4, 5
Unsecured short-term financing, 550, 571
Unsophisticated capital budgeting technique, 355
Unsystematic risk, 211
Upward-sloping yield curve, 238, 239, 240

Valuation, 250, 288–298. *See also* Bond valuation
 key inputs to, **250,** 263
Valuation model. *See also* Capital asset pricing model (CAPM)
 basic, 251–253
 key inputs to, 263
Value, estimating, 465. *See also* Valuation
Value Line, 48
Value Line Investment Survey, 213–214
Value maximization, versus EPS maximization, 465–466

Variable costs, 117, 439, 526
Variable-growth model, 293, 301
Variable operating costs, 440
VC limited partnerships, 283
VCs. *See* Venture capitalists (VCs)
Venture capital, 274, 282–283, 301
Venture capital investments, deal structure and pricing for, 283
Venture capitalists (VCs), 282–283, 301. *See also* VC limited partnerships
Vice presidents, 6
Volvo, 489
Voting rights, of holders of common stock, 275, 279

WACC. *See* Weighted average cost of capital (WACC)
Wages, 107, 108
Wall Street Journal, 23, 245–246, 286
WalMart Stores, Inc., 523
Warehouse receipt loans, 567, 571
Warehouse receipts, key short-term financing features of, 569–570
Washington Post, 25
Wealth, maximizing, 2, 30, 31
Wealth maximization framework, 464

Weighted average cost, 405
Weighted average cost of capital (WACC), 294, 415–418, 421, 425, 457, 468
Weighted marginal cost of capital (WMCC), 418–420, 483–484
 calculating, 419–420
 using to make financing/investment decisions, 421, 425
Weighted marginal cost of capital (WMCC) schedule, 418, 419
Weighting schemes, 416–417, 425
Wire transfer, 536, 540
WMCC. *See* Weighted marginal cost of capital (WMCC)
Working capital, 628–629, 639
 net, 328–330
WorldCom, 47, 247, 404

Yield curves, 238–239
 importance of, 238–239
Yield to maturity (YTM), 238, 258–260, 264, 407

Zero-balance accounts (ZBAs), 536, 540
Zero-coupon bonds, 248
Zero-growth model, 291, 301